TRADE MARK LAW IN EUROPE

THIRD EDITION

TRADE MARK LAW IN EUROPE

THIRD EDITION

by

ALEXANDER VON MÜHLENDAHL
Visiting Professor, Centre for Commercial Law Studies, Queen Mary, University of London
Attorney, Bardehle Pagenberg, Munich

DIMITRIS BOTIS
Deputy Director for Legal Affairs, OHIM

SPYROS MANIATIS
Professor of Intellectual Property and Director of the Centre for Commercial Law
Studies, Queen Mary, University of London

IMOGEN WISEMAN
Partner, Cleveland, London

OXFORD
UNIVERSITY PRESS

Great Clarendon Street, Oxford, OX2 6DP,
United Kingdom

Oxford University Press is a department of the University of Oxford.
It furthers the University's objective of excellence in research, scholarship,
and education by publishing worldwide. Oxford is a registered trade mark of
Oxford University Press in the UK and in certain other countries

© Alexander von Mühlendahl, Dimitris Botis, Spyros Maniatis, Imogen Wiseman 2016

The moral rights of the authors have been asserted

Impression: 3

Second Edition published in 2009
Third Edition published in 2016

All rights reserved. No part of this publication may be reproduced, stored in
a retrieval system, or transmitted, in any form or by any means, without the
prior permission in writing of Oxford University Press, or as expressly permitted
by law, by licence or under terms agreed with the appropriate reprographics
rights organization. Enquiries concerning reproduction outside the scope of the
above should be sent to the Rights Department, Oxford University Press, at the
address above

You must not circulate this work in any other form
and you must impose this same condition on any acquirer

Crown copyright material is reproduced under Class Licence
Number C01P0000148 with the permission of OPSI
and the Queen's Printer for Scotland

Published in the United States of America by Oxford University Press
198 Madison Avenue, New York, NY 10016, United States of America

British Library Cataloguing in Publication Data
Data available

Library of Congress Control Number: 2016933492

ISBN 978-0-19-872605-0

Printed and bound by
CPI Group (UK) Ltd, Croydon, CR0 4YY

Links to third party websites are provided by Oxford in good faith and
for information only. Oxford disclaims any responsibility for the materials
contained in any third party website referenced in this work.

The views and opinions set out in the book do not represent the views and opinions of the OHIM/EUIPO,
but are the personal views and opinions of the author.

FOREWORD

Take as your starting point the provisions of the Directive and the Regulation which govern the availability and scope of trade mark protection within and across the European Union. Resist the temptation to interpret and apply them simply as if they were encapsulations of prior national jurisprudence. Remind yourself that the legislation must, so far as possible, be interpreted and applied in conformity with the provisions of the TRIPs Agreement. Turn to the case law of the Court of Justice for guidance as to the way in which the legislation should be interpreted. Then reach for this book.

Why? Because the authors have analysed the law systematically from an EU perspective and provided a comprehensive and coherent exposition of the main rules and principles as they have thus far been developed and refined by the supervising courts in Luxembourg.

That was not an easy task to accomplish. At the macro level, they have had to recognise that judgments of the Court of Justice do not all contribute equally to the development of the law. At the micro level, they have had to recognise that the significance to be attributed to particular passages in judgments of the Court may depend not so much upon what they say, as upon what they do not say in the legal and factual context in which they appear. And as an aspect of that, since the Court is generally not willing to depart in express terms from its own case law, the process of implicit departure can really only be appreciated by focusing upon what is not currently being said as compared and contrasted with what was said before on the same or inter-related topics.

It is to be welcomed that in the course of drilling down into the case law, the authors have taken account of the importance of the role played by the Advocates General in shaping and testing the rulings of the Court. The opinions of the Advocates General do help to identify any perceived need for the existing state of the law to be restated with or without modification or amplification. Their advice as to what is required for a principled determination of the case at hand also provides a statement of position against which to assess the resistance or receptiveness of the Court to the propositions that have formally been put forward for its consideration.

Sometimes that assessment must allow for an extended period of reflection while the Court works out just how far to take a proposition that the Advocate General has presented to it. As can, in retrospect, be seen to have happened in response to the influential observations of Advocate General Ruiz-Jarabo Colomer beginning at point [41] of his opinion in Case C-206/01 *Arsenal Football Club* with the words: 'To state that the registered proprietor may prevent a third party from using "the trade mark as a trade mark" is as good as saying nothing at all. It is therefore necessary to give substance to that indeterminate concept and, in doing so, to keep the functions of a trade mark very much in mind.'

The authors have not shied away from dealing with the expanding role of 'the functions of a trade mark' as a controlling factor in the determination of relative rights. They have considered the nature of 'the functions' and they have considered the somewhat perplexing effect that referencing 'the functions' has had upon the distribution of protection between 'double-identity protection', 'extended protection for marks with a reputation', and 'protection against the existence of a likelihood of confusion'. There will undoubtedly be more to say in future editions of this book as the case law continues to develop in relation to the concepts of harm and adverse effect on 'the functions' for which a trade mark is protected by registration. Among the questions for consideration in the meantime, with the benefit of the authors' analysis of the position thus far reached, would be: Must some level of use resulting in consumer awareness of a trade mark always be deemed to exist for the purpose of assessing whether the functions for which it is protected by registration are liable to be affected by the use of an identical or similar sign? Does the Court intend a defence of fair use to be recognised and accepted as the antithesis of interference with the functions for which a trade mark is protected by registration?

Exclusions from registration on absolute grounds continue to require compartmentalised treatment in accordance with the case law of the Court. The authors have necessarily adhered to that approach in their analysis of the jurisprudence. Their assessment of the judgment in Case C-307/10 *IP Translator* is illuminating as to the delicacy of the task undertaken by the Court in relation to the legal requirement for clarity and precision in the wording of the list of goods or services for which registration is requested. By the time the next edition of this book is published, it may have become apparent whether the Court is actually prepared to accept or reject the proposition that under the first of the absolute grounds for refusal specified in the Directive and the Regulation, the validity of an application for registration depends upon compliance with that legal requirement. More generally, the authors' analysis of the case law points to the need for a question: should the Court move to the position that the legislation mandates 'distinctiveness' (intrinsic or acquired through use) as a fundamental requirement for registration and does not, in doing so, call for any great debate as to whether and where any neat dividing lines should be drawn between the various different reasons why it might be found that a particular sign does not, in fact, fulfil that requirement?

Three things are clear simply on viewing the authors' exposition of the law as a progress report on the work of the Court of Justice. First, the magnitude of the task with which the Court was confronted in giving meaning and content to the words of the Directive and the Regulation as EU legislative instruments for the implementation of EU standards of compliance with the provisions of the TRIPs Agreement relating to trade mark rights. Second, the substantial progress that the Court has made in dealing with that task to date. Third, the extent to which further progress depends upon the adoption of more explanatory reasoning in judgments relating to the practical application of important aspects of the law. Examples of such aspects of the law would include: the meaning and relative nature of 'distinctiveness' as an attribute of identity in a competitive marketplace; the way in which 'similarity' is actually intended to operate as a test for relatedness between marks and signs and as between goods and services; and the extent to which EU-wide protection of a trade mark may be reduced or eliminated as a result of territorially limited exploitation of the protected trade mark.

There is, however, no justification for viewing this book simply as a progress report on the work of the Court of Justice. The authors have gone well beyond that in contextualising and critically appraising the jurisprudence they have addressed. At every point the reader sees points of interest and practical importance identified in the text and wants to know what

Foreword

the authors have said about them. For people who care about the operation of the law of trade marks, it is a pleasure to read their work and decide whether or not to accept that the law as they describe it is following a correct course and whether to agree or disagree with what they say about that.

Geoffrey Hobbs QC
February 2016

ACKNOWLEDGEMENTS

We are delighted to publish the third edition of this work with the Oxford University Press.

The process from commissioning to bringing to the shelves has been seamless. We are grateful to Ruth Anderson for bringing the project in under the aegis of OUP. We would also like to thank Gemma Parsons for masterfully managing the team of authors, Emma Taylor for supporting the book to completion, and Louise Murgatroyd for her passionate marketing.

We are equally grateful to Paul Tompsett at Newgen for leading a fantastic team of professionals that helped us complete our work: Sue Meek, and Janet Walker for their insightful copyediting, Jim Driscoll for his intuitive proofreading, Avril Ehrlich for her thorough indexing, and Mike Leach for his skilful tabling.

As a team, the four authors had great fun working together, and we are already looking forward to the fourth edition.

Finally, we have to thank all those who helped fill in the pieces of the great EU trade mark law puzzle: students, academics, trade mark professionals, practitioners, lawyers, examiners, regulators, judges, trade mark owners and enforcers, who, in one way or another, have to give life to the case-law of the Court in a logically coherent and practically workable manner.

CONTENTS—SUMMARY

Table of Cases   xxiii
Table of Legislation   xlv

1. Introduction   1
2. European Union Trade Mark Law: The Directive and the Regulation   3
3. Trade Marks in Europe and the Court of Justice of the European Union   17
4. Formalities and the Definition of Goods and Services   49
5. Absolute Grounds   101
6. Distinctiveness Acquired Through Use   269
7. Relative Grounds   299
8. Loss of Rights: Requirement of Use, Conversion to Generic Indication   425
9. Scope of Protection, Limitations, and Enforcement   481
10. Parallel Imports   617
11. Trade Marks and Competition Law   723
12. The Interaction with Other Areas of the Law   775
13. The New Trade Mark 'Package'   845
14. Conclusion   855

Index   859

CONTENTS

Table of Cases   xxiii
Table of Legislation   xlv

1. **Introduction**
2. **European Union Trade Mark Law: The Directive and the Regulation**
   - A. Introduction   2.01
   - B. The 'Harmonization' Directive   2.07
   - C. The Community Trade Mark Regulation   2.14
     - (1) The Basic Principles: Unitary Character, Autonomy, Coexistence   2.19
     - (2) Coexistence as Implemented   2.23
     - (3) The Community Trade Mark   2.30
   - D. The Enlargement of the European Union   2.59
   - E. Conclusion   2.62
3. **Trade Marks in Europe and the Court of Justice of the European Union**
   - A. Introduction   3.01
   - B. Forms of Action   3.06
     - (1) Actions against Member States in Breach of Community Law   3.06
     - (2) Actions against a Community Institution for Failure to Act   3.08
     - (3) Annulment Actions   3.09
     - (4) Appeals   3.12
     - (5) References for a Preliminary Ruling   3.13
   - C. Judicial Review and the Community Trade Mark   3.20
     - (1) The Role of the Boards of Appeal and New or Additional Facts and Evidence   3.20
     - (2) Judicial Review: The Nature of Court Proceedings   3.56
     - (3) Scope and Limits of Administrative and Judicial Review   3.60
     - (4) The Special Case of National Law: *Edwin* and *National Lottery*   3.85
     - (5) The Value of Precedents   3.105
   - D. Conclusion   3.111
4. **Formalities and the Definition of Goods and Services**
   - A. Introduction   4.01
   - B. The Provisions of the Directive and the Regulation   4.08
   - C. What is a Sign?   4.11
     - (1) *Dyson*: The Fundamental Question   4.11
     - (2) Pre-*Dyson* Jurisprudence: Setting the Ground   4.15
     - (3) *Dyson*: The Fundamental Requirement   4.26
     - (4) *Apple*: The Apple Store as Registrable Dress   4.63

D.	Capable of Being Represented Graphically	4.76
	(1) *Sieckmann*: The Purpose of Graphical Representation; Non-visual Signs; Scents; the General Conditions	4.77
	(2) *Shield Mark*: Graphical Representation of Sounds; General Policy Considerations	4.106
	(3) *Libertel*: Colour Samples; Public Policy Considerations	4.131
	(4) *Heidelberger Bauchemie*: Abstract Combinations of Colours	4.148
E.	Capable of Distinguishing	4.156
	(1) *Philips*: Setting the Principles	4.156
	(2) Capable of Distinguishing: The Limited Effect of Article 3(1)(a)	4.172
F.	The Definition of the Goods and Services for Which the Mark is Registered	4.176
	(1) *Praktiker*: Registration of Service Marks for Retail Services	4.176
	(2) *IP Translator*: Specification, Clarity, and Precision	4.190
	(3) *Netto*: The Retailing of Services and the Need for Clarity	4.245

5. Absolute Grounds

A.	Introduction	5.01
B.	Guidelines for Interpreting Article 3	5.05
	(1) Public Interest, Independence, and Interdependence	5.05
	(2) The Independence of Each Ground	5.08
	(3) The Link with the Specification, the Relevant Consumer, and Timing	5.11
C.	Article 3(1)(b): Devoid of any Distinctive Character	5.16
	(1) *Companyline*: Article 7(1)(b); Balancing between *Baby-Dry* and *Postkantoor*	5.16
	(2) *SAT.1*: Back to *Baby-Dry*?	5.37
	(3) *BioID*: The Limited Effect of *SAT.1*	5.64
	(4) Appeals Post *SAT.1* and *BioID*	5.82
	(5) NAI and MMF: Distinctiveness of Abbreviations	5.84
	(6) *BORCO-Marken* and *Technopol*: Single Letters and Numerals	5.95
	(7) *Nichols*: No Special Conditions for Surnames	5.129
	(8) Registrability of Slogans	5.146
	(9) *Libertel*: The Distinctiveness of Colours	5.200
	(10) *Heidelberger Bauchemie*: Combinations of Colours; Replaying *Libertel*	5.229
	(11) *KWS*: Colours; Broader Functionality Considerations	5.238
	(12) *Mag*: Distinctive Character of Shapes of Products	5.248
	(13) *Linde, Winward, and Rado*: Product Shapes; a Broader Perspective	5.282
	(14) *Henkel*: The Assimilation of Packaging and Product Shape	5.301
	(15) *Glaverbel*: The Relevance of Alternatives?	5.315
	(16) The Washing Tablets Cases	5.321
	(17) *SiSi-Werke*: Article 7(1)(b) and Packaging	5.389
	(18) *Eurocermex*: Article 7(1)(b), Three-dimensional Shapes, and the 'Concept' Behind a Product	5.427
	(19) *Storck I*: The Shape of a Sweet	5.444
	(20) *Storck II*: The Distinctive Character of Packaging	5.460
	(21) *Freixenet*: The Frosted Bottles Cases	5.484
	(22) Mouse and Rabbit: Absence of Distinctive Characters for Chocolate in Animal Shapes	5.492
	(23) Louis Vuitton's Lock Device Mark: Absence of Distinctiveness	5.496
	(24) BEST BUY: Absence of Distinctiveness for Device Marks	5.501

D. Article 3(1)(c): Descriptive Signs or Indications ... 5.504
  (1) *Windsurfing Chiemsee*: Geographical Names; Setting the General Principles ... 5.504
  (2) *Baby-Dry*: Composite Words; A Permissive Approach ... 5.532
  (3) *Doublemint*: A More Nuanced Approach ... 5.567
  (4) *Postkantoor*: A Parallel Approach ... 5.595
  (5) *Streamserve*: Consolidating *Doublemint* ... 5.633
  (6) *Telefon & Buch*: Following *Doublemint* ... 5.649
  (7) Recent Case Law on Descriptive Signs and Indications ... 5.659
  (8) *BVBA*: Challenging the Procedural Points of *Postkantoor* ... 5.664
  (9) *Matratzen*: Article 3(1)(c) and Free Movement of Goods Considerations ... 5.699
  (10) *Celltech*: Burden of Proof: Technical and Scientific Terms ... 5.707
  (11) *Develey*: Burden of Proof: Consumer Goods ... 5.715

E. Article 3(1)(d): Signs or Indications that Have Become Customary ... 5.723
  (1) *Bravo*: The Link with the Specification ... 5.723
  (2) *Alcon*: Article 7(1)(d) and Acronyms ... 5.745

F. Article 3(1)(e): Functional Shapes ... 5.759
  (1) *Philips*: The Overriding Scope of Article 3(1)(e) ... 5.759
  (2) *Lego*: Revisiting Functionality ... 5.770
  (3) *Pi-Design*: A Broad Interpretation of Shapes ... 5.796
  (4) *Benetton*: Attractiveness v Distinctiveness ... 5.808
  (5) *Hauck*: The 'Nature' of the Goods; 'Substantive Value' ... 5.819

G. Article 3(1)(g): Trade Marks of a Deceptive Nature ... 5.841
  (1) *Elizabeth Emanuel*: Trade Mark Assignments ... 5.841
  (2) Free Movement of Goods and Deceptive Use ... 5.859

H. Article 3(1)(h): State Emblems ... 5.885
  (1) *Maple Leaf*: Applicability of Article 6ter to Services ... 5.885

I. Article 3(2)(d): Bad Faith ... 5.912
  (1) *Lindt & Sprüngli*: What is Bad Faith? ... 5.915
  (2) *Malaysia Dairy*: The Autonomous Nature of Bad Faith ... 5.932

6. Distinctiveness Acquired Through Use

A. Introduction: The Provisions of the Directive and the Regulation ... 6.01

B. The Test for Assessing Acquired Distinctiveness: *Windsurfing Chiemsee* ... 6.04
  (1) The Opinion of Advocate General Cosmas ... 6.07
  (2) The Judgment of the Court ... 6.13

C. Use as a Mark, and the Monopoly Argument: *Philips* ... 6.25
  (1) The Opinion of Advocate General Ruiz-Jarabo Colomer ... 6.27
  (2) The Judgment of the Court ... 6.28

D. Combined Use: *Nestlé v Mars (Kit Kat)* ... 6.36
  (1) The Opinion of Advocate General Kokott ... 6.39
  (2) The Judgment of the Court ... 6.49

E. Sales Figures: Amount Spent on Advertising; *Storck I* ... 6.50
  (1) The Judgment of the Court of First Instance ... 6.51
  (2) The Opinion of Advocate General Ruiz-Jarabo Colomer ... 6.57
  (3) The Judgment of the Court ... 6.63

F.	Sales Figures and Territorial Scope of Acquired Distinctiveness	6.73
	(1) The Opinion of Advocate General Ruiz-Jarabo Colomer	6.75
	(2) The Judgment of the Court	6.83
G.	Acquired Distinctive Character in the Benelux: Linguistic and Geographical Considerations; *Europolis*	6.90
	(1) The Opinion of Advocate General Sharpston	6.96
	(2) The Judgment of the Court	6.116
H.	The Relevant Point in Time: Filing or Registration Date; *Pure Digital*	6.121
	(1) Background to the Dispute	6.124
	(2) The Judgment of the Court of First Instance	6.127
	(3) The Judgment of the Court of Justice	6.129
I.	Evidence of Acquired Distinctiveness, Territory of Acquired Distinctiveness: *Lindt & Sprüngli*	6.139
J.	Evidence of Acquired Distinctiveness: Surveys Burden of Proof; *Oberbank and Banco Santander*	6.144
	(1) Facts and Questions	6.144
	(2) The Judgment of the Court	6.147
	(3) Some Conclusions	6.156
K.	Concluding on Absolute Grounds	6.163

7. Relative Grounds

A.	Introduction	7.01
B.	The Provisions of the Directive and the Regulation	7.06
	(1) The Trade Marks Directive	7.06
	(2) The Community Trade Mark Regulation	7.07
C.	*LTJ Diffusion*: Establishing Identity	7.08
	(1) The Opinion of Advocate General Jacobs	7.10
	(2) The Judgment of the Court	7.16
D.	Confusion, Similarity, and Distinctiveness	7.20
	(1) *Sabel*: Confusion and Association: Alternative Concepts?	7.21
	(2) *Canon*: Economic Link, the Purpose of Confusion	7.29
	(3) *Lloyd Schuhfabrik*: Properly Substantiated and Genuine Confusion	7.33
	(4) *Marca Mode*: Revisiting *Sabel*; A Positive Finding on Confusion	7.37
	(5) *Lloyd*: The Distinctiveness Factors	7.45
	(6) *Lloyd*: The Average Consumer	7.48
E.	Establishing Confusion: Global Appreciation	7.49
	(1) The Three Tests	7.49
	(2) *Sabel*: The Test for Confusion	7.50
	(3) *Vedial*: Cumulative Similarity/Identity Conditions	7.55
	(4) *Canon*: Global Appreciation against a Wider Context	7.61
	(5) *Sabel*: The Test for Comparing the Marks	7.66
	(6) *Lloyd*: Aural Similarity	7.72
	(7) *Mühlens*: A Challenge to *Lloyd*	7.75
	(8) *Matratzen I*: Similarity between a Figurative and a Word Mark	7.89
	(9) *Formula One*: The Presumption of Distinctiveness	7.100
	(10) *Flexi Air*: Distinctiveness as Part of a Multifactor Assessment	7.114
	(11) *Wesergold*: The Role of Enhanced Distinctiveness in Likelihood of Confusion	7.126

(12) *Ballons d'Or/Golden Balls*: Foreign Equivalents	7.129
(13) *Seven for all mankind*: Distinctiveness of Word Marks	7.134
(14) *Canon*: Comparing the Goods or Services	7.141

F. The Relevant Points in Time — 7.148
  (1) *Levi Strauss*: The Timing of the Assessment — 7.148
  (2) *Génesis*: The Limits of Priority — 7.166

G. Revisiting Global Appreciation — 7.179
  (1) *Picasso/Picaro*: The Limitations of *Arsenal* — 7.182
  (2) *Rossi*: Protection of Surnames; Global Appreciation; the Community Trade Mark Registration Process — 7.198
  (3) *Medion*: The Importance of Dominant Elements — 7.239
  (4) *Barbara Becker, Bimbo Doughnuts*, and *US Polo*: The Application of the *Medion* Principle — 7.250
  (5) *Praktiker*: A Special Case for Retail Services? — 7.271
  (6) *Travatan*: Pharmaceuticals and the Role of Professionals — 7.284
  (7) *Limoncello—Quicky—La Española*: Composite Marks — 7.297
  (8) *Uniweb v Unifonds etc*: Families of Marks — 7.328
  (9) *Armafoam*: Confusion in Part of the Community — 7.332

H. Well-Known and Reputed Trade Marks — 7.346
  (1) *General Motors*: The Factors for Assessing Reputation — 7.346
  (2) *Fincas Tarragona*: Marks Well Known 'in a Member State' — 7.353
  (3) *Pago*: Reputation 'in the Community' — 7.370
  (4) *Davidoff v Gofkid*: The scope of Article 5(2) — 7.403
  (5) *Fitnessworld*: The Interpretive Limits of *Davidoff* — 7.417
  (6) *Adidas v Fitnessworld*: Global Appreciation in the Context of Article 5(2) — 7.426
  (7) *Adidas v Fitnessworld*: Use as a Trade Mark — 7.432
  (8) *Calvin Klein and Ferrero*: Similarity v Reputation — 7.437
  (9) *Intel*: Proof of Dilution: Chasing the Chimera? — 7.458
  (10) *Enviromental Manufacturing*: The Importance of 'Economic Behaviour' — 7.508
  (11) *Bellure*: Unfair Advantage — 7.525
  (12) *Nasdaq*: Putting *Intel* into Perspective? — 7.548
  (13) *Helena Rubinstein*: Unfair Advantage in Practice — 7.560
  (14) The *Red Bull* Trio: Due Cause; Scope of Protection; Confusion and Unfair Advantage; Goods for Export — 7.583
  (15) *Leidseplein Beheer BV v Red Bull GmbH; Red Bull v Bulldog*; The Concept of Due Cause — 7.584
  (16) *Red Bull v Bulldog*: Conceptual Similarity — 7.597

I. Conclusion — 7.603

8. Loss of Rights: Requirement of Use, Conversion to Generic Indication

A. Introduction — 8.01

B. Requirement of Use — 8.04
  (1) Introduction — 8.04
  (2) The Legislative Contexts — 8.06
  (3) The Case Law — 8.12

C. Genuine Use — 8.14
  (1) The Principles: MINIMAX/*Ansul* — 8.14
  (2) Quantity not Relevant: *La Mer* — 8.44

	(3) *Sunrider*: Evidence of Use; the Burden of Proof	8.58
	(4) Minimal Use Again: *Walzertraum*	8.72
	(5) Use with or without Profit Motive: *Radetzky, Silberquelle, Nasdaq*	8.75
D.	The Territory of Use	8.126
	(1) *Leno Merken/ONEL*	8.126
	(2) *Rivella International*: A Variation on the Theme of Use	8.166
E.	Use of the Mark as Registered, Use Together with Another Mark, Use of an Acceptable Variation	8.171
	(1) Registration of a Variation: *Bainbridge*	8.175
	(2) Registration of the Variation not Relevant: *Rintisch v Eder* (PROTI)	8.183
	(3) Combinations of Marks: *Colloseum*	8.190
	(4) Multiple Marks, the Final Chapter? *Specsavers*	8.196
F.	Use of the Mark for the Goods or Services for which it is Registered	8.207
	(1) Introduction	8.207
	(2) The Special Case of Goods Out of Production—*Ansul*	8.208
G.	Use by the Proprietor or with his Consent	8.216
H.	The Grace Period	8.218
	(1) Introduction	8.218
	(2) *Lidl*: Grace Period	8.219
I.	Justification of Non-Use	8.234
	(1) Introduction	8.234
	(2) *Lidl*: Proper Reasons for Non-use	8.236
	(3) Defensive Registrations	8.252
	(4) Conclusions	8.257
J.	Development into a Generic Indication	8.259
	(1) Introduction	8.259
	(2) The Cases	8.260
K.	Conclusion	8.303

9. Scope of Protections, Limitations, and Enforcement

A.	Introduction	9.01
B.	The Provisions of the Directive and the Regulation	9.02
	(1) The Trade Marks Directive	9.02
	(2) The Community Trade Mark Regulation	9.04
	(3) A Clash between Registered Trade Marks and the Concept of 'Third Party': *Fédération Cynologique*	9.08
	(4) The Starting Point: The Trade Mark as Registered? *Specsavers*	9.20
C.	Identical Signs and Goods or Services: The Effect on the Rights of the Trade Mark Proprietor 'Requirement'	9.30
	(1) *Hölterhoff*: Limiting the Scope of Protection	9.31
	(2) *Arsenal*: A Counterbalancing Exercise	9.41
	(3) *Adam Opel*: Challenging the Limits of Protection	9.59
	(4) 'Availability' and Scope of Protection: *Marca II*	9.84
	(5) Expanding the Scope of Protection: Other than the Essential Functions; *Bellure*	9.102
	(6) Use by Intermediaries: The First Stage; *Smirnoff*	9.115

D.	Trade Marks and the Internet: Function Proliferation; Keyword Advertising	9.122
	(1) *Google*: The Relevance of a New Market Context	9.122
	(2) The Issue of Contributory Infringement	9.144
	(3) The Use of Keywords by Advertisers	9.147
	(4) *Eis.de*: Repeating the Google Principles	9.169
	(5) *BergSpechte*: Keywords Similar to Trade Mark; Extending the *Google* Principles	9.170
	(6) *Portakabin*: Keywords Reproducing Misspelt Trade Marks; Original/Reconditioned Goods; Extending the *Google* Principles Further	9.172
	(7) *L'Oréal v eBay*: Keywords and Electronic Market Platforms	9.186
	(8) *Interflora*: A Comprehensive Review	9.222
	(9) *Frisdranken Industrie Winters BV v Red Bull GmbH*: The *Google France* approach in a Non-Internet Environment	9.262
E.	Limitations to Trade Mark Rights	9.272
	(1) *BMW*: Setting the Principles	9.272
	(2) *Gerolsteiner Brunnen*: The Scope of Article 6(1)(b)	9.308
	(3) *Gillette*: Indicating compatibility	9.327
	(4) *Adam Opel*: A Narrow Analysis	9.351
F.	Conflicts Between Trade Marks and Trade Names: Infringement and Defences	9.362
	(1) *Robelco*: Trade Marks and Trade Names	9.362
	(2) *Céline*: Trade Names Performing a Distinguishing Function	9.373
	(3) An Alternative Line of Defence: Acquiescence and Honest Concurrent Use; *Budweiser VI*	9.391
G.	Enforcing the Community Trade Mark	9.409
	(1) Civil enforcement (Title X of the Regulation)	9.414
	(2) Border Measures	9.485
H.	Import, Export, Transit	9.494
	(1) Introduction: The Law, the Issues	9.494
	(2) *Polo/Lauren*: Transit through a Member State from and to a Non-Member State (2000)	9.499
	(3) *Rioglass*: Transit through a Member State as Trade Mark Infringement? (2003)	9.508
	(4) *Rolex* et al.: Transit as Basis for Detention by Customs (2004)	9.513
	(5) *Class*: Customs-Free Zones, Original Goods (2005)	9.521
	(6) *Montex/Diesel*: Transit as Trade Mark Infringement, Again (2006)	9.536
	(7) *Philips* and *Nokia*: Transit and Customs Seizure Once More, the Final Act? (2011)	9.549
	(8) *Blomqvist*: Importing Counterfeit Products through the Mail (2014)	9.574
I.	Conclusion	9.585

10. Parallel Imports

A.	Introduction	10.01
B.	The General Principles	10.02
	(1) The Legislative Framework	10.02
	(2) Duties and Taxes	10.05
	(3) Quantitative Restrictions	10.15

	(4) The Equality Proviso	10.36
	(5) Public Policy Considerations	10.38
	(6) Protection of Health and Life of Humans	10.46
	(7) *Codacons*: Labelling Requirement; The Residual Power of the Free Movement of Goods Rationale	10.50
	(8) *Commission v Ireland*: Hallmarks and Public Interest	10.55
C.	Free Movement of Goods and Intellectual Property	10.57
	(1) The Existence–Exercise Dichotomy	10.61
	(2) The Specific Subject-Matter of the Right	10.65
	(3) 'Independent' Rights	10.67
D.	Free Movement of Goods and Trade Mark Law	10.71
	(1) The Early Days: The Essential Function and the Specific Subject-Matter of Trade Marks	10.71
	(2) Developing the Concept of Consent	10.73
	(3) *Hag-I*: A Restrictive Approach	10.74
	(4) *Terrapin*: Consent and Independent Rights	10.78
	(5) *Merck v Stephar*: Lack of Protection	10.79
	(6) *Pharmon v Hoechst*: Compulsory Licence	10.81
	(7) *Centrafarm v American Home Products*: Changing Direction	10.83
	(8) *Hag II*: The Concept of Consent, The Role and Function of Trade Marks	10.86
	(9) *Ideal Standard*: Voluntary Assignment	10.92
	(10) Repackaging and parallel imports: *Hoffmann-La Roche*; Setting the Principles	10.98
E.	Free Movement of Goods and the New Trade Mark Regime	10.117
	(1) *Bristol Myers Squibb* and the Related Cases: Article 7 of the Directive and the Free Movement of Goods Rules; The Fifth Repackaging Condition	10.117
	(2) *Pharmacia & Upjohn*: Replacing the Trade Mark; The Requirement of Necessity	10.198
	(3) *Boehringer*: Revisiting Repackaging	10.214
	(4) *Ballantine*: Trade Mark Infringement and Policing Channels of Trade	10.229
	(5) *Dior*: Beyond the Origin Function	10.252
	(6) *Silhouette*: The Territorial Scope of Exhaustion	10.274
	(7) *Sebago*: 'Specific' Consent	10.291
	(8) *Davidoff*: 'Clear' Consent	10.297
	(9) *Makro*: Goods put on the Market in the EEA	10.314
	(10) *Peak Holding*: 'Putting Goods on the Market'	10.318
	(11) *Coty*: Offering Testers and Putting Goods on the Market	10.328
	(12) *Boehringer II*: Revisiting Repackaging, Overstickering, and Re-boxing	10.334
	(13) *Orifarm*: Authorization and Repackaging; the Extent of Disclosure I	10.372
	(14) *Wellcome v Paranova*: Is there a Requirement of Minimum Intervention? The Extent of Disclosure II	10.378
	(15) *Martin y Paz*: The Broader Context I; Consent and Acquiescence	10.386
	(16) *Viking Gas*: The Broader Context II: The Market, The Rights of Consumers, The Rights Of Competitors	10.395
F.	Conclusion	10.409

11. Trade Marks and Competition Law

- A. Introduction — 11.01
- B. Competition Rules — 11.06
  - (1) The Provisions of the Treaty — 11.06
  - (2) The Multiple Tasks of European Competition Law — 11.09
  - (3) Direct Applicability — 11.12
- C. Competition and Trade Marks: The Application of Article 101 — 11.13
  - (1) *Consten and Grundig*: The Interaction with Trade Mark Law: The Starting Point — 11.13
  - (2) *Société Technique Minière*: A Rule of Reason Analysis? — 11.26
  - (3) *Völk v Vervaecke*: Significant Effect — 11.28
  - (4) *Béguelin*: The Relevance of Context — 11.31
  - (5) *Delimitis*: A Web of Agreements; Closer to a Rule of Reason Analysis — 11.33
  - (6) *Groupement de Cartes Bancaires*: Object and Effect Revisited — 11.49
  - (7) *Nungesser* and *EMI*: Existence of a Right and the Way the Right is Exercised — 11.53
  - (8) *Pronuptia de Paris*: The Benefits of Franchising Agreements — 11.60
  - (9) *BAT*: Competition and Trade Mark Law; Delimitation Agreements — 11.69
  - (10) The Position of the Commission on Delimitation Agreements — 11.73
  - (11) *Bayer Dental*: The Commission on Repackaging Bans — 11.76
  - (12) *Campari*: An Example of the Application of Article 101(3) TFEU by the Commission — 11.77
  - (13) *Javico*: The Contrast with *Silhouette* — 11.85
- D. Competition and Trade Marks: The Application of Article 102 — 11.98
  - (1) Dominance — 11.98
  - (2) Dominance and Intellectual Property — 11.115
  - (3) *Der Grüne Punkt*: Dominance and Trade Marks; The Function of the Sign — 11.188
- E. Conclusion — 11.215

12. The Interaction with Other Areas of the Law

- A. Introduction — 12.01
- B. Comparative Advertising — 12.02
  - (1) *Toshiba*: The Interplay between Trade Marks and Comparative Advertising — 12.05
  - (2) *Pippig*: The Contradictions of Article 7(2) of Directive 10-025 84/450 — 12.26
  - (3) *Siemens*: Reconfirming the Court's Permissive Approach — 12.43
  - (4) *De Landtsheer Emmanuel*: Designations of Origin; The Competitive Relationship — 12.54
  - (5) *O2*: Use of a Similar Sign; The Indispensability Challenge — 12.66
  - (6) *L'Oreal v Bellure*: Taking a step back? — 12.78
  - (7) *Lidl*: Comparing 'Shopping Baskets'; The Relevance of Information — 12.93
- C. Geographical Indications — 12.100
  - (1) *Feta*: Consumer Confusion and a Misappropriation Rationale — 12.100
  - (2) *Bavaria*: The Coexistence Between Trade Mark and Geographical Indication Protection — 12.117

		(3) *Grana Padano*: Trade Marks v Geographical Indication; The Concept of Genericity	12.134
		(4) *Cognac II*: Geographical Indications as an Absolute Ground for Refusal	12.138
	D.	Trade Marks and Domain Names	12.153
		(1) *Internetportal*: Generic Terms, Trade Marks, Domain Names, and Bad Faith	12.153
	E.	*Budweiser*: A Play in Six Parts	12.161
		(1) Geographical Indications, Bilateral Agreements, and Free Movement of Goods: *Budweiser I*	12.162
		(2) *Budweiser II*: Replaying *Budweiser I*	12.175
		(3) European Trade Mark Law and the TRIPs Agreement Protecting Trade Names: *Budweiser III*	12.194
		(4) BUD as an Appellation of Origin: *Budweiser IV*	12.213
		(5) The European Court of Human Rights: Geographical Indications, Trade Marks, and Property Rights: *Budweiser V*	12.230
		(6) *Budějovický Budvar/Budweiser VI*: A Trade Mark Epilogue	12.247
	F.	Conclusion	12.248

13. The New Trade Mark 'Package'

A.	Introduction	13.01
	(1) Background	13.01
	(2) The Commission Proposals	13.07
	(3) The Outcome: The April 2015 Compromise	13.15
B.	The 'Trade Mark Package' after the April 2015 Compromise	13.18
	(1) Substantive Law	13.19
	(2) Procedures under the Regulation	13.38
	(3) Procedures under the Directive	13.43
	(4) Cooperation	13.45
	(5) OHIM finances	13.46
	(6) OHIM governance	13.48
C.	Outlook	13.52

14. Conclusion

Index	859

TABLE OF CASES

UK CASES

Arsenal Football Club plc v Matthew Reed [2002] EWHC 2695 .... 9.57
Arsenal Football Club plc v Matthew Reed [2003] EWCA Civ 696 .... 9.57–9.58
Boehringer Ingelheim Pharma KG v Swingward Ltd [2003] EWHC 110 (Ch) 10.335
Boehringer Ingelheim Pharma KG v Swingward Ltd [2004] EWCA Civ 757, CA 10.334–10.335
BP Amoco Plc v John Kelly Ltd and Glenshane Tourist Services Ltd [2001] FSR 21 .... 5.206
British Sugar Plc v James Robertson & Sons Ltd [1996] RPC 281 .... 7.145
Dyson Ltd's TM Application [2003] RPC 47 .... 4.28
Elizabeth Emanuel Trade Mark [2004] RPC 15 .... 5.842
*Interflora Inc, Interflora British Unit v Marks and Spencer Plc, Flowers Direct
   Online Limited* [2009] EWHC 1095 (Ch) 9.222, 9.260
*Interflora Inc, Interflora British Unit v Marks and Spencer Plc, Flowers Direct
   Online Limited* [2010] EWHC 925 (Ch) 9.225–9.226
*Interflora Inc, Interflora British Unit v Marks and Spencer Plc, Flowers Direct
   Online Limited* [2013] EWCA Civ 510 .... 9.260
*Interflora Inc, Interflora British Unit v Marks and Spencer Plc, Flowers Direct
   Online Limited* [2013] EWHC 270 (Ch) 9.260
*Interflora Inc, Interflora British Unit v Marks and Spencer Plc, Flowers Direct
   Online Limited* [2013] EWHC 273 (Ch) 9.260
*Interflora Inc, Interflora British Unit v Marks and Spencer Plc, Flowers Direct
   Online Limited* [2013] EWHC 936 (Ch) 9.260
*Interflora Inc, Interflora British Unit v Marks and Spencer Plc, Flowers Direct
   Online Limited* [2013] EWHC 1484 (Ch) 9.260
*Interflora Inc, Interflora British Unit v Marks and Spencer Plc, Flowers Direct
   Online Limited* [2013] EWHC 1683 (Ch) 9.260
*Interflora Inc, Interflora British Unit v Marks and Spencer Plc, Flowers Direct
   Online Limited* [2013] EWHC 2191 (Ch) 9.260
*Interflora Inc, Interflora British Unit v Marks and Spencer Plc, Flowers Direct
   Online Limited* [2014] EWCA Civ 1403 .... 9.260, 9.261
*Interflora Inc (a company incorporated under the laws of the State of Michigan,
   United States of America), Interflora British Unit v Marks and Spencer plc,
   Flowers Direct Online Limited* [2012] EWHC 1722 (Ch) 9.260
John Lewis of Hungerford Ltd's Trade Mark Application [2001] RPC 28 .... 4.88
Joseph Crosfield & Son Ltd's Application ('Perfection') [1910] 1 Ch 130 .... 5.848
*Marks and Spencer Plc v Interflora Inc (A company incorporated under the laws
   of the State of Michigan, USA), Interflora British Unit* [2012] EWCA Civ 1501 .... 9.260
Philips Electronics NV v Remington Consumer Products Ltd [1998] RPC 283 .... 4.15
Philips Electronics NV v Remington Consumer Products Ltd [1999] RPC 809;
   [1999] ETMR 816 .... 4.156
Wagamama Ltd v City Centre Restaurants Plc [1995] FSR 713 .... 7.26
Zino Davidoff SA v A&G Imports Ltd (No 1) [1999] 2 CMLR 1056 .... 10.297
Zino Davidoff SA v A&G Imports Ltd (No 2) [2000] 2 CMLR 750 .... 10.297, 10.302

OTHER NATIONAL/SUPRANATIONAL CASES

Benelux

Turmac v Reynolds, Case A-80/1 [1981] ECC 346 .... 8.17
Vlaamse Toeristenbond, Case A-2002/2, Judgment of the Benelux court of
   15 December 2003 .... 5.666

France

Baccara C. A de Nancy, PIBD 1980, III, 227 .... 5.521
Cass Commerc, PIBD 1982, No 312, III, 238 .... 5.521
L'Oréal SA v Bellure NV [2006] ECDR 16 C d'A (Paris) 4.88

Germany

'Black/yellow colour mark,' German Federal Court of Justice, 10 December 1998 [1999]
    IIC 809 .... 4.149
Mülhens GmbH & Co KG v Zirh International Corp [2005] ETMR 55 .... 7.83

Netherlands

Marca Mode CV v Adidas AG & Adidas BV [1999] ETMR 791 HR (NL) 7.37–7.38

Sweden

Koninklijke Philips Electronics NV v Rotary Shaver Sweden AB [2005] ETMR 103 HR
    (Stockholm) 4.156

United States

In re Clarke, 17 USPQ 2d 1238 (TTAB 1990) 4.88
Qualitex Co v Jacobson Products Co, 514 US 159 (1995); Registration no 1633711 .... 5.207

EU CASES

Court of Justice of the European Union (CJEU) (arranged by case number)

C-2/62, *Commission v Belgium* [1962] ECR 425 .... 10.05, 10.07
C-28/62, C-29/62, and C-30/62, *Da Costa en Schaake NV, Jacob Meijer NV and
    Hoechst-Holland NV v Nederlandse Belastingadministrotie* [1963] ECR 31 .... 3.17
C-31 and C-33/62, *Milchwerke Heinz Wöhrmann & Sohn KG and Alfons Lütticke
    GmbH v Commission* [1962] ECR 501 .... 3.10
C-6/64, *Costa v Ente Nazionale per l'Energia Elettrica (ENEL)* [1964] ECR 585 .... 3.16
C-56 and C-58/64, *Etablissements Consten SARL and Grundig Verkaufs-GmbH v
    Commission* [1966] ECR 299 .... 9.143, 11.13–11.25, 11.59,
                                                                                                                      11.67, 11.90, 11.93
C-161/64, *Pronuptia de Paris GmbH v Pronuptia de Paris Irmgard Schillgallis* [1986]
    ECR 353 .... 11.60–11.68
C-32/65, *Italy v Commission* [1966] ECR 389 .... 3.09
C-56/65, *Société Technique Minière v Maschinenbau Ulm GmbH* [1965]
    ECR/IBT 235 .... 11.26–11.27, 11.44, 11.90, 11.93
C-19/67, *Bestuur der Sociale Verzekeringsbank v JH van der Vecht* [1967] ECR 345 ...... 7.586, 8.278
C-23/67, *Brasserie de Haecht v Wilkin* [1967] ECR 407 .... 11.35, 11.90
C-24/67, *Parke, Davis and Co v Probel, Reese, Beintema-Interpharm and Centrafarm*
    [1968] ECR 55 .... 11.115–11.117
C-10 and 18/68, *Società 'Eridania' Zuccherifici Nazwnali v Commission*
    [1969] ECR 459 .... 3.08
C-24/68, *Commission v Italy* [1969] ECR 193 .... 10.05
C-5/69, *Völk v Etablissements J Vervaecke SPRL* [1969] ECR 295 .... 11.28–11.30, 11.90, 11.94
C-29/69, *Stauder v City of Ulm* [1969] ECR 419 .... 12.157
C-43/69, *Bilger v Jehle* [1970] ECR 127 .... 11.37
C-40/70, *Sirena SRL v Eda SRL* [1971] ECR 69 .... 10.66
C-78/70, *Deutsche Grammophon v Metro* [1971] ECR 487 ...... 10.61–10.64, 10.67, 10.133, 10.304
C-22/71, *Béguelin Import Co v GL Import-Export SA* [1971] ECR 949 .... 11.31–11.32
C-6/72, *Europemballage Corp and Continental Can Co Inc v Commission* [1973]
    ECR 215 .... 11.100–11.105
C-2/73, *Geddo v Ente Nazionale Risi* [1973] ECR 865 .... 10.16

Table of Cases

C-6 and C-7/73, *Instituto Chemioterapico Italiano SpA and Commercial Solvents Corp v Commission* [1974] ECR 223 .... 11.179
C-34/73, *Fratelli Variola SpA v Amministrazione delle finanze dello Stato* [1973] ECR 981 .... 12.143
C-127/73, *Belgische Radio en Televisie v SV SABAM and NV Fonior* [1974] ECR 51 .... 11.12, 11.45
C-192/73, *Van Zuylen Freres v Hag AG (Hag I)* [1974] ECR 731 .... 10.73–10.77, 10.86–10.90
C-8/74, *Procureur du Roi v Dassonville* [1974] ECR 837 .... 5.862, 5.875, 5.880, 10.16–10.17, 10.103
C-15/74, *Centrafarm BV v Sterling Drug Inc* [1974] ECR 1147 .... 10.65–10.66, 10.72
C-16/74, *Centrafarm BV and Adriaan de Peijper v Winthrop BV* [1974] ECR 1183 .... 9.511, 10.71–10.72, 10.79
C-41/74, *Van Duyn v Home Office* [1974] ECR 1337 .... 10.69
C-51/75, *EMI Records Ltd v CBS UK Ltd* [1976] ECR 811 .... 10.284, 11.55, 11.118
C-119/75, *Terrapin (Overseas) Ltd v Terranova Industrie CA Kapferer & Co* [1976] ECR 1039; [1967] 2 CMLR 482 .... 10.68–10.70, 10.78, 10.87–10.88
C-27/76, *United Brands Co and United Brands Continental BV v Commission* [1978] ECR 207 .... 11.09, 11.98, 11.106–11.108, 11.179
C-53/76, *Procureur de la Republique Besanon v Bouhelier* [1977] ECR 197 .... 10.21
C-19/77, *Miller International Schallplatten GmbH v Commission* [1978] ECR 131 .... 11.93
C-28/77, *TEPEA BV v Commission* [1978] ECR 139 .... 11.56
C-30/77, *R v Bouchereau* [1977] ECR 1999 .... 7.586
C-102/77, *Hoffmann-la Roche & Co AG and Hoffmann-la Roche AG v Centrafarm Vertriebsgesellschaft Pharmazeutischer Erzeugnisse mbH* [1978] ECR 1139 ...... 5.53, 5.418, 7.51, 9.53, 9.315, 9.511, 10.98–10.116, 10.120, 10.133, 10.145, 10.148, 10.178, 10.184, 10.187, 10.201, 10.234, 10.238, 10.342, 10.347–10.348, 10.354
C-3/78, *Centrafarm BV v American Home Products Corp* [1978] ECR 1823 .... 10.83–10.85, 10.134, 10.157, 10.199, 10.201–10.202, 10.211
C-22/78, *Hugin Kassaregister AB and Hugin Cash Registers Ltd v Commission* [1979] ECR 1869 .... 11.109–11.111, 11.120, 11.124
C-92/78, *Simmenthal SpA v Commission* [1979] ECR 777 .... 3.11
C-120/78, *Rewe-Zentral AG v Bundesmonopolverwaltung für Branntwein (Cassis de Dijon)* [1979] ECR 649 .... 5.863, 5.880, 10.30–10.32, 10.35, 10.56
C-152/78, *Commission v France (Adevertising of Alcoholic Beverages)* [1980] ECR 2299 .... 10.46
C-167/78, *Commission v France* [1980] ECR 347 .... 10.08–10.09
C-170/78, *Commission v United Kingdom* [1983] ECR 2265 .... 10.10–10.13
C-258/78, *LC Nungesser KG and Kurt Eisele v Commission* [1985] ECR 2015 .... 11.53–11.59
C-34/79, *R v Henn and Darby* [1979] ECR 3795 .... 10.38–10.39
C-99/79, *Lancôme and Cosparfrance Nederland BV v Etos BV* [1980] ECR I-2511 .... 11.94
C-31/80, *NV L'Oreal and SA L'Oreal v PVBA De Nieuwe AMCK* [1980] ECR 3775 .... 11.112
C-55 and C-57/80, *Musik-Vertrieb Membran v GEMA* [1981] ECR 147 .... 10.266, 10.273
C-66/80, *International Chemical Corp v Amministrozione delle Finanze della Staw* [1981] ECR 1191 .... 3.17–3.18
C-100 to C-110/80, *Musique Diffusion Française v Commission* [1983] ECR 1825 .... 11.94
C-113/80, *Commission v Ireland (Irish Souvenirs)* [1981] ECR 1625 .... 10.25–10.28, 10.40
C-187/80, *Merck v Stephar* [1981] ECR 2063 .... 10.79–10.80
C-212 to C-217/80, *Amministrazione delle Finanze dello Stato v Salumi* [1981] ECR 2735 .... 9.277
C-270/80, *Polydor Ltd v Harlequin Record Shops Ltd* [1982] ECR 329 .... 10.285
C-1/81, *Pfizer Inc v Eurim-Pharm GmbH* [1981] ECR 2913 .... 10.133, 10.138, 10.190
C-144/81, *Keurkoop v Nancy Kean Gifts* [1982] ECR 2853 .... 10.304, 11.121
C-220/81, *Robertson* [1982] ECR 2349 .... 10.56
C-249/81, *Commission v Ireland* [1982] ECR 4005 .... 10.22–10.23
C-266/81, *SIOT v Ministero delle Finanze* [1983] ECR 731 .... 9.510
C-283/81, *Srl CILFIT and Lanijicio di Gavardo SpA v Ministry of Health* [1982] ECR 3415 .... 3.17, 8.266

Table of Cases

C-86/82, *Hasselblad (GB) Ltd v Commission* [1984] ECR I-883 .... 11.93
C-174/82, *Sandoz* [1983] ECR 2445 .... 10.149
C-190/82, *Adam PH Blomefield v Commission* [1983] ECR I-3981 .... 3.107
C-222/82, *Apple and Pear Development Council v KJ Lewis Ltd* [1983] ECR 4083 .... 10.24
C-343/82, *Christos Michael v Commission* [1983] ECR 4023 .... 3.107
C-14/83, *Von Colson and Kamann v Land Nordhein-Westfalen* [1984] ECR 1891 .... 7.425
C-29 and C-30/83, *Compagnie Royale Asturienne des Mines SA and*
  Rheinzink GmbH v Commission [1984] ECR 1679 .... 11.90
C-35/83, *BAT Cigaretten-Fabriken GmbH v Commission of the European Communities*
  [1985] ECR 363 .... 11.69–11.72
C-72/83, *Campus Oil Ltd Minister for Industry and Energy* [1984] ECR 2727 .... 10.44–10.45
C-72/83, *Campus Oil Ltd v Minister for Industry and Energy* [1984] ECR 2727 .... 10.21
C-79/83, *Dorit Harz v Deutsche Tradax GmbH* [1984] ECR 1921 .... 7.425
C-117/83, *Theodor Kohl KG v Ringelhan & Rennet SA and Ringelhan*
  Einrichtungs GmBH [1984] ECR 3651 .... 10.29
C-170/83, *Hydrotherm Gerätebau GmbH v Compact del Dott. Ing. Mario*
  Andreoli & C. Sas. [1984] ECR 2999 .... 11.88
C-188/83, *Witte v Parliament* [1984] ECR 3465 .... 5.38
C-207/83, *Commission v United Kingdom* [1985] ECR 1201 .... 10.24, 10.26
C-229/83, *Leclerc v Au Blé Vert* [1985] ECR 1 .... 10.41
C-231/83, *Cullet v Centre Leclerc* [1985] ECR 305 .... 10.42–10.43
C-246/83, *Claudia de Angelis v Commission* [1986] ECR 1253 .... 3.107
C-294/83, *Les Verts v European Parliament* [1986] ECR I-1339 .... 3.106
C-19/84, *Pharmon BV v Hoechst AG* [1985] ECR 2281 .... 10.81–10.82
C-112/84, *Humblot v Directeur des Services Fiscaux* [1985] ECR 1367 .... 10.07
C-134/84, *Williams v Court of Auditors* [1985] ECR 2225 .... 5.38
C-152/84, *Marshall v Southampton and South-West Hampshire Area Health*
  Authority [1986] ECR 723 .... 9.277
C-232/84, *MPA Pharma GmbH v Rhone-Poulenc Pharma GmbH* [1996]
  ECR I-3671 .... 10.131
C-243/84, *John Walker v Ministeriet for Skatter og Afgifter* [1986] ECR 875 .... 10.14
C-121/85, *Conegate v Commissioners of Customs and Excise* [1986] ECR 1007 .... 10.39
C-184/85, *Commission v Italy* [1987] ECR 2013 .... 10.14
C-355/85, *Ministère Public v Cognet* [1986] ECR 3231 .... 10.19
C-62/86, *AKZO Chemie BV v Commission* [1991] ECR I-3359 .... 11.112–11.114
C-158/86, *Warner Brothers Inc and Metronome Video ApS v Erik Viuff Chrislianse*
  [1988] ECR 2605 .... 10.273
C-222/86, *Heylens* [1987] ECR 4097 .... 5.671, 5.690
C-286/86, *Ministere Public v Deserbais* [1988] ECR 4907 .... 11.137
C-53/87, *Consorzio Italiano della Componentistica di Ricambio per Autoveicoli*
  and Maxicar v Regio Nationale des Usines Renault [1988] ECR 6039 .... 11.125–11.126
C-238/87, *AB Volvo v Eric Veng (UK) Ltd* [1988] ECR 6211 .... 11.119–11.124, 11.150, 11.160
C-279/87, *Tipp-Ex GmbH & Co KG v Commission* [1990] ECR I-261 .... 11.93
C-302/87, *European Parliament v Council* [1988] ECR 5615 .... 3.08
C-382/87, *Buet v Ministère Public* [1989] ECR 1235 .... 5.867
C-2/88 Imm, *J.J. Zwartfeld and others* [1990] ECR I-3365 .... 11.48
C-21/88, *Du Pont de Nemours Italiana SPA v Unita Sanitaria Locale No.2*
  Di Carrara [1990] ECR I-889 .... 10.21
C-41/88, *Mathilde Becker and Josyane Starquit v Parliament* [1989] ECR 3807 .... 3.107
C-125/88, *Nijman* [1989] ECR 3533 .... 12.171
C-150/88, *Parfümerie-Fabrik 4711 v Provide* [1989] ECR 3891 .... 5.867
C-320/88, *Staatssecretaris van Financiën v Shipping and Forwarding Enterprise*
  SAFE BV [1990] 7.36, 8.43
C-10/89, *SA CNL-SUCAL NV v Hag GF AG (Hag II)* [1990] ECR I-3711 .... 4.50, 4.84, 5.726,
                                                    5.732, 5.846, 7.51, 9.300, 9.511, 10.73,
                                                      10.86–10.91, 10.96, 10.135

Table of Cases

C-106/89, *Marleasing SA v La Comercial Internacional de Alimentacion SA*
  [1990] ECR I-4135; [1992] 1 CMLR 305 . . . . 8.278, 9.219, 9.276, 9.291, 9.518, 10.290
C-231/89, *Stergios Delimitis v Henninger Bräu AG* [1991] ECR I-935 . . . . 10.286
C-234/89, *Stergios Delimitis v Henninger Bräu AG* [1991]
  ECR I-935 . . . . 11.04, 11.33–11.48, 11.88, 11.90, 11.92
C-238/89, *Pall Corp v PJ Dahlhausen & Co* [1990]
  ECR I-4827 . . . . 3.111, 5.860–5.865, 5.867, 5.870, 5.880
C-358/89, *Extramet Industrie SA v Council* [1991] ECR I-2501 . . . . 3.15
C-367/89, *Richardt and Les Accessoires Scientifiques* [1991] ECR I-4621 . . . . 9.510
C-2/90, *Commission v Belgium* [1992] ECR I-4431 . . . . 10.20
C-47/90, *Parfümerie-Fabrik 4711 v Provide* [1989] ECR 3891 . . . . 5.867
C-3/91, *Exportur v LOR and Confiserie du Tech* [1992] ECR I-5529 . . . . 12.167, 12.172
C-121/91 and C-122/91, *Ct Control and Jct Benelux v Commission* [1993]
  ECR I-3873 . . . . 9.277
C-126/91, *Schutzverband gegen Unwesen in der Wirtschaft v Yves Rocher*
  [1993] ECR I-2361 . . . . 5.880
C-195/91, *Bayer AG v Commission* [1994] ECR I-5619 . . . . 11.75
C-241/91 and C-242/91 P, *Radio Telefis Eireann (RTE) and Independent Television
  Publications Ltd (ITP) v Commission (Magill)* [1995] ECR I-808 . . . . 11.129–11.137,
    11.141, 11.145, 11.150, 11.162–11.163
C-267/91 and C-268/91, *Keck and Mithouard* [1993] ECR I-6097 . . . . 5.875, 10.33–10.35
C-280/91, *Finanzamt Kassel-Goethestrasse v Viessmann KG* [1993] ECR I-971 . . . . 4.134
C-317/91, *Deutsche Renault AG v AUDI AG* [1993] ECR I-6227 . . . . 10.93
C-37/92, *Vanacker and Lesage* [1993] ECR I-4947 . . . . 12.166
C-53/92 P, *Hilti v Commission* [1994] ECR 667 . . . . 5.450, 7.81, 11.127–11.128
C-91/92, *Faccini Dori v Recreb Srl* [1994] ECR I-3325 . . . . 9.277, 9.291
C-127/92, *Enderby v Frenchay Health Authority and the Secretary of State
  for Health* [1993] ECR I-5535 . . . . 5.677
C-152/92, *Faccini Dori v Recreb Srl* [1994] ECR I-3325 . . . . 9.277
C-250/92, *Gøttrup-Klim Grovvareforeninger v Dansk Landbrugs Grovvareselskab
  AmbA (DLG)* [1994] I-5641 . . . . 11.88, 11.181
C-136/92 P, *Commission v Brazzelli Lualdi* [1994] ECR I-1981 . . . . 5.361
C-199/92 P, *Hills v Commission* [1999] ECR I-4287 . . . . 5.757
C-315/92, *Verband Sozialer Wettbewerb eV v Clinique Laboratoires SNC et Estée
  Lauder Cosmetics GmbH* [1994] ECR I-317 . . . . 5.866–5.871, 5.879
C-393/92, *Gemeente Almelo v NV Energiebedrijf Ijsselmij* [1994] ECR I-1477 . . . . 11.95
C-9/93, *HT Internationale Heiztechnik GmbH and Uwe Danzinger v Ideal
  Standard GmbH and Wabco Standard GmbH* [1994] ECR I-2789 . . . . 7.51, 7.336,
    10.92–10.97, 10.133, 10.316
C-69/93, *Punto Casa SpA v Sindaco Del Commune di Capena* [1994] ECR I-2355 . . . . 10.36
C-70/93, *Bayerische Motorenwerke AG v ALD Auto-Leasing D GmbH* [1995]
  ECR I-3439 . . . . 11.93, 11.97
C-266/93, *Bundeskartellamt v Volkswagen AG and VAG Leasing GmbH* [1995]
  ECR I-3477 . . . . 11.92
C-293/93, *Houtwipper* [1994] ECR I-4249 . . . . 10.56
C-415/93, *Union Royale Belge des Societes de Football Association ASBL v Jean-Marc
  Bosman* [1995] ECR I-4921 . . . . 4.122
C-427, C-429 and C-436/93, *Bristol Myers Squibb v Paranova A/S, CH Boehringer Sohn,
  Boehringer Ingelheim KG and Boehringer Ingelheim A/S v Paranova A/S,* and *Bayer
  Aktiengesellschaft and Bayer Danmark A/S v Paranova A/S* [1996] ECR I-3457 . . . . . 10.117–10.124,
    10.150–10.153, 10.160–10.163, 10.168–10.193, 10.194, 10.200–10.201,
    10.203, 10.210, 10.218, 10.224–10.225, 10.228, 10.235–10.236,
    10.238, 10.240, 10.242, 10.245, 10.250, 10.257–10.260, 10.272,
    10.335, 10.340, 10.342, 10.350, 10.353–10.355, 10.374, 10.382–10.383
C-470/93, *Verein gegen Unwesen in Handel und Gewerbe Köln eV v Mars GmbH*
  [1995] ECR I-1923 . . . . 5.872–5.877, 5.880

C-71 to C-73/94, *Eurim-Pharm Arzneimiltel GmbH v Beiersdorf AG, Boehringer Ingelheim KG,* and *Farmitalia Carlo Erba GmbH* [1996] ECR 1-3603 ... 5.314, 10.125–10.130, 10.145, 10.154–10.157, 10.164–10.166, 10.178, 10.194–10.196
C-122/94, *Commission v Council* [1996] ECR I-881.................................. 12.124
C-232/94, *MPA Pharma GmbH v Rhône-Poulenc Pharma GmbH* [1996] ECR I-3671 .... 10.145, 10.158, 10.167, 10.178, 10.197
C-313/94, *Fratelli Graffione SNC v Ditta Fronsa (COTONELLE)* [1996] ECR I-6039.. 5.704, 5.878–5.884
C-321/94 and C-324/94, *Pistre v France* [1997] ECR I-2343 .... 12.172
C-74 and C-129/95, *X* [1996] ECR I-6609..9.518
C-168/95, *Arcaro* [1996] ECR I-4705..9.518
C-219/95 P, *Ferriere Nord SpA v Commission* [1997] ECR I-4411 .... 8.278, 11.88
C-249/95, *SAM Schiffahrt et Stapf v Germany* [1997] ECR I-4475 .... 7.228
C-251/95, *Sabel BV v Puma AG, Rudolf Dassler Sport* [1997] ECR I-6191 .... 5.386, 5.514, 7.13, 7.21–7.28, 7.35, 7.37–7.39, 7.43–7.44, 7.50–7.54, 7.62, 7.66–7.71, 7.73, 7.122, 7.152, 7.215, 7.403, 7.406, 7.412, 7.417, 7.427, 7.431, 8.265, 9.21, 9.284, 9.340
C-267 and C-268/95, *Merck & Co Ltd v Primecrown Ltd* [1996] ECR I-6285 .... 10.79, 10.306
C-317/95, *Canadane Cheese Trading AMBA and Adelfi G Kouri Anonymos Emoriki Kai Viomichaniki Etaireia v Hellenic Republic* [1997] ECR I-4681 .... 12.107–12.108
C-337/95, *Parfums Christian Dior SA* [1997] ECR I-6013 .... 5.846, 9.181, 9.282, 9.299, 10.252–10.273, 10.308, 10.348, 10.350, 10.352, 10.410
C-349/95, *Frits Loendersloot v George Ballantine & Son* [1997] ECR I-6227 ...... 4.95, 4.163, 5.726, 5.740, 7.157, 9.53, 9.184, 9.291, 9.511, 10.90, 10.116, 10.203, 10.229–10.251, 10.337, 10.342, 10.346, 10.380, 10.385
C-352/95, *Phytheron International SA v Jean Bardon SA* [1997] ECR I-1729 37 .... 10.342
C-4/96, *NIFPO and Northern Ireland Fishermen's Federation* (C-4/96) [1998] ECR I-681.. 12.124
C-53/96, *Hermès v FHT Marketing Choice BV* [1998] ECR I-3603 and C-49/02 *Heidelberger Bauchemie GmbH* [2004] ECR I-6129........................... 4.48, 10.281
C-200/96, *Metronome Musik GmbH* [1998] ECR I-1953 .... 10.303
C-210/96, *Gut Springenheide and Tusky* [1998] ECR I-4657................. 5.261, 5.310, 5.847, 6.32, 7.48, 12.178, 12.187
C-261/96, *Conserchimica v Amministrazione delle Finanze dello Stato* [1997] ECR I-6177 ..... 9.277
C-289/96, *Kingdom of Denmark,* C-293/96, *Federal Republic of Germany,* and C-299/96, *French Republic v Commission* [1999] ECR I-1541 .... 12.104, 12.136
C-306/96, *Javico International and Javico AG v Yves Saint Laurent Parfums SA* [1998] ECR I-1983..10.284, 11.85–11.97
C-355/96, *Silhouette International Schmied GmbH & Co KG v Hartlauer Handelsgesellschaft mbH* [1998] ECR I-4799 .... 10.274–10.290, 10.301, 10.340
C-416/96, *Nour Eddine El-Yassini v Secretary of State for Home Department* [1999] ECR I-1209... 5.853
C-2/97, *Mag Instrument Inc v California Trading Co Norway, Ulsteen* [1998] 1 CMLR 331 EFTA.. 10.280
C-7/97, *Oscar Bronner GmbH & Co KG v Mediaprint Zeitungs- und Zeitschriftenverlag GmbH & Co KG, Mediaprint Zeitungsvertriebsgesellschaft mbH* [1998] ECR I-7791 ....11.141–11.146
C-37/97, *Bayerische Motorenwerke* [1999] ECR I-905................................... 4.95
C-39/97, *Canon Kabushiki Kaisha v Metro-Goldwyn-Mayer Inc.* [1998] ECR I-5507 .... 4.95, 4.143, 5.220, 5.740, 7.29–7.32, 7.44, 7.61–7.65, 7.116, 7.122, 7.141–7.147, 7.205, 7.407, 7.412, 7.431, 7.601, 9.23, 9.284
C-61/97, *FDV v Laserdisken* [1998] ECR I-5171 ....9.511
C-63/97, *Bayerische Motorenwerke AG and BMW Nederland BV v Deenik* [1999] ECR I-905 .... 4.50, 5.726, 9.35, 9.63, 9.76, 9.181, 9.185, 9.272–9.307, 9.317, 9.319, 9.324, 9.335–9.336, 9.339, 9.343, 9.375, 9.380, 10.252, 10.350, 10.352, 10.410, 12.20

C-67/97, *Ditle v Bluhme* [1998] ECR I-8033 .... 10.20
C-87/97, *Consorzio per la tutela del formaggio Gorgonzola v Kaserei Champignon
    Hofmeister and Eduard Bracharz* [1999] ECR I-1301 ..... 5.852, 12.122, 12.147, 12.167, 12.181
C-90/97, *Robin Swaddling v Adjudication Officer* [1999] ECR I-1075 .... 4.134
C-108/97 and C-109/97, *Windsurfing Chiemsee Produktions- und Vertriebs
    GmbH v Boots- und Segelzubehör Walter Huber and Franz Attenberger* [1999]
    ECR I-2779 .... 4.41, 4.84, 4.160, 4.165, 4.171, 5.04, 5.06, 5.54, 5.66, 5.154, 5.224, 5.298,
                    5.375, 5.504–5.531, 5.547, 5.603, 5.605, 5.607, 5.621, 5.658, 5.659, 5.821,
                    6.04–6.24, 6.30, 6.47, 6.78–6.79, 6.83, 6.100–6.102, 6.118, 6.149–6.150,
                                          7.47, 8.272, 8.274, 9.87, 9.316, 9.359, 12.178
C-129/97 and C-130/97, *Chiciak and Fol* [1998] ECR I-3315 .... 12.181
C-158/97, *Coote v Granada Hospitality Ltd* [1998] ECR I-5199 .... 7.425
C-262/97, *Rijksdienst voor Pensioenen v Engelbrecht* [2000] ECR I-7321 .... 9.518
C-265/97, *VBA v Florinex* [2000] ECR I-2061 .... 5.175
C-270/97 and C-271/97, *Deutsche Post AG v Elisabeth Sievers* and *Brunhilde Schrage*
    [2000] ECR I-929 .... 4.162
C-303/97, *Verbraucherschutzverein eV v Sektkellerei GC Kessler GmbH und Co*
    [1999] ECR I-513 .... 5.310
C-342/97, *Lloyd Schuhfabrik* [1999] ECR I-3819 .... 5.155, 5.222, 5.261, 5.310, 5.386, 7.13,
                    7.19, 7.33–7.36, 7.45–7.48, 7.72–7.74, 7.79–7.80, 7.83, 7.85–7.86,
                                          7.122, 7.187, 7.284, 7.427, 8.265, 12.21
C-350/97, *Wilfried Monsees v Unabhängiger Verwaltungssenat für Kärnten*
    [1999] ECR I-2921 .... 9.510
C-375/97, *General Motors Corporation v Yplon SA* (CHEVY) [1999]
    ECR I-05421 .... 6.16, 6.107, 6.116, 7.346–7.352, 7.354, 7.357, 7.367, 7.375, 7.381,
                              7.390, 7.406, 7.428, 7.458, 7.462, 7.484, 7.485, 7.489
C-379/97, *Pharmacia & Upjohn v Paranova A/S* [1997] ECR I-0013 .... 10.198–10.213, 10.348, 10.364
C-17/98, *Emesa Sugar (Free Zone) NV v Aruba* [2000] ECR I-665 .... 5.852
C-84/98, *Commission v Portugal* [2000] ECR I-5215 .... 12.174
C-101/98, *Union Deutsche Lebensmittelwerke GmbH v Schutzverband gegen
    Unwesen in der Wirtschaft eV* [1999] ECR I-8841 .... 10.54
C-117/98, *Comar Srl and Tico Sri v Commission* [2000] ECR I-2193 .... 3.08
C-173/98, *Sebago Inc and Ancienne Maison Dubois & Fils SA v G-B Unie SA*
    [1999] ECR I-4103 .... 10.291–10.296, 10.301, 10.393
C-220/98, *Estée Lauder Cosmetics GmbH & Co OHG v Lancaster Group GmbH*
    [2000] ECR I-117 .... 5.262, 5.310, 12.41, 12.178
C-223/98, *Adidas AG* [1999] ECR I-7081 .... 9.569
C-230/98, *Amministrazione delle Finanze dello Stato v Schiavon* [2000]
    ECR I-3547 .... 5.702
C-287/98, *Luxembourg v Linster* [2000] ECR I-6917 .... 8.34
C-300/98, *Parfums Christian Dior SA v Tuk Consultancy BV* and C-392/98
    *Asseo Geruste GmbH and Rob van Dijk v Wilhelm Layher GmbH & Co KG and
    Layher BV* [2000] ECR I-11307 .... 12.196, 12.199, 12.203, 12.204
C-312/98, *Schutzverband gegen Unwesen In der Wirtschaft eV v Warsteiner Brauerei
    Haus Cramer GmbH & Co KG* [2000] ECR I-9187 .... 12.118, 12.166, 12.170, 12.180, 12.181
C-344/98, *HB Ice Cream Ltd v Masterfoods* [2000] ECR I-11369 .... 11.04
C-352/98, *Laboratoires Pharmaceutiques Bergaderm and Goupil v Commission* [2000]
    ECR I-5291 .... 5.442
C-383/98, *The Polo/Lauren Company v PT Dwidua Langgeng Pratama International
    Freight Forwarders*, ECLI:EU:C:1999:624 .... 9.499–9.507, 9.514, 9.520, 9.539,
                                                          9.542–9.543, 9.548–9.549
C-405/98, *Konsumentombudsmannen v Gourmet International Products*
    [2001] ECR I-1795 .... 10.37, 10.47–10.48
C-425/98, *Marca Mode CV v Adidas AG & Adidas BV* [2000]
    ECR I-4861 .... 3.05, 7.37–7.44, 7.411, 7.427, 7.482, 9.84
C-448/98, *Guimont* [2000] ECR I-10063 .... 12.136, 12.165, 12.171

C-23/99, *Commission v France* [2000] ECR I-7653......................... 9.509, 9.511, 9.561
C-30/99, *Commission v Ireland* [2001] ECR I-4619 .... 5.310, 10.55
C-89/99, *Sehieving-Nijstad VF v Groenveld* [2001] ECR I-5851 .... 12.196, 12.197, 12.203
C-112/99, *Toshiba Europe GmbH v Katun Germany GmbH* [2001]
    ECR I-7945 .... 9.340, 12.05–12.25, 12.35, 12.36, 12.38, 12.47, 12.56, 12.70
C-120/99, *Kik v OHIM* [2003] ECR II-8283 .... 2.35
C-191/99, *Kvaerner plc v Staatssecretaris van Financien* [2001] ECR I-447 .... 4.137
C-193/99, *OHIM v WM Wrigley Jr Co (Doublemint)* [2001] ECR II-417 .... 5.553, 5.567–5.570
C-194/99 P, *Thyssen Stahl v Commission* [2003] ECR I-10821........................... 5.273
C-269/99, *Carl Kühne* [2001] ECR I-9517 .... 12.136
C-280/99 to C-282/99, *Moccia Irme v Commission* [2001] ECR I-4717 .... 5.32
C-299/99, *Koninklijke Philips Electronics NV v Remington Consumer Products Ltd*
    [2002] ECR I-5475 .... 4.21–4.23, 4.43, 4.95, 4.156–4.175, 5.41, 5.53, 5.140, 5.154, 5.157,
                5.204, 5.261, 5.287, 5.289, 5.291, 5.310, 5.418, 5.451, 5.606, 5.627,
                5.759–5.769, 5.793, 5.812, 5.821, 5.839, 6.25–6.35, 6.44, 6.45,
                6.49, 6.66, 6.78, 6.83, 6.102, 6.148, 6.150, 9.88
C-315/99 P, *Ismeri Europa v Court of Auditors* [2001] ECR I-5281 .... 5.280
C-350/99, *Wolfgang Lange v Georg Schunemann GmbH* [2001] ECR I-1061................ 4.134
C-352/99, *Eridania v Council of the European Union* [2001] ECR I-5037 .... 5.361
C-363/99, *Koninklijke KPN Nederland NV v Benelux-Merkenbureau (Postkantoor)*
    [2004] ECR I-1619.......... 4.20, 4.172, 4.229, 4.239, 5.09–5.10, 5.12, 5.14, 5.16, 5.20, 5.23,
                5.41, 5.57, 5.66, 5.117, 5.257, 5.274, 5.314, 5.585, 5.595–5.632, 5.659,
                5.664, 5.666, 5.680, 5.685, 5.689, 5.694, 5.695, 6.98, 6.100, 6.101
C-383/99 P, *Procter & Gamble Co v OHIM (BabyDry)* [2001] ECR I-6251 .... 5.04, 5.16, 5.19, 5.117,
                5.137, 5.255–5.256, 5.532–5.566, 5.570, 5.574,
                5.585, 5.587, 5.607, 5.630, 5.655–5.656, 5.659, 5.701
C-414/99, C-415/99 and C-416/99, *Levi Strauss & Co and Levi Strauss (UK) Ltd v
    Tesco Stores, Tesco Plc, Costco Wholesale UK Ltd and Zino Davidoff v A&G
    Imports Ltd* [2001] ECR I-8691 .... 7.421, 8.21, 8.34, 9.204, 9.527, 9.533,
                10.297–10.313, 10.314, 10.317, 10.332
C-443/99, *Merck, Sharp and Dohme GmbH v Paranova Pharmazeutica Handels
    GmbH* [2002] ECR I-3703....................... 10.214, 10.217–10.218, 10.228, 10.381
C-472/99, *Clean Car Autoservice GmbH v Stadt Wien and
    Republik Österreich* [2001] ECR I-9687 .... 5.677, 5.692, 9.448
C-517/99, *Merz and Krell GmbH & Co v Deutches Patent-und Markenamt
    (Bravo)* [2001] ECR I-6959 .... 4.84, 5.155, 5.156, 5.165, 5.171, 5.172, 5.394, 5.627,
                5.723–5.744, 5.747, 5.754, 8.21, 8.269–8.270
C-2/00, *Hölterhoff v Freiesleben* [2002] ECR I-4187....... 9.30–9.40, 9.45, 9.55, 9.110, 9.315, 12.68
C-13/00, *Commission v Ireland* [2002] ECR I-2943 .... 3.06
C-66/00, *Bigi (Dante)* [2002] ECR I-5917 .... 12.135
C-74 and C-75/00 P, *Falck and Acciaierie di Bolzano v Commission* [2002]
    ECR I-7869 .... 12.140
C-104/00 P, *DKV Deutsche Krankenversicherung AG v OHIM (Companyline)*
    [2002] ECR I-7561 .... 3.12, 3.69, 4.248, 5.09, 5.16–5.36, 5.33, 5.268, 5.273, 5.370,
                5.386, 5.412, 5.416, 5.583, 5.658, 5.755, 7.125, 7.231
C-143/00, *Boehringer Ingelheim Pharma KG v Swingward Ltd* [2002] ECR I-3759 ...... 10.214–10.216,
                10.224–10.227, 10.334, 10.346–10.347, 10.354,
                10.356, 10.362, 10.385, 10.410
C-253/00, *Muñoz and Superior Fruiticola v Frumar Ltd and Redbridge Produce
    Marketing Ltd* [2002] ECR I-7289 .... 12.143
C-265/00, *Campina Melkunie BV v Benelux-Merkenbureau (Biomild)* [2004]
    ECR I-1699 .... 5.45, 5.57, 5.117, 5.659, 6.100
C-273/00, *Sieckmann v Deutsches Patent-und Markenamt* [2002]
    ECR I-11737 .... 4.13, 4.16, 4.25, 4.38, 4.77–4.105, 4.112, 4.115, 4.116,
                4.127, 4.139, 4.145, 4.206, 4.223, 5.801, 8.31

Table of Cases

C-291/00, *LTJ Diffusion SA v Sadas Vertbaudet SA* [2003] ECR I-2799 .... 5.584, 7.08–7.19, 9.174, 9.224, 9.402, 12.208
C-292/00, *Davidoff & Cie SA and Zino Davidoff SA v Gofkid Ltd*
 [2003] ECR I-389 .... 5.402, 7.02, 7.355, 7.389, 7.403–7.416, 7.414, 7.417, 7.421,
7.422, 7.538, 7.546, 7.591, 9.106
C-312/00 P, *Commission v Comar and Tico* [2002] ECR I-11355 .... 7.81
C-323/00 P, *DSG v Commission* [2002] ECR I-3919. .... 5.32
C-363/00 P, *Anheuser-Busch Inc v OHIM* (BUDWEISER/BUDWEISER BUDVAR)
 [2006] ECR II-4255 .... 5.696
C-469/00, *Ravil SARL v Bellon Import SARL and Biraghi SpA* [2003] ECR I-5053 .... 5.702, 12.189
C-23/01, *Robelco NV* [2002] ECR I-10913 .... 5.846, 7.421, 9.362–9.372, 9.384, 12.208
C-25/01 P, *Glencore and Compagnie Continentale v Commission* [2002]
 ECR I-10119 .... 5.280
C-40/01, *Ansul BV v Ajax Brandbeveiliging BV* [2003] ECR I-2439 .... 5.394, 8.14–8.43,
8.34, 8.44, 8.47, 8.69–8.70, 8.75, 8.83, 8.89, 8.101, 8.106,
8.110, 8.113, 8.124, 8.140, 8.147, 8.208–8.215, 8.245
C-44/01, *Pippig Augennptik GmbH & Co KG v Hartlauer Handelsgesellschaft GmbH*
 [2003] ECR I-3095 .... 12.26–12.42, 12.70, 12.95
C-53/01 to C-55/01, *Linde AG* (C-53/01), *Winward Industries Inc* (C-54/01),
 and *Rado Uhren AG* (C-55/01) [2003] ECR I-3161............. 4.41, 4.120, 4.162, 5.08, 5.66,
5.141, 5.154, 5.172, 5.282–5.300, 5.368, 5.451, 5.588, 5.621, 5.627, 6.100
C-100/01, *Gerolsteiner Brunnen GmbH & Co v Putsch GmbH* [2004]
 ECR I-691 .... 9.308–9.326, 12.210
C-104/01, *Libertel Groep BV v Benelux-Merkenbureau* [2003]
 ECR I-3793 .... 4.17–4.19, 4.36, 4.42, 4.112, 4.131–4.147, 4.173, 5.07, 5.13, 5.42,
5.56, 5.60, 5.66, 5.137, 5.158, 5.174, 5.200–5.228, 5.232, 5.236–5.237,
5.244–5.246, 5.274, 5.358, 5.379, 5.620, 5.621, 5.627, 5.669, 6.69,
6.100, 6.102, 6.109, 7.163, 7.434, 9.88
C-111/01, *Gantner Electronic GmbH v Basch Exploitatie Maatschappy BV*
 [2003] ECR I-4207 .... 4.122
C-191/01 P, *OHIM v WM Wrigley Jr Co (Doublemint)* [2003] ECR I-12447........ 5.66, 5.72, 5.165,
5.421, 5.553, 5.567–5.594, 5.630, 5.656, 5.659
C-206/01, *Arsenal Football Club plc v Reed* [2002] ECR I-10273 .... 5.854, 7.16, 7.20, 7.157,
7.189, 7.197, 7.411, 7.434, 8.23–8.24, 9.30, 9.36, 9.41–9.58, 9.63,
9.73, 9.108, 9.109, 9.241, 9.315, 9.375, 12.199, 12.206–12.207
C-216/01, *Budějovický Budvar v Rudolf Ammersin GmbH (Budweiser I)*
 [2003] ECR I-13617.......... 12.162–12.174, 12.175, 12.177, 12.177–12.178, 12.180, 12.184
C-218/01, *Henkel KGaA v Deutsches Patent- und Markenamt* [2004]
 ECR I-1725 .... 5.140, 5.142, 5.154, 5.268, 5.301–5.314, 5.323–5.332, 5.368, 5.402,
5.407, 5.408, 5.416, 5.454, 8.278, 9.88, 12.204
C-247/01, *eCopy v OHIM* (ECOPY) [2002] ECR II-5301 .... 6.127
C-283/01, *Shield Mark BV v Kist* [2003] ECR I-14313 .... 4.106–4.130
C-316/01, *Eva Glawischnig v Bundesministerfur soziale Sicherheit und Generationen*
 [2003] ECR I-5995 .... 10.54
C-326/01 P, *Telefon & Buch v OHIM* [2004] ECR I-1371 .... 5.66, 5.649–5.658, 5.755, 7.125
C-387/01, *Weigel* [2004] ECR I-4981 .... 4.56
C-408/01, *Adidas-Salomon and Adidas Benelux BV v Fitnessworld Trading Ltd*
 [2003] ECR I-12537............ 5.936, 7.417–7.436, 7.449, 7.458, 7.462, 7.464, 7.465, 7.467,
7.482, 7.484, 7.488, 7.538, 7.546
C-418/01, *IMS Health GmbH & Co OHG v NDC Health GmbH & Co KG*
 [2004] ECR I-5039 .... 11.147–11.153, 11.160, 11.162–11.163, 11.171
C-456/01 P and C-457/01 P, *Henkel KGaA v OHIM* [2004]
 ECR I-5089 .... 5.07, 5.43, 5.56, 5.166, 5.170, 5.252, 5.268, 5.323–5.332,
5.345–5.382, 5.406, 5.457
C-468/01 P to C-472/01 P, *Procter & Gamble* [2004] ECR I-5141 .... 5.142, 5.166, 5.172–5.173,
5.268, 5.323, 5.383–5.387, 5.437

C-473/01 P and C-474/01 P, *Procter & Gamble* [2004] ECR I-5173 . . . . 5.323, 5.388
C-498/01 P, *OHIM v Zapf Creation AG* [2004] ECR I-11349 . . . . 9.61, 9.83
C-49/02, *Heidelberger Bauchemie GmbH* [2004] ECR I-6129 . . . . 4.32, 4.38, 4.39, 4.48, 4.142,
     4.148–4.155, 4.174, 4.190, 4.223, 4.248, 5.229–5.237, 5.244, 12.203, 12.210
C-60/02, *Criminal proceedings against X (Montres Rolex SA & Others)* [2004]
 ECR I-00651 . . . . 9.513–9.520, 9.539, 9.542–9.543, 9.548–9.549
C-64/02 P, *OHIM v Erpo Möbelwerk* [2004] ECR I-10031 . . . . 5.76, 5.147–5.177, 5.183–5.184, 6.39
C-115/02, *Administration des douanes et droits indirects v Rioglass SA and
 Transremar SL* [2003] ECR I-12705 . . . . 9.267, 9.508–9.512, 9.561
C-136/02 P, *Mag Instrument Inc v OHIM* [2004] ECR I-9165 . . . . 5.248–5.281, 5.399, 5.406,
          5.408, 5.412, 5.414, 5.442, 5.457, 5.488, 6.69
C-150/02 P, *Streamserve Inc v OHIM* [2004] ECR I-1461 . . . . 5.633–5.648
C-153/02, *Neri v European School of Economics* [2003] ECR I-13555 . . . . 7.538
C-239/02, *Douwe Egberts NV v Westrom Pharma NY. FICS-World BVBA* [2004]
 ECR I-7007 . . . . 10.49
C-245/02, *Anheuser-Busch v Budejovicky Budvar, narodni podnik (Budweiser III)*
 [2004] ECR I-10989 . . . . 9.68, 9.73, 9.176, 9.202, 9.355, 9.362, 9.375, 9.380, 9.388,
                9.390, 12.76, 12.194–12.212
C-259/02, *La Mer Technology Inc v Laboratoires Goemar SA* [2004] ECR I-1159. . . . . . 5.758, 8.44–8.57,
          8.70, 8.74, 8.83, 8.106, 8.140, 8.142, 8.147, 8.160
C-293/02, *Jersey Produce Marketing Organisation Ltd v Jersey* [2005] ECR I-09543 . . . . 10.20
C-329/02 P, *SatellitenFernsehen GmbH v OHIM (SAT.1)* [2004] ECR I-8317 . . . . 5.37–5.63,
       5.66, 5.74, 5.78, 5.154, 5.417, 5.418, 5.438–5.440, 9.88
C-371/02, *Björnekulla Fruktindustrier AB v Procordia Food AB* (BOSTONGURKA)
 [2004] ECR I-5791 . . . . 8.260–8.282, 8.283–8.284, 8.295
C-404/02, *Nichols plc v Registrar of Trade Marks* [2004] ECR I-8499. . . . . 4.24, 5.129–5.145,
                     5.855, 6.149
C-418/02, *Praktiker Bau und Heimwerkermärkte AG v Deutsches Patent- und
 Markenamt* [2005] ECR I-5873 . . . . 3.15, 4.176–4.189, 4.201, 4.222, 4.235, 4.245,
              4.249, 4.254, 4.258, 7.271–7.283, 9.387
C-445/02 P, *Glaverbel SA v OHIM* [2004] ECR I-6267. . . . . 5.141, 5.142, 5.315–5.320, 5.491
C-447/02 P, *KWS Saat v OHIM* [2004] ECR I-10107 . . . . 5.671
C-456/02, *Trojani v Centre Public d'Aide Sociale de Bruxelles* [2004] ECR I-7573 . . . . 12.210
C-465 and C-466/02, *Federal Republic of Germany and Kingdom of Denmark v
 Commission (Feta)* [2005] ECR I-9115 . . . . 12.100–12.116
C-3/03 P, *Matratzen Concord GmbH v OHIM (Matratzen I)* [2004]
 ECR I-3657 . . . . 7.89–7.99, 7.124, 7.244, 7.247, 7.267, 7.303, 7.337
C-16/03, *Peak Holding AB v Axolin-Elinor AB* [2004]
 ECR I-11313 . . . . 9.203, 10.318–10.327, 10.330, 10.332
C-37/03 P, *BioID AG v OHIM (BioID)* [2005] ECR I-7975 . . . . 3.108, 5.64–5.81, 5.415, 5.417,
                     7.86, 7.231, 8.67
C-53/03, *Synetairismos Farmakopoion Aitolias & Akarnanias (Syfait) v GlaxoSmithKline Plc*
 [2005] ECR I-4609 . . . . 11.168–11.176, 11.177–11.178
C-106/03 P, *Vedial SA v OHIM* [2004] ECR I-9573 . . . . 7.55–7.60, 7.442
C-123/03, *Ministero della Salute v Coordinamento delle Associazioni per la Difesa
 dell'Ambiente e dei Diritti degli Utenti e de Consumatori (Codacons)* [2005]
 ECR 1-4167. . . . . 10.50
C-152/03, *Ritter-Coulais v Finanzamt Germersheim* [2006] ECR I-1711 . . . . 4.56
C-192/03 P, *ALCON v OHIM* [2004] ECR I-8993 . . . . 5.14, 5.15, 5.745–5.758, 7.294
C-198/03 P, *Commission v CEVA and Pfizer* [2005] ECR I-6357 . . . . 7.230
C-210/03, *Swedish Match AB v Secretary of State for Health* [2004] ECR I-11893 . . . . 5.852
C-228/03, *The Gillette Company v LA-Laboratories Ltd Oy* [2005] ECR I-2337 . . . . 9.155, 9.175,
                     9.327–9.350, 9.354
C-260/03, *Celltech R&D Ltd v OHIM* [2005] ECR II-1215 . . . . 5.707–5.714, 5.709–5.710
C-321/03, *Dyson Ltd v Registrar of Trade Marks* [2003] ECR I-687. . . . . 3.111, 4.11–4.14,
                     4.26–4.62, 4.190, 4.248

Table of Cases

C-353/03, *Société des Produits Nestlé v Mars UK Ltd (Kit Kat)* [2005]
  ECR I-6135 .... 6.36–6.49, 6.58–6.59, 6.64, 6.66, 6.83, 8.192, 8.201
C-405/03, *Class International v Colgate-Palmolive Co, Unilever NV, SmithKline Beecham Plc and Beecham Group Plc* [2005] ECR I-8735; EU:C:2005:616 .... 6.153, 7.165, 9.267, 9.520–9.535, 9.540, 9.548–9.549, 9.561, 13.23
C-120/04, *Medion AG v Thomson Multimedia Sales Germany & Austria GmbH* [2005]
  ECR I-8551 .... .7.16, 7.239–7.250, 7.253, 7.260, 7.266–7.267, 7.270, 7.303
C-173/04, *Deutsche SiSi-Werke GmbH & Co Betriebs KG v OHIM (STANDBEUTEL)*
  [2006] ECR I-551 .... 3.108, 5.389–5.426, 5.457, 5.488
C-95/04 P, *British Airways v Commission* [2007] ECR I-2331 .... 11.180
C-206/04 P, *Mülhens GmbH & Co KG v OHIM* [2006] ECR I-271 .... 7.75–7.88
C-212/04, *Adeneler and others v Ellinikos Organismos Galaktos* [2006] ECR I-6057 .... 10.371
C-259/04, *Elizabeth Florence Emanuel v Continental Shelf 128 Ltd*
  [2006] ECR I-3089 .... 5.841–5.858
C-286/04, *Eurocermex SA v OHIM* [2005] ECR I-5797 .... 5.427–5.443
C-348/04, *Boehringer Ingelheim KG, Boehringer Ingelheim Pharma GmbH & Co KG, Glaxo Group Ltd v Swingward Ltd and Boehringer Ingelheim KG, Boehringer Ingelheim Pharma GmbH & Co KG, Glaxo Group Ltd, Smithkline Beecham Plc, Beecham Group Plc Smithkline and French Laboratories Ltd, Eli Lilly and Co, The Wellcome Foundation Ltd v Dowelhurst Ltd* [2007] ECR I-3391 .... 6.96, 9.181, 9.193, 10.336–10.371, 10.379, 10.380–10.382, 10.384, 11.168
C-361/04 P, *Ruiz-Picasso v OHIM (CompUSA)* [2006] ECR I-643 .... 5.14, 6.59–6.60, 6.70, 7.81, 7.88, 7.182–7.197, 7.286, 7.291, 7.296, 12.207
C-416/04 P, *The Sunrider Corp v OHIM* [2006] ECR I-04237 .... 8.04, 8.58–8.71, 8.74, 8.140, 8.147, 8.216–8.217
C-421/04, *Matratzen Concord AG v Hukla Germany SA* [2006] ECR I-2303 .... 5.699–5.706, 6.101, 12.160
C-108/05, *Bovemij Verzekeringen NV v Benelux-Merkenbureau (Europolis)*
  [2006] ECR I-7605 .... 6.90–6.120
C-24/05 P, *Storck v OHIM (Storck I)*, ECLI:EU:C:2006:421 .... 5.444–5.459, 5.468, 6.50–6.72
C-25/05 P, *Storck v OHIM (Storck II)*, ECLI:EU:C:2006:422 .... 4.68, 5.460–5.483, 5.488, 5.711, 5.714, 6.73–6.89, 6.117
C-29/05 P, *OHIM v Kaul GmbH—Bayer AG (ARCOL)* [2007] ECR I-02213 ...... 3.22, 3.28–3.29, 3.56–3.58, 3.60
C-48/05, *Adam Opel AG v Autec AG* [2007] ECR I-1017 .... 9.59–9.83, 9.104, 9.108, 9.109, 9.265, 9.351–9.361, 12.68
C-59/05, *Siemens AG v VTPA Geselschaft Fur Visualisierung und Prozess Jautomatisierung GmbH* [2006] ECR I-2147 .... 12.43–12.53
C-132/05, *Commission v Germany* [2008] ECR I-957 .... 12.123, 12.127
C-145/05, *Levi Strauss & Co v Casucci SpA* [2006] ECR I-3703 ...... 7.70, 7.148–7.165, 7.592, 9.399
C-214/05 P, *Rossi SpA v OHIM* [2006] ECR I-7057 .... 3.58, 7.198–7.238
C-235/05 P, *L'Oreal SA v OHIM (Flexi Air)* [2006] ECR I-00057 .... 7.114–7.125
C-239/05, *BVBA Management, Training en Consultancy v Benelux-Merkenbureau*
  [2007] ECR I-1455 .... 3.75, 4.239, 5.664–5.698, 5.717
C-246/05, *Armin Häupl v Lidl Stiftung & Co KG (LE CHEF DE CUISINE)*
  [2007] ECR I-4673 .... 8.218–8.233, 8.236–8.251
C-273/05, *OHIM v Celltech R&D Ltd (CELLTECH)* [2007] ECR I-02883
  ECR I-1455 .... 5.707–5.714, 5.715, 5.719
C-276/05, *The Wellcome Foundation Ltd v Paranova Pharmazeutika Handels GmbH*
  [2009] ETMR 20 .... 10.378–10.385
C-281/05, *Montex Holdings v Diesel SpA* [2006] ECR I-10881 .... 9.267, 9.561, 9.578
C-316/05, *Nokia Corp v Joacim Wärdell* [2006] ECR I-12083 .... 9.437–9.454, 9.460, 9.469, 9.471, 13.23
C-334/05 P, *Rossi SpA v OHIM* [2006] ECR I-7057 .... 7.297–7.304, 7.443
C-381/05, *De Landtsheer Emmanuel SA v Comité Interprofessionnel du Vin de Champagne and Veuve Clicquot Ponsardin SA* [2007] ECR I-0311 .... 12.54–12.65, 12.81

C-412/05 P, *Alcon Inc v OHIM (Travatan)* [2007] ECR I-3569 . . . . 7.289–7.296
C-426/05, *Tele2 Telecommunication v Telekom-Control-Kommission* [2008] ECR I-685. . . . . . . 7.586
C-2/06, *Willy Kempter KG v Hauptzollamt Hamburg-Jonas* [2008] ECR I-411 . . . . 12.187
C-17/06, *Céline SARL v Céline SA* [2007] ECR I-07041. . . . . 9.157, 9.176, 9.265, 9.373–9.390
C-56/06, *Euro Tex Textilverwertung GmbH v Hauptzollamt Duisburg* [2007] ECR I-4859. . . . . 7.586
C-193/06, *Société des Produits Nestlé v OHIM* (QUICKY) [2007]
 ECR I-114 . . . . 7.297–7.298, 7.305–7.313, 7.443
C-196/06 P, *Alecansan SL v OHIM (CompUSA)* [2007] ECR I-00036 . . . . 3.71
C-234/06 P, *Il Ponte Finanziaria Spa/OHIM* (BAINBRIDGE) [2007]
 ECR I-7333 . . . . 3.64, 7.442, 8.170, 8.175–8.182, 8.184,
               8.187, 8.196, 8.198, 8.252–8.253, 8.254
C-238/06 P, *Develey Holding GmbH & Co Beleiligungs KG v OHIM
 (PLASTIKFLASCHENFORM)* [2007] ECR II-811 . . . . 3.69, 3.110, 5.106, 5.715–5.722
C-275/06, *Promusicae v Telefónica de España SAU* [2008] ECR I-271 . . . . 9.218
C-304/06 P, *Eurohypo AG v OHIM (EUROHYPO)* [2008] ECR I-03297 . . . . 3.70
C-328/06, *Alfredo Nieto Nuño v Leonci Monlleó Franquet* (FINCAS TARRAGONA)
 [2007] ECR I-40093 . . . . 7.353–7.369, 7.378
C-347/06, *ASM Brescia v Comune di Rodengo Saiano* [2008] ECR I-05641 . . . . .7.538
C-371/06, *Benetton Group SpA v G-Star International BV* (BENETTON)
 [2007] ECR I-7709 . . . . 5.808–5.818, 5.839
C-468 to C-478/06, *Sot. Lelos kai Sia EE and Others v GlaxoSmithKline AEVE
 Farmakeftikon Proionton, formerly Glaxowellcome AEVE* [2008] ECR I-07139. . . . . . 11.177–11.187
C-514/06 P, *Armacell Enterprise GmbH v OHIM* (ARMAFOAM)
 [2008] ECR I-00128 . . . . 7.332–7.345, 9.473
C-533/06, *O2 Holdings Ltd, O2 (UK) Ltd v Hutchison 3G UK Ltd* [2008]
 ECR I-4231 . . . . 9.26, 9.107, 9.155, 9.265, 12.66–12.77, 12.90
C-102/07, *Adidas AG and Adidas Benelux BV v Marca Mode CV, C&A Nederland, H&M
 Hennes & Mauritz Netherlands BV, and Vendex KBB Nederland BV (MARCA II)*
 [2008] ECR I-2439 . . . . 9.84–9.101
C-212/07 P, *Indorata-Serviços e Gestão, Lda v OHIM* (HAIRTRANSFER),
 ECLI:EU:C:2008:83 . . . . 3.108
C-252/07, *Intel Corp Inc v CPM United Kingdom Ltd* (INTEL) [2008]
 ECR I-08823 . . . . .7.458–7.507, 7.512, 7.514, 7.536, 7.539, 7.541, 7.550,
               7.555–7.559, 7.568, 7.573, 7.592
C-298/07, *Bundesverband der Verbraucherzentralen und Verbraucherverbände*
 [2008] ECR I-7841 . . . . 9.216
C-301/07, *PAGO International GmbH v Tirol Milch registrierte Genossenschaft mbH*
 (PAGO) [2009] ECR I-09429 . . . . .7.370–7.402, 8.139
C-317/07, *Union Investment Privatfonds GmbH v OHIM/UniCredito Italiano SpA (UniWeb)*
 [2011] ECR I-05471. . . . . 7.328–7.331
C-320/07 P, *Antarctica Srl v OHIM* (NASDAQ) [2009] ECR I-00028 . . . . .3.71, 7.507, 7.354,
               7.548–7.559, 7.560, 7.582, 8.115–8.125
C-343/07, *Bavaria NV; Bavaria Italia Srl v Bayerischer Brauerbund eV*
 [2009] ETMR 61 . . . . 12.117–12.133
C-378/08 to C-380/07, *Angelidaki v Organismos Nomarkhiaki Aftodiikisi Rethimnis*
 [2009] ECR I-3071 . . . . 9.219
C-385/07 P, *Der Grüne Punkt-Duales System Deutschland GmbH v Commission of the
 European Communities* [2009] ECR I-6155 . . . . 11.188–11.214
C-442/07, *Verein Radetzky-Orden v Bundesvereinigung Kameradschaft 'Feldmarschall
 Radetzky'* [2008] ECR I-09223 . . . . 8.75–8.95, 8.110, 8.125
C-478/07, *Budejovický Budvar National Corp v Rudolf Ammersin GmbH (Budweiser II)*
 [2009] ECR I-7721 . . . . 12.175–12.193
C-487/07, *L'Oréal SA, Lancôme parfums et beauté & Cie SNC, Laboratoire Garnier & Cie v
 Bellure NV, Malaika Investments Ltd, Starion International Ltd* (BELLURE)
 [2009] ECR I-05185 . . . . 7.112, 7.525–7.547, 7.550, 7.557, 7.568, 7.581, 9.102–9.114,
          9.156, 9.164, 9.202, 9.241, 9.402, 9.580, 12.78–12.92, 13.27

C-495/07, *Silberquelle GmbH v Maselli Strickmode GmbH* [2009]
    ECR I-00137 .... 8.96–8.114, 8.125, 9.208
C-498/07 P, *Aceites del Sur-Coosur SA v Koipe Corporoción* (LA ESPAÑOLA) [2009]
    ECR I-7371 .... 7.297–7.298, 7.314–7.327, 7.443, 9.408
C-529/07, *Chocoladefabriken Lindt & Sprüngli AG v Franz Hauswirth GmbH* [2009]
    ECR I-04893 .... 5.492–5.494, 5.915–5.931, 5.938, 6.139–6.143, 9.397, 12.158
C-542/07, *Imagination Technologies Ltd v OHIM* (PURE DIGITAL) [2001]
    ECR I-04937 .... 6.121–6.138, 6.146
C-39/08 and C-43/08, *Bild digital GmbH & Co KG, formerly Bild.T-Online.de AG &
    Co ZVS Zeitungsvertrieb Stuttgart GmbH v Präsident des Deutschen Patent- und
    Markenamts* [2009] ECR I-00020 .... 3.109
C-57/08 P, *Gateway v OHIM* [2008] ECR I-00188 .... 7.442
C-59/08, *Copad SA v Christian Dior Couture SA* [2009] ECR I-3421 .... 10.407
C-62/08, *UDV North America Inc v Brandtraders NV (SMIRNOFF)* [2009]
    ECR I-01279 .... 9.115–9.121, 9.212
C-89/08 P, *Commission v Ireland and Others* [2009] ECR I-11245 .... 3.103
C-131/08 P, *Dorel Juvenile Group Inc v OHIM* [2009] ECR I-00009 .... 5.177
C-202/08 and C-208/08 P, *American Clothing Associates NV v OHIM (Maple Leaf)* [2009]
    ECR I-6933 .... 5.885–5.911
C-236/08 to C-238/08, *Google France SARL and Google Inc v Louis Vuitton
    Malletier SA* [2010] ECR I-02417 .... 7.112, 9.122–9.168, 9.170, 9.173, 9.186–9.187,
                    9.195–9.196, 9.212, 9.216, 9.227, 9.234, 9.241, 9.243, 9.245, 9.249,
                    9.258, 9.265, 9.269, 9.271, 9.402, 9.470, 10.395, 10.401
C-261/08 and C-348/08, *Zurita García and Choque Cabrera* [2009] ECR I-10143 .... 12.157
C-278/08, *Die BergSpechte Outdoor Reisen und Alpinschule Edi Koblmüller GmbH v Günter
    Guni, trekking.at Reisen GmbH* [2010] ECR I-02517 .... 9.170–9.171, 9.241, 9.249
C-302/08, *Zino Davidoff SA v Bundesfinanzdirektion Südost* (DAVIDOFF III)
    [2009] ECR I-05671 .... 9.485–9.493
C-324/08 P, *Makro Zelfbedieningsgroothandel and Others v Diesel SpA* [2009]
    ECR I-10019 .... 9.203, 10.314–10.317
C-394/08 P, *Zipcar Inc v OHIM* (ZIPCAR) [2009] ECR I-00095 .... 7.340
C-398/08 P, *Audi AG v OHIM* (Vorsprung durch Technik) [2010] ECR I-00535 .... 5.178–5.195
C-408/08 P, *Lancôme parfums et beauté & Cie SNC v OHIM* (CMS Hasche Sigle)
    [2010] ECR I-01347 .... 5.660
C-473/08, *Ingenieurbüro Eulitz GbR Thomas und Marion Eulitz v Finanzamt Dresden I*
    [2010] ECR I-907 .... 12.157
C-558/08, *Portakabin Ltd, Portakabin BV v Primakabin BV* [2010] ECR I-06963 ...... 9.172–9.185,
                                                        9.212, 9.243, 9.245, 10.407
C-569/08, *Internetportal und Marketing GmbH v Richard Schlicht* [2010]
    ECR I-04871 .... 12.153–12.160
C-585/08 and C-144/09, *Pammer and Hotel Alpenhof* [2010] ECR I-12527 .... 9.206
C-48/09, *Lego Juris A/S v OHIM* [2010] ECR I-08403 .... 5.770–5.795, 5.802, 5.832, 5.836
C-51/09, *Barbara Becker v OHIM/Harman International Industries Inc* [2010]
    ECR I-05805 .... 7.251–7.256, 7.330
C-91/09, *Eis.de GmbH v BBY Vertriebsgesellschaft mbH* [2010] ECR I-00043 .... 9.169
C-96/09, *Anheuser-Busch Inc v Budějovický Budvar, národní podnik* (Budweiser IV)
    [2011] ECR I-02131 .... 12.213–12.229
C-127/09, *Coty Prestige Lancaster Group v Simex Trading AG* [2010]
    ECR I-04965 .... 9.192, 9.203, 9.208, 10.328–10.333
C-159/09, *Lidl SNC v Vierzon Distribution SA* [2011] E.C.R. I-07235 .... 12.93–12.99
C-168/09, *Flos SpA v Semeraro Casa e Famiglia SpA* [20011] ECR I-181 .... 7.589
C-197/09, *RX-II Review M v EMEA* [2009] ECR I-12033 .... 3.103
C-221/09, *AJD Tuna v Direttur tal-Agrikoltura u s-Sajd and Avukat Generali*
    [2011] ECR I-01655 .... 9.238
C-229/09, *Hogan Lovells International LLP v Bayer CropScience AG* [2010] ECR I-11335 .... 9.238
C-235/09, *DHL Express France SAS v Chronopost SA* [2011] ECR I-02801 .... 7.112, 9.455–9.473

C-320/09, *AA2A v Commission*, ECLI:EU:C:2011:858 .... 3.74
C-323/09, *Interflora and Interflora British Unit v Marks & Spencer plc and Flowers Direct Online Ltd* [2011] ECR I-08625 .... 7.568, 7.588, 9.227–9.261
C-324/09, *L'Oréal SA, Lancôme parfums et beauté & Cie, Laboratoire Garnier & Cie, L'Oréal (UK) Limited v eBay International AG, eBay Europe SARL, eBay (UK) Limited* 9.186–9.221, 9.561, 10.395
C-214/09 P, *Anheuser-Busch Inc v OHIM/Budejovicky Budvar* [2010] ECR I-07665 .... 3.44–3.47, 13.29
C-254/09 P, *Zafra Marroquineros SL v Calvin Klein Trademark Trust* [2010] ECR I-07989 .... 7.128, 7.437–7.443, 7.448, 7.451–7.457
C-263/09 P, *Edwin Co Ltd v OHIM (Elio Fiorucci)* [2011] ECR I-5853 .... 3.87–3.96, 3.99–3.100, 3.102
C-265/09 P, *OHIM v BORCO-Marken-Import Matthiesen GmbH & Co. KG (BORCO-Marken)* [2010] ECR I-08265 .... 5.95–5.106, 5.109, 5.114–5.115, 5.122–5.128, 6.149
C-332/09 P, *OHIM v Frosch Touristik GmbH—DSR touristik GmbH* (FLUGBÖRSE) [2010] ECR I-00049 .... 6.138
C-369/09 P, *ISD Polska and Others v Commission* [2011] ECR I-02011 .... 12.140
C-400/09, *Orifarm A/S, Orifarm Supply A/S, Handelsselskabet af 5 January 2002 A/S, in liquidation, and C-207/10 Ompakningsselskabet af, and Paranova Danmark A/S, Paranova Pack A/S v Merck Sharp & Dohme Corp., formerly Merck & Co. Inc., Merck Sharp & Dohme BV, Merck Sharp & Dohme* [2011] ECR I-07063 .... 10.372–10.377
C-446 and C-495/09, *Koninklijke Philips Electronics NV v Lucheng Meijing Industrial Company Ltd, Far East Sourcing Ltd, Röhlig Hong Kong Ltd, and Röhlig Belgium NV,* and *Nokia Corporation v Her Majesty's Commissioners of Revenue and Customs* [2011] ECR I-12435 .... 9.549–9.573, 9.578, 9.580
C-482/09, *Budějovický Budvar, národní podnik v Anheuser Busch (Budweiser VI)* [2011] ECR I-08701; EU:C:2009:521 .... 6.149, 6.156–6.157, 7.112, 9.391–9.408, 12.247
C-495/09, *Nokia Corporation v Her Majesty's Commissioners of Revenue and Customs* see C-446/09 .... 9.550
C-552/09 P, *Ferrero SpA v OHIM* [2011] ECR I-02063 .... 7.131, 7.437, 7.444–7.457
C-4 and C-27/10, *Bureau National Interprofessionnel du Cognac v Gust Ranin Oy (Cognac II)* [2011] ECR I-06131 .... 12.138–12.152
C-46/10, *Viking Gas A/S v Kosan Gas A/S, formerly BP Gas A/S* [2011] I-06161 .... 10.395–10.408, 11.219
C-51/10 P, *Agencja Wydawnicza Technopol sp. z o.o. v OHIM* [2011] ECR I-01541 .... 5.95, 5.107–5.128, 5.720
C-92/10 P, *Media-Saturn-Holding GmbH v OHIM (Best Buy)* [2011] ECR I-00002 .... 5.502–5.503
C-119/10, *Frisdranken Industrie Winters BV v Red Bull GmbH* [2011] ECR I-13179 .... 7.583, 9.262–9.271
C-138/10, *DP grup EOOD v Direktor na Agentsia 'Mitnitsi'* [2011] ECR I-0000 .... 9.569
C-190/10, *Génesis Seguros Generales, Sociedad Anónima de Seguros y Reaseguros v Boys Toys SA and Administración del Estado*, ECLI:EU:C:2012:157 .... 7.166–7.178
C-307/10, *Chartered Institute of Patent Attorneys v Registrar of Trade Marks* (IP TRANSLATOR), ECLI:EU:C:2012:361 .... 4.198–4.244, 4.245, 4.253, 4.256, 4.261, 4.264, 13.38, 13.44
C-344/10 P, *Freixenet v OHIM* [2011] ECR I-10205 .... 5.484–5.491
C-457/10 P, *AstraZeneca v Commission*, ECLI:EU:C:2012 .... 11.138–11.140
C-488/10, *Celaya Emparanza y Galdos Internacional* [2012] ECR I-0000 .... 9.11
C-523/10, *Wintersteiger AG v Products 4U Sondermaschinenbau GmbH.*
  Judgment: ECLI:EU:C:2012:220, Opinion: ECLI:EU:C:2012:90 .... 9.434
C-32/11, *Allianz Hungária Biztosító and Others*, EU:C:2013:160 .... 3.77–3.82
C-53/11, *OHIM v Nike International Limited/Aurelio Munoz Molina* 3.77–3.82
C-88/11 P, *LG Electronics Inc. v OHIM* [2011] ECR I-00171 .... 5.661
C-90/11 and C-91/11, *Strigl/GPTO, Securvita/GPTO*, ECLI:EU:C:2012:147 ...... 5.84–5.94, 5.93

C-96/11 P, *August Storck KG v OHIM*, ECLI:EU:C:2012:537 .... 5.495
C-98/11, *Chocoladefabriken Lindt & Sprüngli AG v OHIM*, ECLI:EU:C:
  2012:307 .... 5.492–5.493, 6.139
C-100/11 P, *Helena Rubinstein SNC—L'Oréal SA v OHIM*, ECLI:EU:C:2012:28 ...... 7.560–7.582
C-149/11 P, *Leno Merken BV v Hagelkruis Beheer BV* (ONEL), ECLI:EU:C:2012:816 ... 8.126–8.165
C-196/11 P, *Formula One Licensing BV v OHIM*, 24 May 2012, ECLI:EU:
  C:2012:314 .... 7.100–7.113
C-311/11 P, *Smart Technologies ULC v OHIM*, ECLI:EU:C:2012:460 .... 5.197
C-361/11, *Kik v OHIM* [2003] ECR II-8283 .... 2.35–2.38
C-402/11, *Jager & Polacek GmbH v OHIM* ECLI:EU:C:2012:649. .... 3.48–3.55
C-661/11, *Martin Y Paz Diffusion SA v David Depuydt, Fabriek van Maroquinerie
  Gauquie NV,* not yet published. 10.386–10.394
C-327/11, *US Polo Association v OHIM*, ECLI:EU:C:2012:550 .... 7.257–7.261
C-553/11, *Rintisch v Eder (PROTI)*, ECLI:EU:C:2012:671 .... 8.183–8.189, 8.190,
  8.196, 8.204, 8.254–8.256, 13.35
C-561/11, *Fédération Cynologique Internationale v Federación Canina Internacional
  de Perros de Pura Raza*, ECLI:EU:C:2013:91 .... 7.112, 9.08–9.19
C-609/11 P, *Centrotherm Clean Solutions GmbH & Co. KG v OHIM—Centrotherm
  Systemtechnik GmbH*, ECLI:EU:C:2013:592 .... 3.37–3.38
C-610/11 P, *Centrotherm Systemtechnik GmbH v OHIM—Centrotherm Clean
  Solutions GmbH & Co. KG.*, ECLI:EU:C:2013:593 .... 3.37–3.38, 3.39
C-621/11 P, *New Yorker SHK Jeans GmbH & Co. KG v OHIM—Vallis K.-Vallis A. & Co.
  OE.*, ECLI:EU:C:2013:484 .... 3.37–3.38, 3.42
C-655/11 P, *Seven for all mankind LLC v OHIM/Seven SpA.*, ECLI:EU:C:2013:94 ..... 7.134–7.140
C-12/12, *Colloseum Holding AG v Levi Strass & Co.*, ECLI:EU:C:2013:253 .... 8.190–8.195,
  8.196, 8.198, 8.201, 8.204
C-65/12, *Leidseplein Beheer BV v Red Bull GmbH*, 6 February 2014 .... 7.583–7.596
C-97/12 P, *Louis Vuitton Malletier v OHIM-Friis Group International ApS*,
  ECLI:EU:C:2014:324 .... 4.68, 5.497–5.500
C-120/12 P, *Rintisch v OHIM—Bariatrix Europe Inc.*, ECLI:EU:C:2013:638 ..... 3.42–3.43, 13.35
C-121/12 P, *Rintisch v OHIM—Valfleurs Pâtes alimentaires SA* 3.42–3.43
C-122/12 P, *Rintisch v OHIM—Valfleurs Pâtes alimentaires SA*, ECLI:EU:C:
  2013:639 .... 3.42–3.43
C-252/12, *Specsavers International Healthcare Ltd v Asda Stores Ltd.*, ECLI:EU:
  C:2013:497 .... 8.196–8.206, 9.20–9.29
C-268/12 P, *Cadila Healthcare Ltd v Novartis AG*, ECLI:EU:C:2013:296 .... 3.59
C-320/12, *Malaysia Dairy Industries Pte Ltd v Ankenævnet for Patenter og Varemærker*,
  ECLI:EU:C:2013:435 .... 5.932–5.940, 7.591
C-337/12 to C-340/12 P, *Pi-Design AG and Others/Yoshida Metal Industry Co Ltd
  and Others*, ECLI:EU:C:2014:129 .... 5.796–5.807
C-360/12, *Coty Germany GmbH v First Note Perfumes NV*,
  Judgment: ECLI:EU:C:2014:1318, Opinion: ECLI:EU:C:2013:764 .... 9.421–9.436
C-383/12 P, *Environmental Manufacturing LLP v OHIM (Shape of a wolf's head)*,
  ECLI:EU:C:2013:741 .... 7.508–7.524
C-409/12, *Backaldrin Österreich The Kornspitz Company GmbH v Pfahnl Backmittel
  GmbH* (KORNSPITZ), ECLI:EU:C:2014:130 .... 8.283–8.302
C-410/12 P, *medi GmbH & Co KG v OHIM*, ECLI:EU:C:2013:702 .... 5.83
C-445/12 P, *Rivella International AG v OHIM/Baskaya di Kaskaya Alim e C.Sas*,
  ECLI:EU:C:2013:826 .... 8.166–8.170
C-479/12, *H. Gautzsch Großhandel GmbH & Co KG v Münchener Boulevard Möbel
  Joseph Duna GmbH* EU:C:2014:75. .... 6.153, 9.476–9.484
C-530/12 P, *OHIM v National Lottery Commission (Shape of a hand)*, ECLI:
  EU:C:2013:782 .... 3.87, 3.97–3.104
C-558/12 P, *OHIM/Lidl Stiftung v Wesergold Getränkeindustrie*, ECLI:EU:
  C:2014:22 .... 7.126–7.128
C-591/12, *Bimbo SA v OHIM*, ECLI:EU:C:2014:305 .... 7.262–7.270

C-597/12 P, *Isdin SA v OHIM/Bial-Portela & Ca SA* (ZEBEXIR v ZEBINIX),
    ECLI:EU:C:2013:672 .... 3.73–3.76
C-67/13 P, *Groupement des Cartes Bancaires (CB) v European Commission*,
    11 September 2014, ECLI:EU:C:2014:2204 .... 11.49–11.52
C-70/13 P, *Getty Images (US) Inc. v OHIM*, ECLI:EU:C:2013:875 .... 5.662
C-98/13, *Blomqvist v Rolex SA*, ECLI:EU:C:2014:55 .... 9.574–9.584, 13.25
C-126/13 P, *BSH Bosch und Siemens Hausgeräte GmbH*, ECLI:EU:C:2014:2065 .... 5.663
C-141/13 P, *Reber Holding GmbH & Co. KG v OHIM—Wedl & Hofmann GmbH*
    (WALZERTRAUM), ECLI:EU:C:2015:133 .... 8.72–8.74, 8.207
C-205/13, *Hauck GmbH & Co. KG v Stokke A/S, Stokke Nederland BV, Peter Opsvik,
    Peter Opsvik A/S*, ECLI:EU:C:2014:2233 .... 5.819–5.840
C-217/13 and C-218/13, *Oberbank AG, Banco Santander SA and Santander
    Consumer Bank AG v Deutscher Sparkassen- und Giroverband eV*,
    ECLI:EU:C:2014:2012 .... 6.24, 6.144–6.155
C-285/13 P, *Bimbo SA v OHIM/Café do Brasil SpA* (CAFFE KIMBO v BIMBO),
    ECLI:EU:C:2014:1751 .... 3.84
C-324/13, *Fercal—Consultadoria e Serviços Ld^a v OHIM*, ECLI:EU:C:2014:60 .... 3.65
C-420/13 P, *Netto Marken Discount AG & Co KG v Deutsches Patent- und Markenamt*
    (APPLE), ECLI:EU:C:2014:2069 .... 4.75, 4.245–4.264
C-421/13 P, *Apple Inc v Deutsches Patent- und Markenamt* (APPLE),
    ECLI:EU:C:2014:2070 .... 4.63–4.75
C-448/13 P, *Delphi Technologies Inc v OHIM*, ECLI:EU:C:2014:1746 .... 5.197
C-581 and C-582/13 P, *Intra-Presse SAS v OHIM, Golden Balls Ltd.*,
    ECLI:EU:C:2014:2387 .... 7.129–7.133, 7.431
C-670/13 P, *The Cartoon Network Inc v OHIM*, ECLI:EU:C:2014:2024 .... 3.72
C-20/14, *BGW Beratungs-Gesellschaft Wirtschaft mbH/Scholz* 5.93
C-413/14 P, *Intel Corporation v Commission* 11.167
C-491/14, *Rosa dels Vents Assessoria SL v U Hostels Albergues Juveniles SL*, 10 March 2015 .... 9.08

General Court (GC)

T-30/89, *Hilti v Commission* [1991] ECR II-1439 .... 11.127–11.128
T-69/89, *Radio Telefis Eireann (RTE) v Commission* [1991] ECR II-485 .... 11.130–11.133
T-19 and T-88/92, *Groupement D'Achat Edouard Leclerc v EC Commission* [1996]
    ECR II-1851, [1997] 4 CMLR 995 .... 10.262, 11.85
T-123/97, *Salomon SA v Commission* [1999] ECR II-2925 .... 7.228
T-163/98, *Procter & Gamble v OHIM (BABY-DRY)* [1999] ECR II-2383 .... 3.22, 3.29, 5.204,
                                                                   5.532, 5.535–5.538
T-91/99, *Ford Motor Co v OHIM* [2000] ECR II-1925 .... 6.103, 6.115
T-126/99, *Graphischer Maschinenbau v Commission* [2002] ECR II-427 .... 7.228
T-135/99, *Taurus-Film v OHIM* [2001] ECR II-379 .... 5.152
T-136/99, *Taurus-Film v OHIM* [2001] ECR II-397 .... 5.152
T-331/99, *Mitsubishi HiTec Paper Bielefeld GmbH v OHIM* (GIROFORM)
    [2001] ECR II-433 .... 3.67
T-335/99, *Henkel KGaA* [2001] ECR II-2581 .... 5.324, 5.361
T-336/99, *Henkel KGaA* [2001] ECR II-2589 .... 5.324, 5.361
T-337/99, *Henkel (Rectangular tablet, white and red)* [2001] ECR II-2597 .... 5.322–5.323,
                                                                           5.324, 5.361
T-353/99, *Deutsche Krankenversicherung AG (DKV9)* [2001] ECR II-1645 .... 5.17
T-357/99, *Telefon & Buch v OHIM* [2001] ECR II-1705 .... 5.649–5.658
T-358/99, *Telefon & Buch v OHIM* [2001] ECR II-1705 .... 5.649–5.658
T-359/99, *DKV v OHIM* (EuroHealth) [2001] ECR II-1645 .... 5.709
T-34/00, *Eurocool Logistik GmbH v OHIM (EUROCOOL)* [2002] ECR II-683,
    paragraph 12 .... 3.67
T-87/00, *Bank für Arbeit und Wirtschaft v OHIM* [2001] ECR II-1259 .... 5.152
T-88/00, *Mag Instrument Inc v OHIM* [2002] ECR II-467 .... 5.250–5.253, 5.259, 5.265
T-106/00, *Streamserve Inc v OHIM* [2002] ECR II-723 .... 5.633

T-117/00, *Procter & Gamble* [2001] ECR II-2723...................5.333–5.338, 5.383–5.387
T-118/00, *Procter & Gamble* [2001] ECR II-2731............................5.333, 5.383–5.387
T-119/00, *Procter & Gamble* [2001] ECR II-2761............................5.333, 5.383–5.387
T-120/00, *Procter & Gamble* [2001] ECR II-2769............................5.333, 5.383–5.387
T-121/00, *Procter & Gamble* [2001] ECR II-2777...5.333
T-128/00, *Procter & Gamble* [2001] ECR II-2785........................... 5.339–5.344, 5.388
T-129/00, *Procter & Gamble* [2001] ECR II-2793........................... 5.339–5.344, 5.388
T-138/00, *Erpo Möbelwerk v OHIM* [2001] ECR II-3739.........5.147–5.151, 5.160–5.165, 5.175
T-173/00, *KWS Saat AG v OHIM* [2002] ECR II-3843..................................5.238–5.247
T-187/00, *Gödecke AG/Teva Pharmaceutical Industries Ltd v OHIM* [2001]
    ECR II-00859...3.59
T-323/00, *SatellitenFernsehen GmbH v OHIM (SAT.1)* [2002] ECR II-2839.............5.38, 5.59
T-356/00, *DaimlerChrysler/OHIM* (CARCARD) [2002] ECR II-1963....................5.709
T-388/00, *Institut fur Lernsysteme GmbH v OHIM (ELS)* [2002] ECR II-04301............3.66
T-6/01, *Matratzen Concord GmbH v OHIM* [2002] ECR II-4335.......7.89, 7.91–7.94, 7.99, 7.106
T-19/01, *BioID AG v OHIM (BioID)* [2002] ECR II-5159.............................5.64–5.81
T-36/01, *Glaverbel SA v OHIM* [2002] ECR II-3887.....................................5.315
T-39/01, *Fernandes v OHIM* (HIWATT) [2002] ECR II-5233...........................8.139
T-63/01, *Procter & Gamble v OHIM* (Soap bar shape) [2002] ECR II-5255...............3.29
T-110/01, *Vedial SA v OHIM* [2002] ECR II-5275.......................................7.55
T-122/01, *Best Buy Concepts Inc v OHIM* [2003] ECR II-2235....................5.154, 5.502
T-128/01, *DaimlerChrysler Corp v OHIM* [2003] ECR II-701..........................7.227
T-129/01, *Jose Alejandro SL v OHIM (BUDMEN/BUD)* [2007] ECR II-2251.............3.67
T-130/01, *Sykes Enterprises Inc v OHIM* [2002] ECR II-5179..........................5.154
T-151/01, *Duales System Deutschland GmbH v Commission of the European Communities*
    [2007] ECR II-1607............................11.188, 11.192–11.197, 11.211, 11.214
T-162/01, *Laboratorios RTB v OHIM (BASS)* [2003] ECR II-2821......................7.218
T-237/01, *Alcon Inc v OHIM Dr Robert Winzer Pharma (BSS)* [2003]
    ECR II-411 ....5.745–5.752, 6.47, 7.294
T-247/01, *eCopy Inc v OHIM* [2003] ECR II-5301..............................7.227, 7.228
T-292/01, *Philips-Van Heusen v OHIM* [2003] ECR II-4335.....................7.76, 7.214
T-421/01, *Traunfellner GmbH v Österreichische Autobahnen-und
    Schnellstrassen-Finanzierungs-AG* [2003] ECR I-11941....................4.189, 7.283
T-107/02, *GE Betz v OHIM—Atofina Chemicals* (BIOMATE) [2004] ECR II-1845..........7.574
T-146/02 to T-153/02, *Deutsche SiSi-Werke GmbH & Co Betriebs KG v OHIM*
    (Flat-bottomed pouches) [2004] ECR II-447..............5.389–5.391, 5.398, 5.424–5.426
T-164/02, *Kaul v OHIM—Bayer AG (ARCOL)* [2004] ECR II-3807.............3.29–3.35, 3.39
T-185/02, *Succession Picasso v OHIM (PICASSO)* [2005] ECR II-I739..........3.63, 7.182–7.185,
                                                                            7.191–7.192
T-203/02, *Sunrider Corp v OHIM* [2005] ECR II-2793.........................8.60, 8.62–8.65
T-278/02, *Dyson Limited v OHIM* [2002] OJ C289/28................................4.14
T-355/02, *Mülhens GmbH & Co KG v OHIM* [2004] ECR II-791....................7.75–7.77
T-399/02, *Eurocermex SA v OHIM* [2004] ECR II-1391...................5.427–5.434, 5.437
T-402/02, *Storck v OHIM* [2004] ECR II-3849.....................................5.460–5.466
T-8/03, *El Corte Ingles v OHIM-Pucci* (EMILIO PUCCI) [2004] ECR II-4297............6.127
T-31/03, *Grupo Sada v OHIM—Sadia (Grupo Sada)* [2005] ECR II-01667................9.408
T-57/03, *Société provencale d'achat et de gestion (SPAG) SA v OHIM (HOOLIGAN/OLLY
    GAN)* [2005] ECR II-287...3.59, 3.61
T-81/03, T-82/03, and T-103/03, *Mast-Jägermeister v OHIM—Licorera Zacapaneca*
    (VENADO with frame and Others), EU:T:2006:397..........................7.601
T-112/03, *L'Oreal v OHIM* [2005] ECR II-949...............................7.114–7.120
T-117/03, T-118/03, T-119/03, and T-171/03, *New Look Ltd v OHIM* (NL SPORT, NL
    JEANS, NL ACTIVE, NL COLLECTION) [2005] ECR II-3471..................7.338
T-126/03, *Reckitt Benckiser (España), SL v OHIM/Aladin Gesellschaft für innovative
    mikrobiologische Systeme GmbH* [2005] ECR II-02861........................8.207
T-130/03, *Alcon v OHIM-Biofarma* (TRAVATAN) [2005] ECR II-3859......7.290, 7.292, 7.294–7.295

T-164/03, *Ampafrance SA v OHIM (MONBEBE/BEBE)* [2005] ECR II-1401 .... 3.67, 5.696
T-169/03, *Sergio Rossi* [2005] ECR II-685 .... 7.198, 7.201–7.223
T-185/03, *Fusco v OHIM (PICASSO)* [2005] ECR II-715. .... 7.253
T-194/03, *Il Ponte Finanziaria v OHIM—Marine Enterprise Projects* (BAINBRIDGE)
  [2006] ECR II-00445 .... 8.178, 8.252
T-215/03, *SIGLA v OHIM-Elleni Holding* (VIPS) [2007] ECR II-711 .... 7.505, 7.534
T-291/03, *Consorzio per la tutela del formaggio Grana Padano v OHIM* [2007]
  ECR II-3081 .... 12.134–12.137
T-425/03, *AMS Advanced Medical Services GmbH v OHIM* [2007] ECR II-04265 .... 8.119
T-7/04, *Shaker v OHIM—Limiñana y Botella (Limoncello della Costiera Amalfitana
  shaker)* [2008] ECR II-3085 .... 7.106, 7.300–7.302
T-19/04, *Metso Paper Automation v OHIM (PAPERLAB)* [2005] ECR II-2383 .... 5.77
T-22/04, *Reemark Gesellschaft für Markenkooperation mbH v OHIM* [2005]
  ECR II-1559. .... 7.245
T-74/04, *SSociété des Produits Nestlé v OHIM* 7.306–7.311
T-129/04, *Develey Holding GmbH & Co Beleiligungs KG v OHIM
  (PLASTIKFLASCHENFORM)* [2007] ECR II-811 .... 3.63, 5.715–5.718
T-150/04, *Tosca Blu* [2007] ECR II-02353 .... 7.356
T-201/04, *Microsoft Corp v Commission* [2007] 5 CMLR 11 .... 11.154–11.167
T-256/04, *Mundipharma AG v OHIM* (RESPICUR/RESPICORT),
  ECLI:EU:T:2008:203 .... 7.290
T-262/04, *BIC v OHIM* (Shape of a lighter) [2005] ECR II-5959. .... 6.127
T-305/04, *Eden SARL v OHIM* [2006] ETMR 14, Celex No 604A0305 .... 4.105
T-346/04, *Sadas SA v OHIM* [2006] ETMR 27. .... 7.08
T-353/04, *Ontex NY v OHIM* (CURON/EURON) ECR [2007] ECR II-10 .... 7.290
T-363/04, *Koipe v OHIM-Aceites del Sur* (LA ESPAÑOLA) [2007] ECR 3355. .... 7.318–7.324
T-477/04, *Aktieselskabet af 21 november 2001 v OHIM* (TDK) [2007]
  ECR II-00399 .... 7.506
T-172/05, *Armacell v OHIM* (ARMAFOAM) [2006] ECR II-4061 .... 7.334–7.335, 7.341–7.343
T-181/05, *Citigroup v OHIM* [2008] ECR II-00669. .... 7.504, 7.506, 7.n454
T-407/05, *SAEME v OHIM—Racke* (REVIAN's) [2007] ECR II-4385 .... 7.574
T-434/05, *Gateway, Inc. v OHIM* (ACTIVY MEDIA GATEWAY) [2008]
  ECR I-00188. .... 7.334
T-441/05, *IVG Immobilien v OHIM (I)* [2007] ECR II-1937 .... 5.96
T-458/05, *Tegometall International AG v OHIM*. 5.696
T-47/06, *Antartica Srl/OHIM* (NASDAQ) [2007] ECR II-00042. .... 7.549–7.554, 8.115–8.120
T-70/06, *Audi AG v OHIM* [2008] ECR II-00131 .... 5.179–5.181, 5.185–5.190
T-88/06, *Dorel Juvenile Group Inc v OHIM* [2008] ECR II-00010. .... 5.177
T-93/06, *Mülhens v OHIM-Spa Monopole* (MINERAL SPA) [2008] ECR II-00093 .... 7.506, 7.534
T-128/06, *Japan Tobacco v OHIM-Torrefaccao Camelo* (CAMELO) [2008]
  ECR II-00014. .... 7.534
T-146/06, *Sanofi-Aventis SA v OHIM* (ATURION/URION) [2008] ECR 17 .... 5.177
T-215/06, *American Clothing Associates v OHIM* (Representation of a maple leaf)
  [2008] ECR II-303. .... 5.891–5.894
T-270/06, *Lego Juris A/S v OHIM (Mega Brands)* [2008] ECR II-3117 .... 5.770–5.773, 5.807
T-302/06, *Hartmann v OHIM (E)* ECLI:EU:T:2008:267 .... 5.96
T-304/06, *Paul Reber GmbH & Co KG v OHIM* (MOZART/MOZART) [2008]
  ECR II-01927 .... 3.108
T-21/07, *L'Oreal v OHIM* (SPALINE) [2009] ECR II-00031. .... 7.506
T-36/07, *Zipcar Inc v OHIM* (ZIPCAR/CICAR) () [2009] ECR I-00095 .... 3.71
T-189/07, *Frosch Touristik GmbH v OHIM* (FLUGBÖRSE) [2009] ECR I-01503 .... 6.137
T-435/07, *New Look Ltd v OHIM* (NEW LOOK) 7.339
T-109/08, *Freixenet v OHIM Market (Frosted white bottle)* [2010]
  ECR II-00066 .... 5.484–5.487
T-110/08, *Freixenet v OHIM Market (Frosted black matt bottle)* [2010]
  ECR II-00066. .... 5.484–5.487

T-336/08, *Chocoladefabriken Lindt & Sprüngli AG v OHIM* [2010]
  ECR II-00291 .... 5.492–5.493
T-345 and T-357/08, *Rubinstein and L'Oréal v OHIM—Allergan* (BOTOLIST
  and BOTOCYL), [2010] ECR II-00279 .... 7.562–7.565
T-476/08, *Media-Saturn v OHIM* [2009] ECR II-00240 .... 5.502–5.503
T-10/09, *Formula One Licensing v OHIM—Global Sports Media* (F1-LIVE)
  [2011] ECR II-00427 .... 7.102, 7.106
T-13/09, *August Storck KG v OHIM* [2010] ECR II-00297 .... 5.495
T-286/09, *Intel Corporation v Commission*, ECLI:EU:T:2014:547 .... 11.167
T-355/09, *Reber Holding GmbH & Co. KG v OHIM*, ECLI:EU:T:2013:22 ..... 8.72–8.74
T-427/09, *Centrotherm* [2011] ECR II-06207 .... 3.37
T-434/09, *Centrotherm* [2011] ECR II-06227 .... 3.37
T-523/09, *Smart Technologies v OHIM*, ECLI:EU:T:2011:175 .... 5.197
T-237/10, *Louis Vuitton Malletier v OHIM—Friis Group International ApS* [2011]
  ECR II-00449 .... 5.497
T-331/10, *Yoshida Metal Industry v OHIM—Pi-Design and Others* (Representation
  of a triangular surface with black dots), ECLI:EU:T:2012:220 .... 5.800
T-416/10, *Yoshida Metal Industry v OHIM—Pi-Design and Others* (Representation
  of a surface with black dots), ECLI:EU:T:2012:222 .... 5.800
T-569/10, *Bimbo SA v OHIM/Panrico SA* CLI:EU:T:2012:535 .... 7.263, 7.269
T-570/10, *Environmental Manufacturing v OHIM* (Representation of a wolf's head),
  ECLI:EU:T:2015:76 .... 7.512
T-170/11, *Rivella International AG v OHIM/Baskaya di Kaskaya Alim e C.Sas*,
  ECLI:EU:T:2012:374 .... 8.167
T-460/11, *Scandic Distilleries v OHMI—Bürgerbräu, Röhm & Söhne* (BÜRGER)
  ECLI:EU:T:2012:432 .... 9.408
T-515/11, *Delphi Technologies Inc v OHIM*, ECLI:EU:T:2013:300 .... 5.197
T-567/12, *Kaatsu International Co*, ECLI:EU:T:2014:937 .... 3.59
T-78/13, *Red Bull GmbH v OHIM/Sun Mark Ltd*, ECLI:EU:T:2015:72 .... 7.597–7.602
T-368/13, *Boehringer Ingelheim International GmbH v Lehning Enterprise SARL*,
  ECLI:EU:T:2015:81 .... 3.59

OHIM Boards of Appeal/BoA

R-35/1998-1, *Procter & Gamble v OHIM*, 31 July 1998 .... 5.533
R-46/1998-2, *Giacomelli Sport*, 17 December 1999 .... 4.180, 7.275
R-156/1998-2, *Vennootschap Onder Firma Senta Aromatic Marketing's Application*
  [1999] ETMR 429 .... 4.88
R-122/1998-3, *LIGHT GREEN*, 19 December 1998 .... 4.137
R-506/1999-1, *Procter & Gamble*, 8 March 2000 .... 5.339
R-508/1999-1, *Procter & Gamble*, 8 March 2000 .... 5.339
R-509/1999-1, *Procter & Gamble*, 8 March 2000 .... 5.333
R-516/1999-1, *Procter & Gamble*, 19 April 2000 .... 5.333
R-519/1999-1, *Procter & Gamble*, 29 February 2000 .... 5.333
R-520/1999-1, *Procter & Gamble*, 29 February 2000 .... 5.333
R-529/1999-1, *Procter & Gamble*, 29 February 2000 .... 5.333
R-282/1999-2, *KWS Saat AG v OHIM*, 19 April 2000 .... 5.238–5.242
R-292/1999-2, 24 January 2006 .... 5.175
R-312/1999-2, *SatellitenFernsehen GmbH v OHIM* (SAT.1), 2 August 2000 ..... 5.37
R-423/1999-2, *Streamserve Inc v OHIM*, 28 February 2000 .... 5.633
R-719 to 724/1999-2, *Deutsche SiSi-Werke GmbH & Co Betriebs KG v OHIM*,
  28 February 2002 .... 5.389
R-728 and R-792/1999-2, *Matratzen Concord GmbH v OHIM*,
  31 October 2000 .... 7.89
R-747/1999-2, *Deutsche SiSi-Werke GmbH & Co Betriebs KG v OHIM*,
  28 February 2002 .... 5.389

R-748/1999-2, *Deutsche SiSi-Werke GmbH & Co Betriebs KG v OHIM*,
  28 February 2002 .... 5.389
R-70, 71 nd 73/1999-3, *Henkel KGaA*, 21 September 1999 .... 5.223–5.232
R-351/1999-3, *Telefon & Buch v OHIM*, 21 October 1999 .... 5.649
R-352/1999-3, *Telefon & Buch v OHIM*, 21 October 1999 .... 5.649
R-392/1999-3, *Erpo Möbelwerk v OHIM* [2001] ECR II-3739 .... 5.147
R-127/2000-1, *Vedial SA v OHIM*, 9 March 2001 .... 7.56
R-273/2000-1, *Alcon Inc v OHIM* 5.745
R-111/2000-2, *Ringling Bros v Barnum & Bailey Inc (The Greatest Show on Earth)* 6.47
R-256/2001-2, *Storck v OHIM*, 18 October 2002 .... 5.460
R-247/2001-3, *Picasso v OHIM*, 18 March 2002 .... 7.182
R-396/2001-4, *Storck v OHIM*, 15 January 2003 .... 7.114
R-153/2002-1, *Consorzio per la tutela del formaggio Grana Padano v OHIM*
  [2007] ECR II-3081 .... 12.134
R-188/2002-1, *Eurocermex SA v OHIM*, 21 October 2002 .... 5.429
R-569/2002-1, *Sergio Rossi*, 28 February 2003 .... 7.198
R-0986/2004-4, *Glaverbel SA v OHIM*, 1 March 2004 .... 5.316
R-856/2004-G, *Lego Juris A/S v Mega Brands Inc* [2007] ETMR 11 .... 5.770–5.773
R-107/2012-1, *Red Bull GmbH v OHIM* 7.597

European Commission

Commission Decision 64/566 *(Grundig)* [1964] CMLR 489; [1964] OJ 2545 .... 11.14
Commission Decision 68/376 *(Rieckermann/AEG)* [1968] OJ L 276/25 .... 11.90
Commission Decision 75/297 *(Re the Agreement of Sirdar Ltd)* [1975] OJ L 125/27;
  [1975] 1 CMLR D93; [1975] FSR 492 .... 11.73
Commission Decision 78/253 *(Re the Agreements of Campari-Milano SPA)*
  [1978] OJ L 70/69; [1978] 2 CMLR 397; [1978] FSR 528 .... 11.77–11.84, 11.90
Commission Decision 78/823 *(Breeders' rights—maize seed)* [1978] OJ L 286/23;
  [1978] 3 CMLR 11.53
Commission Decision 82/866 *(Rolled Zinc Products and Zinc Alloys)* [1982]
  OJ L 362/40; [1983] 2 CMLR 285 .... 11.90
Commission Decision 82/897 *(TOLTECS/DORCET)* [1982] OJ L 379/19;
  [1983] 1 CMLR 412 .... 11.70
Commission Decision 89/205 *Magill* [1989] OJ L 78/43 .... 11.129
Commission Decision 90/186 *(Moosehead and Whitbread, Agreement)* [1990]
  OJ L 100/32 .... 11.77
Commission Decision 90/645 *(Re Bayer Dental)* [1990] OJ L 351/46 .... 11.76
Commission Decision 92/33/EEC of 16 December 1991 *(Yves Saint Laurent
  Parfums)* [1992] OJ L12/24 .... 10.262
Commission Decision 92/33 *(Yves Saint Laurent Parfums)* [1992] OJ L 12/24 ..... 11.85
Commission Decision 92/428 of July 24, 1992 *(Parfums Givenchy System
  of Selective Distribution)* [1992] OJ L236/11 .... 10., 10.262
Commission Decision 92/428 of July 24, 1992 relating to a proceeding under
  Article 85 EEC C-IV/ 10.262
Commission Notice under Article 19(3) of Reg 17, *Chanel* [1994] OJ C 334/11 ..... 11.90
Commission Decision 2007/53/EC of 24 March 2004
  (Case COMP/C-3/37.792—*Microsoft* [2007] OJ L 32/23) 11.154
EEC v Bayer AG (Bayo-Nox) [1990] 4 CMLR 930 .... 11.75
EEC v Syntex Corp [1990] 4 CMLR 343 .... 11.75
Re the Persil Trade Mark [1978] CMLR 3952 .... 11.74

European Court of Human Rights

Anheuser-Busch Inc v Portugal (Budweiser V), Application no. 73049/01
  [2006] ETMR 43 .... 3.111, 12.230–12.246
Beyeler v Italy, Application no. 33202/96 [GC] ECHR 2000-i 12.243

British-American Tobacco Co Ltd v The Netherlands A, C-331-A[1996]
  21 EHRR 409 .... 12.243
Broniowski v Poland, Application no. 31443/96 [GC] ECHR 2004-v 12.243
Gratzinger and Gratzingerova v The Czech Republic, Application no. 39794/98
  [GC] ECHR 2002-VII. 12.244
Iatridis v Greece, Application no. 31107/96 [GC] ECHR 1999-11 .... 12.246
Lithgow v UK, Opinion referring to [1986] 8 EHRR 329 .... 12.246
Smith Kline and French Laboratories Ltd v The Netherlands,
  Application no. 12633/87, 4 October 1990, Decisions and Reports (DR) 66 .... 12.243

EFTA COURT

E-3/02, *Paranova AS v Merck & CO Inc and others* [2003] EFTA Court Rep 101 .... 10.335,
10.348, 10.381

INTERNATIONAL CASES

World Trade Organization

United States—Section 211 of the Omnibus Appropriations Act, Appellate Body Report,
  6 August 2001 .... 12.211

TABLE OF LEGISLATION

NATIONAL LEGISLATION

Austria

Markenschutzgesetz (Trade Mark Protection Law)
- § 10a 9.513
- § 33a 8.79, 8.222
- § 60 .... 9.518
- § 60(1) 9.513
- § 60(2) 9.513

Benelux

Uniform Benelux Law on
- trade marks 10.266
- Art 6bis 5.667
- Art 6ter 5.667
- Art 13A(1)(d) 9.363
- Art 13C(1) 6.113

Denmark

Trade Mark Law
- s 15(3)(3) 5.933–5.934

France

Code de la propriété intellectuelle (Intellectual Property Code) 1992
- Art L 713-2 .... 7.14

Germany

Law Against Unfair Competition 5.860, 7.404
- s 3 .... 5.860, 5.872

Law on Foodstuffs and Consumer Items
- s 27 .... 5.860, 5.868

Law on Restraints of Competition
- s 15 .... 5.872

Markengesetz (Trade Mark Law) 7.404
- § 8(2)(3) 5.740
- § 26(3) 8.184

Portugal

New Code on Industrial Property 2003 .... 12.237
- Art 5 .... 12.242
- Protocol 1, Art 1 .... 12.243–12.244

Spain

Law No 17/2001 on Trade Marks
- Art 6(2)(a) 7.169
- Art 6(2)(c) 7.169

Sweden

Trade Mark Law
- Art 37 .... 9.438
- Art 37a 9.445

UK Statutes

Trade Marks Act 1938 .... 9.392
Trade Marks Act 1994
- s 5(3) 7.460
- s 10(1) 7.527–7.528
- s 10(3) 7.527–7.528
- s 76 .... 4.198

UK Statutory Instruments

Civil Procedure Rules
- Art 61 .... 4.162

United States

Omnibus Appropriations Act 1998
- s 211 .... 12.211

Trade Mark Act 1946
- s 43(c) 7.470

Trademark Dilution Revision Act 2006 (TDRA, 15 USC 1051) 7.470

EU INSTRUMENTS

Treaties and Conventions

Agreement on the European Economic Area 1994
- Art 54 .... 11.154

Brussels Convention 1968 .... 2.50

Charter of Fundamental Rights of the European Union 2000
- Art 41(2) 5.265
- Art 47 .... 3.103

European Convention on the Protection of Human Rights and Fundamental Freedoms 1950
- Art 6 .... 5.265
- Art 7 .... 9.518

European Patent Convention 1973
   Art 114 . . . . 3.24
Statute of the European Court of Justice
   Art 21 . . . . .3.65
   Art 23 . . . . .4.219
   Art 36 . . . . 3.72, 3.74, 7.120
   Art 49 . . . . 5.33, 5.539
   Art 53 . . . . 3.72, 3.74, 7.120
   Art 54 . . . . .5.555
   Art 58 . . . . 3.65, 3.69, 3.72, 3.91, 3.93
   Art 61 . . . . 3.38, 3.55, 5.191
Treaty Establishing a Constitution for
   Europe [2004] OJ C310/1 . . . . 3.04
Treaty Establishing the EEC (Treaty
   on the Functioning of the
   European Union, Rome 1958)
   Art 3(g) 11.06
   Art 10 . . . . 7.84, 11.48
   Art 14 . . . . .7.413
   Art 24 . . . . .9.529
   Art 26(2) 8.141
   Art 28 . . . . 10.03, 10.56, 10.136
   Art 30 . . . . 10.03, 10.26, 10.48,
         10.94, 10.120, 10.124, 10.130,
         10.132, 10.136, 10.169
   Art 34 (formerly Art 28) 5.866–5.868,
         5.875, 5.879–5.880, 9.510, 9.512,
         10.04, 10.33, 10.56, 10.169, 10.236,
         10.254, 12.108, 12.165, 12.169,
         12.171, 12.173, 12.175, 12.186
   Art 35 . . . . 10.04, 10.169
   Art 36 (formerly Art 30) 5.866,
         5.879–5.880, 7.98, 9.508, 9.510,
         10.05, 10.41, 10.60, 10.63, 10.87,
         10.94, 10.100–10.101, 10.105,
         10.109, 10.113, 10.115, 10.120,
         10.126, 10.128, 10.139, 10.141–10.143,
         10.169–10.171, 10.174–10.175,
         10.194, 10.199, 10.231, 10.236–10.237,
         10.249, 10.254, 10.265, 10.339,
         11.22, 12.108, 12.164–12.165,
         12.167–12.169, 12.171–12.172,
         12.184–12.186, 12.188
   Art 37 . . . . .10.04
   Art 39 . . . . .12.123
   Art 43 . . . . .12.123
   Art 57 . . . . .4.249
   Art 81 . . . . 11.16
   Art 81(1) 11.75
   Art 82 . . . . 11.148, 11.154, 11.181
   Art 95 . . . . .10.136
   Art 101 . . . . 10.62, 10.97, 10.100, 11.01,
         11.06–11.07, 11.12, 11.15, 11.17,
         11.26, 11.62–11.63, 11.70–11.71
   Art 101(1) 11.07, 11.12,
         11.13, 11.15–11.16, 11.18,
         11.20–11.22, 11.28–11.30, 11.32,
         11.34–11.35, 11.39–11.40, 11.42,
         11.44–11.48, 11.50, 11.52, 11.53,
         11.55, 11.57–11.59, 11.67, 11.75,
         11.76, 11.79–11.82, 11.86–11.87,
         11.88, 11.90–11.95, 11.97, 11.116
   Art 101(3) 11.04, 11.07,
         11.13–11.14, 11.23, 11.25, 11.33,
         11.45–11.47, 11.59, 11.67, 11.76,
         11.84, 11.85–11.86, 11.92
   Art 102 . . . . 10.108–10.109, 11.01,
         11.06, 11.08, 11.12, 11.15,
         11.45–11.46, 11.48, 11.70,
         11.110, 11.114, 11.117,
         11.136, 11.143, 11.148,
         11.154, 11.158, 11.160,
         11.179–11.180, 11.184,
         11.187, 11.196, 11.212
   Art 102(b) 11.162
   Art 105(1) 11.73
   Art 110 . . . . 10.07, 10.13
   Art 113 . . . . .9.505
   Art 114 . . . . 10.281, 10.289
   Art 131 . . . . .9.563
   Art 189 . . . . .9.291
   Art 206 . . . . .9.563
   Art 217 . . . . .2.35
   Art 225 . . . . 3.65, 3.69, 5.273–5.274
   Art 226 . . . . 9.515
   Art 227 . . . . 9.515
   Art 234 . . . . 5.597, 8.43, 8.230, 10.239,
         10.266, 11.176
   Art 235 . . . . 2.04
   Art 252 . . . . .9.238
   Art 258 . . . . 3.06
   Art 260 . . . . .3.07
   Art 263 . . . . 3.03, 3.09, 3.10–3.11
   Art 265 . . . . .3.08
   Art 267 . . . . 3.13, 4.219, 10.256
   Art 267(3) 3.17
   Art 267(b) 4.219
   Art 277 . . . . 3.10, 3.10–3.11
   Art 288 . . . . .12.143
   Art 290 . . . . .13.50
   Art 291 . . . . .13.50
   Art 345 . . . . 10.57, 11.22
   Art 351 . . . . .12.174
   Annex I 12.123
Treaty on European Union
   (Maastricht Treaty 1992)
   Art 3(g) 4.47
   Art 3(m) 4.47
   Art 4(3) 9.471
   Art 6 . . . . 3.106, 5.265
   Art 13 . . . . .3.02
   Art 19 . . . . .3.89

Directives (in chronological order)

Council Directive 76/768/EEC on the Approximation of the Laws of the Member States Relating to Cosmetic Products [1976] OJ L 262/169 .... 5.867, 9.194, 10.298
  Art 6(1) 9.200, 9.209–9.210
  Art 6(2) 5.868
Council Directive 79/112/EEC labelling, presentation and advertising of foodstuffs [1979] OJ L33/1 .... 10.251
  Art 4(2) 10.52
Council Directive 80/777/EEC of 15 July 1980 on the approximation of the laws of the Member States relating to the exploitation and marketing of natural mineral waters, [1980] OJ L229/1 .... 9.323
Council Directive 84/450/EEC (Misleading Advertising Directive) [1984] OJ 1250/17, as amended by Directive 97/55/EC [1997] OJ 1290/18 .... 12.03
  Art 2 .... 12.03, 12.209
  Art 2(1) 12.18
  Art 2(2) 12.03, 12.04, 12.28, 12.36
  Art 2(2a) 9.37, 12.06, 12.07, 12.18–12.19, 12.21, 12.35, 12.55, 12.63, 12.74, 12.81
  Art 2a. 12.03
  Art 3a. 12.19, 12.69, 12.72, 12.77, 12.94
  Art 3a(1). 12.04, 12.08, 12.30, 12.39–12.40, 12.64, 12.67, 12.74–12.75, 12.82–12.83, 12.85, 12.90–12.91
  Art 3a(1)(a). 12.27, 12.29, 12.32–12.34, 12.38
  Art 3a(1)(b) 12.55, 12.63
  Art 3a(1)(c). 12.20–12.21, 12.27, 12.46, 12.99
  Art 3a(1)(d) 12.38, 12.75, 12.90
  Art 3a(1)(e). 12.27, 12.34, 12.38, 12.41, 12.70, 12.90
  Art 3a(1)(f). 12.55, 12.59, 12.65
  Art 3a(1)(g) 12.06, 12.27, 12.38, 12.44, 12.53, 12.65, 12.70, 12.80, 12.86, 12.88, 12.90–12.91
  Art 3a(1)(h) 12.80, 12.90–12.91
First Council Directive 89/104/EEC of 21 December 1988 to Approximate the Laws of the Member States Relating to Trade Marks [1989] OJ L 40 .... 2.02, 2.04–2.13, 2.59–2.60, 2.62, 5.865, 5.867, 13.02

Recital 1. .... 6.101
Recital 2. .... 9.395
Recital 3. .... 5.691, 9.372, 10.136, 10.279
Recital 4. .... 4.201, 5.936
Recital 5. .... 5.691
Recital 7. .... 5.620, 5.766, 8.245
Recital 8. .... 4.201, 4.222, 7.453, 8.05, 8.245
Recital 9. .... 8.245
Recital 10. .... 4.95, 4.163, 4.201, 6.153, 7.54, 9.98, 9.402
Recital 11. .... 7.453, 9.395, 9.396, 9.400
Recital 12. .... 12.12
Recital 13. .... 12.12
Art 1 .... 6.116, 8.230, 12.90
Art 2 .... 4.02, 4.08, 4.13–4.14, 4.18, 4.20, 4.21, 4.24, 4.25, 4.31, 4.37, 4.51, 4.54, 4.56–4.57, 4.61, 4.63, 4.65, 4.67–4.74, 4.95, 4.97, 4.111, 4.123, 4.124, 4.134, 4.135, 4.136–4.137, 4.150, 4.152–4.153, 4.164, 4.168, 4.174–4.175, 4.245, 4.247–4.248, 4.251, 4.257, 4.261, 5.134, 5.140, 5.209–5.210, 5.286, 5.291, 5.305, 6.148, 8.100
Art 3 .... 4.09, 4.63, 4.71, 5.620, 5.668, 5.679, 5.702, 8.100, 8.279, 9.93, 9.94, 12.03, 12.04, 12.36
Art 3(1) 4.15, 4.65, 5.06, 5.12, 6.145, 6.151
Art 3(1)(a) 4.09, 4.22–4.23, 4.157, 4.159, 4.163, 4.164, 4.167–4.168, 4.172, 5.05, 5.204
Art 3(1)(b) 4.02, 4.09, 4.20, 4.23, 4.69, 4.74, 4.132, 4.157–4.158, 4.164–4.165, 4.168, 4.172, 5.05, 5.10, 5.29, 5.56, 5.86–5.87, 5.91, 5.95, 5.133, 5.136–5.140, 5.146, 5.195, 5.200, 5.222, 5.225–5.226, 5.228, 5.282, 5.284–5.285, 5.289, 5.292, 5.301, 5.303, 5.358, 5.379, 5.511, 5.629, 5.706, 5.728, 5.730, 6.06, 6.14, 6.28, 6.37, 6.40–6.41, 6.98–6.99, 6.100, 6.101, 6.103, 6.110–6.111, 6.113, 6.148, 9.86, 9.88, 9.91, 9.522, 12.160
Art 3(1)(c) 3.109, 4.09, 4.23, 4.69, 4.157–4.158, 4.164–4.165, 4.168, 5.06, 5.10, 5.29, 5.86–5.87, 5.91, 5.95, 5.134, 5.146, 5.215–5.217, 5.282, 5.285, 5.289, 5.298–5.300, 5.301, 5.303, 5.307, 5.504, 5.506, 5.508–5.509, 5.511–5.515, 5.521–5.522, 5.525–5.530, 5.601, 5.603, 5.623–5.624, 5.626, 5.629–5.630, 5.632, 5.706, 5.730, 5.742, 5.821, 6.06, 6.14, 6.28,

	6.98–6.101, 6.100, 6.103, 6.110–6.111, 6.113, 6.117, 7.435, 8.272–8.273, 9.86–9.87, 9.90–9.91, 9.316
Art 3(1)(d)	4.09, 4.23, 4.157–4.158, 4.164–4.165, 4.168, 5.282, 5.285, 5.289, 5.511, 5.629, 5.723–5.724, 5.726–5.730, 5.733, 5.735, 5.738–5.742, 6.28, 6.117, 8.268, 8.270
Art 3(1)(e)	4.27, 4.43, 4.45–4.51, 4.161, 5.215–5.217, 5.285, 5.288, 5.289–5.290, 5.295–5.297, 5.301, 5.303, 5.307, 5.601, 5.623, 5.759–5.762, 5.766, 5.769, 5.812, 5.815–5.816, 5.818, 5.820–5.822, 5.820–5.824, 5.827, 5.829–5.830, 5.834–5.835, 5.838–5.839, 6.27, 6.30, 6.44, 7.435, 9.88
Art 3(1)(e)(ii)	5.759–5.760, 5.768
Art 3(1)(e)(iii)	5.808
Art 3(1)(f)	4.09, 5.761
Art 3(1)(g)	4.09, 5.761, 5.841–5.842, 5.851, 5.855–5.858, 12.122, 12.131–12.132, 12.139, 12.149
Art 3(2)	4.09
Art 3(2)(a)	12.139
Art 3(2)(d)	5.915
Art 3(3)	4.09, 4.12, 4.30, 4.44, 4.50, 4.53, 4.159, 4.165, 4.168, 5.222, 5.224–5.226, 5.228, 5.286, 5.289, 5.294, 5.300, 5.621, 5.730, 5.761, 5.766, 5.814–5.816, 5.818, 6.01, 6.13–6.14, 6.17–6.18, 6.26, 6.28, 6.30, 6.34–6.35, 6.36, 6.41–6.42, 6.44, 6.44–6.45, 6.49, 6.90, 6.93, 6.103–6.104, 6.106, 6.117–6.118, 6.121, 6.131, 6.145, 6.148, 6.151, 6.152, 6.155, 8.267, 8.274
Art 3(4)	4.09, 9.275
Art 3a	9.37
Art 4	7.01, 7.06, 7.361, 7.365, 8.100, 12.202
Art 4(1)	4.188, 7.06, 7.282, 7.412, 8.100
Art 4(1)(a)	9.391–9.394, 9.398, 9.402, 9.404
Art 4(1)(b)	4.177, 5.93, 7.06, 7.21, 7.28, 7.31, 7.53, 7.61–7.62, 7.65, 7.69, 7.272, 7.407, 8.265
Art 4(2)	7.06, 9.397
Art 4(2)(b)	7.353, 7.354, 7.364
Art 4(2)(c)	9.401
Art 4(2)(d)	7.368, 9.401, 12.202
Art 4(3)	7.06
Art 4(4)	7.06, 7.403, 7.404, 7.414, 7.416
Art 4(4)(a)	7.06, 7.40, 7.348, 7.354, 7.405–7.407, 7.412, 7.462, 7.464, 7.478, 7.482, 7.484–7.486, 7.495, 7.502
Art 4(4)(b)	7.364, 7.368, 12.202
Art 4(4)(g)	5.912, 5.934–5.937, 5.940, 7.06, 8.02
Art 4(5)	7.06, 9.398
Art 4(6)	7.06, 9.275
Art 5	6.44, 7.164, 7.421, 8.81, 8.86, 8.100, 9.02, 9.50, 9.89, 9.94, 9.152–9.153, 9.169, 9.179, 9.214, 9.241, 9.292, 9.314–9.315, 9.329, 9.399, 9.542, 10.254, 10.267, 10.325, 10.332, 10.339–10.340, 10.392, 10.394, 12.199, 12.209, 13.27
Art 5(1)	4.188, 5.701, 7.149, 7.160, 7.162, 7.282, 7.351, 7.412, 7.415, 7.431, 7.591, 8.100, 9.02, 9.08, 9.34–9.36, 9.38–9.40, 9.44, 9.107, 9.114, 9.119, 9.128, 9.177, 9.265, 9.294, 9.369–9.370, 9.374–9.378, 9.384, 9.522, 9.526, 9.529, 9.532, 9.577, 10.89, 10.279, 10.311, 10.338, 10.389, 10.391, 10.401, 12.73–12.76, 12.79, 12.83
Art 5(1)(a)	7.09, 7.15, 7.17, 7.197, 7.434, 7.527, 7.529, 9.02, 9.40, 9.46, 9.60, 9.69–9.70, 9.72–9.73, 9.76, 9.81, 9.102–9.103, 9.106–9.110, 9.112–9.113, 9.115, 9.148, 9.151, 9.168, 9.190, 9.200, 9.212, 9.224, 9.239, 9.259, 9.263, 9.266, 9.274, 9.280, 9.293, 9.298, 9.373, 9.375, 9.386, 9.402, 9.494, 10.286, 10.398, 12.67–12.68, 12.84, 12.90
Art 5(1)(b)	4.177, 7.17, 7.39–7.41, 7.241, 7.249, 7.272, 7.416, 8.265, 9.02, 9.32, 9.40, 9.95, 9.97, 9.103, 9.107, 9.109, 9.125–9.127, 9.148, 9.151, 9.170, 9.174, 9.263, 9.266–9.267, 9.269–9.270, 9.274, 9.275, 9.284, 9.324, 9.494, 12.67–12.68, 12.75–12.77
Art 5(2)	6.105–6.106, 7.40, 7.348–7.349, 7.351, 7.354, 7.367, 7.385, 7.389, 7.403, 7.404, 7.405–7.406, 7.412, 7.414–7.416, 7.417, 7.421–7.422, 7.423–7.424, 7.427–7.428, 7.430–7.434, 7.462, 7.478, 7.482, 7.502, 7.525, 7.527, 7.530, 7.532–7.533, 7.538, 7.585, 7.586, 7.590–7.591, 7.593, 7.596, 9.02, 9.35, 9.77, 9.99, 9.104, 9.106,

	9.107, 9.111, 9.113–9.114, 9.125, 9.164, 9.212, 9.224, 9.232, 9.258–9.259, 9.274, 9.275, 9.285, 9.294, 9.296, 9.370, 9.377, 9.384, 12.73–12.75, 12.79, 12.83, 12.85
Art 5(3)	7.149, 7.161, 9.02, 9.265, 9.297, 9.377, 9.494, 9.577, 10.323
Art 5(3)(a)	9.494
Art 5(3)(b)	3.109, 9.76, 9.494, 9.531
Art 5(3)(c)	9.494, 9.522, 9.529, 12.122, 12.131–12.132, 12.160
Art 5(3)(d)	9.115, 9.494, 10.255, 10.257, 12.73
Art 5(4)	9.274, 9.275, 9.291
Art 5(5)	7.434, 9.02, 9.35, 9.44, 9.274, 9.286, 9.294, 9.296, 9.363, 9.363–9.371, 9.384, 12.208, 13.27
Art 6	7.421, 9.03, 9.78, 9.89, 9.272, 9.287–9.290, 9.298, 9.307, 9.310, 9.314–9.315, 9.317, 9.329, 10.254, 10.339, 12.83
Art 6(1)	9.37, 9.43, 9.90, 9.177, 9.179, 9.190, 9.289–9.290, 9.324, 9.337, 9.352
Art 6(1)(a)	5.136–5.139, 5.145, 9.03, 9.60, 9.379–9.380, 9.383, 12.210
Art 6(1)(b)	5.521, 5.525, 5.701, 7.529, 9.03, 9.82, 9.90–9.91, 9.94, 9.100–9.101, 9.175, 9.309, 9.311–9.313, 9.316–9.318, 9.322, 9.325, 9.353–9.354, 9.355–9.356, 9.358–9.360
Art 6(1)(c)	9.78, 9.175, 9.304, 9.309, 9.328, 9.329–9.333, 9.342, 9.346, 9.357, 12.15, 12.20
Art 7	7.421, 9.203, 9.274, 9.298–9.299, 9.307, 9.395, 9.399, 10.148, 10.168–10.177, 10.194, 10.199, 10.254, 10.257, 10.267, 10.287–10.289, 10.325, 10.330–10.331, 10.339, 10.392
Art 7(1)	9.190, 9.200, 9.281, 9.400, 10.120, 10.124, 10.146–10.147, 10.171–10.172, 10.257, 10.269, 10.275–10.280, 10.285, 10.290, 10.292, 10.295, 10.303–10.305, 10.307, 10.310, 10.316–10.317, 10.318, 10.322, 10.327, 10.332, 10.338, 12.04, 12.27, 12.29, 12.36, 12.83
Art 7(2)	9.180–9.181, 9.185, 9.190, 9.193, 9.200, 9.282–9.283, 9.299–9.301, 10.120, 10.124, 10.146–10.147, 10.173–10.177, 10.218, 10.236, 10.253, 10.258–10.259, 10.269–10.270, 10.276, 10.295–10.296, 10.298, 10.308, 10.310, 10.338–10.340, 10.352, 10.356, 10.363, 10.365, 10.368, 10.376–10.377, 10.384, 12.27, 12.29–12.30, 12.33, 12.35–12.36
Art 8	10.392
Art 8(1)	10.389
Art 8(2)	11.209
Art 9	8.100, 9.399, 13.27
Art 9(1)	9.391–9.397, 9.399–9.401, 9.577, 10.390
Art 9(2)	9.577
Art 10	4.215, 8.06, 8.100, 8.171, 8.207, 8.245
Art 10(1)	8.06, 8.46, 8.99, 8.112, 8.184, 8.223, 8.228–8.229, 8.231–8.233
Art 10(2)(a)	6.43, 8.06, 8.179, 8.184, 8.186–8.188, 8.256
Art 10(3)	8.06, 8.38
Art 11	8.07, 8.245
Art 12	8.08, 8.81, 8.245, 8.279, 9.94
Art 12(1)	8.08, 8.18, 8.46, 8.56, 8.76, 8.80, 8.86–8.87, 8.89, 8.92, 8.99, 8.112, 8.223, 8.236, 8.238–8.241, 8.247–8.248, 8.251
Art 12(2)	7.164–7.165, 8.08
Art 12(2)(a)	7.159, 8.08, 8.262–8.263, 8.265, 8.267, 8.271, 8.273, 8.282, 8.286, 8.291, 8.296, 9.93
Art 12(2)(b)	5.842, 5.852, 5.858, 5.879, 5.884, 8.08, 12.122, 12.131–12.132
Art 13	5.669, 5.685–5.686, 5.690, 8.09, 8.245
Art 14	8.10, 8.245
Art 15	8.245
Art 15(2)	5.525, 5.547
Art 51	9.382
Council Directive 89/396/EEC on indications or marks identifying the lot to which a food-stuff belongs [1989] OJ L186/21	10.246
Council Directive 90/220/EEC [1996] OJ Ll07/10	10.54
Directive 91/321/EEC on infant formulae and follow-on formulae [1991] OJ L 175	10.53
Council Directive 92/97 on the labelling of medicinal products for human use [1992] OJ L113/8	10.145
Directive 96/5 (EC) on processed cereal-based foods and baby foods	10.53

Council Directive 97/55/EEC
 (Comparative Advertising
 Directive) [1984] OJ 1250/17.......12.03
 Recital 2.............. 12.20, 12.41, 12.51
 Recital 6...........................12.18
 Recital 11........................ 12.08
 Recital 12..........................12.59
 Recital 15................... 12.23, 12.42
 Recital 18..........................12.37
 Art 3a(1)(g) 12.11
 see also Council Directive 84/450/
 EEC (Misleading Advertising
 Directive)
Directive 98/34/EC of the European
 Parliament and of the Council
 of 22 June 1998 (Information
 Society Directive) OJ 1998 L204
 Art 1(2) 9.146
Directive 2000/31/EC of the
 European Parliament and of
 the Council of 8 June 2000
 (E-Commerce Directive), OJ
 2000 L178 ....9.165, 9.215
 Art 6 ....9.213
 Art 12 ....9.198, 9.216
 Art 12(1) 9.224
 Art 13 ....9.198, 9.216
 Art 13(1) 9.224
 Art 14..........9.125–9.127, 9.146, 9.148,
 9.168, 9.198, 9.216–9.217
 Art 14(1) 9.190, 9.200, 9.216, 9.224
 Art 14(a).........................9.217
 Art 14(b) 9.217
 Art 15............................9.216
Directive 2001/29/EC (Copyright
 Directive)
 Art 4(1) 9.577
Directive 2001/83 [2001] OJ L 311/67....11.172
Directive 2004/48/EC of the
 European Parliament and of the
 Council of 29 April 2004 on
 the enforcement of intellectual
 property rights (Enforcement
 Directive), OJ L195 .... 9.474, 9.480
 Art 3 .... 9.220, 9.471
 Art 11..... 9.190, 9.200, 9.218–9.219, 9.464
Directive 2004/127 [2004]
 OJ L 136/34.................... 11.172

Regulations (in chronological order)

Commission Regulation (EC) No
 1984/62 covering agreements
 that were in existence prior to 13
 March 1962 and notified to the
 Commission [1962] OJ L 13/204....11.47

Regulation (EC) No 67/67 [1967]
 OJ L 57/849..................11.68
 Art 2 ....11.68
Commission Regulation (EC)
 No 1983/83 (Block Exemption
 Regulation) [1983] OJ L 173/1......11.88
 Art 1 ....11.97
Commission Regulation (EC)
 No 1984/83 on exclusive
 purchasing agreements [1983]
 OJ L 173/5 ....11.33, 11.43
 Art 6 ....11.33
Commission Regulation (EC) No
 2349/84 on patent licensing
 agreements [1984] OJ L 219/15 .....11.01
Commission Regulation (EC) No
 556/89 on know-how licensing
 agreements [1984] OJ L 219/15 .....11.01
Council Regulation (EC) No 2913/
 92 establishing the Community
 Customs Code [1992] OJ 302 ......9.524
Council Regulation (EC) No 2081/92
 of 14 July1992 on the protection
 of geographical indications
 and designations of origin
 for agricultural products and
 foodstuffs [1992]
 OJ 1208/1 ....5.852, 12.123,
 12.135, 12.164, 12.166
 Art 2 ....5.516
 Art 2(2)(a) 12.101, 12.112–12.113
 Art 2(2)(b) 12.118, 12.170, 12.184
 Art 2(3) 12.101, 12.112
 Art 3 .... 12.136, 12.169
 Art 3(1) 12.102, 12.114, 12.118, 12.127
 Art 6(2) 12.112
 Art 13 ....12.59, 12.122, 12.132, 12.135
 Art 13(1) 12.135
 Art 14(2) 12.131, 12.133
 Art 14(3) 12.118, 12.120, 12.130, 12.133
 Art 17(1).........................12.125
 Art 17(2) 12.118
Council Regulation (EC) No 40/
 94 of 20 December 1993 on the
 Community Trade Mark [1994]
 OJ L 11 (CTMR).......2.02, 2.04–2.05,
 2.14–2.15, 2.59–2.62, 13.02
 Recital 5.........................10.96
 Recital 7.........................5.902
 Recital 7(b) 4.15
 Recital 7(c).......................4.15
 Recital 9............... 5.902, 7.165, 8.20
 Recital 14.......................9.461
 Recital 15.......................9.461
 Recital 16........................7.84
 Title I........................... 2.30

Title II 2.30	5.589–5.593, 5.633–5.634,
Title III 2.30	5.637–5.638, 5.645–5.648,
Title IV 2.30	5.649–5.650, 5.654, 5.655–5.657,
Title V 2.30	6.06, 6.14, 6.123, 6.125, 6.138
Title VI 2.30	Art 7(1)(d) 5.38, 5.41–5.42, 5.76,
Title VII. 2.30	5.170, 5.358, 5.423, 5.543, 5.727,
Title VIII. 2.30	5.745–5.746, 5.749, 5.753, 6.123
Title IX 2.30	Art 7(1)(e). 5.38, 5.41–5.42, 5.358,
Title X 2.30, 2.47, 2.49, 9.410,	5.783, 5.909
9.413–9.420, 9.429	Art 7(1)(e)(ii) 5.770–5.772, 5.774,
Title XI 2.30	5.776–5.777, 5.779, 5.782, 5.789,
Title XII. 2.30	5.791, 5.797, 5.801–5.802, 5.804
Title XIII. 2.30, 9.486	Art 7(1)(h) 5.355, 5.357,
Art 1 . . . . 9.459	5.886–5.887, 5.890–5.891,
Art 1(1) 5.902	5.902–5.903, 5.908–5.911
Art 1(2) 7.336, 8.152, 9.469	Art 7(1)(i). 5.910
Art 3(3) 6.136	Art 7(1)(j). 5.909, 13.02
Art 4 . . . . 4.08, 4.14, 4.169, 5.101, 5.104,	Art 7(1)(k) 5.909
5.115, 5.126, 5.154, 5.365, 5.543,	Art 7(2) 5.09, 5.30, 5.563, 6.81,
5.558–5.559, 5.801	6.82, 6.86, 6.87, 6.108, 7.334
Art 5(4) 9.492–9.493	Art 7(3) 3.22, 5.126, 5.159, 5.251,
Art 7 . . . . 4.10, 5.711, 5.806, 6.137	5.274, 5.276, 5.316, 5.387, 5.434,
Art 7(1) 5.09, 5.347, 5.417, 6.89,	5.445, 5.464, 5.466, 5.534, 5.544,
6.103, 6.108	5.557, 5.745–5.746, 5.753, 6.01,
Art 7(1)(a) 5.38–5.40, 5.154,	6.50, 6.56, 6.81, 6.82, 6.86, 6.103,
5.543–5.544	6.121, 6.125–6.126,
Art 7(1)(b) 4.169, 5.16, 5.20, 5.22,	6.130–6.131, 6.152
5.30, 5.34–5.35, 5.37–5.45, 5.52,	Art 8 . . . . 7.01, 7.07
5.60, 5.63, 5.64, 5.66, 5.74, 5.76,	Art 8(1)(a) 3.45, 3.84, 7.07, 7.134
5.78, 5.84, 5.95, 5.97, 5.100–5.101,	Art 8(1)(b) 3.45, 3.72, 3.74, 3.84,
5.104, 5.108, 5.110, 5.112,	5.396, 6.60, 7.07, 7.102, 7.105,
5.114–5.116, 5.123, 5.146–5.150,	7.107, 7.116, 7.120–7.121, 7.126,
5.154, 5.162, 5.165, 5.170, 5.191,	7.128, 7.131, 7.134–7.136, 7.140,
5.195, 5.244, 5.248–5.252, 5.272,	7.223–7.224, 7.229, 7.257, 7.260,
5.276, 5.279, 5.315–5.316, 5.334,	7.262–7.264, 7.295, 7.317, 7.323,
5.340, 5.345, 5.350–5.351, 5.369,	7.336, 7.437, 7.439, 7.444–7.445,
5.371, 5.378, 5.387, 5.392,	7.447, 7.449, 7.561, 12.213
5.418–5.420, 5.445, 5.451, 5.457,	Art 8(2) 7.07, 7.97, 7.336
5.462, 5.466, 5.478, 5.502, 5.533,	Art 8(2)(a)(ii) 7.106
5.543, 5.557, 5.574, 5.634,	Art 8(2)(c) 3.84, 7.354, 7.356
5.645–5.646, 5.649, 5.654,	Art 8(3) 7.07
5.708, 6.06, 6.14, 6.81, 6.82,	Art 8(4) 3.85, 7.07, 7.561, 12.213,
6.86, 6.123, 6.125, 6.138	12.215–12.217, 12.219, 12.222,
Art 7(1)(c). 3.22, 5.18, 5.20, 5.30,	12.225, 12.227, 13.22
5.38–5.39, 5.41–5.42, 5.45, 5.60,	Art 8(5) 3.84, 7.03, 7.07, 7.102, 7.105,
5.63, 5.64, 5.66, 5.78, 5.84, 5.89,	7.131, 7.134–7.135, 7.262, 7.317,
5.92, 5.95, 5.108, 5.110,	7.354, 7.356, 7.413, 7.437, 7.439,
5.112–5.121, 5.123,	7.441, 7.444–7.445, 7.447,
5.146–5.147, 5.154, 5.165, 5.249,	7.449–7.451, 7.502, 7.504,
5.252, 5.349, 5.352, 5.355,	7.505–7.506, 7.508, 7.509,
5.357–5.358, 5.421–5.423,	7.511–7.513, 7.534, 7.548–7.549,
5.532–5.533, 5.535, 5.538,	7.561–7.562, 7.566, 8.116, 8.118–8.120
5.541, 5.543, 5.545–5.546,	Art 9 . . . . 9.04, 9.152–9.153, 9.214
5.548, 5.554, 5.557–5.558,	Art 9(1) 9.08–9.09, 9.14–9.16,
5.560, 5.563–5.565, 5.567,	9.18–9.19, 9.119, 9.440, 9.470,
5.569, 5.573–5.574, 5.577,	9.522, 9.532

Art 9(1)(a) 9.115, 9.117, 9.125, 9.148, 9.168, 9.190, 9.200, 9.224, 9.259	Art 50 . . . . 8.20
Art 9(1)(b) 9.20, 9.28, 9.125, 9.148, 9.212	Art 51. . . . . 2.31, 2.42, 5.347, 7.380, 8.11, 8.197
Art 9(1)(c) 7.354, 7.370, 7.373–7.374, 7.380, 7.382, 7.384–7.385, 7.387, 7.394–7.395, 7.398, 7.502, 9.04, 9.20, 9.27–9.28, 9.125, 9.148, 9.164, 9.212, 9.224, 9.258–9.259	Art 51(1). 5.746
	Art 51(1)(a). 5.797, 6.137
	Art 51(1)(b) 5.913, 5.915, 6.134
	Art 51(2) 5.746, 6.123, 6.128, 6.129, 6.133–6.134
	Art 52. . . . . 2.31, 2.42, 6.152
Art 9(2) 9.116	Art 52(1) 7.566
Art 9(2)(b) 9.522, 9.531	Art 52(1)(a) 7.444, 7.561
Art 9(2)(c) 9.495, 9.522, 9.529	Art 52(2) 6.162
Art 9(2)(d) 9.115, 9.117	Art 53. . . . . 2.31, 2.42
Art 10. . . . . .9.05	Art 53(1)(c). .3.85
Art 10(1) 8.137, 9.05	Art 53(2) 2.42, 3.85, 3.99
Art 11. . . . . .7.169, 9.06	Art 53(2)(a) 3.87–3.88
Art 12 . . . . 5.137, 5.655, 9.07, 9.16	Art 53(2)(c) 3.87
Art 12(b) 5.29, 5.110, 5.112, 5.120, 5.151, 5.164, 5.174, 5.350–5.351, 5.546, 5.554, 5.558, 5.588, 7.94, 7.97, 9.07	Art 54 . . . . 2.31, 9.14, 9.16
	Art 55. . . . . .5.697
	Art 56 . . . . 8.20
	Art 57 . . . . 8.11, 8.253
Art 13 . . . . 7.169, 9.203, 10.330	Arts 57–64. . . . . 2.44
Art 13(1) 9.200, 10.331	Art 57(1) 3.54
Art 13(2) 9.190, 9.200	Art 57(2) 8.59
Art 14. . . . . .7.83	Art 58 . . . . 3.80–3.81
Art 14(1) 9.446, 9.454, 9.468	Art 59. . . . . 3.22, 3.81
Art 15. . . . . 4.215, 8.11, 8.20, 8.129, 8.133–8.134, 8.153, 8.171, 8.197, 8.207	Art 60(1) 3.22
	Art 60(2) 3.22
	Art 61(2) 3.22
Art 15(1). 8.134, 8.137, 8.143, 8.151–8.152, 8.157, 8.191–8.194, 8.205, 8.218	Art 62 . . . . .5.536
	Art 62(1) 3.22
	Art 63(3) 5.636
Art 15(1)(a). 8.200, 8.202–8.203, 8.205–8.206	Art 63(5) 5.536
	Art 63(6) 5.636
Art 15(2)(a) 8.178–8.179, 8.187	Art 64 . . . . 3.21, 3.31
Art 15(3) 8.67, 8.217	Art 64(1) 3.30
Art 16. . . . . .2.32	Art 64(2) 5.547
Art 17. . . . . .5.845	Art 65. . . . . 2.45, 3.56, 3.67
Art 18(2) 9.474	Art 65(2) 3.90, 3.94
Arts 19–22. . . . . .2.33	Art 73 . . . . .5.463–5.466, 5.481–5.482, 7.237–7.238
Art 26 . . . . .7.169	
Art 26(1)(c) 4.203	Art 74(1) 5.463–5.464, 5.466, 5.470, 5.479, 7.227, 7.236, 12.217
Art 27 . . . . .7.168–7.172, 7.175, 7.178	
Art 28 . . . . 4.204	Art 75 . . . . 2.43, 7.263
Art 32 . . . . .7.177	Art 76. . . . . 2.43, 3.23, 3.63, 5.711, 5.714, 5.716, 7.263
Art 34 . . . . 2.26	
Art 35. . . . . 2.26	Art 76(1) 3.62
Art 38 . . . . .5.29	Art 76(2) 3.22, 3.28–3.29, 3.33–3.35, 3.42, 3.46
Art 42 . . . . .3.34, 5.697, 8.178, 8.253	
Art 42(2) 8.58, 8.168	Art 77 . . . . .3.55
Art 42(3) 3.48, 8.58, 8.168	Art 77a. 3.49
Art 43 . . . . . . 5.695, 8.11, 8.20, 8.72, 12.219	Art 77a(1). 3.50
Art 43(2) 3.47	Art 77a(2). 3.50
Art 43(3) 3.47	Art 78 . . . . 2.43
Art 45. . . . . .5.697	Art 79 . . . . 2.43
Art 46 . . . . .5.697	Art 80 . . . . 2.43

Art 81	2.43
Art 82	2.43
Art 85	2.43
Art 86	2.43
Art 91	9.461
Art 92	2.43
Art 93	2.43
Art 93(5)	9.422–9.423, 9.427, 9.432, 9.433
Art 94	2.50, 9.414, 9.461
Art 94(1)	9.468
Art 95	2.51, 9.415
Art 96	2.51, 9.415
Art 96(7)	7.84
Art 97	2.52, 9.416
Art 97(5)	9.416, 9.420, 9.428
Art 98	2.52, 9.456, 9.459–9.460
Art 98(1)	9.438, 9.438–9.449, 9.451–9.454, 9.464–9.465, 9.469, 9.472
Art 98(5)	9.423–9.424, 9.434
Art 99	2.56, 9.417
Art 99(3)	8.11
Art 100	2.56, 7.84, 9.417
Art 101	2.57, 9.417
Art 101(2)	9.483
Art 102	2.57, 9.418
Art 102(1)	9.420
Art 102(2)	9.474, 9.483
Art 103	2.55, 9.416
Art 105	7.84, 9.415
Art 107	2.29, 7.336
Art 108(2)(b)	7.342
Art 110(2)	2.28
Art 112	2.25
Art 112(2)(a)	8.144, 8.154
Art 113	2.25
Art 114	2.25
Art 115	7.574
Art 115(4)	2.36–2.37
Art 142	12.135
Art 146	9.486
Art 146(2)	9.491
Art 160	8.168
Art 165	2.61, 6.81
Council Regulation (EC) No 3295/94 laying down measures on counterfeit and pirated goods [1994] OJ L 341	9.563, 9.568
Recital 2	9.546
Recital 3	9.546
Art 1	9.500, 9.504–9.506, 9.543–9.545
Art 1(1)(a)	9.504
Art 2	9.513, 9.518–9.519, 9.542
Art 6(1)	9.562, 9.566
Art 6(2)(b)	9.559, 9.566
Art 7	9.559
Art 11	9.514–9.519, 9.518, 9.542, 9.567
Council Regulation (EC) No 3378/94 amending Regulation No 1576/89, OJ 1994 L 366/1	12.142
Commission Regulation (EC) No 2868/95 of 13 December 1995 implementing Council Regulation (EC) No 40/94 [1995] OJ L 303 (CTMIR)	2.15
Rule 2	4.191
Rule 2(1)	4.204
Rule 2(2)	4.203, 4.207, 4.213
Rule 2(4)	4.204
Rule 5	7.176
Rule 8(2)	3.50
Rule 17	3.54
Rule 18	3.54
Rule 18(3)	3.48
Rule 19	3.84
Rule 19(4)	3.25, 3.46
Rule 20	3.28
Rule 20(1)	3.42
Rule 20(2)	3.38
Rule 22	8.119
Rule 22(2)	3.25
Rule 31(6)	3.78
Rule 37	3.88, 3.95, 3.99
Rule 38	7.566
Rule 40(5)	3.38
Rule 49	3.80
Rule 49(1)	3.80–3.81
Rule 49(2)	3.81
Rule 50	3.25
Rule 50(1)	3.25, 3.43
Commission Regulation (EC) No 2869/95 on the fees payable to OHIM [1995] OJ L 303 (Fees Regulation)	2.15
Commission Regulation (EC) No 216/96 of 5 February 1996, Laying down the Rules of Procedure of the Boards of Appeal of OHIM, OJ No L 28	2.15
Art 1(d)	3.68
Commission Regulation (EC) No 240/96 on technology transfer agreements [1996] OJ L 31/2	11.01
Commission Regulation (EC) No 1107/96 on the Registration of Geographical Indications and Designations of Origin [1996] OJ L148/1	12.104, 12.135
Commission Regulation (EC) No 258/97 [1997] OJ lA3/1	10.54

Regulation (EC) No 1139/98 on the
labelling of GMO foodstuffs
[2000] OJ L6/13 .... 10.52–10.53
Art 2(2)(b) 10.50, 10.53
Commission Regulation (EC)
No 2790/99 (Vertical
Agreements Block Exemption)
[1999] OJ L 336 .... 11.01, 11.04
Regulation (EC) No 44/2001
concerning jurisdiction and the
recognition and enforcement
of judgments in civil and
commercial matters (Brussels
I Regulation) 2.50, 9.414, 9.465
Chapter III. 9.471–9.472
Art 5(3) 9.422–9.426, 9.428,
9.433, 9.434
Regulation (EC) No 1347/2001
supplementing the Annex to
Regulation 1107/96, OJ L 182 ..... 12.123
Recital 3. .... 12.121
Recital 4. .... 12.121
Art 13 .... 12.121
Art 14. .... 12.121
Art 14(3) 12.121
Council Regulation (EC) No 6/
2002 of 12 December 2001
(Community Designs
Regulation), OJ L 3 .... 2.14
Art 88(2) 9.482
Art 89 .... 9.474
Art 89(1)(d) 9.475–9.476, 9.478–9.482
Regulation (EC) No 178/2002
establishing the European Food
Safety Authority [2002] OJ L31/1
Art 2 .... 12.118, 12.123
Regulation (EC) No 733/2002 on the
implementation of the .eu Top
Level Domain, OJ 2002 L113 ..... 12.153
Commission Regulation (EC)
No 1829/2002 amending the
Annex to Regulation (EC) 1107/
96 with regard to the name 'Feta'
[2002] OJ L277/101 .... 12.105
Recital 20. .... 12.105
Council Regulation (EC) No 692/
2003 Amending Regulation
(EEC) 2081/92 [2003]
OJL 99/1 .... 12.102
Council Regulation (EC) No 1383/
2003 concerning customs action
against goods suspected of
infringing certain intellectual
property rights [2003]
OJ 1296/7 .... 9.553, 9.563, 9.568

Recital 2. .... 9.570
Art 2 .... 9.486
Art 2(1)(a) 9.554
Art 5(1) 9.486
Art 5(4) 9.486–9.489
Art 9(1) 9.562, 9.566
Art 10(1) 9.566
Council Regulation (EC) No 1992/
2003 to give effect to the
Protocol relating to the Madrid
Agreement 2.14, 2.18, 9.486
Recital 6. .... 9.490
Recital 8. .... 9.490
Regulation (EC) No 1891/2004
laying down provisions for the
implementation of Council
Regulation (EC) No 1383/2003,
OJ EU L 328 .... 9.496
Commission Regulation (EC)
No 772/2004 on categories of
technology agreements [2004]
OJ L 123/11 .... 11.01
Commission Regulation (EC)
No 782/2004 of 26 April 2004. .... 2.15
Regulation (EC) No 874/2004 on
public policy rules concerning
the .eu Top Level Domain OJ
2004 L162 .... 12.153–12.155
Art 10(1) 12.155
Art 11. .... 12.159
Art 21. .... 12.155
Art 21(3)(a)–(e) 12.157
Regulation (EC) No 918/2004
introducing transitional
arrangements for the protection
of geographical indications
[2004] OJ L163/88. .... 12.192
Commission Regulation (EC)
No 2082/2004 of 6 December
2004, OJ No L 360 .... 2.15
Commission Regulation (EC)
No 1041/2005 of 29 June 2005 ...... 2.15
Regulation (EC) No 510/2006 [2006]
OJ L93/12 .... 12.179, 12.181,
12.189–12.190
Art 8 .... 12.190
Regulation (EC) No 864/2007 of
the European Parliament and
of the Council of 11 July 2007
on the law applicable to non-
contractual obligations (Rome II
Regulation), OJ L199. .... 9.477
Art 8(2) 9.474, 9.482
Commission Regulation (EC)
No 110/2008 on the definition,

description, presentation, labelling and the protection of geographical indications of spirit drinks 12.139–12.150
Recital 14........................12.144
Art 14(2) 12.145
Art 15(3) 12.145
Art 15(4) 12.144
Art 16....... 12.139, 12.141, 12.143–12.149
Art 16(a)................... 12.146, 12.148
Art 16(b) 12.147, 12.148
Art 16(c)........................12.147
Art 16(d) 12.147
Art 17...........................12.144
Art 23 ....12.139
Art 23(1) 12.141, 12.143, 12.148, 12.149
Art 23(2) 12.141, 12.148
Annex III........................12.141
Council Regulation (EC) No 207/ 2009 on the Community Trade Mark [2009] OJ L 78.... 2.14, 8.167, 13.02
Art 9(1) 9.575
Art 9(2) 9.575
see also Regulation 40/94
Regulation (EU) No 1215/2012 of the European Parliament and of the Council of 12 December 2012 on jurisdiction and the recognition and enforcement of judgments in civil and commercial matters, OJ L 351 (Brussels II Regulation) 2.50, 9.414
Art 7(2) 9.423–9.425
Art 8 ....9.416
Art 81............................9.414
Regulation (EU) No 608/2013 of the European Parliament and of the Council of 12 June 2013 concerning customs enforcement of intellectual property rights and repealing Council Regulation (EC) No 1383/2003 ....2.47, 9.412, 9.496, 9.499, 9.553
Commission Regulation (EU) No 1316/2014 (TTBER) OJ L 93, 28.03.2014................11.01, 11.03

Other Instruments

Commission Decision 92/428 of July 24 ....10.262
Communication No 4/03 of the President of OHIM of 16 June 2003 concerning the use of class headings in lists for CTM applications and registrations..............4.194–4.198, 4.200, 4.211–4.212, 4.216, 4.216–4.217, 4.220, 4.229–4.230, 4.234, 4.239
Point 3................... 4.195, 4.213
Point 4........................4.196
Community Customs Code............9.524
Art 37 .... 9.544, 9.568
Art 56 ....9.570
Art 58 ....9.570
Art 58(1) 9.529
Art 58(2) 9.530
Art 59...........................9.569
Art 75 ....9.569, 9.570
Art 79 ....9.529
Art 84(1)(a) 9.504, 9.544
Art 91...........................9.561
Art 91(1)........................9.524
Art 92 ....9.524, 9.561
Art 98 ....9.561
Memorandum on the Creation of an EEC Trade Mark, *Bulletin of the European Communities,* Supplement 8/76 .... 2.03–2.04
Rules of Procedure of the Court of First Instance
Art 41(c).........................7.226
Art 44(1)(c) 3.65, 7.226
Art 44(1)(d) 7.226
Art 44(1)(e) 7.226
Art 48(2) 7.238
Art 81...........................7.225
Art 135(4) 8.119
Rules of Procedure of the European Court of Justice
Art 38(1)(c) 3.65
Art 104(3) 9.118
Art 112(1)........................3.65
Art 119..........................5.317
Art 169(2) 3.72

INTERNATIONAL INSTRUMENTS

Agreement on Trade-Related Aspects of Intellectual Property Rights 1994 (TRIPS Agreement) 2.17, 9.505, 13.02
Art 2 .... 12.201, 12.233
Art 2(1) 8.19, 12.194, 12.196, 12.211
Art 7 ....4.48
Art 15.............. 4.152, 12.209, 12.210
Art 15(1)........................4.138
Art 16.................. 12.202, 12.209

Art 16(1) 7.11, 12.194,
            12.196–12.199, 12.203,
            12.205–12.206, 12.211
Art 16(2) 7.363
Art 16(3) 7.348, 7.356
Art 19(1) 8.247
Art 21...........................5.845
Art 23 ....12.142
Art 24 ....12.142
Art 24(5) 12.233
Art 61...........................9.411
Art 69 ....9.564
Art 70 ....12.194
Art 70(1) 12.194, 12.203
Art 70(2) 12.203
Berne Convention for the Protection
   of Literary and Artistic Works
   1886........................11.137
Art 9(1) 11.137
Art 9(2) 11.137
General Agreement on Tariffs and
   Trade (GATT) 1947.............. 2.06
Madrid Agreement Concerning the
   International Registration of
   Marks 1891 ....2.06, 2.18, 4.64
Art 3(4) 8.220
Art 9ter 10.93
Nice Agreement Concerning the
   International Classification of
   Goods and Services 1957 ......4.28, 4.63,
            4.75, 4.191, 4.192, 4.199–4.200,
            4.237, 4.251, 5.618
Art 2(1) 4.204
Art 2(3) 4.226
Paris Convention for the Protection
   of Industrial Property
   1883...................... 4.251, 8.90
Art 5C 8.19
Art 6(3) 10.93
Art 6bis 7.348, 7.363
Art 6ter 5.886–5.887, 5.894,
            5.897, 5.901
Art 6ter(1) 5.888, 5.891
Art 6ter(1)(a) 5.904
Art 6ter(1)(c) 5.897
Art 6quater 10.93
Art 6quinquies....................5.601
Art 6quinquies B(2) 4.133, 5.727
Art 6quinquies C(1) 5.613
Art 6sexies 5.889
Art 8 .... 12.195, 12.201, 12.211
Protocol to the Madrid Agreement
   1989......... 9.485, 9.489–9.490, 13.02
Art 4(1) 9.491
Trade Mark Law Treaty 1994
   Art 16..........................5.889
   Art 19...........................8.19
Trade Mark Registration Treaty 1973 .... 2.06
WIPO Recommendations concerning
   Provisions on the Protection of
   Well-Known Marks 1999..........7.357

BILATERAL TREATIES

1892 Convention between
   Switzerland and Germany on the
   reciprocal protection of patents
   Art 5 ....8.166
   Art 5(1) 8.167
1976 Agreement between Austria and
   Czechoslovakia on the protection
   of indications of the source
   of agricultural and industrial
   products.............. 12.163, 12.168
1986 Agreement between Portugal
   and Czechoslovakia on the
   protection of appellations of
   origin...........12.232, 12.237–12.238

1

INTRODUCTION

1.01 Trade mark law has been growing rapidly in Europe during the last twenty years as a result of the harmonization process and the introduction of the Community trade mark system. Until the introduction of the new European regime, national schemes of protection had been developed following contradictory models, ranging from pure deposit systems to registries that wished to protect consumers and competitors first and trade mark owners second. At the same time national courts had been applying their own distinct and often disparate trade mark law doctrines, whereas for the Court of Justice trade mark rights were primarily potential anti-competitive tools and barriers to intra-Community trade. From the early 1990s onwards, the new European regime has changed all that. National laws have had to adapt to following the same substantive principles and national systems to coexist with a new, and truly federal, competing system of protection.

1.02 As a result, the Court of Justice has been deluged by references from national courts and appeals against the judgments of the Court of First Instance. Within this relatively short period of time, the Court of Justice had to face down persistent legal traditions and build up concepts that took the United States Supreme Court decades to delineate in a much less disparate environment. The Court also found that it had to deal with trade marks in a dual capacity, as an interpretive court but also as a supreme court dealing with appeals.

1.03 The aim of this book is to focus on trade marks from that new angle, the jurisprudence of the Court of Justice, and combine a comprehensive review of case law with an analysis of the conceptual core of European trade mark law. It aspires to provide a comprehensive—though not exhaustive—review of the case law of the Court of Justice on trade marks.

1.04 The judgments of the General Court are examined only to the extent that they have been appealed before the Court of Justice. Some matters of administrative and court procedure are covered to the extent that they have influenced the outcome of a judgment of the Court. Note that it has been attempted to follow developments before the Court of Justice up to September 2014.

1.05 The book starts with three brief introductory chapters. Chapter 2 provides an outline of the European trade mark regime. Chapter 3 looks at the role of the Court of Justice in the legal order of the European Union.

1.06 The second part of the book covers the heart of the European trade mark regime, considering what can be protected and the clash with earlier rights. Chapter 4 discusses formalities, the definitional requirements, and the scope of the specification. Chapter 5 looks at absolute grounds and Chapter 6 at distinctiveness acquired through use, including some concluding remarks on absolute grounds. Chapter 7 examines relative grounds. Chapter 8 looks at the requirements for maintaining trade mark rights. Chapter 9 considers the scope of protection of trade mark rights from an infringement perspective, including the jurisprudence of the Court on transit cases.

1.07 The third part examines the interaction between trade marks and other areas of law. First, it traces the development of trade marks from their early EEC days to their current status within the framework of exhaustion of rights and free movement of goods, in Chapter 10, and competition rules, in Chapter 11. Chapter 12 posits trade marks amidst the broader context of unfair competition, with illustrations from the fields of comparative advertising, the protection of geographical indications and trade names, the human rights/property aspects of a trade mark, and the interaction with the domain name system.

1.08 Chapter 13 is a brief exposition of the current state of reform of the European trade mark edifice.

1.09 Finally, Chapter 14 brings together some key points that have been resurfacing throughout the book.

2

EUROPEAN UNION TRADE MARK LAW

The Directive and the Regulation

A. Introduction

Trade mark law at the European Union (EU) level has developed following two parallel paths. One led to the harmonization of disparate national systems of trade mark protection; the other to the creation of a 'federal' trade mark right, unitary in nature and effective throughout the territory of the European Union. The aim of this chapter is to describe briefly the destinations reached by the 'harmonization' and the 'federal' paths. 2.01

Prior to the creation of EU legislation in the field of trade marks—in 1998 the Directive, and in 1993 the Regulation—the Court of Justice had established in a series of prominent cases that national trade mark rights (the same as national patent or other intellectual property (IP) rights) had to give way, when their exercise was involved, to the basic freedoms of the (then) European Economic Community regarding the freedom of movement of goods and the freedom of providing services. Most notable is the Court's case law establishing the principle of EU-wide exhaustion of national IP rights. Now, with the secondary legislation in place, the Court of Justice has been the focus of interpretation of these acts, in preliminary rulings and in appeals from the EU's trade marks and designs office, the Office for Harmonization in the Internal Market (OHIM). 2.02

The history of 'European' trade mark law starts in the late 1950s with the setting up of a working group to prepare a treaty among the then six original Member States, which led in 1964 to the Preliminary Draft of a Convention for a European Trade Mark that remained unpublished. A period of inactivity, caused by French opposition to integration, ended in 1973 with the publication of the draft.[1] In July 1976 the 'Memorandum on an EEC Trade Mark' was adopted by the Commission.[2] The Memorandum described a European market where national markets in branded goods predominated. 'There is as yet, to the disadvantage of consumers, distributors and manufacturers, no common market for branded goods and thus no internal market for a substantial proportion of goods for sale.'[3] Trade marks 2.03

---

[1] The version in the original four languages—Dutch, French, German, and Italian—was published by the Office of Official Publications. An English translation was published by the Department of Trade and Industry: Proposed European Trade Mark—Unofficial Translation of a Preliminary Draft of a Convention for a European Trade Mark (HMSO, 1973).
[2] Memorandum on the Creation of an EEC Trade Mark, *Bulletin of the European Communities*, Supplement 8/76.
[3] A Memorandum on the Creation of an EEC Trade Mark, *Bulletin of the European Communities*, Supplement 8/76, para 10.

deserved to be protected because they enabled consumers to choose. 'To make the right choice, the consumer needs to be able to identify and distinguish these goods and to recognize a connection between a particular product, its quality and its reputation.'[4]

2.04 The stance taken in the Memorandum was radical. The approach of a treaty among the Member States was abandoned in favour of a genuine Community instrument, a Regulation to be based on what was then Article 235 of the EEC Treaty. In addition, national trade mark systems would be harmonized with a Directive. The Regulation would create a new 'Community trade mark' (CTM) with Community-wide protection. The Memorandum acknowledged that the new Community system should not replace national rights, for which there would be demand and justification: thus, the new system would be characterized by the autonomy of the Community-wide system, which would be unitary, and the coexistence with national trade mark systems, which would be subject to the same substantive rules as the Community trade mark. In a series of eighteen meetings with governmental experts, chaired by the Commission, drafts for the Directive and the Regulation were developed. The Commission presented its proposals to the Council and Parliament in 1980.[5]

2.05 From then it was more than eight years until the Directive was finally adopted in 1988, with the Community by then comprising no longer nine Member States, but twelve, after the accession of Greece in 1981 and Spain and Portugal in 1986. The Regulation took five more years, with the primary obstacles being of a political nature, notably the seat of the Office, which was attributed to Spain in the famous special summit in October 1993, which finally decided on the seat of all EU institutions and awarded, inter alia, the European Central Bank to Germany and the European Medicines Agency to the United Kingdom. The other issue was the question whether the Office should have only a limited number of languages, where many favoured the three languages also adopted for the European Patent Office, but where finally a five-language solution, with all-languages elements, prevailed. Accepting that the Office would have only five languages—Spanish, German, English, French, and Italian—is indeed a singular achievement.

2.06 The setting and the basic principles behind the new approach to European trade mark unification and harmonization were described as follows, shortly after the adoption of the Directive:[6]

> Compared with the situation in the 1950s, when the negotiations began, the picture of trade mark law in Europe has been transformed. New national laws have been adopted (e.g. France, 1964, Benelux, 1970) and the European Community has expanded to include Member States with strong, but different, trade mark traditions (United Kingdom, Ireland, Denmark). Expanding the scope of trade mark law to cover new areas (e.g. service marks) whilst imposing new conditions on their owners (e.g. use requirements) has become an international trend.

> At the international stage, the Trade Mark Registration Treaty has been a disappointment. The Madrid Agreement Concerning the International Registration of Marks has been considering ways of becoming more appealing to new Member States and users of the system.

---

[4] Memorandum on the Creation of an EEC Trade Mark, *Bulletin of the European Communities*, Supplement 8/76, para 11.
[5] New Trade Mark System for the Community-Proposed Directive and Regulation, *Bulletin of the European Communities*, Supplement 5/80.
[6] Alexander von Mühlendahl, 'The Future Community Trade Mark System' (1989) 20 IIC 583.

And finally, at the global level trade mark law has become one of the issues considered under the aegis of the General Agreement on Tariffs and Trade.

Negotiations regarding the Community Trade Mark were focusing on the location of the Office and its working languages. The substance of the new right—and of the harmonisation process—in terms of scope and procedure has been less controversial. The intention was to provide for:

- a broad definition of registrable trade marks;
- an examination system that ex officio would focus exclusively on absolute grounds, leaving Member States the freedom to continue their previous practices;
- opposition proceedings for the owners of prior rights;
- the widening of the definition of the exclusive rights of the trade mark owner to cover the right to prevent importation and exportation;
- the establishment of identity or similarity of the signs and of the goods or services as the decisive criteria for protection;
- broader protection for marks with a 'reputation' in appropriate situations, beyond the scope of similar goods or services;
- exceptions from the scope of protection including exhaustion of trade mark rights, acquiescence, and a fair use provision;
- the introduction of a requirement to use the trade mark;
- the ability to assign a trade mark without the respective business or goodwill; and
- trade mark licensing and infringement in some cases where the terms of a licence agreement have been breached.

B. The 'Harmonization' Directive

2.07 The aim of the Directive[7] is to achieve partial harmonization of the Member States' national trade mark laws. The harmonization focuses on the substantive provisions of national trade mark laws that could impede the completion and effective operation of an internal, single European market, in particular if they diverge from one Member State to another.

2.08 The Recitals also stress the significance of ensuring that a registered trade mark enjoys the same protection under the legal systems of all the Member States. It is the function of a trade mark as an indication of origin that primarily justifies protection and delineates its scope.

2.09 The Directive establishes the provisions which must be transformed into national law, and also provides for a number of options for the Member States.

2.10 The mandatory provisions include the definition of registrable signs, the principal absolute grounds of refusal, earlier rights as obstacles to registration, the scope of protection conferred, limitations (exhaustion, fair use, acquiescence), and the use requirement for maintaining a registration.

2.11 Among the optional provisions are some relating to absolute grounds, which were adopted to take into account the special situation in a number of Member States which were not

---

[7] First Council Directive 89/104/EEC of 21 December 1988 to Approximate the Laws of the Member States Relating to Trade Marks [1989] OJ L 40, p 1. The Directive has been codified without modification by Directive 2008/95/EC of the European Parliament and of the Council of 22 October 2008 to Approximate the Laws of the Member States Relating to Trade Marks [2008] OJ L 299, p 25. Since the content and even the numbers of the Articles have remained unchanged, cases dating from before the codification need no 'translation' to the current version.

willing to go for complete harmonization. As regards earlier rights and scope of protection, while the Community trade mark provides for protection in the absence of likelihood of confusion for marks with reputation, the Directive left it to the Member States whether they wished to introduce this broader protection. In practice, all Member States have actually exercised this option.

2.12 In summary, the Directive deals mainly with the definition of a trade mark; grounds for refusal, revocation, invalidity, and infringement, as well as limitations. It also sets out the principles applicable to licensing agreements.

2.13 The Directive leaves to the discretion of Member States the type of system of registration, the establishment of registry and court procedures, and provisions on ownership, as well as the regulation of rights acquired through use, unfair competition, civil liability, and consumer protection.

C. The Community Trade Mark Regulation

2.14 The Community Trade Mark Regulation (CTMR)[8] was adopted in December 1993. OHIM, responsible for the administration of the CTM system (and since 2003 also for the Community design system under the Community Designs Regulation of 2002[9]), was set up in 1994. CTM applications could be filed from 1 April 1996, with a sunrise period beginning on 1 January 1996.

2.15 Prior to the opening of the Office the Commission adopted the required implementing legislation: a Regulation for the various procedures before the Office,[10] a Regulation for the fees to be paid to the Office,[11] and a Regulation for the procedures before the Boards of Appeal of the Office.[12]

---

[8] Council Regulation (EC) No 40/94 of 20 December 1993 on the Community Trade Mark [1994] OJ L 11, p 1 (the Regulation, also CTMR). The Regulation was codified in 2009 as Council Regulation (EC) No 207/2009 on the Community Trade Mark [2009] OJ L 78, p 1. Unfortunately, the codification also led to a change in the numbers of the Articles. In this edition we are using—primarily—the new numbering. Note that the Community trade mark system has become a member of the Protocol to the Madrid Agreement Council Reg (EC) No 1992/2003 amending Regulation (EC) No 40/94 on the Community Trade Mark to give effect to the accession of the European Community to the Protocol relating to the Madrid Agreement concerning the international registration of marks [2003] OJ L 296, p 1.

[9] Council Regulation (EC) No 6/2002 of 12 December 2001 on Community Designs [2002] OJ L 3, p 1.

[10] Commission Regulation (EC) No 2868/95 of 13 December 1995 implementing Council Regulation (EC) No 40/94 on the Community Trade Mark [1995] OJ L 303, p 1 (the Implementing Regulation). The Implementing Regulation has been amended several times, by Commission Regulation No 782/2004 of 26 April 2004 (applicable as of 1 October 2004) and Commission Regulation No 1041/2005 of 29 June 2005 (in part applicable as of 25 July 2005 and in part applicable as of 10 March 2008). Unfortunately, the codification of the Regulation with the new numbers of Articles is not carried over into the Implementing Regulation. OHIM makes available on its website an annotated version of the Implementing Regulation which facilitates its application. The Implementing Regulation is of great practical importance because the Regulation itself only provides for basic rules which are filled in by the Implementing Regulation.

[11] Commission Regulation (EC) No 2869/95 on the fees payable to the Office for Harmonization in the Internal Market (Trade Marks and Designs), [1995] OJ L 303, p 33 (the Fees Regulation), frequently amended.

[12] Commission Regulation (EC) No 216/96 of 5 February 1996 laying down the rules of procedure of the Boards of Appeal of the Office for Harmonization in the Internal Market (Trade Marks and Designs), OJ No L 28, p 11, amended by Commission Regulation (EC) No 2082/2004 of 6 December 2004, OJ No L 360, p 8.

2.16 Whereas it was estimated at the time, by the Commission as well as by those interested in trade mark protection, that the Office should not expect to receive more than 15,000 to 25,000 applications per year, in the first year alone more than 40,000 applications were filed. By the end of 2014, the annual filing amounted to more than 100,000, and the number of registered CTMs surpassed 1,000,000.

2.17 The CTM system is entirely compatible with the Agreement on Trade-Related Aspects of Intellectual Property Rights (TRIPS Agreement) adopted as part of the Uruguay Round agreements signed in 1994 establishing the World Trade Organization. The provisions on absolute grounds were amended to take into account the absolute protection for geographical indications for wine and spirits pursuant to Article 23 of TRIPS.

2.18 The European Union has become a contracting party of the Protocol to the Madrid Agreement Concerning the International Registration of Marks.[13] This allows CTMs to be the basis for an international registration, and protection of an international registration to be extended not only to the individual Member States of the European Union party to the Madrid System, but also to the European Union as a whole. Currently, some 15% of all new requests for protection in the EU arrive via the Madrid Protocol.

(1) The Basic Principles: Unitary Character, Autonomy, Coexistence

2.19 The Community trade mark system is based on three principles: the principle of the unitary character of the Community trade mark, the principle of autonomy, and the principle of coexistence.

(a) Unitary character

2.20 The essence of the Community trade mark system is the establishment of a unitary right that is effective throughout the territory of the European Union. This right is established by filing an application for registration but finally conferred by registration at OHIM. The Community trade mark is one indivisible entity. It has equal effect throughout the Union. It can be registered, transferred, surrendered, or revoked only for the entirety of the European Union. It can, however, be licensed for parts of the Union. Protection may be obtained for goods and for services, either as an individual mark or as a collective mark.

(b) Autonomy

2.21 Autonomy means that the CTM system, as a creation of the European Union's legislature, is governed by European Union law and principles. National law may be applied to Community trade marks only to the extent that the legislation expressly provides for this.

(c) Coexistence

2.22 Coexistence means that the Community trade mark system coexists with the trade mark systems of the Member States. It also means that the same trade mark may be protected both as a CTM and as a national trade mark. It finally means that CTMs are earlier rights in each national trade mark system, and all earlier national rights are potential obstacles to the protection of a CTM.

---

[13] Council Regulation (EC) No 1992/2003, OJ L 296, p 1.

(2) Coexistence as Implemented

(a) Earlier national rights as relative grounds

2.23 While there was agreement from the beginning that national trade marks should not be abolished and that national trademarks and CTMs were of equal rank, one of the most contentious issues in this context was the manner in which national trade mark rights would be taken into account in the new CTM system.[14] At the national level, there were 'deposit' systems with little examination, typified by the 1970 Benelux law, where conflicts were left for the parties and finally for the courts to resolve, there were 'opposition' systems, where earlier rights needed to be asserted in an office opposition procedure, as was the case in Germany, and then there were systems with a complete examination for absolute grounds and earlier rights, eg in the United Kingdom and Ireland, but also in the Scandinavian countries, in Greece, Portugal, and in Spain. The solution which finally found the agreement of all Member States—at the time the Regulation required unanimity—was a typical compromise: No examination for earlier rights by OHIM, but a mandatory search, to be carried out by OHIM in its register and by national offices in their registers, with information so discovered being given to the applicant and the proprietors of earlier rights. Earlier rights could be asserted in opposition proceedings, and also in invalidity proceedings before OHIM. No obligation to make use of these proceedings—rather, proprietors of earlier rights maintained the possibility of prohibiting the use of a later CTM in their territories.

2.24 This solution was in practice accepted without any major opposition. As against predictions that it would be almost impossible to obtain new CTMs in view of the large number of earlier national marks (and now also CTMs), the reality is that no more than ca 16% of all published CTM applications are actually opposed. Also, the CTM system has served as a model for the reform of national systems—the United Kingdom, Demark, and Spain have given up their *ex officio* examination for earlier rights, and the Benelux, France, and Italy have introduced opposition proceedings.

(b) Conversion

2.25 Articles 112–114 provide that a Community trade mark registration or application that loses its effect may be converted into one or more national trade mark applications. The filing date of the CTM application will be deemed to be the filing date of the national applications. Conversion is not available to particular Member States when the CTM application is rejected or registration is cancelled in a final decision on the basis of obstacles which exist in that Member State. Where the obstacle is EU-wide, no conversion is available. Conversion applications are filed at OHIM, which then communicates with the relevant national offices.

(c) Seniority

2.26 Articles 34 and 35 provide that the proprietor of a national registration may claim the date of the earlier mark (or marks) when applying for an identical CTM for the same goods or services, or subsequent to its registration. Such a seniority claim does not 'extend' the resulting CTM into the national system. Rather, a seniority claim allows the proprietor of

---

[14] Von Mühlendahl (1989) (n 6), p 589

the national mark to abandon or not renew its national mark but still retain all the rights it would have had if the mark had continued on the register.

2.27 The purpose of seniority is to make the Community trade mark an attractive option to those who have already registered a trade mark at the national level and wish to retain rights they enjoyed as a result of a national registration. It allows the proprietor of a CTM to retain the advantages of a national registration without the costs and inconvenience of keeping it alive.

(d) Parallel national rights

2.28 Article 110(2) provides that the Regulation, unless otherwise provided, 'shall not affect the right to bring proceedings under the civil, administrative or criminal law of a Member State or under provisions of Community law for the purpose of prohibiting the use of a Community trade mark to the extent that the use of a national trade mark may be prohibited under the law of that Member State or under Community law'.

2.29 Article 107 deals with prior rights applicable to particular localities. It provides that the proprietor of an earlier right which only applies to a particular locality may oppose the use of the Community trade mark in the territory where its right is protected insofar as the law of the Member State concerned so permits. This right shall cease to apply if the proprietor of the earlier right has acquiesced in the use of the CTM in the territory where its right is protected for a period of five successive years, being aware of such use, unless the CTM was applied for in bad faith. In this case the proprietor of the Community trade mark shall not be entitled to oppose use of the right mentioned above even though that right may no longer be invoked against the CTM.

(3) The Community Trade Mark

2.30 The Regulation is divided into XIII Titles. Titles I and II (Articles 1 to 24 CTMR) contain most of the substantive trade mark law. Titles III to VI deal with the various proceedings before the Office, from filing to opposition, renewal, and invalidity. Title VII deals with appeals. Title VIII deals with collective marks, Title IX with general procedural rules, Title X with litigation concerning CTMs, in particular infringement proceedings, Title XI with the effect of CTMs in national law, Title XII with the Office, and Title XIII with the Madrid Protocol applications and registration.

(a) Substantive law

2.31 The substantive law governing CTMs is essentially the same as that governing national marks under the Directive, without, however, the options available under the Directive. Some provisions of a substantive nature are not found in Titles I or II, namely the grounds for invalidity or revocation, which are established in Articles 51 to 53. Also, the defence of acquiescence is found in the same context (Article 54).

2.32 As the European Union does not have a legal regime governing property rights, it was necessary to determine the applicable national law of the Member States for dealing with CTMs as objects of property: A CTM is dealt with as a national trade mark registered in the State where the proprietor has its seat or domicile on the relevant date. If there is no such State, the law of the State where the proprietor has an establishment will apply, and if there is no such State then Spanish law (as the law of the country where OHIM has its seat) applies (Article 16 CTMR).

2.33 CTMs may be freely assigned, with or without the business to which they belong. They may be licensed, without any obligation to record licenses. CTMs may be given as security and rights in rem may be established, and they are subject to insolvency and forced execution (Articles 19 to 22 CTMR).

(b) Procedural matters: Languages

2.34 Applications for registration may be filed either directly with OHIM or with a national Registry which will then forward the application to OHIM. The application can be filed in any official language of the Union but must indicate a second language from the five Office languages, namely, English, French, German, Italian, or Spanish. The second language is required because *inter partes* proceedings (oppositions, cancellations) are always carried out in one of the OHIM languages, either the first or the second language when both are OHIM languages, or the second language when the first language is not an OHIM language.

2.35 The language rule was challenged before the Court in *Kik*.[15] The Court of First Instance had noted that Article 217 EC empowered the Council to establish and alter language rules for the institutions of the European Union. It accepted that the language rule 'was adopted for the legitimate purpose of reaching a solution on languages in cases where opposition, revocation or invalidity proceedings ensue between parties who do not have the same language preference and cannot agree between themselves on the language of proceedings'[16] and that the Council had made 'an appropriate and proportionate choice, even if the official languages of the Community were treated differently'.[17]

2.36 The Court of Justice first delineated the scope of Article 115(4) CTMR:

> the language of proceedings before the Office is to be the language used for filing the application for a Community trade mark, although the second language chosen by the applicant may be used by the Office to send him written communications. It follows from that provision that the option of using a second language for written communications is an exception to the principle that the language of proceedings be used, and that the term 'written communications' must therefore be interpreted strictly.[18]

2.37 This meant that

> any document that is required or prescribed by the Community legislation for the purposes of processing an application for a Community trade mark or necessary for such processing, be they notifications, requests for correction, clarification or other documents ... must ... be drawn up by [the Office] in the language used for filing the application.[19]

2.38 Following this interpretation (which was subsequently applied by OHIM), the Court accepted the reasoning of the Court of First Instance. In addition, it made a distinction between all citizens and economic operators: 'the Community trade mark was created for

---

[15] C-361/011 *Kik v Office for Harmonisation in the Internal Market (Trade Marks and Designs)* [2003] ECR II-8283. The case was an appeal against the decision of the Court of First Instance in C-120/99 *Kik v Office for Harmonisation in the Internal Market (Trade Marks and Designs)* [2001] ECR I-2235, dismissing an action against the decision of the Board of Appeal in Case R 65/98-3, 19 March 1999.
[16] Paragraph 62.
[17] Paragraph 63.
[18] Paragraph 45.
[19] Paragraph 46.

the benefit not of all citizens, but of economic operators, and that economic operators are not under any obligation to make use of it'.[20] 'Whilst the monopoly right to use a trade mark is recognised by a public authority, the trade mark right is essentially a tool used by economic operators in the context of their professional activities to produce profits. The legislature is therefore free to require that they should bear, in whole or at least in part, the operating costs of a body created to register Community trade marks.'[21] It accepted that the Council was pursuing the legitimate aim of seeking an appropriate linguistic solution to the difficulties arising from the failure of the parties to agree on a common language. And, taking into account the public interest of keeping registration costs at a reasonable level, it added that 'even if the Council did treat official languages of the Community differently, its choice to limit the languages to those which are most widely known in the European Community is appropriate and proportionate'.[22]

(c) Office proceedings (Articles 24 et seq)

2.39 The Office examines the application as to formalities, including classification, seniority claims and priority, and absolute grounds. Before an application is rejected, the applicant must be given an opportunity to submit its observations.

2.40 Compromising between the diverse national examination systems the Regulation provides that a search of the Community register will be conducted. The application will be communicated to national Offices that have declared their intention to conduct a search for prior rights. The results of the searches will be communicated to the applicant who can then decide whether to proceed with the application. This search system has been criticized as ineffective, and proposals have been made to abolish it altogether. Under the most recent amendments of the Regulation, the applicant has the choice of requesting national searches or opting out of the searches. In practice, the very large majority of applicants today do not request national searches.

2.41 Oppositions must be filed within three months following the publication of the application. If the applicant so requests, the proprietor of an earlier registered mark, whether CTM or national, is required to prove use of his/her mark if it has been registered, at the time of the publication, for more than five years.

2.42 Registrations of CTMs may be revoked upon application by any person in the case of absence of genuine use or the mark having become misleading or generic (Article 51 CTMR), or may be declared invalid if registered in spite of the presence of absolute (Article 52 CTMR) or relative (Article 53 CTMR) grounds of refusal or invalidity. Among the relative grounds are earlier rights beyond those entitling opposition, such as copyrights, design rights, and personality rights (Article 53(2) CTMR).

2.43 Title IX has general provisions applicable to all proceedings, such as the obligation of decisions to state reasons (Article 75), the scope of examination by the Office and the effect of late submission of facts and evidence (Article 76), provision of evidence (Article 78), notification (Article 79), revocation of erroneous decisions (Article 80), *restitutio in integrum*

---

[20] Paragraph 88. It can be argued that such statements potentially undermine the wider justificatory basis of trade mark rights.
[21] Paragraph 89.
[22] Paragraph 94.

(Article 81), further processing (Article 82), obligation to pay costs of proceedings (Articles 85 and 86), and professional representation (Articles 92 and 93).

(d) Appeals and review by the General Court and the Court of Justice

2.44 The decisions of the Office are subject to an appeal before the Boards of Appeal (Articles 57 to 64). The Boards currently decide more than 2,500 cases annually.

2.45 Decisions of the Boards of Appeal may be reviewed by the General Court, pursuant to Article 65 CTMR, and upon further appeal, limited to points of law, by the Court of Justice.

2.46 Since the late 1990s, more than 2,500 decisions of the Boards of Appeal have been brought before what was then the Court of First Instance and is now, since the Lisbon Treaties, the General Court, and more than 200 are added each year. Some twenty to thirty cases reach the Court of Justice. Some are decided by Judgments, most are disposed of by Order.

(e) Enforcement: Court proceedings

2.47 Community trade marks must show their true value on the market, in competition with other CTMs and national marks for the same or similar goods or services. An efficient enforcement system is a necessary requirement. Enforcement means not only civil proceedings, with which Title X of the Regulation deals, but also criminal enforcement and administrative measures, notably customs seizure. As regards criminal enforcement, the Regulation is entirely silent. It is up to the Member States to make provisions for penalties for the infringement of CTMs, which must be treated no worse than national marks. As regards customs intervention, the EU's customs legislation allows CTM proprietors to request customs seizure upon entry into the EU.[23]

2.48 As regards civil procedures for enforcing Community trade marks, the European legislator was faced with the same dilemma that had provided an insurmountable obstacle for many years for the creation of a unitary European patent—the absence of a true solution for a genuine European enforcement procedure with competence for infringement and validity. In the field of patents, the Unified Patent Court, a separate jurisdiction created by a treaty among the participating Member States, may, once in force, actually provide a solution. In the 1980s, when the Regulation was negotiated in Brussels, the Member States agreed on a similarly ambitious approach: The Member States should designate among their civil courts a limited number as 'Community trade mark courts'. These courts would have exclusive competence for certain actions concerning CTMs, namely infringement and validity, whereas for any other action involving or concerning CTMs national courts would be competent in the same manner as they are competent for national marks, but they would have to accept the CTM as valid. Validity of CTMs could in principle not be challenged by way of defence, but only by an action before OHIM seeking a declaration of revocation or invalidity, or by a counterclaim in an infringement action. In the latter situation, the Community trade mark court would be competent to declare the asserted CTM revoked or invalid.

---

[23] Regulation (EU) No 608/2013 of the European Parliament and of the Council of 12 June 2013 concerning customs enforcement of intellectual property rights and repealing Council Regulation (EC) No 1383/2003, OJ L 181, p 15.

2.49 Some feared that letting any national court decide on the validity of a CTM would lead to great insecurity. Today, more than twenty years after the entry into force of the Regulation, these fears have not materialized. The enforcement system as provided in Title X of the Regulation actually functions reasonably well, even in the absence of a single appeals instance. The Court of Justice does remain the final arbiter, either when exercising its jurisdiction in preliminary rulings or on appeal from General Court judgments.

2.50 As a general approach, the Regulation provides in Article 94 that for matters of jurisdiction and recognition and execution of judgments, the European rules generally applicable in civil and commercial matters apply, unless otherwise provided in the Regulation. The European rules were first established in the so-called Brussels Convention (1968), but have for some fifteen years been converted to a Regulation, initially Regulation 44/2001, and now recast, applicable since early 2015, as Regulation 1215/2012.[24]

2.51 The Community trade mark courts, established under Article 95, have exclusive jurisdiction for the following subject matter (Article 96):

(a) infringement proceedings;
(b) actions for declaration of non-infringement;
(c) actions for compensation for infringing acts during the application period; and
(d) counterclaims for revocation of Community trade mark registrations or for declarations of their invalidity.

2.52 International jurisdiction of these courts is either EU-wide or limited to the territory of the Member State where the court is located (Articles 97 and 98).

2.53 In the first category are the courts where the defendant has its domicile or, failing a domicile, an establishment; if neither is in the European Union, the courts where the claimant has its domicile or, failing this, an establishment, are competent. Finally, in the case of foreign claimants and foreign defendants, the Community trade mark courts in Spain, the seat of the Office, have jurisdiction. In addition, the parties may agree on jurisdiction, or not dispute it, and multiple defendants may be brought before the court in the Member State where one of them is domiciled.

2.54 In the second category are the courts in the Member State where acts of infringement are committed or threatened.

2.55 For preliminary and provisional relief special rules apply (Article 103).

2.56 Community trade mark courts must accept the validity of the allegedly infringed mark, unless the defendant counterclaims seeking a declaration of revocation or invalidity (Articles 99 and 100). As an exception, the defendant may invoke as a defence that it is proprietor of an earlier right or that the claimant has not made genuine use of the mark.

2.57 Community trade mark courts apply their own procedural rules and their national law applicable to national marks where the Regulation does not provide a rule (Article 101). As regards sanctions, the Regulation provides for injunctive relief, but refers for all other

---

[24] Regulation (EU) No 1215/2012 of the European Parliament and of the Council of 12 December 2012 on jurisdiction and the recognition and enforcement of judgments in civil and commercial matters, OJ L 351, p 1.

questions to the laws of the Member States where acts of infringement have been committed or are threatened (Article 102).

2.58 Special rules are established for related actions: When a cancellation action is pending before OHIM, a later infringement suit is as a rule barred. An earlier cancellation action before OHIM or before a Community trade mark court bars a subsequent cancellation action.

D. The Enlargement of the European Union

2.59 When the Directive was adopted in 1988, the Community consisted of twelve Member States. Before the Regulation became effective in 1996, three more countries had joined (Austria, Finland, and Sweden). On 1 May 2004, ten new Member States—Cyprus, Czech Republic, Estonia, Hungary, Latvia, Lithuania, Malta, Poland, Slovakia, and Slovenia—joined the European Union. These were followed in 2006 by Bulgaria and Romania, and in 2013 by Croatia.

2.60 As regards the Directive, all of the new Member States had to adapt their domestic legislation to what the Directive required. This was part of the 'acquis' they had to accept. In fact, the new Member States had adapted their national laws to the Directive some time prior to accession to the Union.

2.61 As regards the Regulation, obviously, any new Community trade mark filed after the respective accession date became effective immediately in the territory of the whole EU as newly constituted. The languages of the new Member States became languages in which a CTM application could be filed. Also, the new Member States became part of the administration of OHIM (Administrative Board, Budget Committee). More complicated was the question of what should happen with pre-existing CTMs and pre-existing national marks in the new Member States. The solution adopted, found in Article 165 CTMR, consists of an automatic extension of all CTMs to all new Member States, without an application or administrative intervention. These earlier CTMs would not, however, prevail over national marks or any other right in the new Member States acquired prior to the date of enlargement without their owners being entitled to obtain the invalidation of these CTMs. The right to prohibit the use of such a CTM in the territory of a new Member State was not affected. As an interim measure, CTM applications filed up to six months prior to the enlargement date could be opposed by the owner of an earlier national trade mark in a new Member State, provided the earlier right was not obtained in bad faith.

E. Conclusion

2.62 There are two points that must be highlighted at the end of this chapter. First, that the Directive and the Regulation cannot be seen as two distinct pieces of legislation covering parallel areas. They share a common historical background and their common aim is to establish a European trade mark regime. In essence there is no hierarchical distinction between them.

Conclusion

Second, that the new regime has been constructed on the basis of a principle of coexistence. **2.63**
The aim is for the Community trade mark system to become an attractive alternative to national systems of protection rather than take over them. The bigger aim is for national and Community rights to contribute to the creation and functioning of a growing European market.

3

TRADE MARKS IN EUROPE AND THE COURT OF JUSTICE OF THE EUROPEAN UNION

A. Introduction

The purpose of this chapter is to offer an introduction on the role of the Court of Justice and its effect on the development of trade mark law in Europe.[1] **3.01**

The Court of Justice is one of the framework institutions of the European Union that according to Article 13 of the Treaty on European Union (TEU) 'aim to promote its values, advance its objectives, serve its interests, those of its citizens and those of the Member States, and ensure the consistency, effectiveness and continuity of its policies and actions'. **3.02**

The Court has no direct role in the formal legislative process, except in the drafting and, with the approval of the Council, the adoption of its own and the General Court's Rules of Procedure. This distancing of the Court from the formal legislative process has been characterized as 'essential to avoid prejudicing the Court's approach to any future judicial proceedings which might arise'.[2] The role of the Court, however, becomes critical when we turn to the law, the product of the legislative process, and the relationships of institutions of the EU between themselves on the one hand and with the Member States on the other. The Court applies the law directly, interprets the law, and adjudicates on the institutional power struggles. The Court is the judiciary side in the European legislature–government–judiciary triangle; a commanding side, since its decisions cannot be reversed by an act of the legislature. On the contrary, any measure having legal effect can be annulled by the Court if it considers it contrary to the Treaties or other provisions of EU law. The Court can and must enforce the law against the EU institutions but also against the contracting parties to the Treaties.[3] **3.03**

---

[1] The reader should note that the selection of cases is purely illustrative.
[2] Brown and Kennedy (eds), *The Court of Justice of the European Communities*, 5th edn (Sweet and Maxwell, 2000) p ll.
[3] Article 263 TFEU:

> The Court of Justice shall review the legality of acts adopted jointly by the European Parliament and the Council, of acts of the Council, of the Commission and of the ECB, other than recommendations and opinions, and of acts of the European Parliament intended to produce legal effects vis-à-vis third parties. It shall for this purpose have jurisdiction in actions brought by a Member State, the European Parliament, the Council or the Commission on grounds of lack of competence, infringement of an essential procedural requirement, infringement of this Treaty or of any rule of law relating to its application, or misuse of powers. The Court of Justice shall have jurisdiction under the same conditions in actions brought by the Court of Auditors and by the ECB for the purpose of protecting their prerogatives. Any natural or legal person may, under the same conditions, institute proceedings against a decision addressed to that person or against a decision which, although in the form of a regulation or a decision addressed to another person, is

3.04 A ruling of the Court can be reversed only by the Court itself in a subsequent case, or by amendment of the Treaties.[4] Amending the Treaties requires unanimous agreement between the Member States and subsequent ratification by all the Member States. The misfortune of the European 'Constitution'[5] is evidence of the complicated nature of this process:

> Conversely, the political obstacles to amending the Treaties lend added significance to the Court's rulings on their interpretation, especially as the Court ... has been ready to interpret boldly in the face of political deadlock between the Council and the Commission.[6]

3.05 The boldness of the Court can also be evidenced in the exercise of its jurisdiction. In theory, the jurisdiction of the Court is conferred upon it and delineated by the Treaties or by a convention. However, its role as a guardian of the Treaties function enables the Court to assume jurisdiction in a way that, in practice at least, appears to be an intrinsic part of its own nature.[7] For example, the Member States did not intend the Treaty of Rome to confer judicially enforceable rights on private legal entities. Still, the Court inferred rights from provisions such as those requiring Member States to remove national obstacles to intra-Community trade: 'Legal integration is therefore largely a record of how the ECJ has made creative use of its discretionary powers to remake the Treaty, and how private actors, national judges, and political elites have responded to these moves.'[8]

B. Forms of Action

(1) Actions against Member States in Breach of Community Law

3.06 This is the second part of a two-tiered procedure that is available against Member States that are considered to act in breach of EU law;[9] the scope of the action is very wide, it may cover Member States' positive actions, omissions, breaches of the Treaty and secondary legislation, failures in implementing directives, or breaking of any rule that has become part

---

of direct and individual concern to the former. The proceedings provided for in this article shall be instituted within two months of the publication of the measure, or of its notification to the plaintiff or, in the absence thereof, of the day on which it came to the knowledge of the latter, as the case may be.

[4] Indeed, the Court appears impervious regarding the doctrinal debate over the status of its jurisprudence: see Barceló, 'Precedent in European Community Law', in MacCormick and Summers (eds), *Interpreting Precedents: A Comparative Study* (Ashgate/Darlmouth, 1997) pp 420–24.

[5] Treaty Establishing a Constitution for Europe [2004] OJ C310/1.

[6] Brown and Kennedy (2000) (n 2) p 6.

[7] For a view supporting that the Court has inherent jurisdiction see Arnull, 'Does the Court of Justice Have Inherent Jurisdiction?' (1992) 27 CMLRev 683.

[8] Stone Sweet, *The Judicial Construction of Europe* (Oxford University Press, 2004) p 24. Albeit this interpretive and jurisdictional boldness, particularly when combined with national judicial obstinacy and sovereignty apprehension, can make national courts behave in unreceptive ways. See, for example, the judicial debate on confusion and association in C-425/98 *Marca Mode CV v Adidas AG & Adidas BV* [2000] ECR I-4861, discussed in paragraph 7.37, below.

[9] Article 258 TFEU provides:

> [I]f the Commission considers that a Member State has failed to fulfil an obligation under this Treaty, it shall deliver a reasoned opinion on the matter after giving the State concerned the opportunity to submit its observations.
>
> If the State concerned does not comply with the opinion within the period laid down by the Commission, the latter may bring the matter before the Court.

of the Community legal order.[10] The Member State is given the opportunity to respond during a preliminary procedure performed by the Commission. It can explain its position and may opt to change its practice in order to reach a compromise with the Commission. If this informal process is unsuccessful, a formal letter is issued by the Commission and the Member State has another opportunity to respond, and resolve the issue. In the absence of a resolution a reasoned opinion is issued by the Commission and if the Member State does not conform an action may be brought by the Commission before the Court.

3.07 The Court may hold, in a declaratory judgment, that the Member State has infringed the Treaty. Further proceedings can be instituted by the Commission against a Member State that has not complied with such a judgment; the Court may then impose financial penalties against the Member State according to Article 260 of the Treaty on the Functioning of the European Union (TFEU).

(2) Actions against a Community Institution for Failure to Act

3.08 The other side of the coin is the action against a Community institution that can be brought by a Member State, another Community institution, or an individual for its failure to act despite having been prompted to do so on the basis of Article 265 TFEU. If the Court decides that the failure to act has been unlawful, the institution must take the appropriate measures to end its failure.[11] The jurisprudence of the Court of Justice in the *Comitology* case implies that Member States and Community institutions can challenge failure to act even if it is in respect of recommendations or opinions.[12]

(3) Annulment Actions

3.09 Measures taken by Community institutions can be attacked directly or through an action for annulment of the underlying regulation according to Article 263 TFEU. The action can be brought primarily by directly affected individuals, but also by Community institutions and Member States.[13]

3.10 Article 277 TFEU does not create an independent cause of action; rather, it provides an attacking tool to parties to proceedings involving an EU measure.[14] It is clear from the wording and the general scheme of this Article that a declaration of the inapplicability of

---

[10] For example, C-13/00 *Commission v Ireland* [2002] ECR I-2943 concerned a breach in the area of the Community's external competence. See the reviews of Snyder, 'The Effectiveness of European Community Law: Institutions. Processes, Tools and Techniques' (1993) 56 MLR 19; and Rawlings, 'Engaged Elites: Citizen Action and Institutional Attitudes in Commission Enforcement' (2000) 6 EW 4. For a US-based comparative perspective see Pfander, 'Member State Liability and Constitutional Change in the United States and Europe' (2003) 51 Am J Comp L 237.

[11] Applications for compensation for non-contractual liability can be filed with the Court of First Instance.

[12] Case 302/87 *European Parliament v Council* [1988] ECR 5615. See Hartley, *The Foundations of European Community Law* (Oxford University Press, 1998) pp 333–41. In principle an individual has standing to bring an action if it is directly and individually concerned, without it being necessary to be individually addressed by the relevant decision: see C-10 and 18/68 *Società 'Eridania' Zuccherifici Nazwnali v Commission* [1969] ECR 459; and C-117/98 *Comar Srl and Tico Sri v Commission* [2000] ECR I-2193.

[13] See the Opinion of AG Roemer in Case 32/65 *Italy v Commission* [1996] ECR 389, p 414.

[14] Article 277 TFEU provides:

Notwithstanding the expiry of the period laid down in Article 263, sixth paragraph, any party may, in proceedings in which an act of general application adopted by an institution, body, office or agency of the Union is at issue, plead the grounds specified in Article 263, second paragraph, in order to invoke before the Court of Justice of the European Union the inapplicability of that act.

a Regulation is only contemplated in proceedings brought before the Court of Justice itself under some other provision of the Treaty, and then only incidentally and with limited effect.

> More particularly, it is clear from the reference to the time limit laid down in Article [263 TFEU] that Article [277 TFEU] is applicable only in the context of proceedings brought before the Court of Justice and that it does not permit the said time limit to be avoided.
>
> The sole object of Article [277 TFEU] is thus to protect an interested party against the application of an illegal Regulation, without thereby in any way calling in issue the Regulation itself, which can no longer be challenged because of the expiry of the time limit laid down in Article [263 TFEU].[15]

3.11 According to the text of the Treaty only the effect of regulations can be challenged in this way; however, the Court of Justice in *Simmenthal* has ensured that it covers any act which in substance functions as a regulation:

> As the Court ... has already held in connexion with Article 36 of the ECSC Treaty, Article [277 TFEU] gives expression to a general principle conferring upon any party to proceedings the right to challenge, for the purpose of obtaining the annulment of a decision of direct and individual concern to the party, the validity of previous acts of the institutions which form the legal basis of the decision which is being attacked, if that party was not entitled under Article [263 TFEU] to bring a direct action challenging those acts by which it was thus affected without having been in a position to ask that they be declared void.
>
> The field of application of the said article must therefore include acts of the institutions which although they are not in the form of a Regulation, nevertheless produce similar effects and on those grounds may not be challenged under Article [263] by natural or legal persons other than Community institutions and Member States.
>
> This wide interpretation of Article [277] derives from the need to provide those persons who are precluded by the second paragraph of Article [263] from instituting proceedings directly in respect of general acts with the benefit of judicial review of them at the time when they are affected by implementing decisions which are of direct and individual concern to them.[16]

(4) Appeals

3.12 The judgments of the General Court can be challenged on points of law following an appeal to the Court of Justice. The Court will consider the admissibility and the basis of the appeal. If the appeal is valid it will set aside the judgment of the General Court and, according to the nature of the proceedings, will either decide the case itself or refer the case back to the General Court to be reconsidered according to the decision given on appeal.[17] Note that following the introduction of specialist tribunals attached to the Court, the Court of Justice retained for itself the role of reviewing in exceptional circumstances the appeal decisions of the General Court.

(5) References for a Preliminary Ruling

3.13 Here the Court acts as a mentor of national courts and custodian of the Union's legal order. This 'preliminary' function of the Court has transformed it from an ordinary supreme—or

---

[15] Case 31 and 33/62 *Milchwerke Heinz Wöhrmann & Sohn KG and Alfons Lütticke GmbH v Commission* [1962] ECR 501, p 507.
[16] Case 92/78 *Simmenthal SpA v Commission* [1979] ECR 777, paragraphs 39–41.
[17] See, for example, C-104/00 P *DKV Deutsche Krankenversicherung AG v Office for Harmonisation in the Internal Market (Trade Marks and Designs)* [2002] ECR I-7561.

even federal supreme—court to the powerhouse of EU law. It is through Article 267 TFEU that the Court of Justice has developed doctrines such as direct effect and supremacy.[18]

3.14 A dispute between individuals or between an individual and a national authority falls within the jurisdiction of the appropriate national court or tribunal rather than the jurisdiction of the Court of Justice. However, a national court during the administration of justice involving Community law is often confronted with interpretive dilemmas. Does its own national legislation conform with the Community legislation that led to its adoption? Is the relevant Community legislation clear enough to allow a finding on conformity? Is a change of direction required when the national court identifies that in a comparable situation it follows a divergent route from other national courts? Is an act of a Community institution valid? To solve the riddles the national court has to turn to the Court of Justice to clarify a particular point of EU law or consider the validity and interpretation of an act of a Community institution.[19] Note that the Court of Justice is not deciding whether a national law is valid or not; this remains within the jurisdiction of the national court that has to decide the particular case that gave rise to the request.

3.15 Individuals even have the right to demand that the national court considers seeking clarification from the Court of Justice.[20] If the national court considers it appropriate and necessary it will formulate a question, often a long list of questions, in the form of a reference to the Court of Justice seeking a preliminary ruling. The Court of Justice has no other option but to consider the question; only in exceptional cases will the Court of Justice refuse to consider a reference. It cannot ignore it; at most it can rephrase it in order to retrieve—or in some cases bypass—its essence.[21] The parties to the national proceedings, Member States, and the Commission can participate in the proceedings before the Court.[22]

3.16 The Court's response to the national court is neither a decision on the facts of a case nor a simple authoritative opinion on the interpretation of a legal provision. In *Costa v ENEL*, the Court of Justice delineated between the functions of the Court of Justice and the national court: the role of the Court of Justice is not to investigate the facts of the case and the grounds and purpose of the request for a preliminary ruling.[23] The Court of Justice does not function as an appeal court. The response is a judgment, or reasoned order, that sets a principle and binds the referring court. The national court has to decide its case on the basis of its own facts following the interpretive direction chosen by the Court of Justice. In addition, the judgment of the Court of Justice has a wider ambit. Subsequent courts facing analogous factual scenarios have to conform, unless they prefer to ask the Court one more time, maybe longing for a different answer. The position of the Court of Justice has been

---

[18] 'The Court of Justice of the European Union shall have jurisdiction to give preliminary rulings concerning (a) the interpretation of the Treaties; (b) the validity and interpretation of acts of the institutions, bodies, offices or agencies of the Union...' (Art 267 TFEU).

[19] See Craig and de Búrca, *EU Law: Text, Cases, and Materials* (Oxford University Press, 2003) p 435; and Hartley, *The Foundations of European Community Law* (Clarendon Press, 1998) pp 262–65.

[20] For an authoritative comment on this see the Opinion of AG Jacobs in C-358/89 *Extramet Industrie SA v Council* [1991] ECR I-2501.

[21] See, for example, C-418/02 *Praktiker Bau und Heimwerkermärkte AG v Deutsches Patent- und Markenamt* [2005] ECR I-5873, as discussed in paragraph 4.176, below.

[22] For the role of governments in the judicial process at this level, see Everling, 'The Member States of the European Community before their Court of Justice' (1984) 9 ELRev 215; and Granger, 'When Governments Go to Luxembourg... The Influence of Governments on the Court of Justice' (2004) 29 ELRev 3, examining their litigation strategies. Three motives are identified: defence of national interests; promotion of national visions of Europe; and furthering of EU interests.

[23] Case 6/64 *Costa v Ente Nazionale per l'Energia Elettrica (ENEL)* [1964] ECR 585, p 593.

stated clearly in *Da Costa*. Having answered the question in an earlier case does not render a new request inadmissible; if there is no new issue, factor, or argument to be examined, it will simply refer the national court to its earlier judgment.[24]

3.17 This, in turn, means that national courts can rely on the precedents set by the jurisprudence of the Court of Justice. In *CILFIT* and *ICC* the Court elaborated further on its ruling in *Da Costa*:

> It must be remembered ... that in ... Da Costa the Court ruled that 'Although paragraph 3 of Article [267 TFEU] unreservedly requires courts or tribunals of a Member State against whose decision there is no judicial remedy ... to refer to the Court every question of interpretation raised before them, the authority of an interpretation under Article [267] already given by the Court may deprive the obligation of its purpose and thus empty it of its substance. Such is the case especially when the question raised is materially identical with a question which has already been the subject of a preliminary ruling in a similar case'. The same effect, as regards the limits set to the obligation laid down by paragraph (3) of Article [267], may be produced where previous decisions of the Court have already dealt with the point of law in question, irrespective of the nature of the proceedings which led to those decisions, even though the questions at issue are not strictly identical.
>
> However, it must not be forgotten that in all such circumstances national courts and tribunals, including those referred to in paragraph (3) of Article [267], remain entirely at liberty to bring a matter before the Court of Justice if they consider it appropriate to do so.[25]

3.18 In *ICC* the Court strengthened the principle that its judgments constitute precedents that national courts have to follow:

> When the Court is moved under Article [267 TFEU] to declare an act of one of the institutions to be void there are particularly imperative requirements concerning legal certainty in addition to those concerning the uniform application of Community law. It follows from the very nature of such a declaration that a national court may not apply the act declared void without once more creating serious uncertainty as to the Community law applicable.[26]

3.19 The development of precedent in the preliminary rulings process led to the creation of a European judicial system where national courts and the Court of Justice co-operate as 'Community' courts.

C. Judicial Review and the Community Trade Mark

(1) The Role of the Boards of Appeal and New or Additional Facts and Evidence

3.20 Conflicts concerning the registration of Community trade marks involve up to four levels of scrutiny: on the one hand, there is a two-tier administrative examination system within OHIM, whereby parties are entitled to appeal unfavourable decisions of the departments dealing with the case at first instance to the Office's Boards of Appeal, which enjoy independence in the performance of their duties; on the other hand, the Regulation also provides for the subsequent judicial review of the decisions of the Boards by the Community

---

[24] C-28/62, C-29/62, and C-30/62 *Da Costa en Schaake NY, Jacob Meijer NV and Hoechst-Holland NV v Nederlandse Belastingadministrotie* [1963] ECR 31.
[25] Case 283/81 *Srl CILFIT and Lanijicio di Gavardo SpA v Ministry of Health* [1982] ECR 3415, at paragraphs 13–15.
[26] Case 66/80 *International Chemical Corp v Amministrozione delle Finanze della Staw* [1981] ECR 1191.

judicature, initially by the General Court (formerly the Court of First Instance), and finally, limited to points of law, by the Court of Justice.

3.21 The scope of the decision-making powers of the Boards is laid down in Article 64, according to which, in deciding on the appeal, the Boards may 'either exercise any power within the competence of the department responsible for the decision appealed, or remit the case to that department for further prosecution'.

3.22 That formulation, however, does not fully reveal the extent of the Boards' powers of review. In particular, it does not clarify whether the Boards have the right or even the obligation to re-examine the case *ab initio*, for example, by taking into account facts and evidence and arguments or even grounds produced for the first time before them, or whether their jurisdiction is actually confined to a mere re-assessment of the factual and legal matrix on which the first instance decision was based. That issue reached the Court of First Instance for the first time in the very first case appealed to that court, the famous *Baby-Dry* case.[27] The applicant in that case had raised the argument that its mark was registrable on the basis of acquired distinctiveness (Article 7(3)) for the first time before the Board, and the Board had dismissed this argument because its role was limited to reviewing the first instance decision. When Procter & Gamble appealed, and argued that the role of the Board was not so limited, OHIM actually supported the applicant. The Court announced for the first time the oft-repeated principle that the Boards and the first instance units in OHIM are linked by a 'continuity in function'. The Boards are therefore not only authorized but required to undertake a new examination of the case, having the same powers as the first instance. The Court pointed out, however, that the Boards were entitled to apply Article 76(2) (then Article 74(2)) and reject evidence or arguments not presented 'in due time'; in the present case, with no time limits having expired, this case did not arise. The arguments of the Court are reproduced in full in the footnote.[28] They contain already all the elements

---

[27] Judgment of 8 July 1999, T-163/98, *Procter & Gamble v OHIM* (BABY-DRY) [1999] ECR II-2383. A further appeal to the Court of Justice led to the notorious decision holding the mark registrable, discussed under the absolute grounds; the issue discussed here did not reach the Court of Justice until much later, in the *Kaul* case.

[28] 32. Under Article 7(3) of Regulation No 40/94, Article 7(1)(c) 'shall not apply if the trade mark has become distinctive in relation to the goods ... for which registration is requested in consequence of the use which has been made of it'. 33. In this case, it is common ground that the applicant at no time referred to that provision during the procedure before the examiner. In his decision, the examiner found that the term 'Baby-Dry' was ineligible for registration, having regard to the prohibition in Article 7(1)(c) of Regulation No 40/94. 34. In the written statement setting out its grounds of appeal against the examiner's decision, the applicant challenged the examiner's finding. In the alternative, it ended its statement with the words: 'we would wish to submit evidence of acquired distinctiveness to the Office as our "Baby-Dry" diapers are on sale throughout Europe since 1993 and heavily advertised'. 35. At paragraph 22 of the contested decision, the Board of Appeal refused to take account of that argument on the ground that it had not been raised by the applicant in the procedure before the examiner. It stated that a decision cannot be criticised for failing to adopt a position on a ground that was not raised. That would not affect the applicant's right to lodge a fresh application for a Community trade mark, this time adducing evidence of acquired distinctiveness in consequence of use. 36. The Court notes that the Office was established by Regulation No 40/94 to register Community trade marks under the conditions which that regulation lays down. The Community trade mark, which is valid throughout the territory of the Member States, is an important instrument for the completion of the internal market, as the First Recital in the Preamble to the regulation makes clear. 37. The Boards of Appeal, which form part of the Office, also contribute, within the limits set by the regulation, to the application of that instrument. 38. In that sense, there is continuity in terms of their functions between the examiner and the Boards of Appeal. 39. That view is borne out by the close interconnection between their duties, as laid down by the rules governing the lodging and preliminary examination of applications. Thus, if an applicant wishes to contest the examiner's decision, he must first file an appeal 'at the Office' (Article 59 of Regulation

of the debate or dispute, even today not entirely resolved, about the distribution of roles of the first instance units in OHIM and its Boards of Appeal. Also, the attempts of the legislature to resolve these conflicts have so far met with little sympathy from the Court of Justice.

3.23 At the heart of the conflict is the scope of Article 76, which obliges the Office to examine the facts of its own motion, except in relative grounds cases, but which entitles the Office to disregard facts or evidence 'not submitted in due time'. Article 76 reads as follows:

Article 76—Examination of the facts by the Office of its own motion
1. In proceedings before it the Office shall examine the facts of its own motion; however, in proceedings relating to relative grounds for refusal of registration, the Office shall be restricted in this examination to the facts, evidence and arguments provided by the parties and the relief sought.
2. The Office may disregard facts or evidence which are not submitted in due time by the parties concerned.

3.24 That provision, by the way, has its parallel or 'model', as is the case with many other provisions, in Article 114 of the European Patent Convention.[29] Its interpretation has led to confusion because the courts have taken 'in due time' to mean 'outside of a time limit', while what was actually meant with this clause is that the Office may react to dilatory tactics, such as late evidence within an ongoing examination, without this being linked to a missed time limit. The provision was never meant to allow the Office to disregard time limits properly set which, if not observed, necessarily lead to a loss of a right. These 'peremptory' time limits are spread throughout the Regulation and the Implementing Regulation and are frequently set by OHIM on the basis of specific authorizations. The Office itself had

---

No 40/94). The appeal is then submitted to the examiner for 'interlocutory revision' (Article 60(1) of the regulation). Finally, if the decision is not rectified within one month, it is immediately and automatically remitted to the Board of Appeal (Article 60(2) of the regulation). 40. The procedure before the Boards of Appeal is divided into two separate stages; examination and decision. 41. Under Article 61(2) of Regulation No 40/94, 'In the examination of the appeal, the Board of Appeal shall invite the parties, as often as necessary, to file observations, within a period to be fixed by the Board of Appeal, on communications … issued by itself'. 42. Under Article 62(1) of Regulation No 40/94, 'Following the examination as to the allowability of the appeal, the Board of Appeal shall decide on the appeal'. That provision also states that the Board is to determine the appeal either by exercising any power within the competence of the department which was responsible for the decision appealed or by remitting the case to that department for further action. 43. It follows from those provisions and from the scheme of Regulation No 40/94 that it was not open to the Board of Appeal, which enjoys the same powers in determining an appeal as the examiner, simply to reject the applicant's arguments based on Article 7(3) of Regulation No 40/94 solely on the ground that they were not raised before the examiner. Having considered the appeal, it should have either ruled on the substance of that issue or remitted the matter to the examiner. 44. That does not by any means preclude the Board of Appeal, under Article 74(2) of Regulation No 40/94, from disregarding facts or evidence which the parties did not submit to it in due time. But that cannot be the case here. First of all, the applicant clearly indicated at the end of the written statement setting out its grounds of appeal that it intended to rely on Article 7(3) of Regulation No 40/94, and secondly, it was not given any time-limit within which to submit the evidence that it had offered to adduce. 45. In the light of all those factors, the Court finds that, by declaring the applicant's arguments based on Article 7(3) of Regulation No 40/94 to be inadmissible, the Board of Appeal has infringed Article 62 of that regulation.

[29] Article 114—Examination by the European Patent Office of its own motion
(1) In proceedings before it, the European Patent Office shall examine the facts of its own motion; it shall not be restricted in this examination to the facts, evidence and arguments provided by the parties and the relief sought.
(2) The European Patent Office may disregard facts or evidence which are not submitted in due time by the parties concerned.

consistently defended the view that neither the first nor the second instance were entitled to take into account submissions presented after the respective peremptory time limit had expired. The parties, however, which in this way lost their cases consistently, appealed to the General Court and also to the Court of Justice, and the case law of these courts has created the current amalgamation of flexible rules with which the Office and the parties to proceedings have to battle.

3.25 The legislature has intervened in this interpretative battle as well, not at the level of the Regulation, but at the level of the Implementing Regulation, in amendments which came into operation in 2005. First of all, the provisions obliging the rejection of submissions out of time were made explicit, notably in Rule 19(4) as regards late submissions by opponents, which must be disregarded, and in Rule 22(2) as regards submission of proof of use—when no proof is presented, the opposition must be dismissed. In view of the by then well-known court cases, the Implementing Regulation added a provision in Rule 50, dealing with appeals, permitting the Boards of Appeal in opposition cases to take into account additional or supplementary evidence unless they considered that this evidence should be dismissed as not having been presented in due time. The third subparagraph of Rule 50(1) of the Implementing Regulation reads as follows:

> Where the appeal is directed against a decision of an Opposition Division, the Board shall limit its examination of the appeal to facts and evidence presented within the time limits set in or specified by the Opposition Division in accordance with the Regulation and these Rules, unless the Board considers that additional or supplementary facts and evidence should be taken into account pursuant to Article 74(2) [now Article 76(2)] of the Regulation.

3.26 One may ask why the additional possibility was explicitly limited to opposition cases. The reason is that peremptory time limits of the nature applicable in opposition cases were considered not to exist in *ex parte* cases, nor in cancellation cases, where the parties should have ample opportunity to present facts and evidence, in view of the final nature of the respective decisions, whereas opposition proceedings were thought to be speedy and, to some degree, provisional, because an unsuccessful opponent could always bring an invalidity case later. That distinction never made it into the court decisions.

3.27 The various interrelated issues which have by now been—more or less—settled by the Court of Justice are the following:

- When an appeal is filed, must the Board undertake a complete *de novo* examination in all cases?
- Under which circumstances, and in which kind of cases, may the Board refuse to take into account new or additional evidence?
- What is the situation in the first instance units when new or additional evidence is submitted before that instance outside of properly set time limits?

(a) The role of the Boards of Appeal

3.28 The first issue reached the Court of Justice in *Kaul*,[30] by way of an appeal concerning the interpretation of what is now Article 76(2), which provides that the Office 'may disregard facts or evidence not submitted in due time by the parties'. In that case, the appellant had

---

[30] C-29/05 P *OHIM v Kaul GmbH—Bayer AG (ARCOL)* [2007] ECR I-02213.

produced new evidence (concerning enhanced distinctiveness) before the Board of Appeal with a view to remedying the deficiencies in the substantiation of its opposition that had led to its rejection at first instance. The Board dismissed that evidence as belated, on the grounds that it had been filed after the expiry of the peremptory time limits provided for in the Implementing Regulation[31] in relation to opposition proceedings.

3.29 The appellant brought an action before the Court of First Instance seeking the annulment of the Board's decision. The Court of First Instance[32] granted the request. Referring to its settled case law,[33] it recalled that the 'continuity in terms of functions' between the decision-making instances of OHIM actually 'requires the Boards of Appeal to base their decisions on all the matters of fact and of law invoked by the parties either at first instance or, subject only to Article 74(2) CTMR [now Article 76], in the appeal'.

3.30 OHIM appealed to the Court of Justice arguing that what is now Article 64(1) does not permit and even less require the Boards to take into account facts and evidence presented out of time and that such an interpretation of 'functional continuity' would ultimately render the provisions relating to the fixing of time limits devoid of purpose. The Court set the framework for its analysis by referring to the role of the various decision-making instances intervening at each stage of the proceedings and by comparing the scope of the examination performed by OHIM to the judicial review of its decisions carried out by the Community courts.

3.31 Dealing with the nature of the proceedings before the Boards of Appeal, it stated that what is now Article 64 had to be interpreted in the light of the 'institutional architecture' introduced by the Regulation,[34] while stressing that 'in spite of the independence enjoyed by their members, the Boards remain nonetheless departments of OHIM'.[35]

3.32 Thus, the Court considered that, when seized of an appeal, the Board is required to 'give judgment on the case itself by either rejecting the relevant claim or declaring it to be founded, thereby either upholding or reversing the contested decision' and that 'through the effect of the appeal brought before it, the Board of Appeal is called upon to carry out a new, full examination of the merits of the case, in terms of both law and fact'.[36] Accordingly, it found that 'there was no reason of principle related to the nature of the proceedings before the Board that precludes it from taking into account facts produced for the first time at the appeal stage' and that unless otherwise specified, the various decision-making departments of the Office have 'wide discretionary powers' to accept evidence presented late,[37] in particular where 'the material produced late is, on the face of it, likely to be relevant to the outcome', provided however that 'the stage of the proceedings and the surrounding circumstances do not speak against such an acceptance'.[38]

---

[31] Rule 20 of the Implementing Regulation prior to its 1995 amendments.
[32] T-164/02 *Kaul v OHIM—Bayer AG (ARCOL)* [2004] ECR II-3807, paragraphs 25–34.
[33] T-163/98 *Procter & Gamble v OHIM* (BABY-DRY) [1999] ECR II-2383, paragraphs 38–44, referred to above; T-63/01 *Procter & Gamble v OHIM* (Soap bar shape) [2002] ECR II-5255, paragraph 21; and T-63/01 *Henkel v OHIM—LHS (UK)* (KLEENCARE) [2003] ECR II-3253, paragraphs 24–32.
[34] Paragraph 55.
[35] Paragraph 51.
[36] Paragraphs 56–57.
[37] Paragraphs 41–43.
[38] Paragraph 44.

The Court rejected OHIM's position that what is now Article 76(2) did not authorize the **3.33** acceptance of new evidence once the time limits had expired. The Court interpreted that provision to apply as well when specific time limits had expired:

> 41 First, in order to give judgment on the ground of appeal in its entirety, it must be found that, as is apparent from the wording of Article 74(2) of Regulation No 40/94, OHIM may disregard facts which were not submitted or evidence which was not produced in due time by the parties.
>
> 42 Contrary to OHIM's submission, it results from such wording that, as a general rule and unless otherwise specified, the submission of facts and evidence by the parties remains possible after the expiry of the time-limits to which such submission is subject under the provisions of Regulation No 40/94 and that OHIM is in no way prohibited from taking account of facts and evidence which are submitted or produced late.
>
> 43 However, it is equally apparent from that wording that a party has no unconditional right to have facts and evidence submitted out of time taken into consideration by OHIM. In stating that the latter 'may', in such a case, decide to disregard facts and evidence, Article 74(2) of Regulation No 40/94 grants OHIM a wide discretion to decide, while giving reasons for its decision in that regard, whether or not to take such information into account.
>
> 44 Where OHIM is called upon to give judgment in the context of opposition proceedings, taking such facts or evidence into account is particularly likely to be justified where OHIM considers, first, that the material which has been produced late is, on the face of it, likely to be relevant to the outcome of the opposition brought before it and, second, that the stage of the proceedings at which that late submission takes place and the circumstances surrounding it do not argue against such matters being taken into account.

There remained a small escape clause in the statement in paragraph 42, 'unless otherwise **3.34** specified', which became of significance in subsequent cases.

The Court also sided with the Office that upon appeal no new time limits for the submission **3.35** of evidence etc begin to run:

> 61 It follows that, contrary to the finding of the Court of First Instance in paragraph 30 of the judgment under appeal, Article 59 of the regulation cannot be interpreted as starting a new time-limit for the person bringing such an appeal in which to submit facts and evidence in support of his opposition.
>
> 62 Consequently, the Court of First Instance erred in law in finding in that paragraph that the facts and evidence were submitted 'in due time' within the meaning of Article 74(2) and in inferring therefrom that the Board of Appeal was required to take that information into consideration in the decision which it was called upon to give on the appeal brought before it.
>
> 63 It follows from paragraphs 41 to 43 of this judgment that, where, as in the present case, such facts and evidence have not been submitted and produced by the party concerned within the time-limit set to that end under the provisions of Regulation No 40/94, and thus not 'in due time' within the meaning of Article 74(2) of that regulation, that party does not enjoy an unconditional right to have such information taken into account by the Board of Appeal. On the contrary, that board has a discretion as to whether or not to take such information into account when making the decision which it is called upon to give.

(b) Under which circumstances, and in which kind of cases, may the Board refuse to take into account new or additional evidence?

The principle established in cases following *Kaul* is that, with the exception of fixed time **3.36** limits set up by the Regulation or the Implementing Regulation, essentially all other time limits, notably those set by the Office in the various proceedings, are of a nature where additional and supplementary evidence may be admitted by the Boards of Appeal, but may also be rejected as 'late'. In either case, the Board is required to exercise its discretion as to whether or not to admit such evidence, and the review of this discretion by the General Court or the Court of Justice will rarely if ever lead to a reversal.

3.37 This applies not only in opposition cases, as in the *Kaul* case, but also in cancellation cases, as established by the Court of Justice in two decisions of 26 September 2013 in the two parallel *Centrotherm* cases.[39] In these cases, an application by Centrotherm Clean Solutions for revocation of the mark CENTROTHERM, registered in 2001, was based on absence of genuine use. The proprietor (Centrotherm Systemtechnik) provided some evidence within the time limit set by OHIM's Cancellation Division, which found the proof of use insufficient. On appeal by Centrotherm, the Board in part annulled the contested decision, finding that proof of use had been established for some of the goods, and confirmed the revocation for the remaining goods. Additional use evidence was not taken into account by the Board. Each party appealed to the General Court. The appeal by Centrotherm against the partial refusal of revocation was successful before the General Court.[40] The General Court agreed with Centrotherm and found that the evidence supplied by Centrotherm was not sufficient to establish genuine use. This decision was confirmed by the European Court of Justice (ECJ) in Case C-609/11 P.[41] The appeal by Centrotherm was dismissed by the General Court in a separate judgment taken on the same day.[42] The General Court considered that the Board had been correct in not taking into account the additional evidence presented before the Board. This decision was annulled by the ECJ in Case C-610/11 P.

3.38 In Case C-610/11 P the principal issue was whether the Board should have taken into account the additional evidence submitted to it after the Cancellation Division had decided that Centrotherm had failed to prove genuine use. Contrary to the General Court, the ECJ held that the Board should have exercised its discretion whether or not to consider the additional evidence. Just as in opposition cases, also in revocation cases where a party had submitted some relevant evidence of use, the submission of additional evidence was not absolutely excluded. Rule 40(5) of the Implementing Regulation, which is similarly worded as Rule 20(2) of the Implementing Regulation, applicable in opposition proceedings, does not preclude additional evidence absolutely. Having concluded that the Board's decision was based on an erroneous reading of the applicable rules, the ECJ then proceeded, as it is entitled under Article 61 of the Statute of the Court, to decide itself whether the appeal against the Board decision was justified. The ECJ concluded that the Board had committed an error when holding—as an alternative ground for dismissing the appeal—that in the exercise of its discretion it would have rejected the new evidence. The criteria established in *Kaul* were not properly taken into account.[43]

---

[39] C-609/11 P *Centrotherm Clean Solutions GmbH & Co. KG v OHIM—Centrotherm Systemtechnik GmbH*, ECLI:EU:C:2013:592; C-610/11 P *Centrotherm Systemtechnik GmbH v OHIM—Centrotherm Clean Solutions GmbH & Co. KG.*, ECLI:EU:C:2013:593.
[40] T-427/09, [2011] ECR II-06207.
[41] The judgment is not really relevant for the late evidence issue because the ECJ found that Centrotherm had not properly pleaded an error on the part of the Board in not taking into account additional evidence.
[42] T-434/09, [2011] ECR II-06227.
[43] The Court concluded as follows:

> 114 In the present case, relevant circumstances liable to be taken into consideration include the fact that the revocation decision of the Cancellation Division of OHIM was given after initial evidence had been submitted—within the time set by the Cancellation Division—of use of the mark

(c) What is the situation in the first instance units when new or additional evidence is submitted before that instance outside of properly set time limits?

3.39 The ability and even obligation of the Boards of Appeal to accept additional evidence in opposition was clearly established by *Kaul*, and now confirmed in *Centrotherm* for cancellation cases. It is thus inevitable that such additional evidence must also be taken into account by the first instance units; it would be absurd if these units would be precluded, while the Boards were even obliged to consider additional evidence.

3.40 Thus, it is no surprise that the Court of Justice expressly confirmed that discretion regarding additional evidence must also be exercised in first instance cases.

3.41 The first decision to this effect is the *New Yorker* case decided on 18 July 2013.[44] In that case, an opposition based on a Greek figurative mark FISHBONE BEACHWEAR against the word mark FISHBONE for clothing, the applicant had requested proof of use. The proof provided by the opponent was considered inadequate by the applicant, whereupon the opponent provided additional evidence, which was taken into account by the Opposition Division and subsequently by the Board of Appeal in partially upholding the opposition. The applicant's appeal to the General Court was dismissed, and the appeal on points of law to the ECJ was also dismissed as unfounded. According to the ECJ, OHIM's Opposition Division was entitled to consider additional use evidence filed after a first timely submission. Rule 22(2) of the Implementing Regulation, which mandates a rejection of an opposition when no proof of use is provided within the time limit set by OHIM, was not applicable because the opponent had submitted relevant evidence within the time limit. The Court added that OHIM's Opposition Division was not obliged to analyse the acceptance of the late evidence specifically under the aspect of exercise of discretion when the relevance of the evidence and the absence of delay was confirmed.

3.42 A few months later, in three parallel cases involving the same appellant (Mr Rintisch) and different applicants, the Court of Justice established that the obligation under Article 76(2), applicable also to first instance units, extends beyond use evidence also to proof of existence of an earlier mark in an opposition case.[45] In these cases, the opponent had failed to provide proper evidence for the continued validity (renewal) of the marks relied on in three separate opposition proceedings within the time limit set by the Opposition Division in accordance with the Rules of the Implementing Regulation. Such evidence was, however, submitted later. The Opposition Division had dismissed the oppositions,

---

at issue, accompanied by remarks expressing reservations as to confidentiality and containing an offer to furnish additional evidence.

115 Yet it does not seem that the Board of Appeal conducted a proper examination of these aspects, or of any other potentially relevant evidence. Nor does it seem to have considered the potential relevance of the additional evidence submitted by Centrotherm Systemtechnik.

116 Moreover, contrary to what is suggested in paragraph 37 of the contested decision, it is not necessary that the party concerned be unable to submit evidence within the time limit in order for additional evidence of use of the mark submitted after expiry of the time limit referred to in Rule 40(5) of Regulation No 2868/95 to be taken into account.

[44] C-621/11 P *New Yorker SHK Jeans GmbH & Co. KG v OHIM—Vallis K.-Vallis A. & Co. OE*, ECLI:EU:C:2013:484.
[45] C-120/12 P *Rintisch v OHIM—Bariatrix Europe Inc.*, ECLI:EU:C:2013:638; C-121/12 P *Rintisch v OHIM—Valfleurs Pâtes alimentaires SA*; C-122/12 P *Rintisch v OHIM—Valfleurs Pâtes alimentaires SA*, ECLI:EU:C:2013:639.

and the Board of Appeal confirmed the dismissal, considering that the late submission required the oppositions to be dismissed. The Board added that if it did have any discretion in this respect, it would have exercised it by refusing the late evidence. Appeals to the General Court were dismissed as unfounded, the General Court holding that, under the applicable rules, OHIM did not have any discretion regarding whether or not to accept the late evidence. Rather, the exception provided in *Kaul* applied because there was an explicit provision precluding such evidence, namely Rule 20(1) of the Implementing Regulation.

3.43 The ECJ confirmed the rejection of the oppositions by OHIM, albeit on grounds different from those of the General Court. The ECJ concluded that the General Court had committed an error by holding that OHIM's Board of Appeal did not have any discretion in this case because the third subparagraph of Rule 50(1) of the Implementing Regulation expressly mandated such exercise in opposition proceedings. The Court nevertheless confirmed the decisions of the Board of Appeal, finding that the Board had properly justified its exercise of discretion.[46]

---

[46] The following paragraphs, found in all three judgments, explain why the refusal was appropriate:

39 In that regard, the Court has held, inter alia, that where OHIM is called upon to give judgment in the context of opposition proceedings, taking into account facts or evidence produced late is particularly likely to be justified where OHIM considers, first, that the material which has been produced late is, on the face of it, likely to be genuinely relevant to the outcome of the opposition brought before it and, second, that the stage of the proceedings at which that late submission takes place and the circumstances surrounding it do not argue against such matters being taken into account (OHIM v Kaul, paragraph 44, and Centrotherm Systemtechnik v OHIM and Centrotherm Clean Solutions, paragraph 113).

40 In this case, since Mr Rintisch based his opposition, inter alia, on three registered German marks, the evidence of the existence, validity and scope of protection of those marks which he had to submit during the opposition proceedings is set out precisely and exhaustively in Rule 19(2)(a)(ii) of the Implementing Regulation. Mr Rintisch was therefore deemed to be aware, even before filing his opposition, of the precise documents which he had to produce in support of it. Consequently, the Board of Appeal must, in those circumstances, exercise its discretion restrictively and may allow the late submission of such evidence only if the surrounding circumstances are likely to justify the appellant's delay in the submission of proof required of him.

41 In stating the reasons for its decision, the Board of Appeal emphasised in particular that Mr Rintisch was in possession of the proof of renewal of the marks at issue as from 15 January 2007 and that he did not put forward any reasons why he withheld that document until October 2007.

42 It is therefore apparent from the contested decision that the circumstances surrounding the late submission of the evidence of the existence, validity and scope of protection of the marks at issue are not capable of justifying the appellant's delay in the submission of proof required of him.

43 The fact that Mr Rintisch produced, within the time-limit set by the Opposition Division, extracts from the Deutsches Patent- und Markenamt online register referring to the renewal of the marks at issue, in a language other than that of the language of the proceedings, cannot call in question that analysis, since it is clear from Rule 19(4) of the Implementing Regulation that OHIM must not take into account documents that have not been submitted, or that have not been translated into the language of the proceedings, within that time-limit.

44 It follows that the Board of Appeal was justified in refusing to take into account the evidence submitted by Mr Rintisch after the expiry of the periods specified for that purpose by the Opposition Division, and there was no need for it to rule on the possible relevance of that evidence or to determine whether the stage of the proceedings at which that late submission takes place precludes such evidence from being taken into account.

45 Contrary to Mr Rintisch's claims, the Board of Appeal is not required, when exercising its discretion under Article 74(2) of Regulation No 40/94, to examine the three criteria referred to in paragraph 39 above when one of those criteria alone is sufficient to establish that it must not take into account the evidence submitted late at issue (see, to that effect, order of 4 March 2010 in Case C 193/09 P Kaul v OHIM, paragraph 38).

Anheuser[47] concerned an opposition to a CTM application for the word mark BUDWEISER **3.44** in Class 32. The opposition was based on three earlier International Trade Mark registrations for BUDWEISER BUDVAR as well as a number of appellations of origin including the word BUDWEISER. The opponent had been granted an extension to file further evidence and arguments. The applicant subsequently put the opponent to proof of use. The opponent's response referred back to documents submitted to OHIM as part of its further evidence and arguments and stated that evidence relating to the use of the appellations of origin also applied to one of the trade mark registrations relied upon. The opponent also provided with subsequent observations an extract from the World Intellectual Property Organization (WIPO) certifying the renewal of the national registration. The Opposition Division upheld the opposition, finding a likelihood of confusion with one of the earlier international registrations having effect in Austria and France (no 674530).

The applicant appealed to the Board of Appeal, who upheld the appeal on the basis that the **3.45** international registration referred to in the Opposition Division's decision had only been protected in Austria and France after the date of the contested application. The case was therefore referred back to the Opposition Division. The Opposition Division upheld the opposition again, this time on the basis of another international registration (no 614536) with effect in Germany, Austria, Benelux, France, and Italy. The third mark relied upon by the opponent was discounted on the basis that there was considered to be insufficient evidence of use. The applicant appealed to the Board of Appeal, which found that the proof of use had been sufficient for the third registration to have been taken into account and, furthermore, that the application should be refused under Article 8(1)(a) for the identical goods and under Article 8(1)(b) for the similar goods.

The applicant appealed to the General Court, arguing firstly an infringement under Article **3.46** 74(2), on the basis that the certificate of renewal for International Registration no 238203 had been filed outside the relevant time period. However, the General Court found that, since the Board of Appeal had not considered the issue, no infringement of Article 74(2) could be found. The General Court found that, in any event, where a registration is due for renewal after a notice of opposition has been filed, the international registration does not oblige the opponent to submit proof, nor oblige OHIM to exclude such evidence if it is filed late. The General Court also noted that Article 74 permits OHIM discretion to take account of evidence filed after a time limit or otherwise. The General Court also found that provisions introduced in 2005 into Implementing Regulation 2868/95, and in particular Rule 19(4) which states that '[t]he observations filed by the applicant shall be communicated to the opposing party who shall be called upon by the Office, if it considers it necessary to do so, to reply within a period specified by the Office', could not be applied retrospectively.

On appeal, the Court of Justice found that the General Court did not err in law in its finding **3.47** that although OHIM is entitled to require under Implementing Regulation 2868/95 that an earlier mark had been renewed (if such a renewal becomes due after the filing of the notice of opposition), there is merely an entitlement and not an obligation on OHIM to provide such proof on its own initiative. It also found that the opponent's allegation that the General Court had infringed Article 43(2) and (3) was inadmissible. The applicant had

---

[47] C-214/09 P *Anheuser-Busch Inc. v Office for Harmonisation in the Internal Market (Trade Marks and Designs)/Budejovicky Budvar* [2010] ECR I-07665.

based its argument on an allegation that the evidence submitted showed use of another mark, namely International Registration no 674530, not the mark forming the subject of International Registration 238203, but the Court of Justice held that this was not raised in the action before the General Court and constituted a new plea. The applicant argued that the use of a trade mark other than the mark considered by the Board of Appeal was not

> sufficiently connected with the third plea raised before the General Court—which alleged that that evidence failed to satisfy the conditions necessary for the earlier mark at issue to be regarded as having been put to genuine use—and, consequently, that argument cannot be regarded as merely expanding the third plea[48]

and

> [i]n any event, that argument has a different purpose from the third plea in the action before the General Court, since it does not seek to dispute that the earlier trade mark was actually put to commercial use but addresses the question whether evidence relates to one trade mark rather than another.[49]

3.48 Finally, *Jager*[50] concerned a notice of opposition which, because of late payment of opposition fees, was treated as not having been entered. There had, however, been some delay in this being reported because OHIM had originally sent letters to both parties indicating that the opposition was considered admissible and setting appropriate deadlines and had issued a correction letter after having been alerted to the late payment by the applicant. Following a request by the applicant, the Opposition Division issued a formal written decision confirming that the conditions set out in Rule 18(3) had not been met. The opponent filed an appeal, which was dismissed by the Board of Appeal.

> The opposition fee was paid after the expiry of the opposition period, contrary to the provisions of [the second sentence of] Article [42(3) of Regulation No 40/94]. It was also established that the applicant gave the transfer order to its banking establishment only after the expiry of the opposition period, namely on 26 March 2008. Consequently, in accordance with [the second sentence of] Article [42(3) of Regulation No 40/94], the opposition was to be treated as not having been duly entered.[51]

3.49 The Board of Appeal also stated in its decision that OHIM's original letter confirming the admissibility of the opposition did not constitute a decision capable of being revoked under Article 77(a) of Regulation 40/94.

3.50 The opponent appealed to the General Court on the basis of three grounds: firstly, that there had been a breach of Rule 8(2); secondly, that the Opposition Division was not entitled to refuse the opposition on the basis of late payment of the opposition fee; and thirdly, that there had been a breach of Article 77a(1) and (2) of Regulation 40/94 because OHIM's original communication confirming the admissibility of the opposition constituted a decision and could only be revoked within six months of it being issued. The General Court refused all three claims and the opponent appealed to the Court of Justice, relying on this occasion solely on the third claim, namely that there had been a breach of Article 77a(1) and (2).

---

[48] Paragraph 106.
[49] Paragraph 108.
[50] C-402/11 *Jager & Polacek GmbH v Office for Harmonisation in the Internal Market (Trade Marks and Designs)* ECLI:EU:C:2012:649.
[51] Paragraph 17.

(d) The Opinion of Advocate General Bot

3.51 Advocate General Bot agreed with the General Court's view that that letter did not constitute a decision, stating in particular that it did not produce binding legal effects for the appellant. Reviewing the Court of Justice's case law on 'acts that are open to challenge', Advocate General Bot agreed with the General Court that 'only an act capable of producing binding legal effects constitutes a decision capable of being appealed'. He also recognised that a balance had to be struck between ensuring 'effective judicial protection of an individual's rights under EU law' and avoiding 'an increase in the number of actions against preparatory measures, which could paralyse the activity of the institutions'.[52]

3.52 Having reached this view, Advocate General Bot stated that in order to assess whether the General Court were right to conclude that the judgment amounted to 'a mere measure of organisation of the opposition proceedings', it would be necessary to examine the substance of OHIM's letter and the surrounding procedural framework. Reviewing the letter, Advocate General Bot found that although the second part of the letter had the aim of merely informing the parties of time limits and so constituted 'a simple communication to the parties', the first part was intended to inform the opponent that its opposition was 'deemed admissible'. Although Advocate General Bot found that the use of the verb 'deem' indicated that OHIM did in fact rule on the admissibility of the claim, this was not in his view sufficient for the letter to be recognized as being a decision.[53]

3.53 Thus, Advocate General Bot concluded that:

> the act whereby OHIM deems the opposition admissible is therefore not an act adopting OHIM's final decision in the opposition proceedings, but a preparatory procedural act which, in that it initiates the procedure of the examination of the merits of the opposition, takes place at the beginning of the preparation, in stages, of the final decision.
>
> Nor, to my mind, does that act entail any binding legal effect. It enables the 'friendly settlement' stage to be initiated between the parties and, in the absence of a friendly settlement, initiates the discussion of the substantive issues connected with the opposition. So far as the opposing party is concerned, the initiation of the opposition proceedings properly places only one obligation on him—if he wishes his opposition to succeed—namely to produce all the evidence and to present all the facts and observations in support of his opposition.[54]

(e) The judgment of the Court

3.54 The Court of Justice held that the General Court's judgment should be set aside. Looking at the Rules, the Court of Justice held that the nature of Rule 17 meant that the examination of admissibility could lead to a decision terminating the proceedings which might be the subject of an appeal and that Rule 18 indicated that the *inter partes* stage commences only when OHIM have confirmed the admissibility of the opposition.[55] The Court of Justice also indicated that Article 57(1) was such that 'there may be measures which, while they are adopted in the course of the proceedings and do not terminate then, nevertheless constitute decisions'.[56]

---

[52] Point 48.
[53] Point 55.
[54] Points 61–62.
[55] Paragraph 49.
[56] Paragraph 52.

3.55 OHIM had argued that a final decision on the admissibility of an opposition can only be made in *inter partes* proceedings, in order to protect the defence. However, confirming the opinion of Advocate General Bot, the Court of Justice held that an opponent would have no interest in contesting a decision finding the opposition admissible and if OHIM errs in finding an opposition admissible, the applicant may assert rights in the *inter partes* proceedings under Article 77 and by appealing the decision at the end of the *inter partes* proceedings.[57] The Court of Justice then took the opportunity to give final judgment on this issue, as allowed by Article 61 of the Statute of the Court of Justice of the European Union. In essence, it found that the Board of Appeal's decision should be annulled since OHIM's letter did amount to a decision and, consequently, the Board of Appeal was wrong to hold that the Opposition Division was entitled to consider whether the opposition was to be treated as not having been entered because of late payment of the fee.[58]

(2) Judicial Review: The Nature of Court Proceedings

3.56 The Court in *Kaul* contrasted the full re-examination performed by the Boards with the judicial review of their decisions, observing that, pursuant to what is now Article 65, the General Court (then the Court of First Instance) may annul or alter a decision of a Board of Appeal of OHIM only on grounds of lack of competence, infringement of an essential procedural requirement, infringement of the Treaty, of the Regulation, or of any rule of law relating to their application, or misuse of power.

3.57 Hence, the Court inferred that the General Court has the power to 'either annul or alter a decision against which an action has been brought only if, at the time that decision was adopted, it was vitiated by one of those grounds for annulment or alteration', which means that the General Court 'may not annul or alter that decision on grounds which come into existence subsequent to its adoption'.

3.58 Accordingly, the Court concluded that the function of the General Court is 'to assess the legality of the decision of the Board by reviewing the application of Community law made by it, particularly in the light of facts which were submitted to the latter; by contrast, that Court cannot carry out such a review by taking into account matters of fact newly produced before it'.[59]

3.59 This has been the consistent approach of the General Court and the Court of Justice, with only minor additions or corrections.[60] The most significant of these variations is that the courts have taken into account agreements between the parties settling their disputes after having brought the case before the Luxembourg courts, with the courts regularly making 'no need to adjudicate' orders. Such an approach has also been adopted when the opposition was withdrawn or the applicant renounced its CTM application.[61] The Courts have also

---

[57] Paragraphs 56–57 and 61–63.
[58] Paragraph 76.
[59] Paragraph 54, citing C-214/05 P *Rossi v OHIM* [2006] ECR I-7057.
[60] T-57/03 *Société provencale d'achat et de gestion (SPAG) SA v OHIM* (HOOLIGAN/OLLY GAN) [2005] ECR II-287, paragraph 21.
[61] Eg Order 6 March 2001, T-187/00 *Gödecke AG/Teva Pharmaceutical Industries Ltd v OHIM* [2001] ECR II-00859. The courts have not been entirely consistent in this respect; for example, even though an earlier mark raised in an opposition was subsequently invalidated, after the Board decision and while the case was pending in Luxembourg, the General Court and subsequently the court of Justice refused to close the case, eg, ECJ Order 8 May 2013, C-268/12 P *Cadila Healthcare Ltd/Novartis AG*, ECLI:EU:C:2013:296, paragraphs 31–35.

taken into account a change in the parties, resulting, for example, from a transfer of the opposed or opposing or otherwise contested mark.[62] Finally, submitting court judgments has been taken as admissible.[63]

(3) Scope and Limits of Administrative and Judicial Review

It follows from *Kaul* that the jurisdictional differences between the Office and the Courts in trade mark registration cases are a direct consequence of their distinct institutional roles. While the subject matter of proceedings before the Office is the complete examination of a ground of refusal pursuant to the Regulations, the object of the dispute before the Court is the Office's decision and the control of its legality, as delimited by the application for annulment. **3.60**

(a) *The scope of the administrative proceedings*

In that regard, the General Court has referred to the scope of the 'full' examination conducted by OHIM by stressing that: **3.61**

> the criteria for applying a relative ground for refusal or any other provision relied on in support of arguments put forward by the parties are naturally part of the matters of law submitted for examination by OHIM. It should be borne in mind in this regard that a matter of law may have to be ruled on by OHIM even when it has not been raised by the parties if it is necessary to resolve that matter in order to ensure a correct application of the Regulation having regard to the facts, evidence and arguments provided by the parties.[64]

Thus, although Article 76(1) of the Regulation requires the Office, at least when dealing with relative grounds of refusal, to 'restrict its examination to the facts, evidence and arguments provided by the parties and the relief sought', this does not relieve it from the obligation to examine all the points of law and fact necessary for adjudicating on the matter pending before it. **3.62**

In addition, the Court has held that Article 76 does not preclude OHIM (or, *mutatis mutandis*, the Court) from also basing its conclusions, where appropriate, on 'generally known facts arising from common experience, or on facts which may be obtained from generally accessible sources',[65] a statement equally valid for both absolute and relative grounds examination. **3.63**

(b) *The scope of judicial review*

On the other hand, the control of legality exercised by the judicature is more closely linked to the claims and pleas put forward in the action or in the appeal, while its main features are defined by the Courts' Rules of Procedure. In that sense, the Courts are not called upon to conduct a new, full examination of the case, by addressing points that were not raised in the application, but rather only to review the legality of the contested decision within the confines of, and for the reasons contained in, the application for annulment. As stressed **3.64**

---

[62] Eg, T-567/12 *Kaatsu International Co.*, ECLI:EU:T:2014:937.
[63] Eg, T-368/13 *Boehringer Ingelheim International GmbH/Lehning Enterprise SARL*, ECLI:EU:T:2015:81.
[64] T-57/03 *Société provencale d'achat el de gestion (SPAG) SA/OHIM (HOOLIGAN/OLLY GAN)* [2005] ECR II-287, paragraph 21.
[65] T-129/04 *Develey Holding GmbH & Co Beleiligungs KG/OHIM (PLASTIKFLASCHENFORM)* [2007] ECR II-811, paragraphs 19–22; and T-185/02 *Succession Picasso/OHIM (PICASSO)* [2005] ECR II-I739, paragraph 29.

by the Court, 'if the applicant does not precisely indicate the contested elements which he seeks to have set aside, or give clear reasons and arguments to that effect, the relevant points cannot be examined'.[66]

3.65 That obligation to clearly delimit the subject matter of the dispute to the points raised in the action for annulment is imposed by Article 225 EC and Article 58 of the Statute of the Court, in conjunction with Article 112(1) of its Rules of Procedure. Moreover, according to Article 21 of the Statute and Article 38(l)(c) of the same Rules (which is identical to Article 44(1)(c) of the Rules of the Court of First Instance), the statement of the grounds of appeal must be sufficiently clear and precise to enable the defendant to exercise its right of defence and the Court to perform its control, without having recourse to extraneous information or supporting documents. Rather, all the essential matters of law and fact must be apparent from the text of the action itself. Note that the Court tends to apply those requirements quite literally, considering that its role is not to 'take the place of the applicant, or his counsel, by trying to locate and identify itself among the documents on the file the information which it might regard as supporting the claims formulated in the application'.[67]

3.66 Exceptionally, however, the Court may annul a decision for reasons not raised by the claimant, notably when the contested decision is vitiated by a defect that infringes against procedural rules or principles relating to public order. In those cases, the Court not only can, but actually must raise the relevant ground of its own motion. Such types of inherent vice typically include formal deficiencies and the breach of the duty to state reasons, as well as all sorts of substantial procedural violations and omissions.[68]

3.67 The judicial review carried out by the Courts is also limited as to its effects by virtue of Article 63(6) CTMR (now Article 65), according to which the Office is required to take 'all the necessary measures in order to comply with the judgments of the Community Courts'. This means that although the Court has the competence to control the legality of the Office's decisions and to either annul or amend them, as the case may be, it cannot take directly administrative measures or issue orders to the Office to perform a specific act, other than those clearly inherent in the annulment of its decision.[69]

3.68 Rather, it is for the Office to take the appropriate measures for complying with the Court's judgment, by deciding whether a separate decision of the Boards or another department is necessary to that effect. In practice, that means that where a decision of the Boards is

---

[66] C-234/06 P *Il Ponte Finanziaria Spa/OHIM (BAINBRIDGE)* [2007] ECR I-7333, paragraph 44.
[67] C-56/92 *Koelman v Commission* [1993] ECR II-1267, paragraph 23. See also C-324/13 *Fercal—Consultadoria e Serviços Ld^a v Office for Harmonisation in the Internal Market (Trade Marks and Designs) (OHIM)*, ECLI:EU:C:2014:60, that concerned an appeal which was filed against a decision of the Opposition Division allowing an opposition against the trade mark PATRIZIA ROCHA. Although the appellant had filed its notice of appeal by the deadline, the statement of grounds was sent by post and arrived after the deadline and the Board of Appeal dismissed the appeal on the basis that it was inadmissible. The appellant appealed to the General Court, which upheld the Board of Appeal's decision. The appellant appealed again to the Court of Justice, which overturned the General Court's decision, finding that the appeal was admissible. In particular, the Court observed that the appellant had accurately identified the articles and rules of Regulation No 40/94 and the Implementing Regulation 2868/95 which were being challenged in the appeal and had done so with sufficient precision to enable the Court to carry out its review of legality.
[68] T-388/00 *Institut fur Lernsysteme GmbH/OHIM (ELS)* [2002] ECR II-04301 paragraphs 58–59.
[69] T-331/99 *Mitsubishi HiTec Paper Bielefeld GmbH/OHIM (GIROFORM)* [2001] ECR II-433, paragraph 33; T-34/00 *Eurocool Logistik GmbH/OHIM (EUROCOOL)* [2002] ECR II-683, paragraph 12; T-129/01 *Jose Alejandro, SL/OHIM (BUDMEN/BUD)* [2007] ECR II-2251, paragraph 22; T-164/03 *Ampafrance SA/OHIM (MONBEBE/BEBE)* [2005] ECR II-1401, paragraph 24.

annulled, but the Court has not fully and finally adjudicated on the substance of the dispute, the Office is bound to reopen the file and continue the prosecution of the case.[70]

(c) The appeal to the Court of Justice

The scope of the appeal to the Court of Justice is defined by Article 225 EC and the first paragraph of Article 58 of its Statute, according to which an appeal is limited to points of law only. As repeatedly stressed by the Court, it is the exclusive jurisdiction of the Court of First Instance to make findings of fact and to appraise the evidence when exercising its powers of review. Moreover, the Court has made clear that 'that assessment does not, save where the clear sense of the evidence has been distorted, constitute a point of law which is subject, as such, to review by the Court of Justice on appeal'.[71]   **3.69**

Such a distortion occurs where the corresponding findings are demonstrably inaccurate and lead to errors of assessment capable of materially affecting the outcome. In that regard, the Court has pointed out that the resulting inaccuracy, omission, or contradiction 'must be obvious from the documents on file, without it being necessary to undertake a fresh assessment of the facts'.[72] In other words, the alleged distortion can only become actionable if it is objectively manifest from the contents of the file, or where it is in apparent contradiction with facts or circumstances which are well known to everyone.   **3.70**

The Court of Justice considers as questions of fact not only matters that are strictly connected to the factual sub-stratum of the case, but also assessments of mixed character, like those concerning the similarity between the signs or the goods, the existence of a reputation, and the fulfilment of the requirement of genuine use, as well as the existence of a likelihood of confusion, detriment, or unfair advantage.[73]   **3.71**

The strict application by the Court of Article 58 of the Statute, and its widespread tendency to summarily dismiss as inadmissible claims that relate to virtually every kind of assessment made in the context of trade mark examination, has led to the rejection of a high number of appeals filed against judgments of the Court of First Instance in intellectual property cases without addressing their merits. It follows that while the review carried out by the General Court effectively involves a genuine reassessment of the findings of the Board, the role of the Court of Justice is strictly limited to examining whether the General Court has reached its decision by applying the correct legal norms, without   **3.72**

---

[70] See in that connection Article 1(d) of Commission Regulation (EC) No 216/96 of 5 February 1996, Laying down the Rules of Procedure of the Boards of Appeal of OHIM, according to which

if pursuant to Article 63(6) of the Regulation, the measures necessary to comply with a Judgment of the Court of Justice annulling all or part of a decision of a Board of Appeal or of the Grand Board include re-examination by the Boards of Appeal of the case which was the subject of that decision, the Presidium shall decide if the case shall be referred to the Board which adopted that decision, or to another Board, or to the Grand Board.

[71] C-104/00 P *DKV v OHIM* [2002] ECR I-7561, paragraph 22; and C-238/06 P *Develey Holding GmbH & Co Beteiligungs KG/OHIM (shape of a plastic bottle)* [2007] ECR I-9375, paragraph 97.

[72] C-304/06 P *Eurohypo AG v OHIM (EUROHYPO)* [2008] ECR I-03297.

[73] See, for instance, C-196/06 P *Alecansan SL/OHIM (CompUSA)* [2007] ECR I-00036; C-394/08 *Zipcar Inc. v OHIM (ZIPCAR/CICAR)* () [2009] ECR I-00095; and C-320/07 P *Antarctica Srl v OHIM (NASDAQ)* [2009] ECR I-00028. That question is particularly important in view of the harmonizing objective of the Directive and its close similarity to the Community Trade Mark Regulation, especially since the parallel existence of Community and national trade mark rights covering the same sign often gives rise to a plurality of disputes within the European Union which have, essentially, the same subject matter.

however entering into the question whether the relevant rules are consistently applied to the facts.[74] Rather, that assessment can only be invalidated if the judgment under appeal has failed to give sufficient reasons in support of its conclusions, or if its findings are manifestly inconsistent.

3.73 An example of a failure is *Isdin*.[75] The case concerned an opposition to a CTM application for ZEBEXIR based on an earlier registration of ZEBINEX, which had been refused by both the Opposition Division and the Board of Appeal on the basis that the marks were not sufficiently similar to result in a likelihood of confusion. The Board of Appeal's decision was, however, annulled on appeal to the General Court on the basis that although there were some differences between the respective marks, these were not sufficient to offset the visual and phonetic similarities, particularly in view of the fact that the relevant goods (in Classes 3 and 5) would be chosen after a visual examination by the relevant consumer.

> However, contrary to what the Board of Appeal found, the signs at issue have an average degree of similarity, particularly visually. In that respect, account must also be taken of the fact that the goods in Class 3 and a large proportion of the goods in Class 5 (namely food for babies, materials for dressings, disinfectants; preparations for destroying vermin; fungicides, herbicides), designated by the marks at issue, are normally marketed on display in supermarkets and therefore chosen by the consumers after a visual examination of their packaging, which means that the visual similarity of the signs is especially important. It must therefore be found that there is a likelihood of confusion between the mark applied for and the earlier mark.[76]

---

[74] See, for instance, C-670/13 P *The Cartoon Network Inc. v Office for Harmonisation in the Internal Market (Trade Marks and Designs) (OHIM)*, ECLI:EU:C:2014:2024 on Articles 36 and 53 of the Statute of the Court of Justice, and Article 169(2) of the Rules of Procedure of the Court of Justice, identifying points and distortion of facts. *The Cartoon Network* concerned an opposition to an application for the word mark BOOMERANG covering services in Classes 38 and 41. The opposition was based on an earlier CTM registration for the figurative mark BOOMERANG in Class 41 and claimed a likelihood of confusion under Article 8(1)(b). The Opposition Division upheld the opposition refusing the application in its totality, a decision which was upheld by the Board of Appeal which found that there was a likelihood of confusion, even though consumers might have a higher level of attention. Evidence produced by the applicant did not in the Board's view demonstrate the coexistence of the marks in the market. The applicant appealed to the General Court, claiming an infringement of Article 8(1)(b). The General Court rejected the appeal, also holding, like the Opposition Division and Board of Appeal, that there was a likelihood of confusion. However, in relation to the issue of the average consumer, the Court found that the Board of Appeal should have assessed the likelihood of confusion solely with regard to professionals in the advertising sector, even though the services also targeted the general public. The applicant appealed to the Court of Justice. In the first place, the applicant claimed that the General Court had infringed Articles 36 and 53 of the Statute of the Court of Justice of the European Union because it had not provided a proper statement explaining its reasons for concluding that the relevant public consisted solely of professionals. The Court of Justice analysed the General Court's decision, finding that they had made an assessment of the average consumer for both the earlier trade mark and the contested application and that, in the absence of arguments from the applicant to support its assertions, the General Court had therefore provided a proper statement for its reasons. Consequently, the first ground of appeal was rejected. The applicant also claimed that the General Court had distorted the facts relating to the relevant public and, in the alternative, that the Court was wrong to find that the professional public could have experienced confusion. However, the Court of Justice found that the Court had not distorted the facts by finding the relevant public to be professionals, and secondly that the applicant had not identified the points in the judgment which were considered to have been infringed and that it was consequently inadmissible under Article 169(2) of the Rules of Procedure of the Court of Justice.

[75] C-597/12 P *Isdin SA v Office for Harmonisation in the Internal Market (Trade Marks and Designs)/Bial-Portela & Ca SA* (ZEBEXIR v ZEBINIX), ECLI:EU:C:2013:672.

[76] T-366/11 *Isdin SA v Office for Harmonisation in the Internal Market (Trade Marks and Designs)/Bial-Portela & Ca SA* [2015], paragraph 40.

3.74 The applicant appealed to the Court of Justice on a number of grounds, including a claim that the General Court had failed to provide reasons in its assessment of Article 8(1)(b). Noting that although there was a duty incumbent on the General Court under Articles 36 and 53 of the Statute of the Court of Justice to state reasons, the Court also noted that this did not require the Court to provide an exhaustive account of each of the arguments raised by the parties and that the Court's reasoning may be implicit, provided it allows the parties to know the grounds on which the decision is based and provides the Court of Justice with sufficient material to review an appeal.[77]

3.75 However, the Court found that whilst the General Court had looked at the marketing conditions for certain goods in Class 5 (ie foods for babies, materials for dressings, disinfectants, preparations for destroying vermin, fungicides, and herbicides), it had not looked at the other Class 5 goods covered by the contested application[78] but had nonetheless annulled the Board of Appeal's decision for all Class 5 goods. Citing the Court's decision in *BVBA Management*,[79] the Court noted that the grounds of refusal must be examined for each of the goods or services covered by the contested application, except where they form a homogenous category.

> In the present case, the General Court itself drew a distinction between goods within the same class of the Nice Agreement on the basis of the conditions under which they are marketed. Consequently, it was incumbent on the General Court to set out reasons for its decision with regard to each group of goods which it had established within that class.
>
> Since such reasoning is lacking with regard to the goods in Class 5 other than those listed in paragraph 40 of the judgment under appeal—namely food for babies, materials for dressings, disinfectants, preparations for destroying vermin, fungicides, herbicides—that judgment does not enable the persons concerned to know the grounds on which the General Court based, in that regard, its annulment of the contested decision or provide the Court of Justice with sufficient material for it to exercise its powers of review within the context of the present appeal.[80]

3.76 Consequently, the decision was annulled and the case was referred back to the General Court.

3.77 In *Nike*,[81] the opponent, DL Sports, had filed an opposition against a CTM application for R10, based on unregistered rights in an identical mark. The opponent had failed to file evidence substantiating the earlier right by the deadline, but Nike's attorneys had subsequently informed the Opposition Division that their clients had acquired a number of DL Sports' trade marks and would be pursuing the opposition and that they should therefore be noted as representative. The Opposition Division rejected the opposition, on the basis that the opponent had not substantiated the earlier right. Nike appealed, but the Board of Appeal dismissed the appeal as inadmissible because Nike had not provided proof of its status as a party to the opposition proceedings, either before the Opposition Division or before the Board of Appeal. Consequently, the Board of Appeal held that Nike was not entitled to appeal.

---

[77] *Isdin* (n 76) paragraph 21, citing C-320/09 *A2A v Commission*, ECLI:EU:C:2011:858, paragraph 97.
[78] Ibid, paragraphs 22–23.
[79] C-239/05 *BVBA Management, Training en Consultancy v Benelux-Merkenbureau* [2007] ECR I-1455, paragraph 34.
[80] *Isdin* (n 77) paragraphs 28–29.
[81] C-53/11 P *Office for Harmonisation in the Internal Market (Trade Marks and Designs) v Nike International Limited/Aurelio Munoz Molina*.

3.78 On appeal, the General Court upheld Nike's argument that the Board of Appeal had made a decision on the basis of an interpretation of the transfer agreement on which Nike had not had an opportunity to submit observations and the decision was furthermore in breach of Rule 31(6) of Implementing Regulation 2868/95 because Nike had not had an opportunity to correct deficiencies in relation to the proof of transfer.

3.79 In relation to the first of these, the General Court pointed to OHIM's Guidelines, part 1, C, E.VIII.131, which state that if the new owner of the earlier national right 'informs [OHIM] of the transfer, but does not submit (sufficient) evidence thereof, the opposition proceedings have to be suspended while the new owner is given two months to provide evidence of the transfer'. The Court furthermore found that although those provisions relate explicitly to the transfer of registered national marks, they should also apply to national non-registered trade marks. Furthermore, the Court stated that, even though the guidelines related to opposition proceedings at first instance, the provisions were equally applicable to proceedings before the Board of Appeal. The General Court also found that:

> The Court cannot accept OHIM's arguments seeking to justify this approach taken by the Board of Appeal and asserting that the applicant applied to be substituted for the original opponent after the closure of the opposition proceedings. It must be observed that, even on the assumption that the substitution application made by the assignee of the earlier national mark between closure of the opposition examination procedure and adoption of the Opposition Division's decision could not be accepted and could even be entirely disregarded without specifically being rejected as inadmissible, that circumstance cannot deprive that assignee of the right to bring an appeal against the Opposition Division's decision. As the owner of the trade mark relied on in support of the opposition, the assignee necessarily has locus standi with regard to the decision by which the opposition proceedings are concluded (see, to that effect and by analogy, CANAL JEAN CO. NEW YORK, cited in paragraph 17 above, paragraphs 18 and 19), irrespective of whether it made a substitution application to the Opposition Division and whether such an application was admissible. While the Board of Appeal is indeed required to satisfy itself that the assignee is actually the owner of the earlier mark, its examination must be carried out in accordance with the applicable procedural rules, including the OHIM Guidelines.[82]

3.80 OHIM appealed to the Court of Justice, alleging, firstly, an infringement of Rule 49 of Implementing Regulation 2868/95 and Article 58 of Regulation 40/94 and, secondly, an infringement of the OHIM Guidelines and Rule 49(1) of Implementing Regulation 2868/95.

3.81 The Court of Justice found that the General Court had infringed Article 58 and Rules 49(1) and (2). In particular, the Court stated:

> It follows that a person who brings an appeal before the Board of Appeal of OHIM must show that he has locus standi within the four month period provided for in Article 59 of Regulation No 40/94, otherwise the appeal will be declared inadmissible. That person has the right to remedy, on its own initiative, any ground of inadmissibility within the same period. Therefore, if there has been an assignment of the sign on which the opposition was based without that assignment being taken into account during the procedure before the Opposition Division of OHIM, the assignee must adduce, within the four month period provided for in Article 59 of Regulation No 40/94, before the Board of Appeal of OHIM the

---

[82] T-137/09 *Office for Harmonisation in the Internal Market (Trade Marks and Designs) v Nike International Limited/Aurelio Munoz Molina* [2010] ECR II-05433.

necessary proof that he became the owner of that sign by transfer in order to show that he has locus standi otherwise the appeal will be declared inadmissible.[83]

3.82 The Court of Justice therefore set aside the General Court's judgment and referred the case back.

3.83 Finally, note too that the appeal to the Court of Justice must be based on issues that have been raised before the General Court.

3.84 For instance, *Bimbo*[84] concerned an opposition to a figurative mark containing the words CAFFE KIMBO in Class 30 under Articles 8(1)(a), 8(1)(b), and 8(5). The opposition was based on a Spanish registration for the word BIMBO, also covering goods in Class 30, in relation to which the opponent claimed a reputation in Spain. The opponent also claimed to have a well-known mark in Spain under Article 8(2)(c). The Opposition Division upheld the opposition under Article 8(1)(b) for some of the goods in the contested application, namely 'flour and preparations made from cereals, bread, pastry and confectionery; ices; yeast baking-powder', but allowed the application to proceed for others. The applicant appealed to the Board of Appeal which partially annulled the Opposition Division's decision, allowing the application to proceed for a wider range of goods, but confirming the Opposition Division's decision in relation to 'preparations made from cereals, bread, pastry'. The opponent appealed to the General Court, which rejected the appeal. The opponent then appealed to the Court of Justice on a number of grounds, which included an alleged breach of Rule 19 of Implementing Regulation 2868/95 and Article 8(1). In relation to the first of these claims, which was based on a contention that the Opposition Division should have considered the opponent's earlier Spanish registration, as well as their well-known mark, the Court of Justice found that the appeal was inadmissible, on the basis that this assertion had never been raised by the opponents before the General Court. In relation to the second ground of appeal, the Court of Justice found that the opponent was asking the Court to substitute its own assessment of the facts concerning the comparison of goods for that of the General Court and that it must therefore also be rejected as inadmissible.

(4) The Special Case of National Law: *Edwin* and *National Lottery*

3.85 The Community Trade Mark Regulation provides in Articles 8(4) and 53(1)(c) that a Community trade mark may be refused registration or, if registered, be declared invalid on the basis of an earlier unregistered trade mark or other sign used in the course of trade, where and to the extent that, 'pursuant to the Community legislation or the law of the Member States', that sign confers on its proprietor the right to prohibit the use of the contested Community trade mark. Similarly, Article 53(2) of the Regulation stipulates that a Community trade mark shall be declared invalid where its use may be prohibited pursuant to another earlier right 'under Community or national law', such as: (a) a right to a name; (b) a right to a personal portrayal; (c) a copyright; or (d) another industrial property right.

3.86 These provisions require the direct application by OHIM and, on appeal, by the EU judicature of legal provisions which are not part of Community law and which, for the most

---

[83] *Nike* (n 82) paragraphs 54–55. See also C-193/09 *Kaul v OHIM* [2010] ECR I-00027, paragraphs 58 and 66.
[84] C-285/13 P *Bimbo SA v Office for Harmonisation in the Internal Market (Trade Marks and Designs)/Café do Brasil SpA* (CAFFE KIMBO v BIMBO), ECLI:EU:C:2014:1751.

part, are not harmonized. In turn, this raises the question of how the national law is to be integrated in the context of the examination: Does this *renvoi* to national legislation render national provisions part of EU law, over which EU bodies have full powers of review, or is it to be assumed that those rules remain an extraneous body of law with all the interpretative and practical complications that this entails?

3.87 The Court of Justice dealt with these questions in *Edwin*[85] and *National Lottery*,[86] two appeals concerning the application of, respectively, Article 53(a) and (c) CTMR, which presented it with the opportunity to clarify the status of national law within the EU trade mark system and to lay down detailed guidelines concerning the scope of the review which OHIM and the EU Courts are called upon to conduct in disputes relating to Community trade marks. The appeal in *Edwin* concerned the latitude of the Court's jurisdiction to review the interpretation of national law made by lower instances. The case arose from a dispute between the fashion designer Elio Fiorucci, who sought to invalidate the registration of a trade mark consisting of his name and surname by a Japanese company to which he had previously transferred all his 'creative assets', including a number of trade marks containing the word 'Fiorucci', on the basis of rights conferred on him by Italian law. The Boards of Appeal of OHIM and the General Court reversed the decision of the Cancellation Division, which had initially upheld the request, based on a different interpretation of the applicable provisions. Mr Fiorucci appealed to the Court of Justice pleading infringement of the relevant national rules.

3.88 Before addressing the main question regarding the powers of review of the Court, Advocate General Kokott[87] set out to investigate the position of national law in the various stages of the proceedings. Starting from the administrative phase before OHIM, she observed that Article 53(2)(a)[88] CTMR takes a twin-track approach by juxtaposing European and national law as clearly distinct entities, considering this a strong indication to the effect that national law is neither assimilated to, nor absorbed by, EU law. She also read Rule 37 of the Implementing Regulation, according to which the applicant must furnish 'particulars showing that ... he is entitled under the applicable national law to lay claim to that right', as shifting the national legal position towards the submission of the facts. She saw this assimilation of national law to a question of fact in a positive light both because she found it to be in conformity with the classic principles of private international law and because it resolved in an efficient manner the practical difficulties inherent in establishing *ex officio* the contents and conditions of application of the applicable law in each particular case.[89]

3.89 The Advocate General then examined how this peculiarity of national law affected the jurisdiction of EU Courts, starting with the general observation that the tasks of the Courts of the Union as listed in Article 19 TEU do not include the interpretation of national

---

[85] C-263/09 P, *Edwin Co. Ltd/Office for Harmonisation in the Internal Market (Elio Fiorucci)* [2011] ECR I-5853.
[86] C-530/12 P, *Office for Harmonisation in the Internal Market/National Lottery Commission (Shape of a hand)*, ECLI:EU:C:2014:186.
[87] Opinion of Advocate General Kokott of 27 January 2011, Case 263/09 P, *Edwin Co. Ltd/Office for Harmonisation in the Internal Market (Elio Fiorucci)* [2009] ECR II-1375.
[88] Which, at the time of the dispute, was Article 52(2)(a) CTMR.
[89] Points 42–48 and 50–56.

provisions, which led her to the preliminary conclusion that, at least in principle, national legislation is amenable only to a limited judicial review before the EU Courts.[90]

She noted, however, that the wording of Article 65(2) CTMR,[91] according to which an action may be brought before the General Court, among other grounds, on an 'infringement of the Treaty, of this Regulation or *of any rule of law relating to their application*', is broad enough to encompass not only provisions of EU law but also of national law. Therefore, she took the view that an incorrect interpretation of national law by OHIM may be challenged at any rate before the General Court, without however this meaning that the General Court is required to go beyond the evidence adduced by the parties or engage in further investigations of its own.[92]

3.90

She found, however, that the position before the Court of Justice is different, since the wording of Article 58 of the Statute of the Court, which expressly states that the scope of the appeal is limited to the infringement of 'Union law', is compelling in this regard. She also found this exclusion of national law from the scope of the appeal to be fully consistent with the classification of national law as a question of fact, the assessment of which is not the task of the appellate jurisdiction.

3.91

Based on these considerations, the Advocate General concluded that, in disputes relating to Community trade marks, a first instance plea based on the infringement of national law is admissible, but a ground of appeal raising such issue is, in principle, inadmissible.[93]

3.92

The Court of Justice agreed that its powers of review are limited by Article 58 of the Statute to infringements of EU law, which clearly places the interpretation of national law outside the scope of the appeal. Thus, it held that its jurisdiction was confined to determining: (a) whether the General Court distorted the wording of the national provisions or of the case law and academic writings relating to them; (b) whether the General Court made findings that were manifestly inconsistent with their content; and (c) whether the General Court, in examining all the particulars, attributed to one of them a significance which is not appropriate, where that is manifestly apparent from the documentation on file.[94]

3.93

The Court also agreed with the Advocate General that the expression 'infringement of any rule of law' in Article 65(2) of the Regulation empowers the General Court to make a full review of the legality of OHIM's assessment of the particulars submitted by the applicant in order to establish the contents of the national law.

3.94

However, with regard to the administrative review carried out by OHIM, the Court took a more nuanced approach. Even though it agreed with the Advocate General that Rule 37 of the Implementing Regulation requires an invalidity applicant to provide particulars establishing the content of the national law of which he/she is seeking application, it avoided drawing the conclusion that this assimilates national law to a question of fact. Rather, it held that once the claimant has discharged its burden of proof, the competent OHIM

3.95

---

[90] Points 49 and 60.
[91] At the time of the dispute, Article 63(2) CTMR.
[92] Points 56, 61–67, and 82.
[93] Points 79–80.
[94] Paragraphs 45–48 and 53.

bodies must 'assess the authority and scope of the particulars submitted by the applicant in order to establish the content of that rule'.[95]

3.96 Although this statement suggests that OHIM is not obliged to accept the elements submitted by an invalidity applicant at face value, the brevity of the Court's language left open the question of whether OHIM could verify their accuracy by conducting a further investigation of its own or if it could only rely on the submissions of the other party in order to rebut the applicant's allegations.

3.97 That question was finally settled in *National Lottery*, an appeal from a case where the General Court had conducted precisely such an investigation, in the course of which it encountered elements that led it to annul OHIM's decision by derogation from the principle that, in ordinary circumstances, the General Court lacks the powers to examine facts submitted for the first time before it, or raise such facts of its own motion.

3.98 As a preliminary point, Advocate General Bot[96] summarized the case law of the General Court in the matter as follows: As a general rule, the General Court regards the national law as an element of fact which it is for the claimant to prove. It does, however, temper that principle significantly by requiring OHIM to obtain, 'of its own motion and by whatever means it considers appropriate', information about the national law by regarding the same as a 'well-known fact', in particular when such information is necessary for the purposes of assessing the applicability of a ground for refusal or the correctness of the facts submitted by the parties. This opens the door for the General Court to determine, by exercising its full powers of review, whether the Board of Appeal 'has construed the relevant law correctly'.[97]

3.99 However, Advocate General Bot distanced himself both from the position of the General Court and from the analysis of Advocate General Kokott in *Edwin*, arguing that the overall scheme of the Regulation does not have the effect of equating national law to a question of fact. He took the view that although Article 53(2) CTMR does not assimilate national law to EU law, it 'undeniably affords it a certain degree of legal status' and interpreted Rule 37 of the Implementing Regulation as not intending 'to enshrine a purely adversarial perception of proceedings, which would make the courts mere arbiters and would leave the reins fully in the hands of the parties'. Moreover, he observed that the investigative powers afforded to OHIM by the provisions dealing with the taking of evidence show that administrative proceedings relating to Community trade marks 'are not dominated by the principle of neutrality or passivity'.[98]

3.100 These considerations led the Advocate General to conclude that, 'even though the adage *juria novit curia* does not extend to national law, of which the EU judicature is not deemed to be aware, and although the content of that law is regarded—for procedural purposes—as a fact which the parties bear the burden of claiming and proving, the fact remains that for the purposes of the [correct] resolution of the dispute, that law has the same standing as any rule of law, irrespective of its origin'. He found that view to be fully consistent with the

---

[95] Paragraphs 49–52.
[96] Opinion of Advocate General Bot of 28 November 2013, Case 530/12 P, *Office for Harmonisation in the Internal Market/National Lottery Commission (Shape of a hand)*, ECLI:EU:C:2013:782 for the Opinion and ECLI:EU:C:2014:186 for the Judgment.
[97] Points 50–56.
[98] Points 61–66.

position taken by the Court in *Edwin*, which required OHIM and the General Court to 'assess the authority and scope' of the particulars submitted by the parties by using an expression which differs from that normally used to refer to the review carried out on points of fact.[99]

3.101 Advocate General Bot added that this solution is the only one that serves the need to give practical effect to the grounds for refusal provided in the Regulation and to safeguard the principle of effective judicial protection. Conversely, these requirements would be rendered meaningless if the examination was restricted to the possibly incomplete or even misleading submissions of the parties, which could result in the incorrect application of the relevant national rules. However, he introduced the caveat that the power to obtain information *ex officio* about the true content of the national provisions is by no means intended to compensate for any shortcoming on the part of the applicant in discharging its burden of proof.[100]

3.102 The Court concurred with the Advocate General about the need to safeguard the *effet utile* of national law and to provide effective judicial protection to the parties, confirming that paragraphs 50 to 52 of *Edwin* do not mean that national law should be treated as a purely factual matter, but intend to emphasize that it is incumbent on OHIM and the General Court to assess the authority and scope of the particulars submitted by the parties 'by exercising a power of verification regarding the relevance of the law invoked that involves, if necessary, obtaining information of their own motion on the conditions of application of the rules relied upon'.[101]

3.103 Finally, the Court of Justice referred to Article 47 of the Charter of Fundamental Rights of the European Union, which warrants the right to a fair trial, recalling that the right to be heard does not merely confer on a party to the proceedings the right to be apprised of the observations made by the other party and to discuss them, but also extends to matters raised by the adjudicating bodies of their own motion.[102] Accordingly, the Court added that, in trade mark disputes under the Regulation, the duty of decision-making authorities to verify the contents of the national law is coupled with an obligation to invite the parties to take a position on any new matter of fact or law raised by them *ex officio*, if this element is decisive for the outcome of the proceedings.

3.104 The judgments in *Edwin* and *National Lottery* served to settle a long-standing uncertainty as regards the status of national law in trade mark disputes. It is now clear that national law cannot be treated as a matter of pure fact, exclusively governed by the submissions of the parties. On the other hand, the investigative powers conferred on OHIM and on the General Court do not require them to take the place of the parties in connection with the taking of evidence. Rather, their duty to obtain is more limited in scope, in that it merely seeks to determine the accuracy of the particulars provided by an opponent or invalidity applicant. Consequently, the exercise of that capacity does not have the effect of altering the subject matter of the dispute, but simply enables examining authorities to verify the

---

[99] Points 71–80.
[100] Points 89–94.
[101] Paragraphs 35–44.
[102] Citing C-89/08 P *Commission v Ireland and Others* [2009] ECR I-11245, paragraphs 51, 53, and 56, and C-197/09 *RX-II Review M v EMEA* [2009] ECR I-12033, paragraphs 41 and 42.

(5) The Value of Precedents

3.105 Another issue arising from the interaction between Community and national trade mark law is the extent to which prior decisions of administrative or judicial authorities in trade mark cases are binding on other such bodies dealing with identical or similar cases in the same or another Member State, or at Community level. It has even been argued[103] that insofar as trade mark examination is inevitably encumbered by a considerable degree of subjectivity, the coherent application of trade mark law can only be guaranteed by extensively relying on the general principles of equality and legitimate expectations when deciding subsequent cases. That view thus advocates in favour of a strict adherence to precedents as the only possible means of achieving a maximum degree of legal certainty and harmonization under the Directive.

3.106 The Court, however, tends to take a more orthodox view: In a series of judgments, it has made it abundantly clear that the principles of legitimate expectations and equal treatment cannot be given precedence over the correct application of the relevant legal provisions; first and foremost, the European Union is a community based on the rule of law, as clearly recognized by Article 6 of the EC Treaty and as repeatedly confirmed by the Court of Justice.[104]

3.107 Hence, the application of the principle of equal treatment in trade mark conflicts and, by extension, the idea that the authority is always bound by its own acts, finds its limits in the rule of law, in the sense that there can be no equality in injustice. Applying this maxim in administrative practice, the Court has also held that the publication of guidelines based on precedents cannot override legally binding provisions and that erroneous decisions can therefore not oblige the authority to apply the same standard in the future.[105]

3.108 As regards specifically the registration of Community trade marks, the Court has consistently held that 'the decisions that OHIM is called on to take under the Regulation are adopted in the exercise of circumscribed powers and are not a matter of discretion' and that, accordingly, the legality of those decisions 'must be assessed solely on the basis of the Regulation, as interpreted by the Community judicature and not on the basis of the previous decision-making practice of either OHIM or its Boards of Appeal'.[106] As a result, the Court systematically rejects claims based on the alleged violation of the principle of equal treatment by the Office or by the Court of First Instance as manifestly unfounded, without even addressing their merits.[107]

---

[103] See David T Keeling, 'Equal before the Law? Not if you Want to Register a Trade Mark' in Anthony Arnull, Piet Eeckhout, and Takis Tridimas (eds), *Continuity and Change in EU Law; Essays in Honour of Sir Francis Jacobs* (Oxford University Press, 2008) pp 283, 294.

[104] C-294/83 *Les Verts/European Parliament* [1986] ECR I-1339.

[105] C-190/82 *Adam PH Blomefield/Commission* [1983] ECR I-3981; C-343/82 *Christos Michael/Commission* [1983] ECR 4023; C-246/83 *Claudia de Angelis/Commission* [1986] ECR 1253; C-41/88 *Mathilde Becker and Josyane Starquit/Parliament* [1989] ECR 3807.

[106] C-37/03 P *BioID AG/OHIM (BioID)* [2005] ECR I-7975, paragraph 47; C-173/04 P *Deutsche SiSi-Werke GmbH & Co Betriebs KG/OHIM (STANDBEUTEL)* [2006] ECR I-551, paragraph 48.

[107] C-212/07 P *Indorata-Serviços e Gestão, Ld^a/OHIM (HAIRTRANSFER)*, ECLI:EU:C:2008:83, paragraph 44.

3.109 Similarly, the General Court has held that precisely because precedents are not binding, but mere factors that may be taken into consideration in assessing whether a sign is suitable for registration, the Boards of Appeal are not required to give specific reasons for the fact that they departed from a previous decision by another Board in an identical or similar case.[108]

3.110 Essentially the same issue, but this time concerning national practice under the Directive, was brought before the Court of Justice in *Volkshandy*,[109] a request for a preliminary ruling asking whether national trade mark authorities are compelled, when applying an absolute ground of refusal, to give decisive value to prior registrations of signs composed of similar or identical elements. The Court was not impressed. Answering by way of reasoned order, it merely made reference to its settled case law on the matter, before stressing once more that the competent authority:

> is not entitled to disregard the grounds of refusal laid down by Article 3(1)(b) and (c) of the Directive, or to accept the mark merely on the grounds that the sign applied for is structured in an identical or comparable manner to another mark that has already been registered by the same authority.

As concerns, finally, the interaction between Community and national law, the Court has additionally pointed out that national decisions cannot constitute valid precedents for Community authorities also because the regime introduced by the CTMR is 'an autonomous system with its own set of objectives and rules peculiar to it, that applies independently of any national system'. Consequently, 'the mark must be examined only on the basis of the relevant Community rules and the national decision can under no circumstances call in question the legality of either the contested decision or the judgment under appeal'.[110] The Court therefore takes the view that a prior decision can constitute a valid precedent only if it was correct in its own right; while the legality of the second decision eventually depends on its correct application of the law and not on its alignment with prior decisions. In the end, if the first decision is correct, it should be followed for that reason only and not because it is prior or binding; whereas if it is wrong, it simply must not be followed. Thus, by practically reserving the final word in all legal matters for itself, the Court has effectively assumed the role of the absolute guardian of Community trade mark law, to whom the privilege to shape up future developments and the responsibility to provide Europe with a harmonized system of trade mark law ultimately belongs.

D. Conclusion

3.111 To illustrate the interaction of the principles described above with the application of trade mark law the reader should consider, for example, the importance of the principle of legal certainty for the graphical representation requirement,[111] the trade mark proprietor's

---

[108] T-304/06 *Paul Reber GmbH & Co KG/OHIM (MOZART/MOZART)* [2008] ECR II-01927, paragraph 53.
[109] C-39/08 and C-43/08 *Bild digital GmbH & Co. KG, formerly Bild.T-Online.de AG & Co. ZVS Zeitungsvertrieb Stuttgart GmbH/Präsident des Deutschen Patent- und Markenamts* [2009] ECR I-00020.
[110] C-238/06 P *Develey Holding GmbH & Co. Beteiligungs KG v Office for Harmonisation in the Internal Market (Trade Marks and Designs) (OHIM)* (shape of a plastic bottle) [2007] ECR I-9375, paragraphs 66–67.
[111] See, for instance, the Opinion of the Advocate General in C-321/03 *Dyson Ltd v Registrar of Trade Marks* [2003] ECR I-687; the Opinion was posted on the website of the Court of Justice on 14 September 2006. This issue is discussed in Chapter 4.

reliance on the right of property in cases like *Anheuser-Busch*,[112] or the catalytic application of proportionality in cases involving consumer protection from deceptive use of distinctive signs.[113]

3.112 In setting the background for the analysis of the trade mark jurisprudence of the Court, three particular points discussed in this chapter must be underlined.

3.113 First, the provisions of the Directive and the Regulation can only be examined and interpreted in their specific and wider legislative contexts. The aim of a provision, its interrelationship with fundamental principles, its place within the Directive or the Regulation, and the broader rationale of trade mark law within the European project could be equally important as its literal wording.

3.114 Secondly, in an integrated European Union the Directive and the Regulation should be seen as two parts that interact and complete the European trade mark regime according to the architecture of coexistence mentioned in Chapter 2. Accordingly, the essentially identical substantive provisions of the Directive and the Regulation should be interpreted and applied by the Court in the same way. In addition, the Court would be expected to interpret the provisions of the Directive in a way that would bring the national trade mark regimes closer to each other and the Community Trade Mark Regulation.

3.115 Thirdly, the Court often relies on repeating statements, using them as paving stones to build a judgment. As we will see in the case of trade marks, their function has been the most commonly used one.

---

[112] *Anheuser-Busch Inc v Portugal* [2006] ETMR 43, discussed in paragraph 12.232, below.
[113] See, for instance, C-238/89 *Pall Corp. v P.J. Dahlhausen & Co.* [1990] ECR I-4827.

4

FORMALITIES AND THE DEFINITION OF GOODS AND SERVICES

A. Introduction

4.01 This chapter is the first of a series of three that will examine the jurisprudence of the Court on formalities and specification (Chapter 4), on absolute grounds for refusing registration (Chapter 5), and on acquired distinctiveness through use (Chapter 6), as a means of of overcoming some of the objections discussed in Chapters 4 and 5.

4.02 The provisions of the Directive appear quite permissive: there is no definition of the concept of a sign and the list in Article 2 is open-ended. The key to obtaining trade mark protection is distinctiveness; nevertheless, the concept possesses a split personality. Article 2 requires the sign to be capable of distinguishing, whereas Article 3(1)(b) demands that the trade mark made up of the sign that is capable of distinguishing must not be devoid of any distinctive character. At the same time distinctiveness acquired through use can overcome an objection based on Article 3(1)(b) but not one based on Article 2.

4.03 There is also a special provision dealing with shapes, aiming to maintain 'functional' shapes outside the scope of exclusive trademark rights.

4.04 Historically, in many European jurisdictions the ability to obtain trade mark registration was limited to certain signs, to the exclusion of others, such as 2D signs or colours. The Directive and the Regulation were designed to be open-ended, the two limitations being graphic representability and capacity to distinguish. Non-traditional trade marks, which include colours and shapes as well as non-visual signs (sound marks, olfactory marks, etc), were often in the forefront of academic discussions, although statistically they were always and continue to be insignificant. Nevertheless, some types of these 'non-traditional' marks have occupied the Court of Justice for some time and in significant numbers, notably 3D marks.

4.05 From a historical perspective, the Court of Justice had to deal for a limited period with references from national courts that wished to apply their trusted principles rather than adopt a liberal approach. Some were concerned about the combination of a broader scope of protection with an expansive list of signs, sensing that this could lead to more conflicts and uncertainty in the marketplace.

4.06 At the same time the Court must function as the ultimate arbiter for Community trade mark applications; it has to consider legal issues rather than facts, though it has often found it difficult to separate legal principles from factual context.

4.07 This series of chapters develops around a logical rather than historical structure, following the text of the Directive.

B. The Provisions of the Directive and the Regulation

4.08 The definition of a trade mark is provided in Article 2 of the Directive; the equivalent provision in the Regulation is Article 4.

Article 2—Signs of which a Trade Mark may consist

A trade mark may consist of any sign capable of being represented graphically, particularly words, including personal names, designs, letters, numerals, the shape of goods or of their packaging, provided that such signs are capable of distinguishing the goods or services of one undertaking from those of other undertakings.

4.09 Article 3 of the Directive lists the grounds for which an application may be refused or a registration declared invalid.

Article 3—Grounds for Refusal or Invalidity

1. The following shall not be registered or if registered shall be liable to be declared invalid:
   a. signs which cannot constitute a trade mark;
   b. trade marks which are devoid of any distinctive character;
   c. trade marks which consist exclusively of signs or indications which may serve, in trade, to designate the kind, quality, quantity, intended purpose, value, geographical origin, or the time of production of the goods or of rendering of the service, or other characteristics of the goods;
   d. trade marks which consist exclusively of signs or indications which have become customary in the current language or in the bona fide and established practices of the trade;
   e. signs which consist exclusively of
      — the shape which results from the nature of the goods themselves, or
      — the shape of goods which is necessary to obtain a technical result, or
      — the shape which gives substantial value to the goods;
   f. trade marks which are contrary to public policy or to accepted principles of morality;
   g. trade marks which are of such a nature as to deceive the public, for instance as to the nature, quality or geographical origin of the goods or service; and
   h. trade marks which have not been authorised by the competent authorities and are to be refused or invalidated pursuant to Article 6ter of the Paris Convention for the Protection of Industrial Property, hereinafter referred to as the 'Paris Convention'.
2. Any Member State may provide that a trade mark shall not be registered or, if registered, shall be liable to be declared invalid where and to the extent that:
   a. the use of that trade mark may be prohibited pursuant to provisions of law other than trade mark law of the Member State concerned or of the Community;
   b. the trade mark covers a sign of high symbolic value, in particular a religious symbol;
   c. the trade mark includes badges, emblems and escutcheons other than those covered by Article 6ter of the Paris Convention and which are of public interest, unless the consent of the appropriate authorities to its registration has been given in conformity with the legislation of the Member State; and
   d. the application for registration of the trade mark was made in bad faith by the applicant.

3. A trade mark shall not be refused registration or be declared invalid in accordance with paragraph 1(b), (c) or (d) if, before the date of application for registration and following the use which has been made of it, it has acquired a distinctive character. Any Member State may in addition provide that this provision shall also apply where the distinctive character was acquired after the date of application for registration or after the date of registration.
4. Any Member State may provide that, by derogation from the preceding paragraphs, the grounds of refusal of registration or invalidity in force in that State prior to the date on which the provisions necessary to comply with this Directive enter into force, shall apply to trade marks for which application has been made prior to that date.

Article 7 is the equivalent provision of the Regulation.   **4.10**

Article 7—Absolute grounds for refusal
1. The following shall not be registered:
   (a) signs which do not conform to the requirements of Article 4;
   (b) trade marks which are devoid of any distinctive character;
   (c) trade marks which consist exclusively of signs or indications which may serve, in trade, to designate the kind, quality, quantity, intended purpose, value, geographical origin or the time of production of the goods or of rendering of the service, or other characteristics of the goods or service;
   (d) trade marks which consist exclusively of signs or indications which have become customary in the current language or in the bona fide and established practices of the trade;
   (e) signs which consist exclusively of:
      (i) the shape which results from the nature of the goods themselves; or
      (ii) the shape of goods which is necessary to obtain a technical result; or
      (iii) the shape which gives substantial value to the goods;
   (f) trade marks which are contrary to public policy or to accepted principles of morality;
   (g) trade marks which are of such a nature as to deceive the public, for instance as to the nature, quality or geographical origin of the goods or service;
   (h) trade marks which have not been authorized by the competent authorities and are to be refused pursuant to Article 6ter of the Paris Convention;
   (i) trade marks which include badges, emblems or escutcheons other than those covered by Article 6ter of the Paris Convention and which are of particular public interest, unless the consent of the appropriate authorities to their registration has been given;
   (j) trade marks for wines which contain or consist of a geographical indication identifying wines or for spirits which contain or consist of a geographical indication identifying spirits with respect to such wines or spirits not having that origin;
   (k) trade marks which contain or consist of a designation of origin or a geographical indication registered in accordance with Regulation (EEC) No 2081/92 when they correspond to one of the situations covered by Article 13 of the said Regulation and regarding the same type of product, on condition that the application for registration of the trade mark has been submitted after the date of filing with the Commission of the application for registration of the designation of origin or geographical indication.
2. Paragraph 1 shall apply notwithstanding that the grounds of non-registrability obtain in only part of the Community.
3. Paragraph 1(b), (c) and (d) shall not apply if the trade mark has become distinctive in relation to the goods or services for which registration is requested in consequence of the use which has been made of it.

C. What is a Sign?

(1) *Dyson*: The Fundamental Question

4.11 Until *Dyson*,[1] a reference from the High Court of the United Kingdom, the Court of Justice had not dealt directly with what constitutes a sign.

4.12 The contested sign was described in the broadest possible terms as a 'transparent bin or collection chamber forming part of the external surface of a vacuum cleaner as shown in the representation'; what it showed was a representation of Dyson's vacuum cleaners. Vacuum cleaners were included in the specification of the application. The High Court sought from the Court an interpretation of Article 3(3) of the Directive, ie the requirements for showing acquired distinctiveness.

4.13 However, the Commission in its intervention submitted that the application should be rejected for failing the fundamental requirement of being a sign under Article 2; it covered a concept rather than a sign; a clear collection chamber for a vacuum cleaner that was not capable of perception by one of the five senses. In addition it claimed that the representations of the concept did not satisfy the *Sieckmann*[2] requirements for graphical representation since, in principle, they did not correspond to any particular shape.

4.14 The Court decided to stay proceedings in the interests of the proper administration of justice because the Court of First Instance was dealing with the same issue regarding two parallel applications for Community trade marks, and Article 2 of the Directive and Article 4 of the Regulation had to be given the same interpretation.[3] As the applications were withdrawn, the Court of First Instance decided not to adjudicate,[4] and the Court revived the original case.

(2) Pre-*Dyson* Jurisprudence: Setting the Ground

4.15 Elements of this fundamental, at least in terms of theory,[5] question, had already been considered: first, in its general discussion on the structure of Article 3(1);[6] and, second, through its attempts to clarify the relationship between signs that are 'not capable of distinguishing' and signs that are devoid of any distinctive character.[7]

---

[1] C-321/03 *Dyson Ltd v Registrar of Trade Marks* (CLEAR BIN) [2007] ECR I-687.
[2] C-273/00 *Sieckmann v Deutsches Patent-und Markenamt* [2002] ECR I-11737.
[3] Case 321/03 R [2004] WL 3168965, paragraph 14.
[4] T-278/02 *Dyson Limited v Office for Harmonisation in the Internal Market (Trade Marks and Designs)* [2002] OJ C289/28.
[5] In *Philips Electronics NV v Remington Consumer Products Ltd* [1998] RPC 283, Jacob J asked the question: 'What is a "sign"? Can the thing itself also be a "sign"? If one is not careful one is likely here to end up discussing metaphysical points—hardly the sort of thing appropriate for a law designed for men of commerce. I think a "sign" is anything which can convey information. I appreciate that this is extremely wide, but I can see no reason to limit the meaning of the word.... What I conclude is confirmed by recital 7(b), which emphasises the necessity to list the examples of "sign"—note the contrast with recital 7(c) which sets out the need to list the grounds of invalidity "in an exhaustive manner". You need the examples of a sign to see just how wide the meaning is. What the examples have in common is the ability to convey information. At this point it does not matter what sort of information is conveyed. It is the proviso to recital 7(b), "capable of distinguishing", which serves to limit the sort of sign which can be registered. Here, on my findings of fact, the picture does convey a message ... So it is a "sign".'
[6] See paragraph 4.156 and following below.
[7] See paragraphs 5.16 and following below.

4.16 In *Sieckmann*[8] there were two further points linked with the question of what constitutes a sign. The first was made by AG Ruiz-Jarabo Colomer, indicating that, in principle, any message capable of sensory perception could function as a trade mark.[9] And, in its judgment the Court found that a chemical formula was not a sufficient representation of a scent, partly because it represented the substance itself rather than its odour;[10] a distinction that had not been identified as a relevant condition.

(a) Libertel: The relevance of 'context'

4.17 In *Libertel*,[11] considering the registrability of a colour per se, AG Léger had remarked that although the questions submitted to the Court centred on the interpretation of Article 3, the starting point should be whether a colour per se fell within the meaning of Article 2.[12] Colour was a sensation rather than a pre-existing objective reality; its perception would vary according to the circumstances of its experience. In addition, colour functioned as a language, provoking feelings and conveying information. Also, in all cases, colours were the attributes of something else; they did not exist independently.

4.18 The Court accepted that it was necessary to start its analysis from Article 2, which set the three conditions for a colour to be registered as a trade mark.[13]

4.19 It ruled that a colour carried within it the potential to satisfy the 'sign' requirement. 'Normally a colour is a simple property of things. Yet it may constitute a sign. That depends on the context in which the colour is used. None the less, a colour per se is capable, in relation to a product or service, of constituting a sign.'[14]

(b) Postkantoor: Article 2 and signs in abstract

4.20 In *Postkantoor*[15] the Court adopted another stance. The difference is immaterial against the broader structure of the Directive where the sign rediscovers its context in Article 3(1)(b). Still, the wording appears contradictory:

> The purpose of Article 2 … is to define the types of signs of which a trade mark may consist, irrespective of the goods or services for which protection might be sought. It provides that a trade mark may consist inter alia of words and letters, provided that they are capable of distinguishing the goods or services of one undertaking from those of other undertakings.[16]

(c) Philips: Linking the concept of the sign with graphical representation and distinctiveness

4.21 *Postkantoor* should be read in the light of the earlier judgment in *Philips*,[17] where the Court provided a comprehensible framework for interpreting Article 3(1). Part of it was the recognition that Article 2 provided that all signs that satisfied its two requirements, capable of distinguishing and of being represented graphically, were in principle registrable.

---

[8] C-273/00 *Sieckmann* [2002] ECR I-11737.
[9] Point 21 of the Opinion of AG Ruiz-Jarabo Colomer.
[10] *Sieckmann* (n 2) paragraph 69.
[11] C-104/01 *Libertel Groep BV v Benelux-Merkenbureau* [2003] ECR I-3793.
[12] Point 35 of the Opinion of AG Léger.
[13] The Court agreed with the AG that the Joint Declaration OHIM OJ 5/96, p 607, did not affect the interpretation of the provision. See paragraphs 25 and 26 of the judgment.
[14] Libertel (n 11) paragraph 27.
[15] Case C-363/99 *Koninklijke KPN Nederland NV v Benelux-Merkenbureau (Postkantoor)* [2004] ECR I-1619.
[16] *Postkantoor* (n 15) paragraph 80.
[17] C-299/99 *Koninklijke Philips Electronics NV v Remington Consumer Products Ltd* [2002] ECR I-5475.

4.22 Article 3(1)(a) excluded 'signs which are not generally capable of being a trade mark and thus cannot be represented graphically and/or are not capable of distinguishing the goods or services of one undertaking from those of other undertakings'.[18]

4.23 To provide a meaning for the term 'generally' it linked Article 3(1)(a) with Article 3(1)(b), (c), and (d): 'Article 3(1)(a) ... like the rule laid down by Article 3(1)(b), (c) and (d), precludes the registration of signs or indications which do not meet one of the two conditions imposed by Article 2 of the Directive, that is to say, the condition requiring such signs to be capable of distinguishing the goods or services of one undertaking from those of other undertakings'.[19]

(d) Nichols: The 'list of examples'

4.24 The list in Article 2 should not be seen as limiting the types of signs that can function, and as a result be protected, as trade marks. In *Nichols*,[20] where the Court considered the conditions for the registration of surnames, it stated:

> Article 2 ... contains a list, described as a 'list of examples' in the seventh recital in the preamble to that directive, of signs which may constitute a trade mark, provided that such signs are capable of distinguishing the goods or services of one undertaking from those of other undertakings, that is to say to fulfil the trade mark's function as an indicator of origin.[21]

(e) Sieckmann: The non-exhaustive character of the list

4.25 In *Sieckmann*,[22] the first case that tested the registrability of a non-visual sign, the Court added that the Article 2 list was a list of examples, thus not exhaustive

> as is clear from the language of both Article 2 of the Directive and the seventh recital in the preamble thereto, which refers to 'a list [of] examples' of signs which may constitute a trade mark, that list is not exhaustive. Consequently, that provision, although it does not mention signs which are not in themselves capable of being perceived visually, such as odours, does not, however, expressly exclude them.[23]

(3) *Dyson*: The Fundamental Requirement

(a) The legal background

4.26 The Court came back to the reference of the High Court once the Community trade mark applications were withdrawn. By then it had ample opportunity to consider distinctiveness and functionality in relation to almost every type of sign. Overall, but not without contradictions, the Court appeared to adopt a more restrictive approach with functionality concepts, exercising a broader influence touching both distinctiveness and graphical representation.

4.27 *Dyson* posed a dilemma: would the Court enhance and formalize this approach transforming Article 3(1)(e) into a public policy doctrine; would it confront the question of what constitutes a sign; or would it choose to decide the case on the basis of the graphical representation requirement?

---

[18] Philips (n 17) paragraph 37.
[19] Philips (n 17) paragraph 38.
[20] C-404/02 *Nichols plc v Registrar of Trade Marks* [2004] ECR I-8499.
[21] *Nichols* (n 20) paragraph 22.
[22] C-273/00 *Sieckmann* [2002] ECR I-11737.
[23] *Sieckmann* (n 2) paragraph 44.

4.28 The case came before the Court as a reference from the English High Court.[24] Dyson had applied for the registration of a sign consisting of a transparent plastic container that was the central element of its bagless vacuum cleaners functioning as a dirt collector. There were two applications that shared a common description: 'The mark consists of a transparent bin or collection chamber forming part of the external surface of a vacuum cleaner as shown in the representation'. However, each application showed a different Dyson model. The specification covered 'apparatus for cleaning, polishing and shampooing floors and carpets; vacuum cleaners; carpet shampooers; floor polishers; parts and fittings for all the aforesaid goods' in Class 9 of the Nice Agreement.

4.29 The applications were rejected at the Trade Mark Registry, which considered the signs to be devoid of any distinctive character and serving to designate the kind and the intended purpose of the specified products. Dyson appealed before the High Court, which agreed with the Registry and raised an additional point regarding the monopoly that Dyson would obtain in the event of a successful application. Looking at the evidence of distinctiveness acquired through use it noted that consumers associated the container with the product in a market where Dyson enjoyed a *de facto* monopoly; inevitably this created a link with Dyson. However, the sign as such had never been promoted as a trade mark.

4.30 The High Court stayed proceedings and referred the following questions to the Court:

1. In a situation where an applicant has used a sign (which is not a shape) which consists of a feature which has a function and which forms part of the appearance of a new kind of article, and the applicant has, until the date of application, had a de facto monopoly in such articles, is it sufficient, in order for the sign to have acquired a distinctive character within the meaning of Article 3(3) of Directive 89/104/EEC, that a significant proportion of the relevant public has by the date of application for registration come to associate the relevant goods bearing the sign with the applicant and no other manufacturer?
2. If that is not sufficient, what else is needed in order for the sign to have acquired a distinctive character and, in particular, is it necessary for the person who has used the sign to have promoted it as a trade mark?[25]

(b) The Opinion of Advocate General Léger

4.31 Advocate General Léger started his analysis by taking up an issue raised by the Commission: was the particular mark applied for capable of constituting a trade mark in the first place under Article 2 of the Directive?

4.32 **(i) The first requirement: What constitutes a sign** He noted that 'the purpose of that requirement is in particular to prevent the abuse of trade mark law in order to obtain an unfair competitive advantage'.[26]

4.33 He found the bin to be 'first and foremost functional and utilitarian',[27] it replaced vacuum cleaner bags and filters, and in addition functioned as an indicator of fullness. It also possessed an aesthetic function to the extent that it formed an integral part of the appearance of a product.

---

[24] *Dyson Ltd's TM Application* [2003] RPC 47.
[25] Reproduced under point 24 of the Opinion of AG Léger.
[26] Point 44, citing in particular paragraph 24 of C-49/02 *Heidelberger Bauchemie GmbH* [2004] ECR I-6129.
[27] Point 46.

4.34 He agreed with the Commission that what Dyson sought to protect was in essence a concept for collecting, storing, and emptying waste. Looking for the meaning of 'concept'—a general and abstract mental representation of an object[28]—he noted that 'when a concept is developed, it can lead to the creation of a wide range of objects'.[29]

4.35 The application sought to obtain exclusive rights over all possible appearances of a functional feature; indeed, the two representations of the mark applying for registration on the two application forms showed two distinct containers.

> The protection claimed is not limited to a shape, a composition, or a particular arrangement since this feature must only form part of the external surface of the vacuum cleaner and allow the user to see through the container. There are many possibilities as regards the shape, the dimensions, the presentation and even the composition of that collection chamber in relation to the product in question, depending not only on the vacuum cleaner models developed by the applicant, but also on technological innovations. As far as transparency is concerned, it allows many colours to be used.[30]

4.36 The Advocate General accepted that a concept appealed to our unconstrained imagination rather than our senses. The potential forms a concept could take were in conflict with the essential function of a trade mark that required a stability that a concept could not satisfy. A trade mark had to enable the consumer, without any possibility of confusion, to distinguish the marked product or service from others which have another origin; this objective could not

> be achieved by a sign which is capable of being perceived by human beings in such diverse ways. As a result, a concept cannot, in my opinion, constitute an indication for the consumer and, consequently, cannot be a sign capable of fulfilling a trade mark's distinguishing function.[31]

4.37 He appeared to admit that the particular concept could be a sign in the first place; however, he linked the sign requirement with the distinguishing function in order to deny trade mark protection based on the lack of the most fundamental requirement of Article 2: 'a functional feature like that at issue in the present case is not capable of constituting a sign within the meaning of Article 2'.[32]

4.38 **(ii) The second requirement: Graphical representation** Advocate General Léger agreed that the applications also failed the graphical representation requirement. According to *Sieckmann*,[33] the representation had to be clear, precise, self-contained, easily accessible, intelligible, durable, and objective.[34]

4.39 Instead of identifying the conditions that were not satisfied, he referred to *Heidelberger Bauchemie*,[35] which had distilled part of them into a requirement that a sign should be

---

[28] Le Petit Robert, *Dictionnaire de la Langue Française* (Paris, Éditions Dictionnaires Le Robert, 2004).
[29] Point 48.
[30] Point 51 of the Opinion of AG Léger.
[31] Point 54. Note that in C-104/01, *Libertel* [2003] ECR I-3793 he had remarked that for colours we employ our feelings to conceive them.
[32] Point 55.
[33] C-273/00 *Sieckmann* [2002] ECR I-11737.
[34] The Advocate General had made the point in C-49/02 *Heidelberger Bauchemie GmbH* [2004] ECR I-6129. that the graphical representation requirement had a dual objective: first, to allow the competent authorities to know with clarity and precision the nature of the signs in order to carry out the examination of an application for registration and maintain an appropriate and precise register; and, second, to enable third parties to identify with clarity and precision what is already protected.
[35] Ibid, paragraph 31 in particular.

represented unambiguously and uniformly. This, together with the durability requirement, was what such a functional feature failed to fulfil:

> the functionality for whose registration Dyson is applying can clearly take on a multitude of different shapes and appearances which will depend not only on the vacuum cleaner models developed by the applicant, but also on technological developments. In so far as the protection conferred by the trade mark right can be for an unlimited duration ... it is highly likely, in my view, that the appearance of the transparent collecting bin and the way in which it is integrated into the vacuum cleaner will change over the years.[36]

4.40 The imprecision on how the bin would actually be integrated into the product went against the principle of legal certainty.

4.41 **(iii) The third requirement: Capable of distinguishing** Advocate General Léger suggested that the application should also fail the distinctiveness requirement. Here, his analysis was based on the distinction between distinctive character in general[37] and intrinsic distinctive character, depending solely on whether the sign was capable in itself of having a distinctive character. He viewed the latter as what Article 2 required.

4.42 Functionality was again the determinative factor. What had to be assessed was whether the functional feature served to convey precise information as to the origin of the product. The answer should be negative for two reasons. It was not possible to determine with any certainty how 'that functionality will be integrated into the products for which registration is sought ... an assessment of whether or not a sign is capable of having a distinctive character requires that one should be able to know exactly what the sign is'.[38] And, the 'functionality' in question would not be able to indicate product origin. The application sought to protect a concept or, at least, all possible appearances the product could take.[39]

4.43 **(iv) Functionality: The application of Article 3(1)(e)** The Advocate General added that the functionality provision of the Directive, Article 3(1)(e), would also preclude registration. Article 3(1)(e) was intended to prevent the extension of trade mark protection beyond signs which served to distinguish a product from those offered by competitors, 'so as to form an obstacle preventing competitors from freely offering for sale products incorporating such technical solutions or functional characteristics in competition with the proprietor of the trade mark'.[40]

4.44 The second indent required that 'a shape whose essential characteristics perform a technical function is not reserved to one undertaking alone and may be freely used by all'.[41] The availability of other shapes that could achieve the same result would not affect the application of that ground; the Court had also precluded the application of Article 3(3) for signs originally covered by Article 3(1)(e).

---

[36] Point 62.
[37] Citing Joined Cases C-108/97 and C-109/97 *Windsurfing Chiemsee Produktions- und Vertriebs GmbH v Boots- und Segelzubehör Walter Huber and Franz Attenberger* [1999] ECR I-2779 and Joined Cases C-53/01 to C-55/01 *Linde AG* (C-53/01), *Winward Industries Inc.* (C-54/01), and *Rado Uhren AG* (C-55/01) [2003] ECR I-3161.
[38] Point 70, citing his Opinion in C-104/01, *Libertel* [2003] ECR I-3793.
[39] Point 73.
[40] C-299/99, *Koninklijke Philips Electronics NV v Remington Consumer Products Ltd* [2002] ECR I-5475; point 83 of the Opinion of AG Léger.
[41] Point 84.

4.45 **(v) Article 3(1)(e): Beyond shapes?** Expanding the scope of the provision beyond three dimensional signs he stated:

> ... it is clear that this reasoning applies legitimately to a functional feature which forms part of the appearance of a product. Although that article refers only to signs which consist exclusively of the shape of a product, I think that the general interest which underlies that provision requires that registration of a functionality like that at issue in the main proceedings be refused.[42]

He followed three lines of supporting arguments.

4.46 First, registration of the particular 'functionality' would mean that the trade mark proprietor could reserve for itself the exclusive use of a technical solution, potentially without any time limitation. The effect in this case would be 'a monopoly on a technical and functional feature which a consumer is likely to seek in bagless vacuum cleaners manufactured by competing undertakings'.[43]

4.47 Second, since the exclusive right would cover a multitude of shapes the functional feature might take, competing undertakings would be unable to determine precisely whether and how they might still use that feature, restricting their freedom in 'a sector where technical progress is based on a process of ongoing improvement of earlier innovations'.[44] Ultimately, such a monopoly might prevent new players from entering the particular product market, wipe out competition in innovative ideas, and harm free competition.[45]

4.48 Third, according to TRIPs and the case law of the Court in Hermès,[46] the second indent of Article 3(1)(e) should be interpreted in the light of the wording and purpose of TRIPs. Article 7 of TRIPs provided that:

> The protection and enforcement of intellectual property rights should contribute to the promotion of technological innovation and to the transfer and dissemination of technology, to the mutual advantage of producers and users of technological knowledge and in a manner conducive to social and economic welfare, and to a balance of rights and obligations.

The wider context drawn for intellectual property rights by that provision precluded the protection of such a feature under trade mark law.

4.49 **(vi) Trade marks and other IP rights: Policy considerations** Trade mark registration 'could result in a situation where exclusive rights are acquired or perpetuated through trade mark law over inventions which are in reality patentable, contrary to the legitimate objective pursued by Article 3(1)(e), second indent, of the directive'.[47] The application of trade mark law should not result in an 'unfair competitive advantage';[48] the function of a trade mark was not to create a monopoly in new developments in technology.

4.50 He added that the jurisprudence of the Court viewed trade marks as an essential element in the system of undistorted competition envisaged by the Treaty and the Directive.[49] However,

---

[42] Point 88.
[43] Point 90.
[44] Point 92.
[45] Citing, in particular, Article 3(g) and (m) EC referring, respectively, to 'a system ensuring that competition in the internal market is not distorted' and the 'the strengthening of the competitiveness of Community industry'.
[46] C-53/96 *Hermès v FHT Marketing Choice BV* [1998] ECR I-3603 and C-49/02 *Heidelberger Bauchemie GmbH* [2004] ECR I-6129.
[47] Point 95 of the Opinion of AG Léger.
[48] Point 96.
[49] C-10/89, *SA CNL-SUCAL NV v Hag GF AG* [1990] ECR I-3711 and C-63/97, *Bayerische Motorenwerke AG and BMW Nederland BV v Deenik* [1999] ECR I-905.

trade mark protection was unlimited in terms of duration and some owners might attempt to circumvent the time limitations of other intellectual property rights through trade mark rights. Technological innovations should be achieved through the grant of a patent and not through a trade mark. He concluded that 'Article 3(1)(e), second indent, of the directive precludes the registration as a trade mark of a functional feature which forms part of the appearance of a product'.[50] Article 3(3) could not affect the application of Article 3(1)(e).

(vii) **The conclusions of the Advocate General** Advocate General Léger concluded that: **4.51**

(1) A visible functional feature of a product which is capable of taking on a multitude of appearances does not fulfil the necessary conditions to constitute a trade mark within the meaning of Article 2 of [the Directive] since it does not constitute a sign capable of being represented graphically and capable of distinguishing goods and services of one undertaking from those of other undertakings.
(2) In any event, Article 3(1)(e), second indent, of [the Directive] precludes the registration as a trade mark of a visible functional feature of a product.[51]

Note the reference to 'visible functional features' rather than three dimensional signs.   **4.52**

(c) The judgment of the court

(i) **Resetting the ground** The High Court had sought from the Court of Justice an in-   **4.53**
terpretation of Article 3(3) of the Directive. However, the Court turned to the definition of a trade mark. Reciting the factual background of the case, it highlighted that consumers recognized the transparent bin as an indication of a bagless vacuum cleaner. Advertising and the lack of rival products indicated that bagless vacuum cleaners were manufactured by Dyson but, in itself, the bin had not been actively promoted as a trade mark.

It had become clear during the hearing that the trade mark application covered all conceiv-   **4.54**
able shapes of a transparent collecting bin as part of the product's external surface and the Court decided to focus on Article 2:

> As Dyson has stated on a number of occasions ... the application does not seek to obtain registration of a trade mark in one or more particular shapes of transparent collecting bin—the shapes represented graphically on the application form being only examples of such a bin—but rather to obtain registration of a trade mark in the bin itself. It is, moreover, common ground that those marks consist not of a particular colour, but rather in the absence of any particular colour, namely transparency, which enables the consumer to see how much dust has been collected in the collecting bin and to know when the bin is full.[52]

The Court should not be precluded from providing the national court with all the elements   **4.55**
for the interpretation of Community law that might contribute to the adjudication of the case pending before it.[53]

(ii) **The 'sign' requirement** The Court repeated that the Article 2 list was purely indica-   **4.56**
tive. However, 'if that condition is not to be deprived of all substance, it cannot be accepted that the subject-matter of any trade mark application necessarily constitutes a sign'.[54] The

---

[50] Point 102.
[51] Point 106.
[52] *Dyson* (n 1) paragraph 19.
[53] Citing C-387/01 *Weigel* [2004] ECR I-4981 and C-152/03 *Ritter-Coulais* [2006] ECR I-1711.
[54] *Dyson* (n 1) paragraph 33.

purpose of the requirement was in particular to prevent the abuse of trade mark law in order to obtain an unfair competitive advantage.

4.57 In this case, the subject matter of the application consisted of all the conceivable shapes of a collecting bin. Accordingly, it was not capable of being perceived visually; the two representations were, as accepted by Dyson, examples of the subject matter rather than specific signs. The Court considered relevant for the interpretation of Article 2 the multitude of different appearances the subject matter could take rather than its inability to be visually perceived. The Court noted that the purpose of Article 2 was, in particular, to prevent the abuse of trade mark law in order to obtain an unfair competitive advantage.

4.58 Turning to the facts of the case it stressed that the subject matter of the application in the main proceedings was not a particular type of transparent collecting bin but, in a general and abstract manner, all its conceivable shapes.

4.59 The two graphic representations could not be assimilated to the subject matter of the application because 'they are merely examples of it'.[55] The subject matter of the application 'is capable of taking on a multitude of different appearances and is thus not specific'.[56]

4.60 What could make the subject matter specific—ie its shape, dimensions, presentation, and composition—depended on the models developed by Dyson and technological innovations. Transparency on the other hand meant that a variety of colours could be used. An exclusive right over such non-specific subject matter would give an unfair competitive advantage to its owner, who would be entitled to prevent competitors from marketing vacuum cleaners incorporating any kind of transparent bin on their external surface.

4.61 The Court concluded that Article 2

> is to be interpreted as meaning that the subject-matter of an application for trade mark registration, such as that lodged in the main proceedings, which relates to all the conceivable shapes of a transparent bin or collection chamber forming part of the external surface of a vacuum cleaner, is not a 'sign' within the meaning of that provision and therefore is not capable of constituting a trade mark within the meaning thereof.[57]

4.62 Despite the Court's extensive discussion of the concept of the sign and its contextualization against a functionality background, the final outcome of *Dyson* is a negative description of what does not constitute a sign based on the very specific facts of the case.

(4) *Apple*: The Apple Store as Registrable Dress

(a) The facts in the main proceedings and the order for reference

4.63 In *Apple*[58] the Court explored whether the representation of the layout of a retail store by means of a design could be registered as a trade mark for 'services' connected with the products on sale in that outlet, within the meaning of Articles 2 and 3 of the Directive. The request was made in proceedings between Apple Inc. (Apple) and the Deutsches Patent- und Markenamt (German Patent and Trade Mark Office, DPMA) concerning the rejection of an application for registration of Apple's trade mark. Apple had obtained in the

---

[55] Paragraph 36.
[56] Paragraph 37.
[57] Paragraph 40.
[58] C-421/13, *Apple Inc./Deutsches Patent- und Markenamt* (APPLE), ECLI:EU:C:2014:2070.

United States the registration of a 'three-dimensional trade mark', consisting of the representation of its flagship stores, in respect of the following services in Class 35 of the Nice Agreement: 'retail store services featuring computers, computer software, computer peripherals, mobile phones, consumer electronics and related accessories and demonstrations of products relating thereto'. That representation was described by Apple as 'the distinctive design and layout of a retail store'.

4.64 Apple sought to extend this trade mark internationally under the Madrid Agreement. This was accepted in some states, like Spain, Italy, and Poland, and refused in others. The DPMA refused the extension to Germany on the ground that the depiction of the space devoted to the sale of the undertaking's products was nothing other than the representation of an essential aspect of that undertaking's business, with the result that consumers would see it not as an indication of commercial origin, but at best as an indication of the quality and price bracket of the products so sold, in particular since the store depicted in the application was not sufficiently distinguishable from the stores of other providers of electronic products.

4.65 Apple appealed to the Bundespatentgericht, which took the view that, contrary to the findings of the DPMA, the layout in question had features that distinguished it from the usual layout of retail stores in the electronic sector. In view, however, of the importance of the questions at stake, the Bundespatentgericht decided to stay the proceedings and to refer the following questions to the Court:

(1) Is Article 2 of the Directive to be interpreted as meaning that the possibility of protection for the 'packaging of goods' also extends to the presentation of the establishment in which a service is provided?
(2) Are Articles 2 and 3(1) of the Directive to be interpreted as meaning that a sign representing the presentation of the establishment in which a service is provided is capable of being registered as a trade mark?
(3) Is Article 2 of the Directive to be interpreted as meaning that the requirement for graphic representability is satisfied by a representation of a design alone or with such additions as a description of the layout or indications of the absolute dimensions in metres or of relative dimensions with indications as to proportions?
(4) Is Article 2 of the Directive to be interpreted as meaning that the scale of the protection afforded by a trade mark for retail services also extends to the goods produced by the retailer itself?

(b) The judgment of the court

4.66 As a preliminary matter, the Court clarified that the expression 'presentation of the establishment in which a service is provided' in the first and second questions, essentially refers to the registration of a sign consisting of the depiction of a retail store for services offered in that store. Accordingly, it understood the first three questions as asking whether the representation, by a design alone, of the layout of a retail store may be registered as a trade mark for services aimed at inducing the consumer to purchase the products of the applicant for registration and, if so, whether such a presentation may be treated, for the purposes of trade mark law, in the same way as 'packaging'.[59]

4.67 In that connection, the Court observed that it was obvious from the inclusion of designs among the categories of signs capable of graphic representation that a depiction such as the

---

[59] Paragraphs 15–16.

one at issue in the main proceedings satisfies the first two conditions laid down in Article 2 of the Directive, namely that the subject matter of any application for registration must be a sign and that that sign must be capable of graphic representation. Hence, a representation which depicts the layout of a retail store by means of an integral collection of lines, curves, and shapes may constitute a trade mark, without it being necessary either to attribute any relevance to the fact that the design does not contain any indication as to the size and proportions of the retail store that it depicts, or to examine whether such a design could be treated in the same way as 'packaging'.[60]

4.68 The Court also held[61] that such a representation is also capable of distinguishing the products or services of one undertaking from those of other undertakings and, hence, of satisfying the third condition laid down in Article 2 of the Directive, since it cannot be ruled out that the layout of a retail outlet may allow the products or the services for which registration is sought to be identified as originating from a particular undertaking, as could be, for instance, the case when the depicted layout departs significantly from the norm or customs of the economic sector concerned.[62]

4.69 However, the Court recalled that the fact that a sign is, in general, capable of constituting a trade mark within the meaning of Article 2 of the Directive, does not mean that it necessarily has a distinctive character for the purposes of Article 3(1)(b) in respect of the products or services for which registration is sought, or that it may not be descriptive of the characteristics of those goods or services within the meaning of Article 3(1)(c) of the Directive; whether or not this is the case must be assessed *in concreto* by reference to the goods or services in question and the perception of the relevant public, bearing always in mind that the assessment criteria to be employed in relation to designs depicting the layout of a retail store do not differ from those used for other types of sign.[63]

4.70 Finally, as regards the question whether services intended to induce the consumer to purchase the products of the applicant themselves can constitute 'services' within the meaning of Article 2 of the Directive, the Court held that a sign depicting the layout of the flagship stores of a goods manufacturer may legitimately be registered, not only for the goods themselves but also for services falling within one of the Nice classes covering services, where those services do not form an integral part of the offer for sale of those goods, noting in that regard that, at least the services that relate to 'demonstrations by means of seminars' of the products displayed in the same store, can themselves constitute remunerated services falling within the concept of 'services'.[64]

4.71 On those grounds, and after dismissing the fourth question as inadmissible due to the fact that it bore no ostensible relation to the subject matter of the main proceedings, the Court ruled that Articles 2 and 3 of the Directive must be interpreted as meaning that the representation, by a design alone, without indicating the size or the proportions, of the layout of a retail store, may be registered as a trade mark for services consisting in services relating

---

[60] Paragraphs 17–19.
[61] Paragraph 20.
[62] Applying by analogy C-25/05 P *Storck v OHIM*, ECLI:EU:C:2006:422 and C-97/12 P *Vuitton Malletier v OHIM*, ECLI:EU:C:2014:324.
[63] Paragraphs 21–24.
[64] Paragraphs 25–26.

to those goods but which do not form an integral part of the offer for sale thereof, provided that the sign is capable of distinguishing the services of the applicant for registration from those of other undertakings and that registration is not precluded by any of the grounds for refusal set out in that Directive.

(c) Conclusions

4.72 Although the ruling in *Apple* is not groundbreaking as regards the interpretation of Article 2 of the Directive (indeed there is nothing novel in the finding that a design consisting of the layout of a retail outlet can function as an indication of commercial origin), it is nevertheless important in economic terms as it paves the way for protecting as a trade mark in the European Union, where the circumstances so permit, a retailer's trade dress, with the caveat that, in this context, trade dress should be understood in the narrow sense, ie as being limited to elements that can be represented graphically and not as including variable or dynamic elements concerning the way business is run, like, for instance, the way attendants act or behave.

4.73 Still, there are a couple of secondary points in the judgment that are not entirely clear and call for a more detailed comment.

4.74 First, the position of the Court as regards the possible analogy between the layout of a retail outlet and 'product packaging' is somewhat ambiguous and confusing. On the one hand, the Court considered that such an analogy was not appropriate in the context of Article 2 of the Directive, since the equation with a 'design' rendered the reference to 'packaging' unnecessary. On the other hand, when it comes to the distinctive capacity of such signs, the Court referred to the criteria traditionally used in respect of 'shape marks' by holding that the layout of a retail outlet may allow the products or the services for which registration is sought to be identified as originating from a particular undertaking when the depicted layout departs significantly from the norm or customs of the economic sector concerned. Thus, although the Court seems to be negating the direct analogy between signs consisting of the external appearance of a retail store and signs consisting of the external appearance of the goods or their packaging, *de facto* it applied the same criteria to both insofar as concerns the assessment of their distinctiveness. Moreover, according to the Court's case law with regard to Article 3(1)(b) of the Directive, the capacity of shape marks to distinguish, provided they depart from the established norms of the sector, is based on the assumption that although the criteria to be applied in the assessment of distinctiveness are the same for all types of marks, the perception of the public may differ for certain kinds of signs. This last part, however, was not repeated in the Court's judgment in relation to signs consisting of the layout of a retail store, not even in the discussion of Article 3(1)(b), although that point was precisely the reason that had led the DPMA to refuse the mark in the first place. Was this a conscious choice of the Court, implying that signs consisting of the layout of a retail store are a 'special case' of shape marks, or was it just an omission of the obvious, in the sense that once the analogy is established, however indirectly, it must work all the way through? The latter interpretation would indeed seem more sensible, as there is no overriding legal or economic consideration for treating the two cases differently.

4.75 Secondly, the Court remained again very cautious when it comes to the question of whether the concept of 'services' extends to the retailing of the applicant's own goods. As in *Netto*, the Court refrained from taking a clear position, merely stating that services intended to induce the consumer to purchase the products of the applicant are acceptable where they 'do not form an integral part of the offer for sale of [the applicant's] goods' and that, in any event, at least 'the services in the application that relate to demonstrations by means of seminars of the products displayed in the same store, can themselves constitute remunerated services'. The relevance of seminars came up at the hearing and infiltrated the Court's judgment, although, at least from a classification point of view, such an extension does not seem justified, considering that, strictly speaking, the 'provision of seminars' would fall within Class 41 of the Nice Classification, as a specific form of training, and not within Class 35. However, if the services relating to seminars are excluded for that reason, the question regarding the acceptability of the rest of the services remains open and could affect the registrability of the sign as a whole, in particular since it is doubtful whether the mere 'demonstration' of products can be regarded as not forming part of their sale. Moreover, the reference of the Court to 'remunerated services' only in relation to seminars, raises the question of whether the 'services that do not form an integral part of the offer for sale of the goods' must also be offered for a remuneration, whether direct or indirect, a point that the Court seems to have left unanswered.

D. Capable of Being Represented Graphically

4.76 The first requirement that a sign has to satisfy is to be capable of being represented graphically. The Court has considered the conditions for satisfying this requirement in cases involving both visual and non-visual signs.

(1) *Sieckmann*: The Purpose of Graphical Representation; Non-visual Signs; Scents; the General Conditions

4.77 The Court took four interpretive steps. First, it described the underlying reasoning and the function of the graphical representation requirement; second, it unequivocally accepted that non-visual signs could be represented graphically; third, it looked at ways for representing scents; and, fourth, in doing so, it came up with the general conditions that had to be satisfied in order to fulfil the requirement.

4.78 *Sieckmann*[65] was a reference by the German Federal Patents Court (Bundespatentgericht). Sieckmann, a trade mark practitioner, had applied to register a scent as a trade mark for services in Classes 35, 41, and 42, including 'legal services', 'advertising', 'education', 'entertainment and sporting and cultural activities', 'providing of food and drink', 'medical, hygienic and beauty care', and 'veterinary and agricultural services'.

4.79 The sign was described in a number of ways:

> the pure chemical substance methyl cinnamate (= cinnamic acid methyl ester), whose structural formula is set out below. Samples of this olfactory mark can also be obtained via local laboratories listed in the Gelbe Seiten (Yellow Pages) of Deutsche Telekom AG or, for example, via the firm E. Merck in Darmstadt.
> A chemical formula:
>
> '$C_6H_5 - CH = CHCOOCH_3$'.[66]

---

[65] C-273/00 *Sieckmann* [2002] ECR I-11737.
[66] Reproduced in paragraph 11.

A verbal description of the scent as 'balsamically fruity with a slight hint of cinnamon' **4.80** had been added to the application and a container with a sample of the scent had also been attached. A declaration of consent to an inspection of the files relating to the deposited mark had also been filed together with the application.

The application was originally rejected because the sign: (i) was not capable of constituting **4.81** a trade mark and of being represented graphically; and (ii) lacked distinctive character. On appeal the Bundespatentgericht took a more liberal approach and held that, in principle, scents might be capable of distinguishing but referred to the Court of Justice two questions regarding graphical representation.

First, it enquired whether the graphical representation requirement of Article 2 of the **4.82** Directive allowed the registration only of signs that could be reproduced directly in their visible form rather than signs, like odours, that could not be perceived visually per se but could be reproduced indirectly.

Second, in case the more liberal approach were to be followed by the Court, whether the **4.83** same requirement would be satisfied: (a) by a chemical formula; (b) by a description; (c) by means of a deposit; or (d) by a combination of the above-mentioned reproductions.

(a) The Opinion of the Advocate General

Advocate General Ruiz-Jarabo Colomer viewed the two questions as a plea to clarify the **4.84** concept of a 'sign capable of being represented graphically', in particular the possibility and the conditions for registering an odour as a trade mark. He started with a review of the functions of a trade mark from a wider than purely legal perspective, linking capability to distinguish with consumer's freedom to choose and effective competition.[67] From a consumer's perspective, this meant identifying goods and services according to origin and quality.[68]

(i) Trade marks: Fiats of communication   Trade marks were communicators: **4.85**

> The matter is thus one of establishment of a dialogue between manufacturer and consumer ... A trade mark is in reality communication. Communication means one person imparting something that he knows to another. Consequently, every act of communication requires a sender, a message, a medium or channel for its transmission, and a recipient who can decipher or decode it. The code in which it can be expressed depends on the type of decoder the recipient uses to receive, comprehend and assimilate it ... perception of signs by consumers can be as varied as the senses at their disposal.[69]

---

[67] Citing C-10/89 *SA CNL-SUCAL NV v Hag GF AG* [1990] ECR I-3711 and C-517/99 *Merz and Krell GmbH & Co v Deutches Patent-und Markenamt* [2001] ECR I-6959 as precedents on the function of a trade mark.

[68] He cited the Opinion of AG Cosmas in Joined Cases C-108/97 and C109/97 *Windsurfing Chiemsee Produktions- und Vertriebs GmbH v Boots- und Segelzubehör Walter Huber and Franz Attenberger* [1999] ECR I-2779 and, in more general terms, Fernández Novoa, *Fundamentos de Derecho de Marcas* (Editorial Montecorvo, 1984) pp 46–49 and Baylos Corroza, *Tratado de derecho industrial*, 2nd edn (Editorial Civitas, 1993) p 817, who linked the distinguishing function with the origin function by supporting that the aim is not to identify a product with one undertaking in particular, but to indicate that all products bearing the same trade mark originate from the same manufacturer, regardless of that manufacturer's identity.

[69] Points 19, 20, and 21. He referred, amongst others, to Maniatis, 'Scents as Trademarks: Propertisation of Scents and Olfactory Poverty' in Bently and Flynn (eds), *Law and the Senses–Sensational Jurisprudence* (Pluto Press, 1996) pp 217–35 and Polasso, 'La Comunicación Inteligente in Humaniora', website of the Faculty of Arts at the University of Göteborg (<http://www.hum.gu.se>), p 61 and following on to how humans communicate and the communicative value of trade marks.

4.86 (ii) **The viewpoint of the individual sensing the sign** Any message capable of perception by the senses could function as a trade mark.[70] However, because taste and touch were inextricably linked with the article they referred to and could not be perceived independently, Advocate General Ruiz-Jarabo Colomer limited the signs that prima facie could function as trade marks to those that can be perceived independently and spatially: visual, auditory, and olfactory signs.[71] He suggested that tactile, visual, and auditory signs were easier to comprehend because they related to the concept of shape and form, whereas taste and olfactory signs lacked precise rules for determining their content.[72]

4.87 He warned against sweeping generalizations because, at the end of the day, the description of all signs depended on the perception of the individual sensing them. He hinted, for example, that, because of their numerous variations, both colours and scents would pose similar problems.

4.88 (iii) **Visual and olfactory signs** The difference between visual and olfactory signs was that whereas 'the eye sees not just colours, but also shapes, the sense of smell only permits perception of the colour of an odour and never its outline. The sense of sight operates over a wider range and therefore has a wider range of perception'.[73] Still, there was no doubt that the sense of smell could fulfil an identification function.[74] The obstacle that a scent could not overcome was the graphical representation requirement of Article 2.

4.89 (iv) **Legal certainty: The reasoning underlying the graphical representation requirement** The public register had to depict the 'nature and scope of the signs ... the symbols so claimed must be known very precisely so that other people may be properly guided. For reasons of legal certainty, the requirement of graphical representation is thus linked with the identification function, the primary and essential function of trade marks',[75] that also justified the exclusive nature of the right.

---

[70] Through a reference to Goethe's Preface for his *Theory of Colours* (republished by MIT Press, 1970) the AG describes the interplay between our senses and the variety of ways that we can perceive nature.

[71] Perot-Morel, 'Les Difficultés Relatives aux Marques de Forme et à quelques Types Particuliers de Marques dans le Cadre Communautaire', *Rivista di Diritto Industriale*, Year XLV (1996) Part 1, 247, had made that distinction.

[72] Referring to Laligant, 'Des Oeuvres aux Marches du Droit d'Auteur: les Oeuvres de l'Esprit Perceptibles par l'Odorat, le Goût et le Toucher', *Revue de Recherche Juridique, Droit Prospectif* [1992] No 1.

[73] Point 28, referring to 'Diderot's Notes on Painting' in *Diderot on Art–1* (Yale University Press, 1995) at p 196.

[74] Advocate General Ruiz-Jarabo Colomer mentioned Baudelaire's poem *Le Parfum* (from *Les Fleurs du Mal* (Ed Gallimard, La Pléiade, 1971)) p 39, the sensory triggers behind Proust's *À la Recherche du Temps Perdu*, Bloom (ed, *Remembrance of Things Past* (Chelsea House Publishers, 1987), and, in particular, the scent of madeleines (Doubrousky, *La Place de la Madeleine: Écriture et fantasme chez Proust* (Mercure de France, 1974)) or the scent of public toilets in the Champs-Élysées (Beckett, *Proust* (Nostromo, 1975)). From a more practical legal perspective the Advocate General mentioned the 'plumeria blossom' and registration for sewing thread and embroidery yarn granted in the United States (see *In Re Clarke*, 17 USPQ 2d 1238 (TTAB 1990)), the one-off registration of the smell of freshly-cut grass as a Community trade mark (see Case R156/199862 *Venootschap onder Firma Senta Aromatic Marketing's Application* [1999] ETMR 429), the change in the position of the United Kingdom's Patent and Trade Mark Office that had registered scents for car tyres and dart flights but rejected the scent of cinnamon for furniture (*John Lewis of Hungerford Ltd's Trade Mark Application* [2001] RPC 28), the more permissive approach of the Benelux Trade Mark Registry that allowed the registration of scents for cosmetic products, and the possibility of protecting a fragrance under copyright in France (see *L'Oréal SA v Bellure NV* [2006] ECDR 16 C d'A (Paris)).

[75] Point 36.

(v) The conditions for fulfilling the graphical representation requirement The concept of 'graphical representation' required drawing the sign on paper 'in a comprehensible manner, since comprehension is a precondition of discernment'.[76] It must be 'complete, clear and precise ... and intelligible to those persons having an interest in inspecting the register, in other words other manufacturers and consumers'.[77] Alas, a scent could not be drawn on paper. **4.90**

(vi) Representing a scent Examining the alternatives indicated in the reference he noted that the chemical formula represented the substance itself rather than the odour of the substance. In addition, it lacked clarity and precision and it would be intelligible by very few individuals. Finally, according to concentration, the ambient temperature, or the substance bearing the odour, the same substance could emit different scents according to the circumstances. **4.91**

Describing the sign in written language would fail the requirements of clarity and precision. The description of scents was subjective and therefore relative.[78] The terms 'balsamically' and 'fruity' exemplified this. A longer, more detailed description would face similar problems. Language on its own was unable to objectively describe a scent. **4.92**

Depositing did not constitute a graphical representation; and in any case the scent of the sample would change with time. **4.93**

The combination of all these ways would only create more uncertainty. However, he refrained from excluding scents as such. 'It is not necessary expressly to exclude certain signs from legal provisions regarding trade marks. They exclude themselves, because they are unable to comply with the requirements of trade mark law.'[79] **4.94**

(b) The judgment of the Court

(i) The context of Article 2 The Court started its analysis from Article 2; according to the Tenth Recital 'the function of the protection afforded by a trade mark is in particular to guarantee the mark as an indication of origin'.[80] The essential function of a trade mark was to guarantee the identity of the origin of the marked product; the trade mark should offer a guarantee that all the goods or services bearing it had been manufactured or supplied under the control of a single undertaking which was responsible for their quality.[81] **4.95**

Registration was the key of trade mark protection. 'The registration system constitutes an essential element of their protection, which contributes, in respect of both Community law and the different national laws, to legal certainty and sound administration.'[82] **4.96**

---

[76] Point 37. Distinctive character and graphical representability shared a common purpose: enabling the products on the market to be selected by potential buyers on the basis of their origin. The graphical representation of distinctive signs had to be such as to allow users of the register to distinguish between the protected signs.
[77] Point 38.
[78] For example, the same wine was described in different ways: fn 56 of the Opinion.
[79] Point 45.
[80] C-273/00 *Sieckmann* [2002] ECR I-11737, paragraph 34.
[81] Citing C-349/95 *Frits Loendersloot v George Ballantine & Son* [1997] ECR I-6227, C-39/97 *Canon Kabushiki Kaisha v Metro-Goldwyn-Mayer Inc.* [1998] ECR I-5507, and C-299/99 *Koninklijke Philips Electronics NV v Remington Consumer Products Ltd* [2002] ECR I-5475.
[82] Paragraph 37.

4.97 **(ii) Article 2: Non-visual signs** Within this context the Court had to consider whether Article 2 covered signs not capable of being perceived visually. It was clear from the language of Article 2 and the Seventh Recital that the list was not exhaustive and did not exclude non-visual signs. A trade mark 'may consist of a sign which is not in itself capable of being perceived visually, provided that it can be represented graphically'.[83]

4.98 **(iii) The underlying reasons and the conditions for the graphical representation requirement** The main requirement the Court set for graphical representation was that it had to enable the sign to be represented visually, particularly by means of images, lines, or characters, so that it could be precisely identified. The Court gave a number of reasons, establishing the eight conditions a graphical representation has to satisfy.

4.99 *Clear and Precise.* The first two were clarity and precision. Graphic representation defined the mark in order to determine the precise subject of protection and its inclusion in a public register informed the competent authorities—that had to fulfil obligations regarding examination, publication, and maintenance of a register—and the public, particularly economic operators, that should be able to locate information about the rights of their competitors.

4.100 *Self Contained, Accessible, and Intelligible.* The second set, that the graphical representation had to be self-contained, easily accessible, and intelligible, aimed to enable users of the register determine the precise nature of a mark on the basis of its registration.

4.101 *Durable.* Durability, the sixth condition, was linked with the indication of origin function of a trade mark. Trade marks rights were potentially perpetual and the signs that constitute them must always be perceived unambiguously and in the same way.

4.102 *Unequivocal and Objective.* The last two were that graphical representation had to be unequivocal and objective; they intended to avoid any element of subjectivity in the process of identification and perception of the sign.

4.103 **(iv) Representing olfactory scents** The chemical formula was rejected by the Court because, first, it would not be sufficiently intelligible, second, it represented the substance itself rather than its odour, and, third, because it was not sufficiently clear and precise.

4.104 Note that the second ground appears to be essentially new; perhaps an indication of how the Court would deal with the question of what constitutes a sign.

4.105 The description of the odour was graphic, but lacked in clarity, precision, and objectivity. The deposit of the sample did not constitute a graphic representation and was not sufficiently stable—again something not directly mentioned in the general framework—or durable. The combination of the above would fail to satisfy the requirements set by the Court, in particular the conditions of clarity and precision.[84]

---

[83] Paragraph 45.
[84] In T-305/04 *Eden SARL v Office for Harmonisation in the Internal Market (Trade Marks and Designs)* [2006] ETMR 14, Celex No 604A0305 the Court of First Instance considered the 'smell of ripe strawberries'. Combining a description with a photograph was not sufficient.

> The image represented only the fruit which emitted the smell of strawberries, not the smell itself. Furthermore, contrary to what the applicant claims, the image adds no additional information in relation to the description in words. The information purportedly added, that is, the state of ripeness in which a strawberry emits the smell in question, is already contained in the description given, since that description states that it is the smell of 'ripe' strawberries. Thus, since the two

(2) *Shield Mark*: Graphical Representation of Sounds; General Policy Considerations

4.106 The next type of signs was sounds. The Court followed the *Sieckmann* conditions; however, wider policy considerations, like the scope of protection, the expansion of protectable types of signs, or the relation between trade mark and copyright law, are gaining relevance when applying the graphical representation requirement. Shield Mark[85] was a reference from the Hoge Raad (Supreme Court of the Netherlands). Shield Mark was the owner of a number of trade marks registered in the Benelux consisting of sounds; the specifications varied from, amongst others, computer software to business management, education, training, and legal services.

4.107 A number of marks consisted of the first nine notes of Beethoven's *Für Elise*,[86] represented in a variety of ways: a musical stave with the notes; the words 'the first nine notes of Für Elise'; the sequence of musical notes. Some were accompanied by explanatory notes indicating a sound mark, and the medium—a piano—on which the melody would be played.

4.108 Two trade marks consisted of the denomination Kukelekuuuuu, with one of them indicating that the sign constituted an onomatopoeia suggesting, in Dutch, a cockcrow.

4.109 Another registration consisted of a cockcrow with the explanatory statement: 'Sound mark, the trade mark consists of the cockcrow as described'.

4.110 The *Für Elise* signs were used in Shield Mark's advertising; the cockcrow was incorporated as a sound in software marketed by Shield Mark. Shield Mark started trade mark infringement and unfair competition proceedings against Kist, a communications consultant involved with the organization of intellectual property seminars and publishing, who used in his advertising a melody consisting of the first nine notes of *Für Elise* and sold a computer program which emitted a cockcrow when starting up.

4.111 The case reached on appeal the Hoge Raad, which referred the following questions to the Court for a preliminary ruling:

1. (a) Must Article 2 of the Directive be interpreted as precluding sounds or noises from being regarded as trade marks? (b) If the answer to question 1(a) is in the negative, does the system established by the Directive require that sounds or noises must be capable of being regarded as trade marks?
2. (a) If the answer to question 1(a) is in the negative, what requirements does the Directive lay down for sound marks as regards the reference in Article 2 to the need for the sign to be capable of being represented graphically and, in conjunction therewith, as regards the way in which the registration of such a trade mark must take place? (b) In particular, are the requirements referred to in (a) satisfied if the sound or the noise is registered in one of the following forms: musical notes; a written description in the form of an onomatopoeia; a written description in some other form; a graphical representation such as a sonogram; a sound recording annexed to the registration form; a digital recording accessible via the internet; a combination of those methods; some other form and, if so, which?[87]

---

elements in the representation convey the same information, their combination cannot amount to more than the sum of the two parts and cannot overcome the criticisms raised against each of them individually (paragraph 46).

[85] C-283/01 *Shield Mark BV v Kist* [2003] ECR I-14313.
[86] Originally composed to be played by a child, as the AG indicated in his Opinion citing Kinderman, *Beethoven* (Oxford University Press, 1995) p 146.
[87] Reproduced in paragraph 25.

(a) The Opinion of Advocate General Ruiz-Jarabo Colomer

4.112 Advocate General Ruiz-Jarabo Colomer linked the case with *Sieckmann*[88] and *Libertel*[89]—
—that was then still pending—and started by answering the question whether sounds functioned as trade marks.

4.113 (i) **Limiting the scope of the reference** Expressing his dislike of speculative doctrinal references he stated:

> The ... request that, irrespective of the facts of the case and in the abstract, the Court of Justice should rule on different forms of representation of a sound ignores the nature of the judicial process, the purpose of which is to provide an answer which will be useful to the determination of the dispute. Furthermore, the very nature of that procedure and the absence of expert evidence would make it difficult to rule on questions of a highly technical content.[90] Accordingly the Court should not deal with sonograms, spectrograms, and sound and digital recordings that were outside the factual scenario of the case before the Hoge Raad.

4.114 (ii) **Sounds as trade marks** Sounds were perceived by our senses, could communicate messages, and possessed the capacity to distinguish.[91] In principle, auditory messages could constitute trade marks, although not specifically mentioned in the Directive.[92] Indeed, a number of Member States specifically listed sounds as signs that might serve as trade marks.[93]

> In so far as the Directive has not precluded sounds, no Member State can prevent a message of that type from being registered as a trade mark, on the clear understanding that it satisfies the mandatory requirements: capacity to distinguish and capability of being represented graphically.[94]

4.115 (iii) **The importance of precision** Precision was the key issue in the graphical representation requirement, linking the subject of protection with the scope of protection: 'If an undertaking reserves certain signs and references for itself in order to distinguish its goods and services from those of other undertakings, the symbols so claimed must be known very precisely.'[95]

4.116 (iv) **Graphical representation of sounds** Following *Sieckmann*, with some hesitation,[96] he found that sounds could be represented graphically. Given the link between written and oral communications, he believed that in the abstract, the capacity of sounds to be

---

[88] C-273/00 *Sieckmann* [2002] ECR I-11737.
[89] C-104/01 *Libertel Groep BV v Benelux-Merkenbureau* [2003] ECR I-3793.
[90] Point 34.
[91] Citing Proust and Schopenhauer, he discussed music's ability to identify as a result of its evocative intensity, converting sounds into a specific language or interpreting the intimate essence of things: Proust, *À la Recherche du Temps Perdu, La Prisonniere* (Ed Gallimard, La Pleiade, 1988) Vol III, at 762–63 and Schopenhauer, *Le Monde Comme Volonte et Comme Representation* translated by Burdeau (1888), revised and corrected by Roos (Ed Presses universitaires de France, 1966) at 340.
[92] He noted, though, that words in essence are sounds capable of being represented graphically. Indicatively, he referred to the Spanish, French, English, and German definitions of 'word' as a combination of sounds that is expressive of an idea.
[93] Germany, Austria, Spain, France, Greece, Italy, and Portugal.
[94] Point 21.
[95] Point 26; reiterating the point expressed in Case C-273/00 *Sieckmann v Deutsches Patent- und Markenamt* [2002] ECR I-11737.
[96] Point 32, where he characterized his answer as more nuanced than the negative one he delivered in *Sieckmann*, definitely not a categorically positive response.

reproduced in writing was undeniable. He stressed that the adequacy of the representation in each actual case was an issue that the national courts had to determine.

Musical notation formed part of the case and the Advocate General found it an acceptable way for representing a sound provided that the notes were set on a musical stave. This would ensure that the sound of the notes: **4.117**

> are perfectly recognisable and leave no room for doubt … With that universal language, the diffused drawing consisting of the sequence of notes, called by name, seems to be clear, with its precise contours to identify it, differentiating it from others. The notes written on the stave, together with the key, which determines the tonality, the time signature, which determines the rhythm, and the relative value of each note, and also an indication of the instruments which are to interpret them, are a faithful photograph of the sequence of sounds which are represented; if I may say so, they are their fingerprint.[97]

He accepted that the majority of those viewing musical notation would be unable to decipher it; still he stressed that once the score is read by an expert, the uninformed would be enabled to understand the sign without confusing its identity. **4.118**

Other ways of describing sounds, including onomatopoeia and reference to the title of the composition, appeared vague and lacking in clarity and precision, in particular in a trade mark system based on registration.[98] Normally they would be insufficient, but this was a matter to be determined on a case-by-case basis. **4.119**

(v) **Wider policy considerations** Advocate General Ruiz-Jarabo Colomer perceived 'monopolization' of the sign as a significant factor in the interpretation of trade mark law, noting that 'particular care must also be exercised when a person is granted the exclusive use on the market of a sign, whatever sense it is perceived by'.[99] The public interest that certain signs should be left free to be used by other traders covered natural indications and signs that were a direct manifestation of nature[100] but also creations of the mind that had become part of the universal cultural heritage. He did not accept that such signs 'should be appropriated indefinitely by a person to be used on the market in order to distinguish the goods he produces or the services he provides with an exclusivity which not even its author's estate enjoys'.[101] **4.120**

(vi) **Trade mark rights and copyright** The last point—the juxtaposition between copyright and trade mark rights—led the Advocate General to remark that when a sign constituted a trade mark and at the same time is an original work protected by copyright, then it was necessary to regulate their reciprocal interrelations.[102] **4.121**

(b) The judgment of the Court

(i) **Limiting the scope of the reference** Before responding to the second question the Court considered its own jurisdiction. Citing *Bosman*,[103] it accepted that where the **4.122**

---

[97] Point 39.
[98] Citing Tarzan's cry as an example of a sign that had acquired distinctiveness through use in the US.
[99] Point 50 of the Opinion of AG Ruiz-Jarabo Colomer.
[100] Citing point 19 and following of his Opinion in Joined Cases C-53 to C-55/01 *Linde AG* (C-53/01), *Winward Industries Inc.* (C-54/01) and *Rado Uhren AG* (C-55/01) [2003] ECR I-3161.
[101] Point 52.
[102] Citing Bercovitz, *Marcas y Derecho de Autor*, (Revista de Derecho Mercantil, 2001) Nos 240, 405–19.
[103] C-415/93 *Union Royale Belge des Societes de Football Association ASBL v Jean-Marc Bosman* [1995] ECR I-4921.

questions submitted by the national court concerned the interpretation of Community law, the Court was, in principle, bound to give a ruling. However, the Court could examine the conditions in which the case was referred to it, because the

> spirit of co-operation which must prevail in the preliminary-ruling procedure requires the national court, for its part, to have regard to the function entrusted to the Court of Justice, which is to assist in the administration of justice in the Member States and not to deliver advisory opinions on general or hypothetical questions,[104]

and refuse to consider hypothetical problems.[105] Representations in the form of a sonogram, a sound recording, a digital recording, or a combination of those methods were not relevant in this case and would not be examined by the Court.

4.123 (ii) **Sounds as trade marks** The first issue was whether sounds constituted signs. The Court repeated that the list in Article 2 was not exhaustive and did not exclude non-visual signs. Further, sound signs were not 'by nature incapable of distinguishing'.[106] Accordingly, sounds could constitute a trade mark and Member States could not preclude their registration as a matter of principle.

4.124 (iii) **Sounds—the general framework** The Court repeated its interpretation of Article 2 in *Sieckmann* and ruled that the same conditions were 'also binding on sound signs, which, like olfactory signs, are not in themselves capable of visual perception'.[107] National courts would have to apply the conditions and determine registrability on a case-by-case basis.

4.125 The Court of Justice felt that in this case it could provide guidance regarding the relevant types of representation, albeit in a prescriptive manner.

4.126 (iv) **The application must indicate the type of sign** First, the Court required emphatically that the application had to indicate that the sign was a sound sign. Otherwise, the sign would have to be examined as a word or figurative mark.

4.127 (v) **Ways for representing sounds** Second, although the Court would not preclude the possibility that the representation of a sound sign by a description in written language might satisfy the *Sieckmann* conditions, it held that a graphical representation such as the first nine notes of *Für Elise* or the word 'cockcrow' lacked precision and clarity.

4.128 Third, it found a lack of consistency between the onomatopoeia itself, as pronounced, and the actual signified sound. So, it would remain questionable whether the registration covered the pronunciation of the onomatopoeia itself or the signified sound. Further, it could be perceived differently by different individuals or in different Member States. The national variations in the onomatopoeia of a cockcrow were indeed a good example.

4.129 Fourth, a sequence of notes without more detail would be neither clear, nor precise, nor self-contained.

4.130 However, a stave divided into bars and showing, in particular, a clef, musical notes, and rests whose form indicates the relative value and, where appropriate, accidentals might constitute a faithful representation of the sequence of sounds forming the relevant melody. The Court accepted that such a representation would not be immediately intelligible; still, it

---

[104] *Shield Mark* (n 85) paragraph 52.
[105] C-111/01 *Gantner Electronic GmbH v Basch Exploitatie Maatschappy BV* [2003] ECR I-4207.
[106] Paragraph 36.
[107] Paragraph 56.

found that it could become 'easily intelligible'[108] allowing traders, in particular, to identify the sound sign with precision.

(3) *Libertel*: Colour Samples; Public Policy Considerations

4.131 *Libertel*[109] considered colours and because it involved questions on distinctiveness as well as graphical representation, public policy considerations found their way into the discussion of the graphical representation requirements almost by osmosis. The case was a reference by the Hoge Raad (Supreme Court of the Netherlands). Libertel, a telecommunications company, had applied to register as a trade mark for telecommunications goods and services in the Benelux a shade of orange. On the application form the mark was described as 'orange', without a reference to the usual colour coding systems, and reproduced by an orange rectangle.

4.132 The application was rejected as devoid of distinctive character. On appeal, the Hoge Raad referred the following questions to the Court for a preliminary ruling:

(1) Is it possible for a single specific colour which is represented as such or is designated by an internationally applied code to acquire a distinctive character for certain goods or services within the meaning of Article 3(1)(b) of the Directive?
(2) If the answer to the first question is in the affirmative:
   (a) in what circumstances may it be accepted that a single specific colour possesses a distinctive character in the sense used above?
   (b) does it make any difference if registration is sought for a large number of goods and/or services, rather than for a specific product or service, or category of goods or services respectively?
(3) In the assessment of the distinctive character of a specific colour as a trade mark, must account be taken of whether, with regard to that colour, there is a general interest in availability, such as can exist in respect of signs which denote a geographical origin?
(4) When considering the question whether a sign, for which registration as a trade mark is sought, possesses the distinctive character referred to in Article 3(1)(b) of the Directive, must the Benelux Trade Mark Office confine itself to an assessment in abstracto of distinctive character or must it take account of all the actual facts of the case, including the use made of the sign and the manner in which the sign is used?[110]

(a) *The Opinion of Advocate General Léger*

4.133 Advocate General Léger started his review of relevant law from the Paris Convention, 'the text on which all international rules governing industrial property rights are based',[111] but which did not contain any definition of signs capable of constituting a trade mark.[112]

4.134 The starting point should be the issue of whether a colour per se fell within the meaning of Article 2. He suggested that the Court should thus expand the scope of the enquiry[113] and

---

[108] Paragraph 63.
[109] C-104/01 *Libertel* [2003] ECR I-3793.
[110] Reproduced in paragraph 20.
[111] Point 3 of the Opinion of AG Léger.
[112] Article 6quinquies B(2).
[113] This was feasible because, according to the Court's case law, it is its duty to interpret all provisions of Community law which referring courts need in order to decide the actions pending before them, even if those provisions are not expressly indicated in the questions referred to it: C-280/91 *Finanzamt Kassel-Goethestrasse v Viessmann KG* [1993] ECR I-971, C-350/99 *Wolfgang Lange v Georg Schunemann GmbH* [2001] ECR I-1061, and C-90/97 *Robin Swaddling v Adjudication Officer* [1999] ECR I-1075.

'consider whether [Article 2] ... should be interpreted as meaning that a colour per se, without any shape or contour, constitutes a sign capable of being represented graphically and of distinguishing the goods and services of one undertaking from those of other undertakings'.[114]

4.135 Libertel, the Commission, the Benelux Trade Mark Office, and the Governments of The Netherlands and the United Kingdom supported the argument that a colour per se could be registered as a trade mark as it constituted a visual statement and possessed communicative characteristics.[115]

4.136 The Advocate General maintained that a colour per se failed both Article 2 requirements.

4.137 **(i) The function of graphical representation** Graphical representation was the first he considered, looking at the text of the provision but taking also into account the context and the objectives of Article 2.[116]

4.138 The open-ended wording of the provision—resulting from the combination of the expression 'any sign' with an indicative rather than exhaustive list of signs—had resulted in diverse approaches at the national level.[117] The ambiguity could not be resolved by reference to the joint declaration of the Council and the Commission because there was no reference to it in the provision.[118] And, turning again to the wider legislative picture, he remarked that Article 15 of TRIPs—to which both the EU[119] and its Member States have acceded—referred only to 'combinations of colours'.[120]

4.139 Graphical representation was a critical requirement. Following registration, it allowed immediate protection without use but also acted as the point of reference for determining whether the trade mark proprietor had put the mark into actual use.

> It therefore follows from the scheme of the Directive that it is the graphic representation of the sign set out in the application for registration that allows an assessment to be carried out

---

[114] Point 35.

[115] Support for this position was also sought from the joint declaration of the Council of the European Union and the Commission at the meeting of the Council adopting the Directive. It stated that Article 2 does not exclude the possibility of registering as a trade mark a combination of colours or one colour alone (OJ OHIM No 5/96, p 607 and the position adopted by OHIM's Third Board of Appeal in case R-122/1998-3, *LIGHT GREEN*, 19 December 1998).

[116] Citing C-191/99 *Kvaerner plc v Staatssecretaris van Financien* [2001] ECR I-447.

[117] At the time, German law allowed the registration of colours; Portuguese law allowed only combinations of colours; French law referred to shades of colours; and Italian law to chromatic tonalities. The laws of the Benelux, Denmark, Greece, Ireland, Austria, Finland, Sweden, Spain, and the United Kingdom were silent.

[118] Citing C-292/89 *Antonissen v Council and Commission* [1991] ECR I-745 and C-329/95 *VAG Sverige AB* [1997] ECR I-2675. In any case, he noted the Declaration clearly stated in its Preamble: 'The declarations of the Council and the Commission set out below not forming part of the legislative text, they do not seek to pre-empt the interpretation of the latter by the Court of Justice of the European Communities.'

[119] Council Decision 94/800, [1994] OJ L336/1.

[120] Article 15(1):

> Any sign, or any combination of signs, capable of distinguishing the goods or services of one undertaking from those of other undertakings, shall be capable of constituting a trademark. Such signs, in particular words including personal names, letters, numerals, figurative elements and combinations of colours as well as any combination of such signs, shall be eligible for registration as trademarks. Where signs are not inherently capable of distinguishing the relevant goods or services, Members may make such registrability depend on distinctiveness acquired through use. Members may require, as a condition of registration, that signs be visually perceptible.

The AG also mentioned the legislative history of Article 15: its original version referred to colours, however its scope as adopted appeared to be narrower.

as to whether all the conditions relating to the acquisition of rights to the trade mark are complied with and which determines the rights and obligations conferred by its registration.[121]

Since, at the time, the Court had not adopted the *Sieckmann*[122] criteria AG Léger cited with approval the Opinion of AG Ruiz-Jarabo Colomer and set two broader conditions.

4.140 First, the representation had to be clear and precise; second it had to be intelligible.

4.141 **(ii) Graphical representation of colours** Colours failed both these requirements irrespective of whether the representation was by reproduction of the colour as such or by reference to codes. The second route was rejected outright because it demanded unreasonable effort from a consumer or a competitor that would like to determine what the protected sign is. Reproduction failed because a colour did not possess an independent existence and it would not be possible to determine how it would appear on the goods or the documents or objects related with the services.

4.142 The trade mark monopoly would be too broad.[123] It would also be difficult to determine: first, whether in practice the colour formed part of a composite sign; second, whether it was purely ornamental; and third, whether there was a likelihood of confusion between shades of the same colour. The difficulty of competitors in determining what remained outside the scope of trade mark protection by inspecting the register was an additional point.

4.143 Citing *Canon*,[124] recognizing the importance of the principle of legal certainty in the field of trade marks, he found that graphical representation of colours as such, without shape or contour, would fail this requirement irrespective of the form or method of representation.

(b) The judgment of the Court

4.144 The Court accepted that it was necessary to start its analysis from Article 2 and noted that '[N]ormally a colour is a simple property of things. Yet it may constitute a sign. That depends on the context in which the colour is used. None the less, a colour per se is capable, in relation to a product or service, of constituting a sign.'[125]

4.145 **(i) Graphical representation of colours** Graphical representation had to satisfy the *Sieckmann*[126] requirements. Depositing a mere sample of a colour would fail in particular the durability requirement, because the shade could change with the passage of time. A verbal description of a colour had to be examined according to the circumstances of each individual case, though in principle it could satisfy the *Sieckmann* standards. Accordingly, the combination of a sample with a verbal description could also satisfy the same standards.

4.146 In cases where the above combination failed, lacking for example precision, this 'could be remedied by adding a colour designation from an internationally recognised identification code'.[127]

---

[121] Point 60.
[122] C-273/00 *Sieckmann* [2002] ECR I-11737.
[123] C-49/02 *Heidelberger Bauchemie* GmbH [2004] ECR I-6129.
[124] C-39/97 *Canon Kabushiki Kaisha v Metro-Goldwyn-Mayer Inc.* [1998] ECR I-5507.
[125] Paragraph 27.
[126] C-273/00 *Sieckmann* [2002] ECR I-11737.
[127] Paragraph 38.

4.147 As part of its conclusion regarding the first question the Court ruled that a colour could be capable of functioning and being protected as a trade mark 'provided that, inter alia, it may be represented graphically in a way that is clear, precise, self-contained, easily accessible, intelligible, durable and objective. The latter condition cannot be satisfied merely by reproducing on paper the colour in question, but may be satisfied by designating that colour using an internationally recognised identification code'.[128]

(4) *Heidelberger Bauchemie*: Abstract Combinations of Colours

4.148 The Court considered abstract combinations of colours in *Heidelberger Bauchemie*.[129] The DPMA had refused to register a colour combination as a trade mark for goods used in the building trade. On the form the sign had been reproduced by a rectangular piece of paper, the upper part of which was blue and the lower half yellow and described in the following terms: 'The trade mark applied for consists of the applicant's corporate colours which are used in every conceivable form, in particular on packaging and labels. The specification of the colours is: RAL 5015/HKS 47—blue RAL 1016/HKS 3—yellow.'[130] The product specification included adhesives, solvents, paints, and insulating materials.

4.149 Originally, the German Office had rejected the application, holding that the sign was not capable of constituting a trade mark, was not capable of being represented graphically, and was devoid of any distinctive character. However, at a later stage,[131] it reviewed its position as to the first two grounds but considered that the sign still lacked distinctive character.

4.150 The case reached the Federal Patents Court (Bundespatentgericht), which queried whether graphical representation of abstract signs satisfied the precision and legal certainty principles that it deemed Article 2 to encapsulate. Accordingly, it referred the following questions to the Court of Justice:

> Do colours or combinations of colours which are the subject of an application for registration as a trade mark, claimed in the abstract, without contours and in shades which are named in words by reference to a colour sample (colour specimen) and specified according to a recognised colour classification system, satisfy the conditions for capability of constituting a trade mark for the purposes of Article 2 of [the Directive]?
>
> In particular, for the purposes of Article 2 of the Directive, is such an (abstract) colour mark:
> (a) a sign,
> (b) sufficiently distinctive to be capable of indicating origin,
> (c) capable of being represented graphically?[132]

(a) *The Opinion of Advocate General Léger*

4.151 Advocate General Léger delivered another sceptical Opinion. He started by reiterating the requirements set by the Court in *Libertel*,[133] *Sieckmann*,[134] and *Shield Mark*.[135]

---

[128] Paragraph 68.
[129] C-49/02 *Heidelberger Bauchemie* GmbH [2004] ECR I-6129.
[130] Reproduced in paragraph 10.
[131] And following the decision in *Farbmarke gelb/schwarz*' [1999] IIC 809 of the German Federal Court of Justice of 10 December 1998.
[132] Reproduced in paragraph 14.
[133] C-104/01 *Libertel* [2003] ECR I-3793.
[134] C-273/00 *Sieckmann* [2002] ECR I-11737.
[135] C-283/01 *Shield Mark* [2003] ECR I-14313.

(i) Colour combinations as trade marks He agreed that the current case was not covered **4.152**
by the recent jurisprudence of the Court because it covered colour combinations rather than single colours as such. Article 2 of the Directive was silent, whereas Article 15 of TRIPs referred to 'combinations of colours'; however, this should not infer that abstract combinations of colours as such could become protectable signs. He also noted that linguistically the term could refer to distinct concepts. In English and Spanish, for example, the terms 'combination' and 'combinaciones' did not imply a special arrangement or organization; in French, though, the term 'combinaison' was narrower, requiring a specific arrangement of the combined elements.

The interpretation given to Article 2 in relation to a single colour should cover combinations **4.153**
of two or more colours; thus, it would appear that colour combinations could be protected. Even so, he disapproved of the existing case law and asked the Court to look again at the reasoning developed in his Opinion in *Libertel* and chose to concentrate here on why two colours should not be protected.

(ii) Representing abstract colour combinations He doubted whether the designation of **4.154**
two colours through identification codes could enable national authorities and economic operators to determine with certainty whether a trade mark consisting of two colours per se was identical or similar to another such sign: 'the competent authorities would have the greatest difficulty in making such a comparison where the trade mark consists of two colours per se. In reality, such a trade mark may assume very different forms. It is undeniable that, depending on the arrangement in which the colours appear and, in particular, the proportion of each colour in relation to the other, the overall impression created by the trade mark, as well as its distinctive and dominant elements, may be very different.'[136]

(b) The judgment of the Court

The Court adapted its ruling in *Libertel*,[137] and required that a graphic representation of two **4.155**
or more colours, designated in the abstract and without contours, should be 'systematically arranged by associating the colours concerned in a predetermined and uniform way'.[138] Looking at it from a negative perspective it found that the

> mere juxtaposition of two or more colours, without shape or contours, or a reference to two or more colours 'in every conceivable form', as is the case with the trade mark which is the subject of the main proceedings, does not exhibit the qualities of precision and uniformity required by Article 2 of the Directive.[139]

E. Capable of Distinguishing

(1) *Philips*: Setting the Principles

Capability of distinguishing was first considered by the Court in a case that involved a three- **4.156**
dimensional sign. In *Philips*[140] the Court of Appeal of England and Wales had to resolve an

---

[136] Point 60.
[137] Case C-104/01 *Libertel Groep BV v Benelux-Merkenbureau* [2003] ECR I-3793.
[138] *Heidelberger Bauchemie* (n 26) paragraph 33.
[139] *Heidelberger Bauchemie* (n 26) paragraph 34.
[140] C-299/99 *Koninklijke Philips Electronics NV v Remington Consumer Products Ltd* [2002] ECR I-5475. See also, as concerns functionality, paragraphs 5.759 to 5.769, below.

infringement case. The Philips trade mark consisted of a two-dimensional representation of the three-dimensional shape of an electric razor, the shape of a Philishave.[141] Remington marketed a similar shaver. The Court of Appeal referred to the Court of Justice a list of seven questions in an attempt to clarify the 'functionality' provisions of the Directive, but also to obtain a framework for determining distinctiveness and the scope of protection.

4.157 The first question had to do with the difference between 'capable of distinguishing' and 'devoid of any distinctive character'. The Court of Appeal wanted to know whether there was a category of signs that did not fail the requirements set by Article 3(1)(b), Article 3(1)(c), or Article 3(1)(d) but nevertheless would be excluded from registration by Article 3(1)(a) of the Directive. The second question focused on shapes from a distinctiveness perspective; when the sign for which registration was sought was the shape of the specified product, did it need to incorporate some capricious addition, an embellishment that had no functional purpose, in order to be capable of distinguishing?

(a) The Opinion of Advocate General Ruiz-Jarabo Colomer

4.158 Article 3(1)(b) covered signs 'which do not fulfil the primary purpose of distinguishing the goods and which, therefore, do not make it possible to identify their origin, that is to say their manufacturer'.[142] Article 3(1)(c) and Article 3(1)(d) excluded signs because of their generic nature or their customary character.

4.159 These specific provisions considered aspects of distinctiveness; they contained 'a partial legal definition of the concept of distinctive character'.[143] The similarity between these three grounds had been recognized by the legislator, who provided through Article 3(3)—acquiring distinctiveness through use—a common route for overcoming them, but not Article 3(1)(a). Having dealt in detail with the 'functionality' question he turned his attention very briefly to the remaining questions that he really considered irrelevant for resolving the matter that concerned the Court of Appeal.

4.160 (i) **Potentiality and actuality** The answer to the first question, he suggested, should be negative. The terminology expressed a distinction between potentiality, expressed by 'capable of distinguishing', and actuality, expressed by 'distinctive character'. He found the Court's approach in *Windsurfing Chiemsee*[144] as supporting his analysis.

4.161 (ii) **Arbitrary addition and technical result** On the second question, he repeated what he had already discussed under the functionality part of his Opinion, that Article 3(1)(e) was not connected with distinctiveness. Still,

> if 'arbitrary addition' means any element the essential features of which do not seek to achieve a technical result, the answer must be in the affirmative. Only if a shape contains an addition of this type will it be appropriate to consider whether it has a distinctive character, assuming that it is not a shape dictated by its nature or which gives substantial value to the goods.[145]

---

[141] For a comparison, see *Koninklijke Philips Electronics NV v Rotary Shaver Sweden AB* [2005] ETMR 103 HR (Stockholm) and *Philips Electronics NC v Remington Consumer Products Ltd* [1999] RPC 809; [1999] ETMR 816.
[142] Point 13.
[143] Point 14.
[144] Joined Cases C-108/97 and C-109/97 *Windsurfing Chiemsee* [1999] ECR I-2779.
[145] Point 47.

(b) The judgment of the Court

4.162 The Court started by ruling on a procedural issue. Philips had requested the reopening of the oral procedure or the joinder of *Linde*[146] in order to take into account the views of the German referring court. The Court dismissed the application because it considered it had all the information necessary to answer the questions referred by the English court.[147]

4.163 **(i) Article 3(1)(a)—the essential function of a trade mark** On the first question, Remington submitted that signs which are not capable of distinguishing, failing Article 3(1)(a), should not be registered, even with evidence of extensive use. Philips submitted the opposite. The analysis of the Court started from the essential function of a trade mark as a guarantee for the consumer of the identity of the origin of the marked product.[148] It stressed that the registrability provisions should be interpreted in view of that essential function.

4.164 **(ii) No distinction between different categories of trade marks** From the wording of Article 2 it was clear that it made no distinction between different categories of trade marks. 'The criteria for assessing the distinctive character of three dimensional trade marks are thus no different from those to be applied to other categories.'[149] According to the analysis of the Court, Article 3(1)(a) was the mirror image of Article 2 expressed in a negative way. Article 3(1)(b), Article 3(1)(c), and Article 3(1)(d) provided specific reasons for which a mark should not be registered.[150]

4.165 Article 3(3) provided that through use a sign that failed Articles 3(1)(b), (c), or (d) could overcome this barrier through evidence of acquired distinctive character. In *Windsurfing Chiemsee*[151] the Court had already observed that this meant that the mark ought to identify the specified product as originating from a particular undertaking, and thus to distinguish that product from goods of other undertakings.

4.166 Perhaps it would have sufficed for the Court to underline the above statement; however, it felt that it had to offer some justification for the obvious textual discrepancy.

4.167 **(iii) The continuum of distinctiveness** On the basis of the language of the provision and the structure of the Directive, it viewed Article 3(1)(a) as excluding 'signs which are not generally capable of being a trade mark and thus cannot be represented graphically and/or are not capable of distinguishing the goods or services of one undertaking from those of other undertakings'.[152]

4.168 However, all the distinctiveness provisions were linked; in a way it viewed them as part of the same continuum.

> Article 3(1)(a) ... like the rule laid down by Article 3(1)(b), (c), and (d), precludes the registration of signs or indications which do not meet one of the two conditions imposed by

---

[146] Joined Cases C-53 to C-55/01 *Linde, Winward*, and *Rado* [2003] ECR I-3161.
[147] Article 61 of the Rules of Procedure; Joined Cases C-270/97 and C-271/97 *Deutsche Post AG v Elisabeth Sievers* (C-270/97), *Brunhilde Schrage* (C-271/97) [2000] ECR I-929.
[148] Citing the Tenth Recital of the Preamble to the Directive; and C-349/95 *Frits Loendersloot v George Ballantine & Son* [1997] ECR I-6227 and C-39/97 *Canon* [1998] ECR I-5507.
[149] *Philips* (n 140) paragraph 48.
[150] Citing joined Cases C-108/97 and C-109/97 *Windsurfing Chiemsee* [1999] ECR I-2779.
[151] Paragraph 46.
[152] Paragraph 37.

Article 2 of the Directive, that is to say, the condition requiring such signs to be capable of distinguishing the goods or services of one undertaking from those of other undertakings.[153]

The Court, as the result of this admittedly unclear statement, concluded that there was no category of marks which was not excluded from registration according to Article 3(1)(b), (c), and (d) and Article 3(3) but could still be excluded under Article 3(1)(a).

4.169 Note that this is a one way only conclusion. In *Henkel*,[154] the Court stressed, in relation to the Regulation: 'The fact that a sign is, in general, capable of constituting a trade mark within the meaning of Article 4 [of the Regulation] does not mean that the sign necessarily has distinctive character for the purposes of Article 7(1)(b) in relation to a specific product or service.'[155]

4.170 **(iv) Three-dimensional signs: No requirement for a capricious addition** The answer to the second question followed the same logic; the Directive made no other distinction between categories of marks. Accordingly, there was no requirement of a capricious addition; the only requirement the shape had to satisfy was to function as a trade mark.

4.171 Note that the submissions of both Philips and Remington had been based on descriptiveness, perhaps influenced by the stance of the Court in *Windsurfing Chiemsee*.[156]

(2) Capable of Distinguishing: The Limited Effect of Article 3(1)(a)

4.172 In its subsequent case law the Court considered distinctiveness overwhelmingly under Article 3(1)(b) and the requirement of distinctive character. The effect of Article 3(1)(a) appears to be quite limited. For example, in *Postkantoor*[157] the Court found that there was 'no reason to find that a word like Postkantoor is not, in respect of certain goods or services, capable of fulfilling the essential function of a trade mark'.[158]

4.173 In respect of colours the Court, having admitted that colours possessed little inherent capacity for communicating specific information, went on to assert that

> that factual finding would not justify the conclusion that colours per se cannot, as a matter of principle, be considered to be capable of distinguishing the goods or services of one undertaking from those of other undertakings. The possibility that a colour per se may in some circumstances serve as a badge of origin ... cannot be ruled out.[159]

4.174 Similarly, in *Heidelberger Bauchemie*[160] it limited further the possibility of a colour functioning as a trade mark. The wording is evidence that the Court views distinctiveness as one issue with many different aspects. Referring to Article 2, it appeared to describe the distinctiveness requirement mentioned therein as initial distinctive character. 'Save in exceptional cases, colours do not initially have a distinctive character, but may be capable of acquiring such character as the result of the use made of them in relation to the goods or services claimed.'[161]

---

[153] Paragraph 38.
[154] Joined Cases C-456/01 P and C-457/01 P *Henkel KGaA v Office for Harmonisation in the Internal Market (Trade Marks and Designs)* [2004] ECR I-5089.
[155] *Henkel* (n 154) paragraph 32.
[156] Joined Cases C-108/97 and C-109/97 *Windsurfing Chiemsee* [1999] ECR I-2779.
[157] C-363/99 *Koninklijke KPN Nederland NV v Benelux-Merkenbureau (Postkantoor)* [2004] ECR I-1619.
[158] *Postkantoor* (n 15) paragraph 81.
[159] C-104/01 *Libertel* [2003] ECR I-3793 paragraph 41.
[160] C-49/02 *Heidelberger Bauchemie GmbH* [2004] ECR I-6129.
[161] *Philips* (n 140) paragraph 39.

Nevertheless, this should not raise an obstacle to registration according to Article 2. **4.175**

> Subject to the above, it must be accepted that for the purposes of Article 2 ... colours and combinations of colours, designated in the abstract and without contours, may be capable of distinguishing the goods or services of one undertaking from those of other undertakings.[162]

F. The Definition of the Goods and Services for Which the Mark is Registered

(1) *Praktiker*: Registration of Service Marks for Retail Services

Trade marks may be registered for goods and services. The acceptance of trade marks for services is relatively recent, beginning in 1946 with the trade mark law of the United States. When the Directive was adopted in 1988, not all EU Member States recognized the registration for services. Differences persisted in properly defining services, and in particular in distinguishing between marks for the sale of goods (marques de commerce) and marks for the service of retailing (or wholesaling, or sales via the Internet, etc). Some thought, as did OHIM initially, that 'retail service' was an imprecise concept, and that it was sufficient to allow registration for the goods which are sold at retail. Others claimed that the 'value-added' service rendered by retailers merited a separate registration of a mark for these services. The issue came before the Court in 2002.[163] **4.176**

(a) The factual setting and the questions referred

Praktiker, a chain of do-it-yourself stores, sought registration in Germany for a mark in Class 35 for 'retail trade in building, home improvement and gardening goods for the do-it-yourself sector'. The German Bundespatentgericht was uncertain about the registrability of such services and referred a series of questions to the Court: **4.177**

1. Does retail trade in goods constitute a service within the meaning of Article 2 of the Directive? If the answer to this question is in the affirmative:
2. To what extent must the content of such services provided by a retailer be specified in order to guarantee the certainty of the subject matter of trade-mark protection that is required in order to (a) fulfil the function of the trade mark, as defined in Article 2 of the Directive, namely, to distinguish the goods or services of one undertaking from those of other undertakings, and (b) define the scope of protection of such a trade mark in the event of a conflict?
3. To what extent is it necessary to define the scope of similarity (Article 4(1)(b) and Article 5(1)(b) of the Directive) between such services provided by a retailer and (a) other services provided in connection with the distribution of goods, or (b) the goods sold by that retailer?[164]

(b) The Opinion of Advocate General Léger

Advocate General Léger first clarified that retailers do not differ from manufacturers who sell their products themselves; they too should be able to distinguish themselves from their competitors. **4.178**

---

[162] *Philips* (n 140) paragraph 40.
[163] C-418/02, *Praktiker Bau- und Heimwerkermärkte AG* (PRAKTIKER) [2005] ECR I-05873.
[164] Reproduced in paragraph 14 of the judgment.

4.179 The essential function of a trade mark became the starting point for his analysis:

> it must be possible for consumers to perceive the activity, as such, for which the applicant is seeking the registration of a mark as constituting a service. This requirement follows from the very function of the mark and its corollary, the principle of speciality, which means that the rights which it confers can be exactly determined. A mark cannot be registered for a service which cannot be perceived as such by consumers, with the result that the scope of protection could not be ascertained.[165]

4.180 Ascertaining some services related to the sale of products, for example, bringing them together for the purposes of selling them, could be difficult. However, developments in marketing meant that 'the conditions under which the act of sale itself takes place may constitute, in the relationship between retailer and consumer, a reason for buying which is just as important as the quality and price of the goods sold'.[166] In many cases it was the selection of goods that attracted consumers rather than the presence of any particular product brand. The same criterion could be applied to a shop selling building, home improvement, and gardening goods.[167] He agreed with the decision of the Board of Appeal in *Giacomelli Sport*,[168] that a service supplied in connection with retail trading may constitute a service for which a trade mark can be registered.

4.181 He suggested that the

> registration of a mark for services supplied in connection with the retail sale of goods should clearly indicate both the specific nature of those services and the goods or types of goods to which they relate ... this dual requirement is justified, in the light of the scheme and purpose of the Directive, by the particular nature of the services supplied in connection with retail trading.[169]

4.182 Advocate General Léger opted for this stricter approach because of the balancing act that trade mark law is asked to perform:

> trade mark law is somewhat paradoxical in conferring upon one retailer in particular exclusive rights in marks which serve the marketing of goods or services in order to promote the free movement of those goods and services. To reconcile the interests of the protection afforded by the mark and free movement, in the trade-mark law registration system the applicant must, in consideration of the exclusive rights which he claims, indicate exactly the mark and the goods and services to which those rights relate.[170]

4.183 Regarding the third question, he accepted that trade mark law should avoid giving retailers extensive protection that cover other services that might be offered in connection with selling goods, as well as all the goods sold by such proprietors.[171]

4.184 However, he was against adopting exceptional set criteria for delimiting the area of similarity between services supplied in connection with the retail sale of goods and the other services which may be offered in the course of marketing in general or the actual goods. The global appreciation test and the interdependence between the factors of the test provided the flexibility that was necessary to deal with this problem. He noted that, according to the

---

[165] Point 47 of the Opinion of AG Léger.
[166] Point 50 of the Opinion of AG Léger.
[167] Referring to Grabrucker, 'Marks for Retail Services—An Example for Harmonising Trade Mark Laws' (2003) 34 IIC 503 for a review of national practices relating to retail services.
[168] Case R 46/1998-2, 17 December 1999.
[169] Point 71 of the Opinion of AG Léger.
[170] Point 79 of the Opinion of AG Léger.
[171] Point 89 of the Opinion of AG Léger.

(c) The judgment of the Court

The Court agreed that the concept of 'services' should be interpreted in the same way throughout the Union, otherwise conditions for the registration of 'service trade marks'[172] could vary according to the laws of each Member State. **4.185**

It described the objective of retail trade as the sale of goods to consumers that **4.186**

> includes, in addition to the legal sales transaction, all activity carried out by the trader for the purpose of encouraging the conclusion of such a transaction. That activity consists, inter alia, in selecting an assortment of goods offered for sale and in offering a variety of services aimed at inducing the consumer to conclude the above-mentioned transaction with the trader in question rather than with a competitor.[173]

The Court found that there was no overriding reason based on the Directive or general principles of Community law precluding the above services from being covered by the concept of 'services' within the meaning of the Directive. In relation to the Regulation it reminded us that the Office had accepted the principle of registration of Community trade marks for retail services. **4.187**

It then rejected the argument that a more restrictive specification of retail services would be required. It accepted that a restrictive approach would 'reduce the protection afforded to the proprietor of the trade mark, so that questions concerning the application of Articles 4(1) and 5(1) of the Directive would arise less often',[174] but this would not be adequate justification. Being more permissive than the Advocate General, the Court held that the applicant should only 'be required to specify the goods or types of goods to which those services relate'.[175] **4.188**

The Court found the third question to be speculative; there was no indication in the reference that the referring court could find it necessary to rule on the concept of 'similarity' in connection with 'likelihood of confusion'. Accordingly, it declined to answer the question. **4.189**

> The Court of Justice has no jurisdiction to answer questions referred for a preliminary ruling where it is obvious that the interpretation of Community law sought bears no relation to the actual facts of the main proceedings or to their purpose, where the problem is hypothetical, or where the court does not have before it the factual or legal material necessary to give a useful answer to the questions submitted.[176]

(2) *IP Translator*: Specification, Clarity, and Precision

The Court had established, in *Dyson*, that a sign must consist of something which is clear and definite, not a mere concept permitting any number of embodiments. With obvious difficulties the Court accepted colours per se as trade marks, without requiring an arrangement in time or space, but made a step back in *Heidelberg Bauchemie* requiring **4.190**

---

[172] *Praktiker* (n 163) paragraph 32.
[173] *Praktiker* (n 163) paragraph 34.
[174] *Praktiker* (n 163) paragraph 46.
[175] *Praktiker* (n 163) paragraph 50.
[176] *Praktiker* (n 163) paragraph 57, citing T-421/01 *Traunfellner GmbH v Österreichische Autobahnen-und Schnellstrassen-Finanzierungs-AG* [2003] ECR I-11941.

for colour combinations the representation to be 'systematically arranged by associating the colours concerned in a predetermined and uniform way'. The issue of clarity and uniqueness is not limited to the sign itself, but arises also with regard to the goods or services for which the mark is to be or is registered. The issue is to what extent it should be possible to generalize, and claim, with one stroke, protection for a whole category of goods or services.

4.191 The Directive has no specific rules on how the goods or services must be indicated, while the Regulation requires a list of goods or services for the obtaining of a filing date, and has specific requirements in Rule 2 of the Implementing Regulation. OHIM must apply the International Classification established by the 1957 Nice Agreement on the International Classification of Good and Services. The goods and services must be indicated in a clear and definite manner allowing them to be grouped into one of the forty-five classes established by the Nice Agreement. OHIM had been very liberal and from the beginning accepted all the terms that are included in the so-called class headings of the forty-five classes, and had further taken the view that using the class headings meant that the applicant obtained protection for all the goods that could be included in the class—in effect OHIM allowed very broad product claims. Some national offices in the EU adopted the same approach, whereas others were more restrictive. Predictably, this led to friction. However, it was only in 2010 that the issue reached the Court of Justice.

(a) Communication No 4/03 of the President of OHIM

4.192 From the beginning of its operations, OHIM followed the approach that the entire heading of each of the classes of the Nice Classification covered all the goods or services encompassed by the respective class. The adoption of that practice was driven by the fact that it was not uncommon amongst early filers of Community applications to claim 'all goods in class X' rather than providing a conventional list. Such claims were at the time acceptable in a number of national offices, with the result that CTM applicants naturally also regarded it as a legitimate way of formulating the list of goods and services in proceedings before the Office.

4.193 However, the adoption of the Trademark Law Treaty (TLT) made this general practice unsustainable, as it was questionable whether such a formula constituted a proper 'list' of goods and services, which is an essential requirement for securing a filing date. In order to deal with that situation and in order to prevent the potential loss of filing dates by its applicants, OHIM decided to convert such claims into the corresponding class heading, with the understanding that the class heading covered all the goods or services falling under the respective class.

4.194 That understanding was formalized by the adoption of Communication No 4/03 of the President of OHIM,[177] which sought to explain and clarify to the users of the system the consequences of the use of class headings when Community trade mark applications or registrations were restricted or partially surrendered or were involved in opposition or cancellation proceedings.

---

[177] Communication No 4/03 of the President of the Office for Harmonization in the Internal Market (Trade Marks and Designs) (OHIM) of 16 June 2003 concerning the use of class headings in lists of goods and services for Community trade mark applications and registrations (OJ OHIM 2003, p 1647).

The main elements of the system were given in points III and IV of that Communication. **4.195** Point III made clear that:

> It constitutes a proper specification of goods and services in an application if the general indications or the whole class headings provided for in the Nice Classification are used... OHIM does not object to the use of any of the general indications and class headings as being too vague or indefinite, contrary to the practice which is applied by some national offices in the European Union and in third countries in respect of some of the class headings and general indications.

Point IV added that: **4.196**

> The 34 classes for goods and the 11 classes for services comprise the totality of all goods and services. As a consequence of this, the use of all the general indications listed in the class heading of a particular class constitutes a claim to all the goods or services falling within this particular class... Similarly, the use of a particular general indication found in the class heading will embrace all of the individual goods or services falling under that general indication and properly classified in the same class.

The adoption of Communication 4/03 thus resulted in two diverging approaches being applied to trademark filings in the European Union. Examining authorities in the majority of the Member States stuck to the rule that the specification 'means what it says', ie it is to be interpreted according to the natural and usual meaning of the terms of which it is composed, whereas a minority of national offices followed OHIM's policy by applying the system that came to be known as 'class-heading-covers-all'. **4.197**

(b) The facts in the main proceedings and the order for reference

The question finally reached the Court of Justice[178] in the form of a preliminary reference from the Person Appointed by the Lord Chancellor under Section 76 of the Trade Marks Act 1994, and presented the Court with the opportunity to establish a uniform set of rules governing the specification of goods or services in trade mark filings made in the European Union and, indirectly, to assess the conformity of Communication No 4/03 with the scheme laid down by the Directive and the Regulation. **4.198**

The reference was made in the course of proceedings between the Chartered Institute of Patent Attorneys (CIPA) and the Registrar of Trade Marks (the Registrar) concerning the latter's refusal to register as a trade mark in the UK the word sign 'IP TRANSLATOR'. To identify the services covered by that registration CIPA used the general terms of the heading of Class 41 of the Nice Classification, namely: 'Education; providing of training; entertainment; sporting and cultural activities'. Deviating from its standard practice, the Registrar interpreted the application in accordance with Communication No 4/03 and inferred that it covered not only the services specifically identified by CIPA, but also every other service falling within Class 41 of the Nice Classification, including 'translation services'. Hence, it rejected the application on the grounds that the sign applied for lacked distinctive character and was descriptive in nature. Tellingly, there was no request by CIPA for 'translation services' to be excluded from its application. **4.199**

---

[178] Case C-307/10 *Chartered Institute of Patent Attorneys v Registrar of Trade Marks* (IP TRANSLATOR), ECLI:EU:C:2012:361.

4.200 CIPA appealed to the Appointed Person, contending that its application did not specify, and therefore did not cover, 'translation services' in Class 41, as a matter of principle. For that reason, it submitted that the Registrar's objections were misconceived and that its application for registration had been wrongly refused. The Appointed Person observed that translation services are not normally regarded as a subcategory of services relating to 'education', 'providing of training', 'entertainment', 'sporting activities', or 'cultural activities', but in view of the varying practices among the trade mark authorities of the Member States and OHIM, it decided to stay the proceedings and to refer the following questions to the Court of Justice for a preliminary ruling:

1. Is it necessary for the various goods or services covered by a trade mark application to be identified with any, and if so what particular, degree of clarity and precision?
2. Is it permissible to use the general words of the class headings of the [Nice Classification] for the purpose of identifying the various goods or services covered by a trade mark application?
3. Is it necessary or permissible for such use of the general words of the Class Headings of [the Nice Classification] to be interpreted in accordance with Communication No 4/03?

(c) The Opinion of Advocate General Bot

4.201 Advocate General Bot recognized that the Directive contains no provision concerning the identification of the goods or services for which registration of a trade mark is sought, but considered that this did not provide sufficient grounds for excluding the rules governing the specification of goods and services from its harmonizing scope. Relying on Recitals 4, 8, and 10 in the Preamble to the Directive, as interpreted by the Court,[179] he recalled that the aim of the Directive is to achieve full harmonization in relation to substantive rules of central importance for the functioning of the internal market, and that the attainment of that aim requires that both the conditions for obtaining a registered trade mark and the rules which serve to determine the scope of its protection are identically interpreted in the legal systems of all the Member States.[180]

4.202 He also observed that, despite the autonomy of the Community trade mark regime, the systems laid down by the Directive and the Regulation are not only based on the same principles and share the same objectives, but they also complement each other and interact throughout the life of a trade mark in a variety of ways. The Advocate General therefore underlined that it was essential for the coherent functioning of the system to adopt a uniform interpretation of the rules governing the identification of goods and services, since otherwise the trade mark registration scheme in the Union may suffer as a result of inconsistencies, significant legal uncertainty, and forum shopping.[181]

4.203 Turning to the first question, Advocate General Bot took the view that, according to the scheme laid down by the Regulation, the identification of the goods or services serves an altogether different purpose from, and must therefore not be confused with, their classification under the Nice Agreement. In this regard, he noted that, under Article 26(1)(c) of the Regulation and Rule 2(2) of the Implementing Regulation, the applicant must draw up

---

[179] Citing Cases C-482/09 *Budějovický Budvar*, paragraph 30 and C-418/02 *Praktiker* (n 163) paragraph 31.
[180] Points 32–36.
[181] Points 37–43.

a list of goods and services which must be worded in such a way as to clearly indicate their nature. He observed, however, that there is no provision in the Regulation either requiring applicants to use the class headings of the Nice Classification for that purpose, or regulating the results of such use, which could possibly serve as a basis for the system instigated by Communication No 4/03.[182]

Conversely, Article 28 of the Regulation and Rule 2(1) and (4) of the Implementing Rules make clear that the classification of goods and services in accordance with the Nice Classification is carried out for exclusively administrative purposes. Similarly, Article 2(1) of the Nice Agreement expressly provides that the Nice Classification has no legal relevance as regards the extent of the protection afforded to a mark, beyond that attributed to it by each country of the Special Union, which encompasses almost all the Member States. On that basis, the Advocate General inferred that the Nice Classification has only a practical value, in that it enables economic operators to conduct more accurate searches and facilitates in general the registration of trade marks, including the proper calculation of class fees. Accordingly, he regarded the classification of goods and services as a mere formality, which must be satisfied for reasons of administration and convenience, and distinguished it from their proper identification, which serves to define the subject matter of the registration.[183] **4.204**

He concluded that the principles governing the preciseness of the specification cannot be derived from the classification system, but can only be based on the rules governing the grant of a trade mark, in a way that enables that mark to perform its essential function in conformity with the principles of legal certainty and sound administration.[184] **4.205**

In that connection, he referred to the principles laid down in *Sieckmann*[185] concerning the need for the graphic representation of the sign to be clear, precise, self-contained, easily accessible, intelligible, durable, unequivocal, and objective, pointing out that the purposes these principles serve, namely enabling the competent authorities to carry out an effective examination and allowing economic operators to obtain relevant information about the rights of third parties, are also applicable to the specification of goods and services, to the extent that the latter contributes with equal force to the determination of the subject matter of the protection conferred by the trade mark.[186] **4.206**

The Advocate General noted, however, that the challenges in each case are quite different, since the requirements laid down in respect of the graphic representation of a sign cannot be applied *stricto sensu* to the verbal description of goods or services, which naturally raises practical problems of an altogether different order. Thus, although it is quite obvious that the need for clarity and precision requires the expressions used to be intelligible and unambiguous, it should not be applied so strictly as to significantly limit the protection which the trade mark confers on its proprietor by requiring him or her to go into excessive detail when describing each of the goods and services concerned by the registration. To avoid this risk, it should be sufficient to draw-up the list of goods and services in such a way as to identify the 'essential objective characteristics and properties' of the designated goods and services, **4.207**

---

[182] Points 46–48.
[183] Points 49–52.
[184] Points 53–61.
[185] Case C-273/00 *Sieckmann* [2002] ECR I-11737, paragraphs 46–55.
[186] Points 62–67.

as is done for instance in similar systems applied in the field of customs classification. That criterion should make it possible to identify objectively the nature of the goods, in accordance with Rule 2(2) of the Implementing Regulation.[187]

4.208 Consequently, the Advocate General proposed to answer the first question to the effect that the Directive and the Regulation must be interpreted as meaning that the identification of the goods and services must be done with sufficient clarity and precision to enable the competent authorities and economic operators to accurately determine the scope of the protection conferred by the trade mark, and added that those requirements may be satisfied by means of 'a specific list of each of the items for which the applicant seeks protection' or 'by identification ... enabling the competent authorities and economic operators to determine the essential characteristics and objective properties of the goods and services concerned'.[188]

4.209 Advocate General Bot considered that those considerations were also applicable to the second question, which sought to clarify whether the applicant may use the general indications in the class headings for the purpose of identifying the goods or services for which he seeks protection. In this regard, he took the view that although the Nice Classification is a practical instrument, and the class headings have no inherent value, nothing precludes the applicant from identifying those goods or services by using the general indications in the class headings if these are clear and specific enough for that purpose. He observed, however, that the assessment of whether this is possible or not can only be made on a case-by-case basis, since some of the general indications are sufficiently clear and precise, whereas others merely indicate, in a general manner, the fields to which the relevant goods or services in principle belong.[189]

4.210 Therefore, the Advocate General proposed to answer the second question to the effect that the Directive and the Regulation are to be interpreted as not precluding an applicant from identifying the goods or services for which he seeks protection by using the general indications of the class headings of the Nice Classification, provided that that identification satisfies the necessary requirements of clarity and precision.

4.211 As concerns the third question, the Advocate General pointed out that Communication No 4/03 is not a legislative text and thus has no binding legal value. Rather, it is an internal organizational document, merely intended to explain and clarify the administrative practice of OHIM and, in so doing, to afford legal certainty to interested parties by establishing a clear and predictable framework as regards the use of class headings. He remarked, however, that there is a fine line between providing explanations and creating actual rules of law, and invited the Court to make sure that that line had not been crossed.[190]

4.212 In that connection, the Advocate General took the clear position that Communication No 4/03 did not comply with the Regulation, giving four reasons in support of that view.

4.213 First, he argued that Point III of that Communication does not comply with Rule 2(2) of the Implementing Regulation, which requires that the list of goods and services be worded in such a way as to clearly indicate their nature, since, by not objecting to the use of any of

---

[187] Points 68–75.
[188] Points 78–80.
[189] Points 81–84.
[190] Points 87–88.

the general indications and class headings, OHIM allows the registration of terms that are too vague or indefinite to observe the need for clarity and precision.

Secondly, he observed that, in practice, the 'class-heading-covers-all' approach affords the applicant almost unlimited exclusive rights over the goods and services covered by a particular class. In this way, however, the scope of the protection conferred by the trade mark becomes indeterminable, almost invisible, to the detriment of the principles of free movement of goods and the freedom to provide services. Hence, he found this approach to be out of line with the speciality principle, as it does not allow for determining with sufficient accuracy the substantive scope of the protection conferred by the trade mark. **4.214**

Thirdly, the Advocate General put forward that such an interpretation does not ensure genuine use of the trade mark within the meaning of Article 10 of the Directive and Article 15 of the Regulation, since the proprietor cannot possibly use the trade mark in relation to all of the goods and services for which protection is sought when the registration has been granted for the entire class. Consequently, the 'class-heading-covers-all' approach ultimately leads to an increase in the total number of registrations and, accordingly, in the number of conflicts which arise between them. Such a practice, however, is not consistent with the principle of sound administration and does not guarantee undistorted competition in the market. **4.215**

Fourthly, the Advocate General found Communication No 4/03 to be at odds with the principle of legal certainty, to the extent that it overlooks the fact that the Nice Classification is an evolving instrument, whose contents change over time. Accordingly, he took the view that the scope of trade mark protection could not possibly depend on a text which may be amended at the whim of an evolving market.[191] **4.216**

In the light of these considerations, he proposed to answer the third question to the effect that Communication No 4/03 does not guarantee the clarity and precision required for the purposes of the registration of a trade mark, whether a national or a Community trade mark. **4.217**

(d) The judgment of the Court

Sitting in Grand Chamber, the Court of Justice addressed first an objection of inadmissibility raised by OHIM in its written observations. Two points were important in that regard. The first had to do with the *locus standi* of OHIM in proceedings for a preliminary ruling, and the second with the argument that the reference was in fact artificial and had no material relevance to the outcome of the main proceedings. **4.218**

The significance of the first point lies in the fact that the Court admitted OHIM's intervention in the proceedings under Article 267 TFEU[192] and Article 23 of the Court's Statute,[193] although, strictly speaking, the 'act' whose legality was at stake was the rejection of the mark 'IP TRANSLATOR' by the UK Office and not a decision of OHIM. **4.219**

---

[191] Points 90–96.
[192] Article 267(b) TFEU provides that the Court of Justice shall have jurisdiction to give Preliminary Rulings concerning 'the validity of acts of the institutions, bodies, offices or agencies of the Union'.
[193] Article 23 of the Statute provides that 'the parties, the Member states, the Commission and, where appropriate, the institution, body, office or agency which adopted the act the validity or interpretation of which is in dispute, shall be entitled to submit statements of case or written observations to the Court'.

4.220 Given the context of the dispute, the Court's acceptance of OHIM's *locus standi* should not come as a surprise. Although the order for reference formally concerned the legality of an administrative act taken by a national office in the context of the TM Directive, its real purpose was to question the conformity of Communication No 4/03 with Community law, as made obvious both by the tenor of the third question and by the Registrar's exceptional decision to apply that Communication to CIPA's application contrary to its standard practice.

4.221 As regards the second point, the Court held that, however artificial, the reference enjoyed a presumption of relevance which had not been rebutted, as it was not obvious from the evidence on file that the interpretation of the EU law sought by it was unrelated to the facts of the main action. The application for registration of the trade mark was actually lodged and the Registrar rejected it, even if in doing so he departed from his usual practice. Accordingly, the Court considered the reference admissible on the grounds that the interpretation of European Union law sought by it 'did actually respond to an objective need inherent in the outcome of a case pending before it'.[194]

4.222 Turning to the merits of the case, the Court agreed with the Advocate General that the absence of any provision in the Directive directly dealing with the identification of goods and services does not mean that this is a matter excluded from its scope. Citing its judgment in *Praktiker*,[195] it recalled that 'the determination of the nature and content of the goods and services eligible for protection is subject, not to the provisions on registration procedures, but to the substantive conditions for acquiring the right conferred by the trade mark', and concluded on that basis that the proper identification of goods and services forms part of the conditions for obtaining and continuing to hold a registered trade mark, which, according to Recital 8 in the Preamble to the Directive, must be interpreted in an identical way in all Member States.[196]

4.223 The Court also observed that the proper application of a number of key provisions in the Directive, like those dealing with the absolute and relative grounds for refusal, depends to a significant extent on whether the goods or services covered by the registration are indicated with sufficient clarity and precision. Moreover, it recalled[197] that the entry of the mark in a public register has the aim of making it accessible to the competent authorities and to the public, particularly to economic operators, since, on the one hand, competent authorities must know with clarity and precision the nature of the sign of which a mark consists in order to be able to perform an accurate examination and to keep an adequate register, while, on the other hand, economic operators must be able to easily obtain relevant information about prior rights of third parties.[198]

4.224 Accordingly, it concluded that, for the purposes of the first question, the Directive requires the applicant 'to identify the goods and services for which protection is sought with sufficient

---

[194] Paragraphs 30–34.
[195] Case C-418/02 *Praktiker Bau- und Heimwerkermärkte*, [2005] ECR I-05873, paragraph 31.
[196] Paragraphs 38–41.
[197] Citing C-273/00 *Sieckmann* [2002] ECR I-11737, paragraphs 49–51 and C-49/02 *Heidelberger Bauchemie* [2004] ECR I-6129, paragraphs 28–30.
[198] Paragraphs 42–48.

clarity and precision to enable the competent authorities and economic operators, on that basis alone, to determine the extent of the protection sought'.

Moving on to the second question, the Court set out to explore the relationship between the requirements of clarity and precision and the use of the Nice Classification. In that regard, it took a more nuanced approach than the Advocate General, refusing to draw, as he had done, a clear distinction between the acts of 'identification' and 'classification' of goods and services. In so doing, it kept the discussion strictly within the confines of the Directive and refrained from either addressing or discussing the relevant provisions of the Regulation.

4.225

Specifically, it noted that although the Directive imposes no obligation or prohibition on Member States with regard to the use of the Nice Classification, Article 2(3) of the Nice Agreement requires the countries of the Special Union to include in their official documents and publications relating to the registration of trade marks the numbers of the classes to which the designated goods or services belong. On that premise, the Court held that the Directive does not preclude the competent national authorities from 'requiring or agreeing that an applicant for a national trade mark should identify the goods and services for which he is seeking the protection conferred by the trade mark by using the Nice Classification'.[199]

4.226

It agreed, however, with the Advocate General that such use of the Nice Classification for identification purposes must, in any event, meet the requisite standards of clarity and precision, sharing also the view that while some of the general indications in the class headings are sufficiently clear and precise, others are not. Still, the Court refrained from citing any examples of terms falling under any of those categories as the Advocate General had done,[200] leaving it up to the competent authorities to make an assessment on a case-by-case basis in order to determine whether the indications used in a specific application for registration meet the relevant requirements.[201]

4.227

Accordingly, the Court answered the second question to the effect that the Directive 'does not preclude the use of the general indications of the class headings of the Nice Classification to identify the goods and services for which the protection of the trade mark is sought, provided that such identification is sufficiently clear and precise'.

4.228

With regard to the third question, the analysis of the Court followed an even more cautious approach. Distancing itself again from the opinion of the Advocate General, it refrained both from directly addressing the compatibility of Communication No 4/03 with the Regulation and from endorsing the Advocate General's main argument that any attempt to designate all goods or services in a given class was doomed to fail the test of clarity and precision. On the contrary, it reiterated its statement in *Postkantoor*[202] that, in fact, 'it is possible to apply for registration of a mark, either in respect of all the goods or services falling within a class, or in respect of only some of those goods or services'.[203]

4.229

---

[199] Paragraphs 50–52.
[200] The cautiousness of the Court in this regard may also be explained by the fact that the clarity of the general indications 'education; providing of training; entertainment; sporting and cultural activities' within the heading of Class 41 was not questioned as such in the main proceedings.
[201] Paragraphs 53–55.
[202] Case C-363/99 *Koninklijke KPN Nederland* [2004] ECR I-1619, paragraph 112.
[203] Paragraph 57.

4.230 Nevertheless, the Court stressed that the parallel existence of two opposite approaches to the use of the general indications in the class headings of the Nice Classification, namely the one followed by Communication No 4/03 and the 'literal' approach, which gives the terms used in those indications their 'natural and usual meaning', may lead to considerable differences in the extent of protection granted to the same mark in different jurisdictions and, hence, is liable to affect the smooth functioning of the system for the registration of trade marks in the European Union. Thus, it found that a situation in which the extent of the protection depends on the interpretation adopted by the competent authority and not on the actual intention of the applicant runs the risk of undermining legal certainty both for the applicant and for third party economic operators.[204]

4.231 Accordingly, the Court held that an application for registration which does not make it possible to establish whether, by using a particular class heading, the applicant intends to cover all or only some of the goods in that class cannot be considered sufficiently clear and precise. It considered, however, that it was for the referring court to determine whether, by using all the general indications in the heading of Class 41 CIPA, it was intended to cover all the services in that class and, in particular, whether or not its application was intended to cover translation services.[205]

4.232 In view of those considerations, the Court ruled that an applicant for a national trade mark who uses all the general indications of a particular class heading of the Nice Classification to identify the goods or services for which protection is sought must specify whether its application is intended to cover all the goods or services included in the alphabetical list of the particular class concerned or only some of those goods or services, and added that in cases where the application concerns only some of those goods or services, the applicant is required to specify which of the goods or services in that class are intended to be covered.

(e) Conclusions

4.233 In *IP Translator* the Court tried to strike a fair balance between its obligation to provide a meaningful answer to the questions asked by the Appointed Person and the need to give as equitable a solution as possible to the division of practices as regards the value to be attributed to the general indications in the class headings of the Nice Classification. At all times, the Court tried to stay as close as possible to the subject of the main proceedings, carefully avoiding the temptation to embark on a full-scale discussion of all the intricacies resulting from the application of the Nice Classification to the specification of goods and services.

4.234 This choice of the Court is attested both by its refusal to extend its analysis to the relevant provisions of the Regulation (it is worth noting that the Regulation is not even mentioned in the judgment) and by the absence of any reference to Communication 4/03 in the operative part of the Judgment. This reluctance of the Court to pronounce itself directly on the validity of Communication 4/03 is consistent with the legal context of the dispute. The UK Office did not (and could not) apply in its own proceedings a practice instruction issued by the President of OHIM, at least not as such, so what it did instead was to transpose some of the basic assumptions of that document to the examination of CIPA's application.

---

[204] Paragraphs 58–60.
[205] Paragraphs 62–63.

Accordingly, even though the Court declared the order for reference admissible, it was right to deal with it only insofar as it concerned the interpretation of the Directive and only to the extent it was necessary to provide the referring court with a workable answer for the purposes of the main proceedings.

4.235 This minimalist approach is already apparent in the Court's treatment of the first question. Although the Court recognized the need for clarity and precision, and briefly referred[206] to its statements in *Praktiker* about the need to go beyond general wording and to specify the goods and services in the application by means 'of other more specific details', it did not follow the suggestion of the Advocate General to provide further guidance as to what those details should consist of. Nor did the Court confirm *expressis verbis* that the only method of complying with the requirement of clarity and precision was to base the identification of goods and services on what it called elsewhere in its judgment the 'literal' meaning of the terms used, ie the meaning derived from their 'natural and usual' connotation.

4.236 All the Court said in this regard was that the applicant is required to identify the goods and services with sufficient clarity and precision to enable the competent authorities and economic operators to determine 'on that basis alone' the extent of the protection sought, which, strictly speaking, is not quite the same thing. Although, admittedly, that proviso implies that the identification of the goods should follow from their description and must be self-contained, in the sense that it cannot be complemented by reference to extraneous considerations, it still leaves room for interpretation, in particular as to whether the Nice class numbers, which are included both in the application and in its publication, could affect the understanding of a given term, or even determine its nature.

4.237 This is more easily understood by reference to an example. Can, for instance, the use of the term 'belts' in Class 9 be understood as 'safety belts' *on that basis alone* (ie by the very fact that in Class 9 there can be no other kind of belts), or does the applicant have to say so expressly? In the absence of a positive statement by the Court that, as a general rule, the Nice Classification has no impact on the specification of goods, both interpretations remain plausible. This is all the more true if account is taken of the statement of the Court made in the context of the second question[207] that the Directive does not preclude the competent authorities from 'requiring or agreeing' that an applicant should 'identify' the goods and services for which protection is sought by using the Nice Classification, which seems to imply that at least the basic rules of the Nice Agreement cannot be entirely ignored in that context.

4.238 Moreover, the answer to the first and second questions should not be understood as contradicting or cancelling the rule in *BVBA*[208] that the designation of the goods and services is not incompatible with their identification by reference to a 'broad category' or 'group'. Following that rule, applicants should continue to be entitled to employ a certain degree of abstraction in their specifications, provided that the nature of the goods and services so listed remains sufficiently clear at all times.

---

[206] Paragraph 45.
[207] Paragraph 52.
[208] C-239/05, *BVBA Management Training & Consulting* (THE KITCHEN COMPANY) [2007] ECR I-1455, points 37 and 38.

4.239 These considerations also explain the approach of the Court as regards the proposition of Communication No 4/03 that the use of the complete heading constitutes a claim to the entire class. In this regard, it seems that the Court felt somehow trapped by the position it had previously taken in *Postkantoor*[209] to the effect that 'it is not impossible to apply for registration of a mark in respect of all the goods or services in a given class'. As that judgment had been taken by a lower chamber, the Court had two choices: either to abandon that approach in view of the apparent impossibility of the task to identify *a priori* and in the abstract all the goods or services possibly falling within a given class, or to stick to its case law and try to reconcile that premise with the need for clarity and precision. Unlike the Advocate General, it opted for the latter.

4.240 Surely, if it is assumed that it is possible to seek protection for all goods or services in a given class, it must also be possible to identify them in the first place, although the judgment in *Postkantoor* did not reveal how this could be done. To solve this riddle, the Court had recourse to the alphabetical list of Nice, holding that an applicant who uses all the general indications of a particular class heading 'must specify whether its application is intended to cover all the goods or services included in the alphabetical list of the particular class concerned or only some of those goods or services'. Of course, the Court cannot have disregarded the fact that the alphabetical list is not an exhaustive record of all the goods contained in a given class. It seems, however, that it regarded that list as the lowest commonly acceptable denominator it could use in order to bridge the distance between the two conflicting approaches without significantly imperilling the need for legal certainty, especially in view of the fact that the terms used in the alphabetical list are generally regarded as acceptable in all European jurisdictions.

4.241 In order to understand the Court's reasoning fully, however, the reference to the alphabetical list should be read in conjunction with paragraph 62 of its judgment, which seems to imply that an application that merely contains a reference to class headings must be objected to with a view to clarifying its scope as a matter of course. As the use of class headings (even in classes where all the general indications are clear and precise per se) cannot lead to any automatic assumption about their semantic value, applicants must be asked to provide clarification as to the exact scope of their claim by reference to the alphabetical list or, for the identity of reason, to any other similar list made available by the examining authority to that effect.

4.242 Of course, the Court's reference to the intention of the applicant as a means of overcoming the danger of conflicting interpretations of the same specification by different authorities does not explain how to interpret past registrations making use of class headings or how to publish the application once the intention of the applicant has been ascertained. Although these matters relate to procedural questions and, as such, fall outside the harmonizing scope of the Directive, the difficulties they raise are considerable and they can be solved in a workable manner only by the close co-operation of trade mark authorities across Europe. It is sufficiently clear, however, that general statements by applicants to the effect that their application was meant to cover all goods or services in the alphabetical list of a given class cannot be entered in the register as such because they cannot amount to a proper 'list of goods and services', as required both by the Regulation and by the TLT.

---

[209] C-363/99 *Koninklijke KPN Nederland* [2004] ECR I-1619, paragraph 112.

4.243 Finally, by not referring to Communication No 4/03 in the operative part of its judgment, the Court apparently tried to avoid the overwhelming consequences the direct declaration of its incompatibility with EU law would have entailed for jurisdictions applying the 'class-heading-covers-all' approach, especially with regard to past registrations. Had the Court done so, the validity of a vast number of registrations using the class heading as a means of extending protection to the entire class would become untenable, without it being possible to reword such registrations, since neither the Directive nor the Regulation include a mechanism specifically designed to deal with this kind of situation. Similarly, such registrations could not be cancelled either, since there is no revocation or invalidity ground foreseen for deficiencies of this type and, even if there was one, it could not be used *ex officio* by the competent authorities to amend or correct the register.

4.244 It would therefore seem fair to conclude that the cautious approach taken by the Court in *IP Translator* led to a pragmatic solution, which attained the objective of realigning the divergent practices applied to the identification of goods and services across Europe, while at the same time maintaining the balance of the system and avoiding the chaos that would have ensued had the Court chosen to directly challenge the validity of registrations granted on the basis of the 'class-heading-covers-all' approach. Given the peculiarities of the case and the complexity of the questions involved, the Court coped as well as it could, leaving it up to trade mark authorities and the legislator to cater for workable solutions to the issues that were left unanswered by its judgment.

(3) *Netto*: The Retailing of Services and the Need for Clarity

(a) *The facts in the main proceedings and the order for reference*

4.245 The reference in *Netto*[210] was the sequel to both *Praktiker* and *IP Translator*. It concerned the question of whether it is possible under Article 2 of the Directive to obtain trade mark protection with respect to retail trade in services and, if so, the degree of clarity and precision with which the services offered in this manner must be described in the application in order to comply with the requisite legal standard. The request was made in the course of proceedings between Netto Marken-Discount AG & Co. KG (Netto) and the DPMA concerning the dismissal by the latter of an application to register the word and device combination 'Netto Marken-Discount' in respect of, among others, the following services in Class 35 of the Nice Classification:

> Services in the retail and wholesale trade, particularly the bringing together, for the benefit of others, of a variety of services enabling customers conveniently to purchase those services, particularly services provided by retail stores, wholesale outlets, through mail order catalogues or by means of electronic media, for example websites or television shopping programmes, in relation to the following services: in Class 35: Advertising; business management; business administration; office functions; in Class 36: Issue of vouchers or tokens of value; in Class 39: Travel arrangement; in Class 41: Entertainment; in Class 45: Personal and social services intended to meet the needs of individuals.

4.246 The DPMA rejected the application on the ground that the wording of the specification did not allow the services in question to be clearly distinguished from other services in either

---

[210] C-420/13, *Netto Marken-Discount AG & Co. KG/Deutsches Patent- und Markenamt* (NETTO), ECLI:EU:C:2014:2069.

their substance or scope, and, thus, did not enable each service to be classified in only one class of the Nice Classification, as required by German law.

4.247 Netto Marken-Discount brought an action for annulment before the Bundespatentgericht, which decided to stay the proceedings and to refer the following questions to the Court for a preliminary ruling:

> (1) Is Article 2 of the Directive to be interpreted as meaning that a service within the meaning of this provision also encompasses retail trade in services?
> (2) If the answer to the first question is in the affirmative, is Article 2 of the Directive to be interpreted as meaning that the content of the services offered by the retailer must be specified in as much detail as the goods that a retailer markets?
>   (a) Does it suffice for the purposes of specification of the services if (i) just the field of services in general or general heading, (ii) just the class(es) or (iii) each specific individual service, is indicated?
>   (b) Do these indications take part in determining the filing date or is it possible, where general headings or classes are stated, to make substitutions or additions?
> (3) If the answer to the first question is in the affirmative, is Article 2 of the Directive to be interpreted as meaning that the scope of trade mark protection afforded to retail services extends even to services provided by the retailer itself?

(b) The judgment of the Court

4.248 The Court set out to address the first question by recalling its case law[211] on the interpretation of Article 2 of the Directive, according to which the subject matter of the application must satisfy three conditions in order to be capable of constituting a trade mark: first, it must be a sign; second, that sign must be capable of graphic representation; and, third, the sign must be capable of distinguishing the 'goods' or 'services' of one undertaking from those of other undertakings.

4.249 The Court pointed out, however, that the concept of 'services' has not been defined by the EU legislature[212] and that, in order to avoid the proliferation of varying national requirements for the registration of trade marks, it is necessary to supply a uniform interpretation of that concept from the perspective of EU law. Citing *Praktiker*,[213] it also recalled that, for the purpose of such an interpretation, services provided in connection with the retailing of goods can constitute services.[214]

4.250 In that regard, the Court observed that the retailing of goods includes, in addition to their sale as such, other activities, such as selecting an assortment of goods offered for sale and a variety of services aimed at inducing the consumer to purchase those goods from the trader in question rather than from a competitor. Taking a market perspective, the Court saw no reason why this business model could not also apply to the retailing of services, considering

---

[211] Citing Cases C-104/01 *Libertel*, paragraph 23, C-49/02 *Heidelberger Bauchemie*, paragraph 22, and C-321/03 *Dyson* (n 1) paragraph 28.

[212] Apparently, the Court does not consider the reference to services in Article 57 TFEU sufficient for the purposes of a proper definition. Article 57 TFEU reads:

> Services shall be considered to be 'services' within the meaning of the Treaties where they are normally provided for remuneration, in so far as they are not governed by the provisions relating to freedom of movement for goods, capital and persons. 'Services' shall in particular include: (a) activities of an industrial character; (b) activities of a commercial character; (c) activities of craftsmen; (d) activities of the professions.

[213] C-418/02, *Praktiker Bau- und Heimwerkermärkte* (PRAKTIKER) paragraphs 28–34.

[214] Paragraphs 31–33.

in particular that it is not uncommon for a market operator to select and offer an assortment of third party services, so that the consumer can choose amongst them from a single point of contact. In such a case, the services rendered consist both of the activities designed to allow the consumer conveniently to compare and purchase those services and of advertising services.[215]

4.251 The Court observed that the provision of such 'bringing together and advertising services' can, where appropriate, fall under Class 35 of the Nice Classification, as follows from both the heading and the explanatory note to that class,[216] and added that this possibility is further supported by the Alphabetical List of the Nice Classification, which includes 'sales (promotion) for third parties' amongst the services in that class. In that regard, the Court held that any supply of services that is covered by one of the classes of the Nice Classification is necessarily covered by the concept of 'services' within the meaning of Article 2 of the Directive, in view of the need for the Directive to be entirely consistent with the Paris Convention and, by extension, with the Nice Agreement.[217]

4.252 Next, the Court noted that, according to the wording of the specification, registration was sought 'particularly' with respect to the bringing together of services offered by third parties, which suggests that those services included, in addition to those offered by other traders, services provided by the applicant itself. However, the Court held that insofar as the application described the activities in question by means of the words 'the bringing together, for the benefit of others, of a variety of services enabling customers conveniently to purchase those services', and that expression is capable of being categorized as a service, the application cannot be rejected on the sole ground that the assortment of services which the applicant intends to provide could also include services offered by itself, as this would prevent the applicant from having that sign registered as a trade mark with respect to such services as a whole.[218]

4.253 Turning to the second question,[219] the Court sought to determine whether the specification in question complied with the principles laid down in *IP Translator* as regards the need to identify the goods and services stated in the application with sufficient clarity and precision to enable the competent authorities and economic operators, on that basis alone, to determine the extent of the protection sought.[220]

4.254 Making a connection with *Praktiker*, the Court pointed out that it is not necessary in that regard to specify in detail each of the activities making up the retail services actually offered, holding that a description such as the one in the main proceedings that refers to 'the bringing together, for the benefit of others, of a variety of services enabling customers conveniently to purchase those services' is sufficiently clear to denote that the application is made in respect of a service which consists in selecting and offering an assortment of other

---

[215] Paragraphs 33–35.
[216] Although the reference to retail services in the explanatory note to Class 35 is limited to the retailing of goods, it is clear from the text of the note that this reference is indicative and not exclusive.
[217] Paragraphs 36–37.
[218] Paragraphs 38–39.
[219] In dealing with the second question, the Court ignored parts 2.a.ii and 2.b, apparently on the assumption that they were hypothetical, since the use of class numbers alone was not an issue in the main proceedings, while the possible loss of filing date did not seem to follow from the facts.
[220] Paragraphs 41–44.

services so that the consumer can choose between them from a single point of contact. On the other hand, the Court made clear that it is still necessary to identify with sufficient clarity and precision the subject of the services so offered, since otherwise it would be near impossible to conduct a meaningful examination of the mark, in particular as regards its possible descriptiveness in respect of one or more of the services the applicant intends to offer.[221]

4.255 In that connection, the Court drew a distinction between services in the application identified by reference to one or more of the general indications included in the heading of the corresponding class of the Nice Classification, and services for the identification of which the entire heading was used.

4.256 With regard to the former, the Court recalled[222] that general indications covering goods or services so variable that they are not capable of satisfying the requirement of clarity and precision are not suitable identifiers. The only cases in which the use without additional description of the general indications is acceptable are where those indications are, in themselves, sufficiently clear and precise. It pointed out, however, that it was for the referring court to assess whether indications such as 'entertainment' and 'personal and social services intended to meet the needs of individuals', are clear and specific enough to satisfy the relevant requirement. Conversely, where the applicant uses all the general indications in the heading of a particular class, he/she must, in any event, specify whether he/she is referring to all the goods or services included in the alphabetical list of that class or only to some of them, since, in the light of the different approaches within the European Union regarding the use of class headings, an application which does not make it possible to establish whether the applicant intends to cover all or only some of the goods or services in the class cannot be considered sufficiently clear and precise.[223]

4.257 Accordingly, the Court answered the questions referred by the Bundespatentgericht to the effect that: (1) services rendered by an economic operator which consist in bringing together services so that the consumer can conveniently compare and purchase them may come within the concept of 'services' referred to in Article 2 of the Directive; and (2) the Directive must be interpreted as imposing a requirement that an application for registration of a trade mark with respect to a service which consists in bringing together services must be formulated with sufficient clarity and precision so as to allow the competent authorities and other economic operators to know which services the applicant intends to bring together.

(c) Conclusions

4.258 Other than confirming the possibility of securing trade mark protection in respect of the retailing of services, the ruling in *Netto* did not do much more than combine the principles previously laid down in *Praktiker* as regards the proper designation of retail services with those laid down in *IP Translator* as concerns the requirements of clarity and precision.

4.259 Still, its main point is significant and shows the ease with which the Court is willing to take in market developments. Although in practice it will not always be easy to distinguish between the retailing of services and more traditional forms of service related transactions,

---

[221] Paragraphs 45–47.
[222] Citing C-307/10, *Chartered Institute of Patent Attorneys*, paragraphs 54–59 and 62.
[223] Paragraphs 47–52.

like the services of commissioning agents, authorized providers, or local licensees, the ruling of the Court opened the door for trade mark protection to business models that combine the access to third parties' services with additional benefits, like the assortment, indexing, or comparison of the various services on offer.

4.260 However, the judgment in *Netto* is also interesting as regards a number of statements it made with regard to the Nice Classification and the impact it has on the interpretation of trade mark specifications.

4.261 The first of those statements concerns the affirmation that any of the expressions included in the alphabetical list of a particular class is acceptable, on that ground alone, for the purposes of Article 2 of the Directive, in view of the need for the latter to comply with the Paris Convention and its derivative instruments, including the Nice Agreement. So radical a view, however, cannot sit comfortably with the voluntary and non-binding nature of the Nice Agreement, however true it may be that, as a matter of fact, the vast majority of terms in the alphabetical list are sufficiently clear and precise to satisfy the relevant requirements. Interestingly enough, that position also seems to assume a much closer relationship between the Nice Classification and the Directive than the one put forward by the Court in *IP Translator*.

4.262 Secondly, the unwillingness of the Court to take a clear position as to whether the retailing of services can consist of services offered by the applicant itself, despite the fact that the words 'in particular' used in the specification literally mean that such services are indeed covered in addition to, and independently of, any other services offered by third parties, results in continued uncertainty about the true scope of the registration, which may prove particularly problematic where the mark is ultimately used only in respect of retailing of services offered by the applicant itself.

4.263 Thirdly, it is not clear why the Court chose to single out the expressions 'entertainment' and 'personal and social services intended to meet the needs of individuals' when asking the referring court to assess the clarity and precision of the terms used in the specification. If that reference implies that the Court disapproves of these expressions as not being clear and precise enough, why did it not say so directly, but took the risk of seeing them interpreted differently in different jurisdictions?

4.264 Finally, the insistence of the Court to consider the use of the entire class heading as a reason for objecting to the application regardless of whether the specification is composed of indications which, in themselves, are sufficiently clear and precise, in view of the 'different approaches within the European Union regarding the use of class headings', seems to be disregarding the fact that, as a result of the judgment in *IP Translator*, the 'class-heading-covers-all' approach has practically been abandoned all around the European Union. It is therefore likely that, despite the significant steps taken by trade mark authorities to converge their practices, the Court will maintain its position as a matter of precaution until the legislator provides a final solution to the questions raised by the use of class headings.

5

ABSOLUTE GROUNDS

A. Introduction

Chapter 4 included an introduction to absolute grounds, the relevant provisions of the Directive and the Regulation, and covered formalities—namely what constitutes a sign, graphical representation requirements, and the concept of 'capable of distinguishing'—as well as the definition of the goods and services for which a trade mark can be registered. **5.01**

Chapter 5 will focus on the jurisprudence of the Court of Justice on specific absolute grounds. **5.02**

Again, the intent for this chapter is to introduce and develop a logical structure following the text of the Directive. **5.03**

Initially, the Court appeared to vacillate between contradictory routes: the first was described in *Windsurfing Chiemsee*;[1] the second, which appeared to be a fast track towards registration, in *Baby-Dry*.[2] **5.04**

B. Guidelines for Interpreting Article 3

(1) Public Interest, Independence, and Interdependence

Despite the limited role Article 3(1)(a) played in the development of the concept of distinctiveness, distinctiveness has become a considerable barrier to registrability as a result of Article 3(1)(b) and the notion that behind each one of the specific provisions of Article 3(1) there is an underlying public interest. **5.05**

The Court has explicitly rejected in *Windsurfing Chiemsee*[3] the need to interpret the provisions of the Directive, and the registrability of a geographical name, according to general policy doctrines; however, it stressed that Article 3(1)(c) had to be interpreted according to the public interest behind it. The same applied to other categories of types of marks and the remaining provisions of Article 3(1). **5.06**

---

[1] C-108/97 and C-109/97 *Windsurfing Chiemsee Produktions- und Vertriebs GmbH v Boots- und Segelzubehör Walter Huber and Franz Attenberger* [1999] ECR II-2779; see paragraphs 5.504 and following.
[2] C-383/99 P *Procter & Gamble Co v Office for Harmonisation in the Internal Market (Trade Marks and Designs)* [2001] ECR I-6251; see paragraphs 5.564 and following.
[3] C-108/97 & C-109/97 *Windsurfing Chiemsee* [1999] ECR I-2779.

5.07 In *Libertel*[4] it ruled that the 'possibility of registering a trade mark may be limited for reasons relating to public interest'.[5] In *Henkel*[6] it added that the public interest underlying each of the grounds of Article 3(1) 'may, or even must, reflect different considerations, depending upon which ground for refusal is at issue'.[7]

(2) The Independence of Each Ground

5.08 In *Linde*[8] it underlined that '[e]ach of the grounds for refusal to register listed in Article 3(1) ... is independent of the others and calls for separate examination'.[9]

5.09 Successfully overcoming one of the grounds would not guarantee the same for the others. In *Postkantoor*[10] the Court ruled that:

> it is not ... open to the competent authority to conclude that a mark is not devoid of any distinctive character in relation to certain goods or services purely on the ground that it is not descriptive of them.[11]

In *Companyline*[12] the Court looking at the equivalent provision of the Regulation, Article 7(1) stressed that 'it is quite evident from the wording of article 7(1) ... that it is sufficient that one of the absolute grounds for refusal listed in that provision applies for the sign at issue not to be registrable as a Community trade mark'.[13]

5.10 However, failing one of the grounds could cause a domino effect. In *Postkantoor*[14] the Court found that a 'word mark which is descriptive of characteristics of goods or services for the purposes of Article 3(1)(c) ... is, on that account, necessarily devoid of any distinctive character with regard to the same goods or services within the meaning of Article 3(1) (b).'[15]

(3) The Link with the Specification, the Relevant Consumer, and Timing

5.11 The assessment of absolute grounds is not an exercise that can be concluded in the abstract. On the contrary, context is everything. We will consider in detail specific contextualization instances, but there are three elements that appear to be common.

5.12 First, registrability is linked with the specification:

> Where registration of a mark is sought in respect of various goods or services, the competent authority must check, in relation to each of the goods or services claimed, that none of the grounds for refusal listed in Article 3(1) of the Directive applies to the mark and may reach different conclusions depending upon the goods or services in question.[16]

---

[4] C-104/01 *Libertel Groep BV* [2003] ECR I-3793.
[5] *Libertel Groep BV* (n 4) paragraph 50.
[6] C-456/01 P and C-457/01 P *Henkel KGaA v Office for Harmonisation in the Internal Market (Trade Marks and Designs)* [2004] ECR I-5089.
[7] C-456/01 P and C-457/01 P *Henkel KGaA* [2004] ECR I-5089, paragraph 46.
[8] C-53/01 *Linde AG*, C-54/01 *Winward Industries Inc*, and C-55/01 *Rado Uhren AG* [2003] ECR I-3161.
[9] *Linde, Winward,* and *Rado Uhren AG* (n 8) paragraph 67.
[10] C-363/99 *Koninklijke KPN Nederland NV v Benelux-Merkenbureau (Postkantoor)* [2004] ECR I-1619.
[11] *Postkantoor* (n 10) paragraph 70.
[12] C-104/00 P *DKV Deutsche Krankenversicherung AG v Office for Harmonisation in the Internal Market (Trade Marks and Designs) (Companyline)* [2002] ECR I-7561.
[13] *Companyline* (n 12) paragraph 29.
[14] C-363/99 *Koninklijke KPN Nederland NV v Benelux-Merkenbureau* [2004] ECR I-1619.
[15] *Postkantoor* (n 10) paragraph 86.
[16] C-363/99 *Koninklijke KPN Nederland NV* [2004] ECR I-1619, paragraph 73.

Second, registrability is considered from the perspective of the specific public that is relevant for the specified goods or services: 'For the purposes of determining whether a sign is registrable as a trade mark it is necessary to take as a standpoint that of the relevant public.'[17] **5.13**

Third, there are two 'timing' points to be made: **5.14**

(i) From the consumer's perspective the Court has indicated that the critical time for determining distinctive character is that of making a choice:

> it is when making his choice between different products in the category concerned that the average consumer exhibits the highest level of attention[18] ... so that the question whether or not the average consumer sees the mark at the time of purchase is of particular importance for determining whether the mark has acquired distinctive character through use.[19]

(ii) From the perspective of the authority administering the system of registration the relevant date for establishing the registrability criteria is the date of filing the application. The Court has indicated this clearly in relation to the Community trade mark regime: 'The date of filing the application for registration of the Community trade mark is the material date for the examination.'[20]

Still, subsequent material could be relevant: 'the Court of First Instance could without inconsistency in its reasoning or error of law take account of material which, although subsequent to the date of filing the application, enabled the drawing of conclusions on the situation as it was on that date.'[21] **5.15**

C. Article 3(1)(b): Devoid of any Distinctive Character

(1) *Companyline*: Article 7(1)(b); Balancing between *Baby-Dry* and *Postkantoor*

In *Companyline*,[22] a post *Baby-Dry*[23] case, the Court reconsidered distinctive character and descriptiveness in the context of composite marks from the perspective of Article 7(1)(b) of the Regulation.[24] **5.16**

(a) The Judgment of the Court of First Instance

The Court of First Instance[25] had dismissed the action against the refusal by the Board of Appeal to allow DKV's application for registration of COMPANYLINE as a Community trade mark for insurance and financial affairs services. The Court of First Instance found the mark to be devoid of distinctive character, consisting of two generic words simply coupled together. **5.17**

---

[17] C-104/01 *Libertel Groep BV* [2003] ECR I-3793, paragraph 45.
[18] Citing C-361/04 P *Ruiz-Picasso v Office for Harmonisation in the Internal Market (Trade Marks and Designs)* [2006] ECR I-643.
[19] C-363/99 *Koninklijke KPN Nederland NV* [2004] ECR I-1619, paragraph 72.
[20] C-192/03 P *ALCON v Office for Harmonisation in the Internal Market (Trade Marks and Designs)* [2004] ECR I-8993, paragraph 40.
[21] *ALCON* (n 20) paragraph 41.
[22] C-104/00 P *DKV Deutsche Krankenversicherung AG* [2002] ECR I-7561.
[23] C-383/99 P *Procter & Gamble Co* [2001] ECR I-6251.
[24] Contrast with C-363/99 *Koninklijke KPN Nederland NV* [2004] ECR I-1619.
[25] T-353/99 *Deutsche Krankenversicherung AG (DKV)* [2001] ECR II-1645.

5.18 It declined to consider the application of Article 7(1)(c) by the Board since failure under one ground would suffice and also rejected a third plea regarding misuse of powers.

(b) The Opinion of Advocate General Ruiz-Jarabo Colomer

5.19 Advocate General Ruiz-Jarabo Colomer distinguished *Baby-Dry* from the current case based on the structure of the two signs: the current comprised two familiar words separated by a hyphen whereas the former involved a 'neologism', a combination of two words.

5.20 Following *Postkantoor*[26] and his 'availability' public interest considerations he attempted to introduce some guiding principles, 'clear pointers'[27] that the legislature had failed to provide, regarding the interpretation of Article 7(1) of the Regulation. The starting point was that all the criteria had to be evaluated separately from each other; and because of the overlap courts had to be cautious in their application:

> the sign could in principle be refused registration on the basis of Article 7(1)(c), and only once it is clear that it is purely descriptive can Article 7(1)(b) be pleaded. In other words, lack of distinctive character is assumed from the sign's descriptiveness and not the other way around. That is how word marks should as a rule be assessed.[28]

5.21 **(i) The way forward: A different view** It is worth mentioning his view about the role of the Court as an appellate court; it should not decide on the registrability of specific signs, contrary to the approach in *Baby-Dry*.[29] Procedural efficiency had to be balanced with the role of the Court as the highest interpreter of Community trade mark law; its function should be to lay down principles of general application, leaving their implementation to the Court of First Instance and the Office. Indeed, procedural efficiency would suffer in the end if large numbers of applications were to be left for the Court to decide.

5.22 **(ii) Distinctive character and perceptible differences** He considered, first, the application of Article 7(1)(b) suggesting that 'a difference should be considered to be perceptible if it affects significant elements either of the appearance of the mark claimed or of its semantic content'.[30]

5.23 **(iii) The perspective for determining registrability** He adopted a pragmatic approach in order to strengthen a point he had already made in *Postkantoor*:

> the standpoint from which the assessment is to be made must move away from formal criteria to reflect the actual characteristics of the class of persons targeted. The fact that there are many applications for trade marks composed of English words in itself shows that applicants assume a certain level of understanding of English, even where consumers have a different mother tongue.[31]

5.24 The whole gamut of possible ways in which such consumers might be expected to respond should be explored before reaching a decision.

5.25 **(iv) Registrability of COMPANYLINE** He agreed that the finding of the Court of First Instance on the nature of the two words was one of fact. He accepted that it had not assessed

---

[26] C-363/99 *Koninklijke KPN Nederland NV* [2004] ECR I-1619.
[27] Point 34.
[28] Point 43.
[29] C-383/99 P *Procter & Gamble Co* [2001] ECR I-6251.
[30] Point 51.
[31] Point 56.

the descriptiveness of the compound sign as such, but there was nothing to suggest that 'taking the expression companyline as a whole invalidates the Court of First Instance's view—rather the reverse is true'.[32] He agreed that the mere coupling of these words failed to generate an additional characteristic that would make the sign 'capable of distinguishing the appellant's services from those of other undertakings'.[33]

(v) Descriptiveness should be assessed first He had some criticism though on the way the Court of First Instance had reached its decision.   **5.26**

> It would have been appropriate to begin by finding that the significant components of the mark claimed were wholly descriptive, and on that basis to declare the mark devoid of any distinctive character. That flaw in logic cannot lead to annulment of the contested decision, since the final assessment is in conformity with law.[34]

(vi) The remaining grounds of appeal The Advocate General agreed that all the remaining grounds should also be dismissed; from his analysis it is worth mentioning here four particular points.   **5.27**

First, he repeated that failing one provision sufficed to reject the application, therefore relying on only one ground 'whilst it may be open to criticism as to expediency, does not give rise to questions of legality'.[35]   **5.28**

Second, Article 12(b) delimited the scope of the right following registration. It did not determine the conditions for registration. Further, disclaimers under Article 38—that the applicant at some stage of the procedure offered to undertake—did not affect the application of Article 3(1) (b) and Article 3(1)(c): 'It is certainly true ... that in BABY-DRY the Court alluded to Article 12 ... when stating the legal basis for its subsequent reasoning. But it did not go on to draw any practical consequence from that provision whatsoever.'[36]   **5.29**

Third, he underlined that Article 7(2) of the Regulation provided that a sign is to be refused registration even where the grounds for refusal obtain in only part of the Community; there was no reason to consider the impression conveyed by that sign to speakers of other Community languages. It would, however, be the opposite   **5.30**

> if they had decided that the sign raised no problems under Article 7(l)(b) or (c) of the Regulation for speakers of the language in which the sign was expressed. Where that is the case, there is ... no reason why a sign's eligibility for registration as a trade mark should not be assessed taking account of the perception of that sign among consumers in other countries.[37]

(vii) The practice of the Office as 'precedent' Fourth, he rejected the claim that the Office had to follow its past decisions. 'The mere fact that the Office treated other signs ending in the suffix line differently, if indeed it did, is no reason to assume that it was exercising a power arbitrarily or to support an allegation of misuse of powers.'[38]   **5.31**

---

[32] Point 64.
[33] Point 65.
[34] Point 69.
[35] Point 76.
[36] Point 82.
[37] Point 92.
[38] Point 96.

(c) The Judgment of the Court

5.32 (i) **Inadmissibility: Appraisal of facts; new pleas** The Court dismissed the appeal, primarily based on the delineation of its jurisdiction that excluded the assessment and appraisal of facts. The actual application of the provisions, as interpreted by the Court, to the facts of the case involved findings of a factual nature and the appraisal of those findings; both were exclusively within the jurisdiction of the Court of First Instance. There were two exceptions: where a substantive inaccuracy in its findings was attributable to the documents submitted to it; and where the clear sense of the evidence before it had been distorted. Only then is there a question of law that allows the Court of Justice to review the appraisal of the facts.[39]

5.33 Partly responding to the reservations of the Advocate General regarding the role of the Court in trade mark appeals, it found the misuse of power plea to be an unsubstantiated 'request for re-examination of the application before the Court of First Instance, which the Court of Justice, by virtue of Article 49 of its EC Statute, has no jurisdiction to entertain'.[40]

5.34 (ii) **The interpretation of Article 7(1)(b)** In terms of substance, first, it accepted that the Court of First Instance was 'entitled to confine itself to considering that [Article 7(1)(b)] question, and was under no obligation to rule on the possible dividing line between the concept of lack of distinctiveness and that of minimum distinctiveness'.[41]

5.35 Then, it found that its interpretation of Article 7(1)(b) was not wrong: 'in examining whether two generic terms coupled together possess any additional characteristic such as to confer on the sign, taken as a whole, a distinctive character, the Court of First Instance did not err in law in its interpretation of Article 7(1) (b)'.[42]

5.36 It also found that the Court of First Instance had considered not only the distinctive character of each individual component but of the compound mark as well.

(2) *SAT.1*: Back to *Baby-Dry*?

5.37 In *SAT.1*[43] the Court appeared to take yet another turn. The appellant had applied to register as a Community trade mark the sign 'SAT.2' for goods in several classes and services in Classes 35, 38, 41, and 42. The specification enumerated the services in detail. The examiner rejected the application in respect of all the services insofar as they referred to satellites or to satellite television in the widest sense. The Second Board of Appeal[44] upheld the examiner's decision in respect of Classes 38, 41, and 42, holding that the sign lacked distinctive character and was descriptive, failing both Article 7(1)(b) and Article 7(1)(c) of the Regulation.

(a) The Judgment of the Court of First Instance

5.38 The Court of First Instance[45] annulled the Board of Appeal's decision to the extent that it had failed to rule on the part of the appeal regarding services in Class 35 and insofar as it

---

[39] Citing C-280/99 to C-282–99 *Moccia Irme v Commission* [2001] ECR I-4717; and C-323/00 P *DSG v Commission* [2002] ECR I-3919.

[40] C-104/00 P *DKV Deutsche Krankenversicherung AG* [2002] ECR I-7561, paragraph 44.

[41] *Companyline* (n 12) paragraph 20.

[42] *Companyline* (n 12) paragraph 21.

[43] C-329/02 P *SAT.1 SatellitenFernsehen GmbH v Office for Harmonisation in the Internal Market (Trade Marks and Designs)* [2004] ECR I-8317.

[44] Case R-312/1999-2, 2 August 2000.

[45] T-323/00 *SAT.1 SatellitenFernsehen v Office for Harmonisation in the Internal Market (Trade Marks and Designs)* [2002] ECR II-2839.

concerned services not connected with satellite broadcasting. Further, whilst the Court of First Instance accepted that the sign was not exclusively descriptive, according to Article 7(1)(c), in respect of all the relevant services, it held that it lacked distinctive character in respect of services that had to do with broadcasting via satellite. According to the Court of First Instance, the absolute grounds for refusal in Article 7(1) subparagraphs (b) to (e) were public interest provisions, ensuring that the signs they covered remained free for all to use. 'SAT.2' lacked distinctiveness because SAT was an established and common abbreviation of a characteristic—a link to satellite broadcasting—of most of the services concerned, and thus devoid of distinctive character. '2' was a number, and numbers were commonly used in trade for the presentation of the same services. And the element '.' was commonly used in trade for the presentation of all goods and services. The sign as a whole was devoid of any distinctive character because of the weaknesses of its constituent elements. In this case, according to the Court of First Instance, there was no evidence that the composite mark was greater than the sum of its parts, a characteristic that could render the mark distinctive. It also rejected the plea that the Office had breached the principle of equal treatment by changing its position regarding alpha numeric signs; a decision wrongly accepting a sign for registration should not be the basis for annulling a later decision to the contrary.[46] The principle of equal treatment should be balanced with the principle of legality.

(b) The Opinion of Advocate General Jacobs

Advocate General Jacobs started his deliberation of the plea on the misinterpretation of Article 7(1)(b) with a general comment on the concept of distinctiveness and the difference between Article 7(1)(a) and Article 7(1)(b). **5.39**

(i) The difference between Article 7(1)(a) and Article 7(1)(b) The answer could be found in Article 7(3), stating that distinctiveness through use is relevant only in the case of Article 7(1)(b). Accordingly, Article 7(1)(a) referred to the abstract capacity to distinguish between products of different origins, whereas Article 7(1)(b) referred to distinctiveness in relation to the class of product in question. **5.40**

(ii) Interpreting Article 7(1)(b): A permissive perspective Advocate General Jacobs accepted that each ground for refusing registration should be interpreted in the light of the underlying public interest, a similar position to that of AG Ruiz-Jarabo Colomer, accepting that Article 7(1)(c), Article 7(1)(d), and Article 7(1)(e) could be interpreted following analogous arguments.[47] **5.41**

Still, according to the Advocate General, some analogous reasoning could not be imposed on Article 7(1)(b), because there was no obvious reason why signs which lacked distinctive character in relation to the specified goods or services should be kept free for general use. Lack of distinctive character did not imply the relationship specified in subparagraphs (c) to (e). He noted that *Libertel* was not about signs to be 'freely used by all' but about 'not unduly restricting' the availability of some types of signs, where there is a limited range of them.[48] **5.42**

---

[46] Citing Case 188/83 *Witte v Parliament* [1984] ECR 3465; Case 134/84 *Williams v Court of Auditors* [1985] ECR 2225.
[47] Citing C-299/99 *Koninklijke Philips Electronics NV v Remington Consumer Products Ltd* [2002] ECR I-5475.
[48] Citing paragraph 47 of the judgment and point 81 of AG Ruiz-Jarabo Colomer's Opinion in C-456/01 P and C-457/01 P *Henkel KGaA* [2004] ECR I-5089.

In this case, he agreed, there was a much wider range of numbers that a consumer could recognize as distinctive.

5.43 Accordingly, he found that the statement at paragraph 36 of the judgment under appeal, 'to the effect that the aim of Article 7(1) (b) is to keep the signs to which it refers available to be freely used by all', went appreciably further than what he considered to be a correct interpretation of the law:

> Although perhaps not decisive in itself, that statement is likely to have influenced the final assessment of the registrability of 'SAT.2'; the application of a test whose aim is to keep signs available to be freely used by all will inevitably be more severe than that of a test aimed simply at not unduly restricting the availability of other types of sign whose range is limited.[49]

5.44 **(iii) Assessing distinctive character** Advocate General Jacobs started by pointing out what he found to be correct in the Judgment of the Court of First Instance: the assessment had to be of the mark as a whole; at an intermediate stage, it might be helpful to examine each one of the components of the mark.

5.45 Regarding the element SAT he agreed that the term was both descriptive and lacking distinctiveness and added that in some cases there was a degree of overlap between the different situations covered by Articles 7(1)(b) and 7(1)(c), whilst the respective aims of the provisions were distinct.[50] He disagreed though, first, with its assessment regarding the element '2', that 'numbers in general, and the number "2" in particular, are commonly used in trade, for the presentation of the services concerned'[51] and therefore lacked distinctive character in that regard. A descriptive element commonly used in trade was very likely to lack distinctiveness; however, this reasoning could not be automatically extended to non-descriptive elements. In some cases use of numbers would be descriptive, for example, when they indicated size, but there was no inherent reason why they should not also distinguish between the products of different suppliers. The approach taken by the Court of First Instance conflated the criterion of distinctiveness in Article 7(1)(b) with that of descriptiveness in Article 7(1)(c).[52]

5.46 There should be no automatic presumption that a mark which consisted exclusively of elements that individually lacked distinctive character lacked itself distinctiveness in the absence of an additional factor.

5.47 **(iv) Registrability of 'SAT.2'** He found that it was possible and in the interests of procedural economy to decide whether the sign 'SAT.2' as a whole lacked distinctive character.

5.48 He characterized the mark as a compound sign of a format that is very common in the field of broadcasting. The presence of a numerical identifier was clearly designed to ensure distinctiveness; the

> very commercial use of these signs to designate television channels and associated products seems ample proof of the success of that approach. If the average consumer of television programmes and spin-offs had difficulty in identifying such signs as differentiating between products and their origins, they would not be used, particularly since the commercial

---

[49] Point 28.
[50] Citing C-265/00 *Campina Melkunie BV v Benelux-Merkenbureau* [2004] ECR I-1699.
[51] *Campina* (n 50) paragraph 46.
[52] Point 42.

pressures of advertising revenue and audience ratings create a powerful need for product loyalty.[53]

5.49 As to the aim of 'not unduly restricting' the availability of certain signs, the number of possible distinctive and distinguishable combinations of a numerical with a non-numerical element was very high.[54]

5.50 **(v) The principle of non-discrimination** He looked briefly at the alternative ground of appeal, the applicability of the principle of equal treatment. If a previous decision of the Office were wrong, it should not be relied on to support the annulment of a subsequent correct decision; no person should be allowed to rely, in support of his/her claim, on unlawful acts committed in favour of another.

5.51 He also stated that the Boards exercise circumscribed, not discretionary, powers when they decide on registrability, but accepted that a degree of subjectivity is inevitable when assessing the distinctiveness of a mark, even if the law had been applied correctly. In this context he emphasized the importance of maintaining consistency.

(c) The Judgment of the Court

5.52 **(i) The five parameters** From the Judgment of the Court we can identify five parameters regarding the application of Article 7(1)(b).

5.53 First, it linked the scope of the provision with the essential function of a trade mark,[55] in particular in view of the extent of protection afforded to a trade mark.[56]

5.54 Second, it held that the viewpoint of the relevant public should determine registrability. In the case of products 'intended for all consumers, the relevant public must be deemed to be composed of the average consumer, reasonably well-informed and reasonably observant and circumspect'.[57]

5.55 Third, distinctive character, like all the other grounds for refusal under Article 7(1), was independent of the others and had to be examined separately from them.

5.56 Fourth, distinctive character should be seen in the light of the 'general interest'[58] specifically underlying the provision. The Court recalled that in *Libertel*[59] Article 3(1) (b) of the Directive was interpreted as aiming at the need not to restrict unduly the availability of colours for other undertakings offering for sale goods or services of the same type. In relation to 'SAT.2', the Court noted:

> Registration of a sign as a trade mark is not subject to a finding of a specific level of linguistic or artistic creativity or imaginativeness on the part of the proprietor of the trade

---

[53] Point 57.
[54] Point 58.
[55] The essential function as described in Case 102/77 *Hoffmann-la Roche & Co AG and Hoffmann-la Roche AG v Centrafarm Vertriebsgesellschaft Pharmazeutischer Erzeugnisse mbH* [1978] ECR 1139 and, after the Directive, in C-299/99 *Koninklijke Philips Electronics NY v Remington Consumer Products Ltd* [2002] ECR I-5475.
[56] *SAT.1* (n 43) paragraph 23.
[57] Paragraph 24. Contrast with C-108/97 and C-109/97 *Windsurfing Chiemsee* [1999] ECR I-2779.
[58] Paragraph 25; citing C-456/01 P and C-457/01 P *Henkel KGaA v Office for Harmonisation in the Internal Market (Trade Marks and Designs)* [2004] ECR I-5089.
[59] C-104/01 *Libertel Groep BV* [2003] ECR I-3793.

mark. It suffices that the trade mark should enable the relevant public to identify the origin of the goods or services protected thereby and to distinguish them from those of other undertakings.[60]

5.57 Fifth, for marks comprising words or a word and a digit, distinctiveness had to be assessed on the basis of the whole comprised by its parts. The fact that each part on its own is devoid of distinctive character did not mean that their combination also lacked distinctive character.[61]

5.58 (ii) **The application of Article 7(1)(b)** The Court found that the Court of First Instance had correctly stated that assessing the distinctive character of a compound trade mark required considering it as a whole; however, it failed to base its decision on such an examination.

5.59 The Court accepted that the findings of the Court of First Instance on the lack of distinctive character of each individual element could not be challenged before the Court.[62] But, the Court of First Instance had erred by relying on a separate analysis of each of the elements of the mark and concluding that 'the fact that a compound trade mark consists only of elements devoid of distinctive character generally justifies the conclusion that that trade mark, considered as a whole, is also capable of being commonly used, in trade, for the presentation of the goods or services concerned'.[63]

5.60 The second error of the Court of First Instance was its position that trade marks which are capable of being commonly used, in trade, for the presentation of the relevant goods or services should not be registered. That, according to the Court, was a criterion relevant for the application of Article 7(1)(c), but it was not the 'yardstick against which Article 7(1)(b) ... should be judged'.[64] The Court failed to describe clearly the public interest behind Article 7(1)(b). It preferred to refer to *Libertel* whilst highlighting the facts that characterized that case.

5.61 (iii) **Registrability of 'SAT.2'** The Court chose to give itself the final judgment regarding the challenge against the decision of the Board of Appeal rather than refer the case back to the Court of First Instance.

5.62 The Office had held that in this case the additional elements were so weak that there could be no comparison with other signs incorporating 'SAT'. The Court disagreed. 'The fact that the element associated with "SAT" is in this case the digit "2" and a point, rather than another verbal element has ... no bearing on that analysis. Furthermore, the Office did not, at any stage in the proceedings, give as a reason for the difference in the treatment afforded to the appellant's application the likelihood of confusion between the sign which the latter sought to register and any previously registered trade mark.'[65]

---

[60] Paragraph 41.
[61] Citing C-265/00 *Campina Melkunie BV* [2004] ECR I-1699; and C-363/99 *Koninklijke KPN Nederland NV* [2004] ECR I-1619.
[62] The Court of First Instance had accepted the decision of the Board of Appeal that 'SAT' lacked distinctive character in respect of services related to broadcasting via satellite and that the elements '2' and '.' were or could be commonly used in trade, for the presentation of the goods or services concerned, and were thus devoid of any distinctive character.
[63] Paragraph 49. T-323/00 *SAT. 1 SatellitenFernsehen* [2002] ECR II-2839.
[64] Paragraph 36.
[65] Paragraph 46.

The Court concluded: 5.63

> In those circumstances, the contested decision must be annulled insofar as the Second Board of Appeal of the OHIM rejected, on the basis of Article 7(1)(b) of the regulation the application to register the term "SAT.2" as a Community trade mark. Since the Court of First Instance has already held, in the contested judgment, that the contested decision could not be based on Article 7(1)(c) of that provision and, second, that the Second Board of Appeal of the OHIM had, in the aforementioned decision, failed to rule in the appeal brought before it so far as concerns the services falling within Class 35, the contested decision must be annulled as a whole.[66]

(3) *BioID*: The Limited Effect of *SAT.1*

The effect of *SAT.1* was tested in *BioID*, another appeal against a Judgment of the Court of First Instance.[67] BioID AG applied to register the sign 'BioID.®' as a Community trade mark for goods and services in Classes 9, 38, and 42 of the Nice Agreement, all in relation to 'the computer-aided identification and/or verification of live organisms based on one or more specific biometric characteristics'. The Bio component of the mark and the full stop after ID were depicted in bold; different fonts were used in respect of the Bio and the ID components. The application was refused on the basis of Articles 7(1)(b) and 7(1)(c). The Board of Appeal confirmed the refusal.[68] 5.64

(a) *The Judgment of the Court of First Instance*

The Court of First Instance found that the relevant public would understand 'BioID' as meaning 'biometrical identification' and that it would be likely to be commonly used in trade for the presentation of the specified goods or services. The typeface and presentation of the sign—Arial in different degrees of boldness—were commonly used in trade for the presentation of all types of goods and services and were equally devoid of any distinctive character. The same applied to the full stop at the end of the sign, a common indication that the word was an abbreviation, as well as the ® symbol. It concluded that the mark was composed of a combination of elements and that each one of them was likely to be used, in trade, to present goods and services in the categories claimed by that trade mark and was therefore devoid of distinctive character in respect of the specified goods or services. However, its consideration of the mark went further than that; it also stated that there was no concrete evidence to indicate that the compound trade mark, taken as a whole, was greater than the sum of its parts. Only then did the Court of First Instance confirm that the trade mark was devoid of any distinctive character. 5.65

(b) *The Opinion of Advocate General Léger*

The Advocate General described the aim of Article 7(1)(c)[69] as intending to leave freely available to all economic operators signs which may be used to designate the specified goods or 5.66

---

[66] Paragraph 48.
[67] C-37/03 P *BioID AG v Office for Harmonisation in the Internal Market (Trade Marks and Designs)* [2005] ECR I-7975; T-91/01 *BioID AG v Office for Harmonisation in the Internal Market (Trade Marks and Designs)* [2002] ECR II-5159.
[68] Case R-538/1999-2, 20 February 2001.
[69] Referring to C-191/01 P *Office for Harmonisation in the Internal Market (Trade Marks and Designs) v WM Wrigley Jr Co* [2003] ECR I-12447; the Order in C-326/01 P *Telefon & Buch v Office for Harmonisation in the Internal Market (Trade Marks and Designs)* [2004] ECR I-1371; C-108/97 and C-109/97 *Windsurfing Chiemsee* [1999] ECR I-2779; C-53/01 *Linde AG*, C-54/01 *Winward Industries Inc*, and C-55/01 *Rado Uhren AG* [2003] ECR I-3161; C-104/01 *Libertel Groep BV* [2003] ECR I-3793; and C-363/99 *Koninklijke KPN Nederland* [2004] ECR I-1619.

services or characteristics of those products or services. Attempting to reconcile *Libertel*[70] with *SAT.1*,[71] he noted that the aim of availability should not be extended as the underlying general interest of Article 7(1)(b) to all the kinds of signs which fell within its scope. Instead, the Court found that the general interest behind Article 7(1)(b) was 'indissociable'[72] from the essential function of the trade mark, precluding from registration signs that were incapable of fulfilling the function of a trade mark for the specified goods and services concerned. Finally, the assessment of distinctive character should consider the overall impression conveyed by the sign,[73] because consumers usually perceive a trade mark as a whole without examining its details. This did not prevent a separate examination of each element; it simply meant that the application of Article 7(1)(b) should not rely exclusively on such an examination.

5.67 Turning to the substance of the appeal, he agreed that identifying the relevant public was a question of fact within the exclusive jurisdiction of the Court of First Instance.

5.68 The Advocate General agreed with BioID that the Court of First Instance had carried out a separate appraisal of the various elements composing the sign and then relied on the presumption that devoid of distinctive character elements could not, once combined, have a distinctive character, examining the overall impression only as a secondary consideration.

5.69 He also believed that the Court of First Instance had wrongly applied in relation to distinctive character a criterion that was relevant in respect of descriptiveness. The criterion was whether the elements composing the sign might be used, in trade, for the presentation of the specified goods and services:

> although that criterion is relevant in respect of an element descriptive of the goods or services covered by the application for registration or of their characteristics, as is the word element 'BioID' in this case, it is not relevant with regard to figurative elements like letters written in the Arial typeface; a simple full-stop or the element °. The fact that those elements, which are not in themselves descriptive of the goods and services concerned, may be used for their presentation in trade does not, in itself, mean that they are devoid of any distinctive character in relation to those goods and services.[74]

5.70 Instead, he suggested a balancing exercise in order to ensure that no proprietary rights would be granted over wholly descriptive words:

> a figurative sign composed of a wholly descriptive word element cannot be regarded as having a distinctive character unless it contains figurative elements which are individually distinctive and have a sufficient impact on the minds of the relevant public to keep their attention instead of that word element, or figurative elements capable of 'overriding' the meaning of that word element, and bestowing a distinctive effect on the overall sign.[75]

5.71 In practice, he admitted, this would be difficult to establish because usually it is easier to remember word rather than figurative elements.

5.72 The second claim of BioID was that the Court of First Instance had failed to take into account that it could not be proved that the contested sign was actually used by the public

---

[70] C-104/01 *Libertel Groep BV* [2003] ECR I-3793.
[71] C-329/02 P *SAT.1 SatellitenFernsehen GmbH* [2004] ECR I-8317.
[72] Point 37 of the Opinion of AG Léger.
[73] Citing C-363/99 *Koninklijke KPN Nederland NV* [2004] ECR I-1619.
[74] Point 79.
[75] Point 75.

or its competitors. The Advocate General recalled that in *Doublemint*[76] the Court had held that it was sufficient that the sign could be used in a descriptive way; it was not necessary to show that the sign was actually used in that way.

(vii) Registration of comparable marks Having proposed to set aside the contested judgment the Advocate General turned to the registrability of the sign. According to the facts of the case it had been established that BioID was wholly descriptive of a characteristic of the specified goods and services. Similarly, he accepted that none of the figurative elements had 'in itself a specific distinctive character'[77] in relation to the same goods and services. Looking at the mark as a whole he found that the interaction between its elements did not give it a distinctive character. The figurative elements accentuated rather than diluted the descriptiveness of the abbreviation. As a result the appeal against the Board of Appeal should be dismissed. **5.73**

(c) The Judgment of the Court

(i) The overall impression The Court repeated that Article 7(1)(b) intended to preclude registration of trade marks which were devoid of distinctive character 'which alone renders them capable of fulfilling' their function.[78] Second, that distinctive character had to be determined from the viewpoint of the relevant public. Third, that for compound marks the distinctive character had to be assessed according to the overall perception of the mark; the distinctive character of each one of the elements might be assessed separately but this should not lead to presumptions about the distinctive character of the compound mark. **5.74**

So the Court of First Instance had 'rightly held that ... [it] is not inconsistent with a successive examination of the different composite elements of the mark to consider that mark as a whole'.[79] And although it had found that a compound mark consisting of elements devoid of distinctive character should be itself presumed to be devoid of distinctive character, it had also directed part of its reasoning to considering the sign's distinctiveness as a whole.[80] **5.75**

(ii) The burden of proof Proving that the trade mark applied for was commonly used by the public or by competitors was relevant under Article 7(1)(d) but not under Article 7(1)(b).[81] In any case the impact of a trade mark on consumers constituted of fact and remained outside the jurisdiction of the Court. **5.76**

(iii) Registration of comparable marks The decisions of the Board of Appeal under the Regulation were 'adopted in the exercise of circumscribed powers and [were] not a matter of discretion'.[82] The legality of the decisions of Boards of Appeal should be assessed solely **5.77**

---

[76] C-191/01 P *Office for Harmonisation in the Internal Market (Trade Marks and Designs) v WM Wrigley Jr. Co.* [2003] ECR I-12447.
[77] Point 104.
[78] *BioID* (n 67) paragraph 27, citing C-329/02 P *SAT.1 SatellitenFernsehen GmbH* [2004] ECR I-8317.
[79] Paragraph 31.
[80] Referring to Paragraphs 42, 43, and 44 of the Judgment of the Court of First Instance.
[81] Citing C-64/02 P *Office for Harmonisation in the Internal Market (Trade Marks and Designs) v Erpo Möbelwerk* [2004] ECR I-10031.
[82] Paragraph 47.

on the basis of the Regulation, as interpreted by the Community judicature, and not on the basis of a previous decision-making practice of the Boards.[83]

> [T]he identity or similarity of the trade mark applied for in relation to another Community trade mark is irrelevant where, as in this case, elements of fact or of law which have been put forward in support of the application for that other mark are not put forward by the appellant for the purpose of showing the distinctive character of the trade mark applied for.[84]

5.78 **(iv) The criterion for the application of Article 7(1)(b)** The Court held that the Court of First instance had wrongly applied a criterion that was relevant in respect of Article 7(1)(c). Each of the grounds listed in Article 7(1) had to be examined and applied on its own according to its own underlying interest. In the case of Article 7(1)(b) the underlying interest was indissociable from the essential function of a trade mark.[85] Restating its stance in *SAT.1*, it held that whether the sign was likely to be commonly used in trade was not the yardstick for interpreting that provision.

5.79 **(v) Registrability of BioID.°** The Court started by breaking down the sign into its elements. The abbreviation was indistinguishable from the goods and services covered by the trade mark application and did not possess the character that could guarantee the identity of the origin of the marked product or service to the consumer or end-user from the viewpoint of the relevant public. Note, here, that there appear to be two audiences that count: first, the consumer or the end-user that is the recipient of the guarantee of origin; and, second, the potentially broader, relevant public that determines whether the sign possesses the character to function as a guarantee of origin.

5.80 Then the Court considered the figurative and graphic features of the sign finding that there was no distinctive element therein that could 'enable the trade mark applied for to guarantee, to the relevant public, the identity of the origin of the goods and services covered by the trade mark application'.[86] This time there was only one relevant audience.

5.81 Considering the overall impression conveyed by the sign it found that the abbreviation BioID was the dominant element of that mark. The additional elements did not possess any feature, 'in particular in terms of fancifulness or as regards the way in which they are combined, allowing that mark to fulfil its essential function in relation to the goods and services covered by the trade mark application'.[87] As a result the sign was devoid of any distinctive character and the action against the decision of the Board of Appeal had to be dismissed.

(4) Appeals Post *SAT.1* and *BioID*

5.82 Word marks or abbreviations which were refused on the basis of absence of distinctiveness have rarely been appealed and the decisions of the Boards of OHIM are routinely confirmed. Even rarer are appeals to the Court of Justice.

5.83 A relatively recent Order dismissing an appeal as manifestly unfounded related to the mark 'medi', sought to be registered for a large number of goods and services. The Court confirmed the decision of the General Court which had in turn confirmed OHIM's decision

---

[83] Citing T-19/04 *Metso Paper Automation v Office for Harmonisation in the Internal Market (Trade Marks and Designs)* (PAPERLAB) [2005] ECR II-2383.
[84] Paragraph 49.
[85] Citing C-329/02 P *SAT.1 SatellitenFernsehen GmbH* [2004] ECR I-8317.
[86] Paragraph 71.
[87] Paragraph 74.

of refusal. 'medi' was properly connected with 'medicine' or 'medical' and thus devoid of distinctiveness.[88]

(5) NAI and MMF: Distinctiveness of Abbreviations

(a) The issue

5.84 It corresponds to the Court's case law (and OHIM practice) that a mark cannot be refused as being contrary to Article 7(1)(b) or (c) CTMR, ie as non-distinctive or descriptive, unless it consists exclusively of a non-distinctive or descriptive sign or indication—adding a distinctive element to a non-distinctive sign overcomes the objection. This principle is undisputed—and unobjectionable—even though it may well be debated whether there should be a *de minimis* rule, or, putting it the other way around, the added element must be more than non-negligible.[89]

5.85 The Court has never made—or even allowed—a distinction to be made between different types of marks; all marks must be examined according to the same principles. It thus came as a surprise that the German Bundespatentgericht (the court with competence to review German Patent and Trade Mark Office (GPTO) decisions) referred two cases to the Court of Justice seeking a preliminary ruling which involved marks consisting of an abbreviation and a series of words the initials of which resulted in the abbreviation, the words themselves being descriptive of the services for which protection was claimed.

(b) The facts and the questions referred

5.86 In Case C 90/11, Mr Strigl had applied for registration of the word mark 'Multi Markets Fund—MMF' at the GPTO for services in Class 36 of the Nice Agreement. The GPTO refused the applications, concluding that the public would understand 'MMF' to stand for 'Multi Market Funds' which in turn was descriptive of the services. Mr Strigl appealed to the Federal Patent Court, which referred the following question to the CJEU:

> Is the ground for refusal under Article 3(1)(b) and/or (c) of the Directive also applicable to a word sign which consists of a descriptive word combination and a non-descriptive letter sequence, if the relevant public perceives the letter sequence as an abbreviation of the descriptive words because it reproduces their initial letters, and the trade mark as a whole can thus be construed as a combination of mutually explanatory descriptive indications or abbreviations?

5.87 In Case C-91/11, Securvita Gesellschaft zur Entwicklung alternativer Versicherungskonzepte mbH had obtained a registration for the word mark 'NAI—Der Natur Aktien Index' for services in Class 36. Öko-Invest Verlagsgesellschaft mbH requested cancellation of the mark, arguing that 'NAI' would be understood as 'Natur Aktien Index' (nature stock index), and thus was descriptive and non-distinctive. The GPTO granted the request, and upon Securvita's appeal, the Federal Patent Court referred the following question to the CJEU:

> Is the ground for refusal under Article 3(1)(b) and/or (c) of the Directive also applicable to a word sign which consists of a letter sequence which is non=descriptive—when considered on its own—and a descriptive word combination, if the relevant public perceives the letter sequence as an abbreviation of the descriptive words because it reproduces their initial

---

[88] Order of 16 October 2013, C-410/12 P *medi GmbH & Co. KG v OHIM*, ECLI:EU:C:2013:702.
[89] See Convergence Programme 3, available following the links at <https://www.tmdn.org/>.

letters, and the trade mark as a whole can thus be construed as a combination of mutually explanatory descriptive indications or abbreviations?

5.88 Thus, the Court was faced with two almost identical questions, the difference being that in the first case the abbreviation followed the words, whereas in the second case the abbreviation came first.[90] The Court therefore joined the cases for purposes of the procedure and the judgment.

(c) The Opinion of Advocate General Jääskinen

5.89 In his Opinion of 16 January 2012,[91] Advocate General Jääskinen proposed as an answer that in the present cases Article 7(1)(c) CTMR was not applicable, and that the referring court should examine the applications under established criteria for determining distinctiveness. The AG pointed out that OHIM's Fourth Board of Appeal had held the same mark registrable (in case R-1630/2008-4), but found the arguments of the Board unconvincing.

(d) The Judgment of the Court

5.90 In its judgment of 15 March 2012,[92] the Court recognized that the letter combinations as such—MMF, NAI—were not descriptive. However, as the public to which the marks were addressed would recognize in the letter combinations the initials of the word elements the marks as a whole would be descriptive.

5.91 The answer to the questions referred is therefore that Article 3(1)(b) and (c) of the Directive must be interpreted as meaning that it is applicable to a word mark which consists of the juxtaposition of a descriptive word combination and a letter sequence which is non-descriptive in itself, if the relevant public perceives that sequence as being an abbreviation of that word combination by reason of the fact that it reproduces the first letter of each word of that combination, and that the mark in question, considered as a whole, can thus be understood as a combination of descriptive indications or abbreviations which is therefore devoid of distinctive character.

(e) Consequences

5.92 The Judgment appears out of step with the general principles referred to above. It might be justified in situations where the letter combination—the abbreviation—is recognized as such by the public as a descriptive term (eg 'XL' as standing for 'extra large', or '4U' for 'for you'). In other situations, such as the present ones, it seems unnecessarily harsh. The Judgment also requires a somewhat unusual reading of 'consist exclusively of' in Article 7(1)(c) of the Regulation, as recognized by the AG. Granting registration would not prevent others from using 'Multi Market Funds' or 'Natur-Aktien-Index', and the applicant's decision to join the abbreviation with the descriptive term for purposes of registration would actually lead to a narrower scope of protection than that obtained by registration of the letters 'MMF' or 'NAI' alone. The Judgment's effects can easily be circumvented by applying for the letter combination without the addition of the words.

5.93 The effects of the Judgment—which may well be an aberration and will not actually be followed by OHIM—are, however, still felt. Recently, the same Federal Patent Court (albeit a

---

[90] Article 3(1)(b) and (c) of the Directive are the same as Article 7(1)(b) and (c) of the Regulation.
[91] ECLI:EU:C:2012:42.
[92] Joined Cases C-90/11 and C-91/11, *Strigl/GPTO, Securvita/GPTO*, ECLI:EU:C:2012:147.

different chamber) was faced with an opposition based on a letter sequence—'BGW'—against a word mark containing the same letter sequence but also words the initials of which made up the letter sequence—'BGW Bundesverband der deutschen Gesundheitswirtschaft'—and under the *Strigl* and *Securvita* judgment the latter mark would be unregistrable. The court felt itself unable to hold the marks confusingly similar because the 'BGW' element in the second mark could not be characterized as independently distinctive or dominant in view of the *Strigl/Securvita* finding that the three-letter combinations in those cases were 'ancillary'.[93] Therefore, the following question was referred to the Court:[94]

> Must Article 4(1)(b) of Directive 2008/95/EC be interpreted as meaning that, in the case of identical and similar goods and services, there may be taken to be a likelihood of confusion for the public if a distinctive sequence of letters which dominates the earlier word/figurative trade mark of average distinctiveness is made use of in a third party's later mark in such a way that the sequence of letters is supplemented by a descriptive combination of words relating to it which explains the sequence of letters as an abbreviation of the descriptive words?

The Opinion of AG Mengozzi became available on 12 March 2015;[95] he seeks to limit *Strigl/Securvita* to its concrete facts, and certainly would not extend its approach to the likelihood of confusion analysis.

5.94

(6) *BORCO-Marken* and *Technopol*: Single Letters and Numerals

In *BORCO-Marken*[96] and *Technopol*[97] the Court dealt with the assessment of the distinctiveness of single letters and numerals under Article 7(1)(b) and (c) of the Regulation (which correspond to Article 3(1)(b) and (c) of the Directive). Taken together, the judgments of the Court provide a useful overview not only of the principles applicable to the registrability of plain letters and numbers, but also of the apportionment of the burden of proof between applicants and examining authorities when it comes to establishing the relevant facts.

5.95

---

[93] Reference is made to paragraph 38 of *Strigl/Securvita* (n 92), which states as follows:

> On the contrary, as the Advocate General has noted in point 56 of his Opinion, the letter sequence which reproduces the initial letters of the words comprising that word combination occupies only an ancillary position in relation to the word combination. As the referring court suggests, each of the letter sequences at issue, although not descriptive when considered in isolation, may be descriptive when combined, within the mark at issue, with a principal expression, which itself is descriptive as such, of which it is perceived to be an abbreviation.

[94] C-20/14, *BGW Beratungs-Gesellschaft Wirtschaft mbH/Scholz*.

[95] ECLI:EU:C:2015:167. The Judgment of the Court, ECLI:EU:C:2015:714, came out at the proofreading stage. The Court held that (42) 'the mere fact that the later mark consists of a sign reproducing the letter sequence that constitutes the only word element of the earlier mark and of a combination of words the initial letters of which correspond to that sequence cannot, on its own, preclude a likelihood of confusion with that earlier mark'. It suggested that the national court (43)

> will have to examine, among other factors, whether the links which the relevant public may establish between the letter sequence and the word combination, in particular the possibility that the former may be perceived as an acronym of the latter, are such that that sequence may be perceived and remembered separately by the relevant public in the later mark. Likewise, it will, if necessary, have to assess whether the elements of which the later mark consists, taken as a whole, form a separate logical unit which has a different meaning from that of those elements taken separately.

[96] C-265/09 P *Office for Harmonisation in the Internal Market/BORCO-Marken-Import Matthiesen GmbH & Co. KG* (*BORCO-Marken*) [2010] ECR I-08265.

[97] C-51/10 P *Agencja Wydawnicza Technopol sp. z o.o./Office for Harmonisation in the Internal Market (Technopol)* [2011] ECR I-01541.

(a) BORCO-Marken: Single letters

5.96 (i) **The different views of OHIM and the General Court**   *BORCO-Marken* concerned an application for the registration as a Community trade mark of the figurative sign 'α' in respect of 'alcoholic beverages (except beers), wines, sparkling wines and beverages containing wine'. OHIM's examiner found that, despite its description as 'figurative', the sign applied for constituted a faithful reproduction of a Greek lower-case letter 'α', without graphical modifications, and that, accordingly, Greek-speaking consumers would see it as a mere letter and not as an indication of commercial origin. The examiner's refusal followed the line taken by the examination guidelines in force at the time of the decision, according to which applications consisting of single letters or numerals were to be objected to as a matter of principle, in view of their limited availability for other traders, unless the sign was stylized in such a way that the overall graphic impression prevailed over the 'mere existence' of a plain letter or number. On appeal, the Fourth Board upheld the rejection, adding further that the reference public 'might' view the letter 'α' as making reference to the quality ('A' quality), size, or type of the alcoholic beverages covered by the application.

5.97 The applicant lodged an application for annulment pleading infringement of Article 7(1)(b). Following the line already taken in previous cases concerning single letters,[98] the General Court[99] annulled the decision of the Board, taking the view that the Office's analysis implicitly but necessarily suggested that single letters lacked, of themselves, the minimum degree of distinctiveness required under Article 7(1)(b), despite the clear position of the Court's case law that registration is not conditional upon the sign applied for having a specific level of creativity.[100]

5.98 The General Court also found that the Board of Appeal had failed to carry out an examination based on the facts and that, apart from 'being of a doubtful nature which renders it valueless', its reasoning did not refer to any specific fact capable of substantiating the assertion that the mark would be perceived as a reference to the quality or to some other characteristic of the goods.[101]

5.99 (ii) **The appeal to the Court of Justice**   OHIM appealed to the Court of Justice, arguing that the *ex ante* nature of the examination did not impose on it an obligation to make a detailed factual assessment linked to the specific characteristics of the goods. Referring to the Court's case law on three-dimensional signs, OHIM contended that the examiner was entitled to rely on general affirmations concerning the consumer's perception and to draw the corresponding inferences about how that perception is conditioned by the nature of the sign at issue.

5.100 Advocate General Bot[102] considered that the appeal raised a question of principle and offered the Court the opportunity to put an end to the enduring disagreement between OHIM and the General Court as regards the correct method of the assessment. Succinctly,

---

[98] See Case T-441/05 *IVG Immobilien/Office for Harmonisation in the Internal Market (I)* [2007] ECR II-1937 and Case T-302/06 *Hartmann/Office for Harmonisation in the Internal Market (E)* ECLI:EU:T:2008:267.
[99] T-23/07 *BORCO-Marken-Import Matthiesen/Office for Harmonisation in the Internal Market (α)* [2009] ECR II-861.
[100] Paragraphs 42 and 43 of the Judgment of the General Court.
[101] Paragraphs 45 and 53–56 of the Judgment of the General Court.
[102] Opinion of Advocate General Bot of 6 May 2010, Case C-265/09 P, *Office for Harmonisation in the Internal Market/BORCO-Marken-Import Matthiesen GmbH & Co. KG* ECLI:EU:C:2010:256.

he reduced the essence of the case to the following question: Is it possible for OHIM to introduce under Article 7(1)(b) an *a priori* exclusion of a non-stylized letter from registration without infringing that Regulation?

The Advocate General took the clear view that the answer should be in the negative. He argued that, to the extent that letters are listed in Article 4 of the Regulation among the signs capable of constituting a trade mark, their general distinctive capacity cannot be questioned and that, in consequence, the assessment of their distinctive character within the meaning of Article 7(1)(b) must be carried out within the context of each specific case, taking into account the particular characteristics of the goods as specified in the application. In this connection, he stressed that, unlike signs consisting of colours, sounds, or smells, for which it might be reasonable to ask whether they are capable of functioning as trade marks, Article 4 creates a clear presumption that a letter is capable of being a sign, that is to say, it is capable, as such, of having a distinctive character.[103]

5.101

The Advocate General pointed out, however, that this is not enough to ensure registration, as OHIM still has to examine whether there are any absolute grounds applicable to the case. That requires a specific examination in connection with which OHIM has particular obligations, as clearly follows from the Court's case law,[104] according to which the examination must be rigorous, thorough, and full, and cannot either be cursory or carried out *in abstracto*. Although the Advocate General admitted that this may prove more difficult for some categories of signs, he stressed that the Court nevertheless refuses to allow those difficulties to be used as an excuse for assuming that such marks are, *a priori*, devoid of any distinctiveness character.[105]

5.102

Accordingly, he found that the reasoning of the Board fell clearly short of meeting the requisite legal standard, being at best hypothetical and at worse irrelevant, and refused to accept that the *a priori* nature of the examination could justify the cursory character of the Board's assessment or explain the 'doubtful tone' of its reasoning. Nor could OHIM claim that it was up to the applicant to rebut the Board's analysis if OHIM had not fulfilled its duty to provide sufficient reasons for its findings in the first place.[106]

5.103

The Court agreed with the Advocate General's argument as regards the presumed distinctive capacity of signs specifically mentioned in Article 4, but stressed that this presumption does not entail a different method of assessment for the purposes of Article 7(1)(b) depending on the type of sign concerned. Recalling its settled case law on single colours, product shapes, and slogans, it reiterated that the maxim requiring distinctiveness to be assessed by reference, first, to the goods or services concerned and, second, to the perception of the relevant public, applies with equal force to all categories of signs, regardless of whether these are expressly listed in Article 4 or not.[107]

5.104

The Court also held that the fact that it may prove more difficult to establish distinctiveness for marks consisting of a single letter than for other word signs does not justify laying down

5.105

---

[103] Points 34–37 and 46–47 of the Opinion of AG Bot.
[104] Citing cases C-363/99 *Koninklijke KPN Nederland* [2004] ECR I-1619, paragraph 31 and C-239/05 *BVBA Management, Training en Consultancy* [2007] ECR I-1455, paragraph 30.
[105] Points 42–45 of the Opinion of AG Bot.
[106] Points 54 and 58–59 of the Opinion of AG Bot.
[107] ECLI:EU:C:2010:508, paragraphs 31–32.

specific criteria supplementing or derogating from the criterion of distinctiveness as interpreted in the case law, or exonerate OHIM from its obligation to assess the distinctiveness of such marks by reference to concrete facts. Nor does the *a priori* character of the assessment preclude the examination from being specific in nature, since the very objective of an *a priori* review would be thwarted if it was open to OHIM, without adequate justification, to rely on conjecture or mere doubts.[108]

5.106 Finally, it found that OHIM could not rely on *Develey*[109] in order to avoid its duty to carry out a full examination, making clear that the applicant's obligation to rebut an objection raised under Article 7(1)(b) only arises after OHIM has duly discharged its burden to conduct an assessment of distinctiveness based on the facts and has provided sufficient reasons in support of its findings.[110]

(b) Technopol: Signs consisting of numerals

5.107 (i) **Background to the dispute** *Technopol*[111] is the flip side of *BORCO-Marken*. This time the Court had to deal not with whether numerals are distinctive per se and the rules governing the burden of proof, but rather with the evidential standard applicable to the examination by OHIM.

5.108 The application concerned the sign '1000' filed in respect of 'brochures, periodicals, including periodicals containing crossword puzzles and rebus puzzles, newspapers', in Class 16 of the Nice Classification. OHIM refused the application under Article 7(1)(b) and (c) of the Regulation on the grounds that the sign '1000' was devoid of any distinctive character and was descriptive of the contents and other features of the goods concerned.

5.109 The Fourth Board of Appeal upheld the rejection.[112] Contrary to *BORCO-Marken*, the Board did not limit its findings to general assertions regarding the distinctive capacity of numerals (although it did include a comment that a sign of this kind was merely laudatory), but gave specific reasons as to why the sign '1000' lacked the requisite distinctiveness, arguing, inter alia, that the relevant public would perceive the number '1000' as a mere indication that a particular publication contains 1000 riddles or rebus puzzles and not as a badge of origin. In support of its findings the Board referred to an Internet search which corroborated that various collections of this kind already existed on the market.

5.110 The applicant brought an action for annulment, claiming infringement of Article 7(1)(b) and (c) of the Regulation. In essence, it submitted that, where the number '1000' is used in isolation and is not coupled with another word explaining what it refers to, it will not be seen as a descriptive indication, since from the point of view of the consumer, no direct and specific link could be made between that sign and the characteristics of the goods. In addition, Technopol pleaded that, by virtue of Article 12(b) CTMR, the registration of the sign '1000' would not deprive third parties of the right to use that figure to designate quantities where such use does not constitute a trade mark infringement, and that there is

---

[108] Paragraphs 33–39 and 44–47.
[109] C-238/06 P *Develey v OHIM* [2007] ECR I-9375.
[110] Paragraphs 55–59.
[111] C-51/10 P, *Agencja Wydawnicza Technopol sp. z o.o. v Office for Harmonisation in the Internal Market* [2011] ECR I-01541
[112] See decision of OHIM's Fourth Board of Appeal of 7 August 2006, Case R-447/2006-4.

5.111 The General Court[113] rejected the action. Although it conceded that descriptive signs are those which may serve in *normal usage* to designate, either directly or by reference to their essential characteristics, the goods or services for which registration is sought, it agreed with the Board that there is a direct and specific link between the sign '1000' and at least some of the characteristics of the goods at issue. Specifically, the Court held that, inasmuch as the sign '1000' alludes to a quantity, it will immediately be perceived by the relevant public as a description of the number of pages, amount of data, or number of puzzles in a collection. It also found that the said conclusion cannot be invalidated by the fact that the mark is composed only of figures, since the missing information may be readily identified by the public, the association between the figure and the designated characteristics of the goods being immediate.[114]

5.112 The General Court further dismissed Technopol's plea based on Article 12(b) as inoperative, holding that the argument concerning availability could not offset the fact that the sign at issue was descriptive. It also dismissed the reference to the acceptance by OHIM of other signs consisting of numerals as irrelevant, holding that the legality of the decisions of the Boards of Appeal must be assessed solely on the basis of the Regulation and not on the basis of OHIM's previous practice. Having thus found that the ground for refusal set out in Article 7(1)(c) was applicable, it considered that there was no need to address the alleged infringement of Article 7(1)(b).[115]

5.113 **(ii) The appeal to the Court of Justice** Technopol appealed to the Court of Justice, pleading infringement of Article 7(1)(c) and criticizing the failure of the judgment under appeal to take account of OHIM's previous practice. More particularly, Technopol put forward that the relevant ground for refusal is subject not only to the 'normal usage' test referred to by the General Court, but also to the condition that the sign must be no different from the 'usual way' of designating the relevant goods or their characteristics.

5.114 Hence, unlike the appeal in *BORCO-Marken*, the dispute in *Technopol* did not concern the distinctiveness of numerals as such, but rather the depth of the examination required for establishing their possible descriptiveness. Notwithstanding, the Court opted for giving a complete overview of the applicable principles, including a reminder on the exact cut-off point between subsections (b) and (c) of Article 7(1) CTMR.

5.115 The Court reiterated at the outset, citing *BORCO-Marken*, that the inclusion of numbers in Article 4 has the effect that a sign composed exclusively of numerals with no graphic modifications and which has not been stylized creatively or artistically, cannot be precluded, for that reason alone, from being registered as a trade mark.[116]

---

[113] T-298/06 *Agencja Wydawnicza Technopol v Office for Harmonisation in the Internal Market (1000)* [2009] ECR II-00217.
[114] Paragraphs 21 and 26–31.
[115] Paragraphs 32–33 of the Judgment of the General Court.
[116] Paragraphs 29–31.

5.116 Moreover, it recalled that, according to settled case law, signs found to be descriptive are also devoid of distinctiveness, which necessarily implies a measure of overlap between the scope of paragraphs (b) and (c) of Article 7(1). However, to the extent that a sign may be devoid of distinctive character for reasons other than the fact that it may be descriptive, it is important for the correct application of Article 7(1) to ensure that the ground for refusal set out in paragraph (c) duly continues to be applied only to the situations specifically covered by that ground for refusal.[117]

5.117 Having set the framework for its analysis, the Court proceeded with the examination of the appellant's pleas under Article 7(1)(c). First, it addressed the argument that by not focusing on whether the sign '1000' represented the 'usual way' of designating the characteristics of the goods in the relevant sector, the General Court had interpreted Article 7(1)(c) in an excessively broad, and therefore incorrect, manner. In this connection, the Court referred to the principles established in *Biomate*[118] and *Postkantoor*[119] that it is not necessary that the sign actually be in descriptive use at the time of the application, being sufficient that it could be used for such a purpose, and that it is, furthermore, irrelevant whether there are other, more usual, signs for designating the same characteristics of the goods. It also took the opportunity to clarify that Paragraph 37 of *Baby-Dry*,[120] according to which a descriptive sign must be 'no different from the usual way of designating the relevant goods or services or their characteristics', cannot be understood as introducing a necessary condition for refusing registration. Accordingly, the Court concluded that Article 7(1)(c) does not require the sign to be the 'usual means' of designation of the goods in order to be objectionable.[121]

5.118 Second, the Court dealt with the argument that the examples given by the General Court regarding the perception of the sign '1000' by consumers as a description of the number of pages or the contents of publications are hypothetical and irrelevant. This gave the Court the chance to clarify that the reference to signs capable of designating a 'characteristic' of the goods is not limited to the properties expressly mentioned in Article 7(1)(c), being clear by the wording of that provision that the relevant list is not exhaustive and that, therefore, any other 'relevant' characteristic of the goods may be taken into account as well. The Court also pointed out that the use of the word 'characteristic' emphasizes that the signs referred to in Article 7(1)(c) are those which serve to designate a property of the goods, provided that it is 'reasonable to believe' that the sign will be recognized by consumers as a description of one of those characteristics.[122]

5.119 The Court then turned to examine the relevance of these principles as regards signs composed exclusively of numerals, observing that, to the extent that such signs are generally equated with numbers, one of the things that they can do in trade is to designate a quantity. Hence, such signs fall foul of Article 7(1)(c) if it is reasonable to believe that, in the mind of the relevant class of persons, the quantity indicated by those numerals characterizes the goods covered by the application. In this context, it held that, at the very least, the finding of the General Court that the sign '1000' designates the number of puzzles contained in a

---

[117] Paragraphs 33–34 and 45–47.
[118] C-265/00 *Campina Melcunie* [2004] ECR I-1699, paragraphs 19 and 38.
[119] C-363/99 *Koninklijke KPN Nederland* [2004] ECR I-1619, paragraphs 57–58.
[120] C-383/99 *Procter & Gamble* [2001] ECR I-6251, paragraph 37.
[121] Paragraphs 34–40.
[122] Paragraphs 41–50.

publication is not unreasonable and, for that reason, it is not incompatible with the scope of Article 7(1)(c).[123]

As to the remainder, the Court agreed with the findings of the judgment under appeal: first, that Article 12(b) does not have a decisive bearing on the interpretation of Article 7(1)(c) and that, therefore, it plays no intrinsic role in its application; and, second, that the General Court was under no obligation to carry out an exhaustive analysis of the right to keep free.[124]

5.120

As regards the second ground of appeal, relating to OHIM's previous practice, the Court conceded that, as a rule, OHIM has the obligation to exercise its powers in accordance with the general principles of equal treatment and sound administration and must, therefore, take into account decisions already taken in respect of the same or similar signs, considering with special care whether it should decide the case pending before it in the same way or not. However, the Court also underlined[125] that the way in which these principles are applied must be consistent with the paramount principle of legality, which means that an applicant cannot rely to his advantage on a possibly unlawful act committed to the benefit of someone else. Accordingly, the Court came to the conclusion that from the moment it had been duly established that the application was caught by the ground for refusal laid down in Article 7(1)(c), the appellant could not rely on the outcome of previous decisions of the Office dealing with signs composed of different numerals.[126]

5.121

(c) Conclusions

The judgments in *BORCO-Marken* and *Technopol* give a full picture of the principles at play when dealing with signs consisting of single letters or numerals. As made clear by the Court, such signs are per se capable of performing a trade mark function, provided that their distinctive capacity is not inhibited by lack of distinctiveness or descriptive connotations, being no different in this regard from any other category of sign.

5.122

Thus, the examining authority cannot merely rely on abstract considerations linked to the availability of letters and numbers or on generic assertions regarding their general unsuitability to designate commercial origin. Nor is it possible to disguise statements of this kind as well-known facts, without providing at least a modicum of substantiation. As *Technopol* shows, it will generally be easier to raise an objection on grounds of descriptiveness within the meaning of Article 7(1)(c) CTMR using arguments linked to the properties of the goods, rather than struggling with speculative contentions under Article 7(1)(b), which are vulnerable to being dismissed by the Court as mere conjecture.

5.123

Still, for the objection to prosper it must be based on 'reasonable' deductions, preferably supported by concrete evidence giving sufficient grounds to believe that consumers will not perceive the sign as a badge of origin. It is to be noted that regardless of the final outcome in *Technopol*, the only argument that has apparently convinced the Court was the one connected to the finding that the sign '1000' may be seen as denoting the number of puzzles

5.124

---

[123] Paragraphs 51–56.
[124] Paragraphs 58–65.
[125] Citing Joined Cases C-39/08 and C-43/08, *Bild digital and ZVS*, summary published at [2009] ECR I-20, paragraphs 17–18.
[126] Paragraphs 73–79.

contained in the appellant's publication and not the reference to its laudatory connotations or to the number of pages possibly included in a publication.

5.125 Useful as they may be as regards the method of assessing distinctiveness, however, the judgments in *BORCO-Marken* and *Technopol* are not entirely free of controversy.

5.126 First, the Court's reference to Article 4 in order to bar general assumptions about the distinctive capacity of single letters and numerals has not impeded it in the past from putting forward similarly generic contentions in relation to other types of signs listed in Article 4, like shape marks; the fact that in relation to three-dimensional shapes the Court has mitigated its general pronouncements by referring to specific situations in which such signs may be seen as distinctive does not affect the intrinsic value of the statement that, as a rule, shape marks are not distinctive. By the same token, it is difficult to see how arguments linked to the generally reduced distinctive capacity of letters or numerals would deprive Article 4 of its effect, considering that signs objected to on that basis can always be registered, at the very least, on the basis of distinctiveness acquired through use pursuant to Article 7(3) CTMR.

5.127 Second, the statement of the Court at paragraph 39 of *BORCO-Marken* that it 'may prove more difficult to establish distinctiveness for marks consisting of a single letter' seems quite at odds with the above remarks and with the logic of the rest of the judgment. Moreover, it is inexplicably left incomplete, raising the question why the Court has not explained in more detail what this difficulty actually consists of and how it could possibly affect the examination. Ultimately, this point marks the difference between the case law dealing with single letters and numerals and the cases relating to colours and shapes, for which the Court has accepted that the presumption of their lack of distinctiveness can be rebutted, in the case of colours in 'exceptional circumstances' and in the case of shapes when these are 'significantly removed from the norms of the sector'.

5.128 While it is true that the assessment of such exceptional circumstances can only be based on the facts of each particular case, the fact remains that the barrier against the registration of single letters and numerals has been set significantly lower in comparison, to the extent that the Court has effectively placed the burden of proving that such signs are devoid of distinctiveness squarely on the shoulders of examining authorities without leaving any margin for generalizations of any kind.

(7) *Nichols*: No Special Conditions for Surnames

5.129 The registrability of surnames was considered by the Court in *Nichols*.[127] This was a reference from the High Court of Justice (England and Wales) dealing with a challenge of the practice of the UK's Patent and Trade Mark Office to refuse registration of common surnames without evidence of acquired distinctiveness. A combination of two factors determined commonness, the number of times the name appeared in the London telephone directory—names appearing more than 200 times were considered to be common—and the type and breadth of the specified goods or services.

5.130 The contested application was for the mark 'Nichols' for food and drink products dispensed from vending machines; the sign was considered to be devoid of any distinctive character because Nichols was a common surname and the specification would cover a large number

---

[127] C-404/02 *Nichols Plc v Registrar of Trade Marks* [2004] ECR I-8499.

of products originating from an equally large number of undertakings. Without evidence of use, consumers would view the sign as a surname rather than a trade mark. The sign had been accepted for vending machines because that market was more specialized.

The High Court referred a list of detailed questions to the Court of Justice, seeking clarification in relation to Articles 2 and 3, but also the scope of Article 6 and its interrelation with Article 3.[128]

5.131

(a) The Opinion of Advocate General Ruiz-Jarabo Colomer

Advocate General Ruiz-Jarabo Colomer expressed some sympathy for the position of the English court:

5.132

> The national court, rather than taking a purely theoretical approach, prefers to take a realistic view of the functioning of the registered trade mark system. Accordingly, he [Mr Justice Jacob, as he then was] suggests that attention be paid to the risk of monopolisation deriving from the registration of a common surname to cover a wide range of goods or services. In view of that danger, the possibility, which is costly in terms of time and money, of challenging some of those indications on the ground of non-use, after the expiry of five years following registration, does not seem to be an effective remedy. For the same reasons, it is inappropriate to take account, when analysing the distinctiveness of a trade mark, of considerations concerning the limitation of its effects, even though that seems to be the approach adopted in paragraph 37 of the Baby-Dry[129] judgment. In practice, favourable treatment is accorded to whoever has secured registration.[130]

He examined the first three questions posed by the English court together, simplifying their essence: are common surnames subject to specific distinctiveness conditions, in particular under Article 3(1)(b)?

5.133

(i) Registrability of surnames Article 2 specifically included personal names in its indicative list and, in practice, surnames were frequently used as trade marks. The wording of Article 6(1) and the absence of surnames from the list of Article 3(1)(c) meant that they were not considered in principle to be generic or descriptive. Thus, he rejected the application of 'keep free for other traders to use' considerations. From a more practical perspective the Commission had underlined in its intervention that the policy of the UK Trade Mark Office was arbitrary and at odds with the Directive.

5.134

(ii) Surnames: Distinctive character Determining distinctiveness inevitably involved a degree of subjectivity; however, he was not satisfied with the reasoning, submitted by the United Kingdom in support of its interpretive derogation, that in respect of common surnames recognition of a trade mark in the marketplace was not enough. It submitted that its formula ensured that only surnames that identified the products of an undertaking could be protected as trade marks.

5.135

The Advocate General was willing to accept only that the distinguishing capability of surnames could vary from one sector of the economy to another. These variations were covered by the criteria imposed by the Court, whilst there was no room for a new policy regarding surnames under Article 3(1)(b) 'in an all-embracing or abstract manner'.[131] The

5.136

---

[128] *Nichols* (n 127) paragraph 6.
[129] C-383/99 P *Procter & Gamble* [2001] ECR I-6251.
[130] Point 18.
[131] Point 41.

commonness of the surname would be one of the factors that had to be taken into account, but on its own should not be seen as decisive.

5.137 Considering the interaction between Article 3(1)(b) and Article 6(1)(a) he suggested that the limitations of the latter should not affect the application of the former. 'Nothing in the directive requires a less rigorous examination for the purposes of classification, having regard to the existence of provisions restricting the effects of the trade mark.'[132] The reference to Article 12 of the Regulation—the equivalent of Article 6 of the Directive—in *Baby-Dry*[133] was not relevant because 'that judgment does not draw any practical inference whatsoever from that reference'.[134] This was confirmed in *Libertel*[135] where the Court opted for a stringent and thorough examination at the time of the application ensuring that only signs that deserved trade mark protection would benefit from the broad infringement provisions.

(b) The Judgment of the Court

5.138 The Court considered the first four conditions together:

> the national court seeks essentially to ascertain what conditions apply to the assessment, in the context of Article 3(1)(b) of Directive 89/104, of the distinctiveness or otherwise of a trade mark constituted by a surname, particularly where that surname is common, and whether the fact that the effects of registration of the trade mark are limited pursuant to Article 6(1)(a) of the same Directive has an impact on that assessment.[136]

5.139 Article 6(1)(a) provides that the trade mark shall not entitle the proprietor to prohibit a third party from using, in the course of trade, his own name or address.

5.140 The inclusion of personal names in the Article 2 list combined with the interpretation and assessment of distinctive character under Article 3(1)(b) were the determinative factors. Distinctive character should not be assessed in the abstract, but following a specific assessment in relation to the specified goods or services and from the perspective of the relevant consumer.[137]

5.141 **(i) Same criteria for all types of marks** There was 'no distinction between different categories of trade mark',[138] the same criteria applying to personal names. In an absolute manner the Court stated that stricter criteria could not be applied.

5.142 **(ii) Consumer perception** In the context of the specific assessment it might prove more difficult to find distinctive character for some categories of marks as a result of consumer perception.[139] However, this should not lead to *a priori* assumptions regarding distinctive character or the acquirement of distinctive character through use.

---

[132] Point 49.
[133] C-383/99 P *Procter & Gamble* [2001] ECR I-6251.
[134] Point 50.
[135] C-104/01 *Libertel Groep BV* [2003] ECR I-3793.
[136] Paragraph 17.
[137] Citing C-299/99 *Koninklijke Philips Electronics NV* [2002] ECR I-5475; and C-218/01 *Henkel KGaA v Deutches Patent- und Markenamt* [2004] ECR I-1725.
[138] Paragraph 24, citing C-53/01 *Linde AC*, C-54/01 *Winward Industries Inc*, and C-55/01 *Rado Uhren AC* [2003] ECR I-3161; and C-445/02 P *Glaverbel SA v Office for Harmonisation in the Internal Market (Trade Marks and Designs)* [2004] ECR I-6267.
[139] Citing C-281/01 *Henkel KGaA* [2004] ECR I-1725; C-468/01 P to C-472/01 P *Procter & Gamble* [2004] ECR I-5141; and C-445/02 P *Glaverbel SA v Office for Harmonisation in the Internal Market (Trade Marks and Designs)* [2004] ECR I-6267.

5.143 Note that the Court talks about the distinctive character of marks rather than the capability of some signs to distinguish. In general it appears that distinctiveness questions are more likely to be resolved under Article 3(1)(b).

5.144 **(iii) Competition considerations** The Court also rejected the argument that registration would give an advantage to the first of those bearing the same surname to apply. First, because the Directive contained 'no provision to that effect, regardless, moreover, of the category to which the trade mark whose registration is sought belongs'.[140]

5.145 In any case, the Court added, Article 6(1)(a) limited the right following registration, 'that is to say after the existence of the mark's distinctive character has been established. It cannot therefore be taken into account for the purposes of the specific assessment of the distinctive character of the trade mark before the trade mark is registered'.[141] Article 6(1)(a) should have no impact on the assessment of distinctive character.

(8) Registrability of Slogans

5.146 Slogans do not make up a distinct category of trade marks. In practice, however, they play an important role in advertising, and they are also often used as identifiers, ie as trade marks. They are mostly composed of several words, taken from the common language, and the question under trade mark law therefore is whether they display the required minimum degree of distinctiveness under Article 3(1)(b) of the Directive or Article 7(1)(b) CTMR. When the individual words and the words taken together are descriptive of the goods or services, they are judged under Article 3(1)(c) of the Directive or Article 7(1)(c) CTMR and do not present any particular problems. Similarly, when the slogan contains a trade mark or the distinctive name of the advertiser, the fact that it also contains other words does not affect its registrability. The question here is rather whether such slogans, which are usually perceived as laudatory phrases, are judged under criteria which are different from other word marks. Clearly, the fact that a slogan is also laudatory or a sales message cannot mean that it is not a trade mark. Trade marks have these functions as their primary functions, in addition to indicating commercial origin. But the limits have remained blurred. Cases before the Court of Justice are limited to appeals from decisions of the Court of First Instance/General Court. There have been no references seeking interpretation from national courts.

(a) Erpo Möbelwerke: DAS PRINZIP DER BEQUEMLICHKEIT

5.147 For the first time, registrability of slogans came before the Court[142] as an appeal against a decision of the Court of First Instance,[143] annulling a decision of the Board of Appeal that had rejected the application for registering as a Community trade mark the slogan 'DAS PRINZIP DER BEQUEMLICHKEIT' (the principle of comfort) for land vehicles, and parts therefor, and household furniture on the basis of Article 7(1)(b) and 7(1)(c).[144]

5.148 **(i) The Judgment of the Court of First Instance** The Office's appeal targeted the interpretation of Article 7(1)(b) by the Court of First Instance which had stated that the:

---

[140] *Nichols* (n 127) paragraph 31.
[141] *Nichols* (n 127) paragraph 33.
[142] C-64/02 *Office for Harmonisation in the Internal Market v Erpo Möbelwerk* [2004] ECR I-10031.
[143] T-138/00 *Erpo Möbelwerk v Office for Harmonisation in the Internal Market* [2001] ECR II-3739.
[144] Case R-392/1999-3, 23 March 2000. The refusal was only partial: the Board had accepted the registrability of the slogan for hand-operated tools and cutlery.

dismissal, on the basis of Article 7(1)(b) [CTMR], of the appeal brought before the Board of Appeal would have been justified only if it had been demonstrated that the combination of the words 'das Prinzip der …' ('the principle of …') alone with a term designating a characteristic of the goods or services concerned is commonly used in business communications and, in particular, in advertising. The contested decision does not contain any finding to that effect and neither in its written pleadings nor at the hearing has the Office asserted that such a usage exists.[145]

5.149 The Board of Appeal had appeared to require specifically for slogans an additional element of imagination.

5.150 The Office contended that the criterion applied by the Court of First Instance—that the Office must prove that the sign in question is commonly used in the relevant commercial circles—was a rule which found no support in Article 7(1)(b) CTMR. The Office also argued, as had the Board, that slogans, like colours and three-dimensional marks, had to incorporate something additional in order to gain the necessary distinctive character because, in most cases, they fulfilled an advertising function.

5.151 Erpo, on the other hand, viewed the contested decision as simply stating that the Board's decision did not contain an objective statement of the reasons for refusing registration rather than imposing a new criterion. Further, it stressed that Article 12(b) CTMR would ensure that competition would not suffer as a result of a liberal policy regarding the registration of slogans.

5.152 **(ii) The Opinion of Advocate General Poiares Maduro** Advocate General Poiares Maduro noted that the paragraph challenged by the Office should not be seen in isolation; the preceding paragraphs provided a fuller picture.[146]

5.153 He started by exploring the correct criteria for the interpretation and application of the provision. The next steps would be to determine the compatibility, first, of the contested statement of the Court of First Instance and, second, of the position of the Board of Appeal with the criteria adopted by the Court.

5.154 Before concentrating on Article 7(1)(b), however, he commented on the relationship between Article 7(1)(b) and Article 7(1)(c) and noted that the two provisions may, but need not necessarily, overlap. A purely descriptive trade mark would in principle be devoid of

---

[145] Judgment of the Court of First Instance, paragraph 46.

[146]
43. Furthermore, the Board of Appeal again noted, in paragraph 30 of the contested decision, that in order to be able to serve as marks, slogans must possess an additional element … of originality and that the term at issue had such originality.

44. In that regard, it is clear from the case-law of the Court of First Instance that lack of distinctiveness cannot be found because of lack of imagination or of an additional element of originality (Case T-135/99 *Taurus-Film v Office for Harmonisation in the Internal Market (Trade Marks and Designs)* [2001] ECR II-379, paragraph 31; Case T-136/99 *Taurus-Film v Office for Harmonisation in the Internal Market (Trade Marks and Designs)* [2001] ECR II-397, paragraph 31; and Case T-87/00 *Bank für Arbeit und Wirtschaft v Office for Harmonisation in the Internal Market (Trade Marks and Designs)* [2001] ECR II-1259, paragraphs 39 and 40). Furthermore, it is not appropriate to apply to slogans criteria which are stricter than those applicable to other types of sign.

45. To the extent that the Board of Appeal, in paragraph 31 of the contested decision, again points out the lack of any conceptual tension which would create surprise and so make a striking impression, it must be stated that that point is really only a paraphrase of the Board of Appeal's finding of additional element of imagination.

distinctive character. But failing or passing the obstacle of Article 7(1)(c) should not be seen as an indication of lack or existence of distinctive character. Concurring with AG Jacobs,[147] he agreed that Article 7(1)(b) did not simply repeat the 'capable of distinguishing' requirement of Article 4 and Article 7(1)(a). The 'distinctive character' requirement covered distinctiveness in relation to the specified products; it did not refer to the general, absolute, and abstract capacity to distinguish.[148]

5.155 He described the 'criterion' for assessing distinctive character as a two-tiered process, referring first:

> to the goods or services in respect of which registration is sought and which it is intended to distinguish and, secondly, to the perception of the relevant persons, namely the consumers of the goods or services in question. That means that it must be examined in the light of the presumed perception of an average consumer of the category of goods or services in question, who is reasonably well informed and reasonably observant and circumspect.[149]

5.156 Regarding slogans in particular, the Court of Justice had already ruled in *Merz & Krell*[150] (relating to the mark BRAVO) that registration of a sign or indication also used as an advertising slogan was not excluded as such. Here, though, the question was whether there should be different requirements for the registration of slogans.

5.157 Advocate General Poiares Maduro rejected the adoption of stricter criteria for slogans. The Court of Justice had ruled that there should be no distinction made between different categories of trade marks.[151] In practice, registrability of any trade mark had to be specifically assessed for each particular case and this did entail considering the nature and the particular characteristics of each individual mark.

5.158 Some types of signs, for example, colours,[152] were perceived in different ways by consumers; the same should be applied to slogans conveying a promotional message:

> In those circumstances, an average consumer will not perceive the combination of words praising the quality of a product as an indication of the commercial origin of that product as distinct from another product in the same category produced by a different undertaking. This does not apply to word combinations of a different sort, such as invented terms (for example, XTP033) which have no inherent meaning such as to commend qualities generally associated with all the products in a certain category. Nor does it apply to cases where the slogan includes an element which enables the average consumer to distinguish the commercial origin of the product for which registration is sought from other products in the same category but of a different commercial origin.[153]

---

[147] C-329/02 P *SAT.1 SatellitenFernsehen GmbH* [2004] ECR I-8317.
[148] Joined Cases C-108/97 and C-109/97 *Windsurfing Chiemsee* [1999] ECR I-2779; C-299/99 *Koninklijke Philips Electronics NV* [2002] ECR I-5475; C-53/01 *Linde AG*, C-54/01 *Winward Industries Inc* and C-55/01 *Rado Uhren AG* [2003] ECR I-3161; and C-218/01 *Henkel KGaA* [2004] ECR I-1725, confirmed this link with the goods or services specified in the application. The Court of First Instance followed the same route in cases such as T-130/01 *Sykes Enterprises Inc v Office for Harmonisation in the Internal Market (Trade Marks and Designs)* [2002] ECR II-5179; and T-122/01 *Best Buy Concepts Inc v Office for Harmonisation in the Internal Market (Trade Marks and Designs)* [2003] ECR II-2235.
[149] Point 29, codifying the principles of, amongst others, C-342/97 *Lloyd Schuhfabrik* [1999] ECR I-3819 and C-517/99 *Merz & Krell GmbH & Co v Deutsches Patent- und Markenamt* [2001] ECR I-6959.
[150] C-517/99 *Merz & Krell* [2001] ECR I-6959.
[151] He cited *Philips* (n 47).
[152] Citing C-104/01 *Libertel Groep BV* [2003] ECR I-3793.
[153] Point 37.

5.159 Slogans originally lacking the necessary distinctive character could still obtain it through use and the application of Article 7(3) of the Regulation.

5.160 He believed that the Court of First Instance had failed to follow the criteria ascertained in the case law of the Court.

5.161 The Court of First Instance had rightly decided that a slogan should not be rejected merely because it did not display any additional element of imagination; however, it was wrong to suggest that, in assessing in practice the distinctive character of a slogan, the competent authority might not find that it lacked any additional element of imagination that would render it capable of distinguishing products according to origin.[154]

5.162 He found that the burden of proof the Court of First Instance imposed on the Office violated Article 7(1)(b). Having to prove that 'that combination of words is commonly used in trade'[155] was a requirement incompatible with the 'criterion' identified by the Advocate General.

5.163 The Advocate General also mentioned approvingly the argument that such slogans should be left free for competing undertakings to use.

5.164 Article 12(b) of the Regulation would not always provide a compensating mechanism once the mark has been registered following the adoption of a broad registrability criterion. New competitors 'ought to be free to invoke the same qualities in presenting their products, without any legal constraints'.[156]

5.165 Referring to *Doublemint*,[157] he transposed the interpretation of Article 7(1)(c) regarding potentially descriptive terms to Article 7(1)(b). The Office was right to underline that requiring proof of use in business communications and advertising in order to refuse registration was in conflict with Article 7(1)(c). The Court of First Instance had added to Article 7(1)(b) what in reality should be examined under Article 7(1)(d).[158]

5.166 (iii) **The Judgment of the Court** The Court of Justice agreed with AG Poiares Maduro and the Court of First Instance that it was inappropriate to apply to slogans stricter criteria than those applied to other types of sign. However, citing *Henkel* and *Procter & Gamble*,[159] it added that in applying those criteria, it might become apparent that the relevant public's perception is not necessarily the same for each of those categories. In practice, it could prove more difficult to establish distinctiveness for some categories of marks.

5.167 For slogans the difficulty arose from their promotional function that the Office had brought to the fore. It would be more difficult to find distinctiveness for a slogan:

> in particular if it were established ... that it served a promotional function consisting, for example, of commending the quality of the product in question and that the importance of that function was not manifestly secondary to its purported function as a trade mark, namely that of guaranteeing the origin of the product.

---

[154] Point 46.
[155] Point 51.
[156] Point 54.
[157] C-191/01 P *WM Wrigley Jr Co* [2003] ECR I-12447.
[158] Citing C-517/99 *Merz & Krell GmbH & Co* [2001] ECR I-6959.
[159] C-456/01 P and C-457/01 P *Henkel KGaA* [2004] ECR I-5089.

Indeed, in such a case, the authorities may take account of the fact that average consumers are not in the habit of making assumptions about the origin of products on the basis of such slogans.[160]

This though should not lead to the adoption of 'specific criteria supplementing or derogating from the criterion of distinctiveness'.[161] **5.168**

The Court of First Instance was right to annul the decision of the Board of Appeal because it had imposed a different and stricter criterion for advertising slogans (originality or imagination). **5.169**

It was wrong to adopt a new criterion for the application of Article 7(1)(b), a criterion that was adapted to assist in the application of another provision, Article 7(1)(d). The Court repeated that each of the grounds for refusal listed in Article 7(1) was independent of the others and called for separate examination.[162] **5.170**

Turning to the registrability of slogans, the Court noted that the fact that they might also function as advertising slogans should not automatically lead to rejection.[163] **5.171**

The real issue was whether the slogan made it possible to identify the specified product 'as originating from a given undertaking and therefore to distinguish the product from those of other undertakings and, therefore, is able to fulfil the essential function of the trade mark'.[164] **5.172**

The assessment of distinctiveness was a two-tiered exercise. According to *Procter & Gamble* (the washing tablets cases),[165] distinctiveness had to be assessed, first, in relation to the specified goods or services and, second, in relation to the perception of them by the relevant public. This should be the only applicable test. **5.173**

Erpo's argument that the effect of Article 12(b) should also be taken into account was rejected.[166] **5.174**

Concluding, in this domino of errors, the Court accepted that the Judgment of the Court of First Instance was vitiated by an error of law, albeit this did not alter the outcome of the dispute, since the Court of First Instance had also held, correctly this time, that the decision of the Board should be annulled. The operative part of the contested judgment remained justified.[167] **5.175**

Interestingly, the mark 'DAS PRINZIP DER BEQUEMLICHKEIT' is registered today for goods in Class 20, 'Furniture for the home, in particular upholstered furniture, seats, chairs, tables, furniture in kit form, and office furniture', for which it was originally rejected **5.176**

---

[160] *Erpo* (n 81) paragraph 35.
[161] Paragraph 36.
[162] C-456/01 P and C-457/01 P *Henkel KGaA* [2004] ECR I-5089.
[163] C-517/99 *Merz & Krell GmbH* [2001] ECR I-6959.
[164] *Erpo* (n 81) paragraph 42; C-468/01 P to C-472/01 P *Procter & Gamble* [2004] ECR I-5141; C-517/99 *Merz & Krell GmbH & Co* [2001] ECR I-6959; and C-53/01 *Linde AG*, C-54/01 *Winward Industries Inc* and C-55/01 *Rado Uhren AG* [2003] ECR I-3161.
[165] C-468/01 P to C-472/01 P *Procter & Gamble* [2004] ECR I-5141.
[166] Repeating what the Court had already ruled in C-104/01 *Libertel Groep BV* [2003] ECR I-3793.
[167] The Court cited C-265/97 P *VBA v Florinex* [2000] ECR I-2061 as an example of its case law stating that if the grounds of a Judgment of the Court of First Instance revealed an infringement of Community law but the operative part appeared well founded on other legal grounds, the appeal should be dismissed.

(CTM 806620). This happened because the Board of Appeal, after the case was returned with the annulment of the initial decision having become final, now found the slogan registrable.[168]

(b) The case law following Erpo Möbelwerke

5.177 In the substantial number of cases following the judgment in *Erpo Möbelwerke*, the applicants seeking to overturn a refusal of registration were routinely unsuccessful before the Court of First Instance/General Court. Only one case of these many refusals was appealed to the Court of Justice, relating to the mark 'SAFETY 1st', sought to be registered for a series of goods in Classes 12, 20, 21, and 28. By Order of 30 January 2009 in Case C 131/08 P, *Dorel Juvenile Group Inc. v OHIM*,[169] the Court dismissed an appeal against the Judgment of the Court of First Instance of 24 January 2008 in Case T 88/06,[170] as in part manifestly inadmissible because it was seeking to challenge factual findings of the Court of First Instance, and in part manifestly unfounded.

(c) Audi AG: Vorsprung durch Technik

5.178 It took another year before the next slogan case was decided by the Court.[171] The case related to the mark 'Vorsprung durch Technik' ('Advancement through Technology'), which was sought to be registered for a series of goods and services in Classes 9, 12, 14, 16, 18, 25, 28, 35 to 43, and 45.

5.179 **(i) OHIM and Board of Appeal** OHIM had rejected the application as lacking in distinctive character, and the Board of Appeal had confirmed for all goods except those in Class 12 for which the Board accepted that Audi had shown distinctive character acquired through use, as evidenced in particular by an earlier registration of the same mark in Class 12. The Board argued essentially that nearly all the goods and services relate, even if only remotely, to technology; technology even plays an important role in the clothing sector. A manufacturer of such goods whose technology is advanced has a great advantage as compared with competing businesses. The slogan 'Vorsprung durch Technik' thus conveys an objective message to the effect that technological superiority enables better goods and services to be manufactured and supplied. A combination of words which does no more than convey that banal objective message is, in principle, devoid of distinctive character. Given that, apart from the goods in Class 12, the applicant has provided no evidence that the slogan 'Vorsprung durch Technik' has become a trade mark in the minds of the public, the application must be refused insofar as it relates to goods and services in other classes.

5.180 **(ii) General Court** Audi's appeal to the General Court failed.[172]

5.181 When giving its reasons for the dismissal of Audi's appeal based on an infringement of Article 7(1)(b),[173] the General Court stated first that the fact that the mark was a laudatory or advertising slogan did not as such preclude its registration. The proper standard was that such a slogan was distinctive only if it could be immediately perceived as an indication of the commercial origin of the goods or services in question, or a mere banal objective

---

[168] Decision R-292/1999-2, 24 January 2006.
[169] [2009] ECR I-00009.
[170] [2008] ECR II-00010.
[171] C-398/08 P *Audi AG v OHIM* (Vorsprung durch Technik) [2010] ECR I-00535.
[172] T-70/06 *Audi AG v OHIM* [2008] ECR II-00131.
[173] Paragraph 34 et seq.

message which would be perceived by the relevant public as laudatory. The Court considered that 'Vorsprung durch Technik' can have a number of meanings, or constitute a play on words, or be perceived as imaginative, surprising, and unexpected and, in that way, be easily remembered, but that this nevertheless does not mean that it is distinctive. The mark would be distinctive only if it were perceived immediately by the relevant public as an indication of the commercial origin of the goods and services which it covers. In the case before it, the relevant public would in practice perceive that mark, first and foremost, as a promotional formula. The General Court concluded that the mark 'Vorsprung durch Technik' does not contain elements likely to enable the relevant public to remember the expression easily and immediately as a distinctive mark for the goods and services covered, over and above its obvious promotional meaning.

(iii) Appeal to the Court of Justice   Audi appealed to the Court of Justice. To the great surprise of OHIM, the nominal defendant, and perhaps also of Audi, and certainly of the general public interested in trade mark law and practice, the Court of Justice reversed, in a judgment of its First Chamber, with Judge Ilešič as Rapporteur,[174] without an Opinion by the Advocate General (Bot), and with a judgment not only overturning the first instance, but also deciding the case on the merits, as the Court is empowered to do under Article 61 of the Statute of the Court.   **5.182**

The Court analysed the issue in traditional terms, referring primarily, as is its habit, to its own case law. The Court stated: 'As regards marks made up of signs or indications that are also used as advertising slogans, indications of quality or incitements to purchase the goods or services covered by those marks, registration of such marks is not excluded as such by virtue of such use.'[175] The Court added: 'As regards the assessment of the distinctive character of such marks, the Court has already held that it is inappropriate to apply to slogans criteria which are stricter than those applicable to other types of sign',[176] citing the *Erpo Möbelwerk* judgment.   **5.183**

The Court next agreed that it may be more difficult for some marks to demonstrate inherent distinctiveness than for others, even though the standards for all marks are the same. However, this does not justify laying down specific criteria supplementing or derogating from the criterion of distinctiveness as established by the Court in, inter alia, its *Erpo Möbelwerk* judgment. Therefore an advertising slogan cannot be required to display 'imaginativeness' or even 'conceptual tension which would create surprise and so make a striking impression' in order to have the minimal level of distinctiveness required under Article 7(1)(b) of the Regulation.   **5.184**

The Court then criticized the General Court's approach, which it considered to derive from an erroneous interpretation of the relevant principles: **5.185**

> even though the General Court stated in paragraph 36 of the judgment under appeal that it is clear from the case law that registration of a mark cannot be excluded because of that mark's laudatory or advertising use, it went on to explain that the reason for its finding that the mark applied for lacks distinctive character was, in essence, the fact that that mark is

---

[174] Readers will no doubt be aware that many of the recent leading trade mark judgments of the Court have Judge Ilešič as their Rapporteur.
[175] Paragraph 35.
[176] Paragraph 36.

perceived as a promotional formula: that is to say, its finding was made precisely on the basis of the mark's laudatory or advertising use.[177]

5.186 The Court added that the mere fact that a mark is perceived by the relevant public as a promotional formula, and that, because of its laudatory nature, it could in principle be used by other undertakings, is not sufficient, in itself, to support the conclusion that that mark is devoid of distinctive character.

5.187 Quite appropriately, the Court pointed out that many marks—and certainly all marks if seen under the perspective of marks being a 'tool' for selling goods or services—have an advertising or promotion element, or an element which applauds the characteristics of the goods or services for which the mark is used. That, however, as the Court correctly noted:

> does not mean that it cannot be appropriate for the purposes of guaranteeing to consumers the origin of the goods or services which it covers. Thus, such a mark can be perceived by the relevant public both as a promotional formula and as an indication of the commercial origin of goods or services. It follows that, in so far as the public perceives the mark as an indication of that origin, the fact that the mark is at the same time understood—perhaps even primarily understood—as a promotional formula has no bearing on its distinctive character.[178]

5.188 As regards the considerations of the General Court that the mark 'Vorsprung durch Technik' can have a number of meanings, or constitute a play on words or be perceived as imaginative, surprising, and unexpected and, in that way, be easily remembered, but that this alone was not sufficient to confer distinctiveness on the mark, the Court held that although the existence of such characteristics is not a necessary condition for establishing that an advertising slogan has distinctive character, the fact remains that, 'as a rule, the presence of those characteristics is likely to endow that mark with distinctive character'.[179]

5.189 The Court next criticized the General Court for holding that 'the mark "Vorsprung durch Technik" does not contain elements which, beyond the obvious promotional message of the mark, could enable the relevant public to commit the expression to memory easily and immediately as a distinctive mark for the goods and services covered' because 'not only is that finding wholly unsupported by the reasoning which precedes it but, moreover, it is contradicted to a certain extent by the finding made in paragraph 41 of that judgment'.[180]

5.190 Thus, concluding that the General Court had applied the wrong criteria, the Court proceeded to decide the case on its own.

5.191 **(iv) The decision on the merits** When deciding a case under Article 61 of the Statue, the Court of Justice essentially acts as the General Court would act, ie it has all the powers and competences that the General Court has when reviewing OHIM decisions. The Court considered that the expression 'Vorsprung durch Technik' was a widely known slogan which Audi had been using for years to promote the sale of its motor vehicles. It was registered in 2001 as a Community trade mark for goods in Class 12 on the basis of proof that that slogan was widely known in German speaking regions. As regards the goods and services in question, other than those in Class 12, the Board of Appeal based its refusal of registration

---

[177] Paragraphs 41 and 42.
[178] Paragraph 45.
[179] Paragraph 47.
[180] Paragraph 48.

on the fact that the slogan 'Vorsprung durch Technik' conveys an objective message to the effect that technological superiority enables the manufacture and supply of better goods and services. According to the Board of Appeal, a combination of words which limits itself to that banal objective message is, in principle, devoid of any inherently distinctive character and cannot therefore be registered unless it is shown that the public has come to perceive it as a trade mark. In view of the reasons for annulling the first instance judgment, the Court concluded that this reasoning is incompatible with Article 7(1)(b) of the Regulation.

5.192 The Court concluded (to the obvious applause of the trade mark community) that all marks made up of signs or indications that are also used as advertising slogans, indications of quality, or incitements to purchase the goods or services covered by those marks convey by definition, to a greater or lesser extent, an objective message. The Court continued that it is clear, however, from the case law that those marks are not, by virtue of that fact alone, devoid of distinctive character. Thus, insofar as they can express an objective message, even a simple one, they are still capable of indicating to the consumer the commercial origin of the goods or services in question. Turning to the case at hand, the Court went on to say that the capacity to indicate commercial origin may be the more possible where those marks are not merely an ordinary advertising message, but possess a certain originality or resonance, requiring some reflection in the way of interpretation by the relevant public, or setting off a cognitive process in the minds of that public.[181]

5.193 The Court added in conclusion:

> Even if it were to be supposed that the slogan 'Vorsprung durch Technik' conveys an objective message to the effect that technological superiority enables the manufacture and supply of better goods and services, that fact would not support the conclusion that the mark applied for is devoid of any inherently distinctive character. However simple such a message may be, it cannot be categorised as ordinary to the point of excluding, from the outset and without any further analysis, the possibility that that mark is capable of indicating to the consumer the commercial origin of the goods or services in question. In that context, it should be pointed out that that message does not follow obviously from the slogan in question. As Audi observed, the combination of words 'Vorsprung durch Technik' exhibits a certain originality and resonance which makes it easy to remember. Inasmuch as it is a widely known slogan which has been used by Audi for many years, it cannot be excluded that the fact that members of the relevant public are used to establishing the link between that slogan and the motor vehicles manufactured by that company also makes it easier for that public to identify the commercial origin of the goods or services covered.[182]

5.194 In conclusion, not only the General Court's judgment but also the decision of the Board of Appeal were annulled, and the slogan was and continues to be registered for all the goods and services claimed by Audi (CTM 30162892).

(d) What happened after 'Vorsprung...'?

5.195 The judgment in *Audi* sounded like it required a new approach to examining slogans for registrability under Article 3(1)(b) of the Directive or Article 7(1)(b) of the Regulation. Not surprisingly, therefore, since the *Audi* judgment, applicants have consistently invoked the criteria of that decision, notably the conclusion that where a phrase can have 'a number

---

[181] Paragraph 57.
[182] Judgment, paragraph 58 and 59.

of meanings, or constitute a play on words or be perceived as imaginative, surprising and unexpected and, in that way, be easily remembered', while this alone is not sufficient to confer distinctiveness on the mark, the 'existence of such characteristics, [while not] a necessary condition for establishing that an advertising slogan has distinctive character, the fact remains that, as a rule, the presence of those characteristics is likely to endow that mark with distinctive character'.

5.196 The record is, however, almost 100% in favour of OHIM. We are not aware of any General Court decision having reversed a decision of a Board of Appeal confirming denial of registration when the contested mark was a slogan, and all of these General Court decisions have been confirmed by the Court of Justice when the Judgment was appealed to the Court, which is of course only rarely the case. That does not mean that slogans are not registrable. There are probably hundreds if not thousands of CTMs—and national marks—on the registers which we could qualify as slogans. What this means is that it depends essentially on the first OHIM or national office instance whether or not a particular slogan is accepted.

5.197 For the record, there are two Court of Justice decisions subsequent to *Audi* with protection claimed in vain for a slogan:

(i) *Smart Technologies ULC v OHIM*,[183] appeal against Judgment of the General Court in *Smart Technologies v OHMI*,[184] relating to the mark WIR MACHEN DAS BESONDERE EINFACH ('We Make the Special Simple'), sought to be registered for a series of goods in Class 9.

(ii) *Delphi Technologies, Inc. v OHIM*,[185] appeal against the Judgment of the General Court in *Delphi Technologies v OHIM*,[186] relating to the mark INNOVATION FOR THE REAL WORLD, sought to be registered for a series of goods in Classes 7, 9, 10, and 12.

5.198 There are in addition a large number of General Court judgments which have upheld a refusal of registration.

5.199 In conclusion, the case law on slogans is, as is the case law on 3D marks, an example of the difficulties faced by trade mark practitioners when seeking to establish distinctiveness of their marks in order to overcome an Office objection. Just as with colours and 3D shapes, slogans also fall into the group of signs or marks which, as held by the courts, are not of a kind where the public is accustomed to make a connection between the mark and the commercial origin of the goods or services which it designates. Showing surprising combinations, imagination, or originality, while not required, certainly helps and may often be decisive.

(9) *Libertel*: The Distinctiveness of Colours

5.200 In *Libertel*,[187] the referring court had focused on whether colours could have sufficient distinctive character to function and be protected as trade marks. It referred the following questions to the Court:

---

[183] Judgment of 12 July 2012, C-311/11 P *Smart Technologies ULC v OHIM*, ECLI:EU:C:2012:460.
[184] Case T-523/09 *Smart Technologies v OHMI*, ECLI:EU:T:2011:175.
[185] Order of 12 June 2014, C-448/13 P, *Delphi Technologies, Inc. v OHIM*, ECLI:EU:C:2014:1746.
[186] Case T-515/11 *Delphi Technologies v OHIM*, ECLI:EU:T:2013:300.
[187] C-104/01 *Libertel Groep BV* [2003] ECR I-3793.

(1) Is it possible for a single specific colour which is represented as such or is designated by an internationally applied code to acquire a distinctive character for certain goods or services within the meaning of Article 3(1)(b) of the Directive?
(2) If the answer to the first question is in the affirmative: (a) in what circumstances may it be accepted that a single specific colour possesses a distinctive character in the sense used above? (b) does it make any difference if registration is sought for a large number of goods and/or services, rather than for a specific product or service, or category of goods or services respectively?
(3) In the assessment of the distinctive character of a specific colour as a trade mark, must account be taken of whether, with regard to that colour, there is a general interest in availability, such as can exist in respect of signs which denote a geographical origin?
(4) When considering the question whether a sign, for which registration as a trade mark is sought, possesses the distinctive character referred to in Article 3(1)(b) of the Directive, must the Benelux Trade Mark Office confine itself to an assessment in abstracto of distinctive character or must it take account of all the actual facts of the case, including the use made of the sign and the manner in which the sign is used?[188]

5.201 As an introductory consideration, the concept of a colour was characterized as a sensation rather than a pre-existing objective reality; its perception would vary according to the nature and intensity of light and the eye of the observer.[189]

5.202 Advocate General Léger focused on the limited number of available colours, starting from Newton's seven principal colours and the three primary colours of painters and finishing with the limited number of words that originally refer to colours.[190] Despite the millions of industrially produced shades or tonalities defined according to chromatic dictionaries, like the Pantone or the Acoat Colour Codification systems, the human eye can distinguish only a limited number of shades with certainty.[191]

5.203 A second observation was that colour was a language, provoking feelings and conveying information. These were 'purely cultural phenomena ... based on conventions';[192] colours did not exist independently, instead they were the attributes of something else.

5.204 A colour per se failed the intrinsic distinctiveness requirement:[193] first, the application for its registration 'would not allow determination of the sign actually appearing on the goods or in association with the services in question';[194] and, second, as a result, it would be unable to fulfil the task of indicating the origin of goods or services without any possibility of confusion. 'It follows that a colour can only be clearly defined if it is seen in the context of a particular shape or design.'[195]

---

[188] Reproduced in paragraph 20.
[189] Citing 'La Couleur', *Dossier pour la Science* No 27 and *Manuel de la Couleur* (Solar, 2001).
[190] White, red, black, green, yellow, blue, grey, brown, pink, violet, and orange. Other words are borrowed from different contexts, for example, lemon or rust.
[191] Up to 200, but commonly under 100 shades, citing M Pastoureau, *Dictionnaire des Couleurs de Notre Temps* (Bonneton, 1999).
[192] Point 45.
[193] Citing the interpretation of the Court of First Instance in T-163/98 *Procter & Gamble (Baby-Dry)* [1999] ECR II-2383; and of the Court of Justice in C-299/99 *Koninklijke Philips Electronics NV* [2002] ECR I-5475 that linked distinctiveness with the specification of the application, and, in the case of *Philips*, that Article 3(1)(a) precluded the registration of signs which were not generally capable of being a trade mark.
[194] Point 85 of the Opinion of AG Léger.
[195] Point 87, referring to an example given by Klinkenberg in 'Qu'est-ce que le Signe?' in Dorties (ed), *Le Langage* (Editions Sciences Humaine, 2001) at 105: in the context of the highway code, red in a round shape signified a prohibition, red in a triangular shape signified a danger.

5.205 Reviewing a number of decisions of the Office to accept the registration of a colour as such[196] he noted that they have been granted in very exceptional cases and questioned whether they truly functioned as trade marks.

5.206 He would have required evidence that the colours on their own would lead consumers to a purchasing decision.[197] He therefore accepted the logic of national registrations in the United Kingdom and Ireland of colours applied on premises or uniforms.[198]

5.207 He also noted that in *Qualitex* the Supreme Court of the United States of America accepted that a particular shade of a colour applied on the external surface of a specific product could be protected as a trade mark following evidence of distinctiveness acquired through use, a practice followed by the United States Patent and Trade Mark Office.[199] The reference to US jurisprudence and practice is evidence of openness to foreign law and practice. The Advocate General submitted that all these cases showed that a colour that functioned as a trade mark could be protected without having to be registered as such; unfair competition, civil liability, and consumer protection laws could also play a part.

(a) Competition considerations

5.208 In addition, protection of a colour per se raised competition questions; for example, because of its indeterminate representation, protection of a particular shade of blue would in the end result in an exclusive right to the colour blue. The limited number of colours that were actually used in practice for particular goods or services combined with the growing use of colours to attract the attention of consumers rendered the competition issue even more pertinent. 'It would thus be enough for several colours per se to be registered as trade marks to confer a real monopoly of use of the colour on a few traders. Such a monopoly could distort competition.'[200] It 'could even stop new traders entering a particular market'.[201]

5.209 So, having found that colour per se did not satisfy the conditions of Article 2 AG Léger decided he did not have to look at the Article 3 questions referred by the Court.

(b) The Judgment of the Court

5.210 The Court accepted that it was necessary to start its analysis from Article 2.

5.211 **(i) Distinctiveness of colours** Regarding distinctiveness of colours the Court remarked that although colours were capable of conveying certain associations of ideas and arousing feelings, they possessed 'little inherent capacity for communicating specific information'.[202] However, this would not justify a blanket conclusion. In some circumstances a colour per se might function as a trade mark.

---

[196] Lilac for chocolate, Registration of 27 October 1999, No 31336; magenta for telecommunication goods and services, Registration of 3 August 2000, No 212787; and yellow for anti-corrosion products, Registration of 9 January 2001, No 396176.
[197] Point 91.
[198] Respectively: *BP Amoco Plc v John Kelly Ltd and Glenshane Tourist Services Ltd* [2001] FSR 21; and a United Parcels Service in the USA registration no 221818, 27 October 1998.
[199] *Qualitex*, 514 US 159 (1995); Registration no 1633711.
[200] Point 101.
[201] Point 103.
[202] *Libertel Groep BV* (n 4) paragraph 40.

(ii) Registrability of colours: The general interest; Article 3(1)(c) and Article 3(1)(e) considerations Having reached the opposite conclusion from the Advocate General the Court turned to consider whether in order to determine registrability recourse had to be given to the general interest that a particular colour had to remain available for other competitors to use.   **5.212**

The right angle for resolving this was the perspective of the average consumer, reasonably well-informed and reasonably observant and circumspect,[203] rather than the availability or not of a large number of colours. From that perspective, the   **5.213**

> number of colours which that public is capable of distinguishing is limited, because it is rarely in a position directly to compare products in various shades of colour. It follows that the number of different colours that are in fact available as potential trade marks to distinguish goods or services must be regarded as limited.[204]

The Court repeated that trade marks constitute an essential element in the system of undistorted competition which the EC Treaty seeks to establish and maintain;[205] this, together with the fact that trade mark rights are potentially perpetual, had to be taken into account when considering the rights and powers they confer.   **5.214**

Citing *Philips*[206] the Court reiterated that the public interest might limit trade mark rights and Article 3 should be interpreted according to the public interest underlying each one of the grounds of the provision. The public interest under Article 3(1)(c) was that signs and indications descriptive of the categories of goods or services for which registration is sought may be freely used by all whereas under Article 3(1)(e) shapes whose essential characteristics perform a technical function and were chosen to fulfil that function may be freely used by all.[207]   **5.215**

For colours the Court raised a general objection based on their nature and linked with the aims of Article 3(1)(c) and 3(l)(e).   **5.216**

It opted to adopt the colour depletion theory holding that the registration of colours per se, not spatially delimited, coupled with the limited number of actually available colours meant that: **5.217**

> a small number of trade mark registrations for certain services or goods could exhaust the entire range of the colours available.
>
> Such an extensive monopoly would be incompatible with a system of undistorted competition, in particular because it could have the effect of creating an unjustified competitive advantage for a single trader. Nor would it be conducive to economic development or the fostering of the spirit of enterprise for established traders to be able to register the entire range of colours that is in fact available for their own benefit, to the detriment of new traders.[208]

---

[203] According to C-342/97 *Lloyd Schuhfabrik* [1999] ECR I-3819.
[204] Paragraph 47.
[205] Citing C-10/89 *SA CNL SUCAL NV* [1990] ECR I-3711; and C-63/97 *Bayerische Motorenwerke AG* [1999] ECR I-905.
[206] C-299/99 *Koninklijke Philips Electronics NV* [2002] ECR I-5475.
[207] C-299/99 *Koninklijke Philips Electronics NV* [2002] ECR I-5475; and C-53/01 *Linde AG*, C-54/01 *Winward Industries Inc* and C-55/01 *Rado Uhren AG* [2003] ECR I-3161.
[208] Paragraph 54.

5.218   The public interest was 'in not unduly restricting the availability of colours for the other operators who offer for sale goods or services of the same type as those in respect of which registration is sought'.[209]

5.219   Broad specifications would exacerbate the conflict with the public interest.

5.220   The contention of the Commission that Article 6 covered that public interest was rejected. The Court, aware of the historical development of the German doctrine, resisted the shift in terms of time and competence from the time of examining the application to the time of enforcing the right; the Directive necessitated a review prior to registration, not *posteriori*.

> It must be a stringent and full examination, in order to prevent trade marks from being improperly registered. As the Court has already held, for reasons of legal certainty and good administration, it is necessary to ensure that trade marks whose use could successfully be challenged before the courts are not registered.[210]

5.221   It concluded that:

> in assessing the potential distinctiveness of a given colour as a trade mark, regard must be had to the general interest in not unduly restricting the availability of colours for the other traders who offer for sale goods or services of the same type as those in respect of which registration is sought.[211]

5.222   **(iii) Distinctive character of a colour per se**   The Court then considered the issue of distinctiveness of a colour per se under Article 3(1)(b) and Article 3(3) based on the essential function of guaranteeing the identity of the origin of the marked products, adding that 'regard must be had both to the ordinary use of trade marks as a badge of origin in the sectors concerned and to the perception of the relevant public',[212] in this case an average consumer, reasonably well-informed and reasonably observant and circumspect, who only rarely has the chance to make a direct comparison between the different marks but must place his/her trust in the imperfect picture of them that s/he has kept in his/her mind.[213]

5.223   **(iv) The importance of public perception**   The Court contrasted between word and figurative signs on the one hand and colours per se on the other:

> While the public is accustomed to perceiving word or figurative marks instantly as signs identifying the commercial origin of the goods, the same is not necessarily true where the sign forms part of the look of the goods in respect of which registration of the sign as a trade mark is sought. Consumers are not in the habit of making assumptions about the origin of goods based on their colour or the colour of their packaging, in the absence of any graphic or word element, because as a rule a colour per se is not, in current commercial practice, used as a means of identification. A colour per se is not normally inherently capable of distinguishing the goods of a particular undertaking.[214]

5.224   So, in principle a colour per se would require distinctiveness acquired through use according to Article 3(3) as interpreted in *Windsurfing Chiemsee*.[215] The Court left open a very

---

[209] Paragraph 55.
[210] Paragraph 59, citing C-39/97 *Canon Kabushiki Kaisha* [1998] ECR I-5507.
[211] Paragraph 60.
[212] Paragraph 62.
[213] Citing C-342/97 *Lloyd Schuhfabrik* [1999] ECR I-3819 and C-291/00 *LTJ Diffusion SA v Sadas Vertbaudet SA* [2003] ECR I-2799.
[214] Paragraph 65.
[215] C-108/97 and C-109/97 *Windsurfing Chiemsee* [1999] ECR I-2779.

narrow gap for 'exceptional circumstances, and particularly where the number of goods or services for which the mark is claimed is very restricted and the relevant market very specific'.[216]

Concluding on the first question the Court ruled that: **5.225**

> a colour per se, not spatially delimited, may, in respect of certain goods and services, have a distinctive character within the meaning of Article 3(1)(b) and Article 3(3) of the Directive, provided that, inter alia, it may be represented graphically in a way that is clear, precise, self-contained, easily accessible, intelligible, durable and objective. The latter condition cannot be satisfied merely by reproducing on paper the colour in question, but may be satisfied by designating that colour using an internationally recognised identification code.[217]

On question 2 (a) the Court ruled that: **5.226**

> a colour per se may be found to possess distinctive character within the meaning of Article 3(1)(b) and Article 3(3) of the Directive, provided that, as regards the perception of the relevant public, the mark is capable of identifying the product or service for which registration is sought as originating from a particular undertaking and distinguishing that product or service from those of other undertakings.[218]

The answer on question 2(b) stressed that, in the case of colours, the breadth of the specification was relevant in assessing: **5.227**

> both the distinctive character of the colour in respect of which registration is sought, and whether its registration would run counter to the general interest in not unduly limiting the availability of colours for the other operators who offer for sale goods or services of the same type as those in respect of which registration is sought.[219]

The fourth question confirmed that trade mark law is linked with what is happening in the marketplace. An application for registration should not be examined in the abstract for distinctiveness. Distinctiveness is determined according to the specification of the application and **5.228**

> in assessing whether a trade mark has distinctive character within the meaning of Article 3(1)(b) and Article 3(3) of the Directive, the competent authority for registering trade marks must carry out an examination by reference to the actual situation, taking account of all the circumstances of the case and in particular any use which has been made of the mark.[220]

(10) *Heidelberger Bauchemie*: Combinations of Colours; Replaying *Libertel*

In *Heidelberger Bauchemie*[221] AG Léger adapted the arguments he had developed in *Libertel* to the fact that this application was for a combination of colours. **5.229**

The intention of Heidelberger Bauchemie was to protect the two colours in relation to the specified products irrespective of any arrangement between them. Such a combination would not be capable of distinguishing in the sense of Article 2 because the number of combinations between them would be unlimited. **5.230**

---

[216] Paragraph 66.
[217] Paragraph 68.
[218] Paragraph 69.
[219] Paragraph 71.
[220] Paragraph 77.
[221] C-49/02 *Heidelberger Bauchemie GmbH* [2004] ECR I-6129.

5.231 The trade mark proprietor would be given the exclusive right to use them as blue and yellow ribbons appearing on the surface of the product or coloured geometrical shapes, for instance, a blue circle on a yellow background.

5.232 However, their ability to distinguish would differ according to the way they would appear on the relevant product. So, and given that the Court had accepted in *Libertel* that colours can communicate specific information only to a limited degree, two colours would be capable of distinguishing only in the context of a specific arrangement.

5.233 Granting trade mark protection to the colours as such would equate to granting protection to a number of letters because in a particular combination the same number of letters forms a word that can be protected as a trade mark.[222]

5.234 He also rejected the possibility that a colour combination in a particular, specified, arrangement would satisfy the distinctiveness requirement:

> to accept that two colours per se are capable of having distinctive character on the ground that they may satisfy that condition, but only in the context of certain specified arrangements, would amount, in my view, to misinterpreting the very purpose of the application for registration, which seeks exclusive rights in all the possible forms in which those colours may appear. In the case of a word mark, that would amount to accepting that a number of letters may have distinctive character and that each of them may be the subject of exclusive rights on the ground that, where those letters form a certain word, they are capable of having distinctive character.[223]

(a) The Judgment of the Court

5.235 The Court approached the issue of distinctiveness by asking 'whether or not those colours or combinations of colours are capable of conveying precise information, particularly as regards the origin of a product or service'.[224]

5.236 It reiterated its approach in *Libertel*[225] and added that subject to the conditions raised therein 'it must be accepted that for the purposes of Article 2 of the Directive colours and combinations of colours, designated in the abstract and without contours, may be capable of distinguishing the goods or services of one undertaking from those of other undertakings'.[226]

5.237 It then stressed that the registration authority would also have to examine whether the mark applied for satisfied Article 3 taking into account the public interest described in *Libertel*.

(11) *KWS*: Colours; Broader Functionality Considerations

5.238 The case came before the Court as an appeal against a Judgment of the Court of First Instance.[227] KWS Saat AG (KWS) had applied for the registration of a shade of orange, using the standard reference 'Orange HKS7', as a Community trade mark for treatment installations for seeds, agricultural, horticultural and forestry products, and technical and business consultancy in the seed sector. The Second Board of Appeal found the mark devoid

---

[222] Point 47.
[223] Point 49.
[224] *Heidelberger Bauchemie* (n 221) paragraph 37.
[225] C-104/01 *Libertel Groep BV* [2003] ECR I-3793.
[226] Point 40 of the Opinion of AG Léger.
[227] T-173/00 *KWS Saat AG v Office for Harmonisation in the Internal Market (Trade Marks and Designs)* [2002] ECR II-3843.

of any distinctive character under Article 7(1)(b) of the Regulation since it was common practice to use colourants to identify treated seed.[228]

(a) The Judgment of the Court of First Instance

The Court of First Instance upheld in part the application brought by KWS, finding that with regard to consultancy services the shade of orange per se was capable of enabling the relevant public to distinguish the services concerned from those of a different commercial origin when they come to make a choice for a subsequent purchase. For treated seed it found that use of colours, including the contested shade of orange or very similar shades, was common. The sign applied for would not enable the relevant public immediately and with certitude to distinguish the applicant's goods from those of other undertakings in other shades of orange. Similarly, for treatment installations, it concurred with the Board of Appeal that it was not rare to come across machines in that or a similar colour. Orange had become a commonplace colour that the relevant public would perceive as an element of the finish of the installations. **5.239**

KWS appealed further to the Court of Justice in relation to the goods covered in the specification. The Office expressed doubts, but did not bring a cross-appeal regarding the consultancy services. **5.240**

The first three grounds were about the judicial process before the Board of Appeal and the Court of First Instance. **5.241**

The fourth ground introduced the argument that the distinctive character of a colour should be assessed in the same way as with word and figurative signs. The availability of other colours to indicate product characteristics should be irrelevant. Public perception would be a more appropriate consideration. If competing undertakings use distinct colours to indicate particular characteristics, consumers would see each colour as indicating two things. Accordingly, the Court of First Instance had erred, applying a more stringent criterion for colours. **5.242**

(b) The Opinion of Advocate General Léger

Regarding the fourth ground in particular, AG Léger reminded the Court that in *Libertel*[229] and *Heidelberg Bauchemie*[230] he had held that a colour per se did not satisfy Article 2 of the Directive. **5.243**

The Court of First Instance had followed the Judgment of the Court in *Libertel*; it did not err in holding that although Article 7(1)(b) of the Regulation did not differentiate between types of signs, the relevant public did not necessarily perceive in the same way a sign consisting of a colour per se and a sign that is independent from the external appearance of the product in relation to which it is used.[231] **5.244**

To the contrary, he criticized the finding of the Court of First Instance regarding the consultancy services, submitting that it had not applied the *Libertel* criteria in their entirety **5.245**

---

[228] Case R-282/1999-2, 19 April 2000.
[229] C-104/01 *Libertel Groep BV* [2003] ECR I-3793.
[230] C-49/02 *Heidelberger Bauchemie GmbH* [2004] ECR I-6129.
[231] Point 77.

(c) The Judgment of the Court

5.246 Regarding the fourth ground the Court repeated its position in *Libertel*.[233] '[W]hile the public is accustomed to perceiving word or figurative marks immediately as signs identifying the commercial origin of the goods, the same does not necessarily hold true where the sign forms part of the external appearance of the goods'.[234]

5.247 It is suggested that the reference to the external appearance of the goods carries the seeds of a European theory of functionality that is much broader than the provisions on shapes.

(12) *Mag*: Distinctive Character of Shapes of Products

5.248 Distinctiveness of shapes was reconsidered by the Court in *Mag*.[235] The applicant had unsuccessfully applied to register as Community trade marks five cylindrical shapes of torches for: 'Accessories for apparatus for lighting, in particular for flashlights (torches)'; and 'Apparatus for lighting, in particular flashlights (torches), including parts and accessories for the abovenamed goods' in Classes 9 and 11 of the Nice Agreement. The shapes were the actual shapes of torches marketed by Mag. The applications were rejected for failing Article 7(1)(b).

5.249 The Board of Appeal rejected the appeal. The decision stated that in order for the shape of a product alone to function as an indication of its origin it had to display some features that were different from the usual shape of the specified goods so that a prospective consumer would perceive the shape as an indication of origin rather than a representation of the goods themselves. In the latter case the shape would be descriptive and fall within the scope of Article 7(1)(c) of the Regulation. It added that attractiveness did not render a sign inherently distinctive and that a mere trace of distinctive character would not confer upon the sign the distinctiveness that is necessary to overcome the objections based on Article 7(1)(b).

(a) The Judgment of the Court of First Instance

5.250 The applicant claimed before the Court of First Instance that the Board had infringed Article 7(1)(b). The Court of First Instance dismissed the application.[236]

5.251 It held that the provision did not make any distinctions between categories of signs; accordingly, the distinctiveness criteria should be the same. It found that the distinctive characteristic of the torches was their cylindrical shape, a common shape for torches, indicating their nature rather than their origin. The aesthetic qualities and original design of the product simply rendered the shape a variant of a common torch shape rather than a shape capable of differentiating them from other torches. It left open the possibility of applying Article 7(3), noting that the applicant had chosen not to invoke the provision, despite the fact that its arguments pointed towards this, rather than the inherent form of distinctiveness.

---

[232] Point 86.
[233] C-104/01 *Libertel Groep BV* [2003] ECR I-3793.
[234] *Libertel Groep BV* (n 4) paragraph 78.
[235] C-136/02 P *Mag Instrument Inc v Office for Harmonisation in the Internal Market (Trade Marks and Designs)* [2004] ECR I-9165.
[236] T-88/00 *Mag Instrument Inc v Office for Harmonisation in the Internal Market (Trade Marks and Designs)* [2002] ECR II-467.

(b) The Opinion of the Advocate General

5.252 Advocate General Ruiz-Jarabo Colomer started his analysis by stating that, although the Court of Justice had to consider only the applicability of Article 7(l)(b), on which the decision of the Court of First Instance was based, he still felt Article 7(1)(c) constituted a better starting point for determining the registrability of shapes.[237] He classified the grounds under three parts: misappraisal of specific distinctiveness, misappraisal of the facts relating to distinctiveness, and infringement of the right to a hearing.

(i) Misappraisal of specific distinctiveness

5.253 *Misappraisal of the distinctiveness of the sign as a whole* The appellant argued that the Court of First Instance had failed to take into account the detailed description of the visual and aesthetic aspects specific to each one of the torches. Seeing them from an overall perspective the Court should hold that the signs were not devoid of any distinctive character. The Office counterclaimed that the appellant's detailed descriptions failed to perceive each sign as a whole; instead, they separated them into their component parts.

5.254 The Advocate General considered that this claim should be rejected, since the Court of First Instance had not undertaken an examination of all the parts of the signs in question without addressing the impression they conveyed as a whole. It had simply stated that the, usual for torches, cylindrical shapes did not enable the consumer to differentiate the product or to associate it with any particular commercial origin.

5.255 *Misappraisal of distinctiveness as a result of applying excessively stringent criteria* According to the appellant, and in respect of shape marks, any perceptible difference compared to usual goods should confer upon the sign the necessary distinctiveness. Following *Baby-Dry*,[238] a 'variant' of the ordinary shape should be accepted for registration.

5.256 The Advocate General rejected this ground as a misinterpretation both of the judgment under appeal and *Baby-Dry*. The term 'variants' in the Judgment of the Court of First Instance meant, according to the Advocate General, 'manifestations' of that common shape. It had also found that the signs 'correspond to shapes commonly used by other torch manufacturers on the market'.[239] He also attacked the test of 'any perceptible difference' as minimal, because it would comprise 'any difference however small' and thus would fail to 'guarantee that the trade marks fulfil their identificatory function'.[240]

5.257 Repeating the position expressed in *Postkantoor*[241] on the form of a sign, he stated that a difference should be regarded truly perceptible only if it affected important components of either the form of the sign or its meaning; a sign could be refused trade mark protection even if it comprised certain differences compared with the usual presentation of the specified products.

---

[237] Referring to his views expressed in C-456/01 P and C-457/01 P *Henkel KGaA* [2004] ECR I-5089 he stated that this would allow the examiner to consider whether the sign 'essentially conveys the idea of the goods formed by the average consumer and if not he would have to refuse it registration on the basis of Article 7(1)(c) because it constitutes a new graphic description of the goods' (paragraph 20).
[238] C-383/99 P *Procter & Gamble* Co [2001] ECR I-6251.
[239] T-88/00 *Mag Instrument Inc* [2002] ECR II-467, paragraph 36.
[240] Point 30 of the Opinion of AG Ruiz-Jarabo Colomer.
[241] C-363/99 *Koninklijke KPN Nederland NV* [2004] ECR I-1619.

5.258 He concluded that the Court of First Instance had not applied more stringent criteria than those applied in the case of other categories of trade mark.

5.259 *Misappraisal of distinctiveness as a result of taking the view that the shapes were usual shapes* According to the appellant, the finding of the Court of First Instance that 'the average consumer is accustomed to seeing shapes similar to those at issue here in a wide variety of designs'[242] should lead to the conclusion that the average consumer perceived the variants as an indication of origin.

5.260 Again, the Advocate General found that the appellant had misconstrued the meaning of a statement that really meant that the signs were not sufficiently different from other torches.

5.261 (ii) **Misappraisal of the facts relating to distinctiveness** The Advocate General discussed together the second, fourth, and fifth grounds because all three of them were based on an incorrect interpretation of the way in which the Court assessed a sign's distinctiveness. This had been settled in *Gut Springenheide and Tusky*,[243] where it had adopted a uniform criterion of general application. The applicability of this criterion in trade mark cases has been endorsed in *Lloyd Schuhfabrik*[244] and for shapes in particular in *Philips*.[245]

5.262 So, if

> a sign's capacity to distinguish can be assessed on the basis of a presumption as to what the average consumer who is reasonably well informed, reasonably circumspect and observant is capable of perceiving, it would seem to be unnecessary to undertake further investigations, analytical or comparative studies, expert's opinions or statistical research. Nor, further, do any of those forms of evidence by their existence relieve the Examiner or the Court of the need to exercise their own discretion based on the yardstick of the average consumer as defined by Community law.[246]

5.263 This was the correct criterion, he argued, in particular in respect of signs intended for the general public, because it 'does not entail actual comparison of the signs sought to be registered with those in current use but with an ideal model composed of elements which naturally convey to the mind an image of the shape of the product'.[247] Only when the relevant authorities were in doubt or the case involved specialist goods or services should they seek outside evidence such as studies or opinions.

5.264 Finally, in respect of the second ground of appeal in particular, he noted that it referred to evidence which in fact should not be considered material.

5.265 (iii) **Infringement of the right to a hearing** With the third ground the appellant submitted that the Court of First Instance, because of its failure to examine the facts and the relevant evidence, had infringed its right to be heard contrary to the second paragraph of Article 6 TEU in conjunction with Article 6 of the European Convention on the

---

[242] T-88/00 *Mag Instrument Inc* [2002] ECR II-467, paragraph 37.
[243] C-210/96 *Gut Springenheide and Tusky* [1998] ECR I-4657.
[244] C-342/97 *Lloyd Schuhfabrik Meyer* [1999] ECR I-3819.
[245] C-299/00 *Koninklijke Philips Electronics NV* [2002] ECR I-5475.
[246] Point 48, citing AG Fennelly in C-220/98 *Estée Lauder Cosmetics GmbH & Co OHG v Lancaster Group GmbH* [2000] ECR I-117.
[247] Point 49.

Protection of Human Rights and Fundamental Freedoms and the first indent of paragraph 2 of Article 41 of the Charter of Fundamental Rights of the European Union.

The Advocate General suggested that his findings under Pt B meant that this ground was inadmissible. **5.266**

(c) The Judgment of the Court

The Judgment of the Court considered all the grounds of appeal following the route indicated by the Advocate General. **5.267**

(i) The first ground: Overall impression The Court repeated that distinctive character should be assessed by reference, first, to the specified goods or services and, second, to the perception of the relevant public,[248] adding that the average consumer normally perceived a mark as a whole without analysing its various details. This is why distinctive character should be assessed according to the overall impression conveyed by the sign.[249] **5.268**

It found that the Court of First Instance had not sought to separate each of the marks into their component parts; rather, it had correctly considered the overall impression given by each one of them. **5.269**

(ii) The sixth ground: The criteria for assessing distinctive character for 'product shape' marks The Court restated that the criteria for assessing the distinctive character of three-dimensional marks consisting of the shape of the product itself were the same as those applicable to other signs, however: **5.270**

> for the purpose of applying those criteria, the relevant public's perception is not necessarily the same... Average consumers are not in the habit of making assumptions about the origin of products on the basis of their shape or the shape of their packaging in the absence of any graphic or word element and it could therefore prove more difficult to establish distinctiveness in relation to such a three-dimensional mark than in relation to a word or figurative mark.[250]

Accordingly, the Court required the shape to depart significantly from the norm or customs of the relevant sector. Being a 'variant' of a common shape for that type of product would not be sufficient to establish registrability. The expert's evidence had also been taken into account and the Court of First Instance had found that the excellence of the design and the aesthetic and functional qualities of the torches did not show that the marks possessed distinctive character ab initio; it was capable only of demonstrating that they might become distinctive through use. **5.271**

Regarding the international recognition enjoyed by the designs the Court noted that 'the fact that goods benefit from a high quality of design does not necessarily mean that a mark consisting of the three-dimensional shape of those goods enables ab initio those goods to be distinguished from those of other undertakings for the purposes of Article 7(1)(b)'.[251] **5.272**

---

[248] Citing C-218/01 *Henkel KGaA* [2004] ECR I-1725, paragraph 50 and the case law cited there; see also C-456/01 P and C-457/01 P *Henkel KGaA* [2004] ECR I-5089, paragraph 35 and the case law cited there.
[249] Citing C-104/00 P *DKV Deutsche Krankenversicherung AG* [2002] ECR 1-7561; and, in relation to shapes, C-468/01 P to C-472/01 P *Procter & Gamble* [2004] ECR I-5141.
[250] Paragraph 30.
[251] Paragraph 68.

5.273 (iii) **The seventh ground: Appraising facts**   Regarding the seventh ground, it found that the Court of First Instance had not taken the view that consumers would, as a matter of principle, fail to recognize the shape of goods as an indication of their origin. In addition, examining the appellant's argument would constitute an appraisal of the facts of the case and remained outside the jurisdiction of the Court according to Article 225.[252]

5.274 (iv) **The fourth ground: Evidence of distinctive character**   The Court clarified that Article 7(1)(b) was concerned with the ab initio distinctive character of a trade mark whereas Article 7(3) was concerned with the distinctive character that might be acquired as a result of use.[253] However, for assessing distinctive character, the Court of First Instance 'must have regard to all the relevant facts and circumstances'.[254]

5.275 Accordingly, 'evidence based on the actual perception of the mark by consumers may, in certain cases, provide guidance'.[255]

5.276 The Court went further and identified what that evidence had to show. The trade mark had to immediately enable consumers to distinguish the marked goods or services from those of competing undertakings. Showing that consumers had become accustomed to the mark would be relevant for Article 7(3) but not for Article 7(1)(b); otherwise Article 7(3) would become redundant.

5.277 Since the evidence in the case considered the perception of consumers at a time when the torches had been on the market for a long period of time, the Court of First Instance was entitled to find that it could be relevant for establishing acquired—but not ab initio—distinctive character.

5.278 (v) **The second ground: The meaning of the evidence**   The Court divided the evidence into consumer and expert evidence. It repeated that the Court of First Instance had taken the consumer evidence and had decided, as it was entitled to, that it was not relevant for the purposes of Article 7(1)(b). The expert's evidence had also been taken into account and the Court of First Instance had found that the excellence of the design and aesthetic and functional qualities of the torches did not show that the marks possessed distinctive character ab initio; these were capable only of demonstrating that they might become distinctive through use.

5.279 Regarding the international recognition enjoyed by the designs, the Court noted that 'the fact that goods benefit from a high quality of design does not necessarily mean that a mark consisting of the three-dimensional shape of those goods enables ab initio those goods to be distinguished from those of other undertakings for the purposes of Article 7(1)(b)'.[256]

5.280 (vi) **The third ground: The right to be heard**   The first part of this ground revisited what the appellant had submitted in the second ground and was accordingly rejected. On the second part regarding the expert evidence, the Court stressed that 'the Court of First

---

[252] Citing C-104/00 P *DKV Deutsche Krankenversicherung AG* [2002] ECR I-7561; and C-194/99 P *Thyssen Stahl v Commission* [2003] ECR I-10821.
[253] Citing C-104/01 *Libertel Groep BV* [2003] ECR I-3793, it noted that 'the normal process of familiarising the relevant public' (paragraph 47) could be one of the ways for acquiring distinctive character.
[254] Paragraph 48, citing C-363/99 *Koninklijke KPN Nederland NY* [2004] ECR I-1619.
[255] Paragraph 49.
[256] Paragraph 68.

(vii) **The fifth ground: General propositions** The Court stated that average consumers **5.281** were not in the habit of making assumptions about origin on the basis of the shape of a product or the shape of its packaging in the absence of any graphic or word element. The Court of First Instance had simply accepted that the nature of the mark might influence the perception of the relevant public. The remaining arguments again required the appraisal of facts, which belonged in the jurisdiction of the Court of First Instance.

(13) *Linde, Winward, and Rado*: Product Shapes; a Broader Perspective

In Joined Cases *Linde, Winward Industries, and Rado Uhren*[258] the Court considered three- **5.282** dimensional marks, first, from the perspective of distinctiveness and, second, in relation to the balance between Article 3(1)(e) on the one hand and Article 3(1)(b), Article 3(1)(c), and Article 3(1)(d) on the other. They came before the Court as a reference from the Bundesgerichtshof dealing with the decisions of the Federal Patent Court that, in turn, considered the Deutsches Patent- und Markenamt's (the German Patent and Trade Mark Office) refusal to register the following marks:

(1) In *Linde*, the shape of a vehicle, as a three-dimensional trade mark, for 'motorised trucks and other mobile works vehicles, particularly fork-lift trucks', for lack of distinctive character. The Bundespatentgericht concurred with the Office holding that what the trade saw in the representation of the product was the product itself. The particular shape did not go beyond the parameters of modern industrial design in its non-technical aspects; accordingly it was not so different from standard shapes in order to become a distinctive sign rather than a variation of a familiar shape.
(2) In *Winward*, the shape of a torch, as a three-dimensional trade mark, for torches, again for lack of distinctive character. The shape, according to the Bundespatentgericht, possessed some elegance but was still a typical torch shape with minimal differences compared to competing products on the basis of which even an observant consumer would be unable to identify a particular manufacturer from memory.
(3) In *Rado*, the shape of a wristwatch as a three-dimensional trade mark for watches, again for lack and distinctiveness but also because there was a need to preserve availability of shapes in a product market characterized by the variety of shapes and designs.

The Bundespatentgericht added that protection could be conferred only where an original **5.283** design could overcome the need to preserve the availability of the elementary shape of the product and its lack of distinctive character.

> A fairly strict test must be applied for the purposes of establishing the originality of the product or its parts because they themselves are the most important means of description, and if they are monopolised there is a risk that competitors will be impeded in the design of their products and it is at least conceivable that there is a need to preserve availability.[259]

---

[257] Paragraph 76, citing C-315/99 P *Ismeri Europa v Court of Auditors* [2001] ECR I-5281 and C-24/01 P and C-25/01 P *Glencore and Compagnie Continentale v Commission* [2002] ECR I-10119.
[258] C-53/01 *Linde AG*, C-54/01 *Winward Industries Inc*, and C-55/01 *Rado Uhren AG* [2003] ECR I-3161.
[259] *Linde, Winward*, and *Rado Uhren AG* (n 8) paragraph 16.

5.284 The Bundesgerichtshof, however, disagreed with this approach, holding that the criteria should be the same for all marks. The 'interest in keeping graphic shapes generally available for use should not affect specific distinctiveness within Article 3(1)(b) of the Directive in any way, although that requirement may nevertheless be relevant in the context of Article 3(1)(c)'.[260]

5.285 Accordingly, it submitted the following questions to the Court:

(1) In determining whether a three-dimensional trade mark which depicts the shape of a product has a distinctive character within the meaning of Article 3(1)(b) of the Directive is there a stricter test for distinctive character than in the case of other forms of trade marks?

(2) In the case of three-dimensional trade marks which depict the shape of the product, does Article 3(1)(c) of the Directive have any significance independently of Article 3(1)(e)? If so, when considering Article 3(1)(c)—or alternatively Article 3(1)(e)—must regard be had to the interest of the trade in having the shape of the product available for use so that registration is, at least in principle, ruled out, and is possible as a rule only in the case of trade marks which meet the requirements of the first sentence of Article 3(3) of the Directive?[261]

(a) The Opinion of Advocate General Ruiz-Jarabo Colomer

5.286 (i) **The first question** Advocate General Ruiz-Jarabo Colomer noted that the Directive did not contain any provision suggesting that three-dimensional product shapes had to be treated differently in respect of the assessment 'as to whether they possess actual distinctive character',[262] making a distinction with 'capable of distinguishing or potential distinctive character (Article 2 of the Directive) or acquired distinctive character (Article 3(3))'.[263]

5.287 He accepted that there were public interest reasons that favoured the application of different rules according to the relevant type of sign. This was reflected in other provisions of the Directive, but the Court had made it clear in *Philips*[264] that the criteria for assessing the distinctive character of three-dimensional trade marks were no different from those to be applied to other categories of trade mark.

5.288 Whether in practice it would be harder to demonstrate distinctive character for three-dimensional shapes constituted a practical difficulty linked with the nature of such signs and consumer idiosyncrasies, but this did not mean that the Court followed a stricter approach in the assessment of distinctive character.[265]

5.289 (ii) **The second question: Setting a roadmap** The Advocate General based his analysis on *Philips*.[266] According to his analysis there were three obstacles product shapes had to overcome before reaching registration: first, they ought to satisfy the abstract requirements

---

[260] Paragraph 24.
[261] Reproduced in paragraph 26.
[262] Point 10.
[263] Footnote 5.
[264] C-299/99 *Koninklijke Philips Electronics NV* [2002] ECR I-5475.
[265] He noted (point 12) that Article 3(1)(e) would preclude the registration of functional shapes but added 'inasmuch as shape is dictated by function and similar products are therefore usually similar in appearance, it can be difficult for the original shape to be distinctive, although it may none the less acquire distinctiveness through use, in accordance with Article 3(3) of the Directive. In any event, it is unlikely that the average consumer will perceive minor differences as an indication of the product's origin'.
[266] C-299/99 *Koninklijke Philips Electronics NV* [2002] ECR I-5475.

of Article 2; second, avoid falling within the scope of Article 3(1)(e); and, third, satisfy the requirements of Article 3(1)(b), Article 3(1)(c), and Article 3(1)(d). Also, although he described the ambit of Article 3(1)(e) in very broad and forceful terms, he also stressed that avoiding its application should not automatically mean satisfying the remaining grounds of Article 3(1). Finally, Article 3(3) provided a potential fourth step, bypassing the obstacles raised by Article 3(1)(b), Article 3(1)(c), and Article 3(1)(d) but not Article 3(l)(e). In the end, he acknowledged, many three-dimensional shape of product signs would probably fall before reaching registration.

(iii) **The ambit of Article 3(1)(e)** The Advocate General stressed that under Article 3(1)(e): 5.290

> the purpose of excluding from trade mark protection three dimensional signs which are exclusively dictated by the nature of the product, by the need for a technical result or by the need to give substantial value, reflects the paramount concern not to permit individuals to use trade marks to perpetuate exclusive rights over natural forms, technical developments or aesthetic designs. In keeping with that logic, the legislature did not include subparagraph (e) among the grounds for refusal which may be cured by virtue of the first sentence of Article 3(3). Natural, functional and ornamental shapes are incapable, by express intention of the legislature, of acquiring distinctive character ... It cannot be denied that that interpretation means that many unadorned signs ... will never be eligible for registration but ... that consequence is not disproportionate: the public interest should not have to tolerate even a slight risk that trade mark rights unduly encroach on the field of other exclusive rights which are limited in time, whilst there are in fact other effective ways in which manufacturers may indicate the origin of a product (addition of arbitrary features to a three-dimensional shape, innovative arrangement of the whole, word and figurative marks).[267]

(b) The Judgment of the Court

(i) **The first question** The Court of Justice noted that for the purposes of Article 2 a three-dimensional shape of product sign could in principle constitute a trade mark.[268] 5.291

Moving to Article 3(1)(b) it added that distinctiveness meant that the trade mark served to identify to the relevant persons the specified product as originating from a particular undertaking, distinguishing it from products of other undertakings. The criteria should be the same for all types of marks.[269] 5.292

Article 3(1)(e) was characterized by the Court as a preliminary obstacle that cannot be overcome even with evidence of acquired distinctiveness through use. 5.293

However, the Court also accepted that, in practice, it might be more difficult to establish distinctiveness in relation to a product shape than a word or figurative mark. In these cases Article 3(3) would become relevant. 5.294

(ii) **The second question: The Court's roadmap** The Court repeated that Article 3(1)(e) constituted a preliminary obstacle. After this, the remaining provisions had to be applied; each one was independent of the others and called for separate examination. 5.295

---

[267] Point 29.
[268] Citing C-299/99 *Koninklijke Philips Electronics NV* [2002] ECR I-5475.
[269] *Philips* (n 47) paragraph 48 and C-210/96 *Gut Springenheide and Tusky* [1998] ECR I-4657, paragraph 31.

5.296 Further, it held that the Article 3 grounds for refusing registration had to be interpreted in the light of the public interest underlying each one of them.

5.297 Elaborating on the second situation envisaged by the referring court it added that for certain three-dimensional shape of product signs, it had already held that the rationale of the grounds for refusing registration laid down in Article 3(1)(e) is to prevent the grant of a monopoly on technical solutions or functional characteristics of a product which a user is likely to seek in the products of competitors.[270]

5.298 Whereas the public interest behind Article 3(1)(c) was to ensure that descriptive signs or indications relating to the characteristics of the specified goods or services could be freely used by all, eg as collective marks or as part of complex or graphic marks.[271]

5.299 Regarding the application of Article 3(1)(c), the Court called again for a balanced approach: robust examination without predetermined outcomes.

> The competent authority called upon to apply Article 3(1)(c) of the Directive to such trade marks must determine, by reference to the goods or services for which registration is sought, in the light of a concrete consideration of all the relevant aspects of the application, and in particular the public interest referred to above, whether the ground for refusing registration in that provision applies to the case at hand. The same concrete examination is required in the case of an application for registration of a three dimensional shape of product mark. The authority may not, however, refuse such an application as a matter of principle.[272]

5.300 There was no differentiation from the above in respect of three-dimensional shape of product marks, so the answer to the second limb of the second question must be that:

> when examining the ground for refusing registration in Article 3(1)(c) of the Directive in a concrete case, regard must be had to the public interest underlying that provision, which is that all three-dimensional shape of product trade marks which consist exclusively of signs or indications which may serve to designate the characteristics of the goods or service within the meaning of that provision should be freely available to all and, subject always to Article 3(3) of the Directive, cannot be registered.[273]

(14) *Henkel*: The Assimilation of Packaging and Product Shape

5.301 In *Henkel KGaA v Deutsches Patent- und Markenamt*[274] the Court considered the registrability of packaging of goods which are normally traded in packaged form mainly under Article 3(1)(b) and Article 3(1)(c) of the Directive, but also the relationship of those provisions with Article 3(1)(e).

5.302 The case was a reference from the Bundespatentgericht. Henkel had applied for the registration of a coloured three-dimensional trade mark consisting of a tall bottle, narrowing towards the top, with an integral handle, a small pouring opening, and a two-level stopper which could also be used as a measuring cup, for liquid wool detergent. The application was rejected by the Deutsches Patent- und Markenamt for lack of distinctive character. Henkel attacked the decision before the Bundespatentgericht claiming that the combination of the

---

[270] Citing C-299/99 *Koninklijke Philips Electronics NV* [2002] ECR I-5475.
[271] C-108/97 and C-109/97 *Windsurfing Chiemsee* [1999] ECR I-2779.
[272] Paragraph 75.
[273] Paragraph 77.
[274] C-218/01 *Henkel KGaA* [2004] ECR I-1725.

shape with the colours of the container created a distinctive overall impression, in particular in a product market that was accustomed to perceive containers as indicators of origin as evidenced in a survey it had commissioned.

The German court found that there was no ground for the application of Article 3(1)(e). **5.303** However, it queried whether the public interest behind Article 3(1)(c) precluded the registration of such a container. It also sought to clarify the criteria for establishing distinctive character under Article 3(1)(b).[275]

(a) The Opinion of Advocate General Ruiz-Jarabo Colomer
Advocate General Ruiz-Jarabo Colomer identified two main issues, first whether packag- **5.304** ing should be equated with content and, second, the test to be applied for the assessment of distinctive character in that case. The effect of registration of comparable marks in other Member States upon the assessment was the third point he had to answer.

(i) **Packaging and content** The Advocate General, however, viewed packaging as a com- **5.305** ponent of the product: the only visible, distinguishable element of the product. Accordingly, it constituted the only component that was relevant for the purposes of trade mark law. He accepted that according to Article 2 packaging appeared to be a separate item from the product. However, he suggested approaching the issue from a teleological perspective taking into account the aim of the Directive.

He suggested that packaging was the only shape that consumers could identify as the shape **5.306** of the product in relation to materials that were devoid of a clearly defined size and form, like liquids, gases, and granulated or highly brittle materials: 'For the purpose of trade mark law, the three-dimensional shape of such substances is the shape of the packaging in which they are displayed; therefore, in this context, goods should be taken to mean the container in which they are traded.'[276] From a marketing perspective, he added, packaging was often a decisive factor. 'The size of the packaging determines the quantity of goods available; its shape, their function; and its material, their weight. In the eyes of a consumer, those characteristics may even be more important than the real or presumed attributes of the liquid itself'.[277]

So, when applying the provisions of the Directive, including Article 3(1)(c) and Article **5.307** 3(1)(e), this link between the product and its packaging should not be ignored. The public interest underlying Article 3(1)(e) in particular would be easily circumvented if the product and its packaging were considered to be distinct from each other.

Concluding, he suggested the following reply to the German court: 'for the purpose of **5.308** Community trade mark law, where goods are normally traded in packaged form, the term three-dimensional goods should be taken to mean the shape of the packaging'.[278]

(ii) **The test for assessing distinctive character** The Advocate General did not come up **5.309** with a multifactor test for determining whether the mark possesses distinctive character. Instead, he reconfirmed the perspectives from which distinctive character should be judged.

---

[275] Reproduced in paragraph 19.
[276] Point 12.
[277] Point 13.
[278] Point 17.

5.310 First, citing *Gut Springenheide and Tusky*,[279] he stated that the national court should make the assessment by reference to the presumed expectations of an average consumer who is reasonably well-informed and reasonably observant and circumspect. In principle, there should be no need to resort to experts' reports or consumer research polls unless the court is unable to make the assessment on its own.

5.311 Second, he stressed the link of the trade mark with the marked product. Protection was limited to the goods or services specified in the application. Accordingly, the assessment of distinctive character should be made from the point of view of an average consumer of the same type of goods or services.

5.312 Third, he introduced to the assessment the element of territoriality. Trade mark rights were territorial; the assessment should be made from the point of view of an average consumer in the territory in which the application was filed. Regarding the type of the particular sign in question he noted that there was no reason to depart from that line of reasoning; the assessment should be made from the same perspective.

5.313 (iii) **The effect of registrations in other Member States** It is worth referring here to the stance of the Commission that had argued that registrations in other Member States should be useful but not binding in assessing distinctive character because it is 'in trade mark law that the effective approximation of trade usage and that of consumers in the internal market can be effectively taken into account'.[280]

5.314 The Court restated its holding that the competent authorities must apply and interpret the relevant national law, as far as possible, in the light of the wording and the purpose of the Directive so as to achieve the result it has in view and comply with Article 249 TEC.[281] The competent authority of a Member State could take account of the decision on registration in another Member State of an identical trade mark for identical products or services but would not be bound by that decision.[282] Distinctive character should be assessed solely on the basis of national trade usage.

(15) *Glaverbel*: The Relevance of Alternatives?

5.315 The interpretation of Article 7(1)(b) by the Court of First Instance was challenged again in *Glaverbel*.[283] Glaverbel had applied for registration as a Community trade mark of 'a design applied to the surface of the goods' for glass products for building and for the manufacture of sanitary installations. The actual sign was an abstract design.

---

[279] C-210/96 *Gut Springenheide and Tusky* [1998] ECR I-4657. The same approach has been consistently adopted by the Court, for example, in C-303/97 *Verbraucherschutzverein eV v Sektkellerei GC Kessler GmbH und Co* [1999] ECR I-513; C-220/98 *Estée Lauder Cosmetics GmbH & Co OHG v Lancaster Group GmbH* [2000] ECR I-117; and C-30-99 *Commission v Ireland* [2001] ECR I-4619; and, in the field of trade mark law, C-342/97 *Lloyd Schuhfabrik Meyer & Co GmbH* [1999] ECR I-3819; and C-299/99 *Koninklijke Philips Electronics NV* [2002] ECR I-5475.
[280] Paragraph 58.
[281] Citing C-71/94 to C-73/94 *Eurim-Pharm Arzneimittel GmbH v Beiersdorf AG* [1996] ECR I-3603 and C-37/97 *Bayerische Motorenwerke* [1999] ECR I-905.
[282] Citing C-363/99 *Koninklijke KPN Nederland NV* [2004] ECR I-1619.
[283] C-445/02 P *Glaverbel SA v Office for Harmonisation in the Internal Market (Trade Marks and Designs)* [2004] ECR I-6267; the appeal was against the Judgment of the Court of First Instance in T-36/01 *Glaverbel SA v Office for Harmonisation* in *the Internal Market (Trade Marks and Designs)* [2002] ECR II-3887.

5.316 The application was rejected for lack of distinctive character under Article 7(1)(b) of the Regulation. The Board of Appeal dismissed the appeal[284] and the case reached the Court of First Instance, which rejected the plea alleging infringement of Article 7(1)(b) but upheld another plea on the basis of Article 7(3) and annulled the contested decision. Glaverbel persisted and brought the Article 7(1)(b) part of the case before the Court.

5.317 The Court rejected the appeal by reasoned Order under Article 119 of the Rules of Procedure: where the appeal is clearly inadmissible or clearly unfounded, the Court may at any time, acting on a report from the Judge Rapporteur and after hearing the Advocate General, dismiss the appeal by reasoned Order.

5.318 The most interesting and challenging part of the appeal was Glaverbel's claim regarding the function of the design applied on the surface of the glass. The Court of First Instance had found that the design, which consisted of countless tiny strokes applied throughout the surface of the sheet of glass, constituted part of the appearance of the product and embodied obvious characteristics of the product. It functioned, and accordingly was perceived in the same way, as a technical means of rendering the glass opaque. It added that the complexity and fancifulness of the design was the result of its ornamental and decorative nature and made its perception as a distinguishing sign difficult and improbable.

5.319 Glaverbel argued that there were thousands of patterns that could make a sheet of glass opaque. It accepted the aesthetic nature of the design by claiming that consumers chose a glass sheet on the basis of its design. However, it viewed this as a counterargument regarding the technical function described by the Court of First Instance, and submitted that the complexity and fancifulness of the design would make consumers recognize it and perceive it as a distinguishing sign when seeing it elsewhere.

5.320 The Court did not get drawn into this discussion of aesthetic functionality for the purposes of distinctive character. Instead, it agreed with the Office and rejected the plea as inadmissible because it saw it as a request to reassess findings of fact.

(16) The Washing Tablets Cases

5.321 In the washing tablets cases the Court took a strict approach regarding the application of Article 7(1)(b). The cases involved a number of appeals against judgments of the Court of First Instance on the distinctive character of the shape of a number of washing tablets as Community trade marks for 'washing or dishwashing preparations in tablet form'. Another issue in these cases was the timing for the determination of distinctive character.

5.322 The Court of First Instance had bypassed this question in *Henkel*,[285] where it had decided that the shapes' lack of distinctive character and their inability to indicate the origin of the product was not affected by the number of similar tablets already on the market.

5.323 Consequently, it was not necessary to decide whether their distinctive character should be assessed by reference to the date on which the application for registration was filed or the date of actual registration. Advocate General Ruiz-Jarabo Colomer examined all

---

[284] Case R-0986/2004-4, 1 March 2004.
[285] T-337/99 *Henkel* (Rectangular tablet, white and red) [2001] ECR II-2597.

the appeals jointly in one Opinion; the Court considered the appeals in three separate judgments.[286]

(a) The Judgments of the Court of First Instance

5.324 (i) *Henkel*: **The two-layered tablets** The trade marks in the *Henkel* judgments[287] consisted of two-layered, rectangular tablets. The colours of the layers were white and red in the first mark and white and green in the second.

5.325 The applications were rejected for lack of distinctive character. The Board of Appeal confirmed the rejection, holding that in the case of a three-dimensional mark that was simply a reproduction of the product, the shape mark had to be sufficiently unique to imprint itself easily on the mind of the relevant consumer and to stand out from what was considered to be normal in the trade. The Board also contrasted between trade mark law and the law of utility models and designs, noting that the standard for assessing distinctive character should be higher under trade mark law because of the broad and potentially perpetual scope of trade mark rights.[288]

5.326 The Court of First Instance linked distinctive character with the function of the trade mark as an indicator of origin: the mark should enable

> members of the public concerned to distinguish the product or service that it designates from those which have a different trade origin and to conclude that all the products or services that it designates have been manufactured, marketed or supplied under the control of the owner of the mark and that the owner is responsible for their quality.[289]

5.327 It added: 'Whilst the public is used to recognising the latter marks instantly as signs identifying the product, this is not necessarily so where the sign is indistinguishable from the appearance of the product itself.'[290] It also agreed with the Board on the level of consumer attention for everyday goods; setting it in a negative way it found that the level was not high.

5.328 Analysing the overall impression conveyed by the sign, it examined first each one of its elements, which also constituted features of the product.

5.329 Its shape was one of the basic geometrical shapes, obvious for such a product. Regarding colours it added that consumers were used to seeing different colour features in detergent preparations; indeed, the use of basic colours like blue and green was typical in that sector, whereas the use of other basic colours was found to be one of the most obvious variations on the typical design of these products.

5.330 Note that the Court of First Instance perceived colours as elements of the overall product design, indirectly introducing into the debate broader functionality arguments.

---

[286] C-456/01 P and C-457/01 P *Henkel KGaA* [2004] ECR I-5089; C-468/01 P to C-472/01 P *Procter & Gamble* [2004] ECR I-5141; and C-473/01 P and C-474/01 P *Procter & Gamble* [2004] ECR I-5173. For the Opinion of the AG, see *Henkel* (n 6).
[287] T-335/99 *Henkel KGaA* [2001] ECR II-2581 and T-336/99 *Henkel KGaA* [2001] ECR II-2589. For the English version of these cases, see the almost identical T-337/99 *Henkel* (Rectangular tablet, white and red) [2001] ECR II-2597.
[288] Case R-70/1999-3, Case R-71/1999-3, and Case R-73/1999-3, 21 September 1999.
[289] Paragraph 43.
[290] Paragraph 47.

5.331 It conceded that consumers might get into the habit of recognizing the product from its colours, but this should only be relevant for the application of Article 7(3).

5.332 Then it looked at the mark as a whole: 'a combination of obvious features typical of the product concerned'[291] that failed to enable consumers to distinguish the specified products according to origin.

5.333 (ii) *Procter & Gamble*: **The speckled tablets** The first set of the *Procter & Gamble* cases concerned five square tablets with slightly rounded edges and corners. Two consisted of two layers (white and pale green,[292] white with green speckles and pale green);[293] the remaining three of a single layer incorporating speckles (white with yellow and blue speckles,[294] white with blue speckles,[295] and white with green and blue speckles[296]). The specified products were 'washing and bleaching preparations and other substances for laundry use; cleaning, polishing, scouring and abrasive preparations; preparations for the washing, cleaning and care of dishes; soaps'.

5.334 The applications were rejected on the basis of Article 7(1)(b) of the Regulation. The Board of Appeal upheld the decision of the examiner finding that the basic geometric shapes were the most obvious shapes for such tablets, there was nothing arbitrary or fanciful in a square tablet as a shape for solid detergents, and that colours failed to confer distinctive character. Looking at them from a 'functionality' angle, it noted that white was associated with cleanliness and was a traditional colour for soap powders; green, apart from being a basic colour, was attractive and associated with environmental protection. The Board had also referred to the need of competitors to use similar shapes and colours for their own tablets.

5.335 Before the Court of First Instance, Procter & Gamble stated that it brought the action because the registrability of these signs was an issue that had to be clarified rather than because it believed they deserved trade mark protection.

5.336 The Court of First Instance[297] was again uncompromising:

> the use of basic colours, such as blue or green, is commonplace and is even typical of detergents. The use of other basic colours, such as red or yellow, is one of the most obvious variations on the typical design of these products. The same is true of the various shades of those colours. For that reason, the applicant's argument that the mark applied for is distinctive because one of the layers of the tablet is 'pale green' must be dismissed.[298]

---

[291] Paragraph 54.
[292] T-117/00 *Procter & Gamble* [2001] ECR II-2723; the appeal was against the decision of the Board of Appeal in Case R-509/1999-1, 8 March 2000.
[293] T-118/00 *Procter & Gamble* [2001] ECR II-2731; the appeal was against Case R-516/1999-1, 3 March 2000, 437. T-119/00 *Procter & Gamble* [2001] ECR II-2761; the appeal was against Case R-519/1999-1, 29 February 1999.
[294] T-119/00 *Procter & Gamble* [2001] ECR II-2761; the appeal was against Case R-519/1999-1, 29 February 1999.
[295] T-120/00 *Procter & Gamble* [2001] ECR II-2769; the appeal was against Case R-520/1999-1, 29 February 2000.
[296] T-121/00 *Procter & Gamble* (T-121/00) [2001] ECR II-2777; the appeal was against Case R-529/1999-1, 29 February 1999.
[297] T-117/00 *Procter & Gamble* [2001] ECR II-2723.
[298] *Procter & Gamble* (n 292) paragraph 64.

5.337 In an attempt to discourage further applications based on different combinations it added that although it was possible to vary the basic geometric shapes and add other basic colours as a layer or as speckles, such differences would not suffice to transform the tablets to indications of the product's origin, 'inasmuch as those differences are, as in the present case, obvious variations on the product's basic shapes'.[299]

5.338 From a doctrinal perspective, it acknowledged that the Board had partially based its decision on the general interest in preventing trade mark law from conferring a monopoly over a product, a criterion that the Court of First Instance did not consider to be directly applicable in relation to Article 7(1)(b); the Board, however, had not automatically precluded the registration of such signs, but required them to display sufficiently unusual and arbitrary features to render them distinctive.

5.339 (iii) *Procter & Gamble*: **The inlaid tablets** The second set of the *Procter & Gamble* cases concerned two tablets—one square[300] and the other rectangular[301]—with chamfered edges, bevelled or slightly rounded corners, speckles, and inlays on the upper surface.

5.340 The Board of Appeal confirmed the decision of the Office to refuse registration according to Article 7(1)(b), adding this time that the use of 'shouldered' corners, bevelled edges, concave centres, and colours did not confer distinctive character on the trade marks.[302]

5.341 The Court of First Instance underlined that here the applicant had not claimed a colour. The applicant therefore had to establish that 'the average consumer, when he sees a rectangular tablet with chamfered edges, speckles and a triangular inlay, will recognise it irrespective of its colour and associate all products presented in that way with the same origin'.[303]

5.342 It found that the additional elements did not assist the shape in gaining distinctive character, irrespective of the fact that there were no other tablets on the market with the same combination of shapes—rectangular tablet/triangular inlay.

5.343 Interestingly, the Court of First Instance continued employing 'functionality' arguments. It found the slightly rounded corners to be dictated by practical considerations and viewed the chamfered edges as a barely perceptible variant on the basic shape.

5.344 Considering the speckles it added that consumers were used to light and dark features in detergent preparations because powder was usually very light grey or beige and appeared to be almost white. Often it contained particles of one or more colours, darker or lighter than its basic colour, which suggested the presence of various active ingredients. Similarly, the inlays were seen as one of the most obvious solutions for combining various ingredients in a tabular washing product. The form of the inlays, a slight depression in the tablet's centre in a geometrical shape, and the combined effect of their shape with the shape of the tablet were equally obvious. The Court of First Instance, however, required something additional that would have an impact on consumers' perception.

---

[299] *Procter & Gamble* (n 292) paragraph 73.
[300] T-128/00 *Procter & Gamble* (Square tablet with inlay) [2001] ECR II-2785.
[301] T-129/00 *Procter & Gamble* (Rectangular tablet with inlay) [2001] ECR II-2793.
[302] Case R-506/1999-1 and Case R-508/1999, 8 March 2000.
[303] T-128/00 *Procter & Gamble* [2001] ECR II-278, paragraph 55.

(b) The Opinion of Advocate General Ruiz-Jarabo Colomer

AG Ruiz-Jarabo Colomer covered all the appeals jointly[304] since they all involved the interpretation and application of Article 7(1)(b). He started his analysis by considering the 'procedural' question of the timing of the assessment of distinctive character. 5.345

(i) The critical time for assessing distinctive character The Advocate General agreed with the Office's position that the sign applied for had to meet the requisite conditions, both at the time of filing the application and on registration. This would preclude the registration of signs that lost their distinctive character during the process of the examination. 5.346

This was, first, based on a joint reading of Article 7(1) with Article 51, providing that a trade mark registered in breach of the provisions of Article 7 should be invalidated. 5.347

Second, he accepted the Office's 'undertaking' that in order to avoid denying registration to a sign that had been systematically copied in the course of the examination procedure, it would exclude from its analysis distinctive character cases where the sign was used solely for that purpose. 5.348

Third, from a doctrinal perspective, he suggested that frequent use of the same elements would be relevant only if the contested judgments had been based on the criterion of relative originality or currency of the signs, which could be more relevant when considering the general interest in preserving the availability of a mark in the context of Article 7(1)(c).[305] 5.349

(ii) The interpretation and application of Article 7(1)(b) The Advocate General divided the remaining grounds of appeal into four categories: first, the significance of the existence of similar products in the marketplace and the relationship between Article 7(1)(b) and Article 12(b); second, the angle for viewing and examining distinctive character; third, the relevance of actual distinctive character; and, finally, the relevance of the need to preserve availability. 5.350

The significance of similar products—Article 12(b) First, Henkel argued that searching for similarities with other comparable products should not be an issue under Article 7(1)(b) because it would introduce into the examination of registrability a concern that was relevant for determining the scope of protection. The Advocate General found that this claim targeted an aspect of the Court of First Instance's reasoning that had no impact on the outcome and, in any case, on its own this possibility would not suffice to make the sign distinctive. 5.351

Procter & Gamble also submitted that if there were no similar tablets on the market at the time of assessment of the sign's distinctive character then it would be appreciably different and possess distinctive character. Again, he rejected the argument: 5.352

> first, what is decisive is not the number of products on the market but the way in which the average consumer perceives them; second, nor is the number of products on the market capable of counteracting, for example, the descriptive nature of their appearance for the purposes of Article 7(1)(c) of the Regulation.[306]

---

[304] *Henkel* (n 6).
[305] Point 47.
[306] Point 57.

5.353 *The average consumer's level of attention*   The Advocate General found that assessing the precise way consumers perceived a product was a matter of fact, outside the jurisdiction of the Court. In any case he found the Court of First Instance's assertion to be the correct inference to be drawn from the proposition that, as regards the relevant public's perception of the trade mark, the attention of the average consumer varied according to the category of products or services in question.

5.354 *Actual distinctive character*   Advocate General Ruiz-Jarabo Colomer categorically supported the approach taken by the Court of First Instance:

> the test used by the Court of First Instance is not only correct, but is also more appropriate, than the test proposed by the appellants. When the signs for which registration is sought are compared, not with those already current, but with a paradigm composed of features which spring to mind if the shape of the product is imagined, the test performed, although based on objective criteria, does not lean so heavily on the vagaries of the market.[307]

5.355 The Court of First Instance had simply adapted the method for assessing distinctive character to take into account the particular features of this type of sign. This would also ensure that no one undertaking could protect under trade mark law features that its competitors would like to use. Nevertheless, he found that since it remained uncertain whether the need to preserve availability could be raised under Article 7(1)(h) of the Regulation, the best way of dealing with such concerns would be under Article 7(1)(c), which excluded signs that were nothing more than the representation of a graphic description of the product. Article 7(1)(c) also allowed the consideration of factors pertaining to the future.

5.356 The second set of claims focused on the significance of specific peculiarities, for example, the arrangement of colours or the rounded edges in relation to some of the tablets. The Advocate General considered these issues to be matters of fact.

5.357 *The need to preserve availability*   The final set of grounds attacked the apparent inclusion in the analysis of the Court of First Instance of the need to preserve the availability of some signs for other undertakings, something that fell within the scope of Article 7(1)(c), which was not applicable in this case. For the Advocate General, the purpose of Article 7(1)(h) was

> to prohibit the registration of signs which are devoid of any real distinctive character, that is to say, those signs which the average consumer, who is reasonably well informed and reasonably observant and circumspect, cannot identify as reliably indicating the commercial origin of the product.[308]

5.358 Preventing the appropriation of three-dimensional shapes that were useful from an aesthetic or technical point of view, or the monopolization of descriptive signs, was covered by Article 7(1), subparagraphs (c) and (e); Article 7(1)(d) protected the general interest in keeping available for all signs that were customary in the current language or in the bona fide and established practices of the trade. In *Libertel*[309] the Court of Justice had taken into account the monopolization of colours in the application of Article 3(1)(b) of the Directive, but this should be seen in the particular context of that case.[310]

---

[307] Point 68.
[308] Point 78.
[309] C-104/01 *Libertel Groep BV* [2003] ECR I-3793.
[310] Point 81.

5.359 The Court of First Instance, 'in using the notion of an obvious shape, it assessed distinctive character by reference to an ideal paradigmatic concept of the product or, in other words, to how it instinctively comes to mind, instead of by reference to products already available on the market'.[311]

5.360 He found the test applied by the Court of First Instance to be an objective one, when properly executed. 'In the present case, it is significant that the appellants, who claim that the shapes of the washing tablets were not customary at the time when the application was filed, accept that they are now.'[312]

(c) The Judgment of the Court in Henkel KGaA

5.361 In the first of the three washing tablets cases[313] the Court considered jointly the appeals against two judgments of the Court of First Instance[314] covering four separate issues: the distinctive character of the trade marks; the relevance of the need to preserve the availability of a sign; the assessment of the average consumer's level of attention; and the date for assessing distinctive character. Henkel also claimed that the Office had already accepted that comparable signs possessed distinctive character; the Court rejected the claim because it had not been raised before the Court of First Instance:

> To allow a party to put forward for the first time before the Court of Justice a plea in law which it has not raised before the Court of First Instance would be to allow it to bring before the Court, whose jurisdiction in an appeal is limited, a case of wider ambit than that which came before the Court of First Instance. In an appeal the Court's jurisdiction is thus confined to review of the finding of law on the pleas argued before the Court of First Instance.[315]

5.362 (i) **Assessing the distinctive character of a trade mark** What mattered when assessing distinctive character was whether the features of the tablets were different from those in that product market or whether they were the result of technical requirements; colours were perceived as individual features of the get-up of a particular product; and, the Court of First Instance had failed to take into account that Henkel was the only player in that market using red on its tablets, which allowed the public to make the link as to origin between the product and Henkel.

5.363 The Office's response was based on the functional nature of the product and the requirement for such marks to be original, unusual, or arbitrary. Trade mark protection should be granted only if there was evidence of distinctive character acquired through use. Regarding colour combinations in particular, it held that they were perceived by consumers as indications of ingredients with different properties rather than conveyors of detailed information regarding the composition and effect of each product in that form.

5.364 The Court held that the Court of First Instance had rightly followed the path mapped by the Court in its earlier jurisprudence. There were, however, surprises in the Court's statements.

---

[311] Point 82.
[312] Point 84.
[313] C-456/01 P and C-457/01 P *Henkel KGaA* [2004] ECR I-5089.
[314] T-335/99 *Henkel* (Rectangular tablet, red and white) [2001] ECR II-2581 and T-336/99 *Henkel* (Rectangular tablet, green and white) [2001] ECR II-2589. For the English version, see the almost identical T-337/99 *Henkel* (Rectangular tablet, white and red) [2001] ECR II-2597.
[315] *Henkel* (n 6) paragraph 50, citing C-136/92 P *Commission v Brazzelli Lualdi* [1994] ECR I-1981; and the Order in Case C-352/99 *Eridania v Council of the European Union* [2001] ECR I-5037.

5.365 First, in principle and according to Article 4, the shape and colours of products could constitute a trade mark provided they were capable of being represented graphically and capable of distinguishing. However, 'the fact that a sign is, in general, capable of constituting a trade mark within the meaning of Article 4 … does not mean that the sign necessarily has distinctive character for the purposes of Article 7(1)(b) in relation to a specific product or service'.[316]

5.366 Second, in order to possess distinctive character a mark had to identify a specified product as originating from a particular undertaking, and thus distinguish that product from those of other undertakings; and distinctive character should be assessed, first, by reference to the specified product or services and, second, by reference to the perception of the relevant public.

5.367 Third, the criteria for assessing distinctive character were the same for all types of trade marks.

5.368 Fourth, for the purposes of those criteria, the relevant public's perception was not necessarily the same in relation to a three-dimensional mark consisting of the shape and colours of the product itself as it would be in relation to a word or figurative mark consisting of a sign independent from the appearance of the products it denoted. Average consumers were not in the habit of making assumptions about the origin of products on the basis of their shape or the shape of their packaging in the absence of any graphic or word element and it could therefore prove more difficult to establish distinctiveness in relation to such a three-dimensional mark.[317]

5.369 This meant that the more closely the shape for which registration is sought resembled the shape most likely to be taken by the specified product in question, the greater the likelihood of the shape being devoid of any distinctive character for the purposes of Article 7(1)(b) of Regulation No 40/94: 'Only a trade mark which departs significantly from the norm or customs of the sector and thereby fulfils its essential function of indicating origin, is not devoid of any distinctive character for the purposes of that provision'.[318]

5.370 How those criteria were applied in a particular case remained in the exclusive jurisdiction of the Court of First Instance because it involved findings of a factual nature. The Court could intervene on appeal only in cases of distortion of the evidence produced before the Court of First Instance.[319]

5.371 **(ii) Article 7(1)(b) and the need to preserve the availability of a sign** Henkel's arguments and the Office's riposte had both taken up the 'functionality' point insinuated in the Judgment of the Court of First Instance. The appellant argued that the Court of First Instance had overly relied on its finding that the shapes and colours of the tablets were both 'basic'. This led to the claim that it had taken into account 'need to preserve the availability of a sign' considerations that were relevant only for the application of Article 7(1)(b).

---

[316] *Henkel* (n 6) paragraph 32.
[317] Citing C-53/01 *Linde AG*, C-54/01 *Winward Industries Inc* and C-55/01 *Rado Uhren AG* [2003] ECR I-3161; and C-218/01 *Henkel KGaA v Deutsches Patent- und Markenamt* [2004] ECR I-1725. Henkel (n 6) paragraph 39, citing C-218/01 *Henkel KGaA v Deutsches Patent- und Markenamt* [2004] ECR I-1725.
[318] *Henkel* (n 6) paragraph 39, citing C-218/01 *Henkel KGaA v Deutsches Patent- und Markenamt* [2004] ECR I-1725.
[319] Citing C-104/00 P *DKV Deutsche Krankenversicherung AG* [2002] ECR I-7561.

5.372 Henkel went further and queried whether the 'need to preserve the availability of a sign' considerations would preclude the registration of the contested signs. The shape of the tablet was determined freely by the manufacturer; it only had to observe some universal technical requirements that did not dictate the details of the actual shape. From a technical point of view there was no compelling ground for a competitor to use that particular shape.

5.373 The same applied to the colour combinations that, it stressed, followed a specific arrangement. Consumers would not perceive them as indications or technical product characteristics but as a manifestation of the individuality of the product.

5.374 It concluded that if there was no need to maintain the availability of each one of the elements of the sign, the same should apply to the combination of those elements.

5.375 The Office held that Henkel's overall approach was wrong because it had misinterpreted the Judgment of the Court in *Windsurfing Chiemsee*.[320] In addition, it suggested that Henkel's own account of the product development of washing tablets showed that from their early stages competing undertakings had been using rectangular and circular two-layered and two-coloured shapes for their tablets. This should be seen as evidence of the need to ensure that these elements would also remain available to other competitors.

5.376 Note that the Office had also submitted, first, that the test for distinctive character suggested by Henkel was appropriate for determining the distinctive character of a design but not of a trade mark and, second, that a Community trade mark registration should not be used to give a priority right over an obvious product configuration; the story would be different if there was evidence of distinctiveness acquired through use.

5.377 The response of the Court was twofold. First, it rejected the basis of Henkel's claim, finding that the Court of First Instance had founded its judgment on lack of distinctive character. Second, and more important from a doctrinal perspective, it held that 'even on the assumption that the Court of First Instance did include considerations pertaining to the public interest in its assessment of distinctive character, it did not make an error of law in that regard'.[321]

5.378 But to which public interest did the Court refer? This remained a moot point. The Court noted: 'Each of the grounds for refusal to register listed in Article 7(1)(b) of Regulation No 40/94 is independent of the others and calls for separate examination. Furthermore, the various grounds for refusal must be interpreted in the light of the public interest underlying each of them'.[322]

5.379 The public interest underlying each of those grounds 'may, or even must, reflect different considerations, depending upon which ground for refusal is at issue'.[323] Decontextualizing *Libertel*[324] from its factual background reminded the Court that there it had ruled that Article 3(1)(b) of the Directive was directed at the need not to restrict unduly the availability of colours for other traders. And, looking at the registrability of the contested signs from a

---

[320] C-108/97 and C-109/97 *Windsurfing Chiemsee* [1999] ECR I-2779.
[321] *Henkel* (n 6) paragraph 44.
[322] *Henkel* (n 6) paragraph 45.
[323] Paragraph 46.
[324] C-104/01 *Libertel Groep BV* [2003] ECR I-3793.

negative perspective, it added: 'there is no public interest in conferring the benefit of the full protection ... on a trade mark which does not fulfil its essential function'.³²⁵

5.380 Accordingly, it rejected Henkel's claim as inadmissible.

5.381 (iii) **The average consumer's level of attention** The Court ruled that this involved findings of fact that were not subject to review by the Court of Justice on appeal.

5.382 (iv) **The date for assessing distinctive character** The Court chose to ignore the substance of this question. Functioning as a true court of appeal rather as an interpretive court, it accepted that the Court of First Instance was correct in finding that it was not necessary to decide this point since its judgment on distinctive character was not affected by the number of similar tablets on the market.

(d) The Judgment of the Court in the speckled tablets Procter & Gamble *cases*

5.383 In the first *Procter & Gamble*³²⁶ case the Court considered the appeals against the judgments of the Court of First Instance in the square speckled tablets cases.³²⁷ Procter & Gamble claimed that the Court of First Instance had misinterpreted Article 7(1)(b) focusing on five issues: the distinctive character of the trade marks; the assessment of the consumer's level of attention; the date for assessing distinctive character; the need to consider the trade mark as a whole; and the criterion concerning use of a trade mark.

5.384 The Court followed its judgment in *Henkel* regarding the first three issues, so here we will concentrate on the need to consider the mark as a whole and the criterion concerning use of the mark.

5.385 (i) **Considering the mark as a whole** Procter & Gamble argued that the Court of First Instance had examined each one of the individual components but failed to analyse the overall impression produced by the specific combinations. The Office responded that the Court of First Instance and examination authorities were entitled to start the examination of a trade mark with a separate analysis of the individual components of the marks.

5.386 The Court repeated its findings in cases that dealt with conflicts between signs. The average consumer normally perceived a mark as a whole and did not proceed to analyse its various details.³²⁸ Accordingly, the overall impression given by the mark should be considered in order to assess distinctive character.³²⁹ However, this did not mean that the competent authorities 'may not first examine each of the individual features of the get-up of that mark

---

³²⁵ Paragraph 50.
³²⁶ C-468/01 P to C-472/01 P *Procter & Gamble v Office for Harmonisation in the Internal Market (Trade Marks and Designs)* [2004] ECR I-5141.
³²⁷ T-117/00 *Procter & Gamble v Office for Harmonisation in the Internal Market (Trade Marks and Designs)* (Square tablet, white and pale green) [2001] ECR II-2723; T-118/00 *Procter & Gamble v Office for Harmonisation in the Internal Market (Trade Marks and Designs)* (Square tablet, white with green speckles and pale green) [2001] ECR II-2731; T-119/00 *Procter & Gamble v Office for Harmonisation in the Internal Market (Trade Marks and Designs)* (Square tablet, white with yellow and blue speckles) [2001] ECR II-2761; T-120/00 *Procter & Gamble v Office for Harmonisation in the Internal Market (Trade Marks and Designs)* (Square tablet, white with blue speckles) [2001] ECR II-2769; and T-121/00 *Procter & Gamble v Office for Harmonisation in the Internal Market (Trade Marks and Designs)* (Square tablet, white with green and blue speckles) [2001] ECR II-2777.
³²⁸ C-251/95 *Sabel BV* [1997] ECR I-6191 and C-342/97 *Lloyd Schuhfabrik* [1999] ECR I-3819.
³²⁹ C-251/95 *Sabel BV* [1997] ECR I-6191; and C-104/00 P *DKV Deutsche Krankenversicherung AG* [2002] ECR I-7561.

in turn. It may be useful, in the course of the competent authority's overall assessment, to examine each of the components of which the trade mark concerned is composed'.[330] This is what the Court of First Instance had done in this case. It examined the shapes of the tablets and their colour arrangements separately and then assessed the overall impression deriving from them.

(ii) The criterion concerning use of a trade mark The Court summarily rejected Procter & Gamble's argument that use of or advertising for other signs could influence the public to view colours as indicators of origin and that this use should be considered under Article 7(1)(b) rather than Article 7(3) by simply stating that the Court of First Instance had correctly applied Article 7(1)(b).

5.387

(e) The Judgment of the Court in the inlaid Procter & Gamble *tablets*

In the second *Procter & Gamble* case[331] the Court considered the appeals against the judgments of the Court of First Instance concerning the inlaid tablets.[332] The claims were the same as those developed in the first *Procter & Gamble* case. The Court rejected the appeal following the same line it had drawn in the first case.

5.388

(17) *SiSi-Werke***: Article 7(1)(b) and Packaging**

In *SiSi-Werke*[333] the Court looked at the application of Article 7(1)(b) of the Regulation in relation to packaging. The case was an appeal against a Judgment of the Court of First Instance[334] dismissing the actions against the decisions of the Second Board of Appeal[335] refusing registration of eight three-dimensional trade marks consisting of various pouches for 'fruit drinks and fruit juices'. The applications were rejected under Article 7(1)(b). The Board of Appeal confirmed the decisions of the examiner, holding that consumers would see the pouches purely as packaging rather than indications of origin. The Board also noted that granting such a registration would be against the interests of packaging manufacturers and beverage producers from a competition perspective.

5.389

(a) The Judgment of the Court of First Instance

The Court of First Instance agreed with the Board. It rejected the applicant's argument that marketing fruit juices in such a type of packaging was, in itself, unusual:

5.390

> This kind of packaging for liquids for human consumption is devoid of distinctive character regards each of the products within that category and, in particular, the beverages concerned in this instance. The expected development of this type of packaging confirms, if confirmation were needed, that its use is unexceptional.[336]

---

[330] *Procter & Gamble* (n 139) paragraph 45.
[331] C-473/01 P and C-474/01 P *Procter & Gamble v Office for Harmonisation in the Internal Market (Trade Marks and Designs)* [2004] ECR I-5173.
[332] T-128/00 *Procter & Gamble v Office for Harmonisation in the Internal Market (Trade Marks and Designs)* (Square tablet with inlay) [2001] ECR II-2785; and T-129/00 *Procter & Gamble v Office for Harmonisation in the Internal Market (Trade Marks and Designs)* (Rectangular tablet with inlay) [2001] ECR II-2793.
[333] C-173/04 *Deutsche SiSi-Werke GmbH & Co Betriebs KG v Office for Harmonisation in the Internal Market (Trade Marks and Designs)* [2006] ECR I-551.
[334] T-146/02 to T-153/02 *Deutsche SiSi-Werke v Office for Harmonisation in the Internal Market (Trade Marks and Designs)* (Flat-bottomed pouches) [2004] ECR II-447.
[335] Cases R-719/1999-2 to R-724/1999-2, R-747/1999-2, and R-748/1999-2, 28 February 2002.
[336] *Deutsche SiSi-Werke* (n 334) paragraph 42.

5.391 Then it considered all the individual elements of the pouches and the over impression produced by their combined appearance and found that the pouches were devoid of any distinctive character.

(b) The Opinion of Advocate General Ruiz-Jarabo Colomer

5.392 Advocate General Ruiz-Jarabo Colomer noted from the outset that the jurisprudence of the Court had already dealt with most of the issues regarding the distinctive character of three-dimensional signs. The outcome was the delimitation of the relevant context for verifying whether a three-dimensional sign was capable of fulfilling the essential function of a trade mark. In addition, he criticized the way the appellant approached the appeal process. It had invoked three pleas regarding the interpretation of Article 7(1)(b) but went on to present its arguments without specifying the ground that each one of them referred to. The Advocate General divided the appeal into five parts.

5.393 (i) **The context for determining distinctive character** The Advocate General submitted that taking account of the packaging of a broader category of products rather than those specified in the application was a more pertinent option. He found the appellant's analysis of the relevant case law of the Court to be rather simplistic. If the relevant goods or services affect the perspective from which the distinctive character is assessed, and this was indeed the case according to the jurisprudence of the Court, then the goods and services that would have to be examined should not be exclusively those actually mentioned in the form but equally all those that belonged to the same class, or the same type, or the same species. In other words, all those goods or services that could compete in terms of product choice either because they travelled through similar channels of distribution or because they targeted the same consumers.

5.394 Citing his views already expressed in *Merz & Krell*[337] and *Ansul*,[338] he stressed that in the assessment of distinctive character it was necessary to take into account the structure of the relevant sector and the channels of commercialization; in essence, AG Ruiz-Jarabo Colomer suggested that we should introduce factors that would also be relevant in competition considerations. It was essential, he added, to examine the whole range of products confronting the consumer. In this particular context we should include all alimentary products in a liquid form.

5.395 He agreed too with the submission of the Office regarding the perception of a consumer who would see for the first time in relation to a particular product a type of packaging that had been used until then only for some other product. It would still function as packaging rather than as an indication of origin.

5.396 He also suggested that consumer perception in the entirety of the Community should be relevant following the same logic as that underlying Article 8(1)(b) of the Regulation regarding likelihood of confusion.

5.397 (ii) **The assessment of the marks as 'basic geometric shapes'** On the same basis the appellant had challenged the finding of the Court of First Instance that the pouches were

---

[337] C-517/99 *Merz & Krell GmbH & Co* [2001] ECR I-6959.
[338] C-40/01 *Ansul BV v Ajax Brandbeveiliging BV* [2003] ECR I-2439.

'basic geometric shapes'. In the absence of other pouches there should not be any basic shape for them.

5.398 The Advocate General found that to a certain extent the plea involved the assessment of evidence. He looked only at the argument that, according to the appellant, the Court of First Instance had wrongly incorporated into the assessment the fact that the pouches could be used frequently as packaging for fruit juices as part of the general interest behind the provision. However, he found that the Court of First Instance had simply stated that because the particular type of packaging had been commonly used in relation to liquid alimentary products, the sign did not present the necessary exceptionality.[339]

5.399 **(iii) The level of the distinctiveness requirement for three-dimensional trade marks** The Advocate General found that even if the same criteria were to be applied this would not change the finding that, because of the nature of the sign, ordinary consumers would not normally understand the form of the product as an indication of origin and that, in order to be able to function as a trade mark, the three-dimensional design would need to be sufficiently distant from the form of the product. Since the packaging of a liquid product would reflect the image of the product, a simple variation of the ordinary form of packaging would not possess the necessary distinctive character.[340]

5.400 He added that it would be helpful to revert to empirical principles in order to compare the forms and the containers existing on the market, in particular in relation to products that consumers encountered in their everyday lives. He believed that the attention of consumers would veer towards the label rather than the form of the packaging. Accordingly, the examination of commonly used containers and of basic structures was relevant and did not imply the application of a stricter criterion.

5.401 He indicated that the Court of First Instance had respected all of those rules in its assessment. It had examined all of the essential characteristics individually, considered the overall impression, and found that the sign lacked distinctive character.

5.402 **(iv) The absence of justification** The Advocate General noted that, following *Henkel*,[341] it was clear that registration of a trade mark for a particular product in one Member State did not imply that the same mark should be accepted or rejected in another Member State. The same reasoning should apply to applications for Community trade mark registrations. He noted that registration was subject to specific rules applied to certain concrete circumstances and this is exactly what the Court of First Instance had decided.

5.403 The Court of First Instance had also shown why past practice of the Office should not be viewed as binding; registrability of a mark could be assessed only on the basis of the relevant Community legislation. In any case, he added, the applications SiSi-Werke referred had been filed and decided at a later date than the date of the contested decisions of the Board. Accordingly, SiSi-Werke would have been unable to rely on them.

---

[339] Referring to T-146/02 to T-153/02 *Deutsche SiSi-Werke v Office for Harmonisation in the Internal Market (Trade Marks and Designs)* (Flat-bottomed pouches) [2004] ECR II-441, paragraph 42.
[340] Citing C-136/02 P *Mag Instrument Inc* [2004] ECR I-9165.
[341] C-218/01 *Henkel KGaA* [2004] ECR I-1725.

5.404 **(v) The interests of competitors** The Advocate General found that the Court of First Instance had referred to the risk of monopolization in order to confirm that the marks could not fulfil the essential function of a trade mark.

(c) The Judgment of the Court

5.405 The Court followed a slightly different pattern in the building up of its judgment, in particular in relation to the first ground. It divided its judgment into three parts: first, it looked at the context of the assessment, the first part of the first plea; then, it reviewed the distinctive character requirements for three-dimensional marks, the second plea; and, third, it combined the second part of the first plea and the third plea that focused on the interests of third parties.

5.406 **(i) The context of the assessment** The Court repeated that the parameters of the assessment should be set according to the specification and the perception of the marks by the relevant public[342] and that the criteria for assessing distinctive character should be the same for all categories of trade marks. However, the relevant public's perception would not necessarily be the same in the case of a three-dimensional mark consisting of the appearance of the product itself as it would be in the case of a word or figurative mark.[343]

5.407 For products in a liquid form, it added, packaging had to enable average consumers of the products, who were reasonably well informed and reasonably observant and circumspect, to distinguish the product concerned from those of other undertakings without conducting an analytical or comparative examination and without paying particular attention.[344]

5.408 Accordingly, the Court of First Instance was right in holding that the average consumer would see the form of drinks packaging as an indication of origin only if it might be perceived immediately as such; it did not hold that the packaging of liquid goods could never have a distinctive character. The Court then referred to its case law stating that 'only a mark which departs significantly from the norm or customs of the sector and thereby fulfils its essential function of indicating origin is not devoid of any distinctive character'.[345]

5.409 In relation to this the Court reinforced and clarified two particular points. First, that it was not necessary 'systematically to restrict the sector for the purposes of comparison to the actual goods in respect of which registration is sought'. It could not be excluded that consumers might be influenced, 'in their perception of the trade mark which the product bears, by the marketing methods used for other goods which they also use'.[346] Depending on the nature of the goods and the trade mark applied for, it might be necessary to take into account a wider sector.

5.410 The current case was characterized by two facts that made this expansion necessary. One was that the product had to be packaged in order to be marketed; and, after *Henkel*,[347] the packaging imposed its shape on the product and had to be assimilated to the shape of the

---

[342] Citing C-456/01 P and C-457/01 P *Henkel KGaA* [2004] ECR I-5089.
[343] Citing C-136/02 P *Mag Instrument Inc* [2004] ECR I-9165.
[344] Citing C-218/01 *Henkel KGaA* [2004] ECR I-1725.
[345] *Deutsche SiSi-Werke* (n 333) paragraph 31, citing C-218/01 *Henkel KGaA v Deutsches Patent-und Markenamt* [2004] ECR I-1725; and C-136/02 P *Mag Instrument Inc v Office for Harmonisation in the Internal Market (Trade Marks and Designs)* [2004] ECR I-9165.
[346] Paragraph 32.
[347] Paragraph 32.

product. Accordingly, the relevant norm or customs applying 'in the sector of the packaging of goods which are of the same type and intended for the same consumers as those goods in respect of which registration is sought'[348] may be relevant. The second was a negative assumption more than a fact.[349]

In essence, the Court held that we should not assume that consumers would be aware of what constituted trade knowledge. At the same time it did not preclude the possibility that the packaging could function as a trade mark even in such a factual scenario. Everything, it appears, is a question of fact. **5.411**

Indeed, this was the second clarificatory point made by the Court: 'restriction of the sector in which the comparison is to be made falls within the appraisal of the facts',[350] and this, in turn, fell within the jurisdiction of the Court of First Instance.[351] **5.412**

Rejecting the first part of the first plea, the Court concluded that the Court of First Instance could take into consideration the types of packaging used on the European market for liquids for human consumption in general in order to determine whether the use of any one of the contested pouches enabled the average consumer of fruit drinks and fruit juices to distinguish, without conducting an analytical or comparative examination and without paying particular attention, the appellant's goods from those of other undertakings. Further it could also refer to the 'standard shape', the 'basic shape', the 'standard form', or the 'standard appearance' of the pouches on the basis of stand-up pouches used for the marketing of liquids for human consumption on the European market. **5.413**

(ii) The level of the distinctive character requirement for three-dimensional 'shape of product marks': The powers of the Board of Appeal Regarding the first part of the second plea, the Court repeated that in order to possess distinctive character a mark had to identify the specified goods or services as originating from a particular undertaking, and thus to distinguish them from those of other undertakings.[352] Following its analysis above, the Court found the claim to be unfounded, to the extent that it challenged the findings regarding the perception of three-dimensional marks consisting of the appearance of the product. To the extent that it challenged the assessment of the Court of First Instance regarding the specific characteristics of the marks the plea was inadmissible. **5.414**

In relation to the second part of the second plea, the Court noted that the decisions of the Board were taken under the Regulation in the exercise of circumscribed powers rather than as a matter of discretion. It concurred with the Court of First Instance that the legality of those decisions should be assessed solely on the basis of the Regulation rather than previous practice.[353] **5.415**

It added that registrations made in Member States were factors that might merely be taken into consideration, without being given decisive weight.[354] Indeed, there was no **5.416**

---

[348] Paragraph 33.
[349] Paragraph 34.
[350] Paragraph 35.
[351] Citing C-104/00 P *DKV Deutsche Krankenversicherung AG* [2002] ECR I-7561; and C-136/02 P *Mag Instrument Inc* [2004] ECR I-9165.
[352] Citing C-136/02 P *Mag Instrument Inc* [2004] ECR I-9165.
[353] Citing C-37/03 P *BioID AG* [2005] ECR I-7975.
[354] Citing C-218/01 *Henkel KGaA* [2004] ECR I-1725.

provision in the Regulation requiring the Office or the Court of First Instance to come to the same conclusions on registrability as those reached by national authorities in similar circumstances.[355]

5.417 (iii) **The monopolization argument** The Court looked at the second part of the first plea and the third plea together, since both regarded the interest of possible competitors. It noted that each one of the Article 7(1) grounds was independent of the others and required separate examination and, further, should be interpreted in the light of the general interest specifically underlying each one of them.[356] In order to readdress the interest behind the provision it linked it with the essential function of a trade mark.

5.418 The combination of the citations of the Court regarding the general interest behind Article 7(1)(b) is revealing as to its continuous efforts to strike a balance between the rights of trade mark proprietors and their competitors. It chose *Hoffmann-La Roche*,[357] from its earlier, pre-harmonization, free movement of goods jurisprudence; *Philips*,[358] the first case where the Court considered the registrability of shapes from a number of diverse perspectives and followed a restrictive approach; and *SAT.1*,[359] where it appeared to be more permissive.

5.419 According to the above, Article 7(1)(b) intended to preclude registration of trade marks:

> which are devoid of distinctive character which alone renders them capable of fulfilling the essential function of a trade mark, which is to guarantee the identity of the origin of the marked product or service to the consumer or end-user by enabling him, without any possibility of confusion, to distinguish the product or service from others which have another origin.[360]

5.420 It added that, in view of the extent of protection, the general interest underlying Article 7(1)(b) was 'manifestly, indissociable from the essential function of a trade mark'.[361]

5.421 Article 7(1)(c) on the other hand pursued 'an aim which is in the public interest, namely that such signs or indications may be freely used by all. That provision accordingly prevents such signs and indications from being reserved to one undertaking alone because they have been registered as trade marks'.[362]

5.422 The reference to the 'public interest' rather than a 'general interest' could be seen as evidence of a stronger basis for Article 7(1)(c), however in the German original text the same term is being used.[363]

---

[355] Citing C-104/00 P *DKV Deutsche Krankenversicherung AG* [2002] ECR I-7561.
[356] Citing C-329/02 P *SAT.1 SatellitenFernsehen GmbH* [2004] ECR I-8317; and C-37/03 P *BioID AG* [2005] ECR I-7975.
[357] Case 102/77 *Hoffmann-la Roche & Co AG and Hoffmann-la Roche AG* [1978] ECR 1139.
[358] C-299/99 *Koninklijke Philips Electronics NV* [2002] ECR I-5475.
[359] C-329/02 P *SAT.I SatellitenFernsehen GmbH* [2004] ECR I-8317.
[360] *Deutsche SiSi-Werke* (n 333) paragraph 60.
[361] Paragraph 61.
[362] Paragraph 62, citing C-191/01 P *WM Wrigley Jr Co* [2003] ECR I-12447.
[363] Imprecise translations are often a problem; see also C-292/00 *Davidoff & Cie SA and Zino Davidoff SA v Gofkid Ltd* [2003] ECR I-389 discussed in Ch.7 at 7.403 et seq, where the term 'well-known' marks is used instead of marks with a reputation.

5.423 In any case, the Court reiterated that:

> the criterion according to which trade marks which are capable of being commonly used, in trade, for the presentation of the goods or services in question may not be registered is relevant in the context of Article 7(1)(c) of Regulation No 40/94 but it is not the yardstick by which Article 7(1)(b) must be interpreted.[364]

5.424 The Court referred in detail to the relevant part of the Judgment of the Court of First Instance, stating that trade marks devoid of any distinctive character were in particular those that were commonly used for the presentation of the specified goods or services 'or with regard to which there exists, at the very least, concrete evidence justifying the conclusion that they are capable of being used in that manner'.[365] The Court of First Instance had found that there was indeed concrete evidence that the pouches were capable of being used in that way and concluded that the expected development of this type of packaging confirmed that its use was unexceptional.

5.425 The Court found that the Judgment of the Court of First Instance had reached its decision on the basis of the trade marks being devoid of distinctive character:[366]

> The Court of First Instance thus reached that conclusion on the basis not of the possibility that stand-up pouches may be commonly used in future in the sector of liquids for human consumption—which it used as the framework for its analysis—but of the finding that they are already commonly used. In so doing, the Court of First Instance based its conclusion on a proper criterion.[367]

5.426 The statement that the pouches were capable of being used in future by competitors of the appellant was, according to the Court, made for reasons of completeness. The Court of First Instance had accepted that the interest of competitors in itself would not suffice to refuse registration under Article 7(1)(b);[368] in its analysis of distinctive character it had, properly 'limited itself to determining whether those trade marks enable the average consumer of fruit drinks and fruit juices to distinguish, without any possibility of confusion, the goods of the appellant from those of a different commercial origin'.[369]

(18) *Eurocermex*: Article 7(1)(b), Three-dimensional Shapes, and the 'Concept' Behind a Product

5.427 *Eurocermex*[370] was another appeal against a Judgment of the Court of First Instance;[371] it involved a sign that could be seen from two perspectives, as a three-dimensional trade mark but, and perhaps even more than that, as a product concept.

5.428 Eurocermex was the distributor of the Mexican beer CORONA in Europe, popularly drunk with an added slice of lime. It applied to register as a Community trade mark a

---

[364] Paragraph 63.
[365] Paragraph 64, referring to paragraph 31 of the Judgment of the Court of First Instance, T-146/02 to T-053/02 *Deutsche SiSi-Werke* [2004] ECR II-447.
[366] Referring to paragraph 42 of the Judgment of the Court of First Instance, *Deutsche SiSi-Werke* (n 334).
[367] Paragraph 67.
[368] Judgment of the Court of First Instance, *Deutsche SiSi-Werke* (n 334) paragraph 32.
[369] Paragraph 70.
[370] C-286/04 P *Eurocermex SA v Office for Harmonisation in the Internal Market (Trade Marks and Designs)* [2005] ECR I-5797.
[371] T-399/02 *Eurocermex SA v Office for Harmonisation in the Internal Market (Trade Marks and Designs)* [2004] ECR II-1391.

three-dimensional mark consisting of a three-dimensional shape of a transparent bottle, filled with a yellow liquid, having a long neck in which a slice of lemon with green skin has been plugged. The pictures of a beer bottle with a piece of lime from three different aspects accompanied the description. The specification was for 'paper, cardboard and goods made from these materials; printed matter, bookbinding materials, photographs; stationery; adhesives for stationery or household purposes; office requisites, except furniture; plastic materials for packaging (not included in other classes); printers' type; printing blocks' in Class 16; 'clothing of all kinds, undershirts, shorts and all kinds of trousers; footwear of all kinds; headgear of all kinds' in Class 25; 'beers, mineral and aerated waters, fruit juices' in Class 32; and 'restaurants, bars, snack bars' in Class 42.

5.429 The examiner refused the application for the goods in Class 32 and the services in Class 42 for being devoid of any distinctive character, also finding that Eurocermex had failed to produce evidence that the mark had become distinctive through use. The First Board of Appeal[372] set aside the part of the examiner's decision relating to 'mineral waters' and upheld the remainder. Eurocermex brought an action before the Court of First Instance in respect of 'beers, aerated waters, fruit juices' and 'restaurants, bars, snack bars'.

(a) The Judgment of the Court of First Instance

5.430 The Court of First Instance found that the mark was devoid of any distinctive character. Before looking at the details of the application it made two general points. First, it repeated its statement that, in particular, the trade marks which were commonly used, in trade, for the presentation of the goods or services concerned or with regard to which there existed, at the very least, concrete evidence justifying the conclusion that they were capable of being used in that manner were devoid of any distinctive character. Second, that in order to assess the distinctive character of the mark, it had to be considered as a whole. However, this was not incompatible with an examination of its individual features.

5.431 Before concluding on distinctive character in relation to the contested goods the Court of First Instance appeared to make another general point, stating that:

> if a composite mark comprises only features devoid of any distinctive character in respect of the products and services concerned, it may be concluded that the overall mark is likewise likely to be commonly used, in trade, to present those goods and services ... That would only not be the case if concrete evidence, such as, for example, the way in which the various features are combined, were to indicate that the composite trade mark, taken as a whole, is greater than the sum of its parts.[373]

5.432 In the absence of such evidence the Court of First Instance found that the mark was devoid of distinctive character in relation to the specified goods. It is worth noting here the reference to the absence of alternatives:

> The trade mark applied for, which is essentially distinguished by the combination of the three-dimensional shape of a bottle with the colours yellow and green, together with a slice of green lemon, is capable of being commonly used, in trade, for the presentation of the products referred to in the application for registration. With more particular reference to the structure of the mark applied for, which is distinguished by the fact that the slice of lemon is plugged in the neck of the bottle, it is difficult to imagine other ways of combining those

---

[372] Case R-188/2002-1, 21 October 2002.
[373] Paragraph 31.

elements in a single three-dimensional form. Furthermore, it represents the only way in which a drink can be decorated with a slice or a piece of lemon when the drink is consumed directly from the bottle. It follows that the manner in which the elements of the composite mark in question are combined is not capable of giving it a distinctive character.[374]

5.433 In relation to the part of the specification covering 'restaurants, bars, snack bars', the Court of First Instance found that they were very closely linked with 'beers, aerated waters, fruit juices':

> it should be noted that the particular aim of those services is the commercialisation of the products concerned. As was stated above, the mark applied for is capable of being commonly used, in trade, for the presentation of those products. That is concrete evidence that that mark is also capable of being commonly used, in trade, for the presentation of those services. It thus lacks a distinctive character in relation to them.[375]

5.434 The Court of First Instance then found that the mark had not acquired distinctive character through use according to Article 7(3). One of the weaknesses of the evidence identified in the judgment was that it related to use of branded bottles of beer rather than the bottle appearing on the application form: 'all bear a label on which appear words such as "corona", "corona extra", "coronita" or even "estrella" '.[376]

(b) The Judgment of the Court

5.435 The Court heard Advocate General Ruiz-Jarabo Colomer and decided to proceed without an Opinion.

5.436 **(i) The overall impression** In the first part of the first plea Eurocermex argued that the Court of First Instance had not taken account of the overall impression conveyed by the mark.

5.437 The Court noted that, according to *Procter & Gamble*,[377] examination authorities could examine each of the individual features of the mark in the course of their overall assessment. The Court of First Instance had assessed each individual characteristic; in respect of their combined effect it had made the point that it was likely that a mark comprising only features devoid of any distinctive character would be commonly used, in trade, to present those goods and services.[378]

5.438 The Court then referred to *SAT.1*[379] as requiring that, in assessing whether a composite mark had distinctive character, the overall perception of the mark by the average consumer should be relied upon; it rejected presumptions that combinations of features individually devoid of distinctive character could not display such character. There, the Court had found that the Court of First Instance had examined the overall impression only secondarily.

5.439 Here, however, the Court of First Instance had continued its analysis 'by investigating in detail whether or not the mark, taken as a whole, displayed such character'.[380] The Court

---

[374] Paragraph 32.
[375] Paragraph 36.
[376] Paragraph 50.
[377] C-468/01 to C-472/01 P *Procter & Gamble* [2004] ECR I-5141.
[378] In paragraph 31 of T-399/02 *Eurocermex SA* [2004] ECR II-1391.
[379] C-329/02 P *SAT.1 SatellitenFernsehen GmbH* [2004] ECR I-8317.
[380] *Eurocermex SA* (n 371) paragraph 28.

found the statements included in paragraph 32 and paragraph 33 of the Judgment of the Court of First Instance to constitute sufficient bases for the Court of First Instance to reach the conclusion that the mark as applied for did not have the necessary distinctive character.

5.440 It is suggested that the Court appears once again to take a more cautious approach compared with *SAT.1*. Accordingly, this part was rejected as unfounded.

5.441 **(ii) Setting the parameters for an appeal** With the second part of the first plea the appellant claimed that it was apparent from the documentation referred to by the Board of Appeal that the trade mark was capable of enabling consumers to identify the origin of the products bearing it.

5.442 The Court found this claim to be inadmissible. Setting some useful parameters that prospective appellants have to conform to, the Court made two particular points: first, it reminded us that an appeal should indicate precisely the contested elements of the judgment that the appellant sought to have set aside and the legal arguments specifically advanced in support of the appeal;[381] and, second, it stressed that an appeal was possible only on a point of law, whereas the Court of First Instance had exclusive jurisdiction to find and appraise the relevant facts and to assess the evidence.[382]

5.443 In this case, the appellant had asserted that the Court of First Instance had wrongly reached its conclusion without specifying the error it had made in its interpretation and application of the Regulation. In the absence of a distortion of the facts and evidence by the Court of First Instance the claim of the appellant was inadmissible. The Court applied the same reasoning to the third part of the first plea, according to which the reasons for rejecting the trade mark for 'restaurants, bars and snack bars' had not been substantiated; the appellant had merely reproduced the line of argument followed at first instance. Similarly, the second plea of the appeal, claiming infringement of Article 7(3), was rejected because it would involve a reassessment of the evidence.

(19) *Storck I*: The Shape of a Sweet

5.444 The two *Storck* cases offered the Court the opportunity to elaborate further not only on the distinctive character of three-dimensional signs but also on the differences between the shape of a product—the three-dimensional shape of a sweet, the Werther's Original—on the one hand and the packaging of a sweet—a gold wrapper—on the other. Both cases reached the Court as appeals against judgments of the Court of First Instance.

5.445 The Court dealt first with the appeal against the judgment regarding the shape of the product. August Storck KG (Storck) had applied to register as a Community trade mark for 'confectionery' a three-dimensional sign in the form of a light-brown sweet. The pictures of a sweet from three different aspects appeared on the application. The application was rejected under Article 7(1)(b); the examiner also found that the mark had not acquired distinctive character as a result of use according to Article 7(3). The Board of Appeal confirmed the decision. Storck brought an action before the Court of First Instance claiming that the Board had infringed both Article 7(1)(b) and Article 7(3).

---

[381] Citing C-352/98 P *Laboratoires Pharmaceutiques Bergaderm and Goupil v Commission* [2000] ECR I-5291.
[382] Citing C-136/02 P *Mag Instrument Inc* [2004] ECR I-9165.

Article 3(1)(b)—Devoid of Distinctive Character

(a) The Judgment of the Court of First Instance

5.446 The Court of First Instance concurred with the Board on the lack of distinctive character and accepted the following general points made by the Board.

5.447 In the case of mass consumer goods, consumers did not pay much attention to their shape and colour. As a result it was unlikely that the choice of the average consumer would be determined by the shape of such a product.

5.448 Regarding the particular shape, it accepted that consumers were accustomed to confectionery products, including sweets, being round, circular, oval, elliptical, or cylindrical and that they commonly had rounded sides regardless of their configuration for functional reasons. The two potentially distinguishing criteria, the circular depression in the middle of the sweet and its flat lower surface, were weak as indicators of origin because they did not substantially alter the overall impression given by the shape. Equally common was the colour.

5.449 The Court of First Instance rejected the argument that the particular shape and colour differed from those of other confectionery products and also found that the mark as a whole did not enable the average consumer to distinguish the products concerned according to origin.

(b) The Opinion of Advocate General Ruiz-Jarabo Colomer

5.450 (i) **Admissibility considerations** Advocate General Ruiz-Jarabo Colomer, agreeing with the submissions of the Office, suggested that a number of grounds were inadmissible because they were seeking from the Court the substitution of its own findings for those of the Court of First Instance[383] and because they had not been presented before the Court of First Instance.

5.451 (ii) **The criterion for the application of Article 7(1)(b)** The Advocate General accepted that the wording of Article 7(1)(b) seemed to suggest clearly that any sign with a minimum degree of distinctiveness should be eligible for registration. However, the Court's case law on three-dimensional marks had been consistently repeating that although the criteria for assessing the distinctive character of signs consisting of the shape of the product were the same as those applicable for any other type of sign, in practice, it was more difficult to prove distinctive character than in relation to a name or figurative mark.[384]

5.452 The Court had also recognized that the perception of the average consumer was not necessarily the same in relation to a three-dimensional sign as with other types of signs that were distinguishable from the appearance of the goods that they covered, since consumers were not accustomed to making assumptions about the origin of goods according to their shape, independently of graphic or word elements.

5.453 The Court of First Instance had clearly followed the case law of the Court and the first part of the first ground of appeal should be rejected as unfounded.

---

[383] Citing C-53/92 P *Hilti v Commission* [1994] ECR 667.
[384] Citing C-299/99 *Koninklijke Philips Electronics NV* [2002] ECR I-5475; and C-53/01 *Linde AG*, C-54/01 *Winward Industries Inc* and C-55/01 *Rado Uhren AG* [2003] ECR I-3161.

5.454 Note that the Advocate General remarked that the dividing line between minimum distinctive character and absolute lack of distinctiveness remained an issue in relation to graphic and name marks.

(c) The Judgment of the Court

5.455 The Court agreed with the Advocate General's suggestions regarding admissibility and found that the second part of the first ground and the second and third grounds were inadmissible.

5.456 **(i) Article 7(1)(b): Three-dimensional signs** The first ground of appeal was considered in some detail. The Court focused on Storck's two main arguments that had to do with the reference to the need for the mark to be markedly different from other forms of product presentation in the relevant product market. This meant that the Court of First Instance had imposed stricter requirements for three-dimensional marks than for word or figurative marks and that it had introduced likelihood of confusion issues into the assessment of distinctive character.

5.457 It repeated its general mantra on the assessment of distinctive character,[385] with the 'in practice' proviso regarding three-dimensional signs,[386] and the assumptions regarding consumer perception regarding the shape of a product or the shape of its packaging.[387] The outcome was that only a mark which departed significantly from the norm or customs of the sector and thereby fulfilled its essential function of indicating origin should be considered as not devoid of any distinctive character for the purposes of Article 7(1)(b).[388]

5.458 Accordingly, the Court of First Instance had not erred in its interpretation. The 'markedly different' condition did not go further than the 'significant departure' case law of the Court:

> It is apparent ... that the Court of First Instance relied on the finding that the mark applied for consists of a combination of presentational features which come naturally to mind and which are typical of the goods in question, that it is a variation of certain basic shapes commonly used in the confectionery sector, that, since the alleged differences are not readily perceptible, it follows that the shape in question cannot be sufficiently distinguished from other shapes commonly used for sweets and that it does not enable the relevant public to distinguish immediately and with certainty the appellant's sweets from those of another commercial origin.[389]

5.459 The Court also rejected the claim that the Court of First Instance had required that the mark applied for be markedly different from similar marks which might exist in the confectionery sector, finding that it was based on an incorrect interpretation of its judgment.

---

[385] Citing, however, cases where it had appeared to take a stricter approach: *Henkel* (n 137).
[386] C-456/01 P and C-457/01 P *Henkel KGaA* [2004] ECR I-5089; and C-173/04 P *Deutsche SiSi-Werke & Co Betriebs KG* [2006] ECR I-551. Citing *Henkel*; C-136/02 P *Mag Instrument* [2004] ECR I-9165.
[387] Citing the same cases as above: *Mag Instrument Inc* [2004] ECR I-9165 and C-173/04 P *Deutsche SiSi-Werke & C. Betriebs* KG [2006] ECR I-551.
[388] Citing the same cases as above; note that in the judgment it referred to a mark in general rather than a three-dimensional mark.
[389] C-24/05 P *August Storck KG v Office for Harmonisation in the Internal Market (Trade Marks and Designs) (Storck I)*, ECLI:EU:C:2006:421, paragraph 29.

(20) *Storck II*: The Distinctive Character of Packaging

5.460 The second *Storck* case[390] dealt with packaging. It came before the Court as an appeal against the Judgment of the Court of First Instance dismissing an action for annulment of the decision of the Board of Appeal[391] refusing registration of a figurative mark as a Community trade mark for sweets for being devoid of any distinctive character. The mark consisted of a two-dimensional representation in perspective of a sweet in a gold-coloured wrapper with twisted ends.

(a) *The Judgment of the Court of First Instance*

5.461 The Court of First Instance followed a parallel route to that followed in the shape of the product *Storck* case. It accepted the Board of Appeal's finding that the configuration of the mark, 'twisted wrapper, light brown or gold coloured', was a normal and traditional shape for a sweet wrapper that did not fundamentally stand out against the other usual presentations in that trade and that the average consumer would perceive the sign as a sweet wrapper rather than an indication of origin.

5.462 It also accepted that the Board of Appeal:

> was entitled to refer... to the risk of monopolisation of the wrapper in question for sweets, since its findings confirmed the lack of distinctive character of that wrapper for those goods, reflecting the general interest underlying the absolute ground for refusal founded on Article 7(1)(b).[392]

5.463 Storck had also raised, unsuccessfully, two procedural points before the Court of First Instance, based on Article 74(1) and Article 73.

5.464 On the first point it stressed that:

> under the maxim ultra posse nemo obligatur (no one is obliged to do the impossible), and notwithstanding the rule in the first sentence of Article 74(1) of Regulation No 40/94 whereby OHIM 'shall examine the facts of its own motion', OHIM is not bound to examine facts showing that the mark claimed has become distinctive through use within the meaning of Article 7(3) of Regulation No 40/94 unless the applicant has pleaded them.[393]

5.465 Regarding the Article 73 point, the Court of First Instance viewed the proceedings before the Office as a unified process. The examiner had highlighted the weaknesses of the evidence regarding sale volumes, but Storck failed to produce any additional evidence before the Board regarding the overall size of the market for sweets. Offering to provide the information to the Court of First Instance was futile since it could not consider new evidence, and viewing the proceedings before the Office as a unified process it added that the applicant did have the opportunity to present its views.

5.466 Before the Court of Justice the applicant raised four grounds of appeal claiming that the Court of First Instance had infringed Article 7(1)(b), Article 74(1), Article 73, and Article 7(3) of the Regulation.

---

[390] C-25/05 P *August Storck KG v Office for Harmonisation in the Internal Market (Trade Marks and Designs) (Storck II)*, ECLI:EU:C:2006:422.
[391] T-402/02 *Storck* [2004] ECR II-3849, dismissing the action fur annulment of the decision of the Second Board of Appeal of the Office for Harmonisation in the Internal Market (Trade Marks and Designs) of 18 October 2002, Case R-256/2001-2.
[392] *Storck II* (n 390) paragraph 60.
[393] *Storck II* (n 390) paragraph 96.

(b) The Opinion of Advocate General Ruiz-Jarabo Colomer

5.467 (i) **Article 7(1)(b): Reassessment of facts**   Advocate General Ruiz-Jarabo Colomer suggested that the third part of the first ground, a claim that the Court of First Instance had not fully considered the effect of the colour on the wrapping and wrongly assessed the behaviour of the average consumer, was inadmissible because its examination would involve the reassessment of the facts of the case.

5.468 (ii) **The application of Article 7(1)(b)**   With the first part of the first ground Storck argued that the Court of First Instance had imposed a stricter criterion regarding the distinctive character of three-dimensional marks. The Advocate General, in essence, repeated the line of argument he developed in *Storck I*, without distinguishing between the shape of the product and its packaging, and submitted that the Court should reject that part as unfounded.

5.469 The Advocate General accepted the Office's submission that the Court of First Instance had referred to the monopolization risk as an additional and confirmatory statement. Before making it, however, the Board had already established that the sign lacked the necessary distinctive character.

5.470 (iii) **Article 74(1) and Article 73**   The second and the third grounds were examined together. In the second ground, the appellant submitted that the Board had undertaken its own assessment of the market situation without giving Storck the opportunity to examine concrete examples of wrappers that were identical to its own according to the Board. By sanctioning this tactic the Court of First Instance had failed to take into account Article 74(1). The Office responded that Article 74(1) required the Office to examine the facts—indeed the Office had the exclusive responsibility for examining the facts—without requiring it to support its findings with concrete examples.

5.471 The third ground followed from the second: Storck had been deprived of the opportunity to prove that its wrappers differed substantially from those on which the Board had built its conclusions. The Office retorted that the third ground was manifestly unfounded. The Board had properly analysed Storck's arguments before rejecting them, and Storck had had the opportunity to present its views on this since it had admitted before the Court of First Instance that it had dealt with shapes commonly used for wrappers for sweets.

5.472 The Advocate General suggested that Storck had misinterpreted the principles behind the two provisions. The procedure before the Office required the examiners and the Board of Appeal to examine the facts of their own motion and establish their accuracy irrespective of the claims of the parties. However, some limitations were to be imposed on this general principle. For example, the parties were under an obligation to co-operate with the Office; or, from another perspective, the Office was entitled to determine the extent to which a simple objective assessment of the facts would suffice in deciding the case. In addition, the Office had to take into account facts arising from practical experience generally acquired from the marketing of general consumer goods, as the Court of First Instance had remarked. Otherwise, the Office would risk overlooking facts that could influence the outcome of a case.

5.473 He stressed that the Court should recognize that the Boards had the option to use facts that were well known to all as part of the examination of absolute grounds without having to assess their accuracy; the burden of proof should pass to the party wishing to challenge them (*res ipsa loquitur*). Accordingly, even if the Court were to accept that Storck had missed the opportunity to express its views before the Board for facts that were well known to all, it should hold that it had been given that opportunity by the Court of First Instance, which had subsequently decided that its observations were not sufficient to overturn the decision of the Board.

Accordingly, the second and the third grounds should be rejected as unfounded. **5.474**

(c) The Judgment of the Court

(i) Article 7(1)(b): Requirements Looking at the first part of the first ground of appeal, the Court followed closely its findings in the shape of the product *Storck* case,[394] failing to make a distinction between product shapes and packaging, and rejected it as unfounded. **5.475**

Indeed, the only new point made by the Court reflected the assimilation of a two-dimensional representation of a three-dimensional sign with the three-dimensional sign itself, but also the potential assimilation between product shapes and packaging. The case law, **5.476**

> which was developed in relation to three-dimensional trademarks consisting of the appearance of the product itself, also applies where, as in the present case, the trade mark applied for is a figurative mark consisting of the two-dimensional representation of that product. In such a case, the mark likewise does not consist of a sign unrelated to the appearance of the products it covers.[395]

(ii) Article 7(1)(b): General interest The Court followed the Advocate General's suggestion that the Court of First Instance had not based its conclusion on the risk of monopolization of the wrapper applying for registration. It referred to it in a purely confirmatory way. The second part of the first ground was rejected as unfounded. **5.477**

(iii) Article 7(1)(b): Reassessment of facts The Court noted that since it had found that the Court of First Instance had not erred in law in its application of Article 7(1)(b), assessing the distinctive character of the mark or the perception of the relevant consumers would involve assessment of the facts. Accordingly, the third part of the first ground was rejected as inadmissible. **5.478**

(iv) Article 74(1) Under Article 74(1), examiners and the Board of Appeal were required to examine the facts of their own motion whilst considering an application for registration under Article 7 and they might reach decisions based on facts that had not been alleged by the applicant. In principle, they would have to establish the accuracy of such facts in their decisions. However, when they relied on facts that were well known it was the applicant who would have to challenge their accuracy. Whether the facts were well known or not was a factual assessment that remained within the jurisdiction of the Court of First Instance. The second ground of appeal was therefore dismissed as unfounded. **5.479**

(v) Article 73 The third ground of appeal was divided by the Court into two parts. **5.480**

The Article 73 ground had not been raised before the Court of First Instance in relation to the proceedings before the Board; to that extent the claim was rejected as inadmissible because a plea could not be introduced for the first time before the Court of Justice. **5.481**

---

[394] *Storck I* (n 389).
[395] *Storck II* (n 390) paragraph 29.

5.482 Then, the Court dealt with that ground in relation to the proceedings before the Court of First Instance. It ruled that Article 73:

> is to be complied with by bodies of OHIM in the context of assessment of applications for registration, but not in the context of proceedings before the Court of First Instance, which are governed by the Statute of the Court of Justice and by the Rules of Procedure of the Court of First Instance.[396]

5.483 In any case, it added, the appellant was in a position to challenge before the Court of First Instance the Board's assertions, and its broader rights of defence, including its right to be heard, were observed. Accordingly, the third ground was rejected as being partly inadmissible and partly unfounded.

(21) *Freixenet*: The Frosted Bottles Cases

(a) Background to the dispute

5.484 The Judgment in *Freixenet*[397] is a complement to the series of cases relating to the distinctiveness of the shape of the goods or their packaging and raises the question whether patterns applicable to the texture of the surface of the packaging are subject to the same rules and method of assessment.

5.485 The case concerned two applications for Community trade marks filed by Freixenet SA in the category 'other' and regarding the 'shape or presentation of a product'. Freixenet claimed the colours 'golden matt' and 'black matt' and described the marks as a 'white polished bottle which when filled with sparkling wine takes on a golden matt appearance similar to a frosted bottle' and a 'frosted black matt bottle' respectively. It also annexed a declaration stating that it '[did] not want to obtain restrictive and exclusive protection for the shape of the packaging but for the specific appearance of its surface'. Both applications were filed in respect of 'sparkling wines' in Class 33 of the Nice Classification.

5.486 OHIM dismissed the applications on the ground that the signs were devoid of distinctive character and that the evidence put forward by Freixenet did not lead to the conclusion that those marks had acquired a distinctive character through use. The Fourth Board of Appeal upheld the refusals and dismissed the appeals brought by Freixenet. Following a first round before the General Court, which quashed the decisions of the Board on the grounds that the applicant's rights of defence had been infringed, the case was remitted to the First Board which again rejected the appeals, holding that the signs applied for could not function as trade marks, since the essential element allowing consumers of wine to identify the origin of the product is the label affixed to the bottle, rather than the shape of the bottle itself or its appearance, and that the importance of this factor could be assumed to be known to everyone, including Freixenet.

5.487 Freixenet brought actions for annulment, pleading, inter alia, infringement of Article 7(1)(b). The General Court[398] dismissed the applications, sharing the Board's view that invariably wines are not sold without a label and that Freixenet's use of the word 'FREIXENET'

---

[396] *Storck II* (n 390) paragraph 64.
[397] Judgment of 20 October 2011, Case C-344/10 P *Freixenet/Office for Harmonisation in the Internal Market* [2011] ECR I-10205.
[398] Case T-109/08 *Freixenet/Office for Harmonisation in the Internal Market (Frosted white bottle)* and T-110/08 *Freixenet/Office for Harmonisation in the Internal Market (Frosted black matt bottle)* [2010] ECR II-00066.

on the very bottles for which it sought registration confirmed the inference drawn from practical experience that the matting of the glass could not function as a trade mark. The General Court also noted that although the originality of the marks was not disputed, the fact remained that the majority of consumers do not perceive the appearance of the bottles as a useful factor in determining the origin of the sparkling wine contained in them, but prefer to have recourse to the label instead.

(b) The Judgment of the Court

5.488 The Court of Justice dismissed that reasoning as fundamentally misconceived and set aside both judgments under appeal on the grounds that they were tainted by the same error in law, insofar as they had taken the view that the presence of a label prevented the appearance of the bottles from performing a distinguishing function. Referring to its settled case law with regard to three-dimensional marks,[399] the Court observed that the principles developed in relation to marks consisting of the appearance of the product itself or of its packaging, 'also apply where the mark for which registration is sought is an "other" mark consisting of the specific appearance of the surface of the packaging of a liquid product', taking into account particularly that liquids have to be packaged for obvious reasons linked to their nature and that the sign at issue is not independent of the appearance of the necessary packaging of the products it designates.[400]

5.489 Consequently, it criticized the line taken by the General Court which, instead of establishing whether the signs at issue varied significantly from the norm or customs of the sector as required by the case law, merely relied on the fact that wines are always sold with a label, in order to come to the erroneous conclusion that the colour and matting of the bottle could not function as a trade mark for sparkling wine when not used in conjunction with a word element. The Court stressed that such an assessment could not be sustained in law, as it effectively meant that marks consisting of the appearance of the packaging of the product that do not contain a verbal inscription would be excluded automatically from the protection conferred by the Regulation.[401]

(c) Conclusions

5.490 The judgment in *Freixenet* is a natural extension of the Court's case law on three-dimensional marks. The application of the principles pertaining to shape marks to the 'frosted effect' used by Freixenet on its cava bottles came all the more naturally since the pattern at issue was not merely affixed on the surface of the packaging as an additional decorative element, but effectively determined the appearance of the packaging itself.

5.491 However, it is not so clear if the same rules should also apply in cases were an embellishing design or other ornamental motif is added to the whole or part of the surface of the goods in a way that does not become so closely assimilated with the configuration of the packaging itself, but merely performs an independent decorative or similar function. Admittedly, the dividing line will not always be clear,[402] but it would seem that in situations where

---

[399] Citing Cases C-136/02 P *Mag Instrument v OHIM* [2004] ECR I-9165, paragraphs 29–31; C-25/05 P *Storck v OHIM* [2006] ECR I-5719, paragraphs 25–29; and C-173/04 P *Deutsche SiSi-Werke v OHIM* [2006] ECR I-551, paragraphs 27–31.
[400] Paragraphs 45–48.
[401] Paragraphs 49–51.
[402] See, for instance, C-445/02 P *Glaverbel* [2004] ECR I-6267.

the pattern dominates the appearance of the goods or their get-up the solution given in *Freixenet* marks the path to follow.

(22) Mouse and Rabbit: Absence of Distinctive Characters for Chocolate in Animal Shapes

(a) Rabbit

5.492 The Swiss chocolatier Lindt & Sprüngli Chocoladefabriken sought registration of its widely used chocolate Easter Bunny (*Goldhase* in German)—not the bunny with the name 'Lindt' and other distinctive elements on it, which was the subject of the litigation in Austria (and elsewhere) leading to the Court of Justice judgment on bad faith[403]—a rabbit or hare in gold foil with a red ribbon and a little bell. Refusal by the examiner and confirmation by the Board led to an appeal to the General Court, which dismissed the application for annulment.[404]

5.493 The appeal on points of law before the Court of Justice was dismissed as unfounded.[405] The applicant had argued, inter alia, that the inherent distinctiveness of the shape was demonstrated by the fact that the mark was registered in fifteen Member States. The Court simply referred to its previous case law and the factual nature of the General Court's judgment.

5.494 As regards the claim based on an infringement of Article 7(3) of the Regulation, we refer to the analysis of the case in the following chapter on acquired distinctiveness.

(b) Mouse

5.495 August Storck KG, having failed to obtain trade mark protection for its well-known Werther caramel sweets, also sought to obtain protection for a chocolate bar in the shape of a mouse in Class 30. Refusal by the examiner and conformation of the refusal by the Board led to an appeal to the General Court, which—predictably—also confirmed.[406] Storck's appeal to the Court of Justice also failed.[407] The Court justified its dismissal of the appeal essentially by pointing out that the General Court had analysed the contested mark in accordance with the rules established by the case law and had, in particular, not disregarded the rule that marks must be examined as a whole. Other procedural challenges were also dismissed.

(23) Louis Vuitton's Lock Device Mark: Absence of Distinctiveness

(a) The mark and its goods, the OHIM decisions

5.496 The mark consisted of a two-dimensional representation of a locking device, well known to connoisseurs of Louis Vuitton products. Registration was sought, and granted, for a number of goods in Classes 9, 14, 8, and 25. Friis Group, established in Denmark, brought an application for declaration of invalidity, which was rejected by OHIM's Cancellation Division as unfounded, but found a receptive Board, which declared the mark invalid for the goods in Classes 9, 14, and 18; Friis had not appealed the rejection of its application as regards Class 25.

---

[403] C-529/07 *Chocoladefabriken Lindt & Sprüngli AG v Franz Hauswirth GmbH* [2009] ECR I-04893; analysed hereafter under paras 5.915 et seq.
[404] T-336/08 *Chocoladefabriken Lindt & Sprüngli AG v OHIM* [2010] ECR II-00291.
[405] C-98/11 P *Chocoladefabriken Lindt & Sprüngli AG v OHIM*, ECLI:EU:C:2012:307.
[406] T-13/09 *August Storck KG v OHIM* [2010] ECR II-00297.
[407] C-96/11 P *August Storck KG v OHIM*, ECLI:EU:C:2012:537.

Article 3(1)(b)—Devoid of Distinctive Character

(b) The General Court

5.497 The General Court[408] faulted OHIM for not having made the necessary distinctions between the various goods in the various classes, and upheld the appeal for some of the goods. For the majority, however, the Board decision was confirmed. The Board applied to the figurative representation the rules established by the Court of Justice for three-dimensional marks, and found that the clasp, for most of the goods, did not significantly depart from the norm or custom in the trade, the standard established by the Court of Justice in *Henkel* (referred to above).

(c) The decision of the Court

5.498 The Court[409] dismissed Louis Vuitton's appeal, which had sought to retain its registration also for the remaining goods.

5.499 The Court confirmed that a two-dimensional representation of a shape must be judged according to the same criteria as the three-dimensional shape itself.[410] The Court further confirmed that the rules on three-dimensional shapes must be applied not only when the shape is sought to be registered for the product represented by the shape, but also when the shape is but a part of the total product (here: a lock for a container, a clasp for a belt etc).[411]

5.500 Interestingly, OHIM had brought a cross-appeal to challenge the outcome of the case before the General Court. The cross-appeal was dismissed as unfounded.

(24) BEST BUY: Absence of Distinctiveness for Device Marks

5.501 The rules on distinctiveness or its absence apply to all kinds of marks. Nevertheless, device marks have not figured prominently in the Court's case law, probably because the cases are rather clear-cut: simple geometrical shapes and banal additions to word marks are regularly held to be insufficient to confer distinctiveness on what would otherwise not be distinctive, and refusals, of which there are a substantial number also at the level of the General Court, have rarely reached the Court of Justice.

5.502 An exception is the BEST BUY judgment.[412] The mark consisted of a rectangle with rounded edges with the words 'Best Buy' arranged in the manner that the 'B' in large size appears only once, ie both for 'BEST" and for 'BUY'. Protection was sought for a wide range of goods and services in many classes. Protection was refused by OHIM, invoking Article 7(1)(b) of the Regulation. Appeals to the Board and to the General Court[413] remained unsuccessful.

5.503 The Court concluded that the determinations made by the General Court were in line with the established case law and were not subject to review by the Court because of their factual nature. In particular, the General Court had correctly applied the legal standards and not

---

[408] T-237/10 *Louis Vuitton Malletier v OHIM—Friis Group International ApS* [2011] ECR II-00449.
[409] C-97/12 P *Louis Vuitton Malletier v OHIM—Friis Group International ApS*, ECLI:EU:C:2014:324.
[410] Paragraph 53.
[411] Paragraph 54.
[412] C-92/10 P *Media-Saturn-Holding GmbH v OHIM* [2011] ECR I-00002.
[413] T-476/08 *Media-Saturn v OHIM* [2009] ECR II-00240. In an earlier case, the General Court (then still Court of First Instance) had rejected a similar mark, showing the words BEST and BUY in two lines in a device of a label: judgment of 3 July 2003, T-122/01 *Best Buy Concepts v OHIM* [2003] ECR II-02235.

D. Article 3(1)(c): Descriptive Signs or Indications

(1) *Windsurfing Chiemsee*: Geographical Names; Setting the General Principles

5.504 In *Windsurfing Chiemsee*[414] the Court clarified that geographical names could be registered. It also established two tests: one for determining whether a mark is descriptive and another for establishing distinctive character acquired through use. Dealing with descriptiveness, it considered the German theory that there are some signs that must be left free for other traders to use, rejecting its applicability as a general public policy doctrine. However, elements of this theory resurfaced as specific considerations underlying the scope of Article 3(1)(c).

5.505 The case came before the Court as a reference from the Landgericht München I, that had to decide whether the word 'Chiemse', the name of the largest lake in Bavaria, could be protected as a trade mark. The word 'Chiemsee' as such would have been refused trade mark registration according to German doctrine since it was considered to be a geographical indication that other traders would also want to use. Windsurfing Chiemsee, a company running a shop near the lake selling sports fashion clothing and sports goods, designed locally but manufactured abroad, had registered the word 'Chiemsee' as part of a number of composite 'picture' trade marks combined with graphic design elements; in some cases the word was also accompanied by other words, for example, 'Chiemsee Jeans' or 'Windsurfing-Chiemsee-Active Wear'. Windsurfing Chiemsee started trade mark infringement proceedings to enjoin two other traders, Attenberger and Huber, from selling T-shirts and other similar types of clothing bearing the term 'Chiemsee' combined with other graphic elements.

5.506 Attenberger and Huber attacked the basis of the claim and contended that the term 'Chiemse' was an indication of geographical origin that should be left available for other traders to use. Accordingly, their own use of the term in a different graphic form could not create any likelihood of confusion. Indeed, the referring court explained that, according to German practice, likelihood of confusion could result only from the similarity between the graphic components of the mark if 'Chiemsee' was considered to be descriptive according to Article 3(1)(c).

5.507 The Landgericht wanted to know whether the interpretation of this provision was affected by the 'need to leave free' (Freihaltebedürfnis) doctrine that had been developed by German courts and provided that some signs, including geographical indications, should be left free for other traders to use.

5.508 German courts had elaborated further on this doctrine, applying a more stringent variant when there was a real, current, or serious need, the 'serious need to leave free' doctrine. Were the original doctrine found to be valid then 'Chiemsee' would be automatically covered by Article 3(1)(c). If the variant were to be applied then the national court would have to take into account the fact that there was no textile industry on the shores of the Chiemsee.

---

[414] C-108/97 and C-109/97 *Windsurfing Chiemsee Produktions- und Vertriebs GmbH v Boots- und Segelzubehör Walter Huber and Franz Attenberger* [1999] ECR I-2779.

Accordingly, the Landgericht München I referred the following questions on Article 3(1) **5.509**
(c) to the Court.

> Is Article 3(1)(c) to be understood as meaning that it suffices if there is a possibility of the designation being used to indicate the geographical origin, or must that possibility be likely in a particular case (in the sense that other such undertakings already use that word to designate the geographical origin of their goods of similar type, or at least that there are specific reasons to believe that that may be expected in the foreseeable future), or must there even be a need to use that designation to indicate the geographical origin of the goods in question, or must there in addition also be a qualified need for the use of that indication of origin, for instance because goods of that kind, produced in that region, enjoy a special reputation?
>
> Is it of significance for a broader or narrower interpretation of Article 3(1)(c) with respect to geographical indications of origin that the effects of the mark are restricted under Article 6(1)(b)?
>
> Do geographical indications of origin under Article 3(1)(c) cover only those which relate to the manufacture of the goods at that place, or does trade in those goods at that place or from that place suffice, or in the case of the production of textiles does it suffice if they are designed in the region designated but then manufactured under contract elsewhere?[415]

(a) The Opinion of Advocate General Cosmas

Advocate General Cosmas interpreted the first and the third questions as in essence enquiring whether in principle a geographical indication can be protected as a trade mark and the conditions and scope of any such protection. **5.510**

(i) The context of Article 3(1)   He viewed Article 3(1)(b) as an obstacle based on the lack of any distinctive character. Whilst Article 3(1)(c) and Article 3(1)(d) covered separate grounds, in essence they were partial or more specific or, simply, the most characteristic instances of lack of distinctive character which explained and elucidated the general concept rather than introduced a new genus of, or fundamentally distinct, concepts. Article 3(1)(b) covered cases that were not specifically covered under Article 3(1)(c) and Article 3(1)(d).[416] **5.511**

(ii) The conditions for the application of Article 3(1)(c)   The application of Article 3(1)(c) in particular required three conditions: the trade mark had to consist exclusively of a geographical term; the term had to be capable of serving in trade as an indication of geographical origin; and the geographical origin had to be linked to the characteristics of the product. **5.512**

(iii) The first condition   The exclusivity requirement would bring outside the scope of the provision composite marks with one of their elements functioning in a descriptive way but also incorporating other elements that attributed distinctive character to the mark. **5.513**

The Court had already indicated in a different context that it was the overall impression conveyed by the mark that authorities had to consider.[417] **5.514**

(iv) The second condition   According to the second condition, the Advocate General excluded from the scope of Article 3(1)(c) imaginary, mythical, or non-existent geographical terms. The same applied to historical terms that no longer existed or were known by **5.515**

---

[415] Reproduced in paragraph 17.
[416] Point 29.
[417] Citing C-251/95 *Sabel BV* [1997] ECR I-6191.

a different name. He also suggested that existing geographical terms that no one would associate with the origin of the relevant product were also meant to remain outside the scope of Article 3(1)(c), referring to examples such as Mont Blanc for pens and North Pole for bananas. Under the same logic, geographical terms that remained obscure for the wider public should also be excluded from its application. In all the above cases the geographical term because of its nature or due to the circumstances did not indicate geographical origin and, accordingly, its arbitrary use as a trade mark should be allowed.

5.516 He added that the term should be interpreted by reference to the jurisprudence of the Court in the free movement of goods cases that had culminated in the definitions provided by Article 2 of Regulation 2081/92.[418]

5.517 Excluding a sign from trade mark protection demanded a causal link between the geographical term and the product based on the kind, characteristics, or quality of the product that resulted from its geographical origin.

5.518 (v) **The German doctrine** Acknowledging the existence of the 'need to leave free' doctrine developed by German courts, he stressed that national provisions and practices could not go against the Directive and noted that in Europe there were two schools regarding the registrability of geographical names.

5.519 The German doctrine was ambiguous as to whether the sign should be kept free to be used by others as a trade mark or as an indication of origin. The first option would be unreasonable because the first user of the term as a trade mark would have to surrender it to be used as a trade mark by its competitors. The second option, he noted, was specifically regulated by the Directive.

5.520 (vi) **The third condition** Here, he required something more than a common property or quality; the geographical indication had to characterize and distinguish the product. The identity of the producer or of the place, method, and time of production would be relevant only when they, on their own, were considered to be relevant in trade. He found the term 'Chiemsee' to be evocative or suggestive but nothing more than that; it lacked the strong relevance he would have required.

5.521 (vii) **The interaction between Articles 3(1)(c) and 6(1)(b)** Advocate General Cosmas suggested that Article 6(1)(b) should not influence the interpretation of Article 3(1)(c). The former could only be applied following the application of the latter, ie once the trade mark had been registered. In any case, he remarked, the provision did not give the right to third parties to use the term as a trade mark. It would only allow use of the term in its original geographical meaning.[419]

(b) The Judgment of the Court

5.522 Behind the first set of questions the Court identified two issues: first, whether the application of Article 3(1)(c) depended on whether there was a real, current, or serious need to leave the sign or indication free; and, second, what connection there should be between the geographic allocation and the marked goods.

---

[418] Council Reg (EEC) No 2081/92 of 14 July 1992 on the protection of geographical indications and designations of origin for agricultural products and foodstuffs [1992] OJ 1208/1.

[419] Citing as example the French case of *Baccara C. A de Nancy*, PIBD 1980, III, 227 and Cass Commerc, PIBD 1982, No 312, III, 238 that allowed use of the term as part of the address for a company manufacturing crystal products.

(i) The German doctrine The Court accepted that the provision covered marks composed exclusively of descriptive signs, narrowing the scope of the provision. The Court rejected the applicability of the German doctrine; instead it relied for the interpretation of the provision on the specific public interest behind it. 5.523

(ii) Article 3(1)(c): The public interest The Court described the public interest in the following terms: 'descriptive signs or indications relating to the categories of goods or services in respect of which registration is applied for may be freely used by all, including as collective marks or as part of complex or graphic marks'.[420] Descriptive geographical terms in particular had to remain available 'not least because they may be an indication of the quality and other characteristics of the categories of goods concerned, and may also, in various ways, influence consumer tastes by, for instance, associating the goods with a place that may give rise to a favourable response'.[421] 5.524

(iii) The interaction between Article 3(1)(c) and Article 6(1)(b) Article 15(2) of the Directive indicated further the nature of the public interest the Court had described.[422] The Court also found Article 6(1)(b) to work towards the same general objective. Still, interpretation of Article 3(1)(c) did not rely on Article 6(1)(b). In terms of scope, the latter: 5.525

> does not confer on third parties the right to use the name as a trade mark but merely guarantees their right to use it descriptively, that is to say, as an indication of geographical origin, provided that it is used in accordance with honest practices in industrial and commercial matters.[423]

(iv) The factors for the application of Article 3(1)(c) It is suggested that the broad description of the public interest expands the scope of the provision. The subsequent uncertain balancing exercises, sometimes contracting sometimes expanding the scope of the provision, or the frequent reference to the limitations of the right is evidence of how the Court attempts to find its way between exclusivity and competition in its interpretation of trade mark law. 5.526

In principle, the Court ruled, Article 3(1)(c) 5.527

> does not... preclude the registration of geographical names which are unknown to the relevant class of persons—or at least unknown as the designation of a geographical location—or of names in respect of which, because of the type of place they designate (say, a mountain or lake), such persons are unlikely to believe that the category of goods concerned originates there.[424]

The Court then expanded the scope of the provision—supported by the inclusion in the provision of the verb 'may'—to cover geographical names designating places currently associated with the category of goods concerned but also names in respect of which 'it is reasonable to assume that such an association may be established in the future'.[425] 5.528

In the latter case 'regard must be had more particularly to the degree of familiarity amongst such persons with that name, with the characteristics of the place designated by the name, and with the category of goods concerned'.[426] 5.529

---

[420] Paragraph 25.
[421] Paragraph 26.
[422] It provided that signs or indications which may serve to designate the geographical origin of the goods may constitute connective marks.
[423] Paragraph 28.
[424] Paragraph 33.
[425] Paragraph 31.
[426] Paragraph 32.

5.530 As to types of location that could fall under Article 3(1)(c), the court ruled that even the name of a lake might function as an indicator of geographical origin for products like sports goods if the name is understood to include the shores of the lake or the surrounding area.

5.531 **(v) The link between the product and the geographical indication** Regarding the link between the product and the geographical indication in terms of origin, the Court found that usually it would be based on manufacture. However, it could also depend on other ties. For example, the geographical location where the goods were conceived and designed could also function as their geographical origin.

(2) *Baby-Dry*: Composite Words; A Permissive Approach

5.532 *Baby-Dry*[427] was the first case where the distinctiveness of a word combination was considered by the Court. The case reached the Court as an appeal against a Judgment of the Court of First Instance[428] and carried additional significance as the first such appeal in the field of trade marks. Procter & Gamble had applied for registration of the sign BABY-DRY as a Community trade mark for diapers (disposable diapers and textile diapers). The application was refused under Article 7(1)(c) of the Regulation.

5.533 The Board of Appeal confirmed the decision of the examiner, finding that both Article 7(1)(b) and Article 7(1)(c) were applicable.[429] It found that existing registrations in some Member States were unpersuasive. Linguistic differences could allow registration in some jurisdictions, but for a Community trade mark registration all the languages of the Union had to be taken into account.

5.534 An additional procedural point was that Article 7(3) evidence on distinctiveness acquired through use was not taken into account by the Board because the issue of acquired distinctive character had not been raised before the examiner.

(a) *The Judgment of the Court of First Instance*

5.535 In terms of substantive law, the Court of First Instance focused exclusively on Article 7(1)(c). It found the sign to be composed exclusively of words that may serve in trade to designate the intended purpose of goods; such signs were inherently incapable of distinguishing the specified products according to origin.

5.536 In terms of procedure the Court of First Instance favoured Procter & Gamble, holding that the Board of Appeal had infringed Article 62 of the Regulation.[430]

---

[427] C-383/99 P *Procter & Gamble Co* [2001] ECR I-6251.
[428] T-163/98 *Procter & Gamble Co* [1999] 2 CMLR 1442.
[429] Case R-35/1998-1, 31 July 1998.
[430] Article 62 provides:

   1. Following the examination as to the allowability of the appeal, the Board of Appeal shall decide on the appeal. The Board of Appeal may either exercise any power within the competence of the department which was responsible for the decision appealed or remit the case to that department for further prosecution.
   2. If the Board of Appeal remits the case for further prosecution to the department whose decision was appealed, that department shall be bound by the ratio decidendi of the Board of Appeal, in so far as the facts are the same.
   3. The decisions of the Boards of Appeal shall take effect only as from the date of expiration of the period referred to in Article 63 (5) or, if an action has been brought before the Court of Justice within that period, as from the date of rejection of such action.

The registration process within the Office should be characterized by continuity. There should not be a distinction between the examiner and the Board of Appeal and, accordingly, it annulled the decision of the Board.[431]

5.537

Procter & Gamble contended that the Court of First Instance had misinterpreted Article 7(1)(c). It argued that each trade mark had to be assessed individually taking into account all the facts of the case; even if the words 'baby' and 'dry' were found to designate the purpose of the diapers, the sign applied for, that the Court of First Instance had failed to consider, was Baby-Dry. By referring to signs that were inherently incapable of distinguishing it had erred in its interpretation of Article 7(1)(c).

5.538

(b) The Opinion of Advocate General Jacobs

(i) **The procedural paradox** The procedural paradox, highlighted by AG Jacobs, was that the appellant, Procter & Gamble, had appealed against a judgment that, in the end, had annulled the decision that Procter & Gamble wanted the Court of Justice to annul. He accepted that the limits on the appeal process were set by the permissive provision of Article 49 of the Statute of the Court. Interpreting 'submissions' liberally, he viewed the provision as referring 'in general terms to a failure to obtain what was asked for rather than strictly to a failure to have a particular argument accepted or a particular form of order granted'.[432]

5.539

(ii) **The scope of the appeal: Article 7(1)(c)** The contested judgment raised two issues according to the Advocate General. First, whether there were signs that should, because of their nature, be considered incapable of distinguishing. The second point was the registrability of Baby-Dry as such.

5.540

The distinction between general doctrine and specific application could be particularly useful when the Court functions as a court of appeal. The Opinion and the Judgment of the Court would set the interpretive parameters of Article 7(1)(c) by answering the first question. The application of these parameters on the factual scenario of the case should be a secondary issue.

5.541

(iii) **The scope of Article 7(1)(c)** Given that the Regulation and the Directive brought together provisions with different origins and legal traditions, the main principle he adopted was that 'at least in the context of the present case, the various provisions should be interpreted each within its own sphere'.[433]

5.542

Article 4 defined the signs of which a trade mark might consist. Article 7 covered the absolute grounds for refusal of registration. Article 7(1)(a) was the negative mirror image of Article 4. The grounds in subparagraphs (b) to (d) of Article 7 formed 'a package'[434] imported from the Paris Convention; they overlapped with each other and with Article 7(1)(a) and its mirror image Article 4. Those degrees of overlap had to be accepted.[435]

5.543

---

[431] AG Jacobs did not express a firm view on the methodology of the Court of First Instance since this was not part of the appeal before the Court of Justice. However, he remarked that it should have done more than simply annul the decision of the Board and leave it to the Office to take the necessary measures to comply with its judgment. It should either rule on the substance of the dispute or remand the case to the examiner.
[432] Point 39.
[433] Point 67.
[434] Point 68; the word 'package' was a hint that these grounds, in essence, covered similar territory.
[435] Point 70.

5.544 The existence of one of the grounds would suffice to block registration of a sign; whether more than one ground could be applied was immaterial in practice. The non-applicability of Article 7(3) in the case of Article 7(1)(a) did not alter this conclusion because, in practice, 'if acquired distinctiveness can be established then there must be an underlying capacity to distinguish; if not, the question is immaterial'.[436]

5.545 So, although Article 7(1)(c) was part of a package it had to be interpreted independently of Article 4. This led the Advocate General first to reject Procter & Gamble's argument that Article 7(1)(c) was just an aspect of the 'capacity to distinguish' criterion; and, second, to support that the Court of First Instance had gone too far by holding that the legislature intended to exclude signs that were by their very nature incapable of distinguishing.

5.546 Delineating Article 7(1)(c) further through a process of elimination he referred to the Board's holding that the provision intended to prevent traders from taking out of the public domain terms that belonged there. He conceded that this anti-monopolistic concern was amongst the reasons for adopting the equivalent provision of the Paris Convention. However, in the context of the Regulation, this was achieved through Article 12(b) by limiting the effects of such trademarks:

> In that light, it may be better to think of Article 7(I)(c) ... as intended not to prevent any monopolising of ordinary descriptive terms but rather to avoid the registration of descriptive brand names for which no protection could be available. If this means that the same words have to be interpreted as having a different import from that which they have in, say, the Paris Convention, that is because they appear in a different context.[437]

5.547 (iv) **The public interest of *Windsurfing Chiemsee*** He faced the challenge of distinguishing his approach from that adopted in *Windsurfing Chiemsee*[438] without alienating the Court. He suggested that the reference to the public interest expressed in that judgment had to be viewed in the specific context of that case, which concerned the use of a geographical name rather than the use of descriptive language. Such terms possessed a special status in the Community trade mark protection scheme—being capable of registration as collective marks[439]—but also in the wider Community legal order—through legislation specific to geographical indications.

5.548 The factual context allowed the Advocate General to extract a fundamental legal point and refocus on it from a different wider perspective. Further, he added, the Court had not embraced the German concept of 'real, current or serious need to keep an indication free'. Article 7(1)(c) had to be taken at its face value.[440]

5.549 (v) **Registrability of 'Baby-Dry'** The Advocate General admitted that the words 'baby' and 'dry' were likely to be used in trade to designate the intended purpose of diapers. However, he introduced two qualifications to the perspective from which the sign should be seen for registrability purposes—first impression and hesitation:

> 'it may be doubted whether any reasonably aware person who had not yet encountered the brand name Baby-Dry would think unhesitatingly of diapers when first confronted with it

---

[436] Point 71.
[437] Point 78.
[438] C-109/97 *Windsurfing Chiemsee* [1999] ECR I-2779.
[439] Article 64(2) of the Regulation and Article 15(2) of the Directive.
[440] Point 81.

or, when hearing it used in connection with such goods, would regard it as a designation of their intended purpose.[441]

5.550 Although one of the functions of diapers was to keep babies dry, the term 'baby-dry' was not used in ordinary language to refer to them or to their intended purpose.

5.551 Confronted with the term Baby-Dry for the first time a consumer might think of a number of diverse products, like talcum powder, rain hoods for prams, or even compact tumble dryers, or drinks presented in small bottles. Using cautious language he suggested that this 'might seem to dilute its power to designate with any precision the intended purpose of diapers'.[442]

5.552 Advocate General Jacobs found the interpretation of the scope of the words 'exclusively' and 'may serve, in trade, to designate' by the Board of Appeal and the Court of First Instance rather narrow. They had concluded that the combination of two terms that could be used to indicate the intended purpose of the product meant that the new sign consisted exclusively of indications which may serve in trade to designate its purpose.

(vi) Ellipsis, unusual and opaque grammatical structure, incompleteness, inventiveness That approach, he suggested, did not consider 'the extremely elliptical nature of the indication, its unusual structure or its resistance to any intuitive grammatical analysis which would make the meaning immediately clear'.[443] He also suggested that they had failed to look at the case from the opposite perspective and explore what terms would indicate the intended purpose of diapers. Something more that the mere juxtaposition of the words would be required, noting that Baby-Dry did not as such form part of the English language.[444]

5.554 Concluding that the Court of First Instance had erred in its interpretation of Article 7(1)(c), he listed the following factors that had not been taken into account: 'extreme ellipsis, unusual and opaque grammatical structure, incompleteness as a description and inventiveness'.[445] He repeated, however, that in any case protection would be limited because of Article 12(b).

(vi) The suggested way forward Article 54 of the Statute of the Court provided that in the case of a successful appeal the Court had to quash the decision of the Court of First Instance and then either itself give a final judgment or refer the case back to the Court of First Instance.

5.556 Given the length of the appeal process, the Court could set aside the judgment under appeal, give a final judgment itself, and alter the decision of the Board of Appeal, albeit he considered it inappropriate, 'a wholly unjustifiable interference',[446] for the Court to order

---

[441] Point 84.
[442] Point 86.
[443] Point 90.
[444] The AG appeared to cite with approval the position adopted by the Court of First Instance in C-193/99 *WM Wrigley Jr Co* [2001] ECR II-417; albeit, when that case came before the Court he clarified that he agreed with the broader approach to Article 7(1)(c) exemplified in several decisions of the Boards of Appeal and the Court of First Instance set out in paragraphs 93 to 95 of the Judgment of the Court of First Instance rather than 'endorsing the specific reasoning or result in any of those cases'; point 37 of his Opinion in C-191/01 P *WM Wrigley Jr Co* [2003] ECR I-12447.
[445] Point 96.
[446] Point 108.

(c) The Judgment of the Court

5.557 (i) **Admissibility considerations** The Court found that the appeal was admissible.[447] The Court of First Instance had dismissed Procter & Gamble's principal claim. The Office could consider the application under Article 7(3) without changing its position on Article 7(1)(b) and (c).

5.558 (ii) **The scope of Article 7(1)(c)** To interpret Article 7(1)(c) the Court also took into account Article 12(b) and Article 4:

> It is clear from those two provisions taken together that the purpose of the prohibition of registration of purely descriptive signs or indications as trademarks is, as both Procter & Gamble and the [Office] acknowledge, to prevent registration as trademarks of signs or indications which, because they are no different from the usual way of designating the relevant goods or services or their characteristics, could not fulfil the function of identifying the undertaking that markets them and are thus devoid of the distinctive character needed for that function.[448]

5.559 That, it found, was the only interpretation that could also be compatible with Article 4.

5.560 (iii) **Defining descriptiveness** The Court defined the signs that fall under Article 7(1)(c) as 'those which may serve in normal usage from a consumer's point of view to designate, either directly or by reference to one of their essential characteristics, goods or services such as those in respect of which registration is sought'.[449]

5.561 (iv) **The condition for composite marks: The new whole; any perceptible difference** Following the hint of the Advocate General the Court considered how its general stance on descriptiveness could be applied to composite marks. A composite mark should not be refused registration unless 'it comprises no other signs or indications and, in addition, the purely descriptive signs or indications of which it is composed are not presented or configured in a manner that distinguishes the resultant whole from the usual way of designating the goods or services concerned or their essential characteristics'.[450]

5.562 For marks like Baby-Dry descriptiveness had to be determined in relation to each word on its own but also in relation to the new whole they form, because any perceptible difference between the mark as a new whole and the terms as used in common parlance could confer distinctive character to the mark.

5.563 (v) **The perspective for assessing descriptiveness** Since Article 7(2) provided that Article 7(1) would be applied even if the relevant grounds exist in a part of the Community, the Court found that descriptiveness in one of the 'languages used in trade within the Community'[451] would suffice to trigger Article 7(1)(c):

> In order to assess whether a word combination such as BABY-DRY is capable of distinctiveness, it is therefore necessary to put oneself in the shoes of an English-speaking consumer.

---

[447] C-383/99 P *Procter & Gamble Co* [2001] ECR I-6251.
[448] Paragraph 37.
[449] Paragraph 39.
[450] Paragraph 39.
[451] Paragraph 41; note that the Court referred to languages used in trade within the Community rather than the languages of the Member States.

From that point of view, and given that the goods concerned in this case are babies' nappies, the determination to be made depends on whether the word combination in question may be viewed as a normal way of referring to the goods or of representing their essential characteristics in common parlance.[452]

(vi) Registrability of 'Baby-Dry': Unusual juxtaposition; lexical inventions The Court found that refusing registration based on Article 7(1)(c) was not justified:

5.564

> Whilst each of the two words in the combination may form part of expressions used in everyday speech to designate the function of babies' nappies, their syntactically unusual juxtaposition is not a familiar expression in the English language, either for designating babies' nappies or for describing their essential characteristics.[453]
>
> Word combinations like BABY-DRY cannot therefore be regarded as exhibiting, as a whole, descriptive character; they are lexical inventions bestowing distinctive power on the mark so formed and may not be refused registration under Article 7(1)(c) of Regulation No 40/94.[454]

(d) The next step

The Court did follow the proposition of the Advocate General. It annulled the relevant part of the Judgment of the Court of First Instance and the decision of the Board of Appeal insofar as it dismissed the application for registration of BABY-DRY as a trade mark on the basis of Article 7(1)(c) of Regulation No 40/94[455] without elaborating further on the way forward for the registration of Baby-Dry.

5.565

The mark BABY-DRY, No 200006 with the filing date of 9 April 1996, for goods in Classes 16 and 25, is at this time still pending before OHIM, as it seems to have unresolved opposition.

5.566

(3) *Doublemint*: A More Nuanced Approach

The Court appeared to take a step back in *Doublemint*, another appeal against a Judgment of the Court of First Instance.[456] Wrigley had applied to register DOUBLEMINT as a Community trade mark for a number of products including chewing gum. The application was rejected under Article 7(1)(c) by the examiner and the Board of Appeal, which found the sign to be a combination of two English words with no additional fanciful or imaginative element, descriptive of the mint-based composition and the mint flavour of the goods in question.

5.567

(a) The Judgment of the Court of First Instance

The case came before the Court of First Instance, which found that the mark was not exclusively descriptive.[457] Use of the word 'double' as a term of praise was unusual, compared with words like 'strong' or 'extra'. 'Mint' could refer to spearmint, peppermint, or other types of herbs. The combination of the two words was found to be ambiguous and suggestive rather than exclusively descriptive. It could convey two messages regarding the

5.568

---

[452] Paragraph 42.
[453] Paragraph 43.
[454] Paragraph 44.
[455] Paragraph 46.
[456] C-191/01 P *WM Wrigley Jr Co* [2003] ECR I-12447; C-193/99 *WM Wrigley Jr Co* [2001] ECR II-417.
[457] C-193/99 *Wrigley Jr Co* [2001] ECR II-417.

product; either that it contained twice the usual amount of mint or that it was flavoured with two varieties of mint.

5.569 The Office appealed before the Court contending that the Court of First Instance had erred in its application of Article 7(1)(c), requiring the sign to be exclusively descriptive in order to be excluded from registration.

5.570 Anticipating the argument as to whether the sign was one that should be left free for other traders to use, Wrigley submitted that this condition should apply only where there was a reasonably clear and foreseeable need for competitors to use the contested term to describe features of their products. Finally, it submitted that the sign satisfied the requirements set by the Court in *BabyDry*,[458] a judgment that came after the Judgment of the Court of First Instance in the current case.

(b) The Opinion of Advocate General Jacobs

5.571 The Advocate General welcomed the opportunity for the Court to 'clarify, refine and develop the indications it gave on the interpretation of that provision in Baby-Dry ... since ... the effect of that judgment has been widely misunderstood'.[459]

5.572 **(i) The meaning of 'exclusively'** First, he suggested that the term 'exclusively' qualified the verb 'consist'. It did not refer to the capacity of the elements of the mark to designate characteristics. What the provision required was for all the elements to have a descriptive meaning rather than have no other non-descriptive meaning.

5.573 **(ii) The multiplicity of meanings** Second, he added, the existence of a multiplicity of meanings should not necessarily lead to the conclusion that the sign did not designate the characteristics of a product. The assumption of the Court of First Instance that the multiplicity of meanings automatically meant that the compound term could not designate a characteristic of the specified products wrongly interpreted Article 7(1)(c).

5.574 He considered that Article 7(1)(c) should be viewed independently of Article 7(1)(b):[460]

> It is true that a term which may serve in trade to designate product characteristics will almost certainly be devoid of distinctive character. I nonetheless still consider it preferable, in the legislative context of the Community Trade Mark Regulation, neither to conflate the two criteria nor to view them as inherently interdependent.[461]

5.575 **(iii) A multifactor test for assessing descriptiveness** Going through the Opinion of the Advocate General it becomes apparent that he identified ten factors that should be considered when determining descriptiveness. It is perhaps unfortunate that these factors have not been combined and branded as a multifactor test for determining descriptiveness.

5.576 The first part of the test consists of four factors. First, descriptiveness had to be assessed in relation to the specification of the trade mark application.

---

[458] C-383/99 P *Procter & Gamble Co* [2001] ECR I-6251.
[459] Point 2.
[460] Noting that the Court had appeared to assimilate the concepts of descriptiveness and distinctive character in C-383/99 P *Procter & Gamble Co* [2001] ECR I-6251.
[461] Point 53.

Second, the way in which a term related to the product or its characteristics was important: **5.577**

> The more factual and objective that relationship, the more likely it is that the term may be used as a designation in trade, so that registration will be precluded by Article 7(1)(c); conversely, the more imaginative and subjective the relationship the more acceptable the term will be for registration.[462]

Third, the immediacy of the message was also relevant. Ordinary, definite, and down-to-earth terms would be readily understood as descriptive designations. 'Where at the other extreme the skills of a cryptic-crossword enthusiast are needed in order to detect any connection with the designated characteristic, the grounds for refusing registration are very weak indeed.'[463] **5.578**

Fourth, the significance of the characteristic for the consumer in relation to the product was equally important: **5.579**

> Where the characteristic designated is essential or central to the product, or is of particular importance in a consumer's choice, then the case for refusing registration is compelling; where the designation is of a characteristic that is purely incidental or arbitrary, the case is considerably weaker.[464]

A descriptive term might actually be used in a deceptive manner, and he stressed that the question of precision, accuracy, or factual correctness is not usually relevant to the examination from the above perspectives. **5.580**

(iv) Applying the first part of the test   Doublemint failed from all the three perspectives suggested by the Advocate General in relation to the goods in question: the compound was a factual reference to mint flavour; it was readily perceivable as such; and the flavour was a feature of the product.[465] **5.581**

(v) The second part of the test: Three *Baby-Dry* factors   Dealing with Wrigley's arguments that Doublemint satisfied the three requirements already set by the Court, the Advocate General accepted that the degree of ellipsis, of unusualness, and of resistance to intuitive analysis should also be taken into account. **5.582**

(vi) Applying the second part of the test   Compared with Baby-Dry, Doublemint should also fail the second wave of considerations. The contested sign did not display the Baby-Dry inversion. The combination was neither elliptical not did it resist intuitive grammatical analysis. Finally, the absence of the term from dictionaries did not compensate the limited degree of lexical invention in creating the word.[466] **5.583**

(vii) More than minimal: The wider context of trade mark law; the eighth factor   To support further his application of the second part of the test the Advocate General also referred to the Judgment of the Court in *LTJ Diffusion*[467] and stressed that the differences between descriptive terms and registrable trademarks should be more than minimal from the perspective of relevant consumers and competing traders. **5.584**

---

[462] Point 62.
[463] Point 63.
[464] Point 64.
[465] Point 67.
[466] The AG referred to similar criteria suggested by AG Ruiz-Jarabo Colomer in C-104/00 P *DKV Deutsche Krankenversicherung AG* [2002] ECR I-7561 then pending before the court.
[467] C-291/00 *LTJ Diffusion SA* [2003] ECR I-2799; see paragraph 7.06 et seq.

5.585 **(viii) Adjusting the perspective for viewing descriptiveness: The ninth factor** Following the critical analysis of his position in *Baby-Dry*,[468] suggesting that an anastrophe that appeared unusual in English would not necessarily be seen in the same light in other languages, AG Jacobs accepted that a sign should be assessed in the light of the perception of consumers in all Member States.

5.586 So, the first step should be to look at the sign within the context of its own language. If the sign were found to be descriptive then it would be unnecessary to consider the position of speakers of other languages. 'However, it may be necessary in some circumstances for a sign consisting of terms drawn from one language to be assessed through the eyes (or ears) of a Community consumer whose language is different.'[469]

5.587 **(ix) Keep free for others to use: Article 7(1)(c) and Article 12(b)** Repeating his position expressed in *Baby-Dry* AG Jacobs stated that a trade mark could include signs or indications designating product characteristics but could not consist exclusively of them.[470]

5.588 In the same case the Court had appeared to endorse this position, albeit there has been some criticism regarding that view based on the Court's earlier reference to the public interest in *Windsurfing Chiemsee* that should not be influenced by Article 12(b).[471] He accepted that a defence under Article 12(b) could be less effective because a trade mark registration would place the owner in a comparatively stronger position. However, the danger would be 'obviated'[472] following the more comprehensive interpretation of the criterion of 'perceptible difference' as something more than a minimal difference.

5.589 **(x) Registrations in other jurisdictions: The tenth factor** The Advocate General dismissed Wrigley's argument and noted, with approval, that the Office considered registrations in Member States or non-member countries as evidence of registrability; however, it did not necessarily view those registrations as proof that the conditions imposed by Article 7(1)(c) were met.

(c) The Judgment of the Court

5.590 The Court followed the Opinion of the Advocate General.[473] However, it took a shortcut; it broadened the scope of Article 7(1)(c) but did not explicitly endorse the multifactor test put forward by AG Jacobs.

5.591 **(i) Restating the principles** The Court first reconsidered the scope of Article 7(1)(c) to exclude signs deemed incapable, by their very nature, of fulfilling the indication-of-origin function[474] and the underlying public interest to prevent such signs from being reserved by a single undertaking.[475]

---

[468] He cited the Opinion of AG Ruiz-Jarabo Colomer in C-363/99 *Koninklijke KPN Nederland NV* [2004] ECR I-1619; and Kur, 'Examining Wordmarks after Baby-Dry Still [a] Worthwhile Exercise?' IPR-Info 2001, 12.
[469] Point 85. 'Handy', for example, signified a mobile phone in Germany; similarly, 'smoking' signified a tuxedo in many languages.
[470] Point 92.
[471] Reaffirmed in C-53/01 *Linde AG*, C-54/01 *Winward Industries Inc*, and C-55/01 *Rado Uhren AG* [2003] ECR I-3161.
[472] Point 96.
[473] C-191/01 P *WM Wrigley Jr Co* [2003] ECR I-12447.
[474] Paragraph 30.
[475] Paragraph 31.

(ii) Future and potential use matters The Court then broadened the scope of Article 7(1) (c) by holding that it was not necessary for the mark to be actually used in a descriptive way at the time of the application: 'It is sufficient, as the wording of that provision itself indicates, that such signs and indications could be used for such purposes. A sign must therefore be refused registration under that provision if at least one of its possible meanings designates a characteristic of the goods or services concerned.'[476]

5.592

(iii) Registrability of DOUBLEMINT The Court held that the Court of First Instance had erred as to the scope of Article 7(1)(c) because it applied a test based on whether the mark was exclusively descriptive of the specified goods or services or of their characteristics: 'It thereby failed to ascertain whether the word at issue was capable of being used by other economic operators to designate a characteristic of their goods and services.'[477]

5.593

The Court chose to annul the decision and refer the case back to the Court of First Instance for judgment.

5.594

(4) *Postkantoor*: A Parallel Approach

In parallel with *Doublemint*, a reference from The Netherlands sought further clarifications on the interpretation of distinctive character and descriptiveness under the Directive.[478] Koninklijke KPN Nederland NV (KPN) had applied to register the sign POSTKANTOOR as a Benelux trade mark for a large number of goods and services including paper, card and products manufactured therefrom, postage stamps, and advertising, insurance, construction, telecommunications, transport, education, and technical information and advice services. 'Postkantoor' meant post office in Dutch.

5.595

The Benelux Trade Mark Office rejected the application for lack of distinctive character. KPN brought an action before the Dutch Gerechtshof te's-Gravenhage. The Gerechtshof stayed proceedings and referred nine questions to the Court of Justice and the Benelux Court and fifteen more questions to the Benelux Court alone.[479]

5.596

(a) The Opinion of Advocate General Ruiz-Jarabo Colomer

(i) Limiting the scope of the reference Advocate General Ruiz-Jarabo Colomer lambasted the approach taken by the national court.

5.597

> It is worrying that a court of recognised competence should harbour many doubts concerning the application of Community trade mark provisions. There appears to be a significant distortion within the system, since it is difficult to believe that the work of the European Union legislature could be so lacking in this area, or that those who are responsible for its implementation should fail to understand their role. Regardless of the reason, the Court of Justice is required to supplement and facilitate the work of others within the interpretative role conferred on it under Article 234 EC.[480]

The Court could only consider the registrability criteria and their assessment. Equally, the consideration of the compatibility of the existing pre-Directive national case law with the

5.598

---

[476] Paragraph 32.
[477] Paragraph 35.
[478] C-363/99 *Koninklijke KPN Nederland NV* [2004] ECR I-1619.
[479] Reproduced in paragraph 18.
[480] Point 28.

5.599 **(ii) Balancing functions with scope of protection** The Advocate General started by introducing the requirement of availability:

> The rights of advantage which ownership of a trade mark confers on its owner exist so that consumers will be able to distinguish the marked product or service from products or services of different origins. As such, they may also be subject to restrictions, including restrictions deriving from the fact that it is in the public interest to ensure that certain names remain as widely available as possible (the requirement of availability).[481]

5.600 **(iii) A roadmap for assessing registrability** He then untangled the questions submitted by the Dutch court according to their theme. Following the structure of the Directive he started by discussing how distinctive character should be assessed.

5.601 According to Article 6quinquies of the Paris Convention the assessment of the registrability conditions had to 'be specific in nature, in the sense that a variety of factual circumstances must be taken into consideration',[482] including the possibility that the sign had acquired distinctive character through use and the likelihood of confusion. He drew a roadmap that followed closely the format of the Directive. Each condition was, and should be, examined on its own, independently of the others. The assessment of each condition should be made according to the specification of the application. Some signs would fail more than one condition. To stress the requirement for independent assessment he added that the fact that a sign was not descriptive did not necessarily mean that it possessed distinctive character. Also, the linguistic factor had to be assessed by reference to the average consumer of the specified products.[483]

5.602 **(iv) Registrability: The practices of national offices** Regarding the administration of national trade mark systems, he made two points: first, he noted that there was nothing in the Directive that would preclude the use of disclaimers; and second, he stressed that the practices of one Member State could not bind the authorities of another; the only requirement was that they all applied the same principles of interpretation. Registration in one Member State could only constitute a useful indication for the authorities of another Member State.

5.603 **(v) The scope of Article 3(1)(c)** Article 3(1)(c) precluded the registration of descriptive signs because such signs failed 'to individualise the goods or services to which they relate'.[484] The assessment of whether a sign was descriptive should primarily be made according to the distinguishing function of a trade mark. However, he also admitted that certain public interest considerations should also be taken into account. The Court had already covered this area in *Windsurfing Chiemsee*.[485]

5.604 **(vi) Same reasoning for all types of signs** Although that case covered geographical indications, the same reasoning should apply to all categories of descriptive signs.

---

[481] Point 32.
[482] Point 38.
[483] Point 41.
[484] Point 51.
[485] C-108/97 and C-109/97 *Windsurfing Chiemsee* [1999] ECR I-2779.

(vii) Challenging *Baby-Dry* Expressing his support for the ruling in *Windsurfing Chiemsee*, the Advocate General made the following point: 5.605

> a trade mark creates a privilege which enables an operator to register a sign in order to designate its goods or services. That privilege becomes all the more excessive when it concerns expressions in everyday use. It is fair and natural that a public authority should be able to reward, with a higher level of protection, signs which demonstrate ingenuity or imagination, and that it should require other signs, which merely reflect aspects or attributes of the products in question, to satisfy more rigorous conditions in order to be eligible for registration. Nor do I think it appropriate for economic development and the promotion of commercial initiatives that established operators should be able to register for their own benefit all the descriptive combinations imaginable, or the most effective [of] such combinations, to the detriment of new operators, who are obliged to use invented names which are more difficult to remember and to establish.[486]

The relationship between trade mark and patent law with competition acting as a catalyst is a theme that the Advocate General had also developed in *Philips*.[487]   5.606

Later, in his Opinion, he explained further why he was quite critical of *Baby-Dry*: first, it was uncertain how well it fitted with *Windsurfing Chiemsee*; second, he repeated his point about the linguistic perspective used in that case; third, because it appeared to contain an assessment of factual matters that should remain outside the jurisdiction of an appeal court; and fourth, the test was a 'purely minimum'[488] one. He accepted, though, that the position of the Court at this stage could not be reversed, because 'at issue is a very recent decision, which was, moreover, adopted by the Court in plenary session, for which reason it will probably be of no avail to seek a reversal of precedent'.[489]   5.607

(viii) The peculiarity of the Benelux Finally, on the language considerations in the case of the Benelux, the Advocate General stated: 5.608

> [I]f a particular territory has implemented a system of trade mark registration which covers several linguistic regions, it would be in keeping with the aims of the Directive for an assessment of the distinctive character of a sign to be carried out in relation to each of the languages spoken.[490]

(ix) Neologism: More than the mere sum of its parts; form and meaning Advocate General Ruiz-Jarabo Colomer noted that 'a combination of components, each of which is devoid of distinctive character, can have distinctive character, provided that it amounts to more than just a mere sum of its parts'.[491]   5.609

In order to find a way for determining whether this was the case he proposed the elaboration of the concept of perceptible difference in two ways. First, a difference should be regarded as perceptible if it affected important components of either the form of the sign or its meaning. Interestingly, he linked this proposal with what he had already suggested in *Philips* regarding functionality. Article 3(1)(c) and Article 3(1)(e) had different purposes, though the similarities in their wording necessitated a uniform interpretive approach. There was a common principle in both cases: economic operators should not have to tolerate even the   5.610

---

[486] Point 61.
[487] C-299/99 *Koninklijke Philips Electronics NV* [2002] ECR I-5475.
[488] Point 69.
[489] Point 70.
[490] Point 63.
[491] Point 65.

slight risk of trade mark law encroaching either on what should be protected under patent law or on use of descriptive terms.

5.611 Regarding form, he required the 'neologism' itself to be more important than the sum of the terms of which it was composed, as a result of the unusual or imaginative nature of the word combination. He required whatever was evoked by the composite sign not to be identical to the sum of what was suggested by its descriptive components.[492]

(b) The Judgment of the Court

5.612 The Judgment of the Court is divided into five parts. The first part covers the issues that are linked with the registration process; the second descriptiveness; the third and the fourth the relationship between descriptiveness and distinctive character; and the fifth looks at composite marks.

5.613 (i) **The registration process: The parameters for assessing registrability** The Court based its response on Article 6quinquies C(1) of the Paris Convention, which provided that all the factual circumstances had to be taken into account whilst considering whether a mark was eligible for protection. The Court then described the parameters for assessing registrability.

5.614 First, the competent authority should consider the characteristics peculiar to the mark.[493] Second, the Article 3 grounds had to be assessed specifically by reference to the relevant goods or services. Distinctive character in particular had to be assessed by reference to the goods or services specified in the application but also by reference to 'the perception of them by the relevant public'.[494] In this assessment the competent authority, before adopting a final decision on registrability, should have regard to all the relevant facts and circumstances, including, where appropriate, the results of surveys submitted by the applicant. The same applied to a court having to review a decision on registrability, subject to the limits on the exercise of its powers imposed in each jurisdiction.

5.615 (ii) **The case of the Benelux** Regarding the Benelux linguistic peculiarity—the extension of protection to the translations of the trade mark in all the official languages of the Benelux countries—the Court ruled that the competent authority had to ascertain descriptiveness for each one of those translations.

5.616 (iii) **Registrability in other Member States** On the effect of registration in one Member State, and given the individualistic character of each application, the Court ruled that registration in one Member State could not have any bearing on registrability of a similar mark in respect of similar goods or services in another Member State.

5.617 (iv) **Specification and disclaimers** The Court also considered the question of disclaimers in relation to the specification of a trade mark application.

5.618 The role of the Nice Agreement is to facilitate the administration of a registration system. Applicants can apply for only some of the goods or services covered in each class of the Agreement and, equally, national authorities can reject parts of a class when the application

---

[492] Point 75.
[493] Paragraph 32.
[494] Paragraph 34.

covers it in its entirety. However, the Court ruled that 'where registration is applied for in respect of particular goods or services, it cannot be permitted that the competent authority registers the mark only in so far as the goods or services concerned do not possess a particular characteristic'.[495]

5.619 The potential burden imposed on competitors was the justification behind this ruling. Third parties would not normally be aware of such a limitation and they might refrain from using the contested sign despite the existence of the limitation.

5.620 (v) **The independence of Article 3 grounds: Thorough examination procedures** Finally, the Court ruled that the competent authority of each Member State must refuse to register any mark caught by one of the grounds for refusal laid down by the Directive, in particular in Article 3. The Seventh Recital stated that the conditions for obtaining and maintaining a registration had to be, in general, identical in all the Member States; this is why the absolute grounds for refusal of registration were listed exhaustively in the Directive and had to be adopted by all the Member States. 'In addition, the scheme of the Directive is founded on review prior to registration, even though it also makes provision for ex post facto review.'[496] Citing *Libertel*,[497] the Court repeated that examination had to be thorough and full. Article 3 did not distinguish between marks which cannot be registered and those which manifestly cannot be registered. Accordingly, it is not open for a national authority to reject only signs that are manifestly inadmissible.

5.621 (vi) **Interpreting and applying Article 3(1)(c)** The Court started by clearly reconfirming its position in *Windsurfing Chiemsee*.[498] The public interest described therein required:

> that all signs or indications which may serve to designate characteristics of the goods or services in respect of which registration is sought remain freely available to all undertakings in order that they may use them when describing the same characteristics of their own goods. Therefore, marks consisting exclusively of such signs or indications are not eligible for registration unless Article 3(3) of the Directive applies.[499]

5.622 The Court avoided a detailed test; instead it described in general terms what the competent authority had to do:

> determine whether a trademark for which registration is sought currently represents, in the mind of the relevant class of persons, a description of the characteristics of the goods or services concerned or whether it is reasonable to assume that that might be the case in the future ... If, at the end of that assessment, the competent authority reaches the conclusion that that is the case, it must refuse, on the basis of that provision, to register the mark.[500]

5.623 And without making the Advocate General's explicit link with Article 3(1)(e), it agreed that it was irrelevant whether there were other, more usual, signs or indications for designating the same characteristics. Article 3(1)(c) did not require the contested signs or indications to be the only way of designating those characteristics.

---

[495] Paragraph 114.
[496] Paragraph 123.
[497] C-104/01 *Libertel Groep BV* [2003] ECR I-3793.
[498] C-108/97 and C-109/97 *Windsurfing Chiemsee* [1999] ECR I-2779. By then it had already been reconfirmed in C-53/01 *Linde AG*, C-54/01 *Winward Industries Inc*, and C-55/01 *Rado Uhren AG* [2003] ECR I-3161; and C-104/01 *Libertel Groep BV* [2003] ECR I-3793.
[499] Paragraph 55.
[500] Paragraph 56.

5.624 On the other hand, it did require that the trade mark consisted exclusively of those signs or indications. Similarly, the number of competitors that might have had an interest in using those signs or indications was not decisive; this appeared to be an issue of principle:

> Any operator at present offering, as well as any operator who might in the future offer, goods or services which compete with those in respect of which registration is sought must be able freely to use the signs or indications which may serve to describe characteristics of its goods or services.[501]

5.625 Answering the fifth question the Court repeated that a word had to be refused registration if at least one of its possible meanings designates a characteristic of the goods or services concerned.[502] The existence of synonyms for designating those characteristics was irrelevant.

5.626 It also considered it irrelevant whether the characteristics of the relevant goods or services were commercially essential or merely ancillary. Following a literary interpretive path the Court stressed that the wording of Article 3(1)(c) drew no distinction by reference to the characteristics which might be designated. Public interest required that all undertakings had to able freely to use such signs and indications to describe any characteristic whatsoever of their own goods, irrespective of the commercial significance of that characteristic.

5.627 (vii) **The independent existence of Article 3(1)(b) and Article 3(1)(c)** Citing its rulings in *Linde*[503] and *Merz & Krell*,[504] the Court confirmed that, despite the overlap in terms of scope, each one of the Article 3 grounds was independent of the others and had to be examined separately from the others. In addition, each ground had to be interpreted in the light of the respective underlying public interest.[505] So, not failing one of the grounds was not a guarantee of not failing the others: 'In particular, it is thus not open to the competent authority to conclude that a mark is not devoid of any distinctive character in relation to certain goods or services purely on the ground that it is not descriptive of them.'[506]

5.628 The Court patiently dealt with all the possible combinations raised by the Dutch court. It ruled that it was not open to the competent authority to conclude that a mark was not devoid of any distinctive character in relation to certain goods or services purely on the ground that it was descriptive of the characteristics of other goods or services, even where registration is sought in respect of those goods or services as a whole. Also, the fact that a mark was descriptive of certain goods or services should not be seen as a ground for refusing to register that mark for other goods or services.

5.629 (viii) **The overlap between Article 3(1)(b) and Article 3(1)(c)** The Court, however, in its reinterpretation of the fifth question, also stated that because there was clear overlap between the scope of subparagraphs (b), (c), and (d) of Article 3(1), a descriptive word mark would necessarily also be devoid of any distinctive character. A mark may nonetheless be devoid of any distinctive character without being descriptive.[507]

---

[501] Paragraph 58.
[502] Citing C-191/01 P *WM Wrigley Jr Co* [2003] ECR I-12447.
[503] C-53/01 *Linde AG*, C-54/01 *Winward Industries Inc*, and C-55/01 *Rado Uhren AG* [2003] ECR I-3161.
[504] C-517/99 *Merz & Krell GmbH & Co* [2001] ECR I-6959.
[505] Citing C-299/99 *Koninklijke Philips Electronics NV* [2002] ECR I-5475; and C-104/01 *Libertel Groep BV* [2003] ECR I-3793.
[506] Paragraph 70.
[507] Paragraph 86.

(ix) Composite marks In order to clarify its rulings in *Baby-Dry*[508] and *Doublemint*[509] the Court provided some further guidelines. The starting point was that descriptiveness of the elements of a composite mark did not automatically mean that the composite mark was also descriptive:

5.630

> As a general rule, a mere combination of elements, each of which is descriptive of characteristics of the goods or services in respect of which registration is sought, itself remains descriptive of those characteristics for the purposes of Article 3(1)(c) of the Directive. Merely bringing those elements together without introducing any unusual variations, in particular as to syntax or meaning, cannot result in anything other than a mark consisting exclusively of signs or indications which may serve, in trade, to designate characteristics of the goods or services concerned.[510]

However, and following the Advocate General's rationale regarding conceptual differences and differences as to form between the neologism and its components, the Court held that even POSTKANTOOR might not be descriptive if it created an impression 'sufficiently far removed from that produced by the simple combination of those elements. In the case of a word mark, which is intended to be heard as much as to be read, that condition must be satisfied as regards both the aural and the visual impression produced by the mark'.[511]

5.631

The Court appeared to insist that the conceptual differences were the ones that mattered. The differences relating to form had to create an impression that was detached from the specified goods or services:

5.632

> Thus, a mark consisting of a word composed of elements, each of which is descriptive of characteristics of the goods or services in respect of which registration is sought, is itself descriptive of those characteristics for the purposes of Article 3(1)(c) of the Directive, unless there is a perceptible difference between the word and the mere sum of its parts: that assumes either that, because of the unusual nature of the combination in relation to the goods or services, the word creates an impression which is sufficiently far removed from that produced by the mere combination of meanings lent by the elements of which it is composed, with the result that the word is more than the sum of its parts, or that the word has become part of everyday language and has acquired its own meaning, with the result that it is now independent of its components. In the second case, it is necessary to ascertain whether a word which has acquired its own meaning is not itself descriptive for the purpose of the same provision.[512]

(5) *Streamserve*: Consolidating *Doublemint*

Streamserve[513] consolidated the position of the Court of Justice regarding the interpretation of Article 7(1)(c).

5.633

The contested sign mark was STREAMSERVE as a Community trade mark for 'Apparatus for recording, transmitting and reproducing of sounds and images; data processing equipment including computers, computer memories, viewing screens, keyboards, processors,

5.634

---

[508] C-383/99 P *Procter & Gamble Co* [2001] ECR I-6251.
[509] C-191/01 P *WM Wrigley Jr Co* [2003] ECR I-12447.
[510] Paragraph 98.
[511] Paragraph 99.
[512] Paragraph 100.
[513] C-150/02 P *Streamserve Inc v Office for Harmonisation in the Internal Market (Trade Marks and Designs)* [2004] ECR I-1461, an appeal against the Judgment of the Court of First Instance in T-106/00 *Streamserve Inc v Office For Harmonisation in the Internal Market (Trade Marks and Designs)* [2002] ECR II-723, which in turn had dismissed the action against a decision of the Second Board of Appeal Case: R-423/1999-2, 28 February 2000.

printers and scanners; computer programs stored on tapes, disks, diskettes and other machine-readable media' in Class 9 and 'Listed computer programs; manuals; newspapers and publications; education and teaching material' in Class 16. The examiner rejected the application based on Article 7(l)(b) and Article 7(1)(c) in respect of all the goods except newspapers and publications and education and teaching material.

5.635 The Board of Appeal concurred with the examiner on both grounds. Examining the mark it found it to consist of two English words without any additional element that would render it distinctive; on the contrary, it was descriptive of the intended use of the goods concerned: a method for transferring digital data from a server enabling the data to be processed as a steady and continuous stream (known as streaming).

(a) The Judgment of the Court of First Instance

5.636 **(i) The division of powers between the Office and the Court of First Instance** The Court of First Instance accepted that it remained within the jurisdiction of the Office to take the necessary measures to comply with the Judgment of the Court of First Instance. However, it added that under Article 63(6) of the Regulation the Court of First Instance was not entitled to issue directions to the Office. By remitting the case to the examiner, the Court would not be imposing on the Office any obligation to take, or refrain from taking, action. In addition, one of the measures available to the Board of Appeal was to remit the case to the examiner; accordingly, it fell within the measures that the Court of First Instance could take in the exercise of its power to amend decisions under Article 63(3).

5.637 **(ii) The application of Article 7(1)(c)** The Court of First Instance held that for:

> the purpose of applying Article 7(l)(c) ... it is necessary only to consider, on the basis of the relevant meaning of the word sign at issue, whether, from the viewpoint of the public addressed, there is a sufficiently direct and specific relationship between the sign and the goods for which registration is sought.[514]

5.638 It rejected the claim that the applicant's competitors did not need to use the term to designate the specified goods. The application of Article 7(1)(c) did not depend on there being a real, current, or serious need to leave a sign or indication free. It identified the general interest behind the provision in the following terms:

> Article 7(1)(c) ... prevents the signs or indications referred to in that provision from being reserved to one undertaking alone because they have been registered as a mark. That provision thus pursues an aim which is in the public interest, namely that such signs or indications may be freely used by all.[515]

5.639 The combination of a basic verb with a noun did not appear unusual. In terms of meaning, it referred to a technique for transferring digital data from a server, enabling it to be processed as a steady and continuous stream. The fact that the combination could have other meanings was irrelevant. It was sufficient if at least one of the potential meanings designated a characteristic of the specified goods or services.

5.640 The Court of First Instance then looked at the relationship between the term and the goods included in the specification. It divided the specification into three parts. The first part

---

[514] Paragraph 40.
[515] Paragraph 36.

covered the categories of goods where STREAMSERVE was directly descriptive of their intended purpose: apparatus for recording, transmitting and reproducing of sounds and images; data processing equipment including computers, computer memories, viewing screens, keyboards, processors, printers and scanners; computer programs stored on tapes, disks, diskettes and other machine-readable media; and listed computer programs. For those goods it accepted the submission of the Office that the technique described by the term involved or indeed required their use.

(iii) **Deconstructing the specification: Broad specifications** The second part was a sub-category of specific goods covered by the category '"data processing equipment"—screens, keyboards, processors, printers and scanners—for which it noted that they did not appear as such in the application for registration but were mentioned only as examples of goods falling under the category "data processing equipment"'. It held that they should not be taken into account in the appraisal of the descriptive character of the term. Here, this would work against the applicant; even if it were assumed that a sufficiently direct and specific link between the term and those goods were lacking, the appraisal described above would not be undermined. 5.641

Further, it noted that the applicant had applied for all goods in that category without drawing any distinction between them. It appears that unless a more precise specification is drawn, failing in respect of some of the goods covered under class headings or subheadings would result in the rejection of the entire class or subclass. The third part covered the categories of manuals and publications in respect of which the Court of First Instance found that the Office had failed to prove that the term designated one of their characteristics.[516] 5.642

Accordingly, it upheld the plea only in relation to 'manuals and publications'. 5.643

(iv) **The autonomy of the Community trade mark regime** Finally, it held that the 'the Community trade mark regime is an autonomous system with its own set of objectives and rules peculiar to it; it is self-sufficient and applies independently of any national system'.[517] Registrations of the same sign for the same specification in a Member State or a third country could not bind the Office or the Community courts. 5.644

(v) **The application of Article 7(1)(b)** The Court of First Instance dealt here with the applicant's contention that the term enjoyed a degree of inventiveness and the argument developed by the Office that signs that were descriptive according to Article 7(1)(c) were also devoid of distinctive character under Article 7(1)(b). 5.645

It noted that once one of the Article 7(1) grounds was found to be applicable the application should be rejected; accordingly, in this case it was necessary to consider the substance of the plea only in relation to manuals and publications, since the Board had found the term to fail under Article (1)(b) because it had also failed under Article 7(1)(c). The Court of First Instance underlined that the decision of the Board and the records of the Office had not shown in any way that the term was not distinctive for goods in the categories manuals and publications. Accordingly, the plea was upheld in relation to goods in those two categories. 5.646

---

[516] Paragraph 50.
[517] Paragraph 47.

(b) The Order of the Court

5.647 The Court found the appeal to be clearly unfounded and dismissed it by reasoned Order. The first ground of the appeal, based on *Baby-Dry*,[518] challenged the stance of the Court of First Instance regarding the public interest behind Article 7(1)(c). Streamserve argued that the provision was intended to preclude the registration of descriptive terms rather than prevent the monopolization of descriptive terms. However, the Court disagreed:

> By prohibiting the registration as a Community trade mark of signs or indications which may serve, in trade, to designate the characteristics of the goods or services for which registration is sought, Article 7(1)(c) ... pursues an aim which is in the general interest, namely that such signs or indications may be freely used by all. That provision accordingly precludes such signs or indications being reserved to a single undertaking as a result of the registration of the trade mark.[519]

5.648 It held that the Court of First Instance had not erred in its description of the public interest behind Article 7(1)(c)[520] and that it had taken into account the objectives of the provision. With the second ground, the appellant argued that the Court of First Instance had misinterpreted the facts in holding that the word 'Streamserve' did not appear unusual for the relevant consumers. The Court rejected the second ground because it focused on findings of fact rather than points of law.[521] Furthermore, it held that, based on its findings, the Court of First Instance had correctly applied Article 7(1)(c) by concluding that STREAMSERVE could serve, in trade, to designate a characteristic of most of the specified goods.

(6) *Telefon & Buch*: Following *Doublemint*

5.649 *Telefon & Buch*[522] was one of the first cases that reconsidered the interpretation and application of Article 7(1)(c) following *Doublemint*.[523] It came before the Court as an appeal against a Judgment of the Court of First Instance.[524] Telefon & Buch had applied for the registration as Community trade marks of the words UNIVERSALTELEFONBUCH (universal telephone directory) and UNIVERSALKOMMUNIKATIONSVERZEICHNIS (universal communications directory) for goods in Classes 9 and Class 16 and 'publishing services, in particular the publication of texts, books, magazines, newspapers' in Class 41 and 'editing of written texts' in Class 42.

5.650 The examiner rejected the terms on the basis of Article 7(1)(c) and Article 7(1)(b) in respect of 'recorded memory media for data processing installations and apparatus, in particular tapes, discs, CD-ROMs' in Class 9; 'printed matter, reference works' in Class 16; 'publishing services, in particular the publication of texts, books, magazines, newspapers' in Class 41; and 'editing of written texts' in Class 42. The Board of Appeal confirmed that in

---

[518] C-383/99 P *Procter & Gamble Co* [2001] ECR I-6251.
[519] Paragraph 25.
[520] See paragraph 36 of the Judgment of the Court of First Instance in T-106/00 *Streamserve Inc* [2002] ECR II-723.
[521] Citing C-104/00 P *DKV Deutsche Krankenversicherung AG* [2002] ECR I-7561.
[522] C-326/01 P *Telefon & Buch v Office for Harmonisation in the Internal Market (Trade Marks and Designs)* [2004] ECR I-1371.
[523] C-191/01 P *WM Wrigley Jr Co* [2003] ECR I-12447.
[524] R-357/99 and T-358/99 *Telefon & Buch v Office for Harmonisation in the Internal Market (Trade Marks and Designs)* [2001] ECR II-1705, where the Court of First Instance dismissed the actions against two decisions of the Third Board of Appeal (Cases R-351/1999-3 and R-352/1999-3, 21 October 1999).

German the two words were descriptive of the specified goods and services indicated by the examiner. It also found them to be devoid of distinctive character.

(a) The Judgment of the Court of First Instance

5.651 The Court of First Instance stated that whether the terms were descriptive had to be determined by reference to the goods or services in respect of which registration was sought. It found them to be formed in accordance with the grammatical rules of the German language and composed of common German words. They designated the kind of goods and the intended use of the services concerned; the addition of the adjective 'universal' did not alter its descriptiveness findings, in contrast it functioned as an additional descriptive element.

5.652 It then looked at the target public—average German-speaking consumers, reasonably well informed and reasonably circumspect—and found that they would establish, immediately and without further reflection, a specific and direct association between the terms and the specified goods and services. The fact that the terms constituted neologisms did not affect that conclusion.

5.653 The Court of First Instance also considered future use of the sign, partly responding to the argument that, until that stage, third parties had not been using the signs:

> Even if universal telephone or communications directories, containing worldwide data, are not currently available on the market, it is very likely that they will exist in the near future, either on paper or on electronic media. In any event, the words UNIVERSALTELEFONBUCH and UNIVERSALKOMMUNIKATIONSVERZEICHNIS may, even now, designate directories which cover or which claim to cover universally, that is to say exhaustively, either the whole of a territory (regional, national or supranational) or a whole sector (professional or social).[525]

5.654 It did not consider the arguments based on Article 7(1)(b) given that the application should be rejected on the basis of Article 7(1)(c).

(b) The Order of the Court of Justice

5.655 Before the Court of Justice Telefon & Buch claimed that the Court of First Instance had not taken account of the fact that the terms were not exclusively descriptive. The Court of Justice found the appeal to be clearly unfounded and dismissed it by issuing a reasoned Order. The appellant had employed the language of the Court in *Baby-Dry*[526] in order to strengthen its claims. It argued that the two signs constituted neologisms that consisted of an unusual juxtapositioning of terms. They had no definite meaning and did not convey to the average consumer a clear picture of the goods and services designated by them. Accordingly, it stressed, they were not exclusively descriptive. They were neologisms that remained outside the scope of Article 7(1)(c). It noted that the Office was unable to form a precise idea of the goods in question on the basis of the contested terms and viewed this as evidence that they were not purely descriptive. Proactively, it argued that since the terms had not been used before, they were not subject to the requirement of availability that was behind Article 12 of the Regulation; in any case, the same provision would ensure that third parties would be allowed to use the signs as descriptive indications. The Office took a stricter approach. Article 7(1)(c) covered signs that consumers in the Community would

---

[525] *Telefon & Buch* (n 524) paragraph 30.
[526] C-383/99 P *Procter & Gamble Co* [2001] ECR I-6251.

understand immediately as designating the goods and services referred to in the application or their characteristics. It conceded that, post *Baby-Dry*, where that understanding was not immediate the terms might be registered as trade marks, in particular where the combination of terms was constructed according to an unusual structure. However, it stressed, the fact that the signs were neologisms should not lead to an automatic finding about their descriptiveness. The signs might have had several possible meanings or been constructed according to a slightly different grammatical structure but what mattered was the effect on the decisive factor: 'the way in which the sign is immediately understood and perceived by the public'.[527]

5.656 The Court repeated the basic points of its case law on Article 7(1)(c) until *Doublemint*,[528] failing to cite *Baby-Dry*.[529] Following *Doublemint* it repeated that it

> is sufficient, as the wording of that provision itself indicates, that such signs and indications could be used for such purposes. Thus, under Article 7(1)(c), registration of a word mark must be refused if at least one of its possible meanings designates a characteristic of the goods or services concerned.[530]

5.657 Applying this principle to the current case it held that the Court of First Instance was right to find that:

> for registration of a descriptive sign to be refused on the basis of Article 7(1)(c), it is sufficient that the sign is, in the eyes of the target public, associated with the goods concerned or that it may be reasonably envisaged that such an association will be made in the future and in holding, in paragraph 30 of the judgment under appeal, that the fact that there is currently no market for universal telephone or communication directories does not alter the descriptive character of the words in question.[531]

5.658 This, the Court held, was also in line with the public interest identified in *Windsurfing Chiemsee*.[532] The same applied to the possibility that the terms possessed several meanings. The Court stressed again that it was sufficient that at least one of the possible meanings of that sign was descriptive. The Court concluded that the Court of First Instance had correctly relied on the fact that the terms, in the minds of the public, designated, or were capable of designating, characteristics of the specified goods or services, rather than the fact that they were exclusively descriptive. The part of the claim agreeing that the Court of First Instance was mistaken as to the meaning of the terms was rejected because it was merely its assessment of the facts.[533]

(7) Recent Case Law on Descriptive Signs and Indications

5.659 In the time since the principles of how to examine signs or indications for descriptiveness were established, and the leading cases of *Chiemsee*, *Doublemint*, *Postkantoor*, and *Biomild* have become enshrined in the rules of interpretation, and *Baby-Dry* has been relegated to a footnote in the Court's case law, a number of new cases have come before the Court,

---

[527] Paragraph 22.
[528] C-191/01 P *WM Wrigley Jr Co* [2003] ECR I-12447.
[529] C-383/99 P *Procter & Gamble Co* [2001] ECR I-251.
[530] Paragraph 28.
[531] Paragraph 31.
[532] C-108/97 and C-109/97 *Windsurfing Chiemsee* [1999] ECR I-2779.
[533] Citing C-104/00 P *DKV Deutsche Krankenversicherung AG* [2002] ECR I-7561.

all as appeals from judgments of the General Court (or what was then the Court of First Instance). In all of these cases, the appeal to the Court of Justice was dismissed on the merits, often by Order, ie as manifestly inadmissible or unfounded. Legally, no new theories or sub-rules were developed. Many cases failed because the Court will not review findings of fact by the General Court. The following are cases that should be listed in this category.

(a) COLOR EDITION: Descriptiveness, right to request invalidation

5.660 Judgment of 25 February 2010, Case C-408/08 P[534] *Lancôme parfums et beauté & Cie SNC v OHIM—CMS Hasche Sigle*. The case involved the mark COLOR EDITION, registered for goods in Class 3. The request for a declaration of invalidity was filed by a law firm. That the mark was found to be unregistrable is not particularly surprising. The Court also confirmed that any person has the right to bring an action for a declaration of invalidity, including—as in the present case—a law firm.

(b) KOMPRESSOR PLUS: Descriptiveness

5.661 Judgment of 10 November 2011, C-88/11 P *LG Electronics Inc. v OHIM*. Refusal of the mark KOMPRESSOR PLUS for electrical vacuum cleaners.[535]

(c) PHOTOS.COM: Descriptive and lacking in distinctiveness

5.662 Order of 12 December 2013, C-70/13 P *Getty Images (US) Inc. v OHIM*.[536] Refusal of the mark 'PHOTOS.COM', applied for in relation to goods and services in Classes 9, 42, and 45. The addition of '.com' to descriptive and non-distinctive words does not result in a registrable mark.

(d) ecoDoor: Descriptive for a part of the goods

5.663 Judgment of 10 July 2014, C-126/13 P *BSH Bosch und Siemens Hausgeräte GmbH*.[537] Refusal of the mark 'ecoDoor', applied for, inter alia, for goods in Classes 7, 9, 11. The Court confirmed the refusal on the basis that a mark may be descriptive for certain goods even if it describes only a part of those goods, such as here the doors to refrigerators, washing machines, etc.

(8) *BVBA*: Challenging the Procedural Points of *Postkantoor*

5.664 In *BVBA*,[538] another detailed reference, this time from the Belgian Hof van Beroep (Court of Appeal, Brussels), the Court reconsidered some of the procedural repercussions of *Postkantoor*.[539] BVBA Management Training en Consultancy (BVBA) had applied for the registration in the Benelux of the word mark THE KITCHEN COMPANY for 'ovens with control panels, hot plates, refrigerators, microwave ovens, freeze boxes, deep freezers, boilers, electrical chip friers, ovens, built-in grills, extractor hoods, kitchen sinks, taps' in Class 11; 'wooden and plastic kitchen furniture, kitchen chairs, kitchen work surfaces made of wood, plastic, granite, natural stone or tiled' in Class 20; 'kitchen utensils and household and kitchen equipment made of glass, porcelain, non-precious metals, plastic

---

[534] [2010] ECR I-01347.
[535] [2011] ECR I-00171; available only in French.
[536] ECLI:EU:C:2013:875.
[537] ECLI:EU:C:2014:2065, available only in German and French.
[538] C-239/05 *BVBA Management, Training & Consultancy v Benelux-Merkenbureau* [2007] ECR I-1445 (the Opinion of the AG was delivered on 6 July 2006).
[539] C-363/99 *Koninklijke KPN Nederland NV* [2004] ECR I-1619.

and earthenware' in Class 21; 'the placing and assembly of kitchen furniture and apparatus, maintenance and repair activities' in Class 37; and 'advising in relation to use, nature and application of kitchen apparatus, planning and advising in regard to the installation of kitchens and built-in apparatus, including at the time of purchase' in Class 42. The Benelux Trade Mark Office rejected the application for lack of distinctive character; its decision did not refer in its conclusion specifically to each one of the goods or services listed in the specification; it was based on the finding that the mark was solely descriptive of the kind, quality, origin, or intended purpose of the specified goods and services provided by, for, or in connection with a kitchen company.

5.665 BVBA attacked the decision before the Hof van Beroep that found the mark to be distinctive for 'household and kitchen equipment made of glass, porcelain, non-precious metals, plastic and earthenware' in Class 21, since it did not refer to the intended use of the goods. The Benelux Trade Mark Office, however, objected to this separation because BVBA had not specifically requested the Office to consider registration only for part of the specification.

5.666 The referring court noted that there appeared to be an inconsistency between the jurisprudence of the Court of Justice as expressed in *Postkantoor*[540] and that of the Benelux Court of Justice in *Vlaamse Toeristenbond*.[541] Indeed, this is a good example of how a national court can challenge the position of a higher court before the Court of Justice. The fact that the higher court whose jurisprudence was challenged was the Benelux Court of Justice, a supranational court functioning in its interpretive capacity, adds more weight and intrigue to the approach of the Court. There were three particular points in *Postkantoor* that the referring court found to be relevant: the competent authority had to take into account all the relevant facts and circumstances before taking a final decision on registration; the same applied to the national courts reviewing such decisions, subject to the limits on the exercise of their powers as defined by the relevant national legislation; and the competent authorities must consider registrability in relation to each one of those goods or services, with potentially different outcomes.

5.667 The Benelux court on the other hand had held that, according to Article 6bis[542] and Article 6ter[543] of the Uniform Benelux Law on trade marks, the competent courts of appeal were authorized to order registration of a mark for specific goods or services within a class only if the Benelux Trade Mark Office had specifically ruled on those goods or services as such rather than the class as a whole.

(a) The Opinion of Advocate General Sharpston

5.668 Advocate General Sharpston divided her Opinion into three parts. First, she covered the general question as to whether Article 3 required national authorities to state their conclusions separately for each one of the specified goods or services. Then, she dealt with the time limitations regarding the facts and circumstances that a court reviewing a decision on registrability could take into account. And, third, she considered whether national rules

---

[540] C-363/99 *Koninklijke KPN Nederland NV* [2004] ECR I-1619.
[541] Case A-2002/2, Judgment of the Benelux court of 15 December 2003.
[542] Article 6bis provides that a refusal to register a mark must concern the sign constituting the mark as a whole, but may be limited to one or several of the products which the mark is intended to cover.
[543] Article 6ter(1) provides that an applicant whose mark has been refused registration may, on appeal to the relevant Court of Appeal, seek an order that the mark be registered.

could preclude a court from ruling on the distinctive character of the mark for each one of the goods and services separately.

(i) Article 3: A product-by-product approach? The Advocate General suggested that a trade mark registration authority had to examine an application for registration with regard to each of those goods or services. *Libertel*,[544] she reminded the Court, required a stringent and full examination. 'How else is the trade mark office to determine the goods or services with regard to which the mark may validly be registered, and thereby ensure compliance with Article 13 of the Trade Marks Directive?'.[545]

5.669

Nevertheless, this should not mean that the authority had to state its conclusion regarding an absolute ground for refusal separately for each of those individual goods and services. 'Where registration is refused on that basis for an entire group or category of goods or services, it is sufficient that the decision, whether provisional or definitive, so states and explains adequately why the group or category as such is ineligible for registration.'[546]

5.670

To enable judicial review of the legality of the reasons for the contested decision the decision also had to disclose in 'a clear and unequivocal manner the reasoning followed by the institution ... which adopted the measure in question in such a way as to enable the persons concerned to ascertain the reasons for the measure and to enable the competent court to exercise its power of review'.[547]

5.671

The reasoning did not have to cover all the relevant facts and points of law, since its assessment would take into account not only its wording but also its context and all the legal rules governing the contested issue.

5.672

The Advocate General stated that using general reasoning could also be useful for practical purposes. Registration authorities received a large number of applications each year and the Nice Classification comprised around 11,000 goods and services. She appeared to accept the Benelux Trade Mark Office's assertion that the only workable method of examination was for the office first to regroup the specified goods and services around the apparent core goods and services, in a way that should be readily apparent to the relevant public.

5.673

Once the Office indicated why it considered that an absolute ground applied to that category, then the burden was on the applicant 'to indicate why and demonstrate how the ground for refusal does not hold good for certain specific goods and services ... That will then enable effective judicial review of the decision to be exercised with regard to the office's decision in respect of those goods and services'.[548]

5.674

The detailed procedure regarding the above would unfold according to national rules, but it seemed to be manifestly disproportionate to require national trade mark offices to set out the reason for refusal to register in respect of each and every product and service in a

5.675

---

[544] C-104/01 *Libertel Groep BV* [2003] ECR I-3793.
[545] Point 38.
[546] Point 39.
[547] Point 40; citing Case 222/86 *Heylens* [1987] ECR 4097 on the capacity of the courts to request from authorities presentation of their reasoning and paragraph 65 of C-447/02 P *KWS Saat v Harmonisation in the Internal Market (Trade Marks and Designs)* [2004] ECR I-10107 for the field of trade marks in particular.
[548] Point 42 of the Opinion of AG Sharpston.

situation such as the one described by the referring court, provided that the decision of the national authority satisfied the criteria set by the Advocate General.

5.676 **(ii) Article 3: Timing considerations** The Advocate General examined the second question together with the first part of the third question, as two sides of the same coin: 'The former asks whether, in the light of Article 3, a court of review may take account of intervening facts and circumstances. The latter asks whether, in that light, a court of review may be precluded by national law from taking account of intervening facts and circumstances.'[549]

5.677 She viewed the difference in views as a difference on a question of law rather than one based on an alteration of facts or circumstances, but remarked that the reference was expressed in general terms and she would attempt answering it in general terms. It was for the national court to determine the need for a preliminary ruling.[550]

5.678 She suggested that it was for national law to determine whether a court reviewing a decision of a trade mark authority might take account of facts and circumstances which were not available at the time of the original decision and that it was consistent with Article 3 for national rules to preclude a court reviewing such a decision from taking account of such facts and circumstances.

5.679 **(iii) Article 3: Specification considerations** In the third part, the Advocate General reviewed whether Article 3 was compatible with national rules precluding a court reviewing the decision of a trade mark office from ruling on the distinctive character of the mark for each of the goods and services separately. The question carried an additional charge because the Court's interpretation could affect the judicial freedom not only of the referring court but of all other courts facing a similar scenario.

5.680 The Advocate General highlighted the general principle that, in the absence of Community legislation governing a particular matter, it was for Member States' domestic legal systems to come up with detailed procedural rules governing court actions for safeguarding rights that individuals enjoyed as a result of Community law, provided that the principles of equivalence and effectiveness were respected.[551] This had been repeated in *Postkantoor*[552] in the context of trade mark law.

5.681 She stressed that the Directive did not undertake full approximation, and registration procedures remained in the competence of Member States according to the Fifth Recital, which enjoyed considerable freedom in that respect.

5.682 The starting point for answering the question was that it appeared to be consistent with that freedom to authorize partial registration only when the applicant requested it as an alternative to full registration in its application to the trade mark authority. Equally consistent should be for national rules to preclude a court reviewing the decision of a trade mark office from ruling on the distinctive character of the mark for each of the goods and services separately:

> It does not seem unreasonable or unduly onerous to expect a trade mark applicant which wishes to preserve its right to apply for partial registration to make that clear in its application

---

[549] Point 46 of the Opinion of AG Sharpston.
[550] Citing C-127/92 *Enderby v Frenchay Health Authority and the Secretary of State for Health* [1993] ECR I-5535.
[551] Citing C-472/99 *Clean Car Autoservice GmbH v Stadt Wien and Republik Österreich* [2001] ECR I-9687.
[552] C-363/99 *Koninklijke KPN Nederland NV* [2004] ECR I-1619.

for registration. It is, after all, at that stage that the applicant can best assess its commercial interests ... and decide whether ... it would be content with partial registration of that mark for fewer goods or services, or whether it would prefer to make a fresh application for a different mark for more goods or services.[553]

5.683 She indicated that procedural efficiency would also be better served 'if the question of full versus partial registration is considered at the time of application for registration. A national trade mark office is surely a more appropriate forum than an appellate court for the first evaluation of that issue'.[554]

5.684 The spirit of Article 13 would still be 'accurately reflected provided that national law ensures that trade mark applicants may in the alternative seek partial registration in their application'.[555]

5.685 Finally, she interpreted the dictum of the Court in *Postkantoor*[556] that 'when registration of a mark is sought in respect of an entire class ... the competent authority may, pursuant to Article 13 of the Directive, register the mark only in respect of some of the goods and services belonging to that class'.[557]

5.686 Invoking Article 13 is the basis for giving national trade mark authorities a permissive power. This interpretation allowed her then to suggest that Article 13 did not impose a substantive obligation on a trade mark authority to contemplate partial registration *ex officio* in all cases and find that there was no conflict with national procedural rules requiring an applicant who wanted the trade mark authority to consider partial registration to make that clear in the application.[558]

5.687 In the current case BVBA had failed to make a request for a partial registration at two distinct points of time: when filing its initial application—the provisional stage—and when contesting the provisional decision before the Benelux Trade Mark Office—the final stage. Instead, it made the 'subsidiary' application when the case reached the reviewing court. The Advocate General had no sympathy for such an applicant.

(b) The Judgment of the Court

5.688 The Court largely concurred with the views expressed by the Advocate General.

5.689 (i) **The need for a reasonably specific reasoning** The Court started its analysis by referring to the requirements in *Postkantoor* that the examination of the absolute grounds for refusal must be thorough and full in order to ensure that trademarks are not improperly registered and that insofar as registration is always sought in respect of particular goods and services, the question whether or not any of the grounds for refusal apply must be assessed specifically by reference to each of those goods or services.

5.690 Moreover, it recalled that, according to Article 13 of the Directive, where grounds for refusal of registration of a trade mark exist in respect of only some of the goods or services covered by the application, the refusal is to cover those goods or services only. Accordingly,

---

[553] Point 64.
[554] Point 65.
[555] Point 67.
[556] C-363/99 *Koninklijke KPN Nederland NV* [2004] ECR I-1619.
[557] Ibid, paragraph 113.
[558] Point 68.

the Court concluded, first, that the examination of absolute grounds must be carried out in relation to each of the goods and services for which registration is sought and, second, that the decision refusing registration must, in principle, state reasons in respect of each of those goods or services.[559] This need also arises from the requirement for any decision of a national authority refusing the benefit of a right conferred by Community law to be subject to judicial review, which is designed to secure the effective protection of that right[560] and applies regardless of whether the application for registration contains subsidiary claims relating to specific goods and services.[561] However, the Court emphasized that where that same ground of refusal is given for a category or group of goods or services, the competent authority may use only general reasoning for all of the goods and services falling under that category.[562]

5.691 (ii) **The overriding effect of national rules** The Court then turned to the second part of the third question, dealing with the extent to which the Directive precludes national laws from providing that courts have no competence to consider the various goods and services concerned by the refusal separately. As a starting point, it noted that, according to the Third and Fifth Recitals in its Preamble, the Directive is not intended to bring about full-scale approximation of the trade mark laws of the Member States, giving them extensive freedom to fix the procedural rules governing the registration of trade marks.[563]

5.692 Moreover, it recalled that, according to settled case law, in the absence of specific Community legislation governing a particular matter, it is for the domestic legal system of each Member State to lay down the detailed procedural rules governing court actions for safeguarding rights derived from Community law; however, such rules must not be less favourable than those governing domestic actions (principle of equivalence) and must not render excessively difficult or impossible the exercise of the relevant rights (principle of effectiveness).[564]

5.693 Applying those principles to the case, the Court held that national legislation such as that at issue in the main proceedings, which prevents a court from ruling on the distinctive character of the mark separately for each of the designated goods, cannot be regarded as being contrary to the principle of effectiveness, especially since the interested party could always make a fresh application for registration in case of a partial or total refusal of its mark. It clarified, however, that it is for the referring court to determine whether the principles of equivalence and effectiveness had been observed in the present case.[565]

5.694 (iii) **Time considerations** Finally, with regard to the question whether the Directive precluded national legislation from providing that the reviewing court could not take into account facts and circumstances subsequent to the refusal, it observed that the national court's duty to have regard to all the relevant factors was subject to the limits imposed on its jurisdiction by the national legislation[566] and that, at all events, the lawfulness of the decision under review depended on the facts and circumstances available at the time of its

---

[559] *BVBA* (n 538) paragraph 34.
[560] Citing Case 222/86 *Heylens* [1987] ECR 4097, paragraphs 14–15.
[561] Paragraphs 35–36.
[562] Paragraph 37.
[563] Paragraphs 43–44.
[564] Citing C-472/99 *Clean Car Autoservice* [2001] ECR I-9687, paragraph 28.
[565] Paragraph 46.
[566] Citing *Postkantoor* (n 10) paragraph 36.

adoption.[567] Accordingly, the Court concluded that a national legal order may prevent the court reviewing a decision from taking account of facts and circumstances subsequent to its adoption when exercising the control of its legality.[568]

(iv) The situation as regards Community trade marks A similar situation arises when Community trade mark applications are restricted while the case is pending before the Courts, that is, after the administrative phase of the proceedings has been concluded. OHIM generally considers restrictions filed at that stage to be admissible, given that Article 44 CTMR (now Article 43) enables the owner to withdraw or restrict the application 'at any time', provided of course that the limitation complies with the requirements laid down by the Court in *Postkantoor*.[569] On the other hand, the Court does not pronounce itself as to the acceptability of the request, considering it to be an administrative act over which it has no real competence. Rather, it asks OHIM to confirm its prior acceptance before considering the potential impact of such limitations on the proceedings that are under way.

5.695

Once the Office confirms its acceptance, two situations may be envisaged: if the restriction is effected by merely deleting specific goods or services from the specification, the Court is inclined to take it into account, considering it to be a partial withdrawal of the application that ultimately has a restrictive effect on the subject matter of its own proceedings. Conversely, if the limitation is done by adding one or more qualifying clauses to the specification that change the attributes of the goods as well as reducing their number, the Court tends to disregard the restriction, on the assumption that it unduly changes the subject matter of the dispute, forcing it thus to address facts not examined by the contested decision.[570]

5.696

However, the practical implications of the Court's refusal to consider the second type of restriction for the purposes of its proceedings ultimately depend on its final decision: if the outcome of the Court case is that the application proceeds, it will be registered as restricted; if, on the other hand, the Court upholds a decision of the Boards rejecting the application, the effects of that rejection go back to the date of filing, as follows from Articles 43(5), 45, 46, and 54(2) CTMR (now Articles 42, 45, 46, and 55).

5.697

Hence, in the latter case, the effects of the limitation are in fact overtaken by the retroactivity of the rejection, which means that if the restriction was made by the applicant with a view to reaching an amicable settlement with a third party challenging the application in *inter partes* proceedings, that party will have to withdraw its opposition or cancellation action before the Court's judgment is handed down, so that the settlement of the parties can take effect.

5.698

(9) *Matratzen*: Article 3(1)(c) and Free Movement of Goods Considerations

In *Matratzen*[571] a Spanish court—the Audiencia Provincial de Barcelona—enquired under what conditions a trade mark can be registered in a Member State if it is not distinctive

5.699

---

[567] Paragraph 60.
[568] Paragraph 61.
[569] See C-363/99 *Koninklijke KPN Nederland* [20041 ECR I-1619, paragraph 117, where the ECJ held that it is not acceptable to add to the specification a condition that the goods or services concerned 'do not possess a certain characteristic'.
[570] T-164/03 *Ampafrance SA/OHIM* (MONBEBE/BEBE) [2005] ECR II-1401, paragraphs 20–22; C-363/00 *Anheuser-Busch, Inc/OHIM* (BUDWEISER/BUDWEISER BUDVAR) [2006] ECR II-4255, paragraphs 40–48; T-458/05 *Tegometall International AG/OHIM*.
[571] C-421/04 *Matratzen Concord AG v Hukla Germany SA* [2006] ECR I-2303.

in the language of another Member State but merely denotes or describes the specified product. The case involved registration in Spain of a trade mark incorporating the German word MATRATZEN (translated as 'mattresses' in English). Enforcement of the trade mark registration could become a barrier to the importation of mattresses from Member States using the German word to describe the product and a disguised restriction on trade between Member States contrary to the free movement of goods rules.

(a) The Opinion of Advocate General Jacobs

5.700 Advocate General Jacobs noted that national authorities were applying national trade mark laws and considering registrability according to the meaning of the word in their own jurisdiction. That, however, 'does not necessarily mean ... that ... [they] must never take into account the meaning of a proposed word mark derived from a language which is not the language of the Member State where registration is sought'.[572]

5.701 The Advocate General appeared on the one hand to focus more on the relevant trader and consumer, thus narrowing the circle of the relevant public, but on the other to expand the perimeter so as to cover traders and consumers irrespective of their language. This, he considered to be a better yardstick that has already been adopted by some national authorities. Revisiting a familiar theme,[573] he concluded that national courts must ensure both that Article 5(1) is not abused and that Article 6(1)(b) is properly invoked. Registration does not result in an unlimited right. The owner of MATRATZEN in Spain would not be entitled to prevent its use either outside Article 5(1) or within Article 6(1)(b).

(b) The Judgment of the Court

5.702 In order to respond to the question in a useful way the Court noted that it would have to consider provisions of Community law that the referring court had not mentioned in its reference.[574] It then added that 'in a field which has been exhaustively harmonised at Community level, a national measure must be assessed in the light of the provisions of that harmonising measure and not of those of primary law'.[575] The Court would focus on Article 3 of the Directive rather than the free movement of goods provisions of the Treaties. Article 3 did not include 'any ground ... specifically aimed at trademarks constituted by a term borrowed from the language of a Member State other than the State of registration in which it is devoid of distinctive character or descriptive of the goods or services in respect of which registration is sought'.[576]

5.703 The Court codified its earlier judgments on distinctiveness in the following way:

> In fact, to assess whether a national trade mark is devoid of distinctive character or is descriptive of the goods or services in respect of which its registration is sought, it is necessary to take into account the perception of the relevant parties, that is to say in trade and or amongst average consumers of the said goods or services, reasonably well-informed and reasonably observant and circumspect, in the territory in respect of which registration is applied for.[577]

---

[572] Point 47.
[573] See also C-383/99 *Procter & Gamble Co* [2001] ECR I-6251.
[574] Citing C-230/98 *Amministrazione delle Finanze dello Stato v Schiavon* [2000] ECR I-3547; and C-469/00 *Ravil SARL v Bellon Import SARL and Biraghi SpA* [2003] ECR I-5053.
[575] Paragraph 20.
[576] Paragraph 22.
[577] Paragraph 24.

It added that because of linguistic, cultural, social, and economic differences, a trade mark which is devoid of distinctive character or descriptive in one Member State may not be so in another Member State.[578] The critical issue was whether the relevant parties in the Member State where registration is sought are capable of identifying the meaning of the term, irrespective of its language. Indeed, this was in accordance with the free movement jurisprudence of the Court.[579]

5.704

The Court had already decided in *Matratzen I*[580] that the principle of the free movement of goods did not prohibit registration as a national trade mark in one Member State of a sign that was descriptive of the specified goods or devoid of distinctive character in the language of another Member State. The Court also endorsed the remark of the Advocate General that registration of a sign as a trade mark did not prohibit all other uses of the same sign.[581]

5.705

It concluded that Article 3(1)(b) and (c)

5.706

> does not preclude the registration in a Member State, as a national trade mark, of a term borrowed from the language of another Member State in which it is devoid of distinctive character or descriptive of the goods or services in respect of which registration is sought, unless the relevant parties in the Member State in which registration is sought are capable of identifying the meaning of the term.[582]

(10) *Celltech*: Burden of Proof: Technical and Scientific Terms

In *Celltech*[583] the Court dealt with the evidential standard to be observed by trade mark authorities when determining the descriptiveness of a trade mark. As in the case of lack of distinctiveness, the question whether the sign applied for is descriptive should be assessed by reference to the relevant consumer profile, as defined by the goods concerned and their specific characteristics. The case concerned an appeal brought by the Office against the Judgment of the Court of First Instance annulling the decision of its Board of Appeal, which had refused registration of the word mark CELLTECH in respect of, essentially, pharmaceutical preparations, medical instruments, and biological research in Classes 5, 10, and 42 of the Nice Classification.

5.707

The Board of Appeal held that the term at issue would be immediately and unambiguously understood by the public as designating activities in the field of cell technology, as well as products, apparatus, and equipment used in connection with, or resulting from, those activities. Hence, it concluded that the connection between the goods and services for which protection was sought and the trade mark applied for, was not sufficiently indirect to endow the mark with the minimum level of inherent distinctiveness required under Article 7(1)(b) CTMR.

5.708

---

[578] Citing by way of analogy an earlier, surprisingly pre-harmonization case on misleading trade marks: C-313/94 *Fratelli Graffione SNC v Ditta Fronsa* [1996] ECR I-6039.

[579] Note that the Court, in its short review of Articles 28 and 30 EC in paragraph 28, made it clear once again that the existence/exercise dichotomy has not been abandoned. It repeated that in relation to the principle of the free movement of goods, the Treaty does not affect the existence of rights recognized by the legislation of a Member State in matters of intellectual property, but only restricts, depending on the circumstances, their exercise.

[580] C-3/03 P *Matratzen Concord GmbH* [2004] ECR I-3657, see paragraph see paragraph 7.95 et seq. below.

[581] Contrast with C-363/99 *Koninklijke KPN Nederland NV* [2004] ECR I-1619.

[582] *Matratzen* (n 580) paragraph 32.

[583] C-273/05 P *OHIM v Celltech R&D Ltd* (CELLTECH) [2007] ECR I-02883.

(a) The Judgment of the Court of First Instance

5.709 Although the Court of First Instance[584] recognized that at least one of the possible meanings of the term 'CELLTECH' is indeed 'cell technology', it observed that neither the examiner nor the Board 'had given an explanation of the meaning, in scientific terms, of cell technology', other than producing a dictionary extract showing the definitions of the terms 'cell' and 'tech', failing thus to explain 'in what way those terms give information about the intended purpose and nature of the goods and services and in particular about the way in which they may be applied to cell technology, or result from it'. Referring to its judgments in *Eurohealth*[585] and *Carcard*,[586] the Court further held that the fact that, in view of their medical nature, the goods and services at issue related to bodies composed of cells, did not relieve the Board of the obligation to show that the relevant public would make a 'definite and direct association between the goods and services claimed and the meaning of the expression'. Furthermore, even supposing that the goods and services may be used for functional purposes involving cell technology, that fact is not sufficient for a finding that the word 'Celltech' may serve to designate their intended purpose, since such use constitutes at most one of many possible areas of application, without, however, revealing their exact technical function.

(b) The Judgment of the Court of Justice

5.710 In the first place, the Court observed that the Court of First Instance did not annul the contested decision for failure to state reasons, but rather on the ground that the Board 'had not established that the mark CELLTECH, understood as meaning "cell technology", was descriptive of the goods and services referred to in the application for registration'.[587]

5.711 It then laid down the framework for its analysis by recalling that, under Article 74(1) of the Regulation (new Article 76), the Office is required, when determining whether the sign applied for falls under one of the grounds for refusal provided for in Article 7 of the Regulation, to examine the facts of its own motion. That means not only that OHIM may be led to base its decisions on facts which have not been alleged by the applicant, but also that it must establish in its decisions the accuracy of the facts relied on, unless those facts are well known.[588] Applying those principles to the case, the Court observed that, by stating that the expression 'CELLTECH' will be perceived as designating activities in the field of cell technology, as well as products used in connection with such activities, the Board of Appeal implicitly held, first, that cell technology is a well-known scientific fact and, second, that the activities forming part of that method include the production or manufacture of the designated goods and services.

5.712 It noted, however, that in deciding that the nature of cell technology is not a well-known fact and that it was therefore for the Board of Appeal to establish the correctness of its findings in that regard, the Court of First Instance made a finding of fact which was not subject to review by the Court of Justice on appeal.

---

[584] C-260/03 *Celltech/OHIM* (CELLTECH) [2005] ECR II-1215.
[585] T-359/99 *DKV/OHIM* (EuroHealth) [2001] ECR II-1645, paragraph 35.
[586] T-356/00 *DaimlerChrysler/OHIM* (CARCARD) [2002] ECR II-1963, paragraph 40.
[587] *Celltech* (n 583) paragraph 37.
[588] Citing C-25/05 P *Storck II* [2006] ECR I-5719, paragraphs 50–51.

5.713 Accordingly, the Court concluded that, by not furnishing any evidence that cell technology had the scientific meaning attributed to it, the Board of Appeal did not establish the correctness of the findings on the basis of which it held that the mark 'CELLTECH' was descriptive, noting also that the Board 'made no attempt to establish the soundness of those findings, for example by referring to scientific literature'.[589]

5.714 The judgment in *Celltech* thus refined the scope of the evidential rules laid down in *Storck II*, by clarifying that if the case relates to specialized terms, as is the case with scientific and technical terminology, for example, the relevant facts cannot qualify as being well known within the meaning of the Court's interpretation of Article 74(1) CTMR (now Article 76). It follows that in such cases OHIM bears the procedural burden to provide concrete explanations not only as to the meaning of the relevant expressions, but also as to their specific relationship to the goods and services at issue, if need be by reference to scientific or other specialized literature.

(11) *Develey*: Burden of Proof: Consumer Goods

5.715 The judgment in *Develey*[590] came to complement the evidential principles developed in *Celltech* by clarifying which facts may be regarded as well known in the context of establishing if a given term is either descriptive or devoid of distinctiveness. The case concerned the registration of a three-dimensional sign in the form of a plastic bottle in respect of various foodstuffs and drinks in Classes 29, 30, and 32 of the Nice Classification, including in particular seasonings, sauces, and creams. OHIM rejected the application on the grounds that the sign merely consisted of the representation of a commonplace ketchup dispenser and thus did not significantly depart from the usual shapes in the sector.

5.716 Develey appealed, pleading infringement of Article 74(1) CTMR (now Article 76) in that OHIM ought to have provided proof of the lack of distinctive character when noting that the shape in question would be perceived as a common bottle and not as a badge of origin. The Court of First Instance rejected the action, holding that where the Board of Appeal finds that a trade mark applied for is devoid of distinctive character, it may base its analysis 'on facts arising from practical experience generally acquired from the marketing of general consumer goods which are likely to be known by anyone and are in particular known by the consumers of those goods', stressing also that since the applicant claimed that the mark was distinctive despite the analysis of the Board, it was for him to provide specific and substantiated information showing that the mark was either intrinsically distinctive or had acquired the requisite distinctiveness by use.[591]

5.717 On appeal, the Court of Justice upheld those findings, stating that the Court of First Instance had not erred in its application of the rules relating to the burden of proof by requiring the applicant to prove its claim that the mark was distinctive, when challenging conclusions of OHIM based on well-known facts.[592]

---

[589] *Celltech* (n 583) paragraph 43.
[590] C-238/06 P *Develey Holding GmbH & Co Beteiligungs KG/OHIM* (PLASTIC BOTTLE) [2007] ECR I-09375.
[591] T-129/04 *Develey Holding GmbH Beteiligungs KG/OHIM* (PLASTIC BOTTLE) [2006] ECR II-00811, paragraph 26.
[592] *Develey* (n 591) paragraphs 48–50.

5.718 As regards the complaint that the reasoning of the Court of First Instance made no distinction between the different goods in the application, the Court considered sufficient to that end the observation that the goods at issue were products for everyday consumption and that consumers primarily perceive the bottles in which such goods are contained as a means of packaging. In addition, it held that, since those goods fell within only three classes of the Nice Agreement, there was no need for a more extensive reasoning.[593]

5.719 *Develey* and *Celltech* thus suggest that the question whether the facts relating to the distinctive character of a sign are well known or not mostly depends on the sector concerned: if the goods for which protection is sought are consumer goods targeting the general public, the relevant marketing practices should generally be considered to be known to everyone and, as such, are exempt from proof; if, however, the relevant setting is a more sophisticated one, it is the Office's task to provide specific indications as to the precise meaning of a scientific or technical term and as to its concrete link to the goods.

5.720 The non-binding effect of previous decisions, however, is not entirely without limits. As the Court made clear in *Technopol*[594] with regard to the examination of Community trade marks, the general principles of equal treatment and sound administration create a specific obligation on OHIM to consider its prior practice in identical or materially similar cases and assess their relevance to the facts under examination.

5.721 In order to comply with this duty, OHIM *'must'* take into account decisions already taken in respect of similar applications, considering with *'special care'* whether it should decide the case pending before its decision-making instances in the same way or not. The prescriptive tone of the Court's statements seem to imply that OHIM must always give specific reasons as to why it chooses to deviate from its previous practice and that it cannot dispense with this obligation without running the risk of having its decision overturned due to a substantial procedural violation.

5.722 In any event, it is clear from that case law that the task of elaborating on more detailed rules in that regard belongs to the Court of First Instance, which is alone competent for deciding whether or not a specific set of facts is to be considered as being well known for the purposes of trade mark examination.

E. Article 3(1)(d): Signs or Indications that Have Become Customary

(1) *Bravo*: The Link with the Specification

5.723 In *Bravo*[595] the Court considered the registrability of a laudatory word from the perspective of Article 3(1)(d) of the Directive. The case came before the Court as a reference from the German Bundespatentgericht and it concerned an application to register in Germany the word BRAVO as a trade mark for typewriters. The German Patent and Trade Mark Office

---

[593] Paragraph 91, citing C-239/05 *BVBA* [2007] ECR I-1455.
[594] C-51/10 P, *Agencja Wydawnicza Technopol sp. z o.o./Office for Harmonisation in the Internal Market (Technopol)*, paragraphs 73–79.
[595] C-517/99 *Merz & Krell GmbH & Co (Bravo)* (2001) ECR I-959.

rejected the application on the ground that BRAVO was a term of praise or an advertising slogan for the specified goods.

The case reached the Bundespatentgericht, which referred to the Court of Justice the following question: **5.724**

> Is Article 3(1)(d) ... to be interpreted restrictively, contrary to the wording thereof, as meaning that only signs or indications which directly describe goods and services for which registration has specifically been applied, or the essential characteristics or features thereof, are affected by the bar to registration? Or is the provision to be construed as meaning that, in addition to free signs and generic names, signs or indications which have become customary in the current language or in the bona fide and established practices of the trade in the relevant or a similar sector as advertising slogans, indications of quality or incitements to purchase etc., without directly describing the specific characteristics of the goods or services for which registration has been applied, may likewise not be registered?[596]

(a) The Opinion of Advocate General Ruiz-Jarabo Colomer

(i) **The legislative framework**   Since this was one of the earliest cases referred to the Court following the adoption of the Directive and the Regulation, AG Ruiz-Jarabo Colomer started with a thorough analysis of the legislative context, beginning with the international context under the Paris Convention, which formed the framework to which the laws of its signatories, but also the agreements and treaties entered into by them, had to adhere. From a European perspective, he referred to the free movement of goods rules, the Directive, and the Regulation, noting that trade marks were one of the exceptions to the free movement of goods principle, and the relevant provisions of the Directive and the Regulation. **5.725**

Regarding the function of trade marks and trade mark rights, he cited *Hag II*.[597] Trade mark rights were an essential element in the system of undistorted competition envisaged in the Treaty; the justification of the exclusive right should be found in the function of trade marks as guarantees of origin. All trade mark provisions—including Article 3(1)(d)—should be interpreted according to these objectives and principles. **5.726**

> Regard must therefore be had to two interpretation criteria when responding to the question referred in the present proceedings: the teleological criterion, which centres on the function of the trade mark, and the integration criterion which seeks to provide an integrated interpretation of the relevant rule.[598]

(ii) **The interpretation of Article 3(1)(d)**   He started by highlighting the similarities of the Community provisions with Article 6quinquies(B)(2) of the Paris Convention: 'an almost literal transcription',[599] with the exception of the German version of Article 7(1)(d). He reconciled this discrepancy by focusing on two things: first, on the overwhelmingly identical reading of the same provision in all the other languages;[600] and, second, on that the German wording of Article 7(1)(d) of the Regulation was not relevant to the interpretation of Article 3(1)(d) of the First Directive. **5.727**

---

[596] Reproduced in point 4.
[597] C-10/89 *SA CNL-SUCAL* [1990] ECR I-3711, confirmed by the Court at that stage in C-63/91 *Bayerische Motorenwerke AG* [1999] ECR I-905 and C-349/95 *Frits Loendersloot* [1997] ECR I-6227.
[598] Point 34.
[599] Point 35.
[600] Citing Case 19/67 *Bestuur de Sociale Verzekeringsbank v van der Vecht* [1967] ECR 445; and Case 29/69 *Stander v City of Ulm* [1969] ECR 419.

5.728 He saw the provision as part of a broader attempt to bar from registration trade marks that lack distinctiveness.[601] Article 3(1)(b) precluded signs which were devoid of any distinctive character, 'followed by two specific examples of indications which are not capable of distinguishing goods or services, that is, those which are descriptive (subparagraph (c)) and those which are customary (subparagraph (d))'.[602]

5.729 (iii) **A test for the application of Article 3(1)(d)**   The Advocate General identified two main factors that authorities and courts had to consider before applying Article 3(1)(d): the association between the sign and the specified good or services; and the type and strength of that link.

5.730 *The first factor—association and distinctive character*   The first factor was linked with the primary function of a trade mark:

> 'the raison d'etre of the ground for refusal set out in Article 3(l)(d) ... is that the indications to which it refers do not meet the conditions for qualification as a trade mark laid down in Article 2, namely that they must be capable of distinguishing the goods or services of one undertaking from those of other undertakings'.[603]

Article 3(3), which allowed applicants to overcome the barrier of subparagraphs (b), (c), and (d) with evidence of acquired distinctive character, supported further his interpretation.

5.731 Distinctive character was an imprecise legal concept for the Advocate General that could only be clarified in its particular context, in the light of the circumstances and of the particular nature of each individual case.

5.732 Returning to the essential function of a trade mark and the Judgment of the Court in *Hag II*,[604] he observed that the exclusive right to use the mark was not the final aim of trade mark law but a step towards allowing consumers to choose according to origin and undertakings to retain their customers by virtue of the quality of their offerings. This remark, that appears to be a step back to his earlier broader discussion on trade marks, allowed the Advocate General to introduce to his test the link with the actual goods or services. Trade mark rights facilitated 'the establishment of a bona fide, undistorted system of competition, from which those who seek to gain advantage or to profit from the reputation of others are excluded'.[605]

5.733 In respect of the Directive he concluded:

> Article 3(1)(d) requires that, for registration of a trade mark to be refused, or, where appropriate, for an existing registration to be declared invalid, the signs or indications of which it consists must have become customary in the current language or in the bona fide and established practices of the trade relevant to the goods or services which the mark is intended to identify.[606]

5.734 *The second factor—the type and strength of the association*   The second factor considered the heart of the provision. Advocate General Ruiz-Jarabo Colomer started by identifying the

---

[601] Point 37.
[602] Point 39.
[603] Point 40.
[604] C-10/89 *SA CNL SUCAL* [1990] ECR I-3711.
[605] Point 42. This was reinforced by the scope and limitations of trade mark rights; they extended as far as necessary for the essential function to be fulfilled.
[606] Point 46.

meaning of the word 'describe'. Taking into account its meaning in a number of Community languages, he stated that 'by describing something, one seeks to define it not by its essential predicates but by providing a general idea of its parts or properties'.[607]

5.735 On the basis of this definition, purely descriptive signs were excluded by Article 3(1)(c). Accordingly, Article 3(1)(d) 'merely requires them to be customary in the current language or in the practices of the trade relevant to the goods or services which they are intended to identify, without specifying the degree of association that must exist between them'.[608]

5.736 The examples provided by the Advocate General linked the provision with the essential function of trade marks and the scope and limitations of trade mark rights. It covered

> free signs, generic names and, in general, all graphic representations (whether or not they contain phonemes) which, one way or another, have come to represent in the perception of the public the goods or services to which they refer and which, consequently, may not be appropriated for anyone's exclusive use.[609]

5.737 Based on the meaning of a term the Commission had referred to in its submissions—'connotation'—he concluded that the sign had to be 'automatically—subconsciously even'[610] associated with the goods or services it identified.

5.738 (iv) **Registrability of BRAVO** In principle, the contested sign, that in most Community languages functioned as an exclamation, should not be excluded from trade mark protection for typewriters on the basis of Article 3(1)(d).[611] Registration would be problematic for goods or services in the field of sports where the exclamation was used habitually.

(b) The Judgment of the Court

5.739 (i) **The legislative framework** The Court chose a narrower legal contextualization referring exclusively to the Directive and the national trade mark law. Regarding the language of Article 3(1)(d), the Court noted that only the Danish and Swedish versions of the provision contained a reference to signs and indications which have become customary in the current language or in the bona fide and established practices of the trade for the goods or services. It divided the referred question into two parts. The first part explored the link between the sign and its specification; the second considered the types of signs that should be excluded.

5.740 (ii) **The link with the specification** The Court repeated the analysis of the Advocate General regarding the essential function of trade marks and the aim of trade mark rights.[612] Article 3(1)(d) did not contain the qualification found in Paragraph 8(2)(3) of the Markengesetz. However, this did not mean that the connection between the sign and the goods or services should be disregarded. On the contrary, the 'question whether particular

---

[607] Point 48.
[608] Point 50.
[609] Point 51.
[610] Point 52.
[611] He noted that the Office had already accepted BRAVO as a registered trade mark for diesel engines (Application number 000463919, date of registration: 7 September 1999).
[612] Citing C-349/95 *Frits Loendersloot* [1997] ECR I-6227; and C-39/97 *Canon Kabushiki Kaisha* [1998] ECR I-5507 from its more recent jurisprudence and the Tenth Recital in the Preamble to the Directive.

signs or indications possess distinctive character cannot, however, be considered in the abstract and separately from the goods or services those signs or indications are intended to distinguish'.[613]

5.741 Article 3(1)(d) should be interpreted as

> only precluding registration of a trade mark where the signs or indications of which the mark is exclusively composed have become customary in the current language or in the bona fide and established practices of the trade to designate the goods or services in respect of which registration of that mark is sought.[614]

5.742 (iii) **The types of signs covered by Article 3(1)(d)**   The second part targeted the types of signs excluded by the provision, in particular whether it covered only signs or indications describing the properties or characteristics of the specified goods or services or it extended to signs or indications that function as advertising slogans, indications of quality, or incentives to purchase that did not necessarily function in the same descriptive way as above. The Court acknowledged that there was clear overlap between the scope of Article 3(1)(c) and Article 3(1)(d) of the Directive. Marks 'covered by Article 3(1)(d) are excluded from registration not on the basis that they are descriptive, but on the basis of current usage in trade sectors covering trade in the goods or services for which the marks are sought to be registered'.[615]

5.743 The sole condition was that indicated by the language of the provision: the sign or indication had to become customary in the current language or in the bona fide and established practices of the trade to designate the goods or services in respect of which registration of that mark was sought. It was immaterial whether it described the properties or characteristics of those goods or services.

5.744 The Court added that the exact nature of the contested signs or indications—for example, were they advertising slogans or indications of quality—would be inconsequential once it was established that they fell within the scope of the provision. But this should not be seen as a blanket prohibition from registration of signs or indications that were also used as advertising slogans, indications of quality, or incitements to purchase the goods or services covered by that mark. National courts had to determine whether the contested signs or indications had become customary in the current language or in the bona fide and established practices of the trade to designate the specified goods or services.

(2) *Alcon*: **Article 7(1)(d) and Acronyms**

5.745 In *Alcon*[616] the Court considered the application of Article 7(1)(d) of the Regulation in relation to an acronym. Another contested issue in this case was the application of Article 7(3). The case was an appeal against a Judgment of the Court of First Instance dismissing

---

[613] *Bravo* (n 595) paragraph 29. In C-108/97 and C-109/97 *Windsurfing Chiemsee* [1999] ECR I-2779 the Court had already decided that a sign's capacity to distinguish could only be assessed by reference to the goods or services it was meant to distinguish.
[614] Paragraph 31.
[615] Paragraph 35.
[616] C-192/03 P *Alcon* [2007] ECR I-8993.

an action against a decision of the Board of Appeal[617] on the invalidation of a Community trade mark registration. Indeed, this was the first invalidity case to reach the Court of Justice.

5.746 Alcon had registered the term 'BSS' as a Community trade mark for 'ophthalmic pharmaceutical preparations; sterile solutions for ophthalmic surgery' in Class 5. Dr Robert Winzer Pharma GmbH (Winzer) challenged the registration under Article 51(1) of the Regulation. It claimed that the term *was* an abbreviation for 'balanced salt solution' or 'buffered saline solution' and that the registration should be invalidated as descriptive. The Cancellation Division of the Office invalidated the registration on the basis of Article 7(1)(d); it also found that the mark had not acquired distinctive character according to Article 7(3) and Article 51(2) of the Regulation. Alcon appealed, but the Board of Appeal confirmed the decision of the Cancellation Division, concluding that both in English and German the acronym was used to describe all ophthalmic solutions.

(a) The Judgment of the Court of First Instance

5.747 (i) **The application of Article 7(1)(d)** The Court of First Instance, following the principles set by the Court of Justice in *Merz & Krell*,[618] reviewed the examination of the evidence by the Board and held that it was right to decide that the term had become customary.

5.748 First, it identified the target public by reference to the specified goods, as medical specialists, particularly ophthalmologists and ophthalmic surgeons throughout the European Union, given that English is the technical language in this area.[619]

5.749 For that group the term clearly fell within the scope of Article 7(1)(d). It has become the current generic term for a balanced salt solution.[620]

5.750 (ii) **The application of Article 7(3)** The Court of First Instance also concurred with the Board that BSS had not acquired distinctive character as a result of use. Alcon had relied on a number of documents to establish acquired distinctive character before the Office, including a plan for protecting BSS, titled the Policing BSS schedule, agreements with third parties concerning use of the sign, national trade mark registration certificates of marks containing the letters BSS, and brochures of ALCON BSS and BSS PLUS products, as well as information on turnover and advertising expenditure.

5.751 The Court of First Instance had found that this information failed to establish distinctiveness, noting in particular that 'the applicant has not advanced any argument in the application on the probative value of those documents'.[621]

5.752 In relation to the brochures, the Court of First Instance noted that they 'might at most indicate that it itself considers that the BSS mark has not acquired a sufficient degree of distinctiveness to be used without any additional element to identify the product'.[622]

---

[617] T-237/01 *Alcon Inc v Office for Harmonisation in the Internal Market (Trade Marks and Designs) Dr Robert Winzer Pharma (BSS)* [2003] ECR II-411 dismissing an action against the decision of the First Board of Appeal of the Office for Harmonisation in the Internal Market (Trade Marks and Designs) (Case R-273/2000-1).
[618] C-517/99 *Merz & Krell GmbH & Co* [2001] ECR I-6959.
[619] *Alcon* (n 618) paragraph 42.
[620] Paragraph 43.
[621] Paragraph 58.
[622] Paragraph 59.

(b) The Order of the Court

5.753 The Court found the appeal to be unfounded and issued a reasoned order that can be divided into two parts; the first deals with the legal context of Article 7(1)(d); and the second covers the broader issue of evidence, in relation to both Article 7(1)(d) and Article 7(3).

5.754 **(i) The interpretation and application of Article 7(1)(d)**   The Court was satisfied that the Court of First Instance had followed *Merz & Krell*.[623] First, it had focused on whether the term had become customary rather than descriptive. Second, it had also examined the possibility that the mark might have acquired distinctive character through use. The Court stressed that the decisive criterion was not the descriptive nature of the mark but its current usage in the relevant sectors. Third, the Court of First Instance had correctly adopted the viewpoint of the target public to determine whether the term was customary.

5.755 **(ii) The findings of fact and the assessment of evidence**   The findings that Alcon had not produced the necessary evidence to support its claims were findings of fact within the jurisdiction of the Court of First Instance that could not be challenged on appeal. Similarly, challenging the assessment of the facts without alleging any distortion of the evidence remained outside the scope of an appeal process that covered only points of law.[624]

5.756 The Court also rejected a claim that the Court of First Instance had wrongly taken into consideration documents published in the Unites States of America that did not affect the target public. The Court accepted that evidence outside Europe could be relevant:

> By stating ... that English was the technical language of specialists in the relevant field, and by referring ... to the perception of the term BSS as a generic term by the 'scientific community', the Court of First Instance necessarily considered that those documents, although published outside the European Union, supported the conclusion that the target public regarded that term as having become customary. In so doing it made an assessment of pure fact, which the appellant cannot challenge on appeal.[625]

5.757 Finally, Alcon, despite its complaints regarding the assessment of its own evidence compared with that of Winzer's evidence, had not submitted that the Court of First Instance had misapplied the rules on the burden of proof.[626]

5.758 **(iii) The relevant dates for determining invalidity**   The Court noted that in terms of timing the Court of First Instance and the Board of Appeal had correctly and explicitly stated that the term had become customary at the time of Alcon's application for registration. It agreed with the Office that the date of filing of the application was the material date for the examination of invalidity. However, the Court of First Instance was entitled to take account of material subsequent to that date that enabled the drawing of conclusions on the situation as it was on that date.[627]

---

[623] C-517/99 *Merz & Krell GmbH & Co* [2001] ECR I-6959.
[624] Citing C-104/00 P *DKV Deutsche Krankenversicherung AG* [2002] ECR I-7561 and the Order in C-326/01 P *Telefon & Buch* [2004] ECR I-1371.
[625] *Alcon* (n 618) paragraph 42.
[626] Citing C-199/92 P *Hills v Commission* [1999] ECR I-4287.
[627] Citing the Order in C-259/02 *La Mer Technology Inc v Laboratoires Goemar SA* [2004] ECR I-1159.

F. Article 3(1)(e): Functional Shapes

(1) *Philips*: The Overriding Scope of Article 3(1)(e)

In *Philips*[628] the English Court of Appeal referred to the Court of Justice a list of seven questions, primarily in order to clarify Article 3(1)(e), the 'functionality' provision of the Directive, but also to obtain a framework for determining distinctiveness and the scope of protection. The fourth question was on functionality. Is the existence of other shapes that can obtain the same technical result relevant when we consider whether the sign 'consists exclusively of the shape of goods which is necessary to achieve a technical result' for the purposes of Article 3(1)(e)(ii)? What is the appropriate test for determining when the restriction applies?

5.759

(a) *The Opinion of Advocate General Ruiz-Jarabo Colomer*

As has already been mentioned above, the analysis of AG Ruiz-Jarabo Colomer was influenced by the finding of the national court that the contested trade mark was nothing more than 'a combination of technical features produced to achieve a good practical design'.[629] As a result, he focused on Article 3(1)(e)(ii), which he considered to be primarily relevant to the outcome of the case because it could raise an obstacle that would have to be surmounted before even considering distinctiveness.

5.760

(i) **The legal nature and scope of Article 3(1)(e)** Article 3(1)(e) possessed a distinct legal nature. The exclusion was not linked with distinctiveness; it reflected 'the legitimate concern to prevent individuals from resorting to trade marks in order to extend exclusive rights over technical developments'.[630] This is why the Article 3(3) route was not available:

5.761

> 'Natural, functional or ornamental shapes are incapable, by express intention of the legislature, of acquiring a distinctive character. It is altogether otiose—as well as contrary to the scheme of the Directive—to consider whether or not such shapes have acquired distinctiveness'.[631]

In terms of scope, Article 3(1)(e) was closer to Article 3(1)(f) on signs that were contrary to public policy and Article 3(1)(g) on deceptive signs. All these provisions were not affected by any findings regarding distinctiveness. He therefore considered first and in detail the fourth question submitted by the English court.

(ii) **The relevance of alternatives: Trade marks, patents, and designs** From a literal perspective, there was nothing in Article 3(1)(e) that could suggest that a 'merely functional shape'[632] could be registered if there was, in terms of result, an alternative shape. 'It suffices that the signs of which the trade mark consists should comprise exclusively features which are necessary in order to achieve a particular technical result.'[633] From a teleological perspective, the scope of the provision was to prevent trade mark rights from extending the effect of other intellectual property rights that the legislator has chosen to protect for limited periods of time.[634]

5.762

---

[628] C-299/99 *Koninklijke Philips Electronics NV v Remington Consumer Products Ltd* [2002] ECR I-5475.
[629] Point 10; see paragraphs 5.289 et seq above.
[630] Point 16.
[631] Point 17.
[632] Point 28.
[633] Point 28.
[634] Point 31.

5.763 Further, a comparison between the functionality provisions of the Community regimes on designs and trade marks showed that the level of functionality required had to be higher in the context of design rights, where the existence of alternative designs would be taken into account. On the other hand. 'in so far as the essential features of a shape are necessary in order to fulfil a function, trade mark protection must not be granted without investigating whether that function could also be achieved by other features'.[635] Design rights protect the product; trade marks protect the identity of the origin of the product.

5.764 Accepting that alternatives should be taken into account would raise a number of problems. First, it would be possible for a single undertaking to register all the alternatives. Second, trade mark courts would have to examine whether all the alternatives were equivalent. Third, there would be a risk—however slight—'that trade mark rights might unduly encroach on the field of patents' and he could not 'see why the public interest should tolerate such a risk, since there are other effective ways available to owners of a product to protect their commercial asset, such as adding arbitrary features'.[636] Note here that the Advocate General appeared to accept that an arbitrary feature would be required in order to obtain trade mark protection for the shape of a product.

(b) The Judgment of the Court

5.765 The Court's answer to the fourth question contributed the first building blocks towards a European theory of functionality.

5.766 **(i) Article 3(1)(e): The legal framework; a preliminary obstacle** Contextualizing the provision against its legal framework, the Court first noted that the grounds for refusal in Article 3(1)(e) targeted a particular type of signs, those consisting of the shape of the specified product. According to the Seventh Recital in the Preamble to the Directive, these grounds have been listed in an exhaustive manner. A sign failing Article 3(1)(e) would never acquire distinctive character according to Article 3(3). This meant that Article 3(1)(e) was a preliminary obstacle concerning signs that were not 'such as to constitute trade marks'.[637]

5.767 **(ii) Article 3(1)(e): The public interest** The provision, according to the Court, had to be interpreted according to its underlying public interest to prevent the monopolization through trade mark law of technical solutions or functional characteristics that a user is likely to seek. It was intended to prevent trade mark protection from being extended beyond signs which served to distinguish a product or service from those offered by competitors: 'so as to form an obstacle preventing competitors from freely offering for sale products incorporating such technical solutions or functional characteristics in competition with the proprietor of the trade mark'.[638]

5.768 **(iii) The aim of Article 3(1)(e)(ii)** The aim of Article 3(1)(e)(ii) in particular was to

> preclude the registration of shapes whose essential characteristics perform a technical function, with the result that the exclusivity inherent in the trade mark right would limit the possibility of competitors supplying a product incorporating such a function or at least limit

---

[635] Point 35.
[636] Point 40.
[637] *Philips* (n 628) paragraph 76.
[638] Paragraph 78.

their freedom of choice in regard to the technical solution they wish to adopt in order to incorporate such a function in their product.[639]

5.769 (iv) **The relevance of alternatives**   To respond to Philips' claim that the existence of alternatives should be taken into account, the Court looked at the wording of the provision and ruled that there was nothing there to support it. 'Where the essential functional characteristics of the shape of a product are attributable solely to the technical result, Article 3(1)(e), second indent, precludes registration of a sign consisting of that shape, even if that technical result can be achieved by other shapes.'[640]

(2) *Lego*: Revisiting Functionality

(a) *The background to the dispute*

5.770 *Lego*[641] was an opportunity to revisit the concept of functionality, focusing in particular on the scope of Article 7(1)(e)(ii) of the Regulation. Lego (more accurately Kirkbi, its predecessor in title) had obtained in 1996 a Community trade mark registration of its toy brick (a three-dimensional sign in red) for 'games and playthings' in Class 28. Ritvik, the predecessor of Mega Brands, attacked the registration to the extent it covered 'construction toys'.

5.771 The Cancellation Division declared the mark invalid on the basis of Article 7(1)(e)(ii) of the Regulation, having found that each of the elements of the brick (the existence of the studs, their symmetrical positioning, size, and cylindrical form, their height in relation to the walls of the brick, the way the sides could connect to produce a wall, the hollow skirt that enabled fixing, and the overall shape and size of the brick) and thus the brick as a whole was necessary to obtain a technical result. Subsequently, the Board of Appeal (sitting for the first time as a Grand Board) upheld the decision having itself found that: (i) surveys were irrelevant for the application of that provision; (ii) a minor arbitrary element such as colour should not allow the sign to escape the application of the provision; and (iii) an earlier patent would not by itself bar registration but constituted irrefutable evidence that the features covered by the patent were functional.

5.772 The challenge before the General Court focused first on the relevance of functionally equivalent alternative shapes using the same technical solution. It upheld the decision of the Grand Board noting that:

(i) 'exclusively' was linked with 'essential characteristics which perform a technical function', thus the addition of non-essential characteristics having no technical function did not prevent the application of Article 7(1)(e)(ii) if all the essential characteristics of that shape performed such a function;
(ii) 'necessary to obtain a technical result' did not narrow the scope of the provision to cases where only the contested shape could achieve the intended result; it was sufficient that its essential characteristics combined the characteristics that were technically

---

[639] Paragraph 79.
[640] Paragraph 83.
[641] C-48/09 P *Lego Juris A/S v Office for Harmonisation in the Internal Market (Trade Marks and Designs) (OHIM)* [2010] ECR I-08403; T-270/06 *Lego Juris A/S v Office for Harmonisation in the Internal Market (Trade Marks and Designs) (OHIM) (Mega Brands)* [2008] ECR II-3117; R-856/2004-G *Lego Juris A/S v Mega Brands Inc* [2007] ETMR 11.

causal of, and sufficient to obtain, the intended technical result, and were therefore attributable to the technical result;

(iii) no distinction should be made between shapes using another 'technical solution' and shapes using the same ' technical solution'. Lego also challenged the concept of what constituted an essential characteristic and the assessment of functional nature.

5.773 The General Court also held that:

(iv) the perception of the targeted consumer audience was not relevant to the assessment of functionality; what constituted an essential characteristic had to be determined objectively, on the basis of the trade mark's graphic representation and any descriptions filed at the time of the application; and

(v) the Board had the power to consider the invisible features of the brick and take into account any other evidence, including expert opinions and prior patent specifications and claims.

5.774 Before the Court, Lego argued that: Article 7(1)(e)(ii) covered shapes that would create a monopoly on technical solutions or on functional characteristics; 'essential characteristics' should be interpreted as synonymous with 'dominant and distinctive elements'; the identification of those characteristics should be carried out from the perspective of the relevant public; and the assessment of functionality should be made by comparing the relevant characteristics with alternatives.

(b) The Opinion of the Advocate General: Ruiz Jarabo Colomer and Mengozzi

5.775 From a human perspective, *Lego* was marked by the loss of Advocate General Dámaso Ruiz-Jarabo Colomer, a towering, eloquent, figure in the development of the Court's trade mark jurisprudence; he passed away on 11 November 2009, the day following the hearing in *Lego*. His seat in this case was taken by Advocate General Mengozzi and the published Opinion was attributed to both.

5.776 The Opinion viewed trade mark rights as part of an intellectual property arsenal, access to which should be regulated. The provision should be contextualized against its own legislative framework, but also embedded against the framework of other intellectual property rights combined with competition considerations. It stressed that Article 7(1)(e)(ii) had a dual role: both preventing a monopoly on technical solutions through trade mark law and 'keeping separate trade-mark protection and the protection conferred by other forms of intellectual property'.[642]

5.777 It openly took into account doctrines developed by non-European courts and wished the Court could follow a more doctrinal approach, maintaining a distance from the factual context of each case. Criticizing the approach in *Philips* (a case in which Ruiz-Jarabo Colomer was in the Advocate General role), it noted that there the Court had 'emphasised the grounds on which it was appropriate to *refuse* registration of a mark having those characteristics, but it scarcely set out for undertakings the guidelines for *registering* functional signs as trade marks … the Court … left [the door] ajar … and this appeal must determine the size of the gap'.[643] *Philips*, according to the Opinion, had introduced an element of

---

[642] Point 55.
[643] Point 51.

vagueness that could be resolved by introducing a three-step test for the application of Article 7(1)(e)(ii).

5.778 The first step involved the identification of the most important elements of the shape, with each of the individual features of the get-up being analysed in turn, followed by an assessment of a necessary connection between those characteristics and the technical result that also had to be defined properly. The functionality of each element had to be determined separately, but there should be a presumption in respect of goods that had benefited from patent or design protection that their essential characteristics performed a technical function.[644] If all the essential characteristics of the shape performed a technical function, the shape itself was functional.

5.779 If not, at the second step the Court should choose between two alternative pathways. The first restricted the trade mark right to the essential and distinctive non-functional elements. The second had to 'compare the other compatible market options',[645] subject to the requirement that any industrial property right granted should not lead to a significant non-reputation related disadvantage for competitors vis-à-vis their own signs. Alternatives had to be analysed, taking into account interoperability and the requirement of availability that represents the public interest behind Article 7(1)(e)(ii).

5.780 The assessment of distinctiveness was the third step, and here the overall impression conveyed by the sign, the perspective of the consumer, and the goods or services included in the specification regained their relevance.

5.781 The Opinion also rejected the distinction between technical solution and technical result and, focusing again on the availability requirement, added that functional shapes should be freely used by all; the existence of alternatives was irrelevant for assessing functionality. Finally, it stressed that the rationale behind Article 7(1)(e) is distinct from the essential function of the trade mark and the applicability of the provision had to be ascertained objectively rather than from the perspective of the average consumer.

(c) The Judgment of the Court of Justice

5.782 (i) **The public interest** The Court, accepting the competition and availability issues developed in the Opinion, repeated that the public interest underlying Article 7(1)(e)(ii) was to prevent trade mark law from granting a monopoly on technical solutions or functional characteristics of a product: 'In that connection, the rules laid down by the legislature reflect the balancing of two considerations, both of which are likely to help establish a healthy and fair system of competition.'[646] It viewed trade mark rights as part of a scheme, a system, of rights; accordingly, it had to ensure they were not used 'in order to perpetuate, indefinitely, exclusive rights relating to technical solutions'.[647] Focusing on patents it highlighted that the technical solutions they covered in the European system of rights were protected for a limited period; following their expiration they should become

---

[644] Citing *TrafFix Devices, Inc v Marketing Displays, Inc*, 532 US 23 (2001).
[645] Point 74.
[646] Paragraph 44.
[647] Paragraph 45.

5.783 **(ii) The scope of the provision** Accordingly, first, the provisions of Article 7(1)(e) were strictly set and should be interpreted as precluding from registration even signs that have acquired distinctiveness as a result of use.

5.784 Second, the terms 'exclusively' and 'necessary' ensured that only shapes of goods that incorporate a technical solution, and whose registration as a trade mark would therefore actually impede the use of that technical solution by other undertakings, are not to be registered. In principle, a shape cannot be refused registration when it incorporates a major non-functional element. However:

> [T]he presence of one or more minor arbitrary elements in a three-dimensional sign, all of whose essential characteristics are dictated by the technical solution to which that sign gives effect, does not alter the conclusion that the sign consists exclusively of the shape of goods which is necessary to obtain a technical result.[648]

5.785 Also, 'necessary to obtain the technical result' did not mean that the shape at issue must be the only one capable of obtaining that result. There might be alternative shapes, but in itself that should not imply that registering the shape as a trade mark would have no effect on the availability of the technical solution. After all, trade mark protection covered both identical and similar shapes; the scope of protection had the potential to encompass a significant number of alternative shapes:

> A sign consisting of the shape of a product that, without the inclusion of significant non-functional elements, merely performs a technical function cannot be registered as a trade mark. Such a registration would unduly impair the opportunity for competitors to place on the market goods whose shapes incorporate the same technical solution.[649]

5.786 This applied *a fortiori* in a case like *Lego*, where it had been established that the solution incorporated in the contested shape was the technically preferable solution. Otherwise it would be difficult for competitors to come up with shapes constituting a real alternative: ie not similar shapes that must also be attractive from a functional perspective. The Court added, however, that protection against 'competitors placing on the market slavish copies of the product shape incorporating exactly the same solution ... can, where appropriate, be examined in the light of rules on unfair competition'.[650]

5.787 **(iii) The identification of essential characteristics** The Court agreed with the Opinion that the expression 'essential characteristics' had to be understood as referring to the most important elements of the sign but failed to provide concrete practical guidance. It indicated that identification must be carried out on a case-by-case basis, without a hierarchy that applies systematically between the elements of which a sign may consist, and accepting that the relevant authority might 'either base its assessment directly on the overall impression produced by the sign, or first examine in turn each of the components of the sign concerned'.[651]

---

[648] Paragraph 52.
[649] Paragraph 59.
[650] Paragraph 61.
[651] Paragraph 70.

Similarly, but at least stating that this would depend in particular on the degree of difficulty of each case, the identification may be carried out by means of a simple visual analysis or require a detailed examination, 'in which relevant criteria of assessment are taken into account, such as surveys or expert opinions, or data relating to intellectual property rights conferred previously in respect of the goods concerned'.[652]

5.788

(iv) Non-functional elements Once the essential characteristics had been identified, it was still necessary to ascertain whether they all performed the technical function of the goods at issue: 'Article 7(1)(e)(ii) ... cannot be applicable where the application for registration as a trade mark relates to a shape of goods in which a non-functional element, such as a decorative or imaginative element, plays an important role'.[653]

5.789

In that case, according to the Court, competitors would 'easily' have access to alternative shapes with equivalent functionality and 'there is no risk that the availability of the technical solution will be impaired'.[654] Against the particular factual context, the Court accepted the findings and reasoning of the Grand Board of Appeal and the General Court that, with the sole exception of its colour, all the other elements of the sign constituted by that brick were functional.

5.790

(v) Average consumer perception The Court re-confirmed the distinction between the assessment of distinctiveness on the one hand and functionality on the other. In the first case, the perception of the target public must be taken into account, though 'such an obligation cannot be imposed'[655] in the context of functionality.

5.791

> The presumed perception of the sign by the average consumer is not a decisive element when applying the ground for refusal under Article 7(1)(e)(ii) of Regulation No 40/94, but, at most, may be a relevant criterion of assessment for the competent authority when it identifies the essential characteristics of the sign.[656]

Responding to the last point raised by Lego, the Court held that for establishing functionality once the essential characteristics had been identified, it was necessary only to assess whether those characteristics perform the technical function of the product concerned: 'Clearly, that examination must be carried out by analysing the sign filed with a view to its registration as a trade mark, and not signs consisting of other shapes of goods.'[657] It added that documents relating to previous patents could be part of the evidence.

5.792

(d) An assessment of Lego

Lego re-establishes the clear principles set by the Court in *Philips*. It positions trade marks against a broader scheme of intellectual property rights and in a context of healthy and fair competition. The Court correctly avoids burdening trade mark authorities with competition questions and instead attempts to internalize competition issues within the public interest behind the specific functionality provisions. It also avoids taking a doctrinal stance on the trumping of trade mark rights by patent or design rights.

5.793

---

[652] Paragraph 71.
[653] Paragraph 72.
[654] Paragraph 72.
[655] Paragraph 75.
[656] Paragraph 76.
[657] Paragraph 84.

5.794 Also, despite the fact that the factual context is imperative in the application of trade mark law, the Court attempts to disentangle principles from facts. What it fails to do is provide a clear multifactor test for establishing functionality in an objective way; an example is its vagueness regarding the role of the target consumer in this process. However, this was a case that came before the Court in its capacity as the ultimate court of appeal rather as an interpretive court. Accordingly, it has to be read in the light of the contested decisions of the Grand Board of Appeal and the General Court.

5.795 From an interpretive perspective it appears that what will become critical in functionality cases is the identification of essential characteristics. It is most likely that future cases will focus on the determination of the essential characteristics of a shape, with applicants trying to argue that not all the essential characteristics are functional or that there is even a single essential characteristic that is non-functional and brings a shape outside the scope of the functionality provisions. Would a disclaimer in respect of the functional elements support an application for registration? At a national level the relationship and balancing between protection against unfair competition and registered trade mark protection in relation to 'slavish imitations' of functional get-up is expected to gain resonance.

(3) *Pi-Design*: A Broad Interpretation of Shapes

5.796 The appeals in *Pi-Design*[658] concerned the extent to which examining authorities can construe the scope of an application when confronted with signs the representation of which is open to more than one interpretation, and the degree of liberty they enjoy in establishing the essential elements of these signs and determining whether these elements are capable of performing a technical function.

(a) Background to the dispute

5.797 The case related to two applications for a declaration of invalidity directed against two Community trade mark registrations, consisting, respectively, of the representations of a triangular and a rectangular surface, covered by an identical pattern of black dots, and registered in respect of, among other things, cutlery, knives, and kitchen utensils. When taking into account the designated goods, the signs could be seen as depicting the outlines of knife handles. The grounds for invalidity were, inter alia, those set out in Article 51(1)(a) in conjunction with Article 7(1)(e)(ii) of the Regulation.

5.798 The Cancellation Division rejected the applications. On appeal, the First Board of Appeal annulled the decisions of the Cancellation Division and upheld the invalidity requests in their entirety.

5.799 The Board noted that even though the signs were simply classified as 'figurative', and no further description was provided, the owner had admitted in the course of the administrative proceedings that the sign at issue was a two-dimensional representation of the 'shape of a product', namely the handle of a knife. Moreover, a number of photographs of the products marketed by the proprietor confirmed that the frame surrounding the black dots represented the outline of a knife handle and that those dots represented dents. The Board decided that it was legitimate to take that information into account, considering that 'a

---

[658] Joined cases C-337/12 P to C-340/12 P *Pi-Design AG and Others/Yoshida Metal Industry Co Ltd and Others*, ECLI:EU:C:2014:129.

trade mark must be examined in accordance with the circumstances of the case' and that 'among these circumstances are, of course, the information and the documents voluntarily submitted by the trade mark owner in support of its application'. The Board went on to consider whether the black dots representing dents performed a technical function. Based on information relating to existing patents, it concluded that the dents were necessary to obtain a non-skid effect and that the fact that the same result could be obtained by other shapes did not preclude the application of the ground for refusal in question.

5.800 The proprietor brought applications for annulment. The General Court[659] upheld the actions, taking a narrow approach as regards its powers to reinterpret the sign as registered. After observing that 'the concave character of the black dots is not part of the trade mark as registered, [as] there is nothing in the graphic representation to suggest that the dots in question represent dents rather than a figurative pattern' and that 'in concluding that the dots were concave in character, the Board did not refer to the sign as filed, but to the goods actually marketed by the applicant', it took the view that 'only the shape as reproduced in the application may be the subject-matter of the examination of the mark'. Accordingly, it saw no reason to consider whether the shape at issue performed a technical function.[660]

(b) The Judgment of the Court

5.801 The case reached the Court of Justice. Referring to the principles set out in *Sieckmann*[661] as regards the requirement of graphic representability, the Court recalled, first, that the graphic representation of a mark must be self-contained, easily accessible, and intelligible, so that the sign may always be perceived unambiguously and, second, that the purpose of that requirement is, in particular, to define the mark itself in order to determine the precise subject matter of the protection afforded by the registration. It noted, nevertheless, that, from a policy perspective, the conditions which must be satisfied by the graphic representation within the meaning of Article 4 of the Regulation cannot restrict the competent authority's examination under Article 7(1)(e)(ii) in such a way as might undermine the public interest underlying the latter provision.[662]

5.802 The Court also recalled that in *Lego*[663] it had occasion to make clear that a correct application of Article 7(1)(e)(ii) requires that the essential characteristics of a sign be properly identified, and that this identification must be carried out on a case-by-case basis, there being no hierarchy that applies systematically between the various types of elements of which a sign may consist. Moreover, it noted that *Lego* laid down an open-ended test, by accepting that such identification may, depending also on the degree of complexity of the sign, be carried out by means of a simple visual analysis or, on the contrary, be based on a detailed examination in which material relevant to the assessment is taken into account, such as surveys or expert opinions, or data relating to intellectual property rights conferred previously in respect of the goods concerned.[664]

---

[659] T-331/10 *Yoshida Metal Industry v OHIM—Pi-Design and Others* (Representation of a triangular surface with black dots), ECLI:EU:T:2012:220 and T-416/10 *Yoshida Metal Industry v OHIM—Pi-Design and Others* (Representation of a surface with black dots), ECLI:EU:T:2012:222.
[660] Paragraphs 22–31 of the Judgment of the General Court.
[661] Case C-273/00 *Sieckmann* [2002] ECR I-11737, paragraphs 48–52.
[662] Paragraphs 57–58.
[663] Case C-48/09 P *Lego Juris v OHIM* [2010] ECR I-8403, paragraphs 68–71.
[664] Paragraphs 46–48.

5.803 Thus, the Court concluded that *Lego* clearly empowered the competent authority to take into account any material allowing it to properly identify the characteristics of a sign, in addition to the representation and any descriptions filed by the owner, and that the General Court could not hold, without erring in law, that the relevant provisions precluded it from taking into consideration the circumstances relating to the actual use of the mark.[665]

(c) Repercussions

5.804 Although the permissiveness of the Court's approach seems to be specifically linked to the public interest underlying Article 7(1)(e)(ii) of the Regulation and to finding its justification in the liberty conferred by the case law on examining authorities to conduct a thorough examination in order to identify the essential characteristics of a shape, there is no reason precluding the application of the same principles to the examination of other grounds for refusal as well.

5.805 Indeed, despite the need for the representation to be unequivocal and self-contained, it will often be the case that the exact way in which a sign may be affixed on the goods and function in practice becomes fully apparent only after considering the specific context, as determined by the goods, the norms of the relevant market sector, and the commercial practices of the proprietor, especially when the sign as registered is open to a variety of practical applications (for instance, in the case at issue the dots could equally stand for a flat decorative motif, for concave dents, or for protruding bulges).

5.806 Considering also that the various forms of public interest underlying the grounds of refusal laid down in Article 7 require that the sign be able to perform its essential function in a meaningful way, the gap between a rather abstract representation and real life can only be bridged by allowing examining authorities some margin of interpretation, at least when public policy considerations so dictate. This is all the more necessary, considering that in the Community trade mark system the submission of an accompanying description is not compulsory and that even where such a description is filed it cannot override the contents of the representation.

5.807 However, the possibility of having recourse to extraneous considerations, whether in the context of functionality or other grounds for refusal, should not be carried too far, for obvious reasons of legal certainty. Hence, even though it may be permissible to take such circumstances into account where the representation of the sign may be interpreted in more than one way, these considerations must not depart from the sign as registered, for example, by extending to elements not visible in the representation or to functions not caused by the shape as depicted, as the General Court had the opportunity to underline on a number of occasions.[666]

(4) *Benetton*: **Attractiveness v Distinctiveness**

5.808 *Benetton*[667] was the first case in which the Court dealt with 'aesthetic' functionality, albeit in a very limited context. The question referred to it did not require a full-scale interpretation of Article 3(1)(e)(iii) of the Directive, concerning rather the fine distinction between

---

[665] Paragraphs 54 and 60–61.
[666] See in particular T-270/06 *Lego* [2008] ECR II-03117, paragraphs 73–76 and the case law cited.
[667] C-371/06 *Benetton Group SpA/G-Star International BV* (BENETTON) [2007] ECR I-7709.

(a) The facts in the main proceedings

The reference concerned a dispute in The Netherlands between G-Star International BV **5.809** (G-Star), a designer and manufacturer of clothing (in particular jeans), who markets its products under the homonymous trade mark, and Benetton Group SpA (Benetton) a company managing textile trading undertakings and selling its products through franchisees. G-Star was the proprietor of two shape marks registered in the Benelux in respect of clothing in Class 25 of the Nice Classification. Those marks covered in particular the following distinctive elements of the product's appearance (the so-called Elwood design):

– sloping stitching from hip height to the crotch seam, kneepads, yoke on the seat of the trousers, horizontal stitching at knee height at the rear, band of a contrasting colour or of another material at the bottom of the trousers at the rear, all on one garment;
– seams, stitching, and cuts on the kneepad of the trousers, slightly baggy kneepad.

G-Star brought an action against Benetton before the Rechtbank te Amsterdam (Amsterdam **5.810** District Court) in order to preclude the manufacture and distribution in The Netherlands of a specific design of the latter's trousers. G-Star maintained that Benetton had infringed the trade mark rights attached to its Elwood design by manufacturing and putting on the market trousers with, inter alia, an oval kneepad and two lines of sloping stitching from hip height to crotch height. Benetton responded by bringing a counterclaim, seeking the annulment of G-Star's trade marks under Benelux law, on the ground that the registered shapes 'determined the market value of the goods to a great extent' as a result of their beauty and originality.

The first instance court dismissed both G-Star's claims and Benetton's counterclaim. Both **5.811** parties lodged appeals before the Gerechtshof te Amsterdam (Amsterdam Regional Court of Appeal), which allowed G-Star's appeal and dismissed Benetton's application for annulment. The Gerechtshof found that the Elwood trousers were a great commercial success mainly owing to G-Star's intensive advertising campaigns, which drew particular attention to the trousers' distinctive characteristics and kneepad design. Accordingly, it held that the reputation of the Elwood trousers was largely attributable not to the aesthetic qualities of the shape as such, but rather to the attractiveness resulting from the recognition of that shape as a trade mark.

Benetton lodged an appeal before the Hoge Raad der Nederlanden (Supreme Court of the **5.812** Netherlands) challenging that analysis. The Roge Raad took the view that the Court's finding in *Philips* that signs which cannot be registered under Article 3(1)(e) of the Directive cannot acquire a distinctive character through use did not cover the situation where, prior to the application for registration, the attractiveness of the shape was a consequence of its recognition as a trade mark. Accordingly, it decided to stay the proceedings and refer the following questions to the Court of Justice:

(1) Must Article 3(1)(e), third indent, [of the Directive] be interpreted as meaning that the prohibition contained therein permanently precludes the registration of a shape as a trade mark where the nature of the product is such that its appearance and shaping determine its market value entirely or substantially as a result of their beauty or original character, or does the prohibition not apply where, prior to the application for

registration, the attractiveness of the relevant shape to the public has been determined predominantly by the recognition of it as a distinctive sign?

(2) If the answer to Question 1 is to the latter effect to what extent must this attractiveness have prevailed for the prohibition no longer to apply?

(b) The Judgment of the Court

5.813 The Court found it appropriate to proceed to judgment without an opinion from its Advocate General.

5.814 With regard to the first question, it took the view that the national court essentially asked whether a shape that gives substantial value to a product can nevertheless constitute a trade mark under Article 3(3) of the Directive where, prior to the application for registration, it acquired 'attractiveness' as a result of its recognition as a distinctive sign. The Court therefore considered that the question actually involved a sign which *initially* consisted of a shape giving substantial value to the product and which, *subsequently* and prior to application for registration, acquired recognition through advertising, that is to say on account of the promotional use made of it.[668]

5.815 Thus, the Court held that, contrary to the perception of the Hoge Raad, the shape in question fell squarely under the *Philips* principles that if a sign is caught by Article 3(1)(e), it can no longer be registered by virtue of Article 3(3) of the Directive, and that Article 3(1)(e) should accordingly be regarded as a 'preliminary obstacle' which cannot be overridden by the distinctiveness that sign may have acquired through use.[669]

5.816 The Court's answer therefore was that the third indent of Article 3(1)(e) of the Directive does not allow the shape which gives substantial value to a product to constitute a trade mark under Article 3(3) where, prior to its filing, that shape acquired attractiveness as a result of its recognition as a distinctive sign following advertising campaigns promoting the specific characteristics of the product in question; moreover, in view of that answer, it held that there was no need to address the second question.[670]

5.817 It is worth noting that the national court considered that the promotion of the shape increased not only its distinctiveness, but also its 'attractiveness'. In practice, that meant that, when the shape was applied for as a trade mark, its economic value was not exclusively or substantially due to its aesthetic features, but also to the extra 'appeal' and 'reputation' it had acquired through use. However, the Court was not impressed by that argument. It stressed that if the appearance of the shape is inherently so attractive as to determine the value of the goods to a substantial extent, it is immaterial whether subsequently more value was added to that sign through promotion and advertising. In other words, it was irrelevant whether the use of the sign further increased an already substantial aesthetic value.

5.818 By taking that view, the Court effectively precluded considerations linked to the acquired distinctiveness of the sign to be reintroduced in the analysis of functionality through the back door, by consistently holding that whatever consequences the use of the sign may have on its attractive or distinctive value, these can be taken into account only in the context of

---

[668] Paragraph 22.
[669] Paragraphs 26–27.
[670] Paragraphs 28–29.

Article 3(3) of the Directive and not when assessing the 'preliminary obstacle' of aesthetic functionality. However, that also means that if the value of the shape is principally attributable not to its aesthetic features, but rather on the appeal resulting from its reputation as a 'famous' shape, the shape is not caught by the prohibition of the third indent of Article 3(1)(e) of the Directive.

(5) *Hauck*: The 'Nature' of the Goods; 'Substantive Value'

(a) The background to the dispute

5.819 The first and third part of the provision were tested in *Hauck*.[671] The case came before the Court following a challenge to the validity of a Benelux trade mark consisting of the shape of a children's chair marketed by Stokke since 1972, that reached the Hoge Raad der Nederlanden, the Supreme Court of the Netherlands. The design of the chair according to the referring court had been highly praised and displayed in museums. In 1998 Stokke registered the design as a trade mark for 'chairs, especially high chairs for children'. The validity of the trade mark was challenged during infringement proceedings against a competitor marketing a similar chair.

5.820 The referring court sent the following questions to the Court:

1. (a) Does the ground for refusal or invalidity in [the first indent of] Article 3(1)(e) of [the Trade Marks Directive], namely that [three-dimensional] trade marks may not consist exclusively of a shape which results from the nature of the goods themselves, refer to a shape which is indispensable to the function of the goods, or can it also refer to the presence of one or more substantial functional characteristics of goods which consumers may possibly looks for in the goods of competitors?
(b) If neither of those alternatives is correct, how should the provision then be interpreted?
2. (a) Does the ground for refusal or invalidity in [the third indent of] Article 3(1)(e) [of the Trade Marks Directive], namely, that [three-dimensional] trade marks may not consist exclusively of a shape which gives substantial value to the goods, refer to the motive (or motives) underlying the relevant public's decision to purchase?
(b) Does a 'shape which gives substantial value to the goods' within the meaning of the aforementioned provision exist only if that shape must be considered to constitute the main or predominant value in comparison with other values (such as, in the case of high chairs for children, safety, comfort and reliability) or can it also exist if, in addition to that value, other values of the goods exist which are also to be considered substantial?
(c) For the purpose of answering Questions 2(a) and 2(b), is the opinion of the majority of the relevant public decisive, or may the court rule that the opinion of a portion of the public is sufficient in order to take the view that the value concerned is 'substantial' within the meaning of the aforementioned provision?
(d) If the latter option provides the answer to Question 2(c), what requirement should be imposed as to the size of the relevant portion of the public?
3. Should Article 3(1)(e) of [the Trade Marks Directive] be interpreted as meaning that the ground for exclusion referred to in subparagraph (e) of that article also exists if the [three-dimensional] trade mark consists of a sign to which the content of [the first indent] applies and which, for the rest, satisfies the content of [the third indent]?

---

[671] Case C-205/13, *Hauck GmbH & Co. KG v Stokke A/S, Stokke Nederland BV, Peter Opsvik, Peter Opsvik A/S*, ECLI:EU:C:2014:2233.

(b) The Opinion of Advocate General Szpunar

5.821 Advocate General Szpunar started his analysis by referring to the historical context: '[T]he issue of trade marks which are a reflection of the goods themselves is not new in intellectual property law … in 1858 protection was conferred by a trade mark which was the shape of a chocolate bar.'[672] Turning to the jurisprudential context, he suggested that there was the same public policy underlying Article 3(1)(c) and the three indents of Article 3(1)(e), and that they sought to

> prevent a situation where registration of a trade mark would result in the grant of a monopoly on technical solutions or functional characteristics of a product which a user is likely to seek in the products of competitors. That provision prevents the protection conferred by the trade mark right from forming an obstacle preventing competitors from freely offering for sale products incorporating such technical solutions or functional characteristics.[673]

5.822 This was linked with the 'axiological grounds for the right to trade mark protection'.[674] Following an eloquent discussion of the nature and function of a trade mark—in essence a tool for redressing the informational imbalance between marketers and consumers—against the broader context of other intellectual property rights promoting innovation and creativity, this required a balancing exercise aimed at 'a balance which is struck between the public interest in protecting innovation and creativity, on the one hand, and the economic interest based on the possibility of exploiting the intellectual achievements of other persons to promote future socio-economic development, on the other'.[675] The purpose of Article 3(1)(e) was to address this balance:

> Those criteria, which are contained in Article 3(1)(e) of Directive 89/104, therefore prevent a trade mark right from being exercised for a purpose which is incompatible with it. They serve to protect fair competition by making it impossible to monopolise the basic characteristics of a product which are essential from the point of view of effective competition on the market concerned. In particular, they also serve to maintain the balance of interests which the legislature established by placing a time-limit on the protection conferred by certain other intellectual property rights.[676]

5.823 *(i) The nature of the goods themselves* According to the above broader interpretive guidelines, the Advocate General submitted that 'the first indent of Article 3(1)(e) precludes registration of a shape all of whose essential characteristics result from the nature of the goods concerned and which are therefore determined by the practical function which those goods perform'.[677]

5.824 Distinguishing the first from the second indent that focused on technical effect, he noted that:

> the first indent of Article 3(1)(e) of Directive 89/104 clearly precludes the registration of shapes whose essential characteristics result from the function of the goods concerned. This relates, for example, to legs with a horizontal level in relation to a chair, or an orthopaedic shaped sole with a V-shaped strap in relation to flip-flops. However, that provision may also be of great relevance in considering the registrability of trade marks consisting of the shapes of more complex products, such as the shape of the sailing boat hull or aircraft propeller.[678]

---

[672] Point 1.
[673] Point 28, citing *Windsurfing Chiemsee* (n 1) paragraph 25 and *Philips*, (n 628) paragraphs 78 and 79.
[674] Point 29.
[675] Point 36.
[676] Point 39.
[677] Point 55.
[678] Point 59.

Taking also into account the fact that trade mark protection would cover both identical and **5.825** similar shapes, he stressed that the provision should also cover shapes whose fundamental characteristics were determined exclusively by the practical function of the product concerned. He agreed with the view that the ground covers:

> in relation to all goods—the most accepted shape which most closely expresses the nature of the goods. This concerns signs which are typical of a particular semantic category, in other words, signs which relate to consumers' ideas of the essential characteristics of the goods concerned. The prohibition on registration applies only to the generic features of the product concerned which result from its function. However, the prohibition does not apply to the peculiar features of the product concerned or those which result from the specific use of that product.[679]

Concluding, he suggested that the first indent 'relates to a shape all of whose essential char- **5.826** acteristics result from the nature of the product concerned and the fact that that product can also take a different, alternative shape is irrelevant in that respect'.[680]

(ii) A shape that gives substantial value He accepted from the outset that the third in- **5.827** dent of Article 3(1)(e) had not been clearly worded. He believed that the provision went further than a simple delineation between distinct intellectual property rights:

> [T]he ground contained in the third indent of Article 3(1)(e) is designed to prevent the monopolisation of the external features of goods which do not perform a technical or practical function and at the same time substantially enhance the attractiveness of goods and strongly influence consumer preferences.[681]

The provision went further than categories of goods that were bought because of their aesthetic design, such as jewellery, for example, and extended to 'goods which are not generally regarded as objects which perform a decorative function but in relation to which the aesthetics of the shape play an essential role in a certain limited segment of the market, such as in the case of designer furniture, for example'.[682] After all, most products performed multiple functions.

Distinguishing between distinctiveness on the one hand and descriptiveness and function- **5.828** ality on the other, he submitted that account

> must be taken both of the perception of the sign by the consumers of the goods and the economic effects which will result from reserving the sign concerned to a single undertaking. In other words, it is necessary to consider whether or not registration of the sign will have a negative impact on the placing of competing goods on the market.[683]

The perception of the average consumer for that product market was one of the approaches that had to be taken into account. Other considerations involved:

> the nature of the category of goods under consideration, the artistic value of the shape concerned, its dissimilarity from other shapes in common use on the market concerned, a

---

[679] Point 48, citing H Fezer, 'MarkenG § 3', in H Fezer (ed), *Markenrecht*, 4th edition (Munich, Verlag C.H. Beck, 2009) paragraph 663; G Eisenführ, 'Art 7' in G Eisenführ, D Schennen (eds), *Gemeinschaftsmarkenverordnung*, 3rd edition (Cologne, Wolters Kluwer, 2010) paragraph 197; and A Firth, E Gredley, and S Maniatis, 'Shapes as Trade Marks: Public Policy, Functional Considerations, and Consumer Perception', *European Intellectual Property Review* (2001) Vol 23, p 92.
[680] Point 65.
[681] Point 80.
[682] Point 83.
[683] Point 89.

substantial price difference in relation to other competing products with similar characteristics, and the development by the manufacturer of a promotion strategy emphasising principally the aesthetic characteristics of the goods concerned.[684]

5.829 **(iii) Single purpose: Independent and joint application of the first and third indent** Advocate General Szpunar viewed Article 3(1)(e) of Directive 89/104 as containing three alternative grounds, with each one of them precluding independently registration of the contested sign. Use of the term 'exclusively' favoured this approach from a literal interpretive perspective, but the teleological route pointed to the same direction: the provision served a 'single, general purpose. Each of the three grounds contained in the individual indents serves to prevent a situation where an exclusive right to a particular sign would result in the monopolisation of the essential features of a product which are reflected in its shape'.[685] Accordingly,

> Article 3(1)(e) of Directive 89/104 ... does not preclude a parallel assessment of the same circumstances to determine whether one or more of the grounds referred to in the individual indents obtains. A trade mark can be refused registration or declared invalid only if at least one of those grounds obtains in full.[686]

5.830 Still he added a final proviso:

> the joint application of the grounds contained in Article 3(1)(e) ... must be permitted in the case of signs which are perceived by consumers merely as a collection of different shapes. By that I mean signs which are a combination of several separate objects such as, for example, a sign reflecting the layout of a petrol station or the décor of a retail outlet ... and which do not therefore represent the shape of the goods but rather a physical reflection of the circumstances in which a service is provided.[687]

(c) The Judgment of the Court

5.831 **(i) The scope of the 'nature of the goods': An expansive approach** Looking at the first question, the Court described the immediate aim of the provision as 'to prevent the exclusive and permanent right which a trade mark confers from serving to extend indefinitely the life of other rights which the EU legislature has sought to make subject to limited periods'.[688] As a result, the Court accepted the view of the Advocate General that the first indent had to be interpreted in a way that is consistent with the aims of the other two indents.

5.832 With reference to *Lego*, it found that in order to apply the first indent

> 'it is necessary to identify the essential characteristics—that is, the most important elements—of the sign concerned on a case-by-case basis, that assessment being based either on the overall impression produced by the sign or on an examination of each [of] the components of that sign in turn.[689]

It would not be applicable where the application related 'to a shape of goods in which another element, such as a decorative or imaginative element, which is not inherent to the generic function of the goods, plays an important or essential role'.[690]

---

[684] Point 93.
[685] Point 101.
[686] Point 105.
[687] Point 107.
[688] Paragraph 19, citing *Lego* (n 649) above paragraph 45.
[689] Paragraph 21.
[690] Paragraph 22.

5.833 Otherwise, if the provision was interpreted as applying only to signs which consist exclusively of shapes which are indispensable to the function of the respective goods, it would only cover

> (i) 'natural' products (which have no substitute) and (ii) 'regulated' products (the shape of which is prescribed by legal standards), even though signs consisting of the shapes formed by such products could not be registered in any event because of their lack of distinctive character.[691]

Instead, the right approach would be for a 'shape which results from the nature of the goods themselves' to cover 'shapes with essential characteristics which are inherent to the generic function or functions of such goods'.[692]

5.834 Concluding, the response to the first question was that:

> the first indent of Article 3(1)(e) ... must be interpreted as meaning that the ground for refusal of registration set out in that provision may apply to a sign which consists exclusively of the shape of a product with one or more essential characteristics which are inherent to the generic function or functions of that product and which consumers may be looking for in the products of competitors.[693]

5.835 **(ii) The scope of 'substantial value': Moving towards aesthetic functionality; a multifactor test** The Court distilled the second question as essentially asking whether the third indent of Article 3(1)(e) covered a sign that consisted 'exclusively of the shape of a product with several characteristics each of which may give that product substantial value and if it is necessary to take the target public's perception of the shape of that product into account during that assessment'.[694] Contextualizing the question, the Court highlighted that according to the referring court the shape of the chair gave it significant aesthetic value but at the same time had other characteristics—safety, comfort, and reliability—that gave it essential functional value. The Court accepted that this is not contradictory.

5.836 **(iii) Artistic or ornamental value** Accordingly, substantial value considerations should not automatically be ruled out when, in addition to its aesthetic function, the product design performs other essential functions. Again looking at the antithetical argument, the Court stressed that we should not limit the scope of the third indent to cover product shapes with only artistic or ornamental value, because then products with essential functional characteristics as well as a significant aesthetic element would not be covered.[695] Looking at the same issue from a different aspect, the Court stressed that in *Lego* it had found that the

> presumed perception of the sign by the average consumer is not a decisive element when applying the ground for refusal set out in the third indent of the latter provision, but may, at most, be a relevant criterion of assessment for the competent authority in identifying the essential characteristics of that sign.[696]

5.837 **(iv) Additional factors** The Court agreed with the Advocate General that other assessment criteria should also be taken into account, including:

> the nature of the category of goods concerned, the artistic value of the shape in question, its dissimilarity from other shapes in common use on the market concerned, a substantial

---

[691] Paragraph 24.
[692] Paragraph 25.
[693] Paragraph 27.
[694] Paragraph 28.
[695] Paragraph 32.
[696] Paragraph 34.

price difference in relation to similar products, and the development of a promotion strategy which focuses on accentuating the aesthetic characteristics of the product in question.[697]

5.838 Concluding, the Court held that:

> the answer to the second question is that the third indent of Article 3(1)(e) of the trade marks directive must be interpreted as meaning that the ground for refusal of registration set out in that provision may apply to a sign which consists exclusively of the shape of a product with several characteristics each of which may give that product substantial value. The target public's perception of the shape of that product is only one of the assessment criteria which may be used to determine whether that ground for refusal is applicable.[698]

5.839 (v) *Article 3(1)(e): Three independent grounds*   The Court viewed the third question as essentially asking whether the first and third indents of Article (3)(1)(e) may be applied in combination. Focusing on the language—the use of the word 'exclusively'—and structure of the provision, the Court found that the three grounds operate independently of one another. The Court stressed that it is sufficient to refuse registration if 'any one of the criteria listed in Article 3(1)(e) of the trade marks directive is satisfied'.[699] It also agreed with the Advocate General that 'the public interest objective underlying the application of the three grounds for refusal of registration set out in Article 3(1)(e) . . . precludes refusal of registration where none of those three grounds is fully applicable.'[700]

(d) A first assessment of Hauck

5.840 *Hauck* is important for developing further the concept of functionality. The approach is pragmatic; looking at the nature of the goods concept, the Court appears to be setting a high but broad barrier for the application of the first indent of the provision, linking it with the concept of generics. Turning to essential value, the Court came up with a multifactor test. Finally, it settled that, although there is a single purpose behind the provision, each one of the three indents must be applied, in principle, independently from each other.

G. Article 3(1)(g): Trade Marks of a Deceptive Nature

(1) *Elizabeth Emanuel*: Trade Mark Assignments

5.841 *Emanuel*[701] is the first case where the Court considered the application of Article 3(l)(g). It is also evidence of how unfair competition and trade mark law are inextricably linked. Elizabeth Emanuel, a fashion designer, started using the trade name ELIZABETH EMANUEL in 1990. In 1996 she signed an agreement with Hamlet International Plc; in return for financial support she transferred to a co-owned company her business, together with its goodwill, and an application for a composite mark including her trade name. The mark was registered in 1997. Later in the same year, she assigned once again her business, together with its goodwill and the registered trade mark to another company, Frostprint Ltd, which became Elizabeth Emanuel International Ltd. Emanuel became an employee of that company, a relationship that lasted for only a month. Indeed, the management of the

---

[697] Paragraph 35.
[698] Paragraph 36.
[699] Paragraph 40, citing *Philips* (n 628) paragraph 76 and *Benetton Group* (n 667) paragraph 26.
[700] Paragraph 42.
[701] C-259/04 *Elizabeth Florence Emanuel v Continental Shelf 128 Ltd* [2006] ECR I-3089.

company instructed its employees to be circumspect when answering questions regarding Emanuel. The trade mark registration was assigned to another company which later applied for an amendment of the registration to a simpler version. Emanuel opposed the application and sought the revocation of the trade mark incorporating her name. By the time the joined cases reached the Appointed Person, on appeal, the trade mark registration had been transferred to yet another entity, Continental Shelf 128 Ltd.

The Appointed Person[702] referred a number of questions to the Court seeking in essence the clarification of the provisions relating to deceptive registrations. He highlighted that, prior to the assignment, the trade mark indicated to a significant proportion of the relevant public that a particular person was involved in the design or creation of the relevant goods and that, at the time of the application, after the assignment, a significant portion of the relevant public wrongly believed that use of the trade mark indicated that the particular person was still involved in the design or creation of the relevant goods, and this belief was likely to affect the purchasing behaviour of that part of the public:

1. Is a trade mark of such a nature as to deceive the public and prohibited from registration under Article 3(1)(g) [of Directive 89/104] in the following circumstances:
    (a) the goodwill associated with the trade mark has been assigned together with the business of making the goods to which the mark relates;
    (b) prior to the assignment the trade mark indicated to a significant proportion of the relevant public that a particular person was involved in the design or creation of the goods in relation to which it was used;
    (c) after the assignment an application was made by the assignee to register the trade mark; and
    (d) at the time of the application a significant portion of the relevant public wrongly believed that use of the trade mark indicated that the particular person was still involved in the design or creation of the goods in relation to which the mark was used, and this belief was likely to affect the purchasing behaviour of that part of the public?
2. If the answer to question 1 is not unreservedly yes, what other matters must be taken into consideration in assessing whether a trade mark is of such a nature as to deceive the public and prohibited from registration under Article 3(1)(g) [of Directive 89/104] and, in particular, is it relevant that the risk of deception is likely to diminish over time?
3. Is a registered trade mark liable to mislead the public in consequence of the use made of it by the proprietor or with his consent and so liable to revocation under Article 12(2)(b) [of Directive 89/104] in the following circumstances:
    (a) the registered trade mark and the goodwill associated with it have been assigned together with the business of making the goods to which the mark relates;
    (b) prior to the assignment the trade mark indicated to a significant proportion of the relevant public that a particular person was involved in the design or creation of the goods in relation to which it was used;
    (c) after the assignment an application was made to revoke the registered trade mark; and
    (d) at the time of the application a significant portion of the relevant public wrongly believed that use of the trade mark indicated that the particular person was still involved with the design or creation of the goods in relation to which the mark was used, and this belief was likely to affect the purchasing behaviour of that part of the public?
4. If the answer to question 3 is not unreservedly yes, what other matters must be taken into consideration in assessing whether a registered trade mark is liable to mislead the public

---

[702] David Kitchin QC, as he then was, *Elizabeth Emanuel Trade Mark* [2004] RPC 15.

in consequence of the use made of it by the proprietor or with his consent and so liable to revocation under Article 12(2)(b) [of Directive 89/104] and, in particular, is it relevant that the risk of deception is likely to diminish over time?[703]

(a) The Opinion of Advocate General Ruiz-Jarabo Colomer

5.843 **(i) Admissibility of the reference** Advocate General Ruiz-Jarabo Colomer started by considering an issue that had caused considerable debate in the corridors of English courts. Was the Appointed Person entitled to submit a reference? The affirmative answer was based on two lines of argument. The first related to the post itself: there was statutory provision for the post; there were only two appeal routes from the decisions of the Trade Mark Registry, one to the court and the other to the Appointed Person; and there were provisions ensuring its independence. The second focused on the nature of the proceedings before the Appointed Person: it applied legal rules, it conducted *inter partes* proceedings, and delivered judicial decisions, often acting at last instance.

5.844 **(ii) The commercialization of trade marks** To prepare the ground for answering the questions the Advocate General started with a general analysis of the nature of a registered trade mark as an object of commerce—that could be exploited on its own[704]—noting that trade mark rights could be transferred in a variety of ways together with other assets of an undertaking or on their own.

5.845 The Directive left the management of this area to Member States; the Regulation, however, provided for the independence of the Community trade mark from the entity behind the marked products.[705] In principle, transactions involving trade marks should be viewed from the same perspective as any other contract. 'The logical approach is to accept the consequences of an act of free disposal, provided that there are no grounds such as to justify recovery of what was disposed of.'[706]

5.846 **(iii) The functions of trade marks: Deceptive use** In order to develop what constituted deceptive use the Advocate General looked first at the functions of a trade mark and the purpose of trade mark rights. Citing his Opinion in *Robelco*,[707] he codified the jurisprudence of the Court as an attempt to ensure the integrity of a message. The specific purpose of trade mark rights was 'to safeguard the correctness of the information which the registered trade mark provides concerning the origin of certain property'.[708] Accordingly, deceptive use had to be determined in relation to use of the sign as an indicator of origin. Trade marks did serve other functions, but 'consideration of the concept of deception, as used in the provisions under review, must relate only to the abovementioned essential function'.[709] Regarding the type of sign in this case, the Advocate General had no doubt that, following

---

[703] Reproduced in paragraph 13.
[704] The AG used a Spanish civil law term, 'autonomy of intention', to express the idea that a trade mark constituted an entity that could be exploited on its own.
[705] Article 17; see also Article 21 of TRIPs.
[706] Point 39.
[707] C-23/01 *Robelco NV* [2002] ECR I-10913; the AG had revisited the same theme in C-206/01 *Arsenal Football Club plc* [2002] ECR I-10273.
[708] Point 43; amongst the 'tangential purposes' (point 44) the Court has recognized was that of an indication of quality in C-10/89 *SA CNL-SUCAL NV* [1990] ECR I-3711 and that of a vehicle for advertising in C-337/95 *Parfums Christian Dior SA* [1997] ECR I-6013.
[709] Point 46.

Nicholls,⁷¹⁰ personal names could function as trade marks and that the usual criteria of trade mark law should be applied.

(iv) The perspective for determining deception The Advocate General suggested that deception should be determined according to the standard of the average, reasonably well informed, and reasonably observant and circumspect consumer.⁷¹¹ There should not be a need for experts' reports and consumer research polls; instead, courts and trade mark authorities should exercise their own powers of assessment. 5.847

(v) Interpreting Article 3(1)(g) The meaning of 'deceive' was the critical issue in this case. There are three relevant factors that can be identified in the narrative of the Opinion. First, the mark had to confuse the public by virtue of its qualities, or its intrinsic characteristics as suggested in the intervention of the United Kingdom Government. Second, it had to contain incorrect information, which might prove deceptive. Third, deceptiveness should be determined 'from an objective point of view; in other words, in every reasonably imaginable case its use must give rise to such deception'.⁷¹² 5.848

(vi) The application of Article 3(1)(g) So, should a change in ownership of a trade mark comprising the name of its original owner be considered deceptive? The Advocate General suggested that the answer should be negative, using the above factors as a background rather than applying them directly. Instead, he relied on his earlier points on the commercialization of trade marks and personal names. 5.849

First, he stated that the legislature had made a clear choice in respect of the Community trade mark regime in that, as an entity, a Community trade mark could be transferred on its own, separately from the business behind it, and that the licensing provisions of the Directive pointed in the same direction. If it had been thought that consumers 'were completely remote and incapable of understanding the vicissitudes experienced by undertakings which affect, in particular, trade marks, like any other object of commerce',⁷¹³ transfers and licensing would be regulated in a more prescriptive way. However, he believed consumers knew that individuals bearing a trade marked name would not necessarily be involved in the production of products marketed under that trade mark. Second, there was no reason for granting additional protection to personal names since the Court had clearly indicated with its case law that personal names should be treated in the same way as any other sign under trade mark law. 5.850

Note that in his conclusion regarding the first question he chose to use the terminology of the question. The introduction of 'goodwill' limited the broad scope of his arguments: 5.851

> [T]he answer to the first preliminary question must be that a trade mark made up, at least in part, of a proper name, which has been transferred together with the goodwill of which it formed part, is not liable to deceive the public, within the meaning of Article 3(1)(g) . . . even

---

⁷¹⁰ C-404/02 *Nichols plc* [2004] ECR I-8499.
⁷¹¹ C-210/96 *Gut Springenheide and Tusky* [1998] ECR I-4657.
⁷¹² Point 57, referring to Bender, 'Absolute Eintragungshindernisse–Artikel 7' in Ekey and Klippel, *Markenrecht* (Heidelberg, 2003) p 912; E Gastinel, 'La marque communautaire' (L.G.D.J., Paris, 1998) pp 88–89; and the ORLWOOLA (deceptively suggesting that the product was made of wool) case from the UK as an example of deceptive use: *Joseph Crosfield & Son Ltd's Application ('Perfection')* [1910] 1 Ch 130.
⁷¹³ Point 62.

though it may give the mistaken impression that that person is involved in the design and manufacture of the goods'.⁷¹⁴

Would the answer differ if the transfer was made without the goodwill of the business?

5.852 (vii) **Interpreting Article 12(2)(b)** The remaining questions necessitated the interpretation of Article 12(2)(b).⁷¹⁵ The Advocate General cited *Gorgonzola*,⁷¹⁶ where the court 'opted ... for a restrictive interpretation of revocation, requiring the actual existence, or a sufficiently serious risk, of deceit of consumers'.⁷¹⁷ Following his earlier reasoning, he suggested that the customers' conflicting perception did not deserve to be classified as a case of deceit. However, he also stressed that the national authority had to consider the particular features of the case in evaluating the effect of the use of the contested mark.

(b) The Judgment of the Court

5.853 (i) **Procedural considerations** The Court dealt first with two procedural issues. First, it rejected the observations submitted by Ms Emmanuel following the Opinion of the Advocate General.⁷¹⁸ Second, it found that the Appointed Person could refer questions to the Court as court or tribunal. The Appointed Person was a permanent body enjoying the same guarantees of independence as judges, making findings of law in *inter partes* proceedings, and taking binding decisions that were final subject exceptionally to an application for judicial review.⁷¹⁹

5.854 (ii) **The interpretation of Article 3(1)(g)** Again, the function of the trade mark became the starting point for answering the question:

> [F]or the trade mark to be able to fulfil its essential role in the system of undistorted competition which the Treaty seeks to establish and maintain, it must offer a guarantee that all the goods or services bearing it have been manufactured or supplied under the control of a single undertaking which is responsible for their quality.⁷²⁰

5.855 (iii) **Article 3(1)(g): The public interest; consumer protection** The Court then identified consumer protection as the public interest behind Article 3(1)(g); following *Nichols*,⁷²¹ there was no question that a personal name could perform the role that the Court had described as the function of a trade mark.

5.856 (iv) **The application of Article 3(1)(g)** The problem here was whether the risk that consumers might think that Elizabeth Emanuel, who originally personified the goods bearing the ELIZABETH EMANUEL mark, was still involved with the production of the garments qualified as deceit under Article 3(1)(g). The Court found that the trade mark would still function as a guarantee of quality despite the transfer:

---

⁷¹⁴ Point 65.
⁷¹⁵ He referred to von Mühlendahl, Ohlgart, and Bomhard, *Die Gemeinschaftsmarke* (Munich, Verlag C.H. Beck, 1998) p 173.
⁷¹⁶ C-87/97 *Gorgonzola* [1999] ECR I-1301, a case on free movement of goods and Regulation 2081/92 on the protection of geographical indications and designations of origin.
⁷¹⁷ Point 68.
⁷¹⁸ Citing amongst others C-17/98 *Emesa Sugar (Free Zone) NV v Aruba* [2000] ECR I-665; and C-210/03 *Swedish Match AB v Secretary of State for Health* [2004] ECR I-11893.
⁷¹⁹ It satisfied all the requirements set by the Court in cases like C-416/96 *Nour Eddine El-Yassini v Secretary of State for Home Department* [1999] ECR I-1209.
⁷²⁰ Paragraph 44, citing C-206/01 *Arsenal Football Club plc* [2002] ECR I-10273.
⁷²¹ C-404/02 *Nichols* [2004] ECR 1-8499.

even if the average consumer might be influenced in his act of purchasing a garment bearing the trade mark ELIZABETH EMANUEL by imagining that the appellant in the main proceedings was involved in the design of that garment, the characteristics and the qualities of that garment remain guaranteed by the undertaking which owns the trade mark.[722]

Accordingly, the name as such could not be regarded as being of such a nature as to deceive the public according to Article 3(1)(g). The Court added that it remained in the jurisdiction of the national court to determine whether the trade mark applicant intended to make the consumer believe that Elizabeth Emanuel was still involved with the garments. This might amount to fraud but still it 'could not be analysed as deception for the purposes of Article 3'.[723]

The Court concluded that: 5.857

> a trade mark corresponding to the name of the designer and first manufacturer of the goods bearing that mark may not, by reason of that particular feature alone, be refused registration on the ground that it would deceive the public, within the meaning of Article 3(1)(g) in particular where the goodwill associated with that trade mark, previously registered in a different graphic form, has been assigned together with the business making the goods to which the mark relates.[724]

(v) **The application of Article 12(2)(b)**   The Court found that the conditions of Article 3(1)(g) were mirrored in Article 12(2)(b) and that the analysis of the Court covered both provisions. The reply to the third and the fourth questions was that: 5.858

> a trade mark corresponding to the name of the designer and first manufacturer of the goods bearing that mark is not, by reason of that particular feature alone, liable to revocation on the ground that that mark would mislead the public, within the meaning of Article 12(2)(b) in particular where the goodwill associated with that mark has been assigned together with the business making the goods to which the mark relates.[725]

(2) Free Movement of Goods and Deceptive Use

Further guidance regarding the scope of the provision can be obtained from four judgments that looked at aspects of deceptive use in a trade mark context. All four of them were resolved on the basis of free movement of goods rules but there are useful analogies. 5.859

(a) Pall: Use of the symbol ®

The first of those cases had to do with the use of the symbol ®. In *Pall v Dahlhausen*,[726] a reference from the Landgericht (Regional Court) München I, the Court considered whether the prohibition of use of that symbol in Germany in relation to a trade mark not registered in the jurisdiction constituted a barrier to intra-Community trade. Pall, a producer and marketer of blood filters in Germany, had started proceedings against Dahlhausen who imported blood filters from Italy bearing the trade mark 'Miropore®'. Relying on Section 3 of the German Law against Unfair Competition, that prohibited misleading statements regarding the origin or the source of specific goods,[727] it claimed that consumers would be 5.860

---

[722] Paragraph 48.
[723] Paragraph 50.
[724] Paragraph 51.
[725] Paragraph 53.
[726] C-238/89 *Pall Corp v PJ Dahlhausen & Co* [1990] ECR I-4827.
[727] The German Law against Unfair Competition incorporated a general clause against the use of misleading information. Section 27 of the Law on Foodstuffs and Consumer Items prohibited the marketing of

misled since the mark had not been registered in Germany and sought an injunction against the marketing of the imported filters.

5.861 The Landgericht München I decided that, according to German law, the injunction should have been granted; it queried, however, whether it would amount to a quantitative restriction and referred the following questions to the Court:

> (1) Is the prohibition laid down in the case-law of the courts of the Federal Republic of Germany founded on Paragraph 3 of the Gesetz gegen den unlauteren Wettbewerb (Law on Unfair Competition) on putting goods into circulation in the Federal Republic of Germany with the symbol ® added to the name of the product when there is not trade mark protection in the Federal Republic of Germany tantamount in its effect to a quantitative restriction prohibited by Article [28] of the EEC Treaty if it is also applied to cases in which there is trade-mark protection in another EEC country?
> (2) In the particular circumstances of the case in question, is Paragraph 3 of the Gesetz gegen den unlauteren Wettbewerb applicable for the purpose of protecting the legal interests mentioned in Article [30] of the EEC Treaty?[728]

5.862 (i) **The legislative context** The Court noted that in the absence of a specific rule on use of the symbol in Germany, it would only apply the free movement of goods rules, and reiterated that they applied to all national trading rules capable of hindering, directly or indirectly, actually or potentially, intra-Community trade.[729] The latter could only be accepted if they applied to both domestic and imported products, they were justified as necessary in order to satisfy imperative requirements relating, inter alia, to consumer protection and fair trading, they were proportionate to the objective pursued, and that objective could not be achieved by measures which were less restrictive in respect of intra-Community trade.[730]

5.863 (ii) **The effect on trade and the scope of the prohibition** The Court started with the effect of the prohibition on intra-Community trade and found that it could function as a barrier to trade. It could force the proprietor of a trade mark registered in one Member State but not in another to change its presentation and set up distinct distribution channels according to its marketing destination. Its scope was to prevent error as to the place of registration and was applicable to domestic and imported products alike. It aimed to protect consumers from being misled as to the place of registration. Balancing the two, the Court decided that the prohibition could not be justified. It relied on five main arguments; two had to do with the meaning of the symbol, the remaining three with unfair competition.

5.864 (iii) **The meaning of ®: Proportionality** First, the Court held that it had not been established that in practice the symbol was used and understood as indicating that the trade mark was registered in the country in which the product was marketed, rather than simply as an indication of registration in some countries. So, the starting point for justifying the

---

cosmetic products using misleading names or packaging and, in particular, the attribution to such products of properties that they did not possess. The Law against Unfair Competition had been amended in 1994 and 2004; in 1994 the role of trade associations such as the one involved in this case was restricted, whereas the most recent amendment codified further and, to a certain extent, relaxed the criteria for determining whether a specific act constituted an act of unfair competition but retained a broad provision against misleading acts. A number of more detailed laws regulate specific product markets.

[728] Reproduced in paragraph 5.
[729] Citing Case 8/74 *Procureur du Roi v Dassonville* [1974] ECR 837.
[730] Citing C-120/78 *Rewe-Zentral AG v Bundesmonopolverwaltung für Branntwein* [1979] ECR 649.

prohibition was weak. Second, using a proportionality type of argument, the Court noted that even if consumers might be misled regarding the place of registration, the risk would not justify the considerable effect of the prohibition because consumers were more interested in the qualities of a product than in the place of registration of its trade mark.

(iv) Free movement of goods: Unfair competition   One of the arguments put forward was that use of the symbol in the absence of regulation should be viewed as an act of unfair competition against its competitors. In parallel, if registration in any Member State would be considered sufficient, then marketers would choose to register the sign in the Member State with the most liberal system of registration. The Court found that a prudent economic operator would look at the public register in order to determine the status of the mark rather than rely on the proclamation of registration on the product. As to the aim of registration, it remarked that the principal aim of the proprietor was to obtain legal protection in the Member State where the mark was registered. Use of symbols indicating registration were of an ancillary or supplementary nature. Finally, the Court rejected the argument supported by the German Government that the prohibition could be justifiable under the misleading advertising Directive.[731] Placing the Directive in its broader context, it held that since the prohibition had been found not to be justified by imperative requirements relating to consumer protection or fair trading—note that this was in the context of free movement of goods—it could not find a basis in the Directive.

5.865

(b) Clinique: The meaning of 'Clinique' for cosmetics

In *Clinique*[732] the Court provided further guidelines on misleading character. The case was decided in the context of free movement of goods, but on the fundamental questions as to whether a sign is misleading or not, the Court appeared to take a restrictive approach. The case came before the Court as a reference from the Landgericht (Regional Court) Berlin. A trade association had started proceedings against the subsidiaries of Estee Lauder in France and Germany under the German Law against Unfair Competition and the Law on Foodstuffs and Consumer Items,[733] claiming that the marketing of cosmetic products under the name 'Clinique' could mislead consumers, suggesting that the products had medicinal properties. Until then, Estee Lauder had been marketing the products under 'Clinique' in the rest of the world, whereas in Germany it had using the name 'Linique'. It decided to revert to 'Clinique' in order to reduce its packaging and advertising costs. The Landgericht decided that the outcome of the case could be affected from the determination of whether the ultimate prohibition of 'Clinique' was found to be against the free movement of goods rules and referred to the Court the following question:

5.866

> Are Articles [28] and [30] of the EEC Treaty to be interpreted as precluding the application of a national provision on unfair competition under which the importation and marketing of a cosmetic product which has been lawfully manufactured and/or lawfully marketed in another European country may be prohibited on the ground that consumers would be misled by the product name—Clinique—in that they would take it to be a medicinal product,

---

[731] Council Directive 84/450/EEC Relating to the Approximation of the Laws, Regulations and Administrative Provisions of the Member States Concerning Misleading Advertising [1984] OJ 1250/17.
[732] C-315/92 *Verband Sozialer Wettbewerb eV v Clinique Laboratoires SNC et Estée Lauder Cosmetics GmbH* [1994] ECR I-317.
[733] See paragraphs n 727 above and following below.

where that product is lawfully marketed without any objection under that name in other countries of the European Community?[734]

5.867 (i) **Setting the context** In order to provide a framework for answering the question, the Court looked at the broader picture of Community law. At the time there were two Directives that could prove relevant, one on misleading advertising[735] and the other on cosmetic products.[736] The scope of the misleading advertising Directive was to provide partial harmonization of national laws on misleading advertising by establishing minimum objective criteria for determining misleading character and the minimum requirements for protection against misleading advertising.[737] The cosmetic products Directive aimed to harmonize national rules on the packaging and labelling of cosmetic products.[738] Setting the two Directives into the hierarchical context of Community law, the Court repeated that all secondary legislation should be interpreted in the light of the free movement of goods rules.[739] The general rule of Article 28 of the EEC Treaty was applicable even if national rules that regulated marketing requirements as to designation, form, size, weight, composition, presentation, labelling, and packaging applied to locally produced and imported products alike. In order to tolerate the application of the national rules, the Court required a public interest objective that took precedence over the free movement of goods.[740] Proportionality was the other general principle invoked by the Court: rules had to be proportionate to the goals pursued.[741]

5.868 (ii) **Cosmetics and the public interest** The Court focused on Article 6(2) of Directive 76/768[742]—the Cosmetics Directive—looking for the underlying public interest in the light of proportionality. It required Member States to take

> 'all measures necessary to ensure that in the labelling, presentation for sale and advertising of cosmetic products, the wording, use of names, trademarks, images or other signs, figurative or otherwise, suggesting a characteristic which the products in question do not possess, shall be prohibited'.

Its scope was delineated by its wording, the broader aim of the Directive that was to ensure free trade in cosmetic products, and the case law of the Court of Justice. It

> defines the measures to be taken in the interests of consumer protection and fairness of commercial transactions, which are included among the imperative requirements specified in the case-law of the Court in the context of the application of Article [28] of the Treaty. It also pursues the objective of protecting the health of humans, within the meaning of Article [30] of the Treaty, in so far as misleading information as to the characteristics of such products may have an effect on public health.[743]

---

[734] Reproduced in paragraph 6.
[735] Council Directive 84/450/EEC Relating to the Approximation of the Laws, Regulations and Administrative Provisions of the Member States Concerning Misleading Advertising [1984] OJ 250/17.
[736] Council Directive 76/768/EEC on the Approximation of the Laws of the Member States Relating to Cosmetic Products [1976] OJ L 262/169.
[737] Citing C-238/89 *Pall Corp* [1990] ECR I-4827.
[738] Citing C-150/88 *Parfümerie-Fabrik 4711 v Provide* [1989] ECR 3891.
[739] Citing C-47/90 *Delhaize and Le Lion v Promalvin and AGE Bodegas Unidas* [1992] ECR I-3669.
[740] Citing C-267/91 and C-268/91 *Keck and Mithouard* [1993] ECR I-6097.
[741] Citing C-382/87 *Buet v Ministère Public* [1989] ECR 1235.
[742] Article 6(2) had been introduced into German law through Section 27 of the Law on Foodstuffs and Consumer Items.
[743] *Clinique* (n 732) paragraph 16.

Through the interpretation of the Community provision behind the national legislation, the court reached the conclusion that the application of the national legislation should be consistent with the free movement of goods provisions.

(iii) Unfair competition and free movement of goods: Effect and scope of the prohibition In order to describe what could fall under Section 3 of the Act against Unfair Competition, but still be considered a derogation from the free movement of goods rules, the Court referred directly to its case law in *Pall*.[744] Similarly, it held that the prohibition of the distribution in Germany of cosmetic products under the same name as in other Member States constituted, in principle, an obstacle to intra-Community trade. The scope of the prohibition would be to protect consumers or the health of humans.

On balance, the Court found the prohibition to be unjustifiable; this time for a number of factual reasons. In Germany the Clinique products were sold exclusively in perfumeries and the cosmetic sections of departments stores, not in pharmacies. The products were presented as cosmetic products, not as medicinal products. The presentation of the products, apart from the contested name, did comply with the rules applicable to cosmetic products. There was no evidence that the marketing of cosmetic products under 'Clinique' in other Member States had misled consumers. On the basis of the above, the Court found that the prohibition was not necessary for consumer protection and the health of humans.

(c) Mars: *Advertising messages*

In *Mars*[745] the Court showed again that it would take a restrictive approach towards deceptiveness. The case was a reference by the Landgericht Köln (Regional Court, Cologne). This time the trade mark itself did not constitute the principal issue. One of the unfair competition associations in Germany challenged the marketing of Mars ice cream bars imported from France to Germany. The packaging of the disputed bars included the sign '+ 10%' to indicate that the quantity of the bar had been increased by 10% as part of an advertising campaign effective throughout Europe. The association claimed that this was misleading and that marketing of the bars should be prohibited under Section 3 of the Law against Unfair Competition. It also claimed that it infringed Article 15 of the Law on Restraints of Competition, the competition provision protecting the freedom of retail trade in terms of pricing.

The association used two main arguments. The first, based on both unfair competition and competition laws, was that consumers were bound to assume that the '+ 10%' sign indicated an increase in content at a constant price. In order not to mislead, the retailer should maintain the same price it had been charging before the increase. The second, based on unfair competition, targeted the presentation of the product; the way it had been incorporated on the packaging of the bar through an introduction of a new colour could hint to the consumer that the product had been increased by a quantity matching the surface covered by the new colour, which covered considerably more than 10% of the packaging.

The Landgericht Köln granted an interim injunction, finding that the presentation of the packaging could mean to the consumer that a bigger size, albeit negligibly bigger in quantitative terms, was offered without an increase in price. This restricted freedom of retail trade

---

[744] C-238/89 *Pall Corp* [1990] ECR I-4827.
[745] C-470/93 *Verein gegen Unwesen in Handel und Gewerbe Köln eV v Mars GmbH* [1995] ECR I-1923.

in the matter of the fixing of prices. In order to rule on the substance of the case, however, it referred the following question to the Court:

> Is it compatible with the principles of the free movement of goods to prohibit the marketing in a Member State of ice-cream snacks in a particular presentation which are produced in another Member State and lawfully marketed there in that same presentation, which is described in the application, (1) on the ground that the (new) presentation is liable to give consumers the impression that the goods are offered for the same price as under the old presentation, (2) on the ground that the visual presentation of the new feature '+ 10% ice-cream' gives consumers the impression that either the volume or the weight of the product has been considerably increased?.[746]

5.875 (i) *Article 28 (now Article 34 TFEU): Effect and scope of the prohibition* According to the case law of the Court, the prohibition constituted a barrier to trade because it might require that the marketer match the presentation of the product with its marketing destination, incurring additional packaging and advertising costs.[747] It added that although it applied to all products without distinction, it would hinder by its nature intra-Community trade. It could only be permitted to satisfy an overriding requirement relating, inter alia, to consumer protection and fair trading, provided it was proportionate to the objective pursued and that objective could not be achieved by less intense measures. Turning to the justification of the prohibition, the Court found that there was no evidence that Mars had as a result of the advertising campaign increased its prices, or that retailers had increased prices. 'In any case, the mere possibility that importers and retailers might increase the price of the goods and that consequently consumers may be deceived is not sufficient to justify a general prohibition which may hinder intra-Community trade.'[748]

5.876 In its usual balancing and cautious manner the Court added that that fact did not prevent the Member States from taking action against duly proven actions which had the effect of misleading consumers.

5.877 Regarding price fixing, it found that the constraint imposed on the retailer not to increase prices would actually favour consumers. There was no contractual stipulation imposed on retailers; it applied only during the advertising campaign; and the actual information conveyed by the '+10%' sign ensured that consumers would not be misled. Finally, regarding the visual presentation of the sign, the Court rejected the allegations about its misleading character. It found that a reasonably circumspect consumer would know that there was not necessarily a link between the size of the signs on the packaging, advertising the increase in quantity, and the actual size of that increase.

(d) Cotonelle: The meaning of COTONELLE

5.878 In *Cotonelle*[749] the reference covered deceptive use of a sign, not only from the perspective of free movement of goods rules but also according to the Directive. The starting point of this case was a Judgment of the Corte d'Appello di Milano (Court of Appeal, Milan) that ordered Scott to stop using in Italy the trade mark COTONELLE for toilet paper and

---

[746] Reproduced in paragraph 10.
[747] Citing Case 8/74 *Procureur du Roi v Dassonville* [1974] ECR 837; and C-267/91 and C-268/91 *Keck and Mithouard* [1993] ECR I-6097.
[748] *Mars* (n 745) paragraph 19.
[749] C-313/94 *Fratelli Graffione SNC* [1996] ECR I-6039.

disposable handkerchiefs and invalidated the national registration of the same mark because it found that the mark might mislead consumers into thinking that the two products were made of or contained cotton. Registrations of COTONELLE had also been challenged, without success, in France and Spain. As a result of that judgment Scott stopped distributing COTONELLE products in Italy and Fratelli Graffione SNC (Graffione), a wholesaler dealing in Scott products, notified its own customers that it too would stop distributing these two products.

Graffione started proceedings against Ditta Fransa (Fransa), a supermarket selling imported COTONELLE products in Italy. It argued that this was against Italian unfair competition rules since Graffione could not obtain the products in Italy whereas Fransa did through parallel imports. In its response, Fransa relied on the territorial nature of trade mark rights. The Corte d'Appello judgment concerned the products that were manufactured and marketed in Italy; its products were lawfully marketed in France where it obtained them. An injunction would be against Article 28 EC.[750] It also claimed that under Article 12(2)(b) of the Directive the outcome before the Corte d'Appello would be different. As a result, the Tribunale di Chiavari referred the following questions to the Court: **5.879**

> (1) Are Articles [28] and [30] to be interpreted as precluding restrictive application of national legislation of a Member State which prohibits the movement within its territory of a product from another Member State where that product has been lawfully manufactured and lawfully bears a trade-mark?
> (2) Is Article 12(2)(b) of Directive 89/104 to be interpreted as entailing harmonisation of the national provisions on revocation of trade-mark rights, on the grounds therein indicated, in relation to products distributed at Community level?
> (3) In circumstances such as those at issue here, is the provision referred to in Question 2 above to be interpreted, having regard inter alia to the principle of proportionality, as precluding restrictive application of national legislation of a Member State intended to prevent the movement in that Member State of a product lawfully manufactured and bearing a trade-mark in, and coming from, another Member State?[751]

(i) Article 28 EC (now Article 34 TFEU): Unfair competition; effect and scope of the provision The Court considered first whether Article 28 EC and Article 30 EC precluded the application of a national provision on unfair competition that would block the marketing of a product lawfully marketed in another Member State. The Court repeated that such an injunction would constitute a measure having equivalent effect to a quantitative restriction on imports.[752] The question was whether it could be justified in order, in this case, to satisfy an overriding requirement relating to consumer protection or fair trading.[753] **5.880**

The Court noted that it was for the national court first of all to interpret the Judgment of the Corte d'Appello as to whether it prevented third parties from marketing the contested products. If it targeted exclusively the proprietor of the Italian trade mark, then third parties would not be prevented from importing and marketing the products in Italy **5.881**

---

[750] Citing C-315/92 *Verband Sozialer Wettbewerb eV v Clinique Laboratoires SNC et Estée Lauder Cosmetics GmbH* [1994] ECR I-317.
[751] Reproduced in paragraph 11.
[752] Citing Case 8/74 *Procureur du Roi v Dassonville* [1974] ECR 837.
[753] Citing C-120/78 *Rewe-Zentral* [1979] ECR 649; C-238/89 *Pall v Dalhausen* [1990] ECR I-4827; C-126/91 *Schutzverband gegen Unwesen in der Wirtschaft v Yves Rocher* [1993] ECR I-2361; and C-470/93 *Verein gegen Unwese in Handel und Gewerbe Köln v Mars* [1995] ECR I-1923.

and the injunction sought by Graffione would not be justified. If the marketing in Italy of all COTONELLE products were to be prohibited, then the barrier would have to be justified.

5.882 This remained an open question that the national court had to resolve; the Court provided the parameters:

> The possibility of allowing a prohibition of marketing on account of the misleading nature of a trade mark is not, in principle, precluded by the fact that the same trade mark is not considered to be misleading in other Member States ... it is possible that because of linguistic, cultural and social differences between the Member States a trade mark which is not liable to mislead a consumer in one Member State may be liable to do so in another.[754]
>
> However ... in order to be justified, the measure adopted to protect consumers must really be necessary for that purpose and proportionate to the objective pursued, which must not be capable of being achieved by measures which are less restrictive of intra-Community trade.[755]

5.883 The Court reiterated that 'the risk of misleading consumers cannot override the requirements of the free movement of goods and so justify barriers to trade, unless that risk is sufficiently serious'.[756]

5.884 (ii) **The early days of Article 12(2)(b)** The Court found that Article 12(2)(b) of the Directive was not relevant to the principal issue of the current case. The aim of the Directive was to achieve a partial, rather than complete, harmonization of national trade mark laws. Also, according to the Fifth Recital in the Preamble of the Directive, Member States remained free to determine the effects of revocation or invalidity of trade marks. Further, according to the Sixth Recital, the Directive did not affect the application of provisions relating to unfair competition, civil liability, or consumer protection. Based on the facts of the case, the Court chose to focus on the effect rather than the cause and ruled that Article 12(2) left it to national law to determine whether and to what extent the use of a revoked trade mark ought to be prohibited.

H. Article 3(1)(h): State Emblems

(1) *Maple Leaf*: Applicability of Article 6ter to Services

5.885 *Maple Leaf*[757] is a good example of the Court's readiness to interpret the provisions of the CTMR broadly when this is necessary to plug gaps in the legislation that would otherwise result in patently absurd and inequitable situations.

5.886 That case concerned the interpretation of Article 7(1)(h) CTMR (the equivalent provision of Article 3(1)(h) of the Directive) in conjunction with Article 6ter of the Paris Convention, dealing with the scope of the protection to be afforded to State emblems for the purposes of trade mark law.

---

[754] Paragraph 22.
[755] Paragraph 23.
[756] Paragraph 24.
[757] C-202/08 P and C-208/08 P *American Clothing Associates NV/OHIM* [2009] ECR I-6933

Article 3(1)(h)—State Emblems

(a) Legislative framework

5.887 Article 7(1)(h) CTMR provides that signs which have not been authorized by the competent authorities and are to be refused pursuant to Article 6ter of the Paris Convention cannot be registered as Community trade marks.

5.888 Article 6ter(1) stipulates the following, insofar as is relevant to the case:

> (1) (a) The countries of the Union agree to refuse or to invalidate the registration ... without authorisation by the competent authorities, either as trademarks or as elements of trademarks, of armorial bearings, flags, and other State emblems, of the countries of the Union ... and any imitation from a heraldic point of view.
>
> (b) The provisions of subparagraph (a), above, shall apply equally to armorial bearings, flags, other emblems, abbreviations, and names, of international intergovernmental organisations ...
>
> (c) The countries of the Union shall not be required to apply the said provisions when the use or registration ... is not of such a nature as to suggest to the public that a connection exists [with] the organisation concerned ... or if such use or registration is probably not of such a nature as to mislead the public as to the existence of a connection between the user and the organisation.

5.889 Article 6sexies requires the countries of the Union to protect service marks, without, however, being obliged to also provide for their registration. On the other hand, Article 16 of the Trade Mark Law Treaty, adopted in Geneva on 27 October 1994, provides that the contracting parties shall register service marks and apply to them the provisions of the Paris Convention concerning trade marks.

(b) Background to the dispute

5.890 American Clothing Associates NY (American Clothing) sought to register at OHIM as a Community trade mark a figurative sign consisting of a black and white image of a maple leaf with the letters 'RW' below it, essentially in order to designate leather goods, clothing articles, and tailoring services in Classes 18, 25, and 40 of the Nice Classification. The Office refused the application in its entirety pursuant to Article 7(1)(h) CTMR, stating that the mark was liable to give rise to an impression on the part of the public that it was linked to Canada, inasmuch as the maple leaf reproduced in the trade mark applied for was a copy of the national emblem of that country. American Clothing filed a notice of appeal against the examiner's refusal which was dismissed by the Office's Board of Appeal. American Clothing appealed that decision to the Court of First Instance.

(c) The Judgment of the Court of First Instance

5.891 The Court of First Instance[758] annulled the Office's decision insofar as it related to services in Class 40, on the ground that Article 6ter(l)(a) of the Paris Convention, to which Article 7(1)(h) CTMR directly refers, does not apply to service marks. In doing so, the Court of First Instance applied Article 6ter of the Paris Convention literally, effectively holding that the legal basis for the rejection and, by extension, the conditions for refusal, were to be found not in Article 7(1)(h) CTMR, but rather in Article 6ter directly. Moreover, it held that it was precisely in order to extend to service marks the protection granted by the Paris

---

[758] T-215/06 *American Clothing Associates v OHIM* (Representation of a maple leaf) [2008] ECR II-303.

5.892 The Court of First Instance also held that when adopting the CTMR, the Community legislature was aware of the economic importance of services and could have extended the protection granted by Article 6ter also to service marks, had it considered it appropriate to do so. Accordingly, it was not for the Community judicature to take the place of the legislature and apply an interpretation *contra legem* of those provisions, whose meaning is in no way ambiguous.[760]

5.893 As to the remainder, the Court of First Instance rejected the appeal, holding that registration was correctly refused in respect of the goods in Classes 18 and 25. In reaching that conclusion, it observed that when assessing a complex mark for the purposes of Article 6ter, it was sufficient if any of its components corresponded to a State emblem or was an imitation thereof 'from a heraldic point of view', which meant that it was the 'heraldic description' of the emblem that had to be considered, rather than its 'geometric description'.[761]

5.894 Finally, it noted that the application of Article 6ter is not subject to the existence of a possibility of error on the part of the public as regards the origin of the goods, or as regards the existence of a connection between the proprietor and the State whose emblem appears in the mark.[762] Both American Clothing and the Office appealed that judgment to the Court of Justice, to the extent that it adversely affected their respective positions.

(d) The Opinion of Advocate General Ruiz-Jarabo Colomer

5.895 Advocate General Ruiz-Jarabo Colomer took the view that the Court of First Instance had correctly rejected the mark in respect of the goods applied for, but had erroneously accepted the application insofar as protection was sought for services.

5.896 **(i) Emblems v trade marks: Different functions** In the first place, he observed that American Clothing could not rely on the argument that State emblems should be protected only insofar as their essential function was affected, by applying the same criteria as for trade mark protection by analogy. Unlike trade marks, emblems cannot be viewed as having a commercial function or as indicating origin, other than possibly identifying a country and its inhabitants, or representing its sovereignty. Thus, even on the assumption that emblems had 'essential functions', the role they fulfil is totally different from that of trade marks, which sufficed to render the drawing of analogies between the two entirely inappropriate. In fact; the contrast between the two situations would suffice to justify their different treatment in law.[763]

5.897 **(ii) Emblems v trade marks: Different scope** The Advocate General then observed that the Paris Convention confers an absolute protection on emblems, at least in the following respects: first, Article 6ter applies to all the products and, if the national law so provides, to all the services in the Nice classification; second, the protection is not conditional on the establishment of a link between the mark and the emblem; finally, various limitations

---

[759] Paragraph 31.
[760] Paragraph 32.
[761] Paragraph 72.
[762] Paragraph 77.
[763] Points 63 and 67.

characteristic of commercial symbols, like for instance invalidity and expiry, do not affect national emblems.[764] Indeed, the second sentence of Article 6ter(1)(c) allows the registration or use of a sign if it does not indicate a connection with the *intergovernmental organisation* which is the proprietor of the corresponding emblem; it may therefore be inferred, *a contrario sensu*, that the need for such a connection is not required for State emblems, but only for the insignia of international institutions.[765] Consequently, an exact replica or an imitation of the emblem is enough to unleash the protection afforded to national symbols by Article 6ter.[766]

(iii) **Imitation 'from a heraldic point of view'**   Next, the Advocate General dealt with the dichotomy between 'heraldic' and 'geometric' description. Although he recognized that the protection of emblems is subject to certain restrictions, in the sense that it does not cover the semantic content incorporated in the emblem but only its 'heraldic expression', he did not accept that the applicability of Article 6ter should be based on its geometric description. In fact, so detailed a comparison would practically negate the protection afforded to emblems, since the existence of any nuance or differentiation, however secondary, would be enough to deny the existence of identity between the respective representations. Moreover, he took the view that the need for an 'imitation' did not imply the existence of a likelihood of confusion. Rather, it is sufficient for refusing protection if the copy possesses the 'heraldic connotations' which generally distinguish the emblem from other signs, as expressed in the descriptions which the States communicate to the International Bureau.[767]   **5.898**

(iv) **Confusion as to endorsement**   As to the argument that the Court of First Instance disregarded the overall impression of the sign applied for, Advocate General Ruiz-Jarabo Colomer stressed that the wording of Article 6ter expressly extends to situations in which national symbols are used 'as elements of trademarks'. Hence, that expression would become completely devoid of meaning if it were possible to circumvent the relevant prohibition by simply placing the emblem in a sign with more components.[768]   **5.899**

Furthermore, he pointed out that the application of Article 6ter is not subject to the possibility of an error as regards the origin of the goods, or the existence of a connection between the proprietor of the sign and the State whose emblem it reproduces. Although it may be true that the ratio of Article 6ter lies in the need to prevent the public from erroneously believing that there is an official approval or endorsement of the goods bearing the emblem by that State, the existence of such a link is not a specific condition for its application.[769]   **5.900**

(v) **Applicability of Article 6ter to services**   Finally, the Advocate General took the view that the Court of First Instance had misinterpreted the aim of the Paris Convention and the reference made to it by Article 7 CTMR. As regards the correct interpretation of Article 6ter, he recalled that the essential aim of the Paris Convention is to uphold the principle of national treatment, combining it with minimum rules for the protection of industrial   **5.901**

---

[764] Points 74 and 76.
[765] Citing GHC Bodenhausen, *Guide to the Application of the Paris Convention for the Protection of Industrial Property* (BIRPI, 1969) p 101.
[766] Point 75.
[767] Point 85.
[768] Point 88.
[769] Point 94.

property rights. Accordingly, the Court of First Instance was wrong to seek in that provision the requirements for denying protection. Although, admittedly, that provision does not extend to service marks, it does not concern itself with delimiting the scope of protection afforded to emblems either. Rather, it only requires the contracting States not to register trade marks containing national emblems, while leaving them free to extend protection to service marks should they so wish.[770]

5.902 Therefore, he considered that the question whether the corresponding absolute ground for refusal also applies to services depends on the interpretation of Article 7(1)(h) CTMR. In that regard, he noted that the Seventh and Ninth Recitals in the Preamble to the CTMR refer to both goods and services, as also does Article 1(1), which defines Community trade marks as marks registered for either of them. Additionally, he observed that the CTMR contains no provision which effectively distinguishes between them in any meaningful way.[771]

5.903 Accordingly, the Advocate General concluded that, in view of the equal treatment reserved by the European legislature for both types of signs, the reference in Article 7(1)(h) to the Paris Convention must be understood as only relating to the kind of sign to be protected and not to the scope of its actual protection.[772]

(e) The Judgment of the Court

5.904 (i) **The meaning of 'heraldic imitation'** At the outset, the Court concurred with the Advocate General that both the functions State emblems perform and their treatment in Community and international law are clearly distinct from the role and protectable aspects of trade marks. That is especially true with regard to likelihood of confusion which, unlike its importance for trade mark protection, is not required for the protection of an emblem, since Article 6ter(1)(a) of the Paris Convention makes no reference to it. In particular, it is apparent from the second sentence of that provision that the protection of State emblems is not subject to there being a connection in the mind of the public between the trade mark and the emblem.[773]

5.905 The Court then turned to the interpretation of the expression 'imitation from a heraldic point of view', observing that Article 6ter prohibits the registration and use of a State emblem not only when it is filed as a trade mark as such, but also when it constitutes an element of a trade mark. Furthermore, that provision prohibits the imitation of the emblem in addition to precluding its exact replication. However, the Court noted also that the prohibition applies only to imitations of the emblem from a heraldic perspective, that is to say, is limited to signs which contain heraldic connotations serving to distinguish the emblem from other signs. Moreover, it agreed with the Advocate General that the protection against imitation from a heraldic point of view refers not to the subject matter of the emblem as such, but rather to its heraldic expression. It is therefore necessary, in order to determine whether there is an imitation, to consider the heraldic description of the emblem at issue and not its geometric reproduction, as this would limit the protection only to cases of graphic equivalence, which is already prohibited by the first part of that provision.[774]

---

[770] Point 107.
[771] Point 111.
[772] Point 113.
[773] *Maple Leaf* (n 757) paragraph 45.
[774] Paragraphs 48–49.

Accordingly, it is the perception of the average consumer as to whether an imitation in the above sense exists that should be taken into account. A difference detected by a specialist in heraldic art will not necessarily be perceived by the average consumer who, in spite of differences at the level of certain heraldic details, can still see in the trade mark an imitation of the emblem in question.[775] **5.906**

Furthermore, the Court observed that the heraldic description of the emblem normally contains only certain descriptive graphic elements, and does not necessarily concern itself with particular features of the artistic interpretation. Hence, it held that the Court of First Instance did not err in law by holding that a number of artistic interpretations of one and the same emblem were possible. Lastly, the Court held in that connection that as Article 6ter applies also to individual elements of complex trade marks, it is sufficient for a single component of the mark applied for to imitate such an emblem for that mark to be refused registration. As a result, to the extent the Court of First Instance had found that the maple leaf represented on the sign applied for is an imitation of the Canadian emblem, it did not need to examine the overall impression produced by that mark.[776] **5.907**

(ii) **Application to service marks** As regards the Court of First Instance's refusal to apply Article 7(1)(h) CTMR, the Court again shared the view of Advocate General Ruiz-Jarabo Colomer that the Paris Convention provides for a minimum level of protection for elements falling within its scope, while leaving the contracting States free to extend the scope of its application beyond that bare minimum. Consequently, it inferred that whilst Article 6ter leaves the extension of the protection guaranteed to trade marks also to services to the discretion of the States party to the Convention, it cannot be interpreted as requiring those States to treat these types of marks differently.[777] **5.908**

Moreover, it noted that, as a rule, the CTMR does not differentiate between goods and services and where it wanted to draw such a distinction, as, for example, in Article 7(1)(e), (j), and (k), it did so expressly. Accordingly, Article 7(1)(h) must be regarded as following the rule rather than the exception, the more so since it does not contain any explicit restriction as to the type of mark covered by it.[778] **5.909**

In addition, the Court held that this interpretation of Article 7(1)(h) is further supported by Article 7(1)(i) CTMR, the scope of which is analogous to that of subparagraph (h), insofar as it concerns marks which include badges, emblems, or escutcheons other than those covered by Article 6ter. Given that Article 7(1)(i) applies without distinction to marks for both goods and services, it would be absurd to refuse registration to a service mark containing a badge and not to one imitating a State flag. Indeed, if the legislature wished to grant such protection to badges and escutcheons, it should be assumed that, *a fortiori*, it also intended to grant at least an equivalent level of protection to flags and other emblems of States.[779] **5.910**

Consequently, the Court concluded that the judgment under appeal erred in finding that, by refusing registration of the trade mark applied for in respect of services, OHIM had infringed Article 7(1)(h) CTMR in conjunction with Article 6ter of the Paris Convention. **5.911**

---

[775] Paragraphs 50–51.
[776] Paragraph 59.
[777] Paragraph 73.
[778] Paragraphs 76–77.
[779] Paragraphs 79–80.

I. Article 3(2)(d): Bad Faith

5.912 The CTM Regulation refers to bad faith only as an absolute ground for invalidity, whereas in the Directive bad faith is foreseen as both an absolute ground for refusal and invalidity, and, additionally, as an optional relative ground by virtue of Article 4(4)(g), which provides that:

> Any Member State may, in addition, provide that a trade mark shall not be registered or, if registered, shall be liable to be declared invalid where, and to the extent that … :
> (g) the trade mark is liable to be confused with a mark which was in use abroad on the filing date of the application and which is still in use there, provided that at the date of the application the applicant was acting in bad faith.

5.913 The Regulation refers to bad faith only as an absolute ground for invalidity in Article 52(1)(b). Regardless of where bad faith is provided for and in which procedural context it may arise, the interpretation of the concept has presented national offices, as well as OHIM and the courts, with difficulties, and notably so when the question is whether the knowledge of someone's earlier use of the same or a similar mark is a case of bad faith.

5.914 The Court has dealt with the issue so far in two judgments: *Lindt & Sprüngli* and *Malaysia Dairy*.

(1) *Lindt & Sprüngli*: What is Bad Faith?

5.915 *Lindt & Sprüngli*[780] was the first case in which the Court was asked to provide guidance on the interpretation of the concept of bad faith for the purposes of Community trade mark law. The order for reference concerned invalidity proceedings brought against a registered Community trade mark under Article 51(1)(b) of the Regulation (new Article 52); its findings are equally applicable in the context of Article 3(2)(d) of the Directive.

(a) The facts in the main proceedings

5.916 The national proceedings arose out of a situation in which a number of competing undertakings originally marketed related products (chocolate Easter bunnies) in similar shapes and presentations. One of those undertakings then registered its own particular configuration as a three-dimensional trade mark and used it as a basis for preventing its competitors from marketing products within the European Union resembling that shape. Was that undertaking, however, acting in bad faith when applying for the mark in the knowledge of those circumstances?

5.917 The reference was made by the Austrian Oberster Gerichtshof in the course of a dispute between Chocoladefabriken Lindt & Sprüngli AG (Lindt), a Swiss company, and Franz Hauswirth GmbH (Hauswirth), a company established in Austria. In 2000 Lindt obtained a Community trade mark registration, representing a gold-coloured chocolate bunny, in a sitting position, wearing a red ribbon and a bell, and with the words 'Lindt GOLDHASE' in brown lettering, essentially corresponding to the shape of a chocolate bunny it has marketed since the early 1950s.

---

[780] C-529/07 *Chocoladefabriken Lindt & Sprüngli AG v Franz Hauswirth GmbH* [2009] ECR I-04893.

5.918 Hauswirth has marketed chocolate bunnies since 1962. According to the order for reference, the shape of those bunnies is confusingly similar to the one covered by Lindt's trade mark, despite the fact that a different brand name is affixed on their packaging. Following registration, Lindt brought infringement proceedings against Hauswirth, who counterclaimed that the registration had been made in bad faith and the trade mark should therefore be declared invalid. At first instance, the Handelsgericht (Commercial Court) in Vienna dismissed the main claim and upheld the counterclaim. On appeal, the Oberlandesgericht (Higher Regional Court) partly quashed that judgment, rejecting both the action and the counterclaim. Both parties appealed to the Oberster Gerichtshof (Supreme Court).

5.919 The Oberster Gerichtshof stated that the decision on the counterclaim brought by Franz Hauswirth depended on whether Lindt was acting in bad faith when applying for registering the shape at issue as a trade mark and referred the following questions to the Court for a preliminary ruling:

> (1) Is Article 51(1)(b) CTMR to be interpreted as meaning that an applicant for a Community trade mark is to be regarded as acting in bad faith where he knows, at the time of his application, that a competitor in (at least) one Member State is using the same sign, or one so similar as to be capable of being confused with it, for the same or similar goods or services, and he applies for the trade mark in order to be able to prevent that competitor from continuing to use the sign?
>
> (2) If the first question is answered in the negative:
>
> Is the applicant to be regarded as acting in bad faith if he applies for the trade mark in order to be able to prevent a competitor from continuing to use the sign, where, at the time he files his application, he knows or must know that by using an identical or similar sign for the same goods or services, or goods or services which are so similar as to be capable of being confused, the competitor has already acquired a 'valuable right' ('wertvollen Besitzstand')?
>
> (3) If either the first or the second question is answered in the affirmative:
>
> Is bad faith excluded if the applicant's sign has already obtained a reputation with the public and is therefore protected under competition law?

(b) The Opinion of Advocate General Sharpston

5.920 Advocate General Sharpston started her analysis by observing that the relevant provisions of Community trade mark law do not contain a clear definition of bad faith, or otherwise describe that notion. However, she inferred from the overall scheme of the legislation that bad faith appeared to be an inherent defect in the application (rather than in the trade mark itself), which fundamentally vitiates the registration regardless of other circumstances; that concept, moreover, should be given the same meaning under both the Regulation and the Directive and should apply equally to both Community and national trade marks.[781]

5.921 The Advocate General noted though that bad faith cannot be defined in the abstract or confined to a limited set of circumstances, such as the existence of a particular kind of prior right, a lack of intention to use the mark, or the actual or constructive knowledge of the existing use of a similar mark. Rather, its nature seems to imply a subjective incentive on the part of the applicant in the form of a dishonest intention or other 'sinister motive', which will normally follow from objective criteria, including, but not limited to, those listed by

---

[781] Points 41–42.

the referring court; in short, it involves conduct which departs from accepted principles of ethical behaviour or honest business practices, which can only be identified by reference to the specific facts of each case.[782]

5.922 Accordingly, she concluded that there is no simple, decisive test for establishing whether a trade mark application is made in bad faith, in particular since that notion involved a subjective state of mind linked to an intention incompatible with accepted standards of honest or ethical conduct, which is only ascertainable from objective evidence, and which must be assessed on a case-by-case basis.

5.923 Moreover, she noted that bad faith requires actual or constructive knowledge of the circumstances from which that incompatibility with the accepted standards of honest or ethical conduct may be deduced and that, in the absence of direct evidence to that effect, the existence of such knowledge may be determined by reference to the common state of knowledge in the economic sector concerned.

5.924 As regards, finally, the specific circumstances put forward in the order for reference, Advocate General Sharpston considered that:

- an intention to prevent others from using similar signs in respect of similar products may be incompatible with such standards if the applicant knew that others were already legitimately using those signs, particularly if that use was substantial and long-standing and enjoyed legal protection, and if the nature of the sign was dictated by technical or commercial constraints;
- however, such an intention would not be incompatible with those standards if the applicant's sign had enjoyed similar or greater legal protection and was used in such a way, to such an extent and over such a time, that the use of similar signs could derive unjustified benefit from the applicant's marks, and if third parties were not constrained in their ability to choose dissimilar signs.

(c) The Judgment of the Court

5.925 As a starting point, the Court observed that the relevant time for determining whether there is bad faith on the part of the applicant is the time of the filing of the application; furthermore, whether the applicant is acting in bad faith must be the subject of an overall assessment that takes account of all the factors relevant to the particular case.[783] Turning to the questions referred, it held that a presumption of knowledge by the applicant that third parties use identical or similar signs may be deduced, among other facts, from general knowledge in the economic sector concerned, while that knowledge can be inferred, inter alia, from the duration of such use, in the sense that the more that use is long-standing, the stronger that presumption will be. However, the fact that the applicant knows or must know that a third party has long been using an identical or similar sign is not of itself sufficient to conclude that the applicant is acting in bad faith; consequently, consideration must also be given to the applicant's intention at the time the application is filed.[784]

---

[782] Point 60.
[783] *Lindt & Sprüngli* (n 780) paragraphs 34–35.
[784] Paragraphs 40–41.

5.926 The Court then observed that insofar as that intention is, necessarily, a subjective factor, it will have to be determined by reference to objective indications arising from the facts of the particular case. In that regard, it noted that the intention to prevent other parties from marketing similar products may, in certain circumstances, be indicative of bad faith, in particular when subsequently it becomes apparent that the applicant applied for the mark without intending to use it in accordance with its essential function, his sole objective being to prevent third operators from entering the market.[785] Equally, the fact that a third party has long used a similar sign is also a factor to be taken into consideration, since, in such a case, the applicant's sole aim in obtaining a registration might be to compete unfairly with a competitor whose sign has obtained some degree of legal protection because of characteristics of its own.[786]

5.927 Furthermore, the Court concurred with the Advocate General that the nature of the sign may also be relevant, in that the existence of bad faith might more readily be established where the competitors' freedom to choose the shape of their products is limited by technical or commercial constraints, since, in such a case, the proprietor will be able to prevent not merely the use of identical or similar signs, but actually the marketing of comparable products.

5.928 However, it cannot be excluded that, even in such circumstances, the application may be pursuing a legitimate objective. That may be the case in particular where the applicant knows that a newcomer in the market is trying to take advantage of his/her sign by copying its presentation and seeks to register that sign precisely with a view to preventing such copying.[787]

5.929 Accordingly, consideration should also be given to the reputation the sign may have acquired by the time of its filing, as well as to the extent to which that reputation might justify the applicant's interest in ensuring a wider protection for his/her signing.[788]

5.930 Therefore, the Court ruled that, in order to determine whether the applicant is acting in bad faith, the national court must take into consideration all the factors relevant to the case and, in particular:

– the fact that the applicant knows or must know that a third party is using an identical or similar sign capable of being confused with the sign for which registration is sought;
– the applicant's intention to prevent that third party from continuing to use such a sign; and
– the degree of legal protection enjoyed by the third party's sign and by the sign for which registration is sought.

5.931 Thus, in *Lindt & Sprüngli* the Court seems to be distinguishing between situations of long-lasting and well-established use of similar signs by competitors, which cannot legitimately be discontinued by having recourse to trade mark protection, and parasitic use by newcomers with the sole purpose of exploiting the sign's reputation, which the owner may lawfully prevent by relying on its trade mark rights without acting in bad faith.

---

[785] Paragraphs 43–45.
[786] Paragraphs 46–47.
[787] Paragraphs 48–49.
[788] Paragraphs 51–52.

(2) *Malaysia Dairy*: The Autonomous Nature of Bad Faith

(a) The facts in the main proceedings and the Order for reference

5.932 The ruling in *Malaysia Dairy*[789] was the consequence of a reference from the Højesteret (Denmark) concerning the legal nature and the scope of the concept of bad faith.

5.933 The dispute in the main proceedings concerned the legality of a decision by the Ankenævnet for Patenter og Varemærker (Patents and Trade Marks Appeal Board) to cancel a Danish trade mark registration owned by Malaysia Dairy in respect of a plastic bottle on the ground that, at the time it had applied for registration, the latter knew of the existence of a very similar foreign trade mark owned by Kabushiki Kaisha Yakult Honsha in Japan and a number of Member States of the EU. The Appeal Board based its decision on Section 15(3)(3) of the Danish Law on Trademarks, according to which a trade mark is also excluded from registration if:

> (3) it is identical to or differs only insubstantially from a trade mark which at the time of the application, or as the case may be the time of priority claimed in support of the application, has been brought into use abroad and is still used there for goods or services of the same or similar kind as those for which the later mark is sought to be registered, and at the time of the application the applicant knew or should have known of the foreign mark.

5.934 The Appeal Board took the view that Section 15(3)(3) must be interpreted as meaning that actual or presumed knowledge of a mark in use abroad is sufficient to establish that the applicant is acting in bad faith, even if the applicant had previously acquired a registration for the same mark in another country. On appeal, the Sø- og Handelsretten (Maritime and Commercial Court) confirmed that interpretation and upheld the decision of the Board, basing its judgment on the undisputed fact that Malaysia Dairy knew of Yakult's mark when it filed its trade mark application in Denmark. Malaysia Dairy appealed before the Højesteret (Supreme Court), which decided to stay the proceedings and to refer the following questions to the Court of Justice:

1. Is the concept of bad faith in Article 4(4)(g) an expression of a legal standard which may be filled out in accordance with national law, or is it a concept of European Union law which must be given a uniform interpretation throughout the European Union?
2. If the concept of bad faith in Article 4(4)(g) is a concept of European Union law, must the concept be understood as meaning that it may suffice that the applicant knew or should have known of the foreign mark at the time of filing the application, or is there a further requirement concerning the applicant's subjective position in order for registration to be denied?
3. Can a Member State choose to introduce a specific protection of foreign marks which, in relation to the requirement of bad faith, differs from Article 4(4)(g), for example by laying down a special requirement that the applicant knew or should have known of the foreign mark?

(b) The Judgment of the Court

5.935 (i) **The autonomous character of bad faith** With regard to the first question, the Court recalled that the need for a uniform application of European Union law and the principle of equality require that the terms of a provision which makes no express reference to the law

---

[789] C-320/12 *Malaysia Dairy Industries Pte Ltd v Ankenævnet for Patenter og Varemærker*, ECLI:EU:C:2013:435.

of the Member States for the purpose of determining its meaning must normally be given an independent and uniform interpretation throughout the European Union, taking into account the context of the provision in question and the objective of the relevant legislation.[790] As neither Article 4(4)(g) nor any other provision of the Directive or the Regulation contain a definition of bad faith or make any reference to the law of the Member States, the Court considered that the meaning and scope of that concept had to be determined through a contextual interpretation of Article 4(4)(g) in the light of the objectives pursued by the Directive.[791]

5.936 In that regard, the Court observed that the provisions relating to the concept of bad faith form part of the rules most directly affecting the functioning of the internal market within the meaning of the Fourth Recital of the Directive, which does not preclude the harmonization relating to those rules from being complete, and added[792] that the optional nature of a provision of the Directive has no effect on whether a uniform interpretation must be given to its wording.[793] Accordingly, the Court answered the first question to the effect that Article 4(4)(g) of the Directive must be interpreted as meaning that the concept of bad faith, within the meaning of that provision, is an autonomous concept of European Union law which must be given a uniform interpretation in the European Union.[794]

5.937 **(ii) The inconclusiveness of prior knowledge** With regard to the second question, the Danish Government and Yakult contended that in view of the autonomous character of the Community trade mark system, and for reasons of legal predictability and sound administration, the interpretation of the concept of bad faith given by the Court in the context of the Regulation cannot be transposed to the Directive. The Court dismissed that argument noting that, despite its autonomy, the Regulation supplements European Union trade mark legislation by creating a Union-wide regime for trade marks and pursues the same objective as the Directive, namely the establishment and functioning of the internal market, and held that, in the light of the need for harmonious interaction between the two systems, it is necessary to interpret the concept of bad faith within the meaning of Article 4(4)(g) in the same manner as in the context of the Regulation, in order to ensure a coherent application of the rules relating to trade marks in the legal order of the Union.[795]

5.938 Accordingly, the Court answered the second question by referring to the statements in *Lindt & Sprüngli*[796] that in order to determine the existence of bad faith, it is necessary to carry out an overall assessment of all the relevant factors present at the time of the application, and that the fact that the applicant knows or should know that a third party is using an identical or similar sign is not conclusive in itself to sustain the conclusion that that applicant is acting in bad faith. In addition to such knowledge, consideration must be given to the applicant's intention, a subjective factor which must be determined by reference to the objective circumstances of the case.[797]

---

[790] Citing C-482/09 *Budějovický Budvar* [2011] ECR I-08701, paragraph 29.
[791] Paragraphs 25–26.
[792] Citing C-408/01 *Adidas-Salomon and Adidas Benelux* [2003] ECR I-12537, paragraphs 18–21.
[793] Paragraphs 27–28.
[794] Paragraph 29.
[795] Paragraphs 32–35.
[796] C-529/07 *Chocoladefabriken Lindt & Sprüngli* [2009] ECR I-4893, paragraphs 37 and 40–42.
[797] Paragraphs 36–37.

5.939 (iii) **The binding effect on the national legislator** As concerns, lastly, the question regarding the possibility for Member States to introduce a specific protection of foreign marks based on the fact that the applicant knew or should have known of their existence, the Court stated that the optional character of Article 4(4) merely meant that a Member State's latitude is limited to the choice to transpose or not that ground into its national law as specifically delimited by the Union legislature. The Court based this interpretation on the Eighth Recital in the Preamble to the Directive, according to which the grounds for refusal set out therein are listed in an exhaustive manner, even if some of them are given as an option, which effectively prohibits Member States from introducing grounds for refusal or invalidity other than those specifically foreseen in the Directive.[798]

5.940 Consequently, the Court answered the third question to the effect that Article 4(4)(g) of the Directive does not allow Member States to introduce a system of specific protection of foreign marks which differs from the system established by that provision.

---

[798] Paragraphs 41–42.

6

DISTINCTIVENESS ACQUIRED THROUGH USE

A. Introduction: The Provisions of the Directive and the Regulation

6.01 Trade marks that are not inherently distinctive or that are descriptive or generic may nevertheless be registered if they have, as a result of the use that has been made of them, acquired distinctiveness, or what is called in US American trade mark law, 'secondary meaning'. The legal basis for this basis for registration is found in Article 3(3) of the Directive and in Article 7(3) CTMR. These provisions read as follows:

Directive

3. A trade mark shall not be refused registration or be declared invalid in accordance with paragraph 1(b), (c) or (d) if, before the date of application for registration and following the use which has been made of it, it has acquired a distinctive character. Any Member State may in addition provide that this provision shall also apply where the distinctive character was acquired after the date of application for registration or after the date of registration.

Regulation

3. Paragraph 1(b), (c) and (d) shall not apply if the trade mark has become distinctive in relation to the goods or services for which registration is requested in consequence of the use which has been made of it.

6.02 All the national trade mark systems recognized acquired distinctiveness, but the application of the rule differed from country to country. In particular, there were differences as regards the degree of knowledge among the relevant parts of the public. Questions also arose as to the manner of proving acquired distinctiveness. These issues were not resolved by the legislation, which merely stated the principle, but left the application to the respective authorities and the courts.

6.03 The issues that the Court of Justice had to solve over time related both to issues of substance and procedure. Among the substantive issues were, in particular, the question as to the degree of knowledge and whether differences should be made according to the need of the competition to make use of a particular sign or indication; also, relevant not only to the Community trade mark system but also to other composite or multi-language territories, such as the Benelux, was the territorial scope of acquired distinctiveness. Among the procedural issues were, in particular, the manner of proving acquired distinctiveness, and, as a sub-issue, the relevance of opinion surveys among the relevant public.

B. The Test for Assessing Acquired Distinctiveness: *Windsurfing Chiemsee*

6.04 The starting point for all the cases to follow is the Court's judgment in the Joined Cases C-108/97 and 109/97, *Windsurfing Chiemsee*,[1] relating to the mark CHIEMSEE, which is also the name of a large lake in southern Bavaria and a region for vacations. The case is also the starting point for the examination of marks for descriptiveness, and is thus also included in Chapter 5.

6.05 In the second part of *Windsurfing Chiemsee* the Court established the test assessing distinctive character that had been acquired through use.

6.06 The questions referred by the Landgericht were phrased in relation to the standards applied by German case law, where the relevant criterion was '*Freihaltebedürfnis*', the 'need to keep available/free' by others active in the same field, and where the issue revolved around the degree of distinctiveness that must be shown to overcome the refusal under Article 3(1)(b) or (c) of the Directive or Article 7(1)(b) and (c) CTMR:[2]

> What requirements follow from [Article 3(3)] for the registrability of a descriptive designation under Article 3(1)(c)?
>
> In particular, are the requirements the same in all cases, or are the requirements different according to the degree of the need to leave free?
>
> Is in particular the view hitherto taken in the German case-law, namely that in the case of descriptive designations which need to be left free, trade acceptance in more than 50% of the trade circles concerned is required and is to be demonstrated, compatible with that provision?
>
> Do requirements follow from this provision as to the manner in which descriptive character acquired by use is to be ascertained?[3]

(1) The Opinion of Advocate General Cosmas

6.07 Advocate General Cosmas dealt with the second set of questions briefly, having found that the contested sign should not require evidence of acquired distinctive character. Without any reservation, he accepted the Commission's view that the 'need to leave free' doctrine, in all its variations, should not be taken into account. Instead he suggested a number of criteria.

6.08 First, there should be use of the sign for a reasonably long period of time, testing the durability of the trade mark and giving the opportunity to those opposing registration to act.

6.09 Second, use of the sign should lead the relevant public to perceive the sign as distinguishing the goods or services of a particular undertaking. The relevant public should comprise primarily the respective consumers; the views of traders and manufacturers of similar products should also count; however, the motives behind the views of the trade should be a counterbalancing factor.

---

[1] C-108/97 and C-109/97 *Windsurfing Chiemsee Produktions- und Vertriebs GmbH* [1999] ECR I-2779.
[2] The 'trade circles' referred to in the questions are actually the opinion of the public to which the mark is addressed, in German '*beteiligte Verkehrskreise*', translated by the Court as 'trade circles'.
[3] Reproduced in paragraph 17.

6.10 Third, he accepted the usefulness of evaluating distinctive character on the basis of percentages and set the minimum limit at 50% of the relevant public believing that the product is linked with a particular undertaking.

6.11 Finally, he provided some guidelines on the type of evidence that could show distinctiveness, stressing again that the link with a particular undertaking, rather than the commercial success of the product, had to be established. Accordingly, information regarding advertising expenditure or the market share enjoyed by the marked product did not appear to be useful. The views of the relevant Chamber of Commerce or appropriate experts were more relevant. Courts could also use the findings of consumer surveys—but should not rely exclusively or predominantly on them—provided that they were conducted by a reliable pollster, using an appropriately constructed questionnaire, and targeting the relevant segment of the population.

6.12 He concluded that a trade mark can acquire distinctive character if there is appropriate evidence that its use for a reasonable period of time caused the public to believe that the product derives from a particular undertaking.

(2) The Judgment of the Court

6.13 The Court distilled the second set of questions into being an enquiry about the requirements for acquiring distinctive character through use according to Article 3(3) and whether the 'need to leave free' doctrine affected them.

(a) The meaning of 'distinctiveness acquired through use'

6.14 The Court saw Article 3(3) as a major exception to the rule laid down in Article 3(1)(b), Article 3(1)(c), and Article 3(1)(d). It was clear for the Court that the concept of distinctive character should be given the same meaning throughout Article 3; the mark had to identify the marked product as originating from a particular undertaking. The same rule applied to geographical indications; '[w]here that is the case, the geographical designation has gained a new significance and its connotation, no longer purely descriptive, justifies its registration as a trade mark.'[4]

6.15 The Court, however, failed to provide a definition of when that process—the conversion of a descriptive sign to a mark—was completed. Rather, the Court concluded, without any further explanation, as follows:

> If, on the basis of those factors, the competent authority finds that *the relevant class of persons*, or at least *a significant proportion* thereof, identify goods as originating from a particular undertaking because of the trade mark, it must hold that the requirement for registering the mark laid down in Article 3(3) of the Directive is satisfied. However, the circumstances in which that requirement may be regarded as satisfied cannot be shown to exist solely by reference to general, abstract data such as predetermined percentages.[5]

6.16 What is decisive is that the 'relevant class of persons', or at least a 'significant proportion thereof', identify the maker of the product through the mark. The Court uses here a concept which it was to apply in a subsequent judgment where similar issues arose, namely the degree of knowledge in order for a mark to have a reputation.[6] The Court never went

---

[4] *Windsurfing Chiemsee* (n 1) paragraph 47.
[5] Paragraph 52.
[6] C-375/97 *General Motors Corporation v Yplon SA* (CHEVY) [1999] ECR I-05421, paragraph 26.

beyond this rather Delphic pronouncement, however, and thus left the respective competent authorities to determine whether the requirement was met.

6.17 The Court also rejected the concept developed by the German case law, according to which the degree of distinctiveness that would have to be shown was proportionate to the degree of the need for others to use the contested sign or indication. All marks must be treated the same: 'Article 3(3) does not permit any differentiation as regards distinctiveness by reference to the perceived importance of keeping the geographical name available for use by other undertakings.'[7]

(b) Assessing distinctiveness: The evidence, and an overall assessment

6.18 To make sure that Article 3(3) was viewed as a self-existent provision, the Court came up with a multifactor test for acquired distinctive character. The Court used the overall assessment concept in order to describe the general tenor of the test: 'the competent authority must make an overall assessment of the evidence that the mark has come to identify the product concerned as originating from a particular undertaking'.[8]

6.19 (i) **A multifactor test** It then identified specific factors that had to be considered as part of the overall assessment.

6.20 First, the specific nature of the geographical name; a well-known geographical name would require long-standing and intensive use in order to acquire a new significance, even more so when the name is familiar in relation to the same category of goods. We assume that the nature of the sign or indication would also be taken into account when the contested sign is not a geographical name.

6.21 The Court went on to identify seven more factors: the market share held by the mark; the intensity of use; the geographical spread of use; the longevity of use; the amount invested in promoting the mark; the proportion of the relevant class of persons who, because of the mark, identify goods as originating from a particular undertaking; and statements from chambers of commerce and industry or other trade and professional associations.

6.22 Note that the last factor could bring the views of competitors into the assessment, introducing a competition element. Just as the Court has never made explicit which parts of the 'public' or the 'trade' must be taken into account when determining whether a mark or indication is lacking in distinctiveness or is descriptive, the Court has also never been specific when the question arises whether the recognition of a sign or indication as a mark must be among all relevant circles, ie consumers and the commercial trade.

6.23 The Court did reject though the practice of relying solely on general, abstract data such as predetermined percentages. Opinion polls could be useful where a national authority 'has particular difficulty'[9] in establishing whether a contested sign has acquired the necessary distinctive character. The national authority would then have to rely on the conditions laid down by its own national law regarding the polls. This is an interesting abstinence and reference to national law, which in cases involving Community trade marks would appear to be highly questionable, but which is also questionable as regards national marks, because

---

[7] Paragraph 48.
[8] Paragraph 49.
[9] *Windsurfing Chiemsee* (n 1) paragraph 53.

it contradicts the Court's own assessment that the notion of 'acquired distinctiveness' is a notion of EU law. It also shows that the Court does not seem to have a clear understanding of how such surveys are carried out and what they are actually able to establish.

The issue of evidence and the role of surveys would be revisited in the 2014 judgment in *Oberbank & Banco Santander*.[10]

6.24

C. Use as a Mark, and the Monopoly Argument: *Philips*

The third question referred to the Court in *Philips*[11] targeted the conditions and the method in which distinctive character could be gained through use.

6.25

Where a trader had been the only supplier of a product, would extensive use of a sign that consisted of the shape of the product, and did not incorporate a capricious addition, be sufficient to render the sign distinctive for the purposes of Article 3(3) when a substantial proportion of the relevant trade and public associated the shape with that trader and no other undertaking and believed that goods of that shape came from that trader unless there was a statement to the contrary?

6.26

(1) The Opinion of Advocate General Ruiz-Jarabo Colomer

Advocate General Ruiz-Jarabo Colomer found that the question could be answered by reference to his brief answer to the second question,[12] where he implied that shapes would require an arbitrary addition in order to become distinctive, and his analysis of Article 3(1)(e), in particular the conclusion that it was not in any way connected with distinctiveness.

6.27

(2) The Judgment of the Court

For the Court, Article 3(3) provided that through use, a sign that failed Article 3(1)(b), Article 3(1)(c), or Article 3(1)(d) could overcome the objection through evidence of acquired distinctive character. According to *Windsurfing Chiemsee*[13] this meant that the mark was able to identify the specified product as originating from a particular undertaking, and thus to distinguish that product from goods of other undertakings.

6.28

Philips had argued before the Court that the *de facto* monopoly described in the question should be seen as an advantage towards registration rather than an impediment. Remington, on the other hand, urged the Court to adopt a balanced approach and require evidence that the sign indeed functioned as an indicator of origin.

6.29

The Court chose the middle ground; it referred to the test and the criteria adopted in *Windsurfing Chiemsee* and added that Article 3(3) was irrelevant in relation to a sign that had been refused registration under Article 3(1)(e).

6.30

---

[10] C-217/13 *Oberbank AG*, C-218/13 *Banco Santander SA and Santander Consumer Bank AG v Deutscher Sparkassen- und Giroverband eV*, ECLI:EU:C:2014:2012. See paragraphs 6.144 and following below.
[11] C-299/99 *Koninklijke Philips Electronics NV* [2002] ECR I-5475.
[12] Points 46-47.
[13] C-108/97 and C-109/97 *Windsurfing Chiemsee* [1999] ECR I-2779.

(a) The requirement for specific and reliable data: Use as a mark

6.31 The Court underlined three particular points. First, it repeated that general, abstract data, such as predetermined percentages, would not be useful and added that in order to establish acquired distinctive character, specific and reliable data was required.

6.32 Second, it stressed that acquired distinctiveness must be established with regard to the public addressed by the mark:

> The distinctive character of a sign consisting in the shape of a product, even that acquired by the use made of it, must be assessed in the light of the presumed expectations of an average consumer of the category of goods or services in question, who is reasonably well-informed and reasonably observant and circumspect.[14]

6.33 This was reinforced by the third point made by the Court:

> The identification, by the relevant class of persons, of the product as originating from a given undertaking must be as a result of the use of the mark <u>as a trade mark</u> and thus as a result of the nature and effect of it, which make it capable of distinguishing the product concerned from those of other undertakings.[15]

6.34 So under the circumstances described above the type of use described by the referring court could generate the distinctive character that was necessary to satisfy Article 3(3), provided that the three points made by the Court were satisfied. Verifying this remained within the jurisdiction of the national court.

(b) The 'monopoly' argument

6.35 The Court refused to draw a distinction between multiple and sole users, thus rejecting the notion that it was detrimental to the claim of acquired distinctiveness that the claimant was in fact the only person using the sign or indication:

> In the light of those considerations, the answer to the third question must be that, where a trader has been the only supplier of particular goods to the market, extensive use of a sign which consists of the shape of those goods may be sufficient to give the sign a distinctive character for the purposes of Article 3(3) of the Directive in circumstances where, as a result of that use, a substantial proportion of the relevant class of persons associates that shape with that trader and no other undertaking or believes that goods of that shape come from that trader.[16]

D. Combined Use: *Nestlé v Mars (Kit Kat)*

6.36 The *Kit Kat* case[17] revisited slogans as trade marks from a different perspective. The reference from the English Court of Appeal enquired whether the distinctive character of a mark referred to in Article 3(3) of the Directive could be acquired following, or in consequence of, the use of that mark as part of or in conjunction with another mark.

---

[14] *Philips* (n 11) paragraph 63, citing C-210/96 *Gut Springenheide and Tusky v Oberkreisdirektor des Kreises Steinfurt-Amt für Lebensmittelüberwachung* [1998] ECR I-4657.
[15] Paragraph 64.
[16] Paragraph 65.
[17] C-353/03 *Société des Produits Nestlé v Mars UK Ltd* [2005] ECR I-6135.

6.37 The sign in question was the slogan HAVE A BREAK that Nestlé applied to register as a trade mark in the United Kingdom. Nestlé was already the proprietor of the marks HAVE A BREAK... HAVE A KIT KAT and KIT KAT covering the same specification: chocolate, chocolate products, confectionery, candy, and biscuits. Mars opposed the application, claiming that the mark lacked distinctive character under Article 3(1)(b).

6.38 On appeal the UK court found that the slogan as such was indeed devoid of distinctive character. Registration could be obtained only if Nestlé could prove that the sign had acquired distinctive character through use. The problem was that the expression HAVE A BREAK was used as part of the trade mark HAVE A BREAK... HAVE A KIT KAT rather than as an independent trade mark.

(1) The Opinion of Advocate General Kokott

6.39 Advocate General Kokott reiterated that following *Erpo Möbelwerk*[18] the universally applicable concept of distinctive character[19] precluded specific criteria from being applied in the case of specific types of trade marks.

6.40 She then distinguished between inherent and acquired distinctiveness. Article 3(1)(b) covered inherent distinctiveness, and as 'a matter of principle that examination is to be conducted independently of use of the sign. It has regard only to whether the sign in itself has distinctive character'.[20]

6.41 Article 3(3), however, diluted Article 3(1)(b), allowing the registration of marks that had acquired distinctive character through use. Delineating the scope of her Opinion and the judgment of the Court she stressed that the role of the Court was to express a view on the interpretation of Article 3(3) rather than decide whether HAVE A BREAK had acquired a distinctive character.

6.42 She rejected outright the argument submitted by Mars and supported by the Commission that use of the contested mark as an element of another mark should not be considered under Article 3(3).

6.43 Following a literal interpretive path, she noted that use of a mark meant both independent use of the sign and use as part of another composite trade mark and that Article 10(2)(a) pointed towards the same conclusion. If use of a mark as part of a composite sufficed to maintain the validity of the registration, it had to suffice for obtaining the same registration.

6.44 The Advocate General contrasted the concept of use in the context of Article 5, where the Court had limited protection to cover instances that affect the function of a trade mark as a guarantee of origin, and in that of Article 3(3), where, she claimed, it fulfilled a different function, to describe the manner in which a sign might acquire distinctive character through use. The Court had considered this type of use in *Philips*.[21] It had to be use as a trade mark, but this did not preclude use of the relevant sign as part of a trade mark.

---

[18] C-64/02 P *OHIM v Erpo Möbelwerk* [2004] ECR I-10031.
[19] Point 16.
[20] Point 18.
[21] She cautioned that C-299/99 *Philips* [2002] ECR I-5475 should be read keeping in mind that it dealt primarily with Article 3(1)(e) of the Directive and that the Court did not have to interpret Article 3(3) as well.

6.45 Use under Article 3(3) had to 'be construed from the perspective of the result. Any use which confers on a sign the distinctive character necessary for registration as a mark must be deemed to be use of a mark as a trade mark'.[22]

6.46 She found the view of Mars, also adopted by the United Kingdom, that the risk of extending the protection of the principal mark to cover the derivative mark meant that stricter criteria had to be adopted when only one part of the principal mark was assessed because then a derivative of the derivative could be protected, to be illusory:

> If a primary derivative mark possesses no sufficient distinctive character of its own but acquires distinctiveness only by way of the connection with the principal mark then it is unlikely that a secondary derivative mark will be able to acquire distinctive character on the basis of its connection with the primary derivative mark.[23]

6.47 She added that so far, the practice of the Court, the Court of First Instance, and OHIM was not to refuse trade mark recognition to parts of a trade mark that had themselves acquired a distinctive character.[24] Nevertheless, gathering evidence of distinctiveness acquired through use would not be an easy exercise. It would not be sufficient:

> for the purposes of demonstrating acquisition of distinctive character, as a result of use as a part of a composite mark, to provide documentary evidence of use of the overall mark. Rather it must also be demonstrated that the relevant consumer groups understand the element in question, if used separately, to designate a product as originating from a specific undertaking, thus distinguishing it from products of other undertakings.[25]

6.48 In practice it would be easier to find distinctive character for the essential elements of a primary mark, whereas inessential elements would be less likely to develop a distinctive character.

(2) The Judgment of the Court

6.49 The Court reiterated the parameters of distinctive character. Both inherent and acquired through use distinctive character had to be assessed in relation to the specified goods or services and the presumed expectations of the relevant class of persons. Acquired distinctive character had to be the result of use as a trade mark.[26] Article 3(3) did not indicate any further restriction or requirement. Identification of the specified product or service as originating from a given undertaking,

> and thus acquisition of distinctive character, may be as a result both of the use, as part of a registered trade mark, of a component thereof and of the use of a separate mark in conjunction with a registered trade mark. In both cases it is sufficient that, in consequence of such

---

[22] Point 33. The reference in C-299/99 *Koninklijke Philips Electronics NV* [2002] ECR I-5475 to the nature and effect of a trade mark as the background of use required under Article 3(3) strengthened the interpretive approach of the AG.

[23] Point 36.

[24] Referring by way of example to C-108/97 and C-109/97 *Windsurfing Chiemsee* [1999] ECR I-2779; T-237/01 *Alcon Inc v OHIM* [2003] ECR II-411; and the decision of the Second Board of Appeal of OHIM in Case R-111/2000-2 *Ringling Bros-Barnum & Bailey Inc* (*The Greatest Show on Earth*).

[25] Point 43. She accepted the submission of the United Kingdom Government that it would not be sufficient to show that consumers merely wondered whether the product or service originated from the owner of the primary mark; this, however, would be a consideration for assessing likelihood of confusion.

[26] Citing C-299/99 *Philips* [2002] ECR I-5475.

E. Sales Figures: Amount Spent on Advertising; *Storck I*

Part of the appeal in *Storck I*[28] challenged the findings of the Court of First Instance in relation to the evidence that is required for establishing that distinctive character has been acquired through use under Article 7(3). **6.50**

(1) The Judgment of the Court of First Instance

The Court of First Instance had agreed with the Board of Appeal of OHIM that the sign— the three-dimensional shape of a sweet—had not acquired distinctive character through use, finding that the evidence was insufficient. Sales figures and the amount spent on advertising to promote the product did not establish that the actual shape had become distinctive as a result of use. **6.51**

Storck had argued that samples of plastic bags in which the sweets were sold bearing reproductions of the shape of the sweets constituted a 'primary reference' point for the consumer and that they should be seen as evidence that the shape was the subject of the advertising as the mark of the product. **6.52**

Responding to the argument the Board had stressed that it should not perform an abstract assessment but, instead, consider the probable way in which the average consumer perceived the representation of the sweets. The consumer would first notice the name 'Werther's Original' written in large print over almost half of the packet and surrounded by further details such as a small oval sign bearing the name Storck and the stylized picture of a small village below which might be perceived as a reference to 'Traditional Werther's Quality'. The lower half of the packet depicted a colour photograph of a pile of about fifteen sweets and the statement: 'The classic candy made with real butter and fresh cream.' **6.53**

The Board found that the way the sweets were represented on the packaging served simply as an illustration of its contents rather than as an indication of source. It was a realistic picture of a pile of unwrapped sweets, rather than a representation of the mark applied for, that did not intend to emphasize the two potentially distinctive characteristics of the mark. It highlighted in particular the combination of the statement 'The classic candy made with real butter and fresh cream' with the picture. They complemented each other in that the statement described the nature of the sweets and the picture depicted them. The Board accepted that a product might simultaneously bear multiple marks but this general proposition did not mean that the particular representation on the packaging of the sweets functioned as a trade mark. As a result, the advertising expenditure could not be linked with the use of the mark applied for. The Board found that the surveys submitted to support the application proved that the sweets were sold on the basis of their name, not their shape, functioning as a trade mark. **6.54**

---

[27] *Kit Kat* (n 17) paragraph 30.
[28] C-24/05 P *August Storck KG v OHIM* [2006] ECR I-5677.

6.55 The Court of First Instance added that Storck had stated on the application form that the sweets were not sold loose; they were individually wrapped and sold in a packet. The average consumer would not be able to see the shape of the sweet prior to the sale of the product in order to perceive it as an indication of origin.

6.56 Before the Court of Justice, Storck argued that the Court of First Instance had infringed Article 7(3) of the Regulation in three ways: first, by making the relevant evidence subject to false requirements; second, by wrongly confirming the function of the representation of the mark on the packaging of the product; and, third, by wrongly taking into consideration consumer perception at the time of the decision to buy.

(2) The Opinion of Advocate General Ruiz-Jarabo Colomer

(a) The application of Article 7(3) to three-dimensional signs

6.57 Advocate General Ruiz-Jarabo Colomer made it clear that he would deal only with those elements of the fourth ground that raised legal questions, not with those that involved the possible re-assessment of facts such as the assertions regarding the impression of the sign on the wrapping.

6.58 He referred to *Nestlé*,[29] where the Court held that the acquisition of distinctive character did not necessarily entail independent use of a sign. In the current case, the Court of First Instance had not contradicted this, nor had it attempted to establish a general rule for three-dimensional signs; it had merely assessed the evidence in the case before it.

(b) The relevant point in time for determining distinctiveness: Point of sale, pre-sale, post-sale

6.59 The Advocate General referred again to *Nestlé* and then to *Picasso*[30]. His interpretation of the first case appeared to leave the question of the decisive moment for determining distinctive character unanswered, since the Court had only indicated that it would be sufficient 'that the relevant sectors perceive the product or service, designated exclusively by the mark applied for, as originating from a given undertaking'.[31]

6.60 The second case also appeared to be, to say the least, inconclusive:

> Apart from my feeling that the present discussion would be more appropriate in the context of Article 8(1)(b) of Regulation No 40/94, it is worth noting that in Ruiz-Picasso the Court of Justice endorsed the reasoning of the Court of First Instance on the likelihood of confusion, to the effect that the relevant public also perceives the products and the marks relating to them in circumstances unconnected with any act of purchase, although on such occasions displaying a lower level of attention, which does not prevent taking into account the particularly high level of attention which the average consumer pays when he prepares and makes his choice between different products in the same range.[32]

6.61 Expressing his own view, he veered towards the point of sale and the time of making the purchase, at least in comparison with advertising:

> In a system in which competition is not distorted ... it is plain that the protection for proprietors of the type of intellectual property right in question is concentrated in the culminating

---

[29] C-353/03 *Société des Produits Nestlé* [2005] ECR I-6135.
[30] C-316/04 P *Ruiz-Picasso v OHIM* [2006] ECR I-643.
[31] Point 59.
[32] Point 61.

moment when the consumer makes his decision, the purchase of the product or the engagement of the service, whilst prior advertising is a measure intended to induce that consumer to opt for a particular acquisition, and it is therefore difficult to understand why it should be taken into account on an equal footing with the act of purchasing the product.[33]

6.62 The argument of the appellant based on the post-sale effect of the mark at the time of consumption was rejected by the Advocate General as even less comprehensible.

(3) The Judgment of the Court

6.63 The Court divided the fourth ground of appeal into three parts. The first part related to the claim that the Court of First Instance had wrongly held that a mark made up of the three-dimensional shape of the product could not acquire distinctive character if accompanied by a word or figurative mark. The second part related to the Court's confirmation of the Board's assessment that the representation of the product on the packaging showed merely its contents. The mark and the product were the same thing and accordingly its reproduction functioned as information regarding the contents of the packet but also an indication of origin. The third part related to the claim that the Court had wrongly discounted consumer perceptions before the point of sale, for example, as a result of advertising, and, after the point of sale, when consuming the product.

(a) *Three-dimensional signs*

6.64 The Court accepted that following *Nestlé*,[34] a three dimensional mark might, in certain circumstances, acquire distinctive character through use even if it were used in conjunction with a word mark or a figurative mark. However, its next statement limited that possibility considerably:

> However, it must be stressed that a three-dimensional mark is essentially different from its two-dimensional graphic representation. It follows that where, as in the present case, a picture of the product features on the packaging, consumers do not actually see the mark itself, being the mark consisting of the three-dimensional form of the product.[35]

6.65 And then, in the same paragraph, the Court reduced the effect of the above statement by introducing a new consideration: a classic example of the, sometimes confusing, habit of the Court to rely on balancing exercises:

> It is possible, however, that the two-dimensional representation of such a mark may in certain circumstances facilitate awareness of the mark by the relevant public where it enables the essential elements of the three-dimensional shape of the product to be perceived.[36]

6.66 The Court then reverted to its sceptical original logic by recalling that, according to *Philips*[37] and *Nestlé*,[38] the acquisition of distinctive character through use had to be the result of the use of the mark as a trade mark, ie use of the mark for the purposes of the identification by the relevant class of persons of the product or service as originating from a given undertaking.

---

[33] Ibid.
[34] C-353/03 *Société des Produits Nestlé* [2005] ECR I-6135.
[35] *Storck I* (n 28) paragraph 60.
[36] *Storck I* (n 28) paragraph 60.
[37] C-299/99 *Philips* [2002] ECR I-5475.
[38] C-353/03 *Société des Produits Nestlé* [2005] ECR I-6135.

6.67 Therefore, it added that not every use of the mark, 'a fortiori use of a two dimensional representation of a three-dimensional mark, amounts necessarily to use as a mark'.[39]

(b) The picture of the product

6.68 As regards the argument that the Court of First Instance had committed an error by considering that the representation on the packaging was not use as a mark, the Court held that following a factual assessment the Court of First Instance had found that the representation related to the contents rather than the mark in question. In terms of law, though, it had accepted, by endorsing the relevant statement of the Board, that a product might bear several marks at the same time.

(c) The relevant point in time: Point of sale

6.69 As to the third ground, the Court accepted that distinctive character might be acquired 'inter alia, after the normal process of familiarising the relevant public has taken place'.[40] This meant that 'all the circumstances in which the relevant public may see that mark must be borne in mind. That means not only when the decision to purchase is made, but also before that point, for example as a result of advertising, and when the product is consumed'.[41]

6.70 But the critical time was the point at which the average consumer made a choice:

> It is when making his choice between different products in the category concerned that the average consumer exhibits the highest level of attention[42] ... so that the question whether or not the average consumer sees the mark at the time of purchase is of particular importance for determining whether the mark has acquired distinctive character through use.[43]

6.71 The Court found that the Court of First Instance had not only considered the time when the decision to purchase was made, but also the effect of the packaging on the consumer 'logically, with reference to the actual time of purchase'.[44]

6.72 And, it had rightly found that the surveys failed to distinguish between the various circumstances in which consumers might have seen the mark, and accordingly could not furnish proof that the mark applied for was known.

F. Sales Figures and Territorial Scope of Acquired Distinctiveness

6.73 In *Storck II*[45] the mark consisted of a gold-coloured sweet wrapper. The Court of First Instance agreed with the Board of Appeal of OHIM that the applicant had not established that the mark had acquired distinctive character. The sales figures that had been provided failed to show the share the mark enjoyed in the market in the absence of any information regarding the total volume of the relevant product market. The same applied to advertising costs. In addition, the information provided was patchy and, in some cases, unpersuasive.

---

[39] *Storck I* (n 28) paragraph 62.
[40] *Storck I* (n 28) paragraph 70, citing C-104/01 *Libertel Groep BV* [2003] ECR I-3793; and C-132/02 P *Mag Instrument Inc* [2004] ECR I-9165.
[41] *Storck I* (n 28) paragraph 71.
[42] Citing C-361/04 P *Ruiz-Picasso* [2006] ECR I-643.
[43] *Storck I* (n 28) paragraph 72.
[44] *Storck I* (n 28) paragraph 74.
[45] C-25/5 P *August Storck KG* [2006] ECR I-5719.

The Court of First Instance appeared to require strong data covering the entire Community because the trade mark should have become distinctive through use throughout its territory. As to the surveys produced by the applicant, the Court of First Instance found that they only proved that the sweets were sold because of their name rather than their wrappers. **6.74**

(1) The Opinion of Advocate General Ruiz-Jarabo Colomer

The Advocate General divided his discussion of the Article 7(3) ground of appeal into two parts. First, he dealt with the evidence of use and then, with its geographical extent. **6.75**

(a) Evidence of use

Storck had attacked the Board's finding that the figures relating to sales and advertising expenditure had failed to establish that the mark had acquired distinctive character through use and that additional information regarding the overall size of these markets should therefore be produced. **6.76**

To an extent, Storck replayed the argument that the condition of the market was irrelevant. In the same way that the existence of similar packaging should not be an obstacle to establishing distinctive character, the existence or absence of different packaging should be irrelevant for the acquisition of distinctive character. **6.77**

The Advocate General recalled the factors the Court had established in *Windsurfing Chiemsee*[46] and *Philips*[47] and added that the applicability and evidential value of these factors remained in the jurisdiction of the Court of First Instance. In that case, the Court of First Instance had considered the appellant's assertions but still found that one of the factors, the share of the market in terms of sales, should be decisive. **6.78**

The share in the advertising market, an apparently new factor compared with those mentioned in *Windsurfing Chiemsee*, failed to attract any further discussion by the Court. **6.79**

(b) Geographical extent

Storck argued that requiring evidence of use throughout all Member States went against two of the fundamental objectives of the EU: the abolition of national borders and the creation of a single market. **6.80**

Storck relied, inter alia, on Article 142a(2) of the Regulation (now Article 165), one of the enlargement provisions.[48] **6.81**

The Advocate General followed the line suggested by OHIM. Reading Article 7(1)(b) together with Article 7(2) meant that lack of distinctive character in part of the EU should lead to the rejection of the application for registration. Admittedly, Article 7(3) did not refer **6.82**

---

[46] C-108/97 and C-109/97 *Windsurfing Chiemsee* [1999] ECR I-2779.
[47] C-299/99 *Philips* [2002] ECR I-5475.
[48] Providing that the 'registration of a Community trade mark which is under application at the date of accession may not be refused on the basis of any of the absolute grounds for refusal listed in Article 7(1) [of Reg No 40/94], if these grounds became applicable merely because of the accession of a new Member State'. Article 7(1)(b) provides that 'trade marks which are devoid of any distinctive character' shall not be registered whereas Article 7(2) provides that Article 7(1) 'shall apply notwithstanding that the grounds of non-registrability obtain in only part of the Community' and Article 7(3) provides that Article 7(1)(b) shall not apply if the trade mark has become distinctive in relation to the goods or services for which registration is requested in consequence of the use which has been made of it.

to Article 7(2). It would be illogical though to demand a lower geographical threshold under Article 7(3). He added that the later 'political' enlargement provision should not affect the application of Article 7(3).

(2) The Judgment of the Court

6.83 The Court repeated the test it had established in its earlier case law.[49] All the facts should be taken into account including: the market share held by the mark; how intensive, geographically widespread, and long-standing use of the mark had been; the amount invested by the undertaking in promoting the mark; the proportion of the relevant class of persons who, because of the mark, identified goods as originating from a particular undertaking; and statements from chambers of commerce and industry or other trade and professional associations.

(a) Market share

6.84 The Court remarked that market share was one of the relevant factors:

> Such is the case, in particular, where ... a mark consisting of the appearance of the product in respect of which registration is sought appears to be devoid of any distinctive character because it does not depart significantly from the norm or customs of the sector. It is probable, in such a case, that such a mark is likely to acquire distinctive character only if, following the use which is made of it, the products which bear it have more than a negligible share of the market in the products at issue.[50]

6.85 The same reasoning applied to advertising expenditure. In any case, the relevance of that information for determining whether a mark had acquired distinctive character through use was part of the assessment of the facts of the case.

(b) Geographical extent

6.86 The Court was unequivocal in its approach. Following the same reasoning as that of the Advocate General, it ruled that:

> a mark can be registered under Article 7(3) of Regulation No 40/94 only if evidence is provided that it has acquired, through the use which has been made of it, distinctive character in the part of the Community in which it did not, ab initio, have such character for the purposes of Article 7(1)(b). The part of the Community referred to in Article 7(2) may be comprised of a single Member State.[51]

6.87 Still, the use of 'may' in the final sentence allows certain doubts to be raised. It may seem logical to require proof of acquired distinctiveness in the territory where the obstacle exists. Thus, the proprietor of a mark which is descriptive in Portuguese may need to show acquired distinctiveness in Portugal, the only territory where Portuguese is spoken. But how would this apply to a mark which is descriptive in German, which is spoken in Austria, Germany, parts of Italy, and Belgium, and known by many? Similarly, how would this apply to a mark in English, which is spoken widely everywhere in the Community? Does it therefore really make sense to divide the EU into its Member States? There is also the issue of non-verbal marks, such as shapes and colours, which cannot be said to have defects in a particular

---

[49] C-108/97 and C-109/97 *Windsurfing Chiemsee* [1999] ECR I-2779; C-299/99 *Philips* [2002] ECR I-5475; and C-353/03 *Nestlé* [2005] ECR I-6135.
[50] *Storck II*, (n 45) paragraph 76.
[51] *Storck II*, (n 45) paragraph 83.

Member State, the less so as Article 7(2) of the Regulation refers not to Member States but to 'parts' of the Community.

6.88 We will see later that the Court seems to have some regrets about its statement in *Storck II*.

6.89 The Act of Accession appeared to reinforce the Court's stance:

> As they found it necessary to introduce an express provision to the effect that registration of a Community trade mark which is under application at the date of accession may not be refused on the basis of any of the absolute grounds for refusal listed in Article 7(1) of Regulation No 40/94, if these grounds became applicable merely because of the accession of a new Member State, the authors of the Act of Accession considered that, if that provision did not exist, such an application would have had to have been refused if the mark was devoid of any distinctive character in one of the new Member States.[52]

G. Acquired Distinctive Character in the Benelux: Linguistic and Geographical Considerations; *Europolis*

6.90 In *Europolis*[53] the Court was asked to determine how a trade mark might acquire distinctive character through use, under Article 3(3) of the Directive, in the Benelux, where a single trade mark law has applied throughout the three Benelux countries since 1970. The case had reached the Gerechtshof te 's-Gravenhage (The Hague Court of Appeal) as an appeal against the decision of the Benelux Trade Mark Office to reject an application for EUROPOLIS for 'insurance, financial affairs, monetary affairs, real estate affairs, transport, packaging and storage of goods, and travel arrangements' on grounds of lack of distinctive character, despite evidence that the mark had been used for a ten-year period before the application.

6.91 The Dutch court considered that the mark had no 'intrinsic distinctive character'.[54] As to whether the sign had acquired distinctiveness through use, the Benelux Trade Mark Office required recognition of the sign as a trade mark throughout the Benelux, whereas the applicant contended that it would be enough to be recognized as a trade mark by the relevant public in a substantial part of the Benelux.

6.92 Viewing the issue of acquired distinctiveness from a rather formalistic perspective, the Hague Regional Court of Appeal referred to the Court of Justice a number of questions.

6.93 First, whether Article 3(3) necessitated the sign to be regarded as a trade mark throughout the Benelux.

6.94 Second, if the answer to the first question were negative, whether it would be enough to be regarded as a trade mark by the relevant section of the public in a substantial part of the Benelux, for example, only in The Netherlands.

6.95 The third question had to do with distinctiveness of word marks in regions characterized by their language: the first part of the question enquired whether it was necessary to take into account the language regions—or linguistic communities as AG Sharpston put it—within

---

[52] *Storck II*, (n 45) paragraph 85.
[53] C-108/05 *Bovemij Verzekeringen NV* [2006] ECR I-7605.
[54] Point 20 of the Opinion of AG Sharpston.

the Benelux; the second, if it suffices to be regarded as a trade mark in a substantial part of the language region of the Benelux in which that language is an official language.

(1) The Opinion of Advocate General Sharpston

6.96 The delineation of the subject matter of the case by the Advocate General is quite interesting. Despite the fact that the first two questions referred to trade marks in general rather than word marks, she narrowed the scope of the Opinion to cover only word marks by referring to the subject matter of the proceedings before the Dutch court.[55]

(a) General criteria for applying distinctiveness and descriptiveness

6.97 Having narrowed the overall scope of the Opinion down to word marks, the Advocate General broadened its legal subject matter by examining not only the issue of distinctiveness acquired through use, as requested by the national court, but also the issue of how word marks fit within the Directive and the jurisprudence of the Court, and the basis for determining that they are devoid of any distinctive character.

6.98 Looking at word marks, the Advocate General repeated the position of the Court:

> a word or combination of words may serve to designate some characteristic(s) of a product. Words used for that purpose are not registrable by virtue of Article 3(1)(c). They are similarly necessarily devoid of any distinctive character with regard to that product within the meaning of Article 3(1)(b), as the Court has already held.[56]

6.99 On the other hand, a word or a combination of words 'may identify a product (whether or not in the process they also incidentally describe it). Such a word mark is registrable as a trade mark because it is not caught by either Article 3(1)(b) or Article 3(1)(c).'[57]

6.100 Note that the Advocate General employed the term 'identify' instead of 'distinguish'. It could be argued that the first term is broader. She then referred to the public interest behind Article 3(1)(c), 'that all signs or indications which may serve to designate characteristics of the goods or services for which registration is sought may be freely used by all',[58] but focused in particular on word marks citing *Linde*[59] and *Campina Melkunie*.[60]

> The public interest in not allowing a descriptive combination of words to be registered and protected as a trade mark is clear. Such registration prevents other undertakings (and hence potential competitors) from using obvious terms to describe their products to consumers, thus placing them at a competitive disadvantage.[61]

6.101 She added that it would be against the purpose of the Directive to remove disparities which may impede free movement and distort competition, referring to Recital 1. Registrability under Article 3(1)(b) and Article 3(1)(c) should be assessed according to the perception of

---

[55] Point 25. Contrast with her Opinion in C-348/04 *Boehringer Ingelheim KG, Boehringer Ingelheim Pharma GmbH & Co. KG, Glaxo Group Ltd v Swingward Ltd.*
[56] Point 28, citing C-363/99 *Koninklijke KPN Nederland NV* [2004] ECR I-1619, paragraph 13.
[57] Point 28.
[58] Citing C-265/00 *Campina Melkunie* [2004] ECR I-1699; C-108/97 and C-109/97 *Windsurfing Chiemsee* [1999] ECR I-2779; and C-104/01 *Libertel* [2003] ECR I-3793.
[59] C-53/01 *Linde AG*, C-54/01 *Winward Industries Inc*, and C-55/01 *Rado Uhren AG* [2003] ECR I-3161.
[60] C-265/00 *Campina Melkunie BV* [2004] ECR I-1699.
[61] Point 29. She noted that the Court did not appear to distinguish between the public interest behind Article 3(1)(b) and that behind Article 3(1)(c); in C-363/99 *Koninklijke KPN Nederland NV* [2004] ECR I-1619 the Court assessed distinctiveness under Article 3(1)(b) but referred to the public interest in terms of Article 3(1)(c).

the 'relevant class of person'[62] in the Member State where registration is sought. The linguistic abilities of that class were critical because they ultimately determined registrability:[63]

> Put another way, words that convey meaning through their ability to describe goods or services may not be registered as marks, but where they fail to convey meaning because of linguistic differences, they cannot perform a descriptive function. There is therefore no bar to their registration arising from Article 3(1).[64]

6.102 To determine whether the sign had acquired distinctiveness, the overall assessment test developed in *Windsurfing Chiemsee*[65] should be applied, to establish whether the relevant class of persons, or at least a significant proportion—according to the Advocate General, significant meant a considerable part but not necessarily the majority—thereof identify the products as originating from a particular undertaking because of the mark.[66]

6.103 She also noted that the factors of this test related either to the actual use of the mark or its identification with the product. In essence, Article 3(3) requirements mirror the assessment that had to be made under Article 3(1)(b) and Article 3(1)(c).[67]

6.104 The relevance of the linguistic abilities of that class of persons depended on the original meaning of the words.

> Where the fact that the words normally convey descriptive meaning to the relevant class was a bar to registration, it must then be relevant to examine whether, for those persons, the word mark has nevertheless acquired distinctive character through use and thus qualifies for registration under Article 3(3).[68]

Article 3(3) had to be applied 'within the same parameters as were used to identify the original lack of distinctiveness'.[69]

(b) The territorial scope of the assessment

6.105 After this general assessment she turned to the actual questions referred by the Dutch court. Regarding the territorial scope of assessment, the Court had already held that for the purposes of Article 5(2) (protection of marks with reputation) the territory of the Benelux should be equated with the territory of a Member State.[70]

6.106 If it was enough to have a reputation in a substantial part of the Benelux, which may consist of a part of one of the Benelux countries for Article 5(2), it should similarly be enough to acquire distinctive character through use in a substantial part of the Benelux for Article 3(3).

6.107 The Benelux Trade Mark Office's position that a trade mark should enjoy distinctiveness throughout the Benelux was wrongly based on *General Motors*.[71] This case concerned a

---

[62] Citing C-108/97 and C-109/97 *Windsurfing Chiemsee* [1999] ECR I-2779; and C-363/99 *Koninklijke KPN Nederland NV* [2004] ECR I-1619.
[63] See the Opinion of AG Jacobs in C-421/04 *Matratzen Concord AG* [2006] ECR I-2303.
[64] Point 32.
[65] C-108/97 and C-109/97 *Windsurfing Chiemsee* [1999] ECR I-2779. On how use can lead to distinctiveness she also cited C-104/01 *Libertel* [2003] ECR I-3793, in particular paragraphs 62–67.
[66] C-299/99 *Philips* [2002] ECR I-5475.
[67] Here the AG made a reference to a judgment of the Court of First Instance, Case T-91/99 *Ford Motor Co v OHIM* [2000] ECR II-1925, applying the corresponding provisions of the Regulation, Article 7(1) and Article 7(3). She noted, however, that there are different territorial considerations in the case of Community trade marks because they are conceptually different from national trade marks.
[68] Point 38.
[69] Point 39.
[70] C-375/97 *General Motors Corp v Yplon SA* [1999] ECR I-5421.
[71] Ibid.

Community trade mark—a new Community right rather than a harmonized national right—the unitary character of which made it reasonable to require evidence of distinctiveness over a wider area.

6.108 The Advocate General also highlighted the importance both of the existence of Article 7(2) of the Regulation, providing that Article 7(1) applies notwithstanding that the grounds of non-registrability obtain in only part of the Community, and of the fact that there was no equivalent provision in the Directive:

> Because the Community trade mark is a unitary mark which, if registered, will be effective throughout the territory of the Community, it is right to impose the condition contained in Article 7(2). Such a mark ought not to be registered if there exist, in any part of the Community, grounds for non-registration. The same considerations do not apply to the registration of national trade marks as harmonised by the Trade Marks Directive.[72]

6.109 She agreed, however, with the Benelux Trade Mark Office that linguistic communities in a Member State or in the Benelux should be taken into account in assessing distinctive character acquired through use; this was linked with her earlier discussion on the relevant class of consumers. In this case, the relevant class comprised Dutch speakers for whom EUROPOLIS (as eg an insurance policy) lacked distinctive character. 'It is therefore only within that linguistic community that distinctiveness must be acquired for registration purposes.'[73]

6.110 Finally, on the proportion of the relevant class that must conceive the sign—the Advocate General used the term mark—as a source identifier, she once again started from Article 3(1)(b) and Article 3(1)(c). If the class that viewed the sign as lacking distinctiveness or being descriptive is reasonably large then 'it is statistically likely that one will find some data that are at variance with the norm'.[74]

6.111 But one must look at the totality of the available data. If the class described above constituted a large proportion of the relevant consumers, the authorities should require a significant proportion of that class to perceive the sign 'as identifying, in a distinctive way, the origin of the goods or services to which it is applied'.[75] And registration should not be granted if only a small proportion of the same class perceive the sign as a trade mark. Taking the opposite position would disregard the public interest behind Article 3(1)(c)—note the absence of a reference to Article 3(1)(b)—creating a situation in the marketplace where the sign would be protected even though the majority of consumers still viewed it as descriptive. From an interpretive perspective, it would imply that Article 3(3) could be applied independently from Article 3(1); this, according to the Advocate General, would create the paradox 'that both provisions—which have opposite effects—could be satisfied at the same time in the same territory'.[76]

---

[72] Point 45.
[73] Point 50 and fn 30 citing paragraph 30 of C-104/01 *Libertel Groep BV* [2003] ECR I-3793, requiring that the examination of registrability must be undertaken by reference to the actual situation rather than in the abstract.
[74] Point 52.
[75] Point 52.
[76] Point 55.

6.112 Note that the two provisions share the same aim, that only distinctive signs are registered, from two different perspectives, with use making the difference. They are inextricably linked.

6.113 There was a Benelux peculiarity—not raised in the reference to the Court—that the Advocate General also took into account to support her approach. Article 13C(1) of the Uniform Benelux Law provided that the exclusive right to a trade mark expressed in one of the national or regional languages of the Benelux territory covers its translations in the other languages. This highlighted the 'importance of not overriding the public interest aims of Article 3(1)(b) and Article 3(1)(c) save where acquisition of distinctive character through use is indeed solidly established'.[77]

6.114 The Advocate General required distinctiveness acquired through use throughout the linguistic community in the Member State; otherwise there was a risk that registration could be obtained as a result of use in a sub-part of the linguistic community.

6.115 To demonstrate this, she employed a useful example. If the mark was descriptive in Dutch, distinctiveness acquired through use by Dutch speakers in Flanders should not be enough; the mark should have become distinctive for Dutch speakers throughout the Benelux, covering at least The Netherlands, the Flemish speaking part of Belgium, and the bilingual region of Brussels.[78]

(2) The Judgment of the Court

6.116 In relation to the first two questions, the Court[79] recalled that according to its case law,[80] the Benelux territory must be treated like the territory of a Member State according to Article 1 of the Directive.

6.117 Article 3(3) constituted an exception to Article 3(1)(b) to (d); accordingly, its scope should be 'interpreted in light of those grounds for refusal'.[81] Following *Storck II*,[82] it held that:

> Article 3(3) of the Directive must be interpreted as meaning that the registration of a trade mark can be allowed on the basis of that provision only if it is proven that that trade mark has acquired distinctive character through use throughout the territory of the Member State or, in the case of Benelux, throughout the part of the territory of Benelux in which there exists a ground for refusal.[83]

6.118 The answer to the third question followed the same logic: 'To assess whether a mark has acquired distinctive character through use which would justify disregarding the grounds for refusal under Article 3(3) of the Directive, it is necessary to take into account the part of Benelux where Dutch is spoken',[84] since Dutch was one of the official languages of the Benelux and the trade mark could be descriptive in that language. The competent authority would have to apply the *Windsurfing Chiemsee*[85] test on the relevant class of persons.

---

[77] Point 56.
[78] The Commission had supported a similar interpretation, however, it was based on T-91/99 *Ford Motor Co v OHIM* [2000] ECR II-1925, the relevance of which for this particular point had been rejected by the AG.
[79] C-108/05 *Bovemij Verzekeringen NV v Benelux-Merkenbureau*.
[80] Citing C-375/97 *General Motors Corp* [1999] ECR I-5421.
[81] *Europolis* (n 53) paragraph 21.
[82] C-25/05 P *August Storck KG* [2006] ECR I-5719.
[83] *Europolis* (n 53) paragraph 23.
[84] *Europolis* (n 53) paragraph 26.
[85] See (n 1).

6.119 It is noted that the Court focused on the official languages of, rather than the languages spoken in the relevant Member State.

6.120 What still remains unclear is whether the word 'throughout' in paragraph 23 ('*dans toute la partie*') actually requires proof from everywhere in the respective territory, or whether a somewhat more global assessment is possible.

H. The Relevant Point in Time: Filing or Registration Date; *Pure Digital*

6.121 In *Pure Digital*,[86] the Court had the opportunity to clarify when a mark must have become distinctive for the purposes of Article 7(3) CTMR. It is worth noting at the outset that Article 7(3) CTMR is not worded in exactly the same way as the equivalent provision in the Directive. Indeed, the language of Article 3(3) of the Directive seems to be more restrictive than its counterpart in the Regulation, but at the same time provides for exceptions. Specifically, while Article 3(3) of the Directive states that a trade mark 'shall not be refused registration or be declared invalid ... if, before the date of application ... it has acquired a distinctive character' and adds that 'any Member State may in addition provide that this provision shall also apply where the distinctive character was acquired after the date of application ... or after the date of registration', Article 7(3) CTMR merely provides that a mark shall not be refused registration 'if [it] has become distinctive in relation to the goods or services for which registration is requested in consequence of the use which has been made of it', without clearly stating that this must have happened before the date of the application.

6.122 What is less clear at this point is whether that discrepancy is legally significant.

6.123 The Regulation also contains Article 51(2) which, in respect of invalidity proceedings, stipulates that even where the Community trade mark has been registered in breach of Article 7(1)(b), (c), or (d), 'it may nevertheless not be declared invalid if ... it has after registration acquired a distinctive character in relation to the goods or services for which it is registered'.

(1) Background to the Dispute

6.124 The matter was brought before the Court of Justice in the context of an appeal lodged by Imagination Technologies Ltd (Imagination Technologies) against the judgment of the Court of First Instance[87] that had dismissed its action for annulment of the decision of the Second Board of Appeal of OHIM refusing registration to the word sign PURE DIGITAL.

6.125 Imagination Technologies had sought to register that phrase as a Community trade mark in respect of, essentially, electronic goods and telecommunication services, included respectively in Classes 9 and 38 of the Nice Classification. OHIM rejected the application on the grounds that it was both descriptive and devoid of any distinctive character within the meaning of Article 7(1)(b) and (c) CTMR. It also found that the applicant's evidence of acquired distinctiveness was insufficient for the purposes of Article 7(3).

---

[86] C-542/07 P *Imagination Technologies Ltd/OHIM* (PURE DIGITAL) [2001] ECR I-04937.
[87] T-461/04 *Imagination Technologies Ltd/OHIM* (PURE DIGITAL) [2007] ECR II-122.

That refusal was upheld both by the Boards of Appeal of OHIM and by the Court of First Instance. Imagination Technologies appealed only against the second limb of that refusal, pleading infringement of Article 7(3) CTMR. It contended that the relevant point in time for assessing distinctiveness was not the time of the application, but rather the time of the finalization of the examination by OHIM. **6.126**

(2) The Judgment of the Court of First Instance

The Court of First Instance rejected the applicant's evidence of use on the ground that it related to a date after the application had been filed, referring to its settled case law[88] that a mark must have become distinctive through use before the application was filed. According to the Court of First Instance, that interpretation is the only one compatible with the logic of the system of absolute and relative grounds for refusal, according to which the date of filing of the application for registration determines the priority of one mark over another; moreover it makes it possible to avoid a situation in which the applicant may take undue advantage of the length of the registration procedure in order to prove that his mark has become distinctive subsequent to the filing of the application.[89] **6.127**

Moreover, the Court of First Instance dismissed the applicant's argument based on Article 51(2) CTMR (new Article 52) on the ground that whilst that provision serves to safeguard the legitimate expectations of the proprietor and the investments made in the period which has elapsed since registration, there are no such expectations at the stage of a mere application for registration worthy of any protection.[90] **6.128**

(3) The Judgment of the Court of Justice

Before the Court, Imagination Technologies principally relied on the following two lines of argument. First, it claimed that the very existence of Article 51(2) CTMR (new Article 52) meant that it was not incompatible with the 'logic of the system' to take into account events subsequent to the date of the application, all the more so since that provision does not require that the relevant use should also take place after the registration of the mark. Second, it maintained that the proprietor of a mark registered erroneously cannot be said to entertain any 'legitimate expectations', being perfectly aware of the fragility of its registration. **6.129**

The Court did not agree with the appellant. First, it pointed out that it is apparent from the very wording of Article 7(3) CTMR, and more particularly from the use of the verbs in the past tense in the phrases 'the mark has become' and 'in consequence of the use which has been made of it', that the mark must have acquired the requisite distinctiveness already at the time of filing of the application.[91] **6.130**

Second, it observed that, unlike the second sentence of Article 3(3) of the Directive, Article 7(3) CTMR does not provide for an option to apply that provision to trade marks which acquire distinctive character after the date of application or after the date of registration; this shows that the Community legislature intended to restrict the applicability of Article **6.131**

---

[88] C-247/01 *eCopy v OHIM* (ECOPY) [2002] ECR II-5301, paragraph 36; T-8/03 *El Corte Ingles v OHIM-Pucci* (EMILIO PUCCI) [2004] ECR II-4297, paragraphs 71 and 72; and T-262/04 *BIC v OHIM* (Shape of a lighter) [2005] ECR II-5959, paragraph 66.
[89] Judgment of the CFI, paragraph 77.
[90] Judgment of the CFI, paragraph 78.
[91] *Pure Digital* (n 86) paragraph 42.

7(3) only to marks that have acquired distinctiveness prior to the date of application. Thus, the Court concluded that a literal interpretation of both Article 7(3) CTMR and the first sentence of Article 3(3) of the Directive clearly support the interpretation of the Court of First Instance.[92]

6.132 Third, the Court confirmed the view that such an interpretation is the only one compatible with the logic of the system of absolute and relative grounds for refusal, according to which the application's filing date determines the priority of one mark over another. It noted that if the appellant's view was followed, a trade mark which is devoid of any distinctive character at the time of the application could serve as a basis for an opposition or an invalidity action against a mark with a subsequent filing date, but which was distinctive from the outset. However, such a situation is particularly unacceptable when the second mark has reached the requisite levels of distinctiveness before the first one.[93]

6.133 Fourth, the Court rejected the argument based on Article 51(2) CTMR on the ground that, insofar as that provision establishes an exception to the absolute grounds for invalidity laid down by Article 51(1) CTMR (new Article 52), it should be interpreted restrictively and could therefore not serve as a basis for interpreting Article 7(3) by analogy.[94]

6.134 Fifth, it concurred with the Court of First Instance that although the exception introduced by Article 51(2) CTMR (new Article 52) is justified by the legitimate expectations of the proprietor arising from the registration of its mark and by the investments he may have made in the meantime, such legitimate expectations cannot be said to exist at the time when the application is filed. In particular, it cannot be argued that each and every proprietor of a trade mark registered erroneously has acted in bad faith; if that was the case, Article 51(1)(b) CTMR (new Article 52), which establishes bad faith as an absolute ground for invalidity, would have to be applied in all cases where trade marks were registered erroneously, with the result that Article 51(2) would be rendered meaningless.[95]

6.135 Therefore, the Court of Justice upheld the interpretation of the Court of First Instance that the material point in time for assessing whether the mark has acquired distinctive character in consequence of the use that has been made of it is the time of application and rejected the appeal.

6.136 In view of the Court's reasoning, that conclusion is also clearly transposable to Article 3(3) of the Directive, in the sense that unless there is a clear exception to the contrary in the national law, the first sentence of that provision, requiring that the mark must have become distinctive before the date of the application, is to be taken literally.

6.137 Finally, it is also worth noting that, in a similar case which involved the reverse situation where a mark was registrable at the time of filing but ceased to be registrable by the time the decision on registrability was taken,[96] the Court of First Instance has interpreted Article 51(1)(a) CTMR (new Article 52), which states that a Community trade mark shall be declared invalid if registered contrary to Article 7, to the effect that the only time to be

---

[92] Paragraph 42.
[93] Paragraphs 51–52.
[94] Paragraph 54.
[95] Paragraphs 55–56.
[96] T-189/07 *Frosch Touristik GmbH/OHIM* (FLUGBÖRSE) [2009] ECR I-01503.

taken into account for that assessment is the application's filing date. This means that a loss of distinctiveness between the filing date and registration date may not be held against the applicant.

Interestingly enough, that interpretation ran counter to the practice of OHIM, which required that the mark should comply with Article 7(1)(b) and (c) *both* at the time of filing *and* at the time of registration. To defend its practice, OHIM had appealed that judgment to the Court. The Court dismissed OHIM's appeal by Order,[97] thus permitting situations to arise where a mark that at the time of registration is not distinctive, may nevertheless not be declared invalid because it was distinctive when filed. Loss of distinctiveness is not a ground of invalidity.

6.138

I. Evidence of Acquired Distinctiveness, Territory of Acquired Distinctiveness: *Lindt & Sprüngli*

In *Lindt & Sprüngli*[98] the Court was again called upon to judge whether the General Court had committed errors of law in confirming a refusal of a three-dimensional shape on grounds of absence of inherent distinctiveness and absence of sufficient proof of acquired distinctiveness. This time the sign was a chocolate rabbit wrapped in golden foil and with a red ribbon with a small bell around its neck. This is the same 'Goldhase' which had reached the Court in the reference from the Austrian Supreme Court, which concerned questions of bad faith. In this case, however, the mark was without the word elements on the body of the product which Lindt & Sprüngli call 'Gold Bunny' in English. The Court confirmed the General Court's decision.[99]

6.139

As regards the challenge of the General Court's judgment on the issue of acquired distinctiveness, the applicant argued that the registration of the same mark in fifteen Member States was proof of inherent distinctiveness in these Member States, so that proof should be required only for the other Member States. Further, as Community trade marks were valid in the EU as a whole and had unitary character, proof of acquired distinctiveness Member State by Member State was incompatible with the single market theory.

6.140

The Court dismissed the claims that an error had been made in the assessment of inherent distinctiveness, as not supported by the facts.

6.141

As concerns the geographical extent required for overcoming the deficiency of lack of distinctiveness, the Court appeared to agree with the applicant that proof for each individual Member State was not required; but concluded that the evidence provided was in any event not sufficient.

6.142

> As for the appellant's argument that since the Community trade mark has a unitary character, the assessment of acquisition by a mark of distinctive character through use cannot be based on individual national markets, it should be noted that, even if it is true, in accordance with the case law recalled at paragraph 60 of this judgment, that the acquisition by a mark

---

[97] C-332/09 P *OHIM v Frosch Touristik GmbH—DSR touristik GmbH* (FLUGBÖRSE) [2010] ECR I-00049.
[98] C-529/07, P *Chocoladefabriken Lindt & Sprüngli AG v Franz Hauswirth Gm* [2009] ECR I-04893.
[99] C-98/11 P *Chocoladefabriken Lindt & Sprüngli AG*, ECLI:EU:C:2012:307.

of distinctive character through use must be proved for the part of the European Union in which that mark did not, ab initio, have such character, it would be unreasonable to require proof of such acquisition for each individual Member State.

However, as regards the present case, the General Court did not err in law because, in any event, the appellant has not sufficiently proved the acquisition, by the mark for which registration is sought, of distinctive character through use throughout the European Union.[100]

6.143 The phrase that 'it would be *unreasonable* to require proof … for each individual Member State' (in German: *es ginge 'zu weit'*; in French: *il serait 'excessif'*) clearly marks a departure from any clear Member State-based approach, but the applicable rule remains unstated; 'unreasonable' is just as vague or unspecific as other criteria established by the Court with regard to acquired distinctiveness. Notably absent is any suggestion what would be or might be 'reasonable' and it will be interesting to see how OHIM practice, and practice of the Community trade mark courts, will develop.

J. Evidence of Acquired Distinctiveness: Surveys Burden of Proof; *Oberbank and Banco Santander*

(1) Facts and Questions

6.144 *Oberbank and Banco Santander*[101] are part of ongoing litigation between Deutscher Sparkassen- und Giroverband (DSGV), the association of German public law savings institutions (Sparkassen), and two foreign banks (Austrian and Spanish), concerning the use of the colour red for identifying their institutions or their respective services. DSGV is proprietor of a German registered trade mark for the colour red, obtained on the basis of acquired distinctiveness. Infringement litigation is ongoing between these parties. Both accused infringers brought requests for invalidity, which under German law are not available as a defence or counterclaim before infringement courts but must be brought before the German Patent and Trade Mark Office. That Office rejected the requests, whereupon Oberbank and Banco Santander appealed to the Federal Patent Court.

6.145 It seems that the Court was unconvinced by the present state of the Court of Justice's case law. Whatever the motives, the questions seemed to echo the Court's case law:

> (1) Does Article 3(1) and (3) of [Directive 2008/95] preclude an interpretation of national law according to which, for an abstract colour mark (in this case: red HKS 13) which is claimed for services in the financial affairs sector, a consumer survey must indicate an adjusted degree of association of at least 70% in order to form a basis for the assumption that the trade mark has acquired a distinctive character following the use which has been made of it?
>
> (2) Is the first sentence of Article 3(3) of [Directive 2008/95] to be interpreted to the effect that the time at which the application for the trade mark was filed—and not the time at which it was registered—is relevant in the case where the trade mark proprietor claims, in his defence against an application for a declaration invalidating the trade mark, that the trade mark acquired a distinctive character, following the use made of it, in any event more than three years after the application, but prior to registration?

---

[100] Paragraphs 62–63.
[101] C-217/13 and C-218/13 *Oberbank AG, Banco Santander SA and Santander Consumer Bank AG v Deutscher Sparkassen- und Giroverband eV*. [ECLI:EU:C:2014:2012].

(3) In the event that, under the abovementioned conditions, the time at which the application was filed is also relevant: Is the trade mark to be declared invalid if it is not clarified, and can no longer be clarified, whether it had acquired a distinctive character, following the use made of it, at the time when the application was filed? Or does the declaration of invalidity require the applicant seeking that declaration to prove that the trade mark had not acquired a distinctive character, following the use made of it, at the time when the application was filed?

6.146 The first question sought clarification regarding the degree of distinctiveness required, and whether opinion surveys with a particular result could be required, with a likely answer probably known to the referring court as well. The second question sought clarification as regards the relevant point in time, again already decided by the Court (see above *Pure Digital*, paragraph 6.121), while the third question raised a new issue, namely the burden of proof in acquired distinctiveness cases. Here, the referring court apparently wished to 'trump' the German Supreme Court, which had held earlier that the invalidity applicant bore the burden of proof.

(2) The Judgment of the Court

6.147 The Court, sitting without an Advocate General, analysed the questions with regard to its existing case law and adopted rather concise answers to the questions.

(a) *The first question: Evidence, opinion surveys, percentages*

6.148 On the first question, the Court repeated its previous case law, beginning with *Windsurfing Chiemsee*, and reiterated that even if it would be more difficult to establish acquired distinctiveness for some categories of marks, it was not possible to differentiate as to the degree of distinctiveness. This is the conclusion in the Court's terms:

> However, Article 2 and Article 3(1)(b) and (3) of Directive 2008/95 make no distinction between different categories of trade marks. The criteria for assessing the distinctive character of contourless colour marks, such as the mark at issue in the main proceedings, including whether that mark has acquired a distinctive character following the use which has been made of it, are thus no different from those to be applied to other categories of trade mark (see, by analogy, *Philips* EU:C:2002:377, paragraph 48, and *Nichols* EU:C:2004:538, paragraphs 24 and 25).
>
> The difficulties in establishing distinctive character which may be associated with certain categories of marks because of their nature—difficulties which it is legitimate to take into account—do not therefore justify laying down stricter criteria supplementing or derogating from application of the criterion of distinctiveness as interpreted in the case-law on other categories of marks (see, to that effect, Nichols EU:C:2004:538, paragraph 26, and, by analogy, *OHIM v BORCO-Marken-Import Matthiesen* EU:C:2010:508, paragraph 34).[102]

6.149 The Court also repeated what it had said earlier as regards evidence in general and opinion surveys in particular:

> It should also be stated that Union law does not preclude the competent authority, where it has particular difficulty in assessing the distinctive character acquired though use of the mark in respect of which registration or a declaration of invalidity is sought, from having recourse, under the conditions laid down by its own national law, to an opinion poll as guidance for its judgment (see, to that effect, *Windsurfing Chiemsee* EU:C:1999:230, paragraph

---

[102] Paragraphs 46–47.

53 and the case-law cited). If the competent authority finds it necessary to resort to such a survey, it must determine the percentage of consumers that would be sufficiently significant (see, by analogy, Case C-478/07 *Budějovický Budvar* EU:C:2009:521, paragraph 89).[103]

6.150 The Court added, predictably:

However, the circumstances in which the requirement concerning the acquisition of a distinctive character through use, under Article 3(3) of Directive 2008/95, may be regarded as satisfied cannot be shown to exist solely by reference to general, abstract data such as predetermined percentages (*Windsurfing Chiemsee* EU:C:1999:230, paragraph 52, and *Philips* EU:C:2002:377, paragraph 62).[104]

6.151 The conclusion as to the first question was as follows:

In the light of those considerations, the answer to the first question is that Article 3(1) and (3) of Directive 2008/95 must be interpreted as precluding an interpretation of national law according to which, in the context of proceedings raising the question whether a contourless colour mark has acquired a distinctive character through use, it is necessary in every case that a consumer survey indicate a degree of recognition of at least 70%.[105]

(b) The second question: The relevant point in time

6.152 The answer to the second question was easy to predict in regard to the Regulation where Article 7(3) is not explicit (see paragraph 6.131 above), as the Court had by then unequivocally stated that the filing date is decisive. The Directive specifically requires acquired distinctiveness at the time of filing unless the Member State has made use of the option provided for in Article 3(3).[106] Thus, the Court concluded:

It follows from those considerations that the answer to the second question is that, where a Member State has not exercised the power laid down in the second sentence of Article 3(3) of Directive 2008/95, the first sentence of Article 3(3) of that directive must be interpreted as meaning that, in the context of invalidity proceedings in respect of a mark which is intrinsically devoid of distinctive character, in order to assess whether that mark has acquired a distinctive character through use, it is necessary to examine whether such character was acquired before the date of filing of the application for registration of that mark. It is irrelevant in that regard that the proprietor of the mark at issue maintains that the mark has, in any event, acquired a distinctive character through use after the date of filing of the application for registration, but before the date of registration of that mark.[107]

(c) The third question: The burden of proof

6.153 The third question raised an interesting issue of principle arising from the fact that the Directive does not deal at all with procedural issues. Despite this, the Court had on previous occasions answered questions relating to the burden of proof (in exhaustion cases, and

---

[103] Paragraph 43.
[104] Paragraph 44.
[105] Paragraph 49.
[106] While the referring court explained in the reference that Germany had not made use of the option in Article 3(3) of the Directive, and the answer follows that assumption, the situation is in reality more complex. Under German law, if acquired distinctiveness is shown in the period between filing and registration, the mark may still be registered if the applicant accepts that the date of showing acquired distinctiveness will become the filing date for the purposes of determining in a case of conflict which mark is earlier; for other purposes the filing date will be preserved. German law also provides, as does Article 52 of the Regulation, that a mark cannot be invalidated if it is shown that acquired distinctiveness exists at the time of the decision on invalidation.
[107] Paragraph 61.

in a recent case relating to an unregistered Community design) when the decision on who has the burden of proof, in our words, has in practical effect had the same impact as a substantive rule. Thus, the Court began the analysis by referring to its previous cases:

> If the question of the burden of proof concerning distinctive character acquired by use which has been made of a mark in the context of invalidity proceedings were a matter for the national law of the Member States, the consequence for proprietors of trade marks could be that protection would vary according to the legal system concerned, with the result that the objective of 'the same protection under the legal systems of all the Member States' set out in recital 10 in the preamble to Directive 2008/95, where it is described as 'fundamental', would not be attained (see, by analogy, Case C-405/03 *Class International* EU:C:2005:616, paragraph 73 and the case-law cited, and Case C-479/12 *H. Gautzsch Großhandel* EU:C:2014:75, paragraph 40).[108]

The Court then concluded that the burden of proof must be on the proprietor of the mark and gave two reasons for this conclusion, namely that since acquired distinctiveness was an exception to the general rule, the person invoking the exception must bear the burden of proof,[109] and that the proprietor is in a better position to provide such proof than the invalidity applicant.[110]   **6.154**

Thus, the answer to the third question was as follows: **6.155**

> In the light of the foregoing, the answer to the third question is that where a Member State does not exercise the power laid down in the second sentence of Article 3(3) of Directive 2008/95, the first sentence of Article 3(3) of that directive must be interpreted to the effect that it does not preclude, in the context of invalidity proceedings, the mark at issue from being declared invalid where it is intrinsically devoid of distinctive character and the proprietor of that mark has failed to show that it has acquired a distinctive character following the use which has been made of it before the date of filing of the application for registration.[111]

(3) Some Conclusions

(a) *The first question*

The answer to the first question could be predicted. However, there is an important caveat to that conclusion, because the Court also stated with regard to opinion surveys that: 'If the competent authority finds it necessary to resort to such a survey, it must determine the percentage of consumers that would be sufficiently significant (see, by analogy, Case C-478/07 *Budějovický Budvar* EU:C:2009:521, paragraph 89).'[112]   **6.156**

This statement seems to conflict with the emphasis that the Court places on the outcome of cases, which should not depend on where the case is brought. Also, the reference to one of the many *Budějovický Budvar v Anheuser Busch* cases, this one involving the protection of BUD in Austria as a geographical indication, seems ill-placed, because the issue there was the protection of so-called simple geographical indications for which the Member States remain competent and which is not harmonized or unified at EU level. There are issues concerning whether national authorities should be authorized to set the percentages which   **6.157**

---

[108] Paragraph 67.
[109] Paragraph 69.
[110] Paragraph 70.
[111] Paragraph 74.
[112] Paragraph 43.

are 'significant' and, furthermore, whether percentages are 'significant' anyway when it is expressly prohibited under the interpretation of the Directive for decisions on acquired distinctiveness to be based on percentages alone. It is submitted that the correct rule would be that national authorities must always consider the result of surveys together with other evidence, and take the percentages as what they are—the conclusion that the authority must arrive at in the end is that the relevant sector of the public, or at least a significant proportion thereof, identifies the proprietor of the mark as responsible for the marketing of the goods or services through the use of the sign—here the colour red—as a mark.

(b) The second question

6.158 The answer to the second question—that the filing date is decisive—was expected and so presents no surprises.

(c) The third question

6.159 The answer to the third question leaves the observer dissatisfied. It appears necessary, or in any event preferable, to distinguish between the various situations that may arise.

6.160 In the registration procedure it is for the applicant to assert and prove acquired distinctiveness at the filing date if it is found that the mark is not inherently distinctive or is descriptive. This has been the practice of OHIM and accepted by the courts, and is also the practice in all national trade mark systems in the EU.

6.161 If later a challenge is made, all the evidence previously presented to OHIM or a national Office is available to the challenger, and it should be for the challenger to claim and prove that OHIM or a national Office committed an error in accepting the proof of acquired distinctiveness. If that situation arises, the proprietor would be entitled, and if he wants to prevail, obliged, to counter the results of the examination of the initial evidence.

6.162 Where the proprietor in an invalidity case claims that the mark has become distinctive after registration, as is provided in Article 52(2) CTMR, and also in German trade mark law, it should be for the proprietor to prove what he claims. What remains is the special situation which arose in the present case, namely proof of acquired distinctiveness in the course of the registration procedure but after the filing date, plus the inability to determine whether the required distinctiveness was already present at the filing date—a *non liquet* situation. In such a situation, it would seem preferable to maintain the validity of the mark. Whether such situations are likely to arise in practice and whether the outcome would then depend on the burden of proof is doubtful, even in the present case, where the 70% hurdle has been removed, and where it is likely that the proprietor of the mark is able to prove distinctiveness under the German rule equivalent to Article 52(2) CTMR.

K. Concluding on Absolute Grounds

6.163 The Court has decided a large number of cases on absolute grounds in a relatively short period of time, having to consider the same, in terms of substance, both as an interpretive court, when it considers preliminary references regarding the Directive, and as an appellate court, when it reviews challenges to Community trade marks.

6.164 Attempting to establish concrete interpretive principles, the Court has rejected the application of broad doctrines and instead is looking for the public policy behind each specific provision. The Court is also attempting to internalize competition issues in the way it interprets absolute grounds. The discourse on what constitutes a sign, the graphical representation requirements, the concept of distinctiveness and the functionality provision is evidence of the Court's awareness that more and broader rights will inevitably lead to more friction in the marketplace.

6.165 The Court has taken a cautious approach, probably recognizing that defending against a weak right may prove more uncertain, and potentially more costly, than attempting to enforce a weak right; the public policy context, protecting trade mark proprietors but also consumers and competitors, requires an examination system that is thorough and concrete.

6.166 The contradictions in the Court's jurisprudence can be explained by its willingness to get drawn into the facts of each case, albeit without always systematically considering all of its aspects.

7

RELATIVE GROUNDS

A. Introduction

This chapter considers the case law of the Court of Justice on conflicts with earlier rights at the time of application. They are resolved by Article 4 of the Harmonisation Directive and Article 8 of the Community Trade Mark Regulation. **7.01**

Conflict resolution is based on a general principle that the earlier right shall prevail and the application of three basic rules. When there is identity between the trade marks or signs on the one hand and between the respective goods or services on the other, resolution appears to be almost automatic. When similarity becomes part of the equation, the criterion is 'likelihood of confusion on the part of the public, which includes the likelihood of association'. Trade marks that have obtained 'a reputation' reach another level; they can prevail against similar or identical signs for 'goods or services which are not similar' (as well as identical and similar goods or services, as confirmed in *Davidoff v Gofkid Ltd*),[1] where use of the later trade mark or sign 'without due cause would take unfair advantage of, or be detrimental to, the distinctive character or the repute of the earlier trade mark'. **7.02**

The adoption of the last rule remained optional at the national level. Member States were free to determine its application in relation to their own national rights. In fact, all Member States have made use of this option. The Community trade mark regime chose to introduce it as a ground of opposition under Article 8(5). **7.03**

Another potentially differentiating factor is who can challenge a right. Member States are free to set the participation rules, provided that at least the owner of the earlier right would be able to obtain protection. The Community trade mark regime opted for enabling only the owners of earlier rights to challenge a Community trade mark on the basis of their respective rights. **7.04**

This chapter too is structured around the provisions of the Directive. **7.05**

B. The Provisions of the Directive and the Regulation

(1) The Trade Marks Directive

Article 4—Further grounds for refusal or invalidity concerning conflicts with earlier rights **7.06**

1. A trade mark shall not be registered or, if registered, shall be liable to be declared invalid:

---

[1] C-292/00 *Davidoff & Cie SA v Gofkid* [2003] ECR I-389.

(a) if it is identical with an earlier trade mark, and the goods or services for which the trade mark is applied for or is registered are identical with the goods or services for which the earlier trade mark is protected;

(b) if because of its identity with, or similarity to, the earlier trade mark and the identity or similarity of the goods or services covered by the trade marks, there exists a likelihood of confusion on the part of the public, which includes the likelihood of association with the earlier trade mark.

2. 'Earlier trade marks' within the meaning of paragraph 1 means:
   (a) trade marks of the following kinds with a date of application for registration which is earlier than the date of application for registration of the trade mark, taking account, where appropriate, of the priorities claimed in respect of those trade marks:
       (i) Community trade marks;
       (ii) trade marks registered in the Member State or, in the case of Belgium, Luxembourg or the Netherlands, at the Benelux Trade Mark Office;
       (iii) trade marks registered under international arrangements which have effect in the Member State;
   (b) Community Trade Marks which validly claim seniority, in accordance with the Regulation on the Community Trade Mark, from a trade mark referred to in (a) (ii) and (iii), even when the latter trade mark has been surrendered or allowed to lapse;
   (c) applications for the trade marks referred to in (a) and (b), subject to their registration;
   (d) trade marks which, on the date of application for registration of the trade mark, or, where appropriate, of the priority claimed in respect of the application for registration of the trade mark, are well known in a Member State, in the sense in which the words 'well known' are used in Article 6bis of the Paris Convention.

3. A trade mark shall furthermore not be registered or, if registered, shall be liable to be declared invalid if it is identical with, or similar to, an earlier Community trade mark within the meaning of paragraph 2 and is to be, or has been, registered for goods or services which are not similar to those for which the earlier Community trade mark is registered, where the earlier Community trade mark has a reputation in the Community and where the use of the later trade mark without due cause would take unfair advantage of, or be detrimental to, the distinctive character or the repute of the earlier Community trade mark.

4. Any Member State may furthermore provide that a trade mark shall not be registered or, if registered, shall be liable to be declared invalid where, and to the extent that:
   (a) the trade mark is identical with, or similar to, an earlier national trade mark within the meaning of paragraph 2 and is to be, or has been, registered for goods or services which are not similar to those for which the earlier trade mark is registered, where the earlier trade mark has a reputation in the Member State concerned and where the use of the later trade mark without due cause would take unfair advantage of, or be detrimental to, the distinctive character or the repute of the earlier trade mark;
   (b) rights to a non-registered trade mark or to another sign used in the course of trade were acquired prior to the date of application for registration of the subsequent trade mark, or the date of the priority claimed for the application for registration of the subsequent trade mark and that non-registered trade mark or other sign confers on its proprietor the right to prohibit the use of a subsequent trade mark;
   (c) the use of the trade mark may be prohibited by virtue of an earlier right other than the rights referred to in paragraphs 2 and 4(b) and in particular:
       (i) a right to a name;
       (ii) a right of personal portrayal;
       (iii) a copyright;
       (iv) an industrial property right;

(d) the trade mark is identical with, or similar to, an earlier collective trade mark conferring a right which expired within a period of a maximum of three years preceding application;
(e) the trade mark is identical with, or similar to, an earlier guarantee or certification mark conferring a right which expired within a period preceding application the length of which is fixed by the Member State;
(f) the trade mark is identical with, or similar to, an earlier trade mark which was registered for identical or similar goods or services and conferred on them a right which has expired for failure to renew within a period of a maximum of two years preceding application, unless the proprietor of the earlier trade mark gave his agreement for the registration of the later mark or did not use his trade mark;
(g) the trade mark is liable to be confused with a mark which was in use abroad on the filing date of the application and which is still in use there, provided that at the date of the application the applicant was acting in bad faith.
5. The Member States may permit that in appropriate circumstances registration need not be refused or the trade mark need not be declared invalid where the proprietor of the earlier trade mark or other earlier right consents to the registration of the later trade mark.
6. Any Member State may provide that, by derogation from paragraphs 1 to 5, the grounds for refusal of registration or invalidity in force in that State prior to the date on which the provisions necessary to comply with this Directive enter into force, shall apply to trade marks for which application has been made prior to that date.

(2) The Community Trade Mark Regulation

Article 8—Relative grounds for refusal   7.07

1. Upon opposition by the proprietor of an earlier trade mark, the trade mark applied for shall not be registered:
   (a) if it is identical with the earlier trade mark and the goods or services for which registration is applied for are identical with the goods or services for which the earlier trade mark is protected;
   (b) if because of its identity with or similarity to the earlier trade mark and the identity or similarity of the goods or services covered by the trade marks there exists a likelihood of confusion on the part of the public in the territory in which the earlier trade mark is protected; the likelihood of confusion includes the likelihood of association with the earlier trade mark.
2. For the purposes of paragraph 1, 'Earlier trade marks' means:
   (a) trade marks of the following kinds with a date of application for registration which is earlier than the date of application for registration of the Community trade mark, taking account, where appropriate, of the priorities claimed in respect of those trade marks:
      (i) Community trade marks;
      (ii) trade marks registered in a Member State, or, in the case of Belgium, the Netherlands or Luxembourg, at the Benelux Trade Mark Office;
      (iii) trade marks registered under international arrangements which have effect in a Member State;
      (iv) trade marks registered under international arrangements which have effect in the Community;
   (b) applications for the trade marks referred to in subparagraph (a), subject to their registration;
   (c) trade marks which, on the date of application for registration of the Community trade mark, or, where appropriate, of the priority claimed in respect of the application

for registration of the Community trade mark, are well known in a Member State, in the sense in which the words 'well known' are used in Article 6bis of the Paris Convention.

3. Upon opposition by the proprietor of the trade mark, a trade mark shall not be registered where an agent or representative of the proprietor of the trade mark applies for registration thereof in his own name without the proprietor's consent, unless the agent or representative justifies his action.

4. Upon opposition by the proprietor of a non-registered trade mark or of another sign used in the course of trade of more than mere local significance, the trade mark applied for shall not be registered where and to the extent that, pursuant to the Community legislation or the law of the Member State governing that sign:
   (a) rights to that sign were acquired prior to the date of application for registration of the Community trade mark, or the date of the priority claimed for the application for registration of the Community trade mark;
   (b) that sign confers on its proprietor the right to prohibit the use of a subsequent trade mark.

5. Furthermore, upon opposition by the proprietor of an earlier trade mark within the meaning of paragraph 2, the trade mark applied for shall not be registered where it is identical with or similar to the earlier trade mark and is to be registered for goods or services which are not similar to those for which the earlier trade mark is registered, where in the case of an earlier Community trade mark the trade mark has a reputation in the Community and, in the case of an earlier national trade mark, the trade mark has a reputation in the Member State concerned and where the use without due cause of the trade mark applied for would take unfair advantage of, or be detrimental to, the distinctive character or the repute of the earlier trade mark.

C. *LTJ Diffusion*: Establishing Identity

7.08 The Court considered the criteria for establishing identity between signs in *LTJ Diffusion v Sadas*,[2] a reference from the Tribunal de Grande Instance (Regional Court), Paris that involved a comparison between a registered figurative trade mark, the name 'Arthur' written in a distinctive way and bearing a dot below the first letter A, and the word mark 'Arthur et Felicie'.[3]

7.09 The French Court enquired whether Article 5(1)(a) covers only an identical reproduction, without addition or omission, of the earlier mark or if it can also cover a reproduction of the distinctive element of an earlier mark or a full reproduction of the earlier mark but with the addition of new signs.

(1) The Opinion of Advocate General Jacobs

7.10 Advocate General Jacobs opted for a strict interpretation of the term 'identical' because of its actual meaning—dictionary definitions in all the languages of the Community stressed the sameness of the compared elements—and the scheme, history, and context of the provision.

7.11 Identity conferred absolute, unconditional protection that 'should clearly not be extended beyond those situations for which it was intended if the aim of ensuring freedom of trade

---

[2] C-291/00 *LTJ Diffusion SA v Sadas Vertbaudet SA* [2003] ECR I-2799.
[3] Note that the Court of First Instance found that there would be likelihood of confusion between the signs in T-346/04 *Sadas SA v Office for Harmonisation in the Internal Market (Trade Marks and Designs)* [2006] ETMR 27.

and undistorted competition in the internal market is to be achieved'.[4] This was exceptional because confusion constituted the theoretical and historical backbone of the Directive. The original proposal did not even include this type of protection.[5] From an international perspective, Article 16(1) of the Agreement on Trade-Related Aspects of Intellectual Property Rights (TRIPs) provides only for a presumption of confusion in the case of identity. However, where

> rigorously identical signs or marks are used in the course of trade for identical goods or services, it is difficult if not impossible to conceive of circumstances in which all likelihood of confusion could be ruled out. In such cases, it would be both redundant and extravagant to require proof of that likelihood.[6]

Likelihood of confusion, in the case of identity between marks and products 'can be presumed without further investigation'.[7]

7.12 But absolute identity in every detail is required; 'in principle, any difference, whether it might be viewed as adding, removing or modifying any element, must involve loss of identity'.[8] He excluded differences that are not noticeable.

7.13 He suggested a two-step process. First the national authority had to 'identify what it is that is perceived by the average, reasonably well-informed, observant and circumspect consumer as the relevant marks, or the relevant mark and sign'.[9] Then it should perform the global assessment test, adopted by the Court in *Sabel*[10] and *Lloyd*:[11] 'two marks, will always be identical where in the light of such an assessment any differences are minute and wholly insignificant, so that the average consumer would not find any noticeable difference between the two; otherwise, they can be regarded as no more than similar'.[12]

7.14 Note that the language of the French law differed from that of the Directive. Article L 713-2 of the Code[13] prohibited the 'reproduction, use or affixing of a mark, even with the addition of words such as: formula, style, system, imitation, type or method, or the use of a mark which has been reproduced, in respect of goods or services identical with those for which the mark is registered'. This provision, according to French doctrine, covered cases where a distinctive element of a composite mark is reproduced (*contrefaçon partielle*) or where a distinctive element of a composite mark is reproduced together with additions that do not affect the identity of the mark (*adjonction inopérante*). This explains the way in which the French court expressed the questions posed to the Court.

7.15 He found that Article 5(1)(a) is a provision aiming towards total rather than partial harmonization and only the language of the Directive should delineate the scope of the national implementing provisions.

---

[4] Point 33.
[5] [1960] OJ C 351/1; for the amended proposal see [1985] OJ C 351/4.
[6] Point 37.
[7] Point 39.
[8] Point 41.
[9] Point 49; however, for registered trade marks, arguably, the starting point should be the mark as registered.
[10] C-251/95 *Sabel BV v Puma AG, Rudolf Dassler Sport* [1997] ECR I-6191.
[11] C-342/97 *Lloyd Schuhfabrik Meyer & Co GmbH* [1999] ECR I-3819.
[12] Point 47.
[13] Book VII of the French Code de la propriété intellectuelle (Intellectual Property Code), JORF, 3 July 1992, p 8801.

(2) The Judgment of the Court

7.16 The Court stressed that both Articles of the Directive should be interpreted in the same way. Its interpretive approach was based on the familiar theme, developed below in *Arsenal*,[14] that the essential function of a trade mark is to guarantee the identity of product origin.[15] To ensure that guarantee the proprietor must be protected against 'competitors wishing to take unfair advantage of the status and reputation of the trade mark by selling products illegally bearing it'.[16]

7.17 And whereas Article 5(1)(b) requires a likelihood of confusion, Article 5(1)(a) 'does not require evidence of such a likelihood in order to afford absolute protection in the case of identity of the sign and the trade mark and of the goods or services'.[17]

7.18 The criterion of identity of the sign and the trade mark must be interpreted strictly: 'There is ... identity between the sign and the trade mark where the former reproduces, without any modification or addition, all the elements constituting the latter.'[18]

7.19 Identity should be assessed globally from the perspective of the average consumer described in *Lloyd Schuhfabrik Meyer*,[19] and '[S]ince the perception of identity between the sign and the trade mark is not the result of a direct comparison of all the characteristics of the elements compared, insignificant differences between the sign and the trade mark may go unnoticed by an average consumer.'[20]

D. Confusion, Similarity, and Distinctiveness

7.20 The second conflict scenario involves an element of similarity: similarity of signs and identity of goods or services; identity of signs and similarity of goods or services; or similarity of both signs and goods or services. Here, likelihood of confusion becomes the essential condition for protection. The provision is awkwardly worded, but confusion clearly constitutes the justificatory, almost philosophical, core of trade mark protection. Advocate General Ruiz-Jarabo Colomer suggested that in the case of identity there is only a presumption of infringement that can be rebutted if there is no confusion.[21] To decipher the scope of the provision and the way it is applied the focus in this section is on the concept of confusion. First we will explore the three global appreciations tests and then consider how the tests are applied in practice.

(1) *Sabel*: Confusion and Association: Alternative Concepts?

7.21 *Sabel*[22] involved a comparison between a composite and a pictorial trade mark. Puma, the registered proprietor of two German trade marks depicting felines—both were

---

[14] See also C-120/04 *Medion AG v Thomson Multimedia Sales Germany & Austria GmbH* [2005] ECR I-8551, paragraphs 7.239 and following below.
[15] C-206/01 *Arsenal Football Club plc* [2002] ECR I-10273.
[16] *LTJ Diffusion* (n 2) paragraph 46.
[17] Paragraph 49.
[18] Paragraph 51.
[19] C-342/97 *Lloyd Schuhfabrik Meyer & Co GmbH v Klijsen Handel BV* [1999] ECR I-3819.
[20] Paragraph 53.
[21] C-206/01 *Arsenal Football Club plc* [2002] ECR I-10273.
[22] C-251/95 *Sabel BV v Puma AG, Rudolf Dassler Sport* [1997] ECR I-6191.

abstract figures, the first a leaping big puma and the second a chasing puma—opposed Sabel's application for registration of a trade mark comprising the name SABEL underneath the figure of a spotted chasing feline, a cheetah. There was partial overlap between the product specifications. The case reached the Bundesgerichtshof (Federal Court of Justice) which decided, provisionally, that according to the traditional principles of German trade mark law there was no likelihood of confusion. However, it stayed proceedings in order to ascertain from the Court of Justice the relevance of the common semantic content of the 'chasing felines' signs, given the ambiguity of the language of Article 4(1)(b):

> With reference to the interpretation of Article 4(1)(b)... is it sufficient for a finding that there is a likelihood (Gefahr: risk) of confusion between a sign composed of text and picture and a sign consisting merely of a picture, which is registered for identical and similar goods and is not especially well known to the public, that the two signs coincide as to their semantic content (in this case, a bounding feline)?
>
> What is the significance in this connection of the wording of the Directive, in terms of which the likelihood (Gefahr: risk) of confusion includes the likelihood that a mark may be associated with an earlier mark?[23]

(a) The Opinion of Advocate General Jacobs

7.22 The Benelux Governments submitted that the term 'likelihood of association' should be construed according to its Benelux interpretation: likelihood of association could arise in the following situations: first, where the public confuses the sign and the mark in question (likelihood of direct confusion); second, where the public makes a connection between the proprietors of the sign and those of the mark and confuses them (likelihood of indirect confusion or association); and, third, where the public considers the sign to be similar to the mark and perception of the sign calls to mind the memory of the mark, although the two are not confused (likelihood of association in the strict sense).

7.23 The Commission and the Government of the United Kingdom opposed this sweeping approach. Based on the freedom of movement case law they argued that the scope of trade mark protection should be commensurate with the essential function of a trade mark as a guarantee of origin of the marked product.

7.24 Following a thorough analysis of the Benelux concept of association, Advocate General Jacobs found that it went further than the trade mark laws of other Member States to cover 'non-origin association'.[24]

7.25 The Benelux countries had failed to incorporate this concept of association into the Directive; they succeeded, however, as part of a compromise to obtain a mention of the term, the law referred to 'a likelihood of confusion on the part of the public, which includes the likelihood of association with the earlier trade mark'. The Advocate General recounted the history of the inclusion of the term into the Directive, but doubted whether it was permissible to take it into account and whether, in any case, it carried any relevance in interpreting the provision.

---

[23] Reproduced in paragraph 10.
[24] Point 39.

(b) *The language of the provision and the principles of the Directive*

7.26 Turning to the language of both the provision and the Tenth Recital he found it difficult to 'see how association not involving confusion can be brought within the Directive when the Directive requires a likelihood of confusion which includes the likelihood of association'. As Laddie J had neatly expressed the point in *Wagamama*, an English case on this very issue: it would be 'unconventional use of language to provide that the smaller (i.e. likelihood of confusion) includes the larger (i.e. likelihood of association)'.[25] The inclusion of 'likelihood of association' meant that confusion should be interpreted in a broad sense covering mistaking one product for another but also making a connection between the entities behind the conflicting signs. He concluded that:

> while the likelihood of association with an earlier mark is a factor to be taken into account, registration of a mark cannot be opposed unless it is established that there is a genuine and properly substantiated likelihood of confusion about the origin of the goods or services in question.[26]

(c) *The Judgment of the Court*

7.27 The Court of Justice looked first at the language of the provision, the logical deduction being that likelihood of association is not an alternative to likelihood of confusion but simply serves to define its scope: 'The terms of the provision itself exclude its application where there is no likelihood of confusion on the part of the public.'[27] This was supported by a purposive analysis: the Tenth Recital setting out that the likelihood of confusion constitutes the specific condition of protection.

7.28 The Court concluded its analysis as follows:

> The answer to the national court's question must therefore be that the criterion of 'likelihood of confusion which includes the likelihood of association with the earlier mark' contained in Article 4(1)(b) of the Directive is to be interpreted as meaning that the mere association which the public might make between two trade marks as a result of their analogous semantic content is not in itself a sufficient ground for concluding that there is a likelihood of confusion within the meaning of that provision.[28]

(2) *Canon*: Economic Link, the Purpose of Confusion

7.29 In *Canon*[29] the Court reiterated that association and confusion were not distinct concepts. Metro-Goldwyn-Mayer Inc had applied in Germany for registration of 'Canon' as a trade mark for 'films recorded on video tape cassettes (video film cassettes); production, distribution and projection of films for cinemas and television organisations'. Canon Kabushiki Kaisha (CKK) opposed the application based on its earlier registration of 'Canon' for 'still and motion picture cameras and projectors; television filming and recording devices, television retransmission devices, television receiving and reproduction devices, including tape and disc devices for television recording and reproduction'. The evidence showed that there was no overlap between manufacturers of video recorders and video tape producers and consumers were aware that video recorders and video tapes ordinarily came from different sources; it also established that 'Canon' enjoyed a reputation in Germany.

---

[25] Point 44, referring to *Wagamama Ltd v City Centre Restaurants Plc* [1995] FSR 713.
[26] Point 55.
[27] Paragraph 18.
[28] Paragraph 26.
[29] C-39/97 *Canon Kabushiki Kaisha* [1998] ECR I-5507.

The case reached the Bundesgerichtshof (Federal Court of Justice) which sought from the   7.30
Court of Justice the ascertainment of whether in assessing product similarity the relevant
authority should take into account the distinctiveness of the earlier mark, in particular the
distinctiveness that is the result of its reputation.

(a) The Opinion of Advocate General Jacobs

Advocate General Jacobs submitted that in principle if 'there is no likelihood of the public   7.31
assuming that there is any sort of trade connection between the marks "Canon" and
"CANNON", there is no likelihood of confusion within the meaning of Article 4(1)(b) of
the Directive'.[30] Elaborating on the importance of the 'place of origin' he noted:

> it is not sufficient to show simply that there is no likelihood of the public being confused
> as to the place in which the goods are manufactured or the services performed: if, despite
> recognising that the goods or services have different places of origin, the public is likely to
> believe that there is a link between the two concerns, there will be a likelihood of confusion
> within the meaning of the Directive.[31]

(b) The Judgment of the Court

The Court of Justice dealt first with product similarity and the importance of reputa-   7.32
tion.[32] It then referred directly to the suggestion of the Advocate General[33] and held that
there is a likelihood of confusion if there is a risk that the 'public might believe that the
goods or services in question come from the same undertaking or, as the case may be, from
economically-linked undertakings'.[34]

(3) *Lloyd Schuhfabrik*: Properly Substantiated and Genuine Confusion

In *Lloyd Schuhfabrik*[35] the Landgericht Munchen I (Munich I Regional Court) requested   7.33
further clarification on the concept of likelihood of confusion. Lloyd Schuhfabrik, the
registered proprietor of 'Lloyd' for footwear, claimed that Klijsen's use of 'Loints' constituted trade mark infringement. The German court sought some guidance regarding similarity between the two signs but also regarding the concept of confusion. It submitted a
number of detailed questions, some very closely linked with the facts of the case.

> 2. What is the significance in this connection of the wording of the Directive which provides
>   that the likelihood of confusion includes the likelihood of association between the sign
>   and the trade mark?
> 3. Must a special distinctive character, and hence an extended material scope of protection
>   of a distinguishing sign, already be taken to exist where there is a degree of recognition
>   of 10 per cent in the relevant section of the public? Would that be the case with a degree
>   of recognition of 36 per cent? Would such an extension of the scope of protection lead
>   to a different answer to Question 1, if that question were to be answered by the Court of
>   Justice in the negative?
> 4. Is a trade mark to be taken to have an enhanced distinctive character simply because it has
>   no descriptive elements?[36]

---

[30] Paragraph 30.
[31] Paragraph 30.
[32] See paragraphs 7.122 and following below.
[33] Point 30 of the Opinion of Advocate General Jacobs.
[34] Paragraph 29.
[35] C-342/97 *Lloyd Schuhfabrik Meyer & Co GmbH* [1999] ECR I-3819.
[36] Reproduced in paragraph 10.

(a) The Opinion of Advocate General Jacobs

7.34 Advocate General Jacobs made a specific point conceding that the Court had:

> on occasions at the prompting of national courts given rulings tied closely to the facts of particular cases. The distinction between interpretation and application is not clear-cut—indeed interpretation may be considered an integral part of the process of applying a legal rule. Almost any question, however specific to a particular set of facts, can be formulated in the guise of an abstract question of interpretation.[37]

7.35 However, it is for the Court of Justice to interpret the law and for the national court to decide, according to the facts of the case and applying the law as interpreted by the Court of Justice, whether there is a likelihood of confusion. Regarding the concept of confusion, the Advocate General repeated the relevant parts of the Court's Judgment in *Sabel*.[38] He added that in assessing the likelihood of confusion the national court will apply national rules of evidence, however, the 'standard and criteria to be applied . . . in making that assessment are a matter of Community law'.[39] Accordingly, the 'likelihood of confusion must be properly substantiated and genuine—it must not be merely hypothetical or remote'.[40]

(b) The Judgment of the Court

7.36 The Court of Justice concurred with the Advocate General regarding its own role: it 'is limited to providing the national court with the guidance on interpretation necessary to resolve the case before it, while it is for the national court to apply the rules of Community law, as interpreted by the Court, to the facts of the case under consideration'.[41] Also, it did not take up—at least directly—the point made by the Advocate General regarding the Community standard of likelihood of confusion. Instead, it chose to answer the questions on distinctiveness and similarity.

(4) *Marca Mode*: Revisiting *Sabel*; A Positive Finding on Confusion

7.37 In *Marca Mode*[42] the Supreme Court of The Netherlands attempted, again, to stretch the limits of confusion.[43] Adidas, the proprietor in the Benelux of the three stripes trade mark started infringement proceedings against Marca Mode, a company marketing sports clothes with two parallel stripes running along their length and a white and orange T-shirt bearing three black vertical stripes running in parallel down its entire length, broken up by a medallion comprising a picture of a cat and the word TIM. The case reached the Dutch Supreme Court where Marca Mode argued that after *Sabel* it was necessary to establish a likelihood of confusion rather than a likelihood of association.

7.38 The Advocate General of the Dutch court, AG Bakels, conceded that as a result of the Directive and the case law of the Court of Justice the law has changed and indicated that Benelux courts should apply the new law even if they would have preferred that case law to have gone the other way. Still, the Dutch Supreme Court interpreted *Sabel* as appearing to indicate that the existence of a risk of association is sufficient when the earlier mark has a particularly distinctive

---

[37] Point 9. An interpretive issue that is almost always relevant in trade mark cases.
[38] C-251/95 *Sabel BV* [1997] ECR I-6191.
[39] Point 20.
[40] Point 21.
[41] Paragraph 11, citing C-320/88 *Staatssecretaris van Financiën v Shipping and Forwarding Enterprise SAFE BV* [1990] ECR I-285.
[42] C-425/98 *Marca Mode CV v Adidas AG Adidas Benelux BV* [2000] ECR I-4861.
[43] *Marca Mode v Adidas AG and Adidas Benelux BV* [1999] ETMR 791 HR (NL).

character either per se or as a result of its reputation, since the possibility that the association arising from some semantic or other similarity may create confusion cannot be ruled out and sought from the Court of Justice confirmation as to whether its reading had been correct.

(a) The Opinion of Advocate General Jacobs

Advocate General Jacobs noted that: **7.39**

> the Hoge Raad is in effect asking the Court to reverse the terms of the Directive: confusion … which includes the likelihood of association in Article 5(1)(b) means, in its view, association … which includes the likelihood of confusion. The Court has already considered and expressly rejected that view in SABEL.[44]

Focusing on distinctiveness he stated that, according to the jurisprudence of the Court, 'the fact that the earlier mark is distinctive will often be relevant for determining whether there is in fact a likelihood of confusion'.[45] However, likelihood of confusion had to be proven rather than assumed; distinctiveness and reputation simply constituted factors that courts had to consider. Looking at the overall scheme of protection and taking into account the protection afforded by Article 5(2) he noted: **7.40**

> Granting yet further protection to marks with a reputation in the absence of confusion would amount to granting protection against dilution, namely the blurring of the distinctiveness of a mark such that it is no longer capable of arousing immediate association with the goods for which it is registered and used. To do so by a creative interpretation of Article 5(l)(b) would run counter to the scheme of the Directive, which clearly envisages that such additional protection should be conferred, if at all, by virtue of Articles 4(4)(a) and 5(2) at Member States' option: see the ninth recital in the preamble.[46]

(b) The Judgment of the Court

The Court agreed with the Advocate General; it considered only the questions referred to it, holding that Article 5(1)(b) requires a positive finding on likelihood of confusion even where the protected mark enjoys a particularly distinctive character. **7.41**

It stressed from 'the outset that, even in particular circumstances such as those outlined by the Hoge Raad in its order for reference, a likelihood of confusion cannot be presumed'.[47] **7.42**

Clarifying its judgment in *Sabel* it repeated that the particularly distinctive character of the earlier mark might increase the likelihood of confusion and that the conjunction of conceptual similarity between the earlier mark and the sign with the fact that the mark possessed a particularly distinctive character might contribute to proving likelihood of confusion. **7.43**

But this did not imply a presumption of likelihood of confusion resulting from the existence of a likelihood of association in the strict sense. Likelihood of confusion had to be proven in a positive way: in *Sabel* **7.44**

> the Court referred by implication to the assessment of evidence which the national court must undertake in each case pending before it. It did not excuse the national court from the necessary positive finding of the existence of a likelihood of confusion which constitutes the matter to be proved.[48]

---

[44] Point 31.
[45] Point 42.
[46] Point 44.
[47] *Marca Mode* (n 42) paragraph 39.
[48] Paragraph 33.

The reputation of a mark was one of the elements courts should examine in their global assessment of likelihood of confusion and, according to *Canon*, 'marks with a highly distinctive character, in particular because of their reputation, enjoy broader protection than marks with a less distinctive character ... Nevertheless, the reputation of a mark does not give grounds for presuming the existence of a likelihood of confusion simply because of the existence of a likelihood of association in the strict sense.'[49]

(5) *Lloyd*: The Distinctiveness Factors

(a) *The Opinion of Advocate General Jacobs*

7.45 In *Lloyd Schuhfabrik*[50] Advocate General Jacobs considered what distinctiveness contributed to a trade mark for the purposes of expanding the scope of protection. He justified this expansion by noting that, although it appeared that distinctiveness of a trade mark would make confusion less rather than more likely, the similarity between the distinctive elements of a mark and a sign makes them both distinguishable from other signs but increases the risk of confusion between themselves. As to distinctiveness, market recognition was one of the factors to be taken into account but there was a 'specific threshold beyond which it should be given decisive weight'.[51]

7.46 In terms of inherent distinctiveness he suggested that 'there must be certain aural, visual or conceptual features which particularly distinguish it from other signs'.[52] He added that the absence of descriptive elements may be a factor in assessing the distinctiveness of a mark but it will not necessarily render the mark distinctive: 'despite the absence of descriptive elements, a mark may still lack original features or be commonplace'.[53]

(b) *The Judgment of the Court*

7.47 The Court followed the Advocate General. Citing *Windsurfing Chiemsee*,[54] it repeated that it is not possible to state in general terms when a mark has a strong distinctive character. Instead, it is necessary to make 'an overall assessment of the greater or lesser capacity of the mark to identify the goods or services for which it has been registered as coming from a particular undertaking, and thus to distinguish those goods or services from those of other undertakings',[55] applying the same criteria: account should be taken in particular of the

> inherent characteristics of the mark, including the fact that it does or does not contain an element descriptive of the goods or services for which it has been registered; the market share held by the mark; how intensive, geographically widespread and long-standing use of the mark has been; the amount invested by the undertaking in promoting the mark; the proportion of the relevant section of the public which, because of the mark, identifies the goods or services as originating from a particular undertaking; and statements from chambers of commerce and industry or other trade and professional associations.[56]

---

[49] Paragraph 41.
[50] C-342/97 *Lloyd Schuhfabrik Meyer & Co GmbH* [1999] ECR I-3819.
[51] Point 21.
[52] Point 22.
[53] Point 23.
[54] C-108/97 and C-109/97 *Windsurfing Chiemsee Produktions-und Vertriebs GmbH* [1999] ECR I-2779.
[55] *Lloyd* (n 50) paragraph 22.
[56] Paragraph 23.

(6) *Lloyd*: The Average Consumer

7.48 In *Lloyd Schuhfabrik* the Court adopted the perspective of the average consumer of the products covered by the trade mark as the most relevant for determining whether there is likelihood of confusion. Citing earlier case law,[57] the Court held:

> For the purposes of that global appreciation, the average consumer of the category of products concerned is deemed to be reasonably well informed and reasonably observant and circumspect. However, account should be taken of the fact that the average consumer only rarely has the chance to make a direct comparison between the different marks but must place his trust in the imperfect picture of them that he has kept in his mind. It should also be borne in mind that the average consumer's level of attention is likely to vary according to the category of goods or services in question.[58]

E. Establishing Confusion: Global Appreciation

(1) The Three Tests

7.49 Regarding confusion the Court has developed and applied three distinct tests. In essence there are three steps: the first is based on the test for establishing similarity between the marks; the second on the test for establishing similarity between the products; and at the third step, that can only be taken if the findings in the earlier tests were positive, we apply the test for establishing likelihood of confusion. The last test combines the findings of the similarity tests with any other circumstance that might be relevant to the outcome of the case.

(2) *Sabel*: The Test for Confusion

(a) *Sabel*: Global appreciation; a test for confusion

7.50 In *Sabel*[59] once the Court dealt with the relationship between confusion and association it turned its attention to formulating a test for establishing whether there is a likelihood of confusion.

(b) The Opinion of Advocate General Jacobs

7.51 Linking the case with the earlier pre-harmonization jurisprudence of the Court, AG Jacobs referred to its free movement of goods case law culminating in *Hag II*[60] and *Ideal Standard*.[61] Risk of confusion served as the justification behind the exercise of national trade mark rights, linking the specific subject matter of trade mark rights with the essential function of a trade mark as a guarantee of the identity of the origin of the marked product.[62] The risk of confusion, however, had to be genuine rather than a pretext for arbitrary discrimination or a disguised restriction on intra-Community trade.

---

[57] C-210/96 *Gut Springenheide GmbH v Oberkreisdirektor* [1998] ECR I-4657, a misleading advertising case.
[58] Paragraph 26.
[59] C-251/95 *Sabel BV* [1997] ECR I-6191.
[60] C-10/89 *SA CNL-SUCAL NV* [1990] ECR I-3711.
[61] C-9/93 *HT Internationale Heiztechnik v Ideal Standard* [1994] ECR I-2789.
[62] Case 102/77 *Hoffmann La Roche & Co AG v Centrafarm Vertriebsgesellschaf t Pharmazeutischer Erzeugnisse GmbH* [1978] ECR 1139.

7.52 This review assisted the Advocate General first in rejecting a broad definition of confusion[63] but also in suggesting a narrow test for proving confusion, a test that would enhance the principle of coexistence:

> the Directive must be read as laying down a Common standard on the basis of which trade marks from different national systems are enabled to co-exist. The standard should not therefore be set at too high a level. In that respect the Directive is perhaps different from harmonising measures in other sectors, where a high level of protection may be desirable in the general interest and where what is essential to ensure free trade is merely that the same standard should be set for all Member States. The Trade Marks Directive, if interpreted too stringently, would have the effect of insulating the national markets. In the absence of a clear intention to that effect, the Directive should accordingly not be read as imposing the most restrictive standard found in the laws of Member States.[64]

(c) The Judgment of the Court

7.53 The Court's examination of Article 4(1)(b) of the Directive resulted first in the obvious statement that 'Article 4(1)(b) of the Directive ... provides that a trade mark conflicts with an earlier trade mark if, because of the identity or similarity of both the trade marks and the goods or services covered, there exists a likelihood of confusion.'[65]

7.54 Citing the Tenth Recital and the reference to 'numerous elements' on which confusion depends the Court came up with a new term: 'likelihood of confusion must therefore be appreciated globally, taking into account all factors relevant to the circumstances of the case'.[66]

(3) *Vedial*: Cumulative Similarity/Identity Conditions

7.55 In *Vedial*[67] the Court confirmed that the two similarity/identity requirements are cumulative. The case involved opposition proceedings against the application for registration of a composite mark, incorporating the word HUBERT combined with the bust of a chef, for, amongst other things, 'milk and milk products' and 'vinegar and sauces'. The opposition was based on an earlier registration in France of the word mark SAINT-HUBERT 41 for 'butters, edible fats, cheeses and all dairy products'. The opposition was rejected by the Opposition Division and the Board of Appeal.[68]

7.56 The Court of First Instance found 'dairy products' and 'edible fats' were identical with 'milk and milk products' and similar to 'vinegar and sauces'. However, the two marks were not found to be similar. It held that even though there was identity and similarity between the goods covered by the conflicting marks, the visual, aural, and conceptual differences between the two marks meant that there would be no likelihood of confusion in the mind of the targeted public.

---

[63] See paragraphs 7.21 and following above.
[64] Point 51.
[65] *Sabel* (n 59) paragraph 12.
[66] Paragraph 22.
[67] C-106/03 P *Vedial SA v Office for Harmonisation in the Internal Market (Trade Marks and Designs)* [2004] ECR I-9573, an appeal against the decision of the Court of First Instance in T-110/01 *Vedial SA v Office for Harmonisation in the Internal Market (Trade Marks and Designs)* [2002] ECR II-5275.
[68] Case R-127/2000-1, 9 March 2001.

(a) The Opinion of Advocate General Ruiz-Jarabo Colomer

(i) Delimiting the dispute Advocate General Ruiz-Jarabo Colomer suggested that the claim should be rejected, not because the proceedings were of an administrative nature, but because it would also need to be established that the litigant was 'dominus litis'—that it could claim ownership of the contested asset—and that the subject matter of the proceedings might be freely availed of.[69] In trade mark proceedings there were wider interests that courts had to take into account, including a public interest, primarily protecting consumers, distinct from the interest of the proprietor. Still, in the case of conflicts with earlier rights, and for reasons of efficiency, the legislator had entrusted their owners with protecting that public interest together with their own. The owner of an earlier right remained free to exercise it and institute opposition proceedings. The Office's capacity, on the other hand, as defendant 'is limited to defending the legality of the decision of one of its bodies, namely, the Board of Appeal concerned';[70] it lacked the capacity of 'dominus litis'. 7.57

(ii) The likelihood of confusion test The Advocate General considered the similarity tests as cumulative but distinct from each other: 'From the moment that the Court of First Instance reached the conclusion ... that the signs were not similar to each other ... there is neither the likelihood of confusion nor the likelihood of association to which the appellant refers.'[71] 7.58

(b) The Judgment of the Court

(i) Delimiting the dispute The Court dismissed this ground by focusing on the role of the Court of First Instance; even if the parties were in agreement and shared a particular view 'the Court of First Instance was in no way bound by that view, but had a duty to determine whether, by finding that there was no similarity between the two marks, the Board of Appeal had infringed Regulation No 40/94 in the contested decision'.[72] 7.59

(ii) The likelihood of confusion test The Court held that 7.60

> likelihood of confusion presupposes both that the mark applied for and the earlier mark are identical or similar, and that the goods or services covered in the application for registration are identical or similar to those in respect of which the earlier mark is registered. Those conditions are cumulative.[73]

Having found that the marks were not similar the Court of First Instance had correctly concluded that there was no likelihood of confusion.

(4) *Canon*: Global Appreciation against a Wider Context

(a) The Opinion of the Advocate General

In *Canon*[74] AG Jacobs stated that according to the Tenth Recital a number of factors, including the recognition of the mark, had to be taken into account before deciding whether there is sufficient similarity of goods or services to give rise to a likelihood of confusion and took 7.61

---

[69] Citing Ramos Mendez, *Derecho Procesal Civil* (Bosch, 1986).
[70] Point 50.
[71] Point 59.
[72] *Vedial* (n 67) paragraph 51.
[73] *Vedial* (n 67) paragraph 51.
[74] C-39/97 *Canon Kabushiki Kaisha* [1998] ECR I-5507.

the reference of the Court to global appreciation in *Sabel* to confirm his statement. He attributed to global appreciation a wider significance:

> It is true that that statement was made in a different context: the Court was there considering the question whether conceptual similarity of the marks alone could give rise to confusion within the meaning of Article 4(1)(b), in a situation in which the goods in question were clearly the same. However the statement is one of general application.[75]

(b) The Judgment of the Court

7.62 This time the Court appeared to be more systematic. First, it confirmed that 'the likelihood of confusion on the part of the public, in the absence of which Article 4(1)(b) of the Directive does not apply, must be appreciated globally, taking into account all factors relevant to the circumstances of the case'.[76]

7.63 Second, it elaborated on the meaning of global appreciation or assessment:

> A global assessment of the likelihood of confusion implies some interdependence between the relevant factors, and in particular a similarity between the trade marks and between these goods or services. Accordingly, a lesser degree of similarity between these goods or services may be offset by a greater degree of similarity between the marks, and vice versa. The interdependence of these factors is expressly mentioned in the tenth recital of the preamble to the Directive, which states that it is indispensable to give an interpretation of the concept of similarity in relation to the likelihood of confusion, the appreciation of which depends, in particular, on the recognition of the trade mark on the market and the degree of similarity between the mark and the sign and between the goods or services identified.[77]

7.64 Third, as we have already seen above, it confronted the issue of the relevance of distinctiveness in determining confusion: '[M]arks with a highly distinctive character, either per se or because of the reputation they possess on the market, enjoy broader protection than marks with a less distinctive character.'[78]

7.65 What, however, the Court failed to do is provide a definitive interpretation of global appreciation or assessment; its conclusion was narrowed to conform with the terms of the reference:

> It follows that, for the purposes of Article 4(1)(b) of the Directive, registration of a trade mark may have to be refused, despite a lesser degree of similarity between the goods or services covered, where the marks are very similar and the earlier mark, in particular its reputation, is highly distinctive.[79]

(5) *Sabel*: The Test for Comparing the Marks

(a) The Opinion of Advocate General Jacobs

7.66 In *Sabel*[80] AG Jacobs reviewed the criteria employed by the Bundesgerichtshof for comparing the two marks. The overall impression made by the marks should form the basis of the comparison. However, two additional elements could shift the balance. First, the characterizing force of the trade mark should also be taken into account as a positively correlative

---

[75] Point 40.
[76] Paragraph 16, citing C-251/95 *Sabel BV* [1997] ECR I-6191.
[77] Paragraph 17.
[78] Paragraph 18.
[79] *Canon* (n 74) paragraph 19.
[80] C-215/95 *Sabel BV* [1997] ECR I-6191.

factor; this force could be either intrinsic or the result of the mark's commercial standing. On the other hand, descriptive signs with little imaginative content should face a stricter test of similarity.

7.67 He stated that reliance on the overall impression of the sign is 'perhaps self-evident. Given that the essential criterion is the likelihood of confusion, the Bundesgerichtshof must be correct in considering that what is important is the overall impression conveyed by the mark.'[81] Considering the relevance of the addition of a textual element to a pictorial sign, he suggested that this was essentially a question of fact for the national court. So from the very beginning it becomes apparent that the application of automated rules is discouraged.

7.68 Turning to the relevance of the shared signification of the two signs he submitted that it should be taken into account and may even become the deciding factor; however, he also suggested that it would be 'difficult to establish the likelihood of confusion on the basis of conceptual similarity alone in circumstances in which the earlier mark is not well known, particularly when, as here, the image in question is not particularly creative or unusual'.[82] The critical issue was to establish a genuine and properly substantiated likelihood of confusion as to origin.[83]

(b) The Judgment of the Court

7.69 The Court attempted to provide a systematic test. Similarity of signs must be decided following a global appreciation:

> That global appreciation of the visual, aural or conceptual similarity of the marks in question, must be based on the overall impression given by the marks, bearing in mind, in particular, their distinctive and dominant components. The wording of Article 4(1)(b) of the Directive—'… there exists a likelihood of confusion on the part of the public …'—shows that the perception of marks in the mind of the average consumer of the type of goods or services in question plays a decisive role in the global appreciation of the likelihood of confusion. The average consumer normally perceives a mark as a whole and does not proceed to analyse its various details.[84]

7.70 It went on to hold that the more distinctive the earlier mark, the greater will be the likelihood of confusion and that conceptual similarity 'resulting from the fact that two marks use images with analogous semantic content may give rise to a likelihood of confusion where the earlier mark has a particularly distinctive character, either per se or because of the reputation it enjoys with the public'.[85]

7.71 Turning to the actual circumstances of the case it found that, since the earlier mark was not especially well known and possessed little imaginative content, conceptual similarity would not be enough to give rise to a likelihood of confusion.

(6) *Lloyd*: Aural Similarity

7.72 The test was developed further in *Lloyd Schuhfabrik*.[86] As you recall, the case involved the marks 'Lloyd' and 'Loints'.

---

[81] Point 59.
[82] Point 62.
[83] Repeating a point he had already made: see paragraph 7.26 above; to reinforce its importance his perspective on similarity tests became narrower.
[84] *Sabel* (n 80) paragraph 23.
[85] Paragraph 24; see also C-145/05 *Levi Strauss & Co v Casucci SpA* [2006] ECR I-3703.
[86] C-342/97 *Lloyd Schuhfabrik* [1999] ECR I-3819.

(a) The Opinion of Advocate General Jacobs

7.73 Advocate General Jacobs repeated *Sabel*'s main points and introduced into the comparison the nature of the goods by adding that as part of the global assessment exercise:

> it may ... be relevant ... to consider not only the degree of aural similarity of the mark and the sign but also the degree (or absence) of visual and conceptual similarity. In the absence of visual or conceptual similarity it would be necessary to consider whether, having regard to all the circumstances including the nature of the goods and the conditions in which they were marketed, the degree of any aural similarity would of itself be likely to give rise to confusion.[87]

(b) The Judgment of the Court

7.74 The Court followed the Opinion of the Advocate General. Global appreciation must be based on the overall impression created by the marks 'bearing in mind, in particular, their distinctive and dominant components ... The average consumer normally perceives a mark as a whole and does not proceed to analyse its various details.'[88] It added that the importance attributed to each one of the elements of the similarity test must be evaluated, where appropriate, 'taking account of the category of goods or services in question and the circumstances in which they are marketed';[89] there may be cases where mere aural similarity might cause confusion.

(7) *Mühlens*: A Challenge to *Lloyd*

7.75 *Mühlens*[90] challenged the relevance of the three specific factors courts had to examine in order to assess trade mark similarity. The case also exemplifies that under the architecture of coexistence sometimes courts facing identical facts would reach contrasting conclusions. It came before the Court of Justice as an appeal against a judgment of the Court of First Instance,[91] dismissing the action for annulment against a decision of the Second Board of Appeal that had in turn dismissed the opposition by Mühlens, the owner of a figurative Community trade mark incorporating the word 'Sir' and a heraldic figure for goods in Class 3 ('Perfumery, essential oils, cosmetics, hair lotions, dentifrices, soaps'), against the word mark 'Zirh' for goods and services in Classes 3, 5, and 42.

(a) The Judgment of the Court of First Instance

7.76 The Court of First Instance conducted the global assessment test and found that visually and conceptually the signs were not similar. Phonetically there were similarities, in particular concerning the way the marks would be pronounced in English-speaking countries and Spain. Phonetic similarity alone could lead to a finding of similarity; however, according to its own case law

> phonetic similarities may be counteracted by the conceptual differences between the trade marks in question. For there to be such a counteraction, at least one of the marks at issue must have, from the point of view of the relevant public, a clear and specific meaning so that the public is capable of grasping it immediately.[92]

---

[87] Point 18.
[88] Paragraph 25.
[89] Paragraph 27.
[90] C-206/04 P *Mühlens GmbH & Co KG v Office for Harmonisation in the Internal Mamet (Trade Marks and Designs)* [2006] ECR I-271.
[91] T-355/02 *Mühlens GmbH & Co KG v Office for Harmonisation in the Internal Market (Trade Marks and Designs)* [2004] ECR II-791.
[92] *Mühlens* (n 91) paragraph 49, citing T-292/01 *Phillips-Van Heusen v Office for Harmonisation in the Internal Market (Trade Marks and Designs)* [2003] ECR II-4335.

In this case the word 'Sir' had an obvious meaning understood by the public despite the fact that it had no link with the product. It also accepted the Office's argument that phonetic similarity is less important when at the time of purchase the relevant public sees the marks. The submission that the products covered by the earlier mark were also sold through other channels, for example, beauty salons, did not alter the Court of First Instance's conclusion that the conflicting signs were not sufficiently similar for establishing confusion.

7.77 Before the Court of Justice Mühlens claimed that the Court of First Instance had misconstrued the concept of likelihood of confusion in two ways. First, phonetic similarity should lead to a finding of likelihood of confusion, in particular given the methods of marketing for the specified goods and services. Second, phonetic similarity should not be counteracted by conceptual considerations.

(b) The Opinion of Advocate General Ruiz-Jarabo Colomer

7.78 (i) **Balancing the factors** Advocate General Ruiz-Jarabo Colomer was tempted to consider the first part of the plea as inadmissible because it challenged factual findings. He chose to examine it applying the 'interpretative principle in dubio pro actione'.[93] This is a typical example of the transformation of the functioning of the Court from an interpretive court to a court that is part of an appeals system; the principle aimed for effective judicial protection and called for continuation of the proceedings until a decision on the substance was reached.

7.79 Mühlens relied on a German theory to read *Lloyd* as setting a doctrine that phonetic similarity should be sufficient for the purposes of a confusion test; consumers did not always have the marked products in front of them at the time of purchase; gifts, mail-order and telephone sales, and recommendations were verbal rather than visual.

7.80 The Advocate General agreed that *Lloyd* did not rule out the possibility that phonetic similarity might suffice; still, it did not render phonetic similarity the ultimate confusion arbiter.[94]

7.81 Regarding the importance that channels of trade might give to phonetic similarity he remarked that the Court of First Instance had not overlooked this issue; it found the evidence submitted by Mühlens insufficient. Whether its assessment was right or not was outside the jurisdiction of the Court of Justice.[95] The second part of the plea challenged the concept, and its application, of the balancing suggested by the Court of First Instance and the counteraction of phonetic by conceptual similarity. Advocate General Ruiz-Jarabo Colomer found that the jurisprudence of the Court demanded an overall assessment that took into account all the relevant factors, so as a concept the approach of the Court of First Instance was correct. Its specific application was, again, a question of assessing evidence. On the legality of the 'counteraction' rule he repeated his position expressed in *Picasso*[96] that the Court of Justice could only review it

---

[93] Point 35.
[94] Point 45. To reinforce his reading of C-342/97 *Lloyd Schuhfabrik Meyer & Co GmbH* [1999] ECR I-3819 he looked at the translations of the contested paragraph 28 in a number of languages; all led to the same conclusion.
[95] Citing C-312/00 P *Commission v Comar and Tico* [2002] ECR I-11355.
[96] See the Opinion of the AG in C-361/04 P *Picasso v Office for Harmonisation in the Internal Market (Trade Marks and Designs)* [2006] ECR I-643.

where the contested rule was relied on in an absolute and a priori manner without prior individual analysis of the various components, resulting in its automatic application in a way that conflicted with ... the case-law of the Court of Justice. Of course, it would also be necessary for the appellant to allege distortion of the facts,[97] a possibility not to be taken into account here since no such allegation was made.[98]

7.82 The Court of First Instance had examined all the factors and considered that the conceptual aspect was decisive. There was nothing wrong with the process it had followed.

7.83 (ii) **The 'cohabitation' between the Community trade mark and national rights** The Advocate General then discussed in some detail a judgment of the Landgericht Hamburg[99] that Mühlens had submitted in order to boost the first part of the appeal. The parties, contested signs, and products were the same; still the German court held that there was a likelihood of confusion. According to the Advocate General this was the result of the cohabitation, rather than coexistence, between the Community trade mark system and national rights. The 'correspondence with national law is reflected in cases of infringement of Community trade marks, a field governed by Community law and, on an ancillary basis, the laws of the Member States, as if the principle of subsidiarity had been inverted'.[100]

7.84 In order to avoid conflicting judgments the Community Trade Mark Regulation includes provisions on related actions (Article 100), cases involving circumstances similar to litispendency (Article 105), and counterclaims (Article 96(7)).[101] The essence is that these

> provisions contemplate the possible suspension of proceedings that are pending or inadmissibility of the originating application, declared either by the Community trade mark court or by another national judicial authority, the sole justification for this being the avoidance of conflicting decisions.[102]

The Advocate General accepted that these provisions did not cover the facts of the case before the German court. However, he invoked the general principles of the Community legal order—first the principle of judicial cooperation between national courts and the Court of Justice; second, the principle of effectiveness of Community law; and, third, the principle requiring sincere cooperation under Article 10 EC—to support the application of Community law as interpreted by the Court of Justice. If in doubt the national court should use the preliminary ruling mechanism, rather than apply a Community provision 'in a manner that openly conflicts with the case-law of the Court of First Instance of the European Communalities'.[103] The Advocate General urged German courts to test the validity of their interpretation of the global appreciation test through a reference to the Court of Justice.

---

[97] Citing C-53/92 *Hilti AG v Commission* [1994] ECR I-667.
[98] Point 55.
[99] *Mülhens GmbH & Co KG v Zirh International Corp* [2005] ETMR 55; this was a Community trade mark infringement action between the same parties. The German court rejected the Court of First Instance's interpretation of C-342/97 *Lloyd Schuhfabrik Meyer & Co GmbH* [1999] ECR I-3819 and instead applied a theory developed by the case law of the Bundesgerichtshof (German Supreme Court) that considered in appropriate cases the existence of phonetic similarity sufficient to find infringement.
[100] According to Article 14 of the Community Trade Mark Regulation. He cited E Gastinel, *La Marque Communautaire* (L.G.D.J., 1998) p 197 as the original source of this succinct remark.
[101] Recital 16 states that 'contradictory judgments should be avoided in actions which involve the same acts and the same parties and which are brought on the basis of a Community trade mark and parallel national trade marks'.
[102] Point 69.
[103] Point 74.

(c) The Judgment of the Court

7.85 The Court in its analysis of *Lloyd* stressed that

> it is conceivable that the marks' phonetic similarity alone could create a likelihood of confusion ... However, it must be noted that the existence of such a likelihood must be established as part of a global assessment as regards the conceptual, visual and aural similarities between the signs at issue. In that regard, the assessment of any aural similarity is but one of the relevant factors for the purpose of that global assessment.[104]

7.86 It added that 'one cannot deduce from paragraph 28 of the judgment in Lloyd Schuhfabrik Meyer that there is necessarily a likelihood of confusion each time that mere phonetic similarity between two signs is established'.[105]

7.87 Having rejected the theoretical background of the first part of the appeal and without considering the methodology of the Court of First Instance in detail, it ruled that it had correctly considered the overall impression created by the two signs at issue for the purpose of the global assessment of the likelihood of confusion. As to the link between phonetic similarity and channels of trade or methods of marketing it ruled that the Court of First Instance had exclusive jurisdiction to find and appraise the relevant facts and to assess the evidence. Unless there was a distortion of the facts or evidence the Court had no jurisdiction to reconsider them and there was no such claim in this case.

7.88 The methodology of the Court of First Instance regarding the counteraction of aural similarity was approved by the Court in its consideration of the second part of the appeal. Citing *Picasso*,[106] it repeated that:

> global assessment means that conceptual and visual differences between two signs may counteract aural similarities between them, provided that at least one of those signs has, from the point of view of the relevant public, a clear and specific meaning, so that the public is capable of grasping it immediately.[107]

The Court finally looked at the application of this balancing exercise on the facts of the case, and in particular the claim that the Court of First Instance had wrongly found that the word 'Sir' had a clear and specific meaning and that it had such a meaning only if the word were pronounced in the English way. Again, the Court ruled that this was a finding of fact outside the jurisdiction of the Court of Justice since there was no distortion of fact or evidence.

(8) *Matratzen I*: Similarity between a Figurative and a Word Mark

7.89 In *Matratzen I*[108] the Court considered the similarity between a figurative mark including the word MATRATZEN and the word mark MATRATZEN. It also touched the issue of coexistence. Matratzen had applied to register as a Community trade mark a sign combining the slogan 'MATRATZEN Markt CONCORD' with a drawing of a human figure carrying a mattress. The specification included 'cushions; pillows; mattresses; air cushions

---

[104] *Mühlens* (n 91) paragraph 21.
[105] Distinguishing C-37/03 P *BioID AG* [2005] ECR I-7975.
[106] C-361/04 P *Claude Ruiz-Picasso and Others v Office for Harmonisation in the Internal Market (Trade Marks and Designs)* [2006] ECR I-643; see also 7.182 below.
[107] *Mühlens* (n 91) paragraph 35.
[108] C-3/03 P *Matratzen Concord GmbH (Trade Marks and Designs)* [2004] ECR I-3657 an appeal against the judgment of the Court of First Instance (Fourth Chamber) in T-6/01 *Matratzen Concord GmbH* [2002] ECR II-4335, which in turn had dismissed the action against the decisions of the Second Board of Appeal in Joined Cases R-728/1999-2 and R-792/1999-2, 31 October 2000.

and beds for medical purposes' in Class 10; 'mattresses; air beds; beds; duckboards, not of metal; loose covers; bedding' in Class 20; and 'bed blankets; pillow shams; bed linen; eiderdowns [down coverlets]; cambric covers; mattress covers; sleeping bags' in Class 24. Hukla opposed the application, based on its earlier registration in Spain of the word mark 'Matratzen' for 'All kinds of furniture and, particularly, rest furniture, such as beds, studio couches, camp beds, cradles, couches, hammocks, bunks and carrycots; transformable furniture; wheels for beds and furniture; bedside tables; chairs, armchairs; spring mattresses, straw mattresses, mattresses and pillows' in Class 20.

7.90 The Opposition Division rejected the opposition in respect of the Class 10 goods and upheld it in respect of the goods in Classes 20 and 24. The Board of Appeal found that the two marks would be considered similar in Spain and that the products covered by the marks were either identical or similar and concluded that there would be a likelihood of confusion in respect of all the goods specified in the application.

(a) The Judgment of the Court of First Instance

7.91 The Court of First Instance made a general point on similarity between the marks: 'two marks are similar when, from the point of view of the relevant public, they are at least partially identical as regards one or more relevant aspects'.[109] The existence of 'Matratzen' in both trade marks meant for the Court of First Instance that the earlier trade mark was identical to one of the signs making up the trade mark applied for from a visual and phonetic perspective.

7.92 It added that similarity between some elements of the mark would not suffice; the assessment of similarity should be based on the overall impression created by the marks, taking account of their distinctive and dominant components that in some cases might dominate the overall impression conveyed by a mark.

7.93 Following an analysis of the components of the trade mark applied for it found that the word 'Matratzen' was its dominant element. Despite its meaning in German—mattresses—the Court of First Instance found that there was no evidence that a significant number of consumers in Spain would understand its German meaning. It held 'that considered cumulatively, the degree of similarity between the trade marks in question and the degree of similarity between the goods covered by them are sufficiently high'.[110]

7.94 It added that even if Article 12(b) were to have an effect on the registration procedure, that effect should be limited; in particular since 'Matratzen' was not descriptive in Spain.

(b) The reasoned order of the Court of Justice

7.95 **(i) Global appreciation: Dominant elements** Matratzen claimed that the Court of First Instance had failed to conduct a proper global appreciation by focusing on similarities between specific elements of the marks. It also claimed that the Court of First Instance had erred in law in its assessment of the factual circumstances by holding that the word 'Matratzen' dominated in the trade mark applied for. Instead, it should have found the word 'Concord' to be the dominant element. It was a more familiar word for Spanish speakers, and would remain more clearly and easily fixed in the memory of consumers. In addition, it

---

[109] T-6/01 *Matratzen Concord GmbH* [2002] ECR II-4335, paragraph 30.
[110] Paragraph 38.

alleged that the principles on the limitation of the effects of a trade mark should be applied by analogy, and 'Matratzen' should not be relied on against the application of a composite mark. The Office argued that Matratzen's arguments should be rejected as inadmissible since they involved exclusively findings and assessments of fact.

7.96 Regarding the global assessment part of the claim it held that the Court of First Instance had rightly pointed out that 'the assessment of the similarity between two marks does not amount to taking into consideration only one component of a complex trade mark and comparing it with another mark'.[111] Instead, it had considered each mark as a whole and had held that this did not mean that the overall impression 'created in the mind of the relevant public by a complex trade mark may not, in certain circumstances, be dominated by one or more of its components'.[112] The Court of First Instance had taken all the necessary steps to complete the global appreciation test, and the first part of the plea was rejected as unfounded.

7.97 The Court also agreed with the Court of First Instance that Article 12(b) was irrelevant. Article 12(b) 'concerns the limitation of the effects of the Community trade mark itself... It does not concern the status of an earlier trade mark, within the meaning of Article 8(2) of Regulation No 40/94.'[113]

7.98 (ii) **The exercise of trade mark rights and free movement of goods** Matratzen had argued that the exercise of the Spanish trade mark rights in relation to a term that would be descriptive in Germany went against the second sentence of Article 36 TFEU. The Office responded that, according to the principle of coexistence, a term that was descriptive in one language could very well be registered in a Member State with another language.[114]

7.99 The Court focused on the free movement of goods issue and found that the Court of First Instance had rightly followed the objectives and propositions developed by the jurisprudence of the Court of Justice by holding that the principle of the free movement of goods did not prohibit either a Member State from registering, as a national trade mark, a sign which, in the language of another Member State, was descriptive of the specified goods or services, or the proprietor of such a trade mark from opposing a later Community trade mark application.

(9) *Formula One*: The Presumption of Distinctiveness

(a) *Background to the dispute*

7.100 In *Formula One*[115] the Court was called upon to clarify whether the degree of distinctiveness to be attributed to the earlier sign for the purposes of the comparison of the signs and the assessment of the likelihood of confusion can be influenced by formal considerations such as the fact that the earlier sign is a registered trade mark in force. The appeal concerned an opposition brought by Formula One Licensing BV before OHIM against the registration as a Community trade mark of a figurative sign consisting of the expression 'F1-LIVE'

---

[111] Paragraph 32.
[112] Paragraph 32.
[113] Paragraph 35.
[114] Compare with the position on absolute grounds; see, for example, paragraphs 5.699 and following above.
[115] C-196/11 P, *Formula One Licensing BV/Office for Harmonisation in the Internal Market*, 24 May 2012, ECLI:EU:C:2012:314.

and a dark rectangular background with a circular device in its centre. The application was filed in respect of a range of goods and services relating 'to the field of Formula 1' in classes 16, 38, and 41. The opposition was based on a number of national and Community registrations, including the word sign 'F1' and the stylized combination of the words 'F1' and 'Formula 1'. Formula One Licensing relied on Article 8(1)(b) and (5) of the Regulation, claiming in addition that all of its earlier trade marks were highly reputed.

7.101 The Opposition Division rejected the application holding that the signs were confusingly similar on account of their common component 'F1'. The First Board, however, upheld the appeal brought by the applicant, considering that the fact that the marks coincide in the word element 'F1' is not sufficient to give rise to a likelihood of confusion, because that element will be perceived by consumers as descriptive of a type of racing car.

7.102 Formula One Licensing appealed to the General Court[116] pleading infringement of Articles 8(1)(b) and 8(5). The General Court upheld the view taken by the Board and dismissed the action. With regard to the comparison of the signs and their perception by the relevant public, the General Court considered that the common element 'F1' could not be regarded as dominant in the sign applied for, taking into account that the term 'Formula 1' is used to designate, in generic terms, the sport of motor racing and that 'the abbreviation F1 is just as generic as the term Formula 1'.

7.103 As regards the formal status of the earlier mark, the General Court acknowledged that, in principle, the validity of an international or national registration may not be called into question in proceedings for registration of a Community trade mark, but only in cancellation proceedings brought in the Member State concerned. Nonetheless, it added that the sole fact that the earlier mark is registered does not prevent it from being descriptive or from having only a weak intrinsic distinctive character in relation to the goods and services it covers. Holding those findings to be equally applicable to Formula One Licensing's earlier national and Community marks, the General Court took the view that the relevant public would not perceive the element 'F1' as distinctive, and that this lack of distinctiveness of the common component of the marks under comparison resulted in a lack of visual similarity and only in a limited phonetic and conceptual similarity between them, with the result that consumers would not make a connection between the mark applied for and the activities of the opponent.

7.104 As regards the alleged infringement of Article 8(5), the General Court held that the only mark for which a reputation had been shown was Formula One Licensing's logo, the distinctiveness and repute of which resided in the 'virtual fusion of the letter "F" and the numeral "1" presented in sharply contrasting colours' and that the sole fact that the same letters and numerals were present in the contested sign was insufficient to support the inference that the public would establish a link between the marks.

(b) The Judgment of the Court

7.105 Formula One Licensing appealed to the Court of Justice pleading infringement of Articles 8(1)(b) and 8(5), on the grounds that the judgment under appeal had failed to recognize the acquisition of distinctive character resulting from the use made of its Community trade

---

[116] T-10/09 *Formula One Licensing/Office for Harmonisation in the Internal Market—Global Sports Media* (F1-LIVE) [2011] ECR II-00427.

mark and had unlawfully removed the protection afforded by registration to a registered mark, since the finding that the designation 'F1' is generic entails a *de facto* annulment of the appellant's registration.

7.106 The Court of Justice endorsed the position taken by the General Court[117] that in view of the autonomy of the Community trade mark system the validity of an international or national registration may not be called into question in proceedings before OHIM but only in cancellation proceedings brought before the competent national jurisdiction. It added, however, that this lack of competence of OHIM, and, by extension, of the General Court, effectively meant that it is not possible to raise with regard to a mark protected in a Member State an absolute ground for refusal such as the lack of distinctiveness in opposition proceedings, since 'the characterisation of a sign as descriptive or generic is equivalent to denying its distinctive character'.[118] Accordingly, the Court held that the verification OHIM and the General Court are expected to carry out in the context of opposition proceedings regarding the way in which the relevant public perceives a sign which is identical to a registered trade mark by evaluating, if necessary, the degree of distinctiveness of that sign, is not without limits, in that

> it may not culminate in a finding of absolute lack of distinctive character, since such a finding would be incompatible with Article 8(2)(a)(ii) of the Regulation, which warrants the enforceability of national marks in opposition proceedings against a later Community trade mark.[119]

7.107 In addition, the Court held that such a finding would be detrimental to national trade marks because the registration of a Community trade mark identical with or confusingly similar to them, would bring about a situation likely to render meaningless the protection granted to them by national law, contrary to the statement in the Sixth Recital in the Preamble to the Regulation that European law does not replace the laws of the Member States. Consequently, it concluded that a proper interpretation of Article 8(1)(b) required acknowledgement of 'a certain degree of distinctiveness of an earlier national mark' on which an opposition is based, and that the judgment under appeal was not entitled to find without erring in law either that the element 'F1' was descriptive in the earlier marks or that the same element was devoid of distinctiveness in the sign applied for.[120]

(c) Conclusions

7.108 The rather formalistic approach followed by the Court in *Formula One* and the limits it imposes on the free assessment of distinctiveness of an earlier registration in the context of relative grounds examination call for a number of remarks.

7.109 First of all, the presumption of distinctiveness it has introduced must be understood as working both ways, ie as binding both OHIM when it comes to earlier national registrations and national authorities when it comes to earlier Community trade marks, otherwise

---

[117] Citing T-7/04 *Shaker/Office for Harmonisation in the Internal Market—Limiñana y Botella* (Limoncello della Costiera Amalfitana shaker) [2008] ECR II-3085, paragraph 26 and T-6/01 *Matratzen Concord/Office for Harmonisation in the Internal Market—Hukla Germany* (MATRATZEN) [2002] ECR II-4335, paragraph 55.
[118] Paragraphs 37–41.
[119] Paragraphs 42–44.
[120] Paragraphs 45–47 and 51.

the argument based on the autonomy and coexistence of the respective systems would make no sense.

7.110 Second, its consistent application advocates in favour of a restrictive reading, in the sense that if the earlier registration consists not only of a descriptive component, however prominent, but also of other elements, which contribute to its overall distinctiveness, it is legitimate to declare that component alone devoid of distinctiveness for the purposes of the assessment of likelihood of confusion. If true, however, this gives rise to a grey zone in cases where it will not be certain if the remaining elements are truly negligible or if they somehow influence the distinctiveness of the sign as a whole.

7.111 Third, the application by the Court of the same rule to the sign applied for stretches the consistency of the principle to the limit, since the assessment of the distinctiveness of the various components of the later sign is not subject to any limitations of formal character. On the contrary, the prerogative of the examining authority to determine the degree of distinctiveness of the later sign is subject to the same guarantees of independence as the need to respect the autonomy of the jurisdiction that held the earlier right to be distinctive. Thus, in trying to achieve a certain degree of logical consistency by giving an identical value to the same element irrespective of the mark in which it is incorporated, the Court appears to have restricted the autonomy of the authority examining the opposition without clear basis. This is further supported by the fact that, as the Court itself has repeatedly held, OHIM is not bound when examining the sign applied for under absolute grounds for refusal by decisions taken by national authorities in the same regard. So if OHIM is not bound directly when examining the sign for absolute grounds, how can it be deemed to be bound indirectly when it examines the same sign in the context of relative grounds?

7.112 Last, by obliging the applicant to initiate cancellation proceedings in the jurisdiction that granted the registration used as a basis for the opposition, the Court seems to be following a different approach from the one it took in *Fédération Cynologique*,[121] where it held that it would be disproportionate to expect the owner of a trade mark to cancel a conflicting registration if the essential function of its mark is at stake, especially since that step could take years before yielding results. Similarly, by focusing on formal rather than substantive considerations, it seems to be deviating from the path marked by its settled case law that the exclusive right conferred upon trade mark proprietors is reserved only against acts by third parties that affect or are liable to affect the functions of the trade mark.[122] If, however, an earlier registered sign is manifestly devoid of distinctiveness (for instance, because the national registration was granted as a result of an oversight) and thus its reproduction in the later sign cannot give rise to confusion, it can only be assumed that the essential function of the marks concerned is not affected, which means that the need to cancel the earlier mark is reduced to a moot formality.

7.113 Consequently, the assimilation of the presumption of validity to a presumption of distinctiveness introduced by the Court in *Formula One* should be seen as an important exception

---

[121] C-561/11 *Fédération Cynologique Internationale v Federación Canina Internacional de Perros de Pura Raza*, ECLI:EU:C:2013:91.
[122] See, among others, Joined Cases C-236/08 to C-238/08 *Google France and Google* [2010] ECR I-02417, paragraph 75; C-235/09, *DHL Express France SAS v Chronopost SA* [2011] ECR I-02801, paragraphs 46–48; C-487/07 *L'Oréal and Others* [2009] ECR I-5185, paragraph 58; and Case C-482/09, *Budějovický Budvar, národní podnik* [2011] ECR I-08701, paragraphs 71–75.

to the maxim that without a real and tangible likelihood of confusion in the mind of the public, or without any harm to the functions of the earlier trade mark, the relevant ground of refusal cannot apply.

(10) *Flexi Air*: Distinctiveness as Part of a Multifactor Assessment

In *Flexi Air*[123] the Court looked at the relevance of distinctiveness for assessing likelihood of confusion. The case was an appeal against a judgment of the Court of First Instance dismissing an action against a decision of the Board of Appeal.[124] L'Oreal filed an application for registration of FLEXI AIR as a Community trade mark for 'shampoos; gels, mousses and balms, preparations in aerosol form for hairdressing and hair care; hair lacquers; hair-colouring and hair-decolorising preparations; permanent waving and curling preparations; essential oils' in Class 3. Revlon filed a notice of opposition based on registrations of FLEX in France, Sweden, and the United Kingdom. The specifications of the earlier registrations covered 'bleaching preparations and other substances for laundry use; cleaning, polishing, scouring and abrasive preparations; soaps; perfumery, essential oils, cosmetics, hair lotions; dentifrices' in Class 3 and 'tobacco (raw or manufactured); smokers' articles; matches' in Class 34 in France; 'shampoos; hair balsam, mousse, hair spray and hair gel' in Class 3 in Sweden; and 'shampoos and conditioning preparations, all for hair' in Class 3 in the United Kingdom.

7.114

The Opposition Division of the Office accepted the opposition and rejected L'Oreal's application for registration on the ground that there was a likelihood of confusion between its trade mark and the earlier trade mark registered in the United Kingdom. The Board of Appeal concurred with the Opposition Division. It found that the earlier mark was weak in terms of distinctive character, however, and given the similarities between the two marks, the risk of confusion could not be excluded.

7.115

(a) The Judgment of the Court of First Instance

L'Oreal relied on three grounds in order to challenge the decision of the Board. The first had to do with the proof of genuine use in respect of the Revlon mark. This was rejected on the basis of a number of procedural failures on behalf of L'Oreal. The third claimed that the Board had granted broader protection to the United Kingdom than the protection it would enjoy in the jurisdiction because it had failed to examine the validity of the national right. This was rejected because there was no provision in the Regulation requiring or even allowing the examination of the validity of the national right that formed the basis of the opposition. With the second ground L'Oreal claimed that the Board had infringed Article 8(1)(b). One of the main arguments supporting this claim was that because the earlier mark was weak in terms of distinctive character only a complete reproduction of that mark could give rise to a likelihood of confusion. The Court of First Instance rejected this general proposition:

7.116

> That argument must be rejected. Although the distinctive character of the earlier mark must be taken into account when assessing the likelihood of confusion ... it is only one factor

---

[123] C-235/05 P *L'Oreal SA v Office for Harmonisation in the Internal Market (Trade Marks and Designs)* [2006] ECR I-00057.
[124] T-112/03 *L'Oreal v Office for Harmonisation in the Internal Market (Trade Marks and Designs)* [2005] ECR II-949 dismissing the action against the decision of the Board of Appeal in Case R-396/20014, 15 January 2003.

among others involved in that assessment. Thus, even in a case involving an earlier mark of weak distinctive character, on the one hand, and a trade mark applied for which is not a complete reproduction of it, on the other, there may be a likelihood of confusion on account, in particular, of a similarity between the signs and between the goods or services covered.[125]

7.117 Starting from the comparison between the products it found them either identical or very similar. Regarding the visual similarity between the marks it found that 'FLEX' was the dominant element in the later mark, agreeing with the Board of Appeal.[126]

7.118 It then rejected the argument that two words by definition could not be visually similar to one word: '[I]t must be pointed out, firstly, that there is no reason why a sign consisting of two words and a sign consisting of a single word may not be visually similar.'[127]

7.119 Phonetically, the signs were also similar. The addition of 'I' and the word 'AIR' played an insignificant role. Conceptually, both signs were founded on a common meaning in English.[128] The Court of First Instance then went on to assess whether on the basis of the above the Board was correct in finding that there was a likelihood of confusion, and that consumers could believe that the slight difference between the signs reflected a variation in the nature of the goods or stemmed from marketing considerations.[129]

7.120 Before the Court of Justice L'Oreal argued that the Court of First Instance had infringed Article 8(1)(b) and Article 36 and Article 53 of the Statute of the Court of Justice. The Court found the appeal to be manifestly unfounded and rejected it by issuing a reasoned order.

(b) The reasoned order of the Court

7.121 With the Article 8(1)(b) claim the appellant argued that the Court of First Instance considered the weak distinctive character of the earlier mark when it assessed likelihood of confusion between the marks at issue but not when assessing similarity between the two signs. Further, it submitted that the degree of distinctiveness of each one of the elements of a composite mark was a relative issue. A weak element might still dominate amongst other weaker elements.

7.122 The Court repeated that the principle that 'as the more distinctive the earlier mark, the greater the risk of confusion ... marks with a highly distinctive character, either per se or because of the reputation they possess on the market, enjoy broader protection than marks with a less distinctive character'[130] formed part of the wider principle, there was some interdependence between the factors of the global assessment. The Court of First Instance made a finding about the distinctive character of the earlier mark, compared the products and the signs following the guidelines of the Court, and concluded that there was a likelihood of confusion:

> In that regard, the Court of First Instance cannot be criticised for not having disregarded, in its examination of the similarity of the signs in question, the element "FLEX", which is common to the marks, on the ground that the earlier mark is only of weak distinctive character.[131]

---

[125] *Flexi Air* (n 124) paragraph 61, citing C-39/97 *Canon Kabushiki Kaisha* [1998] ECR I-5507.
[126] Paragraph 64.
[127] Paragraph 66.
[128] Paragraph 78.
[129] Paragraph 81.
[130] *Flexi Air* (n 123) paragraph 36, citing C-251/95 *Sabel BV* [1997] ECR I-6191; C-39/97 *Canon Kabushiki Kaisha* [1998] ECR I-5507; and C-342/97 *Lloyd Schuhfabrik* [1999] ECR I-3819.
[131] Paragraph 39.

The Court, functioning more as an interpretive rather than an appeal court, went on to reject the logic behind the argument of the appellant that rendered distinctive character the decisive factor:

7.123

> The result would be that where the earlier mark is only of weak distinctive character a likelihood of confusion would exist only where there was a complete reproduction of that mark by the mark applied for, whatever the degree of similarity between the marks in question. If that were the case, it would be possible to register a complex mark, one of the elements of which was identical with or similar to those of an earlier mark with a weak distinctive character, even where the other elements of that complex mark were still less distinctive than the common element and notwithstanding a likelihood that consumers would believe that the slight difference between the signs reflected a variation in the nature of the products or stemmed from marketing considerations and not that that difference denoted goods from different traders.[132]

Finally, it repeated the point made in *Matratzen*[133] that a comparison between two marks can only be made by considering each one as a whole.

7.124

The Court raised another ground for rejecting the appeal; the appraisal requested by L'Oreal would require a review of the facts of the case, not of a point of law.[134] Note that the final ground for rejecting the appeal was mentioned at the end of the discussion of the first plea; the Court discussed the substance of the plea and then added that in any case the plea would be inadmissible. The second plea was also rejected by the Court. It was obvious from the analysis of the first plea that the Court of First Instance had carried out an assessment of the likelihood of confusion between the two marks describing throughout the Judgment the reasons for its stance.

7.125

(11) *Wesergold*: The Role of Enhanced Distinctiveness in Likelihood of Confusion

Wesergold[135] concerned an opposition under Article 8(1)(b) to an application for the trade mark WESTERN GOLD, based on earlier registrations of WESERGOLD. The opponent claimed that the marks were similar, the goods (spirits v food and non-alcoholic drinks) were similar, and that there was a likelihood of confusion, especially bearing in mind the enhanced distinctiveness in the earlier mark arising from its use. The Opposition Division allowed the opposition, finding that the marks and the goods were similar enough to result in confusion. The applicant appealed to the Board of Appeal, who annulled the Opposition Division's decision, finding that there was at best only a low degree of similarity between the goods (in Classes 32 and 33 respectively) and that the signs were conceptually different, even though there was a medium degree of visual and phonetic similarity. In relation to the distinctiveness of the earlier mark, the Board of Appeal found that the mark was slightly below average because of the non-distinctive nature of the word GOLD.

7.126

The opponent appealed to the Court of First Instance, which overturned the Board of Appeal's decision and allowed the opposition. The Court of First Instance held that

7.127

---

[132] Paragraph 45.
[133] C-3/03 P *Matratzen Concord GmbH* [2004] ECR I-3657.
[134] Citing also C-104/00 P *DKV Deutsche Krankenversicherung AG* [2002] ECR I-7561; C-326/01 P *Telefon & Buch* [2004] ECR I-1371.
[135] C-558/12 P *Office for Harmonisation in the Internal Market (Trade Marks and Designs) (OHIM)/Lidl Stiftung v Wesergold Getränkeindustrie*, ECLI:EU:C:2014:22.

although the marks were overall dissimilar and the goods only similar to a low degree, the Board of Appeal was under a duty to consider all the arguments put forward to the Opposition Division and had failed to examine a relevant factor in the global assessment.

7.128 The Court of Justice held that enhanced distinctive character could not result in a finding of likelihood of confusion where there is no similarity between the marks (citing *Calvin Klein*[136]) and rejected the assertion that an error had been made in the examination of the Article 8(1)(b) ground without considering the distinctiveness of the earlier mark. There is certainly an element of semantic interpretation in this assessment. Although no amount of distinctiveness can render dissimilar marks similar, there is nevertheless a question of the point at which distinctiveness can render marks, which might be similar to a low degree, sufficiently similar to lead to the application of a likelihood of confusion test.

12. *Ballons d'Or/Golden Balls*: Foreign Equivalents

(a) Factual context

7.129 *Golden Balls*[137] came before the Court as an appeal against two judgments of the General Court.[138] Golden Balls applied to register GOLDEN BALLS as a Community trade mark for goods and services in Classes 9, 28, and 4 and Classes 16, 21, and 24. The application was opposed by Intra-Presse, working with FIFA, on the basis of two earlier CTMs for the word mark BALLON D'OR (GOLDEN BALL in French) for goods in Classes 9, 9, 14, 16, 18, 25, 28, 38, and 41. The oppositions were rejected because the marks were found to be dissimilar, being visually and phonetically different, and slightly similar conceptually. The Board of Appeal upheld the appeal in respect of part of the specification, finding the marks to be conceptually identical or extremely similar. The General Court found the marks to be dissimilar; conceptually they both called to mind the same semantic content but the difference in terms of language allowed the respective anglophone and francophone public to understand them as distinct from each other. The fact that a translation had to be made prevented the public from making an immediate conceptual comparison.

(b) The Judgment of the Court

7.130 **(i) Identifying the relevant public and its characteristics** The Court found that the General Court had not ignored any part of the relevant public and had not focused excessively on the francophone public. As to the characteristics of the relevant public, including its understanding of foreign languages, this was an appraisal of facts and could not be challenged before the Court.

7.131 Turning to Article 8(5) of the CTMR,

the types of injury referred to in Article 8(5) of Regulation No 40/94 may be the consequence of a lesser degree of similarity between the earlier and the later marks, provided that it

---

[136] C-254/09 *Zafra Marroquineros, SL v Calvin Klein Trademark Trust* [2010] ECR I-7989.
[137] Joined Cases C-581/13 P and C-582/13 P *Intra-Presse SAS v OHIM, Golden Balls Ltd.*, ECLI:EU:C:2014:2387.
[138] T-448/11 *Golden Balls v OHIM—Intra-Presse* (GOLDEN BALLS), EU:T:2013:456, and T-437/11, *Golden Balls v OHIM—Intra-Presse* (GOLDEN BALLS), EU:T:2013:441, considering appeals against Case R-1432/2010-1 and Case R-1310/2010-1.

is sufficient for the relevant section of the public to make a connection between those marks, that is to say, to establish a link between them.[139]

And according to *Ferrero*:[140]

> Article 8(5) … like Article 8(1)(b), is manifestly inapplicable where the General Court rules out any similarity between the marks at issue. It is only if there is some similarity, even faint, between the marks at issue that the General Court must carry out an overall assessment in order to ascertain whether, notwithstanding the low degree of similarity between them, there is, on account of the presence of other relevant factors such as the reputation or recognition enjoyed by the earlier mark, a likelihood of confusion or a link made between those marks by the relevant public.

7.132 The low degree of conceptual similarity was 'sufficient, on account of the presence of other relevant factors such as the reputation or recognition enjoyed by the earlier mark, for the relevant public to make a link between those marks.'[141]

7.133 In the circumstance the two cases were remitted back to the General Court.

(13) *Seven for all mankind*: Distinctiveness of Word Marks

7.134 *Seven for all mankind*[142] concerned an opposition under Articles 8(1)(a), 8(1)(b), and 8(5) to an application for the word mark SEVEN FOR ALL MANKIND covering goods in Classes 14 and 18. The opposition was based on two earlier CTM registrations for the stylized marks containing the word SEVEN covering goods in Classes 16, 18, and 25 and an international registration for a stylized version of SEVEN covering goods in, inter alia, Classes 14, 16, 18, and 25. The Opposition Division allowed the opposition, but only in relation to rucksacks, on the basis that the earlier trade marks had acquired a distinctive character on the Italian market for these goods. The opposition was refused for the other goods on the basis that there was only a low degree of similarity between the marks. The opponent appealed, but the Board of Appeal upheld the Opposition Division's decision, on the basis that because of the differences between the marks, there was no likelihood of confusion. For this reason, the Board of Appeal did not address the distinctive character or reputation in the earlier marks and did not review the Article 8(5) ground.

7.135 The opponent appealed to the General Court claiming an infringement of Articles 8(1)(b) and 8(5). The General Court annulled the Board of Appeal's decision, finding that the presence of the element SEVEN in both marks was not insignificant in their overall comparison. Thus, they found that the marks were visually, phonetically, and conceptually similar to some degree.

7.136 The applicant appealed to the Court of Justice, alleging first that the General Court had committed a breach of procedure when assessing the distinctive character of the word SEVEN, and, second, that the General Court had committed an infringement of Article 8(1)(b).

---

[139] Paragraph 72, citing *Ferrero v OHIM*, ECLI:EU:C:2011:177.
[140] Paragraph 73.
[141] Paragraph 76.
[142] C-655/11 *Seven for all mankind LLC v Office for Harmonisation in the Internal Market (Trade Marks and Designs)/Seven SpA*, ECLI:EU:C:2013:94.

7.137 In relation to the first plea, the Court of Justice found that:

> [E]ven if, as the appellant claims, the General Court had committed a breach of procedure by not examining the arguments presented by SAM as to the existence of numerous marks registered in the European Union containing the word 'seven' or the numeral '7', that would not have had any bearing on the General Court's finding.
>
> Furthermore, the mere existence, even in high numbers, of marks which have that characteristic is not sufficient to establish the weak distinctive character of those marks.
>
> For that claim to be relevant to such a finding, it must be shown that there are significant similarities as regards not only the presence of the word 'seven' or the numeral '7' in the earlier marks but also the position, type-face, ornamental presentation, any special font of a particular letter of that word, and the shape of the numeral '7', as well as, if that be the case, the presence of verbal or figurative additional elements before or after that word or number. Furthermore, the marks at issue must refer to the same goods and services.[143]

7.138 In relation to the second plea, which concerned the significance of the element SEVEN in the overall impression of the contested application, the Court of Justice found that the General Court had not merely made a general finding attributing the dominant character to the elements at the beginning of the mark but rather had examined the sign as a whole. In particular, the Court of Justice pointed to the fact that the General Court had noted that the public would pay more attention to elements appearing at the beginning of a mark because they were more easily remembered and so would have a greater impact. The Court of Justice also held that the General Court had also reviewed the distinctive significance of the additional elements in the contested mark and had concluded that these were not sufficient to rule out phonetic similarity. Furthermore, the Court of Justice found that no distortion of the facts and the evidence had been alleged and that the General Court's assessments as to the significance of the common element in the overall impression of the contested mark could not be considered.

7.139 In relation to the applicant's claim that the General Court had failed to take account of the consumer's overall perception of the contested mark, the Court of Justice found that the General Court had conducted a thorough and comprehensive examination of the consumer's overall perception of the contested mark. This was because the General Court had examined the significance of the expression FOR ALL MANKIND, concluded that the conceptual meaning of the contested mark would be defined predominantly by the word SEVEN, analysed the 'linguistic dimension of the mark' (in other words, the average consumer's perception/understanding of English), and concluded that the element SEVEN was not insignificant in the overall impression.

7.140 In relation to the applicant's allegation that the General Court had contradicted itself as to the significance of the additional elements in the later mark, the Court of Justice found that the General Court (in stating that the additional matter was not insignificant in the later mark, but at the same time was not sufficient to obscure the visual similarity between the signs) had merely weighed the various relevant factors as it was required to do in any assessment under Article 8(1)(b). Similarly, the fact that the General Court had noted the additional elements in the contested mark as 'remarkable' and 'philosophical' was not

---

[143] Paragraphs 47–49.

(14) *Canon*: Comparing the Goods or Services

In *Canon*[144] the Court came up with a test for determining whether goods or services are similar: the second step in the three step test for establishing likelihood of confusion. **7.141**

(a) *The Opinion of Advocate General Jacobs*

The gist was whether **7.142**

> it is permissible to consider goods or services to be similar in relation to particularly distinctive marks when such goods or services would not be considered to be similar in relation to other, less distinctive marks? Or should the test for assessing the similarity of goods or services be objective (i.e. unrelated to the nature of the marks in question)?[145]

He described distinctiveness as a matter of degree, attributed to the fact that a mark is well known or possesses an unusual character, and noted that, according to *Sabel*, the 'more well-known or unusual a trade mark, the more likely it is that consumers might be confused into believing there to be a trade connection between goods or services bearing the same or a similar mark'.[146] **7.143**

The Advocate General noted that the Tenth Recital referred to the recognition of the mark as an important element in determining likelihood of confusion, which in turn had to be taken into account in assessing the similarity of goods or services. Objections based on practical problems would not alter the Advocate General's conceptual analysis. To resolve them he suggested a balancing exercise: **7.144**

> [A]lthough in my view the degree of recognition of the mark must be taken into account in deciding whether there is sufficient similarity to give rise to confusion, the requirement of similarity must be given full weight both in assessing the similarity of the marks and in assessing the similarity of the goods or services in question.[147]

So a similarity of goods or services test should be applied in each and every case. 'Objective factors', viewed approvingly by the Advocate General, for such a test had been suggested by the UK and the French Governments. The UK suggested the following non-exhaustive list of factors, all linked with the goods or services themselves: **7.145**

(1) the uses of the respective goods or services;
(2) the users of the respective goods or services;
(3) the physical nature of the goods or acts of service;
(4) the trade channels through which the goods or services reach the market;
(5) in the case of self-serve consumer items, where in practice they are respectively found or likely to be found in supermarkets and, in particular, whether they are, or are likely to be, found on the same or different shelves; and
(6) the extent to which the respective goods or services are in competition with each other; that inquiry may take into account how those in the trade classify goods, for

---

[144] C-39/97 *Canon* [1998] ECR I-5507.
[145] Point 31.
[146] Point 32.
[147] Point 44.

instance, whether market research companies put the goods or services in the same or different sectors.[148]

7.146 The French focused on the nature of the goods or services, their intended destination and clientele, their normal use, and the usual manner of their distribution.

(b) The Judgment of the Court

7.147 The Court of Justice referred to the global assessment of the likelihood of confusion and the interdependence and balancing between the relevant factors. It accepted that the distinctive character of the earlier trade mark 'and in particular its reputation, must be taken into account when determining whether the similarity between the goods or services covered by the two trade marks is sufficient' to give rise to the likelihood of confusion'.[149] In assessing similarity of goods or services it added 'all the relevant factors relating to those goods or services themselves should be taken into account. Those factors include, inter alia, their nature, their end users and their method of use and whether they are in competition with each other or are complementary.'[150]

F. The Relevant Points in Time

(1) *Levi Strauss*: The Timing of the Assessment

7.148 In *Levi Strauss v Casucci*[151] the Court ruled on the relevant time for assessing likelihood of confusion and elaborated on the significance of distinctive character for the purposes of assessing likelihood of confusion. *Levi Strauss* was a reference from the Belgian Cour de Cassation. Levi Strauss, the proprietor of a graphic mark for clothing described as the 'mouette' (seagull) pocket design, had started infringement proceedings against Casucci who marketed jeans applying a somewhat similar design on the pockets. Levi Strauss was unsuccessful at first instance. Before the Brussels Cour d'Appel (Court of Appeal) it argued that a significant factor in the global assessment of the likelihood of confusion should be the highly distinctive character of its trade mark based on its imaginative content and long and widespread use. The court found that there was little similarity between the two signs. It also found that the mark had lost its highly distinctive character, because its components had become common in the clothing market. Levi Strauss appealed further to the Cour de Cassation (Court of Cassation) and submitted that the distinctive character of a mark should be judged at the time when the allegedly infringing sign had come into use and not, as the Cour d'Appel did, at the time of the ruling. Levi Strauss added that the Cour d'Appel had not attributed the weakening of distinctive character to Levi Strauss. Based on those two arguments it argued that the Cour d'Appel was not entitled to hold that the 'mouette' mark was no longer highly distinctive.

7.149 The Cour de Cassation stayed proceedings and referred the following questions to the Court of Justice:

(1) For the purposes of determining the scope of protection of a trade mark which has been lawfully acquired on the basis of its distinctive character, in accordance with Article 5(1)

---

[148] Originally developed by Jacob J in *British Sugar Plc v James Robertson & Sons Ltd* [1996] RPC 281.
[149] *Canon* (n 144) paragraph 24.
[150] Paragraph 23.
[151] C-145/05 *Levi Strauss & Co Casucci SpA* [2006] ECR 3703.

of Directive 89/104, must the court take into account the perception of the public concerned at the time when use was commenced of the mark or similar sign which allegedly infringes the trade mark?
(2) If not, may the court take into account the perception of the public concerned at any time after the commencement of the use complained of? Is the court entitled in particular to take into account the perception of the public concerned at the time it delivers the ruling?
(3) Where, in application of the criterion referred to in the first question, the court finds that the trade mark has been infringed, is it entitled, as a general rule, to order cessation of the infringing use of the sign?
(4) Can the position be different if the claimant's trade mark has lost its distinctive character wholly or in part after commencement of the unlawful use, but solely where that loss is due wholly or in part to an act or omission by the proprietor of that trade mark?[152]

(a) The Opinion of Advocate General Ruiz-Jarabo Colomer

7.150 Advocate General Ruiz-Jarabo Colomer delivered his Opinion on 17 January 2006.[153] He started by noting that, formally, trade mark protection could be perpetuated; however, trade marks were not immune from competition and the changing circumstances in the marketplace. Consumer perception was one of them and its timing was critical for the outcome of this case. As to the economic significance of the case, he remarked that it would suffice to observe casually the number of people wearing jeans at any one time.[154]

7.151 (i) **The relevant time for assessing confusion** The Advocate General considered the first two questions jointly as essentially asking whether confusion should be determined at the time when use of the allegedly infringing sign first started, at some other time thereafter, or at the time of the relevant ruling. Trade mark rights commenced at the time of filing and their publication in the relevant trade mark journal and it would be reasonable to assume that they could be exercised throughout the time they remained effective.

7.152 He concurred with the Commission that, after *Sabel*,[155] the relevant consumer's perception of the trade mark had become a critical factor for determining likelihood of confusion, being the most relevant criterion for determining its distinctive character. Trade mark rights under Article 5 would be fully operative only if they provided *ipso facto* protection to their owner through an action in case of infringement, and infringement would start at the time the products bearing the infringing sign were put on the market and last until such products ceased to exist. Accordingly, the national court should not take as a reference point for determining confusion any time later than the time the infringing act commenced because otherwise it would be restricting the scope of trade mark protection. At the same time, protection should not extend beyond the point of time that the owner of the rights had ceased to enjoy those rights.

7.153 (ii) **The scope of the right** The Advocate General noted that the Directive did not aim to approximate national laws at the procedural level. Still, the introduction of a Directive

---

[152] Reproduced in paragraph 12.
[153] ECLI:EU:C:2006:41.
[154] The AG made a number of references to diverse sources, from <http://www.wikipedia.org> and Encyclopaedia Britannica, stressing the European origin of the fabric back to the sailors of Genova (Genes, jeans) and the city of Nimes (serge de Nimes, denim) to the work of an Afghan novelist, Hosseini, *The Kite Runner* (Riverhead Books, 2003), on the symbolisms of the 'American' way of dressing in 1970s' Kabul.
[155] C-251/95 *Sabel BV* [1997] ECR I-6191.

into the legal order of a Member State should follow the principle of cooperation and the case law of the Court requiring genuine and effective protection of the rights envisaged in the Directive. Article 5(3) of the Directive suggested that cessation of use of an infringing sign would be an effective measure. It remained for the national court to decide whether cessation was indeed the appropriate measure in the current case.

7.154 (iii) **The scope of the right: Loss of distinctive character** The Advocate General viewed the fourth question as a variation on the same theme. There could be instances where loss of the distinctive character of a trade mark could be attributed to factors related to its use by the trade mark owner, its extensive copying by third parties, or consumer behaviour.[156]

7.155 Loss of distinctive character should not be relevant were it to result from the actions of third parties. However, if it were the result of the abuse of the mark by its owner or a shift in consumer perception then competing undertakings would have the option to seek the invalidation or revocation of the registration.

7.156 Concluding, he suggested that the national court should refrain from granting a cessation order only when third parties rely on the widespread use of the trade mark for reasons unrelated to the use of their own signs, and provided that they have sought the invalidation or revocation of the registration of the trade mark.

(b) The Judgment of the Court

7.157 (i) **The relevant time for assessing confusion** The Court took the rights of the trade mark proprietor as its starting point. In order to ensure the essential function of a trade mark 'the proprietor must be protected against competitors wishing to take unfair advantage of the status and reputation of the trade mark by selling products illegally bearing that mark'.[157]

7.158 Member States should ensure that the rights conferred by the mark could be effectively relied upon before the national courts, and the 'proprietor's right to protection of his mark from infringement is neither genuine nor effective if account may not be taken of the perception of the public concerned at the time when the sign, the use of which infringes the mark in question, began to be used'.[158] Assessing the likelihood of confusion at a later time might give the user of the sign an undue advantage, resulting from his own unlawful behaviour, 'by alleging that the product had become less renowned, a matter for which he himself was responsible or to which he himself contributed'.[159]

7.159 The Court then looked at the same picture from the perspective of the competitors of the trade mark proprietor. Their interests were protected by Article 12(2)(a):

> Thus, by balancing the interests of the proprietor against those of his competitors in the availability of signs, the legislator considered, in adopting this provision, that the loss of that mark's distinctive character can be relied on against the proprietor thereof only where that loss is due to his action or inaction. Therefore, as long as this is not the case, and particularly

---

[156] However, the Greek and French translations of the original Spanish text were not entirely clear.
[157] *Levi Strauss* (n 151) paragraph 15, citing C-349/95 *Frits Loendersloot* [1997] ECR I-6227 and C-206/01 *Arsenal Football Club Plc* [2002] ECR I-10273.
[158] Paragraph 17.
[159] Paragraph 18.

when the loss of the distinctive character is linked to the activity of a third party using a sign which infringes the mark, the proprietor must continue to enjoy protection.[160]

It concluded that Article 5(1): 7.160

must be interpreted as meaning that, in order to determine the scope of protection of a trade mark which has been lawfully acquired on the basis of its distinctive character, the national court must take into account the perception of the public concerned at the time when the sign, the use of which infringes that trade mark, began to be used.[161]

(ii) The scope of protection The Court was more forceful in its approach than the Advocate General. It emphasized that where there was a likelihood of confusion the proprietor should be entitled to prevent all third parties not having its consent from using that sign in the course of trade. To achieve this aim, Article 5(3) provided a non-exhaustive list of measures but did not require them to take a particular form; national authorities retained a degree of discretion. In addition, the requirement of genuine and effective protection required national courts to take the most appropriate measures for each particular case in order to safeguard the proprietor's rights and remedy infringements of its mark. An order to cease use of the infringing sign was clearly seen by the Court as a measure which could genuinely and effectively safeguard those rights. 7.161

It concluded that: 7.162

where the competent national court finds that the sign in question constituted an infringement of the mark at the time when the sign began to be used, it is for that court to take such measures as prove to be the most appropriate in the light of the circumstances of the case in order to safeguard the proprietor's rights deriving from Article 5(1) ... such measures may include, in particular, an order to cease use of that sign.[162]

(iii) Scope of protection: The requirement of vigilant conduct The Court referred again to the balancing exercise[163] attempted by the Directive and inferred that protection 'is limited in particular to those cases in which the proprietor shows himself to be sufficiently vigilant by opposing the use of signs by other operators likely to infringe his mark'.[164] Indeed, the Court widened the scope of the above statement to become a general principle. 'The requirement of vigilant conduct is not confined to trade mark protection, in fact, and may apply in other fields of Community law where an individual seeks to benefit from a right deriving from that legal order.'[165] 7.163

Refocusing on the application of this principle to trade mark law, it referred to Article 12(2) and added that inactivity might also take the form of a failure on the part of the proprietor to utilize Article 5 in due time. Establishing the grounds for revocation remained in the jurisdiction of the national court: 7.164

it is for the competent national court to establish revocation, if appropriate, linked in particular to such a failure, including in the context of proceedings seeking protection of the

---

[160] Paragraph 19.
[161] Paragraph 20.
[162] Paragraph 25.
[163] Referring to C-104/01 *Libertel Group BV* [2003] ECR I-3793 as an example of the balancing between the interests of different actors attempted by the Court.
[164] Paragraph 30.
[165] Paragraph 31.

exclusive rights conferred by Article 5 ... and which may have been brought late by the proprietor of the mark.[166]

7.165 However, national courts would have to follow the above guidelines because otherwise the objective of the 'same protection under the legal systems of all the Member States'[167] would be undermined. Once revocation had been established national courts should not issue such an order, even if there was a likelihood of confusion at the time that use of the sign had begun. Concluding, it held that:

> the answer to the fourth question must be that it is not appropriate to order cessation of the use of the sign in question if it has been established that the trade mark has lost its distinctive character, in consequence of acts or inactivity of the proprietor, so that it has become a common name within the meaning of Article 12(2) ... and the trade mark has therefore been revoked.[168]

(2) *Génesis*: The Limits of Priority

(a) The facts in the main proceedings and the order for reference

7.166 In *Génesis*[169] the Court dealt with the rules determining the priority of a Community trade mark application over a national mark and was asked to clarify whether the concept of 'date of filing' also extends to the hour and minute of the presentation of the earlier Community trade mark application, in particular where this information is considered as determinant by the legislation applicable to the filing of the other mark.

7.167 The dispute in the main proceedings concerned an opposition brought before the Oficina Española de Patentes y Marcas (Spanish Patents and Trade Marks Office) (the OEPM) by Génesis Seguros Generales SA on the basis of its two Community trade marks, RIZO and RIZO, EL ERIZO, against the registration of Spanish trade mark application RIZO'S, owned by Boys Toys SA. The opposing marks had been filed with OHIM by electronic means on 12 December 2003, at 11:52 hours and 12:13 hours respectively, whereas the contested application had been submitted to the OEPM on the same day, but at 17:45 hours.

7.168 The OEPM rejected both the opposition and the administrative appeal brought by Génesis on the grounds that, pursuant to Article 27 CTMR, the conditions for obtaining a filing date had been concluded as regards the Community trade marks at issue on 7 January 2004, which was the date on which the full documentation required by that provision was actually submitted, with the result that the opposing marks were actually later than the Spanish trade mark RIZO'. That decision was further confirmed by the Tribunal Superior de Justicia de Madrid (High Court of Justice, Madrid).

7.169 Génesis appealed to the Tribunal Supremo (Supreme Court), arguing that the correct interpretation of Articles 26 and 27 of the Regulation requires regarding the date of filing of the applications as the date on which those applications were transmitted to and received by OHIM, and that, by failing to recognize the priority of the earlier marks, the Tribunal Superior de Madrid had infringed Article 6(2)(a) and (c) of Spanish Law No 17/2001 on trade marks, according to which earlier marks include Community trade marks with 'a

---

[166] Paragraph 35.
[167] Set out in the Ninth Recital; the Court referred here to C-405/03 *Class International BV* [2005] ECR I-8735 in relation to the onus of proving infringement of the proprietor's exclusive rights.
[168] Paragraph 37.
[169] C-190/10 *Génesis Seguros Generales, Sociedad Anónima de Seguros y Reaseguros v Boys Toys SA and Administración del Estado*, ECLI:EU:C:2012:157.

date of filing or priority which is earlier than the date of the application under consideration', read in combination with Articles 11 and 13, which provide in material part that:

> The body competent to receive the application shall record ... the date, hour and minute of its receipt, in the manner to be determined by regulation.
>
> If any of the [receiving] bodies or administrative units fails to record ... the hour of filing, the application shall be assigned the final hour of the day. If the minute has not been recorded, the application shall be assigned the final minute of the hour. If neither the hour nor the minute has been recorded, the application shall be assigned the final hour and minute of the day.

7.170 The Tribunal Supremo noted the contrast between Article 27 of the Regulation, which lays down no other provision to resolve disputes between marks filed on the same day, and Spanish legislation, stating also that if the Regulation was to be interpreted as not allowing relevance to be attached to the hour and minute of filing, the protection of Community trade marks in national proceedings would be weakened, since all applications filed on a given day would be regarded, under Spanish law, as filed in the last minute of the day and, thus, would be treated as later compared to Spanish marks filed on the same day. Considering that the possibility to take into account the time of filing was decisive for the outcome of the main proceedings, the Tribunal Supremo referred the following question to the Court of Justice:

> May Article 27 of the Regulation be interpreted in such a way as to enable account to be taken not only of the day but also of the hour and minute of filing of an application for registration of a Community trade mark with OHIM (provided that such information has been recorded) for the purposes of establishing temporal priority over a national trade mark application filed on the same day, where the national legislation governing the registration of national trade marks considers the time of filing to be relevant?

(b) The Opinion of Advocate General Jääskinen

7.171 Advocate General Jääskinen[170] proposed to answer the question in the negative, taking the view that Article 27 precludes taking into account, in addition to the day of filing, the hour and the minute of the application. He started his analysis by observing that, insofar as Article 27 makes no express reference to the laws of the Member States, the determination of the date of filing of a Community trade mark was governed solely by EU law and that, accordingly, the scope and meaning of that expression had to be sought in the relevant provisions of the Regulation.[171]

7.172 Next, he noted that the system introduced by Article 27, which merely makes reference to the day of receipt, is fully in line with the Paris Convention, which uses the calendar day as the basic unit of calculation when establishing rules regarding the regularity of the filing or the calculation of convention priority. Moreover, he read Article 32 of the Regulation, according to which a CTM application which has been accorded a filing date is deemed to be equivalent to a 'regular national filing', not as amending the EU concept of filing date, but simply as recognizing that applications filed with OHIM are legally equivalent to those filed in national offices.[172]

---

[170] C-190/10 *Génesis Seguros Generales, Sociedad Anónima de Seguros y Reaseguros v Boys Toys SA and Administración del Estado* ECLI:EU:C:2011:202.
[171] Points 40–44.
[172] Points 57–65.

7.173 Finally, he observed that applying real-time priority rather than the concept of the calendar day would give rise to several practical difficulties, stemming from the fact that the territory of the Union comprises four time zones and that Community trade mark applications are deemed to be duly filed when the relevant documents have been received either at OHIM or at any of the competent authorities of the Member States. Thus, real-time priority could result in confusion about the true time of filing to the detriment of legal certainty. Accordingly, the Advocate General concluded that it was preferable to opt for a system based on the calendar day, even if that system would inevitably result in the forced coexistence of marks filed on the same day, accepting, however, that such a solution is an ordinary if not inevitable phenomenon in trade mark law and has always existed in regimes based on the Paris Convention.[173]

(c) The Judgment of the Court

7.174 The Court shared the Opinion of the Advocate General as regards the hierarchy of norms, inferring from the absence of any provisions in the Directive regarding the registration procedure or the date of filing that Member States remain free to determine their own rules on the subject, with the result that the relevant conditions may differ from one Member State to another. It also confirmed that the autonomous character of the Community trade mark system implied that the rules relating to the procedure for filing a Community trade mark must be interpreted in a uniform way, independently of any national provisions.[174]

7.175 Next, the Court reiterated that the meaning and scope of terms for which European Union law provides no definition must be determined by considering their usual meaning in everyday language, also taking into account the context in which they occur and the purposes of the rules of which they form part. Thus, it held that although the various language versions of Article 27 display certain differences, in that some of them refer to the 'day of filing' whereas others to the 'date of filing', that difference was immaterial, since, according to its ordinary meaning, the term 'date' generally designates the day, the month, and the year when an act has been adopted or an event has taken place. Moreover, it observed that an obligation to state the date or the day does not imply that it is necessary to also state the hour and, *a fortiori*, the minute, which shows that information of this kind was not considered necessary by the Community legislature for the purposes of establishing the time of filing of a Community trade mark and hence its priority over another application.[175]

7.176 The Court also contrasted the requirements in Rule 5 of the Implementing Regulation, which details the formalities to be completed by OHIM or the industrial property offices of the Member States upon the filing of an application for a Community trade mark by only establishing an obligation to indicate the date of receipt, with the practice of OHIM to record the time of filing when applications were submitted by electronic means, holding that the practicalities stemming from an administrative practice cannot amend or complement the clear sense of secondary legislation.[176]

7.177 Finally, the Court stressed that the possibility to take the hour and minute of filing into account under national law would not only challenge the autonomy of the Community

---

[173] Points 66–69 and 75–79.
[174] Paragraphs 30–37 and 40.
[175] Paragraphs 41–47.
[176] Paragraphs 48–54.

system, but would also undermine the unitary character of the Community trade mark and the uniform application of EU law, to the extent that the freedom of Member States to determine the priority date would effectively mean that the protection afforded to the same mark might fluctuate from one State to another. It also concurred with the Advocate General that this conclusion is not called into question by Article 32 of the Regulation, which merely recognizes the equivalence of Community trade mark applications to those filed nationally.[177]

7.178 Accordingly, the Court answered the question referred to the effect that Article 27 must be interpreted as precluding account being taken not only of the day but also of the hour and minute of filing of an application for a Community trade mark for the purposes of establishing that trade mark's priority over a national mark filed on the same day, even where, according to the national legislation, the hour and minute of filing are relevant in that regard.

G. Revisiting Global Appreciation

7.179 Once the Court established the basic tests it started considering difficult cases, challenging aspects of the global appreciation approach.

7.180 One of the areas that remained unexplored was the effect of confusion away from the point of sale. To what extent would post-sale confusion, in particular, be considered actionable? Global appreciation would also have to be fine-tuned in relation to particular types of sign, for example, surnames or composite marks.

7.181 The Court would also have to elaborate on the scope of protection of a trade mark for retail services.

(1) *Picasso/Picaro*: The Limitations of *Arsenal*

7.182 The *Picasso/Picaro*[178] case came before the Court in the form of an appeal against a judgment of the Court of First Instance[179] that had dismissed an action for annulment of a decision of the Office's Third Board of Appeal[180] rejecting the opposition by the proprietors of the Community trade mark PICASSO for 'vehicles; apparatus for locomotion by land, air or water, motor cars, motor coaches, trucks, vans, caravans, trailers' against DaimlerChrysler AG's application for registration of the word PICARO for 'vehicles and parts therefor; omnibuses'. The Picasso estate, comprising members of the artist's family, was the proprietor of the PICASSO mark.

(a) *The Judgment of the Court of First Instance*

7.183 The Court of First Instance had found that the signs were visually and, to a lesser degree, phonetically similar. However, it also held that the marks were conceptually dissimilar. PICASSO was overwhelmingly linked with the artist whereas PICARO had no meaning

---

[177] Paragraphs 56–61.
[178] C-361/04 P *Claude Ruiz-Picasso v Office for Harmonisation in the Internal Market (Trade Marks and Designs)* [2006] ECR I-643.
[179] T-185/02 *Claude Ruiz-Picasso* [2004] ECR II-1739.
[180] Case R-247/2001-3 18 March 2002.

outside the Spanish language; in Spanish 'picaro' means a cheeky, roguish, comical, low-life character, featuring in 'picaresque', a particular genre of Spanish literature.[181]

7.184 The Court of First Instance paid significant attention to the meaning of PICASSO for the average consumer: 'The reputation of the painter Pablo Picasso is such that it is not plausible to consider, in the absence of specific evidence to the contrary, that the sign PICASSO as a mark for motor vehicles may, in the perception of the average consumer, override the name of the painter.'[182]

7.185 The Court of First Instance also rejected the argument that the name PICASSO was well known and deserved broader protection; it held that the fact that the artist behind the name is well known does not automatically mean that there is a stronger likelihood of confusion in respect of the relevant goods, in particular since the relevant public would pay significant attention to the product at the time of purchase because of its nature, price, and characteristics. The Court of First Instance, however, did not take into account the perception of the public away from the time and point of sale.[183]

(b) The Opinion of Advocate General Ruiz-Jarabo Colomer

7.186 The Advocate General[184] started by expressing his surprise that the name of Picasso would become the subject matter of mundane litigation: '[I]t is perfectly legitimate to protect such a name against harmful attacks, but its widespread use for purely commercial ends outside the field in which [it] gained its renown could be detrimental to the respect which his extraordinary personality deserves'.[185] His analysis followed the pattern of the appeal, which was divided into four parts.

7.187 **(i) Conceptual similarity** The first part targeted the approach of the Court of First Instance regarding conceptual similarity and the weight it gave to the fact that the name had a meaning outside the context of the specified goods. He found that the Court of First Instance appeared to consider all the elements of the comparison before focusing on the conceptual element that it considered to be particularly relevant. In making the comparison it did not take the further step of considering the goods and the market because there was not enough similarity in the first place, and this was indeed what, according to the Advocate General, the Court had demanded in *Lloyd Schuhfabrik*.[186]

7.188 **(ii) The distinctiveness of PICASSO** The second part of the appeal focused on the distinctiveness of PICASSO and claimed that the Court of First Instance had not followed the Court's jurisprudence that there is a higher risk of confusion when the earlier mark has a higher degree of distinctiveness. The Advocate General though stressed that the Court of First Instance had found that PICASSO had not obtained such distinctiveness as a mark for vehicles.

---

[181] In fn 11 of his Opinion, AG Ruiz-Jarabo Colomer also mentions Hergé's use of the word in *Tintin and the Picaros* (Casterman, Tourai, 1976), describing a band of guerrillas led by General Alcazar.
[182] *Claude Ruiz-Picasso* (n 179) paragraph 57.
[183] *Claude Ruiz-Picasso* (n 179) paragraph 60.
[184] C-361/04 P *Claude Ruiz-Picasso* [2006] ECR I-643.
[185] Point 3.
[186] C-342/97 *Lloyd Schuhfabrik* [1999] ECR I-3819.

(iii) **The post-sale effect of the trade mark** The third ground of appeal focused on the post-sale effect of the mark, mentioned in *Arsenal*,[187] that the Court of First Instance did not take into account. The Advocate General noted: 7.189

> Paragraph 57 admits the possibility that some consumers may interpret the sign as designating Arsenal FC as the undertaking of origin of the goods, particularly once the goods have been sold by Mr Reed and are no longer on the stall where the notice stating that they are not officially endorsed by the club is displayed. Beyond that it does not establish any general rule that the purpose of a trade mark continues after the sale of the items of which it forms part.[188]

According to the Advocate General the post-sale confusion argument simply confirmed that there was a breach of trade mark rights. He went on to suggest that most writers do not accept that post-sale confusion is relevant for determining likelihood of confusion. 7.190

(iv) **Post-sale confusion** Finally, the fourth part of the appeal challenged the distinction drawn by the Court of First Instance between opposition and infringement proceedings regarding the role of post-sale confusion in determining likelihood of confusion. According to the appellants, post-sale confusion should be relevant in both cases, in particular in the case of goods which are permanently on public view. 7.191

The Advocate General read the judgment of the Court of First Instance in a different light: 7.192

> that statement [see paragraph 60 of the judgment of the Court of First Instance cited above] only highlights the distinction between, on the one hand, gauging the degree of attention of the public in order to assess the likelihood of confusion between two signs which are inevitably similar, because if they were identical it would be a case of breach of trade mark rights, and, on the other hand, weighing up the importance of particular circumstances subsequent to sale with a view to ascertaining whether there has been a breach of the industrial property right in question. Paragraph 60 shows that at no time did the Court of First Instance refer to any difference in the analysis of the likelihood of confusion depending on whether the context involves opposition proceedings or infringement proceedings.[189]

(v) **Concluding remarks** The Advocate General concluded first that where a name such as Picasso is used in a completely different context to that in which it was originally used, it will not automatically carry with it its distinctiveness; without use it is doubtful whether the name conveys information regarding the source of the product. Second, there is a general interest in protecting the names of great artists from commercialization. 7.193

(e) The Judgment of the Court

The Court of Justice confirmed that the conceptual differences between two signs may counteract their visual and phonetic similarities. Turning to the contested judgment the Court noted that the Court of First Instance considered that facing the word PICASSO the relevant public would see it as a reference to the artist; this would greatly 'reduce the resonance with which, in this case, the sign is endowed as a mark, among others, of motor vehicles'.[190] It also found that the Court of First Instance had considered the degree of distinctiveness of PICASSO and found it devoid of any highly distinctive character in relation to motor 7.194

---

[187] C-206/01 *Arsenal Football Club Plc* [2002] ECR I-10273.
[188] Point 53.
[189] Point 60.
[190] Paragraph 27.

vehicles. The Court examined together the two parts of the appeal based on the post-sale effect of the sign. It found that the Court of First Instance was entitled to take into account the high level of consumer attention at the time of purchase: 'Where it is established in fact that the objective characteristics of a given product mean that the average consumer purchases it only after a particularly careful examination, it is important in law to take into account that such a fact may reduce the likelihood of confusion between marks relating to such goods at the crucial moment when the choice between those goods and marks is made.'[191]

7.195 On the post-sale effects of the mark the Court found that the Court of First Instance was also entitled to observe that these do not 'prevent the taking into account of the particularly high level of attention exhibited by the average consumer when he prepares and makes his choice between different goods in the category concerned'.[192]

7.196 The Court acknowledged that there will be situations where the public will pay a low degree of attention; however, taking into account the lowest degree of attention 'would amount to denying all relevance, for the purpose of an assessment of the likelihood of confusion, to the criterion relating to the variable level of attention according to the category of goods'.[193] Also, it would be unreasonable to require from the authority assessing likelihood of confusion to determine for each product the average amount of consumer attention subtracting from the level of attention shown in different situations.

7.197 Turning to *Arsenal*[194] it noted that the case involved the application of a sign that was identical to the registered trade mark on identical goods. This should be precluded according to Article 5(1)(a). The Court had referred to the post-sale effect of the sign in order to assert that the message conveyed at the point of sale—regarding the source of the product—did not alter its interpretation. Almost defensively the Court added:

> In doing so, the Court did not in any way express a general rule from which it could be inferred that, for the purposes of an assessment of the likelihood of confusion ... there is no need to refer specifically to the particularly high level of attention displayed by consumers when purchasing a certain category of goods.[195]

Finally, it accepted that the Court of First Instance had not held that likelihood of confusion had to be interpreted differently for the purposes of infringement than for the purposes of opposition. It had only asserted that the degree of attention of the relevant public had to be taken into account.

(2) *Rossi*: Protection of Surnames; Global Appreciation; the Community Trade Mark Registration Process

7.198 The scope of protection of a surname as a trade mark was considered in *Sergio Rossi*,[196] an appeal against a judgment of the Court of First Instance[197] dismissing an action for annulment of the decision of the First Board of Appeal.[198] Sissi Rossi Srl (Sissi Rossi) had applied

---

[191] Paragraph 40.
[192] Paragraph 41.
[193] Paragraph 42.
[194] C-206/01 *Arsenal Football Club Plc* [2002] ECR I-10273.
[195] Paragraph 47.
[196] C-214/05 P *Sergio Rossi SpA* [2006] ECR I-7057.
[197] T-169/03 *Sergio Rossi* [2005] ECR II-685.
[198] R-569/2002-1, 28 February 2003.

for the registration of the word mark SISSI ROSSI as a Community trade mark for 'leather and imitations of leather, and goods made of these materials and not included in other classes; animal skins, hides; trunks and travelling bags; umbrellas, parasols and walking sticks; whips, harness and saddlery' in Class 18.

7.199 Calzaturificio Rossi SpA, a company at a later stage acquired by Sergio Rossi SpA (Sergio Rossi), opposed the application for registration on the basis of earlier registrations, in Italy as a national trade mark registration and in France as an international trade mark registration, of the mark MISS ROSSI for 'footwear' in Class 25. The opposition related to 'leather and imitations of leather, and goods made of these materials and not included in other classes; animal skins, hides; trunks and travelling bags'.

7.200 The Opposition Division refused the application for registration. The Board of Appeal annulled that decision finding, first, that the marks were only vaguely similar and, second, that, on balance, the differences between the goods outweighed their commonalities, and accordingly there was no likelihood of confusion. Looking at the two products that appeared to be closer than the rest, 'women's footwear' and 'women's bags', it held that they were complementary but still not similar. Sergio Rossi brought an action before the Court of First Instance seeking the annulment of the decision, but its arguments targeted the particular part of the decision regarding footwear and bags.

(a) The Judgment of the Court of First Instance

7.201 The Court of First Instance decided, first, to refuse to take into account new evidence submitted by Sergio Rossi. Second, to examine only that part of the appeal that related to women's footwear and bags since Sergio Rossi had failed to produce any argument against the findings of the Board regarding the remaining goods. Third, that a general reference to the entirety of the submissions of Sergio Rossi in the proceedings before the Office was not enough to cover the lack of argument in the application before the Court of First Instance. Fourth, that the claim that all the goods were sold through the same channels and made of the same raw material was inadmissible because it had not been argued before the Office. Fifth, it looked at the substance of the case and found that there was no likelihood of confusion.

7.202 It is worth covering in more detail how it reached its decision on likelihood of confusion, since the Court of Justice found that the assessment of the facts belonged to the jurisdiction of the Court of First Instance.

7.203 **(i) The targeted public** The Court of First Instance started its analysis by limiting the scope of the dispute. The arguments of Sergio Rossi focused exclusively on the similarity between 'women's footwear' and 'women's bags'. Accordingly, the Court rejected the principal head of claim, seeking annulment of the contested decision in its entirety and considered only the alternative claim, seeking partial annulment of the contested decision in respect of 'women's bags'.

7.204 Both products were for everyday consumption and intended for a female public; 'the target public is, essentially, composed of average female consumers',[199] in principle French and Italian since the earlier registrations covered France and Italy.

---

[199] Paragraph 49.

7.205 **(ii) Similarity between the products** Following *Canon*,[200] it accepted that the fact that both products were often made of the same raw material, leather or imitation leather, was a factor that should be taken into account. However, on its own this would not suffice to establish similarity because a large number of goods were made of leather or imitation leather.

7.206 The Court of First Instance then followed a narrow approach regarding the consideration of end consumers as a relevant factor. It noted that the Court in its *Canon* test had expressly referred to the intended purpose of the goods, rather than the end consumers. 'Accordingly, the fact that the end consumers of the goods are identical cannot be regarded as a significant factor in assessing the similarity between the goods.'[201]

7.207 It accepted that the intended purposes of the goods were different; shoes were used to dress feet and bags to carry objects. The goods were not interchangeable and, therefore, not in competition. It rejected the 'aesthetic function' argument, it carried limited value in relation in the clothing and fashion sector, but this alone could not lead the consumer to believe that those two products originated from the same undertaking or from economically linked undertakings; the factor was too general to permit a finding that the goods were similar. In addition, it underlined that women's shoes and bags were not merely luxury items with a primarily decorative function.

7.208 As to the complementary character of the goods, the Court of First Instance adopted the Office's approach:[202] '[C]omplementary goods are goods which are closely connected in the sense that one is indispensable or important for the use of the other so that consumers may think that the same undertaking is responsible for the production of both goods.' Sergio Rossi had failed according to the Court of First Instance to establish that the goods were complementary in this way in terms of their function. Aesthetic complementarity was subjective, 'determined by the habits and preferences of consumers to which producers' marketing strategies or even simple fashion trends may give rise'.[203] The Court of First Instance seemed open to accepting that this aesthetic or subjective complementary nature might be relevant once it had reached the stage of a true aesthetic 'necessity', when consumers would think it unusual or shocking to carry a bag which did not perfectly match their shoes. However, the simple search for aesthetic harmony was considered to be too general a factor to satisfy by itself a finding that all the goods concerned were complementary and, thus, similar.

7.209 In addition, the Court of First Instance doubted whether consumers would necessarily perceive a product that functioned as a complement of or accessory to another to have the same commercial origin with that other product.[204] The applicant had failed to produce evidence showing that in the minds of the relevant public producers of shoes and of bags were usually the same; general assertions were not enough.

7.210 It is suggested, though, that this discussion could be better placed as part of the global assessment of the likelihood of confusion than as a factor for determining product similarity.

---

[200] C-39/97 *Canon Kabushiki Kaisha* [1998] ECR I-5507.
[201] Paragraph 56.
[202] [2005] OHIM, *Opposition Guidelines*, Pt II, Ch 2, paragraph 2.6.1.
[203] Paragraph 61.
[204] Paragraph 63.

Looking at channels of distribution, it accepted the Board's view that the goods in question are sometimes, but not always and not necessarily, sold in the same shops. However, whilst that fact was indeed an indication that the goods in question were similar, it did not suffice to cancel out the differences between those goods.[205] 7.211

It found that Sergio Rossi had failed to establish three things that could have helped its case: that the goods in question were normally sold in the same places; that consumers necessarily expected to find in shoe shops a wide choice of women's bags and vice versa; or that consumers generally expected producers of shoes to sell bags under the same trade mark or vice versa. 7.212

Concluding, the Court of First Instance accepted that the goods did have some things in common, in particular the fact that they were sometimes sold through the same outlets. This time it viewed the differences as not so sufficient to rule out, by themselves, the possibility of a likelihood of confusion, particularly where the mark applied for was identical to an earlier mark which was distinctive to a particularly high degree. This meant that it would also have to examine the similarity between the two marks. 7.213

(iii) **Similarity between the marks** The Court of First Instance appeared to conflate the test for determining similarity between the marks with the global appreciation of the likelihood of confusion. 7.214

> It is settled case-law that, in so far as the visual, aural or conceptual similarity of the marks in question is concerned, the comprehensive assessment of the likelihood of confusion must be based on the impression given by the marks as a whole, account being taken of, inter alia, their distinctive and dominant components.[206]

In any case, the Court of First Instance went on to examine the factors adopted by the Court of Justice in *Sabel*.[207] Visually, the second word of the two marks was identical, whereas the first words shared the three letters 'iss'. However, 'Sissi' was a longer word than 'Miss' and the respective initials, 'S' and 'M', and final 'i' and 's' letters were visually different. Phonetically, the first words of both marks were characterized by the strong sound of the double 's' and by the presence of the sole vowel 'i'. However, the two words had a different number of syllables and in French, unlike in Italian, the stress will be placed on the last syllable. Conceptually, Italian and French consumers alike would perceive the word 'Rossi' as a surname of Italian origin and 'Sissi' as a female forename; the targeted consumers targeted would also understand the word 'Miss' in its English meaning. Sergio Rossi had submitted that both marks would create the impression of a woman with the surname 'Rossi'; the Court of First Instance noted, however, that there was still a conceptual difference between the word 'Miss' and a specific forename. 7.215

The result of these comparisons was inconclusive; the marks resembled each other in some respects but differed in others. Accordingly, the degree of similarity depended on whether 'Rossi', the common element, constituted the distinctive and dominant element of the two marks. 7.216

---

[205] Paragraph 65.
[206] Paragraph 69; citing T-292/01 *Phillips-Van Heusen v Office for Harmonisation in the Internal Market (Trade Marks and Designs)* [2003] ECR II-1335 and the case law cited therein.
[207] C-251/95 *Sabel BV* [1997] ECR I-6191.

7.217 The Court of First Instance highlighted that 'Rossi' occupied the second part of the two marks without being prominent in any way and underlined that this had not been disputed by Sergio Rossi, which only claimed that the Board had wrongly found that the 'Miss' and 'Sissi' were the dominant elements. It concluded that even if the two first words were not the dominant elements but instead had respectively the same impact as 'Rossi', the degree of similarity would only be raised to average from low; it would not become considerable as argued by Sergio Rossi.

7.218 **(iv) Likelihood of confusion** The Court of First Instance defined likelihood of confusion as:

> the likelihood that the public might believe that the goods or services in question originate from the same undertaking or, as the case may be, economically linked undertakings. The likelihood of confusion as to the commercial origin of the goods must be assessed comprehensively, by reference to the perception by the relevant public of the marks and goods in question and taking account of all the factors relevant to the case, in particular the interdependence between the similarity of the trade marks and that of the goods or services.[208]

7.219 It added that the more distinctive the earlier mark, the greater the likelihood of confusion would be. In this case the earlier marks were not highly distinctive. 'Therefore, it need only be examined whether the similarities between the marks are sufficient to outweigh the differences between the goods in question and to give rise to a likelihood of confusion on the part of the target public.'[209]

7.220 Balancing the two the Court of First Instance held that there was no likelihood of confusion between the two marks. It did not elaborate on the mechanics of this balancing exercise; it reached its conclusion by simply referring to the paragraphs of its judgment where the differences between the goods and the differences between the marks were established.

7.221 **(v) 'Likelihood of association'** The Court of First Instance examined separately the claim of Sergio Rossi that there was a likelihood of association 'in so far as the consumer might believe that the goods sold under the marks in question originate from the same undertaking or from economically linked undertakings'.[210] It observed that Sergio Rossi had not challenged the Board of Appeal's finding that the surname 'Rossi' was seen as a very common Italian surname by both Italian and French consumers. It also found that in the clothing and fashion market 'surname' marks were quite common; accordingly 'it may be assumed, as a general rule, that a very common name will appear more frequently than a rare name'.[211]

7.222 **(vi) The scope of the specification** Finally, the argument of Sergio Rossi that it was active in the sector of handbag production served a welcome reminder that registered trade mark law is all about protection of trade marks in relation to the specification of the registration:

> [T]he the fact that the applicant is also active in the sector of handbag production is irrelevant to the assessment of the likelihood of confusion between the earlier marks and the mark applied for. The goods designated by the marks in question must be examined as they are

---

[208] Paragraph 77; citing T/162/01 *Laboratorios RTB v Office for Harmonisation in the Internal Market (Trade Marks and Designs)* (BASS) [2003] ECR II-2821.
[209] Paragraph 79.
[210] Paragraph 81.
[211] Paragraph 83.

protected by those marks. The earlier marks are not registered for 'goods made of leather or imitation leather not included in other classes' but are regarded as registered in respect of 'women's footwear' only. It follows that the applicant is not entitled to rely on the marks in order to protect the line in handbags produced by him.[212]

7.223 Before the Court Sergio Rossi claimed that the Court of First Instance had misapplied its Rules of Procedure and, also, infringed Article 8(l)(b) of the Regulation.

(b) The Opinion of Advocate General Kokott

7.224 Advocate General Kokott divided the case into four parts. She started with Sergio Rossi's two procedural points and then looked at the claims based on Article 8(l)(b) of the Regulation regarding the similarity between the two marks and the respective products.

7.225 **(i) Limiting the scope of the appeal** The first procedural point regarded the decision of the Court of First Instance to reject in an outright manner the principal head of the claim that covered the broader categories of goods and focus exclusively on the part of the appeal that related to women's shoes and bags, arguing that it had infringed Article 81 of its Rules of Procedure[213] because the judgment gave no reasons for dismissing the principal head of claim.

7.226 The Advocate General found that the Court of First Instance had clearly indicated why it had rejected the principal head of the claim. The limitation was justified according to Article 41(c) of the Rules of Procedure.[214] The summary of the pleas had to be sufficiently clear and precise in order to allow the defending party to prepare its defence and the Court of First Instance to exercise its power. The facts and the points of law had to be presented in a coherent and comprehensible way. Sergio Rossi had focused both in terms of factual evidence and points of law on the similarity between women's shoes and bags. These arguments could not be transposed to the other products. The additional arguments presented before the Court of First Instance in essence constituted a new claim broadening the scope of the case.

7.227 **(ii) Rejecting new evidence** Advocate General Kokott noted that according to Article 63 of the Regulation the Court of First Instance had the jurisdiction to review only the legality of the decisions of the Boards. According to Article 74(1) of the Regulation[215] facts that had not been presented before the Office could not be employed to challenge the legality of the decisions of the Board.[216]

7.228 She agreed with the jurisprudence of the Court of First Instance that the legality of the decision could only be reviewed by the Court of First Instance on the basis of facts that were

---

[212] Paragraph 84.
[213] Article 81 requires the Court of First Instance to indicate in the judgment the grounds for its decision.
[214] Article 44(1) of the Rules of Procedure of the Court of First Instance provides: 'An application of the kind referred to in Article 21 of the Statute of the Court of Justice shall state: ... (c) the subject-matter of the proceedings and a summary of the pleas in law on which the application is based; (d) the form of order sought by the applicant; (e) where appropriate, the nature of any evidence offered in support.'
[215] Article 74(1) provides: 'In proceedings before it the Office shall examine the facts of its own motion; however, in proceedings relating to relative grounds for refusal of registration, the Office shall be restricted in this examination to the facts, evidence and arguments provided by the parties and the relief sought.'
[216] Citing, for example, T-247/01 *eCopy Inc v Office for Harmonisation in the Internal Market (Trade Marks and Designs)* [2002] ECR II-5301 and T-128/01 *DaimlerChrysler Corp v Office for Harmonisation in the Internal Market (Trade Marks and Designs)* [2003] ECR II-701.

known and the law that was effective at the date of the decision.[217] Sergio Rossi had the opportunity to present all the pertinent evidence; if the Office throughout the registration process had violated its procedural rights the particular violation as such should have been raised. The subsidiary claim regarding the right to be heard should also be rejected following the same analysis but also because it had been put forward at a late stage.

7.229 (iii) **Article 8(1)(b) considerations** The competence for assessing the facts belonged to the Court of First Instance; the Court could review that assessment only if the Court of First Instance had distorted the evidence. Claims that referred only to the appreciation of the facts by the Board should be inadmissible.

(c) The Judgment of the Court

7.230 (i) **Article 8(1)(b)** The Court found that the Court of First Instance alone had the competence to assess the value that should be attached to the evidence. The only obligation imposed on it was to provide reasons that would allow the Court to exercise its judicial review, in particular whether there had been any distortion of the evidence.[218]

7.231 Assessing the relevance of the fact that a party had refrained from relying on certain facts constituted clearly a part of its competence. In this case the Court of First Instance had conducted an overall assessment of the likelihood of confusion and provided sufficient reasons for its findings. Regarding the outcome of the assessment the Court of Justice could not substitute its own assessment of the facts for that of the Court of First Instance.[219]

7.232 (ii) **Limiting the scope of the appeal** The Court noted that in reality the first ground of appeal challenged the validity of the rejection of the principal head of claim by the Court of First Instance because Sergio Rossi had not included any argument to support it in the application itself.

7.233 Streamlining and tightening the process of challenging decisions of the Boards of Appeal the Court added:

> Since that claim was inadmissible, it is apparent that the appellant was, in reality, putting forward a new plea by relying on matters of law or of fact at the hearing which had the same purpose as that claim. Under Article 48(2) of the Rules of Procedure of the Court of First Instance, no new plea in law may be introduced in the course of proceedings unless it is based on matters of law or of fact which come to light in the course of the procedure. As the appellant has not alleged that that was the case, the Court of First Instance rightly rejected that plea on the ground that those matters were submitted out of time.[220]

7.234 (iii) **The second ground of appeal** Decisions of the Boards of Appeal could be annulled or altered only on a number of specific grounds: lack of competence, infringement of an essential procedural requirement, failure to comply with the EC Treaty, or Reg 40/94, or of any rule of law relating to their application, or misuse of power.

---

[217] Citing *eCopy Inc* (n 216); T-123/97 *Salomon SA v Commission* [1999] ECR II-2925, T-126/99 *Graphischer Maschinenbau v Commission* [2002] ECR II-427; and C-249/95 *SAM Schiffahrt et Stapf v Germany* [1997] ECR I-4475.

[218] C-198/03 P *Commission v CEVA and Pfizer* [2005] ECR I-6357.

[219] C-104/00 P *DKV Deutsche Krankenversicherung AG* [2002] ECR I-7561 and C-37/03 P *BioID AG* [2005] ECR I-7975.

[220] *Rossi* (n 196) paragraph 40.

7.235 Accordingly, the scope of the review of their decisions by the Community Courts was limited to grounds of legality; it was not intended to re-examine the facts that had been assessed during the process before the Office.

7.236 Pursuant to Article 74(1) of the Regulation, in proceedings relating to refusal of registration the Office was restricted in its examination to the facts, evidence, and arguments provided by the parties and the relief sought. Accordingly, the lawfulness of its decisions could not be challenged on the basis of facts that were not relied upon by the parties.

> Contrary to what the appellant maintains, the fact that the Board of Appeal relied on evidence adduced before OHIM to draw conclusions different from those reached by the Opposition Division is irrelevant in this respect, because the appraisal of the evidence conducted by that Board could, in any event, be challenged before the Court of First Instance.[221]

7.237 If the appellant believed that the Board of Appeal had deprived it of the opportunity to present specific evidence in a timely manner it should have put forward a plea based on the second sentence of Article 73 of the Regulation: 'However, any infringement by the Board of Appeal of the appellant's right to present its comments does not mean that the Court of First Instance is obliged to proceed with its own assessment of facts and evidence which were not put forward previously before OHIM.'[222]

7.238 Finally, the Court dismissed the Article 73 claim. According to Article 48(2) of the Rules of Procedure of the Court of First Instance no new plea in law could be introduced in the course of proceedings unless it was based on matters of law or of fact which came to light in the course of those proceedings. The appellant itself had accepted that in the application to the Court of First Instance it did not allege that the Board had infringed Article 73.

(3) *Medion*: The Importance of Dominant Elements

7.239 In *Medion*,[223] a reference from the Oberlandesgericht (Higher Regional Court) of Dusseldorf, the Court of Justice reconsidered the global appreciation test. Medion, the registered proprietor of LIFE for electronic entertainment goods in Germany, brought an infringement action against Thomson, which applied to identical products the sign THOMSON LIFE. In determining whether there was likelihood of confusion in cases of conflicting marks that comprised identical components, German courts applied a technique known as the Pragetheorie. The decisive criterion was the overall impression conveyed by the marks; in particular, courts had to examine whether the common component dominated in the composite mark whereas the remaining components played a minor role in the overall impression. If the common component merely contributed to the overall impression there would be no likelihood of confusion, even if the earlier sign that had been incorporated in the composite mark retained an independent distinctive presence.

7.240 Another aspect of the Pragetheorie was the recognition that individual components of the overall presentation of a product could have a specific function, independent of the distinguishing function of other components. A component that designated the undertaking behind the product rather than the product itself was considered to be a secondary rather than a dominant component of the composite sign. Counterbalancing this assumption,

---

[221] Paragraph 53.
[222] Paragraph 54.
[223] C-120/04 *Medion AG* [2005] ECR I-8551.

courts also had to take into account the peculiarities of each product market; the name of the manufacturer was particularly relevant for fashion products, for example. Accordingly, if such a name formed part of a composite mark it would be considered a dominant or characterizing element. In such cases courts would also weigh the distinctiveness of each element. For example, if the other components were 'normally distinctive' the dominance of the earlier mark would not be challenged; but, if the earlier mark was particularly distinctive, then its dominance would be even stronger.

7.241 The German court referred to the Court of Justice the following question:

> Is Article 5(1)(b) of the Directive to be interpreted as meaning that where the goods or services covered by competing signs are identical there is also a likelihood of confusion on the part of the public where an earlier word mark with normal distinctiveness is reproduced in a later composite word sign belonging to a third party, or in a word sign or figurative sign belonging to a third party that is characterised by word elements, in such a way that the third party's company name is placed before the earlier mark and the latter, though not alone determining the overall impression conveyed by the composite sign, has an independent distinctive role within the composite sign?

(a) The Opinion of Advocate General Jacobs

7.242 Advocate General Jacobs rejected the basic idea that there was a need for a specific theory 'which formally articulates a set of rules to apply automatically in certain cases'.[224] However, he was drawn into a discussion of the German Pragetheorie because he also recognized that such theories could provide guidance on how to apply the basic principles.

7.243 He repeated the familiar position that similarity between the respective marks is 'a necessary but not a sufficient condition';[225] it is one of a number of interdependent factors. Particularly relevant in this case would be four factors. First, that when the goods are identical, 'less similarity between the marks may give rise to a likelihood of confusion';[226] second, that the more distinctive the earlier mark, the greater will be the likelihood of confusion; third, that the average consumer perceives the mark as a whole; and fourth, that the attention of the average consumer varies. Regarding the fourth factor in particular, the Advocate General made a novel assumption, triggered by the factual findings of the German court, that the average consumer's level of attention will tend to be lower because in the market for electronic entertainment goods customers pay particular attention to the designation of the manufacturer.

7.244 He also noted that the Court had by reasoned order dismissed an appeal against a judgment of the Court of First Instance[227] that dealt with similar issues:

> The Court [of First Instance] rightly pointed out … that the assessment of the similarity between two marks does not amount to taking into consideration only one component of a complex trade mark and comparing it with another mark. On the contrary, such a comparison must be made by examining the marks in question, each considered as a whole. It also held that that does not mean that the overall impression created in the mind of the

---

[224] Point 18.
[225] Point 21.
[226] Point 25.
[227] C-3/03 P *Matratzen Concord GmbH* [2004] ECR I-3657.

relevant public by a complex trade mark may not, in certain circumstances, be dominated by one or more of its components.[228]

Furthermore... the Court [of First Instance] ... devoted a significant part of its reasoning to an appreciation of their distinctive and dominant elements and of the likelihood of confusion on the part of the public, a likelihood which it appreciated globally, taking into account all the factors relevant to the circumstances of the case.[229]

According to the Advocate General the Court, as expected within the global appreciation context, had endorsed an approach similar to the Pragetheorie. **7.245**

> The Court's statement ... that the overall impression of a composite mark may, in certain circumstances, be dominated by one or more of its components reflects that proposition. The extent to which the overall impression is so dominated is a question of fact for the national court.[230]

He concluded that the assessment must be based 'on the overall impression given by each mark, bearing in mind, in particular, their distinctive and dominant components, the nature of the public concerned, the category of goods or services in question and the circumstances in which they are marketed'.[231] The concern of the national court that 'a third party can usurp an earlier sign by adding a company name'[232] should be reviewed within the context of unfair competition rather than trade mark law. **7.246**

(b) The Judgment of the Court

The Court reviewed its jurisprudence on global appreciation highlighting the point made in *Matratzen*[233] that the comparison between the two conflicting signs 'must be made by examining each of the marks in question as a whole, which does not mean that the overall impression conveyed to the relevant public by a composite trade mark may not, in certain circumstances, be dominated by one or more of its components'.[234] **7.247**

However, the Court also added that in some cases an earlier mark that had become part of an unconnected, later, composite mark might have an independent distinctive role in the composite mark, without being the dominant component, leading the public to believe that there is an economic link between the two undertakings behind the two marks. Imposing a condition that the earlier mark becomes the dominant component would deprive the owner of the earlier mark of its exclusive right in such a case where the overall impression of the composite sign is not dominated by the earlier mark but might still cause confusion. By way of example, the Court concocted the scenario of an owner of a widely known mark combining it with another unconnected earlier mark in a new composite sign: 'It must therefore be accepted that, in order to establish the likelihood of confusion, it suffices that, because **7.248**

---

[228] Point 32.
[229] Point 33.
[230] Point 33. The Advocate General referred to another similar case decided by the Court of First Instance, T-22/04 *Reemark Gesellschaft für Markenkooperation mbH v Office for Harmonisation in the Internal Market (Trade Marks and Designs)* [2005] ECR II-1559, which found that there would be confusion between WEST and WESTLIFE; however, he reiterated that the Court of First Instance is reviewing the application of established legal principles by the Board of Appeal whereas the Court of Justice is answering questions of law, so a judgment of the Court of First instance should not precipitate a preliminary ruling by the Court of Justice.
[231] Point 39.
[232] Point 40.
[233] C-3/03 P *Matratzen Concord GmbH* [2004] ECR I-3657.
[234] *Medion* (n 223) paragraph 29

the earlier mark still has an independent distinctive role, the origin of the goods or services covered by the composite sign is attributed by the public also to the owner of that mark.'[235]

7.249 Article 51(b) should

be interpreted as meaning that where the goods or services are identical there may be a likelihood of confusion on the part of the public where the contested sign is composed by juxtaposing the company name of another party and a registered mark which has normal distinctiveness and which, without alone determining the overall impression conveyed by the composite sign, still has an independent distinctive role therein.[236]

(4) *Barbara Becker*, *Bimbo Doughnuts*, and *US Polo*: The Application of the *Medion* Principle

7.250 Although the judgment of the Court in *Medion* is set in the context of marks being compared as a whole, the Court's comments that the presence of an identical element having an independent distinctive role might suffice for a finding of a likelihood of confusion perhaps inevitably led to a series of cases testing the flexibility of this principle.

7.251 (i) The case of *Barbara Becker*[237] concerned an opposition under Articles 8(1)(b) and 8(5) to a CTM application for the trade mark BARBARA BECKER. The opposition was based on an earlier registration of BECKER. Both marks covered a range of goods in Class 9, which were accepted by both parties as being either identical or similar.

7.252 The Opposition Division upheld the opposition, finding that the marks were overall similar, being visually and phonetically very similar and conceptually identical. As the goods were identical, there was therefore a likelihood of confusion. However, the Board of Appeal dismissed the opposition, finding that the marks, whilst having some degree of visual and phonetic similarity, were conceptually distinct; in particular, they found that the public would perceive a full name and that the element BECKER was not the dominant and distinctive part of the contested mark.

7.253 On appeal, the Court of First Instance found that the Board of Appeal had been wrong to conclude that the marks were conceptually distinct, finding that the public would attribute greater importance to surnames than forenames (citing *Fusco*[238]) and holding that the celebrity attached to the BARBARA BECKER name did not render the marks dissimilar. Furthermore, in citing *Medion*, the Court of First Instance found that the element BECKER retained an independent distinctive role in the composite mark which was sufficient for a likelihood of confusion. The applicant appealed, alleging an infringement of Article 8(1)(b).

(a) *The Opinion of Advocate General Cruz Villalón*

7.254 Noting that the matter turned on the conceptual similarity between the marks, and the role played by the presence of the forename in the contested mark, Advocate General Cruz Villalón stated that in order to deviate from exercising a global assessment of the likelihood

---

[235] Paragraph 36.
[236] *Medion* (n 223) paragraph 37.
[237] C-51/09 *Barbara Becker v Office for Harmonisation in the Internal Market (Trade Marks and Designs)/Harman International Industries, Inc.* [2010] ECR I-05805.
[238] T-185/03 *Fusco v Office for Harmonisation in the Internal Market (Trade Marks and Designs)/Fusco International* [2005] ECR II-715, paragraph 54.

of confusion, and as such rely definitively on the principles set out in *Medion*, the Court of First Instance:

> had to reason in terms of an exception, that is to say, it had to explain why exceptionally in that case it was necessary to dispense with the general requirement with respect to an application for a composite trade mark to examine the overall impression, bearing in mind, in particular, its distinctive and dominant components. In other words, it should have dealt with, in that context, the possible conceptual similarity between 'barbara becker' and 'becker', because in this case it is not necessary for the component 'becker' to have a dominant position in the mark as a whole.[239]

7.255 In his view, however, the Court's decision did not demonstrate that this process had taken place. In particular:

> there is scarcely any consideration to be found other than that ... 'becker' is a surname, which is not in dispute, and which would be hard to refute. It is on that basis that the Court directly concludes that 'becker' and 'barbara becker' are similar ... and, therefore that the Board of Appeal had erred in law.[240]

In Advocate General Cruz Villalón's opinion, the Court of First Instance's decision might create a rule whereby any full name could be automatically refused on the basis of an earlier registration for the corresponding surname without further analysis.[241] Rather, an assessment of similarity should include an analysis of the distinctiveness of the surname and the effect of the additional matter.[242]

(b) The Judgment of the Court

7.256 In remitting the case back to the Court of First Instance, the Court of Justice found that the Court of First Instance had:

> erred in law in basing its assessment of the conceptual similarity of the marks on general considerations taken from the case-law without analysing all the relevant factors specific to the case, in disregard of the requirement of an overall assessment of the likelihood of confusion, taking account of all factors relevant to the circumstances of the case, and based on the overall impression produced by the marks at issue.[243]

7.257 (ii) The case of *US Polo*[244] concerned an opposition under Article 8(1)(b) to an application for the word mark U.S. POLO ASSOCIATION covering, inter alia, goods in Class 24. The opposition was based on earlier Spanish and CTM registrations for the word mark POLO-POLO covering identical goods. The Opposition Division upheld the opposition, a decision which was maintained by the Board of Appeal. In particular, the Board of Appeal found that the signs were visually, phonetically, and conceptually similar and that, given the identical nature of the goods, there was a likelihood of confusion amongst the average consumer in the EU.

7.258 The applicant appealed, claiming that the Board of Appeal had failed to apply the principles established by the settled case law and that it had furthermore been wrong to find

---

[239] Point 56.
[240] Point 57.
[241] Point 59.
[242] Point 60.
[243] *Barbara Becker* (n 237) paragraph 40.
[244] C-327/11 *US Polo Association v Office for Harmonisation in the Internal Market (Trade Marks and Designs) (OHIM)*, ECLI:EU:C:2012:550.

the respective marks visually, phonetically, and conceptually similar. The General Court refused the appeal, finding that the Board of Appeal was correct to conclude that the relevant public consisted of the average consumers in the European Union who did not demonstrate a high level of attention. Furthermore, the GC rejected the applicant's argument that the Board of Appeal had limited its comparison of the marks to the common element. Rather, the GC found that the Board of Appeal had considered all the elements in the contested mark but had concluded that these additional elements did not remove the similarity.

7.259 The applicant also claimed that consumers in the EU are familiar with its trade mark as a result of its other CTMs in other classes and that this would reduce the likelihood of confusion. The GC accepted that the coexistence of other marks in the market might reduce the likelihood of confusion, but that it was incumbent on the applicant to have demonstrated coexistence and the absence of confusion in the proceedings before OHIM. This obligation had not been met by the mere submission of a list of earlier CTMs standing in the name of the applicant.

7.260 The applicant appealed to the Court of Justice claiming an infringement of Article 8(1)(b). The first argument was that, contrary to the GC's decision, the element POLO did not have an independent distinctive function in the contested mark and that the GC's decision was contrary to the principles set down in *Medion*. The Court of Justice found that the GC's reference to the independent distinctive role of the word POLO in the analysis of the visual similarities between the marks was not inconsistent with the principles set down in *Medion* in that the Court had not set out to apply the *Medion* principles to the case (and in fact had not mentioned the case in its Judgment).

7.261 The Court also rejected the applicant's argument that the GC had attributed too much importance to the common element POLO in the respective marks, finding that the GC had considered the other elements in the contested mark and examined their relative importance but had merely concluded that these were not particularly distinctive. The Court of Justice also commented that insofar as the applicant was seeking to change the way in which the GC assessed those criteria, this would be fateful in its nature and therefore would not be admissible. It was for this reason the Court of Justice also rejected the applicant's third and fourth arguments, namely that the GC had failed to take account of the repetition of the element POLO and that it had reached inconsistent conclusions regarding the additional elements in the contested mark.

7.262 (iii) The case of *Bimbo SA*[245] concerned an opposition under Articles 8(1)(b) and 8(5) to a CTM application for the word mark BIMBO DOUGHNUTS in Class 30, based on an earlier Spanish registration of DOUGHNUTS, also covering goods in Class 30. Both the Opposition Division and the Board of Appeal found that there was a likelihood of confusion and allowed the opposition. In particular, the Board of Appeal found that the word DOUGHNUTS, whilst having a meaning in English, did not exist in Spanish and would be seen as a foreign or 'fantasy' term. Since the word had an average degree of distinctiveness and was almost identically reproduced in the contested mark, the Board of Appeal held that there was a likelihood of confusion.

---

[245] C-591/12 *Bimbo SA v Office for Harmonisation in the Internal Market (Trade Marks and Designs) (OHIM)/Panrico SA*, ECLI:EU:C:2014:305.

7.263 The applicant appealed to the Court of First Instance, claiming an infringement of Articles 75 and 76 CTMR and an infringement of Article 8(1)(b). The appeal was rejected. In essence, the Court of First Instance found that the relevant public was the average Spanish consumer and that the goods were identical, and rejected the applicant's argument that the element DOUGHNUT was descriptive and that the dominant element of the contested mark was the element BIMBO, which was well known in Spain. The Court of First Instance held that even if the applicant had established in evidence the reputation attached to the element BIMBO in Spain, the element DOUGHNUTS could not be regarded as negligible in the overall impression of the later mark and, furthermore, citing *Medion*, that the element DOUGHNUTS played an independent distinctive role in the later mark on the basis that it had average distinctiveness amongst non-English-speaking members of the relevant public and did not combine with the element BIMBO to form a unitary whole or logical unit.[246] These factors, together with the fact that the respective goods were identical, the visual and phonetic similarities between the marks, and the fact that the general public would exercise a lower level of attention, led the Court of First Instance to conclude that the Board of Appeal had correctly concluded that there was a likelihood of confusion between the marks.

7.264 The applicant appealed, claiming an infringement of Article 8(1)(b). The appeal consisted of four parts, the first of which was that the Court of First Instance had incorrectly attributed the element DOUGHNUTS in the contested mark as having an independent distinctive role.

(a) The Opinion of Advocate General Mengozzi

7.265 In his assessment of the case law, Advocate General Mengozzi noted the problems in interpreting the scope of *Medion* and the variety of interpretations that could be given to 'independent distinctive role':

> Although the terminology used by the Court in that paragraph gives the impression that the Court intended to introduce an exception to the well-established principles of the case-law of the European Union relating to the assessment of the likelihood of confusion, such an interpretation does not seem to me to be satisfactory. In my view, there is no plausible justification for basing the assessment of the similarity of marks on different sets of criteria, in such a way as to entail, for an isolated category of composite marks, a derogation from the rules relating to the perception of marks by the public. In particular, the need—which the Court highlights in paragraphs 33 to 35 of *Medion*—to protect the earlier trade mark against possible appropriation by third parties cannot constitute such a justification; that need, however legitimate, has no bearing on the assessment of the likelihood of confusion and, as has already been observed by Advocate General Jacobs in his Opinion in *Medion*, must be met through laws other than those at issue in that case.[247]

7.266 Advocate General Mengozzi stated that a new interpretation of *Medion* was therefore required, and that when viewed as a preliminary ruling absent factual analysis:

> [I]t is above all essential to bear in mind that *Medion* was a judgment delivered in the context of a reference for a preliminary ruling, in which any verification of fact is exclusively a matter for the referring court. In that context, the Court did not take a position on the

---

[246] T-569/10 *Bimbo SA v Office for Harmonisation in the Internal Market (Trade Marks and Designs) (OHIM)/Panrico SA*, ECLI:EU:T:2012:535, paragraph 97.
[247] Point 22.

possible existence of a likelihood of confusion in that particular case (a comparison of the marks THOMSON LIFE and LIFE), but simply answered the question referred, specifying, on the basis of the information provided by the national court, the criteria to be used as a basis for assessing the likelihood of confusion. Viewed in that context, the ruling in *Medion* merely states, in essence, that the possibility of a likelihood of confusion between an earlier trade mark, used by a third party as part of a composite sign, and that sign cannot automatically be ruled out in cases where the earlier trade mark, albeit not the dominant element of the composite sign, retains a role in that sign of such a kind that 'the origin of the goods or services covered by the composite sign is attributed by the public also to the owner of that mark'.[248]

7.267 Rather, *Medion* solely sought to establish that it was appropriate to consider circumstances where a composite mark contains an earlier mark, even if the element does not dominate but 'only significantly contributes to' the impression formed by the mark on the relevant public. As such, the decision in *Medion* was simply seeking to soften the 'rigidity' of some earlier decisions (citing in particular *Matratzen*[249]). However, Advocate General Mengozzi also emphasized that even when the circumstances do require that such a consideration is made, the comparison should include an analysis of the composite mark's components and of their relative weight. For the avoidance of doubt, Advocate General Mengozzi emphasized that such an assessment is necessary even where the facts of the case reflect those in *Medion*, namely where the later mark comprises the earlier mark in combination with the applicant's company name.[250]

7.268 Furthermore, regardless of the role of the earlier mark in the overall impression, it was still appropriate to consider the relevant factors of the case, such as the visual, phonetic, and conceptual similarities between the marks, the similarities between the goods/services, the level of attention of the relevant public, and the habits of the sector concerned.[251]

(b) The Judgment of the Court

7.269 In analysing the Court of First Instance's decision, the Court took note of the fact that the Court of First Instance had assessed the relative distinctiveness of the elements BIMBO and DOUGHNUTS in the contested mark. Although the Court of First Instance had found that the element DOUGHNUTS did perform an independent distinctive role in the composite mark, the Court held that this was not the sole reason why the Court of First Instance had concluded that there was a likelihood of confusion; rather, the Court had based its assessment on a global assessment. The Court clarified that the reason for examining whether any of the components of a composite sign had an independent distinctive role is to determine which of those will be perceived by the target public:[252]

> The determination of which components of a composite sign contribute to the overall impression made on the target public by that sign is to be undertaken before the global assessment of the likelihood of confusion of the signs at issue. Such an assessment must be based on the overall impression produced by the trade marks at issue, since the average consumer normally perceives a mark as a whole and does not proceed to analyse its various details, as

---

[248] Point 23.
[249] Point 24.
[250] Point 25.
[251] Point 26.
[252] *Bimbo SA* (n 246) paragraph 33.

has been stated in paragraph 21 above. Therefore, this does not involve an exception, that must be duly substantiated, to that general rule.[253]

Thus, the test set out in *Medion* is simply seen as one of the relevant factors to be taken into account when assessing the similarity between marks and, despite the use of the word 'suffice' in the Court of Justice's decision, is not intended to trump all other assessments. As such, whilst the Court did not go as far as Advocate General Mengozzi in explicitly identifying the potential problems of applying an overly broad interpretation of *Medion*, the decision has a similar effect. In this case, the applicant's argument that the Court of First Instance had failed to take account of other relevant factors in the case, in particular the reputation attached to the first element in the contested mark (in other words, the element BIMBO) which they claimed had been widely used in Spain, was rejected, and the opposition upheld.

7.270

(5) *Praktiker*: A Special Case for Retail Services?

In *Praktiker*[254] the Court confirmed that a trade mark could be registered for retail services but also considered whether a special, stricter, test had to be applied in the case of trade marks registered for retail services.

7.271

The first question concerned the registrability of services. The second and the third questions referred by the Bundespatentgericht sought clarification regarding the scope of protection:

7.272

> 2. To what extent must the content of such services provided by a retailer be specified in order to guarantee the certainty of the subject matter of trade-mark protection that is required in order to (a) fulfil the function of the trade mark, as defined in Article 2 of the Directive, namely, to distinguish the goods or services of one undertaking from those of other undertakings, and (b) define the scope of protection of such a trade mark in the event of a conflict?
> 3. To what extent is it necessary to define the scope of similarity (Article 4(1)(b) and Article 5(1)(b) of the Directive) between such services provided by a retailer and (a) other services provided in connection with the distribution of goods, or (b) the goods sold by that retailer?[255]

(a) *The Opinion of Advocate General Léger*

Advocate General Léger first clarified that retailers do not differ from manufacturers who sell their products themselves; they, too, should be able to distinguish themselves from their competitors.

7.273

The essential function of a trade mark became the starting point for his analysis:

7.274

> in so far as the purpose of a service mark is to enable consumers to identify the enterprise supplying the service, the registration of the mark implies that the service which it is intended to designate is itself identifiable as such, by means of a mark. In other words, it must be possible for consumers to perceive the activity, as such, for which [the] applicant is seeking the registration of a mark as constituting a service. This requirement follows from the very function of the mark and its corollary, the principle of speciality, which means that the rights which it confers can be exactly determined. A mark cannot be registered for a service which cannot

---

[253] Paragraph 35.
[254] C-418/02 *Praktiker Bauund Heimwerkermärkte AG v Deutsches Patent- und Markenant* [2005] ECR I-5873.
[255] Reproduced in point 22.

be perceived as such by consumers, with the result that the scope of protection could not be ascertained.[256]

7.275 He admitted that ascertaining some services related to the sale of products, for example, bringing them together for the purposes of selling them, could be difficult. However, developments in marketing meant that 'the conditions under which the act of sale itself takes place may constitute, in the relationship between retailer and consumer, a reason for buying which is just as important as the quality and price of the goods sold'.[257] He agreed with the decision of the Board of Appeal in *Giacomelli Sport*,[258] that a service supplied in connection with retail trading may constitute a service for which a trade mark can be registered.

7.276 Regarding the required degree of detail in the specification of retail services, he submitted that for reasons of legal certainty and sound administration a common standard should be adopted throughout the Union. He suggested that the

> registration of a mark for services supplied in connection with the retail sale of goods should clearly indicate both the specific nature of those services and the goods or types of goods to which they relate ... this dual requirement is justified, in the light of the scheme and purpose of the Directive, by the particular nature of the services supplied in connection with retail trading.[259]

7.277 Advocate General Léger opted for this stricter approach because of the balancing act that trade mark law is asked to perform:

> trade-mark law is somewhat paradoxical in conferring upon one retailer in particular exclusive rights in marks which serve the marketing of goods or services in order to promote the free movement of those goods and services. To reconcile the interests of the protection afforded by the mark and free movement, in the trade-mark law registration system the applicant must, in consideration of the exclusive rights which he claims, indicate exactly the mark and the goods and services to which those rights relate.[260]

7.278 Regarding the third question, he accepted that trade mark law should avoid giving retailers extensive protections:

> that cover other services that might be offered in connection with selling goods, as well as all the goods sold by such proprietor. Like the national court, I consider that recognition of the possibility of registering such marks should not have the consequence of permitting them to replace goods marks or of impairing the advantages attaching to them.[261]

7.279 However, he was against adopting exceptional set criteria for delimiting the area of similarity between services supplied in connection with the retail sale of goods and the other services which may be offered in the course of marketing in general or the actual goods.

(b) The Judgment of the Court

7.280 The Court agreed that the concept of 'services' should be interpreted in the same way throughout the Union, otherwise conditions for the registration of 'service trade marks'[262]

---

[256] Point 47.
[257] Point 50.
[258] Case R-46/1998-2, 17 December 1999.
[259] Point 71.
[260] Point 79.
[261] Point 89.
[262] *Praktiker* (n 254) paragraph 32.

could vary according to the laws of each Member State. It described the objective of retail trade as the sale of goods to consumers that:

> includes, in addition to the legal sales transaction, all activity carried out by the trader for the purpose of encouraging the conclusion of such a transaction. That activity consists, inter alia, in selecting an assortment of goods offered for sale and in offering a variety of services aimed at inducing the consumer to conclude the above-mentioned transaction with the trader in question rather than with a competitor.[263]

The Court found that there was no overriding reason based on the Directive or on general principles of Community law precluding the above services from being covered by the concept of 'services' within the meaning of the Directive. In relation to the Regulation, it reminded us that the Office had accepted the principle of registration of Community trade marks for retail services. **7.281**

It then rejected the argument that a more restrictive specification of retail services would be required. It accepted that a restrictive approach would 'reduce the protection afforded to the proprietor of the trade mark, so that questions concerning the application of Articles 4(1) and 5(1) of the Directive would arise less often';[264] however, this would not be adequate justification. Being more permissive than the Advocate General, the Court held that the applicant should only 'be required to specify the goods or types of goods to which those services relate'.[265] **7.282**

The Court found the third question to be speculative, there being no indication in the reference that the referring court could find it necessary to rule on the concept of 'similarity' in connection with 'likelihood of confusion'. Accordingly, it declined to answer the question.[266] **7.283**

(6) *Travatan*: Pharmaceuticals and the Role of Professionals

(a) *The attentiveness variable*

As we have already seen, in *Lloyd Schuhfabrik* the Court reaffirmed the general principle that 'for the purposes of the global assessment the average consumer of the category of products concerned is deemed to be reasonably well-informed, observant and circumspect'. However, those qualities do not make the average consumer impervious to confusion, especially since he 'only rarely has the chance to make a direct comparison between the different marks, but must place his trust in the imperfect picture of them that he has kept in his mind'. Moreover, the Court stressed that this 'average' level of attentiveness may fluctuate depending on the circumstances, since 'the average consumer's level of attention is likely to vary according to the category of goods or services in question and the way they are marketed'.[267] **7.284**

That definition of the relevant consumer profile and levels of attentiveness provides a remarkably flexible tool for adapting the threshold of confusion to the particularities of **7.285**

---

[263] Paragraph 34.
[264] Paragraph 46.
[265] Paragraph 50.
[266] Paragraph 57, citing T-421/01 *Traunfellner GmbH v Österreichische Autobahnen-und Schnellstraßen-Finanzierungs-AG* [2003] ECR I-11941.
[267] C-342/97 *Lloyd Schuhfabrik Meyer* [1999] ECR I-3819, paragraph 26.

each situation and stresses even further the need for a case-by-case approach in assessing the relevant risk.

7.286 In *Picasso*, the Court elaborated further on the above principles, by noting that for the purposes of the assessment of confusion 'account must be taken of the fact that, in view of the nature of the goods concerned and in particular their price and their highly technological character, the average consumer displays a particularly high level of attention at the time of purchase of such goods' and that:

> where it is established in fact that the objective characteristics of a given product mean that the average consumer purchases it only after a particularly careful examination, it is important in law to take into account that such a fact may reduce the likelihood of confusion between marks relating to such goods at the crucial moment when the choice between those goods and marks is made.[268]

7.287 Even though, admittedly, that view has the result of making the enforcement of trade mark rights in specific market sectors subject to stricter conditions, its economic justification is immediately obvious: if in relation to certain products confusion is indeed less likely to occur, it is only natural that trade mark owners in those fields should not be overprotected and that the corresponding rights should be enforced only to the extent that they are actually threatened.

(b) The special case of pharmaceuticals

7.288 Applying that principle to pharmaceutical preparations, the Court of First Instance has consistently held that if the substance concerned is not entirely harmless, but may have relatively important implications for the consumer's health, the attentiveness of the public tends to be higher, and this is irrespective of whether in the particular case the patient is assisted by qualified professionals.[269] The reference to 'professionals' shows that it is also necessary to consider the sophistication of the relevant consumer, which again depends on the characteristics of the goods and which can be particularly important when addressing the semantic content of a mark, as for example when determining the ease with which specialized terms are likely to be understood by professionals, as compared to their perception by the general public.

7.289 A good example of the interaction of those concepts is the sector of prescription pharmaceuticals, with which the Court was confronted in *Travatan*,[270] an appeal dealing with the impact of the mediation of professionals on the definition of the relevant consumer profile and the levels of attentiveness likely to be displayed. That interaction gave rise to two interrelated questions: the first one was who is the relevant consumer, given that in the case of prescription pharmaceuticals the choice of the appropriate substance is usually made by the physician, rather than the patient; the second was how far does the assistance of medical professionals affect the already high levels of attentiveness ordinary consumers are likely to display when confronted with potentially hazardous substances.

7.290 As regards the first point, the Court of First Instance[271] followed its well-established case law[272] that in the case of prescription pharmaceuticals there is more than one consumer

---

[268] C-361/04 P *Ruiz-Picasso v OHIM* [2006] ECR I-643, paragraphs 39–43.
[269] T-146/06 *Sanofi-Aventis SA v OHIM* (ATURION/URION) [2008] ECR 17, paragraph 27.
[270] C-412/05 P *Alcon Inc v OHIM* [2007] ECR I-3569.
[271] T-130/03 *Alcon v OHIM-Biofarma* (TRAVATAN) [2005] ECR II-3859.
[272] T-256/04 *Mundipharma AG v OHIM* (RESPICUR/RESPICORT), ECLI:EU:T:2008:203, paragraph 57 and T-353/04 *Ontex NY v OHIM* (CURON/EURON) ECR [2007] ECR II-10, paragraphs 55–58.

circle involved, that is, the relevant public comprises both the medical professionals who prescribe the remedy and the end consumer who ultimately purchases it. When assessing confusion, however, it did not make a clear distinction between the perception of the respective consumer circles, holding rather that the marks TRAVATAN and TRIVASTAN are likely to be confused by the 'public'.

(c) The Opinion of Advocate General Kokott

7.291 Advocate General Kokott disagreed with the position taken by the Court of First Instance as regards prescription pharmaceuticals, observing that:

> Even if regard is ... had to patients too, because ... they can influence a doctor's prescription, in the case of medicinal products available only on prescription their influence has very little significance when compared with the doctor's responsibility for the decision.
>
> In particular, the possible influence exerted by patients cannot mean that the patient is regarded as the reasonably well-informed and reasonably observant and circumspect consumer of those products. The average consumer must rather be determined by reference to the group that largely determines decisions on the acquisition of medicinal products available only on prescription, that is to say by reference to prescribing doctors.
>
> The risk ... of confusion on the part of a patient who, independently of prescription, is confronted with the mark, is also of little significance, under trade mark law at any rate. In the *Picasso* judgment, the Court of Justice regarded the moment when the choice between the goods and marks is made as crucial for assessing the likelihood of confusion. Other points in time, at which confusion on the part of consumers might be more likely because they display a lesser level of attention, are by contrast of secondary importance.[273]

(d) Findings of the Court

7.292 Notwithstanding that the Court concurred with the Court of First Instance that the relevant public consists both of professionals in the medical field and of the end-users of the substances concerned, stressing that even though prescription drugs are obtained through intermediaries, such as healthcare professionals, who are liable to influence, or even to determine, the choice made by the end-users, this fact is not of itself capable of excluding all likelihood of confusion on the part of the final consumer. This is because end-users will 'eventually be faced with those products, even if that takes place during separate purchasing transactions for each of those individual products, at various times'.[274]

7.293 The Court also observed that since it is undisputed that the whole process of marketing the goods at issue is aimed at the end-user's acquisition of them, the role played by health care professionals:

> must be in part balanced against the high degree of attentiveness which may be shown by those users when such goods are prescribed and, consequently, against those users' ability to make those professionals take into account their perception of the trade marks and, in particular, their requirements or preferences.[275]

7.294 One exception the Court seems to be accepting in this context, however, is when the trade mark relates not to prescription pharmaceuticals sold to end-users through the ordinary distribution channels, but rather to substances directly administered by the doctor, for

---

[273] Points 49–51 of the Opinion of AG Kokott.
[274] *Travatan* (n 270) paragraphs 57–58.
[275] Paragraph 61.

example, substances for use in surgery, in respect of which the relevant public only consists of medical specialists.[276] Moreover, in order to dispel the uncertainty arising from contradictory decisions in the matter and give more authority to its findings, the Court explicitly stressed that the above interpretation is 'the only correct one, and that it cannot be called into question by arguments derived either from decisions of the Boards of Appeal, or from the previous case-law of the Community Courts'.[277]

7.295 As regards the outcome, the Court held that although the Court of First Instance had committed an error of law in not distinguishing between the respective consumer profiles when assessing confusion, its decision could nevertheless stand, considering that even if only end-users are finally confused, this is sufficient to trigger the consequences of Article 8(1)(b) CTMR.

7.296 The judgment in *Travatan* has therefore shed light on a number of questions arising from professional assistance in the acquisition of pharmaceutical products, by clarifying that: (a) as regards prescription drugs, the relevant public consists of both physicians and patients; (b) the mediation of professionals cannot in itself exclude all likelihood of confusion on the part of end-users; (c) those users are likely to be more attentive when dealing with potentially hazardous substances;[278] and (d) in any event, account must also be taken of the end-user's imperfect recollection, especially since confusion may arise during separate transactions, occurring at different points in time.

(7) *Limoncello—Quicky—La Española*: Composite Marks

7.297 In *Limoncello*,[279] *Quicky*,[280] and *La Española*[281] the Court dealt with the importance to be attached to the figurative elements of composite signs in conflicts with other complex marks, or with signs consisting only of verbal elements. A comparative reading of those judgments shows that the impact of the figurative components on the assessment of likelihood of confusion depends less on their prominence in terms of size and position, and more on the interaction of the various components between them, as determined by their relative distinctiveness.

7.298 In the end, the pivotal question is whether any of the components making up the signs can be regarded as negligible, in which case the comparison can legitimately focus only on the other elements, or if, conversely, none of them can be discarded as unimportant, the comparison must perforce be based on all the components of the marks, since they are

---

[276] See *Travatan* (n 270) paragraph 66; as well as T-237/01 *Alcon Inc v OHIM* (BSS/BSS) [2003] ECR II-411, paragraph 42, confirmed by the Order of the Court of Justice of 5 October 2004; C-192/03 P *Alcon Inc v OHIM* (BSS) [2004] ECR I-8993, paragraph 30.

[277] Paragraph 64.

[278] Apparently in the sense that the more dangerous the substance, or the more serious the disease, the higher the degree of attentiveness likely to be employed by the public. That the degree of attentiveness should be proportional to the specific properties of the product concerned follows not only from the conditional formulation in *Travatan* that consumers '*may* be more attentive', but also from the statement in *Picasso* that 'the average consumer displays a particularly high level of attention ... where it is established in fact that the *objective characteristics* of a given product mean that the average consumer purchases it only after a particularly careful examination'.

[279] C-334/05 P *Shaker di Laudato & C Sas v OHIM* (LIMONCELLO) [2007] ECR I-4529.

[280] C-193/06 P *Société des Produits Nestlé v OHIM* (QUICKY) [2007] ECR I-114.

[281] C-498/07 P *Aceites del Sur-Coosur SA v Koipe Corporación* (LA ESPAÑOLA) [2009] ECR I-7371.

(a) Limoncello: *Non-negligible word elements cannot be ignored*

Limoncello concerned an opposition based on the Spanish word mark LIMONCHELO against the registration of a sign composed of the words 'Limoncello della Costiera Amalfitana-Shaker', coupled with the device of an elaborate dish decorated with lemons. Both marks essentially covered alcoholic drinks in Class 33 of the Nice Classification. Both the Opposition Division and the Boards of Appeal of the Office upheld the opposition, on the grounds that the dominant element of the mark applied for was the word 'Limoncello', which was visually and phonetically similar to the earlier word mark.

7.299

The Court of First Instance[282] annulled the decision of the Board holding the following as regards the comparison of the signs:

7.300

> [T]he Board of Appeal had to consider which component of the trade mark claimed was apt, by virtue of its visual, phonetic or conceptual characteristics, to convey, by itself, an impression of that mark which the relevant public keeps in mind, with the result that all the other components of the mark are negligible in that respect ...
>
> However, if the trade mark claimed is a complex mark which is visual in nature, the assessment of the overall impression created by that mark and the determination as to whether there is any dominant element must be carried out on the basis of a visual analysis. Accordingly, in such a case, it is only to the extent to which a potentially dominant element includes non-visual semantic aspects that it may become necessary to compare that element with the earlier mark, also taking into account those other semantic aspects, such as for example phonetic factors or relevant abstract concepts.

Following that approach, the Court of First Instance held that the representation of the round dish decorated with lemons was clearly the dominant component of the mark applied for and that, since the word elements of that mark were not dominant on a visual level, there was no need to analyse the phonetic and conceptual characteristics of those elements, or to adjudicate on the distinctiveness of the earlier mark. In doing so, the Court of First Instance essentially took the view that, in the case of combined word and device marks, the visual prominence of the various elements takes precedence over the assessment of their distinctiveness. In other words, if a part of the sign is visually less striking than others, it automatically becomes negligible and its impact on confusion need not be explored any further.

7.301

The Court of Justice disagreed with that analysis. It held that the Court of First Instance had merely paid lip service to the principle that the global appreciation of the likelihood of confusion must be based on the overall impression created by the signs, but not effectively applied it in practice.

7.302

Referring to the principles established in *Matratzen* and *Medion*, it reiterated that the assessment of the similarity between two marks means more than taking just one component of a composite trade mark and comparing it with the other and that the comparison must be made by examining each of the marks in question as a whole.[283]

7.303

---

[282] T-7/04 *Shaker v OHIM-Limiñana y Botella (Linoncello della Costiera Amalfitana shaker)* [2005] ECR II-2305, paragraphs 53–54, 59, and 68.
[283] Paragraphs 37–43.

7.304 Thus, it held that although in certain circumstances the overall impression conveyed by a composite trade mark may be dominated by one or more of its components, this does not mean that the other elements of the sign can simply be disregarded, without even addressing their possible impact on that impression, not only visually, but also phonetically and semantically.

(b) Quicky: Unclear dominance; all elements count

7.305 In *Quicky*,[284] another opposition case, Nestlé applied to register as a Community trade mark a sign consisting of the stylized word QUICKY, combined with a larger, stylized bunny device. Quick restaurants opposed it based on its earlier French and Benelux registrations of the words QUICK and QUICKIES. The Office upheld the opposition. On appeal, the Board confirmed the rejection of the application holding that, despite the substantial visual differences contributed by the bunny device, the strong phonetic similarities between the words QUICKY and QUICKIES were sufficient to give rise to a likelihood of confusion between the signs, within the meaning of Article 8(1)(b) CTMR.

7.306 The Court of First Instance[285] shared that conclusion. It took the view that to the extent that the verbal elements of the signs were both visually and phonetically similar, the figurative element could only offset that similarity if it was capable of dominating on its own the image kept in the consumer's memory; that, however, could not happen if the visual impact of the device was of equal or inferior 'intensity' to that of the verbal components.

7.307 The Court also remarked that insofar as words are, as a rule, more distinctive than images and the verbal element in the application is at least as prominent as the bunny device, the latter could not overshadow the similarity between the words, or lead to the conclusion that those elements are in fact negligible. Besides, the widespread use of animal characters on foodstuffs rendered the pictorial element quite banal, thus reducing further its relative impact on the overall impression given by the signs.

7.308 The Court of Justice disagreed with the mechanics of that analysis. It stressed that it could not be sustained in law that every time two marks coincide in their verbal elements, which are more than negligible, there is a likelihood of confusion since such a view effectively ignores the possible impact of the figurative element on the visual impression given by the signs as a whole.[286]

7.309 Specifically, the Court held that although the Court of First Instance had rightly examined the relative importance of the bunny device as compared to the significance of the other elements in the application, it could not simply disregard that device when comparing the signs as a whole solely on the ground that it was not dominant.[287]

7.310 It observed also that the mere fact that a component is not dominant does not necessarily imply that it is insignificant or that it should be overlooked for the purposes of the comparison. Actually, such a conclusion can only be reached if it is first established that the element

---

[284] C-193/06 P *Société des Produits Nestlé v OHIM* (QUICKY) [2007] ECR I-114.
[285] T-074/04 *Société des Produits Nestlé* paragraphs 47–59.
[286] *Quicky* (n 284) paragraph 37.
[287] Paragraph 41.

in question is indeed negligible in an independent and positive manner, something that the Court of First Instance had not done in the case at hand.[288]

Accordingly, the Court of Justice set aside the judgment under appeal and remitted the case to the Court of First Instance for further prosecution. 7.311

Quicky in fact shows that it is not appropriate to single out an element of a composite mark and treat it as dominant if the other components are not clearly subordinate to it in terms of prominence and distinctiveness. On the contrary, if all the parts of a complex mark are of more or less equal significance, their collective impact on the overall impression conveyed to the consumer must be assessed carefully before deciding whether there is a likelihood of confusion. 7.312

At the same time, *Quicky* is once more against the use of aprioristic axioms in trade mark examination, such as the abstract generalization that word elements are by definition more distinctive than devices or that animal motifs as a whole are banal in respect of food products. Rather, such findings are only justified if properly substantiated and their application to the case properly explained. 7.313

(c) La Española: *Dominant figurative elements; get-up imitation*

In *La Española*[289] the Court dealt with the similarity between bottle labels for olive oil. The case concerned two quite successful brands of olive oil already present on the Spanish market for some time. When one of those marks was applied for as a Community trade mark, the owner of the other opposed that application on the basis of both its Community and Spanish trade marks. 7.314

Both marks were composite trade marks containing pictorial elements that represented essentially the same theme: a woman dressed in a traditional Spanish costume, sitting in a certain manner, close to an olive branch with an olive grove in the background. Moreover, the respective images did not merely borrow from the same subject, but rather consisted of an almost identical arrangement of spaces, colours, positions for brand names, and style of lettering. The only substantial difference between them lay in the different word elements used in each mark. The brand name of the applicant was 'La Española', whereas the opponent was using the name 'Carbonell'. 7.315

Thus, the overall setting was reminiscent of a classic get-up imitation case, apart from the fact that the applicant was not a newcomer to the market, but rather a prominent player in the sector with a reputation of his own. Moreover, the opponent's Community trade mark could not validly be relied on because it was filed later than the contested sign. 7.316

The opposition division and the Boards of Appeal of the Office dismissed the opposition under both Article 8(1)(b) and (5) CTMR, taking the view that the different names were sufficient to render the marks visually and phonetically distinguishable from each other and, thus, dissimilar as a whole. The opponent appealed to the Court of First Instance. 7.317

The Court of First Instance[290] annulled the Board's decision, holding that the quasi-identical figurative elements of the signs sufficed to render them confusingly similar overall. 7.318

---

[288] Paragraph 44.
[289] C-498/07 P *Aceites del Sur-Coosur SA v Koipe Corporoción* (LA ESPAÑOLA) [2009] ECR I-7371.
[290] T-363/04 *Koipe v OHIM-Aceites del Sur* (LA ESPAÑOLA) [2007] ECR 3355, paragraphs 103–105.

Specifically, it found that 'the elements common to the two marks at issue, seen as a whole, produce an overall visual impression of great similarity, since the mark applied for reproduces very precisely the essence of the message and the visual impression given by the earlier mark', which was not diminished by the use of different brand names, since the expression 'La Española' merely refers to the geographical origin of the goods and, accordingly, has a very weak distinctive character.

7.319 Having thus established that the verbal component of the application was in fact negligible, the Court of First instance refrained from comparing the marks aurally, or from further exploring the impact the differences between the word elements had on the perception of the consumer. The Court justified that approach by stressing that, as regards consumer goods sold in supermarkets, it is the visual impression that primarily determines the consumer's choice.

7.320 The applicant appealed to the Court of Justice raising a number of points: first, it claimed that the judgment under appeal had failed to differentiate between the various Community and Spanish marks relied on by the opponent, thus taking into account marks which were not actually earlier. Second, it argued that by exclusively relying on the device components the Court of First Instance failed to examine the marks in their entirety, its examination being partial and selective. Finally, it contended that the Court had unduly disregarded the coexistence of the marks on the market and the independent reputation of the sign applied for, while also defining the average consumer as extremely careless.

7.321 The Court of Justice dismissed the appeal, holding that the Court of First Instance had not committed any error of law justifying the annulment of its judgment.

7.322 As to the first point, it held that to the extent that the opposition was also based on a number of earlier Spanish registrations which were identical with the Community trade mark complained of, the omission to clearly differentiate between those rights was not material for the result of the appeal. In particular, insofar as the findings of the Court of First Instance clearly referred to the situation on the Spanish market and were based on the perception of the marks by Spanish consumers, that omission did not materially affect the definition of the relevant public, or change anything in the analysis.[291]

7.323 As regards the alleged infringement of Article 8(1)(b) CTMR, it held that the Court of First Instance had not altogether disregarded the impact of the word elements on the assessment of the likelihood of confusion. On the contrary, it is precisely in the context of that appraisal that the judgment under appeal described the element in question as negligible, by holding that, on account of its weak distinctiveness, it could not invalidate the conclusion that the signs were visually similar.[292]

7.324 Moreover, it held that as olive oil is a very common product in Spain and is mostly purchased in establishments where goods are arranged on shelves, the Court of First Instance correctly found that the relevant consumer is guided more by the visual impact of the mark he/she is looking for and that, accordingly, the figurative element of

---

[291] Paragraphs 43–45.
[292] Paragraphs 69–72.

the marks acquires a greater importance, which substantially increases the likelihood of confusion.[293]

7.325 The Court also observed that the coexistence of two marks in the same market may diminish the likelihood of confusion only if it is 'peaceful', which was not the case here. On the contrary, the evidence showed that the matter of the similarity between the two signs had been at issue between the undertakings concerned before the national courts for a number of years.[294]

7.326 Finally, the Court dismissed the arguments concerning the relevant public and the reputation of the applicant's mark, holding, first, that the findings of the Court of First Instance as regards the attention of the consumer were factual in nature and, second, that the reliance on the well-known character of the application was irrelevant in law, as being contrary to the principle that the scope of protection of the earlier mark should be determined by reference to its own distinctiveness.

7.327 Of course, the result in *La Española* is not easily transposable to all kinds of get-up imitation cases. What characterized that case was the very weak distinctive character of the word component as compared to the elaborate and prominent device, a fact that is not likely to be present in similar settings. However, the focus on the strong visual similarity as a factor that substantially increases the risk of confusion suggests that it will not always be so easy for infringers to escape the consequences of their actions by merely adding a different brand name to an otherwise very similar packaging.

(8) *Uniweb v Unifonds etc*: Families of Marks

7.328 *Uniweb*[295] concerned an opposition, under Article 8(1)(b), to an application for the trade mark UNIWEB covering services in Class 36. The opponent relied on three earlier German registrations all containing the prefix UNI which they claimed constituted a family/series of marks. The Opposition Division allowed the opposition, finding that the opponent's marks did constitute a family and that there was a likelihood of confusion. The Board of Appeal upheld the Opposition Division's decision.

7.329 The applicant appealed to the Court of First Instance, which overturned the Board of Appeal's decision, finding that OHIM had not carried out a thorough examination of whether the marks constituted a family, and that the lack of inherent distinctive character of the prefix UNI, coupled with the nature of the opponent's use, could not result in a finding that there is a likelihood of confusion. The opponent appealed to the Court of Justice, alleging an infringement of Article 8(1)(b).

(a) *The Judgment of the Court*

7.330 In terms of the admissibility of the appeal, citing *Barbara Becker*,[296] the Court distinguished between two types of appeal. First, an appeal asserting that the Court had failed to take all relevant factors into account, which amounted to a claim that there had been an error of law

---

[293] Paragraphs 74–76.
[294] Paragraphs 80–83.
[295] C-317/10 *Union Investment Privatfonds GmbH v Office for Harmonisation in the Internal Market (Trade Marks and Designs) (OHIM)/UniCredito Italiano SpA* [2011] ECR I-05471.
[296] C-51/09 *Barbara Becker* [2010] ECR I-05805, paragraph 40.

and which may be raised in the context of an appeal. Second, an appeal alleging that errors had been made as to the evaluation of each of these factors, which was an issue of fact and therefore inadmissible.[297]

7.331 In relation to the substance of the appeal, the Court found that the General Court had distorted the context of the Board's decision and that it had excluded the existence of a likelihood of confusion without taking into consideration all relevant factors.[298] Furthermore, the Court found that the Court of First Instance had not substantiated its assertion that the element UNI did not have the inherent capacity to identify the opponent's series of marks and so did not properly analyse the Board's statement on this point.[299] The Court of Justice set aside the decision of the GC and referred the case back to the General Court.

(9) *Armafoam*: Confusion in Part of the Community

(a) *Linguistic considerations*

7.332 In *Armafoam*[300] the Court dealt with the impact of possible variations in the understanding of a Community trade mark in different parts of the Community and its impact on the assessment of likelihood of confusion. The linguistic diversity of the European Union inevitably leads to fluctuations in the perception of the same term by consumers in different Member States, which become particularly relevant when dealing with the conceptual comparison of the signs, or when assessing which is the dominant or distinctive element of a complex mark in the context of relative grounds for refusal.

7.333 The case concerned an opposition against the registration of the sign ARMAFOAM by the owner of the earlier Community trade mark NOMAFOAM. OHIM had found the signs to be confusingly similar, in particular for European consumers who do not understand English and, thus, are not in a position to grasp the descriptive connotations of the word 'foam' in relation to the goods concerned.

7.334 Referring to its settled case law in the matter,[301] the Court of First Instance concurred with the Board of Appeal that a risk of confusion does not have to be present throughout the entire territory of the European Union and that it suffices if it exists only in part of the Community, thus transposing into the context of relative grounds the rule reflected by Article 7(2) CTMR that an absolute ground of refusal applies even if its effects are limited only to part of the relevant territory.[302]

7.335 Applying that principle to the conceptual comparison, the Court of First Instance noted that, when considered in their entirety, the marks were fanciful constructions that did not convey any coherent meaning and that only English-speaking consumers were likely to perceive automatically the suffix 'foam' as a meaningful term. Accordingly, it held that, at

---

[297] *Uniweb* (n 295) paragraphs 44–47. See also paragraph 3.59 and following above.
[298] Paragraph 56.
[299] Paragraph 58.
[300] C-514/06 P *Armacell Enterprise GmbH v OHIM* (ARMAFOAM) [2008] ECR I-00128.
[301] See T-434/05 *Gateway, Inc. v OHIM* (ACTIVY MEDIA GATEWAY) [2008] ECR I-00188, paragraph 47, and the case law cited.
[302] T-172/05 *Armacell v OHIM* (ARMAFOAM) [2006] ECR II-4061, paragraph 33.

least as far as non-English-speaking consumers were concerned, the marks were visually and phonetically similar and that this overall impression of similarity could not be offset by conceptual considerations.

(b) The unitary character of Community trade marks

The Court of Justice confirmed that view, holding that it was compatible with the unitary character of Community trade marks. It explained that: 7.336

> [According to] Article 1(2) CTMR a Community trade mark has a unitary character. Subject to the exceptions of Article 106, on the prohibition of use, and of Article 107, on prior rights applicable to particular localities, the Community trade mark 'shall have equal effect throughout the Community: it shall not be registered, transferred or surrendered or be the subject of a decision revoking the rights of the proprietor or declaring it invalid, nor shall its use be prohibited, save in respect of the whole Community'.[303]
>
> Under Article 8(1)(b) and (2) [of the Regulation] where the earlier mark relied on in support of opposition proceedings is a Community trade mark, the trade mark in respect of which registration is sought will not be registered if there exists a likelihood of confusion on the part of the public in the Community territory.
>
> It does not follow from Article 8(1)(b) that, for a Community trade mark to be refused registration under that provision, the likelihood of confusion must exist in all Member States and in all linguistic areas of the Community.
>
> In fact, the unitary character of the Community trade mark means that an earlier mark can be relied on in opposition proceedings against any application for registration of a Community trade mark which would adversely affect the protection of the first mark, even if only in relation to the perception of consumers in part of the Community.[304]

It follows that the expression 'equal effects' used to describe the nature of the unitary character of the Community trade mark does not actually mean that the mark should be enforced in a 'uniform' manner. In reality, the Court has indirectly but clearly reaffirmed the rule in *Matratzen* that the application of trade mark law in the internal market is still under the influence of linguistic, even 'cultural', barriers, if not legal ones. 7.337

In practice, that means that if the weakness of a term points away from the existence of a likelihood of confusion, that factor must be present throughout the Community for confusion to be safely excluded. By contrast, if the specific meaning of a term enhances that risk, it suffices that this meaning is clear to consumers in any part of the Community for the corresponding consequences to be triggered.[305] 7.338

Accordingly, the conceptual comparison should not be carried out in the abstract, or by reference to artificial averages. Rather, it must adapt to the linguistic and cultural diversity of the European Union, taking into account the real understanding of the term concerned in the various Member States. Helpfully enough, the Courts have mitigated the practical complexity of that approach by considering that the extent to which a language is spoken or understood in a given territory is a well-known fact that 7.339

---

[303] C-9/93 *IHT Internationale Heiztechnik and Danzinger* [1994] ECR I-2789, paragraph 55.
[304] *Armafoam*, (n 300) paragraphs 54–57.
[305] See in that connection T-117/03, T-118/03, T-119/03, and T-171/03 *New Look Ltd v OHIM* (NL SPORT, NL JEANS, NL ACTIVE, NL COLLECTION) [2005] ECR II-3471.

can be relied on by the competent authority even in the absence of specific evidence or arguments.[306]

7.340 Note also that in *Zipcar*[307] the Court explicitly confirmed that the above rule applies equally to national marks, in the sense that if in a Member State there are various linguistic zones, or if the understanding of foreign languages varies from one area to another, it suffices if there is a likelihood of confusion in any part of the relevant territory. It stressed, however, that this should not be interpreted as establishing an inflexible rule of law, whereby the average consumer is always deemed to have as his/her mother tongue the language that is predominant in the Member State concerned, or to have no particular knowledge of other languages.[308]

(c) The impact on conversion

7.341 Next, the Court addressed the argument that the Court of First Instance should also have compared the marks from the point of view of English-speaking consumers, in order to determine whether the application could at least be converted into national trade marks in territories that were not affected by the rejection.

7.342 Although the Court admitted in that connection that according to Article 108(2)(b) CTMR the grounds on which a Community trade mark is rejected also determine the scope of its possible conversion, it held, nevertheless, that the Court of First Instance was not required to extend its examination to the whole of the European Union, since the purpose of opposition proceedings is 'to provide undertakings with an opportunity to oppose, by way of a single procedure, applications which might give rise to a likelihood of confusion' with their earlier marks, and not 'to resolve in advance possible conflicts at national level'.[309]

7.343 Moreover, it observed that insofar as the Court of First Instance had upheld the decision rejecting the mark only with regard to non-English speakers, its judgment did not prevent the appellant from requesting the conversion of its Community trade mark application into national trade marks in English-speaking countries.[310]

7.344 It is worth noting, however, that this last statement of the Court is contrary to the practice of OHIM to refuse conversion in cases where the rejection is based on an earlier Community trade mark, on the assumption that, due to the unitary character of that right, the ground of rejection extends, as a matter of legal fiction, to the whole of the Community territory, even if in practice there is a likelihood of confusion only in respect of certain languages.

7.345 Admittedly, that statement of the Court qualifies as *obiter dicta* to the extent that the case did not directly concern the conversion of the application at issue into national marks; it is nonetheless interesting to see whether the Court will also maintain the same view in the

---

[306] See in that connection the analysis of the Court of First Instance in T-435/07 *New Look Ltd v OHIM* (NEW LOOK) ECLI:EU:T:2008:535, paragraphs 22–25.
[307] C-394/08 P *Zipcar, Inc v OHIM* (ZIPCAR) [2009] ECR I-00095.
[308] See *Zipcar* (n 307) paragraphs 49–51.
[309] *Armafoam* (n 300) paragraphs 60–61.
[310] Paragraph 62.

H. Well-Known and Reputed Trade Marks

(1) *General Motors*: The Factors for Assessing Reputation

7.346 The first case that tested the requirements for obtaining this expanded form of protection was *General Motors Corp v Yplon SA*.[311]

7.347 The case came as a reference from the Belgian Tribunal de Commerce, Tournai. General Motors, the proprietor of the trade mark 'Chevy' for motor vehicles sought an injunction against Yplon's use of the same sign for cleaning products. The Belgian court wanted to know the extent of reputation required in order to benefit from Article 5(2) of the Directive; in particular, whether reputation within one of the Benelux countries or a part thereof would suffice.

(a) The Opinion of Advocate General Jacobs

7.348 Advocate General Jacobs considered first the relationship between 'marks with a reputation', under Article 4(4)(a) and Article 5(2) of the Directive, and 'well-known' marks, according to Article 6bis of the Paris Convention and Article 16(3) of TRIPs. He noted the exceptional character of the protection of 'well-known' marks that extended even to unregistered marks and suggested that a relatively high standard should be required for marks enjoying such protection. Indeed, all national laws employed different terms for these two concepts.[312] A mark with a 'reputation' he argued 'need not be as well known as a well-known mark'.[313] He submitted that a mark with a reputation had to be known to a significant part of the relevant sectors of the public but advocated against setting fixed criteria. Fixed criteria were potentially arbitrary; instead, courts should apply a variety of criteria including: the degree of knowledge or recognition of the mark in the relevant sectors of the public; the duration, extent, and geographical area of use of the mark; and the scale and scope of investment in promoting the mark.

7.349 Turning to the peculiarities of the Benelux trade mark system that brought protection in three national jurisdictions under the same umbrella, he agreed with the position taken by the Commission that for the purposes of Article 5(2) the Benelux territory should be assimilated to the territory of a single Member State. It would then be sufficient to have a reputation in a substantial part of the Benelux territory which could be part of only one of the Benelux countries. 'That is the sole method of recognising the cultural and linguistic differences which may exist within a Member State; thus a mark may have a regional reputation, for example in the Dutch-speaking part of Belgium.'[314]

---

[311] C-375/97 *General Motors Corp v Yplon SA* [1999] ECR I-5421.
[312] On the other hand, the Advocate General also noted that reference to 'reputation' in English could involve qualitative criteria; the same applied to the French term. See Annette Kur, 'Well-known Marks, Highly Renowned Marks and Marks Having a (High) Reputation—What's it all About?' (1992) 23 IIC 218.
[313] Point 37.
[314] Point 47.

(b) The Judgment of the Court

7.350 The Court of Justice identified a conceptual linguistic difference regarding the terms 'known' and 'reputation'. The German, Dutch, and Swedish versions used words closer to the first term without indicating the extent of knowledge required, whereas the other versions used expressions closer to 'reputation', implying 'at a quantitative level a certain degree of knowledge amongst the public'.[315] This was viewed as simply a nuance since, in the context of a uniform interpretation of Community law and the general scheme of the Directive, 'a knowledge threshold requirement emerges from a comparison of all the language versions of the Directive'.[316]

7.351 Note the language used by the Court in order to indicate the relationship that must be established between the earlier mark and the later sign in order to trigger the application of Article 5(2) and how this relationship is linked with the reputation requirement and the damage envisaged in the provision. The Court uses the term 'association' and at the same time requires a certain degree of knowledge. This degree of knowledge is pivotal because it is considered a condition for making the association and the reason for the damage suffered by the earlier mark. Later in the judgment the Court also observed that 'the stronger the earlier mark's distinctive character and reputation the easier it will be to accept that detriment has been caused to it'.[317]

> Such a requirement is also indicated by the general scheme and purpose of the Directive. In so far as Article 5(2) of the Directive, unlike Article 5(1), protects trade marks registered for non-similar products or services, its first condition implies a certain degree of knowledge of the earlier trade mark among the public. It is only where there is a sufficient degree of knowledge of that mark that the public, when confronted by the later trade mark, may possibly make an association between the two trade marks, even when used for non-similar products or services, and that the earlier trade mark may consequently be damaged.[318]

7.352 The Court then identified the public in relation to which reputation should be considered as the public 'concerned by that trade mark, that is to say, depending on the product or service marketed, either the public at large or a more specialised public, for example traders in a specific sector'.[319] It rejected the adoption of fixed percentages but required that the mark must be 'known by a significant part of the public concerned by the products or services covered by that trade mark'.[320] This should be determined by taking into consideration 'all of the relevant facts of the case, in particular the market share held by the trade mark, the intensity, geographical extent and duration of its use, and the size of the investment made by the undertaking in promoting it'.[321] In terms of territorial coverage the Court held that it would be sufficient to have a reputation in 'a substantial part'[322] of the relevant Member State, and in this case this substantial part could be a part of one of the Benelux countries.

---

[315] Paragraph 21.
[316] Paragraph 22.
[317] Paragraph 30.
[318] Paragraph 23.
[319] Paragraph 24.
[320] Paragraph 26.
[321] Paragraph 27.
[322] Paragraph 28.

(2) *Fincas Tarragona*: Marks Well Known 'in a Member State'

(a) Well-known v reputed marks

In *Fincas*[323] the question referred to the Court did not relate to the notion of 'reputation', but rather to the specific protection afforded to trade marks which are 'well-known in a Member State, in the sense in which the words "well-known" are used in Article 6bis of the Paris Convention', within the meaning of Article 4(2)(b) of the Directive.

7.353

So far, the relationship between 'reputed' and 'well-known' marks has not been fully explored by the Court of Justice. Although in *General Motors*[324] and *Nasdaq*[325] the Court briefly addressed specific facets of the interrelation between them, it refrained from carrying out a full-scale comparison of the relevant provisions of the Directive and the CTMR[326] on the grounds that such a comparative analysis was not strictly necessary for the purposes of those cases.

7.354

On the other hand, the Court seems to be accepting, at least indirectly, that the notions of 'reputation' and 'well-known character' present a number of similar traits which approximate them to a significant extent. It follows from the statements of the Court that these notions are 'kindred concepts'[327] that imply a 'knowledge threshold requirement'[328] and is further stressed by its frequent reference to 'well-known' marks in the context of provisions actually dealing with trade marks with a reputation.

7.355

In that regard, the Court of First Instance seems to have taken a further step towards the full assimilation of 'well-known' and 'reputed' marks by taking the view that the underlying requirements of 'reputation' and 'well-known' character are overlapping, at least insofar as the conditions for the acquisition of the relevant rights are concerned. This can be inferred from the position it adopted in *Tosca Blu*[329] that Article 8(5) CTMR also applies to 'well-known' marks within the meaning of Article 8(2)(c) of that regulation, on the sole condition that the latter have been registered, as also suggested by Article 16(3) of the TRIPs Agreement.

7.356

That is also the practice of OHIM, which although it recognizes that the function and scope of the above provisions are different, nevertheless applies essentially the same criteria in terms of market recognition and brand awareness when determining whether the substantive requirements laid down by them have been met.[330] This is further attested if the wording used by the Court in General Motors for marking the requisite threshold for reputation, namely that the mark must be 'known by a significant part of the [relevant] public',[331]

7.357

---

[323] C-328/06 *Alfredo Nieto Nuño v Leonci Monlleó Franquet* (FINCAS TARRAGONA) [2007] ECR I-40093.
[324] *General Motors* (n 311) paragraphs 13–23.
[325] C-320/07 P *Antartica Srl v OHIM* (NASDAQ) [2009] ECR I-00028, paragraph 51.
[326] These are Articles 4(2)(b) of the Directive and 8(2)(c) CTMR in respect of well-known marks and Articles 4(4)(a) and 5(2) of the Directive and 8(5) and 9(1)(c) CTMR in respect of trade marks with a reputation.
[327] *General Motors* (n 311) paragraph 22.
[328] cf the English version of the judgment in *Gofkid* in C-292/00 *Davidoff* [2003] ECR I-389.
[329] See the judgment of the Court of First Instance in T-150/04 *Tosca Blu* [2007] ECR II-02353, paragraphs 49–61.
[330] See Guidelines Concerning Procedures before the Office for Harmonisation in the Internal Market (Trade Marks and Designs), Pt C: Opposition Guidelines Pt 5: Trade marks with reputation—Article 8(5) CTMR Ch III, s 3.2, pp 375–76, available on the website of the Office: <http://oami.europa.eu>.
[331] *General Motors* (n 311) paragraph 26.

is compared to the very similar expression used by the WIPO Recommendations on the Protection of Well-Known Marks, ie that a trade mark is well known if it is 'known in the relevant sector' of the market.[332]

(b) The facts in the main proceedings

7.358 In *Fincas* the reference concerned a dispute between Mr Nieto Nuño, proprietor in Spain of the word mark FINCAS TARRAGONA, covering 'management of property in sole or joint ownership, letting of property, sale of property, legal advice and property development' in Class 36 of the Nice Classification, and Mr Monlleó Franquet, an estate agent in the city of Tarragona, who had used, over a period of several years, the expression 'FINCAS TARRAGONA', in Spanish, or 'FINQUES TARRAGONA', in Catalán, for the purpose of designating his business. Mr Nieto Nuño brought proceedings under Spanish trade mark law before the Juzgado de lo Mercantil 3 de Barcelona against Mr Monlleó Franquet, arguing that the latter had infringed his registered trade mark.

7.359 Mr Monlleó Franquet maintained in his defence that the name under which he conducted his business was an earlier well-known trade mark, which he had been using prior to the filing of Mr Nieto Nuño's mark and put forward a counterclaim seeking the annulment of that registration.

7.360 The national court observed that the defendant in the main proceedings used his non-registered mark only in the city of Tarragona and its surrounding area, meaning that the relevant public, consisting of Mr Monlleó Franquet's clientele, customers, and competitors, was limited to that territory and, thus, extended neither to the whole of Spain, nor to a significant part of it.

7.361 Against that background, the Juzgado de lo Mercantil 3 de Barcelona decided to stay the proceedings and to refer the following question to the Court of Justice for a preliminary ruling:

> Must the concept of trade marks which are 'well known' in a Member State, referred to in Article 4 of [the Directive] be taken to indicate solely and exclusively the degree of knowledge and establishment in a Member State or in a significant part of the territory of that State, or may the determination of whether a mark is well known be linked to a territorial scope which does not coincide with that of the territory of a State but rather with an autonomous community, region, district or city, depending on the goods or services which the mark covers and the persons to whom the mark is actually addressed, in short, depending on the market in which the mark is used?

(c) The Opinion of Advocate General Mengozzi

7.362 Advocate General Mengozzi started his examination by making an extensive analysis of the relevant provisions of the Directive against the backdrop of the Paris Convention and its derivative Treaties, in order to determine the purpose and function of the corresponding provisions under Spanish Law.

7.363 In particular, he observed that Article 6bis of the Paris Convention, at least within the scope attributed to it by Article 16(2) of the TRIPs Agreement, applies both where the mark has

---

[332] See Article 2(2)(c) of the WIPO Recommendations [1999] concerning Provisions on the Protection of Well-Known Marks, available following the links at <http://www.wipo.int>.

become well known following its use in the territory of the State where protection is sought and where it has become well known without being used there in the strict sense, but rather as a result of the spillover effect of promotional campaigns and advertising carried out in that State or even outside its territory.[333]

7.364 He then suggested that the trade mark rights acquired by virtue of such use are in fact covered both by Article 4(2)(b) and by Article 4(4)(b) of the Directive, respectively relating to well-known and *de facto* trade marks, and that Member States were free not only to grant protection to unregistered trade marks, thus recognizing that the mere use of a sign gives rise to an exclusive right, but also to define the conditions and scope of that protection.[334]

7.365 Based on the premise that such a protection may be available not only where the knowledge of the mark has achieved a particular geographical dimension, but also without any specific requirement as to a minimum awareness of the sign on the part of the public or the territorial extent of its use,[335] Advocate General Mengozzi proposed to answer the question referred to the Court to the effect that Article 4 of the Directive did not preclude the cancellation of a later trade mark on the basis of an earlier unregistered trade mark which is well known not throughout the territory of the State concerned, or a substantial part of it, but only in a more limited geographical area.

(d) The Judgment of the Court

7.366 The Court did not share the view put forward by the Advocate General. First, it noted that the question referred to it was limited to the geographical area in which the mark must be known and not to the overall criteria for assessing whether it is indeed well known, considered in terms of the degree of knowledge of the mark among the public. Second, it observed that, according to the facts in the main proceedings, the mark at issue was not known throughout the territory of the Member State of protection, or in a substantial part of it, but was merely well known in a city and its surrounding area.

7.367 Moreover, it pointed out that although the provision under interpretation lacked a definition in that regard, a trade mark could not be required to be well known 'throughout' the territory of the Member State, being sufficient for it to be well known in a substantial part of it,[336] by analogy to what applied to the kindred concept of 'reputation', which, for the purposes of Article 5(2) of the Directive, had also to be assessed 'in the Member State' concerned.[337]

7.368 The Court stressed, however, that the customary meaning of the expression 'in a Member State' precluded the application of that provision to a situation where the well-known status of the mark is limited to a city and to its surrounding area which, together, do not constitute a substantial part of the Member State.[338] However, this did not preclude the possibility to protect unregistered signs with a local repute pursuant to Article 4(4)(b) of the Directive, covering *de facto* trade marks, or under Article 6(2) thereof, governing the protection of rights that only apply in a particular locality. Accordingly, the Court interpreted

---

[333] Point 41.
[334] Points 42–45.
[335] Point 46.
[336] *Fincas* (n 323) paragraph 17.
[337] As held in *General Motors* (n 311) paragraph 28.
[338] *Fincas* (n 323) paragraphs 18–21.

Article 4(2)(d) of the Directive as meaning that the earlier trade mark must be well known throughout the territory of the Member State of protection or in a substantial part of it and that local knowledge, such as the one limited to a city and to its surrounding area, was not enough if that area does not constitute a substantial part of the Member State in issue.

7.369 Furthermore, apart from clarifying the territorial scope of the expression 'in a Member State' by using the same criteria as those applicable to reputed marks, the judgment in *Fincas* is also important because it clarified that although the mark must be known in the territory of a Member State, the concept of a 'well-known' trade mark under the Directive and the conditions for its protection must be interpreted not according to the legislation of that State, but in a uniform manner throughout the Community, being a notion of European rather than national law.

(3) *Pago*: Reputation 'in the Community'

7.370 *Pago*[339] is the necessary complement to *General Motors* with regard to the territorial scope of reputation; while in *General Motors* and *Fincas* the Court dealt with the geographical extent of the knowledge required for a sign to qualify as a mark with reputation or as a mark well known 'in a Member State', in *Pago* the question was about the meaning of the expression reputation 'in the Community', within the meaning of Article 9(l)(c) CTMR.

(a) *The facts in the main proceedings*

7.371 The order for reference was made in the context of a dispute between PAGO International GmbH ('Pago GmbH') and Tirol Milch registrierte Genossenschaft mbH ('Tirol Milch'). Pago GmbH was the proprietor of a Community trade mark, registered in respect of, inter alia, fruit drinks and fruit juices. Its mark essentially consisted of the representation of a green glass bottle, used by Pago for a number of years in marketing, next to a distinctive label and cap reproducing a device of a full glass of fruit drink and the word 'Pago' in large characters.

7.372 Tirol Milch marketed in Austria a fruit and whey drink called 'Lattella', packaged in glass bottles whose design resembled in several respects (shape, colour, label, cap) the one depicted in the Community trade mark of Pago GmbH. In the advertising for its drink Tirol Milch used a representation which also shows a bottle next to a full glass.

7.373 From the facts set out in the order for reference it appeared that there was no likelihood of confusion between the signs, since the bottle labels used by Pago GmbH and Tirol Milch bore the names 'Pago' and 'Latella' respectively and both names were widely known in Austria. Rather, the parties to the main action proceeded on the basis that the conditions of Article 9(1)(c) CTMR had been met in as much as, first, the sign in dispute was similar to the earlier Community trade mark of Pago GmbH, and, second, the drink marketed by Tirol Milch was not similar to the juice marketed by Pago. Pago GmbH sought an injunction before the Handelsgericht Wien prohibiting Tirol Milch from: (i) promoting, offering for sale, marketing, or otherwise using its drink in the bottles at issue; and (ii) advertising a representation of the bottles together with a full glass. That court granted the injunction

---

[339] C-301/07 *PAGO International GmbH v Tirol Milch registrierte Genossenschaft mbH* (PAGO) [2009] ECR I-09429.

but its decision was reversed by the Oberlandesgericht Wien. Pago appealed to the Oberster Gerichtshof.

The Oberster Gerichtshof took the view that the question whether there had been an infringement of Pago's Community trade mark was to be assessed solely in accordance with the CTMR. However, since Pago's trade mark was widely known in Austria but not necessarily in other Member States, the Oberster Gerichtshof considered that it required guidance as to how the phrase '[has] a reputation in the Community' in Article 9(1)(c) of the Regulation should be construed, and referred the following questions for a preliminary ruling: **7.374**

(1) Is a Community Trade Mark protected in the whole of the Community as a 'trade mark with a reputation' for the purposes of Article 9(1)(c) of the Regulation if it has a 'reputation' only in one Member State?
(2) If the answer to the first question is in the negative: is a mark which has a 'reputation' only in one Member State protected in that Member State under Article 9(1)(c) of the Regulation, so that a prohibition limited to that Member State may be issued?

(b) The Opinion of Advocate General Sharpston

(i) **Reputation 'in the Community'** Should *General Motors* apply by analogy? Advocate General Sharpston observed at the outset of her Opinion that even though the first question is put in a way suggesting that the answer should be either 'yes' or 'no', implying that whichever answer is given will be equally applicable in every case in which the mark has a reputation in a single Member State, it was necessary to approach the issue in a more flexible manner. In any event, she agreed with the parties that *General Motors* provided the starting point for the analysis, to the extent that it had already established that, as a matter of principle, a national trade mark need not have a reputation throughout the territory of the Member State where it is registered and that, accordingly, it is sufficient for a Benelux trade mark to have a reputation in a substantial part of the Benelux territory, which might consist of a part of one of the Benelux countries.[340] **7.375**

However, although she remarked that the first part of that finding was necessarily transposable to the question at issue, she did not agree that asking whether one Member State could be considered as a 'substantial part' of the Community was the right way of approaching the question. The Advocate General stressed that the CTMR is based on the premise that the Community trade mark is unitary in character and that an approach which focused on Member State boundaries when seeking to establish the extent of a Community trade mark's reputation was, in consequence, fundamentally misconceived. Rather, the starting point must be the territory of the Community, regardless of frontiers, as a single and indivisible whole. As a corollary, it is irrelevant whether a reputation exists in one Member State or any given number of Member States. It is likewise irrelevant whether those Member States are 'big', 'medium-sized', or 'small' (on whatever basis those terms are defined).[341] **7.376**

Instead, the Advocate General proposed the following alternative test: As a starting point, it is necessary for the national court to establish whether the trade mark has a 'reputation'; in doing so, it must first identify the public concerned by the trade mark in the context of the Community as a whole, without regard to national borders; second, it should proceed to **7.377**

---

[340] *General Motors* (n 311) paragraphs 28–29.
[341] Point 29.

determine whether the reputation exists amongst a significant part of the public concerned. The national court must then determine whether the trade mark indeed has a reputation 'in the Community', bearing in mind that the trade mark proprietor need not demonstrate that the trade mark has a reputation throughout the Community, but only in a 'substantial part' of it.[342]

7.378 Next, the Advocate General recalled that, in *Fincas*, the Court had established in relation to the kindred concept of 'well-known' marks, what is not a 'substantial part' of the relevant territory, by holding that the city of Tarragona and its surrounding area within Spain were not a substantial part of that Member State. She went on to note that if that reasoning is applied by analogy to the question *sub judice*, it follows that where the 'part' concerned is, in terms of its size and economic weight, paltry in comparison with the entire Community and where the relevant public is more widely spread, that part cannot be deemed to constitute a 'substantial part' of the Community as a whole. She moreover observed that this conclusion is further supported by the ordinary meaning of the term 'substantial' and also accords with common sense.

7.379 Thus, Advocate General Sharpston concluded that, as with the concept of relevant public, the territorial aspect of 'reputation' cannot be defined by reference to an abstract figure or a particular number of Member States. The national court will have to evaluate a number of factors to determine whether a particular trade mark enjoys a reputation in a substantial part of the Community. Such factors will include, but not be limited to, the economic significance of the territory within the Community, the geographical extent of the area where the trade mark has a reputation, and the demographics of the public concerned.

7.380 Finally, the Advocate General dismissed the Article 51 CTMR argument put forward by Pago GmbH that if use in one Member State is sufficient to preserve the rights relating to a Community trade mark, reputation in that State should, by analogy, be sufficient to trigger the protection conferred by Article 9(l)(c), by noting that the different subject matter of the two provisions rendered the drawing of analogies between them quite inappropriate.

7.381 Thus, the main steps of the Advocate General's reasoning can be summed up as follows:[343]

(a) it is not possible to establish whether a Community trade mark has a reputation in the Community on the basis of whether that trade mark has a reputation in any one Member State;

(b) it follows from the unitary character of the Community trade mark that the Community territory should be considered as a whole;

(c) *General Motors* should be applied by analogy to establish what constitutes a substantial part of the Community;

(d) this must be determined in any particular case by taking account of the public concerned by the products or services covered by the trade mark and the importance of the area where the reputation exists, as defined by factors such as its geographical extent, population, and economic significance.

---

[342] Points 30–31.
[343] Point 40.

7.382 She proposed to answer the first question to the effect that a trade mark has a 'reputation in the Community' within the meaning of Article 9(1)(c) CTMR if it has a reputation in a substantial part of the Community, adding that what constitutes a substantial part of the Community for that purpose should not be dependent on national boundaries but must be determined by an assessment of all the relevant circumstances of the case, taking account, in particular, of: (i) the public concerned by the products or services covered by the trade mark and the proportion of that public which knows of the mark; and (ii) the importance of the area in which the reputation exists, as defined by factors such as its geographical extent, population, and economic significance.

7.383 **(ii) Is local reputation sufficient for obtaining an injunction?** In dealing with the second question, the Advocate General observed that the core of the matter is whether a Community trade mark which has a reputation only in one Member State, and thus cannot be said to have a reputation in the Community, is nonetheless protected in that Member State, so that a prohibition against infringement limited to that Member State may be issued.

7.384 In that connection, she considered that it was implicit in the answer to the first question that a trade mark which has a reputation in only one Member State does not qualify as a trade mark with a 'reputation in the Community'. Given that the existence of a 'reputation in the Community' is the specific condition required to trigger Article 9(1)(c), the answer to the second question is obvious: if that condition is not satisfied, no right to protection arises and the national court should not grant relief to enforce a legal right that does not exist.[344] Moreover, she dismissed the argument that, if such limited protection did not exist, the Community trade mark would not be a viable alternative to national trade marks, because its proprietor would be unable to protect his interests in that Member State without also owning a national trade mark.

7.385 First, she noted that although it is true that Community and national trade marks have similar purposes, in as much as the objective of both Article 9(1)(c) CTMR and Article 5(2) of the Directive is to provide protection against damage to reputation, they reach that objective by different routes and operate in different contexts. Contrary to national trade marks, the unitary nature of the Community trade mark means that it is effectively protected throughout the Community and not merely in the part where it was found to have a reputation. Thus, it is precisely because the protection afforded to a Community trade mark is so extensive that the conditions laid down in the Regulation must be satisfied in full before it is triggered.

7.386 Second, even though she admitted that where a Community trade mark has a reputation in a Member State but not in a substantial part of the Community, national registration in that Member State will be necessary in order to protect the reputation of the mark in that territory, she found this to be generally consistent with the concept that the Community trade mark and national trade marks operate at different levels, but in parallel.

7.387 Accordingly, Advocate General Sharpston suggested that the second question should be answered to the effect that a Community trade mark which has a reputation in an area which is not a substantial part of the Community does not enjoy, under Article 9(1)(c)

---

[344] Point 44.

CTMR, protection limited to that area. Consequently, a prohibition against infringement limited to that area may not be issued.

(c) The Judgment of the Court

7.388 The judgment of the Court in *Pago* proved less thrilling than anticipated. Taking a rather cautious approach, the Court stuck closely to the principles derived from its previous case law as regards the territorial extent of reputation, refusing to advance the discussion beyond what was strictly necessary to resolve the dispute in the main proceedings.

7.389 Before dealing with the core of the matter, however, the Court made a short digression to deal with an outstanding matter regarding the similarity of the goods. It noted that even though it was not apparent from the order for reference whether the products at issue (respectively, fruit drinks and juices and a fruit and whey drink) were similar or not, it is clear from *Davidoff*[345] that, notwithstanding the wording of Article 9(1)(c) and in the light of the overall scheme and objectives of the Regulation, the protection afforded to marks with a reputation cannot be less where a sign is used for identical goods and services than where it is used for dissimilar goods.

7.390 Turning then to the first question addressed to it by the Oberster Gerichtshof, the Court observed that it was called upon to decide on two closely interrelated issues: first, to clarify the meaning of the expression 'reputation in the Community' and, second, to state whether that condition is satisfied from a geographical point of view where the Community trade mark has a reputation in only one Member state. The Court answered the first limb by drawing heavily on *General Motors*,[346] considering that the principles already laid down in that judgment with regard to the nature, conditions, assessment, and territorial extent of reputation in relation to Benelux marks were applicable by analogy to the expression 'reputation in the Community'.

7.391 First, it reiterated that the concept of 'reputation' assumes a certain degree of knowledge amongst the relevant public concerned by the Community trade mark, that is to say, depending on the product or service in question, either the public at large or a more specialized public.[347]

7.392 Second, it noted that it cannot be required that the Community trade mark be known by a given percentage of the relevant public and that the requisite knowledge threshold must be considered to have been reached when the mark is known by a 'significant part of the public concerned by the relevant products or services'. It also stressed that, in examining this condition, the examining authority must take into consideration all the relevant facts, in particular the market share held by the trade mark, the intensity, geographical extent, and duration of its use, and the size of the investment made by the undertaking in promoting it.[348] To the extent that this assessment is of a factual nature, the Court held that it was for the referring court to determine, in view of the elements of the main proceedings, whether the Community trade mark PAGO was known by a significant part of the public concerned by the goods.[349]

---

[345] C-292/00 *Davidoff* [2003] ECR I-389, paragraphs 24–25, taken in the context of Article 5(2) of the Trade Mark Directive.
[346] C-375/97 *General Motors* [1999] ECR I-5421.
[347] Paragraphs 21–22.
[348] Paragraphs 23–25.
[349] Paragraph 26.

Third, the Court affirmed that, territorially, the reputation requirement must be considered to be fulfilled when the Community trade mark has a reputation in a 'substantial' part of the Community, in the same way as Benelux trade marks have to be reputed in a substantial part of the Benelux territory, which part may consist of a part of one of the Benelux countries.[350] **7.393**

Then the Court turned to the second limb of the question, namely whether the condition of reputation is satisfied where the Community trade mark has a reputation in a single Member State. In this regard, it confined itself to observing that: **7.394**

> as the present case concerns a Community trade mark with a reputation throughout the territory of a Member State, namely Austria, the view may be taken, regard being had to the circumstances of the main proceedings, that the territorial requirement imposed by Article 9(1)(c) of the regulation is satisfied

and noted that, in view of this answer, there was no need to reply to the second question which had become devoid of purpose.[351]

On those grounds, the Court answered the first question of the Oberster Gerichtshof to the effect that Article 9(1)(c) of the Regulation must be interpreted as meaning that, in order to benefit from the protection afforded in that provision, a Community trade mark must be known by a significant part of the public concerned by the products or services covered by that trade mark, in a substantial part of the territory of the European Community, and that, in view of the facts of the main proceedings, the territory of the Member State in question may be considered to constitute a substantial part of the territory of the Community.[352] **7.395**

(d) Conclusions

The main interpretative challenge in *Pago* is how to accommodate the Court's pronouncements at paragraph 29 about reputation in Austria within the nexus of the principles that precede it. The brevity and elliptic language of this part of the judgment raise a number of questions which call for a closer analysis. **7.396**

The first question is of a systematic nature and has to do with the role performed by territorial considerations in the assessment of reputation. According to paragraphs 25 and 26 of the judgment, it is for the national court to assess whether the mark is known by a significant part of the relevant public, taking into account, among other factors, the geographical extent of the use of the mark. In that assessment, the geographical extent does not seem to occupy any special position or enjoy any primacy vis-à-vis the other factors. As such, it is subject to the interdependence principle, in the sense that a relatively narrow geographical extent could be offset by other circumstances, like a higher intensity or duration of use. Conversely, at paragraphs 27 and 29 of the judgment, the territorial criterion is mentioned in isolation, ie as a stand-alone condition which requires that the mark be known at least in a substantial part of the relevant territory. This seems to imply that the territorial aspect has been detached from the rest of the factors, in order to become a separate condition that is subject to a *de minimis* threshold. The Court, however, does not explain how the same factor can be used with a different value in two parts of the same assessment or why this should be so. **7.397**

---

[350] Paragraphs 27–28.
[351] Paragraphs 29 and 31.
[352] Paragraph 30.

7.398 The second question raises a point of principle and has to do with the importance of national borders. After observing that, for Benelux marks, the relevant territory may consist of a part of one of the Benelux countries, the Court went on to conclude, at paragraph 29, that 'as the case concerns a mark with a reputation throughout the territory of a Member State, namely Austria' and 'regard being had to the circumstances of the main proceedings' the conditions of Article 9(1)(c) are deemed to be fulfilled. Although this statement is clearly of a factual nature and should, as a matter of principle, have been left for the national court to determine, it seems that the Court opted for this solution because it felt the need to provide the Oberster Gerichtshof with a workable solution that would irrevocably settle the dispute in the main proceedings. This derogation from ordinary practice shows a conscious hesitation on the part of the Court to define what constitutes a 'substantial part of the Community' in the abstract.

7.399 Moreover, it is not clear from this double reference whether it was the knowledge throughout Austria, the additional circumstances of the case, or the combination of the two that tipped the balance in favour of the finding that the mark at issue had met the requisite standards. If the reference to the circumstances of the main proceedings is seen as incidental, the first hypothesis would be true and the inference could be drawn that knowledge throughout the area of a Member State is tantamount to knowledge in a 'substantial part of the Community'. This interpretation finds some support in the analogy drawn by the Court between the situation in the Benelux and the Community, as paragraph 28 of the Judgment seems to suggest. If this is indeed the case, it would mean that also knowledge in a 'part of the territory of a Member State' could prove enough to support a finding of reputation.

7.400 However, this reading does not follow unequivocally from paragraph 29 of the Judgment as the additional reference to the remaining circumstances of the case cannot be simply ignored. On the contrary, the conditional language used the operative part of the Judgment, according to which the territory of the Member State in question 'may' be considered to constitute a substantial part of the territory of the Community, 'in view of the facts of the main proceedings', seems to confirm that it was actually the third hypothesis that the Court had in mind.

7.401 If this is true, the Court's omission to specify further which these facts and circumstances are and explain how they specifically affect the assessment comes as a disappointment, all the more so since those facts and circumstances do not seem to be the same as the ones that pertain to the assessment of whether the mark is known by a significant part of the public, considering that this other pillar of the assessment is treated independently from the territorial question. Logically, however, there are no other factors one could imagine to fill the systematic gap. It therefore seems that leaving all possibilities open was the easy way out for the Court, which chose to disengage itself from a highly politicized debate by merely converting the crux of the matter into a question of fact.

7.402 In view of all these uncertainties the judgment in *Pago* is of limited practical value beyond the confines of the specific case. From a systematic point of view, it is unsafe to draw the conclusion that knowledge throughout one Member State is generally enough or, for that matter, that it is required at all. Nor can it be argued that such knowledge is sufficient at least for medium-sized Member States like Austria, but not for other, smaller Member States. For so long as the Court remains silent on this point, it will not be possible to arrive at clear conclusions about the relevance of national borders or the extent to which they can be decisive for the examination of reputation.

(4) *Davidoff v Gofkid*: The scope of Article 5(2)

Despite the fact that the language of the provision was clear, in *Davidoff v Gofkid*[353] the Court was asked to consider whether Article 5(2) and Article 4(4) also covered identical or similar goods or services. *Gofkid* is a peculiar case. First, the Court appears to forego the distinction between marks with a reputation and well-known marks, referring only to well-known marks. Apparently, this was the result of a translational breakdown. Still, the fact that it went unnoticed is perhaps evidence of the conceptual uncertainties trade mark law is facing. Second, the Court did not follow the path indicated by the Advocate General; this is not unusual as such but the Court also avoided a textual analysis of the provision that would be consistent with its interpretive approach in *Sabel*.[354] The case was referred to the Court of Justice by the German Bundesgerichtshof (Federal Court of Justice). Davidoff was the owner of the homonymous trade mark for, inter alia, goods in Classes 14 ('precious metals and their alloys and goods in precious metals or coated therewith, not included in other classes; jewellery, precious stones; homological and chronometric instruments') and 34 ('tobacco; smokers' articles; matches'). It started proceedings against use by Gofkid of the later trade mark 'Durffee' registered in a particular script (the 'D' and 'ff' elements in 'Durffee' were similar to those in 'Davidoff') for goods in Classes 14 and 34.

7.403

The German Court decided that the outcome of the case relied, first, on whether protection of marks with a reputation covered cases where the relevant goods or services are identical or similar, but there is no likelihood of confusion[355] and, second, on whether the additional protection may be granted only in cases where the use of the sign would take unfair advantage of, or be detrimental to, the distinctive character or repute of the earlier mark, or whether other national rules may also be applied. Both questions were triggered by the finding that before the adoption of the new national law in 1995,[356] that transposed the Directive, trade mark law in conjunction with the Act Against Unfair Competition[357] would prevent use of a sign similar to a well-known mark that possessed a particular reputation and prestige value if the sign deliberately and without any overriding necessity resembled the earlier mark.

7.404

(a) *The Opinion of Advocate General Jacobs*

The Advocate General recognized that the literal terms of the Directive appeared to leave a gap regarding the protection of marks with a reputation that could be filled by the proposition that, since Article 4(4)(a) and Article 5(2) enable protection against use on

7.405

---

[353] C-292/00 *Davidoff & Cie SA v Gofkid* [2003] ECR I-389.
[354] C-251/95 *Sabel BV* [1997] ECR I-6191.
[355] Note that the wording of the first question was perhaps wider; however, both the Advocate General and the Court of Justice were satisfied that this is what in essence the German Court wanted to know. The actual question was:

> Are the provisions of Article 4(4)(a) and Article 5(2) to be interpreted (and where appropriate applied) as also entitling the Member States to provide more extensive protection for marks with a reputation in cases where the later mark is used or to be used for goods or services identical with or similar to those in respect of which the earlier mark is registered?

[356] See Fammler, 'The New German Act on Marks: EC Harmonisation and Comprehensive Reform' [1995] EIPR 22.
[357] See <http://www.wipo.int/wipolex/en/details.jsp?id=990> for the text of the 1994 version of the Act; for an example of relevant jurisprudence see *Shell* [1996] EIPR D-45. The current 2010 version can be found at <http://www.wipo.int/wipolex/en/text.jsp?file_id=229699>.

dissimilar products, they must, *a fortiori*, enable such protection where the products are similar.

7.406 (i) **The ambiguities of *Sabel* and *General Motors*** He noted that according to one reading of *Sabel*[358] and *General Motors*[359] the Court had accepted that protection under Article 4(4)(a) and Article 5(2) was an extension of 'a comparable protection available where [the marks] are similar';[360] the Court had stated that protection of a mark with a reputation can be achieved 'even where' or 'when' the later signs are used on non-similar products.

7.407 On another reading, however, 'even where/when' need not necessarily be taken to mean 'including cases where', that is to say 'in cases where products are similar and also in cases where they are not'. It might also be seen as stressing the difference which was highlighted by the Court in *Canon*:[361] 'In contrast to Article 4(4)(a), which expressly refers to the situation in which the goods or services are not similar, Article 4(1)(b) provides that the likelihood of confusion presupposes that the goods or services covered are identical or similar.' Moreover, those statements were not findings of law underpinning the rulings in the two cases in question but rather commentaries on related points; in neither case was the use of the word 'even' by the Court germane to the matter under consideration.[362]

7.408 Accordingly, the Court had to look at the provision from the very beginning.

7.409 (ii) **A literal interpretation** The linguistic clarity of the provision was compelling for the Advocate General:

> Where a legislative provision is clear, it is in principle unnecessary and undesirable to look behind the terms adopted. That having been said, however, in the present case the drafting history of the Directive—which is closely linked to that of the Regulation—tends to support a literal interpretation.[363]

7.410 In the Preamble to the Directive there was no indication that protection of marks with a reputation should encompass similar or identical products. Placing the provision in its historical context he noted that in the original proposal for the Directive protection was limited against use of identical or similar products. The extended protection was the result of the adoption of a provision on marks with a reputation by the Community Trade Mark Regulation; this was intended to be an advantage of the Community trade mark system as opposed to national trade mark systems.[364] In addition, the wording of the Directive was deliberately chosen; despite the suggestion 'that the protection in question should extend to use for both similar and dissimilar goods, the legislature chose a form of words which referred to dissimilar products alone'.[365]

7.411 (iii) **The protection gap** Considering the argumentation for an interpretation to the contrary he found it not to be compelling. Citing *Marca Mode*,[366] he stated that confusion

---

[358] Referring to paragraph 20 of C-251/95 *Sabel BV* [1997] ECR I-6191.
[359] Referring to paragraph 23 of C-375/97 *General Motors Corp* [1999] ECR I-5421.
[360] Point 30.
[361] C-39/97 *Canon Kabushiki Kaisha* [1998] ECR I-5507, paragraph 22.
[362] Point 31.
[363] Point 34.
[364] See Bulletin of the European Communities, 1980 Supplement 5/80, p 13.
[365] Point 36, citing the Opinion of the Economic and Social Committee (1981) OJ C 310/22, recommending that the Directive should follow the Regulation in specifying that signs similar to well-known marks 'may not be used for dissimilar goods either'.
[366] C-425/98 *Marca Mode CV v Adidas AG & Adidas Benelux BV* [2000] ECR I-4861.

cannot be inferred from reputation alone. So, a gap might exist where use of a similar sign makes a link with an earlier mark with a reputation but additional information explicitly denies the connection required for establishing confusion.[367] He suggested that even in such cases there may be in the end a likelihood of confusion.

7.412 But even if there was no confusion the earlier mark could still be protected according to his interpretation of Article 4(1) and Article 5(1), on the one hand, and Article 4(4)(a) and Article 5(2), on the other. The importance of distinctiveness for establishing confusion, recognized by the Court in *Sabel*[368] and *Canon*,[369] provided the key for this continuum of protection. The starting point was that marks 'having a reputation thus do not enjoy a separate and independent system of protection but rather the same general protection as is afforded to all marks, together with a specific, supplementary and optional protection',[370] dependent on specific and distinct confusion criteria. However, a particularly distinctive character, that could be either inherent or the result of reputation, would assist in bridging the gap in the global appreciation of confusion test:

> Thus, although there may be an area in which a trade mark having a reputation is not protected against the use of identical or similar marks or signs—namely where the products in question are similar and there is no likelihood of confusion—the very definition of that area means that it is likely to be insignificant in practice, and its extent is still further limited by the Court's case law. In deliberately not providing for that area, moreover, the legislature may well have been expressing its intention that likelihood of confusion should be the normal criterion for protection. It may also have had in mind that the area of dissimilar products is one in which dishonest operators might well take unfair advantage of a well-known mark unless extra protection is granted, whereas it would be considerably more difficult to take such advantage in the area of similar products without giving rise to a likelihood of confusion.[371]

7.413 He concluded that an interpretation to the contrary would cause legal uncertainty and would limit the pool of potential Community trade marks, since more national trade mark rights could be raised as obstacles according to Article 8(5) of the Regulation. This would go against the objective of Article 14 of the EC Treaty—the achievement of an internal market—that underlined the Directive.

(b) The Judgment of the Court

7.414 The Advocate General had built up an almost foolproof case for a literal interpretation. Confusion as to origin constituted the legitimizing backbone of the Directive and the consistent mantra of the earlier jurisprudence of the Court of Justice. Derogations from the mantra should be interpreted strictly. However, this time, the Court chose a different and much shorter route; it started by observing that Article 5(2)—and, *mutatis mutandis*, Article 4(4)—must be interpreted in the light 'of the overall scheme and objectives of the system of which it is a part'[372] rather than in an exclusively literal manner.

---

[367] He referred to C-206/01 *Arsenal Football Club Plc* [2002] ECR I-10273, which was then pending before the Court, as an example.
[368] C-251/95 *Sabel BV* [1997] ECR I-6191.
[369] C-39/97 *Canon Kabushiki Kaisha* [1998] ECR I-5507.
[370] Point 46.
[371] Point 51.
[372] *Davidoff* (n 353) paragraph 24.

7.415 Hostage to the argument that Article 5(2) provided more rather than different protection compared with Article 5(1), the Court held that it 'cannot be given an interpretation which would lead to marks with a reputation having less protection where a sign is used for identical or similar goods or services than where a sign is used for non-similar goods or services'.[373]

7.416 Linking the scope of protection under the two articles the Court noted that in the absence of confusion, Article 5(1)(b) 'could not be relied on by the proprietor of a mark with a reputation to protect himself against impairment of the distinctive character or repute of the mark'.[374] Accordingly, Article 4(4) and Article 5(2) entitled Member States to provide specific protection for registered trade marks with a reputation against use of similar marks or signs on identical or similar goods or services.

(5) *Fitnessworld*: The Interpretive Limits of *Davidoff*

7.417 In *Adidas v Fitnessworld*[375] the Court looked at three questions referred by the Hoge Raad: first, whether Article 5(2) covered identical and similar as well as dissimilar goods or services and, following the intervention of the United Kingdom, the extent of freedom that national legislatures enjoyed, following the Court's interpretation of Article 5(2) in *Davidoff*;[376] second, whether there was a test, distinct from *Sabel*,[377] for determining similarity between marks for the purposes of Article 5(2); and, third, whether use of a sign as an embellishment constitutes infringement of an earlier similar trade mark.

7.418 Adidas, based on its registration of the 'three stripes' device mark in the Benelux—a mark that was found to be strong and enjoying general recognition—started trade mark infringement proceedings against Fitnessworld, which marketed clothing garments bearing a 'two stripes' motif, applied to the side seams of the garment. Fitnessworld's stripes were running in parallel and in terms of colour were in contrast with the background colour of the garment.

7.419 The Gerechtshof held that there was no trade mark infringement, since there was no likelihood of confusion, and that Fitnessworld used its sign as an embellishment. On appeal, Adidas claimed before the Hoge Road that the case fell under Article 5(2).

7.420 The answer to the first question—whether Article 5(2) covered identical and similar as well as dissimilar good or services—had to conform to *Davidoff*. However, the United Kingdom, testing the limits of the judgment, submitted that the Court ruled that Member States *may* extend protection to identical and similar goods rather than that they are obliged to do so. Member States remained free to follow a literary interpretation of the provision. Since adoption of the provision remained optional, the degree of its implementation should also remain optional.

(a) *The Opinion of Advocate General Jacobs*

7.421 Advocate General Jacobs, despite his doctrinal disagreement with the Court in *Gofkid*, did not support further this line of argument. First, because the Court had clearly stated that

---

[373] Paragraph 24.
[374] *Davidoff* (n 353) paragraph 24.
[375] C-408/01 *Adidas-Salomon AG and Adidas Benelux BV* [2003] ECR I-12537.
[376] C-292/00 *Davidoff* [2003] ECR I-389.
[377] C-251/95 *Sabel BV* [1997] ECR I-6191.

'Article 5(2) cannot be given an interpretation which would lead to well-known marks having less protection where a sign is used for identical or similar goods or services than where a sign is used for non-similar goods or services.'[378] Second, because the Seventh Recital of the Preamble stated that:

> the grounds for refusal or invalidity concerning the trade mark itself ... or concerning conflicts between the trade mark and earlier rights, are to be listed in an exhaustive manner, even if some of these grounds are listed as an option for the Member States which will therefore be able to maintain or introduce those grounds in their legislation.

Third, because the Court had already held that Article 5, Article 6, and Article 7 are provisions that require complete harmonization.[379]

7.422 Finally, since the national legislation challenged in *Gofkid* followed the same wording with Article 5(2), it was unlikely that the Court had simply issued a permissive rather than an obligatory judgment.

(b) The Judgment of the Court

7.423 The Court indeed referred to its earlier judgment in a non-permissive way. It broadened, however, the scope of the question in order to deal with the challenge of the United Kingdom. 'In that regard, it should be noted that where a Member State exercises the option provided by Article 5(2) of the Directive, it must grant to the proprietors of marks with a reputation a form of protection in accordance with that provision.'[380]

7.424 It followed the Opinion of the Advocate General and ruled that if the Member State

> transposes Article 5(2) ... [it] must therefore grant protection which is at least as extensive for identical or similar goods or services as for non-similar goods or services. The Member State's option thus relates to the principle itself of granting greater protection to marks with a reputation, but not to the situations covered by that protection when the Member State grants it.[381]

7.425 In essence, the Court confirmed that national courts are required to interpret national provisions transposing a Directive according to the wording and the purpose of the Directive.[382]

(6) *Adidas v Fitnessworld*: Global Appreciation in the Context of Article 5(2)

7.426 One of the questions in *Fitnessworld*[383] was whether the criteria of similarity between an earlier mark and a later mark or sign under Article 5(2) are the same as those under Article 5(1).

(a) The Opinion of Advocate General Jacobs

7.427 Advocate General Jacobs submitted that the test elaborated in *Sabel*[384] and *Lloyd*[385] should also be applied here. The difference was that it would not be necessary to show that the similarity gives rise to a likelihood of confusion. The Court had already clearly stated in

---

[378] C-292/00 *Davidoff* [2003] ECR I-389, paragraph 25.
[379] C-414/99 *Levi Strauss & Co and Levi Strauss (UK) Ltd v Tesco Stores, Tesco Plc* and C-415/99 *Costco Wholesale UK Ltd* and C-416/99 *Zino Davidoff v A&G Imports Ltd* [2001] ECR I-8691; and C-23/01 *Robelco NV* [2002] ECR I-1093.
[380] *Fitnessworld* (n 375) paragraph 18.
[381] Paragraph 20.
[382] C-14/83 *Von Colson and Kamann v Land Nordhein-Westfalen* [1984] ECR 1891; C-79/83 *Dorit Harz v Deutsche Tradax GmbH* [1984] ECR 1921; and C-185/97 *Coote v Granada Hospitality Ltd* [1998] ECR I-5199.
[383] C-408/01 *Adidas–Salomon AG and Midas Benelux BV v Fitnessworld Trading Ltd* [2003] ECR I-12537.
[384] C-251/95 *Sabel BV* [1997] ECR I-6191.
[385] C-342/97 *Lloyd Schuhfabrik* [1999] ECR I-3819.

Marca Mode[386] that Article 5(2) did not require the existence of a likelihood of confusion. He suggested that the provision should be linked with the effect of the use complained of rather than with a particular state of mind on the part of consumers. Unless the later sign brought the earlier mark to the mind of the relevant public it would not affect the earlier mark in any way.

7.428 In his general analysis of the provision he had identified three types of effect that could possibly fall under Article 5(2): dilution, degradation, or free riding. Preferring to use the term 'connection' rather than 'association'—note that the Commission had submitted that a likelihood of association would be sufficient—he referred to the Court's ruling in *General Motors*:[387]

> It seems obvious that use of a sign cannot have such an effect unless the sign brings the mark in some way to the mind of the relevant public. Thus, considering in the light of the general scheme and purpose of the Directive the requirement in Article 5(2) that the trade mark have a reputation, the Court has stated that it is only where there is a sufficient degree of knowledge of the mark that the public, when confronted by the sign, may possibly make a connection between the two and that the mark may consequently be damaged.[388]

7.429 Specifying the criteria in detail would not be helpful. National courts would be able to decide whether as a result of sensory or conceptual similarity between the two signs the use complained of would take unfair advantage of, or be detrimental to, the distinctive character or the repute of the mark.

(b) The Judgment of the Court

7.430 The Court cited the same cases as the Advocate General and ruled that 'the condition of similarity between the mark and the sign, referred to in Article 5(2) of the Directive, requires the existence, in particular, of elements of visual, aural or conceptual similarity'.[389] It too preferred to use the term 'connection' rather than 'association'; the public must make a connection between the sign and the mark, establish a link between them 'even though it does not confuse them'.[390] The existence of such a link must be appreciated globally taking into account all the factors relevant to the circumstances of the case.

7.431 In essence, the similarity test is the same under both Article 5(1)(b) and Article 5(2).[391] However, in *Fitnessworld* the language of the Court appears to be less detailed and more abstract; there is perhaps a hint that the Court is moving away from the multifactor tests expressed in *Sabel*[392] and *Canon*[393] towards a more conceptual approach. However, subsequent case law has not revealed a departure from the multifactor test.

---

[386] C-425/98 *Marca Mode CV v Adidas AG & Adidas Benelux BV* [2000] ECR I-4861.
[387] C-375/97 *General Motors Corp* [1999] ECR I-5421.
[388] *General Motors* (n 387) paragraph 49.
[389] *Fitnessworld* (n 383) paragraph 28.
[390] *Fitnessworld* (n 383) paragraph 29
[391] The principle has been applied consistently: without some similarity, visually, phonetically, or conceptually, there can be no likelihood of confusion and no detriment to reputation. However, the Court has also expressed that the degree of similarity required for a finding of likelihood of confusion is not the same as that for finding a 'link' within the meaning of the *Fitnessworld* and *Intel* case law, where the degree of similarity may actually be less; see most recently judgment of 20 November 2014, C-581/13 P and C-582/13 P *Intra-Presse SAS v OHIM—Golden Balls Ltd*, paragraph 72; see paragraph 7.129 and following above.
[392] C-251/95 *Sabel BV* [1997] ECR I-6191.
[393] C-39/97 *Canon Kabushiki Kaisha* [1998] ECR I-5507.

(7) *Adidas v Fitnessworld*: Use as a Trade Mark

The third question in *Fitnessworld*[394] dealt with a wider issue of use. The Hoge Road asked the Court of Justice whether the fact that the later sign is viewed as an embellishment is relevant in assessing the similarity between the mark and the sign. The question was in the context of Article 5(2), however the ruling should also be relevant for the purposes of Article 5(1). **7.432**

(a) *The Opinion of Advocate General Jacobs*

Advocate General Jacobs considered that whether the sign was viewed as an embellishment did not assist in the assessment of similarity. It would be relevant, however, in the overall assessment of the applicability of Article 5(2). He rejected a broad claim that a sign that is viewed as a decoration cannot cause a connection with a trade mark. He noted that some trade marks were based on common shapes, patterns, or even colours,[395] and so even merely decorative use of a similar shape, pattern, or colour could remind the public of the earlier trade mark. **7.433**

He added that, from a literal perspective, Article 5(2) did not refer to whether the sign must be viewed as a mark; he found the Commission's claim that Article 5(5)[396] should lead to such an interpretation as unpersuasive since Article 5(5) targets provisions outside trade mark law. However, he believed that if 'the relevant section of the public perceives a given sign as doing no more than embellishing goods, and in no way as identifying their origin, that sign cannot be regarded as used for the purpose of distinguishing those goods'.[397] A sign that functions purely as an embellishment or decoration would not be perceived as a badge of origin. Distinguishing *Fitnessworld* from *Arsenal*,[398] he underlined that the latter was an Article 5(1)(a) case. 'In that context the unauthorised use by a third party of the identical mark on identical goods was plainly trade mark use, notwithstanding that perception.'[399] So, use of the later sign as a trade mark was an implied condition of Article 5(2). **7.434**

To support further his position he referred to the 'public interest' the Court has applied in its interpretation of Article 3(1)(c) and Article 3(1)(e). By analogy, it would be unjustified to employ trade mark law in order to block use of common decorations, motifs, or colours by competitors. **7.435**

(b) *The Judgment of the Court*

The Court followed a much less analytical route to reach the same outcome. It viewed the establishment of the connection between the earlier trade mark and the later sign as the decisive factor. If the sign establishes a link then the fact that it is viewed as an embellishment is not, 'in itself, an obstacle to the protection conferred by Article 5(2)'.[400] However, **7.436**

---

[394] C-408/01 *Adidas-Salomon* [2008] ECR I-12537.
[395] The AG referred in particular to C-104/01 *Libertel Groep BV* [2003] ECR I-3793; earlier in his examination of the second question he had referred to C-273/00 *Sieckmann* [2002] ECR I-11737. This recurring link between what is registered with its scope of protection can become particularly relevant when the enforcement limits of some types of signs are tested in practice.
[396] C-23/01 *Robelco NV* [2002] ECR I-1093.
[397] *Fitnessworld* (n 383) paragraph 60. He referred once again to *Libertel* where the Court stated that a trade mark must distinguish the goods or services concerned as originating from a particular undertaking. This was the essential function of a trade mark, to act as a badge of origin.
[398] C-206/01 *Arsenal Football Club Plc* [2002] ECR I-10273.
[399] Point 62.
[400] *Fitnessworld* (n 383) paragraph 39.

where the relevant public views the sign purely as an embellishment 'it necessarily does not establish any link with a registered mark. That therefore means that the degree of similarity between the sign and the mark is not sufficient for such a link to be established.'[401]

(8) *Calvin Klein and Ferrero*: Similarity v Reputation

7.437 In *Calvin Klein*[402] and *Ferrero*[403] the Court was called upon to clarify whether the requirement regarding the similarity of the signs in Article 8(1)(b) CTMR is of the same nature and implies the same type of assessment as the one laid down in Article 8(5), as well as whether the reputation of the earlier mark is a matter that must be addressed when assessing the similarity of the signs or, conversely, comes into play only after such similarity has been established in the first place.

(a) Calvin Klein: A mechanical approach

7.438 In *Calvin Klein* the appeal concerned an opposition filed by Calvin Klein Trademark Trust against the application as a Community trade mark of the word sign CK CREACIONES KENNYA in respect of goods in Classes 18 and 25 of the Nice Classification. The opposition was based on a range of Community and national marks consisting of Calvin Klein's well-known stylized two-letter logo, either alone or combined with the words 'Calvin Klein' in smaller print, registered in respect of essentially identical goods.

7.439 The Opposition Division and the Boards of Appeal of OHIM dismissed the opposition on the ground of lack of sufficient similarity between the signs for the purposes of Articles 8(1)(b) and 8(5). The General Court[404] similarly dismissed the action brought by Calvin Klein, taking the view that the visual, phonetic, and conceptual differences between the signs precluded a finding of similarity between them.

7.440 More particularly, the General Court pointed out that a compound trade mark cannot be regarded as being similar to another trade mark which is identical or similar to one of its components, unless that common component forms the dominant element within the overall impression created by the compound mark, and observed that, in the case at issue, the words 'creaciones kennya' occupied a much more significant position than the letters 'ck', and formed a syntactical and conceptual unit which dominated the whole, whilst the element 'ck', which corresponds to the initial letters of the words 'creaciones' and 'kennya', occupied only an ancillary position in relation to that expression.[405]

7.441 Next, the General Court held that although, as a general rule, marks with a highly distinctive character enjoy broader protection, the recognition, in the present case, that the earlier marks were reputed cannot call into question the finding that the signs under comparison created overall impressions which were too different to support a finding that there was a likelihood of confusion. Accordingly, it found that there was no need to address Calvin Klein's arguments under Article 8(5).[406]

---

[401] Paragraph 40.
[402] C-254/09 P *Calvin Klein Trademark Trust/Office for Harmonisation in the Internal Market* [2010] ECR I-07989.
[403] C-552/09 P *Ferrero SpA/Office for Harmonisation in the Internal Market* [2011] ECR I-02063.
[404] T-185/07 *Klein Trademark Trust* v *OHIM—Zafra Marroquineros* (CK CREACIONES KENNYA) [2009] ECR II-13237.
[405] Paragraphs 39, 42, and 44.
[406] Paragraphs 53–55.

7.442 The Court of Justice endorsed the position taken by the General Court as regards the role played by the similarity of the signs in the assessment, noting that, according to settled case law,[407] where there is no similarity between the earlier mark and the mark applied for, the reputation of the earlier mark is not sufficient to lead to a finding that there is a likelihood of confusion. As regards the contention that the General Court erred in law by dismissing the action without examining Calvin Klein's arguments in the light of Article 8(5) and without taking account of the reputation of the earlier marks, it held that, in order for that provision to be applicable, the marks at issue must be identical or similar and that, consequently, that ground of refusal is manifestly inapplicable where any similarity between the marks can be ruled out.[408]

7.443 Moreover, it observed that, although the view taken by the General Court to the effect that the existence of a similarity between two marks presupposes that their common component forms the dominant element of the mark applied for was not correct, being sufficient in that connection for the common component not to be negligible,[409] overall, the analysis of the General Court was not vitiated by an error of law, to the extent that it had found, first, that the overall impression created by the mark applied for was dominated by the element 'creaciones kennya' and, second, that the component 'ck' occupied only an ancillary position, which, in essence, amounted to a conclusion that the element in question was negligible. Accordingly, the Court concluded that from the moment that it had ruled out, on the basis of a properly conducted analysis, any similarity between the marks, the General Court was entitled to hold that, notwithstanding the reputation of the earlier marks, there could be no likelihood of confusion.[410]

(b) Ferrero: *Fine-tuning the principles*

7.444 The facts in *Ferrero* were very similar to those in *Calvin Klein*. Ferrero SpA, holder in Italy of the famous word mark KINDER for chocolate confectionery, sought to invalidate the registration as a Community trade mark of a composite sign consisting of the stylized words 'TiMi KiNDERJOGHURT', registered in respect of yoghurt drinks, on the ground of Article 52(1)(a), in combination with Articles 8(1) and 8(5) CTMR. The Cancellation Division of OHIM upheld Ferrero's action and declared the contested registration invalid pursuant to Article 8(5). The Board of Appeal, however, overturned that decision holding that, in view of their substantial visual and phonetic differences, the marks were dissimilar overall, and dismissed the application for a declaration of invalidity on the ground that one of the conditions for the application of Article 8(1)(b) and (5), namely that the signs must be identical or similar, was not satisfied.

7.445 Ferrero brought an application for annulment. In the first place, the General Court[411] reiterated that the existence of similarity between the marks is a precondition for the

---

[407] Paragraph 53, citing cases C-106/03 P *Vedial v OHIM* [2004] ECR I-9573, paragraph 54, C-234/06 P *Il Ponte Finanziaria v OHIM* [2007] ECR I-7333, paragraphs 50–51, and C-57/08 P *Gateway v OHIM* [2008] ECR I-00188, paragraphs 55–56.
[408] Paragraphs 67–68.
[409] Citing cases C-334/05 P *OHIM v Shaker* [2007] ECR I-4529, paragraphs 41–42, C-498/07 P *Aceites del Sur-Coosur v Koipe* [2009] ECR I-07371, paragraph 62, and C-193/06 P *Nestlé v OHIM* [2007] ECR I-00114, paragraphs 42–43.
[410] Paragraphs 56–58.
[411] T-140/08 *Ferrero v OHIM—Tirol Milch* (TiMi KiNDERJOGHURT) [2009] ECR II-3941.

application of both Article 8(1)(b) and Article 8(5) and that that condition requires the existence, in particular, of elements of visual, aural, or conceptual similarity. It noted, however, that, notwithstanding the fact that in the present case the word 'kinder' was present in both signs, there were a number of visual and phonetic features which precluded the signs from being perceived as similar.

7.446 Second, the General Court held that even if the reputation of the earlier mark mattered for the purposes of assessing the likelihood of confusion or the existence of a link, it did not affect the assessment of the similarity of the signs and that, in any event, the lack of similarity between the signs at issue was so pronounced that the undisputed reputation of the earlier mark was incapable of calling into question that lack of similarity.[412]

7.447 Ferrero appealed to the Court of Justice, arguing that, by undertaking a single factual assessment of similarity under Articles (1)(b) and (5), the General Court overlooked that each of those provisions calls for the application of an entirely distinct set of tests, and that, according to a proper interpretation of *Intel*, Article 8(5) requires taking into account in the assessment of similarity of the signs the reputation of the earlier mark.

7.448 Following, essentially, the line taken in *Calvin Klein*, the Court of Justice rejected Ferrero's arguments and dismissed the appeal. Mindful, however, of the importance of the matter, it went on to provide more detailed guidance about the correct way of applying the relevant principles and about the exact interplay between the reputation of the earlier mark and the similarity of the signs.

7.449 The Court stated at the outset that the existence of similarity between the signs is indeed a precondition for the application of both Article 8(1)(b) and 8(5), but observed, citing *Adidas v Fitnessworld*, that those provisions differ in terms of the degree of similarity required. Whereas the protection provided for under Article 8(1)(b) is conditional upon a finding of a degree of similarity capable of giving rise to a likelihood of confusion, the existence of such a likelihood is not necessary for the protection conferred by Article 8(5). Accordingly, the types of injury referred to in that provision may be the consequence of a lesser degree of similarity, provided that such similarity allows the relevant section of the public to establish a link between the marks. It stressed, however, that, contrary to Ferrero's arguments, it is not apparent, either from the wording of those provisions or from the case law, that the similarity between the marks must be assessed in a different way, according to whether the assessment is carried out under the one or the other provision.[413]

7.450 The Court also disagreed with the inferences drawn by Ferrero from *Intel* as regards the impact of the earlier mark's reputation, reaffirming that, for the purposes of the assessment carried out in the context of Article 8(5), the reputation and the distinctive character of the earlier mark constitute relevant factors for the purposes of determining, not whether the marks at issue are similar, but whether the relevant section of the public makes a link between them. In this regard, it explained that even though the global assessment of the existence of a link between the signs implies some interdependence between the relevant factors, and a low degree of similarity between the marks may therefore be offset by the strong distinctive character of the earlier mark, the fact remains that where there is no

---

[412] Paragraphs 53–61.
[413] Paragraphs 51–54.

similarity between the signs, the reputation or recognition enjoyed by the earlier mark is not sufficient for allowing the public to establish a link between them.[414]

Thus, the Court concluded that Article 8(5) is manifestly inapplicable where all similarity between the signs has been ruled out and stressed that 'it is only if there is some similarity, even faint, between the marks at issue that the General Court must carry out a global assessment' in order to ascertain whether that degree of similarity is enough, on account of the reputation enjoyed by the earlier mark, to give rise to a likelihood of confusion or to allow the public to establish a link between those marks.[415] **7.451**

(c) Conclusions

The judgments in *Calvin Klein* and *Ferrero* provided a comprehensive answer to the controversy surrounding the exact role of reputation in the analysis of confusion and detriment. It is now clear that the Court regards the similarity of the signs, in which the reputation of the earlier mark plays no role, and the overall assessment of the existence of a link or of a likelihood of confusion, in the context of which the reputation is taken into account, as two consecutive but independent steps of the same test. **7.452**

The debate was fuelled by the argument that these steps are not as independent as they seem, first and foremost because the comparison of the signs cannot be conducted in a vacuum. Being a sensory test, it needs a cardinal reference to mark when and in which circumstances the signs must be regarded as similar. The Preambles to the Directive and the Regulation seem to confirm that view by stating that 'an interpretation should be given of the concept of similarity in relation to the likelihood of confusion'.[416] This also follows from the Court's admission that inasmuch as the global assessment of the existence of a link implies some interdependence between the relevant factors, a low degree of similarity between the signs may be offset by the strong distinctive character of the earlier mark. **7.453**

Taken literally, that statement means that it is precisely the existence of a link that marks the outer limits of similarity. In other words, it is only where the similarity of the signs is so weak that even if the earlier mark was highly reputed there could be no link between them, that it is possible to conclude that the marks are dissimilar. If, however, it must first be assumed that the reputation would have no impact on the existence of a link, before safely declaring the marks dissimilar,[417] it is arguable that the two parts of the test are more interconnected than what appears at first sight. **7.454**

This also shows that the test propounded by the Court works better as a negative formula, ie when the similarity of the signs is truly minimal. This is where the nuance introduced by the Court at paragraph 66 of *Ferrero*, that even a 'faint' similarity between the signs should trigger the need to carry out a global assessment, becomes important. Indeed, as in any multifactor test, it is only where the value of one of the factors is zero, or bordering zero, that it can effectively condition the outcome by neutralizing the multiplier effect caused by the interdependence between the various factors.[418] **7.455**

---

[414] Paragraphs 55, 58, and 60–61.
[415] Paragraphs 66–68.
[416] See Recital 8 of the Regulation and Recital 11 of the Directive.
[417] As the General Court seems to admit at paragraph 61 of its judgment in *Ferrero*.
[418] See paragraph 7.452 above.

7.456 In turn, this also means that the test proposed by the Court can easily lead to distortions if not applied consistently. This will inevitably happen if examining authorities are too quick to dispense with elements of similarity by allotting undue weight to the differentiating features of the signs. This is so because, by refusing to recognize a low degree of similarity, in particular where the marks partially overlap, there is a danger of effectively doing away with the residual value of similarities which, although not sufficient in themselves to allow the public to establish a link between the signs, they could nevertheless do so if enhanced by the reputation of the earlier mark.

7.457 The facts in *Calvin Klein* and *Ferrero* are good examples of this risk, at the very least because, by coming to the conclusion that the marks were clearly dissimilar in circumstances where the earlier mark was fully reproduced in the later marks, the General Court overlooked the jurisprudential maxim that a partial overlap between the signs is evidence of at least some degree of similarity between them. It is therefore unfortunate that the case of a manifest inconsistency in the application of the relevant criteria was not made before the Court of Justice, so as to test its readiness to set aside findings that could imperil the coherent application of the principles at stake.

(9) *Intel*: Proof of Dilution: Chasing the Chimera?

7.458 *Intel*[419] was an ambitious attempt to settle all the outstanding questions surrounding the condition of 'detriment to the distinctiveness' of a reputed mark with a single stroke. While *General Motors*[420] and *Fitnessworld*[421] had respectively settled the concepts of reputation and similarity and had briefly touched upon the notions and mechanics of detriment and/or unfair advantage, the specific requirements for proving such detriment largely remained uncharted territory.

(a) *The facts in the main proceedings*

7.459 Intel Corp Inc ('Intel') is the proprietor in the United Kingdom of the word mark INTEL, as well as of various other national and Community trade marks consisting of or including that word. Those marks essentially cover computers and computer-related goods and services in Classes 9, 16, 38, and 42 of the Nice Classification. According to the facts, the word INTEL moreover has a 'huge' reputation in the United Kingdom for microprocessor products (chips and peripherals), multimedia, and business software. CPM United Kingdom Ltd (CPM) is the proprietor of the word mark INTELMARK, registered in the United Kingdom for 'marketing and telemarketing services' in Class 35 of the Nice Classification.

7.460 Intel lodged an application for a declaration of invalidity against CPM's registration, claiming that the use of that mark would take unfair advantage of, or be detrimental to, the distinctive character or the repute of its earlier trade mark within the meaning of Section 5(3) of the Trade Marks Act.

7.461 Its application was dismissed both by the Hearing Officer and the High Court. Intel appealed to the Court of Appeal (England and Wales) (Civil Division).

---

[419] C-252/07 *Intel Corp Inc v CPM United Kingdom Ltd* (INTEL) [2008] ECR I-08823.
[420] C-375/97 *General Motors* (CHEVY) [1999] ECR I-5421.
[421] C-408/01 *Adidas-Salomon AG and Adidas Benelux BV* [2003] ECR I-12537.

7.462 Intel argued that both Article 4(4)(a) and Article 5(2) of the Directive seek to protect a trade mark with a reputation against dilution. Relying on *Fitnessworld*, it maintained that any link between the earlier reputed mark and the later sign in the perception of the public was enough to cause detriment. Moreover, by referring to *General Motors*, it submitted that, where the earlier mark is unique and has a strong distinctive character, detriment will be caused to it by virtually any use for other goods or services and that, unless encroachment was stopped at the outset, that mark would suffer a death 'by a thousand cuts'.

7.463 In its statement of the facts, the referring Court found: first, that the mark INTEL consisted of an invented word and was highly reputed and unique, in the sense that it had not been used by anyone for any other goods or services; second, that the marks at issue were similar, but not confusingly so; and, third, that the respective goods and services were dissimilar 'to a substantial degree'.

7.464 However, the Court of Appeal was uncertain whether, in such factual circumstances, the proprietor of an earlier reputed mark was entitled to the protection of Article 4(4)(a) of the Directive. Accordingly, it decided to stay proceedings and refer the following questions to the Court:

(1) For the purposes of Article 4(4)(a) of the [Directive], where:
   (a) the earlier mark has a huge reputation for certain specific types of goods or services,
   (b) those goods or services are dissimilar or dissimilar to a substantial degree to the goods or services of the later mark,
   (c) the earlier mark is unique in respect of any goods or services,
   (d) the earlier mark would be brought to mind by the average consumer when he or she encounters the later mark used for the services of the later mark,
   are those facts sufficient in themselves to establish (i) 'a link' within the meaning of paragraphs 29 and 30 of [*Adidas-Salomon and Adidas Benelux*], and/or (ii) unfair advantage and/or detriment within the meaning of that Article?
(2) If no, what factors is the national court to take into account in deciding whether such is sufficient? Specifically, in the global appreciation to determine whether there is a 'link', what significance is to be attached to the goods or services in the specification of the later mark?
(3) In the context of Article 4(4)(a) [of the Directive], what is required in order to satisfy the condition of detriment to distinctive character? Specifically, (i) does the earlier mark have to be unique, (ii) is a first conflicting use sufficient to establish detriment to distinctive character and (iii) does the element of detriment to distinctive character of the earlier mark require an effect on the economic behaviour of the consumer?

(c) The Opinion of Advocate General Sharpston

7.465 Advocate General Sharpston provided the context for her analysis by referring to the genesis of the dilution doctrine[422] and to the detailed description of that notion by Advocate General Jacobs in *Fitnessworld*.[423] She stressed, however, that the Court's task was not to define dilution in the abstract, but to interpret the relevant provisions of the Directive, with a view to drawing a fair balance between the interests of the owners of famous marks and the need to avoid such rights from being used abusively to the detriment of other, weaker market operators.

---

[422] Citing Frank Schechter, 'The Rational Basis of Trademark Protection' [1927] *Harvard Law Review* 813.
[423] See, in particular, paragraphs 36–39 of the Advocate General's opinion in C-408/01 *Adidas–Salomon AG* n. 383 above.

7.466 She also observed that the questions referred to the Court overlapped to a substantial degree and that, taken together, they asked essentially what factors were to be taken into account and to what extent those factors must be present in order to establish (i) a 'link' between the signs in the mind of the public; (ii) free riding; (iii) detriment to distinctiveness (blurring); and (iv) detriment to repute (tarnishment).

7.467 **(i) Relationship between link and infringement** The Advocate General reiterated that, according to the case law, the establishment of a link in the mind of the public is a necessary condition for the existence of an infringement and that such a link is mainly the consequence of a degree of similarity between the mark and the sign.[424] Moreover, as is clear from the same case law, the existence of such a link must be appreciated globally, that is, by having regard to all the factors relevant to the particular case.[425] However, she considered that even though the factors that are relevant for the assessment of a possible link will also be pertinent when appraising infringement, the mere existence of such a link was not sufficient in itself to prove the existence of detriment or unfair advantage. In other words, not every link is detrimental, in the same manner that not any association between the marks can give rise to a likelihood of confusion.[426]

7.468 Accordingly, the Advocate General took the view that the fact that the earlier mark would be 'brought to mind' by the consumer when encountering the later sign, is tantamount to the existence of a 'link', 'association', or 'connection' within the meaning of the case law; those terms are in fact equivalent, to the extent that they all imply a mental process above the threshold of 'consciousness' that is something more than a 'vague, ephemeral, indefinable feeling or subliminal influence'.[427]

7.469 She remarked, nevertheless, that such a link must be of a 'reasonably substantial nature' since it must be made by a substantial part of the relevant public (apparently in view of the fact that there must be a tangible risk of detriment for protection to be triggered, that is, something more than a remote possibility, confined to a limited number of cases).

7.470 Moreover, the Advocate General referred to the equivalent provision of US law[428] as giving a useful example of the kind of factors that may be taken into account in assessing detriment. According to that provision, in determining whether a mark is likely to cause dilution by blurring, the court may consider all relevant factors, including the degree of similarity between the marks, the degree of inherent or acquired distinctiveness of the famous mark, the extent to which the owner of the famous mark is engaging in substantially exclusive use of the mark, the degree of recognition of the famous mark, and any actual association between the marks.

7.471 Although she observed that that provision naturally has no force in Community law and the factors it enumerates are to be considered when assessing the likelihood of dilution itself, rather than the existence of a link in the mind of the public (which is not an explicit condition in the American legislation), they still seem relevant to establishing whether such a link

---

[424] *Fitnessworld* (n 383) paragraph 29.
[425] *Fitnessworld* (n 383) paragraph 30.
[426] Point 43.
[427] Point 46.
[428] United States Trade Mark Act of 1946 s 43(c), as amended by the Trademark Dilution Revision Act of 2006 (15 USC 1051 et seq).

exists, all the more so since they largely coincide with the test applied by the Court to the assessment of likelihood of confusion.[429]

7.472 Turning, lastly, to the significance of the goods and services concerned for the establishment of a link, she took the view that it was not necessary that their nature should imply an economic connection between the owners of the two marks, as the referring Court seemed to be suggesting. Besides, such a view would practically efface the distinction between the respective conditions under which the basic protection against likelihood of confusion and the extensive protection afforded to famous marks are available.

7.473 The Advocate General accepted, however, that the nature of the goods is important, particularly in one respect: if the goods in conflict are so far apart that the respective consumer circles do not overlap, it is highly unlikely that an association will ever take place. Conversely, where either mark is used for goods or services targeting the general public, or where both are used for related products, the likelihood of an association on the part of the public is correspondingly much stronger.[430]

7.474 (ii) **Free riding** Advocate General Sharpston then observed that the concept of unfair advantage focuses on benefit to the later sign, rather than harm to the reputed mark. That implies some sort of boost given to the later sign by way of its association with the earlier mark. She considered, though, that the facts set out in the first question seemed too flimsy on their own to support a finding of free riding.[431] In general, it would seem that as the reputation of the earlier mark and the similarity of the goods and services covered by the respective marks increase, so will the likelihood that the later sign will derive advantage from its connection with the reputed mark. But usually more will be needed. If the later sign is to derive such advantage, its association with the earlier mark must be such as to enhance its performance.[432]

7.475 Thus, what is finally decisive is the relationship between the prestigious connotations of the earlier mark and the context in which the later mark is used, in the sense that the image and appeal of the reputed mark must somehow be transferable to the latter.

7.476 (iii) **Blurring** Turning to the third question, the Advocate General stressed that, unlike free riding, the notion of blurring focuses on harm to the earlier mark, necessarily implying a lessening of its distinctiveness. Again, she considered the factors listed in the first question to be insufficient, on their own, to support a finding of dilution, although she admitted that they were in no way inconsistent with such a finding.[433]

7.477 In that connection she found that, like all other relevant factors, 'uniqueness' is not essential in itself to lead to dilution. Terms such as 'truly unique' and 'substantially unique' were not only difficult to define but also impractical in their application. What counts in the end is that the more distinctive a mark is, the more likely it becomes that its distinctiveness will be impaired by the presence of other marks.[434]

---

[429] Point 57.
[430] Point 60.
[431] Points 62–63.
[432] Points 65–66.
[433] Points 68–69.
[434] Point 72.

7.478 As regards the standard of proof, she considered that the question whether 'a first conflicting use' is enough was in reality misconceived, since, as a matter of definition, a first conflicting use may not in itself cause detriment, given that the very point of both Article 4(4)(a) and Article 5(2) is to prevent or pre-empt repeated conflicting use which would dilute the earlier mark; as is obvious, a first use cannot produce such an effect on its own, but the likelihood of that being caused by repeated use may still be extrapolated from the overall circumstances.[435]

7.479 Lastly, as to whether an effect on consumers' economic behaviour is required, she expressed the opinion that detriment to distinctiveness need not necessarily involve actual pecuniary damage, so that a change in economic behaviour is not essential. Surely, however, any evidence of actual negative change in consumer behaviour would buttress the case for dilution.[436]

7.480 Consequently, the Advocate General supported a holistic approach, refusing clearly to favour any specific factor over the others, all the more so since blurring will usually be the result of the combined effect of various circumstances and thus can only be evaluated by taking a case-by-case approach.

7.481 **(iv) Tarnishment** Finally, the Advocate General dealt briefly with tarnishment. She observed that that type of infringement again concerns harm to the earlier mark, in the form of detriment to its repute. That form of damage appears to be a step beyond blurring, in that the mark is not merely weakened but actually degraded by the link which the public makes with the later mark. Accordingly, the most important factor in this regard should be whether the connotations of the later mark are indeed such as to harm the repute of the earlier mark. Thus, in cases of alleged tarnishment, it will be necessary to compare the connotations of each mark, in relation either to the goods or services covered or to the broader message which they convey, and to evaluate the damage entailed.

(d) The Judgment of the Court

7.482 **(i) Detriment in the form of dilution by blurring** The Court started its analysis by noting that the condition of detriment or unfair advantage is the specific condition for the protection conferred by Articles 4(4)(a) and 5(2) of the Directive[437] and that any of the three types of injury stipulated in those provisions suffices to trigger that form of protection.

7.483 As regards, in particular, the detriment to the distinctive character of the earlier mark, which the Court also described as 'dilution', 'whittling away', or 'blurring', it concurred with the generally accepted view that such detriment is caused when that mark's ability to identify the goods or services for which it is registered as coming from the proprietor of that mark is weakened by the use of the later sign, which leads to the dispersion of its identity and hold upon the public mind. It also confirmed that this is notably the case when a mark, which used to arouse immediate association with the goods and services for which it is registered, is no longer capable of doing so.[438]

---

[435] Point 73.
[436] Point 74.
[437] Citing, among others, *Marca Mode* (n 386) paragraph 36 and *Fitnessworld* (n 383) paragraph 36.
[438] *Intel* (n 419) paragraph 29.

7.484 The Court moreover reiterated that the types of injury referred to in Article 4(4)(a) of the Directive, where they occur, are the consequence of a certain degree of similarity between the marks, by virtue of which the relevant section of the public makes a connection between the two marks, that is to say, establishes a link between them even though it does not confuse them.[439] It also concurred with the view of the Advocate General that the existence of such a link is not sufficient, in itself, to establish that there is one of the types of injury referred to in Article 4(4)(a) of the Directive.

7.485 **(ii) The relevant public** The Court then observed that the public to be taken into account for the purposes of Article 4(4)(a) varies depending on the type of injury claimed each time and proposed a two-fold test for its definition. In the first place, the mark's reputation must be assessed by reference to the perception of the relevant public, which consists of average consumers of the goods or services for which that mark is registered, who are reasonably well-informed and reasonably observant and circumspect.[440] Second, if what has been claimed is detriment to the distinctive character or the repute of the earlier mark, it is the average consumers of the goods and services for which that mark is registered who must be taken into account; conversely, in cases of unfair advantage, its existence must be assessed by reference to the average consumers of the goods or services for which the later mark is registered and/or used.[441]

7.486 **(iii) Standard and burden of proof** Next, the Court noted that the burden of proving detriment or unfair advantage falls on the proprietor of the earlier mark, who must adduce appropriate evidence to that effect. It stressed, though, that the proprietor is not required to demonstrate actual and present injury to its mark for the purposes of Article 4(4)(a), since, when it is foreseeable that such injury will ensue from the use of the later mark, he cannot be expected to wait for it actually to occur in order to be able to prohibit that use; in any event, however, he must at least establish that there is a serious risk that such an injury will occur in the future.[442]

7.487 The Court then proceeded to apply these general principles to the questions pending before it.

7.488 **(iv) The existence of a link** After reiterating that the possible existence of a link between the marks must be assessed globally, by taking into account all relevant facts and circumstances,[443] it went on to address the significance of the factors specifically singled out by the referring Court.

7.489 As regards the degree of similarity between the marks, it noted that the more similar they are, the more likely it is that the later mark will bring the earlier mark to mind. That is particularly the case where the marks are identical. However, even that fact is not sufficient for concluding that a link will be positively established. Likewise, the stronger the distinctive character of the earlier mark, whether inherent or acquired through use, the more likely it is that such a link will occur. Accordingly, insofar as the mark's ability to identify the goods or services for which it is registered and, therefore, its distinctive character, are all the stronger

---

[439] *General Motors* (n 420) paragraph 23, *Fitnessworld* (n 383) paragraph 29.
[440] *General Motors* (n 420) paragraph 24.
[441] *Intel* (n 419) paragraphs 35–36.
[442] *Intel* (n 419) paragraph 38.
[443] Citing *Fitnessworld* (n 383) paragraph 30.

if that mark is unique, it is particularly relevant to ascertain whether the earlier mark is 'unique' or 'essentially unique'.[444]

7.490 The Court also pointed out that the goods and services of the conflicting marks are directly relevant for the mechanics of association, especially inasmuch as they determine the kind of public to which the earlier mark is known. In that regard, it reiterated that the reputation of the earlier mark may extend to either the public at large or a more specialized public.[445] Accordingly, the following situations can be envisaged.[446]

7.491 First, it is possible that the section of the public concerned by the goods or services of the earlier mark is completely distinct from the public targeted by the later mark, which means that the earlier mark may not be known to the customers of the later mark, despite its reputation. In such a case, the public targeted by each mark may never be confronted with the other so as to establish a link between the two.

7.492 Second, even if the relevant consumer circles are the same or overlap to some extent, those goods or services may be so dissimilar that the later mark is unlikely to bring the earlier mark to the mind of the relevant public if that sign is seen in an entirely different context.

7.493 Third, the reputation of the earlier mark may have spilled over beyond its natural consumer circles either to the general public or, at least, to the customers of the later mark. In such a case, an association cannot be excluded even if the respective sectors are in theory distinct.

7.494 Thus, the Court answered point (i) of the first question and the second question by holding that the existence of a link must be assessed globally and that the fact that the later mark calls the earlier reputed mark to mind is tantamount to the existence of such a link.

7.495 **(v) The assessment of detriment** As regards the relationship between association and damage, the Court held that, just like the appraisal of a possible link between the marks, the existence of detriment must be assessed globally, taking into account all factors relevant to the circumstances of the case. Thus, the mere existence of such a link does not relieve the proprietor of the earlier trade mark from having to prove an actual and present injury to its mark, or a serious likelihood that such an injury will occur in the future. For the same reason, the circumstances referred to by the national court are not necessarily sufficient to trigger the application of Article 4(4)(a) of the Directive.

7.496 However, the Court noted also that the more immediately and strongly the earlier mark is brought to mind by the later sign, the greater the likelihood that detriment or unfair advantage will occur. Similarly, the stronger the earlier mark's distinctive character and reputation the easier it will be to accept that detriment has been caused to it.

7.497 As regards dilution in particular, it is not necessary for the earlier mark to be unique in order to establish such injury or a serious likelihood that it will occur in the future. A trade mark with a reputation necessarily has distinctive character, at the very least acquired through use; therefore, even if that mark is not unique, the use of a later identical or similar mark may still be such as to weaken its distinctive character. However, the more 'unique' the

---

[444] Paragraph 38.
[445] Citing *General Motors* (n 420) paragraph 24.
[446] Paragraphs 48–53.

earlier mark appears, the greater the likelihood that the use of a later identical or similar mark will be detrimental to its distinctive character.[447]

7.498 Finally, the Court held that a first use of an identical or similar mark may suffice, in some circumstances, to cause detriment or to give rise to a serious likelihood that such detriment will occur in the future.[448] Moreover, considering that blurring is caused when the mark's ability to identify the goods or services for which it is registered is weakened because the use of the later mark leads to dispersion of its identity and hold upon the public mind, the proof of dilution requires evidence of a change in the economic behaviour of the consumer consequent to the use of the later mark, or at least a serious likelihood that such a change will occur in the future.[449]

(e) Repercussions

7.499 The core issue in *Intel* is the approach it has taken as regards the evidential standard for proving detriment and, in particular, its statement as regards the need for a change in the 'economic' behaviour of the consumer. A number of questions arise in that connection.

7.500 First, is this standard applicable by analogy also in cases of unfair advantage, or does it only concern detriment, given that the public involved in each case is different?[450]

7.501 Second, does that change in fact mean that the consumer must appear less inclined to buy the designated goods in the future, or does it suffice if he is less capable of immediately recognizing the mark than before? In other words, does the owner of the reputed mark have to prove tangible pecuniary damage in the form of loss of sales, or can he merely rely on a decline of the value inherent in the mark, however imperceptible? The latter surely seems to be more in line with the dilution doctrine, which focuses on the 'aura' of the mark rather than its actual contribution to the selling of the products it distinguishes.

7.502 On the other hand, it is sufficiently clear that the distinction between proof of 'actual' and 'future' detriment does not follow from the difference in the nature of registration and infringement proceedings (compare the conditional wording 'would be detrimental', in Articles 8(5) CTMR and 4(4)(a) of the Directive, to the positive formulation 'is detrimental' in Articles 9(1)(c) and 5(2) respectively).

7.503 This is apparent from the statement of the Court that 'when injury is foreseeable the proprietor of the earlier mark cannot be required to wait for it actually to occur'[451] and that 'a first conflicting use may suffice, in some circumstances' to cause actual detriment or to give rise to a serious likelihood that such detriment will occur in the future.[452] Moreover, if the notion of a 'death by a thousand cuts' is to have any meaning, the likelihood of detriment cannot be required to be perceptible in economic terms before it becomes actionable. In that sense, *Intel* should not be read in an over-restrictive manner. Rather, the pivotal question seems to be whether the detriment can be regarded as foreseeable in view of the overall circumstances of the case.

---

[447] Paragraphs 72–74.
[448] Paragraph 75.
[449] Paragraph 76.
[450] See also in that regard the statement in paragraph 78.
[451] Paragraph 38.
[452] Paragraph 75.

7.504 Another interesting issue is the one raised by the Advocate General in her concluding remarks[453] as regards the standard used by the Court of First Instance in the context of Article 8(5) CTMR, namely that the proprietor 'is not required to prove actual and present harm, but only to adduce prima facie evidence of a future risk which is not hypothetical'.[454] Is that formulation compatible with the standard set out in *Intel*, even though it does not specifically require a change in the economic behaviour of the consumer? At first sight, it would seem that requiring proof of a 'serious likelihood' is not quite the same as establishing a risk which is 'not merely hypothetical'. In fact, the first formulation seems to be closer to the wording of the law, which clearly requires a probability rather than a remote possibility (in the sense that the detriment cannot 'merely be excluded').

7.505 Even the less restrictive view taken by the Court of First Instance in certain cases[455] that 'if the mark applied for does not, at first sight, appear capable of giving rise to one of the three types of risk covered by Article 8(5) CTMR ... the opposition must be rejected unless a non-hypothetical, future risk of detriment or unfair advantage can be established by other evidence' does not seem to be viable any longer. Inasmuch as the Court did not refer to any such exceptional circumstances where detriment would appear immediately obvious, the need to prove the injury claimed is a task that cannot be sidestepped.

7.506 It is also worth noting that even though so far the Court of First Instance has not upheld any opposition purely on the basis of blurring, it has nevertheless accepted the application of Article 8(5) in a number of cases,[456] mainly involving unfair advantage, without actually analysing in detail the economic benefit gained by the infringing sign.

7.507 It is therefore interesting to see whether and to what extent the Court of First Instance will maintain its current practice in the future, or whether it will move towards a more stringent approach in view of the Court's judgment in *Intel*.[457]

(10) *Environmental Manufacturing*: The Importance of 'Economic Behaviour'

7.508 Indeed, in *Environmental Manufacturing*[458] the Court dealt with the evidential standard required when it comes to proving detriment to the distinctive character of the earlier mark within the meaning of Article 8(5) of the Regulation, in particular as regards the need to prove that the use of the later mark would result in a change in the economic behaviour of the average consumer of the goods covered by the earlier mark.

(a) Background to the dispute

7.509 The appeal concerned an opposition by Société Elmar Wolf (Elmar Wolf) against an application by Environmental Manufacturing's predecessor, seeking to register as a Community

---

[453] See Point 85 of the Opinion of AG Sharpston.
[454] See, among others, T-181/05 *Citigroup v OHIM* [2008] ECR II-00669, paragraph 77 and the case law cited therein.
[455] See, in particular, T-215/03 *SIGLA v OHIM-Elleni Holding* (VIPS) [2007] ECR II-711, paragraph 48.
[456] T-477/04 *Aktieselskabet af 21 november 2001 v OHIM* (TDK) [2007] ECR II-00399; T-181/05 *Citigroup* (CITIBANK) [2008] ECR II-00669; T-47/06 *Antartica Srl v OHIM* (NASDAQ) [2007] ECR II-00042; T-93/06 *Mülhens v OHIM-Spa Monopole* (MINERAL SPA) [2008] ECR II-00093; T-21/07 *L'Oreal v OHIM* (SPALINE) [2009] ECR II-00031.
[457] In that connection, see also the discussion of the judgment in C-320/07 P *Antartica Srl v OHIM* (NASDAQ) below paragraph 7.551.
[458] Judgment of 14 November 2013, Case C-383/12 P, *Environmental Manufacturing LLP/Office for Harmonisation in the Internal Market* (Representation of a wolf's head), ECLI:EU:C:2013:741.

trade mark a sign representing a wolf's head in respect of 'machines for professional and industrial processing of wood and green waste; professional and industrial wood chippers and shredders' in Class 7 of the Nice Classification. The opposition was based on a number of earlier French and international word and figurative trade marks, including a composite trade mark combining the words 'Wolf Jardin' with a device of a stylized wolf's head. Among other grounds, Elmar Wolf based its opposition on Article 8(5) CTMR. OHIM rejected the opposition on the ground that Elmar Wolf had not adduced evidence of any detriment to the repute of the earlier marks or any unfair advantage gained from them.

7.510 On appeal, the Second Board annulled the decision of the Opposition Division, holding that the earlier marks were highly reputed in three Member States, that there was some similarity between the marks capable of inducing the relevant public to establish a link between the signs, and that the use of the mark applied for was likely to dilute the unique image of the earlier marks and take unfair advantage of their distinctive character and reputation.

(b) The permissive approach of the General Court

7.511 Environmental Manufacturing brought an action for annulment, pleading infringement of Article 8(5). It argued in particular that the proprietor of the earlier marks had failed to prove that the use of the later mark would have an impact on the behaviour of the consumers and that the Board of Appeal had omitted to assess that impact.

7.512 The General Court[459] dismissed the action as unfounded. As a preliminary point, it took the view[460] that the ground for refusal based on the risk of dilution as provided for in Article 8(5) protects the primary function of the mark, that is to say its capacity to function as an indication of origin, considering that the earlier mark's ability to identify the goods or services for which it is registered is weakened where the use of the later mark leads to the dispersion of its identity and hold upon the public mind. The General Court also reiterated its settled case law as regards the evidential standard in reputation cases, according to which it is sufficient for the proprietor to adduce prima facie evidence of a future risk, which is not hypothetical, and added that such a conclusion may be established, in particular, on the basis of logical deductions made from an analysis of the probabilities and by taking account of the normal practice in the relevant sector as well as all the other circumstances of the case.[461]

7.513 Next, the General Court interpreted *Intel* to the effect that the proprietor cannot be required to show, in addition to a future risk to the distinctiveness or reputation of its mark, that the use of the later sign will have the effect of affecting the economic behaviour of the average consumer, since such a condition is neither set out either in Article 8(5) nor imposed by the Court's judgment in *Intel*. As regards, in particular, paragraph 77 of *Intel*, the General Court stated that it is apparent from the choice of words 'it follows' and from the structure of paragraph 81 that the change in the economic behaviour of the consumer is established if the proprietor has shown, in accordance with paragraph 76 of *Intel*, that the mark's ability to identify the goods or services for which it is registered is weakened. Accordingly, the General Court held that the Board of Appeal was fully entitled to find that the use of

---

[459] T-570/10 *Environmental Manufacturing/Office for Harmonisation in the Internal Market* (Representation of a wolf's head), ECLI:EU:T:2015:76.
[460] C-252/07, *Intel Corporation* [2008] ECR I-8823, paragraphs 29, 37, 38, and 71.
[461] Paragraphs 50–52 of the judgment of the General Court.

the later mark was likely to be detrimental to the distinctive character of the earlier marks without being obliged to address the possible economic effects resulting from the connection between the marks in the mind of the consumer.[462]

(c) The appeal to the Court of Justice

7.514 The Court of Justice disagreed with the reasoning of the judgment under appeal, stating that, according to a proper interpretation of *Intel*, proof that the use of the later mark is, or would be, detrimental to the distinctive character of the earlier mark requires evidence of a change in the economic behaviour of the consumer. Although the Court admitted that paragraph 77 of *Intel* was tainted by a certain ambiguity in that it could be understood as an explanation of the preceding statements of the Court, it noted that the same wording was autonomously reproduced both in paragraph 81 and in the operative part of *Intel*, which ought to make its importance clear. Thus, it concluded that without adducing proper evidence of a change in the economic behaviour of the consumer, the likelihood of detriment to the distinctive character of the earlier mark cannot be properly established.[463]

7.515 The Court then went on to explain that the concept of change in the economic behaviour of the average consumer lays down an objective condition, the fulfilment of which cannot be deduced solely from 'subjective elements linked to the consumer's perception'. The mere fact that consumers 'note the presence of a new sign' similar to an earlier reputed mark is not sufficient to establish the existence of detriment without that similarity causing any confusion in their minds. Hence, it held that, insofar as the General Court had failed to assess that condition, it had committed a clear error of law.[464]

7.516 The Court also disagreed with the findings of the judgment under appeal that 'the fact that competitors use somewhat similar signs for identical or similar goods compromises the immediate connection between the signs and the goods at issue, which is likely to undermine the earlier mark's ability to identify the goods for which it is registered', noting that *Intel* has actually laid down a 'higher standard of proof' in order to find detriment to the distinctive character of the earlier mark and that the criterion put forward by the General Court could lead to a situation in which economic operators improperly appropriate certain signs in a way that could damage free competition.[465]

7.517 The Court acknowledged, however, that, inasmuch as the Regulation and the Court's case law do not require evidence of actual detriment, but also admit the serious risk of such detriment, they allow the drawing of logical deductions from the evidence submitted. Thus, it endorsed, at least at the level of principle, the evidential rules followed by the General Court and OHIM. Nonetheless, it stressed that such deductions must not be the result of mere suppositions but must be founded on 'an analysis of the probabilities and by taking account of the normal practice in the relevant commercial sector as well as all the other circumstances of the case'.[466]

---

[462] Paragraphs 53–54 and 65–66 of the judgment of the General Court.
[463] Paragraphs 34–36.
[464] Paragraphs 37–38.
[465] Paragraphs 39–41.
[466] Paragraphs 42–43.

(d) Repercussions: Back to square one?

7.518 It is clear that the strict approach taken by the Court in *Environmental Manufacturing* has irrevocably closed the door on all attempts to read *Intel* in a permissive manner. The main message is unequivocal: The change in the consumer's economic behaviour cannot be presumed on the basis of mere conjecture or abstract considerations, but its existence must be proved, at least as a tangible likelihood, within the specific framework of each particular case.

7.519 However, the statements of the Court at paragraphs 37 and 40 that the concept of change in the consumer's economic behaviour lays down an 'objective' condition and that *Intel* requires a 'higher standard of proof' in order to admit the existence of blurring, cannot be taken in isolation and should be read against the specific background of the case. In particular, the statement that the change in the economic behaviour of the consumer 'is an objective condition the fulfilment of which cannot be deduced solely from subjective elements linked to the consumer's perception' cannot sensibly be understood as doing away with perceptional considerations altogether. Indeed, if the subject matter of proof is the change in the consumer's behaviour it cannot be ignored that behavioural changes can only be triggered by choices or that the consumer's choices are necessarily driven by his/her perception.

7.520 Rather, what the Court seems to have taken issue with is the failure of the General Court to sanction the unsubstantiated nature of such considerations. Hence, what the Court seems to consider as appropriate evidence are objective elements or indications allowing inference with a reasonable degree of certainty that the consumer's perception has indeed changed in a manner that may affect its economic behaviour or, when available, direct evidence of such a change. Otherwise, the attempt to detach the behaviour of the consumer from its perception becomes logically problematic.

7.521 Similarly, the Court's reference to a 'higher standard' of proof can only be understood as criticizing the automatism that seems to follow from the findings of the General Court that the mere existence of similar signs in the marketplace is sufficient to compromise the immediate connection between the reputed sign and the goods it designates and that this is likely, without anything more, to undermine the earlier mark's distinctive capacity, and not as dismissing the relevance of the criterion of dispersion as such.

7.522 What the Court has therefore stressed is the need to properly substantiate the alleged weakening of the immediate connection between the sign and the goods which lies at the heart of dilution and not merely take it for granted, as this would effectively grant blanket protection to reputed marks against all similar signs. This reading seems to be confirmed by the concession made by the Court at paragraph 42 in the direction of allowing the use of logical deductions as means of evidence, provided that such inferences are plausible in view of the norms of the relevant commercial sector and the overall circumstances of the case.

7.523 That concession is important because it implies that proving a change in the consumer's behaviour does not necessarily require direct evidence capable of showing a clearly quantifiable economic impact on the mark's distinctive capacity. This is consistent with the mechanics of blurring, according to which the erosion of the mark's distinctiveness is the cumulative result of a number of infringing acts (the individual impact of each often hardly perceptible), and becomes clearly visible only when the detriment to the mark's reputation is already irreversible. Hence, the value of inferences is crucial, since, apart from the *ex ante* character of the assessment, the claimant has also to overcome the difficulty of being obliged to rely on probabilities about events that may occur in the future and, at any rate, beyond the confines of the specific case.

7.524 Still, by staying closely focused on the facts pending before it the Court has forfeited the opportunity to elaborate further on the true meaning of 'economic behaviour' and to provide more detailed guidance about how a change in that behaviour can be positively established, ie what an opponent or plaintiff can do in practice to fulfil that requirement. In this sense, the judgment in *Environmental Manufacturing* goes half a step forward from *Intel*, but is definitely not the end of the debate.

(11) *Bellure*: Unfair Advantage

7.525 *Bellure*[467] was another reference for a preliminary ruling from the Court of Appeal of England and Wales (Civil Division), this time dealing, inter alia, with the concept of unfair advantage within the meaning of Article 5(2) of the Directive.

(a) The facts in the main proceedings and the question referred

7.526 The reference was made in the context of a dispute involving L'Oréal SA, Lancôme parfums et beauté & Cie SNC, and Laboratoire Garnier & Cie against Bellure NV, Malaika Investments Ltd, and Starion International Ltd. The claimants are members of the L'Oréal group, which produces and markets fine fragrances. In the United Kingdom, they are proprietors of a number of well-known trade marks for perfumes. Some of the trade marks consist of the commercial names of those products, while others consist of a representation of the perfume bottles or packaging together with the name of the fragrance concerned. The defendants market in the UK imitations of fine fragrances bearing different commercial names but sold in bottles and packaging generally similar in appearance to those of the corresponding products of the claimants. They also make 'comparison lists' available to their retailers, which indicate the fine fragrance to which the specific imitation corresponds by making reference to its trade mark.

7.527 The claimants brought proceedings before the High Court against the defendants alleging infringement of their trade mark rights. They argued that the reproduction of their marks infringed Section 10(1) of the Trade Marks Act (which essentially corresponds to Article 5(1)(a) of the Directive), while the use of similar bottles and packaging was contrary to Section 10(3) of the same Act (corresponding to Article 5(2) of the Directive).

7.528 The High Court granted the application fully insofar as it was based on Section 10(1) and partly inasmuch as it relied on Section 10(3). The defendants appealed to the Court of Appeal, which decided to stay the proceedings and refer a number of questions to the Court for a preliminary ruling.

7.529 As regards the use of the comparison lists reproducing the word marks of the claimants, the referring Court was uncertain whether use in comparative advertising within the meaning of Directive 84/450 may be prevented under Article 5(1)(a) or permitted under Article 6(1)(b) of Directive 89/104.[468]

---

[467] C-487/07 *L'Oréal SA, Lancôme parfums et beauté & Cie SNC, Laboratoire Garnier & Cie v Bellure NV, Malaika Investments Ltd, Starion International Ltd* (BELLURE) [2009] ECR I-05185.

[468] For more about the first to fourth questions in that reference see paragraphs 12.78 and following.

With regard to the use of packaging and bottles similar to those of the fragrances of the **7.530**
plaintiffs, the referring court sought clarification of the concept of 'unfair advantage'
within the meaning of Article 5(2) of the Directive, in the following terms:

> (5) Where a trader uses a sign which is similar to a registered trade mark which has a reputation, and that sign is not confusingly similar to the trade mark, in such a way that:
> (a) the essential function of the registered trade mark of providing a guarantee of origin is not impaired or put at risk;
> (b) there is no tarnishing or blurring of the registered trade mark or its reputation or any risk of either of these;
> (c) the trade mark owner's sales are not impaired; and
> (d) the trade mark owner is not deprived of any of the reward for promotion, maintenance or enhancement of his trade mark;
> (e) but the trader gets a commercial advantage from the use of his sign by reason of its similarity to the registered mark,
> does that use amount to the taking of an 'unfair advantage' of the reputation of the registered mark within the meaning of Article 5(2) of the Directive?

(b) The Opinion of Advocate General Mengozzi

In the first place, Advocate General Mengozzi noted that the referring court was taking the **7.531**
view that, to conclude that there is an unfair advantage where the use of the later mark is
not liable to affect the origin function of the earlier mark, does not tarnish, degrade, or blur
its reputation, and does not have a negative impact on the owner's sales or investment, but
still confers a commercial advantage on the third party, would effectively deprive the word
'unfair' of any meaning.

He then reiterated that, according to the case law, the protection conferred by Article 5(2) **7.532**
also covers situations involving the use of a sign that is similar to the reputed mark for goods
that are identical or similar and is not designed to combat only the likelihood of confusion
on the part of the public. Rather, it presupposes that the similarity between the well-known
mark and the sign enables the public to make a connection between them in a way that is
detrimental to the earlier mark or confers benefit on the later sign. Those conditions, however, are independent from each other, in the sense that either of them may justify in itself
the corresponding type of protection.

Thus, AG Mengozzi concluded that it could not be ruled out on the basis of the circum- **7.533**
stances referred to by the national court that the advantage gained from the use of a sign
that is similar to another person's well-known mark may be classified as unfair within the
meaning of Article 5(2) of the Directive.[469]

Next, the Advocate General turned to the case law of the Court of First Instance on the in- **7.534**
terpretation of Article 8(5) CTMR[470] that the taking of unfair advantage relates to the risk
that the image of the mark with a reputation and the characteristics which it projects are
transferred to the goods covered by the mark applied for, with the result that the marketing
of those goods is made easier by that association, and that there is such an advantage also
where the consumer, without necessarily confusing the commercial origin of the respective

---

[469] Point 97.
[470] T-215/03 *SIGLA v OHIM-Elleni Holding* (VIPS) [2007] ECR II-711, paragraphs 40–42; T-128/06 *Japan Tobacco v OHIM-Torrefaccao Camelo* (CAMELO) [2008] ECR II-00014, paragraphs 46 and 65; and T-93/06 *Mülhens v OHIM-Spa Monopole* (MINERAL SPA), ECLI:EU:T:2010:106, paragraphs 38–40.

products, is attracted by the mark applied for and buys the products covered by it on the ground that they bear a mark which is identical or similar to a mark with a reputation.

7.535 The Advocate General observed though that those two situations were not equivalent; it is one thing to say that the effect of the reputed mark's image on the products identified by the later mark is that the marketing of those goods is made easier, and quite another that it is solely as a result of that effect that the consumer is induced to buy such products in preference to others. He found the latter view to be too restrictive, since it practically means that a reputed mark is protected against free riding only where it can be demonstrated that consumers would not buy the products in question if they didn't bear the specific sign.[471]

7.536 Accordingly, he concurred with the view taken by AG Sharpston in *Intel* that what must actually be established is some sort of boost given to the later sign by its link with the reputed mark.[472] To that effect, it should be sufficient to demonstrate that the later sign carries a particular attraction for the consumer due to its association with the positive qualities projected by the reputation of the earlier mark in such a way as to induce him/her to buy the products bearing that sign.

7.537 But is this sufficient for concluding that the advantage is unfair? To solve that riddle, the Advocate General had recourse to the additional condition in the relevant provisions that protection is not triggered if the defendant can show 'due cause' justifying the advantage. From the very juxtaposition of this redeeming condition to the need for the advantage to be unfair, he inferred that where due cause cannot be shown, such an advantage must be deemed to be unfair. In other words, he considered that where the only apparent purpose of using a sign that is similar to a well-known mark is to exploit its reputation or particular image, the advantage derived by that use is presumed to be unfair; however, that presumption may be rebutted by demonstrating that there is a due cause capable of justifying such use.[473]

(c) The Judgment of the Court

7.538 As a preliminary point the Court noted that it had no jurisdiction to review the legal and factual context of the case, which fell to be determined by the referring court,[474] even if 'it may appear prima facie unlikely' that use by a third party of a sign similar to a trade mark, in order to market goods which imitate those for which that mark is registered, will benefit from its repute without concomitantly causing harm to the image or the marketing of the goods bearing that mark. It also reiterated, referring to *Gofkid* and *Fitnessworld*, that Article 5(2) of the Directive also applies in relation to goods and services identical with or similar to those in respect of which the earlier mark is registered[475] and that the degree of similarity between the signs need not be such as to cause a likelihood of confusion on the part of the public, it being generally sufficient that such similarity causes the public to establish a link between the sign and the mark.[476]

---

[471] Point 101.
[472] Point 62 of her opinion in *Intel* (n 460).
[473] Points 108–109.
[474] C-153/02 *Neri* [2003] ECR I-13555, paragraphs 34 and 35; and C-347/06 *ASM Brescia* [2008] ECR I-05641, paragraph 28.
[475] *Gofkid* (n 353) paragraph 30.
[476] *Fitnessworld* (n 383) paragraphs 29 and 31.

7.539 The Court then proceeded to analyse the notions of 'detriment to repute' and 'unfair advantage', which had not formed part of the dispute in *Intel*.

7.540 It defined the former as the 'tarnishment' or 'degradation' of the earlier mark, caused when the goods or services of the later sign are perceived by the public in such a way that the earlier mark's power of attraction is reduced. It also pointed out that such detriment may arise in particular from the fact that the goods or services of the later mark possess a characteristic or quality which is liable to have a negative impact on the image of the reputed mark.[477] With regard to the concept of 'unfair advantage', also referred to as 'parasitism' or 'free riding', it held that it relates to the advantage taken by a third party as a result of the use of an identical or similar sign and that it covers, in particular, cases where there is clear exploitation on the coat-tails of the reputed mark by reason of a transfer of the image embedded in that mark, or of the characteristics which it projects, to the goods designated by the later sign.[478]

7.541 As regards the appreciation of unfair advantage, the Court referred to the principles laid down in *Intel* and, in particular, to the need for an overall assessment of all the relevant factors.[479] It added, moreover, that although advantage may generally be taken even if the use of the later sign is not detrimental, the fact that there is a likelihood of dilution or tarnishment is a factor that should also be taken into account for the purposes of that global assessment.

7.542 Turning to the facts of the case, it noted that the referring court had established that the defendants used a similar product get-up in order to market 'downmarket' imitations of the luxury fragrances sold by the claimants and that the public was expected to establish a link between the respective packagings which was likely to confer a commercial advantage on the defendants; moreover, the similarity between the products and their packaging was created intentionally, with the aim of facilitating the marketing of the defendants' imitations.

7.543 On the basis of those findings, it stressed that the fact that the marketing strategies of the defendants were intended to take advantage, for promotional purposes, of the repute of the earlier marks should be given particular weight in assessing whether that advantage was unfair.[480]

7.544 Finally, it observed that where a third party attempts to benefit from the power of attraction, the reputation, or the prestige of the earlier mark, and to exploit, without paying any financial compensation and without making any efforts its his own, the marketing expenditure of the proprietor of that mark, the advantage resulting from such use must be considered to have been unfairly taken.[481]

(d) Applying Gofkid *to get-up imitation*

7.545 Apart from giving a detailed definition of the concept of unfair advantage, the judgment in *Bellure* is also significant because it provides a good example of how the provisions on reputed marks can be used in conflicts involving identical or similar goods.

---

[477] *Bellure* (n 467) paragraph 40.
[478] Paragraph 41.
[479] *Intel* (n 460) paragraphs 67–69.
[480] *Bellure* (n 467) paragraph 48.
[481] Paragraph 49.

7.546 Indeed, in cases of get-up imitation the principles developed by the Court in *Gofkid*[482] and *Fitnessworld*[483] seem to find their natural field of application, since, most of the time, the use of a different brand name on a similar product packaging will considerably reduce, if not altogether exclude, the likelihood of confusion. *Bellure*, however, shows that trade mark owners can still have recourse to the provisions on reputed marks as an alternative means of redress against the slavish copying of their product get-up. On the other hand, the fact that in the order for reference the commercial advantage taken by the defendants was taken for granted deprived the Court of the opportunity to address in more detail the standard of proof applicable in cases of unfair advantage, as it did in *Intel* with regard to detriment.

7.547 However, the statement that an intentional imitation aimed at relieving the defendant from the need to promote its products independently is a strong presumption of unfair advantage is particularly useful insofar as it actually suggests that the economic benefit the infringer hopes to derive from the copying is significant enough to be worth the attempt and not just 'hypothetical'.

(12) *Nasdaq*: Putting *Intel* into Perspective?

7.548 *Nasdaq*[484] concerned an appeal from a judgment of the Court of First Instance in a dispute that arose in the context of an opposition brought by The Nasdaq Stock Market, Inc ('Nasdaq Stock Market') against Antartica Srl ('Antartica') under Article 8(5) CTMR. Antartica had sought to register as a Community trade mark a figurative sign essentially consisting of the stylized word 'nasdaq' for a range of goods in Classes 9, 12, 14, 25, and 28 of the Nice Classification. Nasdaq Stock Market opposed the application based on its earlier Community word mark NASDAQ, on the grounds that the use of the mark applied without due cause would take unfair advantage of the distinctive character and repute its earlier mark had acquired in respect of, inter alia, stock exchange price quotation and financial services.

7.549 The Opposition Division of OHIM had rejected the opposition on the grounds that the reputation of the earlier mark had not been properly substantiated. The Office's Boards of Appeal annulled the decision of the Opposition Division on the grounds that both reputation and unfair advantage had been proved. Antartica brought an application for the annulment of that decision before the Court of First Instance, which held that Article 8(5) was indeed applicable to the case and dismissed the action as unfounded. Antartica appealed to the Court of Justice arguing, first, that the Court of First Instance had defined the relevant public wrongly and, second, that it had misapplied the factors to be taken into account when assessing the existence of unfair advantage.

(a) *The Judgment of the Court of First Instance*

7.550 It is useful to take a look at the assessment of unfair advantage made by the Court of First Instance[485] and compare it to the principles laid down in *Intel* as regards proof of detriment, as both Advocates General Sharpston and Mengozzi did in *Intel*[486] and *Bellure*[487] respectively.

---

[482] C-292/00 *Davidoff* [2003] ECR I-389.
[483] C-408/01 *Adidas-Salomon AG* [2003] ECR I-12537.
[484] C-320/07 P *Antartica Srl v OHIM* (NASDAQ) [2009] ECR I-00028.
[485] T-47/06 *Antartica Srl/OHIM* (NASDAQ) [2007] ECR II-00042.
[486] See Point 85 of the Opinion of AG Sharpston in *Intel* (n 460).
[487] See Points 99–100 of the Opinion of AG Mengozzi in *Bellure* (n 467).

7.551 First, the Court of First Instance held that the reputation of the earlier mark had been established in respect of financial and stock exchange price quotation services not only among the professional public, but also with regard to an important sub-section of the general public interested in the financial indices on account of their current or future investments.[488] That finding was further supported by the inherently very distinctive nature of the earlier mark, its omnipresence not only in specialist publications but also in the general press, as well as the interest shown by a large part of the general public in developments in the financial markets.[489]

7.552 The Court then reiterated that the proprietor of the earlier mark is not required to demonstrate actual and present harm to his mark, but merely adduce prima facie evidence of a future risk, which is not hypothetical, of either unfair advantage or detriment. Interestingly enough, it added that such a conclusion may be established, in particular, on the basis of 'logical deductions' resulting from an analysis of the probabilities following from the usual practices in the relevant commercial sector, as well as all the other circumstances relevant to the case.[490]

7.553 Consequently, the Court held that it could be derived from the minutes of the ordinary meeting of Antarctica's shareholders which approved the adoption of the sign at issue as its brand name, first, that its shareholders were aware that the term 'nasdaq' designated 'the American online stock market', and, second, that the word had been chosen because it was regarded as denoting Antarctica's main activity, which consisted of the design, manufacture, and sale of high-tech materials and sports equipment. Therefore, it considered that the high-tech stocks listed on the Nasdaq Stock Market imbued the earlier mark with a certain image of modernity, which was transferrable to the high-tech composite materials marketed by Antarctica.[491]

7.554 Accordingly, the Court of First Instance ruled that there was enough prima facie evidence to establish the existence of a future risk, which was not hypothetical, and that Antartica had not proved the existence of a due cause by arguing that the choice of its mark was due to the fact that it constituted an acronym for the expression 'Nuovi Articoli Sportivi Di Alta Qualita' (New High Quality Sporting Articles).

(b) Findings of the Court

7.555 As regards the part of the plea dealing with the definition of the relevant public, the Court referred to its findings in *Intel* that the public will vary according to the type of injury alleged each time and that with regard to unfair advantage the public to be taken into consideration consisted of the customers of the goods or services designated by the later mark.[492] Thus, it concluded that insofar as the Court of First Instance had held that the reputation of the earlier mark reached further than the professional public specializing in financial information, it had 'implicitly, but clearly' included in its examination the average customer of the goods for which the later mark had been applied for.[493] The Court dismissed

---

[488] Judgment of the Court of First Instance, paragraph 51.
[489] Paragraph 58.
[490] Paragraph 54.
[491] Paragraph 60.
[492] *Intel* (n 460) paragraph 60.
[493] *Nasdaq* (n 484) paragraphs 49–50.

Antartica's arguments as to the existence of unfair advantage by observing that the findings of the Court of First Instance concerned an assessment of a factual nature that was not subject to the Court's review.[494]

(c) Applying Intel *in practice*

7.556 *Nasdaq* is particularly interesting as regards the degree of freedom it allowed to the Court of First Instance in assessing whether detriment or unfair advantage are likely to occur. It is worth noting that the Court of First Instance implied the existence of a detrimental link by reference to circumstantial evidence rather than hard facts. First, its findings in relation to reputation were mostly based on indirect indications suggesting a spillover beyond the financial sector; second, its inferences as to the transferability of Nasdaq's image to the clothing market did not extend to the question whether consumers would actually consider the garments bearing the later sign more attractive, or whether their economic behaviour would be affected, to use the terminology in *Intel*.

7.557 That is not to say that its analysis is not convincing. On the contrary, even if the reference to the Nasdaq stock exchange is not seen as directly indicating clothing made of high-tech materials, its association with the defendant's sign certainly makes it easier to remember and recognize; in that sense, even if the later mark cannot be regarded as benefiting from Nasdaq's image or repute, it surely exploits its attractive powers, that is, its distinctiveness. The fact remains, however, that the Court of First Instance relied more on the (fully proved) fact that the imitation was intentional and less on its economic repercussions. In that sense, its findings are closer to *Bellure* than to *Intel*.

7.558 However, the Court of Justice did not take issue with that assessment. Although all it said was that the task of assessing the facts fell to the Court of First Instance, it still agreed, at least implicitly, with the legal framework within which that assessment was made, including the statement that the overall evaluation of detriment may be based on 'logical deductions resulting from probabilities instead of direct proof'.

7.559 If the Court maintains that approach in future cases, it may finally become apparent that, after all, the evidential standard proposed in *Intel* was not set as high as it seemed at first sight.

(13) *Helena Rubinstein*: Unfair Advantage in Practice

7.560 In *Helena Rubinstein*[495] the Court had the opportunity to explore in more detail the kind of evidence required for proving unfair advantage, including the relationship between an attempted free ride and possible damage to the distinctiveness or repute of the earlier mark. In so doing, it consolidated the principles set out in *Nasdaq*[496] and showed that the conditions applicable in this respect are subject to different rules from those applicable in the context of dilution.

---

[494] Paragraph 53.
[495] C-100/11 P *Helena Rubinstein SNC—L'Oréal SA/Office for Harmonisation in the Internal Market*, ECLI:EU:C:2012:285.
[496] *Nasdaq* (n 484).

(a) Background to the dispute

7.561 The case concerned two applications for a declaration of invalidity brought by Allergan Inc against Helena Rubinstein's Community trade mark registration of the word sign BOTOLIST and L'Oréal's registration of the sign BOTOCYL, both of which had been registered for a range of cosmetic preparations in Class 3 of the Nice Classification. The applications were based on a number of earlier Community and national figurative and word marks, all relating to the sign BOTOX and registered chiefly for goods in Class 5, including pharmaceutical preparations for the treatment of wrinkles. The grounds of invalidity were those referred to in Article 52(1)(a), in conjunction with Article 8(1)(b), (4), and (5) CTMR. The Cancellation Division rejected both applications for invalidity. Allergan filed notices of appeal, both of which were upheld by the First Board under Article 8(5).

7.562 Helena Rubinstein and L'Oréal brought actions for annulment, pleading, among other things, infringement of Article 8(5). The General Court[497] dismissed the actions, limiting its examination to the two earlier UK registrations for the word 'botox', as the United Kingdom was the territory in respect of which most of the evidence had been submitted and considering that reputation in one Member State is sufficient to justify the application of Article 8(5).

7.563 The General Court held that the evidence submitted by Allergan demonstrated:

(i) that BOTOX had a reputation in the relevant territory as attested by the fact that its market share in the United Kingdom was 74.3% in 2003 and that its awareness among the public 75%;
(ii) that the marks were similar on account of their common part 'BOTO-', which was not likely to be understood as a reference to 'botulinum toxin', ie the active ingredient of the pharmaceutical product sold by Allergan; and
(iii) that even if the term 'botox' could be broken down into 'bo' for 'botulinum' and 'tox' for 'toxin', this did not preclude it from having acquired a distinctive character, inherent or through use, at least in the United Kingdom.

7.564 Considering also that the respective goods concerned 'related market sectors', the General Court held that the relevant public would naturally be led to establish a link between the marks, whether or not it would also associate them with the substance botulinum.

7.565 Lastly, the General Court agreed with Allergan that there was a sufficiently serious and real risk that the disputed marks would take advantage of the distinctive character and repute acquired by BOTOX with the effect of decreasing its brand value, in particular since Helena Rubinstein and L'Oréal had acknowledged that, even though their products did not contain the botulinum toxin, they nevertheless intended to profit from the allusion to that substance.

(b) The appeal to the Court of Justice

7.566 Helena Rubinstein and L'Oréal appealed to the Court of Justice, claiming, inter alia, that the General Court infringed Articles 52(1) and 8(5) of the Regulation. They argued that the General Court wrongly: (i) restricted its examination to Allergan's UK registrations;

---

[497] Joined Cases T-345/08 and T-357/08 *Rubinstein and L'Oréal v OHIM—Allergan* (BOTOLIST and BOTOCYL), [2010] ECR II-00279.

(ii) found that the earlier marks were reputed; (iii) accepted the existence of a link between the signs; and (iv) came to the conclusion that the contested registrations actually sought to take advantage of the repute of the earlier marks. The appellants also argued that the judgment under appeal infringed Article 115 of the Regulation in conjunction with Rule 38(2) of the Implementing Regulation to the extent that it had admitted in the proceedings, and had given material value to, means of evidence that had not been translated into the language of the proceedings before the Office.

7.567 Advocate General Mengozzi[498] proposed to reject the appeal, taking the view, first, that the judgment under appeal rightly found that the evidence submitted by Allergan was sufficient, as a whole, to show that the mark BOTOX was reputed in the United Kingdom and, second, that the General Court had relied on a proper examination of the various factors at play before arriving at the conclusion that there was a risk of unfair advantage being taken of that reputation.

7.568 Specifically, the Advocate General noted, referring to the principles laid down by the Court in *Bellure* and *Interflora*,[499] that the existence of a parasitic intent could be inferred from a number of findings which concerned, on the one hand, the fact that Helena Rubinstein and L'Oréal had opted to use a prefix which reproduced almost all of the earlier marks and that this decision of theirs could not be justified by the mere intention to refer to the botulinum toxin which, moreover, did not form part of the goods covered by the contested marks, and, on the other, the characteristics of the earlier mark, that is to say, its strong distinctive character, uniqueness, and reputation, stressing also that, in this state of affairs, the burden was on the appellants to show that they had a due cause for the choice and use of their marks, which, however, they failed to do.[500]

7.569 Moreover, the Advocate General rejected the alleged irrelevance of the examination of the 'specificity' and 'uniqueness' of the mark BOTOX, which, in the appellants' view, were pertinent factors in the case of dilution, but not of parasitism, observing that even though the risk of detriment to the distinctive character of the mark is not a necessary condition to that effect, it constitutes, where it is found, a factor to be taken into consideration in determining whether or not unfair advantage is likely to be taken of the earlier mark's reputation.[501]

7.570 The Court of Justice followed the proposal of the Advocate General and rejected the appeal as partly inadmissible and partly unfounded. In the first place, it held that the General Court was able to confine its review to the earlier national marks registered in the United Kingdom, noting that, contrary to the Cancellation Division, which had based its decision exclusively on Allergan's stylized Community trade mark, the Board of Appeal had found that a reputation had been acquired in respect of both the figurative and the word marks BOTOX, whether Community or national. In consequence, the General Court had not altered the factual basis of the dispute, but had at most restricted the subject matter of the proceedings before the Board in a lawful manner.[502]

---

[498] Opinion of Advocate General Mengozzi of 16 February 2012, Case C-100/11 P *Helena Rubinstein and L'Oréal SA/Office for Harmonisation in the Internal Market*, ECLI:EU:C:2012:285.
[499] Respectively, Case C-487/07 *L'Oréal and Others* [2009] ECR I-5185 and Case C-323/09 *Interflora and Others* [2011] ECR I-08625.
[500] Points 32–36.
[501] Point 37.
[502] Paragraphs 50–53.

Second, the Court held that the judgment under appeal was entitled to find that the earlier **7.571** marks had a reputation without erring in applying the relevant criteria or distorting the clear sense of the evidence. In that regard, it noted that since the earlier mark enjoyed a reputation with the general public on account of the significant media coverage of the products marketed under that mark and the inclusion of the term BOTOX in English language dictionaries, it could not be argued that the mark was not also known to healthcare professionals, who were equally exposed to that information. Moreover, the Court held that the appellants could not rely on the defects of the various items of evidence, taken in isolation, in order to cast doubt on the validity of the evidence as a whole, since that would additionally require determining the weight of the allegedly deficient items for the purposes of the overall assessment. Nor could they admissibly contest the probative force of such evidence on appeal. Lastly, as regards the argument that the General Court could not rely on a decision of the UK Intellectual Property Office taken in proceedings relating to the mark BOTOMASK, it held that the findings set out in that decision constituted, in themselves, a fact which may, if relevant, be taken into consideration by the General Court in the exercise of its absolute discretion in relation to deciding which items were pertinent for its unfettered evaluation of the evidence.[503]

Third, the Court held that the contention that it must be permissible to include in a later **7.572** trade mark an element which forms part of an earlier mark owned by a third party to the extent that that common element is descriptive presupposed that the common element 'bot' or 'boto' would actually be perceived as such; however, that premise was contrary to the conclusions of the General Court that this was not the case and, being a statement of a factual nature, it could not be challenged before the Court of Justice.[504]

Fourth, the Court reiterated[505] that although the proprietor of the earlier mark must prove **7.573** that use of the later mark would take unfair advantage of, or be detrimental to, the distinctive character or the repute of the earlier mark, it is sufficient to that effect to adduce prima facie evidence of a future risk which is not hypothetical, and that such a risk may be established, in particular, on the basis of logical deductions made from an analysis of the probabilities and by taking account of the practices in the relevant commercial sector. Thus, it held that the conclusions of the judgment under appeal about the existence of such a risk were properly substantiated, since it was only after analysing a variety of factors that the General Court had determined the existence of a parasitic intent. That conclusion was sufficiently supported by the findings that:

(i) the prefix 'boto-' was common to the trade marks at issue and could not be regarded as an abbreviation of 'botulinus' or 'botulinum';
(ii) the sign BOTOX had acquired a distinctive character;
(iii) the earlier marks had acquired a substantial reputation;
(iv) the goods concerned fell within 'related market sectors';
(v) the relevant public would establish a link between the signs before even associating them with 'botulinum'; and

---

[503] Paragraphs 65–78.
[504] Paragraphs 83–88.
[505] Citing case C-252/07 *Intel Corporation* [2008] ECR I-8823, paragraphs 37 and 38.

(vi) the appellants had acknowledged that, even if their products did not contain the botulinum toxin, they nevertheless intended to take advantage of the image which was associated with that product, which is to be found in the mark BOTOX.[506]

7.574 As concerns, lastly, the ground of appeal relying on the alleged infringement of Article 115 CTMR, although the Court admitted[507] that, as a rule, the evidence must be submitted in the language of the proceedings or be accompanied by a translation into that language, it found that in the present case that omission had not adversely affected the rights of defence of the appellants, as demonstrated by the fact that they were able to understand and challenge the evidential value of the relevant items before the General Court and had not submitted any objection in this regard in the course of the administrative proceedings before OHIM.[508]

(c) Conclusions

7.575 In *Helena Rubinstein* the Court of Justice confirmed in a more explicit manner the approach taken in *Nasdaq* as concerns the evidential standard required for proving unfair advantage. It also reaffirmed its unwillingness to tamper with the assessment of the facts made by the General Court showing, once again, that it is notoriously difficult to overturn a first instance judgment based on possible inconsistencies in the weighing up of the relevant factors.

7.576 As regards, first, the assessment of reputation, the statement of the Court that it is not sufficient for the appellant to show that certain items of evidence are irrelevant, but that it must also determine the specific weight of the evidence to be disregarded in the overall assessment carried out by the General Court, creates an obstacle that is near impossible to overcome, since most of the time the judgment under appeal is far from clear when it comes to the relative value that it has attributed to each of the factors it took into account.

7.577 The second point of interest in *Helena Rubinstein* is the part confirming that the overall assessment of unfair advantage does not require direct proof, but may be established on the basis of logical deductions made from an analysis of the probabilities. This statement is significant because it formally endorses the approach taken so far by the General Court in the context of free riding and gives it the status of a general evidential principle, considering also that its parallel application in cases of detriment was similarly confirmed in *Environmental Manufacturing*.

7.578 It should be pointed out, however, that there is an important difference between the two tests, inasmuch as in cases of alleged unfair advantage it is not required to show a change in the economic behaviour of the consumer, in order to establish that the use of the later mark will indeed confer an objective advantage on its owner, before pondering on the question of whether that advantage is unfair.

7.579 On the contrary, what seems to weigh more in the Court's mind is the defendant's 'parasitic intent', which is deemed to be established every time there is an attempt to derive a benefit from the earlier mark's reputation by intentionally using an identical or similar sign in

---

[506] Paragraphs 93–97.
[507] Citing cases T-107/02 *GE Betz v OHIM—Atofina Chemicals* (BIOMATE) [2004] ECR II-1845, paragraph 72 and Case T-407/05 *SAEME v OHIM—Racke* (REVIAN's) [2007] ECR II-4385, paragraph 35.
[508] Paragraphs 102–104.

circumstances rendering possible an image transfer. It would therefore seem that the Court has turned the test upside down, in the sense that it understands the attempt to imitate a famous mark as near conclusive evidence of a competitive advantage, apparently on the assumption that if such an economic benefit was not likely, the defendant would not have attempted to imitate the earlier mark in the first place.

However welcome this permissive approach may be for trade mark owners, the fact remains that, at least from a methodological viewpoint, it has the effect of somehow blurring the boundaries between the various steps of the assessment by effectively equating the proof of the existence of a link to the proof of unfair advantage, since the only material difference that remains between the two is the existence of a parasitic intent. In other words, if the creation of a link proves to be intentional, the existence of an unfair advantage is also presumed. Thus, the Court appears to be focusing more on the unfairness than on the advantage itself, in the sense that if there is evidence of an attempt or intention on the part of the defendant to create an association between the signs, the Court is all too ready to presume that there is an advantage and that this advantage is unfairly taken. **7.580**

This also shows that the requirement set forth in *Bellure* to the effect that, for the advantage to be unfair, the defendant must attempt to exploit the prestige of the reputed mark 'without making any efforts of its own' in terms of promotional expenditure, has practically been relegated to the realm of due cause, in the sense that it will generally be up to the owner of the later mark to prove the absence of a parasitic intent by showing a substantial independent effort to promote its mark. **7.581**

Accordingly, the judgments in *Nasdaq* and *Helena Rubinstein* seem to suggest that, at least in cases where an attempt of an intentional imitation can be established, it will generally be easier to rely on free riding than on dilution to stop the encroachment on the earlier mark's distinctive character or repute. **7.582**

(14) The *Red Bull* Trio: Due Cause; Scope of Protection; Confusion and Unfair Advantage; Goods for Export

There are three Red Bull cases covered in this book. The first provides a test for exploring whether there is a 'due cause' defence; the second—a judgment of the General Court—looks at a similar clash, at least in terms of signs, from a likelihood of confusion perspective; and the third has to do with scope of protection in the case of goods destined for export, and is covered in Chapter 9.[509] There is another link between the first and the third cases: the application of the principles developed as part of the 'trade marks on the Internet' jurisprudence of the Court of Justice in a non-Internet environment. **7.583**

(15) *Leidseplein Beheer BV v Red Bull GmbH; Red Bull v Bulldog;* The Concept of Due Cause

(a) The factual background of the dispute

Red Bull, the proprietor of a number of Red Bull trade marks registered for 'non-alcoholic drinks', including an international registration of the 'Red Bull Krating-Daeng' word/figurative composite trade mark, dated 11 July 1983, started infringement proceedings **7.584**

---

[509] C-119/10 *Frisdranken Industrie Winters BV v Red Bull GmbH* [2011] ECR I-13179, discussed at paragraphs 9.262 and following below.

against Mr de Vries, the proprietor of three Bulldog trade marks registered in the Benelux for the same specification: figurative mark 'The Bulldog', registered on 14 July 1983; word mark 'The Bulldog', registered on 23 December 1999; and figurative mark 'The Bulldog Energy Drink', registered on 15 June 2000. Amongst other things, Red Bull was asking Mr de Vries to cease the production and marketing of energy drinks in packaging that displayed the 'Bull Dog' sign or another sign containing the word element 'Bull'. Mr de Vries challenged the claim that his trade marks were confusingly similar to the trade mark registrations of Red Bull and brought a counterclaim in which he applied for the revocation and cancellation in respect of the Benelux countries of the registration of the 'Red Bull Krating-Daeng' based on his earlier use of 'The Bulldog' as a trade name for a hotel and a restaurant.

7.585 Following a number of appeals the case reached the Hoge Raad which, without having ascertained whether there was likelihood of confusion or free riding on Red Bull's reputation, sought from the Court clarification of the concept of due cause from the factual perspective of the case:

> Is Article 5(2) of [the Trade Marks Directive] to be interpreted as meaning that there can be due cause within the meaning of that provision also where the sign that is identical or similar to the trade mark with a reputation was already being used in good faith by the third party/parties concerned before that trade mark was filed?[510]

(b) The Opinion of Advocate General Kokott

7.586 Advocate General Kokott started by acknowledging the differences in terms of language between the Dutch and other versions of Article 5(2) of the Directive. The Dutch version referred to the concept of a 'proper ground' or a 'valid ground', possibly setting a higher standard than the German concept of 'rechtfertigender Grund', the French 'juste motif', or the English 'due cause'. She noted, however, that the concept had to be interpreted uniformly 'by reference to the purpose and general scheme of the rules of which it forms part'.[511]

7.587 Red Bull argued that since the Benelux trade mark system relied exclusively on registration, earlier use of a sign as a trade name in the absence of registration should be irrelevant. Otherwise due cause would lead to the introduction of unregistered trade marks into the Benelux system.

7.588 However, the Advocate General noted that the concept of due cause required a balancing exercise; the Court in *Interflora*[512] had not understood the concept of due cause as requiring a compelling ground. The use in that case came within 'the ambit of fair, healthy competition in the sector for the goods or services concerned and is thus not without "due cause"'.[513] Instead of relying on the absence of any alternative to the use of trade marks with a reputation as keywords, the decision was based 'on the result of a balancing exercise which weighed up

---

[510] Reproduced in point 11 of the Opinion of AG Kokott. *Leidseplein Beheer BV and Hendrikus de Vries v Red Bull GmbH and Red Bull Nederland BV* Opinion ECLI:EU:C:2013:196; Judgment ECLI:EU:C:2014:49.

[511] Point 22, citing Case 19/67 *Van der Vecht* [1967] ECR 345; Case 30/77 *Bouchereau* [1977] ECR 1999; Case C-56/06 Euro Tex [2007] ECR I-4859; and Case C-426/05 Tele2 Telecommunication [2008] ECR I-685.

[512] C-323/09 *Interflora and Interflora British Unit* [2011] ECR I-8625.

[513] Point 32.

the detriment to the trade mark against other legal rights, in particular freedom of competition'.[514] This balancing exercise approach characterized all areas of trade mark law.

The analysis of the Advocate General identified a number of factors that had to be taken into account for determining whether there was a due cause behind the use of a trade mark with a reputation: **7.589**

(i) the goods were identical;
(ii) Bulldog had been registered since 1983, with Red Bull predating it only for a couple of days;
(iii) whether Red Bull had a reputation at that time;
(iv) whether Mr de Vries could rely on the principle of respect for acquired rights as recognized by EU law;[515]
(v) whether the mark had been used for energy drinks before 1997;
(vi) any use on other economic activity in the catering sphere; and
(vii) whether current use functioned as an indication of origin.

The Advocate General concluded that: **7.590**

> In weighing up whether a third party has, within the meaning of Article 5(2) of Directive 2008/95/EC ... taken, without due cause, unfair advantage of the distinctive character or the repute of a trade mark with a reputation by using a sign similar to that trade mark with a reputation, if that third party was already using the sign in good faith for other goods or services before the trade mark with a reputation was filed or gained a reputation, such a fact will be taken into account in that third party's favour.[516]

(c) The Judgment of the Court

(i) A balancing exercise The Court held that the concept should not be interpreted strictly. That concept must therefore be interpreted in the light of the overall scheme and objectives of the system of which it forms part ... (and, in particular, must take into account the context of the provision which contains it.[517] The freedom Member States had in relation to the introduction and application of Article 5(2) of the Directive is limited; once the provision is transposed Member States must grant protection that is at least as extensive for identical or similar goods or services as it is for non-similar goods or services. 'Such a finding, however, cannot mean that the concept of "due cause" should be interpreted by having regard to the scope of Article 5(1) of Directive 89/104'.[518] The two provisions were applied independently from each other. **7.591**

And all this should be seen against a global requirement; the purpose of the Directive is 'generally to strike a balance between the interest which the proprietor of a trade mark has in safeguarding its essential function, on the one hand, and the interests of other economic **7.592**

---

[514] Point 34.
[515] Citing C-168/09 *Flos* [2011] ECR I-181, paragraph 50. The Advocate General noted: 'The exercise of an existing right cannot, in principle, be unfair and without due cause simply because another trade mark subsequently achieves a high degree of recognition, with the result that its scope of protection conflicts with the scope of protection of existing marks' (point 41).
[516] Point 49.
[517] Paragraph 28, citing to that effect C-292/00 *Davidoff* [2003] ECR I-389 and C-320/12 *Malaysia Dairy Industries*, ECLI:EU:C:2013:435.
[518] Paragraph 35.

operators in having signs capable of denoting their products and services, on the other'.[519] Protection is not unconditional. The trade mark proprietor of a trade mark with a reputation carries the onus of showing that unfair advantage of the distinctiveness or reputation of its trade mark has been taken by another party; that party has, then, the onus of showing that there is due cause for using the trade mark.[520] Potentially widening considerably the scope of due cause, the Court noted that it may include 'objectively overriding reasons but may also relate to the subjective interests of a third party using a sign which is identical or similar to the mark with a reputation'.[521]

7.593 It stressed that:

> the concept of 'due cause' is intended, not to resolve a conflict between a mark with a reputation and a similar sign which was being used before that trade mark was filed or to restrict the rights which the proprietor of that mark is recognised as having, but to strike a balance between the interests in question by taking account, in the specific context of Article 5(2) of Directive 89/104 and in the light of the enhanced protection enjoyed by that mark, of the interests of the third party using that sign. In so doing, the claim by a third party that there is due cause for using a sign which is similar to a mark with a reputation cannot lead to the recognition, for the benefit of that third party, of the rights connected with a registered mark, but rather obliges the proprietor of the mark with a reputation to tolerate the use of the similar sign.[522]

7.594 **(ii) The conditions for establishing due cause** There are two factors in particular that must be taken into account: First, 'a determination as to how that sign has been accepted by, and what its reputation is with, the relevant public';[523] and, second, 'the intention of the person using that sign'.[524] Elaborating further on the second factor,

> in order to determine whether the use of the sign similar to the mark with a reputation was in good faith, it is necessary to take account of the degree of proximity between the goods and services for which that sign has been used and the product for which that mark was registered, as well as to have regard for when that sign was first used for a product identical to that for which that mark was registered, and when that mark acquired its reputation.[525]

7.595 Looking at the specificities of the reference, the Court made two additional points. First, there may be cases where earlier use may lead to an understanding that use subsequent to the registration of the trade mark with a reputation is a natural extension of that prior use. Second, the

> greater the repute of the sign used, prior to the registration of a similar mark with a reputation, for a certain range of goods and services, the more its use will be necessary for the marketing of a product identical to that for which the mark was registered, *a fortiori* as that product is close, by its nature, to the range of goods and services for which that sign was previously used.[526]

7.596 Concluding, the Court held:

> Article 5(2) of Directive 89/104 must be interpreted as meaning that the proprietor of a trade mark with a reputation may be obliged, pursuant to the concept of 'due cause' within the

---

[519] Paragraph 41, citing C-145/05 *Levi Strauss* [2006] ECR I-3703, paragraph 29.
[520] Citing C-252/07 *Intel Corporation* [2008] ECR I-8823, paragraph 39.
[521] Paragraph 35.
[522] Paragraph 46.
[523] Paragraph 54.
[524] Paragraph 55.
[525] Paragraph 56.
[526] Paragraph 59.

meaning of that provision, to tolerate the use by a third party of a sign similar to that mark in relation to a product which is identical to that for which that mark was registered, if it is demonstrated that that sign was being used before that mark was filed and that the use of that sign in relation to the identical product is in good faith. In order to determine whether that is so, the national court must take account, in particular, of:

how that sign has been accepted by, and what its reputation is with, the relevant public;

the degree of proximity between the goods and services for which that sign was originally used and the product for which the mark with a reputation was registered; and

the economic and commercial significance of the use for that product of the sign which is similar to that mark.

(16) *Red Bull v Bulldog*: Conceptual Similarity

7.597 It is worth discussing briefly another aspect of the clash between Red Bull and Bulldog[527] that has reached the General Court. This time Red Bull opposed an application for registration of the word sign BULLDOG for non-alcoholic drinks. The opposition was based on a number of earlier trade marks registered for the same specification, including the word marks BULL and RED BULL. The opposition was successful, but the Board of Appeal annulled the decision of the Opposition Division and the case came before the General Court. The Board had found that the signs had a low degree of visual and phonetic similarity and were conceptually different.

7.598 The General Court found the marks BULL and BULLDOG to possess an average rather than low degree of similarity. On the one hand, they shared four identical letters and 'Bull' was incorporated within 'Bulldog'; on the other, a small difference between two short signs may have been significant in preventing the finding of a high degree of similarity.

7.599 Phonetically, the two marks were also found to be similar to an average degree following a similar analysis with the one adopted above. Strong similarity at the beginning but a clearly pronounceable 'dog' at the end on the other.

7.600 Conceptually, taking into account that the public is that of the EU as a whole and that 'Bull' is not such a common English word, the General Court found that the fact that the

> term cannot have a specific meaning for a large part of the relevant public renders nugatory any comparison with the other word sign 'bulldog', notwithstanding the fact that the English word 'bulldog', as the Board of Appeal pointed out, correctly this time, has passed into nearly all official EU languages almost unchanged.[528]

The Court also held that the English-speaking part of the Community would recognize that the signs at issue referred to two separate animals; however, both the bull and the bulldog 'convey the image of animals from which a concentrated force emanates, a great muscular force often expressing itself aggressively towards their fellow creatures or human beings, especially when that power is on display in combat or at bullfights'.[529] The marks were not comparable conceptually in a large part of the EU and had a low degree of similarity for the English-speaking public. An argument focusing on the commonality of the term in other languages, 'Bulle' in German, 'bullis' in Latvian, and 'bul' in Dutch, failed

---

[527] T-78/13, *Red Bull GmbH v OHIM/Sun Mark Ltd*, ECLI:EU:T:2015:72; appeal against the decision of the BoA in R-107/2012-2.
[528] Paragraph 47.
[529] Paragraph 50.

because it would still have required an understanding of the term in English; in any case, other European languages used different etymological terms to describe a bull, for example, 'tavros' in Greek and 'toro' in Italian and Spanish.

7.601 Turning to an overall comparison, the Court found that the two resembled each other. As to whether there was a likelihood of confusion, the General Court highlighted the interdependence between the similarity of the marks and the similarity of the goods or services; 'a lesser degree of similarity between the goods or services may be offset by a greater degree of similarity between the marks, and vice versa'.[530] In this case the Board of Appeal had failed to take into account the fact that the goods were identical. 'Given, first, how important the fact is that they are identical and, second, the conclusion ... above of the overall resemblance of the signs at issue, it must be held that the likelihood of confusion between the marks at issue has been proved.'[531]

7.602 Context is everything in trade mark law and in addition the Court of Justice had made it very clear in the first of the two Red Bull cases above that the two routes for seeking protection, one based on reputation and the other on confusion, are distinct, each with its own purpose and requirements. Still, the contrast is intriguing.

I. Conclusion

7.603 This chapter has explored the three layers of trade mark conflicts at the time of the application of registration; the first two are based on confusion, the third on reputation.

7.604 In the first case, where there is total identity, there is at least a presumption of confusion. In the case of similarity the Court founded its case law on the concept of confusion. The standard appears to be rigorous: confusion must be genuine and properly substantiated. At the same time, the Court has highlighted the link between the function of a trade mark, that continues to serve as the justification behind protection, with the interests of the trade mark proprietor. Conceptually that is a logical consequence, but in terms of semantics it is a telling detail that the trade mark proprietor appears to be a new starting point in the reasoning of the Court. This will be explored further in Chapter 9.

7.605 The test for establishing confusion is a multifactor open-ended test, with trade mark and product similarity being cumulative conditions. The Court has also established that stronger marks, either because they are inherently distinctive or because they have grown in terms of distinctiveness through use, will inevitably enjoy a wider scope of protection; without this meaning product similarity will become redundant in the case of very strong trade marks. A positive finding on likelihood of confusion will always be required.

7.606 To assess distinctiveness and reputation the Court has suggested a number of factors that must be considered and has insisted that there is no need to set specific targets in terms of consumer recognition that a highly distinctive trade mark or a trade mark with a reputation must reach. What needs to be established, however, is that the trade mark has become

---

[530] Paragraph 57, citing C-39/97 *Canon*, EU:C:1998:442, paragraph 17 and T-81/03, T-82/03, and T-103/03 *Mast-Jägermeister v OHIM—Licorera Zacapaneca* (VENADO with frame and Others), EU:T:2006:397, paragraph 74.

[531] Paragraph 60.

Conclusion

distinctive or gained reputation in respect of the particular product rather than as a name in the abstract.

7.607 What the Court is still uncertain about is whether the concept of confusion encompasses confusion away from the point of sale; would, for example, post-sale confusion suffice when, as a result, the behaviour of the consumer is affected at the point of sale, subsequent to and as a result of the post-sale confusion?

7.608 The partial tests for determining trade mark and product similarity comprise a broad variety of questions, with the Court underlining that all the facts of each individual case must be taken into account. Indeed, the trade mark similarity test is applied in respect of all three layers of protection.

7.609 In terms of marks with a reputation, note that the Court has looked for the purpose of the provision in order to interpret it and gone against a strict literal interpretation. Here, the Court appears to require a higher burden of proof in the case of harm to distinctiveness than in the case of a competitor enjoying a free ride on the reputation of the trade mark proprietor. At the same time, the Court has started developing a multifactorial test to determine what constitutes due cause, making it clear that establishing due cause does not require proving the absence of a free ride. After all, if there is no free ride there should not be a need for a competitor to carry the onus for proving due cause.

7.610 The angle that all these questions are considered from is that of the average consumer of the relevant product.

8

LOSS OF RIGHTS

Requirement of Use, Conversion to Generic Indication

A. Introduction

The rights arising from trade mark registration may be lost. First, when registration is not renewed, the registration will be deleted from the register. Second, a registered trade mark is liable to be revoked if it has not been put to genuine use for more than five years. Third, a trade mark is subject to revocation when it has become the generic indication, the 'name' of the product. Fourth, a mark is also subject to revocation when it has become misleading. The last two revocation grounds are the mirror image of the absolute grounds for refusal, the difference being that revocation is available when the mark, although properly registered initially, has become generic or misleading at a later time. The first ground for revocation, absence of genuine use, has no counterpart at the time of filing or registration. Rather, the legislation provides trade mark proprietors with a period of five years following registration after which revocation is possible. **8.01**

Trade mark registrations that have been obtained contrary to an absolute or relative ground may also be challenged and declared invalid. However, note that the Regulation refers to bad faith only as an absolute ground for invalidity, whereas in the Directive bad faith is foreseen as both an absolute ground for refusal and invalidity, and, additionally, as an optional relative ground by virtue of Article 4(4)(g).[1] **8.02**

This chapter deals first with the use requirement, and thereafter with genericness. **8.03**

B. Requirement of Use

(1) Introduction

Using the trade mark is the main requirement that the proprietor of a trade mark right needs to satisfy. Absence of genuine use is a ground for revocation. The principle of 'use' for the purposes of maintaining a registration is also being developed by the Court in cases where the owner of an earlier right must establish use in order to attack a Community trade mark application or registration.[2] **8.04**

---

[1] See Article 52(1)(a) of the Regulation and Articles 3(2)(d) and 4(4)(g) of the Directive.
[2] See C-416/04 P *The Sunrider Corp v Office for Harmonisation in the Internal Market (Trade Marks and Designs)* [2006] ECR I-04237.

8.05 The Eighth Recital states:

> Whereas in order to reduce the total number of trade marks registered and protected in the Community and, consequently, the number of conflicts which arise between them, it is essential to require that registered trade marks must actually be used or, if not used, be subject to revocation; whereas it is necessary to provide that a trade mark cannot be invalidated on the basis of the existence of a non-used earlier trade mark, while the Member States remain free to apply the same principle in respect of the registration of a trade mark or to provide that a trade mark may not be successfully invoked in infringement proceedings if it is established as a result of a plea that the trade mark could be revoked; whereas in all these cases it is up to the Member States to establish the applicable rules of procedure.

(2) The Legislative Contexts

(a) The provisions of the Directive

8.06 Article 10—Use of trade marks

1. If, within a period of five years following the date of the completion of the registration procedure, the proprietor has not put the trade mark to genuine use in the Member State in connection with the goods or services in respect of which it is registered, or if such use has been suspended during an uninterrupted period of five years, the trade mark shall be subject to the sanctions provided for in this Directive, unless there are proper reasons for non-use.
2. The following shall also constitute use within the meaning of paragraph 1:
   (a) use of the trade mark in a form differing in elements which do not alter the distinctive character of the mark in the form in which it was registered;
   (b) affixing of the trade mark to goods or to the packaging thereof in the Member State concerned solely for export purposes.
3. Use of the trade mark with the consent of the proprietor or by any person who has authority to use a collective mark or a guarantee or certification mark shall be deemed to constitute use by the proprietor.
4. In relation to trade marks registered before the date on which the provisions necessary to comply with this Directive enter into force in the Member State concerned:
   (a) where a provision in force prior to that date attaches sanctions to nonuse of a trade mark during an uninterrupted period, the relevant period of five years mentioned in paragraph 1 shall be deemed to have begun to run at the same time as any period of non-use which is already running at that date;
   (b) where there is no use provision in force prior to that date, the periods of five years mentioned in paragraph 1 shall be deemed to run from that date at the earliest.

8.07 Article 11—Sanctions for non-use of a trade mark in legal or administrative proceedings

1. A trade mark may not be declared invalid on the ground that there is an earlier conflicting trade mark if the latter does not fulfil the requirements of use set out in Article 10(1), (2) and (3) or in Article 10(4), as the case may be.
2. Any Member State may provide that registration of a trade mark may not be refused on the ground that there is an earlier conflicting trade mark if the latter does not fulfil the requirements of use set out in Article 10(1), (2) and (3) or in Article 10(4), as the case may be.
3. Without prejudice to the application of Article 12, where a counter-claim for revocation is made, any Member State may provide that a trade mark may not be successfully invoked in infringement proceedings if it is established as a result of a plea that the trade mark could be revoked pursuant to Article 12(1).
4. If the earlier trade mark has been used in relation to part only of the goods or services for which it is registered, it shall, for purposes of applying paragraphs 1, 2 and 3, be deemed to be registered in respect only of that part of the goods or services.

Article 12—Grounds for revocation **8.08**

1. A trade mark shall be liable to revocation if, within a continuous period of five years, it has not been put to genuine use in the Member State in connection with the goods or services in respect of which it is registered, and there are no proper reasons for non-use; however, no person may claim that the proprietor's rights in a trade mark should be revoked where, during the interval between expiry of the five-year period and filing of the application for revocation, genuine use of the trade mark has been started or resumed; the commencement or resumption of use within a period of three months preceding the filing of the application for revocation which began at the earliest on expiry of the continuous period of five years of non-use, shall, however, be disregarded where preparations for the commencement or resumption occur only after the proprietor becomes aware that the application for revocation may be filed.
2. A trade mark shall also be liable to revocation if, after the date on which it was registered:
   (a) In consequence of acts or inactivity of the proprietor, it has become the common name in the trade for a product or service in respect of which it is registered;
   (b) In consequence of the use made of it by the proprietor of the trade mark or with his consent in respect of the goods or services for which it is registered, it is liable to mislead the public, particularly as to the nature, quality or geographical origin of those goods or services.

Article 13—Grounds for refusal or revocation or invalidity relating to only some of the goods or services **8.09**

Where grounds for refusal of registration or for revocation or invalidity of a trade mark exist in respect of only some of the goods or services for which that trade mark has been applied for or registered, refusal of registration or revocation or invalidity shall cover those goods or services only.

Article 14—Establishment a posteriori of invalidity or revocation of a trade mark **8.10**

Where the seniority of an earlier trade mark which has been surrendered or allowed to lapse, is claimed for a Community trade mark, the invalidity or revocation of the earlier trade mark may be established a posteriori.

(b) The provisions of the Regulation

The Regulation has provisions which are broader and more specific, but as to substance essentially mirror those of the Directive. The basic rule corresponding to Article 10 of the Directive is found in Article 15 of the Regulation, the need to prove use in opposition and invalidity proceedings based on earlier registered marks is provided for in Articles 43 and 57 of the Regulation, and revocation is provided for in Article 51 of the Regulation. The defence of non-use is provided for in Article 99(3) of the Regulation. **8.11**

(3) The Case Law

The provisions on the use requirement contain a number of criteria or concepts which are not self-explanatory and which have led and will continue to lead to litigation. The major substantive requirements are: **8.12**

The use must be "genuine"
Use in the territory where the mark is protected, including use in export trade
Use of the mark as registered or of an acceptable variation
Use by the proprietor of the mark or with his consent
Use after expiry of the grace period of five years subsequent to registration
Absence of genuine use may be justified

8.13 In administrative proceedings, including those before OHIM, many of the issues that have arisen are of a procedural nature, such as when a claim for non-use must be brought, what evidence is admitted, how the evidence is to be presented, and what the possibilities are of submitting additional evidence before the various office instances. A substantial body of case law has developed around these questions. The presentation in this chapter focuses, however, on the substantive issues.

C. Genuine Use

(1) The Principles: MINIMAX/*Ansul*

8.14 Ansul[3] was the proprietor of the trade mark 'Minimax' in the Benelux since 1971; the specification covered fire extinguishers and associated products. Ansul stopped marketing fire extinguishers in 1989 but continued selling component parts and extinguishing substances for 'Minimax' fire extinguishers. It also continued checking, maintaining, and repairing 'Minimax' products itself. As a result 'Minimax' had been used on invoices, stickers, and strips with the statement 'Gebruiksklaar Minimax' ('Ready for use Minimax').

8.15 Ajax, the subsidiary of the German manufacturer of fire extinguishers Minimax GmbH, was the proprietor of a composite mark incorporating the word 'Minimax' in the Benelux since 1992; the registration covered fire extinguishers and extinguishing substances, and the installation, repair, maintenance, and refilling of fire extinguishers. When Ajax started using the mark in 1994 Ansul objected by a letter and successfully obtained a registration for 'Minimax' for certain services, including the maintenance and repair of fire extinguishers. Originally the trade mark 'Minimax' was owned by the same German entity in Germany and The Netherlands; it was expropriated after the Second World War and the Dutch registration became Ansul's Benelux registration whereas the German registration passed to Minimax GmbH.

8.16 Ajax attacked both of Ansul's registrations, the first on the basis of non-use and the second on the ground that the application had been filed in bad faith. Ansul resisted the applications and at the same time sought an injunction against use by the German company of the 'Minimax' mark in the Benelux.

8.17 The case reached the Hoge Raad (Supreme Court of the Netherlands). The Dutch court held that all the particular facts and circumstances of each case had to be taken into account in order to show whether the aim of the use was to preserve an outlet for the marked products rather than maintain the trade mark rights, having regard to what would be considered to be usual and commercially justified in the relevant business sector. Referring to the relevant jurisprudence of the Benelux Court of Justice, it added that as a rule account should be taken of the kind, extent, frequency, regularity, and duration of the use, of the kind of relevant goods or service, and the kind and size of the undertaking.[4]

---

[3] C-40/01 *Ansul BV v Ajax Brandbeveiliging BV* [2003] ECR I-2439.
[4] A-80/1 *Turmac v Reynolds* [1981] ECC 346.

However, the Hoge Raad also held that the interpretation of the relevant provision of the Uniform Benelux Law had to conform to the interpretation of Article 12(1) and referred the following questions to the Court for a preliminary ruling: **8.18**

1. Must the words 'put to genuine use' in Article 12(1) of Directive 89/104 be interpreted in the manner [set out above] and, if the answer is in the negative, on the basis of which (other) criterion must the meaning of 'genuine use' be determined?
2. Can there be genuine use as referred to above also where no new goods are traded under the trade mark but other activities are engaged in as set out [above]?

(a) The Opinion of Advocate General Ruiz-Jarabo Colomer

(i) The legislative framework Advocate General Ruiz-Jarabo Colomer started his analysis with an overview of the legislative concepts of the use requirement. He noted that at the international level the Paris Convention adopted Article 5C[5] in 1925 at the revision of The Hague; and that TRIPs Article 2(1) provided that WTO members had to comply with, amongst other things, Article 5C. He also mentioned Article 19 of the Trademark Law Treaty. **8.19**

At the Community level the Eighth Recital in the Preamble to the Directive stated that it was essential to introduce a use requirement in order to reduce the total number of trade marks registered and protected in the Community and the number of conflicts potentially arising between them. The Regulation followed the same approach through the Ninth Recital and Articles 15, 43, 50, and 56. **8.20**

The Uniform Benelux Law was a reference point but he stressed that the definitive answer could only be provided by Community provisions[6] interpreted in an integrationist manner.[7] **8.21**

(ii) Interpreting use Advocate General Ruiz-Jarabo Colomer stressed that a trade mark register should reflect the reality of the marketplace; '[o]nly marks that are used in commercial life should be registered ... defensive and strategic registrations must be refused'.[8] **8.22**

Use and the manner of use justified the exclusive character of trade mark rights but also reconciled the objectives of trade mark law with those of competition. Use was also critical from the contrasting perspective of the alleged infringer, citing *Arsenal*[9] where the Court had to ascertain the circumstances in which a third party was using a distinctive sign as a trade mark. The concept of use should mean the same thing in both situations. **8.23**

---

[5] Article 5C provides:
    (1) If, in any country, use of the registered mark is compulsory, the registration may be cancelled only after a reasonable period, and then only if the person concerned does not justify his inaction.
    (2) Use of a trademark by the proprietor in a form differing in elements which do not alter the distinctive character of the mark in the form in which it was registered in one of the countries of the Union shall not entail invalidation of the registration and shall not diminish the protection granted to the mark.
    (3) Concurrent use of the same mark on identical or similar goods by industrial or commercial establishments considered as co-proprietors of the mark according to the provisions of the domestic law of the country where protection is claimed shall not prevent registration or diminish in any way the protection granted to the said mark in any country of the Union, provided that such use does not result in misleading the public and is not contrary to the public interest.

[6] Point 38.
[7] Point 38, citing paragraph 42 of C-414/99 *Levi Strauss & Co and Levi Strauss (UK) Ltd*; repeating a point he had made in C-517/99 *Merz & Krell* [2001] ECR I-6959.
[8] Point 42.
[9] C-206/01 *Arsenal* [2002] ECR I-10273.

8.24 According to *Arsenal*, first, use had to be commercial use, or as the Directive put it, use in the course of trade. Secondly, use should be 'for the purpose of distinguishing the goods or services by their origin or source, by their quality or by their reputation'.[10]

8.25 **(iii) The 'genuine' requirement** Genuine meant not token: 'Where use is a mere sham, is formalistic or notional, where it is empty of substance and directed solely at avoiding revocation and does not serve to carve out an opening in the market for the goods and services to which it relates, that use does not constitute genuine use.'[11]

8.26 Taking into account the linguistic variations—some Member States referred to normal use, others to serious, genuine, or effective—he concluded that 'the kind of use intended by the Community legislature is what may be described as sufficient in relation to the function performed by a trade mark'.[12]

8.27 From a purposive interpretation use had to be sufficient or appropriate to distinguish the proprietor's goods or services in the market 'so as to create an outlet by free, open and fair competition'.[13]

8.28 He then suggested a number of factors for proving that the use was indeed genuine.

8.29 First, it should involve use of the sign in relation to the goods and services for which the mark was registered.

8.30 Secondly, it had to be use of the sign exactly as it was granted and registered with all its components; exceptionally, it could also cover use with differences affecting elements that did not alter the distinctive character of the mark in the form in which it was registered.

8.31 Thirdly, it would have to be 'public and external, directed at the outside world ... Accordingly there will be genuine use not only where the goods are being sold or the services supplied, but also where the trade mark is being used for advertising with a view to those goods or services being launched in the market'.[14] Private use that did not extend beyond the internal province of the proprietor's undertaking should not be considered sufficient: 'Preparations for the marketing of goods or services do not, therefore, constitute sufficient or effective use, nor does getting them shop-ready or storing them where they do not leave the undertaking's premises.'[15] Affixing the mark to the goods or their packaging for export purposes would be sufficient in exceptional circumstances only, in order to protect undertakings whose main activity would be export trade.

8.32 Fourthly, it had to be appropriate to the aims of a trade mark. On the one hand, use with the sole aim of preventing revocation would not be genuine. On the other, it introduced an element of objectivity into the assessment; even where the aim would be other than to prevent revocation use should be appropriate at least to a minimum degree for fulfilling the functions ascribed to trade marks by the law. This should be determined on the basis of

---

[10] Point 48.
[11] Point 50.
[12] Point 52.
[13] Point 53.
[14] Point 56, citing his Opinion in C-273/00 *Sieckmann* [2002] ECR I-11737 on the advertising function of a trade mark.
[15] Point 57.

the circumstances of each case and it would be for the national court to decide, taking into account the following criteria.

The starting point should be the sale or supply of the goods or services under the trade mark.[16] Irrespective of volume of sales or size of the proprietor's undertaking, use had to be consistent rather than sporadic or occasional. He added that the structure and limits of the relevant market and the average consumer's perception of the product in question should also be taken into account together with the nature of the product. **8.33**

(b) The Judgment of the Court

(i) Uniform interpretation The requirement of uniform application of Community law and the principle of equality state that: **8.34**

> the terms of a provision of Community law which make no express reference to the law of the Member States for the purpose of determining its meaning and scope must normally be given an autonomous and uniform interpretation throughout the Community; that interpretation must take into account the context of the provision and the purpose of the legislation in question.[17]

A review of the relevant Recitals confirmed that the Community legislature intended to subject the maintenance of trade mark rights to the same condition regarding genuine use throughout the Union[18] and the concept of genuine use should be given the same interpretation in Articles 10 and 12 of the Directive.

(ii) The concept of genuine use The first requirement was that according to the Eighth Recital genuine use meant actual use of the mark. The wording used in some national provisions—including the Dutch, Spanish, Italian, and English versions—that referred to effective and genuine use supported that approach. **8.35**

The second requirement was that use should not be merely token, serving solely to preserve the rights conferred by the mark. It had to be consistent with the essential function of a trade mark as a guarantee of the identity of the origin of goods or services. **8.36**

The Court continued as follows: **8.37**

> [P]rotection the mark confers and the consequences of registering it in terms of enforceability vis-à-vis third parties cannot continue to operate if the mark loses its commercial raison d'être, which is to create or preserve an outlet for the goods or services that bear the sign of which it is composed, as distinct from the goods or services of other undertakings. Use of the mark must therefore relate to goods or services already marketed or about to be marketed and for which preparations by the undertaking to secure customers are under way, particularly in the form of advertising campaigns.[19]

Such use could be either by the trade mark proprietor or by a third party with authority to use the mark, according to Article 10(3). **8.38**

Thirdly, the assessment of genuine use should take account of all the relevant facts and circumstances, 'in particular whether such use is viewed as warranted in the economic sector **8.39**

---

[16] Point 61.
[17] *Ansul* (n 3) paragraph 26, citing C-287/98 *Luxembourg v Linster* [2000] ECR I-6917.
[18] Citing Joined Cases C-414/99 *Levi Strauss*, C-415/99 *Costco*, and C-416/99 *Zino Davidoff* [2001] ECR I-8691.
[19] Paragraph 37.

concerned to maintain or create a share in the market for the goods or services protected by the mark'.[20]

8.40 Those included the nature of the goods or services at issue, the characteristics of the market concerned, and the scale and frequency of use of the mark. The Court appeared to indicate that the quantitative dimension of use could also be relevant, albeit not determinative; it should always be seen in correlation with the remaining factors: 'Use of the mark need not, therefore, always be quantitatively significant for it to be deemed genuine, as that depends on the characteristics of the goods or service concerned on the corresponding market.'[21]

8.41 (iii) **Use in respect of 'integral parts'** Use might also be genuine for goods that were no longer available:

> That applies, inter alia, where the proprietor of the trade mark under which such goods were put on the market sells parts which are integral to the make-up or structure of the goods previously sold, and for which he makes actual use of the same mark under the conditions described [above].[22]

8.42 (iv) **Use in respect of directly related goods and services** The same principle applied to goods and services which were directly related to those goods and intended to meet the needs of their customers: 'That may apply to after-sales services, such as the sale of accessories or related parts, or the supply of maintenance and repair services.'[23]

8.43 (v) **The competence of the national court** The assessment of the circumstances of the case belonged to the national court under the division of functions provided for by Article 234 EC,[24] to apply the rules of Community law, as interpreted by the Court, to the individual case before it.

(2) Quantity not Relevant: *La Mer*

(a) The factual setting and the questions referred

8.44 In *Laboratoire de la Mer*[25] the Court reconfirmed the approach it had taken in *Ansul*.[26] Laboratoires Goemar, a French company specializing in seaweed products, was the proprietor of the trade mark 'Laboratoire de la Mer' in the United Kingdom, registered in 1988 in respect of pharmaceutical products, veterinary and sanitary products, and dietetic products for medical use all containing marine products, included in Class 5, and in 1989 in respect of perfumes and cosmetics containing marine products included in Class 3.

8.45 La Mer Technology sought the revocation of those registrations for non-use. At the UK Trade Mark Registry the marks were revoked only for perfumes in Class 3 and pharmaceutical, veterinary, and sanitary products in Class 5. La Mer Technology challenged the part of the decision rejecting its application before the High Court, which accepted the appeal in relation to the remaining products in Class 5; for cosmetics containing marine products

---

[20] Paragraph 37.
[21] Paragraph 39.
[22] Paragraph 41.
[23] Paragraph 42.
[24] C-320/88 *Staatssecretaris van Financien v Shipping and Forwarding Enterprise Safe BV* [1990] ECR I-285.
[25] C-259/02 *La Mer Technology Inc v Laboratoires Goëmar SA* [2004] ECR I-1159.
[26] C-40/01 *Ansul BV* [2003] ECR I-2439.

in Class 3 it found that Laboratoires Goemar had appointed a Scottish company to distribute its products in the United Kingdom and that the low turnover reflected a commercial failure rather that the intention of the Laboratoires Goemar to use the trade mark for maintaining its registration. Indeed, the company was taking measures to reverse that failure.

Accordingly, it stayed proceedings and referred the following questions to the Court: **8.46**

1. What factors should be taken into account when deciding whether a mark has been put to genuine use in a Member State within the meaning of Articles 10(1) and 12(1) of [the Directive]?

In particular:

2. Should the extent of use of the mark in relation to the goods or services for which the mark is registered in the Member State be taken into account?
3. Is any amount of use, however small, sufficient if it was made with no purpose other than commercially dealing in the goods or providing the service concerned?
4. If the answer to the foregoing question is no, what is the test for determining how much use is sufficient, and in particular does that test include a consideration of the nature and size of the business of the registered proprietor?
5. Is token or sham use to be disregarded, and in particular is use whose sole or predominant purpose is defeating a potential claim for revocation to be disregarded?
6. What types of use can be considered, and in particular is it necessary to show that the mark has been used in the course of trade in the Member State concerned and, in further particular, would importation by a single customer into that Member State be sufficient?
7. Is it necessary to disregard use occurring after the filing of the application for revocation even for the purpose of testing whether use during the relevant period was genuine?

(b) The reasoned order of the Court

The Court informed the national court that it found that the answers to the first six questions could be deduced from its judgment in *Ansul*[27] and that the answer to the seventh question could be given by way of reasoned order. The national court withdrew the fifth question but insisted on the remaining questions. **8.47**

The Court decided to respond to all the remaining questions by reasoned order. **8.48**

(i) Genuine use: the criteria and types of use Genuine use meant actual use, use that was not merely token serving solely to preserve the rights conferred by the mark. The use had to be consistent with the essential function of a trade mark and entailed use of the mark on the market for the goods or services protected by that mark and not just internal use by the undertaking concerned. It should relate to goods or services already marketed or about to be marketed and for which preparations by the undertaking to secure customers were under way, particularly in the form of advertising campaigns. Such use might be either by the trade mark proprietor or by a third party with authority to use the mark. And finally, the assessment of genuine use should consider all the relevant facts and circumstances. **8.49**

From all the above the Court concluded that 'the preservation by a trade mark proprietor of his rights is predicated on the mark being put to genuine use in the course of trade, on the market for the goods or services for which it was registered in the Member State concerned'.[28] **8.50**

---

[27] *Ansul* (n 26) [2003] ECR I-2439.
[28] Paragraph 20.

8.51 In some cases, use that was not quantitatively significant might be sufficient to establish genuine use: 'Even minimal use can therefore be sufficient to qualify as genuine, on condition that it is deemed to be justified, in the economic sector concerned, for the purpose of preserving or creating market share for the goods or services protected by the mark.'[29]

8.52 The question whether the use was sufficient to preserve or create a share in the relevant product market depended on the assessment of each individual case by the national court:

> The characteristics of those products and services, the frequency or regularity of the use of the mark, whether the mark is used for the purpose of marketing all the identical products or services of the proprietor or merely some of them, or evidence which the proprietor is able to provide, are among the factors which may be taken into account.[30]

Similarly, the characteristics of the relevant market should also be taken into account.

8.53 The Court found use of the mark by a single client which imported the marked products could be sufficient, provided that the importation had a genuine commercial justification for the trade mark proprietor.

8.54 Accordingly, it was not possible to determine *a priori*, and in the abstract, a quantitative threshold. The national court should appraise all the circumstances of the case rather than apply a prescriptive *de minimis* rule.

8.55 The Court also held that where use of the mark did not have as its essential aim the preservation or creation of market share for the specified goods or services it should not be considered genuine.

8.56 (ii) **Use after the filing of the application for revocation**   Article 12(1) made it clear that the mark should be put to genuine use prior to the filing of an application for revocation; in addition, the commencement or resumption of use of the mark before the filing of an application for revocation would not suffice if it appeared that it occurred only after the proprietor had become aware that an application for revocation might be filed:

> Nevertheless, the Directive does not expressly preclude in assessing the genuineness of use during the relevant period, account being taken, where appropriate, of any circumstances subsequent to that filing. Such circumstances may make it possible to confirm or better assess the extent to which the trade mark was used during the relevant period and the real intentions of the proprietor during that time.[31]

8.57 Where the particular evidence of use should lie remained a question that the national court had to answer.

(3) *Sunrider*: **Evidence of Use; the Burden of Proof**

(a) The legal and factual setting

8.58 In order to facilitate the establishment of the Community trade mark system the Regulation provides in Article 42(2) and (3) that the owners of earlier national trade mark or Community trade mark rights opposing an application for registration of a Community trade mark

---

[29] Paragraph 21.
[30] Paragraph 22.
[31] Paragraph 31.

when challenged by the applicant are required to furnish proof that during the period of five years preceding the date of publication of the Community trade mark application, the earlier trade mark has been put to genuine use in the Community or the relevant Member State in connection with the goods or services in respect of which it is registered and which the party opposing the application cites as justification for the opposition, or that there are proper reasons for non-use, provided the earlier trade mark has at that date been registered for not less than five years. In the absence of such proof the opposition shall be rejected.

8.59 Article 57(2) and (3) introduce the same principle for challenging a Community trade mark once it has been registered in revocation or invalidity proceedings on the basis of an earlier right.

8.60 *Sunrider*[32] was the first relevant case that reached the Court. It was an appeal against the Judgment of the Court of First Instance dismissing the action for annulment of the Board of Appeal rejecting the application for registration of the mark VITAFRUIT as a Community trade mark for goods in Classes 5, 29, and 32 of the Nice Agreement; the specification under Class 32 that covered 'beers; mineral and aerated waters and other non-alcoholic drinks; fruit and vegetable drinks, fruit juices; syrups and other preparations for making beverages; herbal and vitamin beverages' was critical.[33]

8.61 The application was originally rejected by the Opposition Division following proceedings based on the registration of the mark VITAFRUT as a national trade mark in Spain for 'non-alcoholic and non-therapeutic carbonic drinks, non-therapeutic cold beverages of all kinds, gaseous, granulated effervescent; fruit and vegetable juices without fermentation (except must), lemonades, orangeades, cold beverages (except orgeat), soda water, Seidlitz water and artificial ice', in Classes 30 and 32. The evidence of use submitted by the proprietor of the earlier trade mark, Mr Espadafor Caba, opposing the application consisted of six bottle labels and ten invoices with a date earlier than the contested mark's filing date.

(b) The Judgment of the Court of First Instance

8.62 It found, first, that although use of the earlier trade mark had been under the company name Industrias Espadafor SA, the Board of Appeal had been entitled to rely on the presumption that it had taken place with the consent of the proprietor.

8.63 Secondly, that there was sufficient evidence that the earlier use had been genuine. It might have been preferable to have more evidence regarding the nature of use but nevertheless the Court of First Instance accepted that proof of sales during the period from May 1996 to May 1997 of around 300 cases of twelve items each of concentrated juices of various fruits representing sales of approximately €4,800.00 sufficed.

8.64 Thirdly, that the concentrated juices were destined for end-consumers and not for fruit juice manufacturers. Accordingly, the products of both parties targeted the same market.

8.65 Fourthly, that herbal and vitamin beverages and concentrated fruit juices were similar, based primarily on the argument that they were interchangeable because they shared the

---

[32] C-416/04 P *The Sunrider Corp v Office for Harmonisation in the Internal Market (Trade Marks and Designs)* [2006] ECR I-4237.
[33] T-203/02 *Sunrider v Office for Harmonisation in the Internal Market (Trade Marks and Designs)* [2005] ECR II-2793.

same purpose; they were competing nonalcoholic beverages, normally drunk cold, aiming to quench thirst. The fact that their ingredients differed did not alter this finding.

(c) The Judgment of the Court

8.66 The applicant claimed that the Court of First Instance should not rely on probabilities or presumptions regarding use of the earlier trade mark or require the applicant to prove lack of consent when the use was made by a third party. The proprietor of the earlier trade mark had not produced any evidence that he had consented to use by the company Industrias Espadafor SA. The Board and the Court of First Instance had relied on a presumption of consent.

8.67 As regards proof that the earlier mark was used with the consent of the proprietor, as provided for in Article 15(3) of the Regulation, the Court confirmed the decision of the Court of First Instance. Part of his name was incorporated in the name of the company using the mark, and had he not consented to that use it would be unlikely that he would be able to produce any actual proof. Deciding whether the evidence actually proved his consent constituted an assessment of facts and remained within the jurisdiction of the Court of First Instance.[34]

8.68 As regards proof of genuine use, the Court saw the labels as part of the wider evidence submitted by the proprietor of the earlier trade mark. It noted that the findings of the Court of First Instance regarding sales based on the invoices remained unchallenged. Accordingly, the allegation that the labels in themselves failed to prove earlier use was not enough to set aside the judgment under appeal and was rejected as ineffective.

8.69 Sunrider argued that the evidence had shown only token use of the earlier mark, which should not satisfy 'genuine use' requirements, in particular after *Ansul*,[35] focusing on the limited nature, number, and geographical coverage of the transactions involving the trade mark and the character of the goods in question. It characterized the use as at most only sporadic and occasional rather than continuous, actual, and stable.

8.70 The Court repeated its rulings in *Ansul* and *La Mer Technology*[36] and found that the Court of First Instance had followed the assessment path described by the Court in the above cases. First, it had analysed the place, time, extent, and nature of that use; and, secondly, it had sought to determine whether the trade mark had been used in order to create or preserve an outlet for 'concentrated fruit juices' or had to be regarded as token.

8.71 The Court rejected the claim that the fact that use was linked with only one customer should *a priori* negate its genuine character; the territorial scope of the use was only one of several factors that had to be taken into account. Instead, it stressed that for each individual case all the relevant factors should be considered; accordingly, volumes of sales that would suffice in one particular case could be insufficient in another.

---

[34] C-37/03 P *BioID AG* [2005] ECR I-7975.
[35] C-40/01 *Ansul BV* [2003] ECR I-2439.
[36] C-259/02 *La Mer Technology* [2004] ECR I-1159.

(4) Minimal Use Again: *Walzertraum*

8.72 The issue of minimal use came before the Court in a case involving an Austrian applicant and a German opposer, relating to the mark WALZERTRAUM. The opposing party, proprietor of a German mark registered for chocolate products, when required to prove use under Article 43 of the Regulation, had provided evidence of use of the mark annually for *c.* 40 to 50 kg of handmade pralines sold in its shop and cafe in a little town in southern Germany, where the opposing party was headquartered. The rejection of the opposition on the grounds that this did not amount to genuine use was confirmed by the General Court[37] and, on appeal, by Order of the Court of Justice.[38]

8.73 The Court limited itself essentially to finding that the assessment made by the General Court was of a factual nature and would not be disturbed on appeal.

8.74 The decision is, however, still noteworthy because it would seem that the 'minimal use' issue was dealt with by the General Court to the disadvantage of the proprietor of the earlier right, in clear distinction to the way the minimal use issue was approached in *La Mer* and in *Sunrider*.

(5) Use with or without Profit Motive: *Radetzky, Silberquelle, Nasdaq*

8.75 The use of a mark, in order to be recognized as 'genuine', must be made 'in the course of trade', which, as eloquently explained by AG Ruiz-Jarabo Colomer in his Opinion in *Ansul*, excludes purely 'internal' use within the enterprise of the proprietor, as well as 'private' use. In view of these principles, the Court was called upon to decide, in two references from Austrian authorities, whether use which was not made for profit, by a charitable entity, and use of the mark for products which were given away free as a 'gift' with a principal product, could amount to genuine use.

(a) Radetzky: *Use in respect of non-profitable activities*

8.76 In *Radetzky*[39] the Court was asked to clarify whether the use made by a non-profitmaking association of its trade marks in promoting its activities and in fundraising constitutes genuine use within the meaning of Article 12(1) of the Directive. The reference was made in the context of a dispute between Verein Radetzky-Orden ('Radetzky Orden') and Bundesvereinigung Kameradschaft 'Feldmarschall Radetzky' ('BKFR') concerning the revocation of the latter's trade marks on the grounds of non-use.

8.77 BKFR is a non-profit-making association, which does not sell any goods or provide any services for remuneration. Its activity consists, on the one hand, of the preservation of military traditions, such as the organization of memorial services for members of the armed forces who have fallen in combat, remembrance services, military reunions, and the upkeep of war memorials and, on the other, of charitable work, such as the collection of money and donations in kind and their subsequent distribution to the needy.

---

[37] Judgment of the General Court of 17 January 2013, T-355/09 *Reber Holding GmbH & Co. KG v Office for Harmonisation in the Internal Market (Trade Marks and Designs) (OHIM)*, ECLI:EU:T:2013:22.

[38] Order of 17 July 2014, C-141/13 P *Reber Holding GmbH & Co. KG v OHIM—Wedl & Hofmann GmbH*, ECLI:EU:C:2015:133—the Order is available only in German and French.

[39] C-442/07 *Verein Radetzky-Orden v Bundesvereinigung Kameradschaft 'Feldmarschall Radetzky'* [2008] ECR I-09223.

8.78 BKFR is the proprietor of various word and figurative trade marks, representing essentially badges of honour, entered in the register of the Austrian Patent Office in respect of the following services in Classes 37, 41, and 45 of the Nice Classification. BKFR awards orders and decorations corresponding to its marks, which its members wear at various events and when collecting and distributing donations. The marks are also printed on invitations to forthcoming events, on stationery, and on the association's promotional material.

8.79 Radetzky-Orden sought to have BKFR's trade marks cancelled on grounds of non-use pursuant to the relevant provisions of Austrian law.[40] It claimed that BKFR had not used its trade marks commercially over the course of the previous five years.

8.80 The Austrian Patent Office granted Radetzky-Orden's application and cancelled BKFR's trade marks. BKFR appealed against that decision to the Oberster Patent- und Markensenat, which decided to stay the proceedings and refer the following question to the Court for a preliminary ruling:

> Is Article 12(1) of the Directive to be construed as meaning that a trade mark is put to (genuine) use to distinguish goods and services of one undertaking from those of other undertakings in the case where a non-profitmaking association uses the trade mark in announcements for events, on business papers and on advertising material and that trade mark is used by the association's members when collecting and distributing donations inasmuch as those members wear badges featuring that trade mark?

8.81 (i) **The respective arguments** Radetzky-Orden claimed that according to Article 5 of the Directive trade mark protection is closely linked to the supply of goods and services in the course of trade and that trade mark use thus implies a supply for consideration. Accordingly, the term 'genuine use' in Article 12 of the Directive only applies to commercial or entrepreneurial activity carried out for profit; conversely, activities which are exclusively non-profitmaking fall outside the scope of trade mark protection.

8.82 BKFR countered that although charitable organizations are non-profitmaking associations, they compete against each other in their particular field of activity and thus act like entrepreneurs in any other sector, even where their proceeds are not kept as profit, but made available to the needy. Insofar as the signs used for that purpose, such as marks, decorations, insignia, and coats of arms, indicate the origin of their services and allow the public to distinguish them from those of other organisations, they are put to genuine trade mark use. In fact, the award of decorations and distinctions containing the mark to persons outside the organization is a form of advertising or merchandising that actually serves to promote the association's core activities.

8.83 (ii) **The Opinion of Advocate General Mazák** Advocate General Mazák started his analysis by referring to the Court's statements in *Ansul* and *La Mer* that the question of genuine use must be examined by taking into consideration all the relevant circumstances of the case and in particular the nature and characteristics of the market in which the trade mark is used, especially insofar as those characteristics may directly affect the marketing strategy of the proprietor of the mark.

---

[40] Paragraph 33a of the Markenschutzgesetz 1970, BGBL 260/1970: 'the MSchG'.

Genuine Use

Accordingly, he stressed the need to examine the question of genuine use of a trade mark by non-profit-making associations by reference to the purpose and nature of their activities and by taking into account the manner in which such organizations generally supply goods and services.[41]

8.84

Next, the Advocate General observed that when raising funds and distributing donations, non-profit-making associations actually compete with each other in order to attract donations from the public and, thus, engage in business or in commercial activity in the wider sense of those terms. Thus, he concluded that non-profit-making associations are, in principle, market players which acquire and provide goods and services in conformity with the norms prevailing in the relevant sector. Conversely, completely ignoring the commercial or business environment in which such organizations operate would be unrealistic and could potentially undermine their activities.[42]

8.85

Moreover, he noted that Article 5 of the Directive, which enumerates the rights conferred by a trade mark, does not require that goods and services actually be supplied for profit or indeed for consideration. The question of whether the proprietor uses the trade mark for the purposes of personal enrichment is thus not relevant when assessing whether the trade mark is being put to genuine use within the meaning of Article 12(1) of the Directive.[43]

8.86

Accordingly, the Advocate General considered that the use of the sign in fundraising serves as an indication to donors of the identity of the association in question and the purposes for which the funds are collected and thus constitutes genuine use of the trade mark.[44] However, when the sign is used for the announcement or advertisement of purely private ceremonies or events, principally involving existing members of the association, the use is merely internal and thus cannot qualify as genuine for the purposes of Article 12(1) of the Directive.[45]

8.87

Advocate General Mazák therefore proposed to answer the question in the affirmative, but only insofar as the non-profit-making association uses the trade mark in announcements for public fundraising events, or when the sign is used on business papers addressed to members of the public and on advertising material soliciting donations from the public, while leaving it up to the national court to assess whether the facts in the main proceedings corresponded to such use.

8.88

(iii) The Judgment of the Court In establishing the framework for its analysis, the Court referred to its statements in *Ansul* that the use made of the sign is 'genuine' within the meaning of Article 12(1) of the Directive when it is consistent with the essential function of a trade mark, which is to guarantee the identity of the origin of goods or services to the consumer, and that it entails use of the mark on the market for the designated goods or services and not just internal use within the undertaking concerned. It also reiterated that the protection conferred by the mark and its enforceability vis-à-vis third parties cannot continue to operate if the mark loses its commercial raison d'être, which is to create or

8.89

---

[41] Point 25.
[42] Point 27.
[43] Point 28.
[44] Point 29.
[45] Point 30.

8.90 As regards the case at issue, the Court noted that although the financial implications of marks and their use on the market are apparent from the Paris Convention, which refers to them as 'trade marks', the fact that goods or services are offered on a non-profit-making basis is not decisive in itself for ascertaining whether the use is indeed genuine, in the sense that the fact that a charitable association does not seek to make a profit does not mean that its objective cannot be to create and, later, to preserve an outlet for its goods or services.[47]

8.91 In that connection, the Court also observed that, in the modern economy, various types of non-profit-making associations have sprung up which, at first sight, offer their services for free but which, in reality, are financed through subsidies or receive payment in various forms.

8.92 Consequently, trade marks registered by such organizations may have a raison d'être, in that they protect the association against the possible use in business of identical or similar signs by third entities. Thus, as long as the mark is used in order to identify and promote the goods or services for which it has been registered, there is nothing to prevent such use from being regarded as 'genuine' within the meaning of Article 12(1) of the Directive.[48] Moreover, the Court concurred with the view taken by the Advocate General[49] that use in purely private ceremonies or events, or for the advertisement or announcement of such ceremonies or events, constitutes merely internal use of the mark and not 'genuine use' for the purposes of Article 12(1) of the Directive.[50]

8.93 Thus, the Court concluded that where a non-profit-making association uses the mark in its relations with the public, such as in the course of announcements of forthcoming events, on business papers, and on advertising material, or where its members wear badges featuring that mark when collecting donations, it makes genuine use of its registered trade mark. However, it noted that it was for the national court to ascertain whether the marks in the main proceedings were actually used to identify and promote services offered to the general public, or whether the use made of them was merely internal.

8.94 **(iv) Conclusions** In *Radetzky* the Court seems to be taking the broad view that a real and effective exploitation of the mark is not necessarily incompatible with its use in non-profitable activities or with the rendering of services free of charge, provided, first, that such use is outward and external and, secondly, that the use of the mark in this manner complies with the established norms and characteristics of the relevant market sector.

8.95 On the other hand, its view with regard to internal use seems to be quite restrictive, at least insofar as many non-profit-making associations, such as, for example, mutual assistance funds and other professional organizations, actually depend for the financing of their activities on the subscription fees and donations collected from its members, who are in reality its

---

[46] *Ansul* (n 26) paragraphs 35–37.
[47] Paragraphs 15–17.
[48] Paragraphs 18–21.
[49] At point 30 of his Opinion.
[50] Paragraph 22.

(b) Silberquelle: *Use on promotional items*

*Silberquelle*⁵¹ was another reference from the Austrian Oberster Patent- und Markensenat concerning non-profitable use. This time, however, the Court had to deal not with use in the course of activities which, by their nature, are non-profitable, but rather with the offer of promotional items free of charge as a means of enhancing the sales of other goods. **8.96**

(i) **The facts in the main proceedings and the order for reference** The reference was made in the context of an action brought by Silberquelle GmbH ('Silberquelle') against Maselli-Strickmode GmbH ('Maselli') in respect of the partial revocation of the latter's mark for lack of genuine use. Maselli is a manufacturer and seller of clothing. It is the owner, in Austria, of the word mark WELLNESS, registered in respect of, inter alia, the following goods, in Classes 16, 25, and 32 of the Nice Classification: printed matter (Class 16); clothing (Class 25); and alcohol-free drinks (Class 32). In the context of the sale of its clothing, Maselli used its mark to designate an alcohol-free drink which was handed out as a gift in bottles marked WELLNESS-DRINK, along with the clothing sold. In its promotional documents, Maselli made reference to the free gifts labelled with the WELLNESS mark, but had not used its mark for drinks sold separately. **8.97**

Silberquelle, an undertaking which sells alcohol-free drinks, applied for cancellation of the WELLNESS mark in respect of Class 32 products on grounds of non-use. The Austrian Patent Office accepted Silberquelle's request and cancelled the mark for that class. Maselli brought an action against that decision before the Oberster Patent- und Markensenat. **8.98**

The Oberster Patent- und Markensenat took the view that the resolution of the dispute turned on the interpretation of 'genuine use' and decided to refer the following question to the Court of Justice: **8.99**

> Are Articles 10(1) and 12(1) of the Directive to be interpreted as meaning that a trade mark is being put to genuine use if it is used for goods which the proprietor of the trade mark gives, free of charge, to purchasers of his other goods after conclusion of the purchase contract?

(ii) **The Opinion of Advocate General Ruiz-Jarabo Colomer**

Use as a guarantee of origin First, he observed that the Directive contains two categories of provisions, namely those relating to the organization of national trade mark registrations (Articles 2, 3, 4, and 10 to 14) and those relating to the rights conferred by the trade mark (Articles 5 to 9). He further noted that the function of a trade mark as a guarantee of origin, on which Maselli essentially relied, is connected with the second group of provisions, and, in particular, with Articles 4(1) and 5(1), which are closely linked to the likelihood of confusion.⁵² **8.100**

He also stressed that although, in *Ansul*, the Court required that the use of the mark must always be geared to its essential function,⁵³ that requirement was in fact secondary **8.101**

---

⁵¹ C-495/07 *Silberquelle GmbH v Maselli Strickmode GmbH* [2009] ECR I-00137.
⁵² Points 34–35 of the Opinion of AG Ruiz-Jarabo Colomer.
⁵³ *Ansul* (n 26) paragraph 43.

to the need to use the mark 'in order to create or preserve an outlet for those goods or services'. Moreover, it is equally clear from *Ansul* that the essential function of a trade mark is to enable, without any possibility of confusion, a particular product or service to be distinguished from others which have another origin,[54] which draws attention to the connection between the function as a guarantee of origin and the likelihood of confusion.[55]

8.102 The Advocate General then pointed out that the likelihood of confusion only arises where a consumer discovers similar marks at the crucial moment when he/she chooses between competing goods. To the extent, however, that the drinks which Maselli handed out were not made available to the public in the usual soft drink retail establishments, any such comparison was impossible and, therefore, any possibility of confusion on the part of the relevant customers was excluded. Accordingly, Maselli could not rely on the need to protect its advertising strategies if those strategies did not comply with the essential function of the mark, properly understood.[56]

8.103 *The importance of using the mark in the reference market* Secondly, the Advocate General considered that the position taken by Maselli was not compatible with the overall scheme of the Directive, as expressed in its Eighth Recital, which refers to the obligation to provide evidence of the use as a means of reducing the total number of marks registered in the Community and, ultimately, as serving the objective of protecting freedom of competition.[57]

8.104 Thus, the transparency which must prevail both in the market and on the register explains why competitors have the capacity to cancel inactive registrations which do not fulfil the essential function of trade marks, since if the goods are not offered for sale, the mark does not generate any type of economic benefit. Accordingly, a trade mark proprietor must place the goods bearing the mark on the relevant market for those goods, which, in the main proceedings, was the non-alcoholic drinks market; if trade mark proprietors did not act in that manner, their goods would not be distinguishable from others.[58]

8.105 In fact, by receiving the WELLNESS drink as a free gift when purchasing clothing, the consumer did not perform any conscious act of acquiring the drink by comparing it with other similar products and, hence, the trade mark was not strengthened vis-à-vis competitors' marks because of the customer's preference. In practice, this meant that the trade mark remained outside the reference market and, therefore, did not compete with other marks, since it appeared unlikely that someone who took a liking to the drink would be prepared to spend more money on clothes simply to receive the drink.[59]

8.106 *Use in advertising* Lastly, the Advocate General pointed out that although the Court has accepted that use of a mark in advertising qualifies as genuine use, as does use in relation to goods and services which are about to be marketed and for which preparations to secure

---

[54] *Ansul* (n 26) paragraph 36.
[55] Points 36–39.
[56] Points 40–43.
[57] Point 44.
[58] Points 47–48.
[59] Point 49.

customers are under way,⁶⁰ such circumstances are distinguishable from the 'abstract' use of a trade mark, that is, where its use has no specific connection with the market for the goods to which it is fixed.⁶¹

He also remarked that this was precisely the case with the WELLNESS drink mark, since, in the absence of any effective link with the soft drinks market, the beverage bearing the WELLNESS mark became a mere advertising tool which was completely unconnected with the sale of soft drinks, or with the acquisition of a market share in that sector.⁶² **8.107**

Consequently, the Advocate General concluded that a trade mark which does not compete on the market for the goods for which it was registered is not put to genuine use within the meaning of the Directive, even where the goods bearing the mark are an advertisement to promote the sales of other products bearing the same mark.⁶³ **8.108**

(iii) **The Judgment of the Court** The Court noted at the outset that the case in the order for reference was different from one in which the proprietor of a mark sells promotional items in the form of souvenirs or other derivative products. In addition, the revocation proceedings only concerned Class 32, which covered the promotional items at issue, and not Class 25, encompassing the goods actually sold by the trade mark owner, namely clothing. **8.109**

The Court then referred to its judgments in *Ansul* and *Radetzky* and reiterated once more that 'genuine use' within the meaning of the Directive must be understood to denote actual use and that, in view of the number of marks that are registered and the conflicts that are likely to arise between them, it is essential to maintain the rights conferred by a mark for a given class of goods or services only where that mark has been used on the market for goods or services belonging to that class.⁶⁴ **8.110**

The Court considered, however, that those conditions are not fulfilled where promotional items are merely handed out as a reward for the purchase of other goods, that is, in order to promote the sale of the latter, since, in such a situation, those items are not distributed with the aim of penetrating the market for goods in the same class. In fact, using the mark in this manner does not contribute at all to creating an outlet for the designated goods or to distinguishing, in the interest of the customer, those items from the goods of other undertakings.⁶⁵ **8.111**

In the light of these considerations, the Court held that the answer to the question referred should be that Articles 10(1) and 12(1) of the Directive must be interpreted as meaning that, where the proprietor of a mark affixes that mark to items that it gives, free of charge, to purchasers of its goods, it does not make genuine use of that mark in respect of the class covering those items. In reaching this conclusion the Court in substance qualified its Judgment in *Ansul* in two important respects. **8.112**

---

⁶⁰ *Ansul* (n 26) paragraph 37; *La Mer* (n 36) paragraph 19.
⁶¹ Points 51–52.
⁶² Point 53.
⁶³ Point 56 of the Opinion of AG Ruiz-Jarabo Colomer.
⁶⁴ *Ansul* (n 26) paragraphs 35–37; *Radetzky* (n 39) paragraphs 13–14.
⁶⁵ *Silberquelle* (n 51) paragraphs 20–21.

8.113 First, it clarified that the use of the trade mark in advertising cannot be regarded as genuine if it relates to the promotion of goods other than those covered by the registration, since in such a case the use does not concern the marketing of the goods actually sold, or of goods which are about to be marketed and for which preparations to secure customers are under way, as required by *Ansul*.[66]

8.114 Secondly, it effectively denied that the use of the trade mark in respect of promotional items free of charge concerns goods which are 'directly related' to the goods actually marketed by the proprietor within the meaning of that Judgment, unlike the offering of after-sales services or the sale of accessories and spare parts.[67]

(c) Nasdaq: *Complementary services offered free of charge*

8.115 The Court had the opportunity to further explore the notion of genuine use in connection with the free offer of services in *Nasdaq*,[68] a case brought before it on appeal from a judgment of the Court of First Instance.[69]

8.116 *Nasdaq* concerned a dispute that arose in the context of an opposition brought by Nasdaq Stock Market Inc ('Nasdaq Stock Market') against Antartica Srl ('Antarctica') pursuant to Article 8(5) CTMR.[70] Antarctica had sought to register as a Community trade mark a figurative sign essentially consisting of the stylized word 'nasdaq' in respect of a range of goods in Classes 9, 12, 14, 25, and 28 of the Nice Classification.

8.117 Nasdaq Stock Market opposed the application based on its earlier Community word mark NASDAQ, on the grounds that the use of Antarctica's mark without due cause would take unfair advantage of, or be detrimental to, the distinctive character and repute its earlier mark enjoyed in respect of, inter alia, 'stock exchange price quotation services; listings of securities for quotations for sale or information purposes', and 'financial services, amongst others, providing and updating an index of security values', in Classes 35 and 36 of the Nice Classification.

8.118 The Opposition Division rejected the opposition, holding that the reputation of the earlier mark had not been properly substantiated, since the mark NASDAQ had not been used in the Community to the requisite standard. Nasdaq Stock Market appealed to the Board of Appeal of OHIM, which annulled the Opposition Division's decision on the ground that the latter had wrongly considered that the conditions for the application of Article 8(5) CTMR had not been fulfilled. Antartica brought an action for the annulment of that decision before the Court of First Instance contending, for the first time at that stage, that the mere references made to the Nasdaq indices in the Community do not constitute 'genuine use' of the mark NASDAQ and that, as a result, they cannot support the alleged reputation of the earlier mark.

8.119 Although the Court of First Instance reiterated that, according to Article 135(4) of its Rules of Procedure, the parties' pleadings may not change the subject matter of the proceedings

---

[66] See *Ansul* (n 26) paragraph 37.
[67] See *Ansul* (n 26) paragraph 42.
[68] C-320/07 P *Antartica Srl v OHIM* (NASDAQ) [2009] ECR I-00028.
[69] T-47/06 *Antartica Srl v OHIM* (NASDAQ) [2007] ECR II-00042.
[70] Although that case is not concerned with the obligation to use the mark as a means of maintaining the registration, it is relevant here insofar as it deals with the notion of genuine use in general.

before the Board of Appeal, it nevertheless observed that, according to the case law, the reputation of the earlier mark must be determined by the intensity, geographical extent, and duration of its use and that, in order to ascertain whether Article 8(5) CTMR applied to the case, the Board of Appeal was obliged, before determining whether the mark NASDAQ was reputed, to assess first whether that mark had been used at all. Accordingly, it considered that Antarctica's claim did not unduly modify the subject matter of the dispute before the Board of Appeal, taking in substance the view that a plea based on Article 8(5) CTMR tacitly raises, as an additional preliminary issue, the question of whether the mark has been put to genuine use in the first place.[71]

Moreover, the Court of First Instance found that, insofar as the references to the Nasdaq indices related to the stock exchange price quotation and financial services for which the earlier mark was registered in Classes 35 and 36, they constituted genuine use of that mark, and this regardless of the fact that the corresponding information was offered free of charge.[72] Furthermore, the Court of First Instance held that Article 8(5) was applicable to the case and dismissed the action as unfounded. **8.120**

Antarctica appealed, requesting that the Court of Justice set aside the contested judgment on both counts. As regards proof of use, it claimed, essentially, that genuine use can take place only if the mark is used in connection with the sale of goods or services; contrary to that rule, however, Nasdaq Stock Market's indices were available free of charge in the press and on television, while no evidence had been adduced to the effect that those indices were offered for consideration within the Community. Nasdaq Stock Market countered that its financial and stock market services were not offered gratis and that only certain ancillary services, such as those relating to information, were provided to the general public free of charge, following the rule that advertising of this kind is always offered to the public free of charge. **8.121**

The Court, however, did not agree with the view that, as a matter of principle, the concept of genuine use cannot extend to services offered on a non-profit-making basis, or that it is based on the premise that the goods or services for which the trade mark is used are always paid for.[73] Conversely, it noted that, even if part of the services for which the earlier mark is registered are offered free of charge, that does not of itself mean that Nasdaq Stock Market would not seek, by such use of its trade mark, to create or maintain an outlet for those services in the Community, as against the services of other undertakings.[74] **8.122**

Thus, the Court concurred with the judgment under appeal that, inasmuch as the Nasdaq indices referred to the stock exchange price quotation and financial services principally provided by Nasdaq Stock Market, the earlier mark had been put to genuine use in respect of all the services for which it was registered. **8.123**

---

[71] That view of the Court of First Instance seems to be much more generous than the approach it took in T-425/03 *AMS Advanced Medical Services GmbH v OHIM* 2007 ECR II-04265, where it held that the CTM applicant's proof of use defence must be raised at the latest during the proceedings before the Opposition Division. In the meantime, the applicable Rule 22 of the Implementing Regulation provides that the 'defence' of non-use must be raised in the first substantive reply of the applicant to the substantiated opposition.
[72] See paragraph 45 of the judgment of the Court of First Instance.
[73] Paragraph 28.
[74] Paragraph 29.

8.124 Although the Court did not say so expressly, the decisive factor for considering Nasdaq Stock Market's use of its mark in respect of free information services as genuine was the direct link of those services to its main financial activities and their complementary relationship with them, within the meaning of the Court's findings in *Ansul*.[75]

8.125 In that regard, *Nasdaq* must be distinguished from the Court's Judgment in *Silberquelle*. Unlike that case, where the mark was used for goods the sole purpose of which was to promote a different product, *Nasdaq* concerned the free offer of ancillary services that were functionally related to the owner's main activity, in the sense that those services were indispensable for the proprietor's principal business. In that sense, *Nasdaq* is closer to the principles laid down in *Radetzky*, at least to the extent that it held that it is in the *nature* of stock index information services to be offered free of charge to investors, so as to enable them to effectively follow-up their investments and judge whether the time is opportune to enter or leave the market.

D. The Territory of Use

(1) *Leno Merken*/ONEL

(a) *Legal Context*

8.126 The reference in *Leno Merken*[76] brought before the Court a controversy as old as the Community trade mark itself. From the very inception of the Community trade mark system, the peculiar characteristics of this new type of right, and in particular its unitary effect and its complementary relationship with national marks, raised the question of how geographically widespread its use should be in order to justify its much broader territorial coverage and to mark its difference from national marks.

8.127 From the outset, two opposite theories were put forward in that regard. The first focuses on the supranational character of the CTM and advocates that its more extensive scope of protection comes together with a legal obligation to use it in more than one Member State, since, otherwise, there is no clear dividing line between national and Community trade marks. Conversely, the second approach focuses on the unity of the internal market and assumes that a CTM operates in exactly the same way as a national mark in its home territory, with the result that it is sufficient to use it anywhere within the EU, without any particular obligation to cover a pre-defined territory, provided of course that such use is genuine.

8.128 If the first position is taken to the extreme, it would mean that CTMs are reserved for companies which, at the latest after five years from the registration of their marks, have engaged in cross-border activities. In practice, this would deny access to the Community trade mark to companies operating only nationally, however important their size or activities may be. At the same time, such a requirement would elevate the territorial extent of the use to a status of primacy amongst the factors used for the assessment of genuine use, by making all other considerations, including the intensity of use, subordinate to it. If the second position is taken to the extreme, it would have the consequence that any European

---

[75] See *Ansul* (n 26) paragraph 42.
[76] C-149/11, *Leno Merken BV v Hagelkruis Beheer BV*, ECLI:EU:C:2012:816.

trader, manufacturer, or service provider, however small or locally based, is entitled to hold a CTM and enforce it across the Community, provided that the use made of the mark is real and not token.

8.129 The wording of Article 15 of the Regulation gives no clear answer, but seems to be closer to the second interpretation, inasmuch as it does not impose any express obligation to use the mark in cross-border trade, merely requiring 'use in the Community'. The expression 'use in the Community', however, can be stretched to mean use *across* the Community or can be shrunk to mean use *anywhere within* the Community. The accompanying Joint Statement of the Council and Commission sought to clarify the issue by adding that 'use which is genuine within the meaning of Article 15 in one country constitutes genuine use in the Community', clearly militating in favour of the second view.

8.130 The practice of OHIM consistently followed this approach from the outset.

8.131 In the absence of clear guidance by the Court, the question remained controversial over the years, all the more so since the gradual fall in national filings, while the CTM gained steam, gave the debate a political flair, and made the division between the two approaches even more entrenched.

(b) The facts in the main proceedings and the order for reference

8.132 The question finally reached the Court of Justice in the form of a preliminary reference from the Gerechtshof's-Gravenhage (The Hague), one of the three appeal courts competent to judge on appeals against decisions of the Benelux Office for Intellectual Property (BOIP) (the other two being in Belgium and in Luxembourg), in an appeal from a decision of the BOIP taken in opposition proceedings between Leno Merken BV and Hagelkruis Beheer BV.

8.133 Hagelkruis sought to register the word OMEL as a trade mark in the Benelux. Leno relied on its earlier CTM ONEL to oppose Hagelkruis's application. Hagelkruis asked Leno to prove genuine use of its Community trade mark ONEL. Although it was not disputed that the earlier mark had been used for forty years in The Netherlands, the fact that its use was limited to the territory of a single Member State allowed Hagelkruis to raise doubts as to whether such use amounted to 'genuine use in the Community' for the purposes of Article 15 CTMR. Indeed, the BOIP upheld Hagelkruis's argument and rejected Leno's opposition on the grounds that the use of the mark ONEL was not extensive enough to meet the requisite threshold.

8.134 Leno appealed before the Gerechtshof's-Gravenhage which, in view of the unsettled state of the case law, decided to stay the proceedings and to refer the following questions to the Court of Justice for a preliminary ruling:

1. Must Article 15(1) CTMR be interpreted as meaning that use of a Community trade mark within the borders of a single Member State is sufficient to constitute genuine use of that trade mark, given that, had it been a national trade mark, such use would have been regarded as genuine use in that Member State (see Joint Statement No 10 regarding Article 15 of Council Regulation (EC) No 40/94 of 20 December 1993 and the Opposition Guidelines of the OHIM)?
2. If Question 1 is answered in the negative, can the use of a Community trade mark within a single Member State as described above never be regarded as genuine use in the Community as referred to in Article 15(1)?

3. If the use of a Community trade mark within a single Member State can never be regarded as genuine use in the Community, what requirements apply—in addition to the other factors—in respect of the territorial scope of the use of a Community trade mark when assessing genuine use in the Community?
4. Or else—as an alternative to the above—must Article 15 be interpreted as meaning that the assessment of genuine use in the Community should be carried out wholly in the abstract, without reference to the borders of the territory of the Member States (and that, for example, market share (product markets/geographic markets) should be taken as the point of reference)?

(c) The Opinion of Advocate General Sharpston

8.135 Regretting the absence from the order for reference of sufficient details as regards the use of the mark ONEL in The Netherlands, which obliged her to address the questions pending before the Court only in the most general of terms, Advocate General Sharpston[77] set out to interpret the expression 'genuine use in the Community' by reference to the text of the Regulation and the Directive, the purpose of the relevant provisions, and the case law of the Court.

8.136 As a starting point, she pointed out that the inclusion of a requirement of 'genuine use', expressed in identical terms in the Directive and the Regulation, implied that, despite the fact that national and Community marks exist under different jurisdictions, the function of the requirement of 'genuine use' is the same in both cases: It aims to ensure that the register does not contain marks that obstruct, rather than improve, competition in the marketplace. Accordingly, she saw no reason why the case law of the Court taken under the Directive should not also apply to the interpretation of the Regulation.[78]

8.137 On the other hand, she noted that the difference between Article 10(1) of the Directive, which speaks about use 'in the Member State', and Article 15(1) of the Regulation, which refers to use 'in the Community', appears to suggest that whether the use of a Community trade mark has been genuine depends on the assessment of the relevant criteria in a geographical dimension that transcends the territorial context in which the genuine use of a national mark is established.[79]

8.138 The Advocate General stressed, however, that the expression 'genuine use in the Community' should not be read as implying that 'genuine use' and 'in the Community' are cumulative conditions that must be examined separately, as this would run counter to the principle that the territorial scope of the use is only one of the several factors to be taken into account in the determination of whether such use is genuine. Thus, the place of use is neither an independent condition that applies in addition to the requirement of genuine use, nor is it the sole or dominant factor determining what constitutes genuine use in the Community.[80]

8.139 Accordingly, she disagreed both with the view taken by the General Court in *HIWATT*[81] that 'genuine use means that the mark must be present in a substantial part of the territory where it is protected', and with the soundness of the analogy drawn from the Court's Judgment in *Pago*[82] that 'for a Community trade mark to have a reputation it must be

---

[77] Opinion of Advocate General Sharpston of 5 July 2012, Case C-149/11, *Leno Merken BV v Hagelkruis Beheer BV*, ECLI:EU:C:2012:422.
[78] Points 32–33.
[79] Point 34.
[80] Points 37–38.
[81] Case T-39/01 *Fernandes v OHIM (HIWATT)* [2002] ECR II-5233, paragraph 37.
[82] C-301/07, *PAGO* [2009] ECR I-9429.

known in a substantial part of the Community', all the more so since genuine use and reputation are different concepts with distinct legal function and purpose.[83]

8.140 Rather, she thought that the key to the answer was to be found in the statements of the Court[84] that a trade mark is put to genuine use where it is used 'in accordance with its essential function', on condition that such use 'is sufficient to maintain or create market share for the goods or services protected by the mark', and that, in determining whether a mark has been so used, account must be taken of 'all the circumstances of the case, including the characteristics of the economic sector and the market at issue', which stress the importance not only of the geographic dimension of the market concerned, but also of its particular characteristics and of the kind of use made of the mark within that market.

8.141 In this regard, the Advocate General reiterated that the protection conferred by the Community trade mark was established for undertakings that want to deploy or continue activities on a Community level, by enabling them to adapt their activities to the scale of the internal market, which, in accordance with Article 26(2) TFEU, comprises 'an area without internal frontiers in which the free movement of goods, persons, services and capital is ensured'. To that end, Community trade marks are protected throughout the Community, without any distinction based on territorial borders. Hence, in determining whether the condition of genuine use in the Community is satisfied, the borders between Member States, their respective sizes, and whether the mark has been used in one State or several are irrelevant. What matters is the commercial presence of the mark and its impact on the internal market: in particular, whether its use is sufficient to maintain or create market share by contributing to a 'commercially relevant' presence of the goods and services in that market. Conversely, whether that use results in actual commercial success is not relevant.[85]

8.142 The Advocate General also considered that the findings of the Court in *La Mer*[86] that 'it is not possible to determine a priori, and in the abstract, what quantitative threshold should be chosen in order to determine whether use is genuine or not', should equally apply to the territorial extent of the use, since the existence of such a threshold would not allow appraisal of all the circumstances on an equal footing. Moreover, it would overlook the possibility that the local use of a Community trade mark may nonetheless produce effects on the internal market by, for example, ensuring that the goods are known in a market that is larger than the territory where the mark is used.[87]

8.143 Based on these considerations, the Advocate General concluded that genuine use in the Community is use that, when account is taken of the particular characteristics of the relevant market, is sufficient to maintain or create market share in that market for the goods and services covered by the Community trade mark, and proposed that Article 15(1) CTMR be interpreted as meaning that (i) use of a Community trade mark within the borders of a single Member State is not, of itself, necessarily sufficient to constitute genuine use of that trade mark, but (ii) it is possible that, when account is taken of all relevant facts, use of a

---

[83] Points 40–42.
[84] C-40/01 *Ansul* [2003] ECR I-2439, C-259/02 *La Mer* [2004] ECR I-1159, and C-416/04 P *Sunrider* [2006] ECR I-4237.
[85] Points 44–50.
[86] C-259/02 *La Mer* [2004] ECR I-1159, paragraphs 22–25.
[87] Points 51–54.

Community trade mark within an area corresponding with the territory of a single Member State will constitute genuine use in the Community.[88]

8.144 Finally, the Advocate General took the view that reading the requirement of 'genuine use in the Community' in this manner guarantees the freedom of undertakings of all types to choose to register a mark as either a national or a Community trade mark and found that her reading was not contradicted either by the Joint Statement or the guidelines of OHIM. Moreover, she considered that her view did not undermine the *effet utile* of Article 112(2)(a) CTMR, which allows for a deviation from the rule that a Community trade mark may not be converted into a national mark if revoked on the grounds of non-use. Indeed, if use within a single Member State can, when account is taken of all other facts, constitute genuine use in the Community there will be no basis for revoking the mark. By contrast, if use in a Member State is insufficient to constitute genuine use in the Community, it may still be possible to convert the Community trade mark into a national trade mark, applying the exception of Article 112(2)(a), if in that Member State the mark has been put to use which would be considered to be genuine under the laws of that State.[89]

(d) The Judgment of the Court

8.145 Following for the most part the opinion of the Advocate General, the Court[90] gave a clear answer to the last question, confirming that the territorial borders of the Member States should be disregarded in the assessment of whether a trade mark has been put to genuine use 'in the Community'. Notwithstanding this, and despite the negative answer it gave to the first and second questions, it qualified its approach by holding, in addition, that the size of the Community plays a role in itself, and that use in one or more Member States may be enough or not, depending on the circumstances of the case.

8.146 In order to better understand the Court's rationale, it is worth following its analytical thread from the start. The Court first recalled that, although the size of the respective territories may differ, the legal concept of genuine use is the same as regards both Community and national marks. It made this clear by stressing that the requirement of genuine use is an autonomous concept of EU law which must be given a uniform interpretation, and by recalling that such a uniform interpretation is further imposed by the fact that insofar as the requirement of use is concerned, the Regulation and the Directive pursue the same objective.[91]

8.147 Next, the Court referred to its settled case law[92] as regards the requirements that must be present for the use of the mark to be genuine, by repeating its three-fold canon that: (a) the mark must be used in accordance with its essential function, which is to guarantee the origin of the goods covered by the registration, (b) genuine use does not include token use for the sole purpose of preserving the rights conferred by the mark, and (c) the use made of the mark must be aimed at creating or preserving an outlet for the goods in the market concerned.

---

[88] Points 55, 59, and 64.
[89] Points 56 and 60–63.
[90] C-149/11, *Leno Merken BV v Hagelkruis Beheer BV*, ECLI:EU:C:2012:816.
[91] Paragraphs 28 and 31.
[92] Citing C-40/01 *Ansul* [2003] ECR I-2439, paragraph 43, C-259/02 *La Mer* [2004] ECR I-1159, paragraph 27, and C-416/04 P *Sunrider* [2006] ECR I-4237, paragraph 70.

8.148 In the same vein, the Court reaffirmed that the examination must be based on an overall assessment of all the relevant factors, particularly the accepted norms and usages in the relevant economic sector, the characteristics of the market as defined by the nature of the goods and services concerned, the scale of the use of the mark (which must be understood in terms of both territorial scope and intensity), and the frequency (and, for the identity of reason, the duration) of its use.[93]

8.149 Although there is nothing new in these statements, the express confirmation by the Court of the principles governing the assessment of the user requirement is not devoid of legal significance. On the contrary, it shows that the centre of gravity of the assessment of genuine use has not shifted when it comes to Community trade marks. The ultimate criterion remains whether the mark has been put to real and effective use within the European Union, that is, whether it has been used in a way that aims to acquire or secure a 'share' (which in effect means commercial presence) for the products it designates in the internal market.

8.150 In order, however, to give a meaningful answer to the questions referred to it, the Court had to explain in more detail how the examination of the territorial scope of use fitted this classical test in the case of Community trade marks. Its statements on this point may not be groundbreaking, but are still revealing as to the equal weight to be afforded to the territorial extent of the use as against the other factors to be taken into account when assessing its genuine character.

8.151 In that regard, the Court agreed with the Advocate General that, both for national and Community trade marks, the geographical extent of the use cannot be treated independently or be given primacy among the other relevant factors, being just one consideration among many. In practice, this means that the examining authority must conduct a pure 'overall assessment', without focusing, either exclusively, primarily, or decisively, on the territorial aspects alone. Accordingly, the reference to the territory of the Community in Article 15(1) of the Regulation is merely intended to define the geographical market, serving as a reference point for the purposes of the assessment, and cannot be seen as imposing an additional requirement to that effect.[94]

8.152 In order to define the attributes of that market, the Court turned to the objectives pursued by the legislation,[95] reiterating that the Regulation seeks to remove the barrier of territoriality by enabling the holders of Community trade marks to distinguish their goods and services by identical means throughout the entire Community, regardless of frontiers. This is principally achieved by the unitary character of the Community trade mark, enshrined in Article 1(2) of the Regulation, which results in it enjoying uniform protection and having equal effect throughout the entire area of the Community. This led the Court to conclude that the purpose of the Community trade mark system is to offer on the internal market conditions which are 'similar to those obtaining in a national market' and that giving particular significance to the territories of the Member States would be detrimental to the unitary principle. Accordingly, the territorial borders of the Member States should be entirely disregarded in the assessment of 'genuine use in the Community' within the meaning of Article 15(1) of the Regulation.[96]

---

[93] Paragraph 29.
[94] Paragraphs 30 and 33–36.
[95] As expressed in Recitals 2–6 of the preamble to the Regulation.
[96] Paragraphs 37–44.

8.153 The Court further observed that this conclusion cannot be undermined by either the Joint Statement, according to which 'use which is genuine within the meaning of Article 15 in one country constitutes genuine use in the Community', or the Opposition Guidelines of OHIM, which contain in essence the same rule, as neither of these documents can be used for the purpose of interpreting secondary legislation.[97]

8.154 Equally, the Court rejected the argument regarding Article 112(2)(a) of the Regulation that the territorial scope of the use of a Community trade mark cannot under any circumstances be limited to the territory of a single Member State, holding that, whilst there is admittedly some justification for thinking that a Community trade mark should be used in a larger area than the territory of a single Member State, it cannot be ruled out that, in certain circumstances, the market for the goods or services for which a Community trade mark has been registered is in fact restricted to the territory of a single Member State. In such a case, use of the Community trade mark on that territory might satisfy the conditions both for genuine use of a Community trade mark and for genuine use of a national trade mark.[98]

8.155 Furthermore, it found that the case law concerning the extended protection conferred on trade marks that have a reputation or are well known in the Community or in a Member State requiring that the trade mark be known in a substantial part of the relevant territory cannot be transposed by analogy to the requirement of genuine use, in view of the different objective pursued by the respective provisions.[99]

8.156 In that connection the Court also found that, whilst it is again reasonable to expect that a Community trade mark should be used in a larger area than a national mark, it is not necessary that the use should cover an extensive geographic area in order to be deemed genuine. The Court thus considered that the very nature of the assessment of genuine use, which must be carried out by reference to all the relevant facts and circumstances, does not allow determination *a priori*, and in the abstract, what territorial scope should be chosen in order to establish whether the use of the mark is genuine or not. Consequently, it is not possible to lay down a *de minimis* rule without adversely affecting the overall balance of the system.[100]

8.157 In view of these considerations, the Court answered the questions of the Gerechtshof's-Gravenhage to the effect that Article 15(1) of the Regulation must be interpreted as meaning that the territorial borders of the Member States should be disregarded in the assessment of whether a trade mark has been put to 'genuine use in the Community' within the meaning of that provision, and that a Community trade mark is put to 'genuine use' when it is used in accordance with its essential function and for the purpose of maintaining or creating market share within the Community for the goods or services covered by it, adding that it is for the referring court to assess whether the conditions are met, taking account of all the relevant facts and circumstances, including the characteristics of the market, the nature of the goods or services concerned, and the territorial extent of the use, as well as its scale, frequency, and regularity.

---

[97] Paragraphs 45–48.
[98] Paragraphs 49–51.
[99] Paragraphs 52–53.
[100] Paragraphs 54–55.

(e) Conclusions

8.158 In *ONEL* the Court tried—and for the most part succeeded—to avoid the extremes and to draw a steady middle course between the two interpretative approaches it had to choose from. Essentially, it reaffirmed the principles established by its previous case law, with a minimum of fine-tuning that was necessary in order to answer the questions of the referring Court in a meaningful manner and to provide as useful a guidance about the role played by territorial considerations in the assessment of genuine use as the facts of the case permitted.

8.159 The main point made by the Court is the need for the examination to follow a case-by-case approach and to remain genuinely borderless, without paying undue attention to national territories or giving the geographical aspects of the case a primary or disproportionately prominent role. All that matters is whether the mark has been sufficiently used to create a market share in the internal market, all things considered.

8.160 To that end, the Court gave a number of useful hints, by stressing that: (a) the overall size of the EU must be taken as the reference point for setting the geographical extent of the relevant territory, (b) as a matter of principle, the use shown does not necessarily have to be geographically extensive, in the sense that a *de minimis* rule cannot be applied *a priori*, (c) where appropriate, a limited geographical extent could be compensated by a higher intensity, duration, or frequency of use, and (d) use in one Member State will be enough if it can be seen as creating or preserving an outlet for the goods in the internal market (bearing also in mind the rule in *La Mer*[101] that even minimal use can be sufficient when it serves a real commercial purpose).

8.161 These findings also show that the statement of the Court that 'there is some justification in thinking that a CTM must be used in a broader territory than a national mark' cannot be taken out of context or given undue weight. By saying that, in circumstances where the market in question is restricted to the territory of a single Member State, the same conditions for the genuine use of a Community and a national trade mark apply, the Court merely made reference to particular situations where, because of the specificities of the market concerned, the size of the relevant territory will coincide both for national and Community trade marks. Even in the majority of cases, however, where the respective territories will not coincide, nothing prevents the use of a Community trade mark in the territory of a single Member State from satisfying both the European and national requirements if the use is real in both cases.

8.162 Therefore, that statement cannot be read as meaning that the use of a Community trade mark in a single Member State will be enough only in exceptional circumstances. That reading would effectively distort the substance of the Court's argument, since, in such a case, the relevance of territorial borders, the existence of a *de minimis* rule, and the need for an extensive territorial coverage, which were all expressly dismissed by the Court, would come back in through the back door. Such an interpretation would moreover be circular, to the extent that it would effectively advocate that companies operating in locally concentrated markets must have easier access to the CTM system, when in economic terms such operators might not need a Community trade mark at all.

---

[101] Case C-259/02 *La Mer* [2004] ECR I-1159, paragraph 27.

8.163 More importantly, by emphasizing in more than one way that the geographical extent of the use is not decisive in itself, the Court effectively implied that it is pointless to ask in the abstract how much more extensive the use of a Community trade mark must be compared to a national mark. The Court made this plain by insisting on the need to take a case-by-case approach and to make a true overall assessment of all the relevant factors. In this way, it effectively reduced the question of how much use is sufficient in each case to a matter of fact, which seems to suggest that the Court has actually said most of what it had to say and that it is very unlikely to change its position of principle or add anything radically new in the future.

8.164 It would therefore seem that the task of laying down more detailed rules as regards the territorial aspects of the use of Community trade marks will ultimately fall on the shoulders of the General Court, which will be called upon to fine-tune the relevant principles as the practice unfolds, in matters relating to appeals from OHIM decisions, and on national authorities and courts when the issue arises in proceedings before national IP offices, as in the ONEL case, or before the courts when the genuineness of a Community trade mark is contested.

8.165 Finally, it seems that the element of the territorial extent of use is specific to the Community trade mark and is unlikely to arise for national trade marks.

(2) *Rivella International*: A Variation on the Theme of Use

8.166 *Rivella*[102] concerned an opposition to a CTM application for BASKAYA, stylized. The opponent relied on an earlier international registration of a stylized version of PASSAIA, protected in Germany, which was over five years old and therefore subject to proof of use. In support of the registration, the opponent filed evidence showing use of the mark in Switzerland and relied on Article 5 of the 1892 Convention between Switzerland and Germany which states that 'the legal disadvantages which under the law of the contracting parties, occur when a trade mark had not been used within a certain period of time are precluded if the use takes place in the territory of the other party'.[103] The opposition was rejected by both the Opposition Division and the Board of Appeal on the basis that the relevant proof of use of the earlier mark had not been made out.

8.167 The opponent appealed to the General Court arguing that by virtue of Article 5(1) of the 1892 Convention a trade mark is used in Germany if it is used in Switzerland. However, the General Court refused the appeal on the basis that questions relating to proof of use were governed by Regulation 207/2009, irrespective of the domestic law of Member States, and regardless of whether the registrations were national or international in their nature.[104]

8.168 The opponent appealed to the Court of Justice, arguing in the first place that trade marks obtained under international arrangements did not come under the ambit of Article 42(2) and (3), which only refers to Community marks and national trade marks, and that the General Court had therefore erred in law by applying the genuine use requirement to

---

[102] C-445/12 *Rivella International AG v Office for Harmonisation in the Internal Market (Trade Marks and Designs)/Baskaya di Kaskaya Alim e C.Sas*, ECLI:EU:C:2013:826.
[103] Paragraph 7.
[104] T-170/11 *Rivella International AG v Office for Harmonisation in the Internal Market (Trade Marks and Designs)/Baskaya di Kaskaya Alim e C.Sas*, ECLI:EU:T:2012:374, paragraph 26.

its earlier trade mark. However, the Court of Justice took the view that 'earlier national trade marks' under Article 42(3) should be taken to mean trade marks having effect in a Member State regardless of whether they are obtained nationally or internationally.[105] In support of this view, the Court of Justice relied on Recital 10, which makes no distinction (in relation to priority) as to the type of trade mark protected, as well as Article 160, which 'requires use where opposition proceedings are brought on the basis of an international trade mark in the context of determining the date of registration'.[106] Consequently, the General Court was not found to have erred in law by requiring use of the opponent's international trade mark.

8.169 The opponent also claimed that the 'territorial validity' of a national trade mark should be governed exclusively by national law, especially where it has been registered under international arrangements. However, the Court held that the General Court had not erred in its decision and that the concept of use was governed exclusively by EU law. In particular, the Court found that the General Court had been right to take note of the Court of Justice's decision in *Il Ponte*[107] in which the Court had held that defensive trade marks permitted under national law could not be used to oppose a CTM.

8.170 The Court also rejected the opponent's claims that the fact that the use of the contested mark could be prevented under the 1892 Convention could affect the unitary character of the trade mark. In particular, the Court pointed to the fact that the Regulation already allowed exceptions to the principle, such as under Article 111(1).

E. Use of the Mark as Registered, Use Together with Another Mark, Use of an Acceptable Variation

8.171 Article 15 of the Regulation and Article 10 of the Directive require that the mark must be used as registered, or if it is used in a form differing in elements from the form in which it is registered, provided that the difference does not 'alter the distinctive character' of the mark as registered.

8.172 In analysing this provision it is useful to keep in mind that what is involved in these situations is always an enforcement or other assertion of the mark as registered, not the mark as used. Also, there is no reason to apply the rule only to multi-element marks, ie marks composed of more than one element.

8.173 There is so far very little case law of the Court of Justice on the core issue, namely where the line lies between an acceptable and an unacceptable variation. Cases have focused so far on related issues, such as the use of more than one mark and the question of the relevance, if any, of the fact that the variation which is actually used is also registered.

8.174 In fact, that last point spawned three references, two from the German Bundesgerichtshof and one from the Court of Appeal of England and Wales. It is thus appropriate to begin with the issue of registration of the variation before turning to the three cases.

---

[105] Paragraph 37.
[106] Paragraph 40.
[107] C-234/06 *Il Ponte Finanziaria v Office for Harmonisation in the Internal Market (Trade Marks and Designs)* [2007] ECR I-7333.

(1) Registration of a Variation: *Bainbridge*

(a) The factual setting and the contested decisions

8.175 In *Bainbridge*[108] the Court was confronted with the question as to whether the use of a given sign can constitute genuine use also in respect of another very similar mark belonging to the same owner, as well as with the related issue of whether the existence of national provisions allowing for 'defensive registrations' amounted to proper reasons for non-use under Community law. The 'defensive registration' issue will be dealt with in a different context (justification of non-use).[109]

8.176 The case concerned an opposition to the registration of the CTM application BAINBRIDGE, based on a number of earlier Italian registrations consisting of word and figurative versions of the signs BRIDGE, THE BRIDGE, OLD BRIDGE, THE BRIDGE BASKET, FOOTBRIDGE, THE BRIDGE WAYFARER, and OVER THE BRIDGE, which the opponent claimed to have used as a 'family' of marks. The respective marks were filed in respect of identical or similar goods, namely leather products and articles of clothing in Classes 18 and 25 of the Nice Classification.

8.177 The Office rejected the opposition taking the view that the aural and visual dissimilarities of the marks sufficed to rule out any likelihood of confusion. The Board of Appeal confirmed that view. First, it excluded from its assessment five of the eleven earlier registrations on the ground that their use had not been established. Secondly, it refused to classify the six remaining registrations as marks 'in a series' since the number of them that were used in that manner was not sufficient for that purpose. Finally, it confirmed that there was no likelihood of confusion between the marks considered individually, in view of the absence of the minimum degree of similarity required in order to justify the application of the principle of interdependence.

8.178 In the first place, the Court of First Instance[110] held that the six earlier marks that were not subject to the user requirement within the meaning of Article 43 CTMR (new Article 42), because the five-year period following their registration had not yet elapsed, had to be taken into consideration for the purpose of assessing the existence of a likelihood of confusion. However, it also observed that only two of those marks, which had actually been used, could be taken into account when assessing the existence of a 'family of marks'. Secondly, the Court held that the opponent had failed to prove that the earlier registration THE BRIDGE had been used at all. Moreover, with regard to whether the trade mark BRIDGE could be regarded as broadly equivalent to the mark THE BRIDGE, and thus serve as proof of genuine use of the latter, the Court pointed out that Article 15(2)(a) CTMR does not allow the proprietor of a registered trade mark to demonstrate use of that mark by relying on the use of a similar mark, covered by a separate registration.

(b) The Judgment of the Court

8.179 As regards the issue of simultaneous use of similar marks, the Court found that although under Article 15(2)(a) CTMR (which corresponds to Article 10(2)(a) of the Directive) use of

---

[108] C-234/06 P *Il Ponte Finanziaria Spa v OHIM* (BAINBRIDGE)[2007] ECR I-7333.
[109] See paragraph 8.252, below.
[110] T-194/03 *Il Ponte Finanziaria v OHIM—Marine Enterprise Projects* (BAINBRIDGE)[2006] ECR II-00445.

the Community trade mark 'in a form differing in elements which do not alter the distinctive character of the mark in the form in which it was registered' also constitutes use within the meaning of that provision, the appellant could not rely on the use of the mark BRIDGE for the purpose of demonstrating use of the trade mark THE BRIDGE. It explained this as follows:

> [While] it is possible, as a result of [Article 15(2)(a) CTMR], to consider a registered trade mark as used where proof is provided of use of that mark in a slightly different form from that in which it was registered, it is not possible to extend, by means of proof of use, the protection enjoyed by a registered trade mark to another registered mark, the use of which has not been established, on the ground that the latter is merely a slight variation on the former.[111]

(c) Conclusions

8.180 The General Court's bland statement that the registration of the used variant prevented it from being taken into account when seeking to enforce or maintain another registered mark caused consternation among many in the trade mark community, in any event in countries where such a rule was alien, and where in fact trade mark proprietors routinely sought registration for used variations while relying on such variations to protect an existing earlier mark, provided of course that the variation was acceptable.

8.181 The Court of Justice's statement was not as clear-cut, because it dealt with the attribution of use of one mark not only to one registered mark, but also to another registered mark based on the sole reason that the two registered marks were similar.

8.182 Still, the unrest persisted. Thus, it was not surprising that the German Bundesgerichtshof used the first opportunity it had to refer questions to the Court seeking clarification of what the rule should be.[112]

(2) Registration of the Variation not Relevant: *Rintisch v Eder* (PROTI)

(a) The factual setting and the questions referred

8.183 The first reference from the Bundesgerichtshof, *Rintisch v Eder*,[113] concerned a standard case of the use of a variation which was—or was not—an acceptable variation (this was not a question referred to the Court), but where the variation was also separately registered. The Court of Appeal had refused to accept that variation considering itself bound by the Court's *Bainbridge* Judgment.

8.184 The Bundesgerichtshof, squarely confronting the issue, put the following questions before the Court:

1. Must Article 10(1) and (2)(a) of Directive [89/104] be interpreted as meaning that in principle this provision generally precludes a national rule pursuant to which the use of a trade mark (Trade Mark 1) must be presumed even if the trade mark (Trade Mark 1) is used in a form differing from the form in which it was registered, without the differences altering the distinctive character of the trade mark (Trade Mark 1), and if the trade mark in the form used is also registered (Trade Mark 2)?

---

[111] Paragraph 86.
[112] That the reference came from Germany should not be surprising because the German trade mark has an explicit provision prescribing that the registration of the variation is not an obstacle to the attribution of its use to another registered mark.
[113] C-553/11, *Rintisch v Eder*, ECLI:EU:C:2012:671.

2. If question 1 is answered in the negative:
Is the national provision described in the first question compatible with Directive [89/104] if the national provision is interpreted restrictively as meaning that it is not applicable to a trade mark (Trade Mark 1) which is registered only in order to secure or expand the protection of another registered trade mark (Trade Mark 2) that is registered in the form in which it is used?
3. If question 1 is answered in the affirmative or question 2 is answered in the negative:
   (a) Is there no use of a registered trade mark (Trade Mark 1) within the meaning of Article 10(1) and (2)(a) of Directive [89/104]:
      (i) if the trade mark proprietor uses the form of a sign which differs only in elements from the form in which it (Trade Mark 1) and a further trade mark (Trade Mark 2) of the trade mark proprietor are registered but the differences do not alter the distinctive character of the trade marks (Trade Mark 1 and Trade Mark 2);
      (ii) if the trade mark proprietor uses two forms of sign, neither of which corresponds to the registered trade mark (Trade Mark 1), but one of the forms used (Form 1) is the same as another registered trade mark (Trade Mark 2) of the trade mark proprietor and the second form used by the trade mark proprietor (Form 2) differs in elements from both registered trade marks (Trade Mark 1 and Trade Mark 2), without the differences altering the distinctive character of the trade marks, and if this form of sign (Form 2) displays greater similarity to the other trade mark (Trade Mark 2) of the trade mark proprietor?
   (b) Is a court of a Member State permitted to apply a national provision (here the second sentence of Paragraph 26(3) of the [MarkenG]) which conflicts with a provision of a directive (here Article 10(1) and (2)(a) of Directive [89/104]) in cases in which the facts of the case had already occurred prior to a decision of the Court of Justice of the European Union in which indications of the incompatibility of the Member State's legislation with the provision of the directive became apparent for the first time (the judgment of 13 September 2007 in Case C-234/06 P *Il Ponte Finanziaria* v *OHIM* ... [2007] ECR I-7333) if the national court values the reliance of a party to the court proceedings on the validity of his position, secured under constitutional law, more highly than the interest in the implementation of a provision of the directive?

(b) The Judgment of the Court

8.185 The Court, deciding without an Advocate General, but with the same judge as Rapporteur as in the earlier *Bainbridge* case, needed just over a year to set the record straight.

8.186 The Court began by repeating well-known principles about distinctiveness and directly confronted the question:

> 20 It should then be stated that there is nothing at all in the wording of Article 10(2)(a) of Directive 89/104 to suggest that the different form in which the trade mark is used cannot itself be registered as a trade mark. Indeed, the only condition laid down in that provision is that the form in which the trade mark is used may differ from the form in which that trade mark was registered only in elements which do not alter the distinctive character of the mark.
>
> 21 The purpose of Article 10(2)(a) of Directive 89/104, which avoids imposing a requirement for strict conformity between the form used in trade and the form in which the trade mark was registered, is to allow the proprietor of the mark, in the commercial exploitation of the sign, to make variations in the sign, which, without altering its distinctive character, enable it to be better adapted to the marketing and promotion requirements of the goods or services concerned.

22 That purpose would be jeopardised if, in order to establish use of the registered trade mark, an additional condition had to be met, whereby the different form in which that mark is used should not itself have been registered as a trade mark. In fact, the registration of new forms of a trade mark makes it possible, where necessary, to anticipate changes that may occur in the trade mark's image and thus to adapt it to the realities of a changing market.

23 Furthermore, it is clear from the twelfth recital in the preamble to Directive 89/104 that the provisions of the directive must be 'entirely consistent with those of the Paris Convention'. Therefore, Article 10(2)(a) of Directive 89/104 must be interpreted consistently with Article 5.C(2) of the Convention. Nothing in the latter provision suggests that when a sign is registered as a trade mark the consequence is that use of the sign can no longer be relied on to establish use of another registered trade mark from which the sign only differs in a way that does not alter the distinctive character of the trade mark.

24 Accordingly, registration as a trade mark of the form in which another registered trade mark is used, a form which differs from that in which the latter mark is registered, whilst not altering its distinctive character, is not a bar to the application of Article 10(2)(a) of Directive 89/104.

The Court then turned to its earlier *Bainbridge* Judgment, which had caused all the concerns. It distinguished that case as having dealt with the issue of a family of marks, and the use of marks in order to be perceived as a family: **8.187**

25 That interpretation is not at variance with the interpretation resulting from the judgment in *Il Ponte Finanziaria v OHIM*, in particular paragraph 86 thereof, to which the order for reference alludes.

26 In the case which gave rise to that judgment, the proceedings before the Court concerned a dispute in which one party invoked the protection of a 'family' or 'series' of similar trade marks, for the purpose of assessing the likelihood of confusion with the trade mark whose registration was sought. That dispute fell within the scope of Article 15(2)(a) of Council Regulation (EC) No 40/94 of 20 December 1993 on the Community trade mark (OJ 1994 L 11, p. 1), a provision which corresponded, at the material time, to Article 10(2)(a) of Directive 89/104, the wording of those provisions being in essence identical.

27 Having held, in paragraph 63 of the judgment in *Il Ponte Finanziaria v OHIM*, that where there is a 'family' or 'series' of trade marks, the likelihood of confusion results more specifically from the possibility that the consumer may be mistaken as to the provenance or origin of goods or services covered by the trade mark applied for, considering, erroneously, that that trade mark is part of that family or series of marks, the Court concluded that, in order to establish that there is a 'family' or 'series' of trade marks, use of a sufficient number of trade marks capable of constituting that 'family' or 'series' must be shown.

28 The Court went on to hold, in paragraph 64 of *Il Ponte Finanziaria v OHIM*, that no consumer can be expected, in the absence of use of a sufficient number of trade marks capable of constituting a 'family' or a 'series', to detect a common element in such a family or series and/or to associate with that family or series another trade mark containing the same common element. Accordingly, in order for there to be a likelihood that the public may be mistaken as to whether the trade mark applied for belongs to a 'family' or 'series', the earlier trade marks which are part of that 'family' or 'series' must be present on the market.

29 It is in that particular context of a claim that there is a 'family' or 'series' of trade marks that the Court's statement in paragraph 86 of *Il Ponte Finanziaria v OHIM* should be understood, according to which it is not possible, under Article 15(2)(a) of Regulation No 40/94, and consequently under Article 10(2)(a) of Directive 89/104, to extend, by means of proof of use, the protection enjoyed by a registered trade mark to another registered mark, the use of which has not been established, on the ground that the latter is merely a slight variation on the former. The use of one trade mark cannot be relied on in order to prove the use of

another trade mark where the aim is to establish use of a sufficient number of trade marks of a single family.

8.188 The Court concluded as follows on the first question and point (a) of the third question:

Article 10(2)(a) of Directive 89/104 must be interpreted as meaning that the proprietor of a registered trade mark is not precluded from relying, in order to establish use of the trade mark for the purposes of that provision, on the fact that it is used in a form which differs from the form in which it was registered, without the differences between the two forms altering the distinctive character of that trade mark, even though that different form is itself registered as a trade mark.

8.189 The answer to the question of defensive registrations will be dealt with hereafter. An answer to the third question was not necessary, in view of the positive answer to the question of whether the variation could also be registered.

(3) Combinations of Marks: *Colloseum*

(a) Factual setting and questions referred

8.190 A few months after the *PROTI* reference, the Bundesgerichtshof referred another case to the Court with a variation of the *PROTI* situation. Levi Strass & Co had sued Colloseum for infringement of several of its marks showing a 'flag' at the side of the back pocket of their jeans, and the finding of infringement depended on a mark showing just a flag, which had been registered on the basis of acquired distinctiveness, but which was not used as such, but with the words LEVI'S on the flag. By the time of this reference—in November 2011—the *PROTI* reference had not even been argued. It is apparent from the questions and the reasons given by the Bundesgerichtshof that the referring court clearly wished to have a final answer on the multiple marks issue, and perhaps even hoped that the two cases might be dealt with together by the Court. As it was, the *PROTI* reference was decided first, in October 2012, while the Colloseum reference was decided in April 2013.[114]

8.191 The questions referred were as follows:

Is Article 15(1) of Regulation No 40/94 to be interpreted as meaning that:
1. a trade mark which is part of a composite mark and has become distinctive only as a result of the use of the composite mark can be used in such a way as to preserve the rights attached to it if the composite mark alone is used?
2. a trade mark is being used in such a way as to preserve the rights attached to it if it is used only together with another mark, the public sees independent signs in the two marks and, in addition, both marks are registered together as a trade mark?

(b) The Judgment of the Court

8.192 The Court, again deciding without an Opinion by the Advocate General, began by referring to its decisions on distinctiveness, and in particular to the *Nestlé* Judgment (HAVE A BREAK ...) which had held that a mark may acquire distinctive character even if used together with another mark.[115] The Court stated that the holding in *Nestlé* was of general application, and thus also applied in the context of the use requirement.

---

[114] C-12/12, *Colloseum Holding AG v Levi Strass & Co.*, ECLI:EU:C:2013:253.
[115] C-353/03 *Mars v Nestlé*, [2005] ECR I-06135.

8.193 The Court added a caveat—the individual mark, even if used together with another mark, must still be recognized by the public as 'indicative of the origin of the product at issue for that use to be covered by the term "genuine use" within the meaning of Article 15(1)'.[116]

8.194 The Court concluded as follows:

> 36 In the light of the above considerations, the answer to the questions referred is that the condition of genuine use of a trade mark, within the meaning of Article 15(1) of Regulation No 40/94, may be satisfied where a registered trade mark, which has become distinctive as a result of the use of another composite mark of which it constitutes one of the elements, is used only through that other composite mark, or where it is used only in conjunction with another mark, and the combination of those two marks is, furthermore, itself registered as a trade mark.

8.195 Interestingly, the fact of registration of the actually used combination did not even figure in the Judgment as a separate issue, and *PROTI* was not referred to.

(4) Multiple Marks, the Final Chapter? *Specsavers*

(a) *Factual setting and questions referred*

8.196 While *PROTI* and *Colloseum* were still pending before the Court, the Court of Appeal of England and Wales referred another series of questions to the Court, which also had the use of multiple marks and use sufficient to maintain trade mark rights as one of their issues. Here again, the referring court pointed to the *Bainbridge* Judgment as the source of the need for clarity. The case also raised issues of infringement, which are dealt with in a different context.

8.197 Specsavers is a large chain selling eyeglasses in the United Kingdom. Asda, a large retailer, also engaged in the business of selling eyeglasses, began to use signs and advertising clearly directed at Specsavers. In the ensuing litigation, where Specsavers claimed trade mark infringement and passing off, Asda asserted that one of the Specsaver marks, a so-called 'wordless logo' had not been used and should be revoked. The High Court agreed. When the case reached the Court of Appeal, that court referred the following questions to the Court of Justice:

> 1. Where a trader has separate registrations of Community trade marks for
>   (a) a graphic device mark
>   (b) a word mark
>   and uses the two together, is such use capable of amounting to use of the [figurative] mark for the purposes of Articles 15 and 51 of Regulation [No 207/2009]? If yes, how is the question of use of the graphic mark to be assessed?
> 2. Does it make a difference if:
>   (a) the word mark is superimposed over the [figurative element]?
>   (b) the trader also has the combined mark comprising [the figurative element] and [the] word mark registered as a Community trade mark?

---

[116] Paragraph 35.

3. Does the answer to [the first and second questions] depend upon whether the graphic device and the words are perceived by the average consumer as [on the one hand] being separate signs; or [on the other hand] each having an independent distinctive role? If so, how?
4. ...
5. ...[117]

8.198 Question 2(b) raised the *Bainbridge* issue, whereas the other parts of the first three questions raised issues factually quite similar to the *Colloseum* setting. In addition, they raised for the first time the possibility that the Court would address the question of what constitutes an acceptable variation.

(b) The Judgment of the Court

8.199 It took the Court, again sitting without an Advocate General, hardly a year to come out with its decision.[118]

8.200 The Court began by qualifying the use made of the combination of the wordless logo with the superimposed word as use of the wordless logo which differed from the form in which it was registered, and thus fell under Article 15(1)(a) of the Regulation, because the superimposition had the consequence of hiding an element of the figurative mark.

> 19 First of all, it should be pointed out that a situation such as that at issue in the main proceedings, in which a word mark is superimposed over a figurative mark, falls within the scope of the second subparagraph of Article 15(1)(a) of Regulation No 207/2009, namely, use of the trade mark in a form different from that under which that trade mark was registered.

8.201 This conclusion is surprising, because following *Colloseum* and *Nestlé* the conclusion would have been more probable or realistic that what was involved was the use of two different marks, just as in *Colloseum* the use of the word LEVI'S on the little flag did not amount to the use of a variant of the flag, but to the use of two marks.

8.202 Even more surprising is that the Court then analysed Article 15(1)(a) of the Regulation and required, for the condition of that provision to be fulfilled, that the public would still see in the wordless logo itself, ie without the superimposition, a distinctive mark:

> 24 It follows that the use of the wordless logo mark with the superimposed word sign 'Specsavers', even if, ultimately, it amounts to a use as a part of a registered trade mark or in conjunction with it, may be considered to be a genuine use of the wordless logo mark as such to the extent that that mark as it was registered, namely without a part of it being hidden by the superimposed word sign 'Specsavers', always refers in that form to the goods of the Specsavers group covered by the registration, which is to be determined by the referring court.

8.203 A 'normal' reading of Article 15(1)(a) would seem to require a comparison of the mark as registered with the mark as used and then a determination of whether the variations were substantial or insignificant in relation to the mark as registered. That the mark as registered is distinctive would not seem to be the relevant question at all.

8.204 As regards the fact that the combination was also registered, the Court explained that this issue had been finally resolved in *PROTI* and *Colloseum*.[119]

---

[117] The fourth and fifth questions are discussed at paragraph 9.20 and following below.
[118] C-252/12, *Specsavers International Healthcare Ltd v Asda Stores Ltd.*, ECLI:EU:C:2013:497.
[119] Paragraphs 25–30.

The answer given by the Court thus was: **8.205**

> Article 15(1) and Article 51(1)(a) of Regulation No 207/2009 must be interpreted as meaning that the condition of 'genuine use', within the meaning of those provisions, may be fulfilled where a Community figurative mark is used only in conjunction with a Community word mark which is superimposed over it, and the combination of those two marks is, furthermore, itself registered as a Community trade mark, to the extent that the differences between the form in which that trade mark is used and that in which it was registered do not change the distinctive character of that trade mark as registered.[120]

This answer barely reflects the considerations underlying the Court's analysis, as it is limited to an almost verbatim repetition of the language of Article 15(1)(a). **8.206**

F. Use of the Mark for the Goods or Services for which it is Registered

(1) Introduction

Article 10 of the Directive and Article 15 of the Regulation require that the use of the mark must have been for the goods or services for which the mark is registered. This means, conversely, that use outside of the registration must be entirely disregarded. The principal issue that arises in this context is the proper identification of what is used in relation to what is registered. When—as is usually the case—what is used is much narrower than what is registered (eg, handmade pralines vis-à-vis chocolate products, as in the WALZERTRAUM case), in opposition cases it must be decided whether the conflict is judged only with regard to the actual product for which the earlier mark has been used or whether a suitable generic product description is acceptable. Similarly, in a revocation case, the question must be decided whether the mark can remain registered only for the specific product or a broader generic category. The leading case for this problem is a decision of (what was then) the Court of First Instance,[121] which came up with a rather liberal solution of maintaining (or taking into account) a suitable generic product designation under which the product for which the mark was actually used can be grouped. This has become the practice of OHIM, as well as most national offices. What has also been accepted universally is that use outside of the registration is not sufficient. **8.207**

(2) The Special Case of Goods Out of Production—*Ansul*

Ansul,[122] with which this section opened, also presented the issue, perhaps not really appreciated by the Court with all its consequences, of whether use was made by Ansul, which was no longer producing fire extinguishers but continued selling component parts and extinguishing substances for 'Minimax' fire extinguishers to undertakings that were responsible for maintaining them. It also continued checking, maintaining, and repairing 'Minimax' products itself. As a result 'Minimax' had been used on invoices, stickers, and strips with the statement 'Gebruiksklaar Minimax' ('Ready for use Minimax'). **8.208**

---

[120] Judgment, paragraph 31
[121] T-126/03, *Reckitt Benckiser (España), SL v OHIM Aladin Gesellschaft für innovative mikrobiologische Systeme GmbH* [2005] ECR II-02861.
[122] C-40/01 *Ansul BV v Ajax Brandbeveiliging BV* [2003] ECR I-2439.

8.209 Among the questions referred by the Hoge Raad was the question of whether use as described could count as use for the goods for which the mark was registered.

8.210 The Court distinguished between 'use for parts which are integral to the make-up or structure of the goods previously sold' and 'use in respect of directly related goods or services'.

8.211 As regards the first category, the Court held that use of the mark for such parts should be treated as use for the goods themselves.

> 40. Use of the mark may also in certain circumstances be genuine for goods in respect of which it is registered that were sold at one time but are no longer available.
>
> 41. That applies, *inter alia*, where the proprietor of the trade mark under which such goods were put on the market sells parts which are integral to the make-up or structure of the goods previously sold, and for which he makes actual use of the same mark … Since the parts are integral to those goods and are sold under the same mark, genuine use of the mark for those parts must be considered to relate to the goods previously sold and to serve to preserve the proprietor's rights in respect of those goods.

8.212 That means that, for example, the sale of replacement handles for fire extinguishers under the name MINIMAX may constitute use for fire extinguishers. One should add that this applies—or becomes relevant—only when the registration does not include specifically spare and replacement parts for the respective goods.

8.213 As regards the second category, the Court concluded that there may also be genuine use for the goods for which the mark is registered if the mark is used for after-sales services, sales of accessories or related parts, and maintenance and repair services:

> 42. The same may be true where the trade mark proprietor makes actual use of the mark, under the same conditions, for goods and services which, though not integral to the make-up or structure of the goods previously sold, are directly related to those goods and intended to meet the needs of customers of those goods. That may apply to after-sales services, such as the sale of accessories or related parts, or the supply of maintenance and repair services.

8.214 That means that the repair of fire extinguishers, although a service registrable under the respective service class, amounts to the use of the goods 'fire extinguishers' in Class 9.

8.215 With due respect to the Court, this cannot be correct. The Court fails to give any argument for the support of its conclusions. When a party is offering services, such as car repair services, this is not the same as the sale of goods.

G. Use by the Proprietor or with his Consent

8.216 The use of the mark must have been made by the proprietor or with his consent. Typical cases are use by licensees or use within the same group of companies. In office or court proceedings occasionally difficulties can arise in proving that the use was made with the proprietor's consent. In such a situation the Court's Judgment in *Sunrider* may be helpful.

8.217 As regards proof that the earlier mark was used with the consent of the proprietor, as provided for in Article 15(3) of the Regulation, the Court confirmed the decision of the Court of First Instance. Relying on the material adduced by the opposing party it had found that his consent had been proved. Part of his name was incorporated in the name of the company

H. The Grace Period

(1) Introduction

Both the Directive and the Regulation provide for an initial 'grace period' of five years before the obligation to use sets in, and the same five-year period applies when genuine use, once begun, is no longer continued. According to Article 15(1) of the Regulation, the initial five-year period begins with the registration of the mark. Under the Directive, the provision is not as explicit, but sets the beginning at the 'completion of the registration procedure'. This language was adopted because the national registration systems did not all have the same features. For example, in some Member States the opposition followed registration, and thus it would have been inappropriate in these Member States to require the 'running' of the grace period while oppositions were still pending. The situation is even more complicated with Madrid marks extended to any of the Member States because in these situations there is a requirement to apply both the effective registration dates at the international level and the beginning of the grace period at the national level.

8.218

(2) *Lidl*: Grace Period

The (so far only) case where the calculation of the grace period was referred to the Court is the *Lidl/Häupl* case.[123]

8.219

(a) *The facts in the main proceedings and the order for reference*

The reference was made in the context of a dispute between Mr Häupl and Lidl Stiftung & Co KG ('Lidl') concerning the cancellation of Lidl's Austrian part of the international trade mark LE CHEF DE CUISINE on the grounds of non-use. Lidl was the proprietor of the figurative mark LE CHEF DE CUISINE in Germany. The effects of that registration were extended to Austria by virtue of Article 3(4) of the Madrid Agreement. The international registration was published on 2 December 1993, but took effect as of the date of its filing, namely 12 October 1993.

8.220

Lidl operates a supermarket chain established in Germany. It extended its business to Austria by opening its first supermarket there on 5 November 1998. Before that date, Lidl began to store goods bearing the mark which had already been delivered to it, but the actual opening of its Austrian outlets had been delayed by 'bureaucratic obstacles', in particular delays in the issue of the operating licences.

8.221

On 13 October 1998, Mr Häupl sought to have the mark cancelled for the territory of Austria on the ground of non-use. In his view, the five-year period provided for in the relevant provisions of Austrian law[124] began to run from the beginning of the protection

8.222

---

[123] C-246/05 *Armin Häupl v Lidl Stiftung & Co KG* (LE CHEF DE CUISINE) [2007] ECR I-4673.
[124] Paragraph 33a of the Markenschutzgesetz 1970, BGBl 260/1970: 'the MSchG'.

period, namely on 12 October 1993. Lidl countered that that period only began to run on 2 December 1993, with the result that it did not expire until 2 December 1998. On that date, however, it was already displaying for sale goods bearing the mark at issue in its first Austrian supermarket.

8.223 The Austrian Patent Office upheld the request and declared the mark invalid as of 12 October 1998. Lidl lodged an appeal against that decision with the Oberster Patent- und Markensenat, which decided to stay proceedings and refer the following questions to the Court for a preliminary ruling:

1. Is Article 10(1) of the Directive to be interpreted as meaning that the 'date of the completion of the registration procedure' means the start of the period of protection?
2. Is Article 12(1) of the Directive to be interpreted as meaning that there are proper reasons for non-use of a mark if the implementation of the corporate strategy being pursued by the trade mark proprietor is delayed for reasons outside the control of the undertaking, or is the trade mark proprietor obliged to change his corporate strategy in order to be able to use the mark in good time?

8.224 The 'proper reasons' issue will be discussed hereafter.

(b) The Opinion of the Advocate General Ruiz-Jarabo Colomer

8.225 First, AG Ruiz-Jarabo Colomer remarked that it was not appropriate to link, for the purposes of the discussion, the 'end of the registration procedure' to the 'start of the protection period'. In that regard, he pointed out that there is a wide variety of registration systems in the Community, the procedural particularities of which are not fully aligned.

8.226 Despite the fact, however, that the registration formalities are not entirely covered by the scope of the Directive, there is always a common feature in all registration systems, at least insofar as the relevant procedure is concluded each time by the granting of the registration, usually by virtue of an administrative decision of the competent trade mark authorities, which is communicated to the applicant and published for the information of third parties.[125]

8.227 Nevertheless, to the extent that the Directive does not contain an all-encompassing definition of the precise moment when the registration procedure comes to an end, it is up to the legislation of the Member States to determine when that procedure is deemed to be concluded.[126]

8.228 Next, he turned to the specificities of international registrations, stressing that although in accordance with the Madrid Agreement the protection starts from the date of registration, which actually coincides with the date of either the international application or the national application on which the international mark is based, that protection is subject to the expiry of the term of one year within which national trade mark offices may inform the Bureau of their decision to refuse protection in their territory. Notwithstanding this, he considered that the only workable date for the purposes of Article 10(1) of the Directive is the date the international mark is entered in the register.[127]

---

[125] Point 44.
[126] Point 45.
[127] Point 66.

8.229 Therefore, AG Ruiz-Jarabo Colomer's answer to the first question was that the expression 'date of completion of the registration procedure' in Article 10(1) of the Directive does not refer to the start of the period of protection, with which it may coincide, but rather to the moment when the competent authority, in accordance with national rules, concludes the registration procedure, or, in the case of an international mark, when that procedure is completed by the International Bureau.

(c) The Judgment of the Court

8.230 With regard to the first question,[128] the Court first of all pointed out that several legal systems are involved when a trade mark is registered internationally: both the provisions of the Madrid Agreement, which establishes the part of the registration taking place before the International Bureau, and national legal provisions apply. In addition, the latter must also comply with Community law, as also attested by Article 1 of the Directive, which provides that it 'shall apply to every trade mark ... which is the subject of ... an international registration having effect in a Member State'.[129]

8.231 Further, the Court stressed that for the purpose of interpreting Article 10(1) of the Directive, particular account must be taken of its Third and Fifth Recitals, respectively stating that the Directive is not intended to approximate fully the trade mark laws of the Member States and that the latter remain free to fix the procedural provisions concerning trade mark registration. Moreover, it noted that Article 10(1) does not determine in an unambiguous manner the starting point of the five-year period for which it provides, its wording merely defining that starting point in relation to the registration procedure, that is, by reference to an area which is outside the harmonizing scope of the Directive.[130]

8.232 Thus, it took the view that the wording of Article 10(1) actually implied that the Member States are entitled to organize their registration procedure as they deem fit and, in consequence, they can freely decide when that procedure is to be regarded as having been completed.[131]

8.233 Accordingly, the Court answered the first question to the effect that the 'date of the completion of the registration procedure' within the meaning of Article 10(1) of the Directive must be determined in each Member State in accordance with the procedural rules on registration in force in that State.

---

[128] Before answering the questions referred to it, the Court had to determine whether the Oberster Patent- und Markensenat was a court or tribunal within the meaning of Article 234 EC and whether the Court therefore had jurisdiction to rule on questions referred to it by that body. The Court began by stating that the question of whether the body making a reference is a court or tribunal for the purposes of Article 234 EC is a question governed by Community law alone and that, in answering that question, the Court must take account of a number of factors, such as whether the body is established by law, whether it is permanent, whether its jurisdiction is compulsory, whether its procedure is *inter partes*, whether it applies rules of law, and whether it is independent. Following a detailed examination of the relevant provisions of the Austrian Law on Patents, which was the instrument establishing the Oberster Patent- und Markensenat and governing its function, it concluded that the said body was a court or tribunal within the meaning of Article 234 EC and that the Court therefore had jurisdiction to answer the questions submitted to it by that body. It is perhaps an interesting side note to this question that the Oberster Patent- und Markensenat was recently abolished.
[129] Paragraph 25.
[130] Paragraphs 26–27.
[131] Paragraphs 28.

I. Justification of Non-Use

(1) Introduction

8.234 Both the Directive and the Regulation provide that a trade mark proprietor who cannot show genuine use may still prevail if there are 'proper reasons' justifying the absence of use. A typical case where case law and literature are (almost) unanimous include delay in marketing authorization beyond five years from registration, as may occur notably in the field of pharmaceuticals, herbicides and pesticides, or other chemicals. Government-imposed prohibitions are another category. On the other side there seems to be universal agreement that economic difficulties experienced by the proprietor are not 'proper' reasons.

8.235 Another category of situations where non-use may be an issue is the registration of so-called 'defensive' marks. A number of national systems allow registrations of marks which are identical or similar to a registered mark so as to provide additional protection for the primary mark, especially when that mark is well known. Defensive registrations are, however, not a part of the European trade mark legislation. Nevertheless, the Court has been asked on two occasions to deal with defensive registrations.

(2) *Lidl*: Proper Reasons for Non-use

8.236 In *Lidl*[132] the Court dealt not only with the date on which the 'grace period' begins (see paragraph 8.219), but also with the meaning of the expression 'proper reasons for non-use' in Article 12(1) of the Directive.

(a) *The facts in the main proceedings and the order for reference*

8.237 The reference was made in the context of a dispute between Mr Häupl and Lidl Stiftung & Co KG ('Lidl') as explained earlier. It claimed, inter alia, that the opening of a store in Austria, where the goods were displayed and thus the mark actually used, had been delayed by 'bureaucratic obstacles', in particular delays in the issue of the operating licences.

8.238 The Oberster Patent- und Markensenat referred, inter alia, the following question to the Court for a preliminary ruling:

1. ...
2. Is Article 12(1) of the Directive to be interpreted as meaning that there are proper reasons for non-use of a mark if the implementation of the corporate strategy being pursued by the trade mark proprietor is delayed for reasons outside the control of the undertaking, or is the trade mark proprietor obliged to change his corporate strategy in order to be able to use the mark in good time?

(b) *The Opinion of Advocate General Ruiz-Jarabo Colomer*

8.239 AG Ruiz-Jarabo Colomer observed that Article 12(1) merely refers to 'proper reasons for non-use', without giving any examples of such reasons. He therefore turned to Article 19 of TRIPs, which is more explicit in that regard, by stating that only circumstances which are independent of the will of the proprietor and which constitute an obstacle to the use of the mark, as, for example, import restrictions, are valid reasons for non-use.[133]

---

[132] C-246/05 *Armin Häupl v Lidl Stiftung & Co KG* (LE CHEF DE CUISINE) [2007] ECR I-4673.
[133] Point 78.

8.240 He also observed that the administrative procedures invoked by Lidl merely concerned its own commercial decision to sell the goods bearing the mark exclusively in its own supermarkets and, to that extent, did not directly relate to the use of the mark as such. In that sense, the delays in issuing the construction licences for Lidl's outlets were not in the same league as, for example, setbacks in the sanitary clearance of the foodstuffs bearing the mark, or delays in the approval of a pharmaceutical product by the competent authorities. For instance, Lidl could have launched its products on the market notwithstanding the above delays by granting licences to third parties or by distributing its wares through ordinary food stores.[134]

8.241 Accordingly, the Advocate General proposed that Article 12(1) of the Directive should be interpreted as meaning that the reasons justifying the lack of use must be independent of the will of the trade mark owner and must constitute an obstacle to the use of the sign. If these two requirements are met, the bureaucratic formalities fall within the above exception; however, this is not the case when they obstruct the implementation of a corporate strategy, since in such a situation the undertaking conserves the power to adapt its strategy to the administrative requirements.

(c) The Judgment of the Court

8.242 With regard to the second question, the Court noted that, according to the order for reference, the deferment of the sale on the Austrian market of the goods bearing the mark at issue resulted, first, from Lidl's strategy of selling those goods only in its own outlets and, secondly, from the fact that the opening of its first Austrian supermarket was delayed by 'bureaucratic obstacles'.

8.243 It then defined the subject matter of the question as being whether there are proper reasons for non-use if the implementation of the corporate strategy pursued by the trade mark proprietor is delayed for reasons outside its control, or whether the trade mark proprietor is obliged, in such a case, to change that strategy so as to be able to use the mark in good time. The Court started its analysis by asking whether the term 'proper reasons' within the meaning of Article 12(1) should be given a uniform interpretation at all.

8.244 In that respect, it recalled that the need for uniform application of Community law and the principle of equality require that the terms of a provision of Community law which makes no express reference to the law of the Member States for the purpose of determining its meaning and scope must normally be given an autonomous and uniform interpretation throughout the European Community.[135]

8.245 Next, the Court referred to its Judgment in *Ansul* where it was established that the concept of 'genuine use' must be given a uniform interpretation and reiterated that Articles 10 to 15 of the Directive and the Seventh, Eighth, and Ninth recitals in its Preamble actually show that it was the legislature's intention that the maintenance of rights in a trade mark be subject to the same conditions in all Member States, so that the level of protection enjoyed by a trade mark does not fluctuate according to the legal system concerned.[136]

---

[134] Point 79.
[135] C-287/98 *Linster* [2000] ECR I-6917, paragraph 43.
[136] *Ansul* (n 122) paragraphs 27–31.

8.246 Accordingly, it concluded that since the objective of proper reasons is to justify situations in which there is no genuine use, so as to avoid the revocation of the mark, it was obvious that their function is closely linked to that of genuine use and that, as a result, the concept of 'proper reasons' is subject to the same need for a uniform interpretation as the concept of 'genuine use'.

8.247 The Court went on to note, however, that Article 12(1) does not contain any indication of the nature and characteristics of the 'proper reasons' to which it refers and concurred with the Advocate General that the definition in Article 19(1) of the TRIPs Agreement may therefore constitute a factor in the interpretation of the similar concept of proper reasons used in the Directive. Thus, the Court found it appropriate to determine what kind of circumstances constitute an obstacle to the use of the trade mark within the meaning of that provision, noting that although, quite often, circumstances arising independently of the will of the owner are likely at some point to hinder the preparations for the use of the mark, those difficulties can be overcome in a good many cases.

8.248 For that reason and in view also of the principle in the Eighth Recital to the Directive that registered trade marks must actually be used, the Court stated that it would be contrary to the scheme of Article 12(1) to confer too broad a scope on the concept of proper reasons for non-use; in fact, the objective set out in that recital would be jeopardized if any obstacle, however minimal, were sufficient to justify the non-use of the mark, even if it arose independently of the proprietor's will.[137]

8.249 Therefore, the Court held that the obstacles in question should not only be beyond the control of the trade mark proprietor but must, moreover, have a direct relationship with the mark. It considered, however, that the obstacle concerned need not necessarily make the use of the sign 'impossible' in order to be regarded as having a sufficiently direct relationship with the trade mark; it sufficed if it made the use of that sign 'unreasonable', as, for example, where the proprietor of a trade mark is required to sell its goods in the outlets of its competitors, since in such a case, it does not appear reasonable to require the proprietor to change its corporate strategy merely in order to make the use of the mark possible.[138]

8.250 Accordingly, it found that only obstacles having a sufficiently direct relationship with a trade mark by making its use impossible or unreasonable and arise independently of the will of the proprietor may be described as 'proper reasons for non-use', while stressing that it must be assessed on a case-by-case basis whether a change in the strategy of the undertaking to circumvent the obstacle in question would indeed make the use of that mark unreasonable.[139]

8.251 Consequently, the Court ruled that Article 12(1) of the Directive must be interpreted as meaning that obstacles having a direct relationship with a trade mark which make its use impossible or unreasonable and which are independent of the will of the proprietor constitute 'proper reasons for non-use' of that mark and that it was for the referring instance to assess the facts in the main proceedings in the light of that guidance.

---

[137] Paragraph 51.
[138] Paragraph 53.
[139] Paragraph 54.

(3) Defensive Registrations

(a) Bainbridge

8.252 In *Bainbridge*,[140] which has already been discussed in the context of 'multiple marks', the Court was also confronted with the question as to whether the existence of national provisions allowing for 'defensive registrations' amounted to proper reasons for non-use under Community law. The Court of First Instance[141] confirmed that the Board of Appeal was right in rejecting the 'defensive' registrations of those marks as incompatible with Community law.

8.253 As was to be expected, the Court confirmed that the appellant could not rely on the defensive nature, under Italian trade mark law, of certain of the registrations on which the opposition was based and that the Court of First Instance had rightly disregarded those marks for the purposes of the examination. The Court reiterated that under Articles 43 and 56(2) of the Regulation (new Articles 42 and 57) the proprietor of the mark is required, both in opposition and invalidity proceedings, to furnish proof that the earlier trade mark has been put to genuine use if the defendant so requests, and that he cannot shake off the burden placed upon him by relying on 'national provisions which allow the registration of signs not intended to be used in trade, on account of their purely defensive function in relation to another sign which is being commercially exploited'.[142] The Court also pointed out that the concept of 'proper reasons' mentioned in those provisions refers essentially to circumstances preventing the use of the mark which are independent of the proprietor's will, rather than 'to national legislation which makes an exception to the rule that a trade mark that has not been used for a period of five years must be revoked, even where such lack of use is intentional on the part of the proprietor of the trade mark' and that, accordingly, such 'defensive registrations' are incompatible with Community trade mark law.[143]

(b) PROTI

8.254 The *PROTI* reference,[144] which dealt primarily with the question of whether the registration of a variant of a registered mark precluded an attribution of use, as held by the Court of First Instance in *BAINBRIDGE* and not clearly repudiated on appeal to the Court of Justice, also had a question by the referring court on the aspect of defensive registrations. This is peculiar because German law currently does not and never previously has recognized the notion of 'defensive' registrations. It seems that the question was asked only as a fallback position in case the Court actually confirmed its ill-conceived *Bainbridge* Judgment.

8.255 The question in this context was:

> 2. If question 1 is answered in the negative:
>
> Is the national provision described in the first question compatible with Directive [89/104] if the national provision is interpreted restrictively as meaning that it is not applicable to a trade mark (Trade Mark 1) which is registered only in order to secure or expand the protection

---

[140] C-234/06 P *Il Ponte Finanziaria Spa v OHIM* (BAINBRIDGE)[2007] ECR I-7333.
[141] T-194/03 *Il Ponte Finanziaria v OHIM—Marine Enterprise Projects* (BAINBRIDGE) (2006) ECR II-00445.
[142] Paragraph 101.
[143] Paragraphs 102–103.
[144] C-553/11, *Rintisch v Eder*, ECLI:EU:C:2012:671.

of another registered trade mark (Trade Mark 2) that is registered in the form in which it is used?

8.256 The Court had no difficulty in again rejecting the notion that the Directive allowed Member States to operate a system of defensive registrations:

> In that regard, it should be stated that there are no grounds for interpreting Article 10(2)(a) of Directive 89/104 in such a way that it would be inapplicable to a case such as that described in the previous paragraph. The subjective intention prevailing when it is sought to register a trade mark is wholly irrelevant for the purpose of applying that provision and, in this respect, there is no basis in Directive 89/104 or in any other provisions of European law for a concept of 'defensive' trade marks to which that provision does not apply.[145]

(4) Conclusions

8.257 So far the approach of the Court has been pragmatic. It has rejected *de minimis* rules and rigid definitions. The Court has provided the elements of a multifactor test and insisted that the characteristics of the product and the relevant product market should be assessed as part of that test. As regards the territorial scope of use of Community trade marks, the Court has rejected any rule per se, requiring instead that the territorial scope of use must be considered as one of the elements determining whether the use is genuine or not. The 'multiple marks' issue has been solved by the Court, while the criteria for what amounts to an acceptable variation still have to be developed, not necessarily by the Court of Justice. This is so because all of the 'all circumstances' decisions of the Court, beginning with likelihood of confusion and similarity of signs and goods and services, and moving on to reputation, link, detriment, etc, in the end leave it to the fact-finding instance—the General Court and the national instances—to make the ultimate decision.

8.258 As the system matures the Court is increasingly dealing with variations on the same themes. It seems unlikely that the Court will be drawn into the factual details of the questions.

J. Development into a Generic Indication

(1) Introduction

8.259 Among the grounds of revocation is the traditional ground that the mark, while originally distinctive, has lost its distinctiveness and has become the common name for the product or service for which it was originally a trade mark. The death of trade marks through 'genericide' is rare, and when it occurs it is usually as the result of the proprietor's 'negligence' in not pursuing generic usage of the mark, ie not 'policing' the use of the mark. The Regulation (but not the Directive) provides trade mark proprietors with a remedy against the misuse of their trade marks in dictionaries and similar works, as one of the means by which the generic use of marks may be prevented or at least countered. Among the issues arising under the Directive and the Regulation in the few cases that have come before the Court is the question of which 'public' is relevant when determining whether the trade mark 'has become the common name in the trade for a product or service in respect of which it is registered'.

---

[145] Paragraph 32.

While the literal interpretation would point towards the 'trade', and not towards the (end) consumer, we will see that the Court in the end came out in favour of the opposite solution.

(2) The Cases

(a) *The relevant public:* Procordia *(BOSTONGURKA)*

Procordia[146] came as a reference from the Swedish Svea Hovratt (Svea Court of Appeal) that had to consider whether the word mark 'Bostongurka' had become a generic name for chopped pickled gherkins. **8.260**

There were contradictory messages from surveys that focused on consumers and a survey targeting leading operators in the grocery, mass catering, and food stall sectors. The consumer surveys indicated that the majority considered that the term could be used by any producer of chopped pickled gherkins. Half of the questioned market operators, however, understood the sign to be a trade mark for the same product. **8.261**

The Svea Hovratt referred the following question to the Court: **8.262**

> In cases where a product is handled at several stages before it reaches the consumer what is or are, under Article 12 (2) (a) of the Trade Mark Directive, the relevant class or classes of persons for determining whether a trade mark has become the common name in the trade for a product in respect of which it is registered?

(i) The Opinion of Advocate General Léger AG Léger looked at the question from a broader perspective and described the main issue raised by the Swedish court as to whether Article 12(2)(a) of the Directive: **8.263**

> should be interpreted as meaning that in order to assess whether a trade mark has become a common name in the trade for a product in respect of which the mark is registered, with the result that the trade mark may be revoked, account should be taken of the perception only of those in the trade who deal with the type of goods commercially, or whether the perception of consumers of that type of goods is also relevant.[147]

The fact that the product passed several stages before reaching the consumer only made the issue more relevant. **8.264**

The wording of the provision did not identify directly the relevant classes of persons. Procordia and the Swedish Government had highlighted the inclusion of the words 'in the trade' and contrasted Article 12(2)(a) with Articles 4(1)(b) and 5(1)(b) of the Directive where the effect 'on the part of the public' was considered to be decisive. The Advocate General, however, believed that both expressions did not exclude the viewpoint of persons in the trade.[148] **8.265**

He went on to compare the 'in the trade' concept in different languages.[149] In English and Finnish it appeared to refer to a specific class of persons, 'namely persons in the trade who carry on business in a particular commercial or industrial activity, in a specific area or **8.266**

---

[146] C-371/02 *Björnekulla Fruktindustrier AB v Procordia Food AB* [2004] ECR I-5791.
[147] Point 26.
[148] Point 33, citing C-342/97 *Lloyd Schuhfabrik* [19991 ECR I-3819 and C-251/95 *SABEL BV v Puma AG, Rudolf Dassler Sport* [1997] ECR I-6191.
[149] The Court had already ruled that the different language versions are all equally authentic and that a comparison between them was a valid interpretive tool in C-283/81 *Srl CILFIT and Lanificio di Gavardo SpA v Ministry of Health* [1982] ECR 3415.

sector' and to exclude consumers.¹⁵⁰ In Italian and Greek it covered all persons who would use the term in their commercial relations, traders and consumers alike. The remaining versions adopted a similar, but less explicit, perspective referring to the marketplace in general, a term that was considered to be inclusive covering both traders and consumers.

8.267 He then found that the general scheme of the Directive was dominated by the essential function of a trade mark as an indication of origin. This is why distinctiveness was a condition for protection. Distinctiveness could be gained and lost through use. Article 12(2)(a) had the converse effect of Article 3(3). It applied:

> where the use of a trade mark has become so widespread that the sign which constitutes the trade mark in question has come to designate the kind, the type or the nature of the goods or services covered by the registration rather than the specific goods or services originating from a particular undertaking.¹⁵¹

8.268 All these provisions aimed to safeguard the distinctive character of a trade mark as an indication of origin and had to be interpreted in the same way, in particular since the ambiguous concepts were substantially similar. The wording and interpretation of Article 3(1)(d) proved to be a catalyst. The provision referred to signs or indications that have become customary in the current language or in the bona fide and established practices of the trade.

8.269 In *Merz & Krell*¹⁵² the Court held that registration of a trade mark was precluded where it had formed part of the language or the bona fide and established practices of the trade but also become the common name for the goods or services to which it relates. For the Advocate General this expression clearly referred:

> globally both to the perception of the average consumer of the type of goods or services in question (that is to say to the perception of the reasonably well-informed and reasonably observant and circumspect consumer) and to that of persons in the trade who deal with those goods or services commercially.¹⁵³

8.270 Discussing a point also developed in *Merz & Krell*, he suggested that Article 3(1)(d) took into account persons in the trade in two capacities: setting the relevant context but also using the current language, in the manner of the average consumer.

8.271 The same approach should be adopted for the interpretation of Article 12(2) (a) of the Directive. It referred 'implicitly but necessarily, both to the perspective of the average consumer of the type of goods or services concerned and to that of persons in the trade who deal with the type of goods or services in question commercially'.¹⁵⁴

8.272 The product had a widespread pattern of consumption and involved several successive intermediaries; accordingly, the views of the average consumer as well as of persons in the trade who deal with the type of product in question had to be taken into account. *Windsurfing Chiemsee*¹⁵⁵ supported this view. Considering Article 3(1)(c) the Court was

> making it clear that the descriptive character of a trade mark (at the time of its registration) must be assessed globally, taking into account the perspective of all relevant classes of

---

¹⁵⁰ Point 36.
¹⁵¹ Point 50; 'walkman' was one of the examples he mentioned.
¹⁵² C-517/99 *Merz & Krell GmbH & Co* [2001] ECR I-6959.
¹⁵³ Point 58.
¹⁵⁴ Point 62.
¹⁵⁵ C-108/97 and C-109/97 *Windsurfing Chiemsee* [1999] ECR I-2779.

persons, that is to say both that of the average consumer of the type of goods concerned and of persons in the trade who deal with the type of goods concerned commercially.[156]

Since the 'in the trade' concept appeared in both Article 3(1)(c) and Article 12(2)(a), it should be given the same meaning in terms of logic but also for reasons of legal certainty. **8.273**

Regarding Article 3(3) the Court had stated in even clearer terms that the competent authority must make an overall assessment, taking into account, inter alia, statements from chambers of commerce and industry or other trade and professional associations. AG Léger referred to the Opinion of AG Cosmas, who had underlined that the relevant class of persons comprises consumers of the relevant product as well as traders and manufacturers of similar products.[157] 'The same should apply for the purposes of assessing the generic character of a trade mark once it has been registered.'[158] **8.274**

From the opposite perspective, AG Léger viewed distinctive character at the time of the application and distinctive character at the time of revocation as essentially the same issue: two sides of the same coin. He accepted that revocation could have material consequences for the trade mark proprietor, for example, loss of advertising investment. This called for a global approach. **8.275**

Assessing distinctive character only from the perspective of other traders would be contrary to the objectives of the Directive to guarantee the identity of the marked products to the consumer and thus contribute towards an environment of undistorted competition in which undertakings can develop customer loyalty based on the quality of their products: **8.276**

> [T]hat objective might be undermined if it were sufficient to prove that a trade mark had become generic only amongst the persons in the trade who deal with the type of goods or services in question commercially, for the trade mark to be revoked. To adopt such an approach would mean opening the door to certain practices that might distort competition within the market,[159]

for example, the abusive use of revocation proceedings.

Such an approach would be: **8.277**

> to misconstrue this essential function of a trade mark to base the assessment of its generic character on the perspective only of persons in the trade who deal with the goods or services concerned commercially, to the exclusion of that of consumers or end users of that type of goods or services.[160]

(ii) The Judgment of the Court The Court followed the path set by the Advocate General; in interpreting national laws courts had to follow the wording and purpose of relevant directives rather the *travaux preparatoires* for the national rule.[161] It added that the provision must be uniformly interpreted and applied in the light of the versions existing in all the Community languages.[162] **8.278**

---

[156] Point 67 of the Opinion of AG Léger.
[157] Point 72 of C-108/97 and C-109/97 *Windsurfing Chiemsee Produktions- und Vertriebs GmbH* [1999] ECR I-2779.
[158] Point 73 of the Opinion of AG Léger.
[159] Point 81.
[160] Point 87.
[161] Citing C-106/89 *Marleasing SA v La Comercial Internacional de Alimentacion SA* [1990] ECR I-4135; [1992] 1 CMLR 305; C-218/01 *Henkel KGaA* [2004] ECR I-1725.
[162] Case 19/67 *Bestuur der Sociale Verzekeringsbank v Van der Vecht* [1967] ECR 445; and C-219/95 P *Ferriere Nord SpA v Commission* [1997] ECR I-4411.

8.279 It also concurred with the Advocate General that in the majority of the Community languages the provision was not restricted to those in trade and that this was also supported by the general scheme and the objectives of the Directive. It also found that the requirement of distinctiveness, linked with the essential function of a trade mark, was substantiated by, amongst others, Articles 3 and 12.

8.280 However, the delineation of the Court appeared to be narrower than that of the Advocate General:

> If the function of the trade mark as an indication of origin is of primary importance to the consumer or end user, it is also relevant to intermediaries who deal with the product commercially. As with consumers or end users, it will tend to influence their conduct in the market.[163]

8.281 The Court continued:

> [T]he relevant classes of persons comprise principally consumers and end users. However, depending on the features of the product market concerned, the influence of intermediaries on decisions to purchase, and thus their perception of the trade mark, must also be taken into consideration.[164]

8.282 The wording of its conclusion appeared to leave the door open for a broader interpretation in the future. It started by narrowing the scope of the judgment to products the distribution of which involved intermediaries and ended by involving in the assessment of distinctive character all those in the trade who deal with the relevant product commercially, potentially including competitors:

> The answer to the question referred must therefore be that Article 12(2)(a) of the Directive should be interpreted as meaning that in cases where intermediaries participate in the distribution to the consumer or the end user of a product which is the subject of a registered trade mark, the relevant classes of persons whose views fall to be taken into account in determining whether that trade mark has become the common name in the trade for the product in question comprise all consumers and end users and, depending on the features of the market concerned, all those in the trade who deal with that product commercially.[165]

(b) Differences of perception: The end consumer is decisive; KORNSPITZ

8.283 (i) **The factual setting and the questions referred** *Procordia* had left it to the referring court to draw the conclusions from the holding that, at least in the specific case, the opinions of end consumers and of the 'trade' in the narrow sense should be considered.

8.284 The most recent case[166] to arrive at the Court concerned the issue of what the decision should be when, as was the case in *Procordia* as well, the opinion of the consumer public differed from the trade public, the first considering the mark to be generic, the second a trade mark.

8.285 The trade mark proprietor had a registration in Austria for 'Kornspitz' for 'flour and preparations made from cereals; bakery goods; baking agents, pastry confectionary, also

---

[163] Paragraph 23. The role of the intermediaries was to detect and anticipate the demand of the product but also to increase and direct it.
[164] Paragraph 25.
[165] Paragraph 26.
[166] C-409/12 *Backaldrin Österreich The Kornspitz Company GmbH v Pfahnl Backmittel GmbH*, ECLI:EU:C:2014:130.

prepared for baking; pre-formed dough … for the manufacture of pastry confectionary'. It supplied a large majority of all the bakeries in Austria with a mix used by them to produce a roll with pointed ends, called 'Kornspitz'. According to the findings in the proceedings below, where the revocation of the mark was requested by a competitor of the proprietor, it was accepted that the mark was understood as the name of the product by the end consumer, whereas the bakeries knew and understood the term 'Kornspitz' as the trade mark of the proprietor. While the first instance had ordered the revocation of the mark for all the goods, and the referring court had held that the mark could remain registered for goods addressed not at end consumers but at the 'trade', ie the bakeries supplied by the proprietor, the question remained whether the mark should be revoked for goods addressed at the end consumer.

The Oberste Patent- und Markensenat referred the following questions to the Court: **8.286**

1. Has a trade mark become 'the common name [in the trade] for a product or service' within the meaning of Article 12(2)(a) of Directive [2008/95], where
   (a) although traders know that the mark constitutes an indication of origin they do not generally disclose this to [end users], and
   (b) (inter alia) on those grounds, [end users] no longer understand the trade mark as an indication of origin but as the common name for goods or services in respect of which the trade mark is registered?
2. Can the conduct of a proprietor be regarded as 'inactivity' for the purposes of Article 12(2)(a) of Directive 2008/95 simply if the proprietor of the trade mark remains inactive notwithstanding the fact that traders do not inform customers that the name is a registered trade mark?
3. If, as a consequence of acts or inactivity of the proprietor, a trade mark has become the common name for [end users], but not in the trade, is that trade mark liable to be revoked if, and only if, end consumers have to use this name because there are no equivalent alternatives?

(ii) The Opinion of Advocate General Cruz Villalón The case is one of the rare cases in recent years where the Advocate General, in this instance AG Cruz Villalón, participated and submitted an Opinion.[167] **8.287**

On the first question—which are the relevant circles or sectors of the public—the Advocate General pointed to the differing positions advocated by the parties and the participating Member States (France, Germany, Italy) and the Commission, where Germany and France were joined by the Commission in considering also the commercial part (the 'trade') as relevant. **8.288**

Considering the various trade mark functions recognized by the Court, the Advocate General considered that the quality and advertising functions are of no relevance when dealing with 'genericide'.[168] **8.289**

Since neither the language nor the systematic interpretation revealed an answer, the Advocate General turned to the 'purpose' of the provision.[169] Thus, the function of the mark as a communication tool between producer and consumer is decisive. The perspective of the trade **8.290**

---

[167] Opinion of 12 September 2013, ECLI:EU:C:2013:563.
[168] Points 40–46.
[169] Opinion, point 57.

remains relevant when the trade exerts an influence over the consumer's decision, whereas in the absence of such influence the opinion of the end consumer controls.

8.291 In conclusion, the answer to the first question should be:

> Article 12(2)(a) of the Directive must be interpreted as meaning that the relevant class of persons for assessing the question whether a trade mark has become the common name in the trade for the product in respect of which it was registered consists primarily of consumers and end users. Depending on the features of the market, account must also be taken of those persons in the trade who deal with that product commercially. Features indicating that the latter should also be taken into account are present in particular where the relevant traders exert a degree of influence over the end consumer's decision to purchase. In so far as that is not the case, a trade mark has become the common name for the product in respect of which it is registered where it is understood as such by end consumers, even though traders who manufacture the product themselves from a primary product of the trade mark proprietor and sell it under the trade mark with the trade mark proprietor's consent are aware that the name is an indication of origin but do not generally disclose this to the end consumer.[170]

8.292 The Advocate General then turned to the third question, namely whether the decision must depend on the presence of equivalent alternatives to the contested mark or name, ie the ability of consumers to name the product by another generic name. The Advocate General concluded that there is no space for such a consideration.

8.293 As regards the second question, which is characterized as the 'subjective element' of the provision, the Advocate General concluded that the proprietor has the obligation to undertake what is appropriate and reasonable under the circumstances:

> As I see it, this applies not only to defending the trade mark against infringement but also to the risk of a trade mark becoming a generic name. The duty of vigilance requires the trade mark proprietor to observe the market and take reasonable steps to protect his trade mark from developing into a generic name.[171]

8.294 **(iii) The decision of the Court** The Court, in a rather short judgment,[172] concluded that in a case such as the present one the opinion of the end consumer is decisive, that the developments in the present case may be considered as 'inactivity' on the part of the proprietor, and that the presence of acceptable alternative names is irrelevant.

8.295 On the first question, the Court underlined the origin function of marks and considered its loss as decisive.[173] The Court saw no contradiction with its earlier *Björnekulla/Procodia*[174] decision:

> 24 As the referring court has also stated, that perception on the part of end users is due, in particular, to the fact that the sellers of the bread rolls made using that mix do not generally inform their customers that the sign 'KORNSPITZ' has been registered as a trade mark.
>
> 25 The case set out in the order for reference is, in addition, characterised by the fact that the sellers of that finished product do not generally, at the time of sale, offer their customers assistance which includes an indication of the origin of the various goods for sale.

---

[170] Opinion, point 67.
[171] Point 83.
[172] C-409/12, *Backaldrin Österreich The Kornspitz Company GmbH v Pfahnl Backmittel GmbH*, ECLI:EU:C:2014:130.
[173] Judgment, paragraphs 20, 21, and 22.
[174] C-371/02 *Björnekulla Fruktindustrier AB v Procordia Food AB* [2004] ECR I-5791.

26 Clearly, in such a case, the trade mark KORNSPITZ does not, in the trade in respect of the bread rolls known as 'KORNSPITZ', fulfil its essential function as an indication of origin and, consequently, it is liable to revocation in so far as it is registered for that finished product if the loss of its distinctive character in respect of that product is attributable to acts or inactivity of the proprietor of that trade mark.

27 That finding is not contrary to the interpretation of Article 12(2)(a) of Directive 2008/95 given by the Court in paragraph 26 of the judgment in *Björnekulla Fruktindustrier*, according to which, in cases where intermediaries participate in the distribution of a product which is the subject of a registered trade mark, the relevant classes of persons whose views must be taken into account in determining whether that trade mark has become the common name in the trade for the product in question comprise all consumers or end users and, depending on the features of the market concerned, all those in the trade who deal with that product commercially.

28 It is true, as the Court highlighted in that interpretation, that whether a trade mark has become the common name in the trade for a product or service in respect of which it is registered must be assessed not only in the light of the perception of consumers or end users but also, depending on the features of the market concerned, in the light of the perception of those in the trade, such as sellers.

29 However, as the Court pointed out in paragraph 24 of the judgment in *Björnekulla Fruktindustrier*, in general, the perception of consumers or end users will play a decisive role. It must be held, in line with what the Advocate General stated at points 58 and 59 of his Opinion, that in a case such as that at issue in the main proceedings, which is, subject to verification by the referring court, characterised by the loss of distinctive character of the trade mark concerned from the point of view of the end users, that loss may result in the revocation of that trade mark. The fact that the sellers are aware of the existence of that trade mark and of the origin which it indicates cannot, on its own, preclude such revocation.

The Court thus answered the first question as follows:[175] **8.296**

Article 12(2)(a) of Directive 2008/95 must be interpreted as meaning that, in a case such as that at issue in the main proceedings, a trade mark is liable to revocation in respect of a product for which it is registered if, in consequence of acts or inactivity of the proprietor, that trade mark has become the common name for that product from the point of view solely of end users of the product.

As regards the requirement of acts or inactivity on the part of the proprietor, the Court again followed the analysis of the Advocate General: Not only absence of pursuit of infringers is relevant, but also other acts or inaction, such as in the present case the 'proprietor's failure to take any initiative which may encourage those sellers to make more use of that mark'.[176] **8.297**

As regards the third question, the Court concluded that the presence or absence of acceptable alternatives to name the respective product is not relevant. What is decisive is that the mark 'has lost its distinctive character as a result of its transformation into the common name in the trade'.[177] **8.298**

(iv) Conclusions The two decisions of the Court leave the observer somewhat at a loss, in any event in view of the state of the law when the legislation was adopted. It was recognized in the majority of jurisdictions that the conversion or transformation of a mark **8.299**

---

[175] Paragraph 30.
[176] Paragraph 34
[177] Paragraph 39.

into a generic name required that no relevant parts of the relevant public, which included not only end consumers but also the commercial side (wholesalers, retailers, competitors) considered the mark as a mark. Thus, all the relevant sectors needed to be included, and the opinion of all the sectors had to be 'unanimous', ie when there were substantial or not insignificant parts which still considered the mark to be a mark, revocation was excluded. The 'Kornspitz' Judgment, although worded at times as being limited to the specific facts, concluded broadly that the end consumer controls, thus depriving the proprietor of his mark.

8.300 Another question arose as to when the mark is a Community trade mark: Must the development into a generic name have occurred everywhere in the Community, or is the transformation in a (substantial) part of the European Union sufficient?

8.301 And what about action and inaction? The 'Kornspitz' case sends a warning to owners of widely known marks which are widely used by end consumers to name the product. Not only must they do what is possible to enjoin infringements, but they must also otherwise 'police' their marks.

8.302 Fortunately for trade mark owners death by 'genericide' is extremely rare.

K. Conclusion

8.303 So far the approach of the Court has been pragmatic, despite the contradictions that can often be explained by the tendency of the Court to get drawn into factual contextual detail.

8.304 The Court has been developing variations on the basic themes of use and genericness, growing multi-factorial tests that focus on the characteristics of the relevant product, the product market, and, increasingly, the end user.

9

SCOPE OF PROTECTION, LIMITATIONS, AND ENFORCEMENT

A. Introduction

This chapter explores the scope of protection and considers trade mark conflicts from the perspective of trade mark infringement and enforcement. It also considers conflicts between trade mark and other types of rights over commercial indicia. The concepts of use, confusion, and protection of trade marks with reputation together with their related tests have been developed in Chapter 5. In this chapter we revisit them from an infringement perspective where the comparisons courts have to make become more concrete, and market and factual contexts become even more relevant. Issues specific to the enforcement of the Community trade mark are considered towards at the end of this chapter together with a discussion on goods in transit. For the interaction with other areas of the law the reader should also consider Chapter 12, covering comparative advertising, geographical indications, and aspects of domain names. Exhaustion of trade mark rights and the interaction with competition are covered in Chapters 10 and 11 respectively. **9.01**

B. The Provisions of the Directive and the Regulation

(1) The Trade Marks Directive

Article 5 provides: **9.02**

> Article 5—Rights conferred by a trade mark
> 1. The registered trade mark shall confer on the proprietor exclusive rights therein. The proprietor shall be entitled to prevent all third parties not having his consent from using in the course of trade:
>   a. any sign which is identical with the trade mark in relation to goods or services which are identical with those for which the trade mark is registered;
>   b. any sign where, because of its identity with, or similarity to, the trade mark and the identity or similarity of the goods or services covered by the trade mark and the sign, there exists a likelihood of confusion on the part of the public, which includes the likelihood of association between the sign and the trade mark.
> 2. Any Member State may also provide that the proprietor shall be entitled to prevent all third parties not having his consent from using in the course of trade any sign which is identical with, or similar to, the trade mark in relation to goods or services which are not similar to those for which the trade mark is registered, where the latter has a reputation in the Member State and where use of that sign without due cause takes unfair advantage of, or is detrimental to, the distinctive character or the repute of the trade mark.

3. The following, inter alia, may be prohibited under paragraphs 1 and 2:
   a. affixing the sign to the goods or to the packaging thereof;
   b. offering the goods, or putting them on the market or stocking them for these purposes under that sign, or offering or supplying services thereunder;
   c. importing or exporting the goods under the sign;
   d. using the sign on business papers and in advertising.
4. Where, under the law of the Member State, the use of a sign under the conditions referred to in 1 (b) or 2 could not be prohibited before the date on which the provisions necessary to comply with this Directive entered into force in the Member State concerned, the rights conferred by the trade mark may not be relied on to prevent the continued use of the sign.
5. Paragraphs 1 to 4 shall not affect provisions in any Member State relating to the protection against the use of a sign other than for the purposes of distinguishing goods or services, where use of that sign without due cause takes unfair advantage of, or is detrimental to, the distinctive character or the repute of the trade mark.

9.03 Article 6 sets the limitations of the effects of a trade mark.

Article 6—Limitation of the effects of a trade mark
1. The trade mark shall not entitle the proprietor to prohibit a third party from using, in the course of trade,
   a. his own name or address;
   b. indications concerning the kind, quality, quantity, intended purpose, value, geographical origin, the time of production of goods or of rendering of the service, or other characteristics of goods or services;
   c. the trade mark where it is necessary to indicate the intended purpose of a product or service, in particular as accessories or spare parts; provided he uses them in accordance with honest practices in industrial or commercial matters
2. The trade mark shall not entitle the proprietor to prohibit a third party from using, in the course of trade, an earlier right which only applies in a particular locality if that right is recognized by the laws of the Member State in question and within the limits of the territory in which it is recognized.

(2) The Community Trade Mark Regulation

9.04 Article 9 describes the rights conferred by a Community trade mark.

Article 9—Rights conferred by a Community trade mark
1. A Community trade mark shall confer on the proprietor exclusive rights therein. The proprietor shall be entitled to prevent all third parties not having his consent from using in the course of trade:
   (a) any sign which is identical with the Community trade mark in relation to goods or services which are identical with those for which the Community trade mark is registered;
   (b) any sign where, because of its identity with or similarity to the Community trade mark and the identity or similarity of the goods or services covered by the Community trade mark and the sign, there exists a likelihood of confusion on the part of the public; the likelihood of confusion includes the likelihood of association between the sign and the trade mark;
   (c) any sign which is identical with or similar to the Community trade mark in relation to goods or services which are not similar to those for which the Community trade mark is registered, where the latter has a reputation in the Community and where use of that sign without due cause takes unfair advantage of, or is detrimental to, the distinctive character or the repute of the Community trade mark.

2. The following, inter alia, may be prohibited under paragraph 1:
   (a) affixing the sign to the goods or to the packaging thereof;
   (b) offering the goods, putting them on the market or stocking them for these purposes under that sign, or offering or supplying services thereunder;
   (c) importing or exporting the goods under that sign;
   (d) using the sign on business papers and in advertising.
3. The rights conferred by a Community trade mark shall prevail against third parties from the date of publication of registration of the trade mark. Reasonable compensation may, however, be claimed in respect of matters arising after the date of publication of a Community trade mark application, which matters would, after publication of the registration of the trade mark, be prohibited by virtue of that publication. The court seized of the case may not decide upon the merits of the case until the registration has been published.

Article 10 covers a specific case: the reproduction of Community trade marks in dictionaries. **9.05**

Article 10—Reproduction of Community trade marks in dictionaries

If the reproduction of a Community trade mark in a dictionary, encyclopaedia or similar reference work gives the impression that it constitutes the generic name of the goods or services for which the trade mark is registered, the publisher of the work shall, at the request of the proprietor of the Community trade mark, ensure that the reproduction of the trade mark at the latest in the next edition of the publication is accompanied by an indication that it is a registered trade mark.

Article 11 deals with trade marks registered by agents without authorization. **9.06**

Article 11—Prohibition on the use of a Community trade mark registered in the name of an agent or representative

Where a Community trade mark is registered in the name of the agent or representative of a person who is the proprietor of that trade mark, without the proprietor's authorization, the latter shall be entitled to oppose the use of his mark by his agent or representative if he has not authorized such use, unless the agent or representative justifies his action.

Article 12 covers the limitations of the effects of a Community trade mark. **9.07**

Article 12—Limitation of the effects of a Community trade mark

A Community trade mark shall not entitle the proprietor to prohibit a third party from using in the course of trade:

(a) his own name or address;
(b) indications concerning the kind, quality, quantity, intended purpose, value, geographical origin, the time of production of the goods or of rendering of the service, or other characteristics of the goods or service;
(c) the trade mark where it is necessary to indicate the intended purpose of a product or service, in particular as accessories or spare parts,

provided he uses them in accordance with honest practices in industrial or commercial matters.

(3) A Clash between Registered Trade Marks and the Concept of 'Third Party': *Fédération Cynologique*

(a) *The facts in the main proceedings and the order for reference*

In *Fédération Cynologique*[1] the Court was asked to clarify the definition of a 'third party' against which the holder of a registered Community trade mark may bring infringement **9.08**

---

[1] C-561/11 *Fédération Cynologique Internationale v Federación Canina Internacional de Perros de Pura Raza*, Judgment ECLI:EU:C:2013:91.

proceedings within the meaning of Article 9(1) of the Regulation.[2] The main proceedings concerned an action for infringement and a declaration of invalidity brought before the Juzgado de lo Mercantil No 1 de Alicante (Commercial Court No 1 of Alicante) (Spain) by the Fédération Cynologique Internationale, on the basis of its earlier Community trade mark registration consisting of the expression FCI FEDERATION CYNOLOGIQUE INTERNATIONALE and a globe device, against the Federación Canina Internacional de Perros de Pura Raza, holder of a number of national and Community registrations, also combining a globe with the expressions FEDERACIÓN CANINA INTERNACIONAL DE PERROS DE PURA RAZA—F.C.I. and FEDERACIÓN CINOLOGICA INTERNACIONAL—F.C.I. Both marks essentially covered dog exhibitions and shows, as well as services relating to the training, rearing, and breeding of dogs.

9.09 The referring Court observed that Article 9(1) could be read in two different ways: On the one hand, it can be interpreted as meaning that the exclusive right conferred by a Community trade mark does not entitle its proprietor to prohibit the holder of a subsequent registration from making use of that latter mark. This interpretation reflects a doctrine developed by the Tribunal Supremo (Spanish Supreme Court), known as *inmunidad registral* (immunity by virtue of registration), according to which the mere fact that a mark is registered protects it against infringement proceedings brought by holders of earlier rights and, consequently, makes the bringing of such proceedings contingent on a prior declaration of the invalidity of the later registration. On the other hand, Article 9(1) can be interpreted as meaning that the exclusive right conferred on the proprietor can be enforced against any third party, including the proprietors of subsequently registered Community trade marks, even if the latter mark has not previously or simultaneously been declared invalid.

9.10 Considering that this dilemma related to the interpretation of EU law, the Juzgado de lo Mercantil No 1 referred to the Court the following question for a preliminary ruling:

> In proceedings for infringement of the exclusive right conferred by a Community trade mark, does the right to prevent the use thereof by third parties in the course of trade provided for in Article 9(1) extend to any third party who uses a sign that involves a likelihood of confusion or, on the contrary, is the third party who uses that sign which has been registered in his name as a Community trade mark excluded until such time as that subsequent trade mark registration has been declared invalid?

(b) The Opinion of Advocate General Mengozzi

9.11 As a preliminary point, Advocate General Mengozzi[3] recalled that essentially the same question had been brought before the Court in the context of design law in *Celaya*,[4] where the Court opted for an interpretation that was different from the one supported by the doctrine of immunity by virtue of registration, and declared that the right to prevent third parties from using a later design conferred by the Community Designs Regulation extends to any third party who uses an infringing design, including the holder of a registered Community design. The Advocate General took the view that despite the differences

---

[2] The Court dealt with the same question in the context of Article 5(1) of the Directive in C-491/14, *Rosa dels Vents Assessoria SL v U Hostels Albergues Juveniles SL*, where it essentially reiterated its findings in *Fédération Cynologique*, ECLI:EU:C:2015:161.

[3] C-561/11 *Fédération Cynologique Internationale v Federación Canina Internacional de Perros de Pura Raza*, ECLI:EU:C:2012:722.

[4] C-488/10 *Celaya Emparanza y Galdos Internacional*, ECLI:EU:C:2012:88.

between the protection conferred, respectively, by trade mark and design law, there was no reason why the findings of the Court in *Celaya* could not be transposed in the field of trade marks.[5]

9.12 In the opinion of the Advocate General, the solution to the conflict between the *jus excludendi* of the holder of the earlier trade mark and the *jus utendi* of the proprietor of the subsequent registration required that one of the two rights ought to take precedence over the other and that that precedence could only be based on the fundamental principle of temporal priority, which militated in favour of the former. The Advocate General also noted that the same solution followed from a literal, systematic, and teleological interpretation of the Regulation which not only did not include any express limitation of the right holder's rights vis-à-vis the owners of subsequent registrations but also required that the protection conferred by the Community trade mark must be absolute, so as to enable it to perform its essential function without that function being undermined by the prolonged existence of confusingly similar signs on the market, as would be the case if the owner was required to wait until the cancellation of the later mark had become final.[6]

9.13 Moreover, the Advocate General noted that Article 54 of the Regulation only limits the right of the trade mark owner to either have a later mark declared invalid, or prohibit its use, in the event of acquiescence for five consecutive years. He therefore took the view that it could be inferred, *a contrario*, that where that condition is not satisfied, the owner may indeed bring an action against the proprietor of a later confusing registration.[7]

9.14 For the sake of completeness, the Advocate General added that, for reasons of systemic coherence and in view of the need not to deprive Article 9 (1) of its *effet utile*, the solution arrived at in respect of later Community trade marks should extend to national marks as well, regardless of any rules to the contrary set forth in the applicable national provisions, and that the need for the uniform application of Union law in the field of trade marks required that the same interpretation be given to the equivalent provisions in the Directive.[8]

(c) The Judgment of the Court

9.15 The Court shared the view of the Advocate General that Article 9(1) and the general approach of the Regulation enable the proprietor of a Community trade mark to prevent the proprietor of a later Community trade mark from using that mark in the course of trade.

9.16 First, the Court observed that the wording of Article 9(1) is compelling, as it grants the proprietor the exclusive right to prevent 'any third party' from using signs liable to infringe its mark without making any distinction on the basis of whether the third party is the proprietor of a Community trade mark or not. Second, the Court agreed that Article 54 provided a strong argument in support of that reading, by allowing the proprietor, before the limitation in consequence of acquiescence takes effect, both to apply for a declaration of invalidity before the Office for Harmonization in the Internal Market (OHIM) and to oppose its use through infringement proceedings before a Community trade mark court. Third, it pointed out that neither Article 12 of the Regulation, relating to the limitation

---

[5] Points 23–32.
[6] Points 38–46.
[7] Points 50–52.
[8] Points 50–52.

of the effects of a Community trade mark, nor any of its other provisions provide for an express limitation of the exclusive right of the proprietor in favour of the owner of a later registration.[9]

9.17 The Court further observed that that conclusion is not called into question by the fact that the proprietor of a later trade mark also has the benefit of an exclusive right, since by virtue of the priority principle the earlier Community mark takes precedence over the later mark. Although it admitted that the registration procedure of a Community trade mark includes a substantive examination that seeks to determine, prior to registration, whether a later mark fulfils the requirements for protection, it noted that 'it is not entirely inconceivable' that an infringing sign may be registered, as for instance may happen where the proprietor of the earlier mark has not filed a notice of opposition, or where that opposition has not been examined on its merits by reason of its non-compliance with the procedural requirements laid down by the Regulation.[10]

9.18 Finally, the Court agreed with the Advocate General that the exclusive right conferred by Article 9 (1), which serves to preserve the essential function of a Community trade mark, would be significantly weakened if its proprietor was required, in order to prevent the use by a third party of a sign that is liable to affect the functions of its mark, to await the declaration of invalidity of the later registration.[11]

9.19 Accordingly, the Court ruled that Article 9(1) of the Regulation must be interpreted as meaning that the exclusive right of the proprietor of a Community trade mark to prohibit all third parties from using, in the course of trade, signs identical with or similar to its trade mark extends to a third-party proprietor of a later registered Community trade mark, without the need for that latter mark to have been declared invalid beforehand.

(4) The Starting Point: The Trade Mark as Registered? *Specsavers*

(a) *The facts in the main proceedings and the order for reference*

9.20 The first part of *Specsavers*[12] dealt with the concept of use that is adequate to maintain a trade mark on the Register. The second part related to the scope of protection.

> (4) Where a Community trade mark is not registered in colour, but the proprietor has used it extensively in a particular colour or combination of colours such that it has become associated in the mind of a significant portion of the public (in a part but not the whole of the [European Union]) with that colour or combination of colours, is the colour or colours with which the defendant uses the sign complained of relevant in the global assessment of [either the] likelihood of confusion under Article 9(1)(b) [of Regulation No 207/2009], or unfair advantage under Article 9(1)(c) of[that regulation]? If so, how?
>
> (5) If so, is it relevant as part of the global assessment that the defendant itself is associated in the mind of a significant portion of the public with the colour or particular combination of colours which it is using for the sign complained of?[13]

---

[9] Paragraphs 33–37.
[10] Paragraphs 38–46.
[11] Paragraphs 49–51.
[12] C-252/12 *Specsavers International Healthcare Ltd v Asda Stores Ltd.*, ECLI:EU:C:2013:497, see paragraph 8.196 and following.
[13] Reproduced in paragraph 16.

(b) The Judgment of the Court

(i) The fourth question The Court started its analysis by noting that likelihood of confusion has to be assessed globally, taking into account all factors relevant to the circumstances of the case.[14] Against the factual context of the case—involving identical goods—the Court appeared to link likelihood of confusion exclusively with similarity between the marks, stating that:

9.21

> [t]he Court has also held on several occasions that the global assessment of the likelihood of confusion, in relation to the visual, aural or conceptual similarity of the marks in question, must be based on the overall impression given by the marks, bearing in mind, in particular, their distinctive and dominant components. The perception of the marks by the average consumer of the goods or services in question plays a decisive role in the global appreciation of that likelihood of confusion. In this regard, the average consumer normally perceives a mark as a whole and does not proceed to analyse its various details.[15]

Perhaps a more correct approach would have been to recognize that this relates to establishing similarity between the conflicting signs, the first step for establishing likelihood of confusion, the second being establishing similarity or identity between the goods, and the third considering whether, on the back of the two earlier steps and taking into account all additional evidence, there is likelihood of confusion.

9.22

Following the same path the Court added that 'the more distinctive the trade mark, the greater the likelihood of confusion. Therefore, trade marks with a highly distinctive character, either per se or because of the reputation they possess on the market, enjoy broader protection than trade marks with a less distinctive character.'[16]

9.23

The Court added here that at the very least:

9.24

> where there is a trade mark which is registered not in a particular colour or characteristic, but in black and white, the colour or combination of colours in which the trade mark is later used affects how the average consumer of the goods at issue perceives that trade mark, and it is, therefore, liable to increase the likelihood of confusion or association between the earlier trade mark and the sign alleged to infringe it.[17]

Thus,

> it would not be logical to consider that the fact that a third party, for the representation of a sign which is alleged to infringe an earlier Community trade mark, uses a colour or combination of colours which has become associated, in the mind of a significant portion of the public, with that earlier trade mark by the use which has been made of it by its proprietor in that colour or combination of colours, cannot be taken into consideration in the global assessment for the sole reason that that earlier trade mark was registered in black and white.[18]

The Court followed the same logic in its consideration of Article 9(1)(c) of the Regulation. The strength of the mark's reputation and its distinctive character are amongst the factors that must be taken into account, and the stronger that mark's distinctive character and reputation are, the easier it will be to accept that detriment has been caused to it.[19] Turning

9.25

---

[14] Paragraph 34, citing inter alia C-251/95 *SABEL* [1997] ECR I-6191, paragraph 22.
[15] Paragraph 35.
[16] Paragraph 36, citing C-39/97 *Canon* [1998] ECR I-5507, paragraph 18.
[17] Paragraph 37.
[18] Paragraph 38.
[19] Citing C-487/07 *L'Oréal* [2009] ECR I-5185, paragraph 44.

to the facts of the case the Court stated that the fact that Asda used a similar colour to that used by Specsavers with the intention of taking advantage of the distinctive character and reputation of their marks is a factor that should be taken into account to ascertain whether it had taken unfair advantage of the distinctive character or reputation of the trade mark.[20]

9.26 (ii) **The fifth question** The fifth question considered the colour issue from the perspective of the alleged infringer. Again the Court referred to the global nature of the tests assessing likelihood of confusion and unfair advantage. Those assessments must 'take account of the precise context in which the sign which is allegedly similar to the registered trade mark was used'.[21] Accordingly the third party's association with a particular colour that it is using in relation to the trade mark proprietor's sign 'may have a certain importance while determining the existence of a likelihood of confusion or unfair advantage'.[22]

9.27 This time using a more cautious approach the Court found that 'it is not inconceivable'[23] that such a fact could influence the public's perception of the two signs and affect the likelihood of any confusion. Again referring to the facts the Court suggested that Asda's association with a particular shade of green could:

> result in a reduction of the likelihood of confusion or association between those signs and the trade marks of ... Specsavers ... to the extent that the relevant public could perceive that the colour green of those signs is that of Asda, a matter which is to be determined by the referring court.[24]

Second, the association could also support a 'due cause' defence in the case of Article 9(1)(c) of the Regulation.

9.28 Concluding, the Court offered the following ruling:

> 2. Article 9(1)(b) and (c) of Regulation No 207/2009 must be interpreted as meaning that where a Community trade mark is not registered in colour, but the proprietor has used it extensively in a particular colour or combination of colours with the result that it has become associated in the mind of a significant portion of the public with that colour or combination of colours, the colour or colours which a third party uses in order to represent a sign alleged to infringe that trade mark are relevant in the global assessment of the likelihood of confusion or unfair advantage under that provision.
> 3. Article 9(1)(b) and (c) of Regulation No 207/2009 must be interpreted as meaning that the fact that the third party making use of a sign which allegedly infringes the registered trade mark is itself associated, in the mind of a significant portion of the public, with the colour or particular combination of colours which it uses for the representation of that sign is relevant to the global assessment of the likelihood of confusion and unfair advantage for the purposes of that provision.[25]

(c) Conclusions

9.29 Although the ruling focuses exclusively on colours, the logic behind it could be problematic in terms of delineating the area of protection around a registered trade mark. *Specsavers* allows the centre to move following actual use of the trade mark, with the potential of

---

[20] Citing by analogy ibid, paragraph 48.
[21] Paragraph 45, citing C-533/06 *O2 Holdings and O2 (UK)* [2008] ECR I-4231.
[22] Paragraph 46.
[23] Paragraph 47.
[24] Paragraph 48.
[25] Paragraph 51.

a constant shift of the borders of protection that have the registered trade mark as their epicentre. All this appears to fit better under the aegis of unfair competition rather than registered trade mark law.[26]

C. Identical Signs and Goods or Services: The Effect on the Rights of the Trade Mark Proprietor 'Requirement'

9.30 The scope of trade mark protection in the case of identical signs and identical goods or services was considered by the Court in *Hölterhoff*[27] and *Arsenal*.[28] The Court applied analogous principles in both cases; however, their outcomes appear contradictory, perhaps because although both cases were characterized by their facts the Court of Justice could only look at the snippets referred to it by the national courts.

(1) *Hölterhoff*: Limiting the Scope of Protection

(a) The facts in the main proceedings and the order for reference

9.31 In *Hölterhoff*, Freiesleben was the proprietor of two trade marks in Germany, Spirit Sun and Context Cut, covering, respectively, diamonds and precious stones for further processing as jewellery, and precious stones for further processing as jewellery. In reality both signs were weak trade marks because in addition to the information as to product origin they conveyed information regarding product characteristics. The stones were characterized by their distinctive cuts, with the methods for achieving them protected by patents. This was not an issue before the referring German court. Hölterhoff, a dealer in precious stones, offered for sale to a jeweller stones that he described by using the names Spirit Sun and Context Cut. On the sales invoice and the delivery note the stones were described as rhodolites; their packaging and all related documentation made no reference to the two trade marks.

9.32 Freiesleben started trade mark infringement proceedings. The case reached the Oberlandesgericht Düsseldorf on appeal, which referred to the Court of Justice the following question:

> Does an infringement of a trade mark in the sense contemplated in Article 5(1)(a) and (b) of Directive 89/104/EEC occur where the defendant reveals the origin of goods which he has produced himself and uses the sign in respect of which the plaintiff enjoys protection solely to denote the particular characteristics of the goods he is offering for sale so that there can be no question of the trade mark used being perceived in trade as a sign indicative of the firm of origin?[29]

9.33 Note that the German court had established that Hölterhoff had used the trade marks in order to describe the cut rather than the origin of the stones. In Germany there were two views on the effect of use of a sign that is identical to a registered trade mark. Some argued that it would constitute infringement only where the sign is used as a means of distinction, others that any use in trade should suffice.

---

[26] OHIM and National Offices issued a Common Communication on the Common Practice of the Scope of Protection of Black and White ('B&W') Marks, 15 April 2014, available at <https://oami.europa.eu/tunnel-web/secure/webdav/guest/document_library/contentPdfs/about_ohim/who_we_are/common_communication/common_communication_4/common_communication4_en.pdf>.
[27] C-2/00 *Michael Hölterhoff v Ulrich Freiesleben* [2002] ECR I-4187.
[28] C-206/01 *Arsenal* [2002] ECR I-10273.
[29] Reproduced in paragraph 11 of the judgment.

(b) The Opinion of Advocate General Jacobs

9.34 (i) **The Trade Marks Directive analysis** Advocate General Jacobs linked the negative exclusionary rights expressed in Article 5(1) with the positive rights arising from ownership: '[a] trader registers or acquires a trade mark primarily not in order to prevent others from using it but in order to use it himself'.[30] Since the two aspects were inseparably linked the exclusive aspect covered use by other parties of the protected trade mark to identify their goods or services, negating the essential function of a trade mark.

9.35 He viewed Article 5(5) against BMW[31] to support that only use for the purposes of distinguishing goods or services falls under Article 5(1) and (2). Turning to the context of the case he noted that, although the list was not exhaustive, the contested use was not included in the list of Article 5(3). 'Use of that kind is ... simply too far removed from the essential function of a trade mark to entitle a trade mark proprietor to prevent it under Article 5(1).'[32]

9.36 Concluding his analysis on Article 5(1) he stressed that other factual circumstances—attaching the sign to the goods for example, like the factual scenario of *Arsenal*[33]—could open a different approach, making it clear that he did not wish to express a broader than necessary view.

9.37 (ii) **The influence of the Comparative Advertising Directive** The analysis of Article 6(1) was influenced by the Advertising Directive.[34] Under Article 2(2)(a) of the Misleading Advertising Directive, comparative advertising is any advertising which explicitly or by implication identifies a competitor or goods or services offered by a competitor. This, indeed, was what Mr Hölterhoff was doing; he was entitled to do so, provided his actions did not fall under Article 3a of the Advertising Directive in the same way that they should not fall under the proviso in Article 6(1) of the Trade Marks Directive. Otherwise, it would be absurd for the legislator to adopt two directives with contradictory provisions.

(c) The Judgment of the Court

9.38 The analysis of the Court was very much linked to the facts. Seeking the substance of the referred question it stated that it sought 'to ascertain whether, pursuant to Article 5(1) of the Directive, the proprietor of the trade mark may prevent a third party from using the trade mark in a factual situation such as that which the national court describes in detail'.[35]

9.39 The answer to the question was also based on the facts.

> In that regard, it is sufficient to state that, in a situation such as that described by the national court, the use of the trade mark does not infringe any of the interests which Article 5(1) is intended to protect. Those interests are not affected by a situation in which:

---

[30] Point 34.
[31] C-63/97 *Bayerische Motorenwerke AG* [1999] ECR I-905; see, paragraph 9.272 and following.
[32] Point 39.
[33] Case C-206/01 *Arsenal* [2002] ECR I-10273.
[34] Directive 84/450/EEC relating to the approximation of the laws, regulations, and administrative provisions of the Member States concerning misleading advertising, [1984] OJ L250, p 17, as amended by Directive 97/55/EC of the European Parliament and of the Council amending Directive 84/450/EEC concerning misleading advertising so as to include comparative advertising, [1997] OJ L290/18: see the discussion in Chapter 12, following.
[35] Paragraph 13.

— the third party refers to the trade mark in the course of commercial negotiations with a potential customer, who is a professional jeweller,
— the reference is made for purely descriptive purposes, namely in order to reveal the characteristics of the product offered for sale to the potential customer, who is familiar with the characteristics of the products covered by the trade mark concerned,
— the reference to the trade mark cannot be interpreted by the potential customer as indicating the origin of the product.[36]

9.40 The Court concluded that it was not necessary to consider further what constitutes use of a trade mark under Article 5(1)(a) and (b) and that:

> where a third party, in the course of commercial negotiations, reveals the origin of goods which he has produced himself and uses the sign in question solely to denote the particular characteristics of the goods he is offering for sale ... there can be no question of the trade mark used being perceived as a sign indicative of the undertaking of origin.[37]

(2) *Arsenal*: A Counterbalancing Exercise

(a) *The facts in the main proceedings and the order for reference*

9.41 In parallel with *Hölterhoff* the Court considered very similar concepts in *Arsenal*.[38] The case involved the sale by Reed of unofficial football merchandise products. At the point of sale a sign informed prospective customers about their unauthorized nature.

9.42 The passing off claim failed because there was insufficient evidence regarding deception and damage. Looking at the trade mark infringement claim Laddie J linked the absence of evidence of confusion with the function of the unauthorized signs: there was no evidence of confusion because the signs did not indicate trade origin; they were badges of support, loyalty, and affiliation rather than badges of origin.

9.43 Accordingly he sought clarifications from the Court of Justice as to (i) whether use that does not indicate trade origin, and at the same time does not fall within the scope of Article 6(1) of the Directive, constitutes an infringement, and (ii) whether use that could be perceived as a badge of support, loyalty, or affiliation constitutes use indicating trade origin.[39]

(b) *The Opinion of Advocate General Ruiz-Jarabo Colomer*

9.44 The analysis of Article 5 by AG Ruiz-Jarabo Colomer focused on two points: first, the uses that fell under Article 5(1); and second, the protectable interests of the registered proprietor:

> according to Article 5(1) and (2), the proprietor of a trade mark may not prevent any use of a sign, but only uses whose purpose is to distinguish the goods or services to which it relates from those of other undertakings. Otherwise, Article 5(5) would have no raison d'être.[40] In other words, Article 5(1) protects the accuracy of the information which the registered sign provides on the goods or services which it represents and, thus, their identification[41] ... the proprietor may object to the use by a third party of his trade mark as such.[42]

---

[36] Paragraph 16.
[37] Paragraph 17.
[38] C-206/01 *Arsenal Football Club plc v Matthew Reed* [2002] ECR 1-10273.
[39] *Arsenal Football Club plc v Matthew Reed* [2001] RPC 46.
[40] Point 38.
[41] Point 39.
[42] Point 40.

9.45 **(i) The concept of use**   Noting that the Court had refrained from providing a definition in *Hölterhoff*,[43] the Advocate General elaborated on the concept of use. Insisting strictly on origin, he claimed, would be a 'simplistic reductionism'.[44] After all, consumers are often unaware of who is the actual producer; it is enough that the product carries a trade mark that conveys an autonomous message.

9.46 The Advocate General also provided a defence: 'anyone who uses another's trade mark may claim in defence to the proprietor's objection that his use of it does not indicate the origin of the goods or of the services or give rise to confusion over their quality and reputation'.[45] So, protection should not be automatic. On the same theme he repeated that there is a presumption of likelihood of confusion in the case of identity; 'there is a possibility, however remote it may be, that in a specific case use of a sign identical with another registered as a trade mark may not be prevented by the proprietor on the basis of Article 5(1)(a)'.[46] In cases of identity between signs and products there is a 'presumption iuris tantum that the use by a third party of the trade mark is use thereof as such'.[47]

9.47 Considering the uses described by the High Court—that had to determine according to the evidence whether they were in or outside trade—first, he identified uses that were unrelated to the protectable functions of a trade mark. Trade mark rights did not cover use 'outside the course of trade, that is, outside any commercial activity involving the production and supply of goods and services on the market'.[48]

9.48 Trade according to the Advocate General was narrower than economic activity of some sort:

> The use which the proprietor of the trade mark may prevent is not any that might constitute a material advantage for the user, or even a use which is capable of being expressed in economic terms, but only, as expressed more precisely in all the language versions other than the Spanish, use which occurs in the world of business, in trade, the subject of which is, precisely, the distribution of goods and services in the market. In short, use in trade.[49]

Examples of use outside trade for the purposes of trade mark law would be the private use of the BMW mark on a key ring, Warhol's use of the Campbell brand in his paintings, or use for educational purposes.

9.49 He stated that expressing support, loyalty, or affiliation to the club did signify a connection between the goods and the football club. The nature of the link was irrelevant; it sufficed that it influenced consumers to buy the product.[50]

9.50 **(ii) The interests of the trade mark proprietor**   Pointing towards a significant shift in the balances inherent to trade mark law, he proclaimed:

---

[43] C-2/00 *Hölterhoff* [2002] ECR I-4187.
[44] Point 46.
[45] Point 50.
[46] Point 52.
[47] Point 88.
[48] Point 59.
[49] Point 62.
[50] Point 67.

It is not the reason for which a person buys goods or uses services that I must examine but the reason which has led the person who is not the proprietor of the trade mark to place the goods on the market or to provide the service using the same distinctive sign. If, regardless of the reason which motivates him, he attempts to exploit it commercially, then he can be said to be using it as a trade mark and the proprietor will be entitled to object, within the limits and to the extent allowed under Article 5 of the Directive.[51]

9.51 Closing the circle, he turned his attention to the football club and the reasons behind registering its crests as trade marks. Their commercial exploitability proved critical.

(c) The Judgment of the Court

9.52 The Court of Justice[52] accepted that Mr Reed's unauthorized use constituted use in the course of trade: 'the use of the sign identical to the mark is indeed use in the course of trade, since it takes place in the context of commercial activity with a view to economic advantage and not as a private matter'.[53]

9.53 The position of the trade mark proprietor and the function of a trade mark were pivotal in the Court's analysis. The essential function of a trade mark was that of a guarantee of origin: to ensure that guarantee 'the proprietor must be protected against competitors wishing to take unfair advantage of the status and reputation of the trade mark by selling products illegally bearing it'.[54] The Court referred to its judgments in *Hoffmann-La Roche*[55] and *Loendersloot*,[56] however this was the first time that the link was expressed in such strong terms, albeit in a cyclical way.

9.54 **(i) The interests of the trade mark proprietor** First, the Court highlighted the fact that trade mark rights were conferred in order to enable the trade mark proprietor to protect his specific interests as proprietor; that is, to ensure that the trade mark can fulfil its functions. The exercise of that right must therefore be reserved to cases in which a third party's use of the sign affects or is liable to affect the functions of the trade mark, in particular its essential function of guaranteeing to consumers the origin of the goods.[57]

9.55 The mirror argument was that the proprietor might not prohibit uses that could not affect its 'own interests as proprietor of the mark, having regard to its functions'.[58] Referring to *Hölterhoff*, the Court noted that uses for purely descriptive purposes are excluded from the scope of Article 5(1) 'because they do not affect any of the interests which that provision aims to protect, and do not therefore fall within the concept of use within the meaning of that provision'.[59] In this case the signs were used in such a way as to create the impression of a material link in the course of trade between the unauthorized goods and the club as proprietor of the trade mark. The presence of the notice at the point of sale made no difference because even if those who were aware of it would not be confused, there was a possibility that others

---

[51] Point 69.
[52] C-206/01 *Arsenal* [2002] ECR I-10273.
[53] Paragraph 40.
[54] Paragraph 50.
[55] C-102/77 *Hoffmann-la Roche* [1978] ECR 1139.
[56] C-349/95 *Frits Loendersloot* [1997] ECR I-6227.
[57] *Arsenal* (n 52), paragraph 51.
[58] Paragraph 54.
[59] Paragraph 54.

who came across the goods after their sale and away from the stall might perceive the signs as designating the club as the undertaking from which the goods originated:

> there is a clear possibility in the present case that some consumers, in particular if they come across the goods after they have been sold by Mr Reed and taken away from the stall where the notice appears, may interpret the sign as designating Arsenal FC as the undertaking of origin of the goods.[60]

9.56 (ii) **Protecting the consumer** In order to justify its judgment from the consumer's perspective, the Court added that under these circumstances the guarantee that all goods bearing the same 'trade mark have been manufactured or supplied under the control of a single undertaking which is responsible for their quality'[61] would be impaired. Indeed, Mr Reed's products did not come from Arsenal. Following this line of reasoning, the fact that the sign was perceived as a badge of support for or loyalty or affiliation to the proprietor of the mark had become immaterial.

(d) Back to the National Court

9.57 Back to the High Court, Laddie J found that the holding of the Court that, in the circumstances of the case, the claimant should succeed, was a finding of fact rather than law which exceeded its jurisdiction. Applying the law, as interpreted by the Court in the part of the judgment he found binding, he concluded that there was no trade mark infringement.[62] Arsenal appealed and, at the Court of Appeal,[63] Aldous LJ stated that Laddie J would be entitled to disregard the Court's conclusions to the extent that they were based upon a factual background inconsistent with his judgment. Only the ruling upon interpretation was binding.

9.58 According to his interpretation the Court of Justice had relied on whether the right given by registration is likely to be affected by a third party's use rather than whether Mr Reed's use was such that it would be perceived by some customers or users as a designation of origin.[64]

(3) *Adam Opel*: **Challenging the Limits of Protection**

(a) The facts in the main proceedings and the order for reference

9.59 *Adam Opel*[65] was a reference by the Landgericht Nürnberg-Fürth (Germany). Adam Opel AG (Opel) was the registered proprietor in Germany of a figurative mark, known as the 'Opel Blitz', for a number of products including 'toys'. AUTEC AG (Autec) was a marketer of remote-controlled model cars, sold under the brand 'Cartronic'. Opel started trade mark infringement proceedings in Germany targeting the use of its registered trade mark on the grille of a replica of Opel's Astra V8 coupé. On the packaging, the instructions, and the remote control there were various indications linking the product with Autec.

9.60 The Landgericht Nürnberg-Fürth referred the following questions to the Court.

1. Does the use of a protected trade mark, including as a 'toy', constitute use as a trade mark under Article 5(1)(a) when the manufacturer of toy-scale cars produces a scale model of a car that actually exists, including the sign placed on the model of the owner of the brand, and markets this scale model?

---

[60] Paragraph 57.
[61] Paragraph 58.
[62] *Arsenal Football Club plc v Matthew Reed* [2002] EWHC 2695.
[63] *Arsenal Football Club plc v Matthew Reed* [2003] EWCA Civ 696.
[64] *Arsenal Football Club plc v Matthew Reed* [2003] EWCA Civ 696, paragraph 48.
[65] C-48/05 *Adam Opel AG v Autec AG* [2007] E.C.R I-01017.

2. If the answer to question 1 is yes: Does the means of use of the brand described in question 1 constitute a mention relating to the type or quality of the scale-model of the vehicle under the terms of Article 6(1)(a) of the Directive?
3. If the answer to the question under two is yes: What are, in a case of this type, the determining criteria for evaluating whether use of the brand constitutes honest use in commercial or industrial practices? Is there a specific link with such use when the manufacturer of the scale model places on the packaging and on an accessory necessary for the use of the scale model a recognizable sign of its own brand for the public along with an indication of the offices of the company?[66]

(b) The Opinion of Advocate General Ruiz-Jarabo Colomer

9.61 Advocate General Ruiz-Jarabo Colomer noted that a basic characteristic of toys was that they constituted the representation of something else.[67] It would be useful to analyse here whether the copying of a brand—also registered for toys—in order to imitate reality infringed trade mark rights or whether it might be considered as lying outside the limits of trade mark protection.

9.62 The first question concerned whether use of the Opel logo constituted use as a trade mark. Accordingly, he intended to focus on two aspects: use of the sign as a trade mark and use of the sign for other purposes.

9.63 **(i) Use of a sign as a registered trade mark**   Citing *BMW*[68] and his Opinion in *Arsenal*,[69] he stressed that absolute protection meant that there was a *juris tantum* presumption of infringement rather than protection against all parties and in all circumstances.[70] In this case the national court had to conduct a similar evaluation, recognizing the fact that the Opel logo appeared on the body of the toy cars independently of whether the manufacturer was a licensee or a third party.

9.64 **(ii) Other uses of a sign**   Concluding, AG Ruiz-Jarabo Colomer stated that uses outside of the essential function of a trade mark would have to be assessed progressively, on a case-by-case basis. Looking at them from a broader theoretical and justificatory perspective he remarked that, unlike the cases falling under Article 6(1), they did not require a restrictive interpretation because they did not constitute derogations but rather limitations on the use of *jus prohibendi*.

9.65 **(iii) Application to the facts: Article 5(1)(a)**   Having set 'the jurisprudential panorama'[71] he went on to examine how the facts of the case fitted into it. He found that the application of the logo on the toy cars should not be linked with the function of a trade mark for two reasons: first, because of the nature of the product and, second, because of consumer perception. Looking at the product market he noted that miniature cars, trains, ships, and aeroplanes had been marketed widely since 1898; little cars were the 'Proustian madeleine' of adults reliving their childhood experiences. The audience for the product comprised children of different ages but also adult collectors. To satisfy demand the toys had to replicate even the tiniest details of the original car, including the signs appearing on them. The

---

[66] Point 14. See also paragraph 9.351 and following below for the answers to questions 2 and 3.
[67] Citing the Opinion of AG Jacobs in C-498/01 *P Zapf Creation AG* [2004] ECR I-11349.
[68] C-63/97 *Bayerische Motorenwerke AG* [1999] ECR I-905.
[69] C-206/01 *Arsenal* [2002] ECR I-10273.
[70] See paragraphs 9.41 and following, above.
[71] Point 35.

car industry had only recently become involved in this market, primarily in order to build customer loyalty though merchandising and advertising.

9.66 As a result of that product market analysis he concluded that it would be difficult to imagine that the public would automatically associate the signs appearing on the toy cars with the manufacturer.

9.67 Extensive protection would threaten the existence of the toy car market. The licensees of the car manufacturers 'would be the only ones authorized to provide detailed replicas of the authentic vehicles, thereby unjustifiably restricting the freedom of competitors to conduct their business'.[72]

9.68 The Advocate General started his discussion of consumer perception with a reference to *Anheuser-Busch*.[73] In that case the Court had ruled that the identification of possible harm caused by a third party's use depended on the perception of a material link in the course of trade between the third party's products and those of the trade mark proprietor. So, what courts had to do was assess whether the relevant consumers perceived the sign as designating the trade mark proprietor. The referring Court had examined the link created by the sign and found that, as intended by the nature of the product, it established a link between the miniature prototype and the real car, but not with the toy models manufactured by Opel's licensees. This should not constitute trade mark infringement. 'This would only be the case if the consumer associated the Opel sign on the toy cars of third parties with the one figuring on the toy cars marketed by Opel.'[74]

9.69 The toy car and the original car did not belong to the same category of goods, thus they did not constitute identical goods under Article 5(1)(a). Note though that as mentioned earlier, Opel had been trying to exercise its rights based on the registration of its trade mark for toys, not for cars.

9.70 In his concluding suggestion on how the first question should be answered the Advocate General refocused the argument on the importance of use as a trade mark. Use of a registered sign on toys should not constitute use as a trade mark under the terms of Article 5(1)(a) when the manufacturer of a model car reproduced on a smaller scale and marketed a replica of an actual existing model bearing the trade mark of the owner.

9.71 Advocate General Ruiz-Jarabo Colomer decided to look briefly at the remaining two questions, in the hypothetical scenario of a negative answer to the first question, finding that Article 6 would also cover the use made by the toy manufacturer.[75]

(b) The Judgment of the Court

9.72 **(i) Use in relation to toys** The Court observed at the outset that it was not disputed that the sign was used with a view to economic advantage and not as a private matter, without the consent of the trade mark proprietor and, insofar as the Opel logo has been registered for toys, that the use was in respect of identical goods, as envisaged in Article 5(1)(a) of the Directive. Moreover, it noted that the use is 'in relation to goods' within the meaning of

---

[72] Point 41.
[73] Case C-245/02 *Anheuser-Busch* [2004] ECR I-10989, see 12.194 and following, below.
[74] Point 44.
[75] Paragraphs 9.352 and following, below.

that provision, since it concerns the affixing of the sign onto goods and the offering of those goods for sale by putting them on the market or stocking them for the purposes of Article 5(3)(a) and (b) of the Directive.[76]

9.73 Notwithstanding, it held that these facts were not enough to trigger the absolute protection provided for in Article 5(1)(a), insisting on a narrow interpretation of its preventive scope. Following *Arsenal*[77] and *Anheuser-Busch*,[78] it stressed that the exclusive right afforded by that provision had the purpose of enabling the trade mark proprietor to protect his specific interests; that is, to ensure that the mark can fulfil its functions and that, accordingly, the exercise of its rights must be limited to cases where the essential function of the mark was endangered. On that premise, the Court concluded that the affixing of a sign identical to a trade mark registered for toys on scale models of vehicles cannot be prohibited under Article 5(1)(a) of the Directive, unless it affects, or is liable to affect, the functions of that mark.[79]

9.74 The Court also took notice that, according to the facts stated in the order for reference, the average consumer of toy cars in Germany is used to scale models being based on real products and even accords great importance to absolute fidelity to the original, so that he would take the Opel logo appearing on the miniatures as a mere indication that the toy is a reduced-scale reproduction of a real Opel car. On this point, the Court remarked that if by that explanation the referring court implied that the relevant public does not perceive the Opel logo appearing on the scale models as an indication of their origin, it would have to conclude that the use at issue does not affect the essential function of Opel's trade mark for toys.[80]

9.75 However, it stressed that it was for the referring court to determine, by reference to the perception of the average consumer of toys in Germany, whether the use at issue was likely to affect the functions of Opel's logo, noting also in that connection that Opel did not appear to have claimed that said use affected the other functions of its trade mark.

9.76 The Court then assessed the same question in relation to the registration of Opel's mark for motor vehicles. In that regard, it admitted that its Judgment in *BMW*,[81] where the services of repair of vehicles of a particular make had been found to be identical with the cars so repaired, was quite exceptional and could not be applied to the case at issue; to the extent that Autec sells toys and not vehicles, the use of the Opel logo in the present instance cannot be said to cover identical goods, within the meaning of Article 5(1)(a) of the Directive.[82]

9.77 (ii) **Possible threat to other functions** Despite the fact that Opel had not specifically argued that any of the other functions of its trade mark were liable to be affected by Autec's use, the Court went on to also examine the applicability of Article 5(2), pointing out that it is for the Court to provide the national court with all those elements for the interpretation of Community law which may be of assistance in adjudicating on the case. It considered that, at least prima facie, the circumstances of the case did not preclude the application of

---

[76] Citing *Arsenal* [2002] ECR I-10273, paragraphs 40–41.
[77] Ibid, paragraph 51.
[78] *Anheuser-Busch* (n 73), paragraph 59.
[79] *Opel* (n 65), paragraph 22.
[80] Paragraph 24.
[81] C-63/97 *Bayerische Motorenwerke* [1999] ECR I-905.
[82] Paragraphs 27–30.

Article 5(2), provided that it could be established that the use at issue was likely to take unfair advantage of, or be detrimental to, the distinctive character or the repute of Opel's registration for motor vehicles.[83] All the more so, since Opel had argued at the hearing that it has an interest in the quality of scale models of vehicles bearing its trade mark being good, and in those models being absolutely up to date, as otherwise the reputation of its trade mark for motor vehicles would be damaged.

9.78 (iii) **Can a specific toy model be described by reference to the original product?** As regards the question whether the use in issue could be allowed by virtue of Article 6 of the Directive, the Court held, as a preliminary point, that the affixing of Opel's trade mark on scale models could not be authorized on the basis of Article 6(1)(c) because it was not meant to indicate the intended purpose of the toys concerned. It went on to discuss whether use could have been according to honest practices. This is covered below where we discuss limitations to trade mark protection.[84]

(c) Conclusions

9.79 *Adam Opel* suggests that the reproduction of the mark of the original product on toy models does not fall within the scope of Article 5(1)(a) of the Directive, even if the proprietor holds a registration in respect of those goods, on the assumption that in such cases the public will not see the sign as designating origin; nevertheless, such use might still be covered by Article 5(2), to the extent that it takes unfair advantage of the reputation of the trade mark.

9.80 However, the assumption that in the situation *in casu* there is no likelihood of confusion seems to have been made bearing in mind the real business of the plaintiff rather than its registration for toys, since it is difficult to imagine how that conclusion could be escaped if Opel's logo was actually distinguishing toys.

9.81 In that sense, the Court seems to have interpreted the absolute prohibition contained in Article 5(1)(a) of the Directive in a quite restrictive manner in that it did not give sufficient weight to possible future uses of the mark squarely falling within the confines of the registration.

9.82 At the same time, *Adam Opel* seems to be taking a similarly restrictive approach as regards the exception in Article 6(1)(b), at least insofar as it refuses to concede that traders in the toy industry act in accordance with honest practices, apparently on the assumption that toys do not necessarily need to imitate known products without the consent of their manufacturer. Is this view justified, however, even if in the relevant industry the identification of the type of plaything concerned is traditionally made by reference to the original, as the order for reference seems to imply?

9.83 Moreover, that approach does not adequately explain how the public will actually perceive the reproduction of the mark on the toy if it sees it neither as indication of origin nor as an identification of the type of toy concerned.[85]

---

[83] Paragraph 34.
[84] Paragraph 39, see 9.351 and following below.
[85] For instance, that view seems to be stricter than the approach taken by the Advocate General in case C-498/01P *Zapf Creation AG* [2004] ECR I-05173.

(4) 'Availability' and Scope of Protection: *Marca II*

9.84 *Marca II*[86] is the sequel of *Marca Mode*,[87] albeit in a different context. Once again, Adidas challenged on the basis of its well-known three-stripe trade mark the use by competitors of signs consisting of a double stripe in contrasting colours to conceal and strengthen the seams of their garments. The question concerned the application of the requirement of availability for the purposes of defining the scope of trade mark rights.

(a) The facts in the main proceedings and the order for reference

9.85 The dispute arose in the context of proceedings between Adidas AG and its Benelux subsidiary (together 'Adidas'), on the one hand, and Marca Mode CV, C&A Nederland CV, H&M Hennes & Mauritz Netherlands BV, and Vendex KBB Nederland BV ('the defendants'), on the other. In the Benelux, Adidas owns a number of figurative trade mark registrations for sports and leisure clothing, composed of three vertical, parallel stripes of equal width, running the length of the sides, shoulders, sleeves, legs, and side seams of a garment, in contrasting colours.

9.86 On appeal the case reached the Hoge Raad (Supreme Court of the Netherlands), taking the view that the requirement of availability must be taken into account only when examining the application of the grounds for refusal or invalidity provided for in Article 3 of the Directive. The Hoge Raad decided to stay the proceedings and refer the following questions to the Court for a preliminary ruling:

1. In the determination of the extent to which protection should be given to a trade mark formed by a sign which does not in itself have any distinctive character or by a designation which corresponds to the description in Article 3(1)(c) of the Directive … but which has become a trade mark through the process of becoming customary ('inburgering') and has been registered, should account be taken of the general interest in ensuring that the availability of given signs is not unduly restricted for other traders offering the goods or services concerned ('Freihaltebedürfnis')?
2. If the answer to Question 1 is in the affirmative: does it make any difference whether the signs which are referred to therein and which are to be held available are seen by the relevant public as being signs used to distinguish goods or merely to embellish them?
3. If the answer to Question 1 is in the affirmative: does it, further, make any difference whether the sign contested by the holder of a trade mark is devoid of distinctive character, within the terms of Article 3(1)(b) of the Directive … or contains a designation, within the terms of Article 3(1)(c) of the Directive?

(b) The Opinion of Advocate General Ruiz-Jarabo Colomer

9.87 After considering the origins of the Freihaltebedürfnis principle in German case law preceding the Directive and recalling that it concerned a real, current, and serious risk to the availability of signs that ought to remain free for the use of competitors, Advocate General Ruiz-Jarabo Colomer referred to its treatment under Community law and emphasized that although in *Windsurfing Chiemsee* the Court stated that 'the application of Article 3(1)(c) of the Directive does not depend on there being a real, current or serious need to leave [a sign or indication] free',[88] it nevertheless acknowledged the link between that principle and the general interest underlying that provision.[89]

---

[86] C-102/07 *Adidas AG and Adidas Benelux BV/Marca Mode CV, C&A Nederland, H&M Hennes & Mauritz Netherlands BV, and Vendex KBB Nederland BV (MARCA II)* [2008] ECR I-2439.
[87] C-425/98 *Marca Mode CV v Adidas* [2000] ECR I-4681.
[88] C-109/97 *Windsurfing Chiemsee* [1999] ECR I-2779, paragraph 35.
[89] Ibid, paragraphs 26–27.

9.88 Since then, the Court has repeatedly drawn attention to the need to apply the principle when deciding whether a sign is eligible for registration[90] and has also extended its application to Article 3(1)(b) and (e) of the Directive.[91]

9.89 With regard to Article 5, he advanced two arguments militating against its application when determining the scope of protection. The first, related to the origin of the Freihaltebedürfnis principle, is clearly linked to the registration of signs rather than to the exercise of the rights conferred on the holder of the mark. The second was drawn from the overall scheme of the Directive, which places the limitations of those rights under Article 6. Thus, allowing the principle of availability to be taken into account in the framework of Article 5 would entail the addition of an unwritten condition which would be contrary to the principle of legal certainty and to the spirit of the relevant provisions.[92]

9.90 Next, he turned to Article 6(1) of the Directive, noting the similarities in the structure between Article 3(1)(c) on the one hand and 6(1)(b), on the other, which advocates in favour of a comparative analysis of the respective provisions. He also pointed out that the Court has not ruled out the use of the requirement of availability as a criterion for the interpretation of Article 6 and, by extension, as a factor to be taken into account when assessing the limitation of the rights of trade mark proprietors under that provision.[93]

9.91 Based on the similar wording and purpose pursued by Articles 3(1)(c) and 6(1)(b), he concluded that it is necessary to consider the requirement of availability when establishing the scope of protection of a mark composed of one of the indications referred to in Article 3(1)(c) of the Directive, which has been registered on account of the distinctive character it acquired through use, but that it is not appropriate to rely on that principle where a sign inherently devoid of distinctive character, within the meaning of Article 3(1)(b), subsequently acquired such distinctiveness by use.[94]

9.92 Responding to the second question, he considered that the perception by the public of a sign subject to the requirement of availability has only limited relevance in these circumstances. If the average consumer regards the sign as having a merely decorative purpose, he will not identify it as a badge of origin, from which it follows that the sign will not be suitable for performing its essential requirement and, thus, its scope of protection will have to be diminished accordingly; otherwise, the contrary should apply.[95]

(c) The Judgment of the Court

9.93 **(i) The impact of the requirement of availability on the scope of protection** The Court formally recognized the significance of the principle of availability in the system of European trade mark law by confirming that there are public interest considerations, connected in particular with the need for undistorted competition, which require that certain signs should be used freely by all economic operators.[96] The Court recalled that the

---

[90] Citing C-104/01 *Libertel* [2003] ECR I-03793, paragraph 52 and C- 218/01 *Henkel* [2004] ECR I-01725, paragraphs 40–41.
[91] Citing C-329/02 *SAT.1* [2004] ECR I-08317, paragraphs 26–27 and C-299/99 *Philips* [2002] ECR I-05475, paragraph 80.
[92] Point 48.
[93] Point 69.
[94] Point 80.
[95] Points 81–82.
[96] Paragraph 22.

requirement of availability is both the reason underlying certain of the grounds for refusal set out in Article 3 of the Directive and the justification for the sanction set out in Article 12(2)(a), according to which a trade mark is liable for revocation if it has become generic in the relevant sector. In substance, by those provisions the Community legislator sought to balance the legitimate interests of trade mark proprietors against those of competitors in the availability of signs.

9.94 It observed, however, that the case at issue fell outside that framework, since it only raised the question of whether the requirement of availability constitutes a relevant criterion for the purposes of defining the protection to be afforded to trade mark proprietors. As was clear from the facts, the defendants did not seek to have the mark of Adidas either revoked or declared invalid but merely a declaration that they were entitled to use motifs other than the one registered by the trade mark owner, without the consent of the latter.[97] In that sense, the relevance of that argument had to be examined exclusively in the light of Articles 5 and 6(1)(b) of the Directive that specifically delimit the scope of trade mark protection, without having recourse to the purpose and function of Articles 3 and 12.

9.95 As regards, first, Article 5(1)(b), the Court pointed out once more that the protection conferred by it is subject to the existence of a likelihood of confusion, the assessment of which depends on all relevant factors, as set out in the Tenth Recital of the Preamble to the Directive. It stressed, however, that the need for the sign to remain available for other economic operators cannot be one of those factors. Rather, the answer to the question as to whether there is a likelihood of confusion must be based on the perception by the relevant public as to origin and not on considerations extraneous to that perception. If a third party could rely on the requirement of availability to use a sign which is nevertheless similar to an earlier mark without the proprietor of the latter being able to oppose that use, the effective application of Article 5(1) of the Directive would be seriously undermined.[98]

9.96 The Court also emphasized the fact that those considerations apply in particular to stripe motifs. Such motifs are widely available and may be placed in a vast number of ways on sports garments by all operators. Nonetheless, competitors cannot rely on the requirement of availability in order to place on their garments motifs which are so similar to that registered by the trade mark owner that they give rise to a likelihood of confusion in the mind of the public.

9.97 For much the same reasons, the Court held that the perception of the sign as mere decoration cannot constitute a restriction on the protection conferred by Article 5(1)(b) when, despite its decorative nature, that sign is so similar to the registered trade mark that the public is likely to believe that the respective goods have the same commercial origin.[99]

9.98 Accordingly, the national court would have to determine whether the consumer, when confronted with garments featuring stripe motifs in the same places and with similar characteristics as the logo registered by Adidas, except for the fact that they consist of two rather than three stripes, may be mistaken as to the origin of those goods. As is moreover clear from the Tenth Recital in the Preamble of the Directive that appreciation depends not

---

[97] Paragraph 25.
[98] Paragraphs 30–31.
[99] Paragraph 34.

solely on the degree of similarity of the signs but also on the ease with which the sign may be associated with the mark, having regard, in particular, to the recognition of the latter on the market.

9.99 Finally, the Court held that the same line of reasoning applied also to Article 5(2) of the Directive, with the result that the requirement of availability could not influence the assessment of whether the use of the sign takes unfair advantage of, or is detrimental to, the distinctive character or the repute of the trade mark either.[100]

9.100 (ii) **The requirement of availability as a limiting factor**   As regards the interpretation of Article 6(1)(b) of the Directive, the Court concurred with the Advocate General that insofar as that provision seeks to ensure that all economic operators remain free to use descriptive indications in a fair manner, it essentially constitutes an expression of the requirement of availability. However, it observed at the same time that the requirement of availability cannot constitute an independent restriction of the effects of the trade mark, in addition to those expressly provided for in Article 6(1)(b). At any rate, in order for a third party to invoke the exceptions included in that provision, the indication used by it must necessarily relate to one of the characteristics of the goods or services concerned and not merely on its purely decorative nature.[101]

9.101 Consequently, the Court concluded that to the extent that the two-stripe motifs at issue were not meant as an indication of any of the characteristics of the garments on which they were placed but merely served ornamental purposes, the defendants in the main proceedings could not rely on Article 6(1)(b) of the Directive to justify their use.

(5) Expanding the Scope of Protection: Other than the Essential Functions; *Bellure*

(a) The facts in the main proceedings and the order for reference

9.102 In *Bellure*,[102] the Court appeared to relax the criteria developed as part of its earlier jurisprudence on the application of Article 5(1)(a) of the Directive by clearly including in the protected subject matter of that provision functions of the mark other than its essential one. The first and second questions in that Judgment concerned the use by manufacturers of perfumes that smell alike of 'comparison lists', indicating the fine fragrances to which the specific imitations correspond by referring to their registered trade marks.[103]

9.103 By the first question, the referring court asked whether Article 5(1)(a) or (b) of the Directive must be interpreted as meaning that the trade mark proprietor is entitled to prevent the use by a third party in comparative advertising of a sign identical with its mark in relation to identical goods where such use is not capable of jeopardising the essential function of the mark. By the second question, it asked whether the proprietor of a well-known mark can oppose such use under Article 5(1)(a), even where that use is not capable of jeopardizing the function of the mark as a guarantee of origin, or harm its reputation, whether by tarnishment or dilution or in any other way, but nonetheless plays a significant role in the promotion of the goods of the third party.

---

[100] Paragraph 43.
[101] Paragraph 47–48.
[102] *L'Oréal SA, Lancôme parfums et beauté & Cie SNC, Laboratoire Garnier & Cie/Bellure NV, Malaika Investments Ltd, Starion International Ltd (BELLURE)* C-487/07 [2009] ECR I-05185.
[103] For a more detailed account of the facts of that case see paragraph 12.78 and following, below.

(b) *The Opinion of Advocate General Mengozzi*

9.104 The textual analysis of the Directive was inconclusive. Turning to the jurisprudence of the Court he found that *Adam Opel* took a step further towards recognizing that protection is to be afforded not only in respect of a trade mark's essential function but also in respect of other functions, when it stated that the trade mark proprietor is entitled to prevent the use of its mark by third parties 'if that use affects … the functions of the trade mark'.[104] From that formulation the Advocate General inferred that what is ultimately necessary for activating the protection conferred by Article 5(1)(a) is that there must be an adverse effect on any of the functions of the mark, in the sense there is protection of whichever of the functions of the mark is liable to be affected. Nevertheless, he noted that the gradual development in the Court's case law towards the protection of trade mark functions other than as a guarantee of origin did not entirely settle the issue, especially insofar as it left open the question of the identification of those other functions, as well as the question of ascertaining how such protection may be reconciled with the protection of well-known marks under Article 5(2) of the Directive.

9.105 Considering the function of a trade mark in the marketplace, he had a closer look at the way trade marks function in the market, focusing in particular on the quality and communication functions. He defined the former as the guarantee that the trade mark provides as to the consistency (or uniformity) in the quality of products identified by it[105] and the latter as 'a vehicle for providing consumers with various kinds of information on the goods', be it information communicated directly by the sign which the mark consists of (eg information on the product's physical characteristics), or 'accumulated' information relating to non-physical characteristics thereof (eg quality, trustworthiness, reliability, luxury, strength, etc).[106]

9.106 He noted, however, that while such cases confirm that the protection which the trade mark enjoys by virtue of Article 5 of the Directive goes beyond the need to protect its function as guarantee of origin, the question nevertheless remains open as to what extent that protection ought to be conferred by Article 5(1)(a), or covered by the optional provision of Article 5(2) of the Directive, which, as confirmed by the Judgment in *Gofkid*, also applies to identical or similar goods. Notwithstanding, he pointed out that the circumstances of the case rendered it unnecessary to undertake an exhaustive description of the trade mark functions that could be protected under Article 5(1)(a), since the questions referred were based on the finding that the use made by the defendants does not have any effect on the reputation of the earlier marks and, accordingly, on the communication functions carried out by them. Moreover, the mere fact that the use complained of enables the defendants to take unfair advantage of that reputation does not mean that such a use is liable to undermine the functions which the marks in question perform as a result of that reputation.

(c) *Findings of the Court*

9.107 Before addressing the substantive issues relating to the first and second questions, the Court noted that insofar as the comparison lists used by the defendants were aimed at promoting the supply of goods and explicitly identified the products of a competitor, they fell within

---

[104] *Adam Opel* [2007] ECR I-1017, paragraph 37.
[105] Point 53.
[106] Point 54.

the ambit of Articles 2(1) and 2(2a) of Directive 84/450 and, thus, constituted comparative advertising. Citing *O2*, it also recalled that the use of a sign identical with the mark of a competitor in that manner was to be regarded as use for the advertiser's own goods and services and could therefore be prevented by virtue of Article 5(1) and (2) of the Directive, unless it satisfied all the conditions laid down in Article 3a(1) of Directive 84/450, under which comparative advertising is permitted. Moreover, it observed that insofar as the use at issue was for identical signs and concerned identical goods, it fell within the scope of Article 5(1)(a) of the Directive and not that of Article 5(1)(b).

9.108 The Court then reiterated its statements in *Arsenal* and *Adam Opel* that the exercise of the rights conferred by Article 5(1)(a) is reserved to cases in which the functions of the trade mark are likely to be affected, adding however that 'these functions include not only the essential function of the trade mark, but also its other functions, in particular that of guaranteeing the quality of the goods or services in question and those of communication, investment or advertising'.[107]

9.109 In addition, it explicitly clarified that the protection conferred by Article 5(1)(a) is broader than that provided by Article 5(1)(b), the application of which requires a likelihood of confusion, noting that this was also attested by the Tenth Recital to the Directive, which states that in case of identity the protection afforded by the registered trade mark is absolute, whereas in case of mere similarity the existence of a likelihood of confusion constitutes the specific condition for such protection.[108] Notwithstanding, the Court emphasized that 'absolute' protection under that provision does not mean unlimited protection by stressing that a trade mark proprietor cannot oppose the use of an identical sign if that use is not liable to cause detriment to any of the functions of his mark.[109]

9.110 To make this point even clearer, it referred by way of example to its Judgment in *Hölterhoff* where the use served purely descriptive purposes and thus was held not to constitute 'use' for the purposes of Article 5(1)(a). It observed, however, that the situation in the main proceedings was fundamentally different from the facts in *Hölterhoff* in that the marks reproduced in the comparison were used for advertising and not merely for descriptive purposes.

9.111 Accordingly, it stated that it was for the referring court to determine whether the use made by the defendants was liable to affect one of the functions of the earlier marks and, in particular, their functions of communication, investment, or advertising. In the negative, and insofar as the case concerned reputed marks, the national court would also have to examine whether the use complained of was caught by Article 5(2), the applicability of which does not necessarily require a likelihood of detriment, provided of course that an unfair advantage to the repute of that mark could be established.

(d) Conclusions

9.112 Undoubtedly, the Judgment in *Bellure* is a further step in the 'gradual development' of the case law of the Court—to use the expression of Advocate General Mengozzi—towards a broader and more rational trade mark protection. Although the Court refrained from

---

[107] Paragraph 58.
[108] Paragraph 59.
[109] Citing *Arsenal* [2002] ECR I-10273, paragraph 54, and *Adam Opel* [2007] ECR I-1017, paragraph 22.

defining in detail, at least for now, the functions of 'guaranteeing the quality of the goods or services' and of 'communication, investment or advertising' performed by trade marks, it is still important that it formally recognized their existence, as well as the fact that they form part of the protectable subject matter under Article 5(1)(a) of the Directive.

Moreover, by accepting that those further functions are protected by Article 5(1)(a) of the Directive, the Court seems to be suggesting that trade mark proprietors can invoke them even where the earlier mark does not have a reputation. Although it may be true that in the specific case the earlier mark was well known, that conclusion can nonetheless be inferred, first, by the absence of any reference by the Court to the need for the earlier mark to be reputed when generally defining the scope of Article 5(1)(a) and, second, *a contrario sensu* from its statement that 'furthermore, insofar as [the earlier marks] have a reputation, their use … can also be prevented under Article 5(2)'.[110]

9.113

In doing so, the Court actually went one step beyond what was suggested by the Advocate General in the direction of delimiting the relationship between Articles 5(1) and 5(2) of the Directive, by recognizing in essence that at least where the signs and the goods are identical, these provisions partly overlap, differing only inasmuch as that the latter also covers instances where the use of the later sign draws unfair advantage from the repute of the earlier well-known mark. That 'rapprochement' of the two provisions is particularly significant in view of the optional character of Article 5(2), since it caters for protection against detriment unrelated to a likelihood of confusion and this regardless of whether the earlier mark has a reputation or not.

9.114

(6) Use by Intermediaries: The First Stage; *Smirnoff*

(a) *The facts in the main proceedings and the order for reference*

In *Smirnoff*[111] the Court dealt with the right of the trade mark proprietor to prevent the use of an identical sign within the context of Article 9(1)(a) and (2)(d) of the Regulation, the equivalent provisions to Article 5(1)(a) and 5(3)(d) of the Directive. The question arose in the context of a dispute between UDV, proprietor of the Community trade mark 'Smirnoff Ice', registered for, inter alia, 'alcoholic beverages', in class 33 of the Nice Classification, and Brandtraders, a company operating a website on which companies can anonymously place advertisements and negotiate their transactions. In accordance with the relevant terms and conditions, as soon as Brandtraders is informed of an agreement, it concludes with the purchaser a contract of sale for commission acting as the vendor's broker; that is to say, in its own name but on behalf of the vendor.

9.115

Following the sale in that manner of a quantity of goods bearing the mark 'Smirnoff Ice', UDV sought to obtain an injunction against Brandtraders which was accepted by the competent Belgian Court, which held that Brandtraders had infringed Article 9(1) and (2) CTMR on account of the fact that it advertised, purchased, and resold the goods in question. On appeal, the Hof van beroep te Brussel (Court of Appeal, Brussels) annulled the order and dismissed as unfounded UDV's application on the grounds that, inter alia, Brandtraders had not placed the allegedly infringing references on the website itself and had not used the sign in relation to trade in goods in which it was itself a contractual party, given

9.116

---

[110] Paragraph 64.
[111] C-62/08, *UDV North America Inc. v Brandtraders NV (SMIRNOFF)* [2009] ECR I-01279.

that it was merely acting on behalf of a third party; in that sense it had not made use of the sign for the purposes of Article 9(1) and (2) CTMR.

9.117 UDV brought an appeal before the Hof van Cassatie (Court of Cassation) against that Judgment claiming that it is not necessary, for the application of Article 9(1)(a) and (2)(d) CTMR, that the third party concerned act on its own behalf and/or use the sign at issue as an interested party in relation to the sale of goods in which it is itself a contractual party. The Hof van Cassatie decided to stay the proceedings and to refer the following questions to the Court for a preliminary ruling:

> (1) For there to be use of the sign within the meaning of Article 9(1)(a) and (2)(d) [CTMR], is it necessary that a third party, within the meaning of Article 9(1)(a) of [that] regulation:
>   (a) uses the sign on his own behalf?
>   (b) uses the sign as an interested party in relation to trade in goods in which he is himself a contractual party?
> (2) Can a trade intermediary who acts in his own name, but not on his own behalf, be regarded as a third party who uses the sign within the meaning of Article 9(1)(a) and (2)(d)?

(b) The reasoned order of the Court

9.118 Considering that the answer to the questions referred raised no reasonable doubt, the Court reached, in accordance with Article 104 (3) of its Rules of Procedure, its decision by reasoned order. Before the Court, Brandtraders remarked that under Belgian law, a broker acts in his own name but on behalf of a third principal, in this case the vendor, meaning that he does not actually acquire title to the goods when a sales contract is concluded. As a result, it claimed that the use by a third party of a sign which is identical with a registered mark must relate to that third party's own goods in order for that use to be prevented.

9.119 The Court rejected that argument, noting that all the conditions set out in its case law with regard to the concept of 'use' within the meaning of Article 5(1) of the Directive had been fulfilled and that, consequently, the fact that the party at issue used a sign which is identical with a registered mark in relation to goods which are not its own, in that it does not have title to them, is not relevant and can therefore not mean by itself that the use made in this case does not fall under the definition of Article 9(1) CTMR.[112]

9.120 More specifically, it held that the use at issue is clearly in the context of a commercial activity with a view to economic advantage, since Brandtraders acted in the context of a sales contract and received remuneration for that action; the fact that the broker acted on behalf of a third vendor is in that regard irrelevant.[113] In addition, it is clear that said use is in relation to goods because even though it is not a case of affixing the sign to the goods, there is use 'in relation to goods' in the form of using the sign at issue on business papers. Inasmuch as such a link is established, it is irrelevant that the third party uses a sign for the marketing of goods which are not its own, in the sense that it does not acquire title thereto.[114]

9.121 Lastly, the Court held that the use of the sign is likely to create the impression that there is a material link in trade between the goods on which they are affixed and the undertaking from which they originate; indeed, by making such use, the third party 'assumes de facto the essential prerogative that is granted to the proprietor of a mark, namely the exclusive

---

[112] Paragraph 43.
[113] Paragraph 45–46.
[114] Paragraph 47–48.

power to use the sign at issue so as to distinguish goods', that is, clearly makes use of the sign as a trade mark.[115]

D. Trade Marks and the Internet: Function Proliferation; Keyword Advertising

(1) *Google*: The Relevance of a New Market Context

(a) *The facts in the main proceedings and the order for reference*

9.122 *Google France*[116] was the first case where the Court considered the use of trade marks on the Internet in the context of keyword advertising. The case came to the Court as a reference from the French Cour de Cassation. Advocate General Poiares Maduro started by describing the issue in almost poetic terms:

> The act of typing a keyword into an internet search engine has become part of our culture, its results immediately familiar. The actual inner workings of how those results are provided are, it is fair to say, mostly unknown to the general public. It is simply assumed that if you ask, it shall be given to you; seek, and you shall find.[117]

9.123 He went on to describe how the system works in more technical terms. For any keyword typed into a search engine there are two types of results: (i) 'natural results', meaning a range of sites relevant to the keyword; and, (ii) 'ads', advertisements for certain sites. Natural results lists are compiled on the basis of objective criteria, whereas ads appear because search engine providers make keywords available for selection to advertisers; advertisers pay, almost akin to an auction, for the keywords to function as triggers for their sites to feature in response to the keywords.

9.124 The case before the Court comprised three references from the French Cour de Cassation (Court of Cassation), all dealing with 'AdWords', Google's keyword advertising system, and the use as keywords of national and Community trade marks. The national court referred the following questions to the Court.

9.125 C-236/08:

1. Must Article 5(1)(a) and (b) of [Directive 89/104] and Article 9(1)(a) and (b) of [Regulation No 40/94] be interpreted as meaning that a provider of a paid referencing service who makes available to advertisers keywords reproducing or imitating registered trade marks and arranges by the referencing agreement to create and favourably display, on the basis of those keywords, advertising links to sites offering infringing goods is using those trade marks in a manner which their proprietor is entitled to prevent?
2. In the event that the trade marks have a reputation, may the proprietor oppose such use under Article 5(2) of [Directive 89/104] and Article 9(1)(c) of [Regulation No 40/94]?
3. In the event that such use does not constitute a use which may be prevented by the trade mark proprietor under [Directive 89/104] or [Regulation No 40/94], may the provider of the paid referencing service be regarded as providing an information society service consisting of the storage of information provided by the recipient of the service, within the

---

[115] Paragraph 49–51.
[116] Joined Cases C-236/08, C-237/08, and C-238/08 *Google France, Google Inc. v Louis Vuitton Malletier; Google France v Viaticum Luteciel; Google France v CNRRH Pierre-Alexis Thonet Bruno Raboi Tiger, a franchisee of Unicis* [2010] ECR I-02417.
[117] Point 2, paraphrasing Matthew 7:7.

meaning of Article 14 of [Directive 2000/31], so that that provider cannot incur liability until it has been notified by the trade mark proprietor of the unlawful use of the sign by the advertiser?[118]

9.126 C-237/08:

1. Must Article 5(1)(a) and (b) of [Directive 89/104] be interpreted as meaning that a provider of a paid referencing service who makes available to advertisers keywords reproducing or imitating registered trade marks and arranges by the referencing agreement to create and favourably display, on the basis of those keywords, advertising links to sites offering goods identical or similar to those covered by the trade mark registration is using those trade marks in a manner which their proprietor is entitled to prevent?
2. In the event that such use does not constitute a use which may be prevented by the trade mark proprietor under [Directive 89/104] or [Regulation No 40/94], may the provider of the paid referencing service be regarded as providing an information society service consisting of the storage of information provided by the recipient of the service, within the meaning of Article 14 of [Directive 2000/31], so that that provider cannot incur liability before it has been informed by the trade mark proprietor of the unlawful use of the sign by the advertiser?[119]

9.127 Case C-238/08:

1. Does the reservation by an economic operator, by means of an agreement on paid internet referencing, of a keyword triggering, in the case of a request using that word, the display of a link proposing connection to a site operated by that operator in order to offer for sale goods or services, and which reproduces or imitates a trade mark registered by a third party in order to designate identical or similar goods, without the authorisation of the proprietor of that trade mark, constitute in itself an infringement of the exclusive right guaranteed to the latter by Article 5 of [Directive 89/104]?
2. Must Article 5(1)(a) and (b) of [Directive 89/104] be interpreted as meaning that a provider of a paid referencing service who makes available to advertisers keywords reproducing or imitating registered trade marks and arranges by the referencing agreement to create and favourably display, on the basis of those keywords, advertising links to sites offering goods identical or similar to those covered by the trade mark registration is using those trade marks in a manner which their proprietor is entitled to prevent?
3. In the event that such use does not constitute a use which may be prevented by the trade mark proprietor under [Directive 89/104] or [Regulation No 40/94], may the provider of the paid referencing service be regarded as providing an information society service consisting of the storage of information provided by the recipient of the service, within the meaning of Article 14 of [Directive 2000/31], so that that provider cannot incur liability before it has been informed by the trade mark proprietor of the unlawful use of the sign by the advertiser?[120]

(b) The Opinion of Advocate General Maduro

9.128 Advocate General Maduro brought all the questions under a single fundamental question: 'does the use by Google, in its AdWords advertising system, of keywords corresponding to trade marks constitute an infringement of those trade marks? Although the references are formulated somewhat differently, they all ask for an interpretation of Article 5(1) of Directive 89/104 and therefore concern that basic question of whether Google has committed a trade mark infringement.'[121]

---

[118] Reproduced in paragraph 32.
[119] Reproduced in paragraph 37.
[120] Reproduced in paragraph 42.
[121] Point 38.

Having reviewed the arguments of the two sides the Advocate General gave the following preliminary assessment: **9.129**

> The Court is thus being asked to expand significantly the scope of trade mark protection. I shall make clear why I believe that it ought not to do so. My examination of the question whether there is trade mark infringement will reveal, first, that the use in AdWords of keywords which correspond to trade marks does not, in itself, constitute a trade mark infringement, and, secondly, that the connection with other (potentially infringing) uses is better addressed, as it has been hitherto, through the rules on liability.[122]

He categorized a number of overlapping question under three headings: (i) Infringement and Use by the Search Engine; (ii) The Issue of Contributory Infringement; (iii) Use by Advertisers. **9.130**

(i) **Infringement and use by the search engine** The first heading considered the two types of use by the search engine, both inextricably linked because one follows and is the result of the other: (a) when the search engine allows advertisers to select the keywords, and (b) when it displays such ads, alongside the natural results displayed in response to those keywords. Under a separate heading, he also examined (c) whether use by a search engine could be covered under the provisions covering trade marks with a reputation. **9.131**

Having accepted that the trade mark proprietors had not consented to it he identified three additional requirements that had to be established: **9.132**

> whether: (i) that use takes place in the course of trade; (ii) it relates to goods or services which are identical or similar to those covered by the trade marks; and (iii) it affects or is liable to affect the essential function of the trade mark—which is to guarantee to consumers the origin of the goods or services—by reason of a likelihood of confusion on the part of the public.[123]

(ii) **Use by Google in allowing advertisers to select keywords**
First condition Google's use was part of a commercial activity with a view to a gain, hence constituted use in the course of trade. **9.133**

Second condition **9.134**

> The essential factor is ... the link that is established between the trade mark and the good or service being sold. In the traditional example of a use in advertising, the link is established between the trade mark and the good or service sold to the general public ... That is not the case with the use by Google consisting in allowing advertisers to select keywords so that their ads are presented as results. There is no good or service sold to the general public. The use is limited to a selection procedure which is internal to AdWords and concerns only Google and the advertisers ... The service being sold, and to which the use of the keywords corresponding to the trade marks is linked, is therefore Google's own service, AdWords.[124]

It was evident according to the Advocate General that this use was not identical or similar to any of the goods covered by the trade mark.

Third condition Failing the second condition meant that the infringement claim should fail since the conditions were cumulative. In any case, he added that the same failure made it unlikely that the essential function of a trade mark as an indication of origin would have been harmed. **9.135**

---

[122] Point 50.
[123] Point 54.
[124] Point 66.

9.136 **(iii) Use by Google in displaying ads** Before even considering whether such use constituted trade mark infringement according to the above three factors, finding it difficult to distinguish between natural and sponsored results, the Advocate General came up with a general statement regarding the implications of a possible finding of infringement:

> At issue is the display of ads triggered by the use of keywords corresponding to trade marks. However, in the event that such use is held to constitute a trade mark infringement, it may be difficult to prevent that ruling from also applying to the use of keywords in Google's search engine. Despite the fact that the questions referred are confined to AdWords, the parties' pleadings show that they are aware of this risk. They are right that Google's current activity through AdWords is distinguishable from its activity as a provider of a search engine. That said, there is no substantial difference between the use that Google, itself, makes of the keywords in its search engine and the use that it makes of them in AdWords: it displays certain content in response to those keywords.[125]

9.137 He went on to examine the three conditions.

9.138 *First condition* He found that this constituted use in trade, but he had to issue a warning that natural results were also provided in the course of trade, highlighting that the business model of Google would suffer were the Court to find it infringing:

> Natural results are not provided out of charity: they are provided because, as was mentioned above, AdWords operates within the same context by offering some sites added exposure. The value of this exposure depends on the use of the search engine by internet users. Even though Google gets nothing directly from this use, it obviously lies at the root of the income that Google obtains from AdWords, which in turn allows it to support its search engine.[126]

9.139 *Second condition* The second condition was satisfied: Google was displaying ads, linking the keywords and the sites advertised, and these sites were selling goods that were identical or similar to those covered by the trade mark, including counterfeit products. A very similar, if not the same link was established between the same keywords and natural results, according to the Advocate General.

9.140 *Third condition* Looking at whether this second use could affect the essential function of a trade mark, he stressed that he was focusing on the possible risk of confusion resulting from 'the use of the keywords for the display of ads, regardless of the character of those ads and the sites involved'.[127] Again aligning natural results with ads, he noted that 'like the ads displayed, natural results are just information that Google, on the basis of certain criteria, displays in response to the keywords. Many of the sites displayed do not in fact correspond to the sites of the trade mark proprietors'.[128] He viewed Google's engine as a tool establishing a link that in itself would not lead to confusion.

(c) Trade marks with a reputation: The additional functions

9.141 Advocate General Maduro found that if there is confusion then protection is absolute: there will always be a finding of trade mark infringement. 'Beyond the risk of confusion, the conditions for finding an infringement vary.'[129]

---

[125] Point 71.
[126] Point 77.
[127] Point 83.
[128] Point 86.
[129] Point 97. At the top he placed protection of trade marks with a reputation; in the middle protection against use on identical good or services; and, at the bottom, protection against use on similar goods or services.

For the additional functions that aim to protect innovation and investment, he stressed that they had to be calibrated, taking into account freedom of expression and freedom of commerce. Use for purely descriptive purposes was one of the competing uses that had to be tolerated, even in the case of trade marks with a reputation. The same approach should be followed in the case of comparative advertising. In a manner 'comparable to such situations, AdWords creates a link to the trade mark for consumers to obtain information that does not involve a risk of confusion. It does so both indirectly, when it allows the selection of keywords, and directly, when it displays ads.'[130]

9.142

An absolute right of control would not take into account the particular nature of the Internet and the implicit role of keywords. 'Keywords are therefore, in themselves, content-neutral: they enable internet users to reach sites associated with such words. Many of these sites will be perfectly legitimate and lawful even if they are not the sites of the trade mark proprietor.'[131] Citing *Consten and Grundig*,[132] he highlighted the Court's role in establishing that 'the interests of trade mark proprietors were not sufficient to prevent consumers from benefiting from a competitive internal market'.[133] The same stance should be adopted in this case.

9.143

(2) The Issue of Contributory Infringement

The Advocate General noted that trade mark proprietors possessed the tools to bring down sites offering counterfeit products; using them was not always straightforward. This is why, he suggested, they chose to focus on AdWords: 'they believe that the most effective way to stop the message is to stop the messenger'.[134]

9.144

But having identified Google as the messenger he had no problem rejecting, in principle,

9.145

> the notion that the act of contributing to a trade mark infringement by a third party, whether actual or potential, should constitute an infringement in itself. The risks entailed by such contribution are inherent in most systems that facilitate access to and delivery of information; those systems can be used for both good and bad purposes.[135]

Distinguishing between trade mark protection and 'liability rules', he supported the notion that instead of:

> being able to prevent, through trade mark protection, any possible use—including, as has been observed, many lawful and even desirable uses—trade mark proprietors would have to point to specific instances giving rise to Google's liability in the context of illegal damage to their trade marks. They would need to meet the conditions for liability which, in this area, fall to be determined under national law.[136]

He then examined whether Google could be exempted from liability under Article 14 of Directive 2000/31.[137] Search engines and hyperlinks were covered by the Directive as

9.146

---

[130] Point 106.
[131] Point 110.
[132] C-56/64 [1966] ECR 00429.
[133] Point 112.
[134] Point 115.
[135] Point 119.
[136] Point 123.
[137] Directive 2000/31/EC of the European Parliament and of the Council of 8 June 2000 on certain legal aspects of information society services, in particular electronic commerce, in the internal market ('Directive on electronic commerce'), OJ 2000 L178, p 1.

information society services, defined in Article 1(2) of Directive 98/34[138] as 'any service normally provided for remuneration, at a distance, by electronic means and at the individual request of a recipient of services'. However, AdWords did not fall under the exemption. Directive 2000/31 aimed to create a free and open public domain on the Internet. Natural search results would fall under this: 'Google has an interest—even a pecuniary interest—in displaying the more relevant sites to the internet user; however, it does not have an interest in bringing any specific site to the internet user's attention.' In AdWords the opposite was true. 'Google's display of ads stems from its relationship with the advertisers. As a consequence, AdWords is no longer a neutral information vehicle: Google has a direct interest in internet users clicking on the ads' links (as opposed to the natural results presented by the search engine).'[139]

(3) The Use of Keywords by Advertisers

9.147 The selection of keywords by advertisers was the other side of Google's use. 'It would be contradictory to exclude an infringement in the one case and to assert it in the other. That would be tantamount to saying that Google should be permitted to allow the selection of keywords that no one is permitted to select.'[140] But once the trade marks addressed a consumer audience in the ads then trade mark infringement rules should be applied.

9.148 He concluded:

(1) The selection by an economic operator, by means of an agreement on paid internet referencing, of a keyword which will trigger, in the event of a request using that word, the display of a link proposing connection to a site operated by that economic operator for the purposes of offering for sale goods or services, and which reproduces or imitates a trade mark registered by a third party and covering identical or similar goods, without the authorisation of the proprietor of that trade mark, does not constitute in itself an infringement of the exclusive right guaranteed to the latter under Article 5 of First Council Directive 89/104/EEC of 21 December 1988 to approximate the laws of the Member States relating to trade marks.

(2) Article 5(1)(a) and (b) of Directive 89/104 and Article 9(1)(a) and (b) of Council Regulation (EC) No 40/94 of 20 December 1993 on the Community trade mark must be interpreted as meaning that a trade mark proprietor may not prevent the provider of a paid referencing service from making available to advertisers keywords which reproduce or imitate registered trade marks or from arranging under the referencing agreement for advertising links to sites to be created and favourably displayed, on the basis of those keywords.

(3) In the event that the trade marks have a reputation, the trade mark proprietor may not oppose such use under Article 5(2) of Directive 89/104 and Article 9(1)(c) of Regulation No 40/94.

(4) The provider of the paid referencing service cannot be regarded as providing an information society service consisting in the storage of information provided by the recipient of the service within the meaning of Article 14 of Directive 2000/31/EC of the European Parliament and of the Council of 8 June 2000 on certain legal aspects of information society services, in particular electronic commerce, in the internal market ('Directive on electronic commerce').

---

[138] Directive 98/34/EC of the European Parliament and of the Council of 22 June 1998 laying down a procedure for the provision of information in the field of technical standards and regulations, OJ 1998 L204, p 37.
[139] Point 145.
[140] Point 149.

(a) The Judgment of the Court

9.149 The Court divided its response into two parts. First it considered the trade mark aspects of the dispute, and second, it looked at the dispute from the perspective of the service provider.

9.150 (i) **Keywords and trade mark law** The Court clarified that it would consider jointly first the questions involving identical marks and identical, in terms of classification, goods, and second the questions on the rights conferred by reputable trade marks.

9.151 *The first question—Article 5(1)(a) of the Directive and Article 9(1)(a) of the Regulation* The Court considered systematically all the infringement factors against the Internet and keyword advertising context, initially from two perspectives: the advertiser's and the service provider's.

9.152 *Use in the course of trade* This required use in the context of commercial activity with a view to economic advantage rather than as a private matter. The advertiser's use satisfied the requirement; the advertisement triggered by the keyword was critical for reaching this conclusion. The referencing service was involved in a commercial activity with a view to economic advantage. It involved storing as keywords signs which were identical with trade marks and arranging for the display of ads on the basis of those keywords, and it was offered to third parties without the consent of trade mark proprietors. The service provider according to the Court:

> operates 'in the course of trade' when it permits advertisers to select as keywords signs identical with trade marks, stores those signs and displays its clients' ads on the basis thereof, it does not follow, however, from those factors that that service provider itself 'uses' those signs within the terms of Article 5 of Directive 89/104 and Article 9 of Regulation No 40/94.[141]

9.153 The Court added the fact that the service provider was being paid

> by its clients for the use of those signs. The fact of creating the technical conditions necessary for the use of a sign and being paid for that service does not mean that the party offering the service itself uses the sign. To the extent to which it has permitted its client to make such a use of the sign, its role must, as necessary, be examined from the angle of rules of law other than Article 5 Directive 89/104 and Article 9 of Regulation No 40/94.[142]

9.154 *Use 'in relation to goods or services'* This requirement covered 'the affixing of a sign identical to the trade mark onto goods and the offering of the goods, the importing or exporting of the goods under the sign and the use of the sign on business papers and in advertising, constitute use in relation to the goods or services'.[143] It would be clearly satisfied when the trade marks appeared in the ads displayed under the heading 'sponsored links'.

9.155 The Court, however, noted that the list was not exhaustive,[144] holding that in cases where the trade mark used as a keyword does not appear on the screen courts should not automatically assume that use to fall outside the scope of the provision. Following a comparative advertising rationale,[145] but without fully accepting that this was a case of comparative advertising, the Court held that in the situation, 'characterised by the fact that a sign identical with a trade mark is selected as a keyword by a competitor of the proprietor of the mark with the aim of

---

[141] Paragraph 55.
[142] Paragraph 57.
[143] Paragraph 61.
[144] Citing amongst other cases C-228/03 *Gillette* [2005] ECR I-2337, paragraph 28.
[145] Citing *O2 Holdings* [2008] ECR I-4231, paragraphs 35, 36, and 42.

offering internet users an alternative to the goods or services of that proprietor, there is a use of that sign in relation to the goods or services of that competitor'.[146] The Court added that the same principle applied in cases where the advertiser tried to mislead Internet users as to the origin of its goods or services linking them with the trade mark proprietor.

9.156 *Use liable to have an adverse effect on the functions of the trade mark* The requirement here is that use must cause detriment to any of the functions of the trade mark that include the essential function of the trade mark to guarantee origin, and its other functions, 'in particular that of guaranteeing the quality of the goods or services in question and those of communication, investment or advertising'.[147] In this case, the relevant functions were the function of indicating origin and the function of advertising.

9.157 *The origin function* The effect on the origin indication function depended on the content of the advertisement and the manner, according to the Court, in which the advertisement is presented. Here the Court appeared to adapt the likelihood of confusion test in two ways: first by altering the perspective from which the assessment is made, and second by presenting what is required to be proven in a negative way:

> The function of indicating the origin of the mark is adversely affected if the ad does not enable normally informed and reasonably attentive internet users, or enables them only with difficulty, to ascertain whether the goods or services referred to by the ad originate from the proprietor of the trade mark or an undertaking economically connected to it or, on the contrary, originate from a third party.[148]

The Court chose to cite *Céline*,[149] perhaps indicating that it perceived the Internet as an alternative high street with trade marks and trade names competing to capture the attention of the consumer.

9.158 Turning to the factual context of the case to support the argument and noting that transparency in advertising is promoted as a concept in Europe, the Court added that:

> [i]n such a situation, which is, moreover, characterised by the fact that the ad in question appears immediately after entry of the trade mark as a search term by the internet user concerned and is displayed at a point when the trade mark is, in its capacity as a search term, also displayed on the screen, the internet user may err as to the origin of the goods or services in question. In those circumstances, the use by the third party of the sign identical with the mark as a keyword triggering the display of that ad is liable to create the impression that there is a material link in the course of trade between the goods or services in question and the proprietor of the trade mark.[150]

9.159 Following this, the Court appeared to tinker with the definition of the essential function of the trade mark in the Internet environment:

> [A]lthough it thus proves to be the case that advertisers on the internet can, as appropriate, be made liable under rules governing other areas of law, such as the rules on unfair competition, the fact nonetheless remains that the allegedly unlawful use on the internet of signs identical with, or similar to, trade marks lends itself to examination from the perspective of

---

[146] Paragraph 69.
[147] Paragraph 77, citing *L'Oréal* [2009] ECR I-05185, paragraph 58.
[148] Paragraph 84.
[149] *Céline*, paragraph 27 and the case law cited therein.
[150] Paragraph 85.

trade-mark law. Having regard to the essential function of a trade mark, which, in the area of electronic commerce, consists in particular in enabling internet users browsing the ads displayed in response to a search relating to a specific trade mark to distinguish the goods or services of the proprietor of that mark from those which have a different origin, that proprietor must be entitled to prohibit the display of third-party ads which internet users may erroneously perceive as emanating from that proprietor.[151]

9.160 The Court then went further to capture cases where the advertising message appears to be unclear:

where the ad, while not suggesting the existence of an economic link, is vague to such an extent on the origin of the goods or services at issue that normally informed and reasonably attentive internet users are unable to determine, on the basis of the advertising link and the commercial message attached thereto, whether the advertiser is a third party vis-à-vis the proprietor of the trade mark or, on the contrary, economically linked to that proprietor, the conclusion must also be that there is an adverse effect on that function of the trade mark.[152]

9.161 *The advertising function* This would cover cases where use 'adversely affects the proprietor's use of its mark as a factor in sales promotion or as an instrument of commercial strategy'.[153]

9.162 The Court accepted that the nature of keyword advertising required trade mark proprietors to pay the service provider in order to use their own trade marks as keywords. This however was seen as part of the advertising game that does not in itself affect the advertising function of a trade mark.

9.163 The Court also noted that the sponsored ads appeared next to the lists of natural results following the entry of a trade mark as a keyword. The order there was determined by relevance rather than payment of a fee and usually the link to the trade mark proprietor would appear at the top of that list, guaranteeing the visibility of the trade mark proprietor. This meant that the advertising function would not be negatively affected.

9.164 *The Second Question—Article 5(2) of the Directive and Article 9(1)(c) of the Regulation* Here again the Court distinguished between service provider and advertiser. Following its findings in the previous question it was clear that the service provider did not use the trade mark in the course of trade. Advertisers on the other hand could be found to be liable.

The Court has already held, in the case of offers of imitations for sale, that, where a third party attempts, through the use of a sign which is identical with, or similar to, a reputable mark, to ride on the coat-tails of that mark in order to benefit from its power of attraction, its reputation and its prestige, and to exploit, without paying any financial compensation and without being required to make efforts of its own in that regard, the marketing effort expended by the proprietor of that mark in order to create and maintain the image of that mark, the advantage resulting from such use must be considered to be an advantage that has been unfairly taken of the distinctive character or the repute of that mark.[154]

9.165 (ii) **The liability of the service provider** The Court found the service provider to be an intermediary service provider under Directive 2000/31. The exemption from liability covered cases where the referencing service provider played a neutral role 'in the sense that

---

[151] Paragraph 87.
[152] Paragraph 90.
[153] Paragraph 92.
[154] Paragraph 102, citing *L'Oréal and Others* [2009] ECR I-05185, paragraph 49.

its conduct is merely technical, automatic and passive, pointing to a lack of knowledge or control of the data which it stores'.[155]

9.166 According to the facts of the case, the role of the service provider was neutral. Google processed the data entered by advertisers and the advertisements were presented according to an order controlled by Google. The fact the order was determined according to payments received form the advertisers was not considered to be relevant. 'Likewise, concordance between the keyword selected and the search term entered by an internet user is not sufficient of itself to justify the view that Google has knowledge of, or control over, the data entered into its system by advertisers and stored in memory on its server.'[156]

9.167 To the contrary, what would be relevant—and this had to be determined by the national court—was 'the role played by Google in the drafting of the commercial message which accompanies the advertising link or in the establishment or selection of keywords'.[157]

9.168 The Court concluded with the following ruling:

1. Article 5(1)(a) of First Council Directive 89/104/EEC of 21 December 1988 to approximate the laws of the Member States relating to trade marks and Article 9(1)(a) of Council Regulation (EC) No 40/94 of 20 December 1993 on the Community trade mark must be interpreted as meaning that the proprietor of a trade mark is entitled to prohibit an advertiser from advertising, on the basis of a keyword identical with that trade mark which that advertiser has, without the consent of the proprietor, selected in connection with an internet referencing service, goods or services identical with those for which that mark is registered, in the case where that advertisement does not enable an average internet user, or enables that user only with difficulty, to ascertain whether the goods or services referred to therein originate from the proprietor of the trade mark or an undertaking economically connected to it or, on the contrary, originate from a third party.
2. An internet referencing service provider which stores, as a keyword, a sign identical with a trade mark and organises the display of advertisements on the basis of that keyword does not use that sign within the meaning of Article 5(1) and (2) of Directive 89/104 or of Article 9(1) of Regulation No 40/94.
3. Article 14 of Directive 2000/31/EC of the European Parliament and of the Council of 8 June 2000 on certain legal aspects of information society services, in particular electronic commerce, in the Internal Market ('Directive on electronic commerce') must be interpreted as meaning that the rule laid down therein applies to an internet referencing service provider in the case where that service provider has not played an active role of such a kind as to give it knowledge of, or control over, the data stored. If it has not played such a role, that service provider cannot be held liable for the data which it has stored at the request of an advertiser, unless, having obtained knowledge of the unlawful nature of those data or of that advertiser's activities, it failed to act expeditiously to remove or to disable access to the data concerned.[158]

(4) *Eis.de*: Repeating the Google Principles

9.169 In Eis.de GmbH,[159] the Bundesgerichtshof (Germany) asked again whether the AdWords use constituted use of a trade mark under Article 5 of the Directive. The Court noted that this was the first question it had addressed in Google France and repeated its findings.

---

[155] Paragraph 114.
[156] Paragraph 117.
[157] Paragraph 118.
[158] Paragraph 121.
[159] C-91/09 *Eis.de GmbH v BBY Vertriebsgesellschaft mbH* [2010] ECR I-00043.

(5) *BergSpechte*: Keywords Similar to Trade Mark; Extending the *Google* Principles

9.170 In *BergSpechte*,[160] a reference from the Oberster Gerichtshof (Austria) Court considered first whether the *Google France* principles covered use as keywords of words similar as well as identical to a protected trade mark. The Court reiterated these principles and stated that should the

> rule set out in Article 5(1)(b) of Directive 89/104 be applicable to the dispute in the main proceedings, it will be for the national court to hold whether there is a likelihood of confusion when internet users are shown, on the basis of a keyword similar to a mark, a third party's ad which does not enable normally informed and reasonably attentive internet users, or enable them only with difficulty, to ascertain whether the goods or services referred to by the ad originate from the proprietor of the trade mark or an undertaking economically connected to it or, on the contrary, originate from a third party.[161]

9.171 Note that the Court declined to answer the speculative question of whether the scope of protection could be different depending on whether the advertisement of a third party displayed on the basis of a keyword identical with or similar to a trade mark appeared as a 'sponsored link' or elsewhere because it did not correspond to the factual context of the case.

(6) *Portakabin*: Keywords Reproducing Misspelt Trade Marks; Original/Reconditioned Goods; Extending the *Google* Principles Further

9.172 *Portakabin*[162] applied the same principles in a case that concerned keywords that reproduced a trade mark with 'minor spelling mistakes' in relation to goods placed on the market by the proprietor of the trade mark; for example, advertising the sale of second-hand goods. The case involved a dispute between Portakabin, a manufacturer and supplier of mobile buildings, and the proprietor of the Benelux trade mark PORTAKABIN.com, and Primakabin, a company selling and leasing new and second-hand mobile buildings, including used units manufactured by Portakabin.

(a) Original and competing goods

9.173 The Court first accepted that, according to the principles established in *Google France*, the sign selected by an advertiser as a keyword for an internet referencing service is the means used to trigger its ad display and is therefore used 'in the course of trade'; it added that this

> also constitutes a use in relation to the goods and services of the advertiser ... That finding is not invalidated by the fact ... that the sign which is identical to the mark—in the present case, the sign 'portakabin'—is used not only in relation to the goods under that mark—that is to say, for the resale of units manufactured by Portakabin—but also for goods from other manufacturers, such as, in this instance, units manufactured by Primakabin or by other competitors of Portakabin. On the contrary, use by an advertiser of a sign, which is identical with another person's trade mark, to suggest to internet users an alternative to the offer from the proprietor of that mark, is use 'in relation to goods and services'.[163]

---

[160] C-278/08 *Die BergSpechte Outdoor Reisen und Alpinschule Edi Koblmüller GmbH v Günter Guni, trekking.at Reisen GmbH* [2010] ECR I-02517.
[161] Paragraph 39.
[162] C-558/08 *Portakabin Ltd, Portakabin BV v Primakabin BV* [2010] ECR I-06963.
[163] Paragraph 28.

(b) Misspelt trade marks

9.174 The Court added that whether the goods or services referred to in the ad were actually offered for sale in the wording of the ad or on the advertiser's website also referred to in the ad did not affect the approach the national Court should follow. Regarding the use of signs with 'minor spelling mistakes', like 'portacabin', 'portokabin', and 'portocabin', the Court noted that they should be considered as being either identical, in the case of insignificant differences that would go unnoticed,[164] or similar, in which case Article 5(1)(b) should be applied.

(c) Article 6 defences

9.175 The Court then turned to the applicability of Article 6(1)(b) and (c) of the Directive. This, it stressed, had to be assessed and determined by the national court according to the factual context of each case. In relation to Article 6(1)(c) in particular it underlined that its scope extends beyond the case of accessories and spare parts.[165]

> The situations coming within the scope of Article 6(1)(c) must, however, be limited to those which correspond to the objective of that provision. However ... the objective of Article 6(1)(c) ... is to enable providers of goods or services, which are supplementary to the goods or services offered by a trade mark proprietor, to use that mark in order to inform the public of the practical link between their goods or services and those of the proprietor of the mark.[166]

9.176 Elaborating further on this, the Court added that there is also a duty

> to act fairly in relation to the legitimate interests of the trade mark proprietor. The issue of whether that condition has been satisfied must be assessed by, inter alia, taking account of the extent to which the use by the third party is understood by the relevant public, or at least by a significant section of that public, as establishing a link between the third party's goods and those of the trade mark proprietor or a person authorised to use the trade mark, and of the extent to which the third party ought to have been aware of that.[167]

(d) The parameters of the new test

9.177 Against the context of keyword advertising the Court repeated that use by an advertiser of a sign identical with, or similar to, a trade mark for an Internet referencing service comes within Article 5(1) where that use does not enable normally informed and reasonably attentive Internet users, or enables them only with difficulty, to ascertain whether the goods or services referred to by the ad originate from the trade mark proprietor or from an undertaking economically linked to it or, on the contrary, originate from a third party.

> Thus, the circumstances under which a trade mark proprietor is, pursuant to Article 5(1) ... , entitled to prevent an advertiser from using a sign identical with, or similar to, that trade mark as a keyword may ... easily correspond to a situation in which the advertiser cannot claim that it is acting in accordance with honest practices in industrial or commercial matters, and cannot therefore validly rely on the exception provided for in Article 6(1).[168]

9.178 Accordingly,

> it must be held, first, that one of the characteristics of the situation referred to [above] ... lies precisely in the fact that the ad is likely to cause at least a significant section of the target

---

[164] Citing C-291/00 *LTJ Diffusion* [2003] ECR I-2799.
[165] Citing C-228/03 *Gillette* [2005] ECR I-2337.
[166] Paragraph 64.
[167] Paragraph 67, citing C-245/02 *Anheuser-Busch* [2004] ECR I-10989 and C--17/06 *Céline* [2007] ECR I-7041.
[168] Paragraph 69.

public to establish a link between the goods or services to which it refers and the goods or services of the trade mark proprietor or persons authorized to use that trade mark. Second, in the event that the national court finds that the ad does not enable average internet users, or enables them only with difficulty, to ascertain whether the goods or services referred to by the ad originate from the trade mark proprietor or from a third party, it is unlikely that the advertiser can genuinely claim not to have been aware of the ambiguity thus caused by its ad. It is the advertiser itself, in the context of its professional strategy and with full knowledge of the economic sector in which it operates, which chose a keyword corresponding to another person's trade mark and which, alone or with the assistance of the referencing service provider, designed the ad and therefore decided how it should be presented.[169]

Summing up, the Court held that **9.179**

where use by advertisers of signs identical with, or similar to, trade marks as keywords for an internet referencing service is liable to be prohibited pursuant to Article 5 ... those advertisers cannot, in general, rely on the exception provided for in Article 6(1) in order to avoid such a prohibition. It is, however, for the national court to determine, in the light of the particular circumstances of the case, whether or not there was, in fact, a use, within the terms of Article 6(1), which could be regarded as having been made in accordance with honest practices in industrial or commercial matters.[170]

(e) Article 7: Exhaustion considerations

The fact that Primakabin's advertising also referred to the resale of used goods from Portakabin raised a number of exhaustion of rights issues. Having covered the basic exhaustion concepts, the Court held that **9.180**

a trade mark proprietor is not entitled to prohibit an advertiser from advertising, on the basis of a keyword identical with, or similar to, that trade mark, which the advertiser has chosen for an internet referencing service without the consent of the proprietor, the resale of second-hand goods originally placed on the market in the EEA under that trade mark by the proprietor or with his consent, unless there are legitimate reasons, within the meaning of Article 7(2) ... which would justify that proprietor's opposition to such advertising.[171]

Again, the Court embedded its position on keyword advertising against its relevant jurisprudence on exhaustion.[172] **9.181**

The fact that the reseller, through its advertising based on a sign identical with, or similar to, the trade mark, gives the impression that there is a commercial connection between the reseller and the trade mark proprietor, and in particular that the reseller's business is affiliated to the proprietor's distribution network or that there is a special relationship between the two undertakings, also constitutes a legitimate reason within the meaning of Article 7(2) ... Advertising which is liable to give such an impression is not essential to the further commercialisation of goods placed on the market under the trade mark by its proprietor or with his consent or, therefore, to the purpose of the exhaustion rule laid down in Article 7.[173]

---

[169] Paragraph 70.
[170] Paragraph 72.
[171] Paragraph 78.
[172] Citing *Parfums Christian Dior* [1997] ECR I-6013, *BMW* [1999] ECR I-905, and C-348/04 *Boehringer Ingelheim and Others* [2007] ECR I-3391.
[173] Paragraph 80.

9.182 Taking into account the market context behind the sale of second-hand goods, the Court noted that three aspects had to be considered:

> first, the interest of economic operators and consumers that the sales of second-hand goods via the internet should not be unduly restricted; second, the need for clear information as to the origin of such goods; and, third, the fact that Primakabin's ad, referring to 'used portakabins', led internet users not only to offers for the resale of goods manufactured by Portakabin, but also to offers for the resale of goods from other manufacturers.[174]

9.183 It noted that the sale of second-hand goods under a trade mark is a well-established form of business understood by consumers, hence when an advertiser uses a third party's trade mark combined with adequate additional wording to indicate that the goods are resold it cannot be argued that the ad creates the impression that the reseller and the trade mark proprietor are economically linked or that the ad is seriously detrimental to the reputation of that mark.

9.184 Regarding the second aspect, the Court noted that where the reseller

> without the consent of a trade mark proprietor, removes that trade mark from the goods ('de-branding') and replaces it with a label bearing the reseller's name, with the result that the trade mark of the manufacturer of the goods in question is entirely concealed, the trade mark proprietor is entitled to prevent the reseller from using that mark to advertise that resale. In such a case, damage is caused to the essential function of the trade mark, which is to indicate and guarantee the origin of the goods, and the consumer is prevented from distinguishing the goods originating from the proprietor and those originating from the reseller or other third parties.[175]

9.185 Finally, on the third and potentially more controversial aspect, it noted that

> the mere fact that a reseller derives an advantage from using another person's trade mark insofar as advertisements for the sale of goods covered by the mark, which are in other respects honest and fair, lend an aura of quality to his own business does not constitute a legitimate reason within the meaning of Article 7(2).[176]

Going further it added that where a reseller specializes in the resale of goods bearing a third party's trade mark the reseller cannot be prohibited from using that mark in order to advertise the resale activity that includes:

> apart from the sale of second-hand goods under that mark—the sale of other second-hand goods, unless the resale of those other goods risks, in the light of their volume, their presentation or their poor quality, seriously damaging the image which the proprietor has succeeded in creating for its mark.[177]

In its conclusion the Court went further to hold that in order to fall against the 'legitimate reason' hurdle in terms of harm to reputation the ad must be seriously detrimental to the reputation of that mark.

---

[174] Paragraph 83.
[175] Citing C-349/95 *Loendersloot* [1997] ECR I-6227.
[176] Citing *BMW* [1999] ECR I-905.
[177] Paragraph 91.

(7) *L'Oréal v eBay*: Keywords and Electronic Market Platforms

(a) *The facts in the main proceedings and the order for reference*

9.186 *L'Oréal v eBay*[178] revisited some of the issues raised in *Google France*,[179] this time from the perspective of electronic commerce. L'Oréal maintained that counterfeits and products not authorized for sale in the EU were finding their way on to eBay's online marketplace; some of the products were sold outside their original packaging. L'Oréal complained about the use of its own marks as keywords advertising eBay as a marketplace and activity taking place at the marketplace. Some of the perfumes were counterfeits, others were not intended for sale (such as tester or dramming products), and others were intended for sale in North America and not in the European Economic Area (EEA).

9.187 Advocate General Jääskinen set the parameters:

> The main challenge for the Court lies in the double-balancing act the Court is called to undertake. Not only is the Court requested by the national court to give an interpretation of the EU law provisions in this challenging setting, but it should at the same time ensure that the interpretation given of the instruments in question would remain applicable in settings with different parameters. The trade marks in question are well known and the products are luxury products but the applicable EU law provisions do apply to all trade marks and all kinds of goods. Electronic marketplace is global and it has many specific features. While the replies given should take into account the specificities of the case before the national court, they should, at the same time, be based on a global view on how this system should function in general. In my view, this case is more complicated than *Google France and Google* in many aspects.[180]

9.188 Later on in his Opinion he stressed that the Court had to strike a balance between the rights of trade mark proprietors, the rights of consumers, and the rights of online market operator:

> Electronic marketplaces like eBay have created unprecedented opportunities both for businesses and private persons to trade directly with each other with reduced risks relating to delivery and payment. The main proceedings as well as similar litigation in other Member States and third country jurisdictions show that these opportunities can be abused ... and result in copyright and trade mark infringements ... Therefore it is legitimate to ensure that effective legal protection is available to holders of intellectual property rights also in these new environments. Nevertheless, such protection may not infringe the rights of the users and providers of these services.[181]

9.189 In his review of the dispute, the Advocate General identified the following relevant factors:

> both sellers and purchasers had to register themselves with eBay and accept eBay's user agreement;
>
> selling counterfeit products or infringing a trade mark was a breach of the agreement;
>
> eBay had adopted bidding as the primary operating system but also provided for sales without an auction at fixed prices; sellers could create 'online shops' listing all the available for sale products;

---

[178] Case C-324/09 *L'Oréal SA, Lancôme parfums et beauté & Cie, Laboratoire Garnier & Cie, L'Oréal (UK) Limited v eBay International AG, eBay Europe SARL, eBay (UK) Limited* [2011] ECR I-06011.
[179] *Google France* [2010] ECR I-02417.
[180] Point 5.
[181] Point 50.

- sellers were awarded by eBay a 'Power Seller' status based on performance;
- eBay provided 'detailed assistance to sellers in categorising and describing the items they offer for sale, in creating their own on-line shops and in promoting and increasing sales'. eBay thus organises the sale, conducts the auction (including the making of proxy bids), provides a watching service to notify members of items in which they are interested, and promotes and advertises goods through third party websites;[182]
- however, eBay did not act as an agent for the sellers of the goods and was not in any way in possession of the goods;
- eBay had adopted mechanisms to identify breaches of its policies;
- it also operated a 'VeRO' (Verified Rights Owner) programme, in essence a take-down system targeting sellers engaged in intellectual property rights infringement.

9.190 The High Court sent a large number of detailed questions to the Court of Justice.

(1) Where perfume and cosmetic testers (i.e. samples for use in demonstrating products to consumers in retail outlets) and dramming bottles (i.e. containers from which small aliquots can be taken for supply to consumers as free samples) which are not intended for sale to consumers (and are often marked 'not for sale' or 'not for individual sale') are supplied without charge to the trade mark proprietor's authorised distributors, are such goods 'put on the market' within the meaning of Article 7(1) of [Directive 89/104] and Article 13(1) of [Regulation No 40/94]?

(2) Where the boxes (or other outer packaging) have been removed from perfumes and cosmetics without the consent of the trade mark proprietor, does this constitute a 'legitimate reason' for the trade mark proprietor to oppose further commercialisation of the unboxed products within the meaning of Article 7(2) of [Directive 89/104] and Article 13(2) of [Regulation No 40/94]?

(3) Does it make a difference to the answer to question 2 above if:
   (a) as a result of the removal of the boxes (or other outer packaging), the unboxed products do not bear the information required by Article 6(1) of [Directive 76/768], and in particular do not bear a list of ingredients or a 'best before date'?
   (b) as a result of the absence of such information, the offer for sale or sale of the unboxed products constitutes a criminal offence according to the law of the Member State of the Community in which they are offered for sale or sold by third parties?

(4) Does it make a difference to the answer to question 2 above if the further commercialisation damages, or is likely to damage, the image of the goods and hence the reputation of the trade mark? If so, is that effect to be presumed, or is it required to be proved by the trade mark proprietor?

(5) Where a trader which operates an online marketplace purchases the use of a sign which is identical to a registered trade mark as a keyword from a search engine operator so that the sign is displayed to a user by the search engine in a sponsored link to the website of the operator of the online marketplace, does the display of the sign in the sponsored link constitute 'use' of the sign within the meaning of Article 5(1)(a) of [Directive 89/104] and Article 9(1)(a) of [Regulation No 40/94]?

(6) Where clicking on the sponsored link referred to in question 5 above leads the user directly to advertisements or offers for sale of goods identical to those for which the trade mark is registered under the sign placed on the website by other parties, some of which infringe the trade mark and some [of] which do not infringe the trade mark by virtue of the differing statuses of the respective goods, does that constitute use of the sign by the operator of the online marketplace 'in relation to' the infringing goods within the meaning of 5(1)(a) of [Directive 89/104] and Article 9(1)(a) of [Regulation No 40/94]?

---

[182] Point 27.

(7) Where the goods advertised and offered for sale on the website referred to in question 6 above include goods which have not been put on the market within the EEA by or with the consent of the trade mark proprietor, is it sufficient for such use to fall within the scope of Article 5(1)(a) of [Directive 89/104] and Article 9(1)(a) of [Regulation No 40/94] and outside Article 7(1) of [Directive 89/104] and Article 13(1) of [Regulation No 40/94] that the advertisement or offer for sale is targeted at consumers in the territory covered by the trade mark or must the trade mark proprietor show that the advertisement or offer for sale necessarily entails putting the goods in question on the market within the territory covered by the trade mark?

(8) Does it make any difference to the answers to questions 5 to 7 above if the use complained of by the trade mark proprietor consists of the display of the sign on the web site of the operator of the online marketplace itself rather than in a sponsored link?

(9) If it is sufficient for such use to fall within the scope of Article 5(1)(a) of [Directive 89/104] and Article 9(1)(a) of [Regulation No 40/94] and outside Article 7 ... of [Directive 89/104] and Article 13 ... of [Regulation No 40/94] that the advertisement or offer for sale is targeted at consumers in the territory covered by the trade mark:
  (a) does such use consist of or include 'the storage of information provided by a recipient of the service' within the meaning of Article 14(1) of [Directive 2000/31]?
  (b) if the use does not consist exclusively of activities falling within the scope of Article 14(1) of [Directive 2000/31], but includes such activities, is the operator of the online marketplace exempted from liability to the extent that the use consists of such activities and if so may damages or other financial remedies be granted in respect of such use to the extent that it is not exempted from liability?
  (c) in circumstances where the operator of the online marketplace has knowledge that goods have been advertised, offered for sale and sold on its website in infringement of registered trade marks, and that infringements of such registered trade marks are likely to continue to occur through the advertisement, offer for sale and sale of the same or similar goods by the same or different users of the website, does this constitute 'actual knowledge' or 'awareness' within the meaning of Article 14(1) of [Directive 2000/31]?

(10) Where the services of an intermediary such as an operator of a website have been used by a third party to infringe a registered trade mark, does Article 11 of [Directive 2004/48] require Member States to ensure that the trade mark proprietor can obtain an injunction against the intermediary to prevent further infringements of the said trade mark, as opposed to continuation of that specific act of infringement, and if so what is the scope of the injunction that shall be made available?[183]

(b) The Opinion of Advocate General Jääskinen

Advocate General Jääskinen structured his Opinion on the basis of a thematic analysis. **9.191**

(i) Testers and dramming bottles Citing the Court's jurisprudence in *Coty Prestige Lancaster Group*,[184] he supported that given that the testers and dramming bottles were supplied without charge to authorized distributors, were not intended for sale, and were marked 'not for sale' or 'not for individual sale', this should not be understood as the items having been put on the market in the first place. **9.192**

(ii) Unboxing cosmetic products This was a novel issue to be considered by the Court. Advocate General Jääskinen suggested that following the jurisprudence developed in *Boehringer Ingelheim*,[185] Article 7(2) of Directive 89/104 exhaustion was the main, general **9.193**

---

[183] Reproduced in paragraph 50.
[184] C-127/09 [2010] ECR I-04965.
[185] [2007] ECR I-3391.

rule. 'Consequently the possibility for the trade mark proprietor to oppose further commercialisation of his goods after he has already realized the economical value inherent in the trade mark in relation to those goods must be interpreted narrowly.'[186] In the case of cosmetic products there was no blanket interpretation that could be applied. The existence of legitimate reasons had to analysed according to the factual context of each individual case.

9.194 Also taking into account Directive 76/768 on cosmetic products, he suggested that

> the effect of further commercialisation can be presumed as actually or potentially damaging the image of the goods and hence the reputation of the trade mark in all cases where the offers for sale or the sales transactions concerning cosmetic products stripped of their original packages take place in the course of trade as defined by the case-law of the Court. It follows from this that the trade mark proprietor does not have to show it, but the burden of showing the opposite lies with the seller.[187]

He added that selling cosmetic products in numbers greater than one or two items on an electronic marketplace should be seen as part of commercial activity.

9.195 **(iii) Paid Internet referencing service from the perspective of the operator of an electronic marketplace** The Advocate General relied on the jurisprudence of the Court in *Google France*.[188] eBay was an information society service provider providing an electronic marketplace rather than a paid referencing service. eBay was using keyword advertising but was not itself offering any goods for sale. Reviewing the applicability of the conditions developed by the Court in *Google France* the Advocate General supported the argument that

> a party who is in the position of an intermediary or a marketplace operator also uses a sign 'in relation to goods' if he uses a sign which is identical with a trademark for the purpose of distinguishing between goods that are available through the use of his services and those that are not.[189]

This would also cover use by 'electronic marketplaces offering an alternative source of the same goods covered by the trade mark with respect to the distribution network of the trade mark proprietor'.[190]

9.196 As to whether use would adversely affect the functions of a trade mark, he started with the origin function and underlined that it constituted a question of fact

> to be assessed by the national court whether the nature of activities of some electronic marketplaces like eBay is generally so well known that impairment of the origin function is not likely even if the nature of the operator of the marketplace is not explained in the ad[191] ... in the case of unpackaged or non-EEA goods the origin function cannot be affected. These are genuine L'Oréal goods irrespective of whether their offer for sale infringes L'Oréal's trade mark or not. Regarding counterfeit goods the evaluation is the opposite.[192]

However, following the logic of *Google France*, the adverse effect would be the result of the use by the users of the marketplace as part of the 'listing displayed on the electronic marketplace operator's webpage'.[193] In terms of the other functions,

---

[186] Point 73.
[187] Point 81.
[188] [2010] ECR I-02417.
[189] Point 100.
[190] Point 102.
[191] Point 109.
[192] Point 110.
[193] Point 111.

if the nature of an operator as a marketplace is sufficiently clearly communicated in the ad displayed with the search results of an internet search engine, the fact that some users of that marketplace may infringe a trade mark is as such not liable to have an adverse effect on the functions of quality, communication and investment of that trade mark.[194]

(iv) The cross-territorial reach of the Internet The Advocate General opted for a qualified version of the effects doctrine. He accepted that acts committed outside the EU can be covered if they have an effect in the EU. However, in the context of the Internet this had to be qualified, otherwise intellectual property rights would gain unreasonably wide protection. The real issue should be whether the activity targeted consumers in the EU. Seeking guidance from the World Intellectual Property Organization (WIPO) Joint Recommendation of 2001 Concerning Provisions on the Protection of Marks and other Industrial Property Rights in Signs on the Internet,[195] he suggested that use should have commercial effect in the relevant jurisdiction and referred to the multifactorial test suggested therein. 9.197

(v) Liability of the service provider under Directive 200/31 He then considered the liability of the service provider under Directive 2000/3. The aim of the directive was to facilitate the free movement of information society services within the internal market. It has a wide scope of application in terms of areas of law it affects but only targets specific issues; 'the harmonisation it foresees is at the same time horizontal and specific'.[196] Operators of online marketplaces should be seen as information society services. Interestingly, he viewed the provisions on liability as restatements or clarifications of existing law rather than exceptions since in many cases liability would be excluded because of the lack of subjective fault. The role of operators, along the lines of *Google France* and with users uploading lists, brought them within the scope of the Directive despite their involvement in the advertising process. The Advocate General highlighted that neutrality was perhaps not the appropriate term to describe what was required for the Directive to apply; he noted that 9.198

> Articles 12, 13 and 14 of Directive 2000/31 ... intend to create exceptions to certain *types of activity* exercised by a service provider. To my understanding, it is inconceivable to think that they would purport to exempt a *service provider type* as such.[197]

Thus, the service provider should be exempted only for the activities covered by the provisions.

As to operators' duties in relation to future infringements, he balanced expeditious removal of infringing material with the principle of freedom of speech at the national level. A similar balancing exercise should be applied in the case of injunctions against intermediaries. 9.199

> The basic challenge in the interpretation of Directive 2004/48 relates to the balancing between too aggressive and too lax enforcement of intellectual property rights. This task has been compared to Odysseus' journey between the two monsters of Scylla and Charybdis.[198]

---

[194] Point 118.
[195] <http://www.wipo.int/edocs/pubdocs/en/marks/845/pub845.pdf>.
[196] Point 132.
[197] Point 147.
[198] Point 171.

The justification for, and at the same time the distinction from, an injunction against the direct infringer, was linked with the workings of an online marketplace; it is meant to cover cases where the

> infringement is obvious but the infringer is not identified. It is known that a third party is using the services of an intermediary to infringe an intellectual property right but the true identity of that infringer remains unknown. In such cases the legal protection of the rightsholder may require that an injunction can be obtained against the intermediary whose identity is known and who thus can be brought to a court and who is able to prevent continuation of the infringement.[199]

Hence efficacy, dissuasiveness, and proportionality should be the underlying reasoning of the injunction.

9.200 Concluding, he suggested the following response:

(1) Where perfume and cosmetic testers and dramming bottles which are not intended for sale to consumers are supplied without charge to the trade mark proprietor's authorised distributors, such goods are not put on the market within the meaning of Article 7(1) of First Council Directive 89/104/EEC of 21 December 1988 to approximate the laws of the Member States relating to trade marks and Article 13(1) of Council Regulation (EC) No 40/94 of 20 December 1993 on the Community trade mark.

(2), (3) and (4) The trade mark proprietor is entitled to oppose further commercialisation of the unboxed products within the meaning of Article 7(2) of Directive 89/104 and Article 13(2) of Regulation No 40/94 where the outer packaging have been removed from perfumes and cosmetics without the consent of the trade mark proprietor if, as a result of the removal of the outer packaging, the products do not bear the information required by Article 6(1) of Council Directive 76/768/EEC of 27 July 1976 on the approximation of the laws of the Member States relating to cosmetic products, or if the removal of outer packaging can be considered as such as changing or impairing the condition of the goods or if the further commercialisation damages, or is likely to damage, the image of the goods and therefore the reputation of the trade mark. Under the circumstances of the main proceedings that effect is to be presumed unless the offer concerns a single item or few items offered by a seller clearly not acting in the course of trade.

(5) Where a trader operating an electronic marketplace purchases the use of a sign which is identical to a registered trade mark as a keyword from a search engine operator so that the sign is displayed to a user by the search engine in a sponsored link to the website of the operator of the electronic marketplace, the display of the sign in the sponsored link constitutes 'use' of the sign within the meaning of Article 5(1)(a) of Directive 89/104 and Article 9(1)(a) of Regulation No 40/94.

(6) Where clicking on the sponsored link referred to in point 5 above leads the user directly to advertisements or offers for sale of goods identical to those for which the trade mark is registered under the sign placed on the website by other parties, some of which infringe the trade mark and some which do not infringe the trade mark by virtue of the differing statuses of the respective goods, that fact constitutes use of the sign by the operator of the electronic marketplace 'in relation to' the infringing goods within the meaning of Article 5(1)(a) of Directive 89/104 and Article 9(1)(a) of Regulation No 40/94, but it does not have an adverse effect on the functions of the trade mark provided that a reasonable average consumer understands on the basis of information included in the sponsored link that the operator of the electronic marketplace stores in his system advertisements or offers for sale of third parties.

---

[199] Point 179.

(7) Where the goods offered for sale on the electronic marketplace have not yet been put on the market within the EEA by or with the consent of the trade mark proprietor, it is none the less sufficient for the exclusive right conferred by the national or Community trade mark to apply to show that the advertisement is targeted at consumers within the territory covered by the trade mark.

(8) If the use complained of by the trade mark proprietor consists of the display of the sign on the website of the operator of the electronic marketplace itself rather than in a sponsored link on the website of a search engine operator, the sign is not used by the operator of the electronic marketplace 'in relation to' the infringing goods within the meaning of Article 5(1)(a) of Directive 89/104 and Article 9(1)(a) of Regulation No 40/94.

(9) (a) The use referred to in point 5 does not consist of or include 'the storage of information provided by a recipient of the service' by the electronic marketplace operator within the meaning of Article 14(1) of Directive 2000/31/EC of the European Parliament and of the Council of 8 June 2000 on certain legal aspects of information society services, in particular electronic commerce, in the Internal Market, whereas the use referred to in point 6 may consist of or include such storage.

(9) (b) Where the use does not consist exclusively of activities falling within the scope of Article 14(1) of Directive 2000/31, but includes such activities, the operator of the electronic marketplace is exempted from liability to the extent that the use consists of such activities, but damages or other financial remedies may be granted pursuant to national law in respect of such use to the extent that it is not exempted from liability.

(9) (c) There is 'actual knowledge' of illegal activity or information or 'awareness' of facts or circumstances within the meaning of Article 14(1) of Directive 2000/31 where the operator of the electronic marketplace has knowledge that goods have been advertised, offered for sale and sold on its website in infringement of a registered trade mark, and that infringements of that registered trade mark are likely to continue regarding the same or similar goods by the same user of the website.

(10) Where the services of an intermediary such as an operator of a website have been used by a third party to infringe a registered trade mark, Article 11 of Directive 2004/48/EC of the European Parliament and of the Council of 29 April 2004 on the enforcement of intellectual property rights requires Member States to ensure that the trade mark proprietor can obtain an effective, dissuasive and proportionate injunction against the intermediary to prevent continuation or repetition of that infringement by that third party. The conditions and procedures relating to such injunctions are defined in national law.[200]

(c) The Judgment of the Court of Justice

The Court reorganized and answered the questions thematically. 9.201

(i) Private v business sellers The Court noted that: 9.202

> the exclusive rights conferred by trade marks may, as a rule, be relied on only as against economic operators. Indeed, for the proprietor of a trade mark to be entitled to prevent a third party from using a sign identical with or similar to his trade mark, the use must take place in the course of trade.[201]

This principle brings outside the scope of protection use by an individual consumer who is reselling the product s/he bought: 'when an individual sells a product bearing a trade mark through an online marketplace and the transaction does not take place in the context of a

---

[200] Points 183–189.
[201] Paragraph 54, citing C-245/02 *Anheuser-Busch* [2004] ECR I-10989 and C-487/07 *L'Oréal and Others* [2009] ECR I-5185.

commercial activity, the proprietor of the trade mark cannot rely on his exclusive right'.[202] Albeit, this does not cover business activity that is disguised as private; '[i]f, however, owing to their volume, their frequency or other characteristics, the sales made on such a marketplace go beyond the realms of a private activity, the seller will be acting "in the course of trade" within the meaning of those provisions'.[203]

9.203 (ii) **Targeting consumers in the EU** The Court reiterated the basic exhaustion rules. Interestingly, it started by delineating the scope of the exclusive rights viewing the exhaustion rules as the exception to the rule:

> Article 7 of the directive and Article 13 of the regulation have laid down an exception to that rule, providing that the trade mark proprietor's rights are exhausted where the goods have been put on the market in the EEA—or, in the case of a Community trade mark, in the EU—by the proprietor himself or with his consent.[204]

It is essential that the proprietor of a trade mark registered in a Member State can control the 'first placing of goods bearing that trade mark on the market in the EEA'.[205]

9.204 Does the Internet challenge these fundamental principles? eBay argued that the exclusive rights should not cover cases where the goods bearing the trade mark and offered for sale on an online marketplace are located in a third State and would not necessarily be forwarded to the territory covered by the relevant trade mark. The Court, however, accepted the opposite position: 'the rules of Directive 89/104 and Regulation No 40/94 apply as soon as it is clear that the offer for sale of a trade-marked product located in a third State is targeted at consumers in the territory covered by the trade mark'.[206] Otherwise, it noted, electronic commerce operators would escape from EU intellectual property rules. This would undermine their effectiveness (*effet utile*).

9.205 The Court added that the exclusive rights cover use in offers for sale and advertising. Again, the effectiveness of those rules would be undermined if

> they were not to apply to the use, in an internet offer for sale or advertisement targeted at consumers within the EU, of a sign identical with or similar to a trade mark registered in the EU merely because the third party behind that offer or advertisement is established in a third State, because the server of the internet site used by the third party is located in such a State or because the product that is the subject of the offer or the advertisement is located in a third State.[207]

9.206 It accepted, however, that the mere fact that a website is accessible from the territory where the trade mark is protected is not sufficient for concluding that the offers for sale targeted consumers in that territory, otherwise websites and advertisements not targeting the EU but technically accessible from the EU 'would wrongly be subject to EU law'.[208] The Court

---

[202] Paragraph 55.
[203] Paragraph 55.
[204] Paragraph 59, citing C-16/03 *Peak Holding* [2004] ECR I-11313, C-324/08 *Makro Zelfbedieningsgroothandel* [2009] ECR I-10019, and C-127/09 *Coty Prestige Lancaster Group* [2010] ECR I-04965.
[205] Paragraph 60, citing Joined Cases C-414/99 to C-416/99 *Zino Davidoff and Levi Strauss* [2001] ECR I-8691.
[206] Paragraph 62.
[207] Paragraph 63.
[208] Paragraph 64.

cited by analogy its consumer protection cases.²⁰⁹ Note that in these instances the Court had indicated that the following matters, the list of which is not exhaustive, are capable of constituting evidence from which it may be concluded that the trader's activity is directed to the Member State of the consumer's domicile, namely:

> the international nature of the activity, mention of itineraries from other Member States for going to the place where the trader is established, use of a language or a currency other than the language or currency generally used in the Member State in which the trader is established with the possibility of making and confirming the reservation in that other language, mention of telephone numbers with an international code, outlay of expenditure on an internet referencing service in order to facilitate access to the trader's site or that of its intermediary by consumers domiciled in other Member States, use of a top-level domain name other than that of the Member State in which the trader is established, and mention of an international clientele composed of customers domiciled in various Member States.²¹⁰

9.207 It remained for the national court to assess the relevant factors on a case-by-case basis. For example, it would be particularly important to look at whether the offer is accompanied by details of the geographic areas to which the seller is willing to dispatch the product. In the absence of any evidence to the contrary a 'co.uk' site appears to be targeting consumers in the UK.

9.208 (iii) **Testers and dramming products** The Court then turned to the first question. Following Case C-495/07 *Silberquelle* [2009] ECR I-137, it held where items are supplied free of charge, they cannot, as a rule, be regarded as being put on the market by the trade mark proprietor. The same principle applied to items such as perfume testers with the words 'demonstration' or 'not for sale', citing *Coty Prestige Lancaster Group*.

9.209 (iv) **Unboxed goods** Questions 2 to 4 concerned whether the removal of the packaging of the goods infringes the exclusive rights, entitling the proprietor to oppose their resale. The Court accepted that these questions would have to be answered also in light of Article 6(1) of Directive 76/768, under which cosmetic products may be marketed only if the container and packaging mention, inter alia, the identity of the manufacturer or the person responsible for marketing the product, the composition of the product (content and list of ingredients), the use of the product (function and particular precautions to be observed in use), and preservation of the product (date of minimum durability). Stressing the interrelation between different streams of legislation the Court noted that the national court

> seeks, in essence, to ascertain whether the proprietor of a trade mark may, by virtue of its exclusive right under Directive 89/104 or, in the case of a Community trade mark, under Regulation No 40/94, oppose the resale of products bearing that mark when those sales take place without the requirements of Article 6(1) of Directive 76/768 being met.²¹¹

9.210 The Court looked at the question from a broader perspective, accepting that the question must be examined on a case-by-case basis. In some cases, displaying perfumes or cosmetics without packaging may strengthen their prestige. In others it could have the opposite effect: first, when the packaging is as important as the container in terms of the image of the product and the reputation of the trade mark; second, the essential function of a trade mark

---

²⁰⁹ Joined Cases C-585/08 and C-144/09 *Pammer and Hotel Alpenhof* [2010] ECR I-12527.
²¹⁰ Paragraph 69.
²¹¹ Paragraph 76.

as an indication of origin may be affected when information is required as a matter of law; third, it may constitute a criminal offence, according to Article 6(1) of Directive 76/768.

9.211 **(v) Advertising an online marketplace and the products offered for sale** The Court then looked at the fifth and sixth questions and the issue of advertising of an online marketplace and the products offered for sale there, in particular through keyword advertising.

9.212 It referred to its earlier case law and held that:

> (i) eBay's use of keywords corresponding to L'Oréal trade marks to promote its own service of making an online marketplace available to sellers and buyers of products would not constitute use in relation to identical or similar goods but it could be brought under Article 5(2) of Directive 89/104 and Article 9(1)(c) of Regulation No 40/94 'as those provisions establish, for trade marks with a reputation, more extensive protection than that provided for in Article 5(1)(a) or Article 9(1)(b) and cover, inter alia, the situation in which a third party uses signs corresponding to such trade marks in relation to goods or services which are not similar to the goods or services for which those marks are registered';[212]
> (ii) eBay's use of keywords corresponding to L'Oréal trade marks 'to promote its customer-sellers' offers for sale of goods bearing those marks' was use in relation to identical goods adding that 'the words "in relation to goods or services" do not relate solely to the goods or services of a third party which is using signs corresponding to the trade marks but may also refer to the goods or services of other persons';[213]
> (iii) more specifically, 'use of a sign corresponding to the trade mark of another person in order to promote goods which one of its customers is marketing with the assistance of that service' (par. 92) when a link is established between the sign and the service and such a link exists where the 'advertisements create an obvious association between the trade-marked goods which are mentioned in the advertisements and the possibility of buying those goods through' the online marketplace;[214]
> (iv) use of a keyword corresponding would have an adverse effect on the functions of the trade mark 'where that advertising does not enable reasonably well-informed and reasonably observant internet users, or enables them only with difficulty, to ascertain whether the goods or services referred to by the advertisement originate from the proprietor of the trade mark or from an undertaking economically linked to it or, on the contrary, originate from a third party'.[215]

9.213 The Court finally underlined that Article 6 of Directive 2000/31 (e-commerce) required that the natural or legal person on whose behalf a commercial communication which is part of an information society service is made must be clearly identifiable.

9.214 **(vi) Displaying trade marks on an online marketplace** Question 8 considered the display on an online marketplace of signs identical with or similar to trade marks. The Court accepted that although in the process of selling trade marked products the trade marks, 'are used on that site, it is none the less not evident that it is the operator of the online marketplace that is "using" them, within the meaning of Directive 89/104 and Regulation No 40/94'.[216] Use within the meaning of Article 5 of the Directive and Article 9 of the Regulation:

---

[212] Paragraph 90.
[213] Paragraph 91, citing *Google France* [2010] ECR I-02417 and the order in C-62/08 *UDV North America* [2009] ECR I-1279.
[214] Paragraph 93.
[215] Paragraph 94, citing *Google France* [2010] ECR I-02417 and C-558/08 *Portakabin* [2010] ECR I-I-06963.
[216] Paragraph 101.

implies, at the very least, that that third party uses the sign in its own commercial communication. In so far as that third party provides a service consisting in enabling its customers to display on its website, in the course of their commercial activities such as their offers for sale, signs corresponding to trade marks, it does not itself use those signs within the meaning of that EU legislation.[217]

(vii) The liability of the operator The role of the intermediary had to be examined under the light of Directive 2000/31. Turning to the interpretation of Directive 2000/31, the Court distinguished between two cases. **9.215**

First, when the operator of an online marketplace is hosting information provided by the sellers that are its customers, it is for national law to determine liability. However, under Articles 12 to 15, certain situations cannot give rise to liability on the part of intermediary service providers according to *Google France*. Looking at the wording and the context of Article 14(1)[218] the Court found that the mere fact that the operator of an online marketplace stores offers for sale on its server, sets the terms of its service, is remunerated for that service, and provides general information to its customers cannot have the effect of denying it the exemptions from liability. Albeit, where the operator provides assistance which entails, in particular, optimizing the presentation of the offers for sale in question or promoting those offers, **9.216**

> it must be considered not to have taken a neutral position between the customer-seller concerned and potential buyers but to have played an active role of such a kind as to give it knowledge of, or control over, the data relating to those offers for sale. It cannot then rely, in the case of those data, on the exemption from liability referred to in Article 14(1) of Directive 2000/31.[219]

Second, where the operator of the online marketplace possesses 'awareness', it is for the national court to decide whether eBay has satisfied the conditions leading to exemption from liability under Article 14(1)(a) and (b). Where the provider functions as a merely technical and automatic data processor it will be exempted from liability on condition that it does not have 'actual knowledge of illegal activity or information' and, as regards claims for damages, it is not 'aware of facts or circumstances from which the illegal activity or information is apparent', or that, having obtained such knowledge or awareness, it is acting expeditiously to remove, or disable access to, the information. In the last case 'it is sufficient … for it to have been aware of facts or circumstances on the basis of which a diligent economic operator should have identified the illegality in question and acted in accordance with Article 14(1)(b)'.[220] The Court added here that 'if the rules set out in Article 14(1)(a) … are not to be rendered redundant, they must be interpreted as covering every situation in which the provider concerned becomes aware, in one way or another, of such facts or circumstances',[221] strengthening the position of trade mark proprietors. Notification does not automatically preclude exemption 'given that notifications … may turn out to be insufficiently precise or inadequately substantiated' but notification 'represents, as a general rule, a factor of which the national court must take account'.[222] **9.217**

---

[217] Paragraph 102.
[218] Citing by analogy C-298/07 *Bundesverband der Verbraucherzentralen und Verbraucherverbände* [2008] ECR I-7841.
[219] Paragraph 116.
[220] Paragraph 120.
[221] Paragraph 121.
[222] Paragraph 122.

9.218 (viii) **Measures against online marketplace operators: Effective, proportionate, dissuasive, and must not create barriers to legitimate trade**   Looking at the tenth question concerning the measures that should be made available under Article 11 of Directive 2004/48, the Court noted that the word 'injunction' in the third sentence of Article 11 cannot be equated with the words 'injunction aimed at prohibiting the continuation of the infringement' used in the first sentence of the provision. It[223] added that there must be available measures that aim to end infringements but also measures that aim to prevent further infringements.

9.219 Following the principle of effectiveness the measures must be effective and dissuasive. Given that the United Kingdom has not adopted specific rules to implement the third sentence of Article 11 of Directive 2004/48, the referring court will, 'when applying national law, be required to do so, as far as possible, in the light of the wording and the purpose the third sentence of Article 11'.[224]

9.220 In addition, measures must follow the principle of proportionality. For example, a general monitoring obligation would be incompatible with Article 3 of Directive 2004/48 that requires that measures must be fair and proportionate and must not be excessively costly. In addition they must not create barriers to legitimate trade; general and permanent prohibitions on the selling, on that marketplace, of goods bearing the relevant trade marks would probably create such barriers.

9.221 In the end,

> if the operator of the online marketplace does not decide, on its own initiative, to suspend the perpetrator of the infringement of intellectual property rights in order to prevent further infringements of that kind by the same seller in respect of the same trade marks, it may be ordered, by means of an injunction, to do so[225]

and 'the operator of an online marketplace may be ordered to take measures to make it easier to identify its customer-sellers'.[226] In that context, protection of personal data must be protected; however 'the fact remains that when the infringer is operating in the course of trade and not in a private matter, that person must be clearly identifiable'.[227]

(8) *Interflora*: A Comprehensive Review

(a) *The facts in the main proceedings and the order for reference*

9.222 *Interflora* is the most comprehensive review of the Court's case law on trade marks, search engines, and the Internet. The case started at the English courts[228] where Interflora, the operator of the largest flower delivery network in the world, also operating an online flower delivery service, brought a case against Marks and Spencer (M&S), one of Britain's largest retailers. M&S operated through physical stores, but also online, selling and delivering, amongst other products, flowers in competition with Interflora.

---

[223] Following C-275/06 *Promusicae* [2008] ECR I-271.
[224] Paragraph 137, referring by analogy to C-106/89 *Marleasing* [1990] ECR I-4135 and Joined Cases C-378/07 to C-380/07 *Angelidaki* [2009] ECR I-3071.
[225] Paragraph 141.
[226] Paragraph 142.
[227] Paragraph 142.
[228] *Interflora Inc, Interflora British Unit v Marks and Spencer Plc, Flowers Direct Online Limited* [2009] EWHC 1095 (Ch).

9.223 M&S admitted that it had purchased a number of INTERFLORA keywords including variants and combinations that triggered sponsored links like 'M&S Flowers Online www.marksandspencer.com/flowers. Gorgeous fresh flowers & plants. Order by 5pm for next day delivery'. Interflora argued that both Google and M&S infringed its registered trade marks, targeting amongst the following acts: selecting and nominating the Interflora signs as keywords and associating those keywords with M&S's URLs; setting the cost per click in relation to those keywords; using the Interflora signs in business correspondence relting to the invoicing and payment of fees and the management of an AdWords account; presenting the Interflora signs within search bars located at the top and bottom of search results pages that contains M&S's sponsored link; presenting the sign INTERFLORA by way of an alternative suggestion when the user had entered a word similar to Interflora (eg 'inteflora'); and presenting a search results page containing M&S's sponsored links in response to the entering by the user of one of the Interflora signs. It focused on two types of harm: direct costs, resulting for example from its own bidding costs for the keywords, and lost sales. M&S also enjoyed a free ride; for example INTERFLORA was the fifth most frequent 'paid click' driving traffic to M&S's website.

9.224 Arnold J considered that, despite the earlier jurisprudence of the Court, there were two issues that had to be resolved: whether there was 'use' of the INTERFLORA sign and whether it was 'in relation to' identical goods and services, and he referred the following questions:

(1) Where a trader which is a competitor of the proprietor of a registered trade mark and which sells goods and provides services identical to those covered by the trade mark via its website (i) selects a sign which is identical (in accordance with the Court's ruling in Case C-291/00) with the trade mark as a keyword for a search engine operator's sponsored link service, (ii) nominates the sign as a keyword, (iii) associates the sign with the URL of its website, (iv) sets the cost per click that it will pay in relation to that keyword, (v) schedules the timing of the display of the sponsored link and (vi) uses the sign in business correspondence relating to the invoicing and payment of fees or the management of its account with the search engine operator, but the sponsored link does not itself include the sign or any similar sign, do any or all of these acts constitute 'use' of the sign by the competitor within the meaning of Article 5(1)(a) of First Council Directive 89/104/EEC of 21 December 1988 ('the Trade Marks Directive') and Article 9(1)(a) of Council Regulation 40/94 of 20 December 1993 on the Community trade mark ('the CTM Regulation')?
(2) Is any such use 'in relation to' goods and services identical to those for which the trade mark is registered within the meaning of Article 5(1)(a) of the Trade Marks Directive and Article 9(1)(a) of the CTM Regulation?
(3) Does any such use fall within the scope of either or both of:
 (a) Article 5(1)(a) of the Trade Marks Directive and Article 9(1)(a) of the CTM Regulation; and
 (b) (assuming that such use is detrimental to the distinctive character of the trade mark or takes unfair advantage of the repute of the trade mark) Article 5(2) of the Trade Marks Directive and Article 9(1)(c) of the CTM Regulation?
(4) Does it make any difference to the answer to question 3 above if:
 (a) the presentation of the competitor's sponsored link in response to a search by a user by means of the sign in question is liable to lead some members of the public to believe that the competitor is a member of the trade mark proprietor's commercial network contrary to the fact; or
 (b) the search engine operator does not permit trade mark proprietors in the relevant Member State of the Community to block the selection of signs identical to their trade marks as keywords by other parties?
(5) Where the search engine operator (i) presents a sign which is identical (in accordance with the Court's ruling in Case C-291/00) with a registered trade mark to a user within

search bars located at the top and bottom of search pages that contain a sponsored link to the website of the competitor referred to in question 1 above, (ii) presents the sign to the user within the summary of the search results, (iii) presents the sign to the user by way of an alternative suggestion when the user has entered a similar sign in the search engine, (iv) presents a search results page to the user containing the competitor's sponsored link in response to the entering by the user of the sign and (v) adopts the user's use of the sign by presenting the user with search results pages containing the competitor's sponsored link, but the sponsored link does not itself include the sign or any similar sign, do any or all of these acts constitute 'use' of the sign by the search engine operator within the meaning of Article 5(1)(a) of the Trade Marks Directive and Article 9(1)(a) of the CTM Regulation?

(6) Is any such use 'in relation to' goods and services identical to those for which the trade mark is registered within the meaning of Article 5(1)(a) of the Trade Marks Directive and Article 9(1)(a) of the CTM Regulation?

(7) Does any such use fall within the scope of either or both of:
  (a) Article 5(1)(a) of the Trade Marks Directive and Article 9(1)(a) of the CTM Regulation; and
  (b) (assuming that such use is detrimental to the distinctive character of the trade mark or takes unfair advantage of the repute of the trade mark) Article 5(2) of the Trade Marks Directive and Article 9(1)(c) of the CTM Regulation?

(8) Does it make any difference to the answer to question 7 above if:
  (a) the presentation of the competitor's sponsored link in response to a search by a user by means of the sign in question is liable to lead some members of the public to believe that the competitor is a member of the trade mark proprietor's commercial network contrary to the fact; or
  (b) the search engine operator does not permit trade mark proprietors in the relevant Member State to block the selection of signs identical to their trade marks as keywords by other parties?

(9) If any such use does fall within the scope of either or both of Article 5(1)(a) of the Trade Marks Directive / Article 9(1)(a) of the CTM Regulation and Article 5(2) of the Trade Marks Directive / Article 9(1)(c) of the CTM Regulation:
  (a) does such use consist of or include 'the transmission in a communication network of information provided by a receipt of the service', and if so does the search engine operator 'select or modify the information', within the meaning of Article 12(1) of European Parliament and Council Directive 2000/31/EC of 8 June 2000 on certain legal aspects of information society services, in particular electronic commerce, in the Internal Market ('the E-Commerce Directive')?
  (b) does such use consist of or include 'the automatic, intermediate and temporary storage of information, performed for the sole purpose of making more efficient the information's onward transmission to other recipients of the service upon their request' within the meaning of Article 13(1) of the E-Commerce Directive?
  (c) does such use consist of or include 'the storage of information provided by a recipient of the service' within the meaning of Article 14(1) of the E-Commerce Directive?
  (d) if the use does not consist exclusively of activities falling within the scope of one or more of Article 12(1), 13(1) and 14(1) of the E-Commerce Directive, but includes such activities, is the search engine operator exempted from liability to the extent that the use consists of such activities and if so may damages or other financial remedies be granted in respect of such use to the extent that it is not exempted from liability?

(10) If the answer to question 9 above is that the use does not consist exclusively of activities falling within the scope of one or more of Articles 12-14 of the E-Commerce Directive, may the competitor be held jointly liable for the acts of infringement of the search engine operator by virtue of national law on accessory liability?

(b) The dialogue between the CJEU and the national court: Revisiting the questions

The High Court[229] revisited the questions it had referred to the Court of Justice of the European Union (CJEU) following *Google France* and the CJEU's request as to whether the national court wished to maintain its reference. **9.225**

Arnold J characterized this exchange as a helpful step in the dialogue between the CJEU and national courts but went on to plead for a more transparent procedure before the Court. For example, providing copies of written observations filed by the parties, the Commission or the Member States would shed light on how a case had been argued and would make it easier for national courts to delineate the scope of the Court's rulings. He chose to maintain all the referred questions, having clarified that question 3(b) sought **9.226**

> to establish under which circumstances an advertiser which makes use, as an AdWord, of a sign identical to the well-known trade mark of a competitor must be regarded as acting in a manner detrimental to the distinctive character of that trade mark (dilution) and/or as taking unfair advantage of the distinctive character or repute of that trade mark (free-riding) ... this clarification can be effected by simply deleting the parenthesis in question 3(b).[230]

(c) The Opinion of Advocate General Jääskinen

Advocate General Jääskinen,[231] considering Google's liability, noted that following *Google France*,[232] **9.227**

> the attitude of the referencing service provider as to the possibility of the trade mark proprietor to forbid the use of its trade marks as keywords is irrelevant to the answers to be given to questions 1 to 3(a). The only trade mark law relevant point here is that if the referencing service operator gives such possibility to the trade mark proprietors it may in some cases be inferred that there is silent consent of the trade mark proprietor to the use of his trade marks as keywords.[233]

Turning to the notion of use in relation to goods or services, he supported that it was immaterial whether the resulting ad displayed the trade mark or not; 'it is obvious that an adverse effect to the origin function can be excluded if the ad in the sponsored link mentions the trade mark but effectively dissociates the advertiser from it, for example by means of legitimate comparative advertising'.[234] **9.228**

As to the harm to the origin function he added that if the trade mark is not mentioned in the ad: **9.229**

> the significance of that issue depends ... on the nature of goods and services protected by the trade mark taking into account not only the scope of protection registered for the trade mark but also the meaning and repute the trade mark has acquired through use in the minds of the relevant sector of the public.[235]

He found that the Interflora trade mark had gained, in addition to its trade mark meaning, 'a "secondary meaning" denoting a certain commercial network of florists providing a certain

---

[229] *Interflora Inc, Interflora British Unit v Marks and Spencer Plc, Flowers Direct Online Limited* [2010] EWHC 925 (Ch).
[230] Ibid, paragraph 20.
[231] Case C-323/09 *Interflora Inc, Interflora British Unit v Marks & Spencer Plc, Flowers Direct Online Ltd* [2011] ECR I-08625.
[232] [2010] ECR I-02417.
[233] Paragraph 40.
[234] Paragraph 42.
[235] Paragraph 43.

type of delivery service, and the reputation of that trade mark relates to or is identical with the positive associations this meaning has in the minds of the relevant circles of consumers'.[236]

9.230 Interestingly, the 'secondary meaning' concept here relates to an additional reputation that is the result of the nature of the service covered by the trade mark rather than distinctiveness that is the result of its use. Thus, he submitted 'the display of the ad as a consequence of typing "interflora" into a search engine creates in the context of this case an association that Marks & Spencer is part of the Interflora network'.[237]

9.231 Turning to the link between the functions of a trade mark and the concept of dilution he submitted that:

> dilution relates to the idea that the proper purpose of trade mark law should be to protect the efforts and investments made by the trade mark proprietor and the independent value (good will) of the trade mark. This 'property-based' approach to trade marks differs from the 'deception-based' idea that trade mark law primarily protects the origin function with a view to preventing consumers and other end users from erring as to the commercial origin of goods and services. The property-based approach also protects the communication, advertising and investment functions of trade marks with a view of creating a brand with a positive image and independent economic value (brand equity or good will). Consequently, the trade mark can be used for various goods and services having nothing in common apart from being under the control of the trade mark proprietor. The origin and quality functions would be protected as factors contributing to the value of the brand.[238]

9.232 Note that the notion of goodwill as brand equity is perceived as independent of the trade mark itself or, more probably, of the trade mark as an indicator of origin. Accordingly, dilution should be analysed, according to the Advocate General, exclusively on the basis of Article 5(2), independently from the origin function but taking into account all other functions.

9.233 Looking at how keyword advertising works in practice, he noted that in relation to trade marks composed of common or descriptive words, even if they had acquired widespread trade mark significance, it would not be warranted to assume that an Internet user would in every case be looking for them as trade marks rather than common words. Similarly, buying them as keywords could, equally, be the result of their common rather than trade mark significance.

9.234 Still,

> the identity between a keyword and a trade mark can with certainty be assumed as indicating a link between them in the case of truly unique trade marks that are inherently highly distinctive. Similarly an enterprise buying a keyword can be assumed to target an identical trade mark only if the trade mark has those characteristics and the keyword is acquired by a competitor, i.e. an undertaking selling goods or services that compete with those covered by the trade mark. In my opinion these conditions seem to be fulfilled in the rather exceptional case of the INTERFLORA trade mark.[239]

In any case, *Google France* made it clear that whether such use should be allowed was ultimately linked with the advert appearing in the sponsored link.

---

[236] Paragraph 47.
[237] Paragraph 48.
[238] Paragraph 50.
[239] Paragraph 72.

He added that 'an adverse effect to the origin function is possible even if the trade mark **9.235** is not mentioned in the ad displayed in the sponsored link';[240] however he did not accept that 'dilution of a trade mark, i.e. weakening of its meaning as denoting goods or services of a specific abstract commercial origin, could legally be seen as resulting from advertising where the trade mark is not mentioned'.[241]

Harm to distinctiveness would occur where there was a risk of the trade mark turning into a **9.236** generic term. Focusing on free riding he found it obvious that 'Marks & Spencer [was] taking advantage of the repute of Interflora's trade mark, as it is inconceivable that this selection of keywords could be explained with any other motive. Hence, the question that remains relates to the fairness of that use.'[242] Presenting the advertiser's products as alternatives to those carrying the trade mark 'should count as due cause'.[243]

In essence, 'free-riding has to be analysed on the basis of the ad shown in the sponsored **9.237** link. If that ad mentions or displays the trade mark, the acceptability of the use depends on whether we are faced with legitimate comparative advertising or, on the contrary, with riding on the coat-tails of the trade mark proprietor.'[244]

(d) The Judgment of the Court of Justice

(i) **The Opinion of the AG and the oral procedure**   M&S requested the reopening of the **9.238** oral procedure arguing that the Advocate General had gone beyond a pure analysis of the relevant legal provisions moving into their application against their particular factual context that should remain within the exclusive jurisdiction of the referring court. The court did not agree:

> it should be recalled that, under the second paragraph of Article 252 TFEU, it is the duty of the Advocate General, acting with complete impartiality and independence, to make, in open court, reasoned submissions … In carrying out that task, the Advocate General may, where appropriate, analyse a reference for a preliminary ruling by placing it within a context which is broader than that strictly defined by the referring court or by the parties to the main proceedings. The Chamber hearing the case is not bound either by the Advocate General's Opinion or by the reasoning on which it is based.[245]

The same applies to the referring court that is not obliged to follow the Advocate General's reasoning.

(ii) **Revisiting the referred questions**   The Court viewed Questions 1, 2, and 3(a) under **9.239** the light of its earlier relevant jurisprudence as essentially asking whether, according to Article 5(1)(a) of Directive 89/104:

> the proprietor of a trade mark is entitled to prevent a competitor from displaying—on the basis of a keyword which is identical to that trade mark and which has been selected in an internet referencing service by the competitor without the proprietor's consent—an advertisement for goods or services identical to those for which that mark is registered.[246]

---

[240] Paragraph 89.
[241] Paragraph 90.
[242] Paragraph 96.
[243] Paragraph 99.
[244] Paragraph 103.
[245] Paragraph 24, citing C-229/09 *Hogan Lovells International LLP v Bayer CropScience AG* [2010] ECR I-11335 and *AJD Tuna* (C-221/09) [2011] ECR I-01655.
[246] Paragraph 27.

9.240 Question 4 focused on

> whether, in those circumstances, it is relevant (i) that the advertisement concerned is liable to lead some members of the relevant public to believe, incorrectly, that the advertiser is a member of the trade mark proprietor's commercial network and (ii) that the provider of the internet referencing service does not permit trade mark proprietors to prevent signs identical to their trade marks being selected as keywords.[247]

9.241 (iii) **The relevance of functions** The Court reminded that according to its jurisprudence in *Google France* and *BergSpechte*, use as a keyword by the advertiser constituted use as a trade mark, albeit, the proprietor of the trade mark could prevent that use where the conditions of Article 5 of the Directive were met and in addition, citing *Arsenal*[248] as the original authority, it stressed that 'the exercise of the exclusive right conferred by the trade mark must be reserved to cases in which a third party's use of the sign adversely affects, or is liable adversely to affect, the functions of the trade mark, in particular its essential function of guaranteeing to consumers the origin of the goods'.[249] Consequent case law, citing *Google France* and *L'Oreal*, settled that trade mark rights can be relied upon

> where there is, or is liable to be, an adverse effect on one of the functions of the trade mark, irrespective of whether the function concerned is the essential function of indicating the origin of the product or service covered by the trade mark or one of the other functions of the mark, such as that of guaranteeing the quality of that product or service or that of communication, investment or advertising.[250]

9.242 The Court and the legislature have recognized that 'a trade mark is often, in addition to an indication of the origin of the goods or services, an instrument of commercial strategy used, inter alia, for advertising purposes or to acquire a reputation in order to develop consumer loyalty'.[251] The Court acknowledged that a trade mark is always supposed to fulfil the origin function but will only fulfil one of the other functions insofar as it has been used to that end; it remains for the national court to consider whether the condition of an adverse effect on one of the functions of the trade mark is met but there is no reason to presume that only trade marks with a reputation were 'capable of having functions other than that of indicating origin'.[252]

9.243 (iv) **Adverse effect and the origin function** The Court repeated its *Google France* and *Portakabin* findings: (i) the effect on the origin function depends primarily on the manner the advertisement is presented; (ii) the effect would be adverse if the advertisement does not enable the reasonably well-informed and reasonably observant Internet users, or enables them only with difficulty, to ascertain whether the goods or services referred to by the advertisement originate from the proprietor of the trade mark or an undertaking economically connected to it or, on the contrary, originate from a third party.

9.244 It stressed that

> in such a situation, which is, moreover, characterised by the fact that the advertisement appears immediately after the trade mark has been entered as a search term and is displayed

---

[247] Paragraph 28.
[248] *Arsenal* [2002] ECR I-10273.
[249] Paragraph 37.
[250] Paragraph 38.
[251] Paragraph 39.
[252] Paragraph 40.

at a point when the trade mark is, in its capacity as a search term, also displayed on the screen, the internet user may be mistaken as to the origin of the goods or services in question.²⁵³

9.245 Also, when the advertisement suggests 'that there is an economic link between that third party and the proprietor of the trade mark' and

where the advertisement, while not suggesting the existence of an economic link, is vague to such an extent on the origin of the goods or services at issue that reasonably well-informed and reasonably observant internet users are unable to determine, on the basis of the advertising link and the commercial message attached thereto, whether the advertiser is a third party vis-à-vis the proprietor of the trade mark or whether, on the contrary, it is economically linked to that proprietor, the conclusion must be that there is an adverse effect on that function of the trade mark.²⁵⁴

9.246 The Court, taking into account the factual context the referring court relied upon to develop its questions, added that the mention in point (b) of Question 4 that the referencing service provider had not permitted trade mark proprietors to prevent the selection of a sign identical with their trade mark as a keyword was not relevant; however it confirmed that there was no consent.²⁵⁵ And, the fact that some Internet users might be misled could be relevant but was not necessarily sufficient to establish liability.

9.247 The Court added to its earlier case law that the relevant public comprises reasonably well-informed and reasonably observant Internet users. The finding that 'the fact that some internet users may have had difficulty grasping that the service provided by M&S is independent from that of Interflora is not a sufficient basis for a finding that the function of indicating origin has been adversely affected'.²⁵⁶

9.248 In the end, the referring court will:

in the absence of any general knowledge ... have to determine whether or not the use of words such as 'M&S Flowers' in an advertisement ... is sufficient to enable a reasonably well-informed and reasonably observant internet user ... to tell that the flower-delivery service offered does not originate from Interflora.²⁵⁷

9.249 (v) **Adverse effect and the advertising function** Citing *Google France* and *BergSpechte*, the Court repeated that use of a sign identical with a third party's trade mark in a referencing service does not have an adverse effect on the advertising function of a trade mark.

9.250 It is noted here that the Court positions trade mark law and its application against the broader context of a competitive market; it accepts that keyword advertising might oblige a trade mark proprietor to intensify its own adverting, but this

is not a sufficient basis, in every case, for concluding that the trade mark's advertising function is adversely affected. In that regard, although the trade mark is an essential element in the system of undistorted competition which European law seeks to establish ... its purpose is not, however, to protect its proprietor against practices inherent in competition.²⁵⁸

---

²⁵³ Paragraph 44
²⁵⁴ Paragraph 45, citing *Google France* [2010] ECR I-02417 and *Portakabin*.
²⁵⁵ Paragraph 47.
²⁵⁶ Paragraph 50.
²⁵⁷ Paragraph 53.
²⁵⁸ Paragraph 57.

After all, this type of advertising enables competitors to offer alternatives to the goods or services of the proprietors of the trade marks linked with the keywords.

9.251 **(vi) Adverse effect and the investment function**   Expanding the idea of the advertising function the Court added that a trade mark may also be used to acquire or preserve a reputation capable of attracting consumers and retaining their loyalty;[259] this constituted the investment function that reached further than the advertising function because it employed advertising but also other 'commercial techniques'.[260]

9.252 Albeit, here the Court failed to offer a concrete example of a use that would harm the investment function, maintaining only that competing use must substantially interfere 'with the proprietor's use of its trade mark to acquire or preserve a reputation capable of attracting consumers and retaining their loyalty',[261] to be captured as adversely affecting the investment function. The Court again positioned protection of reputation, possibly the aim behind the introduction of the investment function,[262] against the context of a competitive market:

> it cannot be accepted that the proprietor of a trade mark may—in conditions of fair competition that respect the trade mark's function as an indication of origin—prevent a competitor from using a sign identical with that trade mark in relation to goods or services identical with those for which the mark is registered, if the only consequence of that use is to oblige the proprietor of that trade mark to adapt its efforts to acquire or preserve a reputation capable of attracting consumers and retaining their loyalty. Likewise, the fact that that use may prompt some consumers to switch from goods or services bearing that trade mark cannot be successfully relied on by the proprietor of the mark.[263]

9.253 Potentially, this means that when the origin function is not affected, because there is a clear distinction between competing products, then the investment function will also not be affected.

9.254 **(vii) Dilution: distinctiveness**   Given the parameters of the reference, the Court focused on detriment to distinctiveness. According to the Court, harm to reputation falls under 'tarnishment', harm to distinctiveness under 'dilution', and taking unfair advantage under 'free riding'. It found that the selection of a sign identical with or similar to a trade mark as a keyword does not necessarily contribute to dilution.[264]

9.255 Looking at this from the perspective of what does not harm distinctiveness, the Court held that

> when the use, as a keyword, of a sign corresponding to a trade mark with a reputation triggers the display of an advertisement which enables the reasonably well-informed and reasonably observant internet user to tell that the goods or services offered originate not from the proprietor of the trade mark but, on the contrary, from a competitor of that proprietor, the conclusion will have to be that the trade mark's distinctiveness has not been reduced by that use, the latter having merely served to draw the internet user's attention to the existence of an alternative product or service to that of the proprietor of the trade mark.[265]

---

[259] Paragraph 60.
[260] Paragraph 61.
[261] Paragraph 62.
[262] Paragraph 63.
[263] Paragraph 64.
[264] Paragraph 80.
[265] Paragraph 81.

Again, it appears that if the origin function is not affected then it becomes very difficult, if **9.256** not impossible, to establish harm to distinctiveness:

> If ... the referring court were to conclude that the advertising triggered by the use of the sign identical to the INTERFLORA trade mark did not enable the reasonably well-informed and reasonably observant internet user to tell that the service promoted by M&S is independent from that of Interflora and if Interflora were to seek moreover from the referring court, in addition to a finding that the mark's function of indicating origin has been adversely affected, a finding that M&S has also caused detriment to the distinctive character of the INTERFLORA trade mark by contributing to turning it into a generic term, it would fall to the referring court to determine, on the basis of all the evidence submitted to it, whether the selection of signs corresponding to the trade mark INTERFLORA as keywords on the internet has had such an impact on the market for flower-delivery services that the word 'interflora' has come to designate, in the consumer's mind, any flower-delivery service.[266]

(viii) Free ride The court accepted that where a competitor selects another party's trade **9.257** mark with a reputation as a keyword, the purpose of that use is to take advantage of the distinctive character and repute of the trade mark potentially leading to loss of sales if internet users choose the alternative competing product.[267]

But, again, the free ride must be viewed against the concept of a competitive market. First, **9.258** the extent of actionable free ride is relatively narrow: a free ride will be 'particularly likely to be the conclusion in cases in which internet advertisers offer for sale, by means of the selection of keywords corresponding to trade marks with a reputation, goods which are imitations of the goods of the proprietor of those marks'.[268] And second, not harming the origin function appears to push the free ride outside the scope of protection:

> where the advertisement ... puts forward – without offering a mere imitation of the goods or services of the proprietor of that trade mark, without causing dilution or tarnishment and without, moreover, adversely affecting the functions of the trade mark concerned – an alternative to the goods or services of the proprietor of the trade mark with a reputation, it must be concluded that such use falls, as a rule, within the ambit of fair competition in the sector for the goods or services concerned and is thus not without 'due cause'[269]

for the purposes of Article 5(2) of Directive 89/104 and Article 9(1)(c) of Regulation 40/94.

Accordingly the Order of the Court provided that: **9.259**

> 1 Article 5(1)(a) of First Council Directive 89/104/EEC of 21 December 1988 to approximate the laws of the Member States relating to trade marks and Article 9(1)(a) of Council Regulation 40/94 of 20 December 1993 on the Community trade mark must be interpreted as meaning that the proprietor of a trade mark is entitled to prevent a competitor from advertising—on the basis of a keyword which is identical with the trade mark and which has been selected in an internet referencing service by the competitor without the proprietor's consent—goods or services identical with those for which that mark is registered, where that use is liable to have an adverse effect on one of the functions of the trade mark. Such use:
> - adversely affects the trade mark's function of indicating origin where the advertising displayed on the basis of that keyword does not enable reasonably well-informed and reasonably observant internet users, or enables them only with difficulty, to ascertain

---

[266] Paragraph 83.
[267] Paragraphs 86–87.
[268] Paragraph 90, citing *Google France* [2010] ECR I-02417.
[269] Paragraph 92.

whether the goods or services concerned by the advertisement originate from the proprietor of the trade mark or an undertaking economically linked to that proprietor or, on the contrary, originate from a third party;
- does not adversely affect, in the context of an internet referencing service having the characteristics of the service at issue in the main proceedings, the trade mark's advertising function; and
- adversely affects the trade mark's investment function if it substantially interferes with the proprietor's use of its trade mark to acquire or preserve a reputation capable of attracting consumers and retaining their loyalty.

2 Article 5(2) of Directive 89/104 and Article 9(1)(c) of Regulation 40/94 must be interpreted as meaning that the proprietor of a trade mark with a reputation is entitled to prevent a competitor from advertising on the basis of a keyword corresponding to that trade mark, which the competitor has, without the proprietor's consent, selected in an internet referencing service, where the competitor thereby takes unfair advantage of the distinctive character or repute of the trade mark (free-riding) or where the advertising is detrimental to that distinctive character (dilution) or to that repute (tarnishment). Advertising on the basis of such a keyword is detrimental to the distinctive character of a trade mark with a reputation (dilution) if, for example, it contributes to turning that trade mark into a generic term. By contrast, the proprietor of a trade mark with a reputation is not entitled to prevent, inter alia, advertisements displayed by competitors on the basis of keywords corresponding to that trade mark, which put forward—without offering a mere imitation of the goods or services of the proprietor of that trade mark, without causing dilution or tarnishment and without, moreover, adversely affecting the functions of the trade mark with a reputation—an alternative to the goods or services of the proprietor of that mark.

(e) Applying Interflora

9.260 The application of the Court's guidance was not a straightforward exercise.[270] Mr Justice Arnold understood it as an indication of a reversal of the burden of proof; the advertiser would have to show that the advertisement satisfied the standard set by the Court rather than the trade mark proprietor having to prove that the requirements for establishing infringement were met. In addition, the concept of initial interest confusion, at least for trade marks with a reputation, made it more likely that the free ride would be more effective and, to an extent, actionable. All this, combined with challenges to the acceptability of evidence, the conceptualization of an average consumer, and the scope of the injunction, led to prolonged litigation that is outside the scope of this work.

---

[270] *Interflora Inc, Interflora British Unit v Marks and Spencer Plc, Flowers Direct Online Limited* [2009] EWHC 1095 (Ch) was the starting point; *Interflora Inc, Interflora British Unit v Marks and Spencer Plc, Flowers Direct Online Limited* [2010] EWHC 925 (Ch) is the response of the High Court to the CJEU's clarification request; the CJEU gave its ruling in *Interflora Inc, Interflora British Unit v Marks & Spencer Plc, Flowers Direct Online Ltd* Case C-323/09 [2012] ETMR 1; the evidence was challenged in *Interflora Inc (a company incorporated under the laws of the State of Michigan, United States of America), Interflora British Unit v Marks and Spencer plc, Flowers Direct Online Limited* [2012] EWHC 1722 (Ch) and *Marks and Spencer Plc v Interflora Inc (a company incorporated under the laws of the State of Michigan, USA), Interflora British Unit* [2012] EWCA civ 1501 as well as in *Interflora Inc, Interflora British Unit v Marks and Spencer plc, Flowers Direct Online Limited* [2013] EWHC 270 (Ch), *Interflora Inc, Interflora British Unit v Marks and Spencer plc, Flowers Direct Online Limited* [2013] EWHC 273 (Ch), *Interflora Inc v Marks & Spencer Plc* [2013] EWCA Civ 510, and *Interflora Inc, Interflora British Unit v Marks and Spencer plc, Flowers Direct Online Limited* [2013] EWHC 936 (Ch); the judgment of the High Court on the merits of the case is delivered in *Interflora Inc, Interflora British Unit v Marks and Spencer plc, Flowers Direct Online Limited* [2013] EWHC 1291 (Ch), on the scope of the injunction in *Interflora Inc, Interflora British Unit v Marks and Spencer plc, Flowers Direct Online Limited* [2013] EWHC 1484 (Ch) and *Interflora Inc, Interflora British Unit v Marks and Spencer plc, Flowers Direct Online Limited* [2013] EWHC 1683 (Ch); the Court of Appeal remands the case back to the High Court in [2014] EWCA Civ 1403.

However, it is worth citing here Lord Justice Kitchin who, sitting on the UK Court of Appeal, remanded the case back to the High Court relying primarily on the CJEU's positioning of trade mark rights against the context of a competitive market: having stressed that it is not the purpose of trade mark law to protect the proprietor of a trade mark against fair competition, he adds, rejecting the need for the introduction of initial interest confusion into European law, that: **9.261**

> the tests enunciated by the Court therefore incorporate appropriate checks and balances. In particular, the national court is required to consider the matter from the perspective of the average consumer ... and to decide whether the advertiser has enabled that average consumer to ascertain the origin of the advertised goods or services and so make an informed decision. We would emphasise it is not the duty of such advertisers to avoid confusion.[271]

(9) *Frisdranken Industrie Winters BV v Red Bull GmbH*: The *Google France* approach in a non-Internet environment

(a) The facts in the main proceedings and the order for reference

In *Frisdranken Industrie Winters BV v Red Bull GmbH*,[272] the Court considered aspects of what constitutes infringing use. Red Bull GmbH (Red Bull), the proprietor of the trade mark 'Red Bul' for energizing soft drinks in the Benelux had brought an action against Frisdranken Industrie Winters BV (Winters), a company filling cans with soft drinks produced by itself or third parties. In this case, Winters was filling cans on behalf of a third party, Smart Drinks; the empty cans delivered to Winters were bearing the signs BULLFIGHTER, PITTBULL, RED HORN, later changed to LONG HORN, and LIVE WIRE. **9.262**

The case reached the Hoge Raad that referred the following questions: **9.263**

1. (a) Is the mere "filling" of packaging which bears a sign to be regarded as using that sign in the course of trade within the meaning of Article 5 of the Trade Mark Directive, even if that filling takes place as a service provided to and on the instructions of another person, for the purposes of distinguishing that person's goods?
   (b) Does it make any difference to the answer to question 1(a) if there is an infringement for the purposes of Article 5(1)(a) or (b)?
2. If the answer to question 1(a) is in the affirmative, can using the sign then also be prohibited in the Benelux on the basis of Article 5 of the Trade Mark Directive if the goods bearing the sign are destined exclusively for export to countries outside
   (a) the Benelux area or
   (b) the European Union
   and they cannot—except in the undertaking where the filling took place—be seen therein by the public?
3. If the answer to question 2(a) or (b) is in the affirmative, what criterion must be used when answering the question whether there has been trade-mark infringement: should the criterion be the perception of an average consumer who is reasonably well-informed and reasonably observant and circumspect in the Benelux or alternatively in the European Union—who then in the given circumstances can only be determined in a fictional or abstract way—or must a different criterion be used in this case, for example, the perception of the consumer in the country to which the goods are exported?[273]

---

[271] [2014] EWCA Civ 1403 at paragraph 156.
[272] C-119/10 *Frisdranken Industrie Winters BV v Red Bull GmbH* [2011] ECR I-13179
[273] Reproduced under point 15.

(b) The Opinion of Advocate General Kokott

9.264 Advocate General Kokott identified three main questions:

first, whether a service provider which on the instructions of another fills drink into a can bearing a sign similar to a trade mark infringes the rights associated with that mark (Question 1(a)), *second*, whether the mark is also infringed where those goods are intended for export from the area in which the mark is protected (Question 2) and, *third*, the criterion to be used in the case of export goods to determine the likelihood of confusion (Question 3).

9.265 **(i) Filling cans: Question 1(a)**   Article 5(3) of the Directive provided that the affixing of the sign to goods or the packaging thereof constituted use of the mark. She suggested that filling drinks into cans bearing the signs could be seen as using the sign for the purposes of Article 5(1) of the Directive. She added that the 'principal tenor' of the Court's case law was that 'the use of a sign had to be with a view to distinguishing goods and services. That applies in the present case as the signs in question are intended to distinguish the various drinks marketed by Smart Drinks from other drinks.'[274] However, in *Google France* the Court also stressed that 'use, by a third party, of a sign identical with, or similar to, the proprietor's trade mark implies, at the very least, that that third party uses the sign in its *own* commercial communication'.[275] Accordingly, Winters had not committed an infringing act since it was not marketing the goods bearing the signs. It simply provided a service. She accepted that according to the facts of the case, Winters probably must have been aware of the infringing nature of the product itself; however, this was not enough to introduce an exception to the rule because an exception would expose service providers like Winters to disproportionate risks.

9.266 Considering briefly Question 1(b) (mentioned earlier at paragraph 9.263) she added that it does not make a difference to the answer to Question 1(a) if there is an infringement for the purposes of Article 5(1)(a) or (b) of Directive 89/104.

9.267 **(ii) Goods destined to be exported: Question 2**   Having reviewed Article 5(1)(b) of the Directive she found that, in principle, the fact that the goods were destined to be exported should not make a difference; the goods were still intended to be sold. The transit cases[276] did not make a difference since there the goods were under the control of customs authorities. In this case the goods were not subject to customs control and there was a risk they would circulate in the territory where the mark was protected.

9.268 **(iii) The 'criterion' for establishing infringement: Question 3**   The answer to this question followed the same theme; since, in the case of export goods, trade mark infringement would result from the risk that the goods could be marketed in the territory where the trade mark is protected, infringement should be determined from the perspective of an average consumer in that area.

---

[274] Point 23, citing C-48/05 *Adam Opel* [2007] ECR I-1017, Joined Cases C-236/08 to C-238/08 *Google France* [2010] ECR I-2417, C-533/06 *O2 Holdings* [2008] ECR I-4231, and C-17/06 *Céline* [2007] ECR I-7041.

[275] Point 24, citing *Google France*, paragraph 56.

[276] C-115/02 *Rioglass and Transremar* [2003] ECR I-12705, C-405/03 *Class International* [2005] ECR I-8735, and C-281/05 *Montex Holdings* [2006] ECR I-10881.

(c) The Judgment of the Court of Justice

The Court noted that its response would cover exclusively the interpretation of Article 5(1)(b) since the signs were similar, and not identical, with the protected trade mark. Winters operated in the course of trade; it does not follow, however, that 'the service provider itself "uses" those signs within the meaning of Article 5'.[277] The service provider only 'creates the technical conditions necessary for the other person to use them'.[278] The service provided, according to the Court, had no similarity with the products covered by the Red Bull registrations.

9.269

The Court concluded that:

9.270

> Article 5(1)(b) of Directive 89/104 must be interpreted as meaning that a service provider who, under an order from and on the instructions of another person, fills packaging which was supplied to it by the other person who, in advance, affixed to it a sign which is identical with, or similar to, a sign protected as a trade mark does not itself make use of the sign that is liable to be prohibited under that provision.[279]

It added that given its answer to the first question there was no need to consider the second and third questions.

The Court is widening the scope of its jurisprudence in *Google France*. Interestingly, the criteria that were developed in *Google France* and could be seen as the judicial response to the ethereal world of the Internet are brought back and applied in a more physical commercial environment.

9.271

E. Limitations to Trade Mark Rights

(1) *BMW*: Setting the Principles

(a) The facts in the main proceedings and the order for reference

BMW[280] was the first case that came before the Court seeking the interpretation of Article 6. It was a reference from the Hoge Raad (Supreme Court) of The Netherlands. BMW was the registered proprietor of the BMW trade marks—the BMW acronym as such and two figurative trade marks—in the Benelux. The specification covered motor vehicles, engines, spare parts, and accessories. BMW cars were marketed through a network of dealers that were required to meet the standards set by BMW. Deenik run a garage; he specialized in repairing BMW cars and was also trading second-hand BMWs.

9.272

BMW claimed before the Dutch courts that use of its marks in Deenik's advertisements constituted trade mark infringement. The Arrondissementsrechtbank te Zwolle (Tribunal of Zwolle) decided that although a number of statements made by Deenik in advertisements of his business constituted unauthorized use of the BMW marks insofar as they might create the impression that he was part of the BMW's dealer network, Deenik remained free to use in advertisements statements such as 'Repairs and maintenance of BMWs' since it was clear that that statement referred only to products bearing the BMW mark. He could also use statements such as 'Specialist in BMWs'. The decision was confirmed by the Gerechtshof (Court of Appeal), Arnhem.

9.273

---

[277] Paragraph 28, citing *Google France* [2010] ECR I-02417, paragraph 57.
[278] Paragraph 30.
[279] Paragraph 37.
[280] C-63/97 *Bayerische Motorenwerke AG and BMW Nederlard BV v Deenik* [1999] ECR I-905.

9.274 The case reached the Hoge Raad that stayed proceedings and referred the following questions to the Court.

(1) In view of the fact that, with regard to the rights associated with a trade mark, the Directive contains a transitional legal provision only for the purpose of the case described in Article 5(4), are Member States otherwise free to lay down rules on the matter, or does Community law in general, or the objective and tenor of Directive 89/104 in particular, have the effect that Member States are not entirely free in that regard but must comply with specific restrictions, and if so which?

(2) If someone, without the authorisation of the trade mark proprietor, makes use of that proprietor's trade mark, registered exclusively for specified goods, for the purpose of announcing to the public that he;
  (a) carries out repair and maintenance work on the goods which have been placed on the market under that trade mark by the proprietor or with his consent, or that he;
  (b) is a specialist or is specialised with regard to such goods, does this, under the scheme of Article 5 of the Directive, involve:
    (i) use of the trade mark in relation to goods which are identical to those for which it was registered, as referred to in Article 5(1)(a);
    (ii) use of that trade mark in relation to services which must be deemed to constitute use of the trade mark within the meaning of Article 5(1)(a) or use of the trade mark as referred to in Article 5(1)(b), on the assumption that it can be stated that there is an identity between those services and the goods for which the trade mark was registered;
    (iii) use of the trade mark as referred to in Article 5(2); or
    (iv) use of the trade mark as referred to in Article 5(5)?

(3) For the purpose of answering Question 2, does it make any difference whether announcement (a) or announcement (b) is involved?

(4) In the light of the provision in Article 7 of the Directive, does it make any difference, with regard to the question whether the proprietor of the trade mark can prevent use of his trade mark registered exclusively for specified goods, whether the use referred to in Question 2 is that under (i), (ii), (iii) or (iv)?

(5) On the assumption that both or one of the cases described at the start of Question 2 involve the use of the proprietor's trade mark within the meaning of Article 5(1), whether under Article 5(1)(a) or (b), can the proprietor prevent that use only where the person thus using the trade mark thereby creates the impression that his undertaking is affiliated to the trade-mark proprietor's network, or can he also prevent that use where there is a good chance that the manner in which the trade mark is used for those announcements may create an impression among the public that the trade mark is in that regard being used to an appreciable extent for the purpose of advertising his own business as such by creating a specific suggestion of quality?[281]

(b) The Opinion of Advocate General Jacobs

9.275 (i) **The effect of the Directive** Advocate General Jacobs dealt first with the effect of the Directive. The Benelux law was amended according to the Directive on 1 January 1996 whereas the deadline for its implementation was 31 December 1992. The Directive incorporated specific transitional provisions: Article 5(4) provided that where, under the law of the Member State, the use of a sign under the conditions referred to in Article 5(1)(b) or Article 5(2) could not be prohibited before the date on which the provisions necessary to comply with the Directive entered into force in the Member State concerned, the

---

[281] Reproduced under paragraph 12.

rights conferred by the trade mark could not be relied on to prevent the continued use of the sign; Article 3(4) and Article 4(6) stated that Member States might provide that the grounds of refusal of registration or invalidity in force in that State prior to the date on which the provisions necessary to comply with the Directive entered into force should apply to trade marks for which application was made prior to that date. There was no provision dealing with which national law should be applied, the one effective prior to the adoption of the Directive or that following its adoption, in respect of litigation on use of a sign which commenced before the date that the Directive came into force and was still continuing.

9.276 Citing *Marleasing*,[282] the Advocate General suggested that in respect of the continued use of the sign after the date by which the Directive should have been implemented 'whether or not the Directive has been transposed into national law, all provisions of national law must be interpreted as far as possible in accordance with the Directive'.[283]

9.277 If the Directive had not been properly implemented, the question would be whether it could have direct effect in proceedings brought against individuals. In this case, use of the marks during the period before the date for implementing the Directive had passed would be covered under the previous national law. Substantive rules could be interpreted as applying to situations existing before their entry into force only insofar as it clearly followed from their terms, objectives, or general scheme that such an effect should be given to them, but there was no such need in this case.[284]

9.278 The Advocate General concluded that when implementing the Directive in national law, Member States were not free to adopt any transitional provisions other than those expressly provided for by the Directive insofar as such transitional provisions would prejudice the complete and correct transposition of the Directive.

9.279 (ii) **The role of the Court** Before turning to the substantive trade mark issues Advocate General Jacobs noted that BMW's registrations covered motor vehicles and their parts and accessories but not services relating thereto. In his Opinion he considered Deenik's use first in relation to goods and second in relation to services. Further, he suggested that it would not be appropriate for the Court to seek to give guidance on the specific forms of words which were an issue in the national proceedings. Instead, the Court should give guidance on the applicable principles.

9.280 (iii) **Use of the mark in relation to goods: Article 5(1)(a)** He found the advertisements regarding the sale of second-hand BMWs to fall within Article 5(1)(a) since they concerned use of the mark in relation to the genuine article.

> Indeed, even the advertisement of the repairs and maintenance services falls within that provision insofar as it can be read as meaning simply that Mr Deenik's garage is capable of servicing BMW cars and not that the servicing provided there is authorised by BMW ... in that case

---

[282] C-106/89 *Marleasing* [1990] ECR I-4135.
[283] Point 28.
[284] He cited C-152/84 *Marshall v Southampton and South-West Hampshire Area Health Authority* [1986] ECR 723 and C-91/92 *Faccini Dori v Recreb Srl* [1994] ECR I-3325 and Joined Cases 212/80 to 217/80 *Amministrazione delle Finanze dello Stato v Salumi* [1981] ECR 2735 for the specific proposition. The latter was also supported by C-121/91 and C-122/91 *Ct Control and Jct Benelux v Commission* [1993] ECR I-3873 and C-261/96 *Conserchimica v Amministrazione delle Finanze dello Stato* [1997] ECR I-6177.

the mark is being used to describe what can be repaired and serviced and is thus being used 'in relation to' the cars, rather than Mr Deenik's services.[285]

9.281 *Exhaustion of rights* However, since the cars had already been put on the market in the Community by the proprietor or with his consent, he found that BMW's trade marks rights had been exhausted under Article 7(1).

9.282 As to the applicability of Article 7(2) he referred to *Dior*[286] where the Court held that a reseller was free to make use of the trade mark in order to bring to the public's attention the further commercialization of the marked goods, and that the trade mark owner might object to such use only if it were to seriously damage the reputation of the mark. He believed that the same principle should cover the case where

> there is a genuine and properly substantiated likelihood of advertising leading the public to believe that the reseller is an authorised distributor ... in order to prevent the public being misled in that way, even if, because the undertaking in question is competent and respectable, there is thereby no damage to his reputation.[287]

It was the national court that had to carry out the assessment of that likelihood.

9.283 *The aura of quality* Regarding the last question raised by the Hoge Raad Advocate General Jacobs remarked:

> if there is no likelihood of the public being confused into believing that there is some sort of trade connection between the reseller and the trade-mark owner, the mere fact that the reseller obtains an advantage by the use of the trade mark because the sale of the trade-marked goods gives his own business an aura of quality is not ... a legitimate reason within the meaning of Article 7(2) of the Directive for a trade-mark owner to object to the advertising of his own goods. Otherwise it would be unduly difficult for the trader effectively to inform the public of the business in which he is engaged.[288]

(iv) Use of the mark in relation to services

9.284 *Article 5(1)(b)* Use of the mark in relation to the repairs and maintenance could fall under Article 5(1)(b), since goods and services could not be identical to each other. The national court would have to assess the likelihood of confusion according to the relevant case law of the Court;[289] he stressed that:

> with reference to the last question raised by the Hoge Raad, it is accordingly clearly not sufficient for the application of Article 5(1)(b), in the absence of any such confusion, to show simply that the reseller derives advantage from the mere fact that he deals in the trade-marked goods because the trade mark's aura of quality rubs off to some extent, giving his own business a high quality image.[290]

9.285 *Article 5(2)* He also left open the possibility of applying Article 5(2). Again, the applicability of that provision to the facts of the case was an issue the national court had to determine. He agreed though with the submission of the Commission and the UK Government that it seemed unlikely. It would be difficult to hold that advertising legitimate economic activities

---

[285] Point 35.
[286] C-337/95 *Parfums Christian Dior SA v Evora BV* [1997] ECR I-6013.
[287] Point 39.
[288] Point 42.
[289] He cited C-251/95 *Sabel BV* [1997] ECR I-6191 and his Opinion in C-39/97 *Canon* [1998] ECR I-5507.
[290] Point 45.

could be regarded as use without due cause or that it would be detrimental. 'Any detriment to BMW is perhaps caused primarily, as the Commission suggests, by the competition offered by independent garages to BMW's authorised distributors. Such detriment is not material from the point of view of trade-mark protection.'[291]

Article 5(5) Similarly, the applicability of Article 5(5) appeared unlikely, because it required the use to be 'without due cause'. **9.286**

The application of Article 6 Despite the fact that the national court had failed to refer directly to Article 6 in its questions, the Advocate General discussed its potential application in relation to the provision of services by an independent trader since it had been raised by BMW. **9.287**

He characterized BMW's suggestion that Deenik could offer the services of car maintenance and repair without the need to name any specific make of car as unrealistic. If Deenik did in fact specialize in maintaining and repairing BMW cars, it was difficult to see how he could effectively communicate that fact to his customers without using the BMW signs. '[W]hether there is any benefit to Mr Deenik is not the key issue. The issue is the extent to which a trader in his position should be free to describe the nature of the services he is offering.'[292] **9.288**

Article 6(1) precluded the owner of a trade mark from preventing the use of the mark by an independent trader to advertise repair and servicing of the goods covered by the mark, provided that the independent trader did so in accordance with honest practices in industrial or commercial matters. **9.289**

Enabling the trade mark proprietor to prevent such use would be an undue restriction on the trader's freedom, unless the advertising was designed to lead the public to believe that the reseller was authorized by the trade mark proprietor or to damage seriously the reputation of the trade mark. It would not, however, be contrary to honest practices within the meaning of Article 6(1) merely to derive advantage from the use of a mark. **9.290**

(c) The Judgment of the Court

(i) **The effect of the Directive** The Court remarked that the transitional problem actually facing the Hoge Raad was different from that governed by Article 5(4) and that the Directive did not provide a rule for determining the national law applicable in such a situation. It accepted that there was no reason, based on the effectiveness of Community law in general or of the Directive in particular, to opt for any given solution. Accordingly, the national court should determine in the light of the applicable national rules the law that should be applied.[293] In any case the applicable national law should be interpreted, as far as possible, in the light of the wording and purpose of the Directive in order to achieve the result pursued by it and to comply with the third paragraph of Article 189 EC.[294] That obligation covered transitional rules as well. **9.291**

(ii) **The legislative framework** The Court emphasized 'that classifying the mark as falling under one specific provision or another of Article 5, as the case may be, is not **9.292**

---

[291] Point 47.
[292] Point 54.
[293] Citing C-349/95 *Frits Loendersloot* [1997] ECR I-6227.
[294] Citing C-106/89 *Marleasing* [1990] ECR I-4135 and C-91/92 *Faccini Dori v RE.C.R.eb Srl* [1994] ECR I-3325.

necessarily determinant as regards the assessment as to whether the use in question is permissible'.[295]

9.293 (iii) **Unauthorized use to inform the public and Article 5** The Court looked together at the second and the third question. It did not follow the distinction of the Advocate General between use in relation to goods and use in relation to services; instead it ruled that use for the purpose of informing the public that another undertaking carries out the repair and maintenance of goods covered by that mark or that it has specialized or is a specialist in such goods constitutes, in circumstances such as those described in the Judgment making the reference, use of the mark within the meaning of Article 5(1)(a) of the Directive.

9.294 To reach that conclusion it looked first at the applicability of Article 5(5) and emphasized that the scope of application of Article 5(1) and Article 5(2) of the Directive, on the one hand, and Article 5(5), on the other, depended on whether the trade mark was used for the purpose of distinguishing the relevant goods or services as originating from a particular undertaking—as a trade mark as such—or whether it was used for other purposes. In a situation such as that described in the reference, use of the trade mark was intended to distinguish the goods in question as the subject of the services provided by the advertiser. The advertiser would use the BMW marks in order to identify the source of the goods in respect of which the services were supplied, and thus to distinguish those goods from any others in respect of which the same services might have been provided.

9.295 At the same time the Court found that sale of goods constituted a service.

> If the use of the trade mark in advertisements for the service which consists of selling second-hand BMW cars is undoubtedly intended to distinguish the subject of the services provided, it is not necessary to treat any differently the advertisements for the service consisting of repair and maintenance of BMW cars. In that case, too, the mark is used to identify the source of the goods which are the subject of the service.[296]

9.296 The Court also clarified the purpose of the references to unfair advantage and detriment to the distinctive character or repute of the mark in Article 5(2) and Article 5(5). It stressed that they should be taken into account only in relation to those two provisions. 'Those matters are ... to be taken into account, not when classifying use under Article 5, but when assessing the legality of that use in the situations covered by Article 5(2) or (5).'[297]

9.297 Finally, it found the contested use to be 'in the course of trade', noting that Article 5(3) expressly mentioned use of the sign in advertising as an example of use that might be prohibited.

9.298 (iv) **The limitations to the exercise of trade mark rights** The Court noted that since use in the advertisements fell within the scope of Article 5(1)(a), it should be prohibited unless Article 6 or Article 7 were applicable. To consider this question it distinguished between (a) the advertisements for the sale of second-hand cars and (b) the advertisements for the repair and maintenance of cars.

---

[295] Paragraph 30.
[296] Paragraph 39.
[297] Paragraph 40.

(a) The sale of second-hand BMWs advertisements

9.299 Following *Dior*[298] the Court held that it would be contrary to Article 7 of the Directive for BMW to prohibit the use of its mark by another person for the purpose of informing the public that he is a specialist in the sale of second-hand BMWs, provided that the advertising concerned cars that had been put on the Community market under that mark by BMW or with its consent and did not go against Article 7(2).

9.300 Giving the impression of a commercial connection between the reseller and the trade mark proprietor, in particular that the reseller was part of the trade mark proprietor's distribution network or that there was a special relationship between the two undertakings, might constitute a legitimate reason within the meaning of Article 7(2). This was based on a number of arguments: first, such advertising was not essential to the purpose of the exhaustion rule; second, it would be contrary to the Article 7 obligation to act fairly in relation to the legitimate interests of the trade mark owner and it would affect the value of the trade mark by taking unfair advantage of its distinctive character or repute; third, it was incompatible with the specific object of a trade mark, described as the protection of the proprietor against competitors wishing to take advantage of the status and reputation of the trade mark.[299]

9.301 On the other hand,

> the mere fact that the reseller derives an advantage from using the trade mark in that advertisements for the sale of goods covered by the mark, which are in other respects honest and fair, lend an aura of quality to his own business does not constitute a legitimate reason within the meaning of Article 7(2) of the Directive.[300]

9.302 A reseller who sold second-hand BMWs cars and who had genuinely become a specialist in that market would be unable to communicate this to his customers without using the BMW marks.

> In consequence, such an informative use of the BMW mark is necessary to guarantee the right of resale under Article 7 of the Directive and does not take unfair advantage of the distinctive character or repute of that trade mark.[301]

(b) The repair and maintenance of BMWs

9.303 The Court found that in respect of the repair and maintenance of BMWs, the rights of the trade mark proprietor were not exhausted; advertisements relating to car repair and maintenance did not affect further commercialization of the cars in question.

9.304 However, here the Court had to consider whether use of the trade mark might be legitimate under Article 6(1)(c). The example chosen by the Court showed its willingness to expand the scope of the provision.

> Like the use of a trade mark intended to identify the vehicles which a non-original spare part will fit, the use in question is intended to identify the goods in respect of which the service is provided.[302]

---

[298] Case C-337/95 *Parfums Christian Dior* [1997] ECR I-6013.
[299] Citing C-10/89 *Hag II* [1990] ECR I-3711.
[300] Paragraph 53.
[301] Paragraph 54.
[302] Paragraph 59.

9.305 Regarding the necessity condition, it endorsed the view of the Advocate General that if an independent trader carried out the maintenance and repair of BMWs or was in fact a specialist in that field, that fact could not in practice be communicated to his customers without using the BMW marks.

9.306 Finally, the condition requiring use of the trade mark to be in accordance with honest practices in industrial or commercial matters should be regarded as constituting in substance the expression of a duty to act fairly in relation to the legitimate interests of the trade mark owner. Using another analogy, the Court found this to be similar to the duty imposed on a reseller using another's trade mark to advertise the resale of products covered by that mark.[303]

9.307 The Court saw Article 6 as sharing a common scope with Article 7: to reconcile the fundamental interests of trade mark protection with those of free movement of goods and freedom to provide services in the Common Market in such a way that trade mark rights would be able to fulfil their essential role in the system of undistorted competition which the Treaty sought to establish and maintain. As a result, the application of the two provisions would follow a similar reasoning:

> the use of another's trade mark for the purpose of informing the public of the repair and maintenance of goods covered by that mark is authorised on the same conditions as those applying where the mark is used for the purpose of informing the public of the resale of goods covered by that mark.[304]

(2) *Gerolsteiner Brunnen*: The Scope of Article 6(1)(b)

(a) *The facts in the main proceedings and the order for reference*

9.308 In *Gerolsteiner Brunnen*,[305] the Court considered the same provision from a different angle. Gerolsteiner Brunnen ('Gerolsteiner') was the registered proprietor of the word mark GERRI and of a number of figurative marks incorporating the word GERRI in Germany; the specification covered mineral water, non-alcoholic beverages, fruit juice-based drinks, and lemonades. Indeed, Gerolsteiner marketed mineral water and soft drinks with a mineral-water base. Putsch had been marketing in Germany since the mid-1990s soft drinks with the words KERRY SPRING appearing on their labels. The soft drinks were manufactured and bottled in Ballyferriter in County Kerry, Ireland, by Kerry Spring Water, an Irish company using water from a spring called Kerry Spring. Gerolsteiner claimed that this constituted trade mark infringement. Putsch retorted that the contested words had always been used as an indicator of geographical origin.

9.309 The case reached the Bundesgerichtshof that stayed proceedings and referred the following questions to the Court.
1. Is Article 6(1)(b) of the First Trade Mark Directive also applicable if a third party uses the indications referred to therein as a trade mark (*markenmässig*)?
2. If so, must that use as a trade mark be taken into account when considering, pursuant to the final clause of Article 6(1) of the First Trade Mark Directive, whether use has been in accordance with honest practices in industrial or commercial matters?[306]

---

[303] Citing *Hag II* (n 299).
[304] Paragraph 63.
[305] Case C-100/01 *Gerolsteiner Brunnen GmbH & Co v Putsch GmbH* [2004] ECR I-691.
[306] Reproduced in paragraph 10.

(b) The Opinion of Advocate General Stix-Hackl

9.310 The Advocate General started her legal analysis by identifying the main disputed point as 'whether [Article 6] also applies if the use is intended not, or not only, to describe the goods or service, but also to differentiate them from competitors' goods or services'.[307]

9.311 (i) **The wording and context of Article 6(1)(b)** In her textual analysis of the provision she emphasized that Article 6(1)(b) did not distinguish between types of use. It referred simply to 'indications' of geographical origin. The wording was inconclusive since indications of geographical indications could also be protected as trade marks. She added that the Directive also failed to indicate circumstances where a sign was 'used as a trade mark'. 'Making the application of Article 6(1)(b) dependent on the type of use made of a sign distinguishing between descriptive use and use as a trade mark is tantamount to making that application dependent on an unwritten factual ingredient.'[308]

9.312 The historical context of the provision supported the Advocate General's interpretation. The original proposal provided that the limitation of trade mark rights would apply only where the descriptive indication was not used as a trade mark; however, in the amended proposal the provision was amended to its current version. 'The Community legislature thus deliberately refrained from drawing a distinction according to type of use.'[309]

9.313 Finally, she conceded that the corresponding provisions in Greece, Italy, and Spain provided that a sign might not be used as a trade mark but only in a descriptive manner; however, this should not be seen as decisive.

9.314 (ii) **The 'schematic' classification** The next step was to consider the provision against its broader legislative context. The link between Article 5 and Article 6 required that the use in question should also be covered by Article 5. Otherwise, she agreed with the Commission and Putsch, 'reliance on Article 6 would be meaningless if the use in question did not in any case come under Article 5'.[310]

9.315 Advocate General Stix-Hackl found further support in the case law of the Court on Article 5. According to her reading, *Hölterhoff*[311] and *Arsenal*,[312] combined with the essential function of a trade mark established in *Hoffman-la Roche*,[313] made it clear that the 'admissibility of using a sign for purposes other than to distinguish the goods or services of one undertaking from those of another cannot be inferred from Article 6 of the Trade Mark Directive, because such a use does not fall within the protective scope of Article 5'.[314]

9.316 She also rejected the argument submitted by the UK Government on the potential interpretive inconsistency between Article 3(1)(c) and Article 6(1)(b). She reiterated what the Court had held in *Windsurfing Chiemsee*[315] and noted that only registration would be prohibited, not the simple use of the indication of geographical origin. In any case, *Windsurfing Chiemsee*

---

[307] Point 34.
[308] Point 36.
[309] Point 40.
[310] Point 43.
[311] C-2/00 *Hölterhoff* [2002] ECR I-4187.
[312] C-206/01 *Arsenal* [2002] ECR I-10273.
[313] Case 102/77 *Hoffmann-la Roche* [1978] ECR 1139.
[314] Point 45.
[315] Joined Cases C-108/97 and C-109/97 *Windsurfing Chiemsee* [1999] ECR I-2779.

concerned the trade mark registrability criteria for geographical names; here the trade mark for which protection had been sought consisted of an imaginary name.

9.317 (iii) **A teleological analysis of Article 6(1)(b)** The Advocate General then looked for the scope and purpose of the provision. She repeated that Article 6 served as a balancing mechanism between trade mark rights and free movement of goods.[316] 'As a sort of regulating device, therefore, Article 6 ... is closely linked to the exclusive rights set out in Article 5'.[317] She also remarked that the reference to 'honest practices in industrial or commercial matters' ensured that the protective function of the trade mark would not be jeopardized.

9.318 The weighing up of the interests of the trade mark proprietor with those of the third party in each specific case rather than create legal uncertainty would allow the proper balance of interests to be struck, as required by Community law. Accordingly she concluded use of a sign as a trade mark did not constitute a ground for precluding the application of Article 6(1)(b) as a matter of principle.

9.319 (iv) **Use in accordance with honest practices** In *BMW*[318] the Court had described this condition as a duty to act fairly in relation to the legitimate interests of the trade mark owner. Accordingly, the use as a trade mark should be taken into account in the assessment of the condition. She suggested a number of factors that should be taken into account either with regard to the registered trade mark or the way the indications would be used, noting that the interests of all parties should be taken into account.

9.320 First, she identified the distinctive character and the repute of the registered trade mark. Second, deliberately deceiving the public would not accord with honest practices; it appears that the intention of the third party as well as the perception of the public could influence the finding on this factor. Third, the way the sign was used could also be decisive; she suggested that there was a close link between the way the indication was used and the purpose for which it could be used. Amongst the additional factors that should be considered were the degree of similarity of the indication with the registered mark, the degree of emphasis of the indication, including where this went beyond what might be required under Community law, and the public perception of the indication as a trade mark.

9.321 In relation to mineral waters there were specific rules at the Community level;[319] however, the simple use of the name of the spring did not allow any conclusions to be drawn about the purpose of that indication.

(c) The Judgment of the Court

9.322 The Court agreed with the Advocate General that the provision did not distinguish between the possible uses of the indications referred to in Article 6(1)(b). 'For such an indication to fall within the scope of that article, it suffices that it is an indication concerning one of the characteristics set out therein, like geographical origin.'[320]

---

[316] Citing C-63/97 *BMW* [1999] ECR I-905.
[317] Point 49.
[318] C-63/97 *BMW* [1999] ECR I-905.
[319] Council Directive 80/777/EEC of 15 July 1980 on the approximation of the laws of the Member States relating to the exploitation and marketing of natural mineral waters ([1980] OJ L229/1).
[320] Paragraph 19.

It underlined that the trade mark GERRI had no geographical connotation whereas the sign KERRY SPRING referred to the geographical origin of the water, the place where the product was bottled, and the place where the producer was established, noting that the Commission emphasized the geographical nature of the expression KERRY SPRING, and that Kerry Spring was included in the list of mineral waters recognized by Ireland for the purposes of Council Directive 80/777. On the other hand, the referring court had found that there was a likelihood of aural confusion between GERRI and KERRY, accepting that consumers were shortening KERRY SPRING to KERRY. 9.323

The critical question was whether Article 5(1)(b) allowed the trade mark proprietor to prevent a third party from using the indication of geographical origin. Article 6(1) had to be considered, and the only test it provided for was assessing that the indication of geographical origin was used in accordance with honest practices in industrial or commercial matters. This, according to *BMW*,[321] meant that there was a duty to act fairly in relation to the legitimate interests of the trade mark owner. 9.324

The Court concluded that Article 6(1)(b) should be interpreted as meaning that where there existed a likelihood of aural confusion between a word mark registered in one Member State and an indication, in the course of trade, of the geographical origin of a product originating in another Member State, the proprietor of the trade mark might prevent the use of the indication of geographical origin only if that use were not in accordance with honest practices in industrial or commercial matters. This was an issue for the national court to decide, following an overall assessment of all the circumstances of the particular case in that regard. 9.325

Still, the Court held that: 9.326

> the mere fact that there exists a likelihood of aural confusion between a word mark registered in one Member State and an indication of geographical origin from another Member State is ... insufficient to conclude that the use of that indication in the course of trade is not in accordance with honest practices. In a Community of 15 Member States, with great linguistic diversity, the chance that there exists some phonetic similarity between a trade mark registered in one Member State and an indication of geographical origin from another Member State is already substantial and will be even greater after the impending enlargement.[322]

(3) *Gillette*: Indicating compatibility

(a) *The facts in the main proceedings and the order for reference*

Gillette[323] tested the extent to which a trade mark can be used in order to indicate compatibility with the trade-marked product. The case was a reference from the Korkein Oikeus (Supreme Court) of Finland. Gillette was the registered proprietor of the trade marks 'Gillette' and 'Sensor' in Finland; the specification included razors. The actual product put on the market was a razor that consisted of a handle and a blade that could be attached to the handle; the blades were also sold on their own to be used as replacements. LA-Laboratories ('LA') marketed its own razor, also consisting of a handle and a blade under the trade mark 9.327

---

[321] C-63/97 *BMW* [1999] ECR I-905.
[322] Paragraph 25.
[323] C-228/03 *The Gillette Company v LA-Laboratories Ltd Oy* [2005] ECR I-2337.

'Parason Flexor'. Its blades were similar to Gillette's and they too were sold on their own; on the packaging of the blades there was a sticker with the message 'All Parason Flexor and Gillette Sensor handles are compatible with this blade'.

9.328 The national court referred the following questions:

> When applying Article 6(1)(c) of the First Council Directive 89/104/EEC to approximate the laws of the Member States relating to trade marks:
>
> 1) What are the criteria
>   a) on the basis of which the question of regarding a product as a spare part or accessory is to be decided, and
>   b) on the basis of which those products to be regarded as other than spare parts and accessories which can also fall within the scope of the said subparagraph are to be determined?
> 2) Is the permissibility of the use of a third party's trade mark to be assessed differently, depending on whether the product is like a spare part or accessory or whether it is a product which can fall within the scope of the said subparagraph on another basis?
> 3) How should the requirement that the use must be 'necessary' to indicate the intended purpose of a product be interpreted? Can the criterion of necessity be satisfied even though it would in itself be possible to state the intended purpose without an express reference to the third party's trade mark, by merely mentioning only for instance the technical principle of functioning of the product? What significance does it have in that case that the statement may be more difficult for consumers to understand if there is no express reference to the third party's trade mark?
> 4) What factors should be taken into account when assessing use in accordance with honest commercial practice? Does mentioning a third party's trade mark in connection with the marketing of one's own product constitute a reference to the fact that the marketer's own product corresponds, in quality and technically or as regards its other properties, to the product designated by the third party's trade mark?
> 5) Does it affect the permissibility of the use of a third party's trade mark that the economic operator who refers to the third party's trade mark also markets, in addition to a spare part or accessory, a product of his own with which that spare part or accessory is intended to be used?[324]

(b) The Opinion of Advocate General Tizzano

9.329 (i) **The context for the interpretation of Article 6** Advocate General Tizzano started his analysis by considering the essential function of a trade mark as a guarantee of origin.[325] This led to the exclusive right that covered protection against unauthorized use likely to cause confusion. Article 6 imposed limitations to the rights of trade mark proprietors in order to reconcile the fundamental interests of trade mark protection with the principles of free movement of goods and freedom to provide services in the system of undistorted competition envisaged by the Treaty.[326]

> It can therefore be said that, in limiting the exclusive right provided for under Article 5, Article 6(1)(c) of Directive 89/104 seeks to balance the owner's interest in the trade mark being able to perform to the full its function of guaranteeing the product's origin against the interest of other traders in having full access to the market, but leaving the door open—as

---

[324] Reproduced in paragraph 23.
[325] Citing the Tenth Recital to the Preamble and, indicatively, 102/77 *Hoffmann-la Roche* [1978] ECR 1139, C-206/01 *Arsenal* [2002] ECR I-10273, C-40/01 *Ansul* [2003] ECR I-2439.
[326] Citing C-100/02 *Gerolsteiner Brunnen* [2004] ECR I-691.

would appear borne out by the broad reference to free movement in the Court's statement quoted above and as we will see below—for other interests too to come into play.[327]

9.330 **(ii) The fundamental criterion for the application of Article 6(1)(c)** He identified the function of the trade mark as an indicator of the intended purpose rather than the origin of the product as the main condition that had to be satisfied in order for a third party's trade mark to be lawfully placed on a product. This would arise in the case of accessories and spare parts but also in that of products capable of being used together, using the example of a computer and its operating programme to illustrate the second scenario.

9.331 Article 6(1)(c) should cover use in respect of any product if that use would be necessary to indicate its intended purpose. The history and wording of the provision supported this interpretation; accordingly, 'the fundamental factor in all cases is whether the use of the third party's trade mark is necessary in order to indicate the intended purpose of the product (or service) and does not give rise to confusion as to its origin'.[328]

9.332 This was all that the Court presented in response to the first two questions, since there was no need to distinguish main products from accessories and spare parts.

9.333 **(iii) The factors for assessing whether the use was necessary** Delineating the scope of the provision was a difficult exercise. The history and the wording of the provision pointed towards a stricter interpretation, the context of the provision opened the door to a wider set of interests, whereas the case law of the Court appeared to favour a broader interpretation.

> For my part, I have no difficulty accepting that the approach proposed by Gillette appears more in keeping with the letter of Article 6(1)(c) of the directive, which refers to the use of the third party's trade mark not as 'efficient' but as 'necessary', and needless to say the two are not synonymous.[329]

9.334 Advocate General Tizzano sought support from the legislative history of the provision, this time though for limiting its scope. The original proposal covered use 'for the purpose of indicating the intended purpose of accessories or spare parts', the final use 'where it is necessary to indicate the intended purpose '.

9.335 He accepted though that the provision could not be interpreted solely on that basis, 'in fact ... that provision opens the door also to other [other than the trade mark proprietor's] values and interests which it does not expressly mention but which in the broader perspective it would be difficult to ignore';[330] *BMW*[331] was an attempt to reconcile different interests. Still, those interests were directed towards a common purpose: ensuring a system of undistorted competition and the right of consumers to choose from a variety of interchangeable products.

9.336 He focused on the interests of the trade mark proprietor and consumers. *BMW*[332] 'did indeed reconcile the requirement of protecting the trade mark owner with that of protecting the consumer even in terms of maximising competition and providing complete information'.[333]

---

[327] Point 30.
[328] Point 39.
[329] Point 51.
[330] Point 55.
[331] C-63/97 *BMW* [1999] ECR I-905.
[332] ibid.
[333] Point 58.

9.337 Inevitably there was some uncertainty regarding the test of necessity; this, the Advocate General suggested, could be resolved at the stage of examining the circumstances and manner of use of the trade mark according to Article 6(1).

> The less rigorous [the interpretation of necessity] may be, the more stringent will be the scrutiny of the manner of use. At the same time, it is precisely on the more solid ground of that scrutiny that the actual 'necessity' of the use of the mark can be better assessed and such doubts as may always arise in the abstract in that regard dispelled.[334]

9.338 Subject to the above qualifications, he proposed that:

> the Court should answer the third question to the effect that the use of a third party's trade mark is 'necessary' to indicate the intended purpose of a product if it constitutes the only means of providing consumers with complete information as to the possible uses of the product in question.[335]

9.339 (iv) **The concept of 'honest practices in industrial and commercial matters'** According to *BMW*,[336] the condition of 'honest practices in industrial and commercial matters' was interpreted as a duty to act fairly in relation to the legitimate interests of the trade mark owner. The exclusive trade mark right would not be infringed where a third party uses the trade mark in compliance with the conditions laid down by that Directive.

9.340 There were two conditions: the advertisement should not create confusion in the marketplace or seek to take unfair advantage of the reputation of a trade mark of a competitor. Based on the analogies between trade mark law and comparative advertising that the Court had indicated in *Toshiba*,[337] the Advocate General supported the fact that in order to assess the applicability of the two conditions on a particular case, national courts should follow the 'global assessment' route taking into account all the factors that could be relevant to the circumstances of the case.[338]

9.341 (v) **The activities of the advertiser** The fifth question, in essence, enquired whether the assessment of the lawfulness of a comparative advertisement relied on the fact that the advertiser also sold the type of product with which the advertised product was intended to be used. This should not be considered as a new criterion although it could be one of the factors courts had to take into account in their assessment of the two conditions mentioned above.

(c) *The Judgment of the Court*

9.342 (i) **The criteria that make use necessary** The Court considered the first three questions together. They were essentially seeking the criteria for interpreting the requirement of necessity under Article 6(1)(c). The provision did not lay down criteria for determining whether a given intended purpose of a product fell within its scope, but merely required that use of the trade mark be necessary in order to indicate such a purpose. The intended purpose of the products as accessories or spare parts was cited only by way of example. The provision clearly went beyond the distinction between accessories and spare parts and it was not necessary to determine whether a product should be regarded as an accessory or a spare part.

9.343 Its analysis in *BMW*[339] could also be applied in this case. There the information was necessary in order to preserve the system of undistorted competition in the market for that product

---

[334] Point 69.
[335] Point 71.
[336] C-63/97 *BMW* [1999] ECR I-905.
[337] C-112/99 *Toshiba* [2001] ECR I-7945, see paragraph 12.05 and following, below.
[338] C-251/95 *Sabel* [1997] ECR I-6191.
[339] C-63/97 *BMW* [1999] ECR I-905.

or service.³⁴⁰ Here, the Gillette marks were being used by a third party in order to provide the public with comprehensible and complete information as to the intended purpose of the product; in other words, its compatibility with the product bearing those trade marks.

9.344 Such use would be necessary in cases where the information could not in practice be communicated to the public without using the relevant trade marks. This meant that 'use must in practice be the only means of providing such information'.³⁴¹

> In that respect, in order to determine whether other means of providing such information may be used, it is necessary to take into consideration, for example, the possible existence of technical standards or norms generally used for the type of product marketed by the third party and known to the public for which that type of product is intended. Those norms, or other characteristics, must be capable of providing that public with comprehensible and full information on the intended purpose of the product marketed by that third party in order to preserve the system of undistorted competition on the market for that product.³⁴²

9.345 This was an issue that the national court had to determine according to the above requirements but also taking account of the nature of the public for which the product marketed by LA was intended.

9.346 Finally, since Article 6(1)(c) made no distinction between the possible intended purposes of products the criteria would be the same for all the possible intended purposes.

9.347 **(ii) The interpretation of 'honest practices': Introducing a test** The Court identified four instances where use of a trade mark would not comply with honest practices in industrial or commercial matters. First, where use might give the impression of a commercial connection between the reseller and the trade mark proprietor. Second, where it might affect the value of the trade mark by taking unfair advantage of its distinctive character or repute. Third, where it might discredit or denigrate that mark. Fourth, where the third party presented its product as an imitation or replica of the product bearing the trade mark.

9.348 The outcome remained in the jurisdiction of the national court to determine, taking account of

> the overall presentation of the product marketed by the third party, particularly the circumstances in which the mark of which the third party is not the owner is displayed in that presentation, the circumstances in which a distinction is made between that mark and the mark or sign of the third party, and the effort made by that third party to ensure that consumers distinguish its products from those of which it is not the trade mark owner.³⁴³

9.349 There were two outstanding points the Court had to deal with. First, the fact that a third party used a trade mark in order to indicate the intended purpose of its product did not necessarily mean that it was presenting that product as being of the same quality as, or having equivalent properties to, those of the product bearing the trade mark. Resolution of these questions depended on the facts of the case. Second, the fact that the product marketed by the third party had been represented as being of the same quality as, or having equivalent properties to, the product whose trade mark was used was one of the factors the national court had to take into account.

---

[340] Paragraph 33.
[341] Paragraph 35.
[342] Paragraph 36.
[343] Paragraph 46.

9.350 Finally, the Court held that on its own the fact that the third party marketed not only a spare part or accessory but also the product itself with which the spare part or accessory was intended to be used was not relevant, provided that use of the trade mark satisfied the other requirements.

(4) *Adam Opel*: A Narrow Analysis

9.351 In *Adam Opel* the Court also considered whether would use of the Opel sign on toy cars fell under the scope of Article 6.

(a) The Opinion of Advocate General Ruiz-Jarabo Colomer

9.352 **(i) Application to the facts: Article 6(1)**   Advocate General Ruiz-Jarabo Colomer[344] decided to look briefly at the remaining two questions in the hypothetical scenario of a negative answer to the first question. The aim of Article 6(1) was to balance the interests of the trade mark proprietor on the one hand and those of its competitors on the other, seeking to secure the availability of descriptive signs, but since it constituted an exception to the general rules on protection under Article 5, he accepted it had to be interpreted narrowly.

9.353 Accordingly, he found it difficult to argue that the reproduction of the sign on the toy car qualified as an indication of the type or quality of the product. However, since the nature of a model necessitated the accurate and detailed copy of the original, the sign should be considered as falling within the scope of Article 6(1)(b) as describing other characteristics of the product because it achieved two objectives.

9.354 The third question covered the remaining consideration for the application of Article 6(1)(b): had the sign been used in accordance with honest commercial or industrial practices? To answer that question he went back to the jurisprudence of the Court in *Gillette*. The most relevant of the uses mentioned therein would be where the third party presented its product as an imitation or reproduction of the marked product. This would not, however, cover miniature toys because they did not imitate the miniatures manufactured by Opel licensees but the actual car manufactured by Opel.

9.355 According to the Advocate General compliance with honest practices should be determined according to *Anheuser-Busch*[345] by making an overall assessment of the facts of the case and taking into account three particular factors: the extent that use of a commercial name would be understood by the relevant public as indicating a link between the third party's products and the trade mark proprietor; the extent that the third party should have been aware of this; and whether it possessed a reputation from which the third party could benefit in order to market its own products.

9.356 The way AUTEC presented its products warranted the application of Article 6(1)(b); the inclusion of its own trade marks and indications was evidence of honest behaviour in compliance with commercial practice.

(b) The Judgment of the Court

9.357 **(i) Article 6(1)(c)**   As regards the question of whether the use in issue could be allowed by virtue of Article 6 of the Directive, the Court held, as a preliminary point, that the affixing

---

[344] Points 54–61.
[345] C-245/02 *Anheuser-Busch* [2004] ECR I-10989.

of Opel's trade mark on scale models could not be authorized on the basis of Article 6(1)(c) because it was not meant to indicate the intended purpose of the toys concerned.[346]

9.358 Then it turned to the main issue under the second question, namely the applicability to the case of the exception included in Article 6(1)(b).

(ii) Can a specific toy model be described by reference to the original product? **9.359** In that regard, it held that, although this provision is primarily designed to prevent the trade mark proprietor from prohibiting the use by competitors of descriptive terms forming part of his mark in order to indicate certain characteristics of their products,[347] its wording is in no way specific to such a situation. Thus, it cannot be excluded *a priori* that a trade mark may be used for descriptive purposes if its use merely consists in giving indications about the kind, quality, or other characteristics of the relevant products and provided that it is made in accordance with honest practices in industrial or commercial matters.[348]

9.360 In that connection, the Commission had argued that in specific circumstances, the identical reproduction of each and every detail of the original product, including the copying of its trade mark, might constitute an essential characteristic of the reduced replica, so that Article 6(1)(b) of the Directive could apply, as for example when the scale models were intended for collectors. However, the Court took the view that the facts of the case did not support such a scenario. It found that the affixing of a sign identical to a trade mark for motor vehicles to toy scale models in order to reproduce the original faithfully is not intended to provide an indication as to a characteristic of those models, but is merely an element in the faithful reproduction of the real product.[349]

(c) Conclusions

9.361 The Court left open the possibility of applying the exception in sectors where the reproduction of the mark on the replica is somehow inevitable, but the fact remains that in this way a substantial part of the toy industry is made subject to the owner's control, so that the marketing of 'undesired' imitations is effectively avoided. However, it is difficult to see how the cut-off point between 'honest' and 'dishonest' practices is to be drawn in similar situations, if not by reference to the established practices in the relevant sector.

F. Conflicts Between Trade Marks and Trade Names: Infringement and Defences

(1) *Robelco*: Trade Marks and Trade Names

(a) The facts in the main proceedings and the order for reference

9.362 *Robelco*[350] was the first case that the Court looked at the meaning of Article 5(5). Robeco, an asset management company that owned the Benelux trade mark 'Robeco', started trade mark infringement proceedings against Robelco, a business-park property developer,

---

[346] Paragraph 39.
[347] Citing joined cases C-108/97 and C-109/97 *Windsurfing Chiemsee* [1999] ECR I-2779, paragraph 28.
[348] Paragraph 43.
[349] Paragraph 44.
[350] C-23/01 *Robelco NV v Robeco Groep NV* [2002] ECR I-1093; see C-245/02 *Anheuser-Busch v Budejovick\ay Budvar, narodni podnik* [2004] ECR I-10989, paragraphs 12.194 and following, below.

seeking a restraining order against use of the sign 'Robelc', or any other sign similar to 'Robeco', as a trade name or company name.

9.363 The case reached the Hof van Beroep (Court of Appeal) in Brussels, which referred two questions to the Court of Justice regarding the interpretation of Article 5(5): (i) does the provision cover signs that are similar as well as identical to an earlier trade mark? (ii) if the answer is yes, then is there a likelihood of confusion requirement or would likelihood of association suffice?[351]

9.364 The parties agreed that Article 5(5) was not a trade mark law provision. Robeco claimed that the term sign covered identical as well as similar signs and that whether there is a likelihood of confusion or association is irrelevant according to the provision. Robelco, on the other hand, contended that there must be identity between the trade mark and the sign, otherwise it would be necessary to assess in each case whether there exists a likelihood of confusion. The Commission submitted that Article 5(5) was not a harmonization provision; its purpose was to exclude this area of law from harmonization. The national court had correctly established that Article 5(5) was applicable on the facts of the case and it was free to decide how the national provision should be interpreted.

(b) The Opinion of Advocate General Ruiz-Jarabo Colomer

9.365 Advocate General Ruiz-Jarabo Colomer considered that the critical question was whether Article 5(5) is a provision that falls under the scope of Community or national law rather than whether it is a trade mark law provision or not.

9.366 Regarding the second issue, he noted that:

> although it may be appropriate to consider that trade mark law covers only those matters which relate essentially to the distinguishing function of trade marks, it is not unreasonable to imagine a wider category which encompasses the whole range of conflicts which might arise in relation to a trade mark.[352]

9.367 Article 5 established two boundaries, one positive and one negative.

> In the positive sense, the right to prohibit use of identical or similar signs for identical or similar products, where there is a likelihood of confusion, is a harmonised right of trade mark proprietors. In the negative sense, the strengthened protection of the distinctive character and goodwill of trade marks which have a reputation and the rules relating to use of a sign in a way which is not designed to identify the origin of goods or services are not subject to approximation at Community level.[353]

9.368 He found the language of Article 5(5) puzzling. 'Where a sign is not used, directly or indirectly, subliminally or unintentionally, to identify goods or services, I fail to see what relevance it can have to trade for the purposes of trade mark law'[354] unless the provision covered signs that are not used as trade marks in the formal sense. Indeed, this is how the national court and the parties viewed the provision, and the Advocate General, somewhat reluctantly, adopted the same perspective.

---

[351] The national court highlighted the difference between Article 13A(1)(d) of the Uniform Benelux Law and Article 5(5) of the Directive. Article 13A(1)(d) explicitly covered similar signs. So it questioned whether the two provisions were consistent with each other.
[352] Point 29.
[353] Point 31.
[354] Point 32.

9.369 He had no evidence at his disposal that could lead him to an alternative view and the analysis of the questions referred did not force him to conclude otherwise.³⁵⁵ So the

> situation where a sign is used otherwise than for the purpose of distinguishing the origin of goods or services is not covered by Article 5(1), which refers to the identification of goods and services, and is instead specifically caught by the reservation in favour of the legislatures of the Member States laid down in Article 5(5). That area is outside the scope of the Directive, which, furthermore, and for the avoidance of any doubt, confers on the Member States the power to legislate on such matters.³⁵⁶

9.370 Accordingly, Member States were free to legislate as they wished in this area. Imposing restrictions would lead to an unjustified restriction of the freedom of action they enjoy in areas such as unfair competition, consumer protection, and civil liability. From a trade mark law perspective, Article 5(1) and Article 5(2) and all the similarity requirements therein were linked with the function of a trade mark as distinguishing signs; this function was not relevant in the case of Article 5(5). The Benelux legislature did not appear to exceed its powers under Community law.

(c) The Judgment of the Court

9.371 The Court accepted the core of the Commission's submission:

> it is clear from Article 5(5) of the Directive that the harmonisation brought about by Article 5(1) to (4) does not affect national provisions relating to the protection of a sign against use other than for the purpose of distinguishing goods or services, where such use without due cause takes unfair advantage of, or is detrimental to, the distinctive character or the repute of the trade mark.³⁵⁷

The Third Recital confirmed this.

9.372 Member States 'may adopt no legislation in this area or they may, subject to such conditions as they may determine, require that the sign and the trade mark be either identical or similar, or that there be some other connection between them'.³⁵⁸

(2) *Céline*: Trade Names Performing a Distinguishing Function

(a) The facts in the main proceedings and the order for reference

9.373 In *Céline*,³⁵⁹ the Court dealt with trade names not from the perspective of Article 5(1)(a). The novel element was whether a company name is capable of being used in relation to goods or services within the meaning of that provision, opening thus new possibilities as regards the protection against signs performing a trade mark-like function. Céline SA, a high-end clothing and fashion accessories manufacturer, is the owner of the word mark CÉLINE, registered in France in respect of, inter alia, 'clothes and shoes'. Mr Grynfogel, another French trader, operated a ready-to-wear garments business in Nancy, trading as 'Céline', which was subsequently transferred to Céline SARL. Upon being alerted to that state of affairs, Céline SA brought proceedings against Céline SARL, seeking an order prohibiting it from infringing its trade mark by using the company name and shop title 'Céline'.

---

³⁵⁵ Point 33.
³⁵⁶ Point 34.
³⁵⁷ Paragraph 30.
³⁵⁸ Paragraph 35.
³⁵⁹ C-17/06 *Céline SARL v Céline SA* [2007] ECR I-07041

9.374 The Tribunal de Grande Instance de Nancy (Nancy Regional Court) granted the relief sought and prohibited Céline SARL from using the term 'Céline'. On appeal the Cour d'appel de Nancy decided to stay the proceedings and to refer the following question to the Court for a preliminary ruling:

> Must Article 5(1) of [the directive] ... be interpreted as meaning that the adoption, by a third party without authorisation, of a registered word mark, as a company, trade or shop name in connection with the marketing of identical goods, amounts to use of that mark in the course of trade which the proprietor is entitled to stop by reason of his exclusive rights?

(b) The Opinion of Advocate General Sharpston

9.375 Advocate General Sharpston observed that to the extent that the referring court was asking whether the adoption of a company or trade name can constitute use within the meaning of Article 5(1) of the Directive, it was necessary to distinguish between the formal adoption of such a name and the way in which it is subsequently used in the course of trade. According to the Court's case law,[360] the application of Article 5(1)(a) requires that the sign must be used to distinguish goods and that its use must be likely to affect the trade mark's essential function, in particular by creating the impression that there is a material link in trade between the trade mark proprietor and the goods so distinguished. AG Sharpston moved on to apply those principles to the usual function of company names.

9.376 In that regard, she agreed that although the adoption and use of a company and/or trade name was in principle capable of constituting 'use' within the meaning of Article 5(1) of the Directive, this would not 'necessarily and automatically' be true in all cases.[361]

9.377 Moreover, the existence of a non-exhaustive list, in Article 5(3), of types of conduct which may be prohibited under Article 5(1) and (2) does not imply that all instances of such conduct will always fall within the scope of those provisions. It will always be necessary to ascertain, in addition, whether the particular conduct meets the specific requirements triggering that type of prohibition.

9.378 Mere adoption of a company or trade name does not normally constitute use within the meaning of Article 5(1) of the Directive and subsequent use of such a name in the course of trade must be assessed by the competent court on the facts of each case in order to determine whether it constitutes use in relation to goods or services for the purposes of that provision.

9.379 However, she noted also that insofar as the right which Céline SA sought to assert derives from trade mark law and from its status as trade mark proprietor, it was further necessary to address the possible impact on the case of the limitation in Article 6(1)(a), under which the proprietor may not prevent another person from using his own name in the course of trade, if that use is in accordance with honest practices in industrial or commercial matters.

9.380 Citing *Anheuser Busch*[362] and *BMW*,[363] she recalled that Article 6(1)(a) is not confined to names of natural persons and that the condition of honest practices implies a duty to act fairly in relation to the legitimate interests of the trade mark owner. Furthermore, at stake

---

[360] Citing the Judgments in C-63/97 *BMW* [1999] ECR I-905, *Arsenal* [2002] ECR I-10273, and *Anheuser Busch* [2004] ECR I-10989.
[361] Point 34.
[362] C-245/02 *Anheuser-Busch* [2004] ECR I-10989, paragraphs 77–80.
[363] C-63/97 *BMW* [1999] ECR I-905, paragraph 61.

in the main proceedings was whether the adoption of the company name after the registration of the trade mark and its possible use in relation to goods, is in accordance with honest practices; indeed, even if the name had been adopted before registration, the 'honest practices' condition could only become relevant after that registration, although in such a case its relevance would obviously be affected by the relative timing.

The question of knowledge is crucial in that connection, since a person cannot normally be said to be acting in accordance with honest commercial practices if he adopts a name which he knows to be identical or similar to an existing trade mark.[364] Mere ignorance of the existence of the trade mark cannot be sufficient to exonerate that person of all responsibility. In fact, honest practice in the choice of a name implies a reasonable diligence in ascertaining that the name chosen does not conflict with prior trade mark rights, and thus in verifying the existence of any such marks, all the more so since a search in national and Community trade mark registers is not normally particularly difficult or burdensome.[365]

9.381

On the other hand, if the search reveals the existence of similar or identical trade marks, the applicability of the prohibition should depend on the user's subsequent conduct, given that the compliance with honest practices would presumably imply at least contacting the trade mark proprietor and seeking his approval. Such a course of action may relieve the user of all possible responsibility not only if an approval is actually given but also when it results in acquiescence on the part of the owner, which, depending on the circumstances, may be equated with his (tacit) consent, within the meaning of Article 51 of the Directive.[366]

9.382

(c) The Judgment of the Court

The Court followed the approach of the Advocate General and examined the question referred as regards both the rule contained in Article 5 and the corresponding exception included in Article 6(1)(a) of the Directive.

9.383

(i) **The function of company names**   With regard to the former, it stressed that, as follows from the scheme of that provision, use of the sign in relation to goods or services within the meaning of sections 5(1) and 5(2) is use for the purpose of distinguishing those goods and services, whereas section 5(5) dealt with use for other purposes. Then, it referred to its Judgment in *Robelco* that the purpose of a company, trade, or shop name is not, of itself, to distinguish goods and services. Rather, the purpose of a company name is to identify a company, while that of a trade or shop name is to designate a business or the establishment where it is carried out. Accordingly, where the use is limited to those purposes, it cannot be considered as being 'in relation to goods' within the meaning of Article 5(1).[367]

9.384

Conversely, it held that there is use 'in relation to goods' where a third party either affixes the sign constituting his company, trade, or shop name to goods or, even where the sign is not so affixed, where it is used in a way that a link is established between that sign and the goods or services marketed or provided by the third party.[368] The national court had to determine whether the facts of the specific case actually corresponded to such use, or whether the use made of the sign was liable of affecting the essential function of the registered trade mark.

9.385

---

[364] Points 53–54.
[365] Point 55.
[366] Points 57–58.
[367] Paragraph 21.
[368] Paragraphs 22–23.

9.386 It is worth noting that even if the criterion of use 'in relation to goods' is satisfied in the above sense, it is questionable whether the activities carried out under a company or, in particular, shop name will ever be 'identical' with the goods for which the trade mark is protected in the sense of Article 5(1)(a) of the Directive, unless of course the company name is also used as a trade mark in the strict sense by being actually affixed on goods, as in the case of house marks.

9.387 In a traditional analysis under the Nice Classification, activities more indirectly linked to goods would most likely classify as retail services falling under class 35 of the Nice Agreement, within the meaning of the Court's Judgment in *Praktiker*.[369] Thus, however close the link between those activities and the goods to which they relate, it will be very difficult to ignore the fact that the comparison still concerns goods on the one hand and services on the other, which although on occasion may display similarities, cannot be regarded as being identical. Unless one skips the question altogether and only focuses on the nature of the goods to which the use 'relates' one way or another.

9.388 (ii) **The 'honest practices' exception** Next, the Court noted that it is for the Court to provide the national court with all the elements for the interpretation of Community law which may be of assistance in adjudicating on the case pending before it, whether or not that court has specifically referred to them in its questions. Consequently, it went on to examine the impact of the exception provided for in Article 6(1)(a) to the facts, pointing out that the condition of complying with 'honest practices in industrial or commercial matters' stated in that provision basically constitutes an expression of the duty to act fairly in relation to the legitimate interests of the trade-mark proprietor.[370]

9.389 In that regard, it held that in assessing whether the condition of honest practice is satisfied, account must be taken, first, of the extent to which the use of the name is understood by at least a significant section of the public as indicating a link between the third party's goods or services and the trade-mark proprietor, and, second, of the extent to which the third party ought to have been aware of that. Another factor to be taken into account is whether the trade mark enjoys a reputation in the Member State in which it is registered, from which the third party might profit.[371]

9.390 Note that in relation to honest practices the Court focused primarily on objective factors, like the perception of the relevant public and the possible reputation of the earlier mark[372] rather than on the more subjective criteria linked to the knowledge of the third party as to the existence of the earlier mark and the diligence displayed in ascertaining whether such conflicting prior rights actually exist, suggested by the Advocate General.

(3) An Alternative Line of Defence: Acquiescence and Honest Concurrent Use; *Budweiser VI*

(a) The facts in the main proceedings and the order for reference

9.391 *Budějovický Budvar*[373] was 'the war to end all wars' or an attempt to settle the almost forty-year-old dispute between Budějovický Budvar, národní podnik and Anheuser-Busch Inc.

---

[369] C-418/02 *Praktiker Bau* [2005] ECR I-05873.
[370] Citing C-245/02 *Anheuser-Busch* [2004] ECR I-10989, paragraph 82.
[371] Paragraph 34.
[372] Citing C-245/02 *Anheuser-Busch*, paragraph 83.
[373] C-482/09 *Budějovický Budvar, národní podnik v Anheuser-Busch Inc* [2011] ECR I-08701

by testing the limits of the concepts of acquiescence and honest concurrent use before the Court of Justice. The case was a reference from the Court of Appeal (England and Wales), Civil Division, concerning the interpretation of the term 'acquiescence' in Article 9 (1) of the Trade Marks Directive and the compatibility of the UK law doctrine of 'honest concurrent use' with Article 4(1) (a) of the same Directive.

9.392 The dispute in the main proceedings was the latest episode of the saga concerning the mark BUDWEISER in respect of which both companies held trade mark registrations in the UK, Budvar on the basis of an application made in June 1989 and Anheuser-Busch on the basis of an application dating form December 1979. Both marks had been registered on 19 May 2000, following a judgment by the Court of Appeal under the Trade Marks Act 1938 which expressly allowed the concurrent registration of the same or confusingly similar marks in circumstances where there was honest concurrent use or other special circumstances. On 18 May 2005, that is four years and 364 days after the marks were entered in the register, Anheuser-Busch lodged at the United Kingdom Intellectual Property Office an application for a declaration that Budvar's registration was invalid on the grounds that the marks and goods at issue were identical within the meaning of Article 4 (1) (a) and that there was no limitation in consequence of acquiescence because the period of five years prescribed in Article 9 (1) of that directive had not expired.

9.393 The Registrar granted the application made by Anheuser-Busch and declared Budvar's mark invalid. The High Court of Justice (England & Wales) (Chancery Division) dismissed the action brought by Budvar against that decision. Budvar lodged an appeal. The Court of Appeal had doubts about the correct interpretation, first, of Article 9 of the Directive, in particular as regards the meaning of the terms 'acquiescence' and 'period' as referred to in that article and, second, of Article 4 (1) (a) of the Directive, especially as concerns Budvar's argument that, notwithstanding the apparently absolute protection enjoyed by the earlier trade mark against identical marks which designate identical goods, an exception might be admitted in the event of long-established, honest concurrent use of the same sign by different undertakings, considering that in such circumstances the use of identical marks does not have an adverse effect on the origin function of the earlier mark since the signs at issue are not understood as designating the goods of a single company, but as designating the goods of one or the other.

9.394 In those circumstances the Court of Appeal decided to stay proceedings and refer to the Court the following questions for a preliminary ruling:

(1) What is meant by 'acquiesced' in Article 9(1) of the Directive and in particular:
   (a) is 'acquiesced' a Community law concept or is it open to the national court to apply national rules as to acquiescence (including delay or long-established honest concurrent use)?
   (b) if 'acquiesced' is a Community law concept can the proprietor of a trade mark be held to have acquiesced in a long and well-established honest use of an identical mark by another when he has long known of that use but has been unable to prevent it?
   (c) in any case, is it necessary that the proprietor of a trade mark should have his trade mark registered before he can begin to 'acquiesce' in the use by another of (i) an identical or (ii) a confusingly similar mark?
(2) When does the period of 'five successive years' commence and in particular, can it commence (and if so can it expire) before the proprietor of the earlier trade mark obtains actual registration of his mark; and if so what conditions are necessary to set time running?

(3) Does Article 4(1)(a) apply so as to enable the proprietor of an earlier mark to prevail even where there has been a long period of honest concurrent use of two identical trade marks for identical goods so that the guarantee of origin of the earlier mark does not mean the mark signifies the goods of the proprietor of the earlier and none other but instead signifies his goods or the goods of the other user?

(b) The Opinion of Advocate General Trstenjak

9.395 As regards the first part of the first question, Advocate General Trstenjak took the view that it was quite evident from the overall structure and purpose of the Directive that the term 'acquiescence' in Article 9(1) is an autonomous concept of European Union law that must be given a uniform interpretation. He based that view on a combined reading of the Seventh and Eleventh Recitals in the Preamble to the Directive[374] from which he inferred, first, that the defences against infringement provided for in Article 9 are a natural complement to the fully harmonized conditions for obtaining and continuing to hold a trade mark, and, second, that the exclusive rights of the proprietor could be limited only exceptionally and under conditions precisely defined by law, which gives rise to the need for all such limitations to be interpreted in a uniform manner for obvious reasons of legal certainty. Moreover, he observed that, in this sense, acquiescence was no different from the concept of exhaustion in Article 7 of the Directive, which the Court had decreed to be subject to a full harmonization.[375]

9.396 Next, he defined the concept of acquiescence by reference to its usual meaning, noting that the difference between the verbs 'to tolerate' in the Preamble and 'to acquiesce' in Article 9 of the English version of the Directive was not material in this regard. He also observed that the very essence of this term required an individual conduct characterized by a certain forbearance or passivity, without this ruling out the possibility of an implicit consent being deduced from this passive attitude. He stressed, however, that the owner's inactivity should not be due to extraneous or imposed circumstances, for example the legal or factual impossibility of taking measures against the infringement of his rights, since, after all, the concept of 'acquiescence' implies that the person acquiescing was theoretically in a position to do something about an undesired situation, but deliberately did not do it. He also found that imposed passivity was incompatible with the requirement in the Eleventh Recital that the interests of the proprietor be limited only on condition that this was 'equitable' and that it would run counter to the principle that one cannot be legally obliged to do the impossible.[376]

9.397 As regards the other conditions attached to the concept of acquiescence, the Advocate General considered that the wording of Article 9(1) made the commencement of the five-year period dependent on the fulfilment of three cumulative requirements. First, that the later mark is registered; second, that it is used; third, that the proprietor of the earlier mark is aware of that registration and use. Then, he focused on the knowledge requirement which differentiates acquiescence from the notion of prescription of rights that ensues irrespective of the right-holder's state of mind. In the Advocate General's opinion, Article 9(1) was phrased broadly enough to encompass not only actual but also constructive knowledge. Referring to the Judgment in *Lindt & Sprüngli*,[377] he took the view that a presumption of

---

[374] Which in the meantime have become the Eighth and Twelfth Recitals, respectively.
[375] Points 56–59 and 64–65.
[376] Points 68–72.
[377] C-529/07 *Lindt & Sprüngli* [2009] ECR I-4893, paragraph 39.

knowledge may arise from general awareness in the relevant sector of the use in question, or that it may be inferred, inter alia, from its duration, as the more that use is long-standing, the more probable it is that the owner will have knowledge of it. He observed, however, that such a presumption was a rebuttable one, since what mattered in any case was positive knowledge, the existence of which was firmly established in the main proceedings. Finally, based on the reference made by Article 9(1) to Article 4(2) of the Directive, which extends the concept of 'earlier mark' not only to registrations but also to applications and well-known marks, he concluded that the five-year period can begin even before the date of registration of the earlier mark.[378]

Moving on to the compatibility of Article 4(1)(a) with the doctrine of honest concurrent use, the Advocate General observed that, in essence, that doctrine was tantamount to a defence limiting the rights of the trade mark proprietor in a similar manner as acquiescence or the existence of a prior consent provided for in Article 4(5) of the Directive. Therefore, he concluded that, in principle, a mechanism of this kind could not remain within the competence of the Member States, as this would threaten the need for the exclusive rights of the proprietor to be delimited in a uniform manner by a set of exceptions clearly and exhaustively set forth in the Directive. Nonetheless, the Advocate General was ambivalent as to whether Article 4(1)(a) should apply *ratione temporis* to the main proceedings. Although that point had not been raised by the referring court, he observed that applying the Directive in a retroactive manner to facts that occurred before its transposition would seriously upset the balance of interests and the legitimate expectations of the parties, which are primarily attributable to the legal position that existed in the United Kingdom before its entry into force.[379] 9.398

(c) The Judgment of the Court

As regards part (a) of the first question, the Court agreed with the Advocate General that Article 9 effectively complements Articles 5 and 7 of the Directive by bringing about a complete harmonization of the conditions under which the proprietor of a registered trade mark may maintain his rights in case of challenge, referring to the statement in *Levi Strauss*[380] that the purpose of Article 9 is to strike a balance between the interest of the proprietor to safeguard the essential function of his mark and the interests of other economic operators in using signs capable of denoting their goods and services. Bearing also in mind the presence of the same defence in the Community Trade Mark Regulation (CTMR) and the need to construe both provisions in the same manner, it confirmed that 'acquiescence' in Article 9(1) is an autonomous concept of European law that must be given a uniform interpretation.[381] 9.399

The Court also agreed with the definition of acquiescence given by the Advocate General, stating that the usual meaning of the term, when interpreted in the light of the Eleventh Recital in the Preamble to the Directive, made clear that 'acquiescence' is not the same as 'consent' within the meaning of Article 7(1) which requires the intention to renounce a right to be unequivocally demonstrated but rather implies that the person who acquiesces 9.400

---

[378] Points 74–86.
[379] Points 91–97 and 114–115.
[380] C-145/05 *Levi Strauss* [2006] ECR I-3703, paragraphs 28 and 29
[381] Paragraphs 32–37.

remains intentionally inactive when faced with a situation which he would be in a position to oppose. Accordingly, it ruled that the proprietor of an earlier trade mark cannot be held to have acquiesced in the long and well-established use by a third party of a later trade mark, of which he has long been aware, if he was not in a position to oppose that use, and agreed with the Commission that the effect of any administrative or Court action initiated by the proprietor of the earlier trade mark is to interrupt the period of limitation in consequence of acquiescence prescribed in Article 9(1).[382]

9.401 Then the Court turned to examine whether the period of acquiescence can start before the proprietor has had his trade mark registered and, if so, what are the prerequisites attached to the commencement of that period. In this connection, it noted that it was apparent from the reference of Article 9(1) to a later 'registered' mark, that registration constitutes a necessary condition to set the relevant period running and that that period cannot therefore start from the date of the mere use of a later trade mark, even if that mark is subsequently registered. Conversely, in view of the reference of Article 4(2)(c) and (d) to marks which can be considered to be 'earlier' without having been registered, it took the view that the prior registration of the earlier mark does not constitute a condition for the commencement of the term of acquiescence. Thus, it answered part (c) of the first question and the second question to the effect that the prerequisites for the running of the period prescribed by Article 9(1), are first, registration of the later trade mark in the Member state concerned, second, the application for registration of that mark having been made in good faith, third, that the later trade mark is used by its proprietor in the Member state where it has been registered, and fourth, knowledge by the proprietor of the earlier trade mark that the later trade mark has been registered and used after its registration.[383]

9.402 When it came to the last question it decided to sidestep the proposal of the Advocate General concerning the inapplicability *ratione temporis* of the Directive to the main proceedings, although it took full account of the spirit of his remarks as regards the need to respect the established balance of interests between the parties. Even though it acknowledged that, according to the Tenth Recital[384] and Articles 4(1)(a) and 5(1)(a) of the Directive, the protection conferred by the registered trade mark in case of identity is absolute, and that an absolute protection does not require evidence of a likelihood of confusion on the part of the public, it went on to observe, citing its Judgment in *LTJ Diffusion*,[385] that the conditions of application of Article 4(1)(a) essentially correspond to those of Article 5(1)(a), so that the Court's interpretation of the latter is transposable, *mutatis mutandis*, also to the former. That assimilation of the principles applicable to registration and infringement proceedings allowed the Court to have recourse, once again, to its settled case law[386] regarding the functions of the trade mark and to conclude that Article 4(1)(a) must be interpreted as meaning that a later registered mark is liable to be declared invalid where it is identical with an earlier trade mark and the respective goods are also identical, only if 'the use of the later trade mark

---

[382] Paragraphs 39–50.
[383] Paragraphs 53–62.
[384] Which, in the meantime, has become the Eleventh Recital.
[385] C-291/00 *LTJ Diffusion* [2003] ECR I-2799, paragraphs 41 and 43.
[386] Citing C-487/07 *L'Oréal and Others* [2009] ECR I-5185, paragraph 58, and Joined Cases C-236/08 to C-238/08 *Google France and Google* [2010] ECR I-2417, paragraph 77.

has or is liable to have an adverse effect on the essential function of the trade mark, which is to guarantee to consumers the origin of the goods'.[387]

9.403 Having thus paved the way towards an equitable solution of the dispute, the Court noted that the facts referred to by the Court of Appeal corresponded to an exceptional set of circumstances which were capable of supporting the conclusion that the honest concurrent use of two identical marks such as the ones at issue was not liable to adversely affect their essential function, in particular since (a) Anheuser-Busch and Budvar have each been marketing their beers in the United Kingdom under the sign BUDWEISER or under a trade mark including that sign for almost thirty years; (b) they were expressly authorized to register concurrently that trade mark following a Court judgment; (c) both companies have from the beginning used their trade marks in good faith; (d) United Kingdom consumers are well aware of the difference between the beers marketed by Budvar and Anheuser-Busch, since their tastes, prices, and get-ups have always been different; and (e) the respective beers were clearly identifiable as being produced by different companies.[388]

9.404 In the light of the foregoing, the Court answered the third question to the effect that Article 4(1)(a) of the Directive must be interpreted as meaning that the proprietor of an earlier trade mark cannot obtain the cancellation of an identical later trade mark designating identical goods where there has been a long period of honest concurrent use of those two trade marks where, in circumstances such as those in the main proceedings, that use neither has nor is liable to have an adverse effect on the essential function of the trade mark which is to guarantee to consumers the origin of the goods or services.[389]

(d) Conclusions

9.405 *Budějovický Budvar* is a good example of the Court's ability to strike a balance between the consistent application of the principles deriving from its interpretation of the relevant provisions and the need to find equitable solutions when the circumstances so dictate. Its significance lies not so much in the way it dealt with acquiescence as to the inferences that can be drawn from its statements as concerns the viability of the doctrine of honest concurrent use within the context European trade mark law. In this connection three points are particularly pertinent.

9.406 On the one hand, by accepting that under certain circumstances, however exceptional, the parallel use of two identical trade marks in the same territory may circumscribe the exclusive rights of a trade mark proprietor, even if that proprietor has not consented to the registration of the later mark or acquiesced to its use, the Court has effectively recognized that at least some form of honest concurrent use is *de facto* embedded in European trade mark law, and may be used as a valid defence both in registration and infringement proceedings under the Directive and the Regulation.

9.407 On the other hand, the truly exceptional circumstances on which it based its conclusions militate in favour of an extremely narrow application of that doctrine, especially if it is to be assumed that only in situations such as those in the main proceedings is it possible to allow the concurrent use or registration of identical marks. Indeed, the strict reliance of

---

[387] Paragraphs 68–74.
[388] Paragraphs 76–82.
[389] Paragraph 84.

the Court on the particularities of the case does not allow for drawing inferences of a more general nature as to where the possibility of concurrent use starts or ends. In particular, it is not apparent which factor weighed more in the Court's Judgment, for instance if it was the prior judicial endorsement of the parallel use, the duration of the coexistence, or the absence of confusion in the mind of the public that tipped the balance. Nor can the proviso in the operative part that 'such use can only be allowed if it neither has nor is liable to have an adverse effect on the essential function of the trade mark' shed any more light on the right mixture of circumstances, as it does nothing more than define the concept, in the Court's typical fashion, by reference to its consequences.

9.408 Finally, it is uncertain what the relationship is between the doctrine of 'honest concurrent use' and the kindred concept of 'peaceful coexistence' put forward in *La Española*.[390] In that Judgment, the Court accepted that 'the possibility cannot be ruled out that the coexistence of two marks on a particular market might, together with other elements, contribute to diminishing the likelihood of confusion on the part of the relevant public', adding, however, that in such cases 'the absence of a likelihood of confusion may, in particular, be inferred from the peaceful nature of the coexistence of the marks at issue on the market'. Specifically, it is difficult to understand how the need for a 'peaceful' coexistence can be sustained after *Budějovický Budvar* if the parallel use of two identical or similar signs over a long period of time may prove sufficient to rule out all possible harm on the essential function of the earlier mark, even in cases involving a long history of judicial conflicts.

G. Enforcing the Community Trade Mark

9.409 Community trade marks, once registered, grant exclusive rights which are enforceable vis-à-vis third parties using identical or similar signs in the course of trade to the extent that there is either 'double identity' (signs and goods/services identical), or likelihood of confusion, or detriment to marks with reputation. These infringement rights have been discussed previously. As regards the procedures available to enforce the exclusive rights against non-complying infringers, the focus is usually on civil litigation. However, enforcement also includes criminal proceedings, initiated ex officio or upon complaint by the proprietor, and administrative proceedings, among which border seizure is the most prominent.

9.410 The Regulation itself only deals with civil proceedings, which are the subject of Title X of the Regulation.

9.411 Criminal proceedings are not even mentioned in the Regulation, or in any other European Union legislative instrument. It is however recognized that Member States when they provide for criminal penalties for the infringement of national marks (as they must, inter alia because of Article 61 of the Trade-Related Aspects of Intellectual Property Rights (TRIPs) Agreement), must also provide for the same penalties when the infringement of Community trade marks is involved.

---

[390] C-498/07 P *Aceites del Sur-Coosur SA v Koipe Corporacion (La Española)* [2009] ECR I-07371, paragraphs 80–84; see also T-31/03 *Grupo Sada v OHIM—Sadia (Grupo Sada)* [2005] ECR II-01667, paragraph 86, and T-460/11 *Scandic Distilleries v OHMI—Bürgerbräu, Röhm & Söhne (BÜRGER)* ECLI:EU:T:2012:432, paragraphs 60–61.

As regards border measures, the European Union's customs seizure legislation specifically provides for the protection of EU-wide intellectual property rights—that is, for Community trade marks, Community designs, and Community plant varieties—when infringing goods enter the EU.[391]

9.412

In the following sections we will first deal with civil infringement litigation as provided for in Title X of the Regulation, and then with border seizure.

9.413

(1) Civil enforcement (Title X of the Regulation)

Title X of the Regulation consists of Articles 94 to 108. Article 94 prescribes the application of the Regulation on jurisdiction and enforcement of judgments in civil and commercial matters, the so-called Brussels I Regulation,[392] unless the Community Trade Mark Regulation specifically provides for the applicable rules.

9.414

Pursuant to Article 95 Member States must designate from their civil courts a number 'as limited as possible' as Community trade mark (CTM) courts of first and second instance (Article 105), which have exclusive jurisdiction for the actions described in Article 96, essentially infringement actions, declaratory actions for non-infringement, and counterclaims for invalidity. Most Member States (twenty-three) have designated a single court (Austria, Belgium, Bulgaria, Croatia, Cyprus, Czech Republic, Denmark, Estonia, Finland, France, Greece, Hungary, Ireland, Luxembourg, Latvia, Lithuania, Malta, Netherlands, Poland, Romania, Slovenia, Spain, Sweden), while other have designated more than one, beginning with very few, such as Slovakia and Portugal, to substantial numbers, such as Germany, Italy, and United Kingdom.

9.415

International jurisdiction is provided for in Article 97. Jurisdiction of the CTM courts is either EU-wide or limited to the Member State where the court is located. In the first category (Article 97(1)–(4)) are the courts in the Member State where the defendant is domiciled or, failing a domicile, has an establishment, or, failing both, where the claimant has its domicile, or, failing this as well, an establishment. Residually, the courts in Spain, where the OHIM has its seat, are competent EU-wide.[393] With competence limited to the Member State where the court is located, the courts whose jurisdiction is established on the basis where acts of infringement have been committed or are threatened are competent (Article 97(5)). Special competence rules apply for preliminary and provisional measures (Article 103).

9.416

Community trade mark courts must accept the validity of the allegedly infringed mark, unless the defendant counterclaims seeking a declaration of revocation or invalidity

9.417

---

[391] Regulation (EU) No 608/2013 of the European Parliament and of the Council of 12 June 2013 concerning customs enforcement of intellectual property rights and repealing Council Regulation (EC) No 1383/2003, OJ L181 p 15.

[392] Article 94 specifically refers to Council Regulation (EC) No 44/2001 of 22 December 2000 on jurisdiction and the recognition and enforcement of judgments in civil and commercial matters; this Regulation has in the meantime been superseded by a recast version, Regulation (EC) No. 1215/2012 of the European Parliament and of the Council of 12 December 2012 on jurisdiction and the recognition and enforcement of judgments in civil and commercial matters (recast), OJ 2012 L351 p 1, which became applicable, pursuant to its Article 81, on 10 January 2015. References in the Community Trade Mark Regulation to particular Articles of Regulation 44/2001 must be read as references to the equivalent Articles in Regulation 1215/2012.

[393] Additional EU-wide competence may be established by agreement between the parties, or by not challenging jurisdiction, or by joining several parties before the court of the domicile of one of the parties, pursuant to Article 8 No 1 of Regulation 1215/2012. The latter competence has played a significant role in patent cases, but trade mark cases have so far not reached the CJEU.

(Articles 99 and 100). As an exception, the defendant may invoke as a defence that it is proprietor of an earlier right or that the claimant has not made genuine use of the mark asserted to have been infringed.

9.418 Community trade mark courts apply their own procedural rules and their national law applicable to national marks where the Regulation does not provide a rule (Article 101). As regards sanctions, the Regulation provides for injunctive relief, but refers for all other questions to the laws of the Member States where acts of infringement have been committed or are threatened (Article 102).

9.419 Special rules are established for related actions. When a cancellation action is pending before the OHIM, a later infringement suit is as a rule barred. An earlier cancellation action before the OHIM or before a Community trade mark court bars a subsequent cancellation action.

9.420 The Court of Justice has so far only rarely been called upon to interpret these rules. The cases reported and analysed here concern the jurisdiction based on the forum *delicti commissi* in Article 97 (5), *Coty*, injunctive relief pursuant to Article 102 (1), *Nokia*, and the territorial scope of injunctive relief, *DHL*, and finally, although decided under the parallel provisions of the Community Designs Regulation, a case concerning the law applicable to sanctions other than injunctive relief (*Gnautzsch*).

(a) Coty: The effect of national borders

9.421 (i) **Facts and questions** Coty Germany GmbH (Coty) is proprietor of a 3D CTM consisting of the shape of a perfume bottle. It markets Davidoff Cool Water Woman in these bottles. When allegedly infringing products were brought on the German market, Coty sued First Note Perfumes NV (First Note), a Belgian company, for infringement of its CTM and unfair competition, alleging that First Note had sold the infringing products in Belgium to a third party which had brought them into Germany and sold them there. Coty claimed that First Note was liable for participating in the third party's infringement and had committed comparative advertising and misappropriation. The actions were dismissed at first and second instance for lack of jurisdiction over the foreign defendant First Note.[394]

9.422 On appeal to the German Supreme Court the following questions were referred to the Court of Justice:

1. Is Article 93(5) of Regulation No 40/94 to be interpreted as meaning that an act of infringement is committed in one Member State (Member State A), within the meaning of [that provision], in the case where, as a result of an act in another Member State (Member State B), there is participation in the infringement in the first-named Member State (Member State A)?
2. Is Article 5(3) of Regulation No 44/2001 to be interpreted as meaning that the harmful event occurred in one Member State (Member State A) if the tortious act which is the subject of the action or from which claims are derived was committed in another Member State (Member State B) and consists in participation in the tortious act (principal act) which took place in the first-named Member State (Member State A)?

9.423 Article 98(5) CTMR as codified, the provision corresponding to Article 93(5) CTMR in its original version, provides for jurisdiction over a defendant for CTM infringement in the

---

[394] C-360/12 *Coty Germany GmbH v First Note Perfumes NV*, Judgment: ECLI:EU:C:2014:1318, Opinion: ECLI:EU:C:2013:764.

Member State where 'the act of infringement has been committed or threatened'. Article 5(3) of the Brussels I Regulation provides that '[a] person domiciled in a Member State may, in another Member State, be sued: … 3. in matters relating to tort, delict or quasi-delict, in the courts for the place where the harmful event occurred or may occur'. In the recast Brussels-I Regulation this provision has become, without any change in its wording, Article 7(2).

9.424 Case law of the Court has established that the provision in Article 5(3) (now Article 7(2)) allows the claimant in so-called distance delicts, where the Member State where the act leading to the damage occurred is not the same as the Member State where the damage was suffered, the choice between the courts of the one or of the other Member State. The issue in *Coty* was whether the same interpretation should be given to Article 98(5) CTMR with its somewhat different wording 'act of infringement has been committed or is threatened'.

9.425 The second question was intended to find out whether the previous case law on Article 5(3) of the Brussels I Regulation could also apply in the special situation of a participation in an infringement of unfair competition rules. This issue is not dealt with further except to report that the Court agreed that the case law does apply.

9.426 (ii) **The Opinion of Advocate General Jääskinen** Advocate General Jääskinen analysed the first question essentially from a historical and systematic perspective.[395] The legislature chose not to apply Article 5(3) of the Brussels I Regulation or in any event the wording in that provision, but adopted a different wording; thus the CTMR was *lex specialis*[396] to the Brussels I Regulation. Its interpretation must be in view of the objectives pursued, including the need to avoid forum shopping.[397] In any event, granting jurisdiction to the German courts on the basis of an alleged participation of the Belgian defendant in the infringement committed by a German party was excluded. He proposed the following answer to the first question.[398]

9.427 > Article 93 (5) of Regulation (EC) No 40/94 … must be interpreted as not allowing to deduce, from the place of an infringing act relating to a Community trade mark which a supposed infringer is alleged to have committed, the jurisdiction as regards another alleged actor of this infringement who has not acted in the district of the court seized.

9.428 From this answer, which is worded in very fact-specific terms, it does not become evident whether the Advocate General would exclude in general an interpretation of what is now Article 97(5) CTMR in line with the Court's case law on Article 5(3) of the Brussels I Regulation even when the same person is involved whose infringing acts are to be judged.

9.429 The AG's reference to the preparatory work in the 1970s is honourable, but unsatisfactory. Title X was subjected to a major revision during the negotiations in the Council; it would have been more appropriate to refer to the respective Council documents, which in fact do not support the AG's interpretation to the degree that the pre-1980s documents do.

9.430 The AG added as an argument in paragraph 43 of his Opinion (again translated from the German):

> The legislature appears to me to have established priorities in the context of the protection of the unitary title for the intellectual property embodied in the Community trade mark

---

[395] At the time of writing the Opinion is not available in English.
[396] Point 36.
[397] Point 42.
[398] Translated from German.

which are above all connected with the concentration of litigation before the courts of a single Member State, namely that in which the infringement has been committed or is threatened.

Nothing could be further from the truth: The concentration of litigation with EU-wide competence of the court is not where the acts of infringement have been committed, but where the defendant is domiciled, etc. The forum *delicti commissi* does not have EU-wide competence.

9.431 **(iii) The Judgment of the Court** The Court, in a judgment of its Fourth Chamber, rarely called upon to decide issues of this kind, and with Judge Safjan as Rapporteur, essentially followed the reasoning of AG Jääskinen and gave a ruling which leaves no doubt about its breadth and weight.

9.432 The concept of 'the Member State in which the act of infringement has been committed' in Article 93(5) of Council Regulation (EC) No 40/94 of 20 December 1993 on the Community trade mark must be interpreted as meaning that, in the event of a sale and delivery of a counterfeit product in one Member State, followed by a resale by the purchaser in another Member State, that provision does not allow jurisdiction to be established to hear an infringement action against the original seller who did not himself act in the Member State where the court seized is situated.

9.433 While still somewhat fact-specific, the answer in effect means that different from Article 5(3) of the Brussels I Regulation, in cases of infringement of Community trade marks (and Community designs) the forum *delicti commissi* exists only in the Member State where the infringer acted, not where the acts produced their results. The Court based its conclusions[399] on the wording, the context, and the specificities of Community trade mark infringements. The latter apparently means that because of the unitary nature of Community trade marks the effects of an infringing act are actually not limited to a particular Member State but 'localized' everywhere in the EU, which would provide a claimant with basically unlimited forum shopping.[400]

9.434 **(iv) Conclusions** The *Coty* Judgment is unfortunate because it makes the prosecution of infringements of Community trade marks more difficult by limiting the fora where a case based on Article 98(5) CTMR may be brought. Also, the decision makes the enforcement of CTMs more difficult than the prosecution of infringements of national trade marks: The Court has previously judged, applying Article 5(3) of the Brussels I Regulation, that infringements

---

[399] Paragraphs 28–36 of the judgment, culminating in paragraph 37: 'Consequently, jurisdiction under Article 93(5) of Regulation No 40/94 may be established solely in favour of Community trade mark courts in the Member State in which the defendant committed the alleged unlawful act.'

[400] The Court does not actually spell this out in paragraph 36 of the judgment, but refers to paragraphs 28 and 29 of the AG's Opinion. Actually, a proper reference should have been to paragraph 40 of the Opinion, which is, in the German original, as follows:

> 40. Außerdem geben die Vorarbeiten zur Gemeinschaftsmarkenverordnung Grund zur Annahme, dass die Spezialzuständigkeit aus ihrem Article 93 Abs. 5 eng auszulegen ist. Dieser Ansatz ist aus Gründen angebracht, die mit dieser Verordnung selbst zusammenhängen und mit der Schwierigkeit zu tun haben, die Einheitlichkeit des von der Gemeinschaftsmarke gewährten Schutzes(37) und die Gefahr von Verletzungen an mehreren Orten innerhalb der Union(38) miteinander in Einklang zu bringen. First Note Perfumes, die deutsche Regierung und die Kommission weisen zu Recht darauf hin, dass im Fall der Verletzung einer Gemeinschaftsmarke praktisch jeder Mitgliedstaat als Ort der Verletzung angesehen werden könne, da das geschützte Recht seine Wirkungen im gesamten Unionsgebiet entfalte.

of national trademarks may be pursued both in the Member State where the mark is protected (Austria) and in the country where the infringer acted (Germany) in C-523/10 *Wintersteiger*.[401]

Another consequence of the *Coty* Judgment is that in many situations the Member State where the defendant acted will be the Member State where the defendant is domiciled, and thus the bases of jurisdiction would in fact no longer be distinct. **9.435**

Finally, the Court disregards the situation of third country defendants which are not subject to jurisdiction in the third country, where they acted, and apparently also not in the Member State where the damage occurred. This means that, de facto, third country defendants must always be sued in a CTM court with EU-wide jurisdiction. **9.436**

(b) Nokia: Injunctive relief; adequate enforcement

An enforcement perspective of CTMs was considered by the Court in *Nokia*,[402] a reference from the Swedish Högsta Domstolen (Supreme Court). Nokia had brought a trade mark infringement action, based on its Community trade mark registration of NOKIA for mobile telephones, against Joacim Wärdell for importing into Sweden adhesive stickers bearing the sign NOKIA. The Stockholms Tingsrätten (Stockholm District Court) found that Wardell's acts constituted objective acts of infringement and, because there was a risk of repetition, issued a prohibition on continuing infringement. Wardell appealed to the Svea Hovrätten (Court of Appeal, Svea) claiming that use of the trade mark NOKIA had not been deliberate or negligent and that there was no risk of repetition. The Svea Hovrätten found that the importation of the stickers should not be seen as part of a continuing trade mark infringement, given his history and the fact that he could only be accused of being careless. And, although it accepted that the risk of repetition could not be eliminated, it reversed the Judgment of the Stockholms Tingsrätten on that point. **9.437**

Nokia appealed to the Högsta Domstolen that stayed proceedings and referred four questions regarding the interpretation of Article 98(1) of the Regulation[403] and whether it went beyond the parallel provision of the Swedish trade mark law:[404] **9.438**

(1) Is the condition relating to special reasons in the first sentence of Article 98(1) of Council Regulation (EC) No 40/94 of 20 December 1993 on the Community trade mark to be interpreted as meaning that a court which finds that the defendant has infringed a Community trade mark may, irrespective of the other circumstances, refrain from

---

[401] C-523/10 *WintersteigerAGvProducts4USondermaschinenbauGmbH*.Judgment:ECLI:EU:C:2012:220, Opinion: ECLI:EU:C:2012:90. The Court looked at trade mark disputes in particular and ruled (paragraph 41) as follows:

Where conduct occurs via the internet which is liable to infringe a national trade mark registered in a Member State, Article 5(3) of Regulation No 44/2001 must be interpreted as meaning that it attributes jurisdiction:—to the courts of the Member State in which the trade mark is registered,—and to the courts of the Member State where the means necessary to produce an actual infringement of a trade mark registered in another Member State are used.

[402] C-316/05 *Nokia Corp v Joacim Wärdell* [2006] ECR I-12083.

[403] Article 98(1) provides:

Where a Community trade mark court finds that the defendant has infringed or threatened to infringe a Community trade mark, it shall, unless there are special reasons for not doing so, issue an order prohibiting the defendant from proceeding with the acts which infringed or would infringe the Community trade mark. It shall also take such measures in accordance with its national law as are aimed at ensuring that this prohibition is complied with.

[404] Section 37 of the Swedish trade mark law provides that a trade mark infringement that has been committed deliberately or with gross negligence is punishable by a fine or imprisonment; section 37 a provides

issuing a specific prohibition of further infringement if the court considers that the risk of further infringement is not obvious or is otherwise merely limited?

(2) Is the condition relating to special reasons in the first sentence of Article 98 (1) of the Regulation on the Community trade mark to be interpreted as meaning that a court which finds that the defendant has infringed a Community trade mark may, even if there is no such ground for refraining from issuing a prohibition of further infringement as contemplated in Question 1, refrain from issuing such a prohibition on the grounds that it is clear that a further infringement is covered by a statutory general prohibition of infringement under national law and that a penalty may be imposed on the defendant if he commits a further infringement intentionally or with gross negligence?

(3) If the answer to Question 2 is no, must specific measures, by which a prohibition is for example coupled with a penalty, be taken in such a case to ensure that the prohibition is complied with, even where it is clear that a further infringement is covered by a statutory general prohibition of infringement under national law and that a penalty may be imposed on the defendant if he commits a further infringement intentionally or with gross negligence?

(4) If the answer to Question 3 is yes, does this apply even where the conditions for adopting such a specific measure in the case of a corresponding infringement of a national trade mark would not be regarded as fulfilled?[405]

9.439 (i) **The Opinion of Advocate General Sharpston** Advocate General Sharpston divided her Opinion into three parts. First, she considered the meaning of 'special reasons' in Article 98(1); then, whether national provisions could fit into those 'special reasons'; and third, the adequacy of specific measures arising from national provisions the scope of which was to ensure compliance with a prohibition.

9.440 *Article 98(1)—the 'special reasons' condition* The analysis of the Advocate General started with the wording of the provision, expressed in mandatory terms: 'the court shall issue a prohibition order'. It reflected the fundamental right of a trade mark proprietor to prohibit infringement, according to Article 9(1) of the Regulation. This led her to support the view that the general rule was to prohibit continued infringement; the concept of 'special reasons' was a derogation to that principle, and, accordingly, should be interpreted narrowly.

9.441 She then considered the scheme of the Regulation. Leaving Member States leeway to assess the risk of continuation of infringement would lead to different results in different Member States. This would go against the fundamental principle that a Community trade mark should enjoy the same protection throughout the Union.

9.442 Nevertheless, the concept of 'special reasons' was included in the provision; the Advocate General, looking for its purpose, remarked that it would not be appropriate to discuss this in detail, since the national court had not asked for examples of what might constitute 'special reasons' and the pleadings before the Court had not considered that question. She felt she had to set some sort of parameter, however:

> It may be that in exceptional cases the degree of risk of further infringement is one of a number of circumstances which, taken as a whole, are indeed capable of constituting 'special reasons' within the meaning of Article 98(1). However, the national court's question specifically concerns only the degree of risk of further infringement 'irrespective of the other circumstances'.[406]

---

that the court may, on application by the proprietor of the trade mark, prohibit the infringer, under penalty of a fine, from continuing the infringement

[405] Reproduced in point 17.
[406] Point 25.

The final point was probably the strongest as this case involved an identical sign used in **9.443** relation to identical goods:

> In such circumstances the derogation should in principle not apply at all. At the very most, it might perhaps apply where it is materially impossible for the defendant to repeat the infringement, for example (to borrow the illustrations given by Nokia) if the defendant is a company which has been wound up or if the mark in question has expired.[407]

She concluded that the condition relating to 'special reasons' would not be satisfied if a court which found that the defendant had infringed a Community trade mark refrained from issuing a specific prohibition of further infringement solely on the ground that it considered that the risk of further infringement was not obvious or was otherwise merely limited.

'Special reasons' and national provisions The second question focused on the relationship **9.444** between national law and Article 98(1). Assuming that a national court had found infringement of a Community trade mark and that there was no exceptional case for not issuing a prohibition of further infringement, could it still refrain from issuing such a prohibition on the grounds that a further infringement would be covered by a statutory general prohibition of infringement under national law and that a penalty might be imposed on the defendant that committed a further infringement intentionally or with gross negligence? Advocate General Sharpston followed again a strict approach based on the language, context, and scope of the provision.

First, a general provision of national legislation could not by definition be a 'special' reason **9.445** because on a natural reading the term implied that the reason should be special to a particular case, normally relating to facts rather than law. Further, Article 98(1) explicitly required that an order prohibiting further infringement should be the standard measure against infringement. Second, in terms of context, refusing to order prohibition under Article 98(1) because of the existence of a national general prohibition of further infringement would make application of Community law rules dependent on national law, against the primacy of Community law principle and the unitary character of the Regulation. Third, it would in effect deprive Article 98(1) of all meaning, in particular since such an order might often be more effective than a general prohibition on infringement. Indeed, Article 37a of the Swedish law appeared to be quite cumbersome compared with Article 98(1), requiring a separate application to the court and proof that the infringement was intentional or the result of serious negligence. In view of these arguments, it was only logical that the answer to the Swedish court should be in the negative.

The adequacy of 'national' measures The remaining two questions were examined jointly by **9.446** the Advocate General. Wärdell's argument against an affirmative response was based on Article 14(1) of the Regulation which stated that 'infringement of a Community trade mark shall be governed by the national law relating to infringement of a national trade mark'. He supported that a provision in the national law for a general prohibition of infringement with the possibility of a penal sanction would suffice to fulfil the Article 98(1) requirement.

The Advocate General started with a textual analysis stressing that the same provision **9.447** concluded with the words 'in accordance with the provisions of Title X' that included Article 98(1), a mandatory provision according to her earlier findings. The 'formulation' of

---

[407] Point 27.

Article 98(1) required that 'national law should make available specific measures to back up such a prohibition and thus ensure that it is complied with'. A general statutory prohibition on infringement under national law would not be sufficient. The imposition of the penalty required three additional steps to be taken: it could be imposed only (i) at the national court's option; (ii) on application by the trade mark holder; and only (iii) to a defendant who commits a further infringement intentionally or with negligence.[408]

9.448 The general requirement was that national law should provide for specific and effective measures for the purposes of Article 98(1). The competence of the domestic legal system covered only the detailed procedural rules governing court actions for safeguarding Community trade mark rights with the limitation that these rules should not be less favourable than those governing similar domestic actions, according to the principle of equivalence, and should not render virtually impossible or excessively difficult the exercise of Community trade mark rights, according to the principle of effectiveness.[409] These two principles did not necessarily imply some additional sanction or penalty: 'Rather, the consequences of breaching the prohibition must be clearly laid down, either specifically by the national court in question or more generally by national law.'[410]

9.449 Finally, Advocate General Sharpston suggested that whether the infringement provisions regarding registered trade marks at the national level corresponded to the standard set by Article 98(1) should make no difference to the analysis:

> The principle of equivalence does not require that where Community law confers a high level of protection on a right derived from Community law, equivalent rights derived from national law (even harmonised national law) necessarily enjoy the same level of protection.[411]

(ii) The Judgment of the Court

9.450 *The first question* The Court started its analysis by holding that the term 'special reasons' should be interpreted and applied in the same way throughout the Community. A Community trade mark must have the same effect throughout the Community, if the 'condition relating to "special reasons" were to be interpreted differently in the various Member States, the same circumstances could give rise to prohibitions of further infringement or threatened infringement in some Member States and not in others'.[412]

9.451 Developing how the term should be interpreted, the Court noted that the first sentence of Article 98(1) of the Regulation is drafted in mandatory terms in its different language versions. This meant that the condition relating 'to "special reasons for not doing so"—which the wording of Article 98(1) clearly shows is an exception to that obligation ... must be interpreted strictly'.[413] Next, it noted that Article 98(1) is an essential provision for protecting Community trade marks in the Community. That meant that the term should be interpreted strictly, otherwise the applicant would be required to produce evidence of the risk of recurrence relating to possible future conduct. This would be difficult in practice and

---

[408] Point 41.
[409] Citing C-472/99 *Clean Car Autoservice GmbH v Stadt Wien and Republik Österrich* [2001] ECR I-9687 as an authority for the broader principle.
[410] Point 42.
[411] Point 43.
[412] Paragraph 27.
[413] Paragraph 30.

could risk undermining the exclusive trade mark right. Third, protection must be uniform throughout the entire Community, otherwise protection could vary according to jurisdiction, court, or even action. Counterbalancing this, the Court added that a Community trade mark court was not precluded from not issuing a prohibition in cases where further infringement or threatened infringement was no longer possible, for example in cases where the rights of the trade mark proprietor have been revoked following the commission of the acts in question.

The second question The Court looked at the wording used in different languages to describe the term and found that 'special reasons' relates to factual circumstances specific to a given case. A general prohibition of infringement or penal measures against further infringement at the national level did not possess the specificity the Regulation provision required. Similarly, general provisions adopted according to TRIPs did not constitute 'special reasons'. From a different perspective the Court added that recognizing national provisions as 'special reasons' would mean that an order prohibiting further infringement or threatened infringement would depend on the content of the relevant national law; Community trade mark courts of Member States providing for this type of protection would then be allowed to ignore the specific facts of each case, covered behind the blanket national measures. Article 98(1) of the Regulation would become redundant. This would go against the primacy and uniform application of Community law principles. Finally, general prohibitions lack the dissuasive character of specific court orders. **9.452**

The third question Again, the Court turned first to the meaning of the terms in different languages. The meaning of 'shall … take … measures' in the second sentence of Article 98(1) is mandatory. **9.453**

> Secondly, unlike the obligation to issue an order prohibiting further infringement or threatened infringement—provided for in the first sentence of Article 98(1) of the Regulation—, which is coupled with a derogation in the event of 'special reasons', the obligation to attach to that prohibition measures aimed at ensuring that it is complied with—provided for in the second sentence of that provision—does not allow for any exception.[414]

The fourth question Following its earlier discussion the Court highlighted the mandatory nature of the provision. And under Article 14(1) of the Regulation 'infringement of a Community trade mark shall be governed by the national law relating to infringement of a national trade mark in accordance with the provisions of Title X [of the Regulation]'. There was no room for making such measures contingent on compliance with additional conditions, **9.454**

> the second sentence of Article 98(1) of the Regulation must be interpreted as not referring to national law as regards the conditions for implementing the measures provided for under that law which are aimed at ensuring that the prohibition against further infringement or threatened infringement is complied with, but as requiring that such measures be ordered as soon as an order prohibiting further infringement or threatened infringement has been made. It follows inter alia that Community trade mark courts are required to take such measures without having regard to the conditions necessary for their implementation under the national law applicable.[415]

---

[414] Paragraph 48.
[415] Paragraph 59.

(c) DHL: The territorial scope of the prohibition

9.455 While *Nokia* had established that as a general rule courts must issue an injunction when infringements have been committed or are threatened, the territorial scope of such an injunction in a situation where the Community trade mark court competent to hear the case has EU-wide competence had remained unsettled, in particular the question whether an EU-wide injunction should be issued even if the acts of infringement were territorially limited. The French Cour de cassation was confronted with such a case and took the opportunity to refer relevant questions to the CJEU.

9.456 **(i) The facts in the main proceedings and the order for reference** *DHL*[416] was an order for reference from the Cour de cassation (France), concerning the territorial scope of the prohibition and related coercive measures issued by a Community trade mark court in accordance with Article 98 CTMR,[417] which states:

> Where a Community trade mark court finds that the defendant has infringed or threatened to infringe a Community trade mark, it shall, unless there are special reasons for not doing so, issue an order prohibiting the defendant from proceeding with the acts which infringed or would infringe the Community trade mark. It shall also take such measures in accordance with its national law as are aimed at ensuring that this prohibition is complied with.

9.457 The dispute in the main proceedings concerned an infringement action brought by Chronopost SA before the Tribunal de grande instance de Paris (Regional Court, Paris, France), sitting as Community trade mark court, on the basis of its French and Community trade marks WEBSHIPPING, against DHL International SA and its successor DHL Express France SAS, which were using the signs WEB SHIPPING, 'Web Shipping', and 'Webshipping' for the purposes of designating an express mail-management service accessible via the Internet.

9.458 The Tribunal de grande instance de Paris held, inter alia, that DHL had infringed Chronopost's French trade mark WEBSHIPPING, but it did not consider it necessary to adjudicate upon the alleged infringement of the Community trade mark. On appeal, the Cour d'appel de Paris (Court of Appeal, Paris), acting as a second-instance Community trade mark court, found that the defendant had infringed Chronopost's French and Community trade marks and prohibited DHL, subject to a periodic penalty payment, from continuing to use the signs WEBSHIPPING and WEB SHIPPING in the course of trade. However, it limited the effects of the prohibition exclusively to French territory.

9.459 DHL appealed to the Cour de cassation (Court of Cassation). Chronopost brought a cross-appeal arguing that the Cour d'appel infringed Articles 1 and 98 of the Regulation insofar as it had refused to extend the effects of the prohibition to the entire area of the European Union. The Cour de cassation dismissed DHL's appeal but entertained doubts as to the correct interpretation of Article 98. Accordingly, it decided to stay proceedings and to refer the following questions to the Court of Justice:

> 1. Must Article 98 be interpreted as meaning that the prohibition issued by a Community trade mark court has effect, as a matter of law, throughout the entire area of the European Union?

---

[416] C-235/09 *DHL Express France SAS v Chronopost SA* [2011] ECR I-02801
[417] In the meantime, Article 98 has become Article 102 CTMR. The references in the text reflect the original language of the judgment.

2. If not, is that court entitled to apply specifically that prohibition to the territories of other States in which the acts of infringement are committed or threatened?
3. In either case, are the coercive measures which the court, by application of its national law, has attached to the prohibition issued by it applicable within the territories of the Member States in which that prohibition would have effect?
4. In the contrary case, may that court order such a coercive measure, similar to or different from that which it adopts pursuant to its national law, by application of the national laws of the States in which that prohibition would have effect?'

(ii) The Opinion of Advocate General Cruz Villalón Advocate General Cruz Villalón set the background for his analysis by observing that decisions taken by Community trade mark courts under Article 98 generally comprise three parts, namely the declaratory decision on the existence of an infringement, the corresponding injunctive relief prohibiting its continuation,[418] and, where appropriate, measures of a coercive nature against a further breach of that prohibition which function as both preventive and punitive sanctions. He also observed that the first and second questions were concerned with the scope of the prohibition, whereas the two remaining questions dealt with coercive measures.[419] **9.460**

As regards the first part, he explained that the very purpose of the system of Community trade mark courts is to ensure the uniform application of the substantive rules relating to the Community trade mark by providing a uniform mechanism of judicial protection which is designed to eliminate the risk of contradictory decisions being taken due to the fact that the same dispute is brought before a multitude of adjudicating bodies. He noted that this followed directly from the Fourteenth and Fifteenth Recitals[420] in the Preamble to the Regulation, which require Member States to designate 'as limited a number as possible of national courts having jurisdiction in matters of infringement and validity of Community trade marks' whose decisions must 'have effect and cover the entire area of the Community', and from Articles 91 and 94 of the Regulation,[421] which moreover granted jurisdiction to such courts in respect of acts of actual or threatened infringement committed within the territory of any of the Member States.[422] **9.461**

Accordingly, he reached the interim conclusion that a literal and contextual interpretation of the Regulation confirmed that a decision of a national court which functions as a 'special court' of the Union in the field of Community trade marks is converted into a decision having effect throughout the entire area of the European Union as a matter of law. Nonetheless, he stated that regard should also be had to the overall objectives pursued by the Regulation when it comes to the protection of the individual rights conferred by a Community-wide registration which, in the circumstances, called for a more nuanced approach.[423] **9.462**

In that regard, the Advocate General noted that each dispute is subject to its own peculiar factual and legal circumstances and that, as a result, there may be occasions where an applicant will bring proceedings only against acts committed in one or some Member States, in which case the effects of the decision will be limited accordingly. The same will happen **9.463**

---

[418] Which, as clarified by the Court in C-316/05 *Nokia* [2006] ECR I-12083, can only be dispensed with in exceptional circumstances.
[419] Points 29–33.
[420] Which, in the meantime, have become Recitals Fifteen and Sixteen.
[421] Which, in the meantime, have become Articles 94 and 98.
[422] Points 21–24.
[423] Points 34–36.

when, despite the broader scope of the action, the infringement is deemed to occur in a limited number of Member States, as may be the case where the existence of confusion depends on linguistic considerations. Thus, he took the view that only where such circumstances are not present will the decision of a Community trade mark court have the same effect throughout the entire area of the European Union.[424]

9.464 Turning to the third and fourth questions, the Advocate General first addressed the analytical difficulties resulting from the complex character of coercive measures such as periodic penalty payments, which assume even greater complexity when applied in a cross-border context. He remarked that such penalties implied three possible stages of judicial involvement. First, the adoption of the measure and the fixing of the parameters on which its calculation depends; second, the quantification of the fine in case of continued infringement; and third, the enforcement of the measure in case of non-compliance. Hence, a thorough interpretation of Article 98 required clarifying the rules and procedures applicable to all of these stages. Moreover, he stressed that even though Article 11 of Directive 2004/48 provided for the general adoption of penalty payments as a means of complying with injunctions issued in trade mark disputes, it was possible for Member States to provide for alternative or supplementary measures in their legal systems, and that such measures also fell within the scope of Article 98(1).[425]

9.465 In this connection, the Advocate General took the view that, at least as regards the adoption of the sanction, a literal interpretation of Article 98(1) is compelling in that the expression 'national law' should be understood as referring to the *lex fori* of the Court hearing the substance of the case and issuing the prohibition. The same solution, however, does not necessarily extend to the enforcement phase, as the Regulation is silent regarding the jurisdiction called to apply the sanction in cases where the triggering event occurs in a state other than the forum. Moreover, account should be taken of the fact that the direct effects of the judgment given by a Community trade mark court are perforce limited to the territory of the Member State concerned. In consequence, in cases where the prohibition is breached in a third state, the enforcement of the sanction is a matter for the courts of the state in which this event takes place, in accordance with the rules on recognition laid down in Regulation No 44/2001.[426]

9.466 In view of those considerations, the Advocate General concluded that in cross-border disputes coercive measures must adapt, at least as concerns the phase of their implementation, to the specific nature of each legal system and, therefore, the court responsible for applying the sanction will have not only to recognize the initial judgment but will also have to give effect to it either by enforcing the original sanction, if this is possible under its legal system, or, failing this, by means of equivalent measures foreseen by its national law.[427]

9.467 (iii) **The Judgment of the Court** The Court, sitting in Grand Chamber, considered that the answer to the first question was determined both by the territorial jurisdiction of the Community trade mark court adjudicating on the dispute and by the territorial extent of

---

[424] Points 37–39.
[425] Points 46–50.
[426] Points 61–65.
[427] Points 66–68.

the proprietor's exclusive right insofar as this is affected by the infringement or threatened infringement.

9.468 As regards the first point, the Court noted that Articles 14(1) and 94(1) of the Regulation stipulated that the infringement of a Community trade mark is to be governed by 'the national law relating to the infringement of a national trade mark', and that a Community trade mark court is to have jurisdiction 'in respect of acts of infringement committed within the territory of any of the Member States', which makes clear that the jurisdiction of a Community trade mark court extends to acts of infringement committed or threatened within the territory of one or more Member States or even to the entire area of the European Union.[428]

9.469 As regards the second point, it recalled that, in view of the unitary character of the Community trade mark, enshrined in Article 1(2) of the Regulation, the exclusive right of the proprietor extends, as a rule, to the entire area of the European Union. The Court also referred to the Second, Fifteenth, and Sixteenth Recitals[429] in the Preamble to the Regulation, which confirm that the objective pursued by the CTMR involves the creation of Community arrangements for trade marks which produce their effects throughout the entire area of the European Union and which require that the effects of decisions regarding the validity and infringement of such rights must equally cover the territory of the Union as a whole, in order to prevent inconsistent decisions or contradictory judgments which could undermine the effects of the unitary character of Community trade marks. Referring also to its Judgment in *Nokia I*,[430] in which it had already held that the specific objective of Article 98(1) is the uniform protection of the right conferred by the Community trade mark against the risk of infringement, it came to the conclusion that a prohibition issued by a Community trade mark court must extend, as a rule, to the entire area of the European Union.[431]

9.470 However, the Court stressed that the territorial scope of the prohibition was subject to the same restrictions that were imposed by its case law on the exercise of the proprietor's exclusive right under Article 9(1), namely that it must be available only against acts by third parties that affect or are liable to affect the functions of the trade mark.[432] Thus, it concurred with the Advocate General that if a Community trade mark court finds that the infringement or threatened infringement is limited to part of the territory of the European Union, either because the claimant has restricted the territorial scope of its action and not sought relief beyond this limited territory or because the defendant proves that the use of the sign at issue is not liable to affect the functions of the earlier mark, for example on linguistic grounds, that court must limit the territorial scope of the prohibition accordingly.[433]

9.471 Moving on to the third and fourth questions, the Court referred to its statements in *Nokia I*[434] that the Community trade mark court is required to select, from among the

---

[428] Paragraphs 33–38.
[429] Which, in the meantime, have become the Third, Sixteenth, and Seventeenth Recitals of the Preamble to the CTMR.
[430] C-316/05 *Nokia* [2006] ECR I-12083, paragraph 60.
[431] Paragraphs 39–45.
[432] Citing Joined Cases C-236/08 to C-238/08 *Google France and Google* [2010] ECR I-02417, paragraph 75.
[433] Paragraphs 46–48.
[434] C-316/05 *Nokia* [2006] ECR I-12083, paragraph 49.

sanctions available under its own national law, 'such measures as are aimed at ensuring that the prohibition that it has issued is complied with', adding also that these sanctions can achieve the objective for which they are issued only if they can take effect in the territory in which the prohibition itself has effect. Accordingly, in cases where the breach of the prohibition takes place in a third territory, the courts of that other Member State must recognize and enforce the sanction at issue in accordance with the rules and procedures laid down by the national law under which they operate, by virtue of Chapter III of Regulation No 44/2001. In cases, however, where the latter law does not provide for a coercive measure of a similar nature, these courts must attain the objective pursued by the original sanction by having recourse to measures ensuring that the prohibition issued by the Community trade mark court is complied with in an equivalent manner. According to the Court, that obligation is also derived from the principle of sincere cooperation laid down in Article 4(3) of the Treaty on European Union (TEU), which requires the Courts of the Member States to ensure judicial protection of an individual's rights under European Union law, and, in the trade mark field, from Article 3 of Directive 2004/48, according to which Member States are to provide for effective, proportionate, and dissuasive measures, procedures, and remedies in order to ensure the adequate enforcement of the intellectual property rights covered by that Directive.[435]

9.472 Consequently, the Court answered the third and fourth questions to the effect that Article 98(1) must be interpreted as meaning that a coercive measure, such as a periodic penalty payment, ordered by a Community trade mark court by application of its national law, in order to ensure compliance with a prohibition against further infringement or threatened infringement which it has issued, has effect in Member States to which the territorial scope of such a prohibition extends other than the Member State of that court, under the conditions laid down in Chapter III of Regulation No 44/2001 with regard to the recognition and enforcement of judgments. Where the national law of one of those other Member States does not contain a coercive measure similar to that ordered by the Community trade mark court, the objective pursued by that measure must be attained by the competent court of that other Member State by having recourse to the relevant provisions of its national law which are such as to ensure that the prohibition is complied with in an equivalent manner.

9.473 **(iv) Conclusions** The importance of the Judgment in *DHL* lies not so much in the solutions it provided with regard to the main proceedings as to the confirmation of the rule in *Armacell*[436] that the unitary character of the Community trade mark does not necessarily guarantee a uniform protection throughout the EU, because that protection may fluctuate depending on whether there is a harm to its essential function based, among others, on linguistic considerations. This also underlines the specificity of the Community trade mark, the uniform enforcement of which ultimately finds its limits in the cultural diversity of the internal market. In addition to a voluntary limitation of the scope of relief requested, which is an expression of the claimant's rights to determine the scope of relief requested, the only situation considered so far where the relief should be territorially limited is the absence of likelihood of confusion because of differences at the phonetic or conceptual level between the conflicting marks which are present only in a particular part of the European Union.

---

[435] Paragraphs 53–58.
[436] C-514/06 P *Armacell Enterprise GmbH v OHIM* [2008] ECR I-00128, paragraphs 54–57.

Another case, not mentioned in the Court's Judgment, might be the absence of reputation or detriment to reputation.

(d) Gautzsch (Gartenpavillon): The law applicable to sanctions in case of infringements

9.474 Whereas the right to injunctive relief is provided for in the Regulation, and the Court has established that as a matter of principle injunctive relief must be granted EU-wide by Community trade mark courts having EU-wide jurisdiction, obtaining relief beyond injunction, and in particular collecting damages, but also all other relief mandated by the so-called Enforcement Directive,[437] is not provided directly in the Regulation. Rather, the Regulation refers, in its Article 102(2), to the law of the Member State where the infringement has been committed, including that Member State's international private law. As regards private international law applicable to non-contractual relations, such as torts, in the meantime the EU legislature has adopted uniform rules, in the so-called Rome II Regulation.[438] Under Article 8(2) of that Regulation, the law applicable to the infringement of EU-uniform intellectual property (IP) rights is the law of the Member State where the acts of infringement have occurred, unless the EU's legislative act itself provides for a different rule. A provision which has the same substantive content as Article 102(2) of the Regulation is found in Article 89 of the Community Designs Regulation.[439] When a case reached the German Federal Supreme Court in 2012 where sanctions where sought before a German Community design court with regard to infringements committed in several Member States, the German court seized the opportunity and referred, together with a series of questions dealing with unregistered Community designs, not of relevance here, a question seeking clarification as regards the law applicable to sanctions not provided or in the EU legislation.

9.475 (i) *Gautzsch (Gartenpavillon)* The reference was made on 16 August 2012; the German Federal Supreme Court issued a decision, referring six questions with a number of sub-questions to the Court of Justice of the European Union for a preliminary ruling, related to the establishment, validity, and enforcement of an unregistered Community design right, some of which are applicable to all design rights, and one of which, namely Question 6, has relevance beyond the law of designs also to infringement of Community trade marks.[440] The design questions are not of relevance here. Question 6 reads as follows:

> 6. Is Article 89 (1)(d) CDR to be interpreted as meaning that claims for destruction, disclosure of information and damages by reason of infringement of an unregistered Community design which are pursued in relation to the entirety of the European Union are subject to the law of the Member States in which the acts of infringement are committed?

9.476 The German Supreme Court explained in the Order of reference that two theories were advocated: the 'single law' theory, according to which a single law was to applied to these sanctions, and the 'mosaic' theory, according to which the law of each of the Member States

---

[437] Directive 2004/48/EC of the European Parliament and of the Council of 29 April 2004 on the enforcement of intellectual property rights, as corrected, OJ L195, p 16.
[438] Regulation (EC) No 864/2007 of the European Parliament and of the Council of 11 July 2007 on the law applicable to non-contractual obligations (Rome II), OJ L199, p 40.
[439] Council Regulation (EC) No 6/2002 of 12 December 2001 on Community designs, OJ L3, p 1, as amended.
[440] C-479/12 *H Gautzsch Großhandel GmbH & Co. KG v Münchener Boulevard Möbel Joseph Duna GmbH*, Judgment: ECLI:EU:C:2014:75, Opinion: ECLI:EU:C:2013:537.

where acts of infringement were committed needed to be applied. Obviously, the 'mosaic' theory complicates the situation for claimants who may not have the means of proving to the satisfaction of a local court what the law is in up to twenty-seven other jurisdictions. Regrettably, the question as posed by the German court does nothing more than repeat the governing language of the Community Designs Regulation, which in its Article 89 (1)(d) reads as follows:

> Article 89—Sanctions in actions for infringement
> 1. Where in an action for infringement or for threatened infringement a Community design court finds that the defendant has infringed or threatened to infringe a Community design, it shall, unless there are special reasons for not doing so, order the following measures:
>   (a) an order prohibiting the defendant from proceeding with the acts which have infringed or would infringe the Community design;
>   (b) …;
>   (c) …;
>   (d) any order imposing other sanctions appropriate under the circumstances which are provided by the law of the Member State in which the acts of infringement or threatened infringement are committed, including its private international law.

9.477 (ii) **The Opinion of Advocate General Wathelet** The Advocate General, in his Opinion of 5 September 2013,[441] focused his attention on the (difficult) questions regarding infringement of unregistered Community designs, and barely dealt with Question 6. He began by misunderstanding the question, stating that the issue was whether the law of the Member States where acts of infringement have taken place applies or the law of the forum state.[442] Given these alternatives, it was not difficult to foresee that the Advocate General merely stated that the law(s) of the Member State(s) applied where acts of infringement have been committed or threatened. The 'mosaic' or 'single law' theories were not even mentioned. The Advocate General did however refer to the Rome II Regulation, without however recognizing that Rome II would only apply if the legislative act did not provide for a different rule.

9.478 (iii) **The Judgment of the Court** On 13 February 2014, the CJEU ruled as follows (again here only as regards the answer to Question 6):

> On a proper construction of Article 89(1)(d) CDR, claims for the destruction of infringing products are governed by the law of the Member State in which the acts of infringement or threatened infringement have been committed, including its private international law. Claims for compensation for damage resulting from the activities of the person responsible for the acts of infringement or threatened infringement and for disclosure, in order to determine the extent of that damage, of information relating to those activities, are governed, pursuant to Article 88(2) CDR, by the national law of the Community design court hearing the proceedings, including its private international law.

9.479 The Court, as has been the rule so often, gives hardly any reasons for its conclusions, which in the present case are as follows:

> 51 [Th]e referring court is uncertain whether those claims obey the national law of the Member State in which those rights are invoked or whether Article 89(1)(d) of Regulation

---

[441] Not available in English.
[442] Point 92.

No 6/2002 should be interpreted to the effect that those claims are governed by the law of the Member States in which the acts of infringement were committed. The referring court notes, in that regard, that establishing a link to the law of a single Member State could be justified as being the most effective application of that law, but that Article 89(1)(d) of Regulation No 6/2002 could militate against that approach.

52 First, regarding the claim for destruction of the infringing products, it is clear from Article 89(1) of Regulation No 6/2002, which refers, in subparagraph (a) thereof, to an order prohibiting the defendant from proceeding with the acts which have infringed or would infringe the Community design and, in subparagraphs (b) and (c), to an order to seize the infringing products and to an order to seize materials and implements used in order to manufacture those products, that the destruction of those products falls within the 'other sanctions appropriate under the circumstances' referred to in Article 89(1)(d) of that regulation. It follows that, under Article 89(1)(d) of Regulation No 6/2002, the law applicable to that claim is the law of the Member State in which the acts of infringement or threatened infringement have been committed, including its private international law.

53 Secondly, regarding the claims for compensation for the damage resulting from the activities of the person responsible for the acts of infringement or threatened infringement and for disclosure, in order to determine the extent of that damage, of information relating to those activities, it must be found that the obligation to provide such information and to pay compensation for the damage suffered does not, by contrast, constitute a sanction within the meaning of Article 89 of Regulation No 6/2002.

54 Accordingly, pursuant to Article 88(2) of Regulation No 6/2002, the law applicable to the claims listed in paragraph 53 above is the national law of the Community design court hearing the proceedings, including its private international law. That finding is borne out, moreover, by recital 31 of that regulation, which states that the regulation does not preclude the application to designs protected by Community designs of the laws of the Member States relating to civil liability.

(iv) **Conclusions** The answer of the Court, first of all, makes a (stunning) distinction between claims for damages and attendant relief (information, rendering of accounts), which it qualifies as something other than 'sanctions' and recall of goods and their destruction etc, which fall, in the Court's view, under Article 89(1)(d) Community Design Regulation (CDR). This distinction is unsustainable. Sanctions for IP infringements are currently comprehensively provided for in the so-called Enforcement Directive.[443] There is no reason to differentiate between sanctions provided for in the Directive, which of course include damages. The distinction, which seems to have been advocated by the Commission, was expressly rejected by the Advocate General.[444] **9.480**

Second, the answer does nothing more than repeat what the legislation already provides; the Court obviously did not really understand the underlying issue, perhaps misled by the simple language of Question 6. **9.481**

Does it matter whether Article 88(2) CDR or Article 89(1)(d) CDR is applied to damages? Applying (only) the law of the forum would certainly facilitate claimants, but since Article 88(2) CDR includes a reference to the applicable private international law, we are back at Article 8(2) of the Rome II Regulation, which refers to the law of the Member State of infringements. Thus, there is in effect no difference. This would be different only **9.482**

---

[443] Directive 2004/48/EC of the European Parliament and of the Council of 29 April 2004 on the enforcement of intellectual property rights, as corrected, OJ L195, p 16.
[444] Points 95 and 96.

if the Court's Judgment could be read as providing a clear rule, namely applying the law of the forum, and taking this rule at the same time as an exclusion of the applicable private international law. That, however, is not what the Court says. Therefore, we can today only speculate what the future will bring.

9.483 What the Court held with regard to Community designs is clearly applicable, *mutatis mutandis*, to Community trade marks, with the corresponding provisions being Article 102(2) CTMR and Article 101(2) CTMR.

9.484 The obvious solution, namely having clear rules in the applicable EU legislation providing for sanctions in cases of infringements in line with the Enforcement Directive, is unlikely to become reality for some time to come. The current 'trade mark package' offers nothing on this issue.

(2) Border Measures

(a) Davidoff III: *Seizure of infringing goods*

9.485 *Davidoff III*[445] dealt with a specific interpretation problem as regards the enforcement of Community trade marks, which arose with the accession of the Community to the Protocol relating to the Madrid Agreement concerning the international registration of marks adopted at Madrid on 27 June 1989 ('the Protocol').[446]

9.486 The issue related to the application of Regulation 1383/2003,[447] concerning customs action against goods suspected of infringing intellectual property rights, to international registrations designating the European Community within the meaning of Article 146 CTMR (new Article 151).[448] Article 2 of Regulation 1383/2003 defines infringing goods as, inter alia, counterfeit goods that infringe rights acquired 'under Community law, as provided for by the CTMR or the law of the Member State in which the application for action by the customs authorities is made'. By virtue of Article 5(1) and (4) of said Regulation, a right-holder may apply in writing to the competent customs department of the Member State for action; where the applicant is the holder of a Community trade mark he may, in addition, request action by the authorities of one or more other Member States.

(b) *The facts in the main proceedings*

9.487 The dispute arose in the course of proceedings between Zino Davidoff SA ('Davidoff') and the Bundesfinanzdirektion Südost (South Eastern Federal Revenue Office), when Davidoff lodged an application with the latter under Article 5(4) of Regulation 1383/2003 for border seizure of goods suspected of infringing twelve internationally registered trade marks, of which Davidoff is holder.

9.488 Bundesfinanzdirektion Südost dismissed the action on the grounds that Article 5(4) of Regulation 1383/2003, which extends only to 'right-holders of a Community trademark',

---

[445] C-302/08 *Zino Davidoff SA v Bundesfinanzdirektion Südost* (DAVIDOFF III) [2009] ECR I-05671.

[446] The Community acceded to the Madrid Protocol with effect from 1 October 2004 by virtue of Council Decision 2003/793 [2003] OJ L296/20.

[447] Regulation 1383/2003 concerning customs action against goods suspected of infringing certain intellectual property rights and the measures to be taken against goods found to have infringed such rights [2003] OJ 1296/7.

[448] Article 146 is included in Title XIII, containing provisions specifically relating to the International Registration of marks, which was added to the CTMR by Regulation 1992/2003 [2003] OJ L296/1.

was not amended by the Community legislature despite the Community's accession to the Protocol. Thus, it took the view that the wording of that provision does not cover the owners of internationally registered trade marks.

Davidoff brought an appeal against that decision before the Finanzgericht München, which considered that the provisions at issue pose problems relating to the interpretation of Community law. Accordingly, it stayed the proceedings and referred the following question to the Court for a preliminary ruling: 9.489

> In the light of the accession of the Community to the [Protocol], is Article 5(4) of Regulation [No 1383/2003] to be interpreted as meaning that, despite the use of the term 'Community trademark', marks with international registrations within the meaning of Article 146 et seq. of Regulation [No 40/94], are also covered?

(c) The Judgment of the Court

The Court decided to proceed to judgment without an Advocate General's Opinion. The first point it considered to be of relevance in resolving the question whether the holder of an internationally registered trade mark is entitled to secure action by the customs authorities in the same manner as proprietors of Community trade marks, was that Regulation 1383/2003 had been adopted prior to the accession of the Community to the Madrid Protocol. Accordingly, it turned for its interpretation to the provisions of the Protocol itself and to Regulation No 1992/2003, which, according to the Sixth and Eighth Recitals in its Preamble, introduces measures which are necessary to give effect to the accession of the Community to the Protocol and, in particular, to allow holders of international registrations to apply for protection under the Community trade mark system. 9.490

In that regard, it observed that Article 4(1) of the Protocol provides that the protection of the mark in each of the designated countries is to be the same as if the mark had been filed directly with the trade mark office of that state. Moreover, Article 146(2), inserted to the CTMR by Regulation No 1992/2003, stipulates that the international registration of a trade mark designating the European Community is to have the same effect as a Community trade mark. The Court therefore considered it to be apparent that the Community legislature intended, so far as their practical effects are concerned, to treat internationally registered marks in the same way as Community trade marks. 9.491

Next, it noted that, according to its wording, Article 5(4) of Regulation 1383/2003 only implements a specific procedure for the protection Community trade marks; that is, it merely deals with their effects and not with their definition.[449] 9.492

Thus, in view of the full assimilation of the two types of marks brought about by the above provisions, the Court concluded that Article 5(4) of Regulation No 1383/2003 allowed the holders of International Registrations with effect in the Community to secure action by the customs authorities of one or more Member States, just like the proprietor of a Community trade mark.[450] 9.493

---

[449] Paragraphs 23–24.
[450] Paragraph 26.

H. Import, Export, Transit

(1) Introduction: The Law, the Issues

9.494 Among the exclusive rights expressly granted to trade mark proprietors in Europe are the use of the mark in export or import trade. Article 5 of the Directive provides as follows:

> Article 5—Rights conferred by a trade mark
> 1. The registered trade mark shall confer on the proprietor exclusive rights therein. The proprietor shall be entitled to prevent all third parties not having his consent from using in the course of trade:
>   (a) ...;
>   (b) ....
> 2. ....
> 3. The following, inter alia, may be prohibited under paragraphs 1 and 2:
>   (a) affixing the sign to the goods or to the packaging thereof;
>   (b) offering the goods, or putting them on the market or stocking them for these purposes under that sign, or offering or supplying services thereunder;
>   (c) importing or exporting the goods under the sign;
>   (d) using the sign on business papers and in advertising.

9.495 Proprietors of Community trade marks have the same rights, in accordance with a provision in Article 9(2)(c) of the Regulation which is identical to that in the Directive. Thus, proprietors of trade marks may prohibit third parties from using an infringing sign on or in relation to goods which are imported into the European Union or exported from the European Union.

9.496 The exclusive rights of trade mark proprietors, or, seen from the perspective of infringement, the right to prohibit the use of infringing signs in the course of trade, are secured not only by trade mark law, but also by the European Union's customs regulations. Under these rules, customs authorities have the authority to seize and detain temporarily infringing goods which enter or leave the European Union's customs territory. The customs rules apply not only to national and Community trade marks, but to all other intellectual property rights.[451] The detention takes place at the request of the right holder. If the importer objects, the right holder has to bring an infringement action before the competent tribunals.

9.497 While importing goods under a protected trade mark or exporting such goods have so far not presented any legal problems (of course, combatting infringement and in particular product piracy poses massive technical and logistic problems), the complexities of transit traffic have vexed the IP community. This is indeed understandable. Intellectual property rights are protected within a particular jurisdiction, and not beyond, and transit goods by definition originate from a third country and leave for a third country, seen from the perspective of the country or jurisdiction where the right is protected. Thus, counterfeit or pirated goods or more generally infringing goods cannot be equated with absolutely

---

[451] Regulation (EU) No 608/2013 of the European Parliament and of the Council of 12 June 2013 concerning customs enforcement of intellectual property rights and repealing Council Regulation (EC) No 1383/2003, OJ EU L181 p 15. The Commission has enacted implementing rules, Commission Regulation (EC) No 1891/2004 of 21 October 2004 laying down provisions for the implementation of Council Regulation (EC) No 1383/2003 concerning customs action against goods suspected of infringing certain intellectual property rights and the measures to be taken against goods found to have infringed such rights, OJ EU L 328 p 16.

'prohibited' goods such as drugs, endangered species, etc, which may be seized wherever they are found. The simple statement that transit must be covered by the exclusive rights because it consists of goods entering the territory, that is, importation, and leaving the territory, that is, exportation, is too simplistic to be true. Transit also plays a special role in international trade where the rights of the country of origin, the rights of the country of destination, and the rights of the transit country must be balanced.

9.498 In view of the high stakes involved, it is not surprising that the Court of Justice has been seized repeatedly with questions relating to counterfeit goods and in particular the transit situation, both regarding interpretation of trade mark law and of customs law. These are the subjects of the present section.

(2) *Polo/Lauren*: Transit through a Member State from and to a Non-Member State (2000)

(a) *The factual setting and the questions referred*

9.499 The reference in *Polo/Lauren* arose under the customs regulations then in force, Regulation (EC) No 3295/94, which has by now been replaced by Regulation (EC) No 608/2013. Polo/Lauren, proprietor of Austrian trade marks, requested the detention and seizure of counterfeit T-shirts bearing Polo/Lauren marks in transit through Austria from Indonesia to Poland. The courts where Polo/Lauren had sought an order confirming the detention and seizure considered that they lacked jurisdiction. When the case was brought before the Austrian Oberste Gerichtshof, that court considered that there were solid grounds for holding that the customs regulation did not apply to transit cases. Also, the Oberste Gerichtshof had doubts about the validity of the Regulation—if it applied to transit goods it would constitute a measure not affecting the internal market. The following question was referred to the Court:

9.500 On a proper construction of Article 1 thereof, is Council Regulation (EC) No 3295/94 of 22 December 1994 laying down measures to prohibit the release for free circulation, export, re-export, or entry for a suspensive procedure of counterfeit and pirated goods (Official Journal of the European Communities L341 of 30 December 1994) also applicable to situations in which goods of the type specified in the Regulation are, in the course of transit between two countries not belonging to the European Community, temporarily detained by the customs authorities in a Member State on the basis of that regulation, at the request of a holder of rights who claims that his rights have been infringed and whose undertaking has its registered office in a non-member country?

(b) *The Opinion of Advocate General Ruiz-Jarabo Colomer*

9.501 AG Ruiz-Jarabo Colomer[452] analysed the issue essentially from the perspective of the wording and purpose of the customs regulation. They clearly and unambiguously covered the 'external transit', which the AG characterized as a 'fiction':

> I do not believe that it is possible to assert categorically that the external transit of non-Community goods is an activity completely devoid of effect on the internal market. Like

---

[452] C-383/98 *The Polo/Lauren Company v PT Dwidua Langgeng Pratama International Freight Forwarders* ECLI:EU:C:1999:624, not available in English. He began, as was his habit and for which he was renowned, with remarks going beyond the context of legal analysis:

> In a mythical modern American novel, the character Bateman, on returning to his apartment, finds in his mail a Polo Ralph Lauren catalogue (p. 71) and later buys two pairs of Ralph Lauren

other suspensive customs procedures, external transit is based on a sort of legal fiction. Goods placed under this procedure are subject neither to the corresponding import duties nor to other measures of commercial policy; it is as if they had not entered Community territory. There is no need to extend this fiction any further than necessary. In reality, the goods are imported from a non-member country and pass through one or more Member States before being exported to another non-member country. Thus, in actual fact, like importation, the placing of goods under an external transit procedure constitutes a Community activity. This conclusion is further reinforced by the risk—noted by several of the Parties—of counterfeit goods placed under a transit procedure evading controls and ending up on the European market.

9.502 Also, the Advocate General failed to perceive the inherent conflict with the broad coverage of the customs regulation but their inherent limitation as a result to the reference to substantive intellectual property law as regards the issue of infringement.

(c) The Judgment of the Court

9.503 The Court defined the issues as follows:[453]

> It should be noted at the outset that, in view of the national court's considerations set out in paragraphs 20 and 21 above, the reference for a preliminary ruling raises two distinct questions. The national court is asking, first, whether the Regulation applies in a situation where goods of the type specified in the Regulation are, in the course of transit between two countries not belonging to the European Community, temporarily detained by the customs authorities in a Member State on the basis of that regulation, at the request of a company holding rights which claims that its rights have been infringed and which has its registered office in a non-member country. If the answer is affirmative, the national court asks whether that regulation has an adequate basis in the EC Treaty.[454]

9.504 Then the Court, without spending much effort or time, simply concluded that the customs detention and seizure power explicitly extended to transit goods. It referred to the scope of the Regulation, set out in Article 1(1)(a), which applied to goods placed under a 'suspensive procedure' within the meaning of Article 84(1)(a) of the Community Customs Code. These included goods in so-called external transit, that is, goods from a non-Member State passing through the European Union to another non-Member State:

> According to Article 1(1)(a) of the Regulation, the latter applies where counterfeit or pirated goods are found when checks are made on goods placed under a suspensive procedure within the meaning of Article 84(1)(a) of the Community Customs Code. Under this latter provision, the term [suspensive] procedure designates, inter alia, external transit, that is to say, a customs procedure allowing the movement of non-Community goods from one point to another within the customs territory of the Community without those goods being subject to import duties or other charges under the Community Customs Code.

---

pyjamas (p. 291); at another point, sat in Harry's in New York, he notices that Todd Hamlin is wearing a belt from Ralph Lauren (p. 87); Craig McDermott lunches at the Yale Club wearing a lambswool and cashmere blazer and worsted wool flannel trousers by Ralph Lauren (p. 156); the screams of the unfortunate Bethany are drowned out with a camel-hair overcoat from Ralph Lauren (p. 245); and, finally, Bateman and Evelyn choose huge Polo Ralph Lauren towels for drying themselves after late-night skinny-dipping in the Hamptons (p. 280) (Ellis, B.E., *American Psycho*, Picador, 2000).

[453] C-383/98, *The Polo/Lauren Company LP v PT. Dwidua Langgeng Pratama International Freight Forwarders* [2000] ECR I-02519.
[454] Paragraph 23.

The Regulation is thus expressly designed to apply to goods passing through Community territory from a non-member country destined for another non-member country. It does not matter in this regard whether the holder of the right or those entitled under him have their registered office in a Member State or outside the Community.[455]

As regards the validity of the Regulation, the Court found that it was properly based on Article 113 EC, giving the Community power to regulate trade. The Court added strong language regarding the pursuit of counterfeit and pirated goods and their potential effect on the internal market: 9.505

> In this regard, certain provisions on intellectual property affecting cross-border trade constitute an essential element in international trade legislation. When requested to rule on the question whether or not the Community had exclusive jurisdiction to conclude the Agreement concerning Trade-Related Aspects of Intellectual Property Rights, including Trade in Counterfeit Goods (known as 'the TRIPs Agreement'), annexed to the agreement establishing the World Trade Organisation, the Court held, in Opinion 1/94 of 15 November 1994, [1994] ECR I-5267, paragraph 55, that measures at border crossing points intended to enforce intellectual property rights could be adopted autonomously by the Community institutions on the basis of Article 113 of the Treaty.
>
> So, the Community was empowered, under Article 113 of the Treaty, to introduce common rules for stopping counterfeit goods under a suspensive customs procedure such as the external transit procedure.
>
> After all, the external transit of non-Community goods is not completely devoid of effect on the internal market. It is, in fact, based on a legal fiction. Goods placed under this procedure are subject neither to the corresponding import duties nor to the other measures of commercial policy; it is as if they had not entered Community territory. In reality, they are imported from a non-member country and pass through one or more Member States before being exported to another non-member country. This operation is all the more liable to have a direct effect on the internal market as there is a risk that counterfeit goods placed under the external transit procedure may be fraudulently brought on to the Community market, as several Governments pointed out in their written observations and at the hearing.[456]

The Court answered the question as follows: 9.506

1. Article 1 of Council Regulation (EC) No 3295/94 ... is to be interpreted as being applicable where goods of the type specified in Regulation No 3295/94, imported from a non-member country, are, in the course of their transit to another non-member country, temporarily detained in a Member State by the customs authorities of that State on the basis of that regulation and at the request of the company which holds rights in respect of those goods which it claims have been infringed and whose registered office is in a non-member country.
2. Consideration of the questions raised has revealed no factor of such a kind as to affect the validity of Regulation No 3295/94.

(d) Conclusions

It is interesting to see, in hindsight, that the Court failed to appreciate the conflict between the customs rules and substantive IP legislation, which later led to judgments by the same Court effectively excluding any possibility of permanently seizing and destroying 9.507

---

[455] Paragraphs 26 and 27.
[456] Paragraphs 32–34.

counterfeit goods which are transported from a third country to another third country and which are only temporarily in the European Union.

(3) *Rioglass*: Transit through a Member State as Trade Mark Infringement? (2003)

(a) Facts and question referred

9.508 In *Rioglass*,[457] a case referred to the Court by the French Cour de cassation in 2002, the French customs authorities had seized in France goods made in Spain on their way to Poland, asserting an infringement of French trade mark rights in the goods, which were windows and window screens. The production in Spain and the intended use in Poland were legal. The seizure was held illegal by the Bordeaux Cour d'appel, whereupon the customs authority appealed to the Cour de cassation. This court referred the following question to the Court of Justice:

> Is Article 30 of the Treaty, now Article 28 EC, to be interpreted as meaning that it precludes the implementation, pursuant to the Code de la propriété intellectuelle, of procedures for detention by the customs authorities of goods lawfully manufactured in a Member State of the European Community which are intended, following their transit through French territory, to be placed on the market in a non-member country, in the present case, Poland?

(b) The Opinion of Advocate General Mischo

9.509 The Advocate General Mischo[458] referred to an earlier decision of the Court, *Commission v France*,[459] which had held that France had infringed its obligations under the Treaty by providing for the seizure of goods for infringing French IP rights lawfully placed on the market in one Member State and transported through France with the destination in another Member State, where they could lawfully be marketed. The Advocate General proposed that the same rules should apply when the destination was in a third country (Poland was at the time not yet a Member State). In conclusion, the Advocate General proposed that in the present case Articles 28 and 30 EC precluded the application of detention measures in France.

(c) The decision of the Court

9.510 **(i) Application of the freedom of movement of goods to goods from a Member State transiting through another Member State and destined for a non-Member State** The Court concluded, in view of its established case law, that the prohibition of measures impeding the freedom of movement of goods applied not only when the country of origin, the transit country, and the country of destination were all Member States, but also in a case like the present one, were the transiting goods were on their way to a third country.

> Given that, as is apparent from the file, the present case involves goods lawfully manufactured in one Member State in transit within another Member State, it must be pointed out that, according to settled case-law, the Customs Union established by the EC Treaty necessarily implies that the free movement of goods between Member States should be ensured. That freedom could not itself be complete if it were possible for Member States to impede or interfere in any way with the movement of goods in transit. It is therefore necessary, as a consequence of the Customs Union and in the mutual interest of the Member States, to

---

[457] C-115/02 *Administration des douanes et droits indirects v Rioglass SA and Transremar SL* [2003] ECR I-12705
[458] Opinion of 20 March 2003, Case C-115/02.
[459] Case C-23/99 *Commission v France* [2000] ECR I-07653.

acknowledge the existence of a general principle of freedom of transit of goods within the Community. That principle is, moreover, confirmed by the reference to transit in Article 30 EC (see, to that effect, Case 266/81 SIOT [1983] ECR 731, paragraph 16, and Case C-367/89 Richardt and Les Accessoires Scientifiques [1991] ECR I-4621, paragraph 14).

The Court has moreover already held that Articles 28 EC to 30 EC are applicable to goods in transit through a Member State but intended for a non-member country (see, to that effect, Case C-350/97 Monsees [1999] ECR I-2921 and Richardt and Les Accessoires Scientifiques, cited above).

It follows that, even if goods in transit are intended for a non-member country, they come within the scope of Articles 28 EC to 30 EC and the question referred for a preliminary ruling must accordingly be examined in the light of those provisions.[460]

(ii) No exception for the protection of IP rights The Court then considered whether the measures could be justified under Article 30 EC (now Article 36 of the Treaty on the Functioning of the European Union (TFEU)) as necessary for the protection of intellectual property rights. The Court concluded that such a justification was not possible, as the specific object ('subject matter') of trade mark protection in France would not be affected by goods which were not to be marketed in France: **9.511**

> Therefore, given that the detention under customs control in issue in the main proceedings was carried out on the basis of the Code de la propriété intellectuelle, it is necessary to determine whether the obstacle to the free movement of goods created by that detention under customs control may be justified by the need to ensure the protection of industrial and commercial property referred to in Article 30 EC.
>
> In order to answer that question it is necessary to take account of the purpose of that exception, which is to reconcile the requirements of the free movement of goods and the right of industrial and commercial property, by avoiding the maintenance or establishment of artificial barriers within the common market. Article 30 EC allows derogations from the fundamental principle of the free movement of goods within the common market only to the extent to which such derogations are justified for the purpose of safeguarding rights which constitute the specific subject-matter of such property (see, inter alia, Case C-10/89 Hag GF [1990] ECR I-3711, paragraph 12, Case C-61/97 FDV [1998] ECR I-5171, paragraph 13, and Commission v France, paragraph 37).
>
> According to the judgment for reference, the goods in issue in the present case were detained on suspicion of infringement of trade mark.
>
> With respect to trade marks, it is settled case-law that the specific subject-matter of a trade mark is, in particular, to guarantee to the owner that he has the exclusive right to use that mark for the purpose of putting a product on the market for the first time and thus to protect him against competitors wishing to take unfair advantage of the status and reputation of the trade mark by selling products illegally bearing it (see, in particular, Case 16/74 Centrafarm [1974] ECR 1183, paragraph 8, Case 102/77 Hoffmann-La Roche [1978] ECR 1139, paragraph 7, and Case C-349/95 Loendersloot [1997] ECR I-6227, paragraph 22).
>
> The implementation of such protection is therefore linked to the marketing of the goods.
>
> Transit, such as that in issue in the main proceedings, which consists in transporting goods lawfully manufactured in a Member State to a non-member country by passing through one or more Member States, does not involve any marketing of the goods in question and is therefore not liable to infringe the specific subject-matter of the trade mark.[461]

---

[460] C-115/02, paragraphs 18–20.
[461] Paragraphs 22–27.

9.512 The Court thus concluded:

> Article 28 EC is to be interpreted as precluding the implementation, pursuant to a legislative measure of a Member State concerning intellectual property, of procedures for detention by the customs authorities of goods lawfully manufactured in another Member State and intended, following their transit through the territory of the first Member State, to be placed on the market in a non-member country.

(4) *Rolex* et al.: Transit as Basis for Detention by Customs (2004)

(a) *The factual setting and the question referred*

9.513 In *Rolex*,[462] a reference in a criminal case from a local court in Austria, Landesgericht Eisenstadt, Rolex and a number of other companies had requested from the Landesgericht the initiation of a criminal investigation of a person accused of infringement of Austrian trade mark rights through the transit of infringing goods from Italy through Austria to Poland. The allegedly infringing goods had been detained by the Austrian customs authorities. The Landesgericht had doubts whether the absence of criminal sanctions in the Austrian trade mark law for transit cases was compatible with the customs regulations, and referred the following question to the Court:

> Is a provision of national law, in casu Paragraph 60(1) and (2) of the MSchG, in conjunction with Paragraph 10a thereof, which may be interpreted as meaning that the mere transit of goods manufactured/distributed in contravention of provisions of the law on trademarks is not punishable under criminal law, contrary to Article 2 of Council Regulation (EC) No 3295/94?

(b) *The Opinion of the Advocate General*

9.514 In this case as in the earlier Polo/Lauren case, the Advocate General was D Ruiz-Jarabo Colomer.[463] Not surprisingly, he maintained his view that the customs regulations applied to goods in external transit, as also found by the Court in the *Polo/Lauren* Judgment. The difficulties in the present case were seen in the relationship between the obligation set out in Article 11 of the Customs Regulation to provide penalties for infringement of its prohibitions,[464] and the absence, perceived by the Austrian courts, of penalties of any kind in cases of transit under Austrian trade mark law.

9.515 The Advocate General pointed out that the Austrian Government had asserted that the wording of the infringement provisions of the Austrian Trade Mark law did not exclude their application to transit situations, but that it remained unclear whether this would be specific enough to justify criminal penalties.

> It is clear from the above that, where a Member State does not have in place legislation capable of penalising the types of conduct referred to in Article 11, it will be faced not only with the matter of whether it has complied with Community law but also with the possibility of a complaint that it has failed to fulfil an obligation, which must be dealt with under the procedure outlined in Articles 226 EC and 227 EC. That proposition applies, in particular, to those cases, such as the one currently before the Court, where a lack of adequate legislation

---

[462] C-60/02 *Montres Rolex SA & Others* [2004] ECR I-00651.
[463] AG Ruiz-Jarabo Colomer, Opinion of 5 June 2003.
[464] Apparently it was not recognized that these penalties could only mean infractions of the customs rules themselves, but not infringements of intellectual property rights. Anyway, the AG seemed to assume that these penalties also meant such sanctions for IP rights infringement.

has resulted in a failure to fulfil an obligation. It must, however, be qualified in situations where existing national provisions are contrary to Community law. In such cases, the interpretation of the Court may, in practical terms, be tantamount to a finding that there has been a failure to fulfil an obligation.[465]

The answers proposed by Advocate General Ruiz-Jarabo Colomer were as follows: **9.516**

(1) Article 11 of Council Regulation (EC) No 3295/94 of 22 December 1994 laying down measures to prohibit the release for free circulation, export, re-export or entry for a suspensive procedure of counterfeit and pirated goods is applicable to situations in which goods in transit between two countries not belonging to the European Community are temporarily detained by the customs authorities in a Member State.
(2) The national court must interpret the provisions of national law, within the limits prescribed by its legal system, in the light of the wording and the purpose of the Community measure in order to achieve the result pursued by the latter.
(3) That duty to interpret national law consistently with the Community measure cannot, of itself and independently of a law adopted by a Member State, have the effect of determining or aggravating the liability in criminal law of persons who act in contravention of that measure.[466]

(c) The Judgment of the Court

The Court confirmed its earlier *Polo/Lauren* Judgment and held that the prohibitions of Regulation (EC) No 3295/94 applied to external transit with counterfeit goods.[467] **9.517**

The Court focused primarily on the issue of the absence or presence of criminal sanctions for such transit situations, where it balanced the requirement of an interpretation of national law in accordance with Community obligations[468] and the principle applicable in criminal law that there must be a clear definition of the proscribed conduct. **9.518**

> It must also be recalled that Article 11 of Regulation No 3295/94 requires Member States to introduce penalties for infringements of the prohibition laid down in Article 2 of the regulation on the release for free circulation, export, re-export and placing under a suspensive procedure of counterfeit goods.
>
> Moreover, as the Advocate General correctly observed in point 36 of his Opinion, the interpretation of the scope of that regulation is not conditional upon the type of national proceedings (civil, criminal, administrative) in which that interpretation is relied on.
>
> The national court considers that Article 60 of the MSchG can be interpreted as not applying to the mere transit of goods, which is challenged by the Austrian Government and the complainants in the main proceedings.
>
> It is not for the Court of Justice to rule on the interpretation of national law, which is a matter for the national court alone. If the national court were to find that the relevant provisions of national law do not prohibit and, thus, do not penalise the mere transit of counterfeit goods through the Member State concerned, contrary none the less to the requirements under Articles 2 and 11 of Regulation No 3295/94, it would be proper to conclude that those articles preclude the national provisions in question.

---

[465] Point 38.
[466] Point 49.
[467] C-60/02 [2004] ECR I-00651.
[468] The Court, as did the AG, seemed to assume without further discussion that the penalties prescribed by Article 11 of Regulation (EC) No 3295/94 would have to extend to making certain infringements a crime under trade mark law as well.

Moreover, according to settled case-law, national courts are required to interpret their national law within the limits set by Community law, in order to achieve the result intended by the Community rule in question (see Case C-106/89 Marleasing [1990] ECR I-4135, paragraph 8, and Case C-262/97 Engelbrecht [2000] ECR I-7321, paragraph 39).

If such a compatible interpretation is possible, it will be for the national court, in order to secure for holders of intellectual property rights protection of those rights against abuses prohibited by Article 2 of Regulation No 3295/94, to apply to the transit of counterfeit goods across the national territory the civil-law remedies applicable under national law to other conduct prohibited by that article, provided that they are effective and proportionate and constitute an effective deterrent.

However, a particular problem arises where the principle of compatible interpretation is applied to criminal matters. As the Court has also held, that principle finds its limits in the general principles of law which form part of the Community legal system and, in particular, in the principles of legal certainty and non-retroactivity. In that regard, the Court has held on several occasions that a directive cannot, of itself and independently of a national law adopted by a Member State for its implementation, have the effect of determining or aggravating the liability in criminal law of persons who act in contravention of the provisions of that directive (see, in particular, Pretore di Salò, paragraph 20; Case C-168/95 Arcaro [1996] ECR I-4705, paragraph 37, and Joined Cases C-74/95 and C-129/95 X [1996] ECR I-6609, paragraph 24).

Even though in the case at issue in the main proceedings the Community rule in question is a regulation, which by its very nature does not require any national implementing measures, and not a directive, Article 11 of Regulation No 3295/94 empowers Member States to adopt penalties for infringements of Article 2 of that regulation, thereby making it possible to transpose to the present case the Court's reasoning in respect of directives.

If the national court reaches the conclusion that national law does not prohibit the transit of counterfeit goods across Austrian territory, the principle of non-retroactivity of penalties, as enshrined in Article 7 of the European Convention for the Protection of Human Rights and Fundamental Freedoms, which is a general principle of Community law common to the constitutional traditions of the Member States, would prohibit the imposition of criminal penalties for such conduct, even if the national rule were contrary to Community law.[469]

9.519 The Court thus answered the questions referred as follows:

Articles 2 and 11 of Council Regulation No 3295/94 are applicable to situations in which goods in transit between two countries not belonging to the European Community are temporarily detained in a Member State by the customs authorities of that State.

The duty to interpret national law so as to be compatible with Community law, in the light of its wording and purpose, in order to attain the aim pursued by the latter, cannot, of itself and independently of a law adopted by a Member State, have the effect of determining or aggravating the liability in criminal law of an entity which has failed to observe the requirements of Regulation No 3295/94.[470]

(d) Conclusions

9.520 The Court in *Rolex*, as had the same Court in *Polo/Lauren*, failed to perceive the discrepancy between the customs prohibitions and the trade mark legislation, which came to light only in *Class International*, although the Austrian courts had pointed to the problem from the beginning, both in *Polo/Lauren* and here again in *Rolex*. In hindsight it appears strange that

---

[469] Paragraphs 55–64.
[470] Paragraph 65.

the Court in 2004 still seemed to require Austria to have criminal penalties in place for trade mark infringement in cases of 'external transit'.

(5) *Class*: Customs-Free Zones, Original Goods (2005)
(a) The factual and legal setting, the questions referred

9.521 *Class International*[471] is another transit case with some additional features. GlaxoSmithKline, Colgate Palmolive, and others brought an action against Class International for trademark infringement resulting from the bringing into the EU of original goods (toothpaste), and storing it in a customs warehouse in Rotterdam. Class claimed to be in the transit business with the respective goods, which had never entered free intra-EU circulation and would thus not infringe any national or Community trade mark rights. The case had the additional feature that the goods were 'original' goods placed on the market outside the EU by or with the consent of the trade mark proprietors. This fact, however, would not exclude infringement of their EU rights because under the applicable EU legislation—Directive and Regulation—only a first marketing in the EU or in the EEA leads to an exhaustion of rights. The case is important also because its factual scenario positions the Community in a global trading context where its territory functions as a transit location.

9.522 The referring court, the Gerechtshof te 's-Gravenhage, held that the interpretation of Article 5(1) and (3)(b) and (c) of the Directive and Article 9(1) and (2)(b) and (c) of the Regulation was necessary to decide the case, and sought a preliminary ruling for the following:

9.523 First, whether the proprietor of a trade mark can oppose the introduction of goods from third countries into the territory of a Member State in the context of transit trade. Second, whether 'using a sign in the course of trade' covers the storing, in a customs office or warehouse within the territory of a Member State, of original branded goods which have the customs status of non-Community goods. Third, whether knowledge, or its absence, of the final destination of those goods carries any significance regarding the first two questions. Fourth, whether there are any other additional circumstances that the Court may consider relevant. The fifth question was linked with the first and inquired whether the term 'offering' in the relevant provisions of the Directive and the Regulation covers the offering for sale of original branded goods which are stored in a customs office or warehouse within the territory of a Member State. The final, sixth, question focused on whether the trade mark proprietor or the importer carried the burden of proof.

9.524 Apart from trade mark law, the relevant legislation in this area is the EU's Customs Code, established in Regulation 2913/92, as amended.[472] Article 91(1) provides that the external transit procedure 'shall allow the movement from one point to another within the customs territory of the Community of ... non-Community goods, without such goods being subject to import duties and other charges or to commercial policy measures'. Article 92 provides that the external transit procedure is to end 'when the goods and the corresponding

---

[471] C-405/03 *Class International BV v Colgate-Palmolive Co, Unilever NV, SmithKline Beecham Plc and Beecham Group Plc* [2005] ECR I-8735.
[472] [1992] OJ 302 p 1. Note that the Customs Code has no effect in the European Free Trade Association countries that are part of the European Economic Area. The Court also observed that the Directive, though not the Regulation, is referred to in Annex XVII to the EEA Agreement under the common rules applicable therein.

documents are produced at the customs office of destination in accordance with the provisions of the procedure in question'.

(b) The Opinion of Advocate General Jacobs

9.525 According to Advocate General Jacobs, goods in transit are considered not to have entered the Community, and the essential purpose of customs warehouses is to provide for the storage of goods and not to permit the goods to pass from one stage of marketing to another. On the other hand, the exercise of trade mark rights must be reserved to cases in which a third party's use can affect the functions of the trade mark, in particular its essential function of guaranteeing to consumers the origin of the goods.

9.526 Goods in the transit procedure are not in free circulation within the Community and thus are not liable to affect the functions of the trade mark; thus he concluded that the

> trade mark proprietor may not oppose the entry into the customs territory of the Community without his consent of non-Community goods bearing his trade mark and subject to the Community external transit procedure on the basis that such entry alone constitutes 'using [the mark] in the course of trade' within the meaning of Article 5(1) of the First Council Directive.[473]

9.527 Finally, his conclusion on who carries the burden of proof in infringement cases appears to narrow the scope of *Zino Davidoff*[474] creating a narrower than many would have thought factual and jurisprudential context for the case. In the current state of Community law, where a trade mark proprietor brings infringement proceedings national procedural rules determine which party bears the burden of proof,

> except with regard to the question whether the goods were put on the market in the European Economic Area under that trade mark with the proprietor's consent. The exception is the result of Zino Davidoff where the Court ruled that it was for the trader alleging consent to prove it and not for the trade mark proprietor to demonstrate its absence.[475]

Still, *Zino Davidoff* must be seen as a specific exception to the rule due to 'cogent reasons'. The Court had stated that consent must be expressed in such a way that an intention to renounce the exclusive trade mark rights is unequivocally demonstrated because of consent's serious effect in extinguishing trade mark rights. Thus it was necessary to provide a uniform interpretation. In the current case, however, there were no cogent reasons for a uniform interpretation and national rules on the burden of proof should apply.

(c) The Judgment of the Court

9.528 The Court deliberated sitting as a Grand Chamber. It examined the questions in two stages. Its reasoning followed the pattern of delineating the positions of parallel traders and trade mark proprietors in broad terms, here favouring parallel traders, whilst providing for a special case favouring trade mark proprietors. The final balancing detail would be the rule on the burden of proof.

9.529 (i) The concept of 'importing' First it looked at the scope of the term 'importing' in the context of Article 5(3)(c) of the Directive and Article 9(2)(c) of the Regulation. It started

---

[473] Point 37.
[474] C-414/99 *Levi Strauss*, C-415/99 *Costco Wholesale UK Ltd*, and C-416/99 *Zino Davidoff SA* [2001] ECR I-8691.
[475] Point 79.

by linking it with a requirement that is codetermining the rights of the proprietor: it must entail 'using [the mark] in the course of trade' within the meaning of Article 5(1) of the Directive and Article 9(1) of the Regulation. So 'importing' requires introduction of the goods into the Community for the purposes of putting them on the market therein. For goods coming from non-European Economic Area (EEA) countries this would in turn require their release for free circulation according to Article 24 EC. The Court made a distinction between goods in customs procedures such as external transit, waiting to be transferred to a non-EEA destination, or customs warehousing, stored while awaiting a final destination, on the one hand, and goods in customs procedures leading to their release for free circulation and the conferment of Community goods customs status according to Article 79 of the Customs Code. However, at any stage a trader could switch from one procedure to another under Article 58(1) of the Customs Code:

> As long as that option is not chosen and the requirements of the customs approved treatment or use, other than release for free circulation, under which the goods have been placed are satisfied, the mere physical introduction of those goods into the territory of the Community is not 'importing' … and does not entail 'using [the mark] in the course of trade'[476]

and the trade mark proprietor cannot 'oppose that introduction … or make it conditional on the existence of a final destination already specified in a third country, possibly pursuant to a sale agreement'.[477]

9.530 As to the scope of Article 58(2) of the Customs Code, providing that the choice of customs treatment does not preclude prohibitions or restrictions justified on grounds of industrial and commercial property, the Court viewed the provision under a restrictive light as covering:

> only … cases in which the customs-approved treatment or use would adversely affect industrial and commercial property rights. Placing non-Community goods under a suspensive customs procedure does not make it possible for them to be put on the market in the Community in the absence of release for free circulation. In the field of trade marks, such placing of original goods bearing a mark is not therefore, per se, interference with the right of its proprietor to control the initial marketing in the Community.[478]

9.531 (ii) **The concepts of offering and putting on the market** The Court then moved to the second stage of its analysis, examining whether 'offering' and 'putting on the market' the goods under Article 5(3)(b) of the Directive and Article 9(2)(b) of the Regulation covers:

> respectively, offering and selling original goods bearing a trade mark and having the customs status of non-Community goods, when the offering is made and/or the sale is effected while the goods are placed under the external transit procedure or the customs warehousing procedure.[479]

9.532 Here the Court was more lenient towards trade mark proprietors making what appears to be a practical distinction. The sale to a party in a third country of goods that were in external transit or warehousing did not affect adversely the 'trade mark proprietor's right to control the initial

---

[476] Paragraph 44.
[477] Paragraph 45. The very nature of this process rejected the argument that there was a risk that goods in external transit or customs warehousing would be released for free circulation since this was one of the options available to traders.
[478] Paragraph 47.
[479] Paragraph 51.

marketing in the Community'.[480] This was not the case when the sale 'necessarily entails putting goods bearing the mark on the market in the Community';[481] this would be considered 'using [the mark] in the course of trade' within the meaning of Article 5(1) of the Directive and Article 9(1) of the Regulation and could be opposed by the trade mark proprietor. But trade mark rights should be asserted on the basis of cogent evidence rather than assumptions based on the involvement of the trader in parallel trade. A trade mark proprietor could not 'rely on his right against a trader who offers or sells those goods to another trader on the sole ground that that trader is likely then to put them on the market in the Community'.[482]

9.533 (iii) **The burden of proof** Finally, the Court considered the question of which party carries the burden of proof. Note that the Commission had submitted that it was up to the Member States to establish the applicable rules of procedure, adding though that setting requirements that were too strict would render the right to use the Community as a territory of transit illusory. The Court started from the general position that as long as the conditions of the customs suspensive procedures were complied with, the situation of the trader concerned is, in principle, lawful. It then moved to the stage of 'pleading interference'[483] with the exclusive trade mark rights. It noted that according to its findings in *Zino Davidoff*[484] divergent procedural rules could lead to divergent levels of protection in an area of law that has been described as fundamental. Accordingly, following the principles of *Zino Davidoff*, 'the onus of proving interference must lie with the trade mark proprietor who alleges it. If that is proven, it is then for the trader sued to prove the existence of the consent of the proprietor to the marketing of the goods in the Community'.[485]

(d) *Conclusions*

9.534 *Class* essentially closed the door on any attempt to pursue counterfeit goods in transit through the EU by invoking trade mark infringement. The harshness of the Court's approach is the more surprising as the Court has been very willing to extend the rights of trade mark proprietors, perhaps beyond what standard doctrines would have allowed. It should have been possible for the Court to distinguish between original-goods cases, simple infringements, and cases where counterfeit goods were transported through the EU which could not legally be sold even in the country of destination.

9.535 While there may be some justification for not unduly interfering with 'genuine' transit, permitting transactions relating to such goods to take place in customs-free zones (one could mention in addition to warehouses the customs-free zones in airports etc.) disregards the long-standing principle that intellectual property rights are valid throughout the territory in which they are valid, and that the discrepancy between customs boundaries and territorial boundaries should not be of relevance. Affixing a trade mark in a customs-free zone and conducting transactions thus should be an infringement, regardless of whether the goods are destined for the internal market or for a third country. This would still allow the 'mere' transit to be outside of the trade mark proprietor's exclusive rights.

---

[480] Paragraph 57.
[481] Paragraph 58.
[482] Paragraph 60.
[483] Paragraph 70.
[484] C-414/99 *Levi Strauss*, C-415/99 *Costco Wholesale UK Ltd*, and C-416/99 *Zino Davidoff SA* [2001] ECR I-8691.
[485] Paragraph 74.

(6) *Montex/Diesel*: Transit as Trade Mark Infringement, Again (2006)

(a) *The factual setting and the questions referred*

Montex/Diesel[486] followed quickly after *Class International*. Indeed, there was an overlap. The *Montex/Diesel* reference dated from June 2005, just days after Advocate General Jacobs had delivered his Opinion in *Class International*, and some time before the Judgment in that case, which was delivered on 18 October 2005. *Montex/Diesel* was a trade mark infringement case involving the transit of items of clothing, marked with DIESEL, from Poland through Germany to Ireland. While the Italian Diesel company had trade mark rights in Germany, Diesel could not prevent the marketing in Ireland. **9.536**

The case eventually reached the Bundesgerichtshof, the German Federal Supreme Court, which referred the following questions to the Court: **9.537**

> (1) Does a registered trade mark grant its proprietor the right to prohibit the transit of goods with the sign?
> (2) If the answer is in the affirmative: may a particular assessment be based on the fact that the sign enjoys no protection in the country of destination?
> (3) If the answer to (1) is in the affirmative and irrespective of the answer to (2), is a distinction to be drawn according to whether the article whose destination is a Member State comes from a Member State, an associated State or a third country? Is it relevant in this regard whether the article has been produced in the country of origin lawfully or in infringement of a right to a sign existing there held by the trade-mark proprietor?

The question thus also raised the interesting issue of whether it mattered whether the goods had been lawfully marked in the country of origin. **9.538**

(b) *Opinion of Advocate General Poiares Maduro*

Advocate General Poiares Maduro had no difficulty with *Class International* by the time of his Opinion decided, already decided by the time of his Opinion, and concluded that transit as such did not amount to trade mark infringement, unless there was a genuine risk that the goods would enter the market in the transit country. Also, the fact that there had been an infringement in the country of origin (Poland) did not change the legal situation in the transit country (Germany). The Advocate General spent some effort in seeking to distinguish the earlier *Polo/Lauren* and *X (Rolex)* cases, seeking to explain the outcome in these cases with the risk, supposedly present in those cases, that the good would enter the market in the transit country (Austria). **9.539**

(c) *The Judgment of the Court*

The Court, following the decision in *Class International*, concluded that the transit through Germany in the present case would amount to an infringement of Diesel's German trade mark rights only **9.540**

> if those goods are subject to the act of a third party while they are placed under the external transit procedure which necessarily entails their being put on the market in that Member State of transit.[487]

---

[486] C-281/05 *Montex Holdings Ltd v Diesel SpA* [2006] ECR I-10881
[487] Paragraph 27.

9.541 The outcome is not affected by the existence of trade mark protection in the country of origin: 'Whether the manufacture of the goods in issue was lawful or unlawful is in that respect irrelevant.'[488]

9.542 The Court sought to distinguish the earlier *X (Rolex)* case and *Polo/Lauren*:

> Contrary to Diesel's assertions, such an interpretation of Article 5 of Directive 89/104 is not affected by the judgment in Case C-60/02 X [2004] ECR I-651, regarding, in particular, the interpretation of Articles 2 and 11 of Regulation No 3295/94.

9.543 In that Judgment, the Court pointed out, in paragraph 54, that Article 1 of Regulation No 3295/94 is to be interpreted as being applicable where goods imported from a non-Member State, are, in the course of their transit to another non-Member State, temporarily detained in a Member State by the customs authorities of this latter State on the basis of that regulation and at the request of the company which holds the rights claimed to have been infringed (see also *Polo v Lauren*,[489] paragraphs 26 and 27).

9.544 In that regard, the Court notes that Article 1 of Regulation No 3295/94 lays down first, the conditions under which the customs authorities are to take action where goods suspected of being counterfeit goods are, in particular, found in the course of checks on goods under customs supervision within the meaning of Article 37 of the Customs Code, placed under a suspensive procedure within the meaning of Article 84(1)(a) of that Code, re-exported subject to notification or placed in a free zone or free warehouse under Article 166 thereof.

9.545 Second, Article 1 of Regulation No 3295/94 lays down the measures which can be taken by the competent customs authorities with regard to those goods.

9.546 Third, the Second and Third Recitals of that Regulation, reproduced in paragraph 4 above, refer expressly to the marketing of counterfeit goods or the placing of such goods on the market, and to the need to prohibit the release of such goods for free circulation in the Community.[490]

9.547 The Court concluded:

> It follows that none of the provisions of Regulation No 3295/94 introduces a new criterion for the purposes of ascertaining the existence of an infringement of trade mark law or to determine whether there is a use of the mark liable to be prohibited because it infringes that law.[491]

(d) Conclusions

9.548 The outcome in *Montex/Diesel* was obvious in view of *Class International*. The effort to distinguish *Polo/Lauren* and *X (Rolex)* could not succeed: the Court should have recognized that the link between the customs regulations and substantive trade mark law was not properly appreciated at the time, or that it had been wrong to assume that 'external transit' also fell under the rights of trade mark proprietors.

---

[488] Paragraph 34.
[489] It is interesting for the informed observer to note that the Court thought the *Polo/Lauren* case was between someone called 'Polo' and someone else called 'Lauren'.
[490] Paragraphs 35–39.
[491] Paragraph 40.

(7) *Philips* and *Nokia*: Transit and Customs Seizure Once More, the Final Act? (2011)

9.549 The unresolved conflict between the perceived obligations arising under the customs regulations for the seizure and detention of goods in transit on the one hand, as expressed in *Polo/Lauren* and *Rolex*, and the absence of infringement of national or Community trademarks in cases of transit, unless the goods would 'necessarily' reach the market in the European Union or in the Member State concerned, as expressed in *Class International* and *Montex/Diesel*, and obviously not finally resolved in the latter case, led to the two references in *Philips* and *Nokia*.

(a) Factual settings and questions referred

9.550 Both references, *Philips*[492] and *Nokia*,[493] referred to the Court within a span of three weeks in November 2009, concerned goods which were in the customs situation of 'external transit', within the meaning of Article 91(1)(a) of the Community Customs Code, which allows 'the movement from one point to another within the customs territory of the Community of ... non-Community goods, without such goods being subject to import duties and other charges or to commercial policy measures'. This 'external transit' notion is based on a legal fiction, since the whole procedure unfolds as if the non-Community goods concerned had never entered the territory of a Member State.

9.551 In *Philips*, customs authorities in Antwerp had detained a shipment of shavers from China because of suspected infringement of design rights and copyrights held by Philips. At that time the initial customs regulation on counterfeit and pirated goods, Regulation (EC) No 3295/94, applied, which was superseded by Regulation (EC) No 1383/2003, which again was replaced by the current legislation in 2013.

9.552 The referring court, the court of first instance in Antwerp, referred the following question:

> Does Article 6(2)(b) of Council Regulation (EC) No 3295/94 of 22 December 1994 (the old Customs Regulation) constitute a uniform rule of Community law which must be taken into account by the court of the Member State which, in accordance with Article 7 of the Regulation, has been approached by the holder of an intellectual-property right, and does that rule imply that, in making its decision, the court may not take into account the temporary storage status/transit status and must apply the fiction that the goods were manufactured in that same Member State, and must then decide, by applying the law of that Member State, whether those goods infringe the intellectual-property right in question?

9.553 The Nokia reference involved counterfeit Nokia products detained by customs at Heathrow Airport. The European Union's customs regulation at the time was Regulation (EC) No 1383/2003, the successor to the legislation involved in the Philips reference. Regulation 1383/2003 has since been replaced by Regulation (EC) No 608/2013.

9.554 The Court of Appeal for England and Wales referred to following question to the Court:

> Are non-Community goods bearing a Community trade mark which are subject to customs supervision in a Member State and in transit from a non-Member State to another

---

[492] C-446/09 *Koninklijke Philips Electronics NV v Lucheng Meijing Industrial Company Ltd, Far East Sourcing Ltd, Röhlig Hong Kong Ltd, and Röhlig Belgium NV* [2011] ECR I-12435.
[493] C-495/09 *Nokia Corporation v Her Majesty's Commissioners of Revenue and Customs* [2011] ECR I-12435. The two cases were joined.

non-Member State capable of constituting 'counterfeit goods' within the meaning of Article 2(1)(a) of Regulation (EC) No 1383/2003 if there is no evidence to suggest that those goods will be put on the market in the EC, either in conformity with a customs procedure or by means of an illicit diversion?

9.555 In the first case, *Philips*, the applicant in the main proceedings claimed that, as part of the legal fiction that is the external transit situation, another legal fiction—the so-called production fiction—applies, in accordance with which non-Community goods in transit are treated as though they had been manufactured in the Member State in which they are situated and are, accordingly, subject to the legislation on the protection of intellectual property in force in that Member State. This therefore circumvents the burden of proving that the goods concerned will be traded in the Union, a condition which is, in principle, unavoidable for the purposes of obtaining protection of all forms of intellectual property right.

9.556 In the second case, *Nokia*, the United Kingdom customs authorities refused Nokia's application for seizure of some apparently counterfeit goods, arguing that their destination was Colombia and there was no evidence that they were going to be diverted onto the European Union market. The referring court asked the Court of Justice whether that is a matter which it is essential to establish in order to classify goods as 'counterfeit' for the purposes of the customs legislation and, in short, in order for the customs authorities to be able to detain those goods.

9.557 The two cases were joined for purposes of the oral proceedings and the judgment and thus decided in a single judgment.

(b) Opinion of the Advocate General Cruz Villalón

9.558 Advocate General Cruz Villalón prepared a long Opinion.[494] The conclusions are not surprising, but they allow a separate existence of the customs regulations for the detention of infringing goods and the absence of remedies for counterfeit goods in 'external transit', as found in *Class International*.

9.559 The Advocate General concluded as follows:

[As regards Philips]:
Article 6(2)(b) of Council Regulation (EC) No 3295/94 of 22 December 1994 laying down measures concerning the entry into the Community and the export and re-export from the Community of goods infringing certain intellectual property rights is not to be interpreted as meaning that the judicial authority of the Member State called on, in accordance with Article 7 of that regulation, by the holder of an intellectual property right, may take no account of the status of temporary entry or of transit of the goods in question, or, therefore, as meaning that that authority may apply the fiction that those goods were produced in that same Member State for the purpose of ruling, in accordance with the law of that State, whether or not they infringe the intellectual property right at issue.

[As regards Nokia]:
Non-Community goods bearing a Community trade mark which are subject to customs supervision in a Member State and are in transit from one non-member country to another non-member country may be seized by the customs authorities provided that there are

---

[494] ECLI:EU:C:2011:45.

sufficient grounds for suspecting that they are counterfeit goods and, in particular, that they are to be put on the market in the European Union, either in conformity with a customs procedure or by means of an illicit diversion.[495]

(c) The decision of the Court

Almost two-thirds of the decision was taken up with presenting the applicable legislation and the facts leading up to the questions.[496] **9.560**

The Court, referring to its earlier case law, notably *Class International* and *Montex/Diesel*, explained again that goods in external transit are counterfeit or otherwise infringing goods only if they would reach the market after customs clearance: **9.561**

> As follows from Articles 91, 92 and 98 of the Customs Code, the transit and customs warehousing procedures are respectively characterised by the movement of goods between customs offices and the storage of goods in a warehouse under customs supervision. On any view, those operations cannot, as such, be regarded as the putting of goods on sale in the European Union (see, with regard to intra-Community transit operations, Case C-115/02 Rioglass and Transremar [2003] ECR I-12705, paragraph 27, and Montex Holdings, paragraph 19).
>
> The Court has repeatedly deduced from that fact that goods placed under a suspensive customs procedure cannot, merely by the fact of being so placed, infringe intellectual property rights applicable in the European Union (see inter alia, as regards rights concerning designs, Case C-23/99 Commission v France [2000] ECR I-7653, paragraphs 42 and 43, and, as regards rights conferred by trade marks, Rioglass and Transremar, paragraph 27, Case C-405/03 Class International [2005] ECR I-8735, paragraph 47, and Montex Holdings, paragraph 21).
>
> On the other hand, those rights may be infringed where, during their placement under a suspensive procedure in the customs territory of the European Union, or even before their arrival in that territory, goods coming from non-member States are the subject of a commercial act directed at European Union consumers, such as a sale, offer for sale or advertising (see Class International, paragraph 61, and Case C-324/09 L'Oréal and Others [2011] ECR I-0000, paragraph 67).
>
> Here the Court, it submitted, disregards that commercial operations such as a sale, offer for sale, or advertising takes place in the European Union even if this should happen in a customs-free zone.
>
> The Court continues to recognise that the risk of counterfeit goods actually reaching the market in the European Union is real, and that the customs authorities are entitled (and even obliged) to intervene when there are grounds for such a risk.
>
> As the French, Italian and Polish Governments have pointed out, the placing of goods from a non-member State under a suspensive procedure is often requested in circumstances where the destination of the goods is either unknown or declared in a manner which is unreliable. Having regard, in addition, to the secretive nature of the activities of traffickers of goods which are imitations or copies, the detention by customs authorities of goods which they have identified as being imitations or copies cannot, without reducing the effectiveness of Regulations No 3295/94 and No 1383/2003, be made subject to a requirement for proof

---

[495] Point 113.
[496] Joined Cases C-446/09 and C-495/09 *Koninklijke Philips Electronics and Nokia Corporation* ECLI:EU:C:2011:45. Eight governments had submitted observations; the International Trademark Association had been granted the right to intervene in the case before the Court of Appeal and was thus also present in the case before the Court. The Rapporteur was Judge Ilešič, the primary Rapporteur in recent years in difficult trade mark cases.

that those goods have already been sold, offered for sale or advertised to European Union consumers.

On the contrary, a customs authority which has established the presence in warehousing or in transit of goods which are an imitation or a copy of a product protected in the European Union by an intellectual property right can legitimately act when there are indications before it that one or more of the operators involved in the manufacture, consignment or distribution of the goods, while not having yet begun to direct the goods towards European Union consumers, are about to do so or are disguising their commercial intentions.[497]

9.562 The Court then goes on to highlight elements which may be invoked to justify an intervention:

With regard to the indications required to be before that authority in order for it to suspend release of or detain goods within the meaning of Article 6(1) of Regulation No 3295/94 and Article 9(1) of Regulation No 1383/2003, it is sufficient, as the Advocate General has noted in points 96, 97, 110 and 111 of his Opinion, that there be material such as to give rise to suspicion. That material may include the fact that the destination of the goods is not declared whereas the suspensive procedure requested requires such a declaration, the lack of precise or reliable information as to the identity or address of the manufacturer or consignor of the goods, a lack of cooperation with the customs authorities or the discovery of documents or correspondence concerning the goods in question suggesting that there is liable to be a diversion of those goods to European Union consumers.[498]

9.563 The Court however recognizes the risk of over-eager detentions. The Court also recognizes the central role played by transit goods in international trade, which must remain unimpeded by arbitrary and unjustified national measures:

As the Advocate General has observed in point 106 of his Opinion, such a suspicion must, in all cases, be based on the facts of the case. If that suspicion and the resulting action were capable of being based merely on the abstract consideration that fraudulent diversion to European Union consumers cannot necessarily be ruled out, all goods in external transit or customs warehousing could be detained without the slightest concrete indication of an irregularity. Such a situation would give rise to a risk that actions of the Member States' customs authorities would be random and excessive.

It should be borne in mind, in that regard, that imitations and copies coming from a non-member State and transported to another non-member State may comply with the intellectual property provisions in force in each of those States. In the light of the common commercial policy's main objective, set out in Article 131 EC and Article 206 TFEU and consisting in the development of world trade through the progressive abolition of restrictions on trade between States, it is essential that those goods be able to pass in transit, via the European Union, from one non-member State to another without that operation being hindered, even by a temporary detention, by Member States' customs authorities. Precisely such hindrance would be created if Regulations No 3295/94 and No 1383/2003 were interpreted as permitting the detention of goods in transit without the slightest indication suggesting that they could be fraudulently diverted to European Union consumers.

That consideration is moreover corroborated by the second recital in the preamble to those regulations, stating that the objective of the European Union legislature is restricted to preventing goods infringing intellectual property rights from being 'placed on the market' and to adopting measures for that purpose 'without impeding the freedom of legitimate trade'.[499]

---

[497] Paragraphs 55–60.
[498] Paragraph 61.
[499] Paragraphs 62–64.

The Court also recognizes the relevance of infringements in the country of destination, but points as a remedy to customs cooperation: **9.564**

> Finally, with regard to goods in respect of which there is no indication as referred to in paragraph 61 of this judgment, but in respect of which there are suspicions of infringement of an intellectual property right in the presumed non-member State of destination, it must be noted that the customs authorities of the Member States where those goods are in external transit are permitted to cooperate, pursuant to Article 69 of the TRIPS Agreement, with the customs authorities of that non-member State with a view to removing those goods from international trade where appropriate.[500]

Thus, as concerns the intervention by customs authorities, the Court concludes as follows: **9.565**

> the Court of Appeal (England and Wales) (Civil Division) must examine whether there were indications before HMRC such as to give rise to suspicion for the purposes of that provision, requiring them, in consequence, to suspend release of or detain the goods under that regulation in order to immobilise them pending the determination to be made by the authority competent to take a substantive decision.[501]

The Court then turned to the question of the decisions to be taken on the merits and the theory of the 'manufacturing fiction' advocated by Philips and the Belgian Government. This the Court rejected without much difficulty: **9.566**

> Unlike the decision taken by the customs authority to detain the goods temporarily, by means of the detention provided for in Article 6(1) of Regulation No 3295/94 and Article 9(1) of Regulation No 1383/2003, the substantive decision as referred to in Article 6(2)(b) of Regulation No 3295/94 and the first paragraph of Article 10 of Regulation No 1383/2003 cannot be adopted on the basis of a suspicion but must be based on an examination of whether there is proof of an infringement of the right relied upon.

The Court continues that it is clear that the sanctions envisaged by the customs regulations, such as the destruction of the goods and penalties provided for in Article 11 of the Customs Regulation, cannot be imposed 'on the sole basis of a risk of fraud or on the basis of a fiction such as that proposed by Philips and the Belgian Government'.[502] **9.567**

The Court then takes up the criticism directed at the difficulties in pursuing counterfeit goods created by the case law of the Court. Customs retain the possibility to take measures when it turns out that the goods are not actually sent off to third countries. As regards the possibility of an eventual diversion of counterfeit goods onto EU markets: **9.568**

> The end of detention of goods carried out under Regulations No 3295/94 and No 1383/2003 does not in any way imply that those goods will from then on escape customs supervision. It is apparent from Article 37 of the Customs Code and the implementing provisions of that code that each stage of a suspensive procedure, such as that relating to external transit, must be rigorously monitored and documented by the Member States' customs authorities and that any significant derogation from the data given on the customs declaration may give rise to an action in respect of the goods by those authorities.[503]

---

[500] Paragraph 65.
[501] Paragraph 66.
[502] Paragraph 69.
[503] Paragraph 74.

9.569 As regards the concealment of the real destination or the impossibility of finding the persons responsible for the goods:

> Nor is the combating of unlawful operations impeded by the fact, already found by the Court, that it is impossible for the holder of the intellectual property right to refer the case to the authority competent to take a substantive decision if the operators responsible for the presence of the goods in question in the customs territory of the European Union have conceded [sic! concealed] their identity (Case C-223/98 Adidas [1999] ECR I-7081, paragraph 27). It must be borne in mind, in that regard, that European Union customs law establishes the principle that all goods intended to be placed under a customs procedure must be covered by a declaration (Case C-138/10 DP grup [2011] ECR I-0000, paragraph 33). As is clear from Article 59 of the Customs Code and the implementing provisions of that code, a declaration which does not permit identification since the name or address of the declarant or other relevant operators is concealed will have the consequence that the release of the goods for the purposes provided for by the customs procedure requested cannot be validly granted. Moreover, if the lack of reliable information as to the identity or address of the operators responsible persists, the goods are liable, under Article 75 of the Customs Code, to be confiscated.[504]

9.570 As regards risks to safety and health, brought about by defective or unsafe counterfeit goods:

> As regards, secondly, the risks to consumers' health and safety which goods that are imitations or copies sometimes pose, it is apparent from the file and from recital 2 in the preamble to Regulation No 1383/2003 that those risks are amply documented and their existence recognised by the European Union legislature. Furthermore, as, inter alia, Nokia and the Portuguese Government have pointed out, precautionary considerations may militate in favour of an immediate seizure of goods identified as posing such risks, irrespective of the customs procedure under which they are placed. In such a context, the question whether the operators responsible for the manufacture and distribution of those goods direct them to consumers in the European Union or in non-member States is irrelevant.
>
> [However] … it must be stated that the powers and obligations of the Member States' customs authorities as regards goods posing such risks must be assessed on the basis of other provisions of European Union law, such as Articles 56, 58 and 75 of the Customs Code.[505]

(d) Conclusions

9.571 Goods in 'external transit', as well as goods transiting through Member States where intellectual property rights exist, from one Member State through a second Member State and to a third Member State, do not infringe intellectual property rights unless it is established that the goods necessarily reach the respective domestic market. This conclusion led to the legislative proposals presented hereafter.

9.572 That customs intervention is possible on mere suspicion, duly substantiated, whereas the decision on the merits requires proof of infringement, amounts to an intelligible differentiation between what customs can do and what a decision on the merits requires. However, once the importer comes forward with a claim, duly substantiated, that the goods are meant for a third country, customs must release them. This will change when the substantive law of trade marks as currently proposed changes to include transit situations in the exclusive rights of trade mark proprietors.

---

[504] Paragraph 75.
[505] Paragraphs 76–77.

When that should happen, as currently appears very likely, the underlying issue will remain unsolved for other intellectual property rights, where the interests involved are indeed the same. **9.573**

(8) *Blomqvist*: Importing Counterfeit Products through the Mail (2014)

(a) Factual setting and question referred

Mr Blomqvist ordered a fake Rolex watch from an English website of a Chinese on-line shop. The watch was sent by mail from Hong Kong. Danish customs inspected the package, found the counterfeit watch, and informed Rolex. Rolex requested suspension of customs clearance, which was opposed by Mr Blomqvist. Rolex then brought an action before the Sø-og Handelsretten (Maritime and Commercial Court) seeking an order that Mr Blomqvist allow the suspension of release and the destruction of the watch without compensation. That court granted Rolex's claim. Mr Blomqvist appealed to the Højesteret (Supreme Court). For the referring court, in view of the fact that Mr Blomqvist bought his watch for personal use and did not himself infringe Danish law on copyright and trade marks, the question arose whether the seller infringed copyright or trade mark law in Denmark. **9.574**

Five questions were referred to the Court, the first dealing with distribution to the public, the second and the third dealing with use in the course of trade for national trade marks and for Community trade marks. We reproduce here the third question: **9.575**

> 3. Is Article 9(1) and (2) of Council Regulation No 207/2009 of 26 February 2009 on the Community trade mark to be interpreted in such a way that it must be viewed as constituting '[use] in the course of trade' of a trade mark in a Member State if an undertaking enters into an agreement via a website in a third country for the sale and dispatch of goods bearing the Community trade mark to a private purchaser with an address known to the vendor in a Member State, receives payment for the goods and effects dispatch to the purchaser at the agreed address, or is it also a condition in that situation that the goods must have been the subject, prior to the sale, of an offer for sale or an advertisement targeted at, or shown on a website intended for, consumers in the State in question?

Additional questions were asked as to whether the answer to the first three questions would also apply to the application of the customs regulations. **9.576**

(b) The decision of the Court

The Court,[506] sitting without the benefit of an Opinion of the Advocate General, began by describing the issue to be decided as follows: **9.577**

> the referring court seeks clarification of the term 'distribution to the public' within the meaning of Article 4(1) of the copyright directive and of the term '[use] in the course of trade' within the meaning of Article 5(1) and (3) of the trade mark directive and Article 9(1) and (2) of the Community trade mark regulation, in order to assess, in the main proceedings, whether there was any infringement of an intellectual property right.[507]

The Court, referring to *Philips* and *Montex*, reiterated that customs intervention is premised on an infringement of an intellectual property right, and that the customs regulations did not establish a different concept of infringement. Thus, whether customs were entitled to detain and seize goods depended on whether or not there was an infringement. With regard **9.578**

---

[506] C-98/13 *Blomqvist v Rolex SA* ECLI:EU:C:2014:55.
[507] Paragraph 23.

to trade mark infringement, this required finding 'use in the course of trade', and with regard to copyright infringement, 'distribution to the public'.[508]

9.579 The infringement issue raised one of the many complications that have arisen in the context of trading in infringing goods via the Internet: may the proprietor of an intellectual property right bring an infringement action when infringing goods are sold to a private person residing in the territory of a Member State through an online sales website in a non-Member country, or in terms of trade mark law and copyright law, whether such a sale by means of packages addressed to a private citizens constitutes 'use in the course of trade' or 'distribution to the public'?

9.580 The Court had in fact no difficulty in finding that an infringement has been committed. The Court first established the principles of 'use in the course of trade' and 'distribution to the public'.[509] The Court then considered an analogous domestic situation, the sale through a website in the EU, which clearly would amount to an infringement, and concluded that the answer must be the same when the goods come from abroad:

> Admittedly, the mere fact that a website is accessible from the territory covered by the trade mark is not a sufficient basis for concluding that the offers for sale displayed there are targeted at consumers in that territory (L'Oréal and Others, paragraph 64).
>
> However, the Court has held that the rights thus protected may be infringed where, even before their arrival in the territory covered by that protection, goods coming from non-member States are the subject of a commercial act directed at consumers in that territory, such as a sale, offer for sale or advertising (see, to that effect, Philips, paragraph 57 and the case-law cited).
>
> Thus, goods coming from a non-member State which are imitations of goods protected in the European Union by a trade mark right or copies of goods protected in the European Union by copyright, a related right or a design can be classified as 'counterfeit goods' or 'pirated goods' where it is proven that they are intended to be put on sale in the European Union, such proof being provided, inter alia, where it turns out that the goods have been sold to a customer in the European Union or offered for sale or advertised to consumers in the European Union (see, to that effect, Philips, paragraph 78).
>
> [T]he mere fact that the sale was made from an online sales website in a non-member country cannot have the effect of depriving the holder of an intellectual property right over the goods which were the subject of the sale of the protection afforded by the customs regulation, without it being necessary to verify whether such goods were, in addition, prior to that sale, the subject of an offer for sale or advertising targeting European Union consumers.[510]

9.581 The Court thus answered the questions referred as follows:[511]

> The holder of an intellectual property right over goods sold to a person residing in the territory of a Member State through an online sales website in a non-member country enjoys the protection afforded to that holder by that regulation at the time when those goods enter the territory of that Member State merely by virtue of the acquisition of those goods. It is not necessary, in addition, for the goods at issue to have been the subject, prior to the sale, of an offer for sale or advertising targeting consumers of that State.

---

[508] Paragraphs 24 and 25.
[509] Paragraphs 26–30.
[510] Paragraphs 31–34.
[511] Paragraph 35.

(c) Conclusions

9.582 The finding that commercial sellers from third countries are importing infringing goods into the European Union 'in the course of trade' should actually not come as a surprise. More surprising is that this was apparently doubted by the referring court.

9.583 One of the interesting aspects of the case has to do not with the acts of infringement, but the possibility of actually pursuing such acts. The Danish court stated that Mr Blomqvist himself was not liable, as he was a private person not himself 'in the course of trade', and not himself undertaking a 'distribution to the public'. It seems therefore that Rolex made a clever choice by not bringing an action against Mr Blomqvist for infringement, and not an action against the foreign vendor, who, though liable, would find means to avoid any litigation before a European court, but rather an action requesting Mr Blomqvist not to object to the eventual seizure and destruction of the fake watch. Whether such an infringement action 'in disguise' is available in other jurisdictions remains to be seen.

9.584 The legislative proposals, presented hereafter, to deal with the importation in 'small consignments', would seem to have become superfluous in view of the *Rolex* Judgment. The proposals do not solve the question of who the potential defendant in an infringement action would be.

I. Conclusion

9.585 It would be misleading to draw broad conclusions on the scope of protection from the relevant case law of the Court of Justice.

9.586 Its approach seems to change from case to case, sometimes hinting at broadening the scope of protection, at other times appearing to deny protection even in cases where infringement would appear to be an automatic presumption and being permissive in its approach towards limitations. The Court is often getting involved with the facts of the case and allows factual contexts to delimit its interpretive rulings. It is difficult to identify clear, easily applicable criteria.

9.587 Still, the Court's consistently pragmatic approach must also be acknowledged and appreciated. The Court recognizes that trade marks are tools used by marketers, their competitors, and consumers in a market place that evolves constantly. Trade marks must be protected in order to fulfil their function as a carrier of information; at the same time markets must remain open and competitive. Hence, the Court has so far avoided a doctrinal, macroscopic, interpretive approach. Instead it chooses to focus on the area of protection that is relevant and specific to each individual case. It takes into account the factual and market contexts and views trade mark law as one piece of a bigger market regulation picture.

9.588 After all, context is everything in the interpretation and application of trade mark law. Accepting this more explicitly would allow the Court to reconcile what appear to be inconsistencies in its trade mark jurisprudence.

10

PARALLEL IMPORTS

A. Introduction

Free movement of goods, one of the 'four freedoms' together with free movement of persons, services, and capital covered in the Treaties,[1] is a fundamental principle with two purposes. The first is purely economic; a customs union and common market comprising individual Member States cannot be established unless goods from all the Member States are sold freely and compete effectively in all the Member States. The second is political, if there is to be a single common market then goods must flow freely within its borders. The effect of national measures that block the importation of goods from one Member State to another, make their marketing more difficult, or raise their price, is the distortion of the free flow of goods and competition. Inevitably, in a single market such measures have to be eliminated. **10.01**

B. The General Principles

(1) The Legislative Framework

The principle of free movement of goods has two sides. The first covers duties, charges, and taxes; the second, quantitative import and export restrictions. Article 28 of the Treaty on the Functioning of the European Union (TFEU) provides for: **10.02**

> a customs union which shall cover all trade in goods and which shall involve the prohibition between Member States of customs duties on imports and exports and of all charges having an equivalent effect, and the adoption of a common customs tariff in their relation with third countries.

This covers products originating in Member States and products coming from third countries which are in free circulation in Member States. To achieve this Article 30 TFEU provides that 'customs duties on imports and exports and charges having equivalent effect shall be prohibited between Member States. This prohibition shall also apply to customs duties of a fiscal nature.'

The second side of the free movement of goods principle is found in Articles 34 to 37 TFEU. Article 34 focuses on imports: 'Quantitative restrictions on imports and all measures having equivalent effect shall be prohibited between Member States.' Article 35 covers export restrictions in an identical manner. **10.03**

---

[1] Most of the references follow the renumbering introduced by the Consolidated Version of the Treaty on the Functioning of the European Union, OJ C 326, 26/10/2012, p. 1.

10.04 Possible exemptions can be based on Article 36; prohibitions or restrictions on imports, exports or goods in transit can be justified on grounds of:

- public morality, public policy, or public security;
- the protection of health and life of humans, animals, or plants;
- the protection of national treasures possessing artistic, historic, or archaeological value; or
- the protection of industrial and commercial property.

Article 36 also includes a proviso that such 'prohibitions or restrictions shall not, however, constitute a means of arbitrary discrimination or a disguised restriction on trade between Member States'.

(2) Duties and Taxes

10.05 Considering the first side of the principle the Court of Justice noted that 'the prohibition of new customs duties or charges having equivalent effect, linked to the principle of the free movement of goods, constitutes a fundamental rule which, without prejudice to the other provisions of the Treaty, does not permit of any exceptions'.[2]

10.06 Following a purposive analysis the Court of Justice made clear from the beginning that the criterion for determining the compatibility of a national measure with the principle of free movement of goods is the effect rather than the purpose of the national measure.[3]

(a) The product similarity issue

10.07 Member States must not impose directly or indirectly on the products of other Member States any internal taxation that is in excess of that imposed on similar domestic products.[4] And irrespective of product similarity Member States must not impose any internal taxation affording indirect protection to other products.[5] Article 110 TFEU appears to cover competing but not necessarily similar products. The distinction is a difficult one.[6]

(b) Competition and substitution

10.08 From a trade mark lawyer's perspective this line of cases reveals an interesting analogy with the test for determining similarity between good and services. In *Commission v France*[7] the Court examined the market for spirits in order to determine whether it functioned as a single market or an umbrella for more specific drinks' markets. Following an analysis of the market it drew two conclusions:

---

[2] C-24/68 *Commission v Italy* [1969] ECR 193, paragraph 10.

[3] The Court stressed that any pecuniary charge, irrespective of its size, designation, and mode of application, which is imposed unilaterally on domestic or foreign goods because they cross a frontier constitutes a charge having equivalent effect.

[4] Article 110 mentions any direct or indirect internal taxation of any kind. The Court, once again, has taken a purposive approach in interpreting the provision, see eg C-2/62 *Commission v Belgium* [1962] ECR 425; and C-112/84 *Humblot v Directeur des Services Fiscaux* [1985] ECR 1367 where it found that a punitively higher national French tax imposed on powerful cars was discriminatory because at the time there were no French manufactured cars falling inside the relevant category and as a result the tax was imposed only on imported cars.

[5] 'Furthermore, no Member State shall impose on the products of other Member States any internal taxation of such a nature as to afford indirect protection to other products' (Article 110(2) TFEU).

[6] Indeed, cross elasticity of demand is an issue that is also relevant in competition law, see eg paragraphs 11.96 et seq.

[7] C-168/78 *Commission v France* [1980] ECR 347; see also *Commission v Denmark* (106/84) [1986] ECR 833.

First, there is, in the case of spirits considered as a whole, an indeterminate number of beverages which must be classified as 'similar products' ... although it may be difficult to decide this in specific cases, in view of the nature of the factors implied by distinguishing criteria such as flavour and consumer habits. Secondly, even in cases in which it is impossible to recognize a sufficient degree of similarity between the products concerned, there are nevertheless, in the case of all spirits, common characteristics which are sufficiently pronounced to accept that in all cases there is at least partial or potential competition. It follows that the application of the [provision] ... may come into consideration in cases in which the relationship of similarity between the specific varieties of spirits remains doubtful or contested.[8]

10.09 The Court relied on the competitive and substitution relation between products obtained from distillation. The process of distillation provided the decisive factor for determining similarity, rather than taste, type of use, and distinction according to whether the spirit was obtained from vines or cereals.

(c) Comparing beer with wine

10.10 A classic similarity scenario is the one comparing beer with wine. In *Commission v United Kingdom*[9] the Court found that there was a degree of substitution between them. It also noted that attention

should not be confined to consumer habits in a Member State or in a given region. Those habits, which were essentially variable in time and space, could not be considered to be immutable; the tax policy of a Member State must not therefore crystallize given consumer habits so as to consolidate an advantage acquired by national industries concerned to respond to them.[10]

10.11 At the same time it acknowledged the significant differences between the two products, such as manufacturing processes and natural properties. The Court examined a number of criteria submitted before it: the Commission supported volume and alcohol content, the United Kingdom focused on product price excluding tax, whereas Italy looked at the issue from a negative perspective, considering the types of wine with which a comparison could not be drawn. It was Italy's approach that it found more pertinent:

In view of the substantial differences in the quality and, therefore, in the price of wines, the decisive competitive relationship between beer, a popular and widely consumed beverage, and wine must be established by reference to those wines which are the most accessible to the public at large, that is to say, generally speaking the lightest and cheapest varieties.[11]

10.12 In the end, the Court made an overall assessment and looked at all the criteria. It found that the submission of the United Kingdom—price net of tax—was difficult to follow because of the lack of evidence; all the other criteria, however, indicated to differing degrees that the United Kingdom subjected imported wine to a higher tax burden:

Since such protection is most marked in the case of the most popular wines, the effect of the United Kingdom tax system is to stamp wine with the hallmarks of a luxury product which, in view of the tax burden which it bears, can scarcely constitute in the eyes of the consumer a genuine alternative to the typically produced domestic beverage.[12]

---

[8] Ibid, paragraph 12.
[9] C-170/78 *Commission v United Kingdom* [1983] ECR 2265.
[10] Ibid, paragraph 8.
[11] Ibid, paragraph 12.
[12] Ibid, paragraph 27.

10.13 Concluding, the Court repeated that it is the discrimination against still, light wines made from fresh grapes that made it decide that the United Kingdom had failed its obligations under Article 110.

(d) Comparing whisky with liqueurs, and bananas with other fruits

10.14 In *John Walker*[13] the Court followed a similar but more inclusive route. This time the decisive criteria, for deciding that liqueur fruit wine and whisky were not similar, were alcohol content and method of manufacture. Turning to another market, the Court considered similarities between types of fruit in *Commission v Italy*.[14] Following an analysis of the objective characteristics of bananas on the one hand and other fruits on the other, it decided that they were not similar products because of their organoleptic properties and the distinct consumer needs they satisfied: bananas had low water content, and as a result did not quench thirst, but had high nutritional value. Still, it found that the disproportionate consumption tax imposed on bananas constituted a protectionist measure.

(3) Quantitative Restrictions

10.15 Both import and export quantitative restrictions and measures having an equivalent effect are prohibited. As expected, the Court defined both concepts in broad terms and on the basis of their effect rather than original intention.

(a) The broad principle

10.16 Quantitative restrictions covered 'measures which amount to a total or partial restraint of, according to the circumstances, imports, exports or goods in transit';[15] whereas '[a]ll trading rules enacted by Member States which are capable of hindering directly or indirectly, actually or potentially, intra Community trade are to be considered as measures having an effect equivalent to quantitative restrictions'.[16] The Court introduced some flexibility into the system by noting that in the absence of a Community regulatory regime—in other words, positive harmonization which in this case meant lack of a system guaranteeing the authenticity of a product's designation of origin—a Member State may take measures to prevent unfair practices. '[I]t is however subject to the condition that these measures should be reasonable and that the means of proof required should not act as a hindrance to trade between Member States and should, in consequence, be accessible to all Community nationals'.[17] It accepted that some measures might be justified in principle but should not be applied in a discriminatory way or as a disguised restriction on trade between Member States.

10.17 *Dassonville* also introduces into the picture the figure of the 'parallel importer', the trader who ignores national barriers, buys where it is cheap, offers more choice to the consumer, and undercuts traditional channels of trade. When challenged by national regulations it uses European integration as a defence mechanism.[18]

---

[13] C-243/84 *John Walker v Ministeriet for Skatter og Afgifter* [1986] ECR 875.
[14] C-184/85 *Commission v Italy* [1987] ECR 2013.
[15] C-2/73 *Geddo v Ente Nazionale Risi* [1973] ECR 865, paragraph 7.
[16] C-8/74 *Procureur du Roi v Dassonville* [1974] ECR 837, paragraph 5.
[17] Ibid, paragraph 6.
[18] Belgian law required for products with a 'designation of origin' a certificate, issued by the authorities of the exporting country, that the product lawfully bore the designation. A parallel trader bought Scotch whisky lawfully marketed in France and imported it to Belgium without such a certificate from the United Kingdom. When prosecuted the parallel trader argued that the Belgian regulation constituted a measure equivalent to a quantitative restriction.

(b) The principle, the exception, and the exception to the exception

10.18 In order to police the 'borderline between legitimate and illegitimate national regulation',[19] the Court followed the trusted route of setting a wide principle with a narrow exception, and then introducing an exception to the exception that brings us back to the wide principle.

10.19 From an integrationist's perspective, it adopted a negative, in terms of harmonization, position aiming to break down barriers. The absence of positive harmonization justified exceptions. It then qualified these exceptions by requiring them to be reasonable, a positive requirement, and non-discriminatory, a negative requirement.[20] The Court consistently applied negative harmonization in a way that broadened the scope of the free movement of goods principle. It excluded from the scope of the principle cases where a difference in treatment between imported and domestic goods was not capable of restricting imports or of prejudicing the marketing of imported goods. The aim of the free movement provision was to 'eliminate obstacles to the importation of goods and not to ensure that goods of national origin always enjoy the same treatment as imported or reimported goods'.[21]

(c) Intra-Community and intra-State trade

10.20 Indicative of the Court's conviction and development in juridical rationalization was the answer to the question of whether free movement of goods rules applied against national measures preventing trade within the territory of a single Member State. In *Bluhme*[22] the Court held that such a restriction can violate the free movement of goods principle. Bluhme was accused of keeping on a Danish island a swarm of bees of a species other than the one specified by the Danish Government. The Court found this to be a measure equivalent to a quantitative restriction, albeit a justifiable one. In a later case Advocate General Léger considered *Bluhme* to cover circumstances:

> where local rules that applied to only part of the territory of a Member State affected trade in goods between that part of the national territory and the other Member States and also trade between that part of the national territory and the other parts of the territory of the same Member State.[23]

(d) The effect and scope of the measure

10.21 The Court has been considering the effect the targeted measure had on the market rather than its stated objective in order to determine whether it constituted a quantitative restriction. The objectives of national measures became relevant when the Court examined whether they could be regarded as public policy considerations justifying their adoption. The Court appeared particularly forceful whenever there was an element of discrimination; where the objective was discriminatory even ineffective measures would be caught.[24] For example, public procurement schemes favouring domestic products,[25] special phytosanitary controls and inspections targeting exclusively imported plant products,[26] as well as

---

[19] WPJ Wills, 'The Search for the Rule in Article 30 EEC: Much Ado About Nothing?' (1993) 18 EL Rev 475 at 478.
[20] Ibid, at 476.
[21] C-355/85 *Ministere Public v Cognet* [1986] ECR 3231, paragraph 10.
[22] See C-2/90 *Commission v Belgium* [1992] ECR I-4431 and C-67/97 *Ditle v Bluhme* [1998] ECR I-8033.
[23] C-293/02 *Jersey Produce Marketing Organisation Ltd v Jersey* [2005] ECR I-09543, paragraph 85.
[24] See below paragraph 10.25 et seq.
[25] See, eg, C-72/83 *Campus Oil Ltd v Minister for Industry and Energy* [1984] ECR 2727 and C-21/88 *Du Pont de Nemours Italiana SPA v Unita Sanitaria Locale No.2 Di Carrara* [1990] ECR I-889.
[26] C-4/75 *Rewe-Zentralfinanz v Landwirtschaftskammer* [1975] ECR 843.

additional quality controls provided only for watches destined to be exported[27] were all found to be caught by the principle.

(e) Discrimination based on origin

10.22 Similarly the Court viewed national campaigns supporting domestic products as 'a reflection of the [relevant] government's considered intention to substitute domestic products for imported products on the [national] market and thereby to check the flow of imports from other Member States', rather than an advertising campaign.[28]

10.23 The Court accepted that the campaign did not amount to a binding measure but noted that even measures that do not have binding effect may be capable of influencing the behaviour of consumers and traders in the Member State. It is the effect of the measure that counts rather than its form. But, because in practice the targeted campaign has not been particularly effective, the Court turned back to examine its nature and context:

> it is not possible to overlook the fact that, regardless of their efficacy, those two activities form part of a government programme which is designed to achieve the substitution of domestic products for imported products and is liable to affect the volume of trade between Member States.[29]

10.24 Such broad campaigns must be distinguished from those that appeared to be more targeted and objective. In *Apple and Pear Development,* the promotional campaigns of a 'national development organization' for certain fruit varieties were considered compatible with the free movement of goods rules despite the fact that they were typical of national production; the Court noted, however, that disparaging the purchase of fruits produced in other Member States or encouraging consumers to choose exclusively according to national origin would not be accepted.[30] Another element of the case is the distinction between recommendations regarding product quality and presentation and the imposition of quality standards; the second would be against the free movement of goods provisions, given the state of positive integration in the field of agriculture. The European Union had already developed a system of common quality standards. The Court also dealt with 'origin-marking' national rules. Legislation requiring retail goods to be marked with their country of origin can cover both domestic and imported goods, however 'it has to be recognized that the purpose of indications of origin or origin-marking is to enable consumers to distinguish between domestic and imported products and that this enables them to assert any prejudices which they may have against foreign products'.[31]

---

[27] C-53/76 *Procureur de la Republique Besancon v Bouhelier* [1977] ECR 197.
[28] C-249/81 *Commission v Ireland* [1982] ECR 4005, paragraph 23. The campaign consisted of a 'Buy Irish' sign that the Irish Government encouraged traders to use on goods made in Ireland and an advertising campaign organized by the Irish Goods Council. Two other elements of the campaign, a service informing consumers about goods made in Ireland and retailers stocking them and the organization of exhibitions for Irish goods have been dropped. As to the fact that the Irish Goods Council was not a governmental organization, the Court noted that the Irish Government could not escape liability because it appointed the members of its Management Committee, granted it public subsidies, and defined the aims and outline of its campaign.
[29] Ibid, paragraph 25.
[30] C-222/82 *Apple and Pear Development Council v KJ Lewis Ltd* [1983] ECR 4083; the fruits in question were English and Welsh apple and pear varieties.
[31] C-207/83 *Commission v United Kingdom* [1985] ECR 1201, paragraph 17. The measure covered clothing and textile goods, domestic electrical appliances, footwear, and cutlery.

(f) The concept of origin

10.25 The Court had tolerated 'indication of origin' marking schemes when origin constituted one of the elements of the product either because it indicated a specific and concrete quality or characteristic or because it encapsulated a sociocultural value that is linked with a particular region. In *Commission v Ireland*[32] the challenge concerned two Irish 'Merchandise Marks Orders' requiring imported souvenir jewellery invoking Irishness, like depictions of Irish characters, scenes, shamrocks, etc, to bear an indication of origin or the word 'foreign'.

10.26 The Court stressed that 'the exceptions therein cannot be extended to cases other than those specifically laid down'.[33] Consumer protection and fairness of commercial transactions were not listed in Article 30 and, as a result, did not constitute exceptions. Then it asked a more fundamental question regarding the nature of measures equivalent to quantitative restrictions. Would the argument of the Irish Government bring the Orders outside the scope of the provision? The Court revisited the positive versus negative integration scenario.

10.27 In the absence of positive integration regarding the production and marketing of the relevant product it remained in the competence of Member States to regulate all matters relating to its production, distribution, and consumption. This, however, was subject to the negative integration condition that national regulation should not present an obstacle to intra-Community trade:

> It is only where national rules, which apply without discrimination to both domestic and imported products, may be justified as being necessary in order to satisfy imperative requirements relating in particular … to the fairness of commercial transactions and the defence of the consumer that they may constitute an exception to the [rule]'.[34]

10.28 In this case the Orders fell at the discrimination hurdle since they applied only to imported products. The Court added that local manufacturers could, if they wished, affix their own mark of origin but it remained unnecessary to impose a discriminatory burden on imported products.

10.29 In *Kohl v Ringelhan*,[35] the Court added that an unfair competition provision should not be applied in such a way:

> that it becomes possible to prohibit the use of a distinctive symbol for the sole reason that the public may be misled as to the domestic or foreign origin of the goods, without it being necessary to adduce evidence of other specific factors establishing the existence of unfair competition. In such a case, the provision in question in fact applies only to the marketing of imported products.[36]

(g) Discrimination based on product characteristics

10.30 In *Cassis de Dijon* the Court made clear that measures that discriminated between products on the basis of their characteristics rather than their origin could be caught by the free movement of goods rules.[37] It considered the effect of German laws governing the

---

[32] C-113/80 *Commission v Ireland* [1981] ECR 1625.
[33] C-207/83 *Commission v United Kingdom* [1985] ECR 1201, paragraph 7.
[34] C-113/80 *Commission v Ireland* [1981] ECR 1625, paragraph 10.
[35] C-177/83 *Theodor Kohl KG v Ringelhan & Rennet SA and Ringelhan Einrichtungs GmBH* [1984] ECR 3651.
[36] Ibid, paragraph 15.
[37] C-120/78 *Rewe-Zentrale AG* [1979] ECR 649.

marketing of alcoholic beverages. The authorities had blocked the importation of Cassis de Dijon liqueur from France to Germany because its alcoholic strength was lower than the 25% required for such liqueurs in Germany.

10.31 It conceded that in the absence of common rules relating to the production and marketing of alcohol it was for the Member States to regulate the production and marketing of alcohol and alcoholic beverages at the national level. Disparities in regulation could lead to intra-Community trade obstacles that:

> must be accepted in so far as those provisions may be recognised as being necessary in order to satisfy mandatory requirements relating in particular to the effectiveness of fiscal supervision, the protection of public health, the fairness of commercial transactions and the defence of the consumer.

10.32 Germany argued that the proliferation of alcoholic beverages with low alcohol content could have adverse effects on public health by increasing consumer tolerance to alcohol. The Court was not persuaded, given the extremely wide range of weak alcoholic products on the market. The consumer protection argument was based on the consideration that the lowering of alcohol content could secure a competitive advantage in relation to beverages with higher alcohol content, since alcohol was the most expensive ingredient because of its high rate of tax. The Court found the mandatory fixing of minimum alcohol contents excessive, since 'it is a simple matter to ensure that suitable information is conveyed to the purchaser by requiring the display of an indication of origin and of the alcohol content on the packaging of products'.[38]

(h) Selling arrangements

10.33 The Court reconsidered its position on what is covered under the free movement of goods rules in *Keck*.[39] Two hypermarket managers were prosecuted under French laws prohibiting the resale of products at a loss in order to undercut competition. The national court recognized the potential applicability of Article 34 but noted that traders were increasingly using the provision as a blind weapon against trade regulation at the national level. It asked the Court of Justice to look again at whether measures restricting or prohibiting certain selling arrangements affect trade within the scope of Article 34. In this case the defendants claimed that the national law was incompatible with the free movement of goods rules because it targeted exclusively resale, and not sale by a manufacturer, at a loss.

10.34 The Court followed a pragmatic approach, taking into account how its jurisprudence functioned in the market place.

> In view of the increasing tendency of traders to invoke [the free movement of goods provisions] as a means of challenging any rules whose effect is to limit their commercial freedom even where such rules are not aimed at products from other Member States, the Court considers it necessary to re-examine and clarify its case law on this matter.[40]

10.35 It confirmed its *Cassis de Dijon* principles but added that:

> contrary to what has previously been decided, the application to products from other Member States of national provisions restricting or prohibiting certain selling arrangements is not

---

[38] Ibid, paragraph 13.
[39] C-267/91 and C-268/91 *Keck and Mithouard* [1993] ECR 1-6907.
[40] Ibid, paragraph 14.

such as to hinder directly or indirectly, actually or potentially, trade between Member States within the meaning of Dassonville so long as those provisions apply to all relevant traders operating within the national territory and so long as they affect in the same manner, in law and in fact, the marketing of domestic products and of those from other Member States.[41]

Provided that the above conditions were fulfilled, the national provisions would fall outside the scope of Article 34.

(4) The Equality Proviso

10.36 The Court had proven similarly pragmatic in applying its equality proviso exploiting the flexibility that the balancing of different factors offers. When the Court finds that the factual effect of such a national provision is to protect domestic established market players, it simply chooses not to apply the proviso, whilst repeating that the principle of *Keck* was retained. In *Punto Casa*, Italian legislation restricting retail trading on Sundays was found to apply to all traders operating in Italy; accordingly it did not impede access of imported products to the domestic market compared with access of domestic products.[42]

10.37 In *Gourmet International* the Court applied *Keck* but held that a general prohibition on advertising for alcoholic beverages in the Swedish press, radio, and television would have a discriminatory effect in fact rather than in law. Alcohol consumption was rooted in traditional social practices; consumers were not familiar with non-domestic products and without advertising imported products would be at a comparative disadvantage.[43]

(5) Public Policy Considerations

(a) Public morality

10.38 In *Henn and Darby* the Court accepted that public morality standards vary throughout Europe and it is for each Member State to determine the standards that are applied in its jurisdiction.[44] Accordingly UK customs laws could be used in order to stop the importation of indecent and obscene articles despite the fact that there was a discrepancy between national criminal laws on possession of pornography, against which there was no absolute ban, and importation of pornography, against which an absolute ban was imposed. The purpose of domestic law as a whole was to restrain the creation and marketing of pornography. Thus:

> if a prohibition on the importation of goods is justifiable on grounds of public morality and if it is imposed with that purpose the enforcement of that prohibition cannot, in the absence within the member state concerned of a lawful trade in the same goods, constitute a means of arbitrary discrimination or a disguised restriction on trade contrary to [Article 34].[45]

(b) The relevance of the domestic product market

10.39 The existence or not of the relevant domestic product market proved critical in a subsequent public morality case. In *Conegate* the seized products were inflatable dolls imported from Germany to the United Kingdom. The crucial difference from *Henn and Darby* was that

---

[41] Ibid, paragraph 16.
[42] C-69/93 *Punto Casa SpA v Sindaco Del Commune di Capena* [1994] ECR I-2355.
[43] C-405/98 *Konsumentombudsmannen v Gourmet International Products* [2001] ECR I-1795.
[44] C-34/79 *R. v Henn and Darby* [1979] ECR 3795. The products were imported from The Netherlands to the United Kingdom.
[45] Ibid, paragraph 22.

there was no ban regarding the manufacture or marketing of inflatable dolls within the United Kingdom.[46] The Court was clear in the pronouncement of a general interpretive rule. A 'Member State may not rely on grounds of public morality to prohibit the importation of goods from other Member States when its legislation contains no prohibition on the manufacture or marketing of the same goods on its territory'.[47]

(c) Public policy

10.40 Public policy constitutes a much broader ground for an exception under Article 36. In the free movement of goods context the Court has been wary in its demarcation of the term. Public policy cannot be used as the fiat for introducing grounds that are not specifically enlisted therein. We have seen for example in *Irish Souvenirs* that public policy does not cover consumer protection or fairness in commercial transactions.[48]

10.41 In *Leclerc v Au Blé Vert*[49] the Court added to the list of what does not constitute public policy the protection of creativity and cultural diversity. The Court rejected a derogation under Article 36 based on the need to protect books as cultural media. It reinforced what, by then, had become a mantra: 'Neither the safeguarding of consumers' interests nor the protection of creativity and cultural diversity in the realm of publishing is mentioned in Article [36].'[50]

10.42 A case that evidences the diffidence of the Court in positively describing what constitutes public policy is *Cullet v Centre Leclerc*.[51] The case involved a French scheme imposing minimum retail prices for fuel on the basis of refinery prices and costs existing in France. This meant that the pricing of imported fuel started from a potentially higher minimum price. The Court found that this was a measure equivalent to a quantitative restriction.

10.43 It chose proportionality and insufficient argumentation as the basis of its rejection of the *ordre public* point raised by the French government, stating:

> it is sufficient to observe that the French Government has not shown that an amendment of the regulations in question in conformity with the [free movement of goods] principles ... would have consequences for law and order (ordre public) and public security which the French Government would be unable to meet with the resources available to it.[52]

(d) Public security

10.44 The idea of *ordre public* links public policy with the narrower, and more easily definable, concept of public security. In *Campus Oil*, a case involving an Irish law requiring petrol importers to purchase 35% of the overall quantity of petrol they traded in at fixed prices from a state-owned refinery, the Court commented on the 'public security' defence raised by the Irish Government. Given the lack of a comprehensive and effective network of Community measures that would protect petrol supplies at the national level for each Member State national measures could be tolerated:

---

[46] C-121/85 *Conegate v Commissioners of Customs and Excise* [1986] ECR 1007.
[47] *Henn and Darby* [1979] ECR 3795, paragraph 16.
[48] C-113/80 *Commission v Ireland* [1981] ECR 1625.
[49] C-229/83 *Leclerc v Au Blé Vert* [1985] ECR 1.
[50] Ibid, paragraph 30.
[51] C-231/83 *Cullet v Centre Leclerc* [1985] ECR 305.
[52] Ibid, paragraph 33.

petroleum products, because of their exceptional importance as an energy source in the modern economy, are of fundamental importance for a country's existence since not only its economy but above all its institutions, its essential public services and even the survival of the inhabitants depend upon them. An interruption of supplies of petroleum products, with the resultant dangers for the country's existence, could therefore seriously affect the public security that Article [36] allows States to protect.[53]

10.45 It then narrowed the coverage and applicability of 'public security' both from a negative and a positive perspective. It held that pleading the 'economic difficulties' that the elimination of trade barriers would cause would not as such justify national measures. It then went on to require that even a measure excepted under 'public security' must be 'justified by objective circumstances corresponding to the needs of public security'[54] and 'must not create obstacles to imports which are disproportionate to those objectives'.[55] Note that national security measures can also be taken following Articles 346 to 348.

(6) Protection of Health and Life of Humans

10.46 In *Commission v France*[56] the Court considered advertising restrictions in respect of alcoholic beverages. It found that such restrictions could impede imports because they would affect more directly imported products. The legitimization of the restriction becomes even more problematic if it discriminates against products originating in other Member States. The relevant French legislation had regulated advertising exposure of alcoholic beverages following a codification according to type. The Court found that there were instances of discrimination:

> It is apparent ... that even though it is conceded that an appreciable number of national products are subject to the prohibitions and restrictions on advertising ... nevertheless the fact remains that the classifications which determine the application of those provisions put products imported from other Member States at a disadvantage compared to national products and consequently constitute a measure having an effect equivalent to a quantitative restriction.[57]

The Court recognized the link between advertising and alcohol consumption and accepted the potential applicability of Article 30; however, it stressed that the restrictions should not constitute a means of arbitrary discrimination or a disguised restriction on trade between Member States.

10.47 In *Gourmet International Products*[58] the Court accepted that, in principle, advertising restrictions regarding alcoholic beverages could be tolerated provided they were proportionate to the objective pursued and did not constitute either a means of arbitrary discrimination or a disguised restriction on trade between Member States. The contested national provision was quite restrictive:

> In view of the health risks involved in alcohol consumption, alcoholic beverages should be marketed with particular moderation. In particular, advertisements or other marketing measures must not be insistent, involve unsolicited approaches or encourage alcohol consumption.

---

[53] C-72/83 *Campus Oil Ltd v Minister for Industry and Energy* [1984] ECR 2727, paragraph 34.
[54] Ibid, paragraph 36.
[55] Ibid, paragraph 37.
[56] [1980] ECR 2299.
[57] *Commission v France*, paragraph 14.
[58] *Konsumentombudsmannen (KO) v Gourmet International Products (GIP)* [2001] ECR I-1795 (n 43).

> Advertising may not be used to market alcoholic beverages on radio or television. The same prohibition applies to satellite broadcasts ... Advertising may not be used to market spirits, wines or strong beers either in periodicals or in other publications subject to the Regulation on Press Freedom and comparable to periodicals by reasons of their publication schedule. That prohibition does not however apply to publications distributed solely at the point of sale of such beverages.[59]

10.48 The Court found that an absolute prohibition would impede the marketing of imported products more compared with domestic products that have gained a position in the market place. It accepted though that such a prohibition could fall under Article 36 since there was a direct link between advertising and alcohol consumption. The assessment of proportionality required an examination of the national provisions and the facts that only the national court conduct. The Court noted that there was

> no evidence before the court to suggest that the public health grounds on which the Swedish authorities rely have been diverted from their purpose and used in such a way as to discriminate against goods originating in other Member States or to protect certain national products indirectly.[60]

Accordingly, it held that Articles 30 and 36

> do not preclude a prohibition on the advertising of alcoholic beverages such as that [described in the national legislation] unless it is apparent that, in the circumstances of law and of fact which characterise the situation in the Member State concerned, the protection of public health against the harmful effects of alcohol can be ensured by measures having less effect on intra-Community trade.[61]

10.49 Another, more recent, example is *Douwe Egberts*.[62] The case involved labelling information that incorporated slimming and medical recommendations; this would infringe national laws on advertising and labelling of foodstuffs. The Court found that the challenged advertising and labelling prohibitions constituted an obstacle to imports and held that Article 28 and Article 30 precluded national legislation prohibiting references in the advertising of foodstuffs imported from other Member States to 'slimming' and to 'medical recommendations, attestations, declarations or statements of approval'.

(7) *Codacons*: Labelling Requirement; The Residual Power of the Free Movement of Goods Rationale

10.50 A reference from the Italian Council of State, *Codacons*[63] dealt with another sensitive, in terms of substance, and heatedly debated, in terms of politics, health-related issue. Codacons, the Coordination of the Associations for the Protection of the Environment and of Users' and Consumers' Rights, launched an application for the annulment of an Italian decree implementing community legislation setting that the presence of genetically modified organisms (GMOs) in a proportion not exceeding 1% of the ingredients making up baby foods and follow-on formulae, caused by adventitious contamination, need not be indicated on the labelling of those products. The question referred to the Court focused on

---

[59] Reproduced in paragraph 4.
[60] Ibid, paragraph 32.
[61] Ibid, paragraph 34.
[62] C-239/02 *Douwe Egberts NV v Westrom Pharma NY. FICS-World BVBA* [2004] ECR I-7007.
[63] C-123/03 *Ministero della Salute v Coordinamento delle Associazioni per la Difesa dell'Ambiente e dei Diritti degli Utenti e de Consumatori (Codacons)* [2005] ECR 1-4167.

whether the labelling exemption provided by Article 2(2)(b) of Regulation 1139/98 applied to foodstuffs for infants and young children.[64]

(a) The Judgment of the Court

10.51 The Judgment of the Court shows the residual power of free movement of goods rules. The first part investigated which one of a number of Community legal provisions was applicable in the particular case; the considerations included a contrast between provisions covering a specific product in a vertical sense and provisions covering a type of product in respect of specific consumers. The second part showed how free movement of goods principles could act as a catalyst in assessing the applicability of the principle of precaution developed by the Court in cases involving to risks to human health.

10.52 (i) **Contextualizing the provision: Vertical application** The Court started its analysis by contextualizing the provision within the broader relevant Community legislation. First it referred to Article 4(2) of Directive 79/112[65] by virtue of which the Community provisions applicable to certain specified foodstuffs and not to foodstuffs in general might introduce other compulsory particulars in addition to those listed in the Directive. Regulation No 1139/98, on the other hand, included provisions on labelling which were of a specific nature and applied vertically only to particular foodstuffs: those obtained wholly or in part from certain genetically modified soya beans or certain genetically modified types of maize. According to Article 4 of Directive 89/398, the Commission was responsible for adopting specific directives regarding the labelling, presentation, and advertising of certain products including infant formulae, follow-up milk and other follow-up foods, and baby foods. As a result, Directives 91/321 and 96/5 were adopted, determining the rules on the composition and labelling of infant formulae and follow-on formulae intended for use by infants in good health and processed cereal-based foods and baby foods for infants and young children.

10.53 (ii) **The interrelationship between layers of Community law** Here, the question was how the Regulation and the Directives covering advertising for those types of products interrelated: 'The question therefore arises as to whether the specific labelling requirements of Regulation No 1139/98 also apply to foodstuffs intended for the particular nutritional use of infants and young children.'[66] The Court found that labelling requirements such as those laid down by Regulation 1139/98 applied in principle to foodstuffs intended for nutritional uses within the scope of the Directive unless it was necessary to provide for a derogation from those requirements in order to ensure that the particular nutritional purpose in question was attained.[67] Directives 91/321 and 96/5 did not contain any specific labelling requirements relating to the presence of material derived from GMOs that derogated from the provisions of Regulation 1139/98. The conclusion reached by the Court was that such requirements had not, at least yet, been deemed necessary and Article 2(2)(b) of Regulation 1139/98 had to be interpreted as meaning that the exemption also applied to foodstuffs intended for the particular nutritional use of infants and young children.

---

[64] Regulation 1139/98 [2000] OJ L6/13.
[65] [1979] OJ L33/1.
[66] *Codacons* (n 63), paragraph 52.
[67] C-101/98 *Union Deutsche Lebensmittelwerke GmbH v Schutzverband gegen Unwesen in der Wirtschaft eV* [1999] ECR 1-8841.

10.54 **(iii) The free movement of goods rationale** The Court found that this interpretation was consistent with the precautionary principle developed by the Court for cases involving uncertainty as to the existence or extent of risks to human health. Here the free movement of goods principle acted as a catalyst. The Court remarked that Regulation 1139/98 had a dual purpose: first, to remove potential obstacles to the free movement of products containing genetically modified soya and maize, and, second, to provide the end consumer with information.[68] The Regulation introduced additional labelling requirements to those imposed by Directive 79/112[69] and the Preamble to the Regulation noted that these requirements were intended to ensure that the final consumer was properly informed in relation to products that, as the Court underlined, had been placed on the market being considered safe for human health following the procedures of Directive 90/220[70] and Regulation 258/97;[71] it was to those procedures that the precautionary principle should be applied. Once the authorization process had been completed the free movement of goods rationale should prevail.

(8) *Commission v Ireland*: **Hallmarks and Public Interest**

10.55 In *Commission v Ireland*[72] the Irish Government had imposed extra obligations on the marketing of imported precious metal articles that were lawfully marketed and marked with hallmarks in other Member States but which did not comply with the Irish marking requirements concerning standards of fineness. The importers had to replace the hallmarks with Irish marks certifying the official, lower, Irish standard. They also had to apply to the products a 'sponsor's mark', indicating the relevant maker, worker, or dealer registered with the Irish authorities even when the products had already been marked with the equivalent mark conforming with the legislation of the Member State of origin. In addition, the Irish authorities had adopted different hallmarks for products manufactured in Ireland and for products imported from other Member States.

10.56 The Court started its analysis by noting that at that stage the Community had not adopted common standards of fineness. But, even in the absence of harmonization, obstacles to free movement resulting from rules targeting goods imported from other Member States where they were lawfully put on the market violate Article 28 unless justified by a public interest objective. On the balancing exercise between free movement of goods and effective consumer protection through the application of hallmarks, the Court referred to its earlier jurisprudence that a Member State cannot require a fresh hallmark to be struck on products imported from other Member States when equivalent information is conveyed by the existing hallmark.[73] It found that there was no justification for the hallmarking requirements imposed by Ireland. The same applied to the 'sponsor's mark' requirement. The requirement could be justified only if the product did not bear a hallmark from the Member State of origin. Inevitably, applying different hallmarks according to origin was also found to be against Article 34 TFEU.

---

[68] C-316/01 *Eva Glawischnig v Bundesministerfur soziale Sicherheit und Generationen* [2003].
[69] [1979] OJ L33/1.
[70] [1996] OJ L117/10.
[71] [1997] OJ L43/1.
[72] C-30/99 *Commission v Ireland* [2001] ECR 14619.
[73] C-120/78 *Rewe-Zentrale AG* [1979] ECR 649; C-293/93 *Houtwipper* [1994] ECR I-4249; C-220/81 *Robertson* [1982] ECR 2349.

C. Free Movement of Goods and Intellectual Property

10.57 There are four characteristics of intellectual property that are particularly relevant. The first is the exclusionary essence of intellectual property rights. The second is its territorial existence. The third, linked with territoriality, is the independence of intellectual property rights. The fourth characteristic is its property nature. In Europe, property is considered to be a fundamental right that is left to the authority and control of Member States. Article 345 is clear; the Treaties shall in no way prejudice the rules of Member States governing the system of property ownership.

10.58 The combination of the four characteristics creates two fundamental problems for the free movement of goods. First, the owner of an intellectual property right in a Member State can stop the importation or marketing of products from other Member States that infringe its right. Second, a multi-jurisdictional owner of rights can, in principle, compartmentalize the European market into national markets. How the law deals with this, is linked with the first characteristic of intellectual property mentioned earlier: its exclusionary essence. Intellectual property rights are not absolute rights. Each intellectual property law that creates a right has to settle at which stage in the chain of production and distribution a third party does not require a licence from the owner of the right in order to perform the prescribed acts. Or, from a positive perspective, for each law it 'is necessary to decide which steps in the chain of production and distribution of goods require the licence of the right owner: manufacture, first sale of the manufacturer, subsequent sales and other dealings, export and import, use'?[74] In most cases the intellectual property right is exhausted after the first sale of the product covered by the right by the right owner or with its consent.

10.59 But the problem remains in a world where products cross national borders. Where must the first sale occur in order for the right to be exhausted? Anywhere in the world or in the jurisdiction where the right exists? In the first case the law would opt for international exhaustion, in the second case for domestic exhaustion. In the absence of complete European harmonization in the field of intellectual property, that would involve the abolition of national rights and the adoption in their place of unitary European rights and, given the recognition by the Treaty of Member States' primacy regarding systems of property, free movement of goods rules have been adapted to accommodate intellectual property.

10.60 Article 36 includes intellectual property in the list of grounds that justify prohibitions on imports or exports, subject to the proviso that they do not constitute a means of arbitrary discrimination or a disguised restriction on trade between Member States. Once again, the Court would have to interpret a provision balancing between positive and negative integration; between a general rule, a proviso, and a caveat to the proviso.

(1) The Existence–Exercise Dichotomy

10.61 At first the Court tilted the balance aggressively towards the free movement of goods principle by making, in *Deutsche Grammophon*,[75] an, arguably, artificial distinction between the existence and the exercise of an intellectual property right. Deutsche Grammophon relied

---

[74] W Cornish, *Intellectual Property*. Sweet and Maxwell, 1999, p 41.
[75] C-78/70 *Deutsche Grammophon v Metro* [1971] ECR 487.

on its exclusive right of distribution in Germany, deriving from copyright, in order to stop the marketing of recordings in Germany that it had itself supplied to its French subsidiary. The question referred from the German courts focused on the competition provisions of the Treaty. However, the Court widened the scope of the question, linked competition with free movement, and exported the distinction between existence and exercise of a right from the field of competition to that of free movement of goods.

10.62 If the exercise of the right did not exhibit the elements of contract or concerted practice required by Article 101 it was then necessary to consider its compatibility with the other provisions of the Treaties, in particular those relating to the free movement of goods. The attainment of a single market provided the legitimizing background for linking competition with free movement. The creation of a single market necessitated both the free movement of goods within the borders of the Community and the establishment of rules ensuring that competition was not distorted.

10.63 Moving to Article 36, the Court first accepted that a right related to copyright was covered by the term 'industrial and commercial property', but added:

> [It is] clear from ... Article [36] that, although the Treaty does not affect the existence of rights recognized by the legislation of a Member State with regard to industrial and commercial property, the exercise of such rights may nevertheless fall within the prohibitions laid down by the Treaty. Although it permits prohibitions or restrictions on the free movement of products, which are justified for the purpose of protecting industrial and commercial property, Article [36] only admits derogations from that freedom to the extent to which they are justified for the purpose of safeguarding rights which constitute the specific subject matter of such property.[76]

10.64 Without examining the specific subject-matter of copyright, the Court undermined the effectiveness of the right almost in its entirety. It juxtaposed its exclusive character with the essential purpose of the Treaty—the creation of a single market—and described as repugnant a prohibition that would legitimize the isolation of national markets on the ground that the distribution of the protected product occurred with the consent of the holder of the right, albeit in another Member State. The Court appeared to equate the exercise of the right with an arbitrary discrimination or disguised restriction on trade. It concluded that:

> it would be in conflict with the provisions prescribing the free movement of products within the common market for a manufacturer of sound recordings to exercise the exclusive right to distribute the protected Articles, conferred upon him by the legislation of a Member State, in such a way as to prohibit the sale in that state of products placed on the market by him or with his consent in another Member State solely because such distribution did not occur within the territory of the first Member State.[77]

(2) The Specific Subject-Matter of the Right

10.65 The Court transformed the dichotomy between existence and exercise into a more elaborate and nuanced principle in a patent case, *Centrafarm BV v Sterling Drug Inc*.[78] Centrafarm bought a pharmaceutical product in the United Kingdom and imported it to the Netherlands. The product was protected in both jurisdictions by patents held

---

[76] Ibid, paragraph 11.
[77] Ibid, paragraph 13.
[78] C-15/74 *Centrafarm BV v Sterling Drug Inc* [1974] ECR 1147.

by Sterling Drug, a subsidiary of which had been marketing the product in the United Kingdom. According to Dutch law Sterling Drug could block the marketing of the drug in The Netherlands by enforcing its patent. The Court of Justice had to decide whether this conformed to the free movement of goods rules. The Court found:

> [it] is clear from ... Article [36] ... in particular its second sentence, as well as from the context, that whilst the Treaty does not affect the existence of rights recognized by the legislation of a Member State in matters of industrial and commercial property, yet the exercise of these rights may nevertheless ... be affected by the prohibitions of the Treaty.[79]

10.66 The Court applied the 'derogation from a fundamental rule' analysis; exceptions are admitted 'in fact only ... where such derogations are justified for the purpose of safeguarding rights which constitute the specific subject matter of this property'.[80] But then instead of clearly describing the specific subject-matter of a patent right, it described a broader objective of industrial property,[81] as

> inter alia to ensure to the holder, so as to recompense the creative effort of the inventor, the exclusive right to utilise an invention with a view to manufacture and first putting into circulation of industrial products, either directly or by the grant of licences to third parties, as well as the right to oppose any infringement.[82]

(3) 'Independent' Rights

10.67 *Deutsche Grammophon*[83] involved the exercise of an intellectual property right in order to block the intra-Community cross-border circulation of a product put on the Community market with the consent of the holder of the right. The Court was more perceptive and permissive in cases where conflicting rights in two Member States arose independently from each other.

10.68 In *Terrapin*[84] the Court considered the exercise of trade mark rights. Terranova, a German company, was the holder of a number of 'Terra' marks registered in Germany for building materials. Terrapin, an English company, that manufactured and marketed 'Terrapin' prefabricated houses, had failed to overcome Terranova's opposition and obtain a registration in Germany. Following prolonged litigation between the parties the question referred to the Court of Justice sought to clarify whether the rights of a company in one Member State can be used to stop the marketing of products from another Member State that bear lawfully a distinguishing name which may be confused with the commercial name and trade mark that are protected in the first Member State, when there is no link between the two entities and their national trade mark rights arose 'autonomously' and 'independently' of one another.[85]

---

[79] Ibid, paragraph 7.
[80] Ibid, paragraph 8.
[81] Note the distinction between industrial and intellectual property. In its earlier case law the Court discriminated between rights according to their perceived importance. In C-40/70 *Sirena SRL v Eda SRL* [1971] ECR 69, a competition case, it appeared to place trade mark rights at the bottom of the hierarchy.
[82] C-15/74 *Centrafarm* [1974] ECR 1147, paragraph 9.
[83] C-78/70 *Deutsche Grammophon* [1971] ECR 487.
[84] C-119/75 *Terrapin* [1976] ECR 1039; [1967] 2 CMLR 482.
[85] The timeline of the dispute is indicative of the determination of the parties. Terrapin applied in 1961; litigation regarding the registration went on until 1967 when the Federal Patent Court prohibited registration. In 1968 Terranova brought infringement actions and Terrapin brought an action asking the court to order Terranova to stop objecting to the use of its trade name and trademarks. Appeals and cross appeals culminated in the reference to the Court of Justice dated 31 October 1975. Note that the two companies coexisted in other Member States.

10.69 Advocate General Henri Mayras took a cautious integrationist approach; in the absence of positive integration the crux of the case was identifying the forum and criteria for determining trade mark protection.[86] Following an analysis of the prevailing trade mark theories in Europe he conceded that it was for the Member States to delineate the scope of protection and for national courts to apply it, but the national discretion should still be within the limits imposed by the Treaty: the right could be enforced unless enforcement constituted arbitrary discrimination or a disguised restriction on trade between Member States. His reasoning was analogous to that regarding public policy expressed in *Van Duyn*.[87] The Court concurred with the Advocate General but failed to discuss in any detail the specific subject-matter of trade mark rights. It repeated that the Treaty does not affect the existence of rights arising from national industrial and commercial property legislation but may restrict their exercise, inasmuch as

> it provides an exception to one of the fundamental principles of the Common Market, Article [36] in fact admits exceptions to the free movement of goods only to the extent to which such exceptions are justified for the purpose of safeguarding rights which constitute the specific subject-matter of that property.[88]

10.70 According to the then current state of Community law:

> an industrial or commercial property right legally acquired in a member-State may legally be used to prevent under the first sentence of Article [36] of the Treaty the import of products marketed under a name giving rise to confusion where the rights in question have been acquired by different and independent proprietors under different national laws.[89]

D. Free Movement of Goods and Trade Mark Law

(1) The Early Days: The Essential Function and the Specific Subject-Matter of Trade Marks

10.71 The Court described the essential function of a trade mark and the specific subject-matter of a trade mark right in *Centrafarm v Winthrop*.[90] The essential function is to guarantee the identity of the origin of the marked product and the specific subject-matter of the right is that the owner of a trade mark has the exclusive right to use it when putting the marked product for the first time into circulation. Essentially, protection is against competitors selling products illegally bearing the mark. Sterling Drug held registrations for Negram in the United Kingdom and The Netherlands; the Dutch registration was in the name of one of its subsidiaries, Winthrop. In both jurisdictions the drug was put on the market by subsidiaries of Sterling Drug. Centrafarm, once again, imported Negram to The Netherlands from the United Kingdom. Could Sterling Drug employ the Dutch registration and block the imports?

10.72 The Court referred to the general principle constructed in *Centrafarm v Sterling Drug*[91] and went on to adapt it to fit trade mark law:

---

[86] [1976] 2 CMLR 482 at 495.
[87] C-41/74 *Van Duyn v Home Office* [1974] ECR 1337.
[88] C-119/75 *Terrapin* [1976] ECR 103, paragraph 5.
[89] Ibid, paragraph 7.
[90] C-16/74 *Centrafarm* [1974] ECR 1183.
[91] C-15/74 *Sterling Drug Inc* [1974] EC.R 1147.

> As regards trademarks, the specific object of commercial property is inter alia to ensure to the holder the exclusive right to utilise the mark for the first putting into circulation of a product, and to protect him thus against competitors who would take advantage of the position and reputation of the mark by selling goods improperly bearing the mark.[92]

It then acknowledged that the 'existence' of national provisions 'that the right of the trade mark holder is not exhausted by the marketing in another Member State of the product protected by the mark ... may constitute an obstacle to the free movement of goods'[93] and held that this would not be justified 'when the product has been lawfully put, by the holder himself or with his consent, on the market of the Member State from which it is imported in such a way that there can be no question of abuse or infringement of the mark',[94] because otherwise, the holder would be 'enabled to partition the national markets and thus to maintain a restriction on the trade between the Member States without such a restriction being necessary for him to enjoy the substance of the exclusive right deriving from the mark'.[95] Consent had become the key word.

(2) Developing the Concept of Consent

The two *Hag* cases illustrate two developing trends in the trade mark jurisprudence of the Court of Justice. First, they provide evidence for the growing appreciation of what a trade mark does in the marketplace and the willingness of the Court to adapt protection accordingly and link consent much more accurately with the subject-matter and justification of the right. Second, they depict the continuum applied by the Court in its everlasting balancing between free movement of goods and the establishment of a single market on the one side and trade mark rights on the other. These two trends persuaded the Court to take a sharp turn and depart from its previous rulings, a bold example of admitting rather than disguising change. **10.73**

(3) *Hag-I*: A Restrictive Approach

In *Hag I*[96] registrations of the trade mark 'Hag' for decaffeinated coffee in Belgium, Germany, and Luxembourg were originally held by a German company, Hag AG. In 1927 the rights for Belgium and Luxembourg were transferred to a Belgian subsidiary. German property in Belgium was sequestered following the end of the Second World War, and the subsidiary, according to the Court's terminology, became independent as a result of an act by a public authority. Control passed to Belgian hands and the company was later sold to Van Zuylen Freres who objected to the marketing of Hag coffee originating from the German Hag company on the basis of its trade mark rights. **10.74**

The Court accepted that the competition provisions did not apply because there was no legal, financial, technical, or economic link. It turned to free movement of goods rules and considered the specific subject-matter of trade mark rights from a negative perspective, first, by noting that trade mark laws protect against 'infringement on the part of persons who lack any legal title'[97] and second, by highlighting that the exercise of trade mark rights **10.75**

---

[92] C-16/74 *Winthrop BV* [1974] ECR 1183, paragraph 8.
[93] Ibid, paragraph 9.
[94] Ibid, paragraph 10.
[95] Ibid, paragraph 11.
[96] C-192/73 *Van Zuylen Freres v Hag AG* [1974] ECR 731.
[97] Ibid, paragraph 11.

contributes to the partitioning of markets given, in particular, that they are not subjected to time limitations. In two short paragraphs the Court managed to limit the scope of the right misleadingly and accentuate its territorial effect and life cycle. It overlooked the fact that a legal title can be used to defend against infringement proceedings but does not always trump a trade mark right, and trade mark rights are not unlimited in terms of time; registration can be renewed perpetually but for specified periods of time and non-use renders a registration liable to cancellation proceedings.

10.76 Following its analysis the Court stressed that:

> one cannot allow the holder of a trade mark to rely upon the exclusiveness of a trade mark right—which may be the consequence of the territorial limitation of national legislations—with a view to prohibiting the marketing in a Member State of goods legally produced in another Member State under an identical trademark having the same origin.[98]

It observed that both products were lawfully marketed and although 'the indication of origin of a product covered by a trade mark is useful, information to consumers on this point may be ensured by means other than such as would affect the free movement of goods'.[99]

10.77 It held that:

> to prohibit the marketing in a Member State of a product legally bearing a trade mark in another Member State, for the sole reason that an identical trade mark having the same origin exists in the first state, is incompatible with the provisions providing for free movement of goods within the common market.[100]

The Court also held that if the holder of a trade mark in one Member State could market the marked product in another Member State the same applied to any third party who had duly acquired the product in the first Member State.

(4) *Terrapin*: Consent and Independent Rights

10.78 As we have seen above in *Terrapin*,[101] the Court reconsidered its approach without altering the principles because the 'independence' of the trade marks allowed a more logical outcome. In that case the Court restated that:

> [the] proprietor of an industrial or commercial property right protected by the law of a member-State cannot rely on that law to prevent the importation of a product which has lawfully been marketed in another member-State by the proprietor himself or with his consent It is the same when the right relied on is the result of the subdivision, either by voluntary act or as a result of public constraint, of a trade mark right which originally belonged to one and the same proprietor. In these cases the basic function of the trade mark to guarantee to consumers that the product has the same origin is already undermined by the subdivision of the original right.[102]

Common origin appeared to prevail again over consent. Still, the Court was given the opportunity to reconsider its position on consent in two patent cases.

---

[98] Ibid, paragraph 12.
[99] Ibid, paragraph 14.
[100] Ibid, paragraph 15.
[101] C-119/75 *Terrapin* [1976] ECR 103.
[102] Ibid, paragraph 6.

(5) *Merck v Stephar*: Lack of Protection

In *Merck v Stephar*[103] the pharmaceutical product in question was protected by a patent in The Netherlands held by Merck. The same company marketed the product in Italy where at the time there was no patent protection available for pharmaceutical products. Stephar bought the product in Italy and imported it to The Netherlands. Merck argued that there was a crucial difference from *Centrafarm*.[104] In Italy it did not have the opportunity to enjoy the benefits of exclusivity deriving from patent protection. This in turn meant that its patent rights in The Netherlands had not been exhausted by the circulation of the product in Italy. The Court rejected this line of argument.   **10.79**

Consent prevailed over the absence of protection: **10.80**

> It is for the proprietor of the patent to decide, in the light of all the circumstances, under what conditions he will market his product, including the possibility of marketing it in a Member State where the law does not provide patent protection for the product in question. If he decides to do so he must accept the consequences of his choice as regards the free movement of the product within the Common Market, which is a fundamental principle forming part of the legal and economic circumstances which must be taken into account by the proprietor of the patent in determining the manner in which his exclusive right will be exercised.[105]

(6) *Pharmon v Hoechst*: Compulsory Licence

Pharmon v Hoechst[106] provided a more elaborate factual scenario. Hoechst owned patents for a pharmaceutical product in The Netherlands and the United Kingdom. In the United Kingdom another company, DDSA, obtained a compulsory licence to manufacture and market the product according to the law in the United Kingdom that also provided that the licence was non-assignable and that goods under the licence were not to be exported. DDSA breached the second condition and sold the pharmaceutical product to Pharmon, a Dutch company. Surely, Hoechst argued, there was no consent in this case and its rights in The Netherlands had not been exhausted. Pharmon, on the other hand, argued that there was no difference between a compulsory and a voluntary licence; in both cases the licensor received remuneration.   **10.81**

The Court this time agreed with the patent holder: **10.82**

> It is necessary to point out that where … the competent authorities of a Member State grant a third party a compulsory licence which allows him to carry out manufacturing and marketing operations which the patentee would normally have the right to prevent, the patentee cannot be deemed to have consented to the operation of that third party.[107]

It went on to describe the core of the right:

> the substance of a patent lies essentially in according the inventor an exclusive right of first placing the product on the market so as to allow him to obtain the reward for his creative efforts. It is therefore necessary to allow the patent proprietor to prevent the importation and marketing of products manufactured under a compulsory licence in order to protect the substance of his exclusive rights under his patent.[108]

---

[103] C-187/80 *Merck v Stephar* [1981] ECR 2063; reconfirmed in C-267/95 and C-268/95 *Merck & Co Ltd v Primecrown Ltd* [1996] ECR I-6285
[104] C-16/74 *Winthrop* [1974] ECR 1183.
[105] C-187/80 *Merck* [1981] E.CR 2063, paragraph 11.
[106] C-19/84 *Pharmon BV v Hoechst AG* [1985] ECR 2281.
[107] Ibid, paragraph 25.
[108] Ibid, paragraph 26.

(7) *Centrafarm v American Home Products*: Changing Direction

10.83 In *Centrafarm v American Home Products*[109] the Court favoured the holder of the right. American Home Products was the holder of a number of national trade mark registrations for the same pharmaceutical product; Centrafarm imported the product to The Netherlands under the mark 'Serenid', removed the trade mark affixed to the product and replaced it with the mark 'Seresta' that Centrafarm had registered and had been using in The Netherlands. The Court repeated that,

> [in]relation to trade-marks, the specific subject matter is in particular the guarantee to the proprietor of the trade-mark that he has the exclusive right to use that trade-mark for the purpose of putting a product into circulation for the first time and therefore his protection against competitors wishing to take advantage of the status and reputation of the mark by selling products illegally bearing that trade-mark[110]

and that the essential function of a trade mark is 'to guarantee the identity of the origin of the trade-marked product to the consumer or ultimate user'.[111]

10.84 The Court then linked the essential function of a trade mark with the exclusivity of a trade mark right, finding that only the 'proprietor may confer an identity upon the product by affixing the mark'[112] and the scope of the right, stating that the guarantee of origin would be jeopardized if it were 'permissible for a third party to affix the mark to the product, even to an original product'.[113]

10.85 Accordingly national laws could prevent third parties from 'usurping the right'[114] to affix the trade mark or change the affixed trade mark irrespective of whether 'the different parts of the production, bearing different marks, come from two different Member States'[115] and this would fall within the specific subject-matter of the trade mark. The Court noted that choosing different marks for the same product in different Member States was lawful unless it constituted an attempt to partition national markets artificially. It would then be considered a disguised restriction on intra-Community trade.

(8) *Hag II*: The Concept of Consent, The Role and Function of Trade Marks

10.86 This gradual change of approach culminated in an unequivocal U-turn by the Court that revisited the facts of *Hag I*[116]—this time Belgian coffee found its way into Germany—in *Hag II*.[117]

(a) *The Opinion of Advocate General Jacobs*

10.87 Advocate General Jacobs considered the position adopted in *Terrapin*.[118] He accepted the logic behind the four principles developed by the Court: the existence/exercise dichotomy; the concept of the specific subject-matter; the principle of exhaustion; and the parallel

---

[109] C-3/78 *Centrafarm BV v American Home Products Corp* [1978] ECR 1823.
[110] Paragraph 11.
[111] Paragraph 12.
[112] C-3/78 *American Home Products Corp* [1978] ECR 1823, paragraph 13.
[113] Paragraph 14.
[114] Paragraph 15.
[115] Paragraph 16.
[116] C-192/73 *Van Zuyten Freres v Hag AG* [1974] ECR 731.
[117] C-10/89 *SA CNL-SUCAL NV v Hag GF AG* [1990] ECR I-3711.
[118] C-119/75 *Terrapin* [1976] ECR 103.

application of competition rules. But he questioned the reasoning and justification behind the judicial construct of common origin raised by the Court in *Hag I*,[119] identifying four major flaws. First, the reliance on the second sentence of Article 36 that was not relevant in the case; second, the failure to delineate the specific subject-matter of the right; third, the unwarranted discrimination between trade marks and other intellectual property rights; and fourth, the weakness of the link between reasoning and conclusion, that the Court tried to hide behind the invention of common origin.

Terrapin was: 10.88

> a valiant attempt to legitimise the doctrine of common origin, but the logic on which it is based is … fallacious. It is true that the essential function of a trade mark is 'to guarantee to consumers that the product has the same origin'. But the word 'origin' in this context does not refer to the historical origin of the trade mark; it refers to the commercial origin of the goods. The consumer is not … interested in the genealogy of trademarks; he is interested in knowing who made the goods that he purchases. The function of a trade mark is to signify to the consumer that all goods sold under that mark have been produced by, or under the control of, the same person and will, in all probability, be of uniform quality. That basic function of the 'HAG' mark has never been undermined in Germany, where it has, since its inception, been in the hands of one company. Nor had it been undermined in Belgium and Luxembourg until the Court's judgment in Hag I … throughout its history (until 1974, that is) the mark had, in each territory, been in the exclusive ownership of a single person who had the power either to build up the goodwill associated with it by maintaining the quality of the product or to destroy that goodwill by allowing the quality to deteriorate. Once the owner of the mark is deprived of his exclusive right to its use, he loses the power to influence the goodwill associated with it and he loses the incentive to produce high-quality goods. Looking at matters from the consumer's point of view, the result of all this is thoroughly unsatisfactory because the trade mark no longer acts as a guarantee of origin. At best he is confused; at worst he is misled. In the circumstances, it is difficult not to conclude that the essential function of the mark is compromised, its specific subject-matter is affected and—most seriously of all—its very existence is jeopardised. But none of those consequences ensued from the fragmentation of the 'HAG' trade mark in 1944; they ensued from the Court's judgment in Hag 1.[120]

Given the almost unprecedented call for a change in direction, AG Jacobs attempted to make it more palatable and justify the position of the Court in *Hag I* based on the lack of cases that would allow the Court to develop fully worked out principle. Since that Judgment, however, the Court had developed both the concept of 'specific subject matter'[121] and the principle of exhaustion.[122] Note too that at the time of *Hag II* the Advocate General could also refer to positive integration in the form of a legislative text regulating trade marks. Article 5(1) of the Trade Mark Directive conferred on the proprietor the exclusive right to prevent use of a sign that is confusingly similar with the protected sign without its consent. The European legislator had accepted the principle that trade mark rights can block cross-border trade opting for a broad test involving confusion rather than total identity. How could this be reconciled with the outcome of *Hag I*? His analysis, however, accepted that the Directive did not have direct effect and was inconclusive regarding exhaustion of rights. 10.89

---

[119] C-192/73 *Hag I* [1974] ECR 731, paragraphs 6–15.
[120] Point 24.
[121] See paragraph 10.71 et seq, above.
[122] C-187/80 *Merck v Stephar* [1981] ECR 2063.

The Court would have to reconsider its own jurisprudence rather than hide behind the intent of the legislator.

10.90 He went on to challenge the claim, summarily accepted by the Court in *Hag I*, that two signs could coexist and be distinguished from each other in the same market aided by additional markings. First, he highlighted the historical and doctrinal limitations of the common law doctrine of honest concurrent use that was developed by the courts in a bygone era of localized trade. And second, he discussed in greater detail the actual difficulties of applying additional distinguishing matter. According to the Advocate General 'everything must of course depend on the facts'.[123] In practice, it would be more difficult to distinguish between identical marks, and the nature and style of additional matter should also be taken into account. A sticker placed next to the trade mark disclaiming any connection with another trader's products could be tolerated; a sticker obliterating and replacing the trade mark would create a negative impression for the product.[124]

(b) The Judgment of the Court

10.91 The Court responded to the plea of the Advocate General. It considered the essential function of a trade mark and the specific subject-matter of the right[125] and, linking the factual scenario with its judicial doctrine, noted that in a situation such as that described by the national court:

> the decisive fact is the absence of any element of consent, on the part of the owner of the trade mark right protected by national legislation, to the marketing in another member-State, under a mark which is identical or may cause confusion, of a similar product manufactured and marketed by an enterprise which has no tie of legal or economic dependence with that owner.[126]

The owner of the right should be allowed to exercise the 'option under national law to prevent the importation of the similar product under a name likely to be confused with his own mark'[127] irrespective of whether the offending mark originally belonged to the same owner but changed hands as a result of expropriation. The Court admitted that from the date of expropriation the two marks functioned independently from each other as guarantees of distinct sources in spite of their common origin.

(9) Ideal Standard: **Voluntary Assignment**

10.92 The Court went further and considered the result of a voluntary assignment in *Ideal Standard*.[128] In this case a parent company held, through its subsidiaries, registrations of Ideal Standard covering sanitary fittings and heating equipment in France and Germany. In the process of insolvency proceedings the French subsidiary sold the heating equipment part of the business together with the trade mark registration for heating equipment to another French company. The German subsidiary brought infringement proceedings

---

[123] Point 43.
[124] See C-349/95 *Frits Loendersloot v George Ballantine* [1997] ECR 227, see paragraphs 10.229 and following, below.
[125] See paragraphs 10.71 and following, above.
[126] Paragraph 15.
[127] Paragraph 16.
[128] C-9/93 *IHT Internationale Heiztechnik GmbH and Uwe Danzinger v Ideal-Standard GmbH and Wabco Standard GmbH* [1994] ECR 1-2789.

against the new proprietor for marketing in Germany Ideal Standard products relying on its registration for sanitary fittings.

10.93 It repeated its finding in *Deutsche Renault*[129] that application of national law, in that case the provision for establishing confusion, remained in the jurisdiction of the national court. It had added, however, that the assessment of similarity should not lead to arbitrary discriminations or disguised restrictions. Regarding the territorial split of the rights it accepted the submission that trade mark rights are not only territorial but also independent of each other,[130] and that the French registration could be assigned on its own, without the related business or goodwill, as provided by French law but also without the parallel German registration.[131] As a result the Court looked at the effect of the transfer of the trade mark. If, despite the transfer, control remains in the hands of a single body—the group of companies in the case of products put into circulation by a subsidiary, the manufacturer in the case of products marketed by the distributor, or the licensor in the case of products marketed by a licensee—the origin of the product is the same and the exercise of national trade mark rights would be against the free movement provisions of the Treaty.

10.94 It added that the possibility of control by a single body would suffice; for example, a national law allowing the licensor to oppose the importation of products marketed by the licensee on the basis of their quality would be considered contrary to Articles [30] and [36]; 'if the licensor tolerates the manufacture of poor quality products, despite having contractual means of preventing it, he must bear the responsibility'.[132]

10.95 Unitary control was contrasted with the effect of a transfer to an undertaking which has no economic link with the original holder of the right; 'a contract of assignment by itself, that is in the absence of any economic link, does not give the assignor any means of controlling the quality of products which are marketed by the assignee and to which the latter has affixed the trade mark'.[133] In this case the Court felt that the assignor could exercise its national rights in order to stop the importation of products marketed by the assignee. It rejected the Commission's submission that the assignment implied consent by the assignor and distinguished between consent that is implicit in an assignment and consent that leads to the exhaustion of a right. The latter went together with the ability to determine the products to which the trade mark may be affixed in the exporting State and to control their quality.

10.96 The Court followed the logic of *Hag II*. It reiterated that trade mark rights are territorial, and accordingly the function of a trade mark has to be assessed by reference to the respective territory, and decided that the outcome should be the same irrespective of whether the split in ownership was the result of a voluntary or a mandatory transfer. The Court took into account the development of the Community Trade Mark system highlighting the statement

---

[129] C-317/91 *Deutsche Renault AG v AUDI AG* [1993] ECR 1-6227.
[130] It referred to Article 6(3) of the Paris Convention providing that a mark registered in a country of the Union is independent of marks registered in other countries of the Union.
[131] The Court referred to Article 6quater of the Paris Convention, providing that when according to national law assignment of the relevant goodwill or business is required whenever a trade mark is assigned it suffices to assign the national portion of such business or goodwill, and to Article 9ter of the Madrid Agreement providing that partial, in terms of jurisdictional coverage, assignment of an international registration is possible.
[132] Paragraph 38.
[133] Paragraph 41.

in the Fifth Recital in the Preamble to the Community Trade Mark Regulation that 'the Community law relating to trademarks, does not replace the laws of the Member States on trademarks'.[134] Further, the Regulation empowered the proprietor of an earlier national right with the right to oppose subsequent Community Trade Mark applications. This combination meant that the Regulation did not render void assignments of national trade mark rights. The Court stressed that such a measure could only be introduced by the legislature through the adoption of a Directive, not through case law. It 'would have the effect of imposing on the States a positive obligation, namely to embody in their laws a rule rendering void assignments of national trade marks made for part only of the Community'.[135] It also underlined that competition law could have a role to play in the case of assignments intending to enable a market sharing agreement.

10.97 However, Article 101 of the Treaties should not be applied mechanically to every assignment. 'Before a trade-mark assignment can be treated as giving effect to an agreement prohibited under Article [101], it is necessary to analyse the context, the commitments underlying the assignment, the intention of the parties and the consideration for the assignment.'[136]

(10) Repackaging and parallel imports: *Hoffmann-La Roche*; Setting the Principles

10.98 In *Hoffmann-La Roche*[137] the Court set the foundations of its repackaging case law. The German subsidiary of Hoffmann-La Roche had been marketing Valium Roche (the brand name for Diazepam, a psychopharmacological drug) in Germany in small packets of 20 or 50 tablets; for hospital use five small packets were combined in new packaging containing 100 or 250 tablets. The trade mark 'Valium' was registered in the name of another Hoffmann-La Roche company and its use licensed to the German subsidiary. In the United Kingdom, the local subsidiary marketed Valium in packages of 100 or 500 tablets, at a lower price than in Germany.

10.99 The German subsidiary of Centrafarm bought Valium Roche tablets from its Dutch parent company which, in turn, had purchased them in the United Kingdom and repackaged them in The Netherlands in batches of 1,000 tablets, and started marketing them in Germany. On the new packaging appeared the Valium and Roche signs, in a slightly different format from that used in the United Kingdom and Germany, the registration number of the entry on the German register for pharmaceutical products, the name Centrafarm, and the words 'Marketed by Centrafarm GmbH, 4444 Bentheim-l, Telephone: 05922-2525'. In each packet there was an information leaflet in German, signed 'Hoffmann-La Roche', that repeated the notice that the medicinal preparation was marketed by Centrafarm. Centrafarm also intended to repackage the tablets in smaller packets for sale to individuals. Note that Centrafarm was also manufacturing its own Diazepam preparation.

10.100 Hoffmann-La Roche considered this to constitute trade mark infringement. It obtained an interim injunction and the case reached the Landgericht (District Court) Freiburg that referred the following questions to the Court of Justice:

---

[134] Note that the Court chose to describe the relationship as one where the 'Community trade mark is merely superimposed on the national rights' (paragraph 56), rather than one where they exist in parallel.
[135] Paragraph 57.
[136] Paragraph 59.
[137] C-102/77 *Hoffmann-La Roche* [1978] ECR 1139.

1. Is the person entitled to a trade mark right protected for his benefit both in member-State A and in member-State B empowered under Article [36] of the EEC Treaty, in reliance on this right, to prevent a parallel importer from buying from the proprietor of the mark or with his consent in member-State A of the Community medicinal preparations which have been put on the market with his trade mark lawfully affixed thereto and packaged under this trade mark, from providing them with new packaging, affixing to such packaging the proprietor's trade mark and importing the preparations distinguished in this manner into member-State B?[138]
2. Is the proprietor of the trade mark entitled to do this or does he thereby infringe provisions of the EEC Treaty—in particular those contained in Article [101] thereof—even if he acquires a dominant position within the market in member-State B with regard to the medicinal preparation in question, when prohibition on imports of a repacked product to which the proprietor's trade mark has been affixed has in actual fact a restrictive effect on the market, because different sizes of packages are used in countries A and B and because the importation of the product in another manner has not yet in fact made any appreciable progress on the market, and when the actual effect of the prohibition is that between the member-States there is maintained a substantial—in certain circumstances disproportionate—price differential, without its being possible to prove that the owner of the mark is using the prohibition solely or mainly to maintain this price differential?[139]

(a) The Opinion of Advocate General Capotorti

10.101 Advocate General Capotorti acknowledged that the balance attempted by Article 36 was a delicate and difficult exercise and that the Court had been trying to contribute to the gradual definition of the limits to the protection of individual claims based on trade mark rights, limits that reflected the constraints imposed by Community law on national systems of protection that had been developed independently and preceded the Community legal order. The basic concept was that the Treaty did not prejudice the existence of the rights conferred, but free movement of goods rules impinged on their exercise. The derogation of Article 36 applied only when it was essential to the safeguarding of rights which constituted the specific subject-matter of the mark that was in turn linked with its essential function to guarantee to consumers the identity of the origin of the product.

10.102 The peculiarity of this case, however, was the repackaging of the product; Hoffmann-La Roche would not object to the importation of Valium from the United Kingdom in its original packaging. So according to the principles already developed by the Court what needed to be established in this case was whether there was a necessary connection between the essential function of the mark and the right that German law appeared to grant to Hoffmann-La Roche in Germany to prevent the marketing of the imported tablets on the ground that the importer had, without authorization, altered their packaging and reapplied the trade mark. He found that the injunction sought by the trade mark proprietor would restrict the free movement of the tablets within the Community. Before considering whether the barrier could be justified he rejected two preliminary arguments raised by Hoffmann-La Roche, both linked with consumer protection and perception.

10.103 **(i) Public health and the guarantee of quality function** First, he rejected the argument that the barrier could be justified on the basis of consumer and public health protection. These aims should be obtained in their own proper field, according to the relevant

---

[138] Paragraph 5.
[139] Paragraph 15.

legislation, not by the means of trade mark rights.[140] The second had to do with consumer expectations regarding specific and constant product quality consumer expectations based on trade marks. Seeking support in the views of two prominent academics in this field, Beier and Vanzetti, he concluded that trade mark law protected only the guarantee of origin function, indeed this principle constituted the common element of all the Member States' national systems of protection.[141] Consumer expectations were to be protected under unfair competition and criminal laws. And in any case, the ancillary functions would face the same limitations with those imposed in relation to the primary function.

10.104 **(ii) The position in the Member States** Turning to how Member States would have dealt with unauthorized alterations in the packaging of a product, he found that in most cases the trade mark proprietor would be entitled to object; however, this did not appear to be unconditional but based on confusion as to origin.

10.105 **(iii) The scope of Article 36** But what should be truly decisive was the scope of Article 36 that was linked with the essential function of a trade mark. In general the substitution of packaging could affect the identification of origin, even when the trade mark had been re-affixed. The circumstances of each case did matter; for example, affixing the trade mark on the inner packaging or the product itself would reduce the risk of confusion. However, in order to eliminate all such risks it would be necessary to eliminate any interference with the packaging. This, he found:

> would entail sanctioning restrictions on the movement of goods which seem incommensurate with the objective pursued by Article [36] of the Treaty, that is to protect the essential function of the trade mark. Since, however, the restrictions on the free movement of goods permitted under that provision, which is a derogatory and exceptional provision, must be contained within the limits strictly necessary for that objective, I consider that it is incompatible with Community law to concede a general power to the proprietor of the mark to prohibit the repackaging of the product even where the attainment of the essential objective of the mark is not in fact jeopardised.[142]

10.106 The only concession he was willing to make was in respect of cases that 'having regard to the type of product, any change in the container thereof entails an actual risk of a modification of the essential characteristics of the product itself such as to affect its identity'.[143] The market conditions, for example price discrepancies between Member States and methods of sale, should also be taken into account as counterbalancing factors to a general risk of confusion.

10.107 **(iv) Product quality and liability considerations** Another point raised by Hoffmann-La Roche had to do with the responsibility of the trade mark proprietor for the quality of the product; it should be able to check both the manufacture and packaging of the product. More importantly, once the product was repackaged it should not be answerable for the quality of the product. The Advocate General noted that the party altering the quality of the product should carry the liability burden. He recognized, however, that this was a legitimate concern and suggested that an obligation should be imposed on the importer to indicate on the new packaging that the repackaging was carried out by the importer.

---

[140] C-16/74 *Winthrop BV* [1974] ECR 1183.
[141] F K Beier, 'La Territorialite du Droit des Marques et des Echanges Internationaux' [1971] Journal du Droit International 19; and A Vanzetti, 'La Funzione E la Natura Giuridica del Marchio' [1961] I Rivista del Diritto Commerciale 16.
[142] Point 8.
[143] Ibid.

10.108 **(v) Dominance, trade mark rights, and competition** Advocate General Capotorti underlined that following his submissions in respect of the first question would render the issues raised in the second question superfluous. Still, he proposed some guidelines. First, he suggested that the exercise of trade mark rights should not in itself constitute an abuse under Article 102 TFEU. The exercise of a trade mark within the limits which are necessary to protect its essential function, as has been set out earlier, cannot be precluded for a given undertaking merely because it occupies a dominant position.[144]

10.109 However, should the exercise of the rights exceed the limits set by Article 36 then Article 102 might also be infringed:

> an endeavour to rely on the trade mark right, with regard to a product of the kind in question in the present proceedings, in order to achieve a general and complete prohibition on imports solely on the basis of an alteration in the packaging is not justified under Article [36]. Such unjustified exercise of a trade mark right by an undertaking occupying a dominant position may accordingly, together with other factors, constitute an infringement of Article [102] of the Treaty if it is instrumental in allowing that undertaking to exploit the market in which it operates.[145]

He believed that the situation described in the second question referred to the Court would probably fall under Article 102, since the abuse should not consist merely in restraining competition by the prevention of parallel imports on the basis of trade mark rights. It should be seen in the context of a more complex pattern of behaviour, with the price discrepancy being a decisive factor.

(b) The Judgment of the Court

10.110 **(i) The first question: Repackaging and free movement** The Court repeated that the Treaty did not affect the existence of the rights, but the exercise of those rights might be restricted by the prohibitions contained in the Treaty, and that the exceptions to the fundamental principles should be tolerated only to the extent they were justified for the purpose of safeguarding the rights which constituted the specific subject-matter of that property:

> In relation to trade marks the specific subject-matter is in particular to guarantee to the proprietor of the trade mark that he has the exclusive right to use that trade mark for the purpose of putting a product into circulation for the first time and therefore to protect him against competitors wishing to take advantage of the status and reputation of the trade mark by selling products illegally bearing that trade mark.[146]

The question had to be answered keeping in mind the 'essential function of the trade mark, which is to guarantee the identity of the origin of the trade-marked product to the consumer or ultimate user, by enabling him without any possibility of confusion to distinguish that product from products which have another origin'.[147]

10.111 **(ii) Repackaging and the guarantee of origin** The Court appeared at this stage to take a stance favouring trade mark owners by acknowledging that the guarantee of origin meant that the consumer or ultimate user could be certain that the trade marked product had not been subject to unauthorized interference by a third party at a previous stage of marketing. Preventing this should form part of the specific subject-matter of the right, but the balance

---

[144] Paragraph 11.
[145] Ibid.
[146] Paragraph 7.
[147] Ibid.

shifted once again through the notion of a 'disguised restriction on trade' between Member States. Putting a product on the European market in various packages and employing trade mark rights to prevent repackaging even if it were done in a way that would not affect the identification of origin and the original condition of the product would be such a restriction.

10.112 **(iii) Affecting the original condition of the product** So the critical question for the Court was whether the repackaging was capable of affecting the original condition of the product. This would depend on the circumstances of the case. The Court underlined that the nature of the product and the method of repackaging should be the two decisive factors. There could be cases where the original condition of the product would not be affected, for instance where the manufacturer marketed the product in double packaging and the repackaging affected only the external packaging, leaving the internal packaging intact.

10.113 **(iv) The general rule: The first repackaging condition** Where the essential function of the trade mark to guarantee the origin of the product is thus protected, the exercise of his rights by the proprietor of the trade mark in order to fetter the free movement of goods between member-States may constitute a disguised restriction within the meaning of the second sentence of Article [36] of the Treaty if it is established that the use of the trade mark right by the proprietor, having regard to the marketing system which he has adopted, will contribute to the artificial partitioning of the markets between member-States.[148]

10.114 **(v) The limitations to the general rule: Three additional conditions** The Court accepted that this finding amounted to giving to the importer a certain licence that in normal circumstances would be reserved for the proprietor. Accordingly it should be, first, shown by the importer that the repackaging could not adversely affect the original condition of the product. Second, the importer should give prior notice to the trade mark proprietor. Note that this was viewed as a measure protecting consumers from being misled, although the Court also stated that this would be in the proprietor's interest. Third, the importer should indicate on the new packaging that the product had been repackaged by the importer.

10.115 **(vi) The second question: Article 36 and competition** The Court dealt with the second question in a summary way by observing that to the extent to which the exercise of a trade mark right was lawful in accordance with Article 36, the exercise of trade mark rights would not be contrary to Article 102 on the sole ground that it was the act of an undertaking occupying a dominant position on the market if the trade mark right had not been used as an instrument for the abuse of such a position.

10.116 Accordingly it should be, first, shown by the importer that the repackaging could not adversely affect the original condition of the product. Second, the importer should give prior notice to the trade mark proprietor. Note that this was viewed as a measure protecting consumers from being misled, although the Court also stated that this would be in the proprietor's interest.[149] Third, the importer should indicate on the new packaging that the product had been repackaged by the importer.

---

[148] Paragraph 10.
[149] Compare with the Opinion of AG Jacobs in C-349/95 *Frits Loendersloot v George Ballantine & Son* [199] ECR I-6227, see paragraph 10.229 and following, below.

E. Free Movement of Goods and the New Trade Mark Regime

(1) *Bristol Myers Squibb* and the Related Cases: Article 7 of the Directive and the Free Movement of Goods Rules; the Fifth Repackaging Condition

In *Bristol Myers Squibb*[150] the Court looked at repackaging for the first time after the introduction of the Directive. Advocate General Jacobs delivered a joint Opinion covering a number of cases referred to the Court from Danish and German courts. The Court joined the cases in two judgments.

10.117

(a) The Danish cases

There were three references from Denmark; the first two[151] were references from the Sø- og Handelsret Maritime and Commercial Court, Copenhagen, the third[152] was a reference from the Hojesteret (Supreme Court).

10.118

In the first case,[153] Paranova, an importer and distributor of pharmaceutical products, imported a number of Bristol Myers Squibb products that it had purchased in Member States other than Denmark, repackaged them, and marketed them in Denmark. The repackaging involved the following: repackaging of blisters in new external packaging, bearing the 'Bristol Myers Squibb' logo in yellow and green, application of the names under which the product were sold in Denmark but without the ® symbol, and a statement indicating that the goods were manufactured by Bristol Myers Squibb but imported and repackaged by Paranova, removal of phials from their original padding, application of a label bearing the name of the product without the ® symbol and a similar statement, the phials were then put back into their padding and packed in new external packaging bearing the Bristol Myers Squibb colours and trade marks and the same importation information, the original instructions leaflet was removed and a Danish version with the Bristol Myers Squibb trade marks inserted; removal of flasks from their outer packaging, placement of a similar label as above, repackaging in new external packaging as above but this time together with a spray not manufactured by Bristol Myers Squibb.

10.119

Bristol Myers Squibb brought trade mark infringement proceedings and the Sø- og Handelsret referred the following questions to the Court:

10.120

1. Is Article 7(1) of Council Directive 89/104 to approximate the laws of the Member States relating to trade marks to be interpreted as meaning that unless Article 7(2) applies the proprietor of a trade mark who has put goods into circulation in a Member State under a trade mark cannot prevent a third party from importing the goods into another Member State in order to market the goods there under the same trade mark even if that third party has attached to the inner packaging of the goods labels on which the trade mark is affixed and substituted for the original outer packaging a new packaging on which the trade mark is affixed?

---

[150] C-427/93 *Bristol Myers Squibb v Paranova A/S*, C-429/93 *CH Boehringer Sohn, Boehringer Ingelheim KG and Boehringer Ingelheim A/S v Paranova A/S*, and C-436/93 *Bayer Aktiengesellschaft and Bayer Danmark A/S v Paranova A/S* [1996] ECR I-3457.
[151] C-427/93 and C-429/93.
[152] C-436/93.
[153] C-437/93.

It is stressed that the question does not seek a ruling on cases in which the second sentence of Article [30] of the Treaty might justify repackaging and reaffixing a mark in accordance with the principles set out in Case 102/77 but only on whether Article 7(1) is to be construed as meaning that apart from laying down the general principle of the exhaustion of trade mark rights within the European Community it also entails a general limitation on the rights otherwise conferred on trade mark proprietors regarding use of the trade mark for which the trade mark proprietor has not given his consent.

2. If the answer to Question 1 is affirmative, does Article 7(2) of Directive 89/104, after implementation, entail that the case law of the Court of Justice as set out in Case 102/77 and developed subsequently comes to be of subsidiary importance since the right to repackage will primarily fall to be determined in application of national provisions corresponding to Article 7(2) of the said Directive?

3. On the premise that Article 7(1) of the said Directive is intended to permit parallel importers to reaffix trade marks, must the fact that goods are repackaged be regarded as 'legitimate reasons' for the purposes of Article 7(2)?
In particular, does it make any difference that it is only the outer packaging that has been repackaged and remarked but not the inner packaging?

4. With regard to the derogating provision in the second sentence of Article 36 of the Treaty and in the light of the judgment of the Court of Justice in Case 102/77, what may be described as a partitioning of the market for a specific product and, in particular, what distinguishing factors are to be taken into account in assessing whether an artificial partitioning of markets between the Member States can be said to exist for a specific product in connection with the sales system applied by the trade mark proprietor?[154]

10.121 In the second case[155] Paranova bought products produced by Boehringer in a Member State other than Denmark, and imported, repackaged, and marketed them in Denmark. On the new packaging Boehringer was indicated as the producer and included an informational leaflet in Danish. Note that in this case Paranova had registered the pharmaceutical products with the relevant authorization authorities using the Boehringer names.

10.122 The Sø- og Handelsret referred to the Court two questions with the same wording as the first two questions indicated above.[156]

10.123 The third case[157] involved Bayer products; Paranova followed similar repackaging procedures. One additional complication was that, according to Bayer, a warning to keep the product away from the light was added, following the manufacturer's notification to Paranova. Paranova disputed whether the original packaging bore a warning to that effect.

10.124 The case reached the Hojesteret, which referred the following questions to the Court:

1. Must the possibility for a trade mark proprietor to oppose a parallel importer's action in replacing wholly or in part the original packaging of his goods by new packaging on which the parallel importer reaffixes the trade mark be determined under national trade mark law only in conjunction with Article 7(1) and (2) of the First Council Directive (89/104) to approximate the laws of the Member States relating to trademarks or also in conjunction with the first and second sentences of Article [30] E.C.?

2. In assessing the legal steps that may be taken by the trade mark proprietor, is it significant whether there may be said to exist an 'artificial partitioning of the markets' for trade in the

---

[154] Reproduced in point 15.
[155] C-429/93.
[156] See paragraph 10.120 above and accompanying text.
[157] C-436/93.

goods in question? If so, the Court is asked to specify what is the significance as regards such steps.
3. If Question 2 is answered in the affirmative, is it significant for the rights of the trade mark proprietor whether he had the intention to create or exploit such an artificial partitioning of the markets? If so, the Court is asked to specify what is the significance as regards those rights.
4. In connection with Question 3, must the parallel importer show or else establish a probability that there was intent or must the trade mark proprietor show or establish a probability that there was no intent?
5. Is the reaffixing of the trade mark, as described in Question 1, in itself sufficient 'legitimate reason' within the meaning of Article 7 of the Directive or must the trade mark proprietor in addition show further circumstances, for example that the condition of the goods is changed or impaired when they are put on the market by the parallel importer?[158]

(b) The German cases

10.125 In the first of three cases joined by the Court[159] Beiersdorf manufactured a pharmaceutical product under a licence granted by a French company that was the proprietor of the trade mark in Germany. In France the product was marketed in packages containing two blister strips with fourteen pills each, in order to comply with national legislation. At the back of the blister appeared the days of the week in French, one for each pill. In Germany the standard sizes were packets of 50 or 100 pills. Eurim-Pharm, the parallel importer, bought the product in France, cut some strips in order to achieve the number 50 or 100 (inevitably interrupting the series of week days that appeared at the back), and repackaged them in a new box, some strips still in their own original box and others outside their original box. The new packaging had a small hole from which the original trade mark was visible as it appeared on one of the original packets. On the outer new packaging there was information about the active ingredients and a statement that the goods have been imported, packed, and distributed by Eurim-Pharm. Beiersdorf, authorized by the French company, started infringement proceedings.

10.126 The case reached the Bundesgerichtstshof that referred the following questions to the Court:
1. Is the proprietor of an internationally registered trade mark (I R mark) having effect in Member State A entitled under Article [36] E.C., in reliance upon the trade mark, to prevent an importer from buying medicinal products which have been marketed under the trade mark in Member State B by the proprietor of the trade mark and which require a prescription in Member State A, from repackaging them in conformity with the prescribing practices of medical practitioners in Member State A, which are based on a recommendation by prominent organisations (including those representing the pharmaceutical industry) on therapeutically desirable sizes and which differ from the packaging sizes prescribed by statute in Member State B, and from marketing them in Member State A in external packaging styled by the importer, if such packaging contains an original packet with original blister strips from Member State B and a number of additional blister strips which have been cut up and the new packaging has a window through which the I R mark on the original packaging is visible and displays a reference to the packaging and marketing by the importer but no reference to the manufacturer? Is it of relevance for the purposes of the answer to the question that information printed on the back of the

---

[158] Reproduced in point 21.
[159] C-71/94 *Eurim-Pharm Arzneimiltel GmbH v Beiersdorf AG*, C-72/94 *Boehringer Ingelheim KG*, and C-73/94 *Farmitalia Carlo Erba GmbH* [1996] ECR I-3603.

original blister strip refers (in, for Member State A, a foreign language) to the days of the week for a 14-day period, which when the blister is cut becomes incomplete?

2. Is it sufficient, for the purpose of establishing a disguised restriction on trade between Member States within the meaning of Article [36] E.C., that the use of the national trade mark in conjunction with the marketing system adopted by the proprietor of the I R mark objectively leads to a partitioning of the markets between Member States, or is it necessary for that purpose to show that the proprietor of the I R mark exercises his trade-mark right in conjunction with the marketing system which he employs with the object of bringing about an artificial partitioning of the markets?[160]

10.127 The second case[161] involved Boehringer products marketed in Germany in boxes of 20, 50, or 100 capsules, in blister strips, and in France in boxes of 30 capsules, each containing three blister strips of 10. Eurim-Pharm placed the original French boxes in new outer packaging—adding stickers with information about the active ingredients and the importer details—and made the numbers up to 50 or 100 by adding blister strips that were taken out from their original French packaging. It also included a leaflet with information in German. The packaging had a hole revealing the trade mark that was originally applied on one of the French packets.

10.128 The Bundesgerichtshof referred two questions to the Court:

1. Is the proprietor of an internationally registered trade mark (I R mark) having effect in Member State A entitled under Article [36] E.C., in reliance upon the trade mark, to prevent an importer from buying medicinal products which have been marketed under the trade mark in Member State B by the proprietor of the trade mark and which require a prescription in Member State A, from repackaging them in conformity with the prescribing practices of medical practitioners in Member State A, which are based on a recommendation by prominent organisations (including those representing the pharmaceutical industry) and which differ from the packaging sizes prescribed by statute in Member State B, and from marketing them in Member State A in external packaging styled by the importer, if such packaging contains an original packet with original blister strips from Member State B and a number of additional blister strips which have been cut up and if the new packaging bas a window through which the I R mark on the original packaging is visible and displays a reference to the packaging and marketing by the importer but no reference to the manufacturer?[162]

10.129 The second question was identical to the second question of the first reference reproduced above.[163] In the third case[164] Eurim-Pharm imported Farmitalia products from Portugal and marketed them, repackaging them in packets of 50 or 100 capsules. Similarly as before, the new packets contained some original packets and loose strips to make up the numbers. The difference was that at the back of each strip it added a sticker with the word 'forte' so that the name would correspond with that used in Germany, 'Sernlion forte'. The word 'forte' was printed underneath the hole from which one could see the trade mark as it appeared on the original packet. In the case of imports from Spain, where the product was marketed in packets of 45 capsules, Eurim-Pharm added to the packet a cut strip and placed on the packet a sticker with information about the product and the details of the importer.

---

[160] Reproduced in Point 25.
[161] Case C-72/94.
[162] Reproduced in point 28.
[163] See paragraph 10.126.
[164] Case C-73/94.

10.130 The Bundesgereichtshof referred two questions to the Court, the second being identical with the second question reproduced above:[165]

1. Is the proprietor of an internationally registered trade mark (I R mark) having effect in Member State A entitled under Article [30] E.C., in reliance upon the trade mark, to prevent an importer from buying medicinal products which have been marketed under the trade mark in Member State B by an undertaking belonging to the same group as the proprietor of the trade mark and which require a prescription in Member State A, from repackaging them in conformity with the prescribing practices of medicinal practitioners prevailing in Member State A, which are based on a recommendation by prominent organisations (including those representing the pharmaceutical industry) on therapeutically desirable sizes and which differ from the standard sizes in Member State B and:
    (a) from marketing them in Member State A in external packaging styled by the importer, if such packaging contains an original packet with original blister strips from Member State B and a number of additional original blister strips and the new packaging has a window through which the trade mark on the original packet is visible and displays a reference to the repackaging and marketing by the importer but no reference to the manufacturer, or
    (b) from marketing them in Member State A in the original trademarked packaging from Member State B if it is supplemented by the importer with stickers showing the firm's name and further particulars (batch number, use-by date, registration number, etc.) and with a strip containing five capsules cut from an original blister strip?[166]

10.131 The third German case[167] involved the importation of Rhone-Poulenc products to Germany by MPA. The blister strips were removed from their original packaging and put into new packaging. On the sides of the new packet there was information about the manufacturer, the importer, and the product whereas in the packet itself it introduced a leaflet with information in German.

10.132 The Oberlandesgericht Köln referred two questions to the Court, the first being identical with the second question reproduced above:[168]

2. Is there a presumption of a 'disguised restriction on trade between Member States' within the meaning of the second sentence of Article [30] E.C. where the proprietor of a trade mark protected in Member States A and B relies on its national trade mark in order to prevent an importer from buying medicinal products which have been marketed under the trade mark in Member State B by an undertaking belonging to the same group as the proprietor of the trade mark and which are available only on prescription in Member State A, from repackaging them and marketing them in Member State A in external packaging which the importer designs and to which he affixes the trade mark without the consent of the proprietor of the mark, if the exercise of the trade mark right results in a partitioning of the markets between the Member States, if it is demonstrated that the repackaging cannot impair the original condition of the product and the proprietor of the trade mark was informed in advance of the offering of the repackaged product for sale, and also if not only the manufacturer and importer are indicated on the new packaging, but also the person responsible for the repackaging, even though:
    (a) the information as to who repackaged the product is not set out on the external packaging with sufficient clarity, with the result that it may be overlooked by user groups; and/or

---

[165] See paragraph 10.126.
[166] Reproduced in point 33.
[167] C-232/84 *MPA Pharma GmbH v Rhone-Poulenc Pharma GmbH* [1996] ECR I-3671.
[168] Case C-71/94, paragraph 10.126; the only difference being that it referred to a national rather than an international registration.

(b) neither the information concerning the repackaging itself nor the layout of the external packaging in general indicates that the repackaging was carried out by the importer without the consent of the proprietor of the trade mark or its associated undertaking?[169]

(c) *The Opinion of Advocate General Jacobs*

10.133 (i) **Free movement of goods and repackaging: The basic principles** Advocate General Jacobs started from the principle of exhaustion of rights, referring to *Deutsche Grammophon v Metro*[170] and *Ideal Standard*;[171] a trade mark right could not be invoked in order to prevent the importation and sale of goods which had been placed on the market with the consent of its owner in another Member State. *Hoffmann-La Roche*[172] set out the principles and conditions for repackaging and he cited all the relevant extracts from the Judgment regarding the four conditions. He also referred to *Pfizer v Eurim-Pharm*[173] and identified two additional points made by the Court in that Judgment:

> No use of the trade mark in a manner liable to impair the guarantee of origin takes place in a case such as the one in point where, according to the findings of the national court and the terms of the question submitted by it, a parallel importer had repackaged a pharmaceutical product merely by replacing the outer wrapping without touching the internal packaging and by making the trade mark affixed by the manufacturer on the internal packaging visible through the new external wrapping.[174]

The Court had noted that in such circumstances the original condition of the product would not be affected. The second point was the finding that inserting in the external packaging a leaflet containing information relating to the medicinal product would not affect the above condition.

10.134 The third case he found relevant was *Centrafarm v American Home Products*.[175] A trade mark proprietor was entitled to prevent the marketing of a product by a third party in a Member State even if that product had been lawfully marketed in another Member State under another mark by the same proprietor. The Court accepted that it might be lawful to use different trade marks for the same product in different Member States, but it also stressed that if that choice formed part of a system of marketing intended to partition the markets artificially it would constitute a disguised restriction on intra-Community trade.

10.135 Finally, AG Jacobs referred to *Hag II*,[176] the case that had opened a new direction for the trade mark jurisprudence of the Court since it accepted that trade marks were an essential element in the system of undistorted competition envisaged by the Treaty:

> Under such a system, an undertaking must be in a position to keep its customers by virtue of the quality of its products and services, something which is possible only if there are distinctive marks which enable customers to identify those products and services. For the trade mark to be able to fulfil this role, it must offer a guarantee that all goods bearing it have been produced under the control of a single undertaking which is accountable for their quality.[177]

---

[169] Reproduced in point 36.
[170] C-78/70 [1971] ECR 487.
[171] C-9/93 [1994] ECR I-2789.
[172] C-102/77 [1978] ECR 1139.
[173] C-1/81 [1981] ECR 2913.
[174] Ibid, paragraph 10.
[175] C-3/78 [1978] ECR 1823.
[176] C-10/89 [1990] ECR I-3711.
[177] Ibid, paragraph 13.

(ii) Article 7: Exhaustion of rights and the Directive The Advocate General noted that **10.136**
the epithet 'first' in the title of the Directive as well as the Third Recital of the Preamble showed that the approximation envisaged therein was not complete, but once the Community legislature had adopted specific provisions dealing with exhaustion then the issue should be considered in the terms of the relevant legislation:

> That does not however mean that Articles [28] and [30] of the Treaty may be disregarded entirely. On the contrary, the Directive must be interpreted in the light of the Treaty provisions. If there were any conflict between them and the Directive, the conflict would have to be resolved by giving precedence to the Treaty provisions, which are a primary source of law. Clearly a directive adopted under Article 95 of the Treaty for the purpose of approximating the laws of the Member States could not derogate from the fundamental rules of the Treaty on the free movement of goods.[178]

However, as his Opinion would show, there was no such conflict between the free movement of goods rules and the provisions of the Directive.

(iii) Exhaustion of rights and repackaged goods: A detailed analysis Under the free **10.137**
movement of goods rules the Treaty applied a Community-wide doctrine of exhaustion:

> The justification for that approach is that if the proprietor of the right could preclude the importation and sale of products marketed in another Member State by him or with his consent, he would be able to partition the national markets and thus restrict trade between Member States, even though such a restriction is not necessary to protect the substance of the right ... What matters for the application of the exhaustion principle, according to the case law of the Court, is not whether the owner of the right obtains a fair reward from the sale, but whether he consents to it.[179]

He identified two types of repackaging. In situation A the internal packaging was not altered **10.138**
and the products were placed in a new external packaging on which the importer affixed the trade mark. In situation B the new packaging was designed in such a way that the original trade mark applied on the internal packaging remained visible. The second scenario was examined in *Pfizer v Eurim-Pharm*[180] and found not to impair the trade mark's function as a guarantee of origin; according to his reading of the case, the Court did not even have to consider the application of the second sentence of Article 36. He believed that the same reasoning should be applied in situation A because the crucial factor was not whether the parallel importer affixed the trade mark to the goods or merely allowed the original mark to remain visible, but whether it interfered with the goods in such a way that it is was no longer possible to be certain that their original condition had not been affected. He deduced that:

> the trade mark cannot be used to prevent the sale of repackaged goods where the use of different packages in different Member States has led to a partitioning of the market and where it is established that the repackaging cannot affect the original condition of the goods.[181]

(iv) The scope of Article 36: The fundamental interests protected by trade mark rights In **10.139**
order to identify the scope of Article 36 in a positive way he turned to the justification of trade mark protection. The scope of trade mark systems was twofold: to enable traders to protect the

---

[178] Point 54.
[179] Point 61.
[180] C-1/81 [1981] ECR 2913.
[181] Point 70.

reputation of their goods and prevent the theft of their goodwill by unscrupulous competitors and to enable consumers to make informed purchasing choices on the basis of the assumption that goods sold under the same name emanated from the same source and would, in normal circumstances, be of uniform quality.

> In so far as the trade mark protects the interests of consumers by acting as a guarantee that all goods bearing the mark are of the same commercial origin, that is known, in the Court's terminology, as the essential function of the trade mark. Those two aspects of trade mark protection are of course two sides of the same coin.[182]

10.140 Compartmentalizing the Common Market, on the other hand, was not the purpose of trade mark law. He accepted that trade mark proprietors would feel aggrieved when price differentials were caused by direct or indirect price controls that were outside their control. However, price controls would not justify the exercise of trade mark rights in order to block parallel imports. For trade marks in particular, where the reward issue did not underlie the right in the way it did patents,

> none of the interests protected by a trade mark ... is affected by rules which restrict the trade mark owner's freedom to fix his own selling prices. The trade mark's ability to function as a guarantee of origin is not impaired simply because the exhaustion principle is applied to goods which have been placed on the market at a regulated price.[183]

10.141 **(v) The main criteria for the application of Article 36** The following criteria would be relevant for assessing whether Article 36 should be applied. First, had the condition of the goods been so modified that they could no longer truthfully be described as the goods of the trade mark owner, with the result that the parallel importer would unfairly be taking advantage of the reputation of the trade mark? Second, had the condition of the goods been modified in such a way that their further marketing under the trade mark might unfairly damage the reputation of the trade mark? Third, would consumers be misled, in the sense that they would assume that the goods had been produced under the control of the trade mark owner and so possess the quality normally associated with the trade mark when in fact, as a result of the repackaging, the goods have been interfered with in such a way that their original quality may have been impaired? The answers to these questions would, in the end, provide the answer to the ultimate question: had the trade mark's function as a guarantee of origin been compromised? He suggested that an affirmative answer to any of the three questions would justify the exercise of trade mark rights against parallel imports.

10.142 **(vi) Partitioning the market** Responding to the argument raised by trade mark proprietors that the starting point should be whether they had deliberately chosen different packaging in order to partition the market artificially, AG Jacobs argued that this was a secondary issue.[184]

10.143 It was a mistake to construe the second sentence as an exception to a general rule laid down in the first sentence. A better interpretation would be to read the two sentences of Article 36 jointly, as a whole:

> Either a measure is justified on one of the grounds listed in Article [36] or it is not justified. One of the factors to be taken into account in assessing justification is whether the measure leads

---

[182] Point 72.
[183] Point 76.
[184] Point 81.

to a disguised restriction, in other words whether the measure, though ostensibly intended to safeguard industrial property, is really designed to achieve some other purpose unconnected with trade mark protection. If a trade mark owner uses the trade mark in order to exclude parallel imports of his own goods when the sale of those goods does not threaten the interests protected by the specific subject-matter of the trade mark and does not compromise the essential function of the trade mark by preventing it from acting as a guarantee of origin, then the presumption inevitably arises that the trade mark is being used for some other purpose.[185]

Accordingly, the fact that the partitioning of the markets occurred because of national rules governing size was irrelevant.   10.144

(vii) **Prior notice and indication of repackaging: The additional criteria**   Finally, the Advocate General considered the scope of the last two conditions imposed by Hoffmann-La Roche. Here there were two particular issues he had to examine. Should the repackaged product indicate that the repackaging had taken place without the consent of the proprietor?[186] And should failure to mention the name of the manufacturer on the new packaging justify the exercise of trade mark rights?[187] The Advocate General noted that there might be cases where the prior notice requirement might be superfluous. However, it did appear to be a reasonable requirement, in particular in relation to pharmaceuticals, making it easier for the trade mark proprietor to fight counterfeiters. He suggested that in addition to the notification the parallel importer should also provide the trade mark proprietor with a sample of the new packaging, in order to point out any deficiencies and demand them to be corrected. Otherwise it should be allowed to object to the marketing of the repackaged product.[188] The requirement that the entity responsible for the repackaging should be indicated on the packaging was also justified. Otherwise, consumers would have the impression that the trade mark proprietor was responsible for the repackaging, including defects. However, he did not deem it necessary to indicate that the product had been repackaged without the authorization of the trade mark proprietor. This would taint the product as being not entirely legitimate. Similarly, he suggested that indicating the manufacturer on the product should not be essential, at least where the manufacturer was identified on the original internal packaging.   10.145

(viii) **The position under the Directive: Exhaustion of the rights conferred by a trade mark**   The position would not differ at all under the directive. Article 7 was modelled according to the Advocate General on the free movement of goods rules. Its heading and language confirmed this. Article 7(1) provided the general principle and Article 7(2) recognized that the principle would not apply where there existed 'legitimate reasons ... especially where the condition of the goods is changed or impaired after they have been put on the market'. In addition, the vagueness of Article 7(2) required it to be interpreted following the jurisprudence of the Court in this area. He also suggested that the brevity of the provision was evidence that its purpose was not to codify the existing case law. The Advocate General doubted whether the Council had the authority to 'codify' in the first place; he believed that the Council wanted to let the case law evolve in this area. The word 'especially' strengthened this argument showing the non-exhaustive nature of the provision.   10.146

---

[185] Point 82.
[186] As mentioned in C-232/94 *MPA Pharma GmbH v Rhône-Poulenc Pharma GmbH* [1996] ECR I-3671.
[187] As suggested in Joined Cases C-71/94 to C-73/94.
[188] He noted that some information should, in any case, be provided on the packaging according to Council Directive 92/97 on the labelling of medicinal products for human use and on package leaflets [1992] OJ L113/8.

10.147 He rejected the argument that the Directive had tilted the balance towards trade mark proprietors in that exhaustion covered only goods marketed in their original state. This, he found, would make it difficult to reconcile Article 7(1) with Article 7(2), in particular following his analysis of situations where there would be no legitimate reason for blocking parallel imports, and would disregard the fact that Article 7 had been modelled on the free movement of goods jurisprudence of the Court; finally it would go against the aim of the Directive and raise rather than remove trade barriers.

10.148 **(ix) The burden of proof** Balancing the impact of his Opinion he rejected the submission of the United Kingdom Government that had intervened in the proceedings claiming that Article 7 had reversed the burden of proof. He found both the provision and the free movement of goods case law to be silent on this issue. *Hoffmann-La Roche* appeared to suggest that in principle the trade mark owner had the right to object and would only lose the right in exceptional circumstances. However, he viewed this as an interference with a procedural matter that should remain under the remit of national autonomy, according to the principle of procedural autonomy. In the absence of any specific rules of Community law it was for the domestic legal system of each Member State to determine the conditions governing the implementation of directly effective Community law, provided that the procedural rules applicable to claims founded on Community law were not less favourable than those governing similar actions of a domestic nature and would not render the exercise of rights arising from Community law practically impossible or excessively difficult.[189]

10.149 Considering whether in the cases before the Court the application of rules as to the burden of proof might have the effect of making virtually impossible or excessively difficult the exercise of the right of the trade mark proprietor to prevent unjustified use of its trade mark by a third party compared with the right of the parallel importer to market trade marked goods, provided that no harm was done to the legitimate interests of the trade mark owners he noted that none of the parties should be subject to a *probatio diabolica*: be compelled to prove something which could not be proved or could only be proved with the utmost difficulty. This could be the case for a parallel importer that would have to prove that the repackaging could not affect the original condition of the goods, because proving a negative would be extremely difficult. It would not, however, be unreasonable to be required to show that it had taken adequate safeguards when repackaging goods. On the other hand, a trade mark proprietor of an intellectual property right should do more than make a general reference to the industrial property exception. 'A coherent argument is required, showing precisely how the interest in question will be impaired. I do not think that the Court means to lay down technical rules about the incidence of the burden of proof or about the standard of proof.'[190]

10.150 **(x) Identifying the issues** Having established the basic principles he identified the relevant issues in each particular case. In the first of the Danish cases (C-427/93) Paranova's repackaging affected only the outer packaging of the products; in the two most intrusive instances a label was placed on the inner packaging and a spray manufactured by Paranova was included together with the original product in the new outer packaging. The Advocate

---

[189] For an extensive discussion of this issue see AG Sharpston's Opinion in paragraphs 10.356 and following, below.
[190] Point 105, citing C-174/82 *Sandoz* [1983] ECR 2445, a case concerning the marketing authorization of food products enriched with vitamins in The Netherlands, as an example of the balanced approach sought by the Court.

General suggested that replacing the outer packaging and placing the trade mark on the new packaging did not appear to affect the interests protected by trade mark rights.[191]

10.151 Further, the repackaging did not appear to affect the original condition of the products. The only reservations he had concerned the insertion of a product emanating from a different source; the national court would have to determine, first, whether the statement appearing on the packaging of the product was sufficiently clear to disperse the impression that the products emanated from the same source and, secondly, responsibility for the additional product might still be attributed to the trade mark owner irrespective of the statement.

10.152 In respect of the second of the Danish cases (C-429/93), the Advocate General suggested that the repackaging of the inhalers appeared to be unproblematic. He identified three possible problems that the national court had to consider as questions of fact: the possibility of misprinting the use-by date on the new label; the possibility of mistakes in the translation of the instructions; and the risk of contamination of the inhalers during their repackaging.

10.153 Regarding Case C-436/93, the national court would have to consider the relevance of the non-inclusion of the photo-sensitivity warning, taking into account whether the information appeared on the original packaging.

10.154 In Case C-71/94 the national court would have to focus on three issues. First, the effect that the severed blister packs and the window on the packaging would have on the image of the mark rather than the condition of the product. He accepted that 'part of the function of the trade mark is to enable its proprietor to protect his commercial reputation'[192] and accordingly there could be cases where trade mark law could be relied upon against the marketing of shoddily repackaged products. The type of the product could influence the decision on the presentation of the product. The Advocate General believed this might be more important for luxury than for functional—including pharmaceutical—goods. Another relevant factor would be the way the product reached the consumer; appearance could be less important for a pharmacist dispensing the product than a consumer reaching for the product on a shelf. Second, whether the severing of the blister packs involved a risk of contamination, noting that according to the evidence it appeared that in some cases the severing of the pack occurred too close to the pills themselves. Third, whether the interruption of the series of days of the week at the back of the pack and the repetition of particular days could adversely affect the way the pills were consumed resulting in overdoses.

10.155 The only objectionable issue in Case C-72/94 would be the effect of the window on the image of the trade mark.

10.156 In Case C-73/94, the first issue related to the effect the severing of the packs would have both on the image of the trade mark and the actual condition of the product.

10.157 The second concerned the addition of the word 'forte' as an indication that the imported products corresponded to the stronger version of the locally marketed version. The Advocate General distinguished this case from the third of the Danish cases, *American Home Products*

---

[191] Point 109.
[192] Point 115.

v Centrafarm, because here the starting point was the use of a common trade mark.[193] So, if in principle the parallel imported product could be resold in Germany, then it would indeed be necessary to add the word 'forte' in order to alleviate any possibility of consumer confusion regarding the strength of the product.

10.158 Finally, in Case C-232/94 the Advocate General focused on the information regarding repackaging that appeared on the package. Ultimately the adequacy or not of the content and the presentation of the information was for the national court to decide. Still, he believed that the actual content was sufficient; as to presentation he remarked that if 'the information is written in such a way that a consumer with normal eyesight, exercising a normal degree of attentiveness, would be able to understand who is responsible for the repackaging, that is sufficient'.[194]

10.159 (xi) **Applying the principles** Advocate General Jacobs chose to respond to the questions submitted to the Court by providing first a set of general propositions, a framework that national courts could apply, and only then by suggesting a number of specific rulings. He noted that both were applicable in interpreting both Article 7 of the Directive and the free movement of goods provisions of the Treaty.

10.160 *Joined Cases C-427/93, C-429/93, and C-436/93   The general propositions* The trade mark proprietor should not invoke its rights in order to block the marketing of parallel imported goods placed in new external packaging unless the repackaging was capable of affecting the original condition of the goods or otherwise impairing the reputation of the trade mark.

10.161 In the case of pharmaceuticals, the party carrying out the repackaging of the goods should in principle inform the trade mark proprietor and provide a specimen of the repackaged product. It should also indicate on the repackaged product that it is responsible for the repackaging but did not have to mention the manufacturer of the goods or state that the proprietor of the trade mark has not authorized the repackaging.

10.162 Whether repackaging was capable of affecting the original condition of the goods or otherwise impairing the reputation of the trade mark was a question of fact to be determined by the national court in accordance with its own domestic rules regarding procedural matters, including the burden and the standard of proof and the admissibility of evidence. Those rules should not treat claims founded on Community law less favourably than claims founded on national law or make the enforcement of rights arising from Community law unduly difficult.

10.163 *The specific rulings* In the case of pharmaceuticals originally packaged in blister packs, phials, flasks, or aerosol containers, and where the person responsible for the repackaging simply removed the packs etc from their original external packaging and placed them in new external packaging without cutting or opening them, in suitable premises, with competent staff, and taking all reasonable safeguards, there was not in principle any ground for finding that the original condition of the goods might be affected, and the national court was precluded from making such a finding in the absence of specific evidence. The fact that

---

[193] An issue that has been revisited by AG Jacobs from a different perspective: see paragraphs 10.89 and following, above.
[194] Point 128.

the party responsible for the repackaging used the same colour scheme for the repackaged product as the owner of the trade mark was irrelevant. Where the party responsible for the repackaging inserted in the new packaging additional goods the trade mark proprietor might in principle object to the further marketing of the repackaged goods under the trade mark, unless the origin of the additional material was indicated in such a way as to dispel any impression that the trade mark proprietor was responsible for it.

Joined Cases C-71/94 and C-73/94 8-120 *The general propositions* The Advocate General covered with the same general principles the case where the goods were repackaged in such a way that the trade mark affixed to the internal packaging remained visible. **10.164**

The specific rulings He repeated the first ruling mentioned above, but added that if the blister packs were severed the trade mark proprietor was entitled to object to the further marketing of the goods if the national court considered that practice was capable of affecting the original condition of the goods. The trade mark proprietor was entitled to object to the further marketing of repackaged goods not only where the repackaging affected the technical quality of the goods but also where it gave them a shoddy appearance capable of damaging the reputation of the trade mark. The same would apply where the severing of the blister packs affected information printed on their backs allocating the pills to specific days of the week for a certain period of time, if the national court considered that the interruption of the series of days caused unacceptable confusion for the consumer or endangered his health or was detrimental to the reputation of the trade mark. **10.165**

A trade mark owner that sold two versions of a product in Member State A under the names 'Sermion' and 'Sermion forte' and sold in Member State B under the name 'Sermion' a product which corresponded to 'Sermion forte' in Member State A, could not invoke its trade mark rights in order to prevent the resale in Member State A of goods which it had placed on the market in Member State B, even though the reseller described them as 'Sermion forte'. **10.166**

Case C-232/94 The Advocate General added to the general propositions mentioned above that the indication as to who was responsible for the repackaging should be written in such a way that a person with normal eyesight, exercising a normal degree of attentiveness, would be able to understand it. **10.167**

(d) The Judgment of the Court in joined Cases C-427, 429, and 436/93[195]

The Court constructed its Judgment starting from the basic principles—the relationship between Article 7 and the free movement of goods rules and its interpretation—and then moved to the factual scenarios of the joined cases. Accordingly, it dealt with the questions in a logical rather than formalistic sequence. **10.168**

(i) Article 7 of the Directive and Article 36 EC The Court started its analysis by looking at the first question in Case C-436/93[196] in order to untangle the relationship between Article 7 of the Directive and the free movement of goods rules of the Treaty. It restated that where Community directives provided for the harmonization of measures ensuring the protection of the interests covered by Article 36, 'any national measure relating thereto **10.169**

---

[195] C-427/93 *Bristol Myers Squibb v Paranova A/S*, C-429/93 *CH Boehringer Sohn, Boehringer Ingelheim KG and Boehringer Ingelheim A/S v Paranova A/S*, and C-436/93 *Bayer Aktiengesellschaft and Bayer Danmark A/S v Paranova A/S* [1996] ECR I-3457.
[196] See paragraphs 10.123 and accompanying text.

must be assessed in relation to the provisions of that directive and not Articles [34] to [36] of the Treaty'.[197] Article 7 clearly constituted such a provision—it was worded in general terms and regulated comprehensively the exhaustion of trade mark rights for products traded in the Community,[198] and national exhaustion rules had to be assessed accordingly. Albeit, Article 7 itself had to be interpreted in the light of Article 30, since it constituted part of secondary legislation.

10.170 Accordingly the answer to that question should be that the reliance on trade mark rights in order to prevent intra-Community parallel imports where the importer had repackaged the product and reaffixed the trade mark without the owner's authorization should be assessed on the basis of the combined provisions of national trade mark law and Article 7 of the Directive, interpreted in the light of Article 36.

10.171 (ii) *The interpretation of Article 7(1)* The Court then moved to the interpretation of Article 7 through its answer to the first question in Cases C-427/93 and 429/93.[199] Article 7(1) provided the general rule and it was framed in analogy with Articles 34 and 36 of the Treaty and the case law of the Court that the owner of a trade mark protected by the legislation of a Member State could not rely on that legislation to prevent the importation or marketing of a product which was put on the market in another Member State by the proprietor or with its consent.

10.172 The Court rejected the argument favouring trade mark proprietors that the provision conferred on the parallel importer only the right to resell the products in the form in which the trade mark owner had put them on the market in another Member State and that the proprietor's exclusive right to affix the trade mark was not exhausted. Subjugating the provision to the power of its case law, the Court stressed that the exclusive right to affix a trade mark to a product should in certain circumstances be regarded as exhausted in order to allow parallel imports. To accept the contrary argument would imply a major alteration to the Treaty's free movement of goods rules:

> There is nothing to suggest that Article 7 of the Directive is intended to restrict the scope of that case law. Nor would such an effect be permissible, since a directive cannot justify obstacles in intra-Community trade save within the bounds set by the Treaty rules. The Court's case law shows that the prohibition on quantitative restrictions and measures having equivalent effect applies not only to national measures but also to those emanating from Community institutions.[200]

Accordingly the answer to that question should be that, with the exception of the circumstances defined in Article 7(2), Article 7(1) precluded the owner of a trade mark from relying on its rights to prevent an importer from marketing a product which had been put on the market in another Member State by the owner or with its consent, even if that importer had repackaged the product and reaffixed the trade mark to it without the owner's authorization.

10.173 (iii) *The interpretation of Article 7(2).* The Court brought together the remaining questions in order to define the Article 7(2) circumstances it had mentioned above. It

---

[197] *Bristol Myers Squibb* (n 195), paragraph 25.
[198] Note that the Court avoided stating that Article 7 regulated exhaustion of trade mark rights in general. At this stage it appeared to limit its scope to intra-Community exhaustion.
[199] See paragraphs 10.119 above and accompanying text.
[200] *Bristol Myers Squibb* (n 195), paragraph 36.

considered jointly the second question in Cases C-427/93 and C-429/93, the third and fourth questions in Case C-427/93, and the second, third, fourth, and fifth questions in Case C-436/93.

10.174 It identified three particular issues that troubled the national courts. First, whether the Article 36 case law of the Court remained relevant; second, the significance of the concept of artificial partitioning of the markets; and third, the significance and interpretation of the concept of the adverse effect on the original condition of the product. It added a fourth part where it discussed the remaining conditions that had to be fulfilled. In terms of language analysis the Court highlighted the use of the word 'especially'. This indicated that the situation described in the provision was only an example.

10.175 It then positioned Article 7 in its wider context, in order to delineate properly the role of Article 7(2). Article 7 pursued the same aim with Article 36 EC; it intended to reconcile the fundamental interest in protecting trade mark rights with the fundamental interest in the free movement of goods. As a result the two provisions should be interpreted in the same way and the Article 36 case law of the Court should be the basis for determining the scope of Article 7(2).

10.176 *Article 7(2) and the case law of the court* According to that case law, derogations from the free movement of goods principle were allowed only to the extent they were justified in order to safeguard the rights that constitute the specific subject-matter of the industrial and commercial property in question. For trade marks the Court repeated its findings on their essential function and specific subject-matter it had established in its jurisprudence.

10.177 The effect of this definition of the specific subject-matter was that the owner of a national trade mark right could not rely on the relevant national legislation in order to oppose the importation or marketing of a product which had been put on the market in another Member State by the owner or with its consent. Trade mark rights, the Court stressed, were not intended 'to allow their owners to partition national markets and thus promote the retention of price differences'.[201] It recognized the peculiarities of the market for pharmaceuticals where price differences might be the result of other factors, but repeated that 'distortions ... must be remedied by measures of the Community authorities and not by another Member State introducing measures which are incompatible with the rules on the free movement of goods'.[202]

10.178 Turning to the guarantee of origin function, the Court restated its findings in *Hoffmann-La Roche*[203] and the conditions it had established therein regarding the exercise of trade marks and supplemented in the other two simultaneous parallel import cases.[204]

10.179 *Artificial partitioning of the markets between Member States* The Courts starting point was that blocking the marketing of repackaged products would contribute to the partitioning of markets between Member States, in particular where the owner had placed the same

---

[201] *Bristol Myers Squibb* (n 195), paragraph 46.
[202] Ibid, paragraph 46.
[203] C-102/77 *Hoffmann-La Roche & Co AG and Hoffmann-La Roche AG* [1978] ECR 1139.
[204] C-71/94 *Eurim-Pharm Arzneimittel GmbH v Beiersdorf AG*, C-72/94 *Boehringer Ingelheim KG*, () and C-73/94 *Farmitalia Carlo Erba GmbH* [1996] ECR I-3603; and C-232/94 *MPA Pharma GmbH v Rhône-Poulenc Pharma GmbH* [1996] ECR I-3671.

product on the market in several Member States in various forms of packaging, and the product might be imported from one Member State and put on the market in another by a parallel importer.

10.180 Accordingly, the trade mark proprietor could not oppose repackaging in new external packaging or the modification of the contents of an original external packet when the size of the packaging in the exporting Member State could not be marketed in the importing Member State:

> by reason, in particular, of a rule authorising packaging only of a certain size or a national practice to the same effect, sickness insurance rules making the reimbursement of medical expenses depend on the size of the packaging, or well-established medical prescription practices based, inter alia, on standard sizes recommended by professional groups and sickness insurance institutions.[205]

10.181 The Court went further, holding that the same principle should apply even if the trade mark owner used in the importing Member State a number of sizes of packaging and one of those sizes was also used in the exporting Member State. 'Partitioning of the markets would exist if the importer were able to sell the product in only part of his market.'[206]

10.182 Balancing between the rights of trade mark proprietors and the interests of parallel importers, the Court clarified that repackaging would not gain automatic clearance. The owner could oppose it when the importer could achieve the packaging that might be marketed in the importing Member State by less intrusive means; for example, by affixing to the original external or inner packaging new labels in the language of the importing Member State, by adding new user instructions or information in that language, or by replacing an additional article not capable of gaining approval in the importing Member State with a similar approved article.

> The power of the owner of trade mark rights protected in a Member State to oppose the marketing of repackaged products under the trade mark should be limited only in so far as the repackaging undertaken by the importer is necessary in order to market the product in the Member State of importation.[207]

10.183 Taking a step back, the Court added that 'artificial partitioning' did not require the importer to prove that the trade mark proprietor had deliberately sought to partition the markets by using different forms of packaging. Once again employing the essential function of a trade mark, this time as a tool for limiting protection, the Court added that it had been using the concept with the intention to stress that the owner of a trade mark might always rely on its rights to oppose the marketing of repackaged products when such action was justified by the need to safeguard the essential function of the trade mark. In this case the partitioning would not be artificial.

10.184 *Adverse effect on the original condition of the product* The Court, first, noted that the concept referred to the condition of the product inside the packaging. It recalled that in *Hoffmann-La Roche*[208] it had held that, in order to determine whether there was a risk of

---

[205] *Bristol Myers Squibb* (n 195), paragraph 53.
[206] Ibid, paragraph 54.
[207] Ibid, paragraph 56.
[208] C-102/77 *Hoffman-La Roche & Co AG and Hoffmann-La Roche AG* [1978] ECR 1139.

the product being exposed to tampering or to influences affecting its original condition, account should be taken of the nature of the product and the method of repackaging. Following the principles developed in the same case in respect of pharmaceutical products, the Court ruled that 'the mere removal of blister packs, flasks, phials, ampoules or inhalers from their original external packaging and their replacement in new external packaging cannot affect the original condition of the product inside the packaging'.[209]

10.185 It rejected the specific claims of the trade mark owners—for example, the risk of combining blister packs with different use-by dates in the same outer packaging—outright: 'It is not possible for each hypothetical risk of isolated error to suffice to confer on the trade mark owner the right to oppose any repackaging of pharmaceutical products in new external packaging.'[210] The same applied to the remaining contested operations: the fixing of self-stick labels to flasks, phials, ampoules, or inhalers, the addition to the packaging of new user instructions or information in the language of the Member State of importation, or the insertion of an extra article from a source other than the trade mark owner. It found that they would not affect the original condition of the product inside the packaging.

10.186 Giving some recognition to the arguments of trade mark owners it accepted that:

> the original condition of the product inside the packaging might be indirectly affected where, for example: the external or inner packaging of the repackaged product, or a new set of user instructions or information, omits certain important information or gives inaccurate information concerning the nature, composition, effect, use or storage of the product, or an extra article inserted into the packaging by the importer and designed for the ingestion and dosage of the product does not comply with the method of use and the doses envisaged by the manufacturer.[211]

Ultimately this was a question that the national court had to consider. However, the Court indicated that such problems could be resolved by the parallel importer providing additional information.

10.187 **(iv) The remaining requirements** The Court acknowledged that the above conclusion conferred 'on the importer certain rights which, in normal circumstances, are reserved for the trade mark owner himself'.[212] To safeguard the interests of trade mark proprietors against any misuse of those rights the Court reiterated the requirements it had established in *Hoffmann-La Roche*.[213]

10.188 *Indication of repackaging* It started with the requirement of including an indication on the outer packaging of who was responsible for the repackaging of the product. It agreed with the Advocate General that the national court had to assess whether the indication was printed in such a way as to be understood by a person with normal eyesight, exercising a normal degree of attentiveness.

10.189 It did not, though, consider the content that would satisfy the requirement in a positive way. It simply held that it was not necessary to make a further express statement that the

---

[209] *Bristol Myers Squibb*, paragraph 61.
[210] Ibid, paragraph 63.
[211] Ibid, paragraph 65.
[212] Ibid, paragraph 68; note the language used by the Court: The parallel importer appears to obtain a right rather than a licence to perform some actions that would otherwise constitute an infringement.
[213] C-102/77 [1978] ECR 1139.

repackaging occurred without the authorization of the trade mark owner. Such a statement would imply that the repackaged product was not entirely legitimate. And when an extra article from a source other than the trade mark owner had been added into the packaging, then the parallel importer should ensure that its origin was clearly indicated, dispelling any impression that the trade mark proprietor was responsible for it.

10.190 *Indication of manufacturer* Citing *Pfizer*,[214] it added that it might also be required to incorporate on the external packaging a clear indication as to who manufactured the product. Apart from its informational value this would also serve the interests of the trade mark proprietor ensuring that the consumer of the product would not be led to believe that the importer was the owner of the trade mark or that the product was manufactured under its supervision.

10.191 *The fifth condition—inappropriate presentation and reputation* The Court gave some ground to trade mark proprietors by recognizing that the reputation of a trade mark might suffer from an inappropriate presentation of the repackaged product.

> In such a case, the trade mark owner has a legitimate interest, related to the specific subject-matter of the trade mark right, in being able to oppose the marketing of the product. In assessing whether the presentation of the repackaged product is liable to damage the reputation of the trade mark, account must be taken of the nature of the product and the market for which it is intended.[215]

For pharmaceuticals in particular, the presentation of a product might be capable of inspiring public confidence; 'defective, poor quality or untidy packaging could damage the trade mark's reputation'.[216]

10.192 Taking another step back, this time towards the direction of parallel importers, the Court indicated that the channels of trade for the particular product should also be taken into account. For products sold to hospitals presentation would be of little importance. For those reaching the consumers through pharmacies, presentation would be more significant, even if the product had been prescribed by a doctor.

10.193 *Advance notice* The final requirement was that the parallel importer should give advance notice to the trade mark proprietor. The proprietor might also require to be given a specimen of the repackaged product in order to ensure that the repackaging would not directly or indirectly affect the original condition of the product and that the presentation would not be likely to damage the reputation of the trade mark.

(e) The Judgment of the Court in joined cases C-71/94 to C-73/94[217]

10.194 This time the Court focused on the questions from the perspective of the free movement of goods rules rather than the Directive. In essence, however, the viewpoint remained the same. The national court had not mentioned the Directive in the questions it referred to the Court; still the Court noted that although a directive would not of itself impose obligations on an individual when applying national law, whether adopted before or after the Directive,

---

[214] C-1/81 [1981] ECR 2913.
[215] *Bristol Myers Squibb* (n 195), paragraph 75.
[216] Ibid, paragraph 76.
[217] C-71/94 *Eurim-Pharm Arzneimittel GmbH v Beirsdorf AG*, C-72/94 *Boehringer Ingelheim KG*, and C-73/94 *Farmitalia Carlo Erba GmbH* [1996] ECR I-3603.

the national court that had to interpret that law should do so, as far as possible, in the light of the wording and the purpose of the directive. And in any case the Court had just decided in *Bristol Myers Squibb*[218] that Article 7 of the Directive and Article 36 of the Treaty shared a common purpose but also the same interpretive principles.

10.195 Indeed, the Court repeated the analysis it had followed in *Bristol Myers Squibb* almost verbatim; the distinguishing feature in this case was the way the original trade mark became visible to the public, and the Court found that this did not really make a difference:

> With regard to the arguments raised in these cases, there is no reason in principle to distinguish between the situation where a third party reaffixes the trade mark after repackaging the product, and the situation where, after the product has been repackaged, he uses the trade mark affixed to the original packaging by the manufacturer by leaving it visible through new external packaging or by retaining the original external packaging itself.[219]

In all these cases the critical question remained the same: whether, having regard to the essential function of a trade mark, the power of the owner to oppose the use of the trade mark by a third party after the product had been repackaged fell within the specific subject-matter of the trade mark right.

10.196 The additional point made by the Court in this case was that it was for the national court to ascertain whether the insertion into single external packaging of both original external packaging and loose blister packs constituted an untidy form of packaging liable to damage the reputation of the trade mark. The same applied to the severing of the blister packs.

(f) The Judgment of the Court in Case C-232/94[220]

10.197 Here the Court simply restated the five principles having stressed that the trade mark could not oppose repackaging in new external packaging when the packet size used by the owner in the Member State where the importer purchased the product could not be marketed as a result of a national rule, national practice, sickness insurance rules, or well-established medical prescription practices.

2. *Pharmacia & Upjohn*: Replacing the Trade Mark; The Requirement of Necessity

10.198 The links between free movement of goods and the replacing of a trade mark were re-examined by the Court in *Pharmacia & Upjohn SA v Paranova A/S*,[221] a reference from the Danish Maritime and Commercial Court. The Upjohn Group marketed in the Community the antibiotic clindamycin in a variety of forms using the trade marks 'Dalacin' in Denmark, Germany, and Spain, 'Dalacine' in France, and 'Dalacin C' in the remaining Member States. The variations were due to an agreement concluded in 1968 between the Upjohn Group and American Home Products Corp, another pharmaceutical company. Paranova purchased 'Dalacine' capsules in packets of 100 in France in order to market them in smaller batches in Denmark as 'Dalacin'. Further, it imported 'Dalacin C' injection

---

[218] C-427/93 *Bristol Myers Squibb v Paranova A/S*, C-429/93 *CH Boehringer Sohn, Boehringer Ingelheim KG and Boehringer Ingelheim A/S v Paranova A/S*, and C-436/93 *Bayer Aktiengesellschaft and Bayer Danmark A/S v Paranova A/S* [1996] ECR I-3457.
[219] C-71/94 to C-73/94, paragraph 38.
[220] C-232/94 *MPA Pharma GmbH v Rhône-Poulenc Pharma GmbH* [1996] ECR I-3671.
[221] C-337/95 *Pharmacia & Upjohn v Paranova A/S* [1997] ECR I-0013.

phials from Greece and marketed them as 'Dalacin' in Denmark. When the Upjohn Group initiated trade mark infringement proceedings Paranova argued that the different trade marks used in Denmark, France, and Greece were in essence the same trade mark; this meant that the Upjohn Group's rights had been exhausted. And as a second defence it maintained that a marketing system built on variants of the same mark amounted to artificial partitioning of the markets.

10.199 The Danish court referred the following Questions to the Court.

1. Do Article 7 of Council Directive 89/104/EEC of 21 December 1988 to approximate the laws of the Member States relating to trade marks and/or Articles [34] and [36] of the EC Treaty preclude the proprietor of a trade mark from relying on its right under national trademark law as the basis for opposing a third party's purchasing a pharmaceutical product in a Member State, repackaging it in that third party's own packaging, to which it affixes trade mark X belonging to the trade-mark proprietor, and marketing the product in another Member State, in the case where the pharmaceutical product in question is marketed by the trade mark proprietor or with its consent in the Member State of purchase under trade mark Y and an identical pharmaceutical product is marketed by the trade-mark proprietor or with its consent in the abovementioned second Member State under trade mark X?
2. Does it have any bearing on the reply to Question 1 whether the trade-mark proprietor's use of different trade marks in the country in which the importer purchases the product and in that in which the importer sells the product is attributable to subjective circumstances particular to the trade-mark proprietor? If the answer is yes, is the importer required to adduce evidence that the use of different trade marks is or was intended artificially to partition the markets (reference is made in this connection to the Court's judgment of 10 October 1978 in Case 3/78 Centrafarm v American Home Products Corporation)?
3. Does it have any bearing on the reply to Question 1 whether the trade-mark proprietor's use of different trade marks in the country in which the importer purchases the product and in that in which the importer sells the product is attributable to objective circumstances outside the control of the trade-mark proprietor, including, in particular, requirements of national health authorities or the trade-mark rights of third parties?[222]

(a) The Opinion of Advocate General Jacobs

10.200 Advocate General Jacobs noted that the main reason behind the reference was the uncertainty of the national court regarding the intent of the trade mark proprietor to partition the market, following *Bristol Myers Squibb*.[223]

10.201 **(i) Rejecting the requirement of intention.** Reviewing the case law of the Court, the Advocate General explained that possible inconsistencies between the position in *American Home Products*,[224] where according to one view the Court required some sort of intention to partition the market, and *Hoffmann-La Roche*,[225] where it leaned towards a more objective test, had been resolved by *Bristol Myers Squibb*.[226] For the Advocate General the prevalence of the essential function of the trade mark and the specific subject-matter of the right, compared with the subjective concept of intention, underpinned further the position adopted by the Court. Similarly, the factors that led the trade mark proprietor to adopt different marks in different Member States should be irrelevant when considering whether

---

[222] Reproduced in paragraph 11.
[223] [1996] ECR I-3457.
[224] C-3/78 [1978] ECR 1823.
[225] C-102/77 [1978] ECR 1139.
[226] Point 35.

the importer might affix a different trade mark. It would be illogical to link the legality of the parallel importer's conduct with the subjective behaviour of the trade mark proprietor.

Intention, on the other hand, should be relevant where it could be shown that the trade mark proprietor's practice was indeed intended to partition markets, 'that will in itself be sufficient to preclude reliance by him on his trade-mark rights to oppose affixing of a different mark by the importer'.[227] This was after all what the Court said, or at least meant to say, in *American Home Products*.[228]

10.202

(ii) **The requirement of necessity** The Advocate General observed that on the other hand, the Court had indicated in *Bristol Myers Squibb* and *Ballantine* that the requirement of necessity should act as a balancing factor between the rights of the trade mark proprietor and those of the parallel importer. He suggested that the principle should be applied to rebranding. For repackaging, the Court had already referred to rules or national practices, sickness insurance rules governing the reimbursement of medical expenses, and well-established medical prescription practices as reasons justifying repackaging.

10.203

Necessity and rebranding The same reasoning should apply to rebranding; he suggested, however, that there might be circumstances where repackaging would not be justified, but re-branding could be; 'rebranding will more often be needed in order to avoid confusion in the importing State where *ex hypothesi* an identical product has previously been sold under a different mark'.[229] At the same time there might be circumstances where rebranding would be likely to cause rather than alleviate confusion, for example if the inner and the outer packaging bore different marks.

10.204

He was against rigid categorizations of factors that should be seen as necessary commercial risks rather than reasons necessitating rebranding. Ultimately, the decisive test was 'whether in a given case prohibiting the importer from rebranding would constitute an obstacle to effective access by him to the markets of the importing State'.[230] It was for the national court to assess where each specific factor should be located. He indicated that in general, where the importer used the trade mark applied by the proprietor in the importing Member State for identical products, the criterion should be satisfied, because rebranding would ensure that there would be no confusion.

10.205

The time for assessing necessity He suggested that whether rebranding was necessary should be assessed at the time of the rebranding. He noted that the mere act of registration of a trade mark would not in itself constitute an impediment to importation; it was the exercise of the rights to oppose rebranding by the importer that should count.

10.206

(iii) **Further conditions for rebranding** The Advocate General doubted whether the same conditions that applied to repackaging should also apply to rebranding. Intrusive rebranding—for example, sticking labels with the new trade mark on the inner packaging—that could affect the condition of the product would constitute repackaging rather than rebranding.

10.207

---

[227] Point 42.
[228] According to the AG, paragraph 28 of the Judgment in C-349/95 *Frits Loendersloot v George Ballantine & Son* [1997] ECR I-6227, confirmed this.
[229] Point 50.
[230] Point 54.

10.208   He also rejected the argument that there should be an indication on the outer packaging regarding the identity of the party responsible for the rebranding; such an indication would contribute to customer confusion. He accepted, though, that rebranding should be done in a way that it would not be liable to damage the reputation of the trade mark. Similarly, the importer should give notice to the trade mark proprietor and provide a specimen if required.

10.209   **(iv) The burden of proof**   Here, he referred to his views expressed in *Bristol Myers Squibb*.[231] This was a procedural matter that should be governed by national law, provided that the procedural rules applicable to claims founded on Community law were not less favourable than those governing similar actions of a domestic nature and were not such as to render the exercise of rights flowing from Community law practically impossible or excessively difficult.

(b) The Judgment of the Court

10.210   **(i) The case law of the Court**   The Court referred first to its 'consistent'[232] case law; following a thorough review of its case law on trade mark exhaustion it cited in relation to the concept of artificial partitioning of the markets its Judgment in *Bristol Myers Squibb*: there was no requirement to show that the trade mark proprietor had deliberately sought to partition the markets between Member States. It repeated the argument that reliance on trade mark rights to oppose marketing under the relevant trade mark of products repackaged by a third party would contribute to the partitioning of markets between Member States, in particular where the proprietor had placed an identical pharmaceutical product on the market in several Member States in various forms of packaging and the product might not, in the condition it had been marketed in one Member State, be imported and placed on the market in another Member State by a parallel importer. The power of the trade mark proprietor should be limited only insofar as the repackaging undertaken by the importer was necessary in order to market the product in the importing Member State.

10.211   It then looked at the *American Home Products*[233] Judgment on rebranding. It accepted that it had held that the essential function of the trade mark would be jeopardized if it were permissible for a third party to affix the mark even to the original product and that the right to prohibit any unauthorized affixing of the trade mark fell within the specific subject-matter of the trade mark. It stressed though that it had also held that such a prohibition would constitute a disguised restriction on trade if it were established that using different trade marks for the same product in different Member States was for the purpose of artificially partitioning the markets.

10.212   **(ii) Rebranding and repackaging.**   In its decision as to whether the principles that applied to repackaging covered rebranding, the Court had to examine whether rebranding was different from repackaging. It found that there was no objective difference between re-affixing a trade mark after repackaging and replacing the original trade mark by another that was capable of justifying the condition of artificial partitioning being applied differently. Both practices led to the partitioning of the market on the one hand and unauthorized use of a trade mark by a third party on the other. Accordingly, the condition of artificial

---

[231] [1996] ECR I-3457.
[232] *Pharmacia & Upjohn*, paragraph 13.
[233] [1978] ECR 1823.

partitioning applied to both concepts in the same way. This, the Court found, also meant that there was no requirement to assess the intention of the trade mark proprietor. On the other hand, the replacement of the trade mark had to be objectively necessary. The assessment of this requirement remained in the jurisdiction of the national courts. The Court elaborated on what the national court would have to establish in order to assess the condition of the necessity.

From a positive perspective, it held that it would be: 10.213

> satisfied if, in a specific case, the prohibition imposed on the importer against replacing the trade mark hinders effective access to the markets of the importing Member State. That would be the case if the rules or practices in the importing Member State prevent the product in question from being marketed in that State under its trade mark in the exporting Member State. This is so where a rule for the protection of consumers prohibits the use, in the importing Member State, of the trade mark used in the exporting Member State on the ground that it is liable to mislead consumers.[234]

It would not be satisfied though if the replacement was 'explicable solely by the parallel importer's attempt to secure a commercial advantage'.[235]

(3) *Boehringer*: Revisiting Repackaging

The same motif characterized *Boehringer Ingelheim Pharma KG v Swingward Ltd*[236] and *Merck, Sharp and Dohme GmbH v Paranova Pharmazeutica Handels GmbH*.[237] 10.214

In the first case, capsules and inhalers were repackaged by parallel importers in the United Kingdom that employed a diverse number of tactics such as the application of stickers that did not obscure the trade mark but contained information relevant to the product, marketing in new boxes with a reproduction of the original trade mark, and marketing in new boxes with the generic name but not the original trade mark—parallel importers had not tampered with the original trade mark on the capsules but had covered the trade mark on the inhaler with a sticker bearing a generic name. 10.215

The High Court referred the following questions to the Court: 10.216

1. Can a proprietor of a trade mark use his trade mark rights to stop or hinder the import of his own goods from one Member State into another or to hinder their subsequent marketing or promotion when the importation, marketing or promotion causes no, or no substantial, harm to the specific subject-matter of his rights?
2. Is the answer to the previous question different if the ground relied on by the proprietor is that the importer or subsequent dealer is using his mark in a way which, although not prejudicial to its specific subject-matter, is not necessary?
3. If an importer of the proprietor's goods or a dealer in such imported goods needs to show that his use of the proprietor's mark is necessary, is that requirement met if it is shown that the use of the mark is reasonably required to enable him to access (a) part only of the market in the goods, or (b) the whole of the market in the goods; or does it require that the use of the mark was essential to enabling the goods to be placed on the market and if none of these, what does necessary mean?

---

[234] Paragraph 43.
[235] Paragraph 44.
[236] C-143/00 *Boehringer Ingelheim Pharma KG v Swingward Ltd* [2002] ECR I-3759.
[237] C-443/99 *Merck, Sharp and Dohme GmbH v Paranova Pharmazeutica Handels GmbH* [2002] ECR I-3703.

4. If the proprietor of a mark is, prima facie, entitled to enforce his national trade mark rights against any use of his mark on or in relation to goods which is not necessary, is it abusive conduct and a disguised restriction on trade in accordance with the second sentence of Article [36], to use that entitlement in order to hinder or exclude parallel imports of his own goods which do not threaten the specific subject-matter or essential function of the trade mark?
5. Where an importer or someone dealing in imported goods intends to use the proprietor's trade mark on or in relation to those goods and such use does and will not prejudice the specific subject matter of the mark, must he nevertheless give the proprietor advance notice of his intended use of the mark?
6. If the answer to the previous question is in the affirmative, does that mean that failure of the importer or dealer to give such notice has the effect of entitling the proprietor to restrain or hinder the importation or further commercialisation of those goods even though such importation or further commercialisation will not prejudice the specific subject-matter of the mark?
7. If an importer or someone dealing in imported goods must give prior notice to the proprietor in respect of uses of the trade mark which do not prejudice the specific subject-matter of the mark, (a) does that requirement apply to all such uses of the trade mark, including in advertising, re-labelling and repackaging or, if only some uses, which? (b) must the importer or dealer give notice to the proprietor or is it sufficient that the proprietor receives such notice? (c) how much notice must be given?
8. Is a national court of a Member State entitled, at the suit of the proprietor of trade mark rights, to order injunctions, damages, delivery up and other relief in respect of imported goods or the packaging or advertisements therefor where the making of such an order (a) stops or impedes the free movement of goods placed upon the market within the EC by the proprietor or with his consent but (b) is not for the purpose of preventing harm to the specific subject-matter of the rights and does not help to prevent such harm?[238]

10.217 The second case concerned tablets imported into Austria. The blister packs were being repackaged in new outer boxes on which the original trade mark was reaffixed; the boxes also contained leaflets with information on use and other necessary details for the marketing of the product in Austria.

10.218 The Oberlandesgericht Wien (Higher Regional Court, Vienna) referred the following question to the Court:

> Must Article 7(2) of the First Council Directive of 21 December 1988 to approximate the laws of the Member States relating to trade marks (89/104/EEC) be interpreted as meaning that a trade mark owner may oppose the marketing of a pharmaceutical product put on the market under his trade mark where the importer has repackaged it and reaffixed the trade mark and has complied with the other requirements set forth in the Court of Justice judgment in Joined Cases C-427/93, C-429/93 and C-436/93 (the product inside the packaging must not be affected, the manufacturer and origin must be clearly indicated, the reputation of the trade mark or its owner must not be damaged as a consequence of poor packaging, and the trade mark owner must be given notice before the repackaged pharmaceutical product is put on sale), but the marketability of the product would be jeopardised without such repackaging solely because a significant proportion of the consumers of pharmaceutical products in the State of importation is suspicious of pharmaceutical products which have clearly been produced for the market of another State (in which a different language is spoken) and are inside packagings which have been adapted merely by means of self-stick labels to the domestic provisions governing the sale of pharmaceutical products?[239]

---

[238] Reproduced in Point 58.
[239] Reproduced in Point 61.

(a) The Opinion of Advocate General Jacobs

10.219 Advocate General Jacobs rejected the insinuation that the repackaging requirements set by the Court were inconsistent or incoherent; perhaps such an impression was due to the fact that those requirements were relevant at different stages in the analysis of the question whether a trade mark owner might rely on its trade mark rights to prevent a parallel importer from repackaging trade marked goods.

10.220 **(i) Framing the position of the Court.** Following a review of the case law of the Court, he described its position in the following terms. The trade mark owner was prima facie justified in preventing an importer from affixing the trade mark on the new packaging. However, in certain circumstances the exercise of that right might be unlawful because it would constitute a disguised restriction. The Court had held that it was essential to consider whether the repackaging was objectively necessary in order to market the product in the importing Member State. This requirement would be clearly satisfied in cases of specific rules or national practices, sickness insurance rules on reimbursement of medical expenses, and medical prescription practices. This was in contrast with cases where repackaging aimed to achieve a commercial advantage for the parallel importer. Albeit, in less clear and less extreme cases, the existence and extent of necessity both remained an uncharted territory.

10.221 **(ii) The uncertainties of the necessity requirement.** The Advocate General accepted that the necessity requirement meant that trade mark proprietors might in principle assert their trade mark rights even in the absence of actual harm or risk of harm; hence he described the balancing between the interests of trade mark proprietors and parallel importers the Court aimed to achieve.[240] He emphasized that repackaging in principle constituted a particularly intrusive form of trade mark infringement, and that in most cases, it concerned pharmaceuticals, a type of product that portrayed special features regarding quality and consumer expectations. He also stressed that if it was shown that the trade mark owner's practice of using different marks in different Member States was intended to partition markets, that would in itself be sufficient to preclude the exercise of trade mark rights to oppose affixing of a different mark by the importer.

10.222 Attempting to accommodate these factors within the general principles developed by the Court he added:

> repackaging may correctly be regarded as objectively necessary in other less black and white situations. If the national court finds as fact ... that there is widespread and substantial resistance to over-stickered boxes by the relevant consumers, and if the effect of such resistance is that the parallel importer would be effectively excluded from the market unless permitted to repackage, repackaging would to my mind certainly be regarded as objectively necessary for effective market access in the sense that is reasonably required for such access.[241]

Repackaging on the other hand should not be considered necessary if another, less intrusive, method could be found to give effective market access. The Court should also take account of the peculiarities of each product market.

10.223 **(iii) The advance notice requirement** On the requirement of advance notice the Advocate General suggested that it should be given by the parallel importer in all cases,

---

[240] Point 97.
[241] Point 110.

even where the importation was licensed by the appropriate national authorities dealing with pharmaceutical products. It should not be dependent on whether there was actual prejudice to the specific subject-matter of the mark. Failure to give notice should automatically render the repackaging an infringement. Regarding what would constitute adequate notice he suggested that a three- to four-week period should be reasonable.

(b) The Judgment of the Court in Boehringer

10.224 **(i) The specific subject-matter and the necessity requirement** The Court joined the first, second, fourth, and eighth questions of the English case as essentially seeking clarifications of the concept of the specific subject-matter of the trade mark. It repeated its case law on what constitutes the specific subject and, citing *Bristol Myers Squibb*,[242] it found that:

> it is clear from settled case law that the change brought about by any repackaging of a trade-marked pharmaceutical product—creating by its very nature the risk of interference with the original condition of the product—may be prohibited by the trade mark proprietor unless the repackaging is necessary in order to enable the marketing of the products imported in parallel and the legitimate interests of the proprietor are also safeguarded.[243]

10.225 The third question focused on the circumstances that could render repackaging necessary. The Court first clarified that it was necessary to take account of the circumstances prevailing at the time of marketing in the importing Member State which made repackaging objectively necessary for the product to be placed on that State's market. 'The trade mark proprietor's opposition to the repackaging is not justified if it hinders effective access of the imported product to the market of that State.'[244] It referred to its findings in *Bristol Myers Squibb*;[245] such circumstances could be the result of national rules or practices relating to packaging, or where sickness insurance rules made reimbursement of medical expenses dependent on a certain packaging or where well-established medical prescription practices were based, inter alia, on standard sizes recommended by professional groups and sickness insurance institutions, but not when the repackaging was based solely on the parallel importer's attempt to secure a commercial advantage. In the same case it had held that the trade mark proprietor might oppose replacement packaging where the parallel importer could reuse the original packaging by affixing an additional label to it.

10.226 **(ii) Effective market access** Here though the Court appeared to adopt a more conservative stance. Applying the familiar technique of one step backwards and then another forwards, the Court first remarked that '[r]esistance to relabelled pharmaceutical products does not always constitute an impediment to effective market access such as to make replacement packaging necessary'.[246] Then again, there may exist in a market, or a substantial part of it, such strong resistance from a significant proportion of consumers to relabelled pharmaceutical products that there must be held to be a hindrance to effective market access. In those circumstances, repackaging of the pharmaceutical products would not be explicable solely by the attempt to secure a commercial advantage. The purpose would be to achieve effective market access. National courts would have to determine the applicability of the concept of

---

[242] C-436/93 [1996] ECR I-3457.
[243] Paragraph 34.
[244] Paragraph 46.
[245] C-436/93 [1996] ECR I-3457.
[246] Paragraph 51.

effective access that was linked with the necessity requirement either as a new requirement or, at least, as determining factor.

(iii) **Advance notice** The response to the fifth, sixth, and seventh question was that the purpose of advance notice and furnishing a sample on request was to safeguard the legitimate interests of trade mark proprietors. Fulfilling it should not pose any real practical problems for parallel importers provided that the proprietors reacted within a reasonable time to the notice. If the parallel importer failed to satisfy that requirement, the trade mark proprietor might oppose the marketing of the repackaged pharmaceutical product. As to the method of giving notice, the Court required the parallel importer itself to give notice to the trade mark proprietor of the intended repackaging; notification from another source would not suffice. Finally, regarding the timing of the notice the Court held that it was appropriate to allow a reasonable time for the trade mark proprietor to react to the intended repackaging; on the other hand the parallel importer's interest in actually marketing the pharmaceutical product as soon as possible after obtaining the necessary licence from the competent authority should also be taken into account. The balancing between the two interests was for the national court to achieve, however the Court—referring to the facts of the case—considered that a period of fifteen working days seemed reasonable where the parallel importer had given notice to the trade mark proprietor and supplied simultaneously a sample of the repackaged pharmaceutical product. 10.227

(c) The Judgment of the Court in Merck

Here,[247] the Court took a parallel path with that followed in *Boehringer I*.[248] In this case the problem identified by the Austrian court was that Austrian consumers were not accustomed to pharmaceutical products that had been put on the market in another Member State with a different language. The Court repeated the above analysis and held that it was for the national court to decide whether this resistance made repackaging necessary in order to obtain effective access in the Austrian market. 10.228

(4) *Ballantine*: **Trade Mark Infringement and Policing Channels of Trade**

In *Frits Loendersloot v George Ballantine & Son Ltd*[249] the Court considered a challenge of the whisky producers' practice of affixing identification numbers on the labels, bottles, and packaging of their products. In a way it opened the line of free movement of goods cases under the new European trade mark regime.[250] The Judgment is fundamental as it reconsiders the rapport between trade mark rights and free movement of goods against a background newly dominated by positive integration. 10.229

Whisky producers started trade mark infringement proceedings in The Netherlands against Loendersloot, a transport and warehousing firm active in parallel imports. Loendersloot was removing the labels and, according to the destination market, re-affixing them or replacing them with copies having removed the identification numbers, the word 'pure', and the name of the authorized importer, occasionally substituting it with the name of 10.230

---

[247] C-443/99 [20021] ECR 1-3703.
[248] C-143/00 [2002] ECR I-3759.
[249] C-349/95 [1997] ECR I-6227.
[250] It can be taken as a starting point because any injunction granted by the national court would have taken effect after the effective date of the Directive. See the Opinion of the AG at paragraph 10.236, below.

another importer. The products where then shipped to France, Spain, United States, and Japan. Loendersloot's defence was two-pronged. First, it argued that preventing a third party from removing or reapplying a trade mark was not part of the specific subject-matter of a trade mark right. Second, it placed trade mark law within the context of free movement of goods rules and claimed that the whisky producers exercised their rights in order to eliminate parallel imports. On this second point, the whisky producers counterargued that the application of identification numbers was intended to enable the identification of defective and counterfeit products, and that in any case, it did not raise a barrier in intra-Community trade since the products could circulate within the Community in their original condition.

10.231 The Hoge Road found that Loendersloot's interference with the labels constituted trade mark infringement according to Benelux trade mark law. Still, it stayed proceedings and made a reference to the Court of Justice on the application of Article 36.

1. Is the specific subject-matter of the rights attaching to a trade mark to be regarded as including the possibility afforded to the proprietor of a trade mark under national law to oppose, with regard to alcoholic drinks manufactured by him, the removal by a third party of labels affixed by the proprietor on bottles and on the packaging containing them, and bearing his mark, after the drinks have been placed by him on the Community market in that packaging, and the subsequent reapplication of those labels by that third party or their replacement by similar labels, without thereby in any way damaging the original condition of the product?
2. In so far as the labels are replaced by other similar labels, is the position different where the third party omits the indication 'pure' appearing on the original labels and/or, as the case may be, replaces the importer's name with another name?
3. If Question 1 falls to be answered in the affirmative, but the proprietor of the trade mark avails himself of the possibility referred to in that question in order to prevent the third party from removing the identification marks which the trade mark proprietor has affixed on or underneath the labels in order to enable the trade mark proprietor to detect shortfalls within his sales organisation and thus to combat parallel trade in his products, must such an exercise of the trade mark right be regarded as a 'disguised restriction on trade between Member States' aimed at achieving an artificial compartmentalisation of the markets?
4. To what extent is the answer to Question 3 affected where the trade mark proprietor has affixed those identification marks either pursuant to a legal obligation or voluntarily, but in any event with a view to making a 'product recall' possible and/or in order to limit his product liability and/or to combat counterfeiting, or, as the case may be, solely in order to combat parallel trade?[251]

(a) The Opinion of Advocate General Jacobs

10.232 Advocate General Jacobs viewed this case as a variation on the theme of repackaging, this time covering alcoholic beverages rather than pharmaceutical products. He started by reviewing the principles developed by the Court. It is worth referring to this review in detail as a concise reminder of the case law of the Court until *Ballantine*.

10.233 (i) **The general principles** The exercise of trade mark rights amounted to a measure having equivalent effect to a quantitative restriction on imports or exports, however there were circumstances where a trade mark owner could prevent further marketing. This was linked with the essential function of a trade mark, namely to guarantee the identity of origin of the

---

[251] Reproduced in paragraph 13.

marked product to the consumer or ultimate user by enabling him without any possibility of confusion to distinguish that product from products which have another origin. Trade marks, he added, allowed their owners to attract and retain customers by the quality of their products and services; they made that possible by allowing them to be identified. 'It follows that, notwithstanding the fact that a product bearing a mark has been lawfully marketed by the owner or with his consent, the owner of a trade mark may oppose any use of the mark which is liable to impair the guarantee of origin so understood.'[252]

(ii) The application of the general principles on repackaging In *Hoffmann-La Roche*[253] the Court applied these principles to the repackaging of pharmaceutical products. The starting point in that case was that a trade mark owner could rely on its rights in one Member State to prevent an importer from marketing a product put on the market in another Member State by the owner or with its consent, where that importer had repackaged the product in new packaging to which the trade mark had been reaffixed.

10.234

There was one exception to that principle. The trade mark owner would not be able to rely on his rights, where: (i) it was established that the use of the trade mark right by the owner, having regard to the marketing system which it had adopted, would contribute to the artificial partitioning of the markets between Member States; (ii) it was shown that the repackaging could not adversely affect the original condition of the product; (iii) the owner of the mark had received prior notice before the repackaged product was put on sale; and (iv) it was stated on the new packaging by whom the product had been repackaged. (v) A fifth requirement had been added by the Court in *Bristol Myers Squibb*: the presentation of the repackaged product, in particular defective, poor quality, or untidy packaging, should not damage the reputation of the trade mark.[254] Note that the parallel importer does not appear to enjoy an automatic entitlement to repackage. The trigger is the behaviour of the trade mark proprietor.[255]

10.235

(iii) The legislative context of the Directive The questions referred to the Court focused exclusively on the interpretation of Article 36. The Advocate General suggested that from a procedural perspective the Directive was relevant because any injunction granted by the national court would relate to a post-Directive period. From a substantive perspective, he remarked that the Court had indicated in *Bristol Myers Squibb*[256] that Article 7(2) of the Directive was to be given the same interpretation as that given to Article 34 and Article 36 of the Treaty.

10.236

(iv) The applicability of Article 34 Whether relabelling was necessary or not was a question that the national court had to consider. At this stage:

10.237

> the Hoge Road's questions have to be considered on the hypothesis that parallel trade in the products concerned would not be possible unless they were relabelled. If that hypothesis is correct (which is a matter for the national courts to establish), then reliance by Ballantine and others on their trade mark rights in order to prevent relabelling clearly operates as a barrier to trade which must be justified under Article [36] of the Treaty.[257]

---

[252] Point 17.
[253] C-102/77 [1978] ECR 1139.
[254] C-436/93 [1996] ECR I-3457.
[255] Note that the same point is reiterated by AG Jacobs from the negative starting point of the trade mark proprietor who cannot rely on its rights; see 10.238, below.
[256] C-436/93 [1996] ECR I-3457.
[257] Paragraph 26.

10.238 **(v) The essential principle of the Court's jurisprudence** In order to respond to the questions, the Advocate General delineated the essential principle of *Hoffmann-La Roche* and *Bristol Myers Squibb*:

> a trade mark owner cannot rely on his trade mark rights to prevent a parallel importer from repackaging goods bearing the trade mark and from re-applying the trade mark to the repackaged goods where it is established that the use of the trade mark right by the owner will contribute to the artificial partitioning of the markets between Member States; provided that in the course of such repackaging: (i) the guarantee of origin is not impaired; (ii) the original condition of the product is not adversely affected; and (iii) the reputation of the trade mark is not damaged.[258]

He noted that the third point was also linked with the origin function because consumers confronted with inappropriate packaging might be confused regarding the origin of the product. The remaining two conditions—notice and labelling information—were more specific and more detailed compliance provisions, in particular in relation to pharmaceuticals.[259]

10.239 **(vi) Pharmaceuticals and whisky** The principles of the Court had, until then, been developed in cases involving pharmaceuticals, but there was no reason to make any distinction according to product category in respect of the essential principle. The underlying rationale remained the same. However, the nature of the product would characterize the circumstances of the case, and in some cases particular considerations would be more poignant than in others, for example labelling information could be more critical for pharmaceuticals than alcoholic drinks.

> In any event, this Court would … be going beyond its functions under Article 234 of the Treaty if it were to rule on all aspects of repackaging and relabelling which might be undertaken by parallel importers in relation to different types of product. Once the Court has spelt out the essential principle or principles, it must be left to the national courts to apply those principles in the cases before them.[260]

10.240 **(vii) Reputation considerations** He accepted that for a product like whisky, any form of shoddy repackaging or relabelling would damage the reputation of the trade mark. On the other hand he noted that relabelling would be permissible only to the extent necessary to facilitate parallel imports. This case appeared to involve less interference than in *Bristol Myers Squibb*.[261] The national court would have to conclude that 'there was a significant impairment of the presentation of the product which could affect the reputation of the trade mark'.[262]

10.241 **(viii) Partitioning of the markets** The three specific questions raised by the national court—the omission of the word 'pure' from the relabelled products, the replacement of the importers name with another name, and the removal of identification marks—were linked with the starting point of parallel import cases: artificial partitioning of the markets between Member States.

---

[258] Point 28.
[259] Contrast with the Opinion of AG Sharpston in paragraph 10.350 et seq below.
[260] Point 33. A point that has been made in other cases as well, see, eg, paragraph 10.337 below.
[261] C-427/93 *Bristol Myers Squibb*, C-429/93 *CH Boehringer Sohn, Boehringer Ingelheim KG and Boehringer Ingelheim A/S*, and C-436/93 *Bayer Aktiengesellschaft and Bayer Danmark A/S* [1996] ECR I-3457.
[262] Point 35.

Removal of the word 'pure' Loendersloot had argued that the word 'pure' had to be removed **10.242** from the label for the product to be allowed to circulate in some Member States. The Advocate General referred to *Bristol Myers Squibb* in some detail.[263] The Court had contrasted between two cases. Where repackaging was necessary because the product was marketed in one size in one Member State but could not be marketed in the same size in another Member State, the owner would be unable to rely on its rights. To the contrary: the owner should be able to oppose repackaging in cases where the importer would be able to satisfy the marketing conditions by affixing new labels or adding information in the language of the Member State of importation.

The principle was that the **10.243**

> power of the owner of trade mark rights protected in a Member State to oppose the marketing of repackaged products under the trade mark should be limited only in so far as the repackaging undertaken by the importer is necessary in order to market the product in the Member State of importation.[264]

National courts would have to apply the above principle and determine whether the removal of the word 'pure' was indeed necessary.

Replacement of the importer's name—removal of identification numbers According to the **10.244** basic principles just described:

> it is clear that, subject to compliance with the conditions designed to safeguard the origin, quality and reputation of the product, an importer must be able to relabel products where that is necessary in order to effect parallel trade; otherwise the owner of a trade mark would be able, by relying on his trade mark right, artificially to partition the markets of the Member States. It is for the national courts to determine whether that requirement is met in the present case.[265]

He sought support for his statement from the Court's account of 'artificial partitioning of **10.245** the markets' in *Bristol Meyers Squibb*.[266] The Court did not require a deliberate endeavour to partition the markets between Member States; rather, its intention was to stress that the owner of a trade mark might always rely on its rights when its opposition to parallel imports would be justified by the need to safeguard the essential function of the trade mark, in which case the resultant partitioning could not be regarded as artificial.

'Marking' obligations Responding to the final question, he accepted that at least numbers **10.246** identifying the lot to which a product belonged might serve legitimate public interests, in particular that of consumer protection. Community law had explicitly recognized that for specific product markets:[267]

> However, the extent to which a parallel importer may lawfully remove an identification number ... on the ground that it is used for the purpose of tracking parallel imports is a separate issue ... It is clear that the removal of such identification numbers cannot be resisted by virtue of trade mark rights taken alone.[268]

---

[263] In particular paragraphs 52–56 of C-427/93 *Bristol Myers Squibb*, C-429/93 *CH Boehringer Sohn, Boehringer Ingelheim KG and Boehringer Ingelheim A/S*, and C-436/93 *Bayer Aktiengesellschaft and Bayer Danmark A/S* [1996] ECR I-3457.
[264] *Bristol Myers Squibb*, paragraph 56.
[265] Point 41.
[266] Point 42.
[267] eg Council Directive 89/396 on indications or marks identifying the lot to which a food-stuff belongs: [1989] OJ L186/21.
[268] Point 43.

10.247 Concluding, he suggested that a trade mark proprietor could not exercise its rights in all the instances cases described by the Hoge Raad where it was established that the use of the trade mark right by the proprietor would contribute to the artificial partitioning of the market between Member States. He required that the relabelling should not impair the guarantee of origin, not affect adversely the original condition of the product, and not damage the reputation of the trade mark.

(b) The Judgment of the Court

10.248 The four questions were reformulated by the Court as essentially asking:

> whether Article [36] of the Treaty is to be interpreted as meaning that the owner of trade mark rights may, even if that constitutes a barrier to intra-Community trade, rely on those rights to prevent a third party from removing and then reaffixing or replacing the mark which the owner has himself affixed to products he has put on the Community market, where the original condition of the products is not affected.[269]

10.249 The Court acknowledged that according to the evidence and the position adopted by the Dutch courts Loendersloot's actions constituted infringement under Benelux law, adopted according to the Directive. However, it held that the case should be resolved according to the Directive. The exhaustion provisions of the Directive had the same primary scope as Article 36: to reconcile trade mark protection with free movement of goods. However, they were destined to produce analogous results. It accepted that in principle an injunction would raise a trade barrier. The Court noted that Article 36 allows derogations to the extent that they safeguard the specific subject-matter of the relevant right, which for trade marks was:

> in particular to guarantee to the owner that he has the exclusive right to use that mark for the purpose of putting a product on the market for the first time and thus to protect him against competitors wishing to take unfair advantage of the status and reputation of the trade mark by selling products illegally bearing it.[270]

10.250 This led to the restatement that the holder of a trade mark right in one Member State could not exercise the right to block the importation or marketing of a product that had been put on the market in another Member State by itself or with its consent. Here, the Court relied on its case law on repackaging, adding one additional caveat. The party relabelling the product must also ensure that the reputation of the trade mark was not harmed by 'inappropriate presentation'.[271] The national court should take into account 'in particular the interest of Ballantine in protecting the luxury image of their products and the considerable reputation they enjoy'.[272] This would be in addition to the requirements the Court had set in its earlier jurisprudence.[273] The Court also accepted the finding of the Dutch court that removal of the identification numbers was not necessary for the cross-border trading and marketing of whisky. Where it is established that they impede parallel imports then the parallel trader must turn to the competition provisions of the EC Treaty.

---

[269] *Ballantine*, paragraph 19.
[270] Paragraph 22.
[271] Paragraph 33.
[272] C-436/93 [1996] ECR I-3457.
[273] The trade mark owner must be notified; a specimen must be made available on demand; and the particulars of the person responsible for the relabelling must appear on the product.

Finally, regarding the removal of the word 'pure' and the importer's name from the labels, the Court decided that such acts should be tolerated only if it could be proved that they constituted requirements for the lawful marketing of whisky in a national market, since at this stage the European Union had not reached full harmonization on labelling issues.[274] In such case, re-labelling should cause the minimum possible prejudice to the specific subject-matter of the right. **10.251**

(5) *Dior*: Beyond the Origin Function

The Court reinforced the new approach in *Parfums Christian Dior SA v Evora*,[275] another reference from Dutch courts. The Dior companies held a number of Benelux trade mark registrations for the containers and packaging of cosmetic products and were seeking to enforce their rights against Evora, a company operating a chain of chemists' shops that was not part of Dior's distribution network. Evora's promotional campaign incorporated in advertising leaflets pictures of containers and packaging that related clearly and directly to Dior products offered for sale. This manner of advertising was common amongst similar retailers. **10.252**

Dior complained that the advertising campaign was not in accordance with the luxurious and prestigious image of Dior's brands. It argued that the expression 'condition of the goods' articulated in Article 7(2) of the Directive covered the physical as well as the 'mental condition' of the goods, referring to the 'allure, prestigious image and aura of luxury surrounding the goods, resulting from the manner in which the trade mark owner has chosen to present and advertise the goods using his trade mark rights'.[276] Evora argued, first, that advertising in a manner that was customary to retailers in the relevant sector would not infringe the Dior's rights and, second, that the provisions of the Directive and the free movement of goods provisions of the Treaty should preclude Dior from relying on its rights in order to stop its advertising campaign. **10.253**

The Hoge Road referred a number of questions to the Court of Justice, despite the fact that at the time of the reference the Directive had not yet been implemented into Benelux law. The implementation deadline had passed and it considered that the interpretation of the provisions of the Directive would be of utmost urgency and relevance. **10.254**

(a) Where, in proceedings relating to trade marks in one of the Benelux countries in connection with the interpretation of the Uniform Benelux Act on Trade Marks, a question relating to the interpretation of the First Council Directive 89/104 to approximate the laws of the Member States relating to trade marks arises, is the highest national court or the Benelux Court to be regarded as the court or tribunal of the Member State against whose decisions there is no remedy under national law and which is therefore obliged under the third paragraph of Article [267] EC to make a reference to the Court of Justice?
(b) Is it in keeping with the system of the aforementioned Directive, in particular Articles 5, 6 and 7 thereof, to assume that, where it is a question of the resale of goods which have been put on the market in the Community under a trade mark by the trade mark proprietor or with his consent, the reseller is also free to use that trade mark for the purposes of bringing such further commercialisation to the attention of the public?

---

[274] Council Directive 79/112/EEC [1979] OJ L33/1.
[275] C-337/95 *Parfums Christian Dior SA* [1997] ECR I-6013; see also C-63/97 *BMW* [1999] ECR I-905, paragraphs 9.272 and following.
[276] Point 12.

(c) In the event that question (b) is answered in the affirmative, do exceptions exist to that rule?
(d) In the event that question (c) is answered in the affirmative, is there room for an exception where the advertising function of the trade mark is endangered by the fact that, as a result of the manner in which the reseller uses the trade mark in order to attract public attention in that way, he damages the luxurious and prestigious image of the trade mark?
(e) Can there be said to be 'legitimate reasons' within the meaning of Article 7 (2) of the directive where, as a result of the way in which the reseller advertises the goods, the 'mental condition' of the goods—that is to say, their allure, prestigious image and aura of luxury resulting from the manner in which the trade mark proprietor has chosen to present and advertise the goods using his trade mark rights—is altered or detracted from?
(f) Do the provisions of Articles [34] and [36] E.C. preclude the proprietor of a (picture) trade mark or a holder of copyright relating to the bottles and packaging used for his goods from making it impossible, by invoking the trade mark right or copyright, for a reseller who is free further to commercialise those goods to advertise the goods in a manner customary to retail traders in the relevant sector? Is this the case also where the reseller, as a result of the manner in which he uses the trade mark in his advertising material, damages the luxurious and prestigious image of the trade mark or the publication or reproduction takes place in circumstances such that damage may be done to the person entitled to the copyright?[277]

(a) The Opinion of Advocate General Jacobs

10.255 Advocate General Jacobs described the essential question of the case as whether a trade mark proprietor could prevent the advertising of goods placed on the market by itself or with its consent, 'in circumstances in which such advertising damages the luxurious and prestigious image of his mark. In particular, is the prevention of such advertising possible if the reseller is merely advertising in a manner customary to his trade'?[278] This time the Directive was discussed in greater detail. The Advocate General started by referring to the relevant provisions of the Directive and then turned to the Questions referred by the Hoge Raad. The relevant provisions were Article 5(3)(d) setting the proprietor's right to prevent all third parties not having the proprietor's consent from using the mark in advertising to the rights of the trade mark proprietor; Article 6 providing limitations to the exercise of trade mark rights; and Article 7 on exhaustion.

10.256 **(i) Question 1: A procedural peculiarity** The issue was whether the Hoge Raad, the Dutch court, was bound to refer the questions to the Benelux Court or the Court of Justice. The Advocate General supported that it would suffice for the purposes of Article 267 EC that the national court would adopt a final decision at the national level. It would also be in the interests of procedural economy for the Court to be given the opportunity to rule in advance of the proceedings before the Benelux court.

10.257 **(ii) Question 2: Exhaustion and advertising** Article 7 incorporated into the Directive principles that had already been developed by the Court.[279] The language of the provision precluded a trade mark owner from prohibiting 'use' of a trade mark in relation to goods

---

[277] Reproduced in paragraph 14.
[278] Point 1.
[279] Citing as an example C-427/93 *Bristol Myers Squibb*, C-429/93 *CH Boehringer Sohn, Boehringer Ingelheim KG and Boehringer Ingelheim A/S*, and C-436/93 *Bayer Aktiengesellschaft and Bayer Danmark A/S* [1996] ECR I-3457.

which have been put on the market in the Community under that trade mark by the proprietor or with his consent. If 'a reseller is free to sell products placed on the market by the trade mark owner or with his consent, it must follow that he is free, in principle, to advertise the goods also',[280] otherwise the reseller's entitlement would be rendered virtually meaningless, and even more so if we include point of sale material and displays of the product in the advertising category. The wording of Article 5(3)(d) supported his interpretation. It referred to 'using the sign on business papers and in advertising'. It would be logical to assume that the concept of 'use' in Article 7(1) covered advertising as well. Concluding, he suggested that the answer to the first question should be that a reseller should be free, as a matter of general principle, not only to resell those goods but also to use that trade mark for the purposes of bringing such sale to the attention of the public.

(iii) Questions 3, 4, and 5: The exceptions to the general principle The Advocate General found the *Bristol Myers Squibb* Judgment[281] to be a useful precedent. There the Court found that damage to a trade mark owner's reputation could be a 'legitimate reason' within the meaning of Article 7(2): 'If a trade mark owner is entitled to oppose shoddy repackaging which damages his reputation, I do not see why he should not be entitled in certain circumstances to oppose shoddy advertising which damages his reputation.'[282] Still, he drew some distinctions between the two situations. Repackaging constituted a more direct interference with the rights of the trade mark owner. However, it would only affect the perception of those viewing the repackaged products. Advertising by a reseller could reach a wider audience and have a greater effect on the reputation of the brand. **10.258**

He then found that the word 'commercialization' in Article 7(2) should be seen either as having the same meaning as 'use' in Article 7(1), in the sense that it referred to further marketing of the goods, or as clearly incorporating advertising into its meaning. Accordingly he rejected one of Evora's main arguments. At the same time he disagreed with the argument suggested by Dior that the reference to the 'condition of the goods' in Article 7(2) extended to the 'mental condition' of the goods. The Court in *Bristol Myers Squibb* had indicated that it covered the actual condition of the goods in their packaging. **10.259**

(iv) Reputation and the functions of a trade mark Advocate General Jacobs conceived the protection of reputation as a free standing concern. He agreed with the emphasis the Court placed on the function of a trade mark as an indicator of origin. However, he suggested broadening the framework of protection that was characterized by the function of a trade mark. According to his reading of *Bristol Myers Squibb*[283] the Court had indicated that it would not have necessarily required that consumers believed that the trade mark owner was in any way responsible for or connected with the undertaking which carried out the shoddy repackaging. **10.260**

> It therefore seems reasonable to conclude that, in circumstances such as those of the present case, the trade mark owner need only show risk of significant damage to his reputation, and need not show that the public believe the retailer to be connected to or authorised by him.[284]

---

[280] Point 31.
[281] C-427/93 *Bristol Myers Squibb*, C-429/93 *CH Boehringer Sohn, Boehringer Ingelheim KG and Boehringer Ingelheim A/S*, and C-436/93 *Bayer Aktiengesellschaft and Bayer Danmark A/S* [1996] ECR I-3457.
[282] Point 36.
[283] Referring eg to paragraph 47 of that Judgment.
[284] Point 49.

10.261 His discussion of origin in likelihood of confusion cases remained valid.[285] Choosing the middle ground, he noted that:

> the origin theory, understood more broadly, recognises that marks deserve protection because they symbolise qualities associated by consumers with certain goods or services and guarantee that the goods or services measure up to expectations. It is in that broader sense that the origin function has been understood by the Court ... in HAG II.[286]

All the other functions, be it communication, investment, or advertising, were derivatives of the origin function. 'Accordingly, it follows that the circumstances in which a trade mark owner can invoke his trade mark rights in order to protect his reputation should not be construed too widely.'[287]

10.262 In order to accommodate this middle-ground approach, the Advocate General mediated his willingness to protect the reputation of a trade mark by adding the requirement that there should be a risk of significant damage to it. Concentrating on the market for luxury perfumes he cited a statement of the Commission in a decision exempting a selective distribution network:

> the distribution system notified allows the exclusive character of the contract products to be safeguarded, such exclusive character being the main reason why consumers choose them. The consumer is thus assured that the luxury product will not become an everyday product as a result of the downgrading of its image and a decrease in the level of creation.[288]

Distinguishing this case from selective distribution agreement cases, he noted that here the products had been put on the market by the trade mark owner. As a result, 'trade mark rights may be invoked to object to advertising by parallel traders only if there is a risk of significant damage to the trade mark and that risk is properly substantiated'.[289]

10.263 *Factors for assessing the risk of significant damage* Advocate General Jacobs suggested that the assessment of the risk would be a question of fact for the national court and proposed a number of factors that courts could take into account. First, whether the authorized distributors had advertised in similar ways without a complaint from the trade mark proprietor. Second, evidence that the selective distribution system set up by the trade mark owner would be objectionable under the competition provisions of the Treaty, because it would not be necessary for the relevant type of product in question. Third, the fact that the trade mark proprietor had not attempted to set up a water-tight distribution system. Qualifying further the damage to reputation risk, he noted that trade mark owners 'should not, as a general rule, be entitled to object to respectable advertising by respectable traders, even if it can be shown that there is some damage to the product's luxurious image by virtue of the fact that such advertising is inferior to that of selected distributors'.[290] Towards the other

---

[285] Citing his Opinion in C-251/95 *SABEL* [1997] ECR I-6191.
[286] Point 41.
[287] Point 42.
[288] Commission Decision 92/428 of July 24, 1992 relating to a proceeding under Article 85 EEC C-IV/33.542 *Parfums Givenchy System of Selective Distribution* [1992] OJ L236/11, at p 20 paragraph IIB(3); Commission Decision 92/33/EEC of 16 December 1991 relating to a proceeding under Article 85 EEC IV/33.242 *Yves Saint Laurent Parfums* [1992] OJ L12/24, at pp 32–33 paragraph IIB(3). The position had been upheld by the Court of First Instance in T-19 and 88/92 *Groupement D'Achat Edouard Leclerc v EC Commission* [1996] ECR II.185.
[289] Point 46.
[290] Point 51.

extreme, he accepted that the advertising for sale of luxury perfumes at cut prices joined with rolls of toilet paper and toothbrushes would be objectionable. In some cases, for example a 'novelty' shop in a seedy area, some establishments should not be able to market luxury products.

10.264 Concluding, he submitted that the owner of the trade mark might oppose use of its trade mark by a reseller in advertising that would be liable to damage significantly the reputation of the trade mark and of its owner. In the case of luxury goods such as perfumes, the damage might consist in damage to the luxurious image of the goods. In any case the risk of significant damage to the reputation of the trade mark should be properly substantiated.

10.265 **(v) Question 6: The application of Article 34 and Article 36; copyright considerations** The Advocate General reminded the Court that copyright would fall within the scope of Article 30, in particular when exploited commercially.[291] Both trade mark rights and copyrights should be taken into account in order to prevent advertising liable to damage significantly the reputation of the relevant product. The risk of significant damage to the reputation of the trade mark should be properly substantiated.

(b) The Judgment of the Court

10.266 **(i) Question 1: The admissibility issue** Following an analysis of the respective roles of the Benelux Court and the Hoge Road the Court of Justice held that when a question relating to the interpretation of the Directive was raised in proceedings in one of the Benelux Member States concerning the interpretation of the Uniform Benelux Act on Trade Marks, a court against whose decisions there was no remedy under national law—this covered both the Benelux Court and the Hoge Road—had to make a reference to the Court of Justice under Article 234. However, that obligation would lose its purpose when the question raised was substantially the same as a question which had already been the subject of a preliminary ruling in the same national proceedings.

10.267 **(ii) Question 2: Exhaustion and advertising** For the Court, the second question focused on the link between the resale of parallel imported products and advertising. It asked whether resellers, who are otherwise free to resell them, are also free to use the products' respective trade marks in order to communicate to consumers this further commercialization. The Court of Justice turned to Articles 5 and 7 of the Directive for an answer. It stated unequivocally that the right to prohibit use of a trade mark was exhausted once the marked product has been put on the market by the proprietor or with its consent and that the same should apply to the right to use the trade mark for letting consumers know that the marked product was being resold. Whether the right had been exhausted would be decided according to the Directive; however, Article 7 should be interpreted in the light of the free movement of goods principle. Otherwise, the exhaustion principle set in Article 7 would be undermined.

> When trade-marked goods have been put on the Community market by the proprietor of the trade mark or with his consent, a reseller, besides being free to resell those goods, is also free to make use of the trade mark in order to bring to the public's attention the further commercialisation of those goods.[292]

---

[291] C-55/80 and C-57/80 *Musik-Vertrieb Membran v GEMA* [1981] ECR 147.
[292] Paragraph 38.

10.268 **(iii) Questions 3, 4, and 5: The exceptions to the general principle** The Court then considered the possible exceptions to this rule. According to its interpretation the Hoge Raad wanted to learn whether any exceptions were allowed, in particular:

> where the advertising function of the trade mark is endangered by the fact that the reseller damages the luxurious and prestigious image of the trade mark, as a result of the manner in which he uses the trade mark in order to attract public attention, and where the 'mental' condition of the goods, that is to say the allure, prestigious image and aura of luxury which they have as a result of the manner in which the trade mark owner has chosen to present and advertise the goods using his trade mark rights, is changed or impaired, as a result of the way in which the reseller advertises the goods.[293]

10.269 Note that the reference to the advertising function of a trade mark appeared in the elucidation by the Court of the questions referred by the Hoge Raad rather than in its own interpretation of Article 7(2). Still, the response of the Court appears to broaden the scope of trade mark protection, whilst using a neutral and restrained language. According to Article 7(2) the exhaustion of rights rule of Article 7(1) did not apply where there were legitimate reasons for the proprietor to oppose further commercialization of trade marked goods; altering or impairing the original condition of the goods would constitute one, but the legitimate reasons were not depleted there. The use of the word 'especially' in Article 7(2) combined with the jurisprudence of the Court suggested that alteration or impairment was given only as an example.

10.270 According to the Court, the purpose of Article 7(2) was to reconcile two, now equal, interests; the 'fundamental interest in the protection of trade mark rights with the fundamental interest in the free movement of goods within the common market'.[294] This case involved prestigious, luxury goods and the reseller should 'not act unfairly in relation to the legitimate interests of the trade mark owner'.[295] Expressed positively, this meant that the reseller must endeavour to prevent the relevant advertising from affecting the value of the trade mark 'by detracting from the allure and prestigious image of the goods in question and from their aura of luxury'.[296]

10.271 But the Court then went on to limit the scope of the obligation by adding that a reseller who habitually marketed articles of the same kind—rather than of the same quality or prestige—could use methods of advertising that are customary in the relevant trade sector, even if these methods are not the same with those of the trade mark owner. The final proviso added by the Court expanded again the scope of protection available to the trade mark owner: such advertising would not, in any case, seriously damage the reputation of the trade mark.[297]

10.272 **(iv) The sixth question: The application of Article 34 and Article 36; copyright considerations** The essence of the question according to the Court was whether a prohibition

---

[293] Paragraph 39.
[294] Paragraph 42.
[295] Paragraph 45.
[296] Paragraph 45.
[297] Note that according to the Judgment the exercise of copyright covering an imported product would raise similar concerns; accordingly, the exclusive right of exploitation conferred by copyright should not prevent or restrict, for example, the importation of sound recordings of protected works that have been lawfully marketed in another Member State by the owner of the right or with its consent.

such as that sought in the main proceedings might be allowed under Article 36. Following its analysis above and the ruling in *Bristol Myers Squibb*[298] that Article 7 and the free movement of goods rules should be interpreted in the same way, the Court found that the proprietor of a trade mark might not oppose the use of the trade mark, by a reseller who habitually marketed articles of the same kind, but not necessarily of the same quality, as the trade-marked goods, in ways customary in the reseller's sector of trade, for the purpose of bringing the further commercialization of those goods to the public's attention, unless it was established that, given the specific circumstances of the case, the use of the trade mark for this purpose seriously damages the reputation of the trade mark.

10.273 Regarding copyright it underlined that Article 30 did cover copyright under industrial and commercial property and that commercial exploitation of copyright raised the same issues as that of any other industrial or commercial property.[299] Accordingly, it held that the protection conferred by copyright as regards the reproduction of protected works in a reseller's advertisement should not, in any event, be broader than that conferred on a trade mark owner in the same circumstances and repeated its holding regarding trade marks this time covering copyright.

(6) *Silhouette*: The Territorial Scope of Exhaustion

10.274 *Silhouette*,[300] a reference from the Austrian Oberster Gerichtshof, presented to the Court the scenario of territorial versus international exhaustion. Silhouette, a producer of designer spectacles and spectacle frames exercised its national trade mark rights, arising from registration of 'Silhouette', against Hartlauer, a retailer known for its low prices. Hartlauer had obtained genuine 'Silhouette' frames from a Bulgarian company to which Silhouette had sold part of its out-of-fashion stock. Silhouette had instructed its representative to agree with the purchasers of this stock that it would be made available only in Bulgaria and states of the former Union of Soviet Socialist Republics and not exported to other countries.[301] Silhouette claimed that the frames had not been put on the market of the European Economic Area by itself or with its consent. Hartlauer responded that Silhouette had not sold the frames subject to any prohibition of re-importation.

10.275 The Oberster Gerichtshof posed two questions. First, whether the true meaning of Article 7(1) of the Directive is 'that the trade mark entitles its proprietor to prohibit a third party from using the mark for goods which have been put on the market under that mark in a State which is not a Contracting State', and, second, whether a trade mark proprietor may 'seek an order that the third party cease using the trade mark for goods which have been put on the market under that mark in a State which is not a Contracting State'[302] based exclusively on Article 7(1).

---

[298] C-427/93 *Bristol Myers Squibb* [1996] ECR I-3457
[299] C-55/80 and C-57/80 *Musik-Vertrieb Membran v GEMA* [1981] ECR 147 and C-158/86 *Warner Brothers Inc and Metronome Video ApS v Erik Viuff Chrislianse* [1988] ECR 2605.
[300] C-355/96 *Silhouette International Schmied GmbH & Co KG v Hartlauer Handelsgesellschaft GmbH* [1998] ECR I-4799.
[301] The factual scenario of the case raised a number of uncertainties. First, Austrian courts were unable to establish whether the representative had acted according to its instructions; and, second, the itinerary of the frames from a warehouse in the United Kingdom to Sofia combined with a cloud over where the sale had been concluded meant that the case could be viewed as a case of re-importation of products into the EEA.
[302] Reproduced in paragraph 14.

(a) The Opinion of Advocate General Jacobs

10.276 (i) **Article 7(1): Territorial scope**   The Advocate General demarcated the scope of the first question by assuming that Silhouette had not consented to its products being resold within the European Economic Area (EEA); in addition, the referring court had not suggested that there were any legitimate reasons for Silhouette to oppose the resale of its spectacles in Austria under Article 7(2). The Court had to decide whether the Directive precluded Member States from adopting the principle of international exhaustion.

10.277 *The wording and legislative history of Article 7(1)*   He remarked that according to its wording, Article 7(1) provided only for Community wide, not for international, exhaustion. It did not require Member States to provide for international exhaustion; the ambiguity in its interpretation was whether it allowed Member States to adopt international exhaustion. Turning to the history of the provision he noted that the original proposal provided for international exhaustion; subsequently the Commission changed its stance and limited the scope of the provision to goods that had been put on the market in the Community. The language of the provision indicated that the Directive precluded international exhaustion:

> Article 7(1) spells out the circumstances in which the trade-mark rights are exhausted: it is naturally read as doing so exhaustively. In providing that the rights are exhausted when the goods are marketed in the Community, Article 7(1) is naturally understood as meaning that the rights are not exhausted when the goods are marketed in a third country. It is true that the Directive does not specifically preclude international exhaustion, but that effect can reasonably be inferred from the language. I accept that there are arguments which go the other way, but those arguments derive little support from the language of the Directive.[303]

10.278 Still, only by delineating the scope of Article 7(1) it would become clear what principle the Directive sought. 'Since the terms of the Directive are not conclusive, the aims and scope of the Directive are of crucial significance in interpreting its provisions.'[304]

10.279 *The scope of Article 7(1)—derogating from Article 5(1)*   He viewed Article 7(l) as a derogation from the rights conferred by Article 5(l), and argued that derogations should not be construed broadly: accepting that Article 7(1) allowed international exhaustion would introduce another, implied, derogation.[305] He admitted that the Recitals appeared contradictory; on the one hand the Directive did not aim to undertake full-scale approximation but rather to approximate the national provisions that most directly affected the functioning of the Common Market.[306] On the other, it intended to provide for trade marks the same protection under the legal systems of all the Member States.[307] Proponents of international exhaustion stressed the first element, opponents the second.

10.280 The Advocate General viewed Article 7 as having a broader role rather than that of a simple codification tool of the case law of the Court, which appeared to leave free Member States to choose a principle of exhaustion provided that they respected Community wide exhaustion: 'If the Directive is seen as establishing the essential terms and effects of trade-mark protection, it is difficult to argue that it leaves Member States free to opt for international

---

[303] Point 33.
[304] Point 35.
[305] Regarding the starting point in this debate see also paragraph 10.176 et seq, below.
[306] Point 4.
[307] Citing the Third Recital to the Preamble.

exhaustion. The scope of the exhaustion principle is after all central to the content of trademark rights.'[308] He reached the same conclusion from the perspective of the functioning of the internal market. If some Member States adopted international exhaustion and others did not there would be barriers to trade within the internal market, whereas the aim of the Directive was to remove such barriers. He accepted the argument that if Member States were free to adopt international exhaustion then the same products could be the subject of parallel imports into one Member State but not into another, a result incompatible with the internal market. Accepting that once goods were imported into an international exhaustion Member State, they should be allowed to circulate freely throughout the Community, would indirectly impose international exhaustion on all Member States.[309]

(ii) **The 'competence' of the Directive** He also rejected the submission of the Swedish Government that the choice of an exhaustion principle remained outside the scope of a Directive because it concerned the relations between the Member States and third countries. The Advocate General looked at the Directive from a narrower perspective. Its aim was not to regulate relations between Member States and third states but only to lay down the rights of trade mark proprietors in the Community; precluding international exhaustion would have an effect on external trade but it would not actually regulate it. Internal market measures would affect imports from third countries; this was inevitable. The Swedish argument was supplemented by the claim that the external competence in matters of intellectual property was not exclusive to the Community.[310] Here the Advocate General noted that the issue would arise only if negotiations were to be undertaken with third countries to deal with international exhaustion. Indeed, commercial policy and reciprocity considerations were among the reasons why the original provision for international exhaustion had been amended. These considerations however did not limit the material scope of a measure based on Article 114 of the Treaties.

10.281

(iii) **Commercial policy considerations** The final Swedish argument for international exhaustion was based on the case law of the Court on the function of a trade mark as an indicator of origin. Trade mark rights, it argued, should not become tools for dividing and compartmentalizing the global market. International exhaustion would break down the barriers and promote price competition. He accepted that these arguments were attractive, albeit not persuasive. First, the case law of the Court had been developed in the context of the Community and the development of a common market rather than the global market.[311]

10.282

In a way, the Advocate General admitted that trade mark rights had been limited through the origin function because they impeded the establishment of a common market; the

10.283

---

[308] Point 40.
[309] Contrast with the approach of the EFTA Court that opted for international exhaustion in Case E-2/97 *Mag Instrument Inc v California Trading Co Norway, Ulsteen* [1998] 1 CMLR 331 EFTA.
[310] Opinion 1/94 on the WTO Agreement [1994] ECR I-5267. The AG observed that some Member States and some third countries had not opted for international exhaustion and that had not been held to be contrary to the General Agreement on Tariffs and Trade. Indeed, the World Trade Organisation Agreement left, in Article 6 of the Agreement on Trade-related aspects of Intellectual Property Rights (TRIPs), the exhaustion issue an open question. On how TRIPs affects provisional measures, see C-53/96 *HERMÈS International v FHT Marketing Choice BV* [1998] ECR I-3603.
[311] C-51/75 *EMI Records v CBS United Kingdom* (1976) ECR 811 where the Court had held that its free movement of goods rules case law could not be transposed to imports from third countries.

wider role of trade marks had not really influenced the case law of the Court. International exhaustion, as he had argued, would erect rather than bring down intra-Community barriers and distort price competition within the internal market because only consumers in the international exhaustion Member States would benefit. He accepted that there was a powerful argument for international exhaustion based on the concern for free trade; however this was a commercial policy consideration that remained outside the function of the Court.

10.284 **(iv) Exhaustion and competition policy**   Finally, whatever the Court decided on exhaustion it would not affect the application of the competition provisions of the Treaty. He highlighted the outcome of cases like *EMI v CBS*[312] and *Javico International*.[313]

10.285 **(v) Exhaustion and the Community Trade Mark Regulation**   Since the Community Trade Mark Regulation formed part of the Community Trade Mark regime AG Jacobs noted that Article 13, the exhaustion provision of the Regulation, was worded in identical terms with Article 7 of the Directive. Again, the original proposal provided for international exhaustion but it was then amended to cover only goods that had been put on the market in the Community. Given the nature of the Regulation it was clear that it did not leave the adoption of an exhaustion principle in relation to the Community Trade Mark to the discretion of the Member States. Could the two provisions be interpreted differently?[314] The answer was negative since the Directive and the Regulation shared the same context, the Community's internal market. He concluded that Article 7(1):

> is to be interpreted as meaning that the proprietor of a trade mark is entitled to prevent a third party from using the mark for goods which have been put on the market under that mark outside the territory of the EEA Member States are accordingly precluded from adopting the principle of international exhaustion.[315]

10.286 **(vi) The effect of the Directive in the national legal order**   National legislation had to be interpreted consistently with the Directive. 'Provided that the legislation is capable of being interpreted in that way, the national courts are under a duty to give trade marks the same protection as if each of the provisions of the Directive had been specifically and explicitly transposed into national law.'[316] Austrian courts had to interpret the Austrian legislation in the light of Article 5(1)(a) that indicated that the trade mark proprietor should be entitled to a court order. If such an order were available under national law, even under unfair competition rather than trade mark law, it should also be made available for cases falling under Article 5(1)(a). The Advocate General went further and argued that the Court had also held that interim relief should also be provided for the protection of Community rights even where they would be unable to do so under national law.[317] The same should apply to a final injunction.

---

[312] Ibid.
[313] Citing the Opinion of AG Tesauro in C-306/96 *Javico International and Javico AG v Yves Saint Laurent Parfums SA* (1998) ECR I-1983.
[314] He cited C-270/80 *Polydor Ltd v Harlequin Record Shops Ltd* [1982] ECR 329, as an example of identical provisions being construed differently according to their respective context, the EC Treaty on the one hand and the EFTA Agreement on the other.
[315] Point 63.
[316] Point 69.
[317] C-231/89 *R. v Secretary of State for Transport Ex p. Factortame* [1990] ECR I-2433.

(b) The Judgment of the Court

(i) The territorial scope of Article 7(1) Presenting the context for its answer to the first question, the Court noted that exhaustion of the exclusive rights conferred by registration was subject to two conditions: first, that the goods had been put on the market by the proprietor or with its consent; secondly, that the relevant market was that of the EEA. The second point had been contested by Hartlauer and the Swedish Government that maintained that Article 7 had not resolved comprehensively the issue of exhaustion failing to delineate between EEA and international exhaustion. According to their interpretation, EEA exhaustion should be seen as the minimum required by the Directive, abolishing national exhaustion principles. International exhaustion provided a broader context beyond merely incorporating the EEA.

10.287

The Court though sided with the position of the Commission, supported by Austria, France, Germany, Italy, and the United Kingdom. The Directive, according to its Preamble, demanded harmonization in relation to substantive rules of central importance in the sphere of trade mark law. Accordingly, Articles 5, 6, and 7 should be construed as embodying the principle of complete harmonization and interpreted strictly. Article 7 did not leave Member States free to adopt wider than EEA exhaustion. This interpretation, the Court noted, would also be consistent with the establishment of an internal market.

10.288

The second argument submitted by the Swedish Government that the Directive, adopted according to Article 114 of the Treaties, could not interfere with relations between Member States and non-Member countries was also rejected by the Court. It remarked that Article 7 simply delineated the rights of trade mark proprietors in the Community. Community authorities could in the future conclude international agreements adopting international exhaustion.

10.289

(ii) The effect of the Directive in the national legal order On the second question, regarding the direct applicability of Article 7(1), the Court stated that Directives did not in themselves impose obligations on individuals and, as a result, they should not be relied upon in actions against individuals. National courts, though, applying national law should interpret national law, as far as possible, in the light of the wording and the purpose of the Directive.[318]

10.290

(7) *Sebago*: 'Specific' Consent

The qualitative assessment of consent started with *Sebago Inc and Ancienne Maison Dubois et Fils SA v GB-Unic SA*,[319] a reference from the Brussels Court of Appeal. Sebago, the registered proprietor of 'Sebago' and 'Docksides' for shoes in the Benelux, started trade mark infringement proceedings against GB-Unic which marketed and advertised the sale of Sebago and Docksides shoes in its hypermarkets. The shoes were genuine, manufactured in El Salvador, and supplied to GB-Unic by a parallel trader. Sebago claimed that the unauthorized importation of goods from outside the EEA constituted infringement. GB-Unic supported the fact that once goods that are similar to those imported have been marketed in the EEA by the proprietor or with its consent, then its rights have been exhausted in relation to all goods of that brand. Sebago responded that consent must relate to each individual

10.291

---

[318] C-106/89 *Marleasing* [1990] ECR I-4135.
[319] C-173/98 *Sebago Inc and Ancienne Maison Dubois & Fils SA v G-B Unie SA* [1999] ECR I-4103.

consignment imported at a particular time by a particular importer. GB-Unic's second line of defence was that Sebago had not prohibited the licensee in El Salvador from exporting its products to the Community and that this accounted to implied consent to the marketing of the shoes in the Community.[320]

10.292 The Cour d'Appel (Court of Appeal), Brussels, referred the following questions to the Court:

> Is Article 7 (1) ... to be interpreted as meaning that the right conferred by the trade mark entitles its proprietor to oppose the use of his trade mark in relation to genuine goods which have not been put on the market in the European Economic Community (extended to ... the European Economic Area) by the proprietor or with his consent, where:
>
> -the goods bearing the trade mark come directly from a country outside the European Community or the European Economic Area;
>
> -the goods bearing the trade mark come from a Member State of the European Community or the European Economic Area in which they are in transit without the consent of the proprietor of the trade mark or his representative;
>
> -if the goods were acquired in a Member State of the European Community or of the European Economic Area in which they were put on sale for the first time without the consent of the proprietor of the trade mark or his representative;
>
> -either where goods bearing the trade mark—which are identical to the genuine goods bearing the same trade mark but imported in parallel either directly or indirectly from countries outside the European Community or the European Economic Area—are, or have already been, marketed within the Community or the European Economic Area by the proprietor of the trade mark or with his consent; or
>
> -where goods bearing the trade mark—which are similar to the genuine goods bearing the same trade mark but imported in parallel either directly or indirectly from countries outside the European Community or the European Economic Area—are, or have already been, marketed within the Community or the European Economic Area by the proprietor of the trade mark or with his consent?[321]

(a) The Opinion of Advocate General Jacobs

10.293 Advocate General Jacobs identified two main issues. The first, the territorial scope of exhaustion, had been settled in *Silhouette*. Here the Court would have to resolve the second issue, whether consent in relation to the marketing of one batch of goods meant that the trade mark proprietor had exhausted its rights in relation to other batches of identical or similar goods bearing the same trade mark.

10.294 In order to set the background for answering the question, the Advocate General referred to the relevant exhaustion principle the Court had been applying in an intra-Community context:

> If a trade-mark proprietor places on the market one particular batch of goods it is only that batch of goods which he puts into circulation: obviously he does not thereby put into circulation all other batches of identical (or similar) goods remaining in his warehouse, and so he retains, in respect of those remaining batches, all such rights as he may enjoy to impose conditions of retail sale.[322]

10.295 He then turned to the contested provision and maintained that the loose wording of Article 7(1) should be linked with the reference to 'further commercialization' in Article 7(2). The

---

[320] Interestingly the existence and scope of the licence has not been established before the Belgian courts.
[321] Reproduced in point 10.
[322] Point 21.

French wording '*commercialisation ulterieure*' made it even clearer that it referred to 'subsequent dealings with individual products following first sale'.[323] The Court too had referred to the exhaustion of the 'right of resale' in *Dior*[324] and '*la commercialisation ulterieure*' in *BMW*.[325] Article 7(1) should be interpreted as meaning that where goods 'have been marketed by the trade-mark owner or with his consent within the EEA, he is not thereby precluded from exercising his trade-mark rights to oppose the importation into the EEA of other identical or similar goods bearing his mark'.[326]

(b) The Judgment of the Court

The Court of Justice restated that trade mark rights were exhausted only in respect of the individual items that had been put on the market in the EEA with the consent of the trade mark proprietor who might prohibit the use of the trade mark with regard to other individual items of the same product put on the market in the same territory without its consent. This conclusion according to the Court was justified by the language of Article 7(2) of the Directive referring to the 'further commercialization'. The relevant goods were not the product as an abstract concept but specific individualized goods that had been put on the market with the consent of the trade mark proprietor. The principle of EEA exhaustion would become devoid of substance if the rights were exhausted by the marketing of identical or similar products.

10.296

(8) *Davidoff*: 'Clear' Consent

What constitutes consent had been discussed further in joined cases *Zino Davidoff* and *Levi Strauss*[327] that had brought separately trade mark infringement proceedings in the United Kingdom in order to prevent the sale of products that parallel importers had obtained from distributors outside the EEA The parallel importers maintained that since the two trade mark owners had not specifically restricted their distributors they had implicitly consented to the importation of their products. In *Davidoff*[328] the function of batch code numbers that the importer had removed was also contested. The trade mark owner claimed that this altered the characteristics of the product whereas the importer viewed them as tools for policing trade channels.

10.297

The High Court referred the following questions to the Court of Justice:

10.298

(A) Insofar as the Directive refers to goods being put on the market in the Community with the consent of the proprietor of a mark, is it to be interpreted as including consent given expressly or implicitly and directly or indirectly?

(B) Where:
  (i) a proprietor has consented to or allowed goods to be placed in the hands of a third party in circumstances where the latter's rights to further market the goods are determined by the law of the contract of purchase under which that party acquired the goods, and
  (ii) the said law allows the vendor to impose restrictions on the further marketing or use of the goods by the purchaser but also provides that, absent the imposition by or on

---

[323] Point 22.
[324] C-337/95 *Parfums Christian Dior* [1997] ECR I-6013.
[325] C-63/97 *BMW* [1999] ECR I-905.
[326] Point 31.
[327] C-414/99 *Levi Strauss & Co and Levi Strauss (UK) Ltd*, C-415/99 *Costco Wholesale UK Ltd*, and C-416/99 *Zino Davidoff SA* [2001] ECR I-8691.
[328] See *Zino Davidoff SA (No 1)* [1999] 2 CMLR 1056; and *Zino Davidoff SA (No 2)* [2000] 2 CMLR 750.

behalf of the proprietor of effective restrictions on the purchaser's right to further market the goods, the third party acquires a right to market the goods in any country, including the Community, then, if restrictions effective according to that law to limit the third party's rights to market the goods have not been imposed, is the Directive to be interpreted so as to treat the proprietor as having consented to the right of the third party acquired thereby to market the goods in the Community?

(C) If the answer to Question (B) is in the affirmative, is it for the national courts to determine whether, in all the circumstances, effective restrictions were imposed on the third party?

(D) Is Article 7(2) of the Directive to be interpreted in such a way that legitimate reasons for the proprietor to oppose further commercialisation of his goods include any actions by a third party which affect to a substantial extent the value, allure or image of the trade mark or the goods to which it is applied?

(E) Is Article 7(2) of the Directive to be interpreted in such a way that legitimate reasons for the proprietor to oppose further commercialisation of his goods include the removal or obliteration by third parties (in whole or in part) of any markings on the goods where such removal or obliteration is not likely to cause any serious or substantial damage to the reputation of the trade mark or the goods bearing the mark?

(F) Is Article 7(2) of the Directive to be interpreted in such a way that legitimate reasons for the proprietor to oppose further commercialisation of his goods include the removal or obliteration by third parties (m whole or in part) of batch code numbers on the goods where such removal or obliteration results in the goods in question (i) offending against any part of the criminal code of a Member State (other than a part concerned with trade marks) or (ii) offending against the provisions of Directive 76/768/EEC?[329]

10.299 In *Levi Strauss* it added the following:

(1) Where goods bearing a registered trade mark have been placed on the market in a non-EEA country by the trade mark proprietor or with his consent and those goods have been imported into or sold in the EEA by a third party, is the effect of Directive 89/104/EEC (the Directive) that the trade mark proprietor is entitled to prohibit such importation or sale unless he has expressly and explicitly consented to it, or may such consent be implied?

(2) If the answer to Question 1 is that consent may be implied, is consent to be implied from the fact that the goods have been sold by the proprietor or on his behalf without contractual restrictions prohibiting resale within the EEA binding the first and all subsequent purchasers?

(3) Where goods bearing a registered trade mark have been placed on the market in a non-EEA country by the trade mark proprietor:

[A] to what extent is it relevant to or determinative of the issue whether or not there was consent by the proprietor to the placing of those goods on the market within the EEA, within the meaning of the Directive, that:

(a) the person placing the goods on the market (not being an authorised retailer) does so with the knowledge that he is the lawful owner of the goods and the goods bear no indication that they may not be placed on the market in the EEA; and/or

(b) the person placing the goods on the market (not being an authorised retailer) does so with knowledge that the trade mark proprietor objects to those goods being placed on the market within the EEA; and/or

(c) the person placing the goods on the market (not being an authorised retailer) does so with the knowledge that the trade mark proprietor objects to them being placed on the market by anyone otherwise than an authorised retailer; and/or

---

[329] Reproduced in point 14.

(d) the goods have been purchased from authorised retailers in a non-EEA country who have been informed by the proprietor that the proprietor objects to the sale of the goods by them for the purposes of resale, but who have not imposed upon purchasers from them any contractual restrictions on the manner in which the goods may be disposed of; and/or

(e) the goods have been purchased from authorised wholesalers in a non-EEA country who have been informed by the proprietor that the goods were to be sold to retailers in that non-EEA country and were not to be sold for export, but who have not imposed upon purchasers from them any contractual restrictions on the manner in which the goods may be disposed of; and/or

(f) there has or has not been communication by the proprietor to all subsequent purchasers of its goods (i.e. those between the first purchaser from the proprietor and the person placing the goods on the market in the EEA) of its objection to the sale of the goods for the purposes of resale; and/or

(g) a contractual restriction has or has not been imposed by the proprietor and made legally binding upon the first purchaser prohibiting sale for the purposes of resale to anyone other than the ultimate consumer?

[B] Does the issue of whether or not there was consent by the proprietor to the placing of those goods on the market within the EEA, within the meaning of the Directive, depend on some further or other factor or factors and, if so, which?[330]

10.300 In essence, there were two issues the Court had to decide. First, whether the proprietor's consent to import or sell the product had to be expressed or it sufficed to show implied consent. Second, if implied consent was considered sufficient, what factors could be used to imply consent, in particular whether consent could be implied from indications on the goods, contractual restrictions prohibiting resale binding the first and subsequent purchasers, or knowledge on behalf of the importer or reseller of the position of the trade mark proprietor.

(a) The Opinion of Advocate General Stix-Hackl

10.301 (i) **The existing background** Advocate General Stix-Hackl referred both to *Silhouette*[331] and *Sebago*[332] in order to settle parts of the questions that the Court had covered in those cases but also in order to provide the necessary background. The Directive according to that case law intended to enable trade mark proprietors within the EEA to oppose the importation of goods bearing their trade marks which were first placed on the market outside the EEA; and Articles 5, 6, 7 provided for complete harmonization. In this case the first contested issue was whether the existence of consent should be determined by reference to national law or Community law. Subsequently, the Court would have to elaborate on the type and characteristics of consent that would contribute to exhausting the rights of a trade mark owner.

10.302 (ii) **Consent: A Community concept** The Advocate General noted that in *Davidoff*[333] the national court had assumed that consent had to be defined according to the law that was applicable to the first contract, but this approach would go against the harmonization aim of the Directive and, given the number of transactions along the distribution chain, could reintroduce international exhaustion through a presumption of consent. Moving towards

---

[330] Reproduced in point 24.
[331] C-355/96 *Silhouette* [1998] ECR I-4799.
[332] C-173/98 *Sebago* [1999] ECR I-4103.
[333] *Zino Davidoff SA (No 1)* [1999] 2 CMLR 1056.

a definition of consent by elimination, she suggested that exhaustion had to be determined independently of the question of the national law governing the contract.

10.303 She then rejected the line of parallel importers' arguments based on property and the legitimate expectations following a change of ownership. The sole question is whether he can exploit the products bearing that mark. It is only within that context that the question of protection of legitimate expectations can arise.[334] Further, even the right to property could be restricted in its exercise provided that the restrictions corresponded to Community objectives of general interest and did not constitute a disproportionate and intolerable interference in relation to the aim pursued impairing the very substance of the rights.[335] As a result she proposed that only an interpretation that focused on the meaning and purpose of Article 7(1) would make it possible to provide an answer that took proper account of the content and function of the concept of consent. Consent had to be examined from the perspective of Community law.

10.304 (iii) **Delineating consent** Examining first the wording of the provision, she eliminated its narrow definition as an expression of intent made for the purposes of concluding a contract; 'such a construction would fail to take sufficient account of the distinction in Article 7(1) … between the marketing of goods by the trade mark proprietor and the marketing of such goods with his consent'.[336] Revisiting the development of the concept in the case law of the Court she identified two main characteristics. The first had to do with the territorial extent of consent. The Courts case law 'extended the barrier of exhaustion in the sense that consent to the placing of goods on the market could no longer relate solely to the territory of one Member State but to the entire territory of the Community'.[337] The second, with the qualities of consent: 'consent within the framework of the Courts exhaustion theory does not relate to an expression of intent by the trade mark proprietor concerning transfer but rather to the question of accountability for the sale—or marketing—of the trade-marked products'.[338] What needed to be ascertained in each case was whether the placing of the goods on the EEA market could be attributed to the proprietor.[339] Another essential prerequisite for consent was that the proprietor had, or could have availed itself of, the opportunity to exercise its rights within the EU. On the other hand, there was no need to actually exercise the right one way or the other, the mere possibility that it might have been exercised would suffice.

10.305 The Advocate General then distinguished between goods marketed inside and outside the EEA, from a teleological perspective:

> Indiscriminate application of Article 7(1) … to trade within the Community, on the one hand, and to trade from non-member countries, on the other, would fail to take account of the differences in the respective initial positions: in the case of parallel imports within the Community, transfer of the power of disposal over the trade-marked goods coincides with the placing of those goods on the market within the EEA, whereas these do not coincide in the case of parallel imports into the Community from non-member countries. This

---

[334] Point 62.
[335] C-200/96 *Metronome Musik GmbH* [1998] ECR I-1953.
[336] Point 67.
[337] Point 70.
[338] Point 73, citing C-144/81 *Keurkoop BV v Nancy Kean Gifts BV* [1982] ECR 2853.
[339] Point 73. On the other hand she also noted that consent could be equally linked with entitlement, citing the Opinion of AG Roemer in C-78/70 *Deutsche Grammophon Gesellschaft GmbH v Metro-SB-Grossmärkte*

necessarily gives rise to different possibilities in regard to control over distribution, of which appropriate account must be taken when balancing the requirements of trade mark protection against the interests of free-flowing trade.[340]

Accordingly, the trade mark proprietor's rights would be exhausted in the case of parallel imports from non-member countries if it was able, or could have been able, to control the distribution of the marked goods within the EEA.

10.306 Having explored two possible links that could lead to a presumption of consent—economic links and control—she found that ultimately they related to a single criterion: control over the initial distribution within the EEA. She reminded the Court that it was not the actual exercise of the right that was determinative, but the mere possibility that it might have been exercised.[341]

10.307 **(iv) Assessing consent** Trade mark proprietors had an exclusive right to control the distribution of their goods first marketed outside the EEA unless their conduct at the time of marketing would lead subsequent purchasers justifiably to believe that they had waived their rights. Consent could be implied rather than explicit and its assessment by national courts should be based on Community law and a consideration of all the circumstances of each individual case. She also remarked that in its case law, the Court had constantly been trying to balance between the interests underlying free movement of goods on the one hand,[342] and the rights of trade mark proprietors on the other. She cautioned, though, national courts to apply reasonable standards and resist making 'presumptions of consent'; it should not become practically impossible for the trade mark owner to rely on its exclusive right. Article 7(1), in principle, precluded the application of a national rule which constituted a general presumption of waiver.

10.308 **(v) Damage to reputation: The removal of batch codes** She went on to suggest that where there was a risk of serious damage to the reputation, image, or allure of a trade mark this could be the basis for opposing further commercialization of the marked products under Article 7(2).[343] Finally, in relation to the *Davidoff* code numbers and the argument that their removal could damage its reputation she stated:

> [The] trade mark proprietor has a legitimate interest in being able to remove such products from circulation. Consequently, it would also be necessary in the national proceedings to examine whether the damage to the reputation of the trade mark is rendered sufficiently serious by the removal or obliteration of the prescribed batch code numbers. An infringement of the cosmetics directive would be relevant in the context of trade mark rights only under this aspect.[344]

10.309 Ultimately, the legitimate reasons which might justify a trade mark proprietor in opposing further commercialization of products bearing the trade mark did not include the actions of

---

GmbH & Co KG [1971] ECR 487. It appears that this alternative approach strengthened her view that in the end all the circumstances of each individual case had to be taken into account.

[340] Point 84.
[341] Citing C-267/95 and C-268/95 *Merck & Co Inc, Merck Sharp & Dohme Ltd and Merck Sharp & Dohme International Services BV v Primecrown Ltd and Beecham Group Plc v Europharm of Worthing Ltd* [1996] ECR I-6285.
[342] Note that the AG avoided referring to the 'rights' of parallel importers.
[343] Citing C-337/95 *Parfums Christian Dior* [1997] ECR I-16013.
[344] Point 121.

third parties or circumstances that did not affect the rights constituting the specific subject-matter and essential function of the rights conferred by the trade mark.

(b) The Judgment of the Court

10.310 The Court focused on the questions relating to Article 7(1). Its answers meant that the questions relating to Article 7(2) did not have to be answered, at least at this stage.

10.311 **(i) The Article 7(1) questions: Interpreting the concept of consent** Having repeated the main points it had resolved in its earlier case law the Court focused on the requirements for establishing consent. Before considering whether consent might be implied the Court dealt with the fundamental issue of whether the concept had to be interpreted uniformly throughout the community legal order. Being a major component of Article 7, consent constituted the decisive factor in the extinction of the rights arising from Article 5(1):

> If the concept of consent were a matter for the national laws of the Member States, the consequence for trade mark proprietors could be that protection would vary according to the legal system concerned. The objective of the same protection under the legal systems of all the Member States set out in the ninth recital … would not be attained.[345]

It was clear that consent had to be interpreted uniformly.

10.312 **(ii) The requirements for consent** The first requirement—and in essence the answer to the first question of the *Levi* cases—was that because of its effect consent 'must be so expressed that an intention to renounce those rights is unequivocally demonstrated'.[346] An express statement of consent would normally satisfy this requirement. However, in some cases consent might be inferred from facts and circumstances prior to, simultaneous with, or subsequent to the placing of the goods on the market outside the EEA which, in the view of the national court, 'unequivocally demonstrate that the proprietor has renounced his rights'.[347] The second requirement, that also constituted the answer to the second question in both the *Levi* and the *Davidoff* references, was that consent had to be expressed positively; this led to five more specific requirements ensuring that courts would not find deemed consent to be sufficient. For implied consent this meant that the factors taken into consideration should unequivocally demonstrate that the trade mark proprietor had renounced any intention to enforce his exclusive rights. For the burden of proof, it meant that it was for the trader alleging consent to prove it and not for the trade mark proprietor to demonstrate its absence. Third, it led to the finding that implied consent could not be inferred from the mere silence of the trade mark proprietor. Fourth, implied consent could not be inferred from the fact that a trade mark proprietor had not communicated its opposition to marketing within the EEA or from the fact that the goods did not carry a warning that it was prohibited to place them on the market within the EEA. And finally, consent could not be inferred from the fact that the trade mark proprietor transferred ownership of the goods bearing the mark without imposing contractual reservations or from the fact that, according to the law governing the contract, the property right transferred included, in the absence of such reservations, an unlimited right of resale or a right to market the goods subsequently within the EEA.

---

[345] Paragraph 42.
[346] Paragraph 45.
[347] Paragraph 46.

10.313 The next condition had to do with the consequences of the importer's ignorance of the trade mark proprietor's expressed opposition to the imports, a response to Question 3(a) (ii)–(v) of the *Levi* reference. The Court found that since consent could not be inferred from silence, the exclusive rights of the trade mark proprietor should not depend on an express prohibition of marketing in the EEA or the repetition of such a prohibition in the product's distribution chain. The fact that the importer was unaware of the proprietor's objections should not be relevant in the assessment of consent.

> The national rules on the enforceability of sales restrictions against third parties are not, therefore, relevant to the resolution of a dispute between the proprietor of a trade mark and a subsequent trader in the distribution chain concerning the preservation or extinction of the rights conferred by the trade mark.[348]

(9) *Makro*: Goods put on the Market in the EEA

10.314 *Makro*[349] asked the Court to decide whether the criteria set out in *Zino Davidoff* and *Levis Strauss*[350] could be applied where the goods were first put on the market in the EEA. Diesel was the owner of Benelux registrations for the word mark DIESEL. A Spanish company called Distributions Italian Fashion SA was the distributor of Diesel goods in Spain, Portugal, and Andorra. They had entered into an exclusive distribution agreement with another Spanish company called Flexi Casual SA, which granted Flexi Casual exclusive selling rights in Spain, Portugal, and Andorra for a range of goods, including shoes, and which allowed them to conduct 'market tests' to determine marketing requirements. Distributions Italian Fashion SA granted Flexi Casual a licence authorizing it to manufacture and distribute shoes of its own design so that those goods could be offered to Diesel for distribution or for the 'assignment of the manufacturing licence'. Flexi Casual granted a licence to a Spanish company called Cosmos World SL to manufacture and sell shoes, bags, and belts bearing the Diesel trade mark.

10.315 Makro sold shoes bearing the mark Diesel which they had acquired from two Spanish undertakings which had bought them from Cosmos. Diesel claimed that it had never consented to the marketing of the shoes by Cosmos and brought an action against Makro and one of Makro's partners, Deelnemingmij Nedema BV. The Dutch Court granted the injunction, a decision which was upheld on appeal.

10.316 The applicant appealed to the Hoge Raad claiming that Diesel's rights were exhausted because Cosmos had marketed the shoes with Diesel's consent. The Hoge Raad stayed the proceedings and referred the following questions to the Court for a preliminary ruling:

> (1) In the case where goods bearing a trade mark proprietor's mark have first been placed on the market within the EEA, but not by him or with his express consent, must the same criteria be applied in determining whether this has occurred with the (implied) consent of the trade mark proprietor, within the meaning of Article 7(1) of [Directive 89/104], as are applied in the case where such goods have previously been placed on the market outside the EEA by the trade mark proprietor or with his consent?
> (2) If the answer to Question 1 is in the negative, what criteria—whether or not derived (in part) from the judgment of the Court of Justice in Case C-9/93 *IHT Internationale*

---

[348] Paragraph 65.
[349] C-324/08 *Makro Zelfbedieningsgroothandel CV, Metro Cash & Carry BV and Remo Zaandam BV v Diesel SpA* [2009] ECR I-10019.
[350] C-414/99 to C-416/99 *Zino Davidoff* and *Levi Strauss* [2001] ECR I-8691.

> *Heiztechnik and Danzinger* [1994] ECR I-2789—must be applied in the first case referred to in that question in order to determine whether the trade mark proprietor has given (implied) consent within the meaning of the First Directive relating to trade marks?[351]

10.317 The Court of Justice concluded firstly that there was nothing in the Judgement in *Zino Davidoff* and *Levi Strauss* which was unique to the factual circumstances of that case and that the requirements for proving implied consent set out in that Judgement were expressed in general terms, with no distinction being made whether marketing first occurred outside the EEA or within it. Furthermore, the Court of Justice held that such a distinction would run counter to the system established by Directive 89/104.[352]

> According to the very wording of Article 7(1) of that directive, the Community rule of exhaustion at issue in the present case can apply only to goods which have been put on the market in the EEA with the consent of the proprietor of the trade mark concerned. In other words, for the purposes of the extinction of the exclusive rights of the trade mark proprietor laid down in Article 5 of that directive, what is important is only the fact that the goods in question have been marketed within the EEA.[353]

(10) *Peak Holding*: 'Putting Goods on the Market'

10.318 *Peak Holding AB v Axolin-Elinor*[354] looks at the concept of putting goods on the market for the purposes of Article 7(1) of the Directive following an often intricate itinerary.

10.319 Factory Outlet, a Swedish company controlled by Axolin-Elinor, marketed in Sweden genuine 'Peak Performance' garments, the trade mark held by Peak Holding. The garments belonged to earlier collections and were sold at half their original price. Peak Holding brought trade mark infringement proceedings targeting the marketing conditions of the sale. The case focused on a particular consignment of garments, that according to Peak Holding, consisted of garments that had been originally offered for sale by Peak Holding in Denmark; the garments that were not sold were returned to the warehouse and subsequently sold to COPAD, a French company, under restrictions regarding resale; mainly that the goods were not to be resold in European countries, except Russia and Slovenia, with the further exception of 5 per cent that could be resold in France. Factory Outlet on the other hand supported that it had acquired the consignment from a Swedish company and was not aware of any restrictions regarding resale. According to the evidence of the case the consignment never left the territory of the EEA during the contested period of time.

10.320 The Swedish referring court posed the following questions. First, whether goods are considered to have been put on the market when the trade mark proprietor has imported them into the common market with the intention of selling them but the sale has not materialized. Second, if the answer to the first question is in the affirmative, whether exhaustion can be interrupted by returning the goods to a warehouse. Third, whether goods that have been sold to another company in the common market with a resale restriction are considered to have been put on the common market, and fourth, whether the contractual exception to the resale restrictions should affect the answer to the third question.

---

[351] *Makro*, paragraph 17.
[352] Paragraph 29.
[353] Paragraph 30.
[354] C-16/03 *Peak Holding AB v Axolin-Elinor AB* [2004] ECR I-11313.

In respect of the first question, Peak Holding, supported by the Commission in this, submitted that rights are exhausted by actual sales rather than hypotheses. Axolin-Elinor focused on customs procedures supporting that rights are exhausted by importation, customs clearance, and warehousing of the goods in the EEA with a view to sale; in any case offering for sale, even without success, should suffice. **10.321**

(a) The Opinion of Advocate General Stix-Hackl

The Advocate General examined Article 7(1) first from a literal perspective concluding that internal transactions, for example the transfer of goods bearing the mark to a retail subsidiary, or preparatory acts, like the importation by the proprietor of goods from non-member countries which have been manufactured there on its behalf, did not put the goods on the market. For goods manufactured outside the EEA, she added that the trade mark proprietor might have not yet decided upon importation whether the goods were to be sold for the first time in the EEA; so importing the goods in to the EEA should not necessarily mean putting the goods on the market. **10.322**

To resolve this she turned to a systematic interpretation of the provision linking it with Article 5(3) that inter alia prohibited 'offering the goods, or putting them on the market or stocking them for these purposes under that sign'. Whether the meaning was the same in both provisions remained unanswered and as a last resort she employed a teleological interpretation; in essence a balancing exercise. From an economic point of view the critical point was the disposal of the goods bearing the mark. From a legal perspective the critical point was the transfer of the right of disposal rather than a change in legal ownership. **10.323**

Regarding the third and the fourth question, the Advocate General suggested that once the goods bearing the mark were put on the market in the EEA by the trade mark proprietor itself, exhaustion of rights arose by operation of law, irrespective of the contract between the proprietor and the purchaser. Breach of territorial restrictions on sale which the proprietor might have imposed on purchasers might only give rise to claims under the contract of sale but would be irrelevant under trade mark law. **10.324**

(b) The Judgment of the Court

The Court started its analysis by noting the complete harmonization effect of Articles 5 and 7 of the Directive; whether goods were 'put on the market' was decisive in the application of these provisions and should be interpreted in a uniform manner. And since the wording of the term did not in itself solve the interpretive dilemma the Court had to turn to the scheme and objectives of the Directive. Article 5 provides the general rule, that trade mark rights are exclusive rights that include the prevention of imports; Article 7 is the exception to the general rule providing for exhaustion. The Community legislature allowed the trade mark proprietor to control the initial marketing of the marked goods in the EEA but not their further marketing. **10.325**

The mechanism of exhaustion would be triggered by a 'sale which allows the proprietor to realise the economic value of his trade mark'.[355] Importing the goods with a view to selling them or offering them for sale in the EEA would not be enough: **10.326**

> Such acts do not transfer to third parties the right to dispose of the goods bearing the trade mark. They do not allow the proprietor to realise the economic value of the trade

---

[355] Paragraph 40.

mark. Even after such acts, the proprietor retains his interest in maintaining complete control over the goods bearing his trade mark, in order in particular to ensure their quality.[356]

Offering a product for sale without actually selling it did not satisfy the exhaustion requirements.

10.327 Regarding the third question, the arguments put before the Court contested whether the contractual imposition of a resale prohibition is equivalent to retaining trade mark rights or whether exhaustion takes place by operation by law and breaching the prohibition should be considered simple breach of contract. The Court observed that Article 7(1) of the Directive does not refer to an additional requirement of consent regarding further marketing. 'Exhaustion occurs solely by virtue of the putting on the market in the EEA by the proprietor'.[357] Contractual stipulations do not preclude exhaustion.

(11) *Coty*: Offering Testers and Putting Goods on the Market

10.328 In *Coty*,[358] a request for a preliminary ruling came about as a result of an action brought for trade mark infringement by perfume manufacturers Coty against Simex. As a result of a test purchase, Coty had obtained two 'testers' containing perfume bearing the 'Davidoff Cool Water Man' brand. Although the testers were original bottles, and contained original perfume, they did not include the original seal and were furthermore labelled 'Demonstration'. The packaging of the testers also differed from the original goods; firstly because of the lettering on the box and also because of the presence of the word 'Demonstration' on the front of the box and the statement 'Not for Sale' on one side. Coty's serial numbers indicated that the products had been delivered to one of its authorized specialist dealers established in Singapore and the retail establishment the testers had been bought at had informed Coty that the testers had been obtained from Simex.

10.329 Coty claimed that the testers had been put on the market for the first time in the EEA without their consent. Specifically, they argued that the testers were supplied exclusively to its authorized specialist dealers as advertising material and, as such, were not meant to be passed on to customers. Under the contracts with those dealers, Coty retained ownership of the testers. Simex claimed that the trade mark had been exhausted as the testers had been put on the market in the EEA with Coty's consent.

10.330 The Regional Court dismissed Coty's application on the basis that the trade mark had been exhausted. Even though the testers were marked as not for sale, the Court found that the testers were given to the authorized specialist dealers with the authority to use the perfume they contained, and that consequently the goods were put on the market within the meaning of Article 7 of Directive 89/104 and Article 13 of Regulation No 40/94. The Court held that the principle of exhaustion could not be restricted or invalidated by contractual restrictions. On appeal, the Higher Regional Court, citing in particular the Judgment in *Peak Holding*,[359] queried this decision, noting that the essential conditions for goods to be 'put on the market' are the transfer of the power of disposal of the goods and the realization

---

[356] Paragraph 42.
[357] Paragraph 53.
[358] C-127/09 *Coty Prestige Lancaster Group GmbH v Simex Trading AG* [2010] ECR I-04965.
[359] C-16/03 *Peak Holding AB v Axolin-Elinor AB* [2004] ECR I-11313.

of their economic value. The fact that Coty remained the owners of the testers by virtue of the contracts with their authorized specialist dealers, with only their contents being made available for use, meant that the authorized specialist dealer only had a limited power of disposal and also that Coty could not have realized the economic value of the goods, as no sale had taken place.

In those circumstances, the Higher Regional Court referred the following question to the Court of Justice for a preliminary ruling: **10.331**

> Are goods put on the market within the meaning of Article 13(1) of Regulation (EC) No 40/94 and Article 7 of Directive 89/104/EEC if 'perfume testers' are made available to contractually-bound intermediaries without transfer of ownership and with a prohibition on sale, so that those intermediaries are able to allow potential customers to use the contents of the goods for test purposes, the goods bearing a notice stating that they may not be sold, the recall of the goods by the manufacturer/trade mark proprietor at any time remaining contractually possible and the presentation of the goods being significantly different from the goods usually put on the market by the manufacturer/trade mark proprietor in that it is plainer?[360]

The Court distinguished the case from *Peak Holding*, which had essentially dealt with the question of whether certain acts fell within the meaning of 'being put on the market'.[361] Rather, this case concerned the issue of whether by virtue of their activities Coty had implicitly consented to Simex placing the testers on the market. Citing *Zino Davidoff* and *Levi Strauss*, the Court noted the circumstances in which implied consent could not be inferred, but stated that even though it was therefore for the national court to assess whether there was express or implied consent, 'certain factors' did not indicate a clear renunciation of the exclusive rights provided for in Article 5 of Directive 89/104. In particular, the Court held that the fact that the packaging included the word 'Demonstration' and also the statement 'Not for Sale' reflected Coty's intention and led to a conclusion (in the absence of evidence to the contrary) that Coty had not consented to the goods being put on the market in the EEA within the meaning of Article 7(1) of Directive 89/104.[362] **10.332**

In the circumstances, the Court found that: **10.333**

> In circumstances such as those of the main proceedings, where 'perfume testers' are made available, without transfer of ownership and with a prohibition on sale, to intermediaries who are contractually bound to the trade mark proprietor for the purpose of allowing their customers to test the contents, where the trade mark proprietor may at any time recall those goods and where the presentation of the goods is clearly distinguishable from that of the bottles of perfume normally made available to the intermediaries by the trade mark proprietor, the fact that those testers are bottles of perfume which bear not only the word 'Demonstration' but also the statement 'Not for Sale' precludes, in the absence of any evidence to the contrary, which it is for the national court to assess, a finding that the trade mark proprietor impliedly consented to putting them on the market.[363]

---

[360] Paragraph 26.
[361] Paragraph 33.
[362] Paragraph 48.
[363] Ibid, see also *eBay*, discussed at paragraph 9.201 et seq.

(12) *Boehringer II*: Revisiting Repackaging, Overstickering, and Re-boxing

10.334 The Judgment of the Court in *Boehringer*[364] was not the end of the story. The Court of Appeal came back seeking further clarifications.[365] The High Court, somewhat provocatively, interpreted *Boehringer I* as laying down two propositions:

> first, that damage to the specific subject-matter ... must be assumed to result from repackaging, even where there was in fact no damage either to the quality of the goods or to the mark's function as an indication of origin; and second, that the necessity test applied ... also ... to determine the type of repackaging which was permissible, so that the only permissible repackaging was that which from a trade mark point of view was as unobtrusive as possible. The High Court accordingly concluded that both debranding and cobranding infringed the claimants' trade mark rights.[366]

10.335 The Court of Appeal felt that a number of points regarding the meaning of 'necessary', the burden of proof, and the consequences of failure to give notice, required further clarifications and referred a number of detailed questions to the Court of Justice.

1. Where a parallel importer markets in one Member State a pharmaceutical product imported from another Member State in its original internal packaging but with a new exterior carton printed in the language of the Member State of importation (a 'reboxed' product): (a) does the importer bear the burden of proving that the new packaging complies with each of the conditions set out in [*Bristol Myers Squibb*] or does the trade mark proprietor bear the burden of proving that those conditions have not been complied with or does the burden of proof vary from condition to condition, and if so how? (b) does the first condition set out in [*Bristol Myers Squibb*] as interpreted in [*Pharmacia & Upjohn*] and [*Boehringer I*], namely that it must be shown that it is necessary to repackage the product in order that effective market access is not hindered, apply merely to the fact of reboxing (as held by the EFTA Court in Case E-3/02 *Paranova v Merck*) or does it also apply to the precise manner and style of the reboxing carried out by the parallel importer, and if so how? (c) is the fourth condition set out in [*Bristol Myers Squibb*], namely that the presentation of the repackaged product is not such as to be liable to damage the reputation of the trade mark or its owner, only infringed if the packaging is defective, of poor quality or untidy or does it extend to anything which damages the reputation of the trade mark? (d) if the answer to question 1(c) is that the fourth condition is infringed by anything which damages the reputation of the trade mark and if either. (i) the trade mark is not affixed to the new exterior carton (debranding,) or (ii) the parallel importer applies either his own logo or a house-style or get-up or a get-up used for a number of different products to the new exterior carton ('co-branding') must such forms of box design be regarded as damaging to the reputation of the trade mark or is that a question of fact for the national court? (e) If the answer to question 1(d) is that it is a question of fact, on whom does the burden of proof lie?
2. Where a parallel importer markets in one Member State a pharmaceutical product imported from another Member State in its original internal and external packaging to which the parallel importer has applied an additional external label printed in the language of the Member State of importation (an 'overstickered' product): (a) do the five conditions set out in [*Bristol Myers Squibb*] apply at all? (b) if the answer to question 2(a) is yes, does the importer bear the burden of proving that the overstickered packaging complies with each of the conditions set out in [*Bristol Myers Squibb*] or does the

---

[364] C-143/00 *Boehringer Ingelheim Pharma KG v Swingward Ltd* [2002] ECR I-3759.
[365] [2004] EWCA Civ 757, CA.
[366] Point 26; [2003] EWHC 110 (Ch).

trade mark proprietor bear the burden of proving that those conditions have not been complied with or does the burden of proof vary from condition to condition? (c) if the answer to question 2(a) is yes, does the first condition set out in [Bristol Myers Squibb] as interpreted in [Pharmacia & Upjohn] and [Boehringer I], namely that it must be shown that it is necessary to repackage the product in order that effective market access is not hindered, apply merely to the fact of overstickering or does it also apply to the precise manner and style of overstickering adopted by the parallel importer? (d) if the answer to question 2(a) is yes, is the fourth condition set out in [Bristol Myers Squibb], namely that the presentation of the repackaged product is not such as to be liable to damage the reputation of the trade mark or its owner, only infringed if the packaging is defective, of poor quality or untidy or does it extend to anything which damages the reputation of the trade mark? (e) if the answer to question 2(a) is yes and the answer to question 2(d) is that the fourth condition is infringed by anything which damages the reputation of the trade mark, is it damaging to the reputation of a trade mark for this purpose if either (i) the additional label is positioned so as wholly or partially to obscure one of the proprietors trade marks or (ii) the additional label fails to state that the trade mark in question is a trade mark owned by the proprietor or (iii) the name of the parallel importer is printed in capital letters?
3. Where a parallel importer has failed to give notice in respect of a repackaged product as required by the fifth condition of [Bristol Myers Squibb], and accordingly has infringed the proprietor's trade mark(s) for that reason only: (a) Is every subsequent act of importation of that product an infringement or does the importer only infringe until such time as the proprietor has become aware of the product and the applicable notice period has expired? (b) Is the proprietor entitled to claim financial remedies (i.e. damages for infringement or the handing over of all profits made by infringement) by reason of the importer's acts of infringement on the same basis as if the goods had been spurious? (c) Is the granting of financial remedies to the proprietor in respect of such acts of infringement by the importer subject to the principle of proportionality? (d) If not, upon what basis should such compensation be assessed given that the products in question were placed on the market within the EEA by the proprietor or with his consent?[367]

(a) The Opinion of Advocate General Sharpston

10.336 The reference gave Advocate General Sharpston the opportunity to sum up the current position regarding repackaging and overstickering.[368]

10.337 (i) **The role of the Court of Justice** However, her starting remark was about the role and purpose of the Court of Justice. Once the principles were established, national courts should:

> play their part robustly in applying the principles to the facts before them without further requests to fine-tune the principles. Every judge knows that ingenious lawyers can always find a reason why a given proposition does or does not apply to their client's situation. It should not however in my view be for the Court of Justice to adjudicate on such detail for evermore.[369]

---

[367] Reproduced in point 27.
[368] C-348/04 *Boehringer Ingelheim KG Boehringer Ingelheim Pharma GmbH & Co KG, Glaxo Group Ltd v Swingward Ltd and Boehringer Ingelheim KG, Boehringer Ingelheim Pharma GmbH & Co KG, Glaxo Group Ltd, Smithkline Beecham Plc, Beecham Group Plc Smithkline and French Laboratories Ltd, Eli Lilly and Co, The Wellcome Foundation Ltd v Dowelhurst Ltd* [2007] ECR I-3391.
[369] Point 3, noting that a similar point had been made by AG Jacobs in C-349/95 *Ballantine & Son* [1997] ECR I-6227.

Parallel Imports

10.338 **(ii) The Legal Context:** The Advocate General first constructed the legal framework Regarding the specific subject-matter of a trade mark, she noted that the jurisprudence of the Court had developed two components:

> First, there is the right to use the mark for the purpose of putting products protected by it into circulation for the first time in the EC, after which that right is exhausted. Second, there is the right to oppose any use of the trade mark which is liable to impair the guarantee of origin, which comprises both a guarantee of identity of origin and a guarantee of integrity of the trade-marked product.[370]

These two components were also reflected in the Trade Marks Directive, with Article 7(1) qualifying the application of Article 5(1). She viewed them as counterbalancing provisions rather than an exception to a general rule. Article 7(2) on the other hand should be seen as an exception and should 'not be generously construed;[371] as a result "legitimate reasons" and the notion of the "condition" of the goods being "changed or impaired" should be interpreted narrowly'.

10.339 She suggested that the jurisprudence of the Court on Articles 5, 6, and 7 had settled the following principles: (i) they effected a complete harmonization; (ii) Article 36 should be the basis for the application of Article 7(2), in respect of repackaged products to which the original trade mark had been reaffixed; (iii) the same 'canons of interpretation must apply to other variants of repackaging';[372] and (iv) the Directive should be construed in accordance with the Treaty framework and the core rights developed by the Court. She appeared to indicate however, that since the interpretive principles were settled it was time to move on and look at the Directive rather than Article 36.

10.340 **(iii) Reformulating the *Bristol Myers Squibb* propositions** To achieve this she started by reformulating the propositions of *Bristol Myers Squibb*[373] within the language and structure of the Directive, stressing that, in a post-*Silhouette*[374] reading, Article 7(2) did not create an independent right of action but was linked with the exercise of Article 5:

> To summarise the BMS conditions in a way that fits clearly within the structure and language of the Directive, repackaging—as a necessary condition for preventing him or at least certain types of repackaging—will constitute a 'legitimate reason' within the meaning of Article 7(2) unless (i) the repackaging is necessary for market access; (ii) the repackaging cannot affect the original condition of the product; (iii) the new packaging shows the name of the importer and the manufacturer; (iv) the presentation is not such as to be liable to damage the reputation of the mark and its owner; and (v) the importer gives notice to the owner.[375]

10.341 **(iv) The six questions of 'essence'** The next step was to suggest how these principles should be applied in relation to the questions referred to the Court. She divided her Opinion by providing the answers to six questions that reflected the essence of the reference.

10.342 *The conditions of Bristol Myers Squibb and overstickered products* (1) Do the five conditions set out in *Bristol Myers Squibb* apply to overstickered products? The answer according to the Advocate General should be no. In both *Bristol Myers Squibb* and *Loendersloot*[376] the Court

---

[370] Point 9.
[371] Point 13.
[372] Point 14.
[373] C-427/93 *Bristol Myers Squibb, CH Boehringer* [1996] ECR I-3457.
[374] C-355/96 *Silhouette International Schmied GmbH & Co KG* [1998] ECR I-4799.
[375] Point 20.
[376] C-349/95 *Ballantine* [1997] ECR I-6227.

had hinted that overstickering should be tolerated; this in turn implied that overstickering did not amount to repackaging. Still, *Phytheron*[377] appeared to indicate that some conditions also apply to overstickering, in particular the second and fourth conditions of *Bristol Myers Squibb*. However, in *Bristol Myers Squibb* itself the Court had accepted that the second condition was not breached by overstickering the inner packaging, so it could be validly argued that overstickering the outer packaging should also not be considered a breach; even more so since *Phytheron* was not a pharmaceuticals case. In order to resolve the interpretive contradictions she turned to basic principles. *Hoffmann-La Roche*[378] linked the proprietor's right with impairment of the trade mark as a guarantee of origin.

Looking at the facts of the case she stated: **10.343**

> Whatever the Court's historical approach to the risks attached to replacing external packaging, the overstickering at issue in the present case does not appear to me to constitute such use of the trade mark. The mark is being affixed to genuine goods with no risk of affecting the original condition of the product itself ... In my view, where there is no risk that the guarantee of origin is impaired, as in the case of applying an additional external label to the original external packaging while retaining the original internal packaging, the BMS conditions do not apply.[379]

Attempting to narrow down the scope of the five provisions she added: **10.344**

> That approach to my mind best reflects the appropriate balance between the primary Treaty principle of free movement of goods and the rights of trade mark owners in relation to parallel imports. Where there is no risk to the guarantee of origin as defined by the Court, free movement of goods must prevail. Where on the facts a trade mark owner can demonstrate that overstickering risks impairing the guarantee of origin as so understood, then by way of derogation from the free movement of goods, the trade mark owner's rights may exceptionally prevail. That follows from the Court's definitions of the core rights and specific subject-matter of a trade mark.[380]

Note that the Advocate General based her negative answer primarily on the facts of the case: **10.345**

> I accordingly conclude on question 2(a) that the BMS conditions do not apply where a parallel importer markets in one Member State a pharmaceutical product imported from another Member State in its original internal and external packaging to which the parallel importer has applied an additional external label printed in the language of the Member State of importation.[381]

The necessity requirement and the style of reboxing (2) Does the requirement that repackaging be necessary apply merely to the fact of reboxing or to the precise manner and style of the reboxing, and if so, how? The contrast between the positive position of the High Court and the claimants on the one hand and the negative position of the Court of **10.346**

---

[377] C-352/95 *Phytheron International SA v Jean Bourdon SA* [1997] ECR I-1729 37; the Court had ruled that the addition on the label of a product of information designed to comply with the laws of the Member State where the product is imported would not constitute a legitimate reason within the meaning of art.7(2) of the Trade Marks Directive, if the 'label so altered does not omit important information or give inaccurate information and its presentation is not liable to damage the reputation of the trade mark and that of its owner' (paragraph 23).
[378] C-102/77 *Hoffmann-La Roche* [1978] ECR .1139.
[379] Point 40.
[380] Point 41.
[381] Point 42.

10.347 Here the Advocate General chose to be more provocative. She supported the view that the necessity requirements applied to reboxing itself rather than its precise manner and style; the Court's statement in *Boehringer I* that 'it is the repackaging of the trade-marked pharmaceutical products in itself which is prejudicial to the specific subject-matter of the mark, and it is not necessary in that context to assess the actual effects of the repackaging by the parallel importer'[384] had misread *Hoffmann-La Roche*. The guarantee of origin had been narrowly construed by the Court in *Hoffmann-La Roche*: the trade mark should enable the consumer to be certain that the marked product had not been subject to unauthorized interference by a third party 'such as to affect [its] original condition'.[385] 'That suggests that the precise manner and style of reboxing which affects only the outer packaging would not impair the guarantee of origin.'[386]

Appeals, the defendants, and the Commission on the other, all based on *Boehringer I*[382] and *Loendersloof*,[383] illustrated the ambiguity—real or apparent—of the jurisprudence of the Court on these issues.

10.348 Turning to the *travaux preparatoires* for the Directive she stated:[387]

> the Commission originally intended the necessity requirement to apply to the fact of repackaging; and envisaged that the parallel importer should enjoy a degree of freedom as to how precisely he repackaged, provided that he met the requirements laid down in *Hoffmann-La Roche*. There is nothing to suggest that that intention did not survive the legislative process.[388]

The treatment of *Paranova v Merck*,[389] a relevant decision of the EFTA court, was also relevant in terms of substance but also as an example of the weight EFTA court decisions can carry. The EFTA court decided that once the right to repackage is established and the parallel importer has achieved effective access to the market the necessity requirement should not be decisive for interpreting 'legitimate reasons'. '[I]mposing the necessity requirement on the market conduct of the parallel importer after having gained market access, in particular on its strategy of product presentation, such as advertising or packaging design, would constitute a disproportionate restriction on the free movement of goods'[390] The Advocate General accepted the logic of the proportionality argument and suggested that the Court itself had hinted something similar in *Pharmacia & Upjohn*.[391]

10.349 Finally the Advocate General stressed the burden a stricter interpretation would impose on national courts that would have 'to take numerous decisions on trivial details of pattern and colour which are not obviously within their judicial remit'.[392]

---

[382] C-143/00 *Boehringer Ingelheim Pharma KG* [2002] ECR I-3759.
[383] C-349/95 *Frits Loendersloot* [1997] ECR I-6227.
[384] *Boehringer I*, paragraph 30.
[385] *Hoffmann-La Roche*, paragraph 7.
[386] Point 46.
[387] Explanatory Memorandum to the Proposal for a first Council Directive to approximate the laws of the Member States relating to trade marks (COM(80) 635 final, 19 November 1980), commentary on Article 6.
[388] Point 49.
[389] E-3/02 *Paranova AS v Merck & Co Inc* [2003] 3 CMLR 7.
[390] *Paranova*, paragraph 45.
[391] C-337/95 *Pharmacia & Upjohn v Paranova A/S* [1997] ECR I-6013.
[392] Point 54.

What causes damage to reputation (3) Is the fourth *Bristol Myers Squibb* condition infringed **10.350** only if the packaging is defective, of poor quality, or untidy or does it extend to anything which damages the reputation of the trade mark? Here the Advocate General offered some comfort to the pharmaceutical companies. There was no reason to limit the fourth condition; it was clear that the Court in *Bristol Myers Squibb* referred to defective, poor quality, or untidy packaging as examples of 'inappropriate presentation'. Other cases-like *Dior*[393] and *BMW*[394] went even further and considered inappropriate use and damage to the reputation in advertising.

Damage to reputation—a question of fact (4) Are certain (specified) methods of repackaging **10.351** necessarily damaging to the reputation of a trade mark or is damage to reputation a question of fact? The methods specified by the Court of Appeals were 'debranding', not applying the trade mark to the new packaging, and 'cobranding', adding the parallel importer's to the packaging. Advocate General Sharpston agreed with the position of the Commission that national courts had to carry out a detailed factual appraisal in order to determine whether the repackaging damaged the reputation of the trade mark owner; in principle both debranding—leading to inappropriate presentation of the mark—and cobranding, incorrectly suggesting a commercial link with the trade mark owner, could be damaging.

In *Dior* the Court had held that only serious damage to reputation would amount to a **10.352** legitimate reason under Article 7(2) and in *BMW* that determining whether there is a link between the advertisement and the impression of a commercial connection between the parties was a question of fact. These two rulings should create general principles. 'Whether a given circumstance (e.g. damage to reputation) may in principle constitute a "legitimate reason" is a question of law, but whether in a given case that circumstance obtains is a question of fact'.[395]

The effect of giving notice (5) What is the effect of failing to give notice as required by the fifth **10.353** *Bristol Myers Squibb* condition? Advocate General Sharpston distinguished between the first four conditions that were substantive and based on the Treaty and the fifth condition that was of procedural nature and introduced by the Court.

Initially, the rationale behind it, as developed in *Hoffmann-La Roche*[396] was to reduce the **10.354** risk of consumers being misled. But, as is almost always the case in the development of trade mark and unfair competition law, the Court introduced in *Bristol Myers Squibb*[397] the interests of the proprietor; the notice enabled the proprietor to ensure that the repackaging did not affect the original condition and presentation of the product. And *Boehringer*[398] stressed that it strengthened anti-counterfeiting protection.

Accordingly, she maintained, 'breach of the notice requirement attracts a sanction distinct **10.355** from the sanctions applicable if the other, substantive [*Bristol Myers Squibb*] conditions are breached'.[399] She then distinguished between two scenarios: no or inadequate notice

---

[393] C-337/95 *Parfums Christian Dior SA* [1997] ECR I-6013, one of the few instances that *Dior* has been cited by the Court.
[394] C-63/97 *BMW* [1999] ECR I-905.
[395] Point 65.
[396] C-102/77 *Hoffmann-La Roche* [1978] ECR 1139.
[397] C-427/93 *Bristol Myers Squibb* [1996] ECR I-3457.
[398] C-143/00 *Boehringer Ingelheim Pharma KG* [2002] ECR I-3759.
[399] Point 72 of the Opinion of AG Sharpston.

without breach of the other conditions and no or inadequate notice with breach of one or more of the other conditions. Breaching the notice requirement should be sanctioned in both cases in an effective and dissuasive way, because the breach would, almost always, be deliberate disregard of a straightforward condition. However, it would be disproportionate to apply the same sanction under both scenarios. Finally she suggested a number of balancing parameters national courts would have to explore before determining the appropriate sanction. Where delay in commencing proceedings might be deliberate in order to increase financial awards for infringement, the sanction should not make it practically impossible for the parallel importer to exercise what in essence was a Community right. Deliberate breach of the condition would be an aggravating factor, if it allowed the parallel importer to access the market before the trade mark owner was given a chance to enforce its rights.

10.356 *The burden of proof* (6) The Advocate General acknowledged that the Court's ruling in *Boehringer*[400] that the burden of proof was a procedural matter that remained in the jurisdiction of national court provided that its exercise is non-discriminatory, was insufficiently precise. She suggested a more intricate distinction. The Court should indicate who carried the burden of proof in respect of each of the five conditions. National procedural and evidential rules would then determine how this burden would be discharged. It was essential to differentiate between each condition for conceptual and practical reasons. Requiring the parallel importer to discharge all five conditions would tilt the balance from the principle of free movement of goods to its exception, the recognition of intellectual property rights. On the other hand, requiring the same from the trade mark owner would hinder the exercise of rights under Article 7(2). Further, because the conditions differed in terms of complexity and individual requirements it was worth exploring for which of the two parties would be more practicable to gather the necessary evidence.

10.357 *Necessity* It was implicit in the logic of the requirement that the parallel importer had to demonstrate necessity. The parallel importer would also be familiar with the market conditions and regulatory requirements and had the commercial incentive to research consumer perceptions regarding overstickering and reboxing.

10.358 *No adverse effect on condition of product* The parallel importer again would have to prove this, because it determined and controlled the repackaging process. This would not be a disproportionate burden because the parallel importer would also have to satisfy national regulatory authorities that repackaging would not affect the condition of the original product.

10.359 *Clear identification of importer and manufacturer* Again, the parallel importer determined and controlled the repackaging process and should carry the burden of showing that both the trade mark owner and the parallel importer were clearly identified on the repackaged product.

10.360 *Presentation not damaging to reputation* The trade mark owner was in the best position to assess whether there was such a risk, to consider whether it was serious, and to present the relevant evidence.

10.361 *Notice* The parallel importer controlled whether, when, and how the trade mark owner had been informed and would have to carry the burden of proof.

---

[400] C-143/00 *Boehringer Ingelheim Pharma KG* [2002] ECR I-3759.

(b) The Judgment of the Court

(i) The concept of repackaging It started its specific analysis by examining Question 2(a) and the concept of 'repackaging'. Looking again at *Boehringer*[401] it found that the concept of repackaging included relabelling and that relabelling, just like reboxing, was prejudicial to the specific subject-matter of the mark. Accordingly it was not necessary to assess the actual effects of the activity performed by the parallel importer:

10.362

> The change brought about by any new carton or relabelling of a trade marked medicinal product creates by its very nature real risks for the guarantee of origin which the mark seeks to protect. Such a change may thus be prohibited by the trade mark proprietor unless the new carton or relabelling is necessary in order to enable the marketing of the products imported in parallel and the legitimate interests of the proprietor are also safeguarded.[402]

It followed accordingly that the five requirements should be applied and, if met, prevent the proprietor from opposing further commercialization of a pharmaceutical product.

Accordingly, the answer to Question 2(a) should be that:

10.363

> Article 7 (2) of Directive 89/104 must be construed as meaning that the proprietor may legitimately oppose further commercialization of a pharmaceutical product imported from another Member State in its original internal and external packaging with an additional external label applied by the importer, unless it is established that reliance on trade mark rights by the proprietor in order to oppose the marketing of the overstickered product under that trade mark would contribute to the artificial partitioning of the markets between Member States; it is shown that the new label cannot affect the original condition of the product inside the packaging; the packaging clearly states who overstickered the product and the name of the manufacturer; the presentation of the overstickered product is not such as to be liable to damage the reputation of the trade mark and of its proprietor; thus, the label must not be defective, of poor quality, or untidy; and the importer gives notice to the trade mark proprietor before the overstickered product is put on sale, and, on demand, supplies him with a specimen of that product.[403]

(ii) The manner and style of repackaging: The necessity requirement. The Court then considered Questions 1(b) and 2(c): the application, as regards the manner and style of repackaging, and the condition that there must be a need to repackage the product. The Court described the two approaches on this issue:

10.364

> That condition that repackaging be necessary is fulfilled if the rules or practices in the importing Member State prevent the product in question from being marketed in that State in the same packaging as that in which those products are marketed in the exporting Member State. Conversely, the condition that it be necessary is not fulfilled if repackaging of the product is explicable solely by the parallel importer's attempt to secure a commercial advantage.[404]

The condition was directed only at the fact of repackaging the product, and the choice between a new carton and oversticking, for the purposes of allowing that product to be marketed in the importing State and not at the manner or style in which it had been repackaged.

---

[401] Ibid.
[402] *Boehringer I*, paragraph 30.
[403] *Boehringer II*, paragraph 32.
[404] *Boehringer II*, paragraphs 36–37, citing C-379/97 *Upjohn* [1999] ECR I-6927.

10.365 Accordingly the answer to Questions 1(b) and 2(c) should be that the condition that the repackaging of the pharmaceutical product, either by reboxing the product and re-applying the trade mark or by applying a label to the packaging containing the product, be necessary for its further commercialization in the importing Member State, as one of the conditions which, if fulfilled, prevent the proprietor under Article 7(2) of Directive 89/104 from opposing such commercialization, is directed solely at the fact of repackaging and not at the manner and style of the repackaging.

10.366 (iii) **Damaging reputation: Turning back to *Dior*** The Court found, following the application of the five conditions, that the carton or the label should not be defective, of poor quality, or untidy. However, this referred only to certain cases in which inappropriate presentation of the repackaged product was liable to damage the reputation of the trade mark and of its proprietor. The Court held that:

> a repackaged pharmaceutical product could be presented inappropriately and, therefore, damage the trade mark's reputation in particular where the carton or label, while not being defective, of poor quality or untidy, are such as to affect the trade mark's value by detracting from the image of reliability and quality attaching to such a product and the confidence it is capable of inspiring in the public concerned.[405]

10.367 The answer to Questions 1(c) and 2(d) was that the condition that the presentation of the pharmaceutical product should not be such as to be liable to damage the reputation of the trade mark and of its proprietor—from legitimately opposing further commercialization of a pharmaceutical product, where the parallel importer had either reboxed the product and re-applied the trade mark or applied a label to the packaging containing the product—is not limited only to cases where the repackaging is defective, of poor quality, or untidy. It went on to examine Question 1(d) and Question 2(e) on the circumstances likely to damage the trade mark's reputation.

10.368 The Court here decided that the effect of the specific acts mentioned in the questions was for the national court to determine:

> precisely as with the question whether advertising is liable to create the impression that there is a commercial connection between the reseller and the trade mark proprietor and, therefore, constitute a legitimate reason within the meaning of Article 7(2) of Directive 89/104 ... the question whether the circumstances referred to in the previous paragraph of the present judgment are liable to damage the trade mark's reputation is a question of fact for the national court to decide in the light of the circumstances of each case.[406]

10.369 (iv) **The burden of proof** The Court held that where it was established that the parallel imported medicinal products had been repackaged, it was for parallel importers to prove the existence of the conditions that would prevent proprietors from lawfully opposing further commercialization. As to whether the repackaging affected the original condition of a product inside its packaging, it should be sufficient that the parallel importer furnishes evidence that leads to the reasonable presumption that that condition has been fulfilled:

> This applies a fortiori also to the condition that the presentation of the repackaged product must not be such as to be liable to damage the reputation of the trade mark and of its proprietor. Where the importer furnishes such initial evidence that the latter condition has been fulfilled it will then be for the proprietor of the trade mark, who is best placed to assess whether

---

[405] Paragraph 43.
[406] Paragraph 46.

the repackaging is liable to damage his reputation and that of the trade mark, to prove that they have been damaged.[407]

(v) Prior notice: The requirements In its analysis of the third question the Court held that prior notice was a requirement that the parallel importer had to fulfil. It was not sufficient that the proprietor be notified by other sources. If a parallel importer had failed to give prior notice to the trade mark proprietor concerning a repackaged pharmaceutical product, he would infringe the right of that proprietor on the occasion of any subsequent importation of that product, so long as he had not given the proprietor such notice. **10.370**

(vi) The absence of prior notice: The consequences On the consequences of failure to give prior notice the Court held that where Community law did not lay down specific sanctions it was incumbent on the national authorities to adopt appropriate measures to deal with such a situation. Those measures had to be proportionate, but also sufficiently effective and, in themselves, a deterrent to ensure that Directive 89/104 was fully effective.[408] Accordingly, a national measure under which the trade mark proprietor was entitled to claim financial remedies on the same basis as if the goods had been spurious, would not in itself be contrary to the principle of proportionality. It was for the national court, however, to determine the amount of the financial remedies according to the circumstances of each case, in the light in particular of the extent of damage to the trade mark proprietor caused by the parallel importer's infringement and in accordance with the principle of proportionality. **10.371**

(13) *Orifarm*: Authorization and Repackaging; the Extent of Disclosure I

The joined cases of *Orifarm*[409] were references from the Danish Supreme Court in relation to actions brought by Merck against, in the first case, companies within the Orifarm group, and in the second case, companies in the Paranova group. In both cases, the defendants imported in parallel into the Danish market, branded medicines produced by Merck, but the companies within the group that carried out the repackaging of the product were not the same as those that actually held the authorizations to market and sell the products. The dispute arose because in both cases, the packaging of the goods indicated that they had been repackaged by the company which owned the authorizations rather than the actual repackager. **10.372**

Merck brought actions before the Maritime and Commercial Court of Denmark on the ground that the name of the actual repackager did not appear on the packaging of the medicinal products in question. The Court found that the defendants had infringed Merck's trade mark rights by failing to indicate on the packaging the name of the undertaking which had actually performed the repackaging. **10.373**

On appeal, the Supreme Court stayed the proceedings and referred the following questions to the Court for a preliminary ruling: **10.374**

(1) The Court of Justice is requested to clarify whether [*Bristol-Myers Squibb and Others* and *MPA Pharma*] are to be interpreted as meaning that a parallel importer which is the holder of the marketing authorisation for, and possesses information on, a medicinal

---

[407] Paragraph 53.
[408] C-212/04 *Adeneler* [2006] ECR I-6057.
[409] *Orifarm A/S, Orifarm Supply A/S, Handelsselskabet af 5 January 2002 A/S, in liquidation*, C-400/09 and C-207/10 *Ompakningsselskabet af, and Paranova Danmark A/S, Paranova Pack A/S v Merck Sharp & Dohme Corp., formerly Merck & Co. Inc., Merck Sharp & Dohme BV, Merck Sharp & Dohme* [2011] ECR I-07063.

product imported in parallel, and which issues instructions to a separate undertaking for the purchase and repackaging of a medicinal product, for the detailed design of the product's packaging and for arrangements in relation to the product, infringes the rights of the trade mark proprietor by indicating itself—and not the separate undertaking which holds the repackaging authorisation, has imported the product and has carried out the physical repackaging, including (re)affixing of the trade mark proprietor's trade mark—as the repackager on the outer packaging of the medicinal product imported in parallel.

(2) The Court of Justice is requested to clarify whether it is of significance in answering Question 1 that an assumption might be made that, where the marketing authorisation holder indicates itself as the repackager instead of the undertaking which physically carried out the repackaging to order, there is no risk that the consumer/end user might be misled into assuming that the trade mark proprietor is responsible for the repackaging.

(3) The Court of Justice is requested to clarify whether it is of significance in answering Question 1 that an assumption might be made that the risk of misleading the consumer/end user into assuming that the trade mark proprietor is responsible for the repackaging is excluded if the undertaking which physically carried out the repackaging is indicated as being the repackager.

(4) The Court of Justice is requested to clarify whether it is only the risk that the consumer/end user might be misled into assuming that the trade mark proprietor is responsible for the repackaging which is of significance in answering Question 1, or whether other considerations regarding the trade mark proprietor are also relevant, for example

(a) that the entity which undertakes the importation and physical repackaging and (re)affixes the trade mark proprietor's trade mark on the product's outer packaging potentially on its own account infringes the trade mark proprietor's trade mark by so doing, and

(b) that it may be due to factors for which the entity that physically carried out the repackaging is responsible that the repackaging affects the original condition of the product or that the presentation of the repackaging is of such a kind that it must be assumed to harm the trade mark proprietor's reputation (see, inter alia, … *Bristol-Myers Squibb and Others* …).

(5) The Court of Justice is requested to clarify whether it is of significance in answering Question 1 that the holder of the marketing authorisation, which has indicated itself as being the repackager, at the time of the notification of the trade mark proprietor prior to the intended sale of the parallel imported medicinal product once repackaged, belongs to the same group as the actual repackager (sister company).[410]

10.375 The Court found that Merck had no legitimate interest in the actual repackager appearing on the packaging merely because the repackaging might affect the original condition of the product and might therefore cause harm to its trade mark rights. In particular, the Court found that Merck's interests were sufficiently protected by the requirement that the repackaging cannot affect the original condition of the product, which is the responsibility of the holder of the marketing authorization to show.[411]

10.376 The Court also rejected Merck's argument that consumers have an interest in knowing the identity of the repackager as their national law might entitle them to bring action against both the holder of the marketing authorization and also against the repackager. This is on the basis that the wording of Article 7(2) of Directive 89/104 is specific in limiting the exception to the principle of the exhaustion of the rights to the protection of the legitimate

---

[410] Paragraph 12.
[411] Paragraph 32.

interests of the trade mark proprietor, the specific protection of the legitimate interests of consumers being ensured by other legal instruments.[412]

Consequently, the Court held that: **10.377**

> It follows from all the foregoing that Article 7(2) of Directive 89/104 must be interpreted as not allowing the proprietor of a trade mark relating to a pharmaceutical product which is the subject of parallel imports to oppose the further marketing of that product in repackaged form on the sole ground that the new packaging indicates as the repackager not the undertaking which, on instructions, actually repackaged the product and holds an authorisation to do so, but the undertaking which holds the marketing authorization for the product, on whose instructions the repackaging was carried out, and which assumes liability for the repackaging.[413]

(14) *Wellcome v Paranova*: Is there a Requirement of Minimum Intervention? The Extent of Disclosure II

Two of the *Boehringer* issues were revisited in *The Wellcome Foundation Ltd v Paranova Pharmazeutika Handels GmbH*.[414] This time the reference came from the Austrian Oberster Gerichtshof. Wellcome, the proprietor of the trade mark ZOVIRAX, registered in Austria for pharmaceutical products, started proceedings against Paranova, who had imported ZOVIRAX products from Greece. The product had to be sold in Austria in packs of 60 tablets whereas in Greece it was sold in packs of 70. Paranova repackaged the product in packs of 60. On the new packaging the statement 'Repackaged and imported by Paranova' appeared on the front, in bold type and block capitals. Wellcome was mentioned on the sides and the back in normal type. And a blue strip, commonly used by Paranova, appeared at the edges. Paranova did inform Wellcome regarding the importation of the product in Austria. Wellcome required additional information regarding the State of export and a requested a sample, rather than prints, of the packaging. **10.378**

The case came before the Oberster Gerichtshof, which referred two questions, to an extent overlapping with *Boehringer II,* to the Court. The case was suspended and following the Judgment in *Boehringer II* the national court maintained two sub-questions, that had not been answered in that case, concerning the presentation of repackaging and the importer's obligation to notify the trade mark owner of its intention to repackage. **10.379**

(a) The Opinion of Advocate General Sharpston

(i) Minimum intervention v damage to reputation The Advocate General started her analysis by highlighting the differences between *Loendersloot* and *Boehringer II,* for example that the second concerned a pharmaceutical product, a point specifically recognized in *Loendersloot*. She reiterated the point she had made in *Boehringer II* that the specific subject-matter of a trade mark had two components: the right to use the mark for the purpose of putting products protected by it into circulation for the first time in the EEA, after which that right is exhausted, and the right to oppose any use of the trade mark which is liable to impair the guarantee of origin, which comprised both a guarantee of identity of origin and a guarantee of integrity of the trade-marked product. In the current case the first right had been exhausted. Regarding the second, she noted that the Court had dealt with the **10.380**

---

[412] Paragraph 34.
[413] Paragraph 36.
[414] C-276/05 *The Wellcome Foundation Ltd v Paranova Pharmazeutika Handels GmbH* [2009] ETMR 20.

guarantee of identity of origin in the context of co-branding as an aspect of reputation. 'If the principle of minimum intervention had applied, there would have been no need for such an approach. It would have sufficed to state that co-branding was unlawful per se.'[415]

10.381 Looking at the jurisprudence of the European Free Trade Association (EFTA) Court,[416] *Boehringer II*, and *Merck, Sharpe & Dohme*,[417] she argued that repackaging that went beyond minimum intervention should not be automatically unlawful. She rejected Wellcome's argument that without the principle of minimum intervention the parallel importer would be able to repackage for the sole purpose of obtaining a commercial advantage. Albeit, obtaining such an advantage would not be enough as the Court had already held in *Boehringer II*:

> repackaging solely for a commercial advantage will be neither more nor less permissible depending on whether the principle of minimum intervention is or is not the relevant criterion for determining whether specific repackaging is permissible. Such repackaging is in any event impermissible.[418]

10.382 (ii) **The duty of notification** The Austrian court had also questioned whether the duty of notification required the identification of the State of export and a statement of the precise reasons for the repackaging. She suggested that identifying the State of export was not necessary. The parallel importer had to prove the existence of the five *Bristol Myers Squibb* conditions. *Boehringer II* set that the necessity condition was directed at the fact of repackaging and not at the manner and style of the repackaging. The parallel importer had to give the trade mark proprietor information that objectively demonstrated that the repackaging was necessary. Such information might have to cover the State of export but this was not a requirement as such.

(b) The Judgment of the Court

10.383 The Court too started its analysis by referring to *Bristol Myers Squibb*.[419] It viewed the notification requirement as a condition that enables the proprietor, first, to check that the repackaging does not directly or indirectly affect the original condition of the product and, second, that it is not likely to damage the reputation of the trade mark.

10.384 (i) **The necessity condition: Repackaging and presentation** It added that in *Boehringer II* it had held that the necessity requirement was directed only at the fact of repackaging the product and not at the manner or style in which it had been repackaged. 'Thus, the condition of necessity is directed only at the fact of repackaging the product, inter alia by reboxing it, and not at the presentation of that new packaging.'[420] The Court also held that since the presentation of the new packaging of the product should not be assessed against the condition of necessity for the further marketing of the product, it should also not be assessed against the criterion that the adverse effect on the trade mark rights should be the minimum possible. The trade mark proprietor would be adequately protected by the requirement that the presentation of the repackaged product must not be such as to be liable

---

[415] Point 32.
[416] Case E-3/02 *Paranova v Merck* [2003] EFTA Court Report 2004 1.
[417] C-443/99 *Merck v Paranova* [2002] ECR I-3703.
[418] Point 40.
[419] C-427/93 *Bristol Myers Squibb* [1996] ECR I-3457.
[420] C-276/05 *Wellcome v Paranova* (n 414), paragraph 26.

to damage the trade marks or its proprietor's reputation. Accordingly, Article 7(2) of the Directive should be interpreted

> as meaning that, where it is established that repackaging of the pharmaceutical product is necessary for further marketing in the Member State of importation, the presentation of the packaging should be assessed only against the condition that it should not be such as to be liable to damage the reputation of the trade mark or that of its proprietor.[421]

(ii) Prior notice: The extent of disclosure Here the Court added that following *Boehringer I*[422] and in order to ensure the adequate functioning of the notice system, it presupposed that the interested parties would make sincere efforts to respect each other's legitimate interests. Accordingly it held: **10.385**

> it is for the parallel importer to furnish the proprietor of the trade mark with the information which is necessary and sufficient to enable the latter to determine whether the repackaging of the product under that trade mark is necessary in order to market it in the Member State of importation.[423]

The kind of information required would depend on the factual context of each case and, in exceptional cases, could involve disclosing the Member State of export, where the absence of that information would prevent the proprietor of the trade mark from evaluating the need to repackage. To balance this the Court added that competition provisions of the EC Treaty could cover cases where the details provided by the importer were used by the proprietor to enable him to police his distribution and sale networks and combat parallel trade.[424]

(15) *Martin y Paz*: The Broader Context I; Consent and Acquiescence

The facts of *Martin y Paz*[425] are complex, but in essence, the dispute arose as a result of the fact that the original owner of the trade mark, Mr Baquet, sold rights associated with the name NATHAN to two unrelated parties. In the first place, in 1990, he sold the name of an insolvent Belgian company to Martin y Paz. This sale included a guarantee of the exclusive use of the name NATHAN in connection with the manufacture and sale of small leather goods and an undertaking not to manufacture or sell small leather goods under the NATHAN name. Second, in 1995, Mr Baquet sold the business relating to the sale of handbags to Mr Depuydt (the manager of 'FVMG'). This sale included the sale of the Benelux trade mark registration for NATHAN. Both parties started using independently the name NATHAN in conjunction with a 'stretched' letter N. In 1998, Martin y Paz approached FVMG suggesting greater cooperation between the companies, including collaboration on aspects of the goods and also an exchange of customer lists. Around the same time, Martin y Paz obtained registrations in Benelux for the 'stretched' letter N and a stylized version of the word 'Nathan' ('the figurative mark Nathan') for goods in inter alia classes 18 and 25. In 2002, both parties were also using the trade mark 'Nathan Baume' and around this time, Martin y Paz obtained a Benelux registration for that mark in classes 18 and 25. **10.386**

It seems that during this time, the companies sold goods to each other and displayed them in their shops but in 2005, Mr Depuydt and FVMG issued proceedings in **10.387**

---

[421] *Wellcome* (n 414), paragraph 30.
[422] C-143/00 *Boehringer Ingelheim Pharma KG* [2002] ECR I-3759.
[423] *Wellcome* (n 414), paragraph 34.
[424] Citing C-349/95 *Frits Loendersloot* [1997] ECR I-6227.
[425] C-661/11 *Martin y Paz Diffusion SA v David Depuydt, Fabriek van Maroquinerie Gauquie NV* ECLI:EU:C:2013:577.

Belgium to have Martin y Paz's Benelux registrations declared invalid or, in the alternative, limited to cover only small leather goods. The Tribunal de Commerce de Nivelles dismissed the action. In 2007, Martin y Paz issued proceedings against FVMG for trade mark infringement. FVMG counterclaimed trade mark infringement. Martin y Paz's application was dismissed but FVMG's action was allowed in relation to Martin y Paz's use of the marks 'N', 'Nathan' and 'Nathan Baume' on handbags. Martin y Paz appealed to the Court of Appeal; Brussels and FVMG cross-appealed. FVMG's appeal extended not only to the Court's recent Judgment but also the earlier Judgment regarding the validity of Martin y Paz's Benelux registrations. In relation to the cross actions for infringement, the Court of Appeal ordered that FVMG could not use the marks 'N' or 'Nathan Baume' on goods other than handbags and shoes and that Martin y Paz could not use the mark 'N', the figurative mark 'Nathan', and the mark 'Nathan Baume' for handbags and shoes. The Court also dismissed FVMG's appeal against the earlier judgement.

10.388 The Court of Appeal held that Martin y Paz's approaches to FVMG for collaboration amounted to 'irrevocable consent' to FVMG's use of the trade marks on handbags and shoes. It held that by seeking a prohibition of that use, Martin y Paz had abused the exclusive right conferred by its marks, and, secondly, that Martin y Paz's use of the marks on handbags and shoes constituted unfair competition. Martin y Paz appealed. In the first place, claiming that although it had consented, for an indeterminate period, to FVMG's use on handbags and shoes, the Court erred in law in holding that the consent was 'irrevocable' and that rather than being abusive, its action was a legitimate exercise of the exclusive right conferred upon it by its marks. They also claimed that the Court's order preventing them from using the trade marks on handbags and shoes deprived it of its exclusive right.

10.389 The Court of Cassation rejected Martin y Paz's argument that its application for an injunction could not be categorized as abusive and that the Court of Appeal's decision was based not only on the consent which that company had given, but also on the terms in which it had formulated its application for an injunction and on the underlying motivation of retaliation. However, the Court stayed the proceedings and referred the following questions to the Court of Justice for a preliminary ruling:

(1) (a) Must Article 5(1) and Article 8(1) of [Directive 89/104] be interpreted as meaning that the exclusive right conferred by the registered mark can definitively no longer be asserted by its proprietor against a third party, in respect of all goods covered by it at the time of registration:
— where, for an extended period, the proprietor has shared the use of that mark with that third party in a form of co-ownership for part of the goods covered;
— where, when that sharing was agreed, the proprietor gave the third party its irrevocable consent to use of that mark by the third party in respect of those goods?
(b) Must those articles be interpreted as meaning that application of a national rule, such as that according to which the proprietor of a right cannot exercise that right in a wrongful or abusive manner, can lead to a definitive prohibition on the exercise of that exclusive right for part of the goods covered or as meaning that that application must be restricted to penalising the wrongful or abusive exercise of that right in another way?
(2) (a) Must Article 5(1) and Article 8(1) of [Directive 89/104] be interpreted as meaning that, where the proprietor of a registered mark ends its undertaking to a third

party not to use that mark for certain goods and thus intends to recommence that use itself, the national court can none the less definitively prohibit it from recommencing that use of the mark on the ground that it amounts to unfair competition because of the resulting advantage to the proprietor of the publicity previously made for the mark by the third party and possible confusion in customers' minds, or must they be interpreted as meaning that the national court must adopt a different penalty which does not definitively prohibit the proprietor from recommencing use of the mark?

(b) Must those articles be interpreted as meaning that a definitive prohibition on use by the proprietor is justified where the third party has, over a number of years, made investments in order to bring to the attention of the public the goods in respect of which the proprietor has authorised it to use the mark?[426]

(a) The Opinion of the Advocate General Cruz Villalón

10.390 Advocate General Cruz Villalón looked towards the Court of Justice's parallel import cases for a meaning of consent, citing[427] '[t]he statements of the Court suggest that consent requires the (unequivocal) expression of the intention to renounce the trade mark rights. It is a voluntary legal transaction between the owner and the person receiving the consent.'[428] As such, Advocate General Cruz Villalón highlighted the view that licences are the most common form of consent but distinguishes between consent on the one hand and acquiescence on the other. 'The distinction between "acquiescence" used in Article 9(1) and "consent" also is instructive. Whereas the first term implies passivity in the sense of not preventing the use of a later trade mark, the latter requires the expression of an intention to renounce the right.'[429]

10.391 He was of the view that '[e]ven though irrevocable consent does, hence, not exist, it could still be impermissible to exercise the exclusive trade mark rights against the person with whom use was shared over an extended period of time both prior and after the registration of the trade marks'.[430] As such, Advocate General Cruz Villalón concluded that:

> In the light of the foregoing considerations … the Court should answer the questions referred to it as follows:
>
> — Under Article 5(1) of First Council Directive 89/104/EEC of 21 December 1988 to approximate the laws of the Member States relating to trade marks the proprietor of a registered trade mark cannot give its consent to the use of its trade mark irrevocably. After the revocation of such consent, the exclusive right conferred by a registered trade mark can be asserted against the party that used the mark with the consent of the proprietor, even though the proprietor and that party shared the use of the trade mark—each for different goods, for which the mark was registered—over an extended period of time.
>
> — National law on the wrongful or abusive exercise of rights may not permanently prevent the proprietor of a trade mark from exercising its rights with respect to some of the goods for which the trade mark is registered. This notwithstanding, Directive 89/104 does not prevent national law from providing for a different remedy.

---

[426] *Martin y Paz* (n 425), paragraph 35.
[427] Point 61.
[428] Point 62.
[429] Point 56 of the Opinion of AG Cruz Villalón, citing C-482/09 *Budějovický Budvar* [2011] ECR I-8701, paragraphs 43–44.
[430] Point 67.

— Article 5(1) of Directive 89/104 does not allow national courts to definitively prevent the proprietor of a registered trade mark from recommencing the use of the mark after terminating an undertaking to a third party not to use that mark for certain goods by way of the law of unfair competition based on benefits of the proprietor from and investments by the third party in the publicity of the trade mark as well as the confusion of consumers. This notwithstanding, Directive 89/104 does not prevent national law from providing for a different remedy.[431]

(b) The Judgment of the Court

10.392 The Court held that, except for specific cases governed by Article 8 of the Directive, (ie exclusive and non-exclusive licences), a national court may not limit the exclusive right in a manner which exceeds the limitations arising from Articles 5 to 7 of the Directive.[432]

10.393 The Court went on to hold that the facts of the case did not amount to any of the limitations allowed for in Article 6 of the Directive. However, the Court held that Martin y Paz's consent to FVMG's use of the trade marks did amount to an exhaustion of its exclusive right within the meaning of Article 7 of the Directive in relation to the individual items that were first put on the market in the EEA (citing *Sebago* and *Maison Dubois*).[433] However, the Court held that the wording of Article 7 and the resulting case law was such that the party receiving the consent was not entitled to claim exhaustion once that consent was withdrawn.[434]

10.394 Thus the Court concluded that:

Article 5 of Directive 89/104 precludes a proprietor of trade marks which, in a situation where there has been use shared with a third party, had consented to the use by that third party of signs which are identical to its marks in respect of certain goods in classes for which those marks are registered and which no longer consents to that use, from being deprived of any possibility of asserting the exclusive right conferred upon it by those marks against that third party and of itself exercising that exclusive right in respect of goods which are identical to those of that third party.[435]

(16) *Viking Gas*: The Broader Context II: The Market, The Rights of Consumers, The Rights Of Competitors

10.395 As highlighted throughout this book, trade mark law internalizes competition considerations by setting distinctiveness thresholds, raising functionality barriers, or adopting first sale exhaustion principles. There are cases, however, where competition considerations also influence the way a court rationalizes as a whole the application of trade mark law. We have seen this for example in *Google France*[436] and *eBay*[437] where the Court appeared reluctant to interfere with the way a business was conducted or a marketplace functioned. In *Viking Gas A/S v Kosan Gas A/S (Viking Gas)*[438] the Court followed the same approach looking at a much more mundane marketplace.

---

[431] Point 93.
[432] Paragraph 55.
[433] C-173/98 *Sebago* [1999] ECR I-4103, paragraphs 19–20.
[434] Paragraph 57.
[435] Paragraph 62.
[436] Discussed at paragraph 9.122 et seq.
[437] Discussed at paragraph 9.186 et seq.
[438] Case C-46/10, *Viking Gas A/S v Kosan Gas A/S, formerly BP Gas A/S*, Court of Justice of the European Union, 14 July 2011.

The case came before the Court as a reference from the Danish Supreme Court. Kosan **10.396** produced and marketed bottled gas in 'composite' (lightweight) bottles; it also refilled the bottles for a separate charge. The shape of the bottles was protected as a three-dimensional trade mark both for gas and gas bottles. The shape departed from the norm and its validity did not constitute an issue, either from a functionality or from a distinctiveness perspective. Viking, a competitor that sold but did not itself produce gas, offered a refilling service for the Kosan bottles. Viking attached to the bottles an adhesive label bearing its name and the filling station number without the Kosan marks being removed or covered. Kosan claimed that a competitor should not be free to reuse Kosan's protected packaging for its own product.

(a) The Opinion of Advocate General Kokott

Advocate General Kokott indirectly stressed the relevance of the functionality of the bottle **10.397** in the introductory statement to the case:

> May a company fill the used packaging of a competitor with its own product and offer it for sale in that form where that packaging is protected as a trade mark? That is the question in the present case. In that regard, if one thinks, for example, of the well-known Coca Cola bottle, the answer appears obvious. However, does the same apply in relation to an innovative gas bottle for which a customer has paid more than for the gas it contains?[439]

Later in the Opinion, the relevance of the market and competition contexts becomes **10.398** apparent:

> If one were to examine the wording of art.5(1)(a) of Directive 89/104 in isolation, Kosan would be entitled thus to prohibit Viking from selling refilled composite bottles. However, on closer examination, it is clear that the right associated with the mark is subject to considerable restrictions. To that extent, a distinction must be made between the sale of the bottle and the sale of the gas.[440]

Looking at the gas bottle first, the Advocate General made the point that a second hand **10.399** product, be it a car or a gas bottle, may be damaged. This is a risk understood by consumers and 'where the goods have not been changed or impaired, a proprietor cannot oppose the resale of goods identified with its mark'.[441] And in the absence of a defect Kosan could not even rely on product liability laws.

Turning to the trade mark registration covering gas, and in particular the effect of the addi- **10.400** tional labelling on the origin function, the Advocate General focused on the perception of the consumer and sale practices:

> Crucial to that assessment will be the question of how the average consumer of that kind of product perceives the labelling ... and, thus, also the sales practices in the market for bottled gas. If ... consumers are accustomed to the fact that gas bottles are refilled by companies which did not initially place them on the market, the likelihood of a mistake is reduced.[442]

Linked with the origin function is the Advocate General's view on the guarantee of quality function; if 'the labelling of the bottles excludes any connection to the proprietor of the

---

[439] Point 1.
[440] Point 20.
[441] Point 26.
[442] Point 42.

trade mark, consumers have no reason to presume in the present case that the proprietor of the trade mark acts as a guarantor for the quality of the gas'.[443]

10.401 A different approach is followed regarding the additional functions the Court came up with in *Google France*.[444] Having acknowledged that there are circumstances that the advertising, investment, or communication function might be affected the Advocate General introduced a counterbalancing consideration, 'not every adverse affect on those functions justifies the application of art.5(1) of Directive 89/104. The protection of those functions on the basis of that provision, *first*, must not undermine the requirements of specific protective rules and, *secondly*, must respect overriding other interests'.[445] In this case, the 'the consumer's property rights in the composite bottle and the protection of competition outweigh the affected functions of the trade mark'.[446] Consumers would not be free to exercise their property rights in the bottle; to the contrary they would find themselves tied to a single supplier. Competitors should, in principle, be allowed to use the bottle in the same way a car mechanic should be allowed to advertise its own services in relation to a branded car.

(b) The Judgment of the Court

10.402 The Court held that, to allow the owner of a trade mark right constituted by the shape of the composite bottle to prevent those bottles from being refilled would unduly reduce competition in the downstream market for the refilling of gas bottles. This would even create the risk of that market being closed off if Kosan was to succeed in imposing its bottle because of its specific technical characteristics.

10.403 The Court paid less attention to the fact that the specification covered both gas and gas bottles. It focused on the nature of the protected trade mark as a product in itself:

> the composite bottles, which are intended for re-use a number of times, do not constitute mere packaging of the original product, but have an independent economic value and must be regarded as goods in themselves. When the consumer first purchases such a bottle filled with gas from one of Kosan Gas's dealers, he must pay not only for that gas, but also for the composite bottle, the price of which is higher than that of standard steel gas canisters, in particular on account of their specific technical characteristics, and than the price of the gas which they contain.[447]

10.404 It went on, with considerable clarity, to identify and describe all the interests that must be taken into account. Note, here, the holistic reference the Court made to the interest of the proprietor, its licensee, its competitors, and its consumers:

> In those circumstances, a balance must be struck between, on the one hand, the legitimate interest on the part of the licensee of the right to the trade mark constituted by the shape of the composite bottle and the proprietor of the marks affixed to that bottle in profiting from the rights attached to those marks and, on the other, the legitimate interests of purchasers of those bottles, in particular the interest in fully enjoying their property rights in those bottles, and the general interest in maintaining undistorted competition.[448]

---

[443] Point 46.
[444] Discussed at paragraph 9.122 et seq.
[445] Point 59.
[446] Point 65.
[447] Paragraph 30.
[448] Paragraph 31.

10.405 The first sale realized for their proprietors the economic value of the marks relating to the bottles. However, the property rights of the purchasers of the bottles would not be fully enjoyed if they were 'restricted by the related trade mark rights even after the sale of those bottles by the proprietor or with his consent'.[449] The market itself could suffer; not allowing third parties to refill the bottles would:

> unduly reduce competition on the downstream market for the refilling of gas bottles, and would even create the risk of that market's being closed off if the licensee and proprietor were to succeed in imposing its bottle because of its specific technical characteristics, the protection of which is not the purpose of trade mark law. That risk is, moreover, increased by virtue of the fact that the cost of the composite bottle is much more than the gas and that the purchaser, in order to regain a free choice of gas supplier, would have to forgo the initial outlay made in purchasing the bottle, the recouping of which requires the bottle to be reused a sufficient number of times.[450]

10.406 Accordingly, the sale of the bottle should exhaust the rights to the trade mark constituted by the shape of the composite bottle. It went on to state that the trade mark proprietor

> transfers to the purchaser the right to use that bottle freely, including the right to exchange it or have it refilled, once the original gas has been consumed, by an undertaking of his choice, that is to say, not only by that licensee and proprietor, but also by one of its competitors. The corollary of that right on the part of the purchaser is the right of those competitors, within the limits set out in art.7(2) of Directive 89/104, to refill and exchange the empty bottles.[451]

10.407 Cases where the condition of the goods was changed or impaired after they had been put on the market[452] or use would seriously damage the reputation of the mark, or would give the impression of a commercial connection between the party using the mark and the trade mark proprietor could potentially fall within these limits.[453] Note too that the Court focused exclusively on the origin function when it provided some practical advice on what the national court should be looking for whilst considering the impression the additional labelling would give to consumers.

> The labelling of the composite bottles and the circumstances in which they are exchanged must not lead the average consumer who is reasonably well informed and reasonably observant and circumspect to consider that there is a connection between the two undertakings at issue in the main proceedings or that the gas used to refill those bottles comes from Kosan Gas. In order to assess whether such an erroneous impression is precluded, it is necessary to take into account the practices in that sector and, in particular, whether consumers are accustomed to the gas bottles being filled by other dealers. Furthermore, it appears to be reasonable to assume that a consumer who goes directly to Viking Gas either to exchange his empty gas bottle for a full bottle or to have his own bottle refilled is more readily in a position to be aware that there is no connection between Viking Gas and Kosan Gas.[454]

Indeed the fact that Kosan Gas trade marks remained visible following the additional labelling seemed to rule out that Viking's labelling altered the condition of the bottles by masking their origin.

---

[449] Paragraph 33.
[450] Paragraph 34.
[451] Paragraph 35.
[452] Citing C-59/08 *Copad SA v Christian Dior Couture SA* [2009] ECR I-3421.
[453] Citing C-558/08 *Portakabin Ltd v Primakabin BV* [2010] ETMR 52.
[454] Paragraph 40.

10.408 The case makes it clear that:

> First, trade mark law is not applied in a vacuum: factual, market, and competition contexts affect not only the internalised interpretation of legal provisions and doctrines but also their application when the external to trade mark law reality of the market place is taken into account. Second, the role of the consumer is becoming increasingly more nuanced either as the test case for establishing infringement or as a market player whose interests are taken more directly into account. And, third, obtaining a trade mark right has become ostensibly an easier exercise following objective and comparable for all criteria. Enforcing them though is a different game; specific for each product market competition concerns introduce a much more complex and subjective spectre for trade mark proprietors.[455]

F. Conclusion

10.409 This chapter looked at the interaction between free movement of goods rules and the exercise of trade mark rights. This has been an area where the Court has willingly undertaken a policy role. At the early stages the balance tilted heavily towards the free movement principle; but as the common market grew in strength the Court started acknowledging the beneficial effects of trade mark rights.

10.410 The free movement principle remains the starting point throughout the jurisprudence of the Court in free movement and exhaustion cases; it is the rule to which the property right over a trade mark is an exception that must be interpreted narrowly, even in the most recent cases involving repackaging and rebranding. At the same time, though, the Court has recognized that both trade mark rights and the free movement of goods rules are there to protect fundamental interests, and gradually it has started accommodating the idea of trade marks deserving to be protected not only as indications of origins but also as indicators of reputation and prestige. Note that in *Boehringer I*[456] the Court chose to refer to *Dior*[457] in order to describe the reputation interests of the proprietor.

10.411 Looking at the exhaustion provisions of the Directive and the Regulation the Court followed the rationale it had developed in its free movement of goods case law. It opted for a territoriality principle: the general rule is that the right is exhausted once the marked product is put on the market within the EEA. At the same it developed a set of conditions for establishing whether and delineating the extent to which trade mark rights can still be used in order to stop intra-Community trade.

10.412 The last two cases show how the interpretation and application of trade mark law in Europe become increasingly cohesive. Consent first becomes a tool for interpreting the concept of acquiescence and second positions the exhaustion of rights at the centre of the debate on the extent of protection trade marks should enjoy in a competitive market.

---

[455] V Liakatou and S Maniatis, 'Red soles, gas bottles, and ethereal market places: competition, context, and trade mark law', EIPR 2012, 34(1).
[456] C-143/00 *Boehringer Ingelheim Pharma KG* [2002] ECR I-3759.
[457] C-337/95 *Parfums Christian Dior SA* [1997] ECR I-6013; see also C-63/97 *Bayerische Motorwerke AG and BMW Nederland BV* [1999] ECR I-905.

11

TRADE MARKS AND COMPETITION LAW

A. Introduction

In this chapter we will examine briefly the formal interaction between trade marks and competition law. We have seen that competition questions were raised in the previous chapter in respect of the potential function of trade mark rights as tools for compartmentalizing the common European market into national markets. We have also highlighted the competition arguments and rationale considered by the Court first in determining what constitutes a protectable trade mark and second in delineating the scope of protection.[1] Here, the focus shifts to how trade mark rights and agreements involving trade marks are weighed up by competition law. The two primary competition rules that are described below deal with anti-competitive collusion (Article 101 TFEU, previously Article 81 EC) and abuse of market dominance (Article 102 TFEU, previously Article 82 EC). For the purposes of competition law, and Article 101 in particular, there is another legal tool that we must also take into account, that of block exemptions; a mechanism that European law has employed often in order to ease the tension between the exclusive nature of intellectual property rights and competition principles. Historically, the exemptions covered specific rights or types of agreement, for example, Regulation 2349/84[2] covered patent licences whereas Regulation 556/89[3] followed the same route for know-how licences. Gradually the scope of the exemptions broadened, in parallel with the growing completion of the common market project and responding to changes in economic thinking. Regulation 240/96[4] amalgamated the two exemptions mentioned above and became known as the Technology Transfer Regulation for patent, know-how, and mixed patent and know-how licences. The Commission, feeling that its approach had become too formalistic, expanded further the ambit of the exemptions by adopting Regulation 2790/99,[5] the vertical agreements block exemption, and Regulation 772/2004.[6] The most recent version of the Regulation was adopted in 2014.[7]

11.01

---

[1] See, for example, the opinion of the AG in C-321/03 *Dyson Ltd v Register of Trade Marks* [2007] 2 CMLR 14, discussed in Chapter 5.
[2] Commission Regulation 2389/84 [1984] OJ L 219/15.
[3] Commission Regulation 556/89 [1989] OJ L 61/1.
[4] Commission Regulation 240/96 [1996] OJ L 31/2.
[5] Commission Regulation 2790/99 on the application of Article 81(3) of the Treaty to categories of vertical agreements and concerted practices [1999] OJ L 336.
[6] Commission Regulation 772/2004 on the application of Article 81(3) of the Treaty to categories of technology agreements [2004] OJ L 123/11.
[7] Commission Regulation (EU) No 316/2014 of 21 March 2014 on the application of Article 101(3) of the Treaty on the Functioning of the European Union to categories of technology transfer agreements (TTBER) OJ L 93, 28.03.2014, pp 17–23 and Communication from the Commission—Guidelines on the application of Article 101 of the Treaty on the Functioning of the European Union to technology transfer agreements OJ C 89, 28.03.2014, pp 3–50.

11.02 Intellectual property transactions might also fall under the umbrella of other block exemptions relating to specific types of agreements or specific product markets. Note that only one block exemption may apply to any agreement.

11.03 Transactions involving trade marks will have to satisfy the requirements of the relevant block exemption in order to benefit from its application. For example, trade mark licensing is not covered by the Technology Transfer Regulation, unless and to the extent that the trade marks are directly related to the exploitation of the licensed technology and do not constitute the primary objective of the agreement. Still, signs that constitute trade marks but also enjoy design protection can be covered directly by the Regulation.

11.04 The general principle is the same for all the block exemptions: agreements that satisfy the conditions of the relevant regulation are automatically exempted under Article 101(3). To avoid abuse of the system there are market thresholds above which the exemptions do not apply and lists of clauses that would not be exempted in any case. For example, under the Vertical Agreements Block Exemption, setting maximum or recommended prices would be allowed, but fixing or setting minimum prices would not be tolerated. National authorities should always take into account the Guidelines and other Notices issued by the Commission, part of a system of cooperation between the Commission, on the one hand, and the national courts and competition authorities, on the other, established by the Court in cases like *Delimitis*[8] and *HB Ice Cream*.[9]

11.05 Finally, a cautionary note. The cases discussed below aim to give the reader a flavour of the interface between trade marks, or by way of example other intellectual property rights, and competition from a European competition law angle; the perspective, however, remains that of a trade mark lawyer. They do not purport to be an authoritative, or even comprehensive, picture of European competition law.

B. Competition Rules

(1) The Provisions of the Treaty

11.06 Article 3(g) of the EC Treaty stated that one of the deeds of the Community is the establishment of a system ensuring that competition in the internal market is not distorted. The primary tools for achieving this are provided by the joint application of Article 101 TFEU and Article 102 TFEU.

11.07 Article 101 TFEU is the provision that aims to stop anti-competitive collusion between market players:

    1. The following shall be prohibited as incompatible with the common market; all agreements between undertakings, decisions by associations of undertakings and concerted practices which may affect trade between Member States and which have as their object or effect the prevention, restriction or distortion of competition within the common market, and in particular those which:
       (a) directly or indirectly fix purchase or selling prices or any other trading conditions;
       (b) limit or control production markets, technical development, or investment;

---

[8] C-234/89 *Stergios Delimitis v Henninger Bräu AG* [1991] ECR I-935.
[9] C-344/98 *HB Ice Cream Ltd v Masterfoods* [2000] ECR I-11369.

(c) share markets or sources of supply;
(d) apply dissimilar conditions to equivalent transactions with other trading parties, thereby placing them at a competitive disadvantage; and
(e) make the conclusion of contracts subject to acceptance by the other parties of supplementary obligations which, by their nature or according to commercial usage, have no connection with the subject of such contracts.

Any agreements or decisions prohibited pursuant to this Article shall be automatically void.

The provisions of paragraph 1 may, however, be declared inapplicable in the case of: any agreement or category of agreements between undertakings; any decision or category of decisions by associations of undertakings; and any concerted practice or category of concerted practices, which contributes to improving the production or distribution of goods or to promoting technical or economic progress, while allowing consumers a fair share of the resulting benefit, and which does not
(a) impose on the undertakings concerned restrictions which are not indispensable to the attainment of these objectives; and
(b) afford such undertakings the possibility of eliminating competition in respect of a substantial part of the products in question.

Article 102 targets the concentration of economic power when combined with abusive behaviour:

11.08

Any abuse by one or more undertakings of a dominant position within the common market or in a substantial part of it shall be prohibited as incompatible with the common market in so far as it may affect trade between Member States. Such abuse may, in particular, consist in:
(a) directly or indirectly imposing unfair purchase or selling prices or unfair trading conditions;
(b) limiting production, markets or technical development to the prejudice of consumers;
(c) applying dissimilar conditions to equivalent transactions with other trading parties, thereby placing them at a competitive disadvantage; and
(d) making the conclusion of contracts subject to acceptance by the other parties of supplementary obligations which, by their nature or according to commercial usage, have no connection with the subject of such contracts.

(2) The Multiple Tasks of European Competition Law

The Court of Justice has described the negative effect of monopolies, in *United Brands*,[10] as: **11.09**

a position of economic strength enjoyed by an undertaking which enables it to prevent effective competition being maintained on the relevant market by giving it the power to behave to an appreciable extent independently of its competitors, customers and ultimately of its consumers.[11]

Competition law in a 'national market' environment aims to inject into trade an efficiency catalyst that benefits both consumers and marketers. Resources are allocated productively and efficiently, consumer welfare is enhanced, and the dynamism of smaller players is protected from the abuse of stronger opponents. In Europe competition law has undertaken an additional role, to facilitate the creation of a single market. **11.10**

From a historical perspective the application of the competition provisions of the Treaty can be divided into three stages that broadly correspond with the establishment, development, and **11.11**

---

[10] Case 27/76 *United Brands Co and United Brands Continental BV v Commission* [1978] ECR 207.
[11] *United Brands* (n 10) paragraph 2.

strengthening of the common market.[12] The system adapted, accepting broad policy trends but without conforming to a strict hierarchy of objectives and each case has to be viewed within its own economic and historical context. Market regulation when the cost of failure is not acceptable is another aim of competition law but in Europe competition policy is not only about efficiency; it affects trade integration, the approximation of the economies of the Member States, the development of targeted sectors of the European economy and specific geographical regions, and, ultimately, the creation and support of an integrated European economy.

(3) Direct Applicability

11.12 Articles 101 and 102 are directly applicable. In *BRT*[13] the Court ruled that they had direct effect in the national legal orders, they apply to relationships between individuals, and create rights directly in respect of the individuals concerned which national courts must safeguard. Articles 101(1) and 102 are therefore part of the national legal order and can be pleaded before a national court either as a case of action and/or as a defence.[14]

C. Competition and Trade Marks: The Application of Article 101

(1) *Consten and Grundig*: The Interaction with Trade Mark Law: The Starting Point

11.13 *Consten and Grundig*[15] is the starting point in the interaction between competition and trade mark law in Europe. It was also the first time that a Decision of the Commission regarding the application of Article 101(1) and Article 101(3) on an individual case was challenged before the Court. Consten was the sole distributor of Grundig products in France and had undertaken not to stock competing products. It provided an after-sales service and was responsible for the national marketing campaigns in France. In order to protect the territorial integrity of the licence Consten had also undertaken not to sell Grundig products outside the territory covered by the licence.

11.14 Grundig, the German manufacturer of electronic products, had similar arrangements with other 'national' distributors in Europe. To enable the enforcement of these agreements Grundig had assigned to Consten the registration of the trade mark GINT in France. UNEF, a parallel importer, who bought Grundig products in Germany and imported them into France, responded to Grundig's trade mark infringement action by claiming that the agreement between Grundig and Consten violated Article 101 and complained to the Commission. Grundig too notified to the Commission the sole agency agreements. The Commission found that the contract concluded between Grundig and Consten constituted an infringement of Article 101 and refused to grant an exemption under Article 101(3).[16] The Decision was challenged before the Court of Justice.

---

[12] For intellectual property rights in particular, see Rosa Greaves, 'Herschel Smith Lecture 1998: Article 86 [82] of the EC Treaty and Intellectual Property Rights' [1998] EIPR 379 and Imelda Maher, 'Competition Law and Intellectual Property Rights: Evolving Formalism' in Craig and de Búrca (eds), *The Evolution of EU Law* (Oxford: Oxford University Press, 1999).
[13] Case 127/73 *Belgische Radio en Televisie v SV SABAM and NV Fonior* [1974] ECR 51, paragraph 16.
[14] Greaves (n 12) 380.
[15] Joined Cases 56 and 58/64 *Etablissements Consten SARL and Grundig Verkaufs-GmbH v Commission* [1966] ECR 299.
[16] Commission Decision 64/566 (*Grundig*) [1964] CMLR 489; [1964] OJ 2545.

(a) The interpretation of Articles 101 and 102 TFEU: Vertical agreements

The Court started its consideration by noting that Articles 101 and 102 did not have distinct areas of application. Article 101 could be applied to an agreement between competitors as well as to an agreement between non-competing entities operating at different levels of the supply chain, even if the latter did not constitute an abuse of a dominant position. Competition might be distorted by agreements limiting competition that might take place between one of the parties to the agreement and third parties. It held that sole distribution agreements should be examined under the light of Article 101(1), excluding, in principle, only cases where a sole undertaking integrated its own distribution network into its business organization.

11.15

Revealing the Court's priorities it added that:

11.16

> an agreement between producer and distributor which might tend to restore the national divisions in trade between Member States might be such as to frustrate the most fundamental objections of the Community. The Treaty, whose preamble and content aim at abolishing the barriers between states, and which in several provisions gives evidence of a stern attitude with regard to their reappearance, could not allow undertakings to reconstruct such barriers. Article 101(1) is designed to pursue this aim, even in the case of agreements between undertakings placed at different levels in the economic process.[17]

(b) Capable of constituting a threat

As to whether an agreement affects trade between Member States, the factor triggering the application of Community rather than national law, the Court identified as particularly important 'whether the agreement is capable of constituting a threat, either direct or indirect, actual or potential, to freedom of trade between Member States in a manner which might harm the attainment of the objectives of a single market between states'.[18] It followed that an agreement preventing, first, undertakings other than the sole distributor from importing Grundig products into France, and then the sole distributor from re-exporting Grundig products from France to other Member States, fell within the scope of Article 101. The Court, however, equated to such an agreement limitations that 'might ensue for third parties from the registration in France by Consten of the GINT trade mark'.[19]

11.17

(c) The relevant product market

The Court then considered the relevant product market. Grundig and the German Government submitted that the Commission had failed to follow a 'rule of reason' analysis by looking only at the market for Grundig products rather than the market for similar products of different makes. Vertical sole distributorship agreements would increase rather than harm competition between different brands. The Court disagreed.

11.18

> The principle of freedom of competition concerns the various stages and manifestations of competition. Although competition between producers is generally more noticeable than that between distributors of products of the same make, it does not thereby follow that an agreement tending to restrict the latter kind of competition should escape the prohibition of Article [101](1) merely because it might increase the former.[20]

---

[17] *Consten and Grundig* (n 15) 340. The reader should note that the Court viewed Article 81 as a tool for breaking down barriers between States.
[18] Ibid 341.
[19] Ibid.
[20] Ibid 342.

(d) Object and effect

11.19 Also, against a 'rule of reason' analysis, the Court added that for an agreement that had as its object the prevention, restriction, or distortion of competition there was no need to take account of its concrete effects. Still, it considered the agreement within its economic and legal context, concluding that it aimed to isolate the French market for Grundig products and maintain artificially separate national markets within the Community. The Court stressed that this would be in relation to products of a very well-known brand. It rejected the relevance of economic data, including price differences between France and Germany, the character of the considered products, and the level of Consten's overheads, in potentially justifying the agreement from a commercial perspective, as well as the possibility of other beneficial effects. It also decided that although it was desirable for the Commission to take into account the views of other parties affected by its Decision, for example, other Grundig licensees, this did not mean they had a right to be party to the Consten and Grundig proceedings.

(e) The validity of the agreement

11.20 The only concession the Court made was deciding that only the parts of the agreement that went against Article 101(1) should be considered automatically void, unless those parts were not severable from the overall agreement, in which case it should be considered void in its totality. Thus, the Commission had to justify its Decision specifically in respect of each one of the clauses of the agreement.

(f) The effect of the trade mark registration

11.21 Part of the argument against the Decision of the Commission was based on the role of the trade mark registration. The argument was that the effect on competition was the result of the trade mark registration; the contested Decision would take away from Consten the power to assert its trade mark rights. The Court, however, took a step back noting that the French registration was the result of the agreement between Grundig and Consten, which should be prohibited according to Article 101(1). Allowing Consten to use the trade mark registration assigned to it by Grundig to achieve the objective of the agreement would render the prohibition ineffective.

(g) Property, Article 36, and the competition provisions

11.22 The Court then considered the Treaty provisions relied upon by Consten and Grundig. Article 36 TFEU was linked with the liberalization of trade rather than competition, and could not limit the application of Article 101. Further, there was no conflict with Article 345, providing that the Treaty shall not prejudice the rules in Member States governing the system of property ownership, because the Decision did not interfere with the grant of property rights but only limited

> their exercise to the extent necessary to give effect to the prohibition under Article [101](1). The power of the Commission to issue such an injunction ... was in harmony with the nature of the Community rules on competition which have immediate effect and are directly binding on individuals.[21]

It concluded that such 'a body of rules, by reason of its nature described above and its function, does not allow the improper use of rights under any national trade-mark law in order to frustrate the Community's law on cartels'.[22]

---

[21] Ibid 345.
[22] Ibid 346.

(h) The exemption requirements

11.23 The Court then looked at the grounds for applying Article 101(3). The Court recognized that, as a matter of good administration, the Commission had to contribute to the process of determining whether an exemption is justified rather than expect the parties to prove that the requirements have been fulfilled. The ultimate decision on this involved complex economic evaluations and the Court in its judicial review confined itself to an examination of the relevance of the facts on which the evaluations were based and of the legal consequences which the Commission deduced from those facts. The Court—looking once again at the wider picture—decided that the existence of a compensating improvement in the production or distribution of the relevant goods could only be decided in the spirit of Article 101; the advantages had to be generally indisputable, render the agreement indispensable in all respects, and be appreciable and objective.

(i) The quality function

11.24 One specific argument linked with the quality function of a trade mark was that the Commission did not examine whether it would be possible to provide guarantee and after-sales services without absolute territorial protection, taking into account Grundig's reputation in respect of these services. Allowing parallel imports could compel Consten to refuse them in respect of parallel imported products, whereas those provided by parallel importers could be unsatisfactory. Here, the Court took another step back and looked at the actual marketplace, finding that UNEF's services were comparable to Consten's and their services did not seem to have harmed Grundig's reputation. It added that Consten could inform potential consumers about the advantages of dealing with the official distribution network.

11.25 As to the need to compensate Consten through exclusivity for taking the risk for launching the products onto the French market, the Court found that this was linked with its decision to accept the agreement but not with the improvement in distribution mentioned in Article 101(3). Similarly, the Court rejected the argument that Consten deserved exclusivity because some of the products were specially adapted for the French market; indeed, the Court considered this to be an advantage for a sole distributor.

(2) *Société Technique Minière*: A Rule of Reason Analysis?

11.26 *Société Technique Minière*[23] offers a contemporaneous comparative context for comprehending the effect and limitations of *Grundig*. Again, the contested contract covered an 'exclusive right of sale' agreement. Société Technique Minière was the exclusive distributor in France of grading equipment produced by Maschinenbau Ulm. Typically, the validity of the contract according to Article 101 became an issue when a dispute arose between the parties. The crucial difference with *Grundig* was that the French market had not been compartmentalized: Société Technique Minière could export to other Member States, parallel imports could reach the French market, and intellectual property rights were not raised as cross-border barriers. Accordingly, the Court felt comfortable enough to consider the benefits of such an agreement. It noted that according to Article 101 'object' and 'effect' are alternative rather than cumulative conditions and described a two-step analysis.

---

[23] Case 56/65 *Société Technique Minière v Maschinenbau Ulm GmbH* [1965] ECR 235.

11.27 The precise purpose of the agreement had to be sought within its economic context. This examination followed the principles of a 'rule of reason' analysis:

> The competition in question must be understood within the actual context in which it would occur in the absence of the agreement in dispute. In particular it may be doubted whether there is an interference with competition if the said agreement seems really necessary for the penetration of a new area by an undertaking. Therefore, in order to decide whether an agreement containing a clause 'granting an exclusive right of sale' is to be considered as prohibited by reason of its object or of its effect, it is appropriate to take into account in particular the nature and quantity, limited or otherwise, of the products covered by the agreement, the position and importance of the grantor and the concessionnaire on the market for the products concerned, the isolated nature of the disputed agreement or, alternatively, its position in a series of agreements, the severity of the clauses intended to protect the exclusive dealership or, alternatively, the opportunities allowed for other commercial competitors in the same products by way of parallel re-exportation and importation.[24]

(3) *Völk v Vervaecke*: Significant Effect

11.28 In *Völk v Vervaecke*[25] the Court considered an exclusive distribution agreement for washing machines covering the territories of Belgium and Luxembourg. The agreement provided that only if the distributor failed to sell the agreed number of products would the manufacturer supply other traders in the same territory. The Oberlandesgericht Munich sought from the Court clarification as to whether, in order to assess the application of Article 101(1), the part of the market which the plaintiff in fact held or had sought to win in the relevant Member States, the ceded territory, should be taken into account.

11.29 The Court held that to be capable of affecting trade between Member States:

> the agreement must, on the basis of a collection of objective legal or factual factors, permit a reasonably probable expectation that it could exercise an influence, direct or indirect, actual or potential, on the trade trends between member-States in a direction which would harm the attainment of the objectives of a single market between States. Furthermore, the prohibition in Article [101(1)] may apply only on condition that the agreement in question also has the object or effect of preventing, restricting or distorting competition in the Common Market. These conditions should be understood by reference to the actual context in which the agreement exists.[26]

11.30 From the opposite perspective, an agreement would escape Article 101(1) if it only affected the market insignificantly, taking into account the weak position of the parties in the relevant product market. It found that it was possible that 'an exclusive concession agreement, even with absolute territorial protection, may in view of the weak position of the parties on the market in the products in question in the territory which is the subject of the absolute protection escape the prohibition'.[27]

(4) *Béguelin*: The Relevance of Context

11.31 In *Béguelin*[28] the Court again considered the overall context of the agreement rather than the agreement in isolation. On the one hand, it required from the national courts

---

[24] Ibid 250.
[25] Case 5/69 *Völk v Etablissements J Vervaecke SPRL* [1969] ECR 295.
[26] Ibid, paragraph 3.
[27] *Völk* (n 25) paragraph 3.
[28] Case 22/71 *Béguelin Import Co v GL Import-Export SA* [1971] ECR 949.

examining not only the rights and obligations derived from the clauses of the agreement but also its economic and legal context, and particularly the possible existence of similar agreements concluded by the same producer with concessionaires established in other Member States.

> More particularly, an exclusive agency agreement is capable of affecting trade between member-States and may have the effect of hindering competition where the concessionnaire can prevent parallel imports from other member-States into the conceded territory by means of a combination of the agreement with the effects of national law on unfair competition.[29]

11.32 However, for Article 101 to apply 'the agreement must affect noticeably the trade between member-States and competition'.[30] Courts should consider the relevant factors 'in the real context in which they would be in the absence of the agreement in the case'.[31] The Court added that in assessing whether the agreement could escape the application of Article 101(1) courts should look at:

> the nature and limited or unlimited quantity of the products covered by the agreement, the position and importance of the grantor, the position and importance of the concessionnaire on the market in the products in question, the isolated nature of the agreement in question or its place among a network of agreements, the severity of the clauses intended to protect the exclusive right or the possibilities left open to other commercial dealings in the same products through re-export or parallel imports.[32]

(5) *Delimitis*: A Web of Agreements; Closer to a Rule of Reason Analysis

11.33 *Delimitis*[33] offered the Court the opportunity to deal with the effect of restrictive practices adopted by a network of similar beer supply agreements. The case is also relevant from the aspect of market definition, contrasting between beer supplied through retail channels and beer supplied through public houses and restaurants. Note that at the time the Commission had adopted Regulation 1984/83[34] on the application of Article 101(3) to certain categories of exclusive purchasing agreements, including long-term exclusive purchasing agreements for the resale of beer in premises used for the sale and consumption of drinks. Article 6 of the Regulation defined the agreements eligible for block exemption as agreements between only two undertakings (a supplier and a reseller), whereby the reseller agreed with the supplier to purchase only from the supplier certain beers, or certain beers and certain other drinks specified in the agreement, for resale in designated premises in consideration for special commercial or financial advantages. According to a Notice issued by the Commission the drinks covered in such agreements should be specified by brand or denomination.

11.34 The contested agreement was between Henninger, the supplier, and Delimitis, the reseller. The supplier let a cafe to Delimitis who undertook to obtain, exclusively, draught, bottled, and canned beer from Henninger and soft drinks from its subsidiaries. The purchase of beers and soft drinks from other undertakings established in the Federal Republic of Germany or from undertakings established in non-Member States was prohibited. However, the agreement allowed the tenant to purchase beer and soft drinks from undertakings in other

---

[29] Paragraph 14.
[30] Paragraph 16.
[31] Paragraph 17.
[32] Paragraph 18.
[33] *Delimitis* (n 8).
[34] [1983] OJ L 173/5.

Member States. Once again, the validity of the agreement was challenged upon termination. Henninger deducted from the initial deposit an amount that it considered it was owed by Delimitis. Delimitis disagreed and contended that the contract was contrary to Article 101(1) and was not covered by the block exemption. The case reached the Oberlandesgericht (Higher Regional Court) Frankfurt am Main that referred a number of questions to the Court on the interpretation of Article 101(1) and the Block Exemption Regulation.

(a) Object and effect

11.35 The Court repeated that even if the agreements did not have the object of restricting competition within the meaning of Article 101(1), it remained necessary to ascertain whether they had the effect of preventing, restricting, or distorting competition. Citing *Brasserie de Haecht*,[35] it noted that they had to be assessed in the context in which they occurred; this included the issue whether they might combine with others to have a cumulative effect on competition. In order to ascertain the effects of beer supply agreements the Court first defined the relevant market and then looked at the function and effect of the supply agreements.

(b) The definition of the relevant market

11.36 The starting point was identifying the nature of the economic activity in question, in this case the sale of beer. The second step was to identify the channels of trade: retail channels and premises for the sale and consumption of drinks, in particular public houses and restaurants. The second method of sale was distinguished from the first on the basis of price elasticity; consumption was not necessarily dependent on price because the sale of beer was linked with the provision of services. 'The specific nature of the public house trade is borne out by the fact that the breweries organise specific distribution systems for this sector which require special installations, and that the prices charged in that sector are generally higher than retail prices.'[36] It accepted that there was some overlap between the two channels, in particular that retail sales allowed new players to get into the wider market for beer, make their brands known, and then use their reputation to gain access into the second market, but found that it had to define the relevant market narrowly as to the market for beer distribution in premises for the sale and consumption of drinks. The third step was to identify the geographical limits of the relevant market. Since most beer supply agreements covered the national level, it concluded that account was to be taken of the national market for beer distribution in premises for the sale and consumption of drinks.

(c) The object and effect of the agreements

11.37 The fourth step was to examine the nature and extent of the beer supply agreements in their totality, comprising all similar contracts tying a large number of points of sale to several national producers:[37]

> The effect of those networks of contracts on access to the market depends specifically on the number of outlets thus tied to national producers in relation to the number of public houses which are not so tied, the duration of the commitments entered into, the quantities of beer to which those commitments relate, and on the proportion between those quantities and the quantities sold by free distributors.[38]

---

[35] Case 23/67 *Brasserie de Haecht v Wilkin* [1967] ECR 407.
[36] *Delimitis* (n 8) paragraph 16.
[37] Citing Case 43/69 *Bilger v Jehle* [1970] ECR 127.
[38] *Delimitis* (n 8) paragraph 19.

(d) A multifactor Article 101(1) test

11.38 However, the existence of a bundle of agreements would not in itself be enough for a finding that the relevant market was inaccessible. The Court saw the bundle as one amongst a number of factors that had to be considered in the examination of

> whether there are real concrete possibilities for a new competitor to penetrate the bundle of contracts by acquiring a brewery already established on the market together with its network of sales outlets, or to circumvent the bundle of contracts by opening new public houses.[39]

The factors included the legal rules and agreements on the acquisition of companies and the establishment of outlets, the minimum number of outlets necessary for the economic operation of a distribution system, and the presence of beer wholesalers not tied to producers.

11.39 The fifth step, in essence a parallel enquiry, should consider the actual conditions under which competitive forces operated on the relevant market. This covered the number and the size of producers present in the market, the degree of market saturation, brand loyalty, and the trend in beer sales in the retail trade. If the above examination revealed that it was difficult to gain access to the relevant market then—and this would be the sixth step—'it is necessary to assess the extent to which the agreements entered into by the brewery in question contribute to the cumulative effect produced in that respect by the totality of the similar contracts found on that market'.[40] According to the competition rules of the Community the responsibility for closing off the market would fall on the breweries which made an appreciable contribution thereto. Agreements by breweries with an insignificant contribution to the cumulative effect would remain outside the scope of Article 101(1). The critical question for this assessment would be the market position of the contracting parties, determined by the market share held by the brewery and any group to which it might belong and the number of tied outlets in relation to the total number of premises for the sale and consumption of drinks in the relevant market.

11.40 However, courts would also have to consider the contribution of the individual contracts. Here, their duration would be the most important issue. If it were manifestly excessive in relation to the average duration of such agreements generally in the relevant market, the individual contract would fall within the prohibition under Article 101(1). 'A brewery with a relatively small market share which ties its sales outlets for many years may make as significant a contribution to a sealing off of the market as a brewery in a relatively strong market position which regularly releases sales outlets at shorter intervals.'[41]

(e) The relevance of the access clause

11.41 The Court then looked at the relevance of the access clause authorizing the reseller to obtain supplies from other Member States. It accepted that it mitigated the scope of the prohibition in favour of beers from other Member States. However, the scope of the clause should be assessed in the light of its wording and its economic and legal context. It noted that the wording of the actual clause appeared limited, allowing the reseller to purchase competing beers in other Member States but not to sell beers imported from other Member States by other undertakings.

---

[39] Paragraph 21.
[40] Paragraph 24.
[41] Point 26.

11.42 The economic and legal context encompassed questions about the minimum quantity of beer the reseller was obliged to obtain from the supplier and the overall sales it could achieve. This would reveal whether the access clause had any practical meaning, in particular where failure to reach the target also meant payment of financial penalties. If the effect of the clause was non-existent or insignificant, the agreement would be treated in the same way as a classic supply agreement without an access clause for the purposes of Article 101(1). If, on the other hand, the clause could give a national or foreign supplier of beers from other Member States a real possibility of supplying the relevant outlet, then the agreement would fall outside the scope of Article 101(1).

(f) Block exemptions: Exemptions to the rule

11.43 The Court found that an agreement could not benefit from Regulation 1984/83 if it failed to identify specifically the beers and drinks it related to. An agreement that referred to a list of products which might be unilaterally altered by the supplier would fail to satisfy the above requirement.

(g) The validity of the agreement

11.44 Citing *Société Technique Minière*,[42] the Court repeated that in principle only those aspects of the agreement that were prohibited by Article 101(1) would be void. The agreement as a whole would be void only if those parts were not severable from the agreement itself. It added that according to the Community legal order an agreement that did not enjoy the protection of a block exemption regulation could always be exempted individually.

(h) The role of the national court

11.45 The national court had also sought guidance in relation to the division of competences. What should a national court do in regard to an agreement that did not satisfy the conditions for the application of Regulation 1984/83, since the Commission was responsible for the implementation of competition policy? The Court held that it was for the Commission to adopt, subject to review by the Court of First Instance and the Court of Justice, individual decisions; this entailed complex economic assessments, in particular in order to assess whether an agreement fell under Article 101(3). At the same time the Commission shared with national courts the competence to apply Article 101(1) and Article 102.[43] 'Articles [101](1) and [102] produce direct effect in relations between individuals and create rights directly in respect of the individuals concerned which the national courts must safeguard.'[44]

11.46 The same principle applied to Block Exemption Regulations; however, in the case of such Regulations, courts could not extend their application to agreements not covered by them because any extension 'whatever its scope, would affect the manner in which the Commission exercises its legislative competence'.[45] The problem as identified by the Court has a significance wider than just competition law:

> It now falls to examine the consequences of that division of competence as regards the specific application of the Community competition rules by national courts. Account should here be taken of the risk of national courts taking decisions which conflict with those taken or envisaged by the Commission in the implementation of Articles [101](1) and [102], and also

---

[42] Case 56/65 *Société Technique Minière v Maschinenbau Ulm GmbH* [1965] ECR 235.
[43] Citing Case 127/73 *Belgische Radio en Televisie v SV SABAM and NV Fonior* [1974] ECR 51.
[44] *Delimitis* (n 8) paragraph 45.
[45] Paragraph 46.

of Article [101](3). Such conflicting decisions would be contrary to the general principle of legal certainty and must, therefore, be avoided when national courts give decisions on agreements or practices which may subsequently be the subject of a decision by the Commission.[46]

11.47 The agreement was clearly outside the scope of Regulation 17/62[47] and so did not enjoy provisional validity. Still the Court held that in order to avoid conflicting decisions the national court should consider a number of alternatives whilst applying Article 101. First, if the conditions for the application of Article 101(1) were clearly not satisfied and there was not a genuine risk of the Commission taking a different decision, the national court might continue the proceedings and rule on the agreement in issue. The same principle should apply where the agreement was clearly contrary to Article 101(1), and according to the exemption regulations and the decision practices of the Commission the agreement 'may on no account be the subject of an exemption decision under Article [101](3)'.[48]

11.48 The second option would cover agreements that satisfied the formal requirements and that the national court considered, again according to the rules and practices of the Commission, that they could be the subject of an exemption decision. The court might then decide to stay proceedings or adopt interim measures. The court should follow the same route when it envisaged a risk of conflicting decisions in the context of the application of Articles 101(1) and 102. A parallel option would be to contact the Commission regarding the state of any proceedings undertaken by it or in order to obtain the necessary economic and legal information. The Commission would be bound to assist the national court according to the duty of sincere cooperation.[49] The final option available to the national court would be to stay proceedings and make a reference to the Court for a preliminary ruling.

(6) *Groupement de Cartes Bancaires*: Object and Effect Revisited

11.49 In *Groupement de Cartes Bancaires*[50] the Court reconfirmed the multifactorial test that must be applied to assess whether coordination between undertakings is harmful to competition, taking into account, in particular, the nature of the services and the functioning and structure of the market against their economic and legal context.

11.50 The court noted that according to its case law there are certain types of coordination between undertakings that reveal a sufficient degree of harm to competition and as a result there may be no need to examine their effects.[51] When this is not the case, in order to:

> determine whether an agreement between undertakings or a decision by an association of undertakings reveals a sufficient degree of harm to competition that it may be considered a restriction of competition 'by object' within the meaning of Article [101(1) TFEU], regard must be had to the content of its provisions, its objectives and the economic and legal context of which it forms a part. When determining that context, it is also necessary to take into consideration the nature of the goods or services affected, as well as the real conditions of the functioning and structure of the market or markets in question.[52]

---

[46] Paragraph 47.
[47] Regulation 17/62 [1962] OJ L 13/204, covering agreements that were in existence prior to 13 March 1962 and notified to the Commission.
[48] Point 50.
[49] According to Article 10 EC; C-2/88 *Imm J.J. Zwartfeld* [1990] ECR I-3365.
[50] C-67/13 P *Commission v Groupement des Cartes Bancaires (CB) v European Commission*, 11 September 2014, ECLI:EU:C:2014:2204.
[51] Citing C-32/11 *Allianz Hungária Biztosító and Others*, EU:C:2013:160.
[52] *Groupement des Cartes Bancaires* (n 50) paragraph 53.

11.51 In addition the intention of the parties may also be taken into account.

11.52 The Court added that the concept of infringement by object should not be given a strict interpretation because the Article 101(1) list was not exhaustive.

(7) *Nungesser* and *EMI*: Existence of a Right and the Way the Right is Exercised

11.53 In *Nungesser*[53] the Court considered the exercise of plant breeders' rights. The French Institut National de la Recherche Agronomique (INRA) had given Eisele exclusive propagating and selling rights over certain varieties of hybrid maize seeds it had developed, in respect of Germany. Eisele and, through Eisele, Nungesser enjoyed absolute territorial protection in Germany: INRA had undertaken not to sell the seeds to other undertakings in Germany, and through its agreements with other national distributors similar to Eisele would ensure that they too would not export the seed to Germany. Eisele could enforce the restriction outside the contractual agreement through the exercise of German plant breeders' rights assigned to him by INRA. In return, Eisele had undertaken not to sell the seeds outside Germany. The Commission found that the agreement infringed Article 101(1).[54]

11.54 Note that under the relevant German legislation, an owner of breeders' rights established outside Germany would be unable to enjoy them in Germany. Thus, the assignment of the rights to a German entity appeared to be objectively necessary outside the context of the licensing agreement. The Court considered that all the agreements between INRA and Eisele should be considered as part of an indivisible whole. In economic terms, Eisele was INRA's exclusive licensee in Germany. Challenging the Commission's Decision before the Court, Eisele and INRA argued that the exclusive licence was commercially essential to allow INRA to enter a new national market and compete with products that were not identical but comparable. INRA would be unable to find a licensee without guaranteeing protection from competition from itself, as licensor, and other licensees. A further argument raised by the applicants was that the exclusive licence constituted the most appropriate means of attaining the objectives of the Common Agricultural Policy, leveraging one fundamental European policy against another.

(a) Rights and contract: Existence and exercise

11.55 The Court repeated its two familiar distinctions: first, between the contractual agreement and plant breeders' rights, and, secondly, between the existence and the exercise of the rights developed in cases like *EMI*.[55] There, the Court had found that cross-licensing of trade marks between competitors leading to market sharing should be prohibited. A trade mark right as such would not fall under the concept of a concerted practice. Still, the exercise of that right might fall within the ambit of the competition prohibitions 'if it were to manifest itself as the subject, the means, or the consequence of a restrictive practice'.[56] In *Nungesser* the Court had confirmed that an 'industrial or commercial property right, as a legal entity, does not possess those elements of contract or concerted practice referred to in Article [101](1)[TFEU] … but the exercise of that right might fall within the ambit of the

---

[53] Case 258/78 *L.C. Nungesser KG and Kurt Eisele v Commission* [1985] ECR 2015.
[54] Commission Decision 78/823 (*Breeders' rights—maize seed*) [1978] OJ L 286/23; [1978] 3 CMLR.
[55] Case 51/75 *EMI Records* [1976] ECR 811.
[56] Ibid, paragraph 27.

prohibitions contained in the Treaty if it were to manifest itself as the subject, the means or the consequence of an agreement'.[57]

In particular: **11.56**

> an agreement granting exclusive rights to utilize an industrial or commercial property right in a certain territory, in conjunction with an agreement appointing the licensee sole distributor for that territory, has the effect of ensuring absolute territorial protection for the licensee by preventing parallel imports.[58]

Turning to the nature and economic characteristics of the product, the Court acknowledged that the development of new seeds involved considerable financial risks; however, it limited their relevance by finding that they were encountered at the time of production of the basic seeds. Once the new variety had reached the stage that the seeds were capable of being officially certified and marketed, trade rules, including competition provisions, should in principle be applied. According to the Court, the technical complications were not dissimilar to those encountered in the field of food or pharmaceutical products, possibly protected by patent or trade mark rights, and were not sufficient to justify a special system for breeders' rights in relation to other industrial or commercial property rights.

(b) Open exclusive and exclusive licences

The Court then looked at the nature of the agreement. It distinguished between an open **11.57** exclusive licence, the case where the licensor undertakes not to compete with the licensee in a defined territory directly or indirectly by granting licences to others, and an exclusive licence with absolute territorial protection, providing the means for eliminating all competition by third parties. It was therefore necessary to examine the situation between licensor and licensees, asking whether 'the exclusive nature of the licence, in so far as it is an open licence, has the effect of preventing or distorting competition within the meaning of Article [101](1) [TFEU]'.[59] At this more specific stage the Court appeared willing to look at the substantive arguments it had rejected as grounds for treating plant breeders' rights separately from other commercial and industrial property rights.

The product took years of research and experimentation and it was unknown to German **11.58** farmers before INRA and Eisele started cooperating. 'For that reason the concern … as regards the protection of new technology is justified.'[60] It accepted that assurances regarding competition might be necessary for the licensee to take the risk of cultivating and marketing that product; not granting licences 'would be damaging to the dissemination of a new technology and would prejudice competition in the Community between the new product and similar existing products'.[61] It concluded that having:

> regard to the specific nature of the products in question … in a case such as the present, the grant of an open exclusive licence, that is to say a licence which does not affect the position of third parties such as parallel importers and licensees for other territories, is not in itself incompatible with Article [101](1) [TFEU].[62]

---

[57] *Nungesser* (n 53) paragraph 28.
[58] Ibid, paragraph 29, citing Case 28/77 *TEPEA BV v Commission* [1978] ECR 139.
[59] *Nungesser* (n 53) paragraph 54.
[60] Paragraph 56.
[61] Paragraph 57.
[62] Paragraph 58.

11.59 However, the position of the Court shifted when it introduced into the picture the position of third parties not bound by the contractual agreement, in particular parallel importers. It repeated its findings in *Grundig*[63] that 'absolute territorial protection granted to a licensee in order to enable parallel imports to be controlled and prevented results in the artificial maintenance of separate national markets, contrary to the Treaty'.[64] For example, the clauses of the agreement seeking to prevent third parties buying seeds in France and exporting them to Germany were found to be contrary to Article 101(1). The Court then considered what was required in order to grant an exemption under Article 101(3). This time the importance of the product was used by the Court as an argument against the grant of an exemption. The seeds would be used by a large number of farmers for the production of maize, an important foodstuff. Accordingly, 'absolute territorial protection manifestly goes beyond what is indispensable for the improvement of production or distribution or the promotion of technical progress'.[65]

(8) *Pronuptia de Paris*: The Benefits of Franchising Agreements

11.60 In *Pronuptia de Paris*[66] the Court looked at a franchising agreement for wedding dresses and accessories within the context of competition rules. It was the nature of the agreement that the Court considered of particular importance.

(a) *Franchising agreements*

11.61 According to the agreement the franchisor undertook: to grant the franchisee the exclusive right to use the 'Pronuptia de Paris' trade mark for a specified area for marketing the relevant products; not to open any other Pronuptia shops or to provide goods or services to third parties in that area; and to assist the franchisee in successfully setting up and operating the franchise and with the commercial aspects of the business, advertising, staff training, fashion and products, purchasing and marketing, and other aspects of the business. The franchisee remained the owner of its business but undertook: to sell the relevant products using the 'Pronuptia de Paris' trade mark only in the shop specified in the contract, and to maintain the shop according to the franchisor's instructions; to purchase from the franchisor 80% of wedding dresses and accessories; to pay the franchisor a royalty on sales; to regard the prices suggested by the franchisor as recommended retail prices, but retaining its freedom to fix its own prices; to advertise in the contract territory only with the franchisor's agreement; to apply the business methods imparted by the franchisor; and to refrain from competing in any way with other Pronuptia shops. Following a dispute between the parties, the franchisee challenged the validity of the agreement on the back of the competition provisions. The Court highlighted the variety of franchising agreements and distinguished in particular between: service franchises, where the franchisee offers a service under the business name or trade mark and in accordance with the instructions of the franchisor; production franchises, where the franchisee manufactures products according to the instructions of the franchisor and sells them under the franchisor's trade mark; and distribution franchises, where the franchisee sells products in a shop with the franchisor's business name or symbol.

(b) *The relevance of the specific agreement*

11.62 The contested agreement fell under the third category, but the Court stressed that its compatibility with Article 101 should be determined on the basis of its specific provisions

---

[63] *Consten and Grundig* (n 15).
[64] *Consten and Grundig* (n 15) paragraph 61.
[65] *Nungesser* (n 53) paragraph 77.
[66] C-161/64 *Pronuptia de Paris GmbH v Pronuptia de Paris Irmgard Schillgallis* [1986] ECR 353.

rather than its categorization. It recognized the benefits of this type of agreement, which was something more than a simple method of distribution. From the franchisor's perspective it was a way for an undertaking to derive financial benefit from its expertise without investing its own capital. For the franchisee, it gave a trader without the necessary experience the opportunity to exploit the franchisor's proven business methods and reputation.

> Franchise agreements for the distribution of goods differ in that regard from dealerships or contracts which incorporate approved retailers into a selective distribution system, which do not involve the use of a single business name, the application of uniform business methods or the payment of royalties in return for the benefits granted. Such a system, which allows the franchisor to profit from his success, does not in itself interfere with competition.[67]

11.63 The Court then found that there were two conditions that had to be met for a franchise agreement to work and not violate Article 101.

(c) Essential clauses

11.64 First, the franchisor should be able to support the franchisee without the risk that its know-how might benefit competitors, directly or indirectly. This would cover clauses that were essential to avoid that risk, including clauses that prohibit the franchisee during the term of the agreement and for a reasonable period after its termination from opening a similar shop in an area covered by a member of the franchise, and prohibit the franchisee from transferring its shop without the approval of the franchisor.

11.65 Secondly, the franchisor must be able to maintain the identity and reputation of the network bearing its business name or symbol. This would cover provisions which establish the means of control necessary for that purpose, including clauses that require the franchisee to: apply the franchisor's business methods and know-how; follow the franchisor's specifications regarding the location and appearance of its shop and seek approval for all advertising; seek authorisation regarding assignment of the franchise; and sell only products supplied by the franchisor or by selected suppliers, but without preventing the franchisee from obtaining those products from other franchisees, in order to enable the public to find at the franchises products of the same quality and the franchisor to protect the reputation of the network. Note the open-ended language of the Court; it simply described some types of clauses that appeared to be essential, linking them with the purpose they ought to fulfil, without providing a closed list.

(d) Anti-competitive clauses

11.66 The Court then went on to consider provisions that restrict competition between members of the network without being necessary for satisfying the two conditions mentioned above, in particular those that share markets between the franchisor and the franchisees or between franchisees or prevent price competition between franchisees.

11.67 By way of example, the Court considered the effect of a clause prohibiting a franchisee from opening a second shop combined with the franchisor's obligation to ensure that the franchisee has the exclusive use of the indicia identifying the network—ie business names, symbols, and trade marks—within the context of the web of agreements of the franchising network. They could result in the sharing of markets and the restriction of competition

---

[67] *Pronuptia de Paris* (n 66) paragraph 15.

within the network. Following *Grundig*,⁶⁸ 'a restriction of that kind constitutes a limitation of competition for the purposes of Article [101](1) if it concerns a business name or symbol which is already well-known'.⁶⁹ It added that even if such agreements covered the territory of a single Member State they were liable to affect trade between Member States if they prevent franchisees from establishing themselves in other Member States. Extrapolating on the viability of the franchise network without such provisions became for the Court an issue for the national courts to determine from the perspective of Article 101(3). Similarly, price guidelines should not become a concerted network practice to set prices.

11.68 Finally, the Court decided that franchising agreements did not fall within the scope of Regulation 67/67⁷⁰ by underlining four characteristics of the block exemption established in the Regulation. First it covered contracts defined by reference to obligations of supply and purchase, which might or might not be reciprocal, and not by reference to the franchising factors analysed by the Court. Secondly, the wording of Article 2 expressly covered only exclusive dealing agreements. Thirdly, Article 2 listed the restrictions and obligations of the exclusive distributor rather than those that were imposed on franchisors. Fourthly, Article 2 did not include the obligation to pay royalties or other obligations pertaining to franchising.

(9) *BAT*: Competition and Trade Mark Law; Delimitation Agreements

11.69 In *BAT*⁷¹ the Court of Justice held that trade mark law should not be used improperly to undermine European competition law. BAT, the proprietor of the trade mark 'Dorcet' that had been registered in Germany but not used commercially, opposed the registration of 'Toltecs' by Segers. Segers entered into negotiations and signed an agreement with BAT regarding the specification of his application without challenging BAT's registration on the basis of non-use.

11.70 At a later stage BAT and Segers disagreed regarding the definition of the products covered by the agreement. Segers did not apply to the German courts to rectify the ambiguity because, according to the Commission, he was not in a position to risk costly litigation with BAT. Because of the ongoing difficulties with BAT, Segers stopped using the trade mark in Germany and applied to the Commission claiming that BAT had infringed Articles 101 and 102. The Commission issued a Decision against BAT,⁷² which it challenged before the Court of Justice. According to the Court the scope of the agreement was objectively ambiguous as a result of the wording suggested by Segers himself. BAT took advantage of this ambiguity in order to block Segers from marketing in Germany the only kind of tobacco he produced. According to BAT the agreement constituted a 'delimitation' agreement that contained a no-challenge clause 'intended to consolidate the position of the Dorcet mark even after it had ceased to be legally protected'⁷³ and its validity should be judged according to German law.

---

⁶⁸ *Consten and Grundig* (n 15).
⁶⁹ *Pronuptia de Paris* (n 66) paragraph 24.
⁷⁰ Regulation 67/67 [1967] OJ L 57/849.
⁷¹ Case 35/83 *BAT Cigaretten-Fabriken GmbH v Commission of the European Communities* [1985] ECR 363.
⁷² Commission Decision 82/897 (*TOLTECS/DORCET*) [1982] OJ L 379/19; [1983] 1 CMLR 412.
⁷³ *BAT* (n 71) paragraph 26.

(a) Risk of confusion and competition

11.71 The Commission had found that there was no 'serious' risk of confusion between the two marks and accordingly no basis for the agreement, whereas BAT argued that according to the principles of German law there was a real risk of confusion. The German Government supported BAT's general argument; in relation to confusion it claimed that there was a real risk because of the phonetic similarity between the signs. The Court accepted that delimitation agreements are:

> lawful and useful if they serve to delimit, in the mutual interest of the parties, the spheres within which their respective trade marks may be used, and are intended to avoid confusion or conflict between them. That is not to say, however, that such agreements are excluded from the application of Article [101] of the Treaty if they also have the aim of dividing up the market or restricting competition in other ways.[74]

However, the relevant agreement imposed obligations on Segers in return for an obligation on behalf of BAT that proved to be fictitious. Without even considering the confusion criteria the Court noted that

> on the one hand, Segers is the proprietor of a trade mark legally acquired and used in a Member State and BAT, on the other, is the proprietor of an unused, dormant, trade mark which is liable to be removed from the register upon application by any interested party. BAT's opposition, as part of its efforts to control the distribution of Segers's products, constitutes an abuse of the rights conferred upon it by its trade mark ownership.[75]

11.72 BAT's overall aggressiveness confirmed that it aimed to prevent Segers from entering the German market rather than protect its dormant trade mark.

(10) The Position of the Commission on Delimitation Agreements

11.73 Note that the position of the Commission on delimitation agreements varied according to the effect of the agreement. In *Sirdar*[76] an agreement between a French and an English undertaking not to use their trade marks in each other's respective territory was found to infringe Article 105(1) TFEU. The French trade mark was LE PHIL D'ART (and its phonetic equivalent PHILDAR) whereas the UK registration was for SIRDAR. The agreement covered PHILDAR and SIRDAR for knitting yarns and its validity was challenged by the French firm following the accession of the United Kingdom to the EEC. The Commission noted that the two signs coexisted in all the other Member States and found that the object of the agreement was to restrict competition in the common market, rejecting the argument that the French company could import its products into the UK market under a different trade mark. Use of another trade mark would deprive the French company of the impact of its advertising campaign and would be financially impossible for other prospective importers to undertake since the yarn was sold in 50 gram packs contained in larger packages. The Commission stressed that even likelihood of confusion between the two signs would not justify market sharing between the two companies. It rejected the claim that the agreement deserved to be exempted, holding that in fact it hindered distribution of the relevant products by obstructing cross-border trade and harmed consumers by denying them choice between competing products.

---

[74] Paragraph 33.
[75] Paragraph 35.
[76] Commission Decision 75/297 (*Re the Agreement of Sirdar Ltd*) [1975] OJ L 125/27; [1975] 1 CMLR D93; [1975] FSR 492.

11.74 In *Persil*,[77] however, where ownership of the same trade mark throughout Europe had been split between two undertakings, an agreement to allow each other's products to circulate freely subject to distinctive colouring was found not to infringe the competition provisions. The agreement covered only the appearance of the two trade marks and aimed to ensure that there could be no confusion about the difference between the relevant products; this, according to the Commission, allowed the products to circulate freely within Europe without either party having to give up a well-established trade mark.

11.75 In *EEC v Syntex*[78] the Commission reconfirmed that it remained within the jurisdiction of Member States to decide whether there was a risk of confusion between different trade marks. However, Article 101(1) would still be applicable to trade mark delimitation agreements where it was evident that the holder of an earlier trade mark could have recourse to national law to prevent the holder of the later mark from using it in one or more Member States, and in particular where the result was to divide the territory of the Union into various territories.[79] Similarly, an agreement that provided for field of use restrictions could also fall under Article 101(1). In *Bayonox*[80] a German chemical producer distributed additives for animal feedstuffs direct to the feed manufacturers through local subsidiaries or licensees. The Commission held that an agreement with its German customers that they would use supplies of a particular additive exclusively for their own feedstuff production in return for reduced prices was against Article 101(1). The selective distribution network would not be objectionable only if there was freedom to trade within the network.

(11) *Bayer Dental*: The Commission on Repackaging Bans

11.76 In *Bayer Dental*[81] the Commission found excessive repackaging bans to be against Article 101(1); even if notified they would not be exempted under Article 101(3). Dental, a division of Bayer AG, was the distributor of Bayer's dental products in a number of Member States either directly, in Germany and to an extent in Denmark, or through wholly owned subsidiaries, in other Member States. In its wholesale price lists in Germany it incorporated the following objectionable clauses: (1) original packages of the seller bearing a registered trade mark could be supplied to a third party only in unopened form; (2) the preparations were intended for distribution solely within the Federal Republic of Germany. Their resale abroad might therefore constitute an infringement of industrial property rights. The Commission found Bayer Dental's subsequent amendments acceptable; however, it issued a Decision in order to indicate that irrespective of the intention of the parties a provision would still infringe Article 101(1) if its effect, objectively considered, would be to restrict exports of the products concerned.

---

[77] *Re the Persil Trade Mark* [1978] CMLR 395.
[78] *EEC v Syntex Corp* [1990] 4 CMLR 343.
[79] In this particular case the Commission considered that the risk of confusion between the trade marks of two pharmaceutical companies did not justify a delimitation agreement that covered the United Kingdom and other non-member countries and that it should be caught by Article 81(1). It closed its investigation once the companies agreed to amend the agreement, allowing their trade marks to coexist in all Member States.
[80] *EEC v Bayer AG (Bayo-Nox)* [1990] 4 CMLR 930; the Decision of the Commission was challenged, without success, before the Court of Justice in C-195/91 P *Bayer AG v Commission* [1994] ECR I-5619.
[81] Commission Decision 90/645 (*Re Bayer Dental*) [1990] OJ L 351/46.

(12) *Campari*: An Example of the Application of Article 101(3) TFEU by the Commission

Campari[82] is another Decision of the Commission. Campari-Milano was the holder of the international trade marks Bitter Campari and Cordial Campari for aperitifs that were manufactured using special mixtures of crushed herbs. To promote its aperitifs Campari set up a network of exclusive product and trade mark licences that proved to be quite successful. Bitter Campari was the only product manufactured both by the licensor and its licensees at that stage. The alcoholic strength and quality of ingredients varied from country to country. The bottles used for the product followed the same design but varied in terms of size. **11.77**

The agreements were notified to the Commission, which went on to examine them according to Article 101. Its views on trade mark licensing appeared restrictive. 'The proprietor of a trade mark has the exclusive right to use the distinctive mark on first sale and to protect the product against infringement of the mark. The proprietor of the trade mark may by licence authorise the use of the protected mark by third parties.' However, if it undertakes only to allow one single undertaking to use its trade mark in a particular territory and to refrain itself from manufacturing products bearing its trade mark there, it loses its freedom to respond to other requests for licences and the competitive advantage to be gained from manufacturing itself within that territory. In the case in point, the exclusive nature of the licence entailed a restriction upon Campari-Milano's freedom to use its marks, as well as preventing third parties, particularly manufacturers of alcoholic beverages, from using them as licensees, however much they may find it in their interests to do so.[83] **11.78**

Accordingly, the Commission found that the obligation on licensees not to handle competing products for the duration of the licensing agreement restricted competition under Article 101(1). The same applied to a ban on the licensor and the licensees engaging in active sales outside their territories, although passive sales were permitted, and the obligation on the licensees to supply the grantor's Campari product rather than their own Campari to diplomatic customers, ships' provision suppliers, and other organizations with duty-free facilities. **11.79**

> The ban on engaging in an active sales policy outside their respective territories prevents Campari-Milano and its licensees from freely disposing throughout the Common Market of the Bitter they have manufactured, restricting them to their exclusive territories, and thus affects international trade in the product. The obligation to supply certain consumers with the original Italian product rather than that which they themselves manufacture means that the licensees have to obtain supplies of Bitter Campari from Italy and thus affects international trade in the product.[84]

It found though that a prohibition on licensees exporting that product to countries outside the European Union would not affect competition under Article 101(1) where reimportation was unlikely because of economic factors. A similar approach was taken in relation **11.80**

---

[82] Commission Decision 78/253 (*Re the Agreements of Campari-Milano SPA*) [1978] OJ L 70/69; [1978] 2 CMLR 397; [1978] FSR 528. See also Commission Decision 90/186 (*Moosehead and Whitbread, Agreement*) [1990] OJ L 100/32, where a restriction imposed on the licensee not to produce or promote any other beer identified as a Canadian beer (when the licensed Moosehead beer was a Canadian beer) was exempted by the Commission. The same applied to a no challenge clause regarding the validity of a trade mark.
[83] *Campari* (n 82) paragraphs 51–52.
[84] Paragraph 56.

to export prohibitions to EFTA States. The Commission deemed reimportation unlikely because potential buyers could obtain the product within the borders of the Union directly from the licensor or its licensees. In addition, economic factors such as the accumulation of trade margins and the combination of excise duties and taxes on alcohol levied by importing countries with the duties charged on crossing the borders of the Union made reimportation financially unattractive. Restriction of a manufacturing licence to plants that were capable of guaranteeing the quality of the product was not covered by Article 101(1) provided that it did not go beyond a legitimate concern for quality control; indeed, the licensor could object only on the basis of product quality criteria.

11.81 The Commission appeared to have been influenced by the link between quality control and the licensed trade marks. This contributed to making the obligation on licensees to follow the licensor's instructions regarding the manufacture of the product and the quality of the ingredients and to buy certain secret raw materials from the licensor compatible with Article 101(1). Note that the agreements covered only the ingredients that were essential for the qualities of the product. The Commission accepted that the qualities of the licensed product had to be controlled by the licensor, who had marketed the original product in the first place. Further, the licensor should not be required to reveal its trade secrets to its licensees.

11.82 Similarly, an obligation on licensees not to divulge the licensed manufacturing process to third parties was compatible with Article 101(1). The obligation on licensees to maintain continuous contact with customers and to spend a standard minimum sum on advertising also passed the hurdle of Article 101(1). The same applied to the prohibition on licence assignments. The licensor was simply safeguarding its freedom to select its licensees. The Commission found that the exclusivity granted by Campari-Milano benefited the production and distribution of Campari Bitter and could be exempted under Article 101(3). The Commission was influenced by the evidence showing that the web of licensing agreements had been successful in practice in creating a decentralized and rational system of production within the Union.

11.83 Note that even the obligation to supply certain customers with Campari-Milano's product was accepted by the Commission. The Commission accepted that there might be taste variations between the products; the purpose of the clause was to ensure product consistency for the customers who had to move frequently from one country to another. In essence, it multiplied rather than restricted choice:

> By restricting licensees' freedom to supply the products they manufacture themselves it makes sure that particular categories of consumers, who are deemed to be outside the licensee's territory and are usually required to move frequently from one territory to another, can always purchase the same original product with all its traditional features as regards both composition and outward appearance. Even though quality standards are observed, it is impossible in particular to avoid differences in taste between the products of the various manufacturers. This obligation is thus designed to prevent these consumers from turning to other competing products and to ensure that they continue to buy Bitter Campari, with the facility of being able to obtain stocks from their local dealer. Further, such consumers are not prevented from freely obtaining the licensees' own products even though any such purchase would be on the normal trading conditions applicable to non-duty-free purchasers.[85]

---

[85] Paragraph 74.

Finally, in respect of arbitration clauses and awards the Commission, in granting an exemption under Article 101(3), required that it be informed of any relevant arbitral awards. It was concerned that the agreements might be interpreted without regard for the Commission's Decision and that the Commission might have to amend it:

11.84

> There is a greater risk at arbitration than in the ordinary courts that interpretation of the agreement may go beyond the limits imposed by the exemption, particularly where the arbitrators, whose function, as in this case, is to produce an amicable settlement, are not bound by the substantive law. Furthermore, review of arbitral awards for their compatibility with Articles [101] and [102], inasmuch as these fail to be regarded as part of EEC public policy, is not necessarily available in non-member-States.[86]

(13) *Javico*: The Contrast with *Silhouette*

Javico[87] is evidence of how much the legislative context of a case can influence its outcome. Despite the apparent analogies with *Silhouette*,[88] the competition context led to a different conclusion. The case came before the Court as a reference from the Cour d'Appel, Versailles. Yves Saint Laurent Parfums (YSL) had set up a selective distribution network for its products in the European Union that was granted an exemption under Article 101(3).[89] For Eastern European markets YSL had concluded with Javico, a company that was not part of YSL's selective distribution network, two distribution contracts, one for Russia and Ukraine and the other for Slovenia, which was not then a member of the Union.

11.85

The Russia and Ukraine agreements included a number of detailed provisions aiming to ensure that the YSL products covered therein were destined solely for those markets. The Slovenia agreement included a more general clause to that effect. Neither agreement was notified to the Commission for the purposes of Article 101(3). Once YSL had spotted in the EU market products originally sold to Javico it terminated the contracts and sought compensation before the French courts. The case reached the Cour d'Appel where Javico argued that the relevant clauses infringed Article 101(1) and that the exemption granted by the Commission was irrelevant.

11.86

The French court stayed proceedings and referred the following questions to the Court.

11.87

> (1) Where an undertaking (the supplier) situated in a Member State of the European Union by contract entrusts another undertaking (the distributor) situated in another Member State with the distribution of its products in a territory outside the Union, must Article [101](1) of the Treaty establishing the European Community be interpreted as prohibiting provisions in that contract which preclude the distributor from effecting any sales in a territory other than the contractual territory, and hence any sale in the Union, either by direct marketing or by re-exportation from the contractual territory? (2) In the event that the said Article [101](1) prohibits such contractual provisions, must it be interpreted as not being applicable where the supplier otherwise distributes his products on the territory of the Union by means of a

---

[86] Paragraph 87.
[87] C-306/96 *Javico International and Javico AG v Yves Saint Laurent Parfums SA* [1998] ECR I-1983.
[88] C-355/96 *Silhouette International Schmied GmbH & Co KG v Hartlauer Handelsgesellschaft mbH* [1998] ECR I-4799.
[89] Commission Decision 92/33 (*Yves Saint Laurent Parfums*) [1992] OJ L 12/24. Part of the decision was declared void by the Court of First Instance in T-19/92 *Leclerc v EC Commission* [1996] ECR II-1851, [1997] 4 CMLR 995 but this related to a provision unrelated to the current case and the remaining parts of the Decision were upheld by the Court of First Instance.

selective distribution network which has been the subject of an exemption decision under Article [101](3)?[90]

(a) The Opinion of Advocate General Tesauro

11.88 (i) **The interpretation of Article 101(1)**   Advocate General Tesauro identified two distinct obligations imposed on Javico through the contested clauses. The first was to export the products to the specified countries; the second was a prohibition on marketing outside the contractual territories. He found that the Block Exemption Regulation 1983/83[91] was irrelevant, since Article 1 clearly provided that it only covered agreements relating to the whole or parts of the European Union; this was viewed by the Court as an essential condition.[92] Accordingly, the object and effect of the clauses had to be examined under the light of Article 101(1).[93] The intention of the parties was clearly to prevent the distribution in the Common Market of the products sold to Javico. 'That allows YSL to oppose parallel imports into the Common Market, where it operates through a selective distribution network whose efficacy might be undermined by the presence on the market of products distributed by resellers not belonging to the network.'[94]

11.89 The Advocate General found that the clauses pursued an essentially anti-competitive aim and in order to gauge their necessity he looked at the two agreements rather than YSL's selective distribution network:

> those clauses are not in fact necessary to ensure that the distribution contract fulfils the economic function assigned to it: that of facilitating penetration of [YSL] products into the East European market. The export clauses must therefore in principle be regarded as prohibited as far as their purpose is concerned.[95]

11.90 The next step was to consider whether the agreements had an appreciable effect on competition in the Common Market.[96] In order to discern the factors the national court had to take into account, AG Tesauro looked at the Decisions of the Commission regarding destination clauses: the impact of the customs duties which must be paid on the product upon reimportation into the European Union; the existence of a difference between the prices charged within the Union and in non-Member States large enough to cover the greater costs of transport and the profit margins of those involved in reimportation and distribution within the Union; and the level of inter-brand competition within the Community.[97] The

---

[90] Reproduced in *Javico* (n 87) paragraph 9.
[91] [1983] OJ L 173/1.
[92] Citing Case 170/83 *Hydrotherm Gerätebau GmbH v Compact del Dott. Ing. Mario Andreoli & C. Sas.* [1984] ECR 2999.
[93] He cited C-250/92 *Gøttrup-Klim Grovvareforeningen v Dansk Landbrugs Grovvareselskab AmbA (DLG)* [1994] I-5641; and C-234/89 *Stergios Delimitis v Henninger Bräu AG* [1991] ECR I-935. The object and effect were considered as alternatives not cumulatively according to C-219/95 P *Ferriere Nord SpA v Commission* [1997] ECR I-4411.
[94] Point 10 of the Opinion of AG Tesauro.
[95] Point 10, citing the analogies in Joined Cases 29 and 30/83 *Compagnie Royale Asturienne des Mines SA and Rheinzink GmbH v Commission* [1984] ECR 1679; Commission Decision 82/866 (*Rolled Zinc Products and Zinc Alloys*) [1982] OJ L 362/40; [1983] 2 CMLR 285; and Commission Decision 68/376 (*Rieckermann/ AEG*) [1968] OJ L 276/25.
[96] Case 56/65 *Société Technique Minière v Maschinenbau Ulm* [1966] ECR 235; Case 23/67 *Brasserie de Haecht v Wilkin* [1967] ECR 407; C-234/89 *Stergios Delimitis v Henninger Bräu AG* [1991] ECR I-935; and 5/69 *Völk v Ets Vervaecke SPRL* [1969] ECR 295.
[97] He referred to a number of decisions including Commission Decision 78/253 (*Re the Agreements of Davide Campari-Milano SpA*) [1978] OJ L 70/69; [1978] 2 CMLR 397; [1978] FSR 528 and the Commission Notice under Article 19(3) of Reg 17 in *Chanel* [1994] OJ C 334/11.

additional requirement for the application of Article 101(1) was the finding of an adverse impact on trade between Member States.[98]

The applicability or not of Article 101(1) remained in the jurisdiction of the national court, though the Advocate General believed that the lack of parallel imports from outside the Community was anti-competitive: 11.91

> in this case, the possibility and economic advantage of reimporting the contractual products is not in doubt, if only because reimportation has in fact occurred. It is undisputed that large volumes of the contractual products are present on the market in the United Kingdom, Belgium and the Netherlands, and are being distributed at significantly lower prices by resellers outside the [YSL] distribution system, a fact which clearly indicates the advantageousness, and therefore the possibility, of parallel imports.[99]

(ii) **The interpretation of Article 101(3)** The exemption of the selective distribution network under Article 101(3) did not require or mean that it should remain immune to competition and parallel imports.[100] On the contrary, the Advocate General viewed parallel imports as a way 'for tempering excess rigidity of the system, particularly as regards prices'.[101] The Advocate General was a strong supporter of parallel trade: 11.92

> parallel trade—far from being the result of a sort of perverse economic opportunism, still less unlawful opportunism, as many tend maliciously to depict it—is a guarantee of the overall vitality of the distribution system which, alongside selective networks, ultimately is beneficial to the final consumer, whose interests are in any event (at least) one of the objectives of Article [101](1) and (3).[102]

Apart from that general stance the Advocate General added a more concrete argument. The exemption decision could not cover distribution agreements that had not been themselves examined by the Commission; it was a derogation from the fundamental rule of Article 101(1) and should be construed restrictively.[103] That approach would also ensure that the Commission would be able to fulfil its role as competition enforcer,[104] a competence that belonged to the Commission rather than the national court.

(b) *The Judgment of the Court*

(i) **The interpretation of Article 101(1)** The Court repeated that Article 101(1) covered agreements between economic operators at different levels of the economic process.[105] The Court had already decided that agreements that were destined to apply within the Community and deprived a reseller of its commercial freedom were against Article 101(1).[106] The same applied to agreements with the aim of exclusion of parallel imports within the Community and consequently of restriction of competition in the common market.[107] 11.93

---

[98] Citing Joined Cases 56 and 58/64 *Consten and Grundig*.
[99] Point 14.
[100] Citing C-376/92 *Metro SB-Großmärkte GmbH v Cartier SA* [1994] ECR I-15.
[101] Point 18.
[102] Ibid.
[103] Citing C-266/93 *Bundeskartellamt v Volkswagen AG and VAG Leasing GmbH* [1995] ECR I-3477.
[104] Citing C-234/89 *Stergios Delimitis v Henninger Bräu AG* [1991] ECR I-935.
[105] Citing 56/65 *Société Technique Miniére* [1966] ECR 235 and Joined Cases 56/64 and 58/64 *Consten and Grundig*.
[106] Citing Case 86/82 *Hasselblad (GB) Ltd v Commission* [1984] ECR I-883 and C-70/93 *Bayerische Motorenwerke AG v ALD Auto-Leasing D GmbH* [1995] ECR I-3439.
[107] Citing C-279/87 *Tipp-Ex GmbH & Co KG v Commission* [1990] ECR I-261.

Accordingly, '[s]uch provisions, in contracts for the distribution of products within the Community, therefore constitute by their very nature a restriction of competition'.[108]

11.94 For Article 101(1) to apply, these agreements should also be capable of affecting trade between Member States in a significant way.[109] The position and importance of the parties in the relevant market were significant factors in that assessment.[110] Here, the Court had to determine whether similar considerations applied to agreements covering a territory outside the Community, for which the starting point was different. The Court also considered the purpose of such agreements but reached a different conclusion from the Advocate General:

> [i]n the case of agreements of this kind, stipulations of the type mentioned in the question must be construed not as being intended to exclude parallel imports and marketing of the contractual product within the Community but as being designed to enable the producer to penetrate a market outside the Community by supplying a sufficient quantity of contractual products to that market. That interpretation is supported by the fact that, in the agreements at issue, the prohibition of selling outside the contractual territory also covers all other non-member countries.[111]

11.95 Accordingly, an undertaking to sell the contractual products on a market outside the Community should not be regarded as having the object of appreciably restricting competition within the common market or as being capable of affecting, as such, trade between Member States. 'Similarly, the provisions of the agreements in question, in that they prohibit direct sales within the Community and re-exports of the contractual product to the Community, cannot be contrary, by their very nature, to Article [101](1) of the Treaty.'[112] Article 101(1) would still be applied if, according to the national court, the agreements had the effect of preventing, restricting, or distorting competition within the common market irrespective of their object. This was an assessment for the national court that should also take account of their economic and legal context.[113]

11.96 The Court underlined the following issues that should be seen as part of that context. First, whether the relevant market was an oligopoly; secondly, whether there was an appreciable difference between the Community and the non-Community prices of the contractual products; and, thirdly, if there was an effect it had to be an appreciable effect on the pattern of trade between the Member States such as to undermine attainment of the objectives of the common market. 'In that regard, intra-Community trade cannot be appreciably affected if the products intended for markets outside the Community account for only a very small percentage of the total market for those products in the territory of the common market.'[114]

11.97 **(ii) The interpretation of Article 101(3)** The Court underlined that the individual exemption decision related only to standard YSL selective distribution contracts for the

---

[108] *Javico* (n 87) paragraph 14, citing Case 19/77 *Miller International Schallplatten GmbH v Commission* [1978] ECR 131.
[109] Case 5-69 *Völk v Ets Vervaecke SPRL* [1969] ECR 295.
[110] Case 99/79 *Lancôme and Cosparfrance Nederland BV v Etos BV* [1980] ECR I-2511 and Joined Cases 100/80 to 103/80 *Musique Diffusion Française v Commission* [1983] ECR 1825.
[111] Paragraph 19.
[112] Paragraph 21.
[113] Citing C-393/92 *Gemeente Almelo v NV Energiebedriff Ijsselmij* [1994] ECR I-1477.
[114] Paragraph 26.

retail sale of its products in the Community; it could not affect agreements concerning their distribution outside the Community. Indeed, Article 1 of Regulation 1983/83 made it clear that the block exemption could not even apply to such agreements. As to whether the contested provisions could escape Article 101(1) because their aim was to protect an exempted selective distribution network the response of the Court was categorically negative. The Decision provided for an exemption to the fundamental rule and should be interpreted restrictively so as to ensure that its effects would not be extended to situations that it was not intended to cover.[115]

D. Competition and Trade Marks: The Application of Article 102

(1) Dominance

The Court of Justice described dominance as 'a position of economic strength enjoyed by an undertaking which enables it to prevent effective competition being maintained on the relevant market by affording it the power to behave to an appreciable extent independently of its competitors, customers and ultimately of its consumers'.[116] **11.98**

(a) Identifying the relevant product market

From a trade mark law perspective identifying dominance is a particularly topical issue because the primary issue is identifying the relevant product market. **11.99**

(i) *Continental Can*—**the interchangeability criterion**   In *Continental Can*[117] the Court indicated that interchangeability of products was the decisive criterion: '... the possibilities of competition can only be judged in relation to those characteristics of the products in question by virtue of which those products are particularly apt to satisfy an inelastic need and are only to a limited extent interchangeable with other products'.[118] **11.100**

The Commission had failed to show why and how three markets for food containers—'light containers for canned meat products', 'light containers for canned seafood', and 'metal closures for the food packing industry'—differed from each other in the first place and, second, from the general market for 'light metal containers, namely the market for metal containers for fruit and vegetables, condensed milk, olive oil, fruit juices and chemico-technical products'. **11.101**

The Court added that: **11.102**

> in order to be regarded as constituting a distinct market, the products in question must be individualized, not only by the mere fact that they are used for packing certain products, but by particular characteristics of production which make them specifically suitable for this purpose. Consequently, a dominant position on the market for light metal containers for meat and fish cannot be decisive, as long as it has not been proved that competitors from other sectors of the market for light metal containers are not in a position to

---

[115] Citing C-70/93 *Bayerische Motorenwerke AG v ALD Auto-Leasing D GmbH* [1995] ECR I-3439.
[116] Case 27/76 *United Brands Co and United Brands Continental BV v Commission* [1978] ECR, paras 65 and 66.
[117] *Europemballage Corp and Continental Can Co Inc v Commission* [1973] ECR 215.
[118] *Continental Can* (n 117) paragraph 32. Greaves (n 12) p 380: 'Interchangeability is established by looking primarily at the demand side substitutability (e.g. physical characteristics; price; intended use) but the supply substitutability should also be considered.'

enter this market, by a simple adaptation, with sufficient strength to create a serious counterweight.[119]

11.103 Further, the Court took into account the argument that competition from containers made of other material was possible, opening up the concept of the relevant product market. It also looked at potential competition in a geographical context. Parts of the case focused on the German market and the Court rejected as unsubstantiated the Commission's argument that plants in neighbouring countries should not be considered as competitive because they were located too far away from most German consumers. And, finally, it considered the potential for competition from large consumers of containers, food producers who were manufacturing their own containers.

11.104 Once the market is identified, the most common criteria for establishing dominance are market share, whether market power constitutes a sufficient barrier to entry, and the conduct of the undertaking.

11.105 The Court accepted that superior technology, access to financial resources, and intellectual property rights can function as barriers to entry.

(b) United Brands: The market for bananas

11.106 *United Brands*[120] considered whether bananas were part of a larger market for fresh fruit or constituted a market of their own. United Brands argued that the cross elasticity of demand between bananas and other fresh fruit was high; the Commission argued that it was low.

11.107 The Court started its analysis by noting that establishing whether there was a distinct market for bananas rested on whether it was possible for the banana 'to be singled out by such special features distinguishing it from other fruits that it is only to a limited extent interchangeable with them and is only exposed to their competition in a way that is hardly perceptible'.[121] One of its characteristics was that ripening took place the whole year round so it was always available in sufficient quantities. The Court therefore had to examine whether it could be replaced by other fruits throughout the year.

11.108 The Court looked at the market for seasonal fruits and found that limited substitutability existed between bananas, on the one hand, and peaches and table grapes, on the other, in only one Member State; this meant that there was some—but minimal—price interaction. It then considered oranges and apples, which were also available throughout the year, finding that there was no link with oranges and only a limited one with apples. After the analysis of the market conditions it attempted to identify the reasons behind them, focusing on the product's special characteristics. 'The banana has certain characteristics, appearance, taste, softness, seedlessness, easy handling, a constant level of production which enable it to satisfy the constant needs of an important section of the population consisting of the very young, the old and the sick.'[122] It concluded that the banana market is a market which is sufficiently distinct from the market for other fresh fruits.

---

[119] *Continental Can* (n 117) paragraph 33.
[120] Case 27/76 *United Brands Company and United Brands Continental BV v Commission* [1978] ECR 207.
[121] *United Brands* (n 120) paragraph 22.
[122] *United Brands* (n 120) paragraph 31.

(c) Hugin: *The market for spare parts*

The delineation of the relevant product market in *Hugin*[123] is particularly topical from a trade mark law perspective.[124] **11.109**

According to the Commission, Hugin, a manufacturer of cash registers, was in breach of Article 102 because it refused to supply spare parts to Liptons, a company that competed with Hugin in the market for servicing Hugin registers. The Commission had defined the relevant market as the market for spare parts for Hugin cash registers required by independent repairers, where Hugin was by definition the dominant player. Hugin submitted that the product market should be the wider market for cash registers, a much more open and competitive market, and argued that charging anti-competitive prices for its spare parts would influence negatively its position as a manufacturer of cash registers. The Court agreed with the Commission. It started its analysis by the finding of fact that the servicing of Hugin registers was a specialist job: **11.110**

> there exists a separate market for Hugin spare parts at another level, namely that of independent undertakings which specialize in the maintenance and repair of cash registers, in the reconditioning of used machines and in the sale of used machines and the renting out of machines. The role of those undertakings on the market is that of businesses which require spare parts for their various activities. They need such parts in order to provide services for cash register users in the form of maintenance and repairs and for the reconditioning of used machines and for re-sale and renting out. Finally, they require spare parts for the maintenance and repair of new or used machines belonging to them which are rented out to their clients. It is, moreover, established that there is a specific demand for Hugin spare parts, since those parts are not interchangeable with spare parts for cash registers of other makes.[125]

Hugin admitted that in this narrow market it had a monopoly in new spare parts, but submitted nevertheless that the purchase and dismantling of used machines constituted an alternative source of supply. The Court held that this was not a sufficient alternative. **11.111**

(d) *Crossing market boundaries*

In *L'Oreal*[126] the Court described the definition of the market as an issue of fundamental significance. **11.112**

> Indeed, the possibilities of competition must be judged in the context of the market comprising the totality of the products which, with respect to their characteristics, are particularly suitable for satisfying constant needs and are only to a limited extent interchangeable with other products.[127]

In *AKZO*[128] the Court applied this test in a case where the Commission had found AKZO dominant in a particular market, the organic peroxides market (including the benzoyl peroxide used in the plastics industry) because that was the market from which AKZO sought to exclude, in the long run, one of its competitors, submitting that, alternatively, abuse also occurred in the flour additives market (including the benzoyl peroxide used in the milling sector) in the United Kingdom and Ireland. The Court concurred with the

---

[123] Case 22/78 *Hugin Kassaregister AB and Hugin Cash Registers Ltd v Commission* [1979] ECR 1869.
[124] See paragraphs 11.120 and following, below.
[125] *Hugin* (n 123) paragraph 7.
[126] Case 31/80 *NV L'Oreal and SA L'Oreal v PVBA De Nieuwe AMCK* [1980] ECR 3775.
[127] *L'Oreal* (n 126) paragraph 25.
[128] C-62/86 *AKZO Chemie BV v Commission* [1991] ECR I-3359.

Commission primarily because the same organic peroxide was used in both markets. In addition, AKZO's competitor historically had been more active in the flour additives sector, which was of limited importance to AKZO as it was able to subsidise its losses in that market with its profits from the plastics sector.

11.113 According to the evidence, AKZO's intention was to preserve its position in the plastics sector by preventing its competitor from entering this market. 'The Commission was in those circumstances justified in regarding the organic peroxides market as the relevant market, even though the abusive behaviour alleged was intended to damage ECS's main business activity in a different market.'[129] The Court also rejected the argument that the definition of the market was not precise enough because the category of organic peroxides contained more than one product:

> organic peroxides may, indeed, be individualized with regard to their formula, their concentration or their presentation in order to meet the particular requirements of customers. Nevertheless, 90% of their use is in various operations in the plastics industry and they are therefore suitable for satisfying constant needs … Moreover, they are not exposed to competition from other products, such as sulphur-based compounds used in the limited field of vulcanization of synthetic rubber, since the latter products cannot replace them completely as they do not have all the technical properties required.[130]

(e) Derivative markets

11.114 Note that the Court had already considered the effect of dominance in one market amongst other derivative markets in *Commercial Solvents*.[131] There, the Court found that abuse of a dominant position in a market for raw materials—aminobutanol—could have anti-competitive effects in the market on which derivatives are sold—ethambutol, an anti-tuberculosis drug—that should be taken into account regarding the applicability of Article 102 TFEU. Commercial Solvents had also argued that ethambutol was only one amongst a number of anti-tuberculosis drugs but the Court held that its holding covered even the case of a second market that did not constitute a self-contained market. The particular facts of the case were relevant to the outcome because Commercial Solvents was active only in the market for raw materials before deciding to start manufacturing the derivative pharmaceutical product and thus compete with its former customers:

> an undertaking which has a dominant position in the market in raw materials and which, with the object of reserving such raw material for manufacturing its own derivatives, refuses to supply a customer, which is itself a manufacturer of these derivatives, and therefore risks eliminating all competition on the part of this customer, is abusing its dominant position within the meaning of Article [102].[132]

(2) Dominance and Intellectual Property

(a) Exclusivity and dominance

11.115 Because of their exclusive nature, intellectual property rights can lead to dominance. However, exclusivity should not lead to automatic conclusions. In *Parke, Davis v Probel*[133] the Court

---

[129] *AKZO* (n 128) paragraph 45.
[130] *AKZO* (n 128) paragraph 52.
[131] Joined Cases 6/73 and 7/73 *Instituto Chemioterapico Italiano SpA and Commercial Solvents Corp v Commission* [1974] ECR 223.
[132] *AKZO* (n 128) paragraph 25.
[133] Case 24/67 *Parke, Davis and Co v Probel, Reese, Beintema-Interpharm and Centrafarm* [1968] ECR 55.

considered whether in itself the existence of an intellectual property right constituted a problem for competition. The referring Dutch court had noted that the owner of a patent could block all commercial dealings in a Member State in the product covered by the patent coming from another Member State that did not grant an exclusive right to manufacture and sell that product, and that the price of the patented product was higher than that of a similar product not covered by a patent. The Judgment was partly based on the fact that at that stage there was no harmonization of the national rules relating to industrial property and drew from analogies with free movement of goods cases; for 'similar reasons, the exercise of the rights arising under a patent granted in accordance with the legislation of a Member State does not, of itself, constitute an infringement of the rules on competition laid down by the Treaty'.[134]

In respect of Article 101(1), in particular, a patent taken by itself and independently of any agreement of which it may be the subject: **11.116**

> is the expression of a legal status granted by a state to products meeting certain criteria, and thus exhibits none of the elements of contract or concerted practice required by Article [101](1). Nevertheless it is possible that the provisions of this Article may apply if the use of one or more patents, in concert between undertakings, should lead to the creation of a situation which may come within the concepts of agreements ... within the meaning of Article [101](1).[135]

Regarding Article 102, it added that although a **11.117**

> patent confers on its holder a special protection at national level, it does not follow that the exercise of the rights thus conferred implies the presence together of all the three [dominance, abuse, and effect on trade between Member States] elements in question. It could only do so if the use of the patent were to degenerate into an abuse of the abovementioned protection.[136]

Price differences between patented and unpatented products did not necessarily constitute an abuse.

In *EMI* the Court adopted the same principle in respect of trade marks: **11.118**

> Although the trade-mark right confers upon its proprietor a special position within the protected territory this, however, does not imply the existence of a dominant position within the meaning of the abovementioned Article, in particular where, as in the present case, several undertakings whose economic strength is comparable to that of the proprietor of the mark operate in the market for the products in question and are in a position to compete with the said proprietor.[137]

(b) Volvo v Veng: Spare parts and intellectual property

Volvo v Veng[138] reconsiders the markets for spare parts, only this time an intellectual property right is involved. Volvo, the car manufacturer, employed its UK registered design right for body panels against Veng, an importer of infringing panels. The Patents Court referred three questions to the Court of Justice: did a car manufacturer in Volvo's position hold a dominant position in the relevant market for spare parts; would refusal to license third parties to supply spare parts in return for a reasonable royalty constitute prima facie an abuse of **11.119**

---

[134] *Parke, Davis and Co.* (n 133) 71.
[135] *Parke, Davis and Co.* (n 133) 71.
[136] *Parke, Davis and Co.* (n 133) 72.
[137] Case 51/75 *EMI Records* [1976] ECR 811.
[138] Case 238/87 *AB Volvo v Eric Veng (UK) Ltd* [1988] ECR 6211.

a dominant position; and would this be considered to affect trade between Member States where the parts derived from another Member State?

11.120 Advocate General Mischo, without mentioning *Hugin*,[139] suggested that Volvo indeed held a dominant position. A Volvo owner simply had to buy a body panel identical to the original Volvo panel and any substitutable product would infringe Volvo's design right. The combination of these two facts meant that potential competitors faced a barrier that was impossible to mount. In essence, Volvo enjoyed a double monopoly, one over the car as a whole and another over the parts of the car as spare parts.

11.121 **(i) Reversing the order** The Court, however, chose a different route. Instead of considering first the issue of dominance and then the question of abuse—as a proper economic analysis would require—it started and finished its analysis by focusing on the second question of the Patent Court. It highlighted the absence of harmonization of national laws in this particular field and repeated its earlier holding that in such cases national laws determine the subject matter and scope of protection.[140] So, given the scope of the national right,

> an obligation imposed upon the proprietor of a protected design to grant to third parties, even in return for a reasonable royalty, a licence for the supply of products incorporating the design would lead to the proprietor thereof being deprived of the substance of his exclusive right, and that a refusal to grant such a licence cannot in itself constitute an abuse of a dominant position.[141]

11.122 The Court then went further and identified hypothetical types of conduct by the proprietor of an industrial design that would still constitute an abuse, to the extent that they affected trade between Member States: the arbitrary refusal to supply spare parts to independent repairers; the fixing of prices for spare parts at an unfair level; and a decision to stop the production of spare parts for car models still in circulation in substantial numbers.

11.123 Irrespective of the actual outcome of the case the anomaly in the judicial reasoning is obvious. It appears that, uncharacteristically, the Court felt uneasy with the antagonistic relationship between national intellectual property rights and European competition law and chose to hide behind the lack of harmonization. However, it then immediately rediscovered its interventionist appetite and identified hypothetical anti-competitive situations. Keeling expresses his disbelief in the following words:

> The Court's performance in *Volvo v Veng* was extraordinary. The question whether a dominant position exists is surely preliminary to the question whether a dominant position is abused. Presumably the Court thought that the question whether ownership of an intellectual property right could by itself give rise to a dominant position was so horrendously controversial and difficult that it was preferable to say that, even if a dominant position existed, it was not abused simply because the owner of an exclusive right exercised it. If anything though, the latter question was surely the more controversial of the two. Moreover, if the Court was anxious to avoid making unnecessary pronouncements in this field, why did it choose to identify certain forms of conduct not mentioned by the national court and condemn them as abusive of a (purely hypothetical) dominant position?[142]

---

[139] *Hugin* (n 123).
[140] Referring to Case 144/81 *Keurkoop v Nancy Kean Gifts* [1982] ECR 2853.
[141] *Volvo v Veng* (n 138) paragraph 8.
[142] David T Keeling, *Intellectual Property Rights in EU Law—Volume I* (Oxford, Oxford University Press, 2003) p 373.

It is suggested that the Court, facing a difficult judicial and political dilemma, attempted **11.124**
another balancing exercise, choosing to ignore the route that a court facing a competition
question would normally take, like it did in *Hugin*.[143] It is worth repeating that even in the
more orthodox approach of the Advocate General there was no reference to *Hugin*. *Volvo v
Veng* is perhaps the most telling example of the difference an intellectual property right can
make, but also of the willingness of the Court to take into account the ever-changing nature
of the European project in its judicial reasoning.

(c) Renault: A lenient approach

Renault[144] reconfirmed that, per se, the sale of components protected by an industrial prop- **11.125**
erty right at a higher price than that charged for the same components by independent
manufacturers is not deemed to be an abuse. The Italian referring court had underlined
that a return for the proprietor of the rights was already guaranteed by the exclusive rights
covering the bodywork as a whole and suggested that protection of the components of the
bodywork was unjustified.

The Court of Justice held that a higher price for the protected component than its unpro- **11.126**
tected equivalent 'does not necessarily constitute an abuse, since the proprietor of protective
rights in respect of an ornamental design may lawfully call for a return on the amounts
which he has invested in order to perfect the protected design'.[145]

(d) Hilti: *Anti-competitive exploitation of a patent*

In *Hilti*[146] the Court confirmed on appeal the decision of the Court of First Instance[147] **11.127**
identifying one instance of abuse: Hilti held a patent and protracted the process for granting to a competitor a licence of right, available according to UK law, by making excessive
royalty demands:

> As far as [Hilti's] policy on the grant of licences of right is concerned ... it is clear ... that ...
> Hilti was not prepared to grant licences on a voluntary basis and that during the proceed-
> ings for the grant of licences of right it demanded a fee approximately six times higher than
> the figure ultimately appointed by the Comptroller of Patents. A reasonable trader, as Hilti
> claims to have been, should at least have realized that by demanding such a large fee it was
> needlessly protracting the proceedings for the grant of licences of right, and such behaviour
> undeniably constitutes an abuse.[148]

It also agreed with the Court of First Instance that the relevant market was consumables, **11.128**
nails and cartridge strips, for Hilti nail guns rather than the wider market of nail guns as
submitted by Hilti.

(e) Magill:*Copyright, exclusivity, and dominance*

In *Magill*[149] the Court revisited the issue of whether the exercise of an intellectual property **11.129**
right can constitute an abuse of a dominant position. Magill published a weekly television

---

[143] *Hugin* (n 123).
[144] Case 53/87 *Consorzio Italiano della Componentistica di Ricambio per Autoveicoli and Maxicar v Regio Nationale des Usines Renault* [1988] ECR 6039.
[145] *Volvo v Veng* (n 138) paragraph 17.
[146] C-53/92 *Hilti AG v Commission* [1994] ECR I-667.
[147] T-30/89 *Hilti AG v Commission* [1991] ECR II-1439.
[148] *Hilti* (n 146) paragraph 99.
[149] C-241/91 P and C-242/91 P *Radio Telefis Eireann (RTE) and Independent Television Publications Ltd (ITP) v Commission* [1995] ECR I-808.

guide listing the programmes of British and Irish broadcasters without seeking their authorization. The latter claimed copyright in the listings of their programmes and refused to license Magill to publish them. Note that they too were publishing separate weekly television guides. The gap in the market was obvious: broadcasters had become publishers of guides that did not compete with each other since each guide was based on the content of its own broadcaster/publisher. They only allowed daily newspapers to publish daily guides, or information for forty-eight hours when the next day was a public holiday, and weekly highlights. Magill introduced a new product combining the listings of all broadcasters and competing with all the existing guides. Magill's complaint that the broadcasters' refusal constituted an abuse of a dominant position was upheld by the Commission, which considered the market for advance weekly listings as the relevant market, in which the broadcasters/publishers enjoyed a dominant position that they abused by refusing to license Magill to publish the listings.[150]

11.130 The broadcasters/publishers challenged the Commission's decision before the Court of First Instance. They submitted that the relevant market was the market for all advance programme information, both weekly and daily, and there was a high degree of substitutability between the various information platforms. Indeed, the majority of viewers relied on daily newspapers rather than weekly listings.

11.131 The Court of First Instance concurred with the Commission.[151] It characterized the markets for weekly and daily listings as sub-markets of a wider market for television programme information and found that there was a specific demand for information on a weekly basis.

11.132 The Court of First Instance clearly acknowledged that copyright in their listings transformed the broadcasters/publishers into dominant players; the applicant:

> enjoyed, as a consequence of its copyright in its programme listings, the exclusive right to reproduce and market those listings. It was thus able, at the material time, to secure a monopoly over the publication of its weekly listings in ... [its own] magazine specializing in its own programmes. Consequently, the applicant clearly held at that time a dominant position both on the market represented by its listings and on the market for the magazines in which they were published.[152]

11.133 RTE and ITP appealed further to the Court of Justice.

11.134 (i) *De facto* **monopoly** The Court recognized the competition issues but, in order to avoid considering the potential conflict between national copyright law and European competition law, it chose to take a step back and stated that the dominance of the broadcasters/publishers was due to their 'de facto monopoly over the information used to compile listings for the television programmes'.[153]

11.135 It repeated that mere ownership of an intellectual property right cannot confer a position of dominance. Greaves notes that the Court 'did its utmost to distance itself from the controversial issue of reconciling national copyright law with the Community's competition rules

---

[150] Commission Decision 89/205 *Magill* [1989] OJ L 78/43.
[151] T-69/89 *Radio Telefis Eireann (RTE) v Commission* [1991] ECR II-485.
[152] *Magill* (n 150) paragraph 63.
[153] Paragraph 47.

... The fact that [basic information] was not available from another source, mainly because of the copyright, was conveniently ignored'.[154]

(ii) Factors establishing abusive conduct However, the Court added that the exercise of an intellectual property right could still be reviewed under the light of Article 102. Turning to the facts of the case, it agreed with the Court of First Instance that the following constituted abusive conduct: 11.136

(a) there was no actual or potential substitute for a weekly television guide offering information on the programmes for the week ahead whilst 'there was a specific, constant and regular potential demand on the part of consumers';[155]
(b) the broadcasters/publishers, 'who were, by force of circumstance, the only sources of the basic information on programme scheduling ... gave viewers wishing to obtain information on the choice of programmes for the week ahead no choice but to buy the weekly guides for each station, and draw from each of them the information they needed to make comparisons';[156]
(c) the broadcasters/publishers' refusal 'to provide basic information by relying on national copyright provisions ... prevented the appearance of a new product ... which the appellants did not offer and for which there was a potential consumer demand';[157]
(d) 'there was no justification for such refusal either in the activity of television broadcasting or in that of publishing television magazines';[158] and
(e) the broadcasters/publishers 'by their conduct, reserved to themselves the secondary market of weekly television guides by excluding all competition on that market ... since they denied access to the basic information which is the raw material indispensable for the compilation of such a guide'.[159]

The Court also rejected the plea that the Commission's decision would violate the obligations of the Member States under the Berne Convention,[160] based on its jurisprudence regarding the effect of international agreements, without having to examine the substance of the argument. The Community was not a member of the Berne Convention and the provisions of an agreement concluded prior to entry into force of the Treaty or prior to a Member State's accession cannot be relied on in intra-Community relations if the rights of non-Member countries are not involved.[161] 11.137

(f) AstraZeneca: Prolonging patent rights

In *AstraZeneca*[162] the Court held that the misuse of patent and regulatory procedures can be seen as an abuse of a dominant position where the aim is to block new entrants, in particular generic companies, from entering the market. AstraZeneca was involved in ten parallel trade lawsuits filed by Greek wholesalers of pharmaceuticals before the Greek authorities. AstraZeneca had provided misleading information regarding the first authorization date 11.138

---

[154] Greaves (n 12) p 381.
[155] *Magill* (n 150) paragraph 52.
[156] Paragraph 53.
[157] Paragraph 54.
[158] Paragraph 55.
[159] Paragraph 56.
[160] In particular, Article 9(1) conferring an exclusive right of reproduction and Article 9(2) allowing a signatory State to permit reproduction only in certain special cases, provided that such reproduction did not conflict with normal exploitation of the work and did not unreasonably prejudice the legitimate interests of the copyright owner.
[161] Referring to Case 286/86 *Ministere Public v Deserbais* [1988] ECR 4907.
[162] C-457/10 P *AstraZeneca v Commission*, ECLI:EU:C:2012.

for one of its most popular products, Losec, treating gastrointestinal diseases, leading to longer patent protection; in addition, it switched from marketing the product in capsules to tablets.

11.139 The CJEU found the arguments around the legality of the misrepresentations to be:

> tantamount to an argument that where an undertaking in a dominant position considers that it can, in accordance with a legally defensible interpretation, lay claim to a right, it may use any means to obtain that right and even have recourse to highly misleading representations with the aim of leading public authorities into error.[163]

This was 'manifestly not consistent with competition on the merits' or with the specific responsibility of a dominant undertaking not to prejudice effective and undistorted competition in the EU.[164] It added that although the conduct of a dominant undertaking cannot be abusive in the absence of any anti-competitive effect, it is not essential for the anti-competitive effect to be concrete. 'It is sufficient to demonstrate that there is a potential anti-competitive effect in order for there to be an abuse'.[165]

11.140 The second abuse involved misusing the rules and procedures applied by national regulatory authorities by withdrawing the marketing authorizations for the product in its capsule form and switching to tablets. The effect was to prevent generic manufacturers from proving their product functioned in the same way in order to obtain marketing authorization. The CJEU reiterated that a dominant undertaking has a responsibility not to use regulatory procedures in such a way as to prevent or make more difficult the entry of competitors, in the absence of grounds related to 'competition on the merits' or in the absence of objective justification.[166]

(g) Bronner: *Exporting the principles of Magill*

11.141 *Bronner*[167] is not an intellectual property and competition law case but it relied on *Magill*[168] and provided a new perspective that the Court used in subsequent judgments involving intellectual property rights. The reference was from an Austrian court, the Oberlandesgericht Wien, and involved the refusal by the publisher of the biggest national newspapers, that also operated the only home delivery scheme in Austria, to allow access to the scheme to Bronner, a smaller rival competitor.

11.142 The Court accepted that this could be seen as a national rather than Community competition law case but this would not preclude it from considering the reference; it was also possible for the same situation to fall under both national and Community law. The circumstances concerning the applicability of Article 102 to the factual situation of the main proceedings fell within the scope of the assessment by the national court; they were irrelevant for determining admissibility.

11.143 Bronner argued that postal delivery did not constitute an alternative to Mediaprint's home delivery scheme because it took place later and that it would be entirely unprofitable to

---

[163] *AstraZeneca* (n 162) paragraph 98.
[164] Paragraph 98.
[165] Paragraph 112.
[166] Paragraph 133.
[167] C-7/97 *Oscar Bronner GmbH & Co KG v Mediaprint Zeitungs- und Zeitschriftenverlag GmbH & Co KG, Mediaprint Zeitungsvertriebsgesellschaft mbH* [1998] ECR I-7791.
[168] *Magill* (n 150).

set up a competing delivery service, on its own or in collaboration with other publishers, because of its small number of subscribers. Bronner sought access to Mediaprint's service, characterized as an 'essential facility', for a reasonable fee. Mediaprint argued that, irrespective of its dominant position, in principle it was entitled to decide freely to whom it wished to allow access to its facilities and that there were no exceptional circumstances leading to the application of Article 102. In any case its refusal was justified because opening the scheme to its rivals would be a challenge for its capacity.

The Court started its analysis by defining the relevant market. In principle, it comprises all the products or services which are particularly suited to satisfying constant needs and are only to a limited extent interchangeable with other products or services, but it remained for the national court to decide whether home delivery schemes constituted a separate market from other methods for selling newspapers. The next step would be to establish whether Mediaprint's refusal deprived its competitor 'of a means of distribution judged essential for the sale of its newspaper'.[169] **11.144**

Revisiting *Magill* it read it as an intellectual property case and held that: **11.145**

> even if that case-law on the exercise of an intellectual property right were applicable to the exercise of any property right whatever, it would still be necessary ... not only that the refusal of the service comprised in home delivery be likely to eliminate all competition in the daily newspaper market on the part of the person requesting the service and that such refusal be incapable of being objectively justified, but also that the service in itself be indispensable to carrying on that person's business, inasmuch as there is no actual or potential substitute in existence for that home-delivery scheme.[170]

Turning to the facts of *Bronner* the Court found that other methods of distribution did exist. Perhaps they were less advantageous but this would not be enough. Further, there were no technical, legal, or economic obstacles capable of making it impossible or unreasonably difficult for any other publisher to establish, alone or in cooperation with others publishers, its own nationwide home delivery scheme. The argument that such a scheme would not be economically viable because of the small circulation of the newspapers to be distributed was not enough for the Court. It accepted the view of AG Jacobs that in order to regard access to the scheme as indispensable 'it would be necessary at the very least to establish ... that it is not economically viable to create a second home-delivery scheme for the distribution of daily newspapers with a circulation comparable to that of the daily newspapers distributed by the existing scheme.'[171] **11.146**

(h) IMS Health: *Importing the principles of Bronner*

Following *Bronner*, the attitude of the Court of Justice towards the balance between intellectual property rights and competition is reflected in the *IMS* case,[172] a reference from the Landgericht Frankfurt am Main. IMS provided information on sales of pharmaceutical products in Germany using a brick structure. Each brick corresponded to a geographic area and its boundaries were set according to a variety of criteria relevant to the market for pharmaceuticals, eg postcodes, distribution of pharmacies, and distribution of doctors' **11.147**

---

[169] *Bronner* (n 167) paragraph 37.
[170] Paragraph 41.
[171] Paragraph 46.
[172] C-418/01 *IMS Health GmbH & Co OHG v NDC Health GmbH & Co KG* [2004] ECR I-5039.

surgeries. There were two brick formats, the basic consisting of 1,860 bricks and a secondary consisting of 2,847 bricks. At an early stage IMS and other users of the formats had collaborated in developing the formats. IMS marketed the two formats to its clients but also distributed them free of charge to pharmacies and surgeries to the extent that they had become the industry standard to which its clients adapted their information and distribution systems.

11.148 A former employee of IMS set up a company, marketing similar information. He used a format consisting of 2,201 bricks. Potential clients, however, had become accustomed to the IMS model and he switched to two formats of 1,860 and 3,000 bricks similar to the IMS ones. His company was acquired by NDC. German courts described the formats as databases protectable under copyright law and granted an order prohibiting NDC from using formats deriving from the basic 1,860 brick format. The referring court, however, held that IMS should not be allowed to exercise its right if it acted in an abusive manner, according to Article 82, by refusing to grant a licence to NDC. So, in essence, it sought from the Court of Justice an indication as to whether IMS's behaviour fell within the scope of Article 102.

11.149 Referring to *Bronner*, the Court noted that in order to establish that a product is indispensable for enabling an undertaking to operate in a particular market it must be determined whether there are products that offer alternative, even less advantageous, solutions and whether there are technical, legal, or economic obstacles capable of making it impossible or at least unreasonably difficult to create these alternatives, possibly in cooperation with others. This remained within the jurisdiction of the national court; in this case the court should take into account the fact that pharmaceutical laboratories had contributed substantially to the improvement of the basic brick format. This had created a dependency that could render competition, through use of an alternative format, unviable.

11.150 As to whether refusal to grant a licence in such circumstances constituted an abuse the Court referred to *Volvo* and *Magill*, stating that the exclusive right of reproduction, being part of an intellectual property right, meant that in itself refusal did not constitute an abuse. Additional circumstances, however, could reverse this finding: 'it is sufficient that three cumulative conditions be satisfied, namely, that that refusal is preventing the emergence of a new product for which there is a potential consumer demand, that it is unjustified and such as to exclude any competition on a secondary market'.[173]

11.151 The Court looked at the third condition first. Deciphering *Bronner* the Court noted that in order to assess indispensability it is relevant to distinguish between an upstream market, constituted by the product or service in question, and a secondary, downstream, market 'on which the product or service in question is used for the production of another product or the supply of another service'.[174] It is sufficient that a potential or even hypothetical market can be identified, but it is 'determinative that two different stages of production may be identified and that they are interconnected, inasmuch as the upstream product is indispensable for the supply of the downstream product'.[175]

---

[173] Paragraph 38.
[174] Paragraph 42.
[175] Paragraph 45.

11.152 In, admittedly, one of its most impenetrable holdings, the Court concluded that transposed 'to the facts of the case in the main proceedings, that approach prompts consideration as to whether the 1,860 brick structure constitutes, upstream, an indispensable factor in the downstream supply of German regional sales data for pharmaceutical products'[176] and left it to the national court to decide whether IMS's refusal constituted an abuse.

11.153 As to the first condition, relating to the emergence of a new product, the Court held that the balance will tilt from intellectual property towards competition when refusal to grant a licence prevents the development of the secondary market to the detriment of consumers: the undertaking which requested the licence must intend to offer, 'on the market for the supply of the data in question, new products or services not offered by the owner of the intellectual property right and for which there is a potential consumer demand'.[177] So, according to the Court, intellectual property prevails when the potential competitor intends to duplicate what the owner of the intellectual property right is already offering. The statement is significant because the Court appears to accept as uncontroversial the exclusivity that lies at the heart of the intellectual property right. In respect of the second condition, the Court stated only that it is for the national court to examine whether the refusal of the request for a licence is justified by objective considerations.

(i) Microsoft: *Interoperability, bundling, and intellectual property*

11.154 The Court of First Instance considered the concept of interoperability and revisited the friction between intellectual property rights and Article 102 in *Microsoft*.[178]

11.155 The case goes back to the end of 1998 when the Commission started investigating Microsoft following a complaint by Sun Microsystems (Sun), and found it had abused its market dominance in the client PC operating systems market and in the work group server operating systems market by (i) restricting interoperability between Windows and non-Microsoft work group servers; and (ii) tying its own media player with its personal computer operating system. The Commission imposed a record fine, an obligation to bring an end to infringement, a requirement to divulge all necessary interface information, and a requirement to update the disclosed information in parallel with the circulation of new versions of its relevant products. From an intellectual property perspective, information protected by copyright would be given to competitors under a compulsory licence, with reasonable remuneration calculated on non-discriminatory terms. In 2006 the Commission imposed a further fine for non-compliance.

11.156 The Court of First Instance stated from the outset that it would focus on the decision from the perspective of checking the accuracy of the facts, the completeness of the evidence, and whether the evidence supported the conclusions; however, insofar as the Commission's decision was the result of complex technical appraisals, Community Courts should not substitute their own assessment of matters of fact for the Commission's.

---

[176] Paragraph 46.
[177] Paragraph 52.
[178] T-201/04 *Microsoft Corp v Commission of the European Communities* [2007] 5 CMLR 11. This was an application for annulment of Commission Decision 2007/53/EC of 24 March 2004 relating to a proceeding pursuant to Article 82 EC and Article 54 of the EEA Agreement against Microsoft Corp (Case COMP/C-3/37.792—*Microsoft* [2007] OJ L 32/23).

11.157 **(i) The indispensability requirement** The first part of the Judgment focused on the indispensability of the interface protocols. Following an essential facilities reasoning, the Court of First Instance concurred with the Commission that Microsoft's operating system had become the *de facto* standard and access to it was necessary for the operators in the market for work servers. Consequently, the Court accepted that there was a risk of eliminating competition in the market for work servers.

11.158 **(ii) The applicable standard** Here, Microsoft had argued that in cases involving intellectual property rights a stricter test had to be applied requiring a 'high probability' of eliminating competition. The court rejected the argument:

> Microsoft's complaint is purely one of terminology and is wholly irrelevant. The expressions 'risk of elimination of competition' and 'likely to eliminate competition' are used without distinction by the Community judicature to reflect the same idea, namely that Article 102 TFEU does not apply only from the time when there is no more, or practically no more, competition on the market. If the Commission were required to wait until competitors were eliminated from the market, or until their elimination was sufficiently imminent, before being able to take action under Article 102, that would clearly run counter to the objective of that provision, which is to maintain undistorted competition in the common market and, in particular, to safeguard the competition that still exists on the relevant market.[179]

11.159 The Court of First Instance added that because the market was characterized by significant network effects the elimination of competition would be difficult to reverse. Further, what had to be established was the likelihood of eliminating all effective competition on the market; 'a marginal presence in certain niches on the market cannot suffice to substantiate the existence of such competition'.[180]

11.160 **(iii) Refusal to license an intellectual property right** Revisiting the *Volvo v Veng* and *IMS Health* discussion, the Court of First Instance accepted that:

> the fact that the holder of an intellectual property right can exploit that right solely for his own benefit constitutes the very substance of his exclusive right. Accordingly, a simple refusal, even on the part of an undertaking in a dominant position, to grant a licence to a third party cannot in itself constitute an abuse of a dominant position within the meaning of Article 102 EC. It is only when it is accompanied by exceptional circumstances such as those hitherto envisaged in the case-law that such a refusal can be characterised as abusive and that, accordingly, it is permissible, in the public interest in maintaining effective competition on the market, to encroach upon the exclusive right of the holder of the intellectual property right by requiring him to grant licences to third parties seeking to enter or remain on that market. It must be borne in mind that it has been established above that such exceptional circumstances were present in this case.[181]

11.161 The Court of First Instance also rejected an argument based on the secrecy of the relevant technology. It accepted the finding of the Commission that it was normal practice for operators in the industry to disclose to third parties the information which would facilitate interoperability with their products and Microsoft itself had followed that practice until it was sufficiently established on the work group server operating systems market.

---

[179] Paragraph 561.
[180] Paragraph 563.
[181] Paragraph 691.

11.162 Note, too, the broad approach followed by the Court of First Instance in relation to the new product argument:

> The circumstance relating to the appearance of a new product, as envisaged in *Magill* and *IMS Health* … cannot be the only parameter which determines whether a refusal to license an intellectual property right is capable of causing prejudice to consumers within the meaning of Article [102(b) TFEU]. As that provision states, such prejudice may arise where there is a limitation not only of production or markets, but also of technical development.[182]

11.163 In any case the Court of First Instance had also stressed that the existence of potential consumer demand could satisfy the new product condition. It found that Microsoft had not demonstrated the existence of any objective justification for its refusal to disclose the interoperability at issue and that the exceptional circumstances identified by the Court of Justice in *Magill* and *IMS Health* were also present in this case.

11.164 **(iv) The media player bundling** The Court of First Instance accepted the Commission's finding that software developers who wrote applications that relied on a media player had incentives to write foremost to Windows Media Player. The ubiquity of the Windows Media Player, by virtue of the bundling, also had effects on adjacent markets, such as media players on wireless information devices, set-top boxes, DRM solutions, and online music delivery.

11.165 The Court of First Instance also paid attention to the considerable rise in the market share of the media player that had contributed to the bundling.

11.166 In short, it accepted that Windows was used as a distribution channel to ensure a significant competitive advantage on the media players market; because of the bundling, Microsoft's competitors were *a priori* at a disadvantage even if their products were inherently better than Windows Media Player; Microsoft interfered with the normal competitive process which would benefit users by ensuring quicker cycles of innovation as a consequence of unfettered competition on the merits; bundling increased the content and applications barriers to entry, which protected Windows, and facilitated the erection of such barriers for Windows Media Player; Microsoft shielded itself from effective competition from vendors of potentially more efficient media players who could challenge its position, and thus reduced the talent and capital invested in the innovation of media players; through bundling, Microsoft could expand its position in adjacent media-related software markets and weaken effective competition to the detriment of consumers; and, through bundling, Microsoft sent signals which deterred innovation in any technologies in which it might conceivably take an interest and which it might tie in with Windows in the future.

11.167 Following a similar analysis to the one regarding interoperability the Court rejected Microsoft's argument that its behaviour could be objectively justified.[183]

(i) Syfait: Refusal to supply

11.168 As we have already seen in the chapter on parallel imports[184] the market for pharmaceutical products continues to challenge the efficacy of the common market and test both the

---

[182] Paragraph 647.
[183] C-413/14 P *Intel Corporation v Commission*, currently before the CJEU, provides an opportunity to revisit rebates. The case is an appeal against T-286/09, ECLI:EU:T:2014:547.
[184] See, for example, the Opinion of AG Sharpston in C-348/04 *Boehringer Ingelheim KG v Dowelhurst Ltd* [2007] ECR I-03391 discussed in paragraphs 10.336–10.361, below.

functions and the limitations of intellectual property rights in Europe. There are still wide price variations between Member States. This has meant increased activity from parallel importers and a significant body of European jurisprudence in this area. The same applies to the Court's jurisprudence on competition.

11.169 In *Syfait v GlaxoSmithKline*[185] the Court considered the applicability of Article 82 to GlaxoSmithKline's refusal to supply wholesalers in Greece with its products branded under Irnigran, Lamictal, and Serevent. Because the prices in Greece were significantly lower, these wholesalers were parallel exporting the products to other Member States. The wholesalers complained to the national Greek Competition Commission which referred two questions to the Court of Justice.

11.170 The first question asked whether a dominant player's refusal to supply constitutes an abuse of its dominant position in all cases, even where the relevant national market is distorted by State intervention. If this was not an abuse in all cases, the second question sought to clarify the criteria for establishing whether it constituted an abuse in specific cases, referring, for example, to the percentage of exported products relative to national demand, the loss of the manufacturer relative to its turnover, the benefit to the patient, or the interest of national insurance bodies.

11.171 Following *IMS*,[186] Advocate General Jacobs suggested that refusal to supply, even where the intention behind it is to limit parallel trade, does not necessarily constitute an abuse of a dominant position. The ultimate question should be whether 'such a refusal is in all circumstances justified'.[187] Turning to the second question he identified three relevant factors: regulation of price and distribution, impact on manufacturers, and impact on purchasers and patients.

11.172 Regarding regulation of price and distribution he noted that Member States influence the price of pharmaceutical products leading to price differences between Member States. At the same time there are obligations imposed on manufacturers and wholesalers under national and Community[188] laws to guarantee the availability of pharmaceutical products. These obligations influence both the manufacturers' ability to refuse to supply a market and the wholesalers' ability to parallel export. The Advocate General then conducted a thorough economic analysis of the market for pharmaceuticals in order to delineate the second factor. The price of pharmaceuticals reflects the relatively low marginal cost of production but also the high fixed costs of research and development, including risk. It can be uniform or it can vary between markets.

> It is therefore rational for an undertaking to supply its products on any market where the price is fixed above variable cost. The mere fact that a product is marketed on a given market at a given price does not mean that a pharmaceuticals undertaking could recoup its total costs if that price were generalised across the whole of the Community.[189]

11.173 Manufacturers may accept a lower price in certain markets, but will not do so if the products are then exported to a higher price market, because parallel exports would undermine

---

[185] C-53/03 *Synetairismos Farmakopoion Aitolias & Akarnanias (Syfait) v GlaxoSmithKline Plc* [2005] ECR I-4609.
[186] C-418/01 *IMS Health GmbH & Co OHG v NDC Health GmbH & Co KG* [2004] ECR I-5039.
[187] Point 71 of the Opinion of AG Jacobs.
[188] Directive 2001/83 [2001] OJ L 311/67 as amended by Directive 2004/127 [2004] OJ L 136/34.
[189] Point 89.

recoupment of the fixed costs by higher priced sales. He recognized that forcing manufacturers to supply wholesalers in lower price markets would lead to higher prices, withdrawal of products, or delays in product launches in these markets. Consumer welfare would suffer in such cases.

The finding on consumer welfare led to the Advocate General's finding in respect of the third factor, the impact on purchasers and patients. He noted that distributors benefit more than consumers or purchasers from parallel trade. Purchasers are often public bodies that can set prices and parallel trade may undermine the agreed prices. The consumers are patients who often and to varying degrees do not pay for pharmaceutical products directly; for them the impact from parallel trade is limited. 11.174

Advocate General Jacobs concluded that 'a restriction of supply by a dominant pharmaceutical undertaking in order to limit parallel trade is capable of justification as a reasonable and proportionate measure in defence of that undertaking's commercial interests'.[190] He stressed though that this conclusion was 'highly specific to the pharmaceutical industry in its current condition and to the particular type of conduct at issue in the present proceedings'.[191] In particular, it was highly unlikely that restrictions of supply could be justified in other sectors; even in the pharmaceutical sector conduct 'which more clearly and directly partitioned the common market would not be open to a similar line of defence'.[192] 11.175

Unfortunately, the Court chose not to look at the substance of the questions. The case fell at the first obstacle, as the Court did not follow the finding of the Advocate General that the Greek Competition Commission constituted a court or a tribunal under Article 234. The Commission was not wholly independent of the Greek Government and its proceedings would not lead to a decision of a judicial nature. 11.176

(k) Lelos: Revisiting Syfait

The issue of refusing to supply wholesalers engaged in parallel imports resurfaced in *Lelos v GlaxoSmithKline*.[193] As described above in *Syfait*,[194] GSK, the Greek subsidiary of GlaxoSmithKline, was the holder of marketing authorizations in Greece for a number of pharmaceutical products, including Imigran, Lamictal, and Serevent, available in Greece on prescription only. Lelos and the other appellants were buying the GSK products for distribution in Greece and other Member States. GSK at some point stopped supplying the appellants—claiming there were shortages for which it was not responsible—and started supplying the Greek market itself. At a later stage GSK started supplying the appellants again but with limited quantities. GSK had applied to the Competition Commission for a negative clearance according to Greek law, whereas the appellants had also applied for a declaration that GSK's policy constituted an abuse of a dominant position. 11.177

Following court proceedings and the intervention of the National Organization for Medicines, a case came before the Efetio Athinon (Court of Appeal, Athens). In the 11.178

---

[190] Point 100.
[191] Point 101.
[192] Point 103.
[193] Joined Cases C-468/06 to C-478/06 *Sot. Lelos kai Sia EE and Others v GlaxoSmithKline AEVE Farmakeftikon Proionton, formerly Glaxowellcome AEVE* [2008] ECR I-07139.
[194] C-53/03 *Synetairismos Farmakopoion Aitolias & Akarnanias (Syfait) v GlaxoSmithKline Plc* [2005] ECR I-4609.

meantime, the Competition Commission had referred the *Syfait* questions that the Court had declined to answer. The Court of Appeal, however, decided to stay the proceedings and refer the following questions:

1. Where the refusal of an undertaking holding a dominant position to meet fully the orders sent to it by pharmaceuticals wholesalers is due to its intention to limit their export activity and, thereby, the harm caused to it by parallel trade, does the refusal constitute per se an abuse within the meaning of Article 82 EC? Is the answer to that question affected by the fact that the parallel trade is particularly profitable for the wholesalers because of the different prices, resulting from State intervention, in the Member States of the European Union, that is to say by the fact that pure conditions of competition do not prevail in the pharmaceuticals market, but a regime which is governed to a large extent by State intervention? Is it ultimately the duty of a national competition authority to apply Community competition rules in the same way to markets which function competitively and those in which competition is distorted by State intervention?
2. If the Court holds that limitation of parallel trade, for the reasons set out above, does not constitute an abusive practice in every case where it is engaged in by an undertaking holding a dominant position, how is possible abuse to be assessed?
   In particular:
   (a) Do the percentage by which normal domestic consumption is exceeded and/or the loss suffered by an undertaking holding a dominant position compared with its total turnover and total profits constitute appropriate criteria? If so, how are the level of that percentage and the level of that loss determined (the latter as a percentage of turnover and total profits), above which the conduct in question may be abusive?
   (b) Is an approach entailing the balancing of interests appropriate, and, if so, what are the interests to be compared?
   In particular:
     (i) is the answer affected by the fact that the ultimate consumer/patient derives limited financial advantage from the parallel trade and
     (ii) is account to be taken, and to what extent, of the interests of social insurance bodies in cheaper medicinal products?
   (c) What other criteria and approaches are considered appropriate in the present case?[195]

11.179 **(i) The Opinion of Advocate General Ruiz-Jarabo Colomer** Advocate General Ruiz-Jarabo Colomer characterized the case as a boomerang that came back to the Court and expressed his trepidation about having to write a second Opinion that appeared to be 'the second part of somebody else's novel'.[196] The Advocate General started by expressing some criticism regarding the formulation of the questions. First, there was an issue as to whether GSK indeed held a dominant position in relation to some of the products concerned. According to the view of the Advocate General the Court should move back from a broader theoretical context to that characterised by the circumstances that gave rise to the legal questions. Accordingly, he attempted a practical reformulation of the questions by introducing headings and providing a broader legal contextual analysis. He started by considering the relevant Community case law, highlighting the parallels between the current case and *Commercial Solvents* on the one hand[197] and *United Brands* on the other.[198] The case law showed that a dominant undertaking which avoided supplying goods, particularly when

---

[195] *Lelos* (n 193) paragraph 23.
[196] Point 3.
[197] Joined Cases 6/73 and 7/73 *Instituto Chemioterapico Italiano SpA and Commercial Solvents Corp v Commission* [1974] ECR 223.
[198] Case 27/70 *United Brands Co and United Brands Continental BV v Commission* [1978] ECR 207.

there are no substitutes, and reserved to itself the parallel export market, is committing an abuse under Article 102 TFEU.

11.180 To determine whether this constituted an abuse per se he considered a number of factors. He accepted that abuse was an objectively assessed concept according to the case law of the Court. Still, subjective elements could indicate that an anti-competitive outcome was being sought and, also, in order to demonstrate that a breach of Article 102 had taken place it was sufficient to prove that the abusive conduct of the dominant undertaking tended to restrict competition or, in other words, was capable of having such an effect.[199] 'Therefore, the closer the undertaking in a dominant position is to hindering competition in the market, the stronger the presumption of abuse.'[200]

11.181 Despite the strong inference of infringement he went on to identify a methodology for recognizing abuse. There were three types of behaviour that the Court had considered in its jurisprudence to be anti-competitive: imposing exclusive supply obligations on purchasers by a dominant company; loyalty rebates; and predatory pricing. The Court had always been prepared to listen to arguments defending the above.[201] 'However, apart from specific statements focusing on the circumstances of each individual case, the Court has not given any general rules indicating that abuses per se do not fall within the article of the Treaty dealing with abuse of a dominant position.'[202] He then went on to try and identify and delineate some relevant rules.[203] Following this analysis he suggested that the answer to the first question should be that 'abusive conduct per se does not sit well with Article 82 EC, and consequently the first question put by the Efetio Athinon should not be answered in the affirmative'.[204]

11.182 In order to respond to the second question, he suggested three routes that had to be explored: grounds relating to the market in which they are operating; the legitimate protection of their business interests; and proof of net positive economic effect. Accordingly, the answer to that question should be that:

> when an undertaking in a dominant position reduces the number of wholesalers' orders which it processes to the levels necessary to meet demand in a domestic market, with the intention of preventing parallel imports to other Member States by such wholesalers, this in principle constitutes an abuse of a dominant position within the meaning of Article 82 EC. However, the potentially abusive undertaking can point to any matters it considers relevant in order to justify its behaviour objectively.[205]

11.183 (ii) **The Judgment of the Court** The Court, sitting in Grand Chamber, accepted that the refusal by an undertaking occupying a dominant position on the market of a given product to meet the orders of an existing customer constituted abuse of that dominant position 'where, without any objective justification, that conduct is liable to eliminate a trading party as a competitor'.[206] This would also cover cases involving exports to other Member States and the Court underlined the pro-parallel import stance it had often adopted.

---

[199] Citing C-95/04 P *British Airways v Commission* [2007] ECR I-2331.
[200] Point 51 of the Opinion of AG Ruiz-Jarabo Colomer.
[201] Citing, for example, C-250/92 *Gøttrup-Klim Grovvareforeningen v Dansk Landbrugs Grovvareselskab* [1994] ECR I-5641.
[202] Point 61.
[203] Point 65.
[204] Point 76.
[205] Points 121–22.
[206] Paragraph 34.

Parallel imports enjoy a certain amount of protection under Community law because they encourage trade and help reinforce competition. It was willing, however, to consider the peculiarities of the market for pharmaceutical products. It turned first to the consequences of parallel trade for the ultimate consumers of medicinal products and accepted that:

> even in the Member States where the prices of medicines are subject to State regulation, parallel trade is liable to exert pressure on prices and, consequently, to create financial benefits not only for the social health insurance funds, but equally for the patients concerned, for whom the proportion of the price of medicines for which they are responsible will be lower. At the same time, as the Commission notes, parallel trade in medicines from one Member State to another is likely to increase the choice available to entities in the latter Member State which obtain supplies of medicines by means of a public procurement procedure, in which the parallel importers can offer medicines at lower prices.[207]

11.184 It then considered the other side of the coin, the impact of State price and supply regulation in the pharmaceuticals sector. It highlighted that this remained a non-harmonized area but also acknowledged that the control exercised by Member States over the selling prices or the reimbursement of medicinal products did not entirely remove the prices of those products from the law of supply and demand. It also reiterated that market integration was amongst the objectives of the Treaty. Therefore:

> there can be no escape from the prohibition laid down in Article [102 TFEU] for the practices of an undertaking in a dominant position which are aimed at avoiding all parallel exports from a Member State to other Member States, practices which, by partitioning the national markets, neutralise the benefits of effective competition in terms of the supply and the prices that those exports would obtain for final consumers in the other Member States.[208]

11.185 Balancing its approach it added that the application of competition rules could not be precluded; nevertheless, State intervention was one of the factors triggering parallel trade.

11.186 It concluded that even if

> the degree of regulation regarding the price of medicines cannot prevent any refusal by a pharmaceuticals company in a dominant position to meet orders sent to it by wholesalers involved in parallel exports from constituting an abuse, such a company must nevertheless be in a position to take steps that are reasonable and in proportion to the need to protect its own commercial interests.[209]

For the appraisal of whether the refusal by a pharmaceuticals company to supply wholesalers involved in parallel exports constituted a reasonable and proportionate measure in relation to the threat that those exports represented to its legitimate commercial interests, it had to be ascertained whether the orders of the wholesalers were out of the ordinary. Within the context of the pharmaceutical industry the Court held that:

> although a pharmaceuticals company in a dominant position, in a Member State where prices are relatively low, cannot be allowed to cease to honour the ordinary orders of an existing customer for the sole reason that that customer, in addition to supplying the market in that Member State, exports part of the quantities ordered to other Member States with higher prices, it is none the less permissible for that company to counter in a reasonable and proportionate way the threat to its own commercial interests potentially posed by the

---

[207] Paragraph 56.
[208] Paragraph 66.
[209] Paragraph 69.

activities of an undertaking which wishes to be supplied in the first Member State with significant quantities of products that are essentially destined for parallel export.[210]

The answer to the questions as a whole should be that: **11.187**

> Article [102 TFEU] must be interpreted as meaning that an undertaking occupying a dominant position on the relevant market for medicinal products which, in order to put a stop to parallel exports carried out by certain wholesalers from one Member State to other Member States, refuses to meet ordinary orders from those wholesalers is abusing its dominant position. It is for the national court to ascertain whether the orders are ordinary in the light of both the size of those orders in relation to the requirements of the market in the first Member State and the previous business relations between that undertaking and the wholesalers concerned.[211]

(3) *Der Grüne Punkt*: Dominance and Trade Marks; The Function of the Sign

A case involving a logo, *Der Grüne Punkt-Duales System Deutschland GmbH v Commission of the European Communities*,[212] is one of the most recent cases in which the Court dealt with the abuse of a dominant position. The case came before the Court as an appeal against a judgment of the Court of First Instance.[213]   **11.188**

Under German law manufacturers and distributors of packaging were required to take back the packaging they had placed on the German market. Duales System Deutschland (DSD) provided such a service and allowed them to benefit from an 'exemption system' rather than 'self-manage' packaging as provided in the relevant Ordinance. The 'exemption system' had to be approved by the relevant State authority. To benefit from the exemption system they had to place the Der Grüne Punkt logo (DGP)—a registered trade mark—on their packaging and pay DSD a fee. DSD's exemption system covered the entire territory of Germany through a number of subcontractors; it employed a standard trade mark agreement covering use of the logo and payment of the corresponding fee that was calculated on the basis of the weight and volume of the packaging and the type of material used. The fee aimed to cover collection, sorting, recovery, and administrative costs.   **11.189**

Following proceedings before the Commission, DSD had committed to measures assuring that users of alternative exemption systems or those who self-managed their packaging would not have to pay the fee; however, it required evidence in cases of part recovery of packaging. According to the Commission, the fact that the fee charged by DSD was not determined according to actual use of its system but calculated on the basis of the number of packages bearing the DGP trade mark constituted an abuse of a dominant position, since in a number of possible scenarios involving both DSD and another exemption or self-management system, manufacturers and distributors would have to place the logo on all the packaging and pay the fee for the whole packaging although DSD would only recover part of it or provide for separate production lines and distribution channels.   **11.190**

Accordingly, the principal measure imposed on DSD was the requirement not to charge any licence fee for quantities of packaging put into circulation in Germany carrying the DGP logo for which the exemption service was not used and for which the obligations imposed by   **11.191**

---

[210] Paragraph 71.
[211] Paragraph 77.
[212] C-385/07 P *Der Grüne Punkt* [2009] ECR I-6155.
[213] T-151/01 *Duales System Deutschland v Commission* [2007] ECR II-1607, which concerned a challenge to a decision of the Commission on an Article 82 proceeding: Case COMP D3/34493—*DSD* (2001) OJ L 166/1.

the Packaging Ordinance had demonstrably been fulfilled in another way. DSD challenged the decision before the Court of First Instance without success and appealed further to the Court of Justice. The Court had to consider a number of issues, focusing from a substantive perspective on whether DSD could rely on the logo to justify the fee and from a procedural perspective on whether the CFI had failed to decide the case within a reasonable time since the proceedings covered a period of five years and nine months.

(a) The Opinion of Advocate General Bot

11.192 Following a thorough review of the factual context and the Judgment of the Court of First Instance, Advocate General Bot looked at the abuse of the dominant position issue.

11.193 Reviewing the Judgment of the Court of First Instance he agreed that the DGP logo had an economic value and that merely placing that logo on packaging was likely to have a price; however, a distinction had to be made between a fee that covered only the costs associated with the actual use of the system and a fee for merely using the DGP logo, 'which, being different in nature, is merely a possibility for negotiation in a completely different sphere and extraneous to the matter before the Court of First Instance'.[214]

11.194 **(i) The trade mark agreement** Specifically as to the trade mark agreement he adopted the Court of First Instance's position that it was the fee that was considered to be abusive not the requirement that the manufacturer or distributor wishing to use the DSD system had to affix the DGP logo to each piece of notified packaging; in particular, the imbalance between the fee and the service actually provided, since DSD charged a fee even where certain packaging was taken back by a competitor's system. According to the system, the fee should cover the costs of collecting, sorting and recovering the packaging, and administrative costs.

11.195 The Court of First Instance, according to the Advocate General, had not interpreted the trade mark agreement as having the effect of granting a licence to use the DGP logo to the participating undertakings for the packaging not taken back or recovered by the DSD system. Indeed, the logo bore no relation to the trade mark agreement; it merely played an identifying role and informed the consumer as to what he/she had to do with the packaging.

11.196 The peculiar function of the logo meant that it could coexist with other logos, allowing manufacturers or distributors to participate in other exemption or self-management programmes, meaning that the decision of the Commission did not constitute 'a disproportionate impairment of the trade mark right or, in any event, an impairment which is not justified by the need to prevent an abuse of a dominant position within the meaning of Article [102 TFEU]'.[215]

11.197 DSD had argued against coexistence and in favour of exclusivity, claiming that consumers would be deceived as a result of contradictory information appearing on the packaging. However, the trade mark agreement concerned manufacturers and distributors of packaging rather than consumers. DSD further argued that if packaging not disposed of by its own system was allowed to carry the DGP logo there was a risk that the logo would lose its distinctiveness. Advocate General Bot agreed with the Court of First Instance regarding the function of the logo. The possibility of cumulative marking simply meant that DSD and another system could be applied to the same piece of packaging.

---

[214] Point 97.
[215] Point 132.

(ii) The effect of trade mark law: The function of the logo Turning his attention more closely to the effect of trade mark law, the Advocate General said that the specific object of trade mark law was, in particular, to guarantee to the owner that it had the exclusive right to use that mark for the purpose of putting a product on the market for the first time and thus to protect it against competitors wishing to take unfair advantage of the status and reputation of the trade mark by selling products illegally bearing it. This was linked with the exclusive rights of the trade mark proprietor entitling it to stop third parties from using identical or similar signs.

11.198

However, in this case the undertakings participating in the DSD system for only part of their packaging or for packaging placed on the market of another Member State could not be regarded as competitors of DSD or as third parties improperly selling goods covered by the DGP logo. In the first two cases the manufacturers and distributors had entered into an agreement with DSD; in the third case they were holders on the territory of another Member State of a licence to use the logo. This was the essence of the system as devised by DSD.

11.199

In practice, here, the essential function of the logo was to ensure that the packaging could be taken back by the DSD system. The logo did not fit into the classic scheme of trade mark law that allowed consumers to choose between products. He accepted that it could be closer to the scheme if it indicated a characteristic of the product, for example, that it was recyclable.

11.200

(iii) The competition issues The Advocate General highlighted that, according to the Court of First Instance, the abuse consisted in requiring payment of a fee for the total quantity of packaging carrying the DGP logo and put into circulation in Germany. Accordingly, the obligations imposed by the Commission did not amount to an obligation to grant a licence to use the mark 'but merely to require it not to charge a fee on the total amount of packaging bearing [that] logo where it is shown that all or only some of that packaging has been taken back or recovered through another system'.[216] He also agreed with the Court of First Instance that there was no need to insert an explanatory text on the packaging according to the principle of proportionality. The function of the sign combined with the unpredictability characterizing consumer behaviour would render it irrelevant.

11.201

(iv) The 'reasonable time' claim He accepted that 'where the stakes are high in financial terms, the case must ... be dealt with rapidly'.[217] In this case, however, DSD had not been fined by the Commission and the decision had not affected its activities. 'The importance of the case is therefore ... real for DSD, as it necessarily has an impact on that undertaking, but it is not fundamental, as it does not threaten the economic survival of its activity.'[218]

11.202

On the other hand, the complexity of the case did not justify the length of the proceedings, and the behaviour of DSD had contributed, albeit not drastically, to the delay. Overall, the period of the delay should be considered unreasonable.

11.203

Failure to observe the reasonable time requirement could only give rise to a claim for compensation for the harm caused. Here, though, there was no economic harm. The only satisfaction DSD could enjoy was the recognition of breach of a Community principle. DSD, he accepted, could still bring an action for compensation before the Court of First Instance.

11.204

---

[216] Point 224.
[217] Point 273.
[218] Point 279.

(b) The Judgment of the Court

11.205 The Court delivered its Judgment sitting in a Grand Chamber and considering systematically all the grounds of appeal.

11.206 First, it rejected the claim that there were contradictions in the Judgment of the Court of First Instance considering the fee charged by DSD. It found that the fee that DSD might charge for use of the logo on its own was a separate issue from the fee it charged in respect of the packaging that was actually taken back and recovered by DSD under the trade mark agreement.

11.207 It also accepted the Court of First Instance's reading of the trade mark agreement and the fact that its provisions concerning the fee were regarded to be abusive. The Decision of the Commission had not criticized the requirement that manufacturers or distributors wishing to use the DSD system had to affix the logo to each piece of notified packaging intended for domestic consumption.

11.208 Thirdly, it agreed with the Court of First Instance that the question whether an item of packaging did, or did not, bear the DGP logo was not determinative; the only point at issue was whether the quantities of material for recovery put into circulation by the manufacturer or distributor were actually taken back and recovered. It also found that DSD had not established that the affixing of the DGP logo to packaging processed under a different system ran counter to that objective of transparency.[219] The affixing of that logo to packaging notified to DSD indicates clearly to consumers and to the relevant authorities, irrespective of the question as to whether that packaging will actually be processed under that system or under another system, that the packaging in question is no longer covered by the obligation that it be taken back at points of sale or in the immediate vicinity of them but has been notified to DSD.[220] In essence, this was the function of the logo.

11.209 **(i) The exclusive trade mark use argument** The fourth plea concerned the challenges based on Community trade mark law. Here, the Court elaborated further on use and distinguished between the use of the DGP logo by DSD's contractual partners and its possible use by other third parties. In relation to the first type of use the Court noted that Article 5 of Directive 89/104 did not cover circumstances in which a third party uses a trade mark with the consent of its proprietor. Clearly, DSD could not rely on that provision. The Court noted that, according to Article 8(2) of Directive 89/104, a trade mark proprietor might invoke its rights against a licensee contravening the terms of the licensing agreement. However, in this case DSD itself had set up the system serviced by the trade mark agreement.

11.210 Further, it rejected the claim that the measures imposed by the Commission allowed partial free use of the logo. The decision had targeted solely the fee charged for services not provided by DSD. Also, in the end, if there was a price for the application of the logo on its own this could be negotiated between the parties.

11.211 Finally, the Court noted, use of the DGP logo by third parties was not covered in the Commission's decision and the Judgment of the Court of First Instance.

11.212 **(ii) The competition argument** The fifth ground of appeal was based on Article 102 TFEU. The Court reiterated that setting a disproportionate value for the services provided

---

[219] Paragraph 118.
[220] Citing 226/84 *British Leyland v Commission* [1986] ECR 3263 as an example.

fee was an abuse of dominance. Charging a fee for a service that was not provided should be seen in the same light.

11.213 Also, obliging DSD not to charge any licence fee for partial quantities of sales packaging bearing the DGP logo and put into circulation in Germany, but for which (i) the exemption service was not used and (ii) the obligations imposed by the German authorities had demonstrably been fulfilled in another way, was the consequence of the finding of an abuse of a dominant position and of the exercise of the Commission's power to put an end to the infringement. This did not constitute a compulsory licence since it did not affect DSD's freedom to choose the parties with which it entered into a trade mark agreement.

11.214 (iii) **The principle of proportionality** The Court repeated that there was no obligation imposed on DSD to grant the licence to use the DGP logo. It also agreed with the Court of First Instance that it was impossible to make the *a priori* distinction DSD wanted to make between packaging bearing the logo that would be processed by the DSD system on the one hand and mixed or self-managed systems on the other. It was impossible to determine in advance the route that an item of packaging would follow.

E. Conclusion

11.215 There are four particular points that need to be highlighted.

11.216 First, that the starting point in the antagonistic relationship between trade mark law on the one hand and free movement of goods and competition rules on the other was competition. The fact that the majority of subsequent cases have been decided under the free movement rules does not mean that competition has become redundant. Following the case law of the Court, the existence of intellectual property rights, including trade marks, is not in itself anti-competitive. The Court also appears to increasingly accept that there are benefits that the owner of intellectual property rights enjoys, for example, the opportunity to charge a higher price, that in themselves are not anti-competitive. What counts is whether the way in which these rights are exercised falls under what the Court would consider to be infringing the rules on competition.

11.217 Secondly, that a particular factual scenario could be decided one way under trade mark rules but another under competition rules.

11.218 Thirdly, that a number of competition considerations have been internalized within trade mark law. For example, as we have seen in Chapter 5, whether a functional product feature or a geographical name can be protected as a trade mark is, ultimately, a competition question, the answer to which can be found in trade mark law.

11.219 And finally, *Viking Gas*[221] is evidence of the current unwillingness of the Court to interfere with how a market functions using the tools provided by trade mark law.

---

[221] C-46/10, *Viking Gas A/S v Kosan Gas A/S, formerly BP Gas A/S* [2011] I-06161.

12

THE INTERACTION WITH OTHER AREAS OF THE LAW

A. Introduction

Competition law and the free movement of goods principles have guided the development of trade mark law in Europe. This chapter will examine other relationships. The first part considers the use of trade marks in comparative advertisements. We have seen in Chapter 7 how comparative advertising has delineated the limits of trade mark law. Here the other side of the relationship is examined. Chapter 5 considered whether a geographical name can function and be protected as a trade mark and the limits of such protection. The second part of this chapter gives a flavour of the system of protecting product designations as geographical indications of origin. The third part looks at the clash between trade marks and domain names and the catalysing role of the concept of bad faith. The fourth part is a good example of how one dispute between distinguishing signs can become the common theme of distinct plots performed before different European audiences; this part was a trilogy in the first edition, it became a tetralogy in the second, and grew to a play in six parts in the third.   **12.01**

B. Comparative Advertising

Member States had adopted divergent perspectives on comparative advertising, with Germany the most restrictive, and post-1994 United Kingdom the most liberal, occupying antithetical corners.   **12.02**

In 1997 the Misleading Advertising Directive (84/450) was amended by the Comparative Advertising Directive (97/55) in order to allow and regulate comparative advertising.[1] Being the result of a compromise the amendments could be read either way. Article 2 defines advertising as 'the making of a representation in any form in connection with a trade, business, craft or profession in order to promote the supply of goods or services, including immovable property, rights and obligations'. Article 2a defines comparative advertising as 'any advertising which explicitly or by implication identifies a competitor or goods or services offered by a competitor'. According to Article 2(2) misleading advertising is 'any advertising which in any way, including its presentation, deceives or is likely to deceive the persons to whom it is addressed or whom it reaches and which, by reason of its deceptive   **12.03**

---

[1] Council Directive 84/450/EEC relating to the approximation of the laws, regulations, and administrative provisions of the Member States concerning misleading advertising [1984] OJ 1250/17 as amended by Directive 97/55/EC amending Directive 84/450/EEC concerning misleading advertising so as to include comparative advertising [1997] OJ 1290/18.

nature, is likely to affect their economic behaviour or which, for those reasons, injures or is likely to injure a competitor'. Article 3 includes a list of factors that should, in particular, be considered for determining whether the advertisement is misleading; the list covers information regarding:

> (a) the characteristics of goods or services, such as their availability, nature, execution, composition, method and date of manufacture or provision, fitness for purpose, uses, quantity, specification, geographical or commercial origin or the results to be expected from their use, or the results and material features of tests or checks carried out on the goods or services; (b) the price or the manner in which the price is calculated, and the conditions on which the goods are supplied or the services provided; (c) the nature, attributes and rights of the advertiser, such as his identity and assets, his qualifications and ownership of industrial, commercial or intellectual property rights or his awards and distinctions.

12.04 Article 3(a)(1) provides that comparative advertising shall, as far as the comparison is concerned, be permitted when the following conditions are met:

(a) it is not misleading according to Articles 2(2), 3, and 7(1);
(b) it compares goods or services meeting the same needs or intended for the same purpose;
(c) it compares one or more material, relevant, verifiable, and representative features of those goods and services, which may include price, objectively;
(d) it does not create confusion in the market place between the advertiser and a competitor or between the advertiser's trade marks, trade names, other distinguishing marks, goods, or services and those of a competitor;
(e) it does not discredit or denigrate the trade marks, trade names, other distinguishing marks, goods, services, activities, or circumstances of a competitor;
(f) for products with designation of origin, it relates in each case to products with the same designation;
(g) it does not take unfair advantage of the reputation of a trade mark, trade name, or other distinguishing marks of a competitor or of the designation of origin of competing products;
(h) it does not present goods or services as imitations or replicas of goods or services bearing a protected trade mark or trade name.

(1) *Toshiba*: The Interplay between Trade Marks and Comparative Advertising

12.05 *Toshiba*[2] came before the Court as a reference from the Landgericht Dusseldorf (Regional Court, Dusseldorf). Toshiba manufactured and marketed spare parts and consumables for its photocopiers. Katun used Toshiba's product numbers for its own products, equivalent to Toshiba's, that could be used with Toshiba photocopiers. In its catalogues it listed next to Toshiba's order numbers (displayed in a column under the heading 'OEM Product Number' with OEM being used as an acronym for 'Original Equipment Manufacturer') its own order numbers (under the column 'Katun Product Number'); the third column listed the description of each product, and the fourth referred to the photocopier models for which the product was intended. For some products the catalogues included advertising statements regarding price and performance like 'you can reduce your costs without loss of quality or performance'.

---

[2] C-112/99 *Toshiba Europe GmbH v Katun Germany GmbH* [2001] ECR I-7945.

12.06 Toshiba relied on German jurisprudence and claimed before the German courts that the listing of its own product numbers next to Katun's product numbers should not be allowed. The German court stayed proceedings and referred the following questions to the Court.

1. Is advertising by a supplier of spare parts and consumable items for an equipment manufacturer's product to be regarded as comparative advertising within the meaning of Article 2(2a) of the Directive if the advertising indicates the manufacturer's product numbers (OEM numbers) for the relevant original spare parts and consumable items for reference purposes in order to identify the supplier's products?
2. If Question 1 is to be answered in the affirmative:
   (a) Does the display of the equipment manufacturer's product numbers (OEM numbers) alongside the supplier's own order numbers constitute a comparison of goods permissible under Article 3a(1)(c) of the Directive, in particular a comparison of the prices?
   (b) Are the product numbers (OEM numbers) distinguishing marks of a competitor within the meaning of Article 3a(1)(g)?
3. If Question 2 is to be answered in the affirmative:
   (a) What are the criteria to be used when assessing whether an advertisement within the meaning of Article 2(2a) takes unfair advantage of the reputation of a distinguishing mark of a competitor within the meaning of Article 3a(1)(g)?
   (b) Is the fact that the equipment manufacturer's product numbers (OEM numbers) appear alongside the supplier's own order numbers sufficient to justify an allegation that unfair advantage is being taken of the reputation of the distinguishing mark of a competitor within the meaning of Article 3a(1) (g), if the third party competitor could instead indicate in each case the product for which the consumable item or spare part is suitable?
   (c) When assessing unfairness, does it matter whether a reference (solely) to the product for which the consumable item or spare part is suitable, rather than to the product number (OEM number), is likely to make sale of the suppliers products difficult, particularly because customers generally go by the equipment manufacturers product numbers (OEM numbers)?

(a) The Opinion of Advocate General Léger

12.07 (i) **'Delineating' comparative advertising** Without attempting to define the concept of advertising, Advocate General Léger found that the catalogues were created with a view to the promotion and sale of Katun's products, by providing consumers—the term included both end consumers and trade customers—with information on replacement parts and consumable items required to operate Toshiba photocopiers. He then opted for a broad interpretation of the concept of comparative advertising based on the wording and the purpose of the Directive. Article 2(2a) referred to any advertising which explicitly or by implication identified a competitor or goods or services offered by a competitor. There was no reference to a requirement of an express comparison. 'It may be concluded that a comparison, in the broadest sense, begins where two competing economic operators are associated in an advertisement, even in a non-descriptive way.'[3] There was no requirement that the competitor be expressly identified. It remained in the jurisdiction of the national court to determine whether the advertising complained of constituted comparative advertising, however the Advocate General suggested that there was an at least implicit identification of a competitor

---

[3] Point 30.

in the eyes of an ordinary well-informed person in the form of a reference to the trade mark TOSHIBA and product numbers.

12.08 (ii) **Objective comparisons** According to the Eleventh Recital the conditions of Article 3a(1) were cumulative and should be respected in their entirety. Advocate General Léger divided the provisions into positive and negative, with the requirement of making an objective comparison belonging to the first category. What he found problematic was that Katun had not included any comparative description of the relevant products. In Katun's advertising, he noted, 'one sees the double justification for comparative advertising improving the information available to consumers and stimulating competition'.[4] It was the absence of any indication that the suggestion was not objective that counted: 'A competitor who has been harmed can show perfectly well that the prices actually charged rebut the statements in the advertisement. Consumers can also verify the truth of this information by recourse to other sources, such as price lists issued by the two competing suppliers.'[5]

12.09 What was missing was a wider comparison of the characteristics of the products:

> The passive juxtaposition of the products is an invitation to treat as equivalent characteristics which are not all capable of being identified. If one ignores the price or the purpose of the supplies in question, the advertising appears to convey a desire by the advertiser to confer on his product all the virtues of the competing product, including those which belong to the competitor's trade mark itself.[6]

12.10 The advertisement suggested that the quality of the competing products was identical; however, it lacked the necessary information to back up the suggestion. Having identified one of the problem areas, he noted:

> The objectivity of the information is masked by the impossibility of listing the features on which the comparison is based, and consequently of verifying the merits claimed for them. Seen from this perspective and having regard to the documents before the Court, advertising of this kind does not appear ... to comply with the requirement for an objective presentation of the goods.[7]

He required the advertisement to provide 'a precise and concrete description of the merits or deficiencies of the advertised products, such as their durability, reliability or ease of use'.[8] He added that claiming that the products were of the same quality without indicating the verifiable features supporting that claim would render an advertisement even less objective.

12.11 (iii) **The misuse of reputation** The remaining questions introduced trade mark law considerations. The Advocate General noted that by its nature, comparative advertising involved use of a competitor's trade marks that could in turn lead to an unfair advantage. Article 3a(1)(g) of Directive 97/55 sought to eliminate this risk. To interpret the provision the Advocate General looked first at the concept of 'distinguishing marks'.

---

[4] Point 45.
[5] Point 53.
[6] Point 56.
[7] Point 59.
[8] Point 60.

The concept of distinguishing marks The Advocate General referred first to the Trade Marks Directive. Citing the Twelfth and Thirteenth Recitals he noted that the approach of the Community legislature was to favour objective comparisons between goods or services while at the same time maintaining trade mark rights. For comparative advertising on the other hand reference to a competitor's trade mark or trade name appeared indispensable. In order to avoid 'parasitic business conduct'[9] he suggested that the concept of 'distinguishing marks' should be interpreted very broadly. Accepting the opposite view could strip of legal protection identifying signs that competitors might use for their comparisons without directly referring to a trade mark. Indeed, the provision referred to a trade mark, trade name, or other distinguishing marks. So the national court would have to establish whether the order numbers allowed the identification of Toshiba; if they did they should be considered to be distinguishing marks.

12.12

Unfair advantage Comparative advertising included the risk of the advertiser taking a share of its competitor's reputation. Accordingly, the provision prohibited only the 'unfair' taking of reputation. He indicated that if the only aim of the advertiser was to take advantage of the reputation of its competitor then the advertising should be considered unfair. But there would not be an unfair advantage where the content of the advertisement could be justified by reference to certain conditions. From his perspective the right to use a competitor's distinguishing marks was an exception that should be interpreted narrowly.[10]

12.13

The lawfulness of use should be determined according to a test of necessity: when the reference itself to the competitor or the manner in which it is done is not necessary in order to inform customers of the respective qualities of the goods compared the advertisement would be unlawful; if the comparison could not be made without making reference to the competitor it would be lawful. The Advocate General characterized the indication of order numbers alongside one another as an ambiguous method of advertising. On the one hand it indicated the purpose of the products, on the other it might also be perceived as suggesting that the products were in fact interchangeable, but without indicating in what respect this is so. The Advocate General disapproved the aggressiveness of such advertising: 'there is a risk of presenting the products as being equal which is not permissible if not justified by the informative purpose of the advertising'.[11]

12.14

The indication of compatibility with the Toshiba photocopiers did not necessitate a comparative advertisement; it could be achieved in other descriptive ways that would fall under the permitted uses of Article 6(1)(c) of Directive 89/104. Note that the Advocate General used that provision in order to limit the scope of allowable comparative advertising.

12.15

The necessity factors The Advocate General referred to two of the factors that should be examined as part of the assessment of the necessity test. First, the purpose of the products, where he balanced between effective communication of information on the one hand and limited use of the competitor's reputation on the other. He concluded that 'account may be taken of the consequences of not being able to refer to the product number of the competing product only if no other solution is available whereby the advertiser may use comparative advertising'.[12]

12.16

---

[9] Point 68.
[10] Point 84.
[11] Point 89.
[12] Point 106.

The second was price. He required the advertisement to specify the relative prices explicitly, 'comparative advertising whose aim is price comparison may not use the distinguishing mark of a competitor without explicitly mentioning the prices of each of the products compared'.[13]

(b) The Judgment of the Court

12.17 The Court too made the link between trade mark law and comparative advertising; however, this led to diametrically opposing conclusions from those of the Advocate General.

12.18 **(i) Defining comparative advertising** The Court noted that according to Article 2(1) of Directive 84/450 'advertising' meant 'the making of a representation in any form in connection with a trade, business, craft or profession in order to promote the supply of goods or services, including immovable property, rights and obligations'. This broad definition meant that advertising, including comparative advertising, could take different forms. The comparative element of the concept was described in equally broad terms by reference to Article 2(2a) and the Sixth Recital of the Preamble to Directive 97/55, which stated that the intention was to introduce a broad concept of comparative advertising that would cover all its forms:

> [I]t is therefore sufficient for a representation to be made in any form which refers, even by implication, to a competitor or to the goods or services which he offers. It does not matter that there is a comparison between the goods and services offered by the advertiser and those of a competitor.[14]

12.19 **(ii) The conditions for comparative advertising** The Court moved away from a literal interpretation and looked at the provisions from a teleological perspective, showing how practical it could become in interpreting the law:

> It follows from a comparison of Article 2(2a) of Directive 84/450 as amended, on the one hand, and Article 3a of that Directive, on the other, that, on a literal interpretation, they would render unlawful any reference enabling a competitor, or the goods or services which he offers, to be identified in a representation which did not contain a comparison within the meaning of Article 3a. That would have to be the case where there were mere mentioned of the trade mark of the manufacturer of the original models or of the reference numbers of models for which the spare parts and consumable items are manufactured.[15]

12.20 Article 6(1)(c) of the Trade Marks Directive became the interpretive catalyst; the relevant case law of the Court clearly provided that use of another party's trade mark might be legitimate where it was necessary to inform the public of the nature of the products or the intended purpose of the services offered.[16] Because a literal interpretation of Directive 84/450 would result in a contradiction with Directive 89/104 that the Community legal order would not tolerate, the Court held that it was necessary to take account of the objectives of Directive 84/450 as amended. Those were indicated in the Second Recital of the Preamble to Directive 97/55 stating that comparative advertising would help demonstrate objectively the merits of the various comparable products and thus stimulate competition between suppliers of goods and services to the consumer's advantage: 'For those reasons, the conditions

---

[13] Point 116.
[14] Paragraph 31.
[15] Paragraph 33.
[16] C-63/97 *BMW* [1999] ECR I-905.

required of comparative advertising must be interpreted in the sense most favourable to it.'[17] Following this analysis the Court concluded that displaying the product numbers of the equipment manufacturer alongside a competing supplier's product numbers enabled the public to match precisely the corresponding products:

> Such an indication does, however, constitute a positive statement that the two products have equivalent technical features, that is to say, a comparison of material, relevant, verifiable and representative features of the products within the meaning of Article 3a(1)(c) of Directive 84/450 as amended.[18]

(iii) **The answer to question 1 and question 2(a)** Note that the actual answer of the Court was very heavily based on the facts of the case:

> The answer to Question 1 and Question 2(a) must therefore be that, on a proper construction of Articles 2(2a) and 3a(1) (c) of Directive 84/450 as amended, the indication, in the catalogue of a supplier of spare parts and consumable items suitable for the products of an equipment manufacturer, of product numbers (OEM, numbers) by which the equipment manufacturer designates the spare parts and consumable items which he himself sells may constitute comparative advertising which objectively compares one or more material, relevant, verifiable and representative features of goods.[19]

12.21

(iv) **The concept of distinguishing marks** The Court referred to its case law on trade mark distinctiveness in order to support its holding that a sign used by an undertaking may be a 'distinguishing mark' 'if the public identifies it as coming from a particular undertaking'.[20] It expressed doubts as to whether the alphanumeric combinations in question would be seen as distinguishing signs without the OEM reference at the top of the column. Still, this was for the national court to decide once it had considered the perception of an average individual, reasonably well informed and reasonably observant and circumspect. It added that the average individual should reflect the persons targeted by the advertisement, in this case specialist traders who would be much less likely to associate the reputation of the equipment manufacturer's products with those of the competing supplier.

12.22

(v) **Unfair advantage** In the case that the national court would find the codes to be distinguishing marks it would also have to have regard to the Fifteenth Recital of the Preamble to Directive 97/55, stating that use of a trade mark or distinguishing mark did not breach the right to the mark where it complied with the conditions of Directive 84/450 as amended, 'the aim being solely to distinguish between the products and services of the advertiser and those of his competitor and thus to highlight differences objectively'.[21] From that the Court concluded that an advertiser should not be considered as taking unfair advantage of the reputation of his competitor's distinguishing marks if effective competition on the relevant market was conditional upon a reference to them. The Court also reminded us that it had already held that one of the ways that a third party's use of a mark might take unfair advantage of the distinctive character or the reputation of the mark or be detrimental to them could be by giving the public a false impression of the relationship

12.23

---

[17] Paragraph 37.
[18] Paragraph 40.
[19] Ibid, citing C-342/97 *Lloyd Schuhfabrik Meyer & Co. GmbH* [1999] ECR I-3819.
[20] Paragraph 49.
[21] Paragraph 53.

between the advertiser and the trade mark owner. It repeated that the way the codes were displayed could be seen as a positive statement that the technical features of the two products were equivalent; however, the national court would also have to determine whether the public would associate the equipment manufacturer with the competing suppliers, in that the public might associate the reputation of that manufacturer's products with the products of the competing supplier. The Court held that the overall presentation of the advertising at issue should be considered. For example, the manufacturer's product number might be one of several combined indications relating to that manufacturer and his products, or the trade mark of the competing supplier might be highlighted 'in such a way that no confusion or association is possible between the manufacturer and the competing supplier or between their respective products'.[22]

12.24 In this case it appeared, first, that Katun would have difficulty in comparing its products with Toshiba's without referring to the order numbers and, second, that a 'clear distinction is made between Katun and Toshiba Europe, so that they do not appear to give a false impression concerning the origin of Katun's products'.[23]

12.25 (vi) **The answer to Question 2(b) and Question 3** Again it is worth reproducing here the actual answer of the Court, as its wording was influenced by the facts of the case:

> In the light of those considerations, the answer to be given to Question 2(b) and Question 3 is that, on a proper construction of Article 3a(1)(g) of Directive 84/450 as amended, where product numbers (OEM numbers) of an equipment manufacturer are, as such, distinguishing marks within the meaning of that provision, their use in the catalogues of a competing supplier enables him to take unfair advantage of the reputation attached to those marks only if the effect of the reference to them is to create, in the mind of the persons at whom the advertising is directed, an association between the manufacturer whose products are identified and the competing supplier, in that those persons associate the reputation of the manufacturer's products with the products of the competing supplier. In order to determine whether that condition is satisfied, account should be taken of the overall presentation of the advertising at issue and the type of persons for whom the advertising is intended.[24]

(2) *Pippig*: The Contradictions of Article 7(2) of Directive 10-025 84/450

12.26 The Court reconfirmed its pro-comparative advertising stance in *Pippig*[25] where the case was a reference from the Oberster Gerichtshof (Supreme Court) of Austria. Pippig Augenoptik (Pippig) was a specialist optician firm running three shops in Linz. Hartlauer was a retailer that sold spectacles that were usually obtained through parallel trade at low prices and conducted a twofold advertising campaign. First it used in a marketing campaign a leaflet highlighting the price differences between its own prices and those charged by specialist opticians like Pippig; the general claim was supported by the more specific claim that for a clear Zeiss lens, opticians made a profit of 717%. The advertising leaflet also contained a direct comparison between Pippig's prices for a particular frame fitted with Zeiss lenses and the price charged by Hartlauer for the same model, albeit with lenses of another brand; the comparison was based on a test purchase. Second, the latter price comparison was also

---

[22] Paragraph 58; note the reference to 'confusion or association'.
[23] Paragraph 59; note here the insistence on 'impression concerning the origin'.
[24] Paragraph 60.
[25] C44/01 *Pippig Augennptik GmbH & Co KG v Hartlauer Handelsgesellschaft GmbH* [2003] ECR I-3095.

used in television and radio advertisements. The television advertisements showed one of Pippig's shop fronts.

12.27 Pippig claimed before the Austrian courts that Hartlauer's advertising was misleading and discrediting; it argued that the price difference between the identical models was largely due to the price of the Zeiss lenses for that particular model and that the same model was made available at Hartlauer's at a later date and only in a limited number of colours. The case reached the Oberster Gerichtshof which stayed proceedings and referred the following questions to the Court

(1) Is Article 7(2) ... to be interpreted to the effect that comparative advertising, as far as the comparison is concerned means the statements regarding the product offered by the advertiser himself, the statements regarding the product offered by the competitor and the statements regarding the relationship between the two products (the result of the comparison)? ... Is the reference in Article 3a(1)(a) of the directive to Article 7(1) of the directive a lex specialis in relation to Article 7(2) of the directive? Is Article 3a(1)(a) of the directive to be interpreted as meaning that the comparison of the price of a brand-name product with the price of a no-name product of equivalent quality is not permitted where the name of the manufacturer is not indicated, or do Article 3a(1)(c) and Article 3a(1)(g) of the directive preclude indication of the manufacturer? Is the image of a (brand-name) product a feature of the product/service within the meaning of Article 3a(c) of the directive? Does it follow from a (possible) negative answer to this question that any (price) comparison of a brand-name product with a no-name product of equivalent quality is not permitted?
(2) Is Article 7(2) ... to be interpreted as meaning that differences in the procurement of the product/service whose features are compared with features of the advertiser's product/service must also be assessed solely on the basis of Article 3a of the directive? ... [is] a (price) comparison permitted only if the compared goods are procured through the same distribution channels and are thus offered by the advertiser and his competitor(s) in a comparable selection?
(3) Is comparison ... to be construed as including the creation of the bases for comparison through a test purchase? ... [does] the deliberate initiation of a (price) comparison which is favourable to the advertiser through a test purchase which is made before the beginning of the advertiser's own offer and is arranged accordingly make ... the comparison unlawful?
(4) Is a comparison discrediting ... if the advertiser selects the goods purchased from the competitor in such a way that a price difference is obtained which is greater than the average price difference and/or if such price comparisons are repeatedly made with the result that the impression is created that the prices of the competitor(s) are generally excessive? Is Article 3a(1)(e) ... to be interpreted as meaning that the information on the identification of the competitor must be restricted to the extent absolutely necessary?[26]

(a) The Opinion of Advocate General Tizzano

12.28 **(i) Indicating the names of manufacturers** Advocate General Tizzano considered each of the issues raised by the Austrian Court. He agreed that the brand of the lenses was one of the factors influencing consumers; comparing prices without indicating the brand names of the respective lenses appeared to be misleading. He noted that according to Article 2(2), a likelihood of deceiving consumers would suffice to render the advertisement unlawful.

---

[26] Reproduced in paragraph 21.

Turning to the facts of the case he found it obvious that comparing the retail price whilst stating that the frames were the same and the lenses had the same features, but not indicating that the lenses had different brand names, one more known to the public than the other, would be misleading. On the basis of the particular facts he rejected the claim that such a finding would require, for example, indicating the manufacturers of all the parts and accessories of two cars when comparing their prices and would make it very difficult to use comparative advertising.

12.29 (ii) **Stricter national standards** The wording of this part of the first question was so imprecise that it could be rejected as hypothetical and inadmissible; still, in the spirit of cooperation between the Court and national courts, he offered his views. There appeared to be a contradiction between Article 3a(1)(a) of the Directive, which referred to Article 7(1) in defining the conditions permitting comparative advertising, and Article 7(2), which precluded the application of Article 7(1) 'to comparative advertising as far as the comparison is concerned'. His starting point was that the primary purpose of Directive 84/450 was to protect consumers and traders against misleading advertising. For that reason Article 7(1) did not preclude more extensive protection. Article 3a(1)(a) provided that comparative advertising should not be misleading according to the relevant provisions of the Directive or to any stricter national provisions adopted according to Article 7(1). At the same time the amendments introduced by Directive 97/55 and Directive 84/450 itself aimed to lift the national barriers to trade that could be raised as a result of comparative advertising's regulatory differences. This is why Article 3a was added, providing that comparative advertising was, 'as far as the comparison is concerned', to be permitted in all the Member States according to the conditions specified in that article. This was also reflected by Article 7(2).

12.30 He suggested that Article 7(2) did not preclude the application to comparative advertising of a national standard that would be stricter than the Community rules in respect of the definition of comparative advertising.[27] The conditions of Article 3a(1) precluded misleading advertising and the concept of 'misleading' could vary according to stricter national standards.

12.31 His suggested solution would resolve the contradiction and reconcile the purposes of the Directive, rejecting the opposite view expressed by Hartlauer and the Commission as assuming without

> any objective justification that consumers, traders and the general public are being afforded different and less extensive protection against the danger of anything misleading in advertising material only in cases where the material makes a comparison between competing products or services.[28]

12.32 (iii) **The relevance of channels of trade: A challenge to parallel imports** The Advocate General noted that there was no provision in Article 3a setting that price comparisons should cover only goods following the same trade channels; it seemed obvious that 'Member States cannot indiscriminately prohibit any advertising that compares the price charged for certain products by competing traders who obtain their supplies through different distribution channels'.[29] He admitted though that in some cases such a comparison could be misleading under Article 3a(1)(a).

---

[27] Point 44.
[28] Point 46.
[29] Point 50.

(iv) The context of the test purchase: Acceptability of additional conditions Advocate 12.33
General Tizzano repeated that Article 7(2) provided that Member States could not subject
the permissibility of comparative advertising to conditions additional to those prescribed
by Article 3a. The comparison could not be regarded as misleading merely because it was
based on a test purchase, made before the products concerned were offered for sale by the
advertiser, or because the products selected were being sold at different prices by competitors. However, he suggested that the advertisement would be misleading under Article 3a(1)
(a) were the advertisement to be released before the products were offered at the price quoted
or where the comparison was presented in such a way as to suggest falsely that the price difference also applied to other products.

(v) The context of price comparisons In relation to the third question, the Advocate 12.34
General repeated that comparison between the prices charged for certain products by two
or more competing traders might be misleading under Article 3a(1)(a) if it gave the false
impression that the price difference indicated also applied to other products. 'Comparing
products sold by different traders at very different prices is in itself likely to create the
impression that the same difference applies to other products.'[30] The frequency of the advertisement would not in itself be likely to create that impression. Finally, he suggested that the
content and presentation of the advertisement would determine whether it was discrediting
or not, but identifying a competitor by pictures of a shop or a company logo should not as
such be considered discrediting under Article 3a(1)(e).

(b) The Judgment of the Court

(i) The interpretation of article 7(2) Once again the Court appeared to be more supportive of comparative advertising. It stressed that in *Toshiba* it had already held that Article 12.35
2(2)(a) provided a broad definition of comparative advertising, a statement referring even by
implication to a competitor or to the goods or services offered by a competitor would suffice.
Its approach was pragmatic:

> All comparative advertising is designed to highlight the advantages of the goods or services
> offered by the advertiser in comparison with those of a competitor. In order to achieve that,
> the message must necessarily underline the differences between the goods or services compared by describing their main characteristics. The comparison made by the advertiser will
> necessarily flow from such a description.[31]

Accordingly it was not necessary 'to establish distinctions in the legislation between the
various elements of comparison, that is to say the statements concerning the advertiser's
offer, the statements concerning the competitor's offer, and the relationship between those
two offers'.[32]

As to the scope of the Comparative Advertising Directive, the starting point for the Court 12.36
was different from that of the Advocate General. In relation to comparative advertising its
objective was the establishment of conditions in which comparative advertising should be
regarded as lawful in the context of the internal market. Article 3(a) included amongst the
conditions to be satisfied that the comparative advertisement should not be misleading
according to Article 2(2), Article 3, and Article 7(1). It conceded that Article 7(1) allowed

---

[30] Point 66.
[31] Paragraph 36.
[32] Paragraph 37.

Member States to apply stricter national standards since the harmonization undertaken by the Directive was minimal. However, it observed, Article 7(2) expressly provided that Article 7(1) did not apply to comparative advertising in respect of the comparison. It acknowledged the 'apparent textual contradiction'[33] and in order to resolve it held that the provisions had to be interpreted in such a way as to take account of the objectives of Directive 84/450 and in the light of *Toshiba* where the Court had held the conditions required of comparative advertising should be interpreted in the sense most favourable to it.

12.37 The Preamble to Directive 97/55 underlined that differences in the recognition (or not) of comparative advertising at the national level could raise obstacles to the free movement of goods and distort competition. The Eighteenth Recital excluded stricter national provisions on misleading advertising:

> It follows that Directive 84/450 carried out an exhaustive harmonisation of the conditions under which comparative advertising in Member States might be lawful. Such a harmonisation implies by its nature that the lawfulness of comparative advertising throughout the Community is to be assessed solely in the light of the criteria laid down by the Community legislature. Therefore, stricter national provisions on protection against misleading advertising cannot be applied to comparative advertising as regards the form and content of the comparison.[34]

12.38 (ii) **Indicating the names of manufacturers** The Court underlined that Directive 84/450 allowed an advertiser to state the brand of a competitor's product in comparative advertising. This was made clear in the Preamble to Directive 97/55 and through the application of Article 3a(1)(d), (e), and (g) of Directive 84/450, 'where the comparison does not have the intention or effect of giving rise to such situations of unfair competition, the use of a competitor's brand name is permitted by Community law'.[35] The Court had also accepted this in *Toshiba*. Now, the omission of such a statement might also be capable of misleading:

> In cases where the brand name of the products may significantly affect the buyer's choice and the comparison concerns rival products whose respective brand names differ considerably in the extent to which they are known, omission of the better-known brand name goes against Article 3a(1)(a) of Directive 84/450, which lays down one of the conditions for comparative advertising to be lawful.[36]

This was for the national court to decide taking into account the presumed expectations of an average consumer who is reasonably well informed and reasonably observant and circumspect.[37]

12.39 (iii) **The relevance of the channels of trade** The conditions comparative advertising had to satisfy were set out in Article 3a(1). The requirement that the products had to be obtained through the same distribution channels was not amongst them; in addition, such a requirement would be against the objectives of the internal market and Directive 84/450. Parallel imports prevented the compartmentalization of national markets and comparative advertising empowered consumers to exploit the opportunities offered by the internal market.

---

[33] Paragraph 42.
[34] Paragraph 44.
[35] Paragraph 49.
[36] Paragraph 53.
[37] Citing C-220/98 *Este Lauder GmbH & Co OHG v Lancaster Group GmbH* [2000] ECR I-117.

(iv) **Test purchases**   Again, since a test purchase by the advertiser before putting on the   **12.40**
market its own competing product was not in itself prohibited, the advertisement would be
unlawful only if it failed to comply with one of the Article 3a(1) conditions.

(v) **The context of price comparisons**   The Court started by accepting that price com-   **12.41**
parison was at the core of comparative advertising. Accordingly, in itself it did not constitute discrediting or denigration of a competitor within the meaning of Article 3a(1)
(e). Restricting price comparisons to the average prices of the products offered by the
advertiser and those of its competitor would, according to the Court, be contrary to the
objectives of the Community legislature. Based on objectivity, a requirement for comparative advertising identified in the Second Recital in the Preamble to Directive 97/55, the
Court concluded that the audience of the advertisement should be capable of knowing the
actual price differences between the compared products rather than merely the average
differences.

(vi) **Delineating the exclusive trade mark rights**   Finally, regarding the use of the picture   **12.42**
of the competitor's shop front and logo, the Court noted that according to the Fifteenth
Recital in the Preamble to Directive 97/55, use of another's trade mark, trade name, or other
distinguishing marks would not breach the respective exclusive right where it complied
with the conditions laid down by the Directive.

(3) *Siemens*: Reconfirming the Court's Permissive Approach

Siemens[38] confirmed the Court's approach. Siemens manufactured and marketed program-   **12.43**
mable controllers under the name 'Simatic' using a system of alphanumeric combinations
as order codes for the controllers and their add-on components. VIPA manufactured and
marketed components that were compatible with 'Simatic' controllers; the codes were identical with those used by Siemens, with the only difference being that VIPA used its own
acronym in the first part of the codes. For example, whereas a Siemens product carried
the code 6ES5 928-3UB21 the VIPA equivalent displayed VIPA 928-3UB21. The codes
were also used in VIPA's trade catalogue. In the catalogue VIPA linked the codes with the
Siemens products. It stated: 'Please check the order number of the memory modules you
require in the handbook for your module or call us. The order numbers correspond to those
of Siemens programme modules.'[39]

Siemens claimed before the German courts that VIPA took unfair advantage of the repu-   **12.44**
tation of its products. The case reached the German Bundesgerichtshof (Federal Court of
Justice) that stayed proceedings and referred to the Court the following questions in relation to the interpretation of Directive 84/450:

(1) Is the reputation of an 'other distinguishing mark' within the meaning of Article 3a(1)
(g) of Directive 84/450/EEC taken advantage of unfairly where an advertiser adopts in
identical form the core elements of a distinguishing mark of a competitor (in this case,
a system of order numbers) which is known in trade circles, and refers to those identical
elements in advertising?

---

[38] C-59/05 *Siemens AG v VTPA Geselschaft Fur Visualisierung und Prozess Jautomatisierung GmbH* [2006] ECR I-2147.
[39] Paragraph 9.

(2) In determining whether unfair advantage is taken of a reputation for the purposes of Article 3a(1)(g) of Directive 84/450/EEC, is the benefit to the advertiser and the consumer procured by the adoption of the identical system a relevant factor?[40]

(a) The Judgment of the Court

12.45 The Court decided to proceed without requiring an Opinion and looked at the two questions jointly. The link between comparative advertising and trade mark law was considered by the Court as settled case law:

> the use of a trade mark or distinguishing mark does not breach the right to the mark where it complies with the conditions laid down by Directive 84/450, the aim being solely to distinguish between the products and services of the advertiser and those of his competitor and thus to highlight differences objectively.[41]

12.46 It was clear that a manufacturer would not take unfair advantage of the reputation of its competitor's marks by referring to them if that was a condition for effective competition. From the opposite perspective there would be an unfair advantage if the reference gave the public a false impression about the relationship between the two entities. In this case it was apparent that VIPA was using the codes for the purpose of informing the public that the products had equivalent technical features to the Siemens products. The Court viewed this as a comparison within the meaning of Article 3a(1)(c) of Directive 84/450. Still, it went on to consider whether the adoption of the code would associate VIPA and its products with the reputation of Siemens products. There were three reasons for giving a negative answer.

12.47 *The importance of the relevant public* Following *Toshiba* it found that given that the products were intended for a specialist public it would be much less likely for that public, rather than final consumers, to associate the reputation of Siemens products with VIPA's products.

12.48 *Use of VTPA's acronym* The use of its own acronym combined with the statement in the catalogue would ensure further that there would be no false impression either as to the origin of VIPA products or of an association between those two companies.

12.49 *The relevance of the technical function* Finally, the technical nature of the codes weakened the argument of Siemens further. The codes had to be programmed into the assembly system in order to operate the controller.

12.50 **(i) The significance of the benefits of comparative advertising** The reference to the benefits to the advertiser and the consumer allowed the Court to elaborate further on the policies underlying comparative advertising.

12.51 *The benefits to the consumer* The Court reiterated the fact that it had consistently held that comparative advertising was designed to enable consumers to make the best possible use of the internal market and that the Second Recital to the Preamble of the Directive 97/55 indicated that amongst the aims of comparative advertising was that of stimulating competition between suppliers of goods and services, to the consumer's advantage: 'It follows that the benefit of comparative advertising to consumers must necessarily be taken into account

---

[40] Paragraph 11.
[41] Paragraph 14.

in determining whether an advertiser is taking unfair advantage of the reputation of a trade mark, trade name or other distinguishing marks of a competitor.'[42]

The benefits to the advertiser The benefits to the advertiser, although self-evident, 'cannot alone be determinative of whether the conduct of such an advertiser is lawful'.[43]   **12.52**

(ii) **The importance of the circumstances of the case**   *Siemens* was another case where the Court was unable to untangle its response from the factual scenario of the case. It found that if a different code was used by VIPA the users of the components would have to refer to comparative listings. That would be disadvantageous, both to consumers and to VIPA. From that it deduced that the possibility that there would be restrictive effects on competition in the market for add-on components to the controllers manufactured by Siemens could not be excluded. The Court concluded that: **12.53**

> Article 3(1) (g) of Directive 84/450 must be interpreted as meaning that, in circumstances such as those in the main proceedings, by using in its catalogues the core element of a manufacturer's distinguishing mark which is known in specialist circles, a competing supplier does not take unfair advantage of the reputation of that distinguishing mark.[44]

(4) *De Landtsheer Emmanuel*: Designations of Origin; The Competitive Relationship

De Landtsheer Emmanuel SA[45] reached the Court as a reference from the Cour d'Appel de Bruxelles (Brussels Court of Appeal). De Landtsheer had been marketing beer varieties in Belgium under the trade mark MALHEUR. One of its beers, 'Malheur Brut Reserve' was brewed according to a method for producing sparkling wine. On the label and the packaging of the product a number of statements highlighted this particular characteristic: 'The First BRUT Beer in the World', 'Light Beer Produced according to the Traditional Method, Reims-France', and a reference to the wine-growers of Reims and Épernay. Whilst presenting the beer the company often used the term 'Champagnebier', a reference to the champagne method used for the production of the beer. The company also referred to the qualities of the beer in the media using champagne comparisons or contrasts. The Comité Interprofessionnel du Vin de Champagne (CIVC) and Veuve Clicquot brought an action based on the Belgian law concerning misleading and comparative advertising. They got a partial injunction, covering references to 'Reims–France' and the 'Traditional Method' and any other reference to Champagne producers and product characteristics.   **12.54**

De Landtsheer appealed and the Brussels Court of Appeal referred the following questions to the Court: **12.55**

1. Does the definition of comparative advertising cover advertisements in which the advertiser refers only to a type of product, so that in those circumstances such advertisements must be regarded as referring to all undertakings which offer that type of product, and each of them can claim to have been identified?

---

[42] Paragraph 24.
[43] Paragraph 25.
[44] Paragraph 27.
[45] C-381/05 *De Landtsheer Emmanuel SA v Comité Interprofessionnel du Vin de Champagne and Veuve Clicquot Ponsardin* SA [2007] ECR I-0311.

2. With a view to determining whether there is a competitive relationship between the advertiser and the undertaking to which reference is made ... : (a) ... should any undertaking which can be identified in the advertising be regarded as a competitor within the meaning of Article 2(2a), whatever the goods or services it offers? (b) ... is it necessary to consider the current state of the market and drinking habits in the Community or is it necessary also to consider how those habits might evolve? (c) Must any investigation be confined to that part of the Community territory in which the advertising is disseminated? (d) Is it necessary to consider the competitive relationship in relation to the types of products being compared and the way in which those types of products are generally perceived ... ? (e) Are the criteria by which a competitive relationship ... can be established identical to the criteria for verifying whether the comparison satisfies the condition referred to in Article [3a(1)(b)]?
3. Does a comparison of Article 2(2a) of Directive 84/450 with Article 3a of that directive mean that, (a) either any comparative advertising is unlawful which enables a type of product to be identified where a competitor or the goods offered by him cannot be identified from the wording? (b) or the lawfulness of the comparison must be considered in the light only of national legislation other than that by which the provisions of the directive on comparative advertising are transposed, which could lead to reduced protection for consumers or undertakings offering the type of product being compared with the product offered by the advertiser?
4. If it should be concluded that there has been comparative advertising within the meaning of Article 2(2a), must it be inferred from Article 3a(1)(f) of the Directive that any comparison is unlawful which, in respect of products without designation of origin, relates to products with designation of origin?

(a) The Opinion of Advocate General Mengozzi

12.56 **(i) The first question: Reference to a type of product** The Advocate General supported the claim that the broad nature of the definition of comparative advertising should not of itself be conclusive for answering the question. He turned instead to the Recitals to the Directive and the Judgment of the Court in *Toshiba:* comparative advertising should identify, explicitly or by implication, a competitor or goods or services offered by a competitor. He acknowledged that whether the Directive covered types of as well as specific products was not clear. A literal reading would probably not agree with a teleological approach. A compromise would be to decide that 'the test for comparative advertising must be that the message refers, albeit only by implication, to one or more specific competitors or the corresponding goods or services'.[46] An oligopolistic market might facilitate such a finding but in the end it was for the national court to decide whether the contested signs functioned in that way.

12.57 **(ii) The second question: The competitive relationship** The Advocate General supported the argument that the language of the provision was clear: 'in order for comparative advertising to exist, the advertising must make it possible to identify a competitor undertaking (or the related goods or services) and not just any undertaking (or its related goods or services)'.[47] The products of the two parties had to be identified and taken

---

[46] Point 46.
[47] Point 61.

into account. He added that there was no need for competition between the products. 'What matters is that the advertising make it possible to identify that there is competition between the advertiser and the other undertaking (or its product) in relation to any part of the range of goods or services they each offer'.[48] He argued against taking a narrow approach focusing on defining product markets according to competition law principles; instead the Court should embrace a broader interpretation taking into account a contemporary view of advertising and its functions. Actual or potential competition in relation to segments of the relevant markets or even a degree of demand substitutability could suffice.

(iii) The third question: The scope of the Directive The Advocate General strongly supported the argument that advertising which did not meet the requirements to be classified as comparative advertising should not be considered automatically illegal pursuant to the provisions of Directive 84/450; it would simply fall outside its scope. **12.58**

(iv) The fourth question: Article 3(a)1(f) He referred to the Twelfth Recital in the Preamble to Directive 97/55 stating that the conditions for comparative advertising: **12.59**

> should include, in particular, consideration of the provisions resulting from Council Regulation (EEC) No 2081/92 of 14 July 1992 on the protection of geographical indications and designations of origin for agricultural products and foodstuffs, and in particular Article 13 thereof, and of the other Community provisions adopted in the agricultural sphere.

Accordingly, Article 3a(1)(f) should 'be interpreted as meaning that comparative advertising which relates to a product with designation of origin is lawful only if the comparison refers to another product with the same designation of origin'.[49]

(b) The Judgment of the Court

(i) The first question: Reference to a type of product The Court repeated that a statement relating even by implication to a competitor or to the goods or services which it offered could suffice to render the advertisement comparative. 'The mere fact that an undertaking solely refers in its advertisement to a type of product does not mean that the advertisement in principle falls outside the scope of the directive.'[50] It went on to hold that it should be irrelevant that the reference to a type of product might, given the circumstances of the case and, in particular, the structure of the market in question, enable a number of competitors, or the goods or services that they offer, to be identified. **12.60**

(ii) The second question: The competitive relationship To answer the first part of the question, the Court noted that identification of a 'competitor' of the advertiser or of the goods and services which it offered was the key element of comparative advertising. The competitive relationship depended on the substitutable nature of the goods or services that they offered on the market. The specific assessment of the degree of substitution depended on a number of factors and fell within the jurisdiction of national courts. It was necessary to consider not only the present state of the market but also the possibilities for development within the context of free movement of goods at the Community level and the further potential for the substitution of products for one another which could be revealed by intensification of trade. **12.61**

---

[48] Point 63.
[49] Point 125.
[50] Paragraph 18.

12.62 In short, the following should be considered: the current state of the market and consumer habits and how they might evolve; the part of the Community territory in which the advertising is disseminated, without, however, excluding, where appropriate, the effects which the evolution of consumer habits seen in other Member States may have on the national market at issue; and the particular characteristics of the product which the advertiser seeks to promote and the image which it wishes to impart to it.[51]

12.63 Regarding the third part of the question the Court accepted that Articles 2(2a) and 3a(1)(b) served different purposes. The first delimited the scope of the Directive, the second provided one of the conditions that had to be satisfied. Accordingly the criteria for their application should be distinct.

12.64 (iii) **The third question: The scope of the Directive** The Court held that the conditions set out in Article 3a(1) were applicable only to advertisements which are comparative in character. The question of the permissibility of an advertisement which referred to a type of product without, however, identifying a competitor or the goods offered by that competitor did not fall within the scope of comparative advertising. National law and Community law on misleading advertising should then be taken into account.

12.65 (iv) **The fourth question: Article 3a(1)(f)** The Court held that for products without a designation of origin, any comparison which related to products with a designation of origin should not be impermissible. The Court added that Article 3a(1)(f) had to be read in conjunction with Article 3a(1)(g).

> Where all the other conditions governing whether such advertising is permissible are met, protection of designation of origin which would have the effect of prohibiting absolutely comparisons between products without designation of origin and others with designation of origin would be unwarranted and could not be justified under the provisions of Article 3a(1)(f) of the directive.[52]

(5) *O2*: Use of a Similar Sign; The Indispensability Challenge

12.66 In *O2*[53] the Court considered the conditions for comparative advertising focusing on whether a sign similar to a competitor's trade mark can be used in a comparative advertisement. O2, a mobile telephone services provider, had been using bubble images in their advertising and had registered two pictures of bubbles for telecommunication services and apparatus. They brought a trade mark infringement action against Hutchison 3G (H3G) targeting a television advertisement with price comparisons. The advertisement began by using the name 'O2' and moving black-and-white bubble imagery, followed by 'Threepay' and '3' imagery (H3G's trade marks), together with a message on price differences. O2 accepted that the comparisons were true and the advertisement was not misleading, however they maintained that use of the bubble imagery was unnecessary. The action was dismissed, O2 filed an appeal, and the English Court of Appeal referred three questions to the Court.

12.67 The first question regarded the concept of use in the context of Article 5(1) of the Trade Mark Directive. The second and the third questions queried whether there was an indispensability requirement.

---

[51] Paragraph 42.
[52] *De Landtsheer* (n 45), paragraph 70.
[53] C-533/06 *O2 Holdings Ltd, O2 (UK) Ltd v Hutchison 3G UK Ltd* [2008] ECR I-4231.

1. Where a trader, in an advertisement for his own goods or services, uses a registered trade mark owned by a competitor for the purpose of comparing the characteristics (and in particular the price) of goods or services marketed by him with the characteristics (and in particular the price) of the goods or services marketed by the competitor under that mark in such a way that it does not cause confusion or otherwise jeopardize the essential function of the trade mark as an indication of origin, does his use fall within either (a) or (b) of Article 5[(1)] of Directive 89/104?
2. Where a trader uses, in a comparative advertisement, the registered trade mark of a competitor, in order to comply with Article 3a [(1)] of Directive 84/450 ... must that use be 'indispensable' and if so what are the criteria by which indispensability is to be judged?
3. In particular, if there is a requirement of indispensability, does the requirement preclude any use of a sign which is not identical to the registered trade mark but is closely similar to it?[54]

(a) The Opinion of Advocate General Mengozzi

12.68 Advocate General Mengozzi conceded that there had been, at least at first sight, inconsistencies in the case law of the Court on the interpretation of Article 5(1)(a) and (b) of the Directive. As an example he contrasted the approach taken in *BMW*[55] with that followed in *Hölterhoff*[56] and *Adam Opel*:[57]

> the use of another's trade mark by a third party to distinguish the goods or services supplied by the proprietor of the trade mark, which does not cause confusion regarding the origin of those goods or services and the third party's goods or services, may apparently fall within the ambit of Article 5(1) of Directive 89/104 on the basis of BMW, and may escape it on the basis of Hölterhoff and Adam Opel, while ... in order to determine whether or not the said use is caught by that provision, it must be ascertained whether it is liable to affect a function of the trade mark other than the essential function of providing a guarantee of origin.[58]

12.69 Instead, the Advocate General chose to focus on the regulation of comparative advertising and the exhaustive harmonization introduced by Directive 84/450. He supported the view that the use of a competitor's trade mark in a comparative advertisement was specifically and exhaustively covered by Article 3a of Directive 84/450.[59] Since the use complained of fell clearly within the scope of Directive 84/450 and Directive 97/55 there was little point in wondering whether that conclusion would also have been reached in the absence of Directive 97/55, because that use did not in any case fall within the scope of Article 1 of Directive 89/104.

12.70 **(i) The indispensability requirement** He supported the view that there was no indispensability requirement. He recalled that in *Pippig* the Court had concluded that Article 3a(1)(e) of Directive 84/450 did not prevent the competitor's logo and a picture of its shop front if the advertising complied with the conditions laid down by Community law. Article 3a, which provided an exhaustive harmonization of the conditions for comparative

---

[54] Reproduced in paragraph 28.
[55] *BMW* (n 16).
[56] C-2/00 *Hölterhoff v Freiesleben* [2002] ECR I-4187.
[57] C-48/05 *Adam Opel AG v Autec AG* [2007] ECR I-1017.
[58] Point 26.
[59] Point 34.

advertising, did not refer to indispensability. Article 3a(1)(g) prohibited only taking unfair advantage of the reputation of a trade mark or other distinguishing marks of a competitor or of the designation of origin of competing products. In *Toshiba*,[60] Advocate General Léger had discussed a condition of necessity, however the Court appeared to disregard this and take a narrower approach as to when there is an unfair advantage covering only cases where the effect of the references to create in the mind of the targeted audience an association between the manufacturer whose products were identified and the competing supplier, in that they associated the reputation of the manufacturer's products with the products of the competing supplier.

12.71 The same considerations should also apply to use of a sign which is not identical but similar to a competitor's trade mark. Turning to the factual context of this case he added:

> [I]f a link with the competitor is already established by means of the reference to O2's trade mark, without any objection on the subject from O2, I do not see what unfair advantage H3G could gain from the additional use in the advertisement at issue of signs similar to the bubbles trade marks likewise owned by O2.[61]

12.72 The fact that the H3G bubbles were a distorted version of the O2 bubbles was irrelevant unless it did not comply with the Article 3(a) conditions. He noted that Article 3a did cover discrediting or denigration and the taking unfair advantage of the reputation of a trade mark. If the distortions were presenting the O2 trade marks or O2's image in a negative light, O2 could complain. He stressed though that Article 3a did not cover the protection of the distinctive character of the trade mark and contrasted this with the approach taken by Directive 89/104 and Regulation 40/94.

> This must represent a deliberate choice by the Community legislature, which clearly considered that it had a duty to prefer the interest in effective comparative advertising which acts as an instrument to inform consumers and a stimulus to competition between suppliers of goods and services ... to the interest of protecting the distinctive character of trade marks.[62]

(b) The Judgment of the Court

12.73 **(i) The relationship between Directives 89/104 and 84/450** The Court started by clarifying the relationship between the two Directives. Article 5(1) and (2) of Directive 89/104 provide for the exclusive rights of the trade mark proprietor. Article 5(3)(d) states that the proprietor may prevent all third parties from using such a sign in advertising. So, use in a comparative advertisement, of a sign identical with, or similar to, a competitor's mark may constitute use within the meaning of Article 5(1) and (2). The aim of Directive 97/55, on the other hand, is to promote comparative advertising and this meant that trade mark rights had to be limited to a certain extent.

> Such a limitation of the effects of the mark for the purposes of promoting comparative advertising appears necessary not only in the case of use, by the advertiser, of a competitor's actual mark, but also in the case of use of a sign similar to that mark.[63]

---

[60] See 12.05–12.25 above.
[61] Point 61.
[62] Point 65.
[63] Paragraph 40.

12.74 The Court added that the broad definition of comparative advertising in Article 2(2a) of Directive 84/450 covered cases where a reference to a competitor or its products was made even by implication.[64] Comparative advertising should also cover use of a sign similar to the mark of a competitor of the advertiser perceived by the average consumer as a reference to that competitor or its goods and services:

> Consequently, in order to reconcile the protection of registered marks and the use of comparative advertising, Article 5(1) and (2) of Directive 89/104 and Article 3a(1) of Directive 84/450 must be interpreted to the effect that the proprietor of a registered trade mark is not entitled to prevent the use, by a third party, of a sign identical with, or similar to, his mark, in a comparative advertisement which satisfies all the conditions, laid down in Article 3a(1) of Directive 84/450, under which comparative advertising is permitted.[65]

12.75 The Court then made the link between Article 5(1)(b) of Directive 89/104 and Article 3a(1)(d) of Directive 84/450 both covering cases where there is a likelihood of confusion. So, Article 5(1) and (2) of Directive 89/104/EEC and Article 3a(1) of Directive 84/450 had to

> be interpreted as meaning that the proprietor of a registered trade mark is not entitled to prevent the use by a third party of a sign identical with, or similar to, his mark, in a comparative advertisement which satisfies all the conditions, laid down in Article 3a(1) of Directive 84/450, under which comparative advertising is permitted.[66]

But, where the conditions required in Article 5(1)(b) of Directive 89/104 were met, then the condition of Article 3a(1)(d) of Directive 84/450 would not be met.

12.76 **(ii) Use of a sign similar to a trade mark** The Court noted that the factual context of the case meant that only Article 5(1)(b) of Directive 89/104 had to be interpreted. However, some concepts had to be clarified in a uniform way for the purpose of Article 5 (1). 'Use' was one of them, and reviewing its case law the Court identified four conditions: that use must be in the course of trade; it must be without the consent of the proprietor of the mark; it must be in respect of goods or services which are identical with, or similar to, those for which the mark is registered; and, it must affect or be liable to affect the essential function of the trade mark, which is to guarantee to consumers the origin of the goods or services, by reason of a likelihood of confusion on the part of the public.[67]

12.77 Turning to the facts of the case the Court made the following remarks: H3G's use was use in the course of trade, without the consent of O2, for services identical with those for which those marks were registered, but did not give rise to a likelihood of confusion. Accordingly, the answer to the first question should be that:

> Article 5(1)(b) of Directive 89/104 is to be interpreted as meaning that the proprietor of a registered trade mark is not entitled to prevent the use, by a third party, in a comparative advertisement, of a sign similar to that mark in relation to goods or services identical with, or similar to, those for which that mark is registered where such use does not give rise to a likelihood of confusion on the part of the public, and that is so irrespective of whether or not

---

[64] Paragraph 42.
[65] Paragraph 45.
[66] Paragraph 51.
[67] Paragraph 57, citing amongst others C-245/02 *Arsenal Football Club; Anheuser-Busch* [2004] ECR I-10989.

the comparative advertisement satisfies all the conditions laid down in Article 3a of Directive 84/450 under which comparative advertising is permitted.[68]

(6) *L'Oreal v Bellure*: Taking a step back?

(a) The factual context

12.78 The Court appears to be taking a step back in the discourse on comparative advertising with its Judgment in *L'Oreal v Bellure*.[69] Bellure and the other respondents referred to the trade marks of the appellants in comparative lists in which they paired, according to similarity of smell, their own much cheaper products with the established luxury perfumes; the lists had been circulated to retailers. Some of the similarly scented products were also sold in packaging similar in terms of appearance to the packaging of their luxury paired perfumes, although it had been accepted that it was unlikely that either retailers or consumers would be misled as to origin.

12.79 The case reached the English Court of Appeal that referred five questions to the Court. In the first four questions, the balancing between the interests of trade mark proprietors and the use of trade marks in comparative advertising was an issue. Questions 1 and 2 primarily covered aspects of Article 5(1) of Directive 89/104; question 5 considered Article 5(2), covered earlier in this book.[70]

12.80 The remaining two questions focused more, either directly or indirectly, on Directive 84/450:

(3) In the context of Article 3a[1](g) of Directive [84/450] what is the meaning of 'take unfair advantage of' and in particular, where a trader in a comparison list compares his product with a product under a well-known trade mark, does he thereby take unfair advantage of the reputation of the well-known mark?

(4) In the context of Article 3a [1] (h) of the said directive, what is the meaning of 'present[ing] goods or services as imitations or replicas' and in particular does this expression cover the case where, without in any way causing confusion or deception, a party merely truthfully says that his product has a major characteristic (smell) like that of a well-known product which is protected by a trade mark?[71]

(b) The Opinion of Advocate General Mengozzi

12.81 Advocate General Mengozzi expressed some reservations in respect of the findings of the Court of Appeal. For example, he doubted whether the parties were real competitors in the market place for perfumes but accepted that following *De Landtsheer Emmanuel*, where he also delivered the Opinion,[72] the acts of the respondents could still constitute comparative advertising since potential competition and how markets and consumers might evolve should also be taken into account. He conceded though that in the absence of clear evidence to the contrary it was necessary to accept the premise adopted by the Court of Appeal that the lists constituted comparative advertising within the meaning of Article 2(2a) of Directive 84/450.

---

[68] Paragraph 69.
[69] C-487/07 *L'Oreal SA, Lancôme Parfums et Beauté & Cie, Laboratoire Garnier & Cie v Bellure NV, Malaika Investments Ltd, Starion International Ltd*. [2009] ECR I-5185.
[70] See paragraphs 7.525 and following.
[71] Reproduced in Point 15.
[72] See 12.56–12.59 above.

(i) The first two questions He then proceeded to remind the Court that they had held in *O2* that use of a third party's trade mark in comparative advertisements could be regarded as use for the advertiser's own goods and services for the purposes of Article 5(1) and (2) of Directive 89/104; however, the trade mark proprietor was not entitled to prevent such use provided it satisfied Article 3a(1) of Directive 84/450.

12.82

According to the Advocate General[73] compliance with the conditions under which comparative advertising is permitted under Article 3a(1) of Directive 84/450 constitutes, in my view, an independent ground of defence, in addition to those in Articles 6 and 7(1) of Directive 89/104, which is capable of defeating an action brought against a comparative advertisement based on national provisions implementing Article 5(1) or (2) of Directive 89/104.

12.83

Focusing on the first two questions the Advocate General noted that elements, and at least the first question, had been answered in terms of principles by *O2* but still felt he had to consider in the light of the factual context. Following an analysis of the jurisprudence of the Court in respect of the essential function of a trade mark, Advocate General Mengozzi suggested that the answer to the first two questions should be that Article 5(1)(a) of Directive 89/104 should be interpreted as meaning that:

12.84

> the proprietor of a trade mark is not entitled to prohibit use by a third party in comparative advertising of a sign that is identical with that mark for goods or services which are identical with those for which the mark is registered where such use does not affect or is not liable to affect the mark's essential function of providing a guarantee of origin or any of the mark's other functions and that is the case even if such use plays a significant role in the promotion of the advertiser's goods and, in particular, permits that advertiser to take unfair advantage of the mark's reputation.[74]

However, the stated use could still be prohibited under Article 5(2) of Directive 8/104 or Article 3a(1) of Directive 84/450. He then went on to discuss questions 3 and 4.

12.85

(ii) The comparative advertising questions Advocate General Mengozzi suggested that the legislature used the word 'unfair' in Article 3a(1)(g):

12.86

> because it considered that the fact that there may be an advantage for the advertiser deriving from the reputation of the competitor's distinctive signs is not sufficient in itself to justify prohibiting comparative advertising … In order for it to be prohibited, it is necessary for that advantage to be classified as 'unfair'.[75]

Accordingly, the second part of the question should be answered in the negative.

Identifying the criteria according to which a comparative advertisement could be classified as unfair, he supported that 'it will be necessary first of all to ascertain whether such advertising may cause the public at whom it is directed to make an association with the reputation of the competitor's mark by way of extension';[76] the overall presentation of the advertising and the type of audience targeted by the advertisement would be factors that should be taken into account. The second step would be to determine whether the advantage was unfair; for this reference to the individual circumstances of each case had to be

12.87

---

[73] Point 25.
[74] Point 61.
[75] Point 66.
[76] Point 74.

made. Even an advertisement with genuine informative content could be found to confer an unfair advantage

> where, when an association with the reputation of another person's mark is made by way of extension, that content is, viewed objectively, of limited value, the competitor's mark enjoys a high degree of brand recognition and the funds invested for the purpose of promoting the advertiser's product are fully utilised in advertising which makes a comparison with the product identified by that mark.[77]

12.88 The assessment was of a factual nature, a matter for the national court to determine. Turning to the fourth question, on Article 3a(1)(g) of Directive 84/450, he suggested that the provision:

> does not even appear to be intended to prohibit a positive statement that the advertiser's product or one of its characteristics and the product protected by another person's mark or one of its characteristics are equivalent. Accordingly, where the advertiser simply states that his product is equivalent (or has an equivalent characteristic) to the product protected by another person's mark (or to one of that product's characteristics), without, however, alluding to the fact that that equivalence is the result of copying the latter mark (or one of its characteristics), it does not seem to me that one product is being presented as an imitation or replica of another.[78]

12.89 Choosing a strict interpretation he added that the provision covered only 'a statement of the fact that the advertised product has been manufactured in a process involving the making of an imitation or replica of the model for the product bearing the protected trade mark'.[79]

(c) The Judgment of the Court

12.90 **(i) The first two questions** The Court concurred with the Advocate General that the broad definitions of advertising and comparative advertising in Article 2(1) of Directive 84/450 could cover varied advertising patterns and made the same points regarding its findings in *O2*. Following a review of its case law on the functions of a trade mark the Court concluded that:

> Article 5(1)(a) of Directive 89/104 must be interpreted as meaning that the proprietor of a registered trade mark is entitled to prevent the use by a third party, in a comparative advertisement which does not satisfy all the conditions, laid down in Article 3a(1) of Directive 84/450, under which comparative advertising is permitted, of a sign identical with that mark in relation to goods or services which are identical with those for which that mark was registered, even where such use is not capable of jeopardising the essential function of the mark, which is to indicate the origin of the goods or services, provided that such use affects or is liable to affect one of the other functions of the mark.[80]

12.91 **(ii) The comparative advertising questions** The Court examined questions 3 and 4 together. It held that the Article 3a(1)(a)–(h) list of factors had to be applied cumulatively and that they should be interpreted in the sense most favourable to permitting advertisements which objectively compare product characteristics. It followed:

---

[77] Point 77.
[78] Point 84.
[79] Point 88.
[80] Paragraph 65.

that the use of a competitor's trade mark in comparative advertising is permitted by Community law where the comparison objectively highlights differences and the object or effect of such highlighting is not to give rise to situations of unfair competition, such as those described inter alia in Article 3a(1)(d), (e), (g) and (h) of Directive 84/450.[81]

Turning to Article 3a(1)(h), the Court found that: 12.92

> it is not only advertisements which explicitly evoke the idea of imitation or reproduction which are prohibited, but also those which, having regard to their overall presentation and economic context, are capable of implicitly communicating such an idea to the public at whom they are directed.[82]

The Court then considered Article 3a(1)(g), taking into account the factual context and its own approach towards Article 3a(1)(h). Accordingly, it held that:

> the answer to the third and fourth questions is that Article 3a(1) of Directive 84/450 must be interpreted as meaning that an advertiser who states explicitly or implicitly in comparative advertising that the product marketed by him is an imitation of a product bearing a well-known trade mark presents 'goods or services as imitations or replicas' within the meaning of Article 3a(1)(h). The advantage gained by the advertiser as a result of such unlawful comparative advertising must be considered to be an advantage taken unfairly of the reputation of that mark within the meaning of Article 3a(1)(g).[83]

(7) *Lidl*: Comparing 'Shopping Baskets'; The Relevance of Information

It is also worth mentioning *Lidl*,[84] because although it is not directly linked with trade mark law it involves trade marks as communicators. The case involved competing claims between supermarket chains. Vierzon, trading as Leclerc, published comparative advertisements that compared the till receipts for a list of everyday items of shopping from different supermarkets, albeit without revealing their brands. 12.93

Lidl, which appeared to be more expensive than Leclerc, brought an action and the French Tribunal de Commerce de Bourges referred the following question: 12.94

> Is Article 3a of Directive 84/450/EEC, as amended by Directive 97/55/EC, to be interpreted as meaning that it is unlawful to engage in comparative advertising on the basis of the price of products meeting the same needs or intended for the same purpose, that is to say, products which are sufficiently interchangeable, on the sole ground that, in regard to food products, the extent to which consumers would like to eat those products, or, in any case, the pleasure of consuming them, is completely different according to the conditions and the place of production, the ingredients used and the experience of the producer?[85]

(a) *The Opinion of Advocate General Mengozzi*

Advocate General Mengozzi focused on the second and third conditions: does the advertisement compare 'goods or services meeting the same needs or intended for the same purpose' and does it 'objectively compare ... one or more material, relevant, verifiable and representative features ... which may include price', and applied them against the context of foodstuffs, that comprised the majority of the compared 'shopping baskets'. He referred to the jurisprudence developed above and stressed that the multifactorial interchangeability 12.95

---

[81] Paragraph 72.
[82] Paragraph 75.
[83] Paragraph 80.
[84] C-159/09 *Lidl SNC v Vierzon Distribution SA* [2011] E.C.R. I-07235.
[85] Paragraph 20.

had to be carried out by the national court on a case-by-case basis. The test, however, should not include a 'total taste equivalence' factor because then any comparison would be impossible. The lack of branding information according to *Pippig*, that set a high threshold, would be relevant only where the brand name would significantly affect the buyer's choice and the comparison concerned brand names that differed considerably. Lack of branding information could also be relevant if it did not allow the identification of the products being compared, but both these issues were for the national court to determine.

(b) The Judgment of the Court

12.96 The Court stressed that there is nothing in the law or its jurisprudence to imply that comparisons cannot be made in relation to food products or that comparisons can only be made in relation to identical food products:

> the fact alone that food products differ in terms of the extent to which consumers would like to eat them and the pleasure to be derived from consuming them, according to the conditions and place of production, their ingredients and who produced them, cannot preclude the possibility that the comparison of such products may meet the requirement laid down in that provision that the products compared meet the same needs or are intended for the same purpose, that is to say, that they display a sufficient degree of interchangeability.[86]

12.97 Turning to whether comparisons of shopping baskets could be misleading, the Court added:

> advertising such as the advertisement at issue could, first, be misleading, as is apparent from case-law, if the referring court were to find that, in the light of all the relevant circumstances of the particular case, in particular the information contained in or omitted from the advertisement, the decision to buy on the part of a significant number of consumers to whom the advertising is addressed may be made in the mistaken belief that the selection of goods made by the advertiser is representative of the general level of his prices as compared with those charged by his competitor and that such consumers will therefore make savings of the kind claimed by the advertisement by regularly buying their everyday consumer goods from the advertiser rather than from the competitor, or in the mistaken belief that all of the advertiser's products are cheaper than those of his competitor.[87]

12.98 The Court noted that in the absence of branding information consumers would probably expect that the baskets would include comparable products. Lack of branding and other relevant information could make the advertisement misleading and potentially problematic to verify. Consumers may be affected in making a choice by relying on the composition or the place of production of a particular product.

> In such cases, the fact that the consumer is not informed of the differences between products being compared in terms of price alone may deceive the consumer as to the reasons for the difference in prices claimed and the financial advantage that can in fact be obtained by the consumer by buying his goods from the advertiser rather than from a given competitor and have a corresponding effect on the consumer's economic behaviour. The latter may thus be led to believe that he will in fact obtain an economic advantage because of the competitive nature of the advertiser's offer and not because of objective differences between the products being compared.[88]

---

[86] Paragraph 39.
[87] Paragraph 50.
[88] Paragraph 55.

Adequate product identification was also relevant for verifying the comparison: **12.99**

> Article 3a(1)(c) of Directive 84/450 is to be interpreted as meaning that the condition of verifiability set out in that provision requires, in the case of an advertisement, such as that at issue in the main proceedings, which compares the prices of two selections of goods, that it must be possible to identify the goods in question on the basis of information contained in the advertisement.[89]

C. Geographical Indications

(1) *Feta*: Consumer Confusion and a Misappropriation Rationale

The Judgment of the court in *Feta*[90] considered a challenge to the European regime for the protection of geographical indications and designations of origin. The issue was whether the term 'feta' constituted a generic description of a type of cheese or a designation of origin. For our purposes the Judgment of the Court reveals the wider applicability of consumer confusion and misappropriation rationales. It also provides the opportunity to compare the Community Trade Mark system with another Community-wide system of protection of distinguishing signs that has to deal with analogous problems, in this case what constitutes a generic description. **12.100**

(a) The framework of protection

The framework of protection based on registration is provided by Council Regulation (EEC) 2081/1992. Article 2(2)(a) defines a designation of origin as: **12.101**

> the name of a region, a specific place or, in exceptional cases, a country, used to describe an agricultural product or a foodstuff originating in that region, specific place or country, and the quality or characteristics of which are essentially or exclusively due to a particular geographical environment with its inherent natural and human factors, and the production, processing and preparation of which take place in the defined geographical area.[91]

Article 2(3) equates to designations of origin certain traditional geographical or non-geographical names designating an agricultural product or a foodstuff originating in a region or a specific place, which fulfils the same conditions.

According to Article 3(1) generic names should not be registered. A name that relates to the place or the region where this product or foodstuff has been originally produced or marketed but has become the common name of an agricultural product or a foodstuff is considered to have become generic. To determine whether a name has become generic all relevant factors are taken into account and, in particular, the existing situation in the Member State in which the name originates, in areas of consumption, and in other Member States, as well as the relevant national or Community laws. A 'Register of Protected Designations of Origin and Protected Geographical Indications' is maintained by the Commission. The process has been subsequently repealed by Council Regulation (EC) No 692/2003.[92] **12.102**

---

[89] Paragraph 64.
[90] C-465/02 and C-466/02 *Federal Republic of Germany and Kingdom of Denmark v Commission* [2005] ECR I-9115.
[91] Council Regulation (EEC) 2081/92 on the Protection of Geographical Indications and Designations of Origin for Agricultural Products and Foodstuffs [1992] OJL 208/1.
[92] Council Regulation (EC) 692/2003 Amending Regulation (EEC) 2081192 on the Protection of Geographical Indications and Designations of Origin for Agricultural Products and Foodstuffs [2003] OJL 99/1.

12.103 A committee of representatives from Member States assists the Commission in respect of measures to be taken according to the Regulation. Disagreement between the Commission and the committee triggers a process that involves the Council. The Commission has also set up a scientific committee to examine technical problems relating to the application of the Regulation.

(b) The history of feta's protection

12.104 'Feta' had been registered as a designation of origin in 1996 according to earlier Regulations,[93] albeit the Court annulled the registration in 1999[94] on the ground that the Commission had not taken into account all the factors it had to consider, in particular the situation in other Member States. Subsequently the Commission conducted a survey on the manufacture, consumption, and reputation of 'feta' in each of the Member States on the basis of which the scientific committee concluded that 'feta' was not generic.

12.105 As a result, the Commission reintroduced 'feta' into the list of protected designations of origin through the adoption of the contested Regulation 1829/2002 (the Regulation)[95] that, to an extent, followed a 'misappropriation' rationale. The finding on consumer confusion was influenced by the evidence of free riding. According to the Twentieth Recital, most 'feta' cheeses made explicit or implicit reference to Greek territory, culture, or tradition, irrespective of their actual origin, by adding text or drawings with a Greek connotation. The link was considered to be 'deliberately suggested and sought as part of a sales strategy that capitalises on the reputation of the original product, and this creates a real risk of consumer confusion'.[96] In addition, the Regulation incorporated a broad range of criteria; legal, historical, cultural, political, social, economic, scientific, and technical information contributed to its justificatory basis. The geographical area covered by the Regulation was broadly delineated: the relevant natural and human factors applied throughout the mainland and the island of Lesvos (or Lesbos). However, the revised product specification submitted by Greek authorities included a balancing limitation: milk used to produce 'feta' must come from ewes and goats of local breeds reared traditionally and whose feed is based on the flora present in the pastures of eligible regions. This, coupled with the traditional method of production, in particular the straining without pressure process, gave to the end product its specific aroma and flavour and as a result its international reputation.

(c) The Opinion of Advocate General Ruiz-Jarabo Colomer

12.106 There were five main points in the substantive analysis of Advocate General Ruiz-Jarabo Colomer.[97]

12.107 First, he described the reasoning behind the protection of geographical names as the reward for the efforts of those manufacturing a product in a particular way that bestows the product a reputation deserving to be protected through an industrial property right. The aim

---

[93] Commission Regulation (EC) 1107/96 on the Registration of Geographical Indications and Designations of Origin under the Procedure laid down in Article 17 of Regulation 2081/92 [1996] OJ L148/1.
[94] C-289/96 *Kingdom of Denmark*, C-293/96 *Federal Republic of Germany*, and C-299/96 *French Republic v Commission* [1999] ECR I-1541.
[95] Commission Regulation (EC) 1829/2002 amending the Annex to Regulation (EC) 1107/96 with regard to the name 'Feta' [2002] OJ L277/10.
[96] Paragraph 21.
[97] The Opinion was available to the author in French and Greek.

is to prevent financial injury but also the unjust enrichment of third parties. Citing his Opinion in *Canadane*[98] he noted that:

> geographical names are legally protected by national laws on industrial and commercial property. The legal protection of a geographical name confers a collective monopoly over its commercial use upon a particular group of producers by reference to their geographical location—in contrast, a trade mark can only be used by the owner.[99]

Reviewing the jurisprudence of the Court in this area he concluded:

> All those judgments reflect the tendency of European legislation to put the emphasis on the quality of the products, within the framework of the common agricultural policy, in order to improve their reputation ... they attribute a dual purpose to appellations of origin: to guarantee the origin of the particular product and act as a barrier against the deceptive use of the appellation and in parallel to protect the industrial and commercial property which has become increasingly more in relation to the principle of free movement of goods.[100]

12.108 Second, he repeated his conclusion in *Canadane* regarding the principle of protecting the designation 'feta':

> (1) Legislation of a Member State which prevents the marketing, under the sales description 'feta', of a cheese lawfully produced and marketed under that name in another Member State is a measure having equivalent effect to a quantitative restriction, contrary to Article [28] of the EC Treaty. (2) Legislation of a Member State which restricts to national products the use of the name 'feta' is not justified on the grounds of consumer protection or fair trading. (3) Legislation of a Member State intended to protect the rights which are the specific subject-matter of a geographical name, such as the name 'feta', is justified on the ground of protection of industrial and commercial property referred to in Article [30] of the EC Treaty.[101]

12.109 Third, he suggested that in ascertaining consumer perception the view of Greek consumers should be taken into account since there was partial overlap between the place of origin and the place of consumption. Greek consumers perceived 'feta' as a domestic product that enjoyed a high degree of reputation, and a large part of consumers in other Member States associated 'feta' with Greece to the extent that the overwhelming majority of labelling of 'feta' included references to the Greek cultural identity.

12.110 Fourth, he suggested that the views of consumers in Germany, Denmark, and France on 'feta'—countries that produced 'feta'-like cheeses using cows' milk—should be taken into account but not dominate the overall assessment that should consider the position throughout the Union and take account of all relevant factors. The situation in other countries, outside the Union, constituted another factor to be taken into account; he suggested though that it should be accorded less relevance in the absence of a specific international agreement. He noted that the use of cows' milk rather than goats' or sheep's milk, as a result of chemical and organoleptic differences, meant that the cheese produced in those countries differed in terms of appearance, taste, and aroma. Fifth, he emphasized the historical context of use, stretching back to Homer's *Odyssey* and the account of the cheese produced by the Cyclops Polyphemus.[102] There was a historical link with Greece that should not be

---

[98] C-317/95 *Canadane Cheese Trading AMBA and Adelfi G Kouri Anonymos Emoriki Kai Viomichaniki Etaireia v Hellenic Republic* [1997] ECR I-4681.
[99] *Canadane* (n 98), point 36.
[100] *Feta* (n 90), point 82.
[101] Point 79 of *Canadane* (n 98).
[102] See the historical analysis in *Canadane* (n 98).

overlooked. Looking at the link from another angle he posed the rhetorical question: 'Why do the manufacturers of white cheese made from cows' milk in brine choose to call it "feta"? Without a doubt, in order to use a designation that means something to consumers … they sought the name that would allow them to maximize sales.'[103]

12.111 Following the consideration of all relevant factors under the light of the five points described above he proposed that the challenge to the Regulation should be rejected.

(d) The Judgment of the Court
(i) The attack against feta: Geographical coverage and genericity
12.112 *Geographical coverage* Article 2(3) of the basic application referred to Article 2(2)(a); their joint application meant that 'the designated area must therefore, present homogenous natural factors which distinguish it from the areas adjoining it'.[104] The relevant Greek legislation identified the geographical area that satisfied the criteria of Article 2(3) and excluded a significant part of the territory of Greece, namely all the islands except Lesvos (Lesbos). It did not cover all Greece. Accordingly, the Court had only to consider whether the designated area was determined in an artificial manner. The Greek legislation provided that: 'the milk used for the manufacture of feta must come from breeds of ewes and goats raised using traditional methods and adapted to the region of manufacture of the feta and the flora of that region must be the basis of their feed'.[105] According to the specifications submitted in 1994 the demarcation of the geographical area was based on its homogeneous geomorphology, climate, and botanical characteristics. The excluded territories did not display the same features. There was evidence that feta was also produced in some of the smaller Aegean islands, however this was not found to constitute a problem since, according to the Commission, those islands were part of the department of Lesvos. On the basis of this the Court rejected the claim that the geographical area was not defined according to Article 6(2) of the Regulation.

12.113 *Geography and product characteristics* Another claim targeting the geographical coverage of the Regulation was that feta's quality and characteristics were not essentially or exclusively due to a particular geographical environment, as required by Article 2(2)(a) of the basic regulation. The Court rejected this claim since the Preamble to the Regulation referred to a list of factors supporting the view that the characteristics of feta were essentially or exclusively due to a particular geographical environment. The specifications submitted by the Greek Government focusing, amongst others, on the amount of sunshine, temperature changes, the practice of transhumance, extensive grazing, and vegetation reinforced the statement in the Preamble.

12.114 **(ii) Genericity and feta** The Court also rejected the plea that the Regulation infringed Article 3(1) of the basic Regulation because 'feta' was a generic name within the meaning of Article 3(1). One of the specific arguments under this plea was that the likelihood of consumer confusion referred to in the Twentieth Recital in the Preamble had no bearing on the issue of whether a name was generic. Another had to do with identifying the party that carried the burden of proof. The Court noted that although white cheeses soaked in brine had been produced for a long time in other countries they were known in those

---

[103] *Feta* (n 90), point 176.
[104] *Feta* (n 90), paragraph 50; the Court cited *Commission v Germany* (12/74) [1975] ECR 181.
[105] Article 2(1)(e) of Ministerial Order No 313025, cited in paragraph 56.

countries under other names than 'feta'. In Greece itself, until 1987, cheese produced from cows' milk and according to non-traditional methods was produced under the name 'feta' and, until 1988, imported under the same name from other countries. If this were to continue inevitably the name would have become generic. Through a number of measures these practices were discontinued, however. The Court accepted that the fact that a product that had been lawfully marketed under a particular name in some Member States might constitute a factor in the assessment of whether that name had become generic. It noted, however, that although the production in the other countries had been relatively large and of substantial duration, the production of feta had remained concentrated in Greece. Lawful production in other countries was only one of the factors that had to be taken into account. Consumption, on the other hand, occurred predominantly in Greece, 85% of Community consumption of feta was concentrated in Greece where the majority of consumers considered the name to carry a geographical rather than a generic connotation. In Denmark, the opposite outcome was reached.

12.115 What weakened the evidence regarding the generic use of 'feta' in Member States other than Greece was that it was commonly marketed with labels referring to Greek cultural traditions and civilisation. It was legitimate to infer that consumers perceived feta as a cheese associated with Greece, irrespective of its place of production.

12.116 All the above suggested that 'feta' was not generic and that it was not incorrect to state that the link between the name 'feta' and Greece was deliberately suggested. Accordingly the German Government contention was unfounded. Even the national legislation in Denmark, the Court remarked, referred to 'Danish feta' rather than 'feta', a fact that suggested that even in Denmark the name had a Greek connotation. Note that the Court did not consider the burden of proof argument, once it found that the statement was correct.

(2) *Bavaria*: The Coexistence Between Trade Mark and Geographical Indication Protection

12.117 In *Bavaria*,[106] the Court considered the coexistence between trademark and protected geographical indication protection. The case came before the Court as a reference from the Italian Corte d'Appello di Torino (Turin Court of Appeal). The questions posed by the Italian court focused on whether the name 'Bayerisches Bier' constituted a valid protected geographical indication (PGI), registered by a German association, and whether such protection would affect the validity and use of existing trade marks for beer incorporating the name 'Bavaria' registered in Italy by a Dutch controlled group of companies.

(a) *The Opinion of Advocate General Mazak*

12.118 (i) **The validity of the PGI registration** Turning to the substantive arguments of the parties, Advocate General Mazak accepted that beer could be considered a 'foodstuff', defined in Article 2 of Regulation No 178/2002[107] as 'any substance or product, whether processed, partially processed or unprocessed, intended to be, or reasonably expected to be ingested

---

[106] C-343/07 *Bavaria NV; Bavaria Italia Srl v Bayerischer Brauerbund eV* [2009] ETMR 61.
[107] Regulation 178/2002 laying down the general principles and requirements of food law, establishing the European Food Safety Authority and laying down procedures in matters of food safety [2002] OJ L31/1.

by humans'. Having rejected all the challenges based on procedural aspects he moved to the crux of the dispute: whether the term was generic and as such should be precluded from registration.[108] The Dutch group supported that the term referred to a widespread method of production rather the origin of the product, highlighting that 'Bavaria' was a common element of company names trade marks in a number of countries, including Germany, and a synonym for beer in Denmark, Sweden, and Finland.

12.119 The term has been accepted for registration because of the particular reputation of beer produced in Bavaria, the result of tradition and legal measures that went back to 1516.

> What is decisive, for the purposes of registering a PGI, is not whether the quality, reputation or other characteristic of a specific type or brand of beer is attributable to its geographical origin, but whether such a link can be established between the beverage 'beer' and the geographical origin concerned. Similarly, PGIs are not designed to distinguish a specific product or producer but can be used by all producers and with regard to all products, in this case by all types of beer, which emanate from the geographical area concerned and which satisfy the relevant product specifications.[109]

Even if the term had become generic at some point it could regain its indication of origin significance; in this case there was evidence 'Bayerisches Bier' functioned as such an indicator after 1940.

12.120 The other critical point of validity was whether use of the term has become misleading in the light of the reputation of the registered trade marks.[110] According to the Advocate General the purpose of Article 14(3) was to 'prevent a product bearing a PGI from being confused by the consumer with a given trade mark product';[111] however, this had already been considered at the time the PGI was registered and there was no evidence that the finding of the Commission was incorrect. Note the point made by the Advocate General that 'the higher the reputation or renown of a mark, and thus the stronger its distinctiveness, the lower will be the likelihood that consumers may be misled to the extent of ascribing a product with a given PGI to that trade mark'.[112]

12.121 **(ii) The effect of the PGI registration on pre-existing trade marks: Another aspect of coexistence** To answer that question, the Advocate General focused on the actual relevant provision of the Regulation No 1347/2001, Article 14, rather than the Recitals in its Preamble.[113] Article 14(3): 'offers ... protection to pre-existing trade marks in so far as it prevents the registration of an indication or designation, the use of which would result in a likelihood of confusion with an earlier trade mark'.[114] It was a barrier to registration and did not cover 'all the situations in which, according to the scope of protection afforded under Article 13 of the regulation, trade marks may encroach on names registered under that regulation'.[115]

---

[108] According to Articles 2(2)(b), 3(1), and 17(2) of Regulation No 2081/92 and citing C-312/98 *Warsteiner* [2000] ECR I-9187.
[109] Paragraph 112.
[110] According to Article 14(3) of Regulation No 2081/92.
[111] Paragraph 128.
[112] Paragraph 133.
[113] See in particular the Third and the Fourth Recitals, referring to the trade marks in question.
[114] Paragraph 151.
[115] Paragraph 153.

Coexistence in this case meant that a trade mark which conflicts with a protected geographical indication or designation of origin for the purposes of Article 13 of Regulation 2081/92 could be continued to be used:

12.122

> only on condition that, first, that trade mark was registered in good faith before the date on which the application for registration of a designation of origin or a geographical indication was lodged and, secondly, provided that there are no grounds for the invalidity or revocation of the trade mark as laid down under Article 3(1)(c) and (g) and Article 12(2)(b) of the Trade Marks Directive.[116]

Whether the facts of the case fell under the provision was for the national court to determine.[117]

(b) The Judgment of the Court

The Court[118] accepted that it cannot be claimed that Bavaria and Bavaria Italia are undoubtedly directly affected by Regulation 1347/2001 and accordingly did not have standing to bring an action for annulment. Given that Regulation 2081/92 does not provide a definition of the term 'foodstuff' the Court found no reason why beer should be excluded. From a positive perspective, the Court added that in other Community legislation beer is covered by the definition of 'foodstuff'[119] and the Court had already decided that Articles 39 and 43 TFEU also apply to products that are not covered in Annex I to the Treaty. Note that the Court also paid attention to the argument that although beer is not expressly mentioned in the annex, most of its ingredients are.

12.123

(i) The social aspects of agriculture   From a social perspective, the Court added:

12.124

> when implementation by the Council or the Commission of the Community's agricultural policy necessitates the evaluation of a complex economic or social situation, their discretion is not limited solely to the nature and scope of the measures to be taken but also, to some extent, to the finding of basic facts. In that context, it is open to the Council or the Commission to rely if necessary on general findings.[120]

Accordingly, and given that the assessment made by the German authorities did not appear to be vitiated by manifest error, the Council or the Commission could rightly assume that the PGI in question satisfied the conditions set out in Article 17(1) of Regulation 2081/92 for registration under the simplified procedure.

12.125

(ii) Genericity considerations   As to whether the term was generic or not, the Court accepted that the German authorities were best placed to make the complex and detailed assessment that had not been challenged before a national court. It also rejected the argument that 'Bavaria' was the name of a state and hence exceptional conditions had to be established in order to be protected as a PGI, finding that it did not constitute the name of

12.126

---

[116] Paragraph 156.
[117] Citing C-87/97 *Consorzio per la tutela del formaggio Gorgonzola v Kaserei Champignon Hofmeister and Eduard Bracharz* [1999] ECR I-1301.
[118] See also C-132/05 *Commission v Germany* [2008] ECR I-957 on the conflict between Parmiggiano Reggiano and Parmesan.
[119] Citing Article 2 of Regulation (EC) No 178/2002 of the European Parliament and of the Council of 28 January 2002 laying down the general principles and requirements of food law, establishing the European Food Safety Authority and laying down procedures in matters of food safety [2002] OJ L31/1.
[120] Paragraph 84, citing C-122/94 *Commission v Council* [1996] ECR I-881 and *NIFPO and Northern Ireland Fishermen's Federation* (C-4/96) [1998] ECR I-681.

a 'country', as indicated in the Regulation, but an infra-State body. Looking at the reasons for granting PGI protection the Court found that neither purity nor the traditional brewing method were in themselves the bases for the registration of the term; 'it was rather the reputation of beer originating in Bavaria that was determinative'.[121] Admittedly, these now widespread qualities have contributed to building up the reputation, but it was also the reputation of Bavarian beer that contributed to the worldwide acceptance of those qualities.

12.127 The Court found those arguments to be more relevant for the claims regarding the generic nature of the term. It repeated that:

> when assessing the generic character of a name, it is necessary, under Article 3(1) of Regulation No 2081/92, to take into account the places of production of the product concerned both inside and outside the Member State which obtained the registration of the name at issue, the consumption of that product and how it is perceived by consumers inside and outside that Member State, the existence of national legislation specifically relating to that product, and the way in which the name has been used in Community law.[122]

Following this it rejected all the specific contentions regarding generics.

12.128 The analysis of the Court regarding the purpose of the PGI registration system to prevent a term becoming generic may, by analogy, also be relevant in trade mark cases. The system is

> designed … to prevent the improper use of a name by third parties seeking to profit from the reputation which it has acquired and, moreover, to prevent the disappearance of that reputation as a result of popularisation through general use outside its geographical origin or detached from a specific quality, reputation or other characteristic which is attributable to that origin and justifies registration … Therefore, as regards a PGI, a name becomes generic only if the direct link between, on the one hand, the geographical origin of the product and, on the other hand, a specific quality of that product, its reputation or another characteristic of the product, attributable to that origin, has disappeared, and that the name does no more than describe a style or type of product.[123]

12.129 Looking at the facts of the case the Court found that the name has not become generic. Note that it considered the existence between 1960 and 1970 of the collective marks 'Bayerisch Bier' and 'Bayrisches Bier' as evidence supporting its findings.

12.130 (iii) **Reputation, trade marks, and PGIs** The Court stated that according to the Third Recital the Council had found that registration of the name 'Bayerisches Bier' was not liable to mislead the consumer as to the true identity of the product and that, consequently, the geographical indication 'Bayerisches Bier' and the trade mark 'Bavaria' were not part of the situation referred to in Article 14(3) of Regulation No 2081/92. It noted that the finding did not appear to be manifestly inappropriate and there was no argument against it. Regarding the effect of the registration of the PGI on the Bavaria trade marks the Court noted that Article 14 of Regulation No 2081/92 specifically governs that relationship. Article 14(3) covers:

> the conflict between a PDO or a PGI and a pre-existing trade mark where registration of the name at issue would, in the light of the trade mark's reputation, renown and the length of time for which it has been used, be liable to mislead the consumer as to the true identity

---

[121] Paragraph 97.
[122] Paragraph 101, citing C-132/05 *Commission v Germany* [2008] ECR I-957.
[123] Paragraphs 106 and 107.

of the product. The consequence provided for in the event of such a conflict is that registration of the name must be refused. This is therefore a rule which implies that there must be an analysis, intended inter alia for the Community institutions, prior to registration of the PDO or PGI.[124]

Its aim is to prevent the possibility of a mistake on the part of the consumer.

On the other hand: **12.131**

Article 14(2) of Regulation No 2081/92 refers to a situation of conflict between a registered PDO or a PGI and a pre-existing trade mark where the use of that trade mark corresponds to one of the situations referred to in Article 13 of Regulation No 2081/92 and the trade mark was registered in good faith before the date on which the application for registration of the PDO or PGI was lodged. The consequence provided for in that situation is that use may continue notwithstanding the registration of the name, where there are no grounds for invalidity or revocation of the trade mark as provided respectively by Article 3(1) (c) and (g) and Article 12(2) (b) of First Directive 89/104. This is therefore a rule which implies that there must be an analysis, intended inter alia for the authorities and courts called upon to apply the provisions in question, after registration.[125]

[The] analysis ... involves ascertaining whether the use of the trade 10-102 mark corresponds **12.132** to one of the situations referred to in Article 13 of Regulation No 2081/92; whether the trade mark was registered in good faith before the date on which the application for registration of the name was lodged; and, if appropriate, whether there are grounds for invalidity or revocation of the trade mark as provided respectively by Article 3(1)(c) and (g) and Article 12(2) (b) of First Directive 89/104.[126]

This requires an examination of facts that the national court must undertake.

According to the Court, the two provisions have separate objectives and functions and are **12.133** subject to different conditions. The fact that the marks according to the Third Recital do not fall under Article 14(3) does not affect the examination of the conditions which make it possible for the mark and the PGI to coexist as set out in Article 14(2). In particular, the fact that 'there is no likelihood of confusion does not mean that it is not necessary to ascertain that the trade mark in question was registered in good faith before the date on which the application for registration of the PDO or PGI was lodged'.[127]

(3) *Grana Padano*: Trade Marks v Geographical Indication; The Concept of Genericity

It is also worth referring to a Court of First Instance case[128] that looks at the concept of **12.134** generics from the geographical indication perspective. The case involved an application by the Consorzio per la tutela del formaggio Grana Padano (the Consorzio) for the invalidation of the Community Trade Mark 'Grana Biraghi' registered for cheese on the basis of the registration of the words 'grana padano' as a protected denomination of origin. The Cancellation Division accepted that the trade mark registration was invalid; Biraghi, the

---

[124] Paragraph 118.
[125] Paragraph 119.
[126] Paragraph 121.
[127] Paragraph 125.
[128] T-291/03 *Consorzio per la tutela del formaggio Grana Padano v Office for Harmonisation in the Internal Market (Trade Marks and Designs) (OHIM)* [2007] ECR II-3081.

trade mark proprietor, successfully appealed against OHIM's decision before the Board of Appeal.[129] The Board based primarily on Italian dictionaries and internet searches found, in turn, that the term 'grana' was generic from a PDO perspective and, as such, did not preclude the registration of the trade mark.

12.135 Before the Court of First Instance the Consorzio argued that 'grana' was not a generic name, since the PDO 'grana padano' was protected under Italian law and at Community level under Regulation 1107/96[130] and Regulation 2081/92. Originally, it argued, the term functioned as a geographical designation for a small stream in Valle Grana and has now become part of the designation 'grana padano'. Further, the Court had already ruled against the argument that mere parts of complex names of origin are generic in nature.[131] OHIM observed that the Board of Appeal did not appear to have consulted the competent Italian or Community authorities or to have carried out an in-depth examination of the Italian market and the markets of other Member States. From a 'jurisdictional' perspective it noted that once a PDO is registered it may not be considered generic unless the Commission or the competent Community or national judicial authorities decided that it has become so. The core of Biraghi's contention was that the term 'grana' was generic, literally describing the granular structure of a type of cheese rather than its geographical origin. The CFI started by Article 142 of Regulation 40/94 providing that the CTM Regulation does not affect the provisions of Regulation 2081/92. Accordingly, OHIM was bound to apply the CTM Regulation 'in such a way as not to affect the protection granted to PDOs by Regulation No 2081/92'.[132] Thus, a CTM registration of a mark covered by Article 13 of Regulation 2081/92 had to be declared invalid. However, according to Article 13(1) of Regulation 2081/92, 'where a registered name contains within it the name of an agricultural product or foodstuff which is considered generic, the use of that generic name on the appropriate agricultural product or foodstuff shall not be considered to be contrary to (a) or (b) in the first subparagraph'.

12.136 The Court of First Instance accepted that the Board of Appeal was competent to determine whether part of the PDO was generic and refuse to grant protection to that part,[133] however the analysis had to verify that a certain number of conditions have been met. This required, to some considerable extent, detailed knowledge both of matters particular to the relevant Member State and also other Member States. In short, the Board of Appeal was required to carry out a detailed analysis of all the factors that could establish a generic character, including legal, economic, technical, historical, cultural and social evidence, consumer surveys, and any other relevant factor including the definition of the name as generic in the *Codex alimentarius*.[134] The Board had overlooked the criteria identified by Community case law and covered in Article 3 of Regulation 2081/92.

12.137 The Court of First Instance then considered in detail the relevant Italian legislation against its historical context. Originally it referred to different granas (parmigiano reggiano,

---

[129] Case R 153/2002-1.
[130] Commission Regulation (EC) No 1107/96 of 12 June 1996 on the registration of geographical indications and designations of origin under the procedure laid down in Article 17 of Regulation No 2081/92 [1996] OJ L148/1.
[131] C-66/00 *Bigi (Dante)* [2002] ECR I-5917.
[132] *Grana Padano* (n 129), paragraph 55.
[133] *Grana Padano* (n 129), paragraph 60.
[134] Citing amongst others C-269/99 *Carl Kühne* [2001] ECR I-9517; C-289/96, C-293/96, and C-299/96 *Denmark v Commission* [1999] ECR I-1541; and C-448/98 *Guimont* [2000] ECR I-10663.

lodigiano, emiliano, lombardo, and veneto), all produced in the area of the plain of the Po. Subsequent legislation introduced the name 'grana padano' and abandoned the earlier names; this indicated that:

> grana is a cheese traditionally produced in numerous areas of the plain of the Po, which the Italian legislature therefore, at a certain point in time, identified by the term 'padano' so as to simplify the framework of rules and to include in one single name the various previous names, all originating in the Padanian Valley.[135]

Note too the point made by the Court of First Instance regarding the use of 'grana' on other cheeses intended for export to countries where the name 'grana' was not protected: 'that argument is irrelevant, in accordance with the principle of territoriality recognised by the Court in the area of intellectual property rights'.[136] The Court of First Instance annulled the decision of the Board of Appeal.

(4) *Cognac II*: Geographical Indications as an Absolute Ground for Refusal

(a) *The facts in the main proceedings and the order for reference*

12.138 *Cognac II*[137] was a reference for a preliminary ruling from the Korkein hallinto-oikeus (Supreme Administrative Court, Finland) concerning the interpretation of Articles 16 and 23 of Regulation 110/2008 on the protection of geographical indications of spirit drinks and its relationship to the Trade Marks Directive as regards the function of geographical indications as absolute grounds for refusing registration to trade marks encroaching on the reputation of protected geographical names. The reference was made in proceedings brought by the Bureau National Interprofessionnel du Cognac (the BNIC) against the registration in Finland of two figurative marks for spirit drinks in the form of bottle labels containing the expressions 'COGNAC L & P HIENOA KONJAKKIA Lignell & Piispanen Product of France 40% Vol 500 ml' and 'KAHVI-KONJAKKI Café Cognac Likööri—Likör—Liqueur 21% Vol Lignell & Piispanen 500 ml', respectively. The goods for which registration was sought were described as 'liqueurs containing "konjakki"' in Class 33 of the Nice Classification. After a first partly successful round before the Patentti- ja rekisterihallitus (Registration Board), which upheld one of the two actions, the BNIC lost both cases before the Patentti- ja rekisterihallituksen valituslautakunta (Board of Appeal) which dismissed both its cancellation requests.

12.139 The BNIC appealed to the Korkein hallinto-oikeus, seeking to annul the decisions of the Board of Appeal on the grounds that the reference made by the contested marks to the protected indication 'Cognac' was infringing Articles 16 and 23 of Regulation 110/2008, insofar as it was liable to mislead the public as to the true geographical origin of the goods covered by the registration. As the Korkein hallinto-oikeus had doubts as regards the applicability *ratione temporis* of Regulation 110/2008 and the extent to which it could be used to oppose the registration of a later trade mark, it decided to stay the proceedings and refer the following questions to the Court:

1. Is Regulation 110/2008 applicable to the assessment of the conditions for registration of a trade mark, containing a geographical indication protected by that regulation, which was applied for on 19 December 2001 and registered on 31 January 2003?

---

[135] Paragraph 77.
[136] Paragraph 80.
[137] Joined cases C-4/10 and C-27/10, *Bureau National Interprofessionnel du Cognac v Gust Ranin Oy* [2011] ECR I-06131.

2. If the answer to Question 1 is affirmative, is a trade mark which inter alia contains a geographical indication of origin which is protected by that regulation, or such an indication in the form of a generic term and a translation, and which is registered for spirit drinks which, inter alia in terms of their manufacturing method and alcohol content, do not meet the requirements set for the use of the geographical indication of origin in question, to be refused as contrary to Articles 16 and 23 of Regulation 110/2008?
3. Regardless of the answer to Question 1, is a trade mark of the type described in Question 2 to be regarded as liable to mislead the public for instance as to the nature, quality or geographical origin of the goods or services, in the way referred to in Article 3(1)(g) of the Directive?
4. Regardless of the answer to Question 1, if a Member state has, on the basis of Article 3(2)(a) of the Directive, provided that a trade mark is not to be registered or, if registered, is to be liable to be declared invalid, if the use of the trade mark can be prohibited by virtue of legislation other than the trade mark law of the Member state in question or of the Community, is the view to be taken that, if the trade mark registration contains elements which infringe Regulation 110/2008, on the basis of which the use of the trade mark can be prohibited, such a trade mark is not to be registered?

(b) The Judgment of the Court

12.140 (i) **The temporal application of Regulation 110/220** With regard to the first question, the Court was basically asked to clarify whether Regulation 110/2008 applies to trade marks registered before its entry into force. To answer that question, the Court turned to the principles governing the retroactive application of Community law, recalling that as a general rule, the principle of legal certainty precludes a legislative measure from taking effect before its publication. It observed, however, that 'it may exceptionally be otherwise where the purpose to be achieved so demands and where the legitimate expectations of those concerned are duly respected', and added that rules of Community law apply to situations existing before their entry into force 'only in so far as it clearly follows from their terms, objectives or general scheme that such effect must be given to them'.[138]

12.141 Applying these principles to the facts, the Court noted that Article 23(1) of Regulation 110/2008 stipulates that the registration of a trade mark which contains a geographical indication listed in its Annex III is to be refused or invalidated if its use would lead to any of the situations referred to in Article 16 without imposing any temporal restriction in this regard. On the contrary, Article 23(2) makes clear that such use can continue, by way of derogation, only so long as the mark was registered before the date of entry into force of the geographical indication concerned in the country of origin or before 1 January 1996. Thus, the Court considered evident from the wording and overall scheme of Regulation 110/2008 that, apart from the marks falling within the temporal limits of Article 23(2), all other marks registered prior to its entry into force may be invalidated in accordance with Article 23(1).

12.142 The Court moreover held that such a temporal application of the relevant provisions is not incompatible with the principles of legal certainty and the protection of legitimate expectations, considering that Regulation 100/2008 is a continuation of the protection already ensured by Regulation 3378/94, which had effectively incorporated into Community law the rules laid down in Articles 23 and 24 of the Trade-Related Aspects of Intellectual Property Rights (TRIPs) Agreement for the protection of geographic indications with

---

[138] Citing Joined Cases C-74/00P and C-75/00P *Falck and Acciaierie di Bolzano v Commission* [2002] ECR I-7869, paragraph 119, and Case C-369/09 P *ISD Polska and Others v Commission* [2011] ECR I-02011, paragraph 98.

(ii) **The scope of the prohibition** The second question sought to clarify whether **12.143** Regulation 110/2008 precludes the registration of a mark which contains a protected geographical indication and its translation where the registration is for spirit drinks which do not satisfy the conditions for the use of that indication. In that connection, the Court observed first, that pursuant to Article 288 TFEU, regulations have a direct and immediate effect and confer rights on individuals which national courts have a duty to protect,[139] and second, that the clear and unconditional wording of Article 23(1) of Regulation 110/2008 requires national authorities to refuse or invalidate the registration of a mark if its use would lead to any of the situations referred to in Article 16 of that regulation.[140]

Turning to the conditions for the application of Article 16, the Court noted that points **12.144** (a) to (d) of that provision refer to various situations in which the marketing of a product is accompanied by an explicit or implicit reference to a geographic indication in circumstances liable to mislead the public as to the origin of the product or, at the very least, to set in train in the mind of the public an association regarding that origin, or to enable a third party to take unfair advantage of the reputation of the geographical indication concerned. Moreover, it held that the protection conferred by Article 16 must be interpreted in the light of the objective pursued by the registration of geographical indications, as stated in the Fourteenth Recital to Regulation 110/2008, namely to enable the identification of spirit drinks as originating in a particular area, and that the extent of that protection must be assessed in the light of the fundamental rule laid down in Articles 15(4) and 17, in accordance with which a geographical indication registered in Annex III may be borne only by spirit drinks which meet all the specifications contained in the technical file provided to the Commission by the Member State of origin.[141]

Next, the Court observed that the second question assumed that the mark at issue had **12.145** been registered for spirit drinks which do not meet the specifications set for the indication 'Cognac', and proceeded to examine the applicability of Article 16 to the facts from that angle. It also noted that the reference of the national Court to a mark 'containing a generic term corresponding to a protected geographical indication and its translation' could not change the fact that Article 15(3) of Regulation 110/2008 prevents the geographical indications registered in Annex III thereto from becoming generic and that Article 14(2) prohibits the translation of such indications on the label of spirit drinks.[142]

As regards the situations referred to in Article 16, the Court recalled that point (a) of that **12.146** provision refers, inter alia, to the direct or indirect commercial use of a geographical indication in respect of products which are not covered by the registration, insofar as those products are 'comparable' to the registered spirit drink. In this regard, it held that, regardless of their various categories, 'spirit drinks' generally include drinks which have common objective characteristics and which are consumed on largely identical occasions. Furthermore,

---

[139] Citing 34/73 *Variola* [1973] ECR 981, paragraph 8, and Case C-253/00 *Muñoz and Superior Fruiticola* [2002] ECR I-7289, paragraph 27.
[140] Paragraphs 40–41.
[141] Paragraphs 46–48.
[142] Paragraphs 50–52.

they are frequently distributed through the same channels and subject to similar marketing rules. Thus, it found Article 16(a) to be applicable to the marks in the main proceedings, which had been registered in respect of liquors that were 'comparable' to the registered spirit drink.[143]

12.147 The Court then proceeded to examine whether the concept of 'evocation', as referred to in Article 16 (b), applied to the case as well. Citing *Gorgonzola*,[144] it recalled that the concept of 'evocation' covers a situation in which 'the term used to designate a product incorporates part of a protected designation, so that when the consumer is confronted with the name of the product, the image triggered in his mind is that of the product whose designation is protected' and that such a situation may occur particularly in the case of products with visual similarities and sales names which are phonetically and visually alike. The Court found it reasonable to transpose those findings to the case, holding that Article 16(b) was applicable to the use of a mark containing the element 'Cognac' for spirit drinks, all the more so since the same provision made clear that the mention of the actual origin of the goods or the use of the geographical indication in translation or together with an expression such as 'like', 'type', 'style', 'made', 'flavour' could not prevent the relevant prohibition form applying. Thus, it let it be understood that the inclusion of the word 'Cognac' in the contested mark, combined with its translation into Finnish, had the effect of evoking the protected goods in the mind of the public. Finally, the Court did not exclude the incompatibility of the contested registration with points (c) and (d) of Article 16, but left it to the referring Court to ascertain whether the mark in the main proceedings is such as to give rise to a false impression as to the origin of the drinks.[145]

12.148 Accordingly, the Court answered the second question to the effect that:

> the competent national authorities must, on the basis of Article 23 (1) of Regulation 110/2008, refuse or invalidate the registration of a mark which contains a protected geographical indication and which is not covered by the temporary derogation provided for in Article 23(2), where the use of that mark would lead to one of the situations referred to in Article 16; a situation such as that referred to in the second question—that is to say, the registration of a mark containing a geographical indication, or a term corresponding to that indication and its translation, in respect of spirit drinks which do not meet the specifications set for that indication—falls within the situations referred to in Article 16(a) and (b) of Regulation 110/2008, without prejudice to the possible application of other rules laid down in Article 16.

12.149 (iii) **Relationship to the Directive** In view of its answer to the second question, the Court considered unnecessary to address in detail the third and fourth questions, limiting itself to two important remarks. First, it stressed that insofar as a mark containing a geographical indication falls foul of Article 16 of Regulation 110/2008, the competent national authorities must refuse or invalidate the registration of such a mark by applying Article 23(1) of that regulation, which renders the question of the parallel application of Article 3(1)(g) of the Trade Mark Directive devoid of relevance. Second, it emphasized that Regulation 110/2008 must apply independently of the rules transposing the Trade Marks Directive into the national legal order, recalling that the direct application of a regulation implies that its application is independent of any measure of reception into national law, strict compliance

---

[143] Paragraphs 53–55.
[144] Case C-87/97 *Consorzio per la tutela del formaggio Gorgonzola* [1999] ECR I-1301, paragraphs 25–27.
[145] Paragraphs 56–60.

with that obligation being an indispensable condition for the simultaneous and uniform application of regulations throughout the European Union.[146]

(c) Conclusions

The Judgment in *Cognac II* provides useful guidance as regards the exact relationship between Community legislation relating to the protection of geographical indications and legislation dealing with trade mark registration both at the national and Community levels. **12.150**

In particular, by conferring on the regulations dealing with geographical indications the status of an autonomous and self-contained ground for refusal, it makes clear that the direct applicability of these norms supersedes any additional conditions or limitations possibly imposed by national laws or by the CTM Regulation, if those requirements have the effect of not ensuring the same level of protection. That interpretation also shows that the Eighth Recital in the Preamble to the Directive, according to which the grounds for refusal or invalidity concerning the trade mark itself should be listed in an exhaustive manner, cannot be read as excluding the possibility of introducing additional grounds for refusal by means of secondary legislation. **12.151**

In *Cognac II* the Court also provided some guidance as concerns the factors to be taken into account when applying the concept of 'comparable goods', which generally includes products which have common objective characteristics, are consumed on largely identical occasions, and are distributed through the same channels. Although these factors replicate a good part of the *Canon* criteria determining the similarity between goods, they do not include others such as, for instance, the ones referring to goods and services which are complementary to or in competition with each other. Thus, despite the fact that the list of factors laid down by the Court in *Cognac II* cannot be regarded as exhaustive, the concept of 'comparable goods' emerging from it appears to be somewhat narrower than the notion of similarity used in the context of the assessment of the likelihood of confusion. **12.152**

D. Trade Marks and Domain Names

(1) *Internetportal*: Generic Terms, Trade Marks, Domain Names, and Bad Faith

In *Internetportal*[147] the Court considered the speculative and abusive registrations of domain names and the interaction between Community trade mark law on the one hand and European law on the introduction[148] and functioning of domain names, including principles governing registration,[149] on the other. **12.153**

(a) The factual context

The Oberster Gerichtshof (Austrian Supreme Court) referred a number of questions, focusing on the interpretation of Regulation No 874/2004, that arose in proceedings between **12.154**

---

[146] Paragraphs 64–66.
[147] C-569/08 *Internetportal und Marketing GmbH v Richard Schlicht* [2010] ECR I-04871.
[148] Regulation (EC) No 733/2002 on the implementation of the .eu Top Level Domain, OJ 2002 L113, p 1.
[149] Regulation (EC) No 874/2004 laying down public policy rules concerning the implementation and functions of the .eu Top Level Domain and the principles governing registration OJ 2004 L162, p 40.

Internetportal und Marketing GmbH, a company operating websites and marketing products on the internet and proprietor of the Swedish trade mark '&R&E&I&F&E&N&' on the one hand and Mr Schlicht, the proprietor of the Benelux trade mark of 'Reifen', primarily for cleaning and bleaching products, on the other, concerning the domain name www.reifen.eu. In German, *'reifen'* means 'tyres'. The argument was that the domain name registration was obtained by Internetportal in bad faith, given that it was based on the Swedish trade mark registration and counted on the elimination of the special character '&' in order to obtain the domain name. Note that Internetportal had submitted applications for the registration of 180 domain names, all consisting of generic terms.

12.155 Article 21 of Regulation 874/2004 provide:

1. A registered domain name shall be subject to revocation, using an appropriate extra-judicial or judicial procedure, where that name is identical or confusingly similar to a name in respect of which a right is recognised or established by national and/or Community law, such as the rights mentioned in Article 10(1), and where it:
   (a) has been registered by its holder without rights or legitimate interest in the name; or
   (b) has been registered or is being used in bad faith

...

3. Bad faith, within the meaning of point (b) of paragraph 1, may be demonstrated where:
   (a) circumstances indicate that the domain name was registered or acquired primarily for the purpose of selling, renting, or otherwise transferring the domain name to the holder of a name in respect of which a right is recognised or established by national and/or Community law or to a public body; or
   (b) the domain name has been registered in order to prevent the holder of such a name in respect of which a right is recognised or established by national and/or Community law, or a public body, from reflecting this name in a corresponding domain name, provided that:
      (i) a pattern of such conduct by the registrant can be demonstrated;
      (ii) the domain name has not been used in a relevant way for at least two years from the date of registration; or
      (iii) in circumstances where, at the time the ADR procedure was initiated, the holder of a domain name in respect of which a right is recognised or established by national and/or Community law or the holder of a domain name of a public body has declared his/its intention to use the domain name in a relevant way but fails to do so within six months of the day on which the ADR procedure was initiated;
   (c) the domain name was registered primarily for the purpose of disrupting the professional activities of a competitor; or
   (d) the domain name was intentionally used to attract Internet users, for commercial gain, to the holder of a domain name website or other on-line location, by creating a likelihood of confusion with a name on which a right is recognised or established by national and/or Community law or a name of a public body, such likelihood arising as to the source, sponsorship, affiliation or endorsement of the website or location or of a product or service on the website or location of the holder of a domain name; or
   (e) the domain name registered is a personal name for which no demonstrable link exists between the domain name holder and the domain name registered.

12.156 One of the questions referred by the Oberster Gerichtshof was whether bad faith

also exist[s] if a domain was registered in the first phase of phased registration on the basis of a trade mark, coinciding with a German-language generic term, which the domain holder acquired only for the purpose of being able to register the domain in the first phase of phased registration and thereby to pre-empt other interested parties, including the holders of rights to the mark?[150]

(b) The Judgment of the Court

12.157 (i) **Bad faith: An open concept: A multifactor test** The Court first looked at whether circumstances capable of establishing bad faith are listed exhaustively in Article 21(3)(a)–(e) of Regulation 874/2004. Underlining the linguistic disparity in the various versions of the provision, it found that that the provision's list of circumstances constituting bad faith 'is merely by way of example'.[151] It then went on to describe the factors and interpretive methods the Court had to take into account for delineating the scope of the provision, in the light of linguistic differences and against the need for a single legal meaning: (1) the real intention of the legislator; (2) the aim it seeks to achieve;[152] (3) the public policy behind the legislation implemented by Article 21; and (4) international best practices in the field, including the relevant World Intellectual Property Organisation (WIPO) recommendations. Determining whether an applicant is acting in bad faith must be the subject of an overall assessment, taking into account all the circumstances relevant to the particular case.[153]

12.158 The Court, against the case's factual context, identified first the factors that had to be taken into account in order to assess the relevant circumstances: (i) the intention of the applicant at the time it filed the application for registration, a subjective factor to be determined according to objective circumstances (noting that applying for registration of a trade mark without the intention to use but hoping to obtain a .eu top level domain name on the back of the registration might indicate bad faith); (ii) the presentation of the mark (highlighting the unusual and irrational, from a semantic and visual perspective, structure and adding that without the special characters the trade mark corresponded to a generic term indicating 'tyres' in German); (iii) the repetitive nature of conduct (noting that the applicant had obtained thirty-three similar registrations corresponding to generic terms in German).

12.159 Second, it considered the conditions under which the domain name registration had been obtained adding the following factors that had to be taken into account: (i) the abusive use of special characters or punctuation marks, within the meaning of Article 11 of Regulation 874/2004 (holding that the special transcription rules of Article 11 of Regulation 874/2004 were 'subordinate to the objective of ensuring that the domain name which it is sought to register and the name in respect of which a prior right is invoked are identical or as close as possible to each other');[154] (ii) registration during the first part of the phased registration, given that Regulation 874/2004 established a procedure for phased registration and that meant that the general opening of registration of .eu top level domain names could not commence until after the end of the period provided for phased registration: 'It thus appears that a domain name such as that at issue in the main proceedings, which corresponds to a generic term sought as such, could have been registered during the first part of the

---

[150] Paragraph 26.
[151] Paragraph 34.
[152] Citing 29/69 *Stauder* [1969] ECR 419, Joined Cases C-261/08 and C-348/08 *Zurita García and Choque Cabrera* [2009] ECR I-10143, and C-473/08 *Eulitz* [2010] ECR I-907.
[153] Citing C-529/07 *Chocoladefabriken Lindt & Sprüngli* [2009] ECR I-4893.
[154] Paragraph 62.

phased registration only by means of the stratagem of a trade mark created and registered for that purpose';[155] (iii) the large number of applications for registration of generic terms as domain names. On the other hand, the Court found that awareness of the respondent in the main proceedings at the time the appellant submitted its application for registration of the domain name was not relevant.

12.160 (ii) **Generic terms as earlier rights** Looking at an argument that directly affects the relationship between trade marks and domain names, the Court found that registration of a generic name as a domain name could affect the rights of third parties, particularly since a generic name might still be protected as a trade mark:

> prior rights can legitimately exist in respect of generic terms ... Article 3(1)(b) and (c) of First Council Directive 89/104/EEC ... does not preclude the registration in a Member State, as a national trade mark, of a term borrowed from the language of another Member State in which it is devoid of distinctive character or is descriptive of the goods or services in respect of which registration is sought, unless the relevant parties in the Member State in which registration is sought are capable of identifying the meaning of the term.[156]

Otherwise, the Court added, the domain name applicant would:

> obtain an unfair advantage to the detriment of any other person interested in the same domain name who cannot rely on a prior right and must therefore await the general opening of registration for .eu top level domain names in order to be able to apply for registration.[157]

E. *Budweiser*: A Play in Six Parts

12.161 The six cases covered here deal with aspects of the same dispute played before different European fora. The *Budweiser* cases present perhaps the best example of the interplay between trade mark and other laws at the Community level. The effect of a bilateral agreement on the free movement of goods, the relationship between European trade mark law and the TRIPs Agreement, and the limitations on the right of property from a human rights perspective have all become factors in a dispute involving distinguishing signs. The potential epilogue, however, has brought the battle back into its trade mark context.

(1) Geographical Indications, Bilateral Agreements, and Free Movement of Goods: *Budweiser I*

12.162 The first *Budweiser* case[158] came before the Court as a reference from the Handelsgericht Wien (Commercial Court, Vienna). The case is important not only because it helped in setting the context regarding the protection of geographical indications but also because the approach of the Court highlighted the critical difference between the system for protecting geographical indications and that for protecting trade marks. Both are centralized systems based on registration and providing uniform protection throughout the Community. Both coexist with national systems of protection. However, the development of trade mark law has been primarily influenced by the Harmonisation Directive that brought national systems of protection closer together.

---

[155] Paragraph 68.
[156] Paragraph 74, citing C-421/04 *Matratzen Concord* [2006] ECR I-2303.
[157] Paragraph 76.
[158] C-216/01 *Budějovický Budvar v Rudolf Ammersin GmbH* [2003] ECR I-13617 (*Budweiser I*).

Budvar, the Czech brewer using the names 'Budejovicky Budvar' and 'Budweiser Budvar', started proceedings in Austria against Ammersin, a company that marketed in Austria a beer called 'American Bud', produced by the US brewer Anheuser-Busch. It claimed first, that the Austrian trade mark 'American Bud' should be annulled on the basis of its own earlier registrations in Austria of 'Budweiser', 'Budweiser Budvar', and 'Bud', and second, that use of the designation 'American Bud' for a beer from a State other than the Czech Republic was contrary to the provisions of a bilateral convention between Austria and Czechoslovakia.[159]

12.163

The Austrian court noted that there had been parallel proceedings in Austria against the importer of the American Bud that highlighted the uncertainties surrounding aspects of the case, in particular whether simple indications of geographical source should be considered to fall under the scope of Article 36 TFEU in the absence of consumer confusion, and referred to the Court four questions, the first two of which are particularly relevant for the purposes of this book.

12.164

(1) Is the application of a provision of a bilateral agreement concluded between a Member State and a non-member country, under which a simple/indirect geographical indication which in the country of origin is the name neither of a region nor a place nor a country is accorded the absolute protection, regardless of any misleading, of a qualified geographical indication within the meaning of Regulation No 2081/92 compatible with Article [34 TFEU] and/or Regulation No 2081/92, if on application of that provision the import of a product which is lawfully put on the market in another Member State may be prevented? (2) Does this apply also where the geographical indication which in the country of origin is the name neither of a region nor a place nor a country is not understood in the country of origin as a geographical designation for a specific product, and also not as a simple or indirect geographical indication?[160]

(a) The Opinion of Advocate General Tizzano

Advocate General Tizzano started by casting away any doubt as to admissibility. The Court was asked to interpret Article 34 TFEU and Article 36 TFEU, rather than the provisions of the bilateral agreement, between a Member State, Austria, and a non-Member State (the Czech Republic joined the Union on 1 May 2004). He also rejected the submission of the Commission that the reference concerned a hypothetical situation. It was for the national court to determine the need for a preliminary ruling and the relevance of the questions to its case; the Court should consider the reference, unless it was obvious that the interpretation of Community law had no relation to the actual nature of the case or the subject-matter of the main action.[161]

12.165

(i) The first question The Advocate General started by considering whether Regulation 2081/92[162] precluded the application of the provisions of the bilateral agreement. He conceded that the classification of the designation required the interpretation of the rule

12.166

---

[159] Agreement on the protection of indications of source, designations of origin, and other designations referring to the source of agricultural and industrial products, Vienna, 11 June 1976; annexed protocol, Vienna, 30 November 1977; BGBl. 1981, 75. The Agreement between Austria and Czechoslovakia provided amongst others that the parties would protect a number of designations, including Bud, Budjovicke pivo, Budjovicke pivo, Budvar, and Budjovicky Budvar, for beer.
[160] Reproduced in paragraph 43.
[161] Citing C-448/98 *Guimont* [2000] ECR I-10663.
[162] Council Regulation (EEC) 2081/92 on the Protection of Geographical Indications and Designations of Origin for Agricultural Products and Foodstuffs, [1992] OJ L208/1.

that implemented the relevant provision of the agreement into Austrian law. The interpretation of national rules remained a matter for the national courts;[163] however, he expressed his support for the view that the agreement provided for absolute protection of a simple geographical indication. This remained outside the scope of Regulation 2081/92.[164]

12.167 The second point concerned the applicability of the free movement of goods rules. All parties accepted that the application of the agreement had the potential to hinder the intra-Community circulation of products that have been placed on the market lawfully in other Member States by precluding their importation into Austria. The challenge lay in the applicability of Article 36 TFEU. He reminded the Court that in *Exportur*[165] the Court had accepted that the provision covered in principle the protection of simple geographical designations provided for in a bilateral international agreement. There it had observed that the aim of such protection was to prevent taking advantage of the reputation attaching to the products of the undertakings in the protected designations, even though no particular or distinctive quality was necessarily linked to the origin of the product. Article 36 TFEU, however, should not be applied when the designations had become, either at the time of the entry into force of the agreement or subsequently, generic in the country of origin.

12.168 The Austro-Czechoslovak agreement pursued the same objective:

> it aims to prevent persons not established in the Czech Republic from using for the marketing of beer a Czech geographical designation, and more precisely an indication which refers to the Bohemian city of Budweis, thus taking advantage of the reputation attaching to the beer produced in that place,[166]

and its compatibility with Article 36 TFEU should be judged following the above stated principles.

12.169 **(ii) The second question** All the parties concurred that if there was no link between the designation and the product then its protection would constitute a quantitative restriction without benefiting from the exemption of Article 36 TFEU. Citing *Exportur* again and using the language of Regulation No 2081/92, the Advocate General asserted that the protection of generic designations could not be justified under Article 34 TFEU. He defined what constitutes a generic designation by referring to Article 3 of the Regulation as an indication which 'although it relates to the place or the region where this product or foodstuff was originally produced or marketed, has become the common name of an agricultural product or a foodstuff'.[167] Expanding on this theme he stated that it covered designations that had either become generic or never been capable of establishing a link between a product and its geographical origin. There would be no public interest in protecting such a designation.

> It is quite clear that, if any possibility of consumers being misled as to the origin of the product can be ruled out, as on the assumption put forward by the national court, the designation

---

[163] Citing C-37/92 *Vanacker* [1993] ECR I-4947.
[164] Citing C-312/98 *Schutzverband gegen Unwesen In der Wirtschaft eV v Warsteiner Brauerei Haus Cramer GmbH & Co KG* [2000] ECR I-9187.
[165] C-3/91 *Exportur v LOR and Confiserie du Tech* [1992] ECR I-5529; also followed in C-87/97 *Consorzio per la tutela del formaggio Gorgonzola v Kdserei Champignon Hofmeister and Eduard Bracharz* [1999] ECR I-1301.
[166] Point 83.
[167] Point 90.

in question would not be able to result in, even potentially, either a luring away of customers or wrongful exploitation of a reputation which, by definition, does not exist.[168]

He doubted whether 'Bud' was such a designation. Being an abbreviation of the name of the city of Budweis, it was capable of evoking the Bohemian origin of the product by associating it with that city. This was a matter for the national court to explore.

(b) The Judgment of the Court

(i) **The first question** The Court started by describing the two hypotheses implied by the wording of the first question. First, that the name 'Bud' constituted a simple and indirect indication of geographical source; a name in respect of which there was no direct link between a specific quality, reputation, or other characteristic of the product and its specific geographical origin.[169] Second, it was not in itself a geographical name but was at least capable of informing the consumer that the product bearing that indication came from a particular place, region, or country. The function of the name was considered relevant for deciding whether Regulation 2081/92 precluded or not protection of a name that fell outside its net. Budvar argued that the distinction was irrelevant because the Regulation itself was irrelevant when considering purely national protection accorded by a bilateral convention. Ammersin on the other hand argued that the Regulation precluded protection at the national level of names that failed to meet its strict requirements. The Court restated its analysis of the scope of the Regulation, originally made in *Warsteiner*.[170] It provided a uniform Community-wide system of protection based on registration, but it coexisted with, rather than replaced, national systems of protection. The absolute nature of the Austrian system that provided protection without requiring evidence of confusion did not affect that interpretation. Accordingly, the Regulation did not preclude the application of a provision of a bilateral agreement between a Member State and a non-Member State under which a simple and indirect indication of geographical origin from that non-Member State was accorded protection in the importing Member State, whether or not there was any risk of consumers being misled, and the import of a product lawfully marketed in another Member State might be prevented.

12.170

However, the outcome could be different from the perspective of Article 34 TFEU. Given the origin of the American Bud—the United States—the Court clarified that Article 34 TFEU and Article 36 TFEU applied without distinction to products originating in the Community and to those admitted into free circulation in any of the Member States, irrespective of the real origin of the latter category,[171] and found the prohibition on marketing beer from countries other than the Czech Republic under the name of 'Bud' in Austria capable of becoming an intra-Community barrier to trade. Such rules, without always precluding in an absolute manner the importation of the 'protected' products into the Member State concerned made their marketing more difficult, impeding trade between Member

12.171

---

[168] Point 93.
[169] Outside the scope of Article 2(2)(b) of Regulation No 2081/92 according to C-312/98 C-3/91 *Schutzverband gegen Unwesen In der Wirtschaft eV v Warsteiner Brauerei Haus Cramer GmbH & Co KG* [2000] ECR I-9187.
[170] C-312/98 *Schutzverband gegen Unwesen In der Wirtschaft eV v Warsteiner Brauerei Haus Cramer GmbH & Co KG* [2000] ECR I-9187.
[171] Citing 125/88 *Nijman* [1989] ECR 3533.

States.¹⁷² The Court then followed Advocate General Tizzano's proposition. It concluded that Article 36 TFEU covered the application of the provisions of the bilateral agreement, unless the name was generic at the date of the entry into force of the agreement or had subsequently become generic in the state of origin.

12.172 (ii) **The second question** The answer to the second question followed the same logic. If the national court found that according to the perception prevailing in the Czech Republic, the name 'Bud' did not directly or indirectly identify any region or place in the territory of that State, then it would fall outside the scope of Article 36 TFEU, at least under the industrial or commercial property exemption.¹⁷³ Note that here the Court appeared to refer to the status of the name in the abstract, as a geographical indication as such, rather than as an indication of source for a specific product. The Court would then have to examine whether the barrier could be justified by an imperative requirement in the general interest such as fairness in commercial transactions or consumer protection. Taking a more neutral stance than the Advocate General, the Court responded using itself taking part in a hypothetical scenario:

> If it were established that the name Bud does not contain any reference to the geographical source of the products that it designates, the Court would have to hold that none of the information supplied to it by the national court shows that protection of that name is susceptible of preventing economic operators from obtaining an unfair advantage or consumers from being misled as to any of the characteristics of those products.¹⁷⁴

12.173 Following the function of the name as a link between the product and its origin, it concluded that Article 34 TFEU precluded the application of a provision of a bilateral agreement between a Member State and a non-Member country under which a name which in that country did not directly or indirectly refer to the geographical source of the product that it designated was accorded protection in the importing Member State, whether or not there was any risk of consumers being misled, and the import of a product lawfully marketed in another Member State might be prevented.

12.174 (iii) **The remaining questions** The Court started by describing the aim of Article 351 TFEU.

> The purpose of that provision is to make clear, in accordance with the principles of international law, that application of the EC Treaty does not affect the duty of the Member State concerned to respect the rights of non-member countries under an earlier agreement and to perform its obligations thereunder.¹⁷⁵

What had to be established was whether that agreement imposed on Austria obligations whose performance might still be required by the Czech Republic. The Court referred to the analysis of the Advocate General and stated that the national court would have to ascertain whether the two parties actually intended to apply the principle of the continuity of treaties to that particular agreement and whether there was any relevant evidence during the period between the date of the break-up and that of the Republic of Austria's accession to the European Union. The national court also had to ascertain whether a possible incompatibility between the Treaty and the agreement could be avoided by interpreting the

---

¹⁷² Citing C-448/98 *Guimont* [2000] ECR I-10663.
¹⁷³ Citing C-3/91 and C-324/94 *Exportur* and *Pistre v France* [1997] ECR I-2343.
¹⁷⁴ Paragraph 110.
¹⁷⁵ Paragraph 145, citing C-84/98 *Commission v Portugal* [2000] ECR I-5215.

agreement, to the extent possible and in compliance with international law, in such a way that it is consistent with Community law. If that was not possible then Austria had to apply the agreement but remained obliged to eliminate the incompatibilities. The Court noted that an obligation to denounce an agreement that could not be reconciled with Community law could not be excluded.

(2) *Budweiser II*: Replaying *Budweiser I*

12.175 The same Budweiser saga was behind a more recent judgment of the Court on geographical indications.[176] The Handelsgericht Wien (Commercial Court, Vienna), referred more questions to the Court following its Judgment in the original *Budweiser I* reference. The Opinion of Advocate General Ruiz-Jarabo Colomer provides a comprehensive summary of the history and disputes between the American and Czech breweries. Following *Budweiser I*, the Austrian court had found that the Czech public did not associate the name 'Bud' with a specific geographical location and that, as a result, it should not be protected as a geographical indication following Article 34 TFEU. The Oberster Gerichtshof (the Austrian Supreme Court) however annulled that Judgment and found that the term was at least capable of conveying a message regarding geographical origin and that the Commercial Court had to determine whether 'Bud' functioned as a simple and indirect geographical indication. The Commercial Court found that it did not function in that way following a consumer survey. There was then a further appeal to the Oberlandesgericht Wien (Higher Regional Court, Vienna), which sent the case back to the Commercial Court suggesting a more focused survey targeting Czech consumers. This triggered the Commercial Court's current round of questions, in particular following the Czech Republic's new membership of the European Union.

(a) *The Opinion of Advocate General Ruiz-Jarabo Colomer*

12.176 The Advocate General started his analysis by commenting on the judicial politics of the reference, suggesting that the Commercial Court had hoped that its own position would be endorsed by the Court.

> However, the Court of Justice should not take up the challenge. In Bud I it expressly made the evaluation in question the responsibility of the national court and there is no reason for it now to change its mind or to bring into play different criteria or clarifications additional to those it made in the past.[177]

12.177 Advocate General Ruiz-Jarabo Colomer also distinguished between 'simple and indirect' geographical indications, on the one hand, and 'qualified' ones, on the other:

> Simple geographical indications do not require products to have any special characteristics or element of renown deriving from the place from which they come, but they must be capable of identifying that place. In contrast, geographical indications which designate a product having a quality, reputation or other characteristic related to its origin are qualified geographical indications. As well as the geographical link, they have another, qualitative, link, less strong than that of designations of origin, which are reserved to products whose particular characteristics are due to natural or human factors relating to their place of origin. Community law protects only designations of origin and qualified geographical indications.[178]

---

[176] C-478/07 *Budějovický Budvar National Corp v Rudolf Ammersin GmbH* (*Budweiser II*).
[177] Point 54. A poignant indirect response to those critics who target the Court's judicial processes and delays but tend to overlook the games played by advocates and national courts.
[178] Point 57.

He noted that whereas in *Budweiser I* the Court had found 'Bud' to constitute a simple geographical indication, the Austrian court employed both concepts in its questions. The Advocate General queried whether the Court should decline responding to what can be seen as hypothetical questions, but given the genuine uncertainty regarding the meaning of 'Bud' in the Czech Republic decided to deal with their substance.

12.178 (i) **The first question: Establishing the association** The first question focused on paragraphs 101–107 of *Budweiser I*. The Advocate General noted that there may be 'indirect' geographical indications, not comprising actual geographical names, that can still indicate to consumers a link between the product and a geographical location. This should suffice; in

> the situation under analysis, it must be ascertained whether 'Bud' makes it clear to Czech citizens that beer with that name comes from the town of Ceske Budejovice, which does not mean that the name performs that role of geographical indication when it is mentioned together with the product in question, and only then.[179]

As to whether the three requirements mentioned in *Budweiser I*[180] must be assessed cumulatively or independently from each other he preferred the first interpretation. Paragraph 101 meant that Czech consumers had to associate 'Bud' with a particular place or region, as stated above, 'without particular "circumstances" having to be present'.[181] On the value of consumer surveys he observed that the Court had accepted such surveys.[182] At the end it was for the national court to determine the value of each evidentiary tool.

12.179 The national court had also enquired whether a geographical indication had to indicate a number of undertakings or a single undertaking. The Advocate General made a distinction between trade marks and geographical indications. Both protected commercial reputation:

> against potential unlawful usurpation by third parties, focussing on its geographical or its business origin respectively. They differ in that a trade mark safeguards a private interest, that of its holder, whereas a geographical indication protects the interests of all producers established in the relevant area.[183]

However, this did not mean it had to be used in parallel by several undertakings. He accepted though that in the Community system there was 'a certain underlying preference for the former, perhaps because they protect the public interest in consumers knowing the provenance and characteristics of goods'.[184] Regulation No 510/2006[185] provided that the application for registration of trade marks will be refused if they correspond to protected designations of origin or geographical indications, whilst trade marks registered earlier or acquired by established use in good faith will coexist with indications subsequently registered in accordance with European law. Furthermore, the Harmonisation Directive and the CTM Regulation prohibit the use of signs which may mislead as to the geographical origin

---

[179] Point 69.
[180] See paragraphs 12.161–12.174 above.
[181] Point 75.
[182] Citing C-210/96 *Gut Springenheide and Tusky* [1998] ECR I-4657, C-220/98 *Estée Lauder Cosmetics* [2000] ECR I-117, and Joined Cases C-108/97 and C-I09/97 *Windsurfing Chiemsee* [1999] ECR I-2779.
[183] Point 82.
[184] Citing amongst others N Resinek 'Geographical indications and trade marks: Coexistence or "first in time, first in right principle?"' [2007] EIPR 446; and A von Mühlendahl, 'Geographical indications and trade marks in the European Union: conflict or coexistence', in A Bakardjieva Engelbrekt, U Bernitz, B Domeij, and A Kur (eds), *Festskrift till Marianne Levin*, Stockholm: Norstedts Juridik, 2008, p 401.
[185] [2006] OJ L93/12.

(ii) The exclusivity of the Community system The second question as to whether national protection for an indication that has not been notified to the Commission becomes void when it is found to be a qualified geographical indication, focused on whether the Community system is exclusive or not. *Budweiser I* and *Warsteiner*[186] had settled the fact that simple geographical indications were considered to be part of 'industrial property' regimes, exempted according to Article 36 TFEU, without being covered by the Community system. 　12.180

> There remain designations of origin and qualified geographical indications, which do satisfy the requirements of the European legislation and may, therefore, be registered and enjoy protection under Regulation No 510/2006. However, unless they are registered at Community level, it is uncertain whether Member States can protect them with their own arrangements or whether that regulation is exclusive and precludes any intervention at State level within the formal and material scope of its application.[187]

12.181

In other words, does the Community system pre-empt national measures? According to the Advocate General, an exclusive Community system is more coherent with the wording of the Community provisions, with their purpose, and with the case law of the Court of Justice in contrast with the trade mark regime where there is a Community system existing in parallel with national systems of protection. Taking into account the history and objectives of the 1992 and the 2006 Regulations and the transitional nature of the Community legislation referring to national measures, he supported the view that they can be achieved only with a single European instrument. Whilst he accepted that the case law of the Court had not fully determined the issue he observed that 'Gorgonzola[188] and Chiciak and Fol[189] highlight the limitations to which Member States are subject from the moment they apply to the Commission to register a name.'[190] And according to *Warsteiner*,[191] the purpose of Regulation No 2081/92 could not be undermined by the parallel application of national rules falling outside its scope.[192] The same principle should cover systems of protection extended bilaterally to another Member State.[193]

Considering the last question posed by the Commercial Court, he supported the argument that: 　12.182

> the fact that a name, unlike other names for the same foodstuff with the same provenance, is not on the list in the Accession Treaty so as to have protection at Community level, is not, in theory, an obstacle to its national or bilateral protection, unless it is a shortened version or a part of any of the notified geographical indications. That assertion has no practical consequences, however, given the exclusive nature of Regulation No 510/2006.[194]

---

[186] C-312/98 *Schutzverband gegen Unwesen In der Wirtschaft eV v Warsteiner Brauerei Haus Cramer GmbH & Co KG* [2000] ECR I-9187.
[187] Point 92.
[188] C-87/97 *Consorzio per la tutela del formaggio Gorgonzola v Kdserei Champignon Hofmeister and Eduard Bracharz* [1999] ECR I-1301.
[189] C-129/97 and 130/97 *Chiciak and Fol* [1998] ECR I-3315.
[190] Point 116.
[191] C-312/98 *Schutzverband gegen Unwesen In der Wirtschaft eV v Warsteiner Brauerei Haus Cramer GmbH & Co KG* [2000] ECR I-9187.
[192] Point 119.
[193] Point 129.
[194] Point 138.

(b) The Judgment of the Court

12.183 (i) **Judicial cooperation** Starting from the perspective of judicial cooperation, the Court described in detail first the ambiguities of its initial Judgment and second the changes in circumstances that made the Commercial Court refer the case back to the Court. It accepted that the approach taken by the national court on whether 'Bud' must be classified as a designation of origin differed from the approach that led to the first reference but also diverged within the current reference between the first question on the one hand and the second and third on the other. However, it rejected the claim that the first question concerned a hypothetical situation:

> the possibility cannot be ruled out that, in reality, those are two distinct and, a priori, possible theories and that, at this stage, the national court does not wish definitively to discard that of a simple and indirect indication of geographical provenance, with the result that it referred the first question in order to allow for the possibility that it might, none the less, accept that theory.[195]

12.184 (ii) **Clarifying** *Budweiser I* The Court adopted a contextual type of analysis. It had considered 'Bud' to be a simple and indirect geographical designation. 'Simple' meant a name in respect of which there was no direct link between a specific characteristic of the product and its specific geographical origin. 'Indirect' meant a designation not in itself a geographical name but at least capable of informing the consumer that the product comes from a particular place, region, or country. A simple and indirect designation fell outside the scope of Article 2(2)(b) of Regulation 2081/92. It had then viewed the bilateral agreement as aiming to ensure fair competition and within the sphere of industrial and commercial property under Article 36 TFEU, provided that the names covered in the agreement had not, at the time of the entry into force of that agreement or subsequently, become generic in the country of origin. Against that background the Court reviewed the contestable elements of paragraph 101 in *Bud weiser I*. First, the reference to factual circumstances and perceptions prevailing in the Czech Republic, had to be understood

> in the particular context of the mechanism for protection of the designation 'Bud' under the bilateral instruments at issue, which rests in the fact that that mechanism … is based on an extension of the protection provided in the Member State of origin, in the present case the Czech Republic, to the importing Member State, here the Republic of Austria.[196]

Accordingly, the national court had to examine the circumstances and perceptions prevailing in the Czech Republic; if the designation was not at least capable of evoking the geographical provenance of the product then its protection could not be justified.

12.185 Second, the reference to the Article 36 TFEU criteria meant that the national court also had to ascertain whether the designation had, at the time of the entry into force of the bilateral instruments or subsequently, become generic in the Czech Republic.

12.186 Third, for a simple and indirect geographical designation that has not become generic Articles 34 and 36 TFEU 'do not preclude national protection … nor, moreover, the extension of that protection by way of a bilateral agreement to the territory of another Member State'.[197]

---

[195] Paragraph 66.
[196] Paragraph 78.
[197] Paragraph 85.

(iii) Consumer surveys: The principles of equivalence and effectiveness The Court   **12.187**
repeated that Community law does not provide for procedural rules in this matter:

> [I]t is for the domestic legal system of each Member State to designate the courts and tribunals having jurisdiction and to lay down the detailed procedural rules governing actions for safeguarding rights which individuals derive from the direct effects of Community law, provided that such rules are not less favourable than those governing similar domestic actions [the principle of equivalence] and that they do not render practically impossible or excessively difficult the exercise of rights conferred by Community law [the principle of effectiveness].[198]

Accordingly it was for the national court to decide whether a consumer survey should be commissioned and to set the parameters for what would be sufficiently significant when assessing its results.[199]

(iv) Use as a designation versus use as a trade mark As to whether the evidence had to   **12.188**
show use as a geographical indication by a number of undertakings and not use solely as a trade mark by a single undertaking, the Court responded that Article 36 TFEU did not contain 'specific requirements as to both the quality and the duration of the use made of a designation'.[200] Once the Article 36 TFEU requirements were satisfied the provision did not preclude the extension, according to the bilateral agreement, of the specific protection for 'Bud' to the territory of another Member State. The provision did not lay down specific requirements as to the quality and the duration of the use of the designation. National law and the bilateral agreements would determine whether any such requirements had to be applied in the context of the specific dispute.

(v) The nature of the Regulation 510/2006 system The Court first noted that the acces-   **12.189**
sion of the Czech Republic meant that bilateral agreements including provisions contrary to the rules of the Treaty could not be applied.[201] From an international perspective it added that the case concerned a designation that was protected as an appellation of origin under the Lisbon Agreement in the Czech Republic. Both the Regulation and the Lisbon Agreement had adopted essentially the same definition for designation of origin under the Regulation, and an appellation of origin under the Lisbon Agreement; however, whether the fact that Regulation 510/2006 was exhaustive in nature precluded protection under the Lisbon Agreement did not arise in this case since Austria was not a member of the Lisbon Treaty. In the absence of an application for registration of the designation under the Regulation, the Court noted that what the national court was seeking to ascertain was whether the exhaustive nature of Regulation 510/2006 precluded national protection and extension of that protection to the territory of another Member State. The Court set the protection of geographical designations within the broader context of protection of industrial and commercial property rights. The aim was to protect against improper use by third parties seeking to profit from their reputation and guarantee that the product bearing them comes from a specified geographical area and displays particular characteristics. The Court made a causative link between the two; the characteristics were the reason for gaining reputation.

---

[198] Paragraph 88, citing C-2/06 *Kempter* [2008] ECR I-411.
[199] Citing C-210/96 *GutSpringenheide and Tusky* [1998] ECR I-4657.
[200] Paragraph 91.
[201] Citing C-469/00 *Ravil* [2003] ECR I-5053.

12.190 According to the Court:

> Regulation No 510/2006, adopted on the basis of Article 37 EC, constitutes an instrument of the common agricultural policy essentially intended to assure consumers that agricultural products bearing a geographical indication registered under that regulation have, because of their provenance from a particular geographical area, certain specific characteristics and, accordingly, offer a guarantee of quality due to their geographical provenance, with the aim of enabling agricultural operators to secure higher incomes in return for a genuine effort to improve quality and of preventing improper use of those designations by third parties seeking to profit from the reputation which those products have acquired by their quality.[202]

> But if Member States allowed the use of indications

> which are reserved, under Article 8 of Regulation No 510/2006, for designations registered under that regulation, on the basis of a national right which could meet less strict requirements than those laid down in that regulation for the products in question, the risk is that that assurance of quality, which constitutes the essential function of rights conferred pursuant to Regulation No 510/2006, could not be guaranteed. That also carries the risk, in the internal market, of jeopardising the aim of fair competition between producers of products bearing those indications or symbols and, in particular, would be liable to harm rights which ought to be reserved for producers who have made a genuine effort to improve quality in order to be able to use a geographical indication registered under that regulation.[203]

12.191 The Court also highlighted the difference between the geographical designation and trade mark regimes in that the first had not adopted the principle of harmonizing national systems in parallel with the creation of a Community system.

12.192 Following the two fundamental reasons favouring the exhaustive nature of the Community system, the Court considered a number of additional grounds. First, the registration procedure was based on powers shared between the Member State concerned and the Commission. 'The national registration procedures are therefore incorporated in the Community decision making procedure and constitute an essential part thereof. They cannot exist outside the Community system of protection.'[204] Second, the Community system provided for transitional arrangements for existing national designations or in Member States where there was no system of protection. In this case Regulation 918/2004[205] was specifically relevant. National protection of existing qualified geographical indications would be permitted subject to conditions, including the condition to submit an application for registration within six months. The Czech authorities had failed to do so.

12.193 Turning back to the broader principle, the Court repeated that the Community system of protection was exhaustive in nature and decided that this precluded the application of a system of protection laid down by agreements between two Member States conferring protection on a designation, recognized under the law of a Member State as constituting a designation of origin, in another Member State despite the fact that an application for registration of that designation had not been made.

---

[202] Paragraph 111.
[203] Paragraph 112.
[204] Paragraph 117.
[205] Commission Regulation of 29 April 2004 introducing transitional arrangements for the protection of geographical indications and designations of origin for agricultural products and foodstuffs in connection with the accession of the Czech Republic, Estonia, Cyprus, Latvia, Lithuania, Hungary, Malta, Poland, Slovenia, and Slovakia [2004] OJ L163/88.

(3) European Trade Mark Law and the TRIPs Agreement Protecting Trade Names: *Budweiser III*

12.194 The third *Budweiser* case[206] concerned the interpretation of Article 2(1),[207] Article 16(1),[208] and Article 70(1)[209] of the TRIPs Agreement. Anheuser-Busch was the proprietor in Finland of the trade marks 'Budweiser', 'Bud', 'Bud Light', and 'Budweiser King of Beers', for beer. The application filing date for 'Budweiser', the earlier of the marks, was 24 October 1980. Budvar had two registrations for the trade marks 'Budvar' and 'Budweiser Budvar' for beer since 21 May 1962 and 13 November 1972, respectively, that had been cancelled for non-use. Budvar had also registered the following trade names in the Czechoslovakian commercial register since 1967: 'Budejovicky Budvar, narodni podnik', 'Budweiser Budvar, National Corporation', and French 'Budweiser Budvar, Entreprise nationale'.

12.195 Anheuser-Busch started infringement proceedings before the Helsingin karajaoikeus (Helsinki District Court); it also sought to stop use of the trade names that Budvar had been using. Budvar counterargued that there was no confusion and, further, that the registration of its trade names constituted an earlier right according to Article 8 of the Paris Convention.[210] The Helsinki District Court found that there was no trade mark infringement and that Budvar was entitled to use its trade names in the way it did—specifically as the trade name of the brewery rather than as a trade mark—because there was evidence that they were well known in the relevant trade circles at the time Anheuser-Busch's marks were registered in Finland. The Helsingin hovioikeus (Helsinki Court of Appeal)

---

[206] C-245/02 *Anheuser-Busch v Budejovicky Budvar, narodni podnik* [2004] ECR I-10989.

[207] Article 2 of TRIPs provides:

  1. In respect of Parts II, III and IV of this agreement, Members shall comply with Articles 1 through 12, and Article 19, of the Paris Convention (1967). 2. Nothing in Parts I to IV of this agreement shall derogate from existing obligations that Members may have to each other under the Paris Convention, the Berne Convention, the Rome Convention and the Treaty on Intellectual Property in Respect of Integrated Circuits.

[208] Article 16(1) of TRIPs provides:

  The owner of a registered trade mark shall have the exclusive right to prevent all third parties not having the owner's consent from using in the course of trade identical or similar signs for goods or services which are identical or similar to those in respect of which the trade mark is registered where such use would result in a likelihood of confusion. In case of the use of an identical sign for identical goods or services, a likelihood of confusion shall be presumed. The rights described above shall not prejudice any existing prior rights, nor shall they affect the possibility of Members making rights available on the basis of use.

[209] Article 70 of TRIPs provides:

  1. This agreement does not give rise to obligations in respect of acts which occurred before the date of application of the Agreement for the Member in question. 2. Except as otherwise provided for in this agreement, this agreement gives rise to obligations in respect of all subject-matter existing at the date of application of this agreement for the Member in question, and which is protected in that Member on the said date, or which meets or comes subsequently to meet the criteria for protection under the terms of this agreement … 4. In respect of any acts in respect of specific objects embodying protected subject-matter which become infringing under the terms of legislation in conformity with this agreement, and which were commenced, or in respect of which a significant investment was made, before the date of acceptance of the WTO Agreement by that Member, any Member may provide for a limitation of the remedies available to the right holder as to the continued performance of such acts after the date of application of this agreement for that Member. In such cases the Member shall, however, at least provide for the payment of equitable remuneration…

[210] Article 8 of the Paris Convention provides: 'A trade name shall be protected in all the countries of the Union without the obligation of filing or registration, whether or not it forms part of a trade mark.'

set aside only the second part of the Judgment of the Helsinki District Court regarding the well-known status of Budvar's trade name. Both parties appealed to the Korkein oikeus (Supreme Court).

12.196 The Supreme Court observed that the Court of Justice had pointed out in *Dior*[211] that it had jurisdiction to interpret a provision of the TRIPs Agreement in cases where the Community had already adopted legislation in the relevant field. Accordingly it referred the following, rather detailed, questions to the Court:

1. If the conflict between a trade mark and a sign alleged to infringe it is situated at a point in time before the entry into force of the TRIPs Agreement, do the provisions of the TRIPs Agreement apply to the question of which right has the earlier legal basis, when the alleged infringement of the trade mark is said to continue after the date on which the TRIPs Agreement became applicable in the Community and the Member States?
2. If the answer to Question 1 is affirmative:
    (a) Can the trade name of an undertaking also act as a sign for goods or services within the meaning of the first sentence of Article 16(1) of the TRIPs Agreement?
    (b) If the answer to Question 2(a) is affirmative, on what conditions may a trade name be regarded as a sign for goods or services within the meaning of the first sentence of Article 16(1) of the TRIPs Agreement?
3. If the answer to Question 2 (a) is affirmative:
    (a) How is the reference in the third sentence of Article 16(1) of the TRIPs Agreement to existing prior rights to be interpreted? May the right to a trade name also be regarded as an existing prior right within the meaning of the third sentence of Article 16(1) of the TRIPs Agreement?
    (b) If the answer to Question 3 (a) is affirmative, how is the said reference in the third sentence of Article 16(1) of the TRIPs Agreement to existing prior rights to be interpreted in the case of a trade name which is not registered or established by use in the State in which the trade mark is registered and in which protection is sought for the trade mark against the trade name in question, having regard to the obligation under Article 8 of the Paris Convention to afford protection to a trade name regardless of whether it is registered and to the fact that the Permanent Appellate Body of the WTO has regarded the reference in Article 2 (1) of the TRIPs Agreement to Article 8 of the Paris Convention as meaning that WTO members are obliged under the TRIPs Agreement to protect trade names in accordance with the latter article? When assessing, in such a case, whether a trade name has a legal basis prior to a trade mark for the purposes of the third sentence of Article 16(1) of the TRIPs Agreement, may it thus be considered as decisive:
        (i) whether the trade name was well known at least to some extent among the relevant trade circles in the State in which the trade mark is registered and in which protection is sought for it, before the point in time at which registration of the trade mark was applied for in the State in question; or
        (ii) whether the trade name was used in commerce directed to the State in which the trade mark is registered and in which protection is sought for it, before the point in time at which registration of the trade mark was applied for in the State in question; or

---

[211] C-300/98 *Parfums Christian Dior SA v Tuk Consultancy BV* and C-392/98 *Asseo Geruste GmbH and Rob van Dijk v Wilhelm Layher GmbH & Co KG and Layher BV* [2000] ECR I-11307. It added that in C-89/99 *Sehieving-Nijstad VF v Groenveld* [2001] ECR I-5851 the Court had ruled that the TRIPs Agreement was applicable insofar as the infringement of intellectual property rights continued beyond the date on which TRIPs became applicable with regard to the Community and the Member States.

(iii) what other factor may decide whether the trade name is to be regarded as an existing prior right within the meaning of the third sentence of Article 16 (1) of the TRIPs Agreement?[212]

(a) The Opinion of Advocate General Tizzano

12.197 Advocate General Tizzano noted that the case raised a number of admissibility issues together with the substantive interpretive questions. The two, however, where interwoven in such a way that they could only be answered together. Regarding the first question, the Advocate General supported that the effect of the TRIPs agreement was *ratione temporis*, covering infringing acts that had started before the agreement but continued after its effective date.[213] In his analysis of the second question he had no doubt that a trade name could constitute a sign for the purposes of Article 16 (1) of TRIPs; the requirements for the application of that provision, however, were less straightforward.

12.198 **(i) The use as a trade mark requirement** He suggested that the function of a trade name was to identify an undertaking whereas the function of a trade mark was to distinguish the products of one undertaking from those of other undertakings. In principle, there should be no risk of confusion between a sign used as a trade name and another used as a trade mark. However, a trade name could also fulfil the essential function of a trade mark, to create a link between the product and the undertaking responsible for its manufacture or distribution; in that case there could be a likelihood of confusion. For the Advocate General, according to Article 16(1) of TRIPs, use of a sign as trade mark constituted one of the essential requirements for the exercise of the exclusive rights arising from registration. When the trade mark and the sign were not identical, the next requirement that had to be satisfied was the establishment of a risk of confusion between the sign and the trade mark.

12.199 **(ii) Compatibility with Community law** The next consideration was the compatibility between Article 16 of TRIPs and Community law. The Court had ruled in *Dior*[214] that although TRIPs provisions do not have a direct effect on the Community legal order, national courts would have to act, to the extent that is possible, according to the letter and the scope of the relevant TRIPs provisions. Article 16 provided the minimum standard of protection that had to be guaranteed by the national laws of the Member States of the World Trade Organisation.[215] Since the Advocate General had found that use of the sign as a trade mark constituted the essential requirement for its application he went on to consider the position of the Court on the function of a trade mark as a guarantee of origin.[216] The national court would have to examine accordingly the nature of the function of the trade name 'Budvar'. If it functioned in that way then the court would have to consider the likelihood of confusion according to its national law following the criteria set by Article 5 of the Trade Marks Directive and the relevant jurisprudence of the Court. The Advocate General expressed his certainty that the Community regime was fully compatible with the minimum standard of protection envisaged by TRIPs. Comparing the respective TRIPs and Trade Mark Directive provisions he noted that even the wording was similar.

---

[212] Reproduced in paragraph 39.
[213] Citing C-89/99 *Schieving-Nijstad VoF v Groeneveld* [2001] ECR I-5851.
[214] C-300/98 *Parfums Christian Dior SA v Tuk Consultancy BV* and C-392/98 *Assco Geruste GmbH and Rob van Dijk v Wilhelm Layher GmbH & Co KG and Layher BV* [2000] ECR I-11307.
[215] See n 211.
[216] Citing C-206/01 *Arsenal Football* [2002] ECR I-10273 as a recent restatement.

(iii) The third question

12.200 *The status of trade names* The first point raised in the third question was whether trade names constituted existing prior rights. The Advocate General believed that earlier rights could be established only in relation to signs that functioned as trade marks; he accepted though that those signs could also function in other ways, for example as trade names. He stressed that there should be an analogy between the scope of protection, discussed above, and the obstacles to gaining that protection. Narrowing the scope of the limitation further he suggested that in order to satisfy the 'existing prior' condition only prior rights based on uninterrupted trade mark registrations should be taken into account. Any other interpretation, he added, would go against the scope of TRIPs, the elimination of trade barriers raised by the differences between national industrial property regimes.

12.201 *Requirements for protecting a trade name* The second point of the third question concerned the availability and the requirements of protection for a trade name that had not been registered or established through use in a Member State of the World Trade Organisation, taking into account Article 2 of TRIPs and Article 8 of the Paris Convention that provides for the obligation of Member States to protect foreign trade names irrespective of registration.

12.202 He explored the criterion for determining relative strength according to Article 16 of TRIPs and Article 4 of the Directive. The priority between the two rights should be established according to the date the trade name, that functioned as a trade mark, became well known in the Member State where protection was sought, based on Article 4(2)(d) of the Directive, or the date that because of its use it gave rise to a right under Article 4(4)(b) of the Directive and according to the relevant legislation of the Member State where protection was sought. This interpretation would also be in accordance with the fundamental principle that priority could only exist between the same types of right. The application of this rule to the facts of the case remained in the jurisdiction of the national court; however he doubted whether the trade name of 'Budvar' had become well known in Finland according to the evidence of the case.

(b) The Judgment of the Court

12.203 (i) **The admissibility issues** Citing *Dior*,[217] the Court reaffirmed that it had assumed jurisdiction to interpret a provision of the TRIPs Agreement when national courts had to apply their national rules with a view to ordering measures for the protection of rights created by Community legislation which fall within the scope of TRIPs; the Community was under an obligation to interpret its trade mark legislation, as far as possible, in the light of the wording and purpose of TRIPs.[218] Accordingly, the interpretation of Article 16(1) fell within the jurisdiction of the Court. It viewed the first question as a further admissibility issue, linked with the temporal applicability of the TRIPs provision. Applying the rule adopted in *Schieving-Nijstad*,[219] it found that the provision was applicable because Budvar's acts commenced in Finland before the date the TRIPs Agreement gained effect but they continued thereafter. Article 70(1) of TRIPs excluded the imposition of obligations in respect of 'acts which occurred' before the Agreements' date of application but it

---

[217] See n 211.
[218] Citing C-49/02 *Heidelberger Bauchemie GmbH* [2004] ECR I-6129.
[219] Citing C-89/99 *Schieving-Nijstad VoF v Groeneveld* [2001] ECR I-5851.

did not exclude such obligations in respect of situations that continued beyond that date. Whereas 'subject matter' that existed at the time TRIPs became effective was specifically covered according to Article 70(2).[220]

(ii) The effect of TRIPs: A balancing exercise On the one hand, the Court repeated that although the TRIPs Agreement did not have direct effect national courts were required, in areas where the Community had already legislated, to take them into account and any relevant measures should be taken, as far as possible, in the light of the wording and purpose of the relevant provisions.[221] On the other, it stressed that the competent authorities had to apply and interpret the relevant national law, as far as possible, in the light of the wording and the purpose of the Harmonisation Directive.[222] Accordingly, the relevant national provisions had to be applied and interpreted, as far as possible, in the light of the wording and purpose of both the TRIPs Agreement and the Directive. 12.204

(iii) Trade marks and trade names The answers to the remaining two questions can be divided into three parts: first, it considered whether a trade name could infringe a trade mark right under Article 16(1) of TRIPs; second, it looked at the limitations of trade mark protection that could be relevant in that case; third, it considered whether a trade name might constitute an earlier right. 12.205

Trade names as 'signs' The question whether a trade name might constitute a sign for the purposes of Article 16(1) of TRIPs was answered by the Court by reference to its Judgment in *Arsenal*,[223] departing from the Opinion of the Advocate General that viewed use of the sign in a trade mark sense as an essential condition: 12.206

> the exclusive right conferred by a trade mark was intended to enable the trade mark proprietor to protect his specific interests as proprietor, that is, to ensure that the trade mark can fulfil its functions and that, therefore, the exercise of that right must be reserved to cases in which a third party's use of the sign affects or is liable to affect the functions of the trade mark, in particular its essential function of guaranteeing to consumers the origin of the goods.[224]

The ambiguities of *Arsenal* became even more apparent by the following statement of the Court: 12.207

> It must be established whether the consumers targeted, including those who are confronted with the goods after they have left the third party's point of sale, are likely to interpret the sign, as it is used by the third party, as designating or tending to designate the undertaking from which the third party's goods originate.[225]

The Court here appeared to include post-sale confusion to the gamut of actionable behaviour, a position from which it pulled back later in *Picasso*.[226] At any rate this is what the national court had to establish, in relation to the labelling used by Budvar in Finland. The

---

[220] Citing, from the World Trade Organization's perspective, the Report of the WTO Appellate Body, Canada—Term of Patent Protection (AB-2000-7), WT/DSI70/AB/R, available following the links at <http://www.wto.org>, paragraphs 69, 70, and 71.
[221] Citing C-300/98 *Parfums Christian Dior SA* and C-392/98 *Assco Geruste*.
[222] Citing C-218/01 *Henkel KGaA* [2004] ECR I-1725.
[223] C-206/01 *Arsenal Football Club Plc* [2002] ECR I-10273.
[224] Paragraph 59, citing paragraphs 51 and 54 of *Arsenal* (n 206).
[225] Paragraph 60, citing paragraphs 56 and 57 of *Arsenal* (n 206).
[226] C-361/04 P *Claude Ruiz-Picasso* [2006] ECR I-643.

Court seemed to take for granted that Budvar's use was 'use in the course of trade' and 'in relation to goods', noting that the national court ultimately needed to confirm these two points.

12.208 The next step would be to determine whether the signs and the goods were identical, in which case protection was absolute, or similar and there was the additional requirement to prove confusion.[227] The Court highlighted that if use of the sign was other than for the purposes of distinguishing goods or services further protection might be available under Finnish law. Article 5(5) of the Directive left to the Member States to decide the availability, extent, and nature of trade mark protection in that case. Note that it failed to mention that Article 5(5) required use to take unfair advantage of without due cause, or be detrimental to, the distinctive character or the repute of the trade mark.[228]

12.209 The Court had then to consider the compatibility of the approach suggested above with the minimum standards of protection set by TRIPs. It approached this from a teleological perspective: the primary objective of TRIPs was to strengthen and harmonize the protection of intellectual property on a worldwide scale and at the same time reduce distortions and impediments to international trade.[229] It found that there was a close link between TRIPs and the Directive. A combined reading of Article 15 and Article 16 of TRIPs led to the conclusion that TRIPs, like Article 2 and Article 5 of the Directive, laid down a guarantee of origin as the essential function of a trade mark. Thus,

> [the] interpretation of the relevant provisions of the national trade-mark law so far as possible in the light of the wording and purpose of the relevant provisions of Community law ... is not prejudiced by an interpretation in keeping with the wording and purpose of the relevant provisions of the TRIPs Agreement.[230]

12.210 *The limitations to trade mark protection* The Court broadened the remit of the original question.[231] It went on to consider Article 17 of TRIPs and the limitations to trade mark protection. Use of a sign in good faith by a third party, in particular where the sign was part of that party's name or address could be fair use of a descriptive term, outside the scope of trade mark protection. A similar provision, Article 6(1)(a), was included in the Directive. The Council of the European Union and the Commission had indicated in a joint declaration that the provision covered only natural persons' names; however, as the declaration itself acknowledged, it had no legal significance since it was not mentioned in the wording of the provision.[232] According to the Court the application of Article 6(1)(a) provided to a third party an entitlement to use a sign for the purpose of indicating its trade name, even if that use would constitute an infringement of a registered trade mark; the only assessment criterion was that such use should be made in accordance with honest practices in industrial or commercial matters.[233] The Court appeared to accept that Budvar in principle was entitled to use its trade name and that the burden of proof was carried by Anheuser-Busch by noting

---

[227] Citing C292/00 *Davidoff & Cie SA and Zino Davidoff SA* [2003] ECR I-389 and C-291/00 *LTJ Diffusion SA v Sadas Vertbaudet SA* [2003] ECR I-2799.
[228] Citing C-23/01 *Robelco* [2002] ECR I-10913.
[229] See also C-89/99 *Schieving-Nijslad VoF v Groeneveld* [2001] ECR I-5851.
[230] Paragraph 70.
[231] Paragraph 75, citing C-456/02 *Trojani v Centre Public d'Aide Sociale de Bruxelles* [2004] ECR I-7573.
[232] Citing C-49/02 *Heidelberger Bauchemie, GmbH* [2004] ECR I-6129 on the non-effect of the declaration.
[233] Citing C-100/01 *Gerolsteiner Brunnen GmbH & Co v Putsch GmbH* [2004] ECR I-691.

that it was for the national court to determine, following an overall assessment of all the relevant circumstances, whether Budvar competed unfairly with Anheuser-Busch. It offered three factors that should be examined together with all the other circumstances. First, the extent to which the use of the third party's trade name was understood by the relevant public, or at least a significant section of that public, as indicating a link between the third party's goods and the trade mark proprietor. Second, the extent to which the third party ought to have been aware of that. Third, whether the trade mark enjoyed a reputation in the relevant Member State from which the third party might profit in selling its own products.

Trade names as prior rights The third sentence of Article 16(1) meant that: **12.211**

> where the proprietor of a trade name has a right falling within the scope of the TRIPs Agreement which arose prior to that conferred by the trade mark with which it is alleged to conflict and which entitles him to use a sign identical or similar to that trade mark, such use cannot be prohibited by virtue of the exclusive right conferred by the trade mark on its proprietor under the first sentence of Article 16(1) of the TRIPs Agreement.[234]

The Court suggested five steps that a national court had to take. First, decide whether the right to a trade name fell within the substantive scope of TRIPs. A joint reading of Article 2(1) of TRIPs with Article 8 of the Paris Convention led to the clear conclusion that members of the World Trade Organisation were under an obligation to protect trade names.[235] The second and the third step dealt with time. It would be for the national court to determine whether the right fell within the temporal scope of the TRIPs Agreement and then whether it was still protected at the time it was relied on by its proprietor. This led to the fourth step: determining whether the right was an 'existing' right. According to Article 8 of the Paris Convention, protection of a trade name should be guaranteed without any registration requirement. However, Article 16(1) did not preclude Finnish law imposing conditions relating to minimum use or minimum awareness of the trade name. The fifth step would be to determine priority. This meant that 'the basis for the right concerned must have arisen at a time prior to the grant of the trade mark with which it is alleged to conflict.'[236]

The approach of the Court diverged from that of the Advocate General. It did not require the trade name to be used in a trade mark way, nor it did it impose the requirement of being well known in the jurisdiction where protection for the competing trade mark was being sought. **12.212**

(4) BUD as an Appellation of Origin: *Budweiser IV*

Budweiser IV[237] concerned an opposition to a CTM for BUD which covered a range of goods and services. The opposition was based on earlier appellations of origin existing under the Lisbon Treaty and bilateral treaties under Article 8(4), as well as an International registration under Article 8(1)(b). The Opposition Division upheld the opposition under Article 8(4) insofar as the application covered restaurant, bar, and pub services in class 42, finding that the opponent had established its rights to the appellation of origin in France, Italy, and Portugal. **12.213**

---

[234] Paragraph 89.
[235] Citing again the Report of the WTO Appellate Body. United States—Section 211 of the Omnibus Appropriations Act, for a similar conclusion from the perspective of the World Trade Organization.
[236] Paragraph 98.
[237] C-96/09 *Anheuser-Busch Inc. v Budějovický Budvar, národní podnik* [2011] ECR I-02131.

However, this was at odds with decisions issued against three other applications, which had refused the oppositions on the basis that the opponent had not demonstrated that the appellations had been used in the course of trade.

12.214 Anheuser appealed the first of these decisions insofar as it refused the application in class 42. Budvar appealed the acceptance of that application in other classes as well as the Opposition Division's decision to allow the other three applications to proceed. The Board of Appeal allowed Anheuser's appeal and refused the appeals filed by Budvar. In essence, the Board of Appeal found that in the first place, it was difficult to see how 'Bud' functioned as an appellation of origin; second, that the opponent's use had been insufficient; and third that the opponent had failed to demonstrate how the appellation of origin would give it the right to prevent use of BUD in France or Austria.

12.215 Budvar appealed to the General Court, alleging an infringement of Article 8(4). The General Court allowed the appeal finding in the first place that the fact that 'Bud' was protected as an appellation of origin could not be challenged in opposition proceedings and that the Board of Appeal had erred in concluding that the word BUD would not amount to an appellation of origin. The fact that the French appellation of origin was under challenge did not entitle the Board of Appeal to conclude that the right was invalid. The most it could do at such a point was suspend the opposition until a final judgment had been issued.

12.216 The General Court also found that the Board of Appeal had been wrong to apply the standard of genuine use to the application of Article 8(4) and that for an opponent to demonstrate use in the course of trade, he need only demonstrate that the sign had been used in the context of a commercial activity. Furthermore, the use only had to predate the publication of the contested application and not their filing. In relation to Anheuser's arguments that the use filed demonstrated use as a trade mark, the Court found firstly that Anheuser had failed to expand on this criticism and that in any event, the fact that the sign was identical to a trade mark did not mean that it was not used in the course of trade.

12.217 Anheuser appealed to the Court of Justice, claiming in the first place, an infringement of Article 8(4) and second, an infringement of Article 8(4) and Article 74(1).

(a) The Opinion of Advocate General Cruz Villalón

12.218 In relation to OHIM's competence to assess the validity of the unregistered right, Advocate General Cruz Villalón did not consider the fact that national trade marks are harmonized and other signs are not relevant:[238] OHIM could only have rejected the opposition if protection had been 'definitively annulled in the Member State concerned (by judicial decision or by the appropriate procedure)'.[239]

12.219 In relation to the requirement of 'use in the course of trade', Advocate General Cruz Villalón considered that there are important differences between 'genuine use' under Article 43 and 'use in the course of trade', and that Article 8(4) establishes 'a special set of conditions which must be interpreted independently of those laid down for the other grounds of opposition'

---

[238] Point 79.
[239] Point 80.

and that the requirement for 'use in the course of trade' is an independent concept which warrants its own interpretation.²⁴⁰

In his view, there must be specific use in a commercial context which mirrors the essential function of the sign, which for geographical indications, would be guaranteeing that the public is able to identify the geographical origin of the product.²⁴¹ **12.220**

Furthermore, Advocate General Cruz Villalón was of the view that the use must be demonstrated by the date of application rather than the date of publication 'to avoid situations where the earlier right is used solely because of opposition proceedings' and also that the use must be in the Member State in which the right was protected. **12.221**

In relation to the requirement 'of more than mere local significance', Advocate General Cruz Villalón was of the view that the General Court had applied an overly literal interpretation of Article 8(4): **12.222**

> The fact is that it is difficult to separate the term 'significance' from the market in which the sign is present and from the use of the sign. It is not by chance that the requirement of use of the sign 'in the course of trade' is mentioned first; although that requirement refers to the sign, the interpretation of it is inextricably linked to the context. The article must be interpreted as a whole.²⁴²

He concluded by stating: **12.223**

> even where a geographical indication like Bud is protected in more than one State under an international agreement, it would not satisfy the requirement of 'more than mere local significance' if (as appears to occur in the instant case) it could be proved only that that geographical indication is known and used in one of the States where it benefits from protection.²⁴³

(b) The Judgment of the Court

The Court essentially agreed with Advocate General Cruz Villalón's analysis, finding that the General Court had erred in its interpretation of the requirement of more than mere local significant and that it had also erred in its assessment of use in the course of trade firstly by applying the tests set out in relation to genuine use of earlier trade mark registrations. **12.224**

The Court refused Anheuser's claim that the General Court was wrong to find that the Board of Appeal had incorrectly found that 'Bud' could not be regarded as an appellation of origin. Furthermore, the Court of Justice held that having found that the earlier rights had not been declared definitively invalid in two Member States when the contested decisions were adopted, the General Court was right to conclude that the Board of Appeal ought to have taken into account the claimed earlier rights without calling in question the actual classification of those rights: **12.225**

> Although it is for OHIM, when it decides upon an opposition based on Article 8(4) of Regulation No 40/94, to take into account decisions of the courts of the relevant Member States concerning the validity or classification of the earlier rights claimed to ensure that those rights continue to produce the effects required by that provision, it is not for it to

---

²⁴⁰ Point 98.
²⁴¹ Points 99–100.
²⁴² Point 132.
²⁴³ Point 141.

substitute its assessment for that of the competent national courts—a power which, in any event, Regulation No 40/94 does not confer on it.[244]

12.226 The Court also rejected Anheuser's claim that the General Court had misinterpreted the meaning of a 'sign used in the course of trade of more than mere local significance'. In the Court's view, the General Court had not made an error of law:

> [...] the sign relied on in opposition must actually be used in a sufficiently significant manner in the course of trade and its geographical extent must not be merely local, which implies, where the territory in which that sign is protected may be regarded as other than local, that the sign must be used in a substantial part of that territory.
>
> In order to ascertain whether that is the case, account must be taken of the duration and intensity of the use of that sign as a distinctive element vis-à-vis its addressees, namely purchasers and consumers as well as suppliers and competitors. In that regard, the use made of the sign in advertising and commercial correspondence is of particular relevance.[245]

12.227 However, the Court found that the General Court had made an error of law in holding that Article 8(4) of Regulation No 40/94 does not require that the sign concerned be used in the territory in which it is protected and that use in a territory other than that in which it is protected may suffice.[246]

12.228 Furthermore, the Court agreed with Anheuser and OHIM and found that use of the sign should be demonstrated at the date of filing of the contested mark and that the General Court had erred in finding that the relevant date was the date of publication of the later mark.

> In view, in particular, of the considerable period of time which may elapse between the filing of an application for registration and its publication, applying that temporal condition provides a better guarantee that the use claimed for the sign concerned is real and not an exercise whose sole aim has been to prevent registration of a new trade mark.[247]

12.229 Thus the General Court was found to have erred in

> holding, first, that the significance of the sign concerned, which cannot be merely local, must be evaluated exclusively by reference to the extent of the territory in which the sign is protected, without taking account of its use in that territory, second, that the relevant territory for the purpose of evaluating the use of that sign is not necessarily the territory in which the sign is protected and, finally, that the use of the sign does not necessarily have to occur before the date of the application for registration of the Community trade mark.[248]

(5) The European Court of Human Rights: Geographical Indications, Trade Marks, and Property Rights: *Budweiser V*

12.230 The fifth case considered the interrelationship between geographical indications and trade mark rights on the one side and the concept of property on the other. This time the battle was played in Portugal, the challenge was based on the rules of the Convention for the Protection of Human Rights and Fundamental Freedoms, and the adjudicator was the European Court of Human Rights.

---

[244] Paragraph 95.
[245] Paragraphs 159–160.
[246] Paragraph 161.
[247] Paragraph 167.
[248] Paragraph 169.

12.231 The Convention for the Protection of Human Rights and Fundamental Freedoms became effective in 1953, drafted by the Council of Europe following the principles set by the 1948 Universal Declaration of Human Rights. The Convention listed a number of civil and political rights and freedoms and provided for a mechanism of collective enforcement that was assigned by the Contracting States to the European Commission of Human Rights, the European Court of Human Rights, and the Committee of Ministers of the Council of Europe (composed of the Ministers of Foreign Affairs of the Contracting States). The European Court of Human Rights (the Court, in this section) was established in 1959.[249] The scope of the Convention and the jurisdiction of the Court expanded through the adoption of a number of Protocols. Recognition of the right of individual application that was originally optional became compulsory according to Protocol 11 and Protocol 2 empowered the Court to give advisory opinion.

12.232 In *Anheuser-Busch Inc v Portugal*,[250] Anheuser-Busch applied for the registration of the trade mark BUDWEISER for beer back in 1981. The application was opposed by Budejovicky Budvar on the basis of its registration of 'Budweiser Bier' as an appellation of origin in Portugal. The parties failed to reach an agreement and the applicant started cancellation proceedings regarding the registration of the appellation of origin in 1989. The Lisbon Court of First Instance cancelled the registration on 8 March 1995 and subsequently the Portuguese Intellectual Property Office granted the trade mark registration on 20 June 1995. Budejovicky Budvar counterattacked on the basis of a bilateral agreement concluded in 1986 between Czechoslovakia and Portugal protecting a number of appellations of origin. The Court of First Instance rejected the claim but the Judgment was reversed by the Lisbon Court of Appeal.

12.233 The case reached the Portuguese Supreme Court where Anheuser-Busch argued that the decision went against Article 2 and Article 24(5) of TRIPs.[251] The Supreme Court rejected the claim on two grounds. First, it found that the applicant had failed to discharge the burden of proving it had acted in good faith, as required by Article 24 (5). Secondly, it ruled that TRIPs, effective since 1 January 1996 in Portugal, did not cover in terms of time the 1986 bilateral agreement.

12.234 Anheuser-Busch also claimed that the bilateral agreement covered the term 'Ceskebudejovicky Budvar' and its translation into Portuguese rather than the German expression 'Budweiser'. The Supreme Court took the intention of the two contracting parties as its starting point. They wanted to protect their respective national products, including cases where a translation of the protected names was used. The appellation of origin 'Ceskebudejovicky Budvar' and its translations in German that indicated a beer coming from that region should be protected.

12.235 Finally, the Supreme Court rejected a third ground of appeal regarding the constitutionality of the agreement.

---

[249] For an overview of proceedings in the ECtHR see Clare Ovey and Robin White, *Jacobs and White: The European Convention of Human Rights* (OUP 2006), ch 24.
[250] *Anheuser-Busch Inc v Portugal* [2006] ETMR 43.
[251] Article 24(5) provides:
> Where a trademark has been applied for or registered in good faith, or where rights to a trademark have been acquired through use in good faith either (a) before the date of application of these provisions in that Member as defined in Part VI; or (b) before the geographical indication is protected in its country of origin; measures adopted to implement this Section shall not prejudice eligibility for or the validity of the registration of a trademark ... on the basis that such a trademark is identical with, or similar to, a geographical indication.

(a) The arguments of the parties

12.236 Before the European Court of Human Rights, Anheuser-Busch supported the claim that the Judgment of the Supreme Court contravened Article 1 of the Protocol to the Convention providing that:

> Every natural or legal person is entitled to the peaceful enjoyment of his possessions. No one shall be deprived of his possessions except in the public interest and subject to the conditions provided for by law and by the general principles of international law. The preceding provisions shall not, however, in any way impair the right of a State to enforce such laws as it deems necessary to control the use of property in accordance with the general interest or to secure the payment of taxes or other contributions or penalties.

12.237 It sought from the Court to set aside the Judgment of the Supreme Court, claiming that the right to use a trade mark fell within the scope of indisputably constituted 'possessions' and should be protected from the date the application for registration was filed back in 1981. It was dispossessed by a subsequent third party right produced by the 1986 bilateral agreement. It noted that the Judgment of the Supreme Court had relied exclusively on the provision of the New Code on Industrial Property that precluded registration when the sign was in conflict with another rule of law but had failed to refer to the Code's provision on confusion.

12.238 In effect, it argued, its mark had been expropriated without any compensation and this interference with its right of property was against the general principles of international law and based on a wrong interpretation of the 1986 agreement, targeting the Supreme Court's willingness to protect against use of a translation of the term in a language other than Portuguese. In any case the interference did not pursue a legitimate aim, in the apparent absence of a risk of confusion, and was disproportionate, failing to strike a fair balance between the general interest and the right of individuals. Finally, it submitted that insisting on the application of the 1986 agreement the Supreme Court had overlooked TRIPs and the Community legal order that could provide the tools for resolving a conflict between a trade mark and an indication of source.

12.239 The Portuguese Government challenged the assertion that the application for registration constituted a 'possession' in the first place prior to registration. In any case, it added, it certainly did not constitute an 'existing' possession that could be protected by the European Court of Human Rights, but even supposing that there had been an interference with the right of property, such interference amounted to control of the use of property rather than deprivation of possessions and was based on an agreement that had become part of the Portuguese legal order. Regarding the risk of confusion argument it supported the view that the Judgment had taken into account in its reasoning the risk of confusion but conceded that it had not relied on the relevant provision of the Code. Even if there was any interference it was entirely proportionate given that states enjoyed a wide margin of appreciation when determining the public interest. The final point made by the Portuguese Government had to do with the function of the European Court of Human Rights. It argued that by granting the remedy sought the Court would transform itself into a court of fourth instance, contrary to the aim and spirit of the Convention.

(b) The analysis of the European Court of Human Rights

12.240 The Court started its analysis with a comparative review of the national laws of the Member States of the Council of Europe regarding the rights linked with an application for a trade mark registration. Then the Court presented the arguments of the parties and moved into its own assessment of the case, answering first whether the applications constituted possessions and then assessing the interference.

(i) The rights arising from an application for trade mark registration The general principle was that trade mark rights were conferred by registration, however an application for registration also conferred a number of rights: in most cases registration conferred retrospective protection going back to the filing date of the application. In some cases the application itself functioned as a provisional registration; international priority was determined according to the application filing date, and in some jurisdictions the mark applied for might be assigned, licensed, or used as security. In terms of procedural steps the Court noted that in most countries a notice of the application was published triggering an opposition period, although in some jurisdictions registration followed immediately the examination of the application as to formalities and substantive requirements. **12.241**

In its consideration of Portuguese law there were three points worth highlighting: the application for registration could be the subject of an assignment, with or without consideration, or a licence; there was a process for third parties adversely affected by the registration to appeal against the decision of the national Office; and, that according to earlier Portuguese jurisprudence the application conferred on the applicant a protectable 'legal expectation',[252] so this last principle had been adopted by Article 5 of the New Code on Industrial Property that afforded provisional protection to an applicant through an action in damages. **12.242**

(ii) Trade mark applications and the concept of 'possessions' The Court reminded us that according to its case law the concept of 'possessions' had an autonomous meaning, not limited to ownership of physical goods and independent from the formal classification in domestic law. 'The issue that needs to be examined in each case is whether the circumstances of the case, considered as a whole, conferred on the applicant title to a substantive interest protected by Article 1 of Protocol 1.'[253] Intellectual property had the status of possessions and enjoyed the protection of Article 1;[254] the status of an application, however, was more uncertain. The Commission had found that an unsuccessful patent application meant that the applicant had been denied a protected intellectual property right but not deprived of its existing property; the case went to the Court that had not examined and ruled on that particular issue.[255] **12.243**

The Court appeared to be influenced by the financial repercussions of the legal position of an applicant for the registration of a trade mark. The particular sign enjoyed an international reputation; the application could be assigned or licensed; Portuguese law, according to case law prior to 1993 and expressly with the New Code on Industrial Property thereafter provided that unlawful or fraudulent use by a third party of a mark applied for registration entitled the applicant to compensation in certain circumstances; and filing the application conferred a priority right. All the above created a pecuniary interest, albeit 'the company's **12.244**

---

[252] In paragraph 31 the Court noted that in a Judgment of 10 May 2001, the Lisbon Court of Appeal held that the mere filing of an application for registration conferred on the applicant a 'legal expectation' that warranted the protection of the law.
[253] *Budweiser V*, paragraph 42, citing as examples C-33202/96 *Beyeler v Italy* [GC] No ECHR 2000-i and C-31443/96 *Broniowski v Poland* [GC] ECHR 2004-v.
[254] C-12633/87 *Smith Kline and French Laboratories Ltd v The Netherlands* 4 October 1990, Decisions and Reports (DR) 66.
[255] C-331-A *British-American Tobacco Co Ltd v The Netherlands A* [1996] 21 EHRR 409.

position in law was not sufficiently strong to amount to a legitimate expectation attracting the protection of Article 1 of Protocol 1'.[256] That provision applied only to existing possessions and according to the Court's case law future income could not be considered 'possessions' unless it had already been earned or was definitely payable. In order to dissolve any doubt that could be raised by the complicated history of the application, the Court added that the hope that a long-extinguished property right might be revived could not be regarded as a 'possession'; the same applied to a lapsed conditional claim.[257] In this case the applicant 'had a conditional right, which was extinguished retrospectively for failure to satisfy the condition, namely that it did not infringe third-party rights'.[258] Budejovicky-Budvar had contested the application from the beginning and Anheuser-Busch had entered into negotiations before challenging the registration of the geographical origin. The Court noted that commercial enterprises always carried an element of risk and Anheuser-Busch was or should have been aware that there was a possibility that its application would be rejected. The Court concluded that a trade mark constituted a 'possession' only after its final registration.

12.245 (iii) **The dissenting opinions** Contrary to the practice of the Court, the dissenting members of the European Court of Human Rights can publicize their opinions. Based on the right of priority the dissenting members in this case supported the view that the applicant company was entitled to expect that its application would be examined in accordance with the priority rule and the other rules governing intellectual property in force at the time of the original application for registration. They viewed the provision of the New Code of Industrial Property regarding the entitlement of an applicant for registration to seek compensation in some cases as strengthening their argument. They believed that Anheuser-Busch had a legitimate expectation that was sufficiently strong to attract the protection of Article 1 of Protocol 1 and that the refusal to register the mark amounted to interference with its right of property. This was not a case of deprivation of ownership but still the effect of the denial to register the mark was to prevent the applicant from using the mark.

12.246 In order to be acceptable the interference had to satisfy three requirements: comply with the rule of law, pursue a legitimate aim, and strike a 'fair balance' between the demands of the general interest of the community and the requirements of the protection of the individual's fundamental rights.[259] Here it was the 'fair balance' requirement that appeared problematic. Its assessment required an overall examination of the interests of all the actors involved. The State had an undisputed right to enter into such international agreements but it also had to take into account the rights of private parties, especially if they are non-nationals, because 'there may well be legitimate reason for requiring nationals to bear a greater burden in the public interest than non-nationals'.[260] By essentially making registration impossible, the Portuguese authorities had passed to Anheuser-Busch an individual and excessive burden that upset the 'fair balance' between the general interest and the protection of the right to the peaceful enjoyment of the individual's possessions.

---

[256] Paragraph 48.
[257] C-39794/98 *Gratzinger and Gratzingerova v The Czech Republic* [GC] ECHR 2002-VII.
[258] *Budweiser V*, paragraph 50.
[259] C-31107/96 *Iatridis v Greece* [GC] ECHR 1999-11.
[260] Opinion referring to *Lithgow v UK* [1986] 8 EHRR 329, paragraph 17.

(6) *Budějovický Budvar/Budweiser VI*: A Trade Mark Epilogue

As shown in Chapter 6, this battle was fought in the English courts and the Court; *Budějovický Budvar*[261] was seen as an attempt to settle the almost forty-year-old dispute between Budějovický Budvar and Anheuser-Busch Inc. The Court looked at the concept of 'acquiescence', the English doctrine of 'honest concurrent use', and the commercial reality of coexistence. It concluded that:

12.247

> the proprietor of an earlier trade mark cannot obtain the cancellation of an identical later trade mark designating identical goods where there has been a long period of honest concurrent use of those two trade marks where, in circumstances such as those in the main proceedings, that use neither has nor is liable to have an adverse effect on the essential function of the trade mark which is to guarantee to consumers the origin of the goods or services.[262]

F. Conclusion

This chapter has continued developing the theme of interaction between trade mark law and other areas of law. The comparative advertising cases have shown how the Court used advertising rules to define the scope of trade mark rights on the one hand and trade mark provisions to establish what should be allowed under comparative advertising on the other. They have also shown that according to the context of the case signs other than trade marks could also function as distinguishing indicia.

12.248

The geographical indication cases have shown how the regulation of another type of distinguishing signs deals with descriptiveness and genericity issues. They have also indicated that messages about the geographical origin of a product can be conveyed by distinguishing signs that do not as such possess a geographical meaning.

12.249

The relationship and clash between domain names and trade marks highlighted the nuances of the trade mark system recognizing potential alternative trade mark space for generic terms and how 'bad faith' can become the catalyst for resolving the clash.

12.250

Following the same line we have seen a geographical name having the potential to function and be protected as a geographical indication, a trade name, and a trade mark. Note that conflicts between trade marks and trade names or geographical indications have also been considered in Chapter 6. Finally, the property element of trade marks highlighted that there is yet another angle under which a trade mark dispute can be perceived.

12.251

---

[261] C-482/09 *Budějovický Budvar, národní podnik v Anheuser-Busch Inc* [2011] ECR I-08701.
[262] Paragraph 84.

13

THE NEW TRADE MARK 'PACKAGE'

A. Introduction

(1) Background

13.01 Trade mark protection in Europe, when the European Economic Community was established in 1957, was territorial in nature, and the respective trade mark systems varied widely. Reforms were undertaken in some of the original six and eventually nine Member States, highlighted by the creation of a uniform trade mark system for the three Benelux countries in 1970, and the introduction of the requirement of use in Germany in 1967.

13.02 The efforts to create a uniform European trade mark law and to harmonize the national trade mark laws of the Member States culminated in the 1988 'First' Trade Marks Directive and the 1993 Community Trade Mark Regulation. Since then, the legislation has not been subject to any major modifications. The Directive was amended in 1992 as regards its transposition deadline and by the European Economic Area Agreement. The Regulation was amended in 1995 to take into account the results of the Uruguay Round as embodied in the TRIPS Agreement (Article 7(1)(j) was added to the Regulation). In 2003 amendments were made to take into account the accession of the EU to the Protocol to the Madrid Agreement. In 2004, the Regulation was amended further as regards some matters of substantive law and procedure. In parallel, a special provision to take account of the accession of new Member States became part of the accession treaties. Both the Directive and the Regulation were codified in 2008 and 2009, respectively,[1] but without any changes of substance.

13.03 Not only has the number of Member States grown from twelve, when the Directive and the Regulation were adopted, to the current twenty-eight, but the business environment has also changed, with the advent of the Internet being the single most notable event. The numbers of trade marks, both at EU level and nationally, has grown beyond original estimates. This has led to a substantial surplus in OHIM's budget, and concerns about imbalances in the system comprising EU-wide protection and overlapping and coexisting national trade mark protection.

---

[1] From the perspective of users of the CTM system, these codifications were entirely useless. The Directive was codified although it had been amended only twice (changing the date for complying with the Directive, and making exhaustion also applicable when first marketing was in the EEA), and the codification actually missed the amendment of Article 7 (exhaustion). The codification of the Regulation resulted in new numbers for familiar Articles at a time when it was already clear that the 'trade mark package' was on its way.

13.04 The Council was seized in 2007 with the issue of OHIM finances, and in its conclusions[2] emphasized the need for an overall assessment of the functioning of the European trade mark system and requested the Commission to undertake a comprehensive review of the system. After some time, the Commission, in its 'IPR strategy for Europe' announced a review of the trade mark system in the European Union. As an initial step, the Munich Max Planck Institute for Innovation and Competition (formerly Max Planck Institute for Intellectual Property and Competition Law) was commissioned to undertake a comprehensive study of the system. On the basis of the interim results of that Study, the Competitiveness Council adopted on 25 May 2010 conclusions on the future revision of the trade mark system in the EU[3] which outlined what the Member States were expecting from the 'package'.

13.05 The results of the Max Planck study were published in February 2011, entitled 'Study on the Overall Functioning of the European Trade Mark System'. The Study consists of the results of interviews with the EU's intellectual property offices, a survey among users of the CTM system carried out by the Allensbach Institute, an economic analysis by INNO-Tec of Munich University, and a comprehensive legal analysis of the trade mark system, looking both at substantive law and procedure before OHIM. The Study came up with concrete proposals of how the Directive and the Regulation could be amended as well as how cooperation between OHIM and national offices could be structured. The Study also suggested a solution for the distribution of some of OHIM's income to national offices. The Study concluded that the European trade mark system, characterized by the coexistence of national and EU-wide rights, was overall properly balanced and should be maintained in its basic structure, while certain amendments and improvements were considered appropriate. Harmonized procedures under the national trade mark legislation was noted as an important objective of the legislation.

13.06 The Study is still available for consultation and download at the Max Planck Institute's website and provides an interesting backdrop to the actual results of the reform effort. Upon reading the Study it will become apparent that the legislature will have missed a unique chance to realign substantive trade mark law, which today shows certain imbalances as a result of a number of controversial judgments of the Court of Justice.

(2) The Commission Proposals

13.07 The Commission took another two years until it was able to present its proposals for a recast of the Directive[4] and for amendments of the Regulation[5] to the European Parliament and to the Council. The proposals were accompanied by a comprehensive Impact Assessment.[6]

---

[2] Council Conclusions of 21 and 22 May 2007, Council Doc 9427/07.
[3] Council Doc 2010/C 140/07.
[4] Proposal for a Directive of the European Parliament and of the Council to approximate the laws of the Member States relating to trade marks (recast), Doc COM(2013) 162 final, 2013/0089 (COD), 27 March 2013.
[5] Proposal for a Regulation of the European Parliament and of the Council amending Council Regulation (EC) No 207/2009 on the Community trade mark, Doc COM(2013) 161 final, 2013/0088 (COD), 27 March 2013.
[6] Commission Staff Working Paper—Impact Assessment—Accompanying document to the Proposal for a Regulation of the European Parliament and of the Council amending Council Regulation (EC) No 207/2009 of 26 February 2009 on the Community trade mark and the Proposal for a Directive of the European Parliament and of the Council to approximate the laws of the Member States relating to trade marks (recast), Commission Doc SWD(2013) 95 final, Council Doc 8066/13 ADD 1, 3 April 2013.

Introduction

The Commission proposals consisted of six different elements of differing impact on the European trade mark system as a whole: **13.08**

(a) Substantive trade mark law

As regards substantive trade mark law some rather radical amendments were proposed in the area of absolute and relative grounds of refusal, such as the suppression of the requirement of graphic representation and the refusal of trade marks in foreign language or script, which, if translated or transliterated in any EU language, would fall foul of the Directive or the Regulation, as well as the scope of protection and limits of the exclusive rights. For goods in transit a right to prohibit transiting counterfeit goods was proposed, as well as a prohibition against importing infringing goods in small consignments with private persons as purchasers. The Directive recast would reduce the options available to Member States as regards absolute and relative grounds of refusal and scope of protection and essentially align them with the provisions of the Regulation. **13.09**

(b) Procedures in Community trade mark law

As regards procedure under the Regulation, some adaptations would be made to take into account experiences over the past twenty years, but overall the OHIM procedures would remain much the same (without prejudice of course to procedural changes that may come about as a result of the future revision of the rules implementing the Regulation). **13.10**

(c) Procedures in national trade mark laws

As regards trade mark proceedings in national law, the Directive would mandate procedures substantially aligned with those of the Regulation and would oblige Member States to abstain from *ex parte* rejection on the basis of earlier rights and have administrative opposition and invalidation procedures. **13.11**

(d) Cooperation between OHIM and national IP offices

As regards cooperation between OHIM and national IP offices, provisions would be made in the Regulation making the obligation to cooperate explicit, and provide a proper legal basis for such cooperation. **13.12**

(e) OHIM finances

As regards OHIM finances, provision was made to create a sustainable source of financing of such cooperation by using part of OHIM income (up to 10%) to support common projects with national IP authorities and to deal with future substantial surpluses. The setting of a new system of OHIM fees was part of the 'package' in the form of a proposal for a Commission Regulation. **13.13**

(f) OHIM governance

As regards OHIM governance the Commission concept was to align OHIM, a first-generation agency with substantial administrative and financial autonomy, with the scheme of EU agencies overall,[7] which should be reflected in the name (European Agency **13.14**

---

[7] As reflected in the Joint Statement of the Commission, the Parliament and the Council of 19 July 2012 and as detailed in the 'Common Approach' document annexed thereto. Note that one of the fundamental principles of the common approach is that the specificities of established agencies ought to be taken into account where appropriate, which raises questions as to why the Commission insisted on a 'one size fits all' approach in the case of OHIM.

for Trade Marks and Designs), the composition of the administrative organs, the appointment of senior staff, etc. The Community trade mark would become the European trade mark. Furthermore, in line with the distribution of legislative and administrative powers between Parliament, Council, and Commission in the Lisbon Treaties, the Commission would get specific powers to adopt delegated acts comprising what is currently in the Implementing Regulation, the Fees Regulation, and the Rules of Procedure of the Boards of Appeal.

(3) The Outcome: The April 2015 Compromise

13.15 The Commission proposals received overall positive reactions. However, in the ensuing deliberations in the European Parliament and in the Council quite significant changes were proposed, with the most important ones at the expense of the Commission, in particular as concerns the finances and governance of OHIM. As regards substantive law, the most intensive debate and lobbying focused on the transit issue and the languages of examination. Member States were also most concerned about the far-reaching harmonization of their procedures and pressed for the conversion of a number of mandatory provisions in the Directive into optional ones.

13.16 The European Parliament, where the Committee on Legal Affairs was responsible, adopted its position on the two proposals in February 2014.[8] The Council considered the proposals in parallel, and reached its Common Position in July 2014.[9] In the subsequent so-called Trialogue—negotiations between the European Parliament, Council, and Commission, a procedure not foreseen in the Lisbon Treaty and frequently attacked for its lack of transparency—an overall agreement among the three participants was reached in April 2015, under the Latvian Presidency of the Council, and with a newly elected Parliament and a new Commission in place.

13.17 While the reduction of the agreements to specific texts was still outstanding at the time of writing this chapter (May 2015), and the actual adoption of the proposals will probably not take place before late in the second half of 2015, the outlines of what the package is likely to consist of are already apparent, even though some of the details still need to be filled in.

B. The 'Trade Mark Package' after the April 2015 Compromise

13.18 Hereafter, the elements of the 'trade mark package' will be summarized as agreed between the European Parliament, Council, and Commission.

(1) Substantive Law

13.19 It appears that substantive trade mark law will be substantially the same in the Regulation and in the Directive, where many of the current options will be mandatory or disappear. It is thus appropriate to deal with substantive trade mark law without (except where necessary) distinguishing between Regulation and Directive.

---

[8] European Parliament Doc P7_TA-PROV(2014)0118 (Regulation); P7_TA-PROV(2014)0119 (Directive).
[9] Council Doc 11826/14, 18 July 2014.

(a) Types of marks

13.20 The Regulation will provide for the registration of certification marks, in addition to the current collective marks. For the Directive, certification marks will be an option.

(b) Formalities: Absolute grounds

13.21 The graphic representation requirement will be replaced by a more flexible obligation to represent the sign objectively and unambiguously, which makes the registration of various types of non-traditional trade marks easier. The absolute grounds based on earlier geographical indications are remodelled and expanded with the inclusion of national rights (where they still exist) and complemented with provisions relating to traditional specialties guaranteed and traditional terms for wines. Earlier plant variety denominations will become absolute grounds for refusal of identical or 'closely related' species. Unexpectedly, the functionality ground is broadened to encompass not only shapes, but also any other characteristic of the goods which is either dictated by the nature of the goods, is necessary to obtain a technical result, or adds substantial value to the products. This would include not only two dimensional signs, but also colours, sounds, etc.

(c) Relative grounds

13.22 The protection of national marks with a reputation will also become mandatory in national trade mark laws, which means that earlier national marks with a reputation will be relative grounds not only under the EU system but also under national systems. This applies also to the scope of protection. A new, specific ground is created for geographical indications, modelled on the provisions of the Regulation dealing with unregistered signs (Article 8(4)) minus the requirement of use in the course of trade of more than mere local significance.

(d) Rights conferred

13.23 **(i) Transit** The most controversial or in any event debated issue was whether and under what conditions trade mark proprietors should have the right to prohibit the bringing into the EU of infringing goods not destined for the EU market but for markets in third countries (transit goods). A legislative solution was necessary because of the unfortunate decisions of the Court of Justice in *Class International, Philips,* and *Nokia*.[10]

13.24 The solution finally adopted consists of the position of the Council and reflects the hotly debated divisions of opinion among Member States: the rights to seize and prohibit counterfeit goods ends when the person responsible for the importation and transit is able to prove that the goods can be marketed in the country of destination without infringing any rights in that jurisdiction—together with the clauses proposed by the European Parliament for the Preamble, which focus on the need to prevent intervention with generic medicines on their way through the territory of the EU to third countries.

13.25 **(ii) Small consignments** The proposals for dealing with small consignments of infringing products sent from abroad to private recipients in the EU was finally deleted in view of the decision of the Court of Justice in the *Blomqvist* case.[11]

---

[10] For more details, see Chapter 9 at paragraphs 9.520 and following and 9.436 and following respectively, and Chapter 6 at paragraph 6.25 and following.

[11] The *Blomqvist* case is also dealt with in detail in Chapter 9 at paragraph 9.571 and following.

13.26 With the absence of any provision, the limitation in the initial proposals to restrict this measure to counterfeit products will no longer apply, and rights will apply to all infringing goods. The issue, however, of how to bring a civil action in such cases remains to be addressed because the private consignee of the goods is not infringing, and bringing the foreign sender before an EU jurisdiction, while possible, will be most difficult in practice.

13.27 (iii) **Other amendments** The exclusive rights of trade mark proprietors will extend to the use of trade names if used for the purposes of distinguishing the origin of goods or services,[12] and to the use of marks in comparative advertising.[13]

13.28 Exclusive rights have also been created in relation to labels and packaging etc prior to their combination with goods.

(e) Exceptions

13.29 (i) **Fair use** The unfortunate Court of Justice judgment in *Anheuser-Busch v Budějovický Budvar* (the Finnish Budweiser case)[14] will be 'overruled' to the extent it held that arbitrarily chosen company names, and not only personal (family) names, were also privileged under the fair use clause.

13.30 The right to use descriptive signs or indications, even if they conflict with an earlier trade mark, will be extended to the use of non-distinctive signs or indications.

13.31 Finally, no provision was made to expressly exclude other uses of a mark which should also be privileged, such as use which is protected by the freedom of expression, contrary to the Parliament's initial proposal.

13.32 (ii) **Exhaustion** Exhaustion under the Regulation will extend to the European Economic Area, as it does already under the Directive. Another effect of the extension of the effects of the Regulation to the EEA is also the right of applicants and professional representatives from those countries to appear before OHIM.

13.33 (iii) **Intervening rights** The Directive and the Regulation currently provide that the use and registration of a later trade mark may not be prohibited or cancelled when the proprietor of the earlier mark has 'tolerated' the use of the later mark for five consecutive years. The Regulation and the Directive further provide that the registration of a later trade mark may not be declared invalid when the later mark was applied for at a time when the earlier mark was subject to revocation on grounds of non-use.

13.34 It is also made explicit that in the absence of use situation referred to, not only can the registration not be invalidated but also the use cannot be prohibited. Furthermore, similar limitations on the right to prohibit the use of a later mark or obtain its invalidation apply when the earlier mark could not have been successfully asserted against the registration

---

[12] This confirms rather than extends the Court of Justice decision in *Celine*. For details see Chapter 9 at paragraph 9.373. This leaves an unfortunate gap in the protection of trade marks against their use as trade names as such, which Article 5(5) of the Directive (which will be maintained) allows Member States to prohibit, but which is not a remedy available under EU trade mark law. The Max Planck Study had proposed adding a provision to Article 9 of the Regulation so as to cover other uses of a protected mark in the manner provided for in Article 5 of the Directive. Neither the Commission nor the Parliament or Council even considered this additional proposal.

[13] This codifies the Court's jurisprudence in *O2* and *Bellure*: see Chapter 7 at paragraph 7.528 for details.

[14] For details on the *Budweiser* case, see Chapter 3 at paragraph 3.43.

of the later mark because of the absence of a relevant conflict at the time, such as because the earlier mark had not yet become particularly distinctive through use or had not yet obtained a reputation.

(f) Requirement of use

13.35 The ability to recognize the use of a variant of a registered mark, even if the variant is itself registered, codifies the Court of Justice judgment in *Rintisch v Eder*.[15]

13.36 In opposition proceedings, the requirement to show genuine use in order to be entitled to prevent the registration of a later mark will apply for the five years preceding the filing (or priority) date of the later mark, and not—as currently—for the five years preceding the publication date of the later mark. This will have the effect that a resumption of use after the priority or filing date, when previously five years of non-use have passed, will no longer entitle an opposition to prevail.

(g) Transfer, rights in rem, licensing

13.37 The Directive will have specific provisions on transfer, rights in rem, levy of execution, and licensing, but not as extensive as the initial proposal of the Commission which was intended to mirror the corresponding provisions in the Regulation.

(2) Procedures under the Regulation

13.38 The most controversial part of OHIM procedures concerned the question of whether or not a transition rule should be introduced to take care of the 'chaos' caused by the *IP Translator* judgment of the Court of Justice.[16] In the end the Council abandoned its opposition to such a rule, which will—probably—allow a period of six months to make CTM registrations *IP Translator* compliant.

13.39 Agreement was reached that separate class fees must be paid for all classes beyond the first class, while currently the basic fee comprises three classes.

13.40 Among the more controversial proposals of the Commission, the obligation to pay the filing fee with the application did not survive the compromise.

13.41 A provision was also added to the effect that the surrender of a registration may not take effect until pending revocation proceedings have been concluded and the mark still survives (ie the surrender does not override the effect of a revocation the effects of which precede the surrender), thus blocking the way to conversion.

13.42 As regards searches, the current system will be maintained—a search for earlier Community trade marks in all cases and an option for applicants to request national searches—but in a much more flexible form, disconnected from the stifling time limits currently in place.

(3) Procedures under the Directive

13.43 Some of the more controversial proposals in the ambitious Commission proposal for the Directive, while supported by the Parliament, did not survive in the Council and in the April 2015 compromise.

---

[15] On the *Rintisch* case and its antecedent, see Chapter 3 at para 3.41.
[16] On the *IP Translator* case, see Chapter 4 at paragraph 4.190.

13.44 Thus, Member States will be entitled to continue *ex officio* examination for earlier rights. While Member States agreed to the obligation to have administrative opposition and cancellation proceedings, for the latter they also obtained a long transition period (up to seven years). The single class fee system was also made optional for the Member States. Interestingly, it seems that no provision is made for a transitional arrangement to comply with the *IP Translator* judgment, which is left to the national legislator to enact where desirable.

(4) Cooperation

13.45 The Regulation will contain a number of provisions dealing with cooperation not only with national trade mark offices, but also between other authorities of the Member States and OHIM. The mandatory nature of some of the proposals has been softened by the introduction of voluntary elements and opt-out clauses.

(5) OHIM finances

13.46 OHIM fees will be provided for in an Annex to the Regulation, as proposed by the European Parliament and also by the Council, which means that any change will require a Commission proposal and the agreement of the European Parliament and of the Council. The fees for renewals, oppositions, cancellations, and appeals will be reduced.

13.47 OHIM income will not be 'diverted', as suggested at different times, to help finance the European School in Alicante or certain activities of the Court of Justice. Certain parts of OHIM revenue will be used to finance cooperation activities, whereas other parts will be paid to Member States to offset costs incurred as a result of the promotion of the European trade mark system and the obligation to grant protection to European Union trade marks in opposition, cancellation, and enforcement proceedings. The overall limit of such contributions is set at 20–25% of OHIM revenues (a 15% cap is foreseen for cooperation activities and another 5+5% is to be paid as 'compensation' on the basis of a distribution key based on the number of trade marks and opposition, cancellation, and enforcement cases originating from each Member State in a given year, except where OHIM finances do not so permit). OHIM will be entitled to keep its substantial reserve funds, and only when there is significant surplus for an extended period of time may the Budget Committee decide, with a two-thirds majority, that such surplus should be paid into the EU budget. Importantly, provision is also made for the creation of a reserve fund, equal to a year's expenditure, in order to safeguard the continuity of operations of the Office.

(6) OHIM governance

13.48 The name of OHIM will become 'European Union Intellectual Property Office', which will result in the acronym EUIPO. The versions in the other twenty-three EU languages are not yet established, but we would expect something like 'OUEPI' in French, or 'EUAGE' (or 'AEUGE') in German. The Community trade mark will become the 'European Union trade mark' (EUTM/MUE/EUM instead of CTM/MC/GM), and the Regulation will be the European Union Trade Mark Regulation (EUTMR/RMUE/EUMV instead of CTMR/RMC/GMV). It will take some time to get used to these new designations, but OHIM and CTM will be forgotten quickly.

13.49 In many respects, the ambitious and controversial proposals of the Commission to align the administration of OHIM with that of other, less self-administered agencies, were rejected.

The appointment of senior management will continue to be made by the Council. There will be no Executive Committee or Board, and the composition of the Administrative Board (rebranded as the Management Board) will remain essentially unchanged beyond extending full membership (that is, with voting rights) to a representative of the European Parliament and an additional member of the European Commission, which will thus have two representatives instead of the current one.

As a result of the distinction in Articles 290 and 291 TFEU, adopting implementing measures to Council regulations has become a new battlefield between the Commission and European Parliament and Council, the Commission always preferring Article 290—'delegated' legislation—which excludes participation of the Member States or the European Parliament, and the latter instead preferring so-called implementing legislation. The EU Trade Mark Regulation will most likely have a set of both types of third-generation legislation, a compromise between the two extremes. We are not aware of the details of the compromise, but it seems accepted that the Regulation itself will contain many more details than previously, because the general delegation of powers to Commission Regulations is no longer permitted under the Lisbon Treaties. **13.50**

From the practitioners' point of view it is hoped that the Commission will be able to adopt the respective acts in time and together with the coming into force of the amended Regulation. **13.51**

C. Outlook

If all goes according to plan, the 'package' may be voted on some time toward the middle or the end of the second half of 2015. The Regulation—EUTMR—could enter into force in April 2016, twenty years after the first CTMs (now EUTMs) could be filed. **13.52**

14

CONCLUSION

The Court of Justice has considered within a relatively short period of time a large number of trade mark cases from two perspectives: as an interpretive court for the purposes of both the Directive and the Regulation and as a supreme court of appeal under the Regulation and its implementing rules. In both contexts it has interpreted and applied provisions that were essentially identical. However, under the Regulation the Court also had to be supportive of the new Union-wide trade mark right and the bodies administering it. For example, by strengthening the role of the Boards of Appeal[1] and streamlining their decision-making trends, the Court could achieve a number of things: make the registration process more efficient, raise the level of dependency on the decision-making instances of OHIM, make the appeal route to the courts in Luxembourg more difficult, and lessen the burden imposed on the General Court (previously the Court of First Instance) and the Court of Justice.

14.01

At the same time the Community trade mark has been a success. Its 'peculiarities', which have been described in Chapter 2—the architecture of coexistence, conversion, and seniority—combined with competitive pricing and membership of the Madrid Protocol have made it a very attractive right. The story appears even more successful if one considers the long history of its inception and, as we have seen in Chapters 5, 6, and 9, the delicate balancing exercises that were aimed at reconciling fundamentally different systems of protection and satisfying a variety of stakeholders—not only the European Union institutions, which have viewed OHIM, because of its independence, with some scepticism, and national authorities, who are represented in OHIM's governing bodies, but also the 'private' sector, including existing trade mark owners, new applicants (European and foreign large corporations but also small enterprises), trade mark lawyers and agents, and courts with heightened national sensitivities. It should also be recalled that the Community trade mark is in essence a federal right in a European Union that shies away from being perceived as a federation. In many ways it is the closest we can get to a European 'national' right, applied by national courts that play the role of Community courts.[2]

14.02

Throughout this analysis of the trade mark jurisprudence of the Court of Justice it has become apparent that it, too, has been attempting to perform two balancing exercises: first, between the rights of trade mark proprietors and the interests of competitors and consumers; secondly, between the subject matter and the extent of protection.

14.03

In terms of registrability there is a body of case law that appears to embrace a broader concept of functionality (albeit not always phrased as such), similar to that applied by the US

14.04

---

[1] See, for example, paragraphs 3.60 and following.
[2] See paragraphs 9.409 and following.

Supreme Court,³ in order to accommodate the interests of competitors. Having initially rejected the direct applicability of general public policy doctrines,⁴ the Court started looking for the public interest or policy behind each specific provision,⁵ sometimes introducing arguments very heavily influenced by the public policy doctrine it had rejected in the first place. Conceptually, there is no inconsistency in that tactic since the Court made it clear that the specific grounds in the registrability provisions had been adopted in response to the same questions that were previously covered by general doctrines; however, the adoption of over-broad policy considerations often dilutes the character of each specific provision. For example, the Court had shown that it takes seriously the provisions on the exclusion of functional three-dimensional signs⁶ and, lacking the tools to expand their rationale to cover signs that are not three-dimensional, relied on the fundamental question of what constitutes a sign and the distinctiveness and graphical representation requirements.⁷ It also had to make assumptions regarding the function of particular types of signs in the marketplace and the way in which consumers react to them by laying down a number of presumptions, mostly in the form of predetermined cognitive and behavioural patterns, as regards consumer habits.⁸

14.05 In the same area of trade mark law the Court has assimilated the appearance of a product with the appearance of its packaging,⁹ following an initially more nuanced distinction based on whether the product had an innate shape or not.¹⁰ That approach seems to expand continuously to cover decorative motifs and ornamental details, the texture of the surface of the goods, and even the layout of retail stores. This is perhaps a rushed conclusion that could make the registration of all those things more difficult without any obvious justification. Again, a clearer position on functionality would make these issues easier to resolve.

14.06 Functionality questions illustrate another issue that will keep on coming before the Court. Chapters 10 and 11 have shown that trade mark law has to some extent internalized competition and free movement of goods questions; for example, there is considerable case law in this field re-establishing the free movement of goods principle and the related case law of the Court as the starting point for the exhaustion cases. From a competition perspective though, what will keep on coming back before the Court is the relationship between trade mark and other intellectual property rights and the effect of simultaneous protection; a policy issue that will require the Court to develop a coherent and economically solid narrative to resolve it in a balanced manner.¹¹

14.07 Turning to relative grounds and the scope of protection, the Court has consistently required evidence of likelihood of confusion. And the hurdle is high: likelihood of confusion must be genuine and substantiated. It has established, in a manner previously unknown, the essential tests for assessing sign and product similarity and views the two similarity conditions as cumulative, before even looking at the likelihood of confusion issue: there must be

---

[3] See paragraphs 5.860 and following and *Two Pesos, Inc v Taco Cabana, Inc* 505 U.S. 763 (1992) from a USA perspective.
[4] See paragraphs 5.05 and following.
[5] See, for example, paragraphs 5.215 and 5.855.
[6] See paragraphs 5.849 and following.
[7] See paragraph 4.11 and following.
[8] See for example *Wal-Mart Stores, Inc v Samara Bros*, Inc, 529 US 205 (2000).
[9] See paragraphs 5.444 and following above and contrast with *Wal-Mart* (fn. 8).
[10] See paragraphs 5.301 and following.
[11] See paragraph 5.793.

some evidence of similarity between the products and between the signs in order to proceed to the overall assessment of confusion. In practice, however, the assessment of confusion remains too heavily dependent on the resemblances of the signs, so much so that any perceptible degree of similarity is oftentimes enough to trigger the application of the relevant provisions. This tendency to overprotect is further demonstrated by the reluctance of the Court to embrace a coherent theory of weak marks or weak elements of composite marks and develop a convincing set of normative considerations to serve as a safety valve against the use by lower courts of arbitrary or unsubstantiated empirical assumptions. Similarly, the tension between 'dominant' and 'distinctive' components remains for the larger part unresolved, as the Court continues to give too much weight to any element that is 'non-negligible', while at the same time refusing to acknowledge the need to downplay the impact of non-distinctive elements on the assessment of the likelihood of confusion.[12]

14.08 The Court also faces particular difficulty in dealing with distinct variations of confusion, or, in other words, scope of protection. In *Arsenal*[13] it appeared to include post-sale confusion in what it found to be actionable. But then in subsequent case law it chose to take a step back.[14]

14.09 The protection of goodwill is another area where the Court has made an arduous effort to define the relevant requirements but the overall picture remains somewhat blurred. The notions of 'reputation' and 'well-known character', the conditions for the existence of a 'link' and the identification and attributes of the relevant public have been discussed at considerable length. The choice of the Court to refrain from imposing inflexible thresholds when it comes to the definition of reputation has rendered the scope of protection more flexible and versatile: more marks can qualify for extended protection, provided that there is detriment or unfair advantage. These concepts, however, seem to be developing in different directions: while proving blurring has become an almost impossible exercise, as the main triggering factor in this regard, namely the 'change in the economic behaviour' of the consumer, is still imperfectly defined, the proof of free riding seems to depend on much more abstract considerations, sketchily transplanted from the area of competition law.

14.10 The distinctions developed by the Court between double-identity protection, where additional trade mark functions are protected,[15] and likelihood of confusion protection lacks in empirical support. This clouds somewhat the Court's pragmatic approach in delineating the scope of protection, taking into account the specific factual context of each case and its wish to counterbalance the expansion of exclusionary rights with the need to keep markets open and competitive, which are factors that explain its reluctance to embrace doctrinally solid but rigid solutions. Instead, the Court so far has opted for a more flexible—but narrower in terms of scope—approach. Its judgments are often embedded against a context that is characterized by the relevant product market, the facts of the case, parallel developments in other areas of law, and the setting of the trade mark within a broader and hierarchical system of rules.

---

[12] See paragraphs 7.144 and following.
[13] See paragraphs 9.55 and following.
[14] See paragraphs 7.182 and following.
[15] See paragraphs 9.53 and following.

14.11 In the future the Court will also have to refine further the types of use that remain outside the scope of protection. The concept of use has served in Chapter 5 as a factor that is determinative of trade mark protection: the way a sign is used will dictate the possibility and scope of protection. In Chapters 5 and 6 the nature of use by the alleged infringer has determined whether there is a question of infringement in the first place and then, even if the conditions of infringement are satisfied, whether there is a defence that can be raised. So far, the Court has been consistent in requiring use in trade and interpreting the defences from a permissive angle.[16] This will probably be challenged further in relation to the extended protection enjoyed by marks with a reputation, with freedom of commercial and political speech arguments being introduced into the debate.

14.12 A parameter of the above is use of trade marks on the Internet. This is another area of law that the Court will have to explore further, taking into account competition considerations and further jurisdictional issues.

14.13 In terms of style the Court appears to favour multi-factor tests. However, these tests are sometimes lost in the narrative of the judgment. This is indicative of a more intricate problem. The Court has proven to be quite pragmatic and practical in its approach, but the difficulty it faces is that it only views snippets, often distorted, of the cases before the referring courts. Also, it has a limited jurisdiction over appeals against the judgments of the General Court. So, often it deals only with an aspect of the case that is sometimes characterized by very particular and specific facts. The wider significance of the judgment of the Court can be lost because the audience focuses on the answer to the specific question or issue under appeal. A solution, proposed to and followed by the Court in a number of cases,[17] is to take a step back, detach itself from the facts of the case, and attempt to give an answer from basic principles. On the other hand, as shown in Chapter 9, context is everything in the interpretation and application of trade mark law. Accepting this more explicitly could allow the Court to reconcile what appear to be inconsistencies in its trade mark jurisprudence and give back to national courts the power to decide how to consistently apply the basic principles established by the Court. In a way, the Court has done so already by qualifying issues as factual rather than legal, and by its many multi-factor tests, which absolves it from deciding the complicated cases itself.

14.14 The Court of Justice does not have the luxury of choosing its cases. Although the high number of trade mark files to be processed and the logistical burden this entails have led the Court to develop a defensive approach, by laying down an extremely narrow interpretation of what it sees as 'questions of law', the wealth of issues that constantly crop up before it could be converted into a blessing for the purposes of further developing European trade mark doctrine. The time is ripe for the Court to move away from its highly detached style and deal more actively and decisively with the fine-tuning of the principles and multi-factor tests it has propounded over the years. Of course, re-establishing, restating, and insisting on the basic principles will continue to be necessary, but if the Court does not move on to devise a more practical approach, focusing not so much on high rules but on the mechanics of the application of the relevant norms, its case law risks becoming more and more irrelevant and it may hold back, instead of pushing forward, the development of a genuinely useful European trade mark law.

---

[16] See, for example, paragraphs 9.308 and following.
[17] See paragraphs 9.94 and following.

INDEX

References to OHIM stand for Office for Harmonization of the Internal Market, while those to IP represent 'intellectual property'. References to 'judgments' are to the Court of Justice of the European Union unless otherwise specified.

abbreviations, distinctiveness 5.84–5.94
    Multi Market Funds (MMF) 5.86, 5.90, 5.92
    Natur-Aktien-Index (NAI) 5.87, 5.90, 5.92
absolute grounds for refusal of registration/ declaration of invalidity
    abbreviations, distinctiveness 5.84–5.94
    acronyms 5.745–5.848
    Advocate General Opinion
        descriptive signs or indications 5.510–5.521, 5.539–5.556, 5.571–5.589, 5.597–5.611, 5.668–5.687, 5.700–5.701
        devoid of any distinctive character 5.19–5.31, 5.39–5.51, 5.66–5.73, 5.89, 5.132–5.137, 5.152–5.165, 5.243–5.245, 5.252–5.266, 5.286–5.290, 5.345–5.360, 5.392–5.404, 5.450–5.454, 5.467–5.474
        signs or indications that have become customary 5.760–5.764, 5.775–5.781, 5.821–5.830
        trade marks of a deceptive nature 5.843–5.852
    appeals
        composite words (permissive approach) 5.540–5.541
        devoid of any distinctive character 5.99–5.106, 5.113–5.121, 5.182–5.190
        single letters and numerals 5.99–5.106, 5.113–5.121
        slogans, registrability 5.182–5.190
    Article 3
        guidelines for interpreting 5.05–5.15
        independence of grounds 5.620
        product-by-product approach 5.669–5.675
        specification considerations 5.679–5.687
        timing considerations 5.676–5.678
    Article 3(1) 5.511
    Article 3(1)(c)
        application 5.621–5.626
        conditions for application of 5.512–5.520
        context 5.511
        factors for application 5.526–5.530
        and free movement of goods 5.699–5.706
        independent existence of Articles 3(1)(b) and 3(1)(c) 5.627–5.628
        interaction with Article 6(1)(b) 5.521, 5.525
        interpretation 5.621–5.626
        overlap between Articles 3(1)(b) and 3(1)(c) 5.629
        public interest 5.524
        scope 5.603
    Article 3(1)(d)
        interpretation 5.727–5.728

        signs or indications that have become customary 5.723–5.758
        test for application 5.729–5.737
        types of signs covered by 5.742–5.744
    Article 3(1)(e)
        aim of Article 3(1)(e)(ii) 5.768
        ambit of 5.290
        and Article 3(1)(c) 5.212–5.221
        functional shapes 5.759–5.840
        independent grounds 5.837–5.838
        legal nature and scope 5.761
        overriding scope 5.759–5.769
        public interest considerations 5.767
    Article 3(1)(g) 5.841–5.973
        application 5.849–5.851, 5.856–5.857
        interpretation 5.584, 5.848
        public interest considerations 5.855
    Article 7(1)(b) 5.16–5.36
        application 5.58–5.60, 5.78, 5.350–5.360, 5.451–5.454, 5.468–5.469, 5.645–5.646
        compared to Article 7(1)(a) 5.40
        criterion for application 5.78, 5.451–5.454
        general interest 5.477
        interpretation 5.40–5.43, 5.350–5.360
        and need to preserve the availability of a sign 5.371–5.380
        and packaging 5.389–5.426
        reassessment of facts 5.467, 5.478
        requirements 5.475–5.476
        three-dimensional signs 5.456–5.459
    Article 7(1)(c)
        application 5.637–5.640
        and Article 12(b) 5.587–5.588
        scope 5.542–5.546, 5.558–5.559
        scope of appeal 5.540–5.541
    Article 7(1)(d)
        and acronyms 5.745–5.848
        application 5.747–5.749
        interpretation and application 5.754
    Article 7(3)
        application 5.750–5.752
    Article 12(2)(b) 5.884
        application 5.858
        interpretation 5.852
    Article 73 5.480–5.483
        and Article 74(1) 5.470–5.474
    Article 74(1) 5.479
        and Article 73 5.470–5.474
    burden of proof
        consumer goods 5.715–5.722
        technical and scientific terms 5.707–5.714

Index

absolute grounds for refusal of registration/
declaration of invalidity (*cont.*):
  case details/order of reference
    abbreviations, distinctiveness 5.86–5.88
    attractiveness versus distinctiveness 5.809–5.812
    broad interpretation of shapes 5.797–5.800
    frosted bottle cases 5.484–5.487
    functionality 5.770–5.774
    nature of goods and substantive
      value 5.819–5.820
    numerals (single), signs consisting of 5.107–5.112
  cases of importance
    Audi AG 5.178–5.199
    Baby Dry 5.16–5.36, 5.37–5.63, 5.532–5.566, 5.549–5.552, 5.605–5.607
    Benetton 5.808–5.818
    BioID 5.64–5.81
    BORCO-Marken 5.95, 5.96–5.106, 5.122, 5.125, 5.127
    Bravo 5.723–5.744
    BVBA 5.664–5.698
    Celltech 5.707–5.714
    Companyline 5.16–5.36
    Cotonelle 5.878–5.884
    Develey 5.715–5.722
    Doublemint 5.567–5.594, 5.633–5.648, 5.649–5.658
    Elizabeth Emanuel 5.841–5.858
    Erpo Möbelwerke 5.147–5.176, 5.177
    Eurocermex 5.427–5.443
    Freixenet 5.484–5.491
    Glaverbel 5.315–5.320
    Hauck 5.819–5.840
    Heidelberger Bauchemie 5.229–5.237
    Henkel 5.301–5.314, 5.324–5.332
    Henkel KGaA 5.361–5.382
    Lego 5.770–5.795
    Linde, Winward Industries, and *Rado Uhren* 5.282–5.300
    Mag 5.248–5.281
    Mars 5.872–5.877
    Matrazen 5.699–5.706
    Nichols 5.129–5.145
    Pall 5.860–5.865
    Philips 5.759–5.769
    Pi-Design 5.796–5.807
    Postkantoor 5.16–5.36, 5.595–5.632, 5.664–5.698
    Procter & Gamble 5.333–5.344
    SAT I 5.37–5.63, 5.64–5.81
    Sisi-Werke 5.389–5.426
    Storck I 5.444–5.459
    Storck II 5.460–5.483
    Streamserve 5.633–5.648
    Technopol 5.95, 5.107–5.121, 5.122, 5.125
    Telefon & Buch 5.649–5.658
    Windsurfing Chiemsee 5.504–5.531, 5.547–5.548
  chocolate in animal shapes
    mouse 5.495
    rabbit 5.492–5.494
  colours, distinctiveness 5.200–5.228
    combinations of colours 5.229–5.237
    competition considerations 5.208–5.209
    distinctive character of colour per se 5.222
    public perception, importance 5.223–5.228
    registrability of colours and general interest 5.212–5.221
  composite trade marks or words 5.630–5.632
    admissibility considerations 5.557
    conditions for composite marks 5.561–5.562
    defining descriptiveness 5.560
    lexical inventions 5.564
    permissive approach 5.532–5.566
    perspective for assessing distinctiveness 5.563
    procedural paradox 5.539
    public interest considerations 5.547–5.548
    scope of appeal 5.540–5.541
    suggested way forward 5.555–5.556
    unusual juxtaposition 5.564
  definition of goods and services 4.09, 4.10
  descriptive signs or indications
    adjusting perspective for viewing 5.585–5.586
    autonomy of Community trade mark regime 5.644
    balancing functions with scope of protection 5.599
    burden of proof 5.707–5.722
    challenging of procedural points 5.664–5.698
    COLOR EDITION 5.660
    Community trade marks 5.695–5.698
    composite trade marks or words 5.532–5.566, 5.630–5.632
    Court orders 5.647–5.648, 5.655–5.658
    deconstructing the specification 5.641–5.643
    defining descriptiveness 5.560
    descriptive and lacking in distinctiveness 5.662
    descriptive for a part of the goods 5.663
    ecoDoor 5.663
    free movement of goods 5.699–5.706
    future and potential use matters 5.592
    general principles, setting 5.504–5.531
    geographical names 5.504–5.531
    German doctrine 5.518–5.519, 5.523
    keeping free for others to use 5.587–5.588
    KOMPRESSOR PLUS 5.661
    limiting scope of reference 5.597–5.598
    link between product and geographical indication 5.531
    meaning of 'exclusively' 5.572
    more than mere sum and its parts neologism 5.609–5.611
    multifactor test 5.573–5.574
    multiplicity of meanings 5.573–5.574
    nuanced approach in *Doublemint* 5.567–5.594
    overriding effect of national rules 5.691–5.693
    parallel approach 5.595–5.632
    peculiarity of Benelux 5.608, 5.615
    Photos.com 5.662
    practices of national offices and registrability 5.602
    public interest considerations 5.524, 5.547–5.548
    recent case law 5.659–5.663
    registrability in other Member States 5.616
    registration process 5.613–5.614

Index

restating the principles 5.591
restrictions in other jurisdictions 5.589
right to request invalidation 5.660
roadmap for assessing registrability 5.600–5.601
same reasoning for all types of sign 5.604
specifications and disclaimers 5.617–5.619, 5.641–5.643
thorough examination procedures 5.620
time considerations 5.694
device marks, absence of distinctiveness 5.501–5.503
Louis Vuitton's lock device mark 5.496–5.500
devoid of any distinctive character 5.16–5.503
absence of justification 5.402–5.404
actual distinctive character 5.354–5.356
alternatives, relevance 5.315–5.320
appeals 5.82–5.83, 5.99–5.106, 5.113–5.121, 5.441–5.443
appraisal of facts and new pleas 5.32–5.33
assessment of distinctive character 5.44–5.46, 5.362–5.370
availability, need to preserve 5.357–5.360
average consumer's level of attention 5.353, 5.381
biometrical identification 5.65
burden of proof 5.76
versus capable of distinguishing 4.157
chocolate in animal shapes 5.492–5.495
colours, distinctiveness 5.200–5.228
combinations of colours 5.229–5.237
considering mark as a whole 5.384–5.386
context for determining distinctiveness 5.393–5.396, 5.406–5.413
criteria concerning use of a trade mark 5.387
critical time for assessing distinctive character 5.346–5.349
date for assessing distinctive character 5.382
definition of goods and services 4.09, 4.10, 4.157
descriptive and lacking in distinctiveness 5.662
descriptiveness, assessing first 5.26
device marks 5.496–5.503
distinctive character and perceptible differences 5.22
distinctiveness of abbreviations 5.84–5.94
effect of registrations in other Member States 5.313–5.314
frosted bottle cases 4.484–4.491
functionality of colours 5.238–5.247
grounds of appeal 5.27–5.30
inadmissibility 5.32–5.33
interests of competitors 5.404
monopolization argument 5.417–5.426
non-discrimination principle 5.50–5.51
overall impression 5.74–5.75, 5.268–5.269, 5.436–5.440
packaging 5.301–5.314, 5.305–5.308, 5.389–5.426, 5.460–5.483
permissive perspective 5.40–5.43
perspective for determining registrability 5.23–5.24
practice of Office as 'precedent' 5.31
registration of comparable marks 5.73, 5.77
responsibility of sign 5.79–5.81
shapes 5.248–5.314, 5.414–5.416, 5.427–5.459
significance of similar products 5.351–5.352
single letters and numerals 5.95–5.128
slogans 5.146–5.199
statutory interpretation 5.34–5.36
surnames, no special conditions for 5.129–5.145
test for assessing distinctive character 5.309–5.312
three-dimensional trade marks, level of distinctiveness required 5.399–5.401
washing tables cases 5.321–5.388
free movement of goods and deceptive use 5.859–5.911
advertising messages 5.872–5.877
cosmetics 5.866–5.871
effect on trade and scope of prohibition 5.863, 5.875–5.877
legislative framework 5.862
proportionality 5.864
symbol, use of 5.860–5.865
unfair competition 5.865, 5.870–5.871, 5.880–5.883
frosted bottle cases 4.484–4.491
functionality of colours 5.238–5.247
geographical indications 12.138–12.152
scope of prohibition 12.143–12.148
temporal application of Regulation 110/220 12.140–12.142
and Trade Marks Directive 12.149
independence
of each ground 5.08–5.10
and interdependence 5.05–5.07
judgments
of Court of First Instance 5.17–5.18, 5.38, 5.148–5.151, 5.239–5.242, 5.250–5.251, 5.324–5.344, 5.390–5.391, 5.430–5.434, 5.446–5.449, 5.461–5.466, 5.535–5.538, 5.568–5.570, 5.636–5.646, 5.651–5.654, 5.709, 5.747–5.752
descriptive signs or indications 5.522–5.531, 5.590–5.594, 5.612–5.632, 5.688–5.698, 5.702–5.706, 5.709, 5.710–5.714
devoid of any distinctive character 5.17–5.18, 5.32–5.36, 5.38, 5.52–5.63, 5.74–5.81, 5.90–5.91, 5.138–5.145, 5.148–5.151, 5.166–5.176, 5.235–5.237, 5.239–5.242, 5.246–5.247, 5.250–5.251, 5.291–5.300, 5.324–5.344, 5.361–5.382, 5.383–5.387, 5.388, 5.390–5.391, 5.405–5.426, 5.430–5.434, 5.446–5.449, 5.455–5.459, 5.475–5.483, 5.488–5.489, 5.496–5.503
signs or indications that have become customary 5.738–5.741, 5.765–5.769, 5.782–5.792, 5.801–5.803, 5.813–5.818, 5.831–5.839
trade marks of a deceptive nature 5.853–5.858
Louis Vuitton's lock device mark
absence of distinctiveness 5.496–5.500
General Court 5.497
judgment 5.498–5.500
OHIM decisions 5.496

absolute grounds for refusal of registration/ declaration of invalidity (*cont.*):
  multifactor test, distinctiveness 5.575–5.580
    first part of test 5.581
    more than minimal 5.584
    second part of test 5.582, 5.583
    wider context of trade mark law 5.584
  new trade mark 'package' after April 2015 13.21
  packaging
    and Article 7(1)(b) 5.389–5.426
    assimilation of 5.301–5.314
    and content 5.305–5.308
    distinctive character 5.460–5.483
  public interest considerations
    independence and interdependence 5.05–5.10
  relevant consumer 5.13
  shapes
    assimilation of packaging 5.301–5.314
    broad interpretation of 5.796–5.807
    broad perspective 5.282–5.300
    character of 5.248–5.281
    criteria for assessing distinctive character 5.270–5.272
    evidence of distinctive character 5.274–5.277
    facts, appraising 5.273
    general propositions 5.281
    infringement of right to hearing 5.265–5.266
    meaning of evidence 5.278–5.279
    misappraisal of facts relating to distinctiveness 5.261–5.264
    misappraisal of specific distinctiveness 5.253–5.260
    right to be heard 5.280
    setting a roadmap 5.289, 5.295–5.300
    substantial value, giving 5.827–5.828, 5.831–5.834
    sweets 5.444–5.459
    three-dimensional 5.414–5.416, 5.427–5.443
  signs or indications that have become customary 5.723–5.758
    acronyms 5.745–5.848
    additional factors 5.837–5.838
    aesthetic functionality 5.835
    artistic or ornamental value 5.836
    association and distinctive character 5.730–5.733
    attractiveness versus distinctiveness 5.808–5.818
    average consumer 5.791–5.792
    broad interpretation of shapes 5.796–5.807
    case assessment 5.793–5.795, 5.840
    Court orders 5.753–5.758
    findings of fact/assessment of evidence 5.755–5.758
    functionality/functional shapes 5.759–5.840
    identification of essential characteristics 5.787–5.788
    legal framework 5.766
    link with specification 5.723–5.744, 5.740–5.741
    nature of goods and substantive value 5.819–5.840
    non-functional elements 5.789–5.790
    public interest considerations 5.767, 5.782
    relevance of alternatives 5.762–5.764, 5.769
    scope of provisions 5.783–5.786
    single purpose 5.829–5.830
    trade marks, patents and designs 5.762–5.764
    type and strength of association 5.734–5.737
  single letters and numerals 5.95–5.128
    appeals 5.99–5.106, 5.113–5.121
    views of OHIM and General Court 5.96–5.98
  slogans, registrability 5.146–5.199
    DAS PRINZIP DER BEQUEMLICHKEIT example 5.147–5.176
    decision on the merits 5.191–5.194
    OHIM and Board of Appeal 5.179
    'Vorsprung durch Technik' example 5.178–5.199
  specification, link with 5.12
  surnames
    competition considerations 5.144–5.145
    consumer perception 5.142–5.143
    distinctive character 5.135–5.137
    no special conditions for 5.129–5.145
    registrability of 5.134
    same criteria for all types of marks 5.141
  sweets, shape 5.444–5.459
    admissibility considerations 5.450
    criterion for application of Article 7(1)(b) 5.451–5.454
  timing issues 5.14
  trade marks of a deceptive nature 5.841–5.973
    admissibility considerations 5.843
    assignment of trade marks 5.841–5.858
    commercialization of trade marks 5.844–5.845
    and free movement of goods 5.859–5.911
    functions of trade marks 5.846
    perspective for determining deception 5.847
    procedural considerations 5.853
    symbol, use of 5.860–5.865
  washing tables cases 5.321–5.388
    inlaid tablets 5.339–5.344, 5.388
    significance of similar products 5.351–5.352
    speckled tablets 5.383–5.387
    two-layered tablets 5.324–5.332
abstract, signs in 4.20
abusive conduct, factors establishing dominance 11.136–11.137
accessibility requirement
  graphical representation 4.38, 4.100
acronyms
  comparative advertising 12.48
  signs or indications that have become customary 5.745–5.848
administrative proceedings, scope 3.61–3.63
admissibility considerations
  Budweiser judgments 12.203
  composite trade marks or words 5.557
  devoid of any distinctive character 5.32–5.33
  sweets, shape 5.450
  trade marks of a deceptive nature 5.843
adverse effect
  and advertising function 9.249–9.250
  and investment function 9.251–9.253
  keywords, use by advertisers 9.156

Index

and origin function 9.243–9.248
on original condition of product 10.184–10.186
advertising
  see also **comparative advertising**
  adverse effect and advertising function 9.249–9.250
  compatibility, indicating 9.341
  display of advertisements 9.136–9.140
  and exhaustion of rights, in new regime 10.257
  free movement of goods 5.872–5.877, 10.257
  function 9.161–9.163
  keywords *see* **keywords, use by advertisers**
  promotional items, genuine use requirement 8.106–8.108
  sales figures and advertising expenditure 6.50–6.72
  second-hand goods 9.299–9.302
  transparency in 9.158
  unclear messages 9.160
aesthetic functionality
  nature of goods 5.835
Agreement on Trade-Related Aspects of Intellectual Property Rights (TRIPS Agreement) *see* **TRIPS Agreement (Agreement on Trade-Related Aspects of Intellectual Property Rights)**
alcohol
  trade marks containing geographical indication 4.10
annulment actions
  Court of Justice of the European Union 3.09–3.11
appeals
  see also **Boards of Appeal; Court of Justice of the European Union (CJEU); General Court**
  to Boards of Appeal 2.44
  cases of importance
    BVBA Management 3.75–3.76
    Isdin 3.73–3.75
    Nike 3.77–3.78
  to Court of Justice 2.45, 2.46, 3.12, 3.69–3.84
    'economic behaviour', importance 7.514–7.517
    single letters and numerals 5.99–5.106, 5.113–5.121
    slogans, registrability 5.182–5.190
    unfair advantage 7.566–7.574
  descriptive signs or indications 5.540–5.541
  devoid of any distinctive character 5.82–5.83, 5.99–5.106, 5.113–5.121, 5.182–5.190, 5.441–5.443
  to General Court 2.45
  grounds of 7.234–7.238
  limiting scope of 7.225–7.226, 7.232–7.233
  setting parameters for 5.441–5.443
appearance
  assimilation with packaging 14.05
  and product shape 5.301–5.314
applications for registration
  see also **absolute grounds for refusal of registration/ declaration of invalidity; Office for Harmonization in the Internal Market (OHIM); registration of trade marks; relative grounds for refusal of registration/declaration of invalidity**
  in bad faith 4.09
  and concept of 'possessions' 12.243–12.244
  conversion 2.25
  Court as ultimate arbiter 4.06
  languages 2.34
  numbers received 2.16
  rights arising from 12.241–12.242
artistic or ornamental value
  nature of goods 5.836
auditory messages *see* **sounds**
Austria
  accession to EU (1995) 2.59
autonomy
  Community Trade Mark Regulation 2.21
availability and scope of protection 9.84–9.101
  availability requirement as a limiting factor 9.100–9.101
  impact of 9.93–9.99

bad faith
  applications for registration in 4.09
  domain names and trade marks 12.155, 12.157–12.159
  as open concept 12.157–12.159
badges
  trade mark including 4.09
Benelux law (1970)
  and Community Trade Mark Regulation 2.23
Benelux Trade Mark Office 4.132
bilateral agreements
  geographical indications and free movement of goods 12.162–12.174
block exemptions
  competition 11.43
blurring
  dilution, proof of 7.476–7.480, 7.482–7.484
Boards of Appeal
  see also **Office for Harmonization in the Internal Market (OHIM)**
  decision stage 3.22
  decisions of reviewed by General Court and Court of Justice 2.46
  ex parte cases 3.26
  examination stage 3.22
  extent of powers of review 3.22
  and first instance units in OHIM 3.22
  late presentation of evidence 3.32, 3.33
  numbers of cases heard annually 2.44
  and OHIM 3.29–3.33
  opposition cases 3.26
  powers 5.414–5.416
  procedure 3.22
  refusal to take into account new/additional evidence, appropriate circumstances/ cases 3.36–3.38
  review of decisions by General Court and Court of Justice 2.45
  role 3.28–3.35
  scope of decision-making powers 3.21
  slogans, registrability 5.179
  time limits 3.30, 3.32, 3.33

863

border measures 9.485–9.493
  see also enforcement proceedings
  national borders, effect 9.421–9.436
  seizure of infringing goods 9.485–9.486
brands, copying of
  challenging limits of protection 9.59–9.83
Brussels Convention (1968)
  and enforcement proceedings 2.50
Budweiser judgments
  admissibility considerations 12.203
  Advocate General Opinion 12.165–12.169, 12.197–12.202, 12.218–12.223
  BUD as appellation of origin (*Budweiser IV*) 12.213–12.229
  Budějovický Budvar/Budweiser IV 12.247
  clarifying *Budweiser I* 12.184–12.186
  compatibility with Community law 12.199
  consumer surveys 12.187
  details of 12.170–12.174, 12.183–12.193, 12.203–12.212, 12.224–12.229
  equivalence and effectiveness principles 12.187
  and European Court of Human Rights 12.230–12.246
  European trade mark law and TRIPS Agreement protecting trade names (*Budweiser III*) 12.194–12.212
  exclusivity of Community system (*Budweiser II*) 12.180–12.182
  'fair balance' requirement 12.246
  geographical indications, bilateral agreements and free movement of goods (*Budweiser I*) 12.162–12.174
  judicial cooperation 12.183
  limitations for trade mark protection 12.210
  nature of Regulation 510/2006 system 12.189–12.193
  replaying of *Budweiser I* (*Budweiser II*) 12.175–12.193
  trade names
    as prior rights 12.211
    protecting 12.194–12.212
    requirements for protecting 12.201–12.202
    status 12.200
    and trade marks 12.205–12.212
  use as a derogation versus use as a trade mark 12.188
  use as a trade mark requirement 12.198
Bulgaria
  accession to EU (2006) 2.59
bundling
  media player 11.164–11.167
burden of proof
  see also evidence
  acquired distinctiveness 6.153–6.155, 6.159–6.162
  consumer goods 5.715–5.722
  descriptive signs or indications 5.707–5.714, 5.715–5.722
  devoid of any distinctive character 5.76
  dilution, proof of 7.486–7.487
  and evidence of use 8.58–8.71
  free movement of goods and new trade mark regime 10.148–10.149, 10.209, 10.369
  technical and scientific terms 5.707–5.714
  transit 9.533

capable of being represented graphically *see* graphical representation
capable of distinguishing
  see also distinctiveness; distinctiveness acquired through use
  versus devoid of distinctive character 4.157
  goods and services, definition 4.02, 4.21–4.23, 4.41–4.42, 4.156–4.175, 4.172–4.175
  principles, setting 4.156–4.171
channels of trade
  comparative advertising 12.32, 12.39
  policing and trade mark infringement 10.229–10.251
    general principles 10.233
    repackaging 10.234–10.235
Charter of Fundamental Rights of the European Union
  judicial review 3.103
chemical formulae
  and scents 4.16, 4.79, 4.103
CJEU *see* Court of Justice of the European Union (CJEU)
clarity requirement
  definition of for which mark registered 4.190–4.244
  graphical representation 4.38, 4.92, 4.99, 4.105, 4.115
co-existence (CTMR)
  conversion 2.25
  earlier national rights as relative grounds 2.23–2.24
  as implemented 2.23–2.29
  parallel national rights 2.28–2.29
  principle 2.22, 2.63, 3.114
  seniority 2.26–2.27
colours
  as attributes of something else 4.17
  combinations 5.229–5.237
    abstract 4.148–4.155
    representing 4.154
    as trade marks 4.152–4.153
  distinctiveness 5.200–5.228
    acquired through use 6.87
    competition considerations 5.208–5.209
    distinctive character of colour per se 5.222
    public perception, importance 5.223–5.228
  functionality considerations 5.238–5.247
  graphical representation 4.141–4.143, 4.145–4.147
  historical ability to obtain registration 4.04
  judgments 4.155
  registrability of colours and general interest 5.212–5.221
  registrability per se 4.17
  as sensations 4.17
  'sign' requirement 4.17, 4.18, 4.19
  trade mark as registered, scope of protection 9.26–9.29
combined use
  distinctiveness acquired through use 6.36–6.49
Comitology case (1987)
  actions against a Community institution for failure to act 3.08

Index

Community trade mark courts
  jurisdiction 2.51–2.54
  Member States, established by 2.48
  procedural rules and national law 2.57
  related actions 2.58
  validity of allegedly infringed mark, acceptance of 2.56

Community Trade Mark Regulation (CTMR) 2.14–2.58
  absolute grounds for refusal of registration 4.10
  adoption (December 1993) 2.14
  and Boards of Appeal 3.22
  co-existence
    conversion 2.25
    earlier national rights as relative grounds 2.23–2.24
    as implemented 2.23–2.29
    parallel national rights 2.28–2.29
    principle 2.22, 2.63
    seniority 2.26–2.27
  definition of a trade mark 4.08
  distinctiveness acquired through use 6.01–6.03
  enforcement proceedings 2.49, 2.50, 9.414–9.486
  enlargement of EU 2.61
  exhaustion of rights, in new regime 10.285
  grace period 8.218
  interaction with Directive 2.62, 3.114
  interpretation of provisions in context 3.113
  justification of non-use 8.234
  and keywords 9.150–9.164
  open-ended nature of 4.04
  political obstacles 2.05
  principles
    autonomy 2.21
    co-existence *see above*
    unitary character 2.20
  reforms 13.38–13.42
  relative grounds for refusal 7.07
  reproduction of Community trade marks in dictionaries 9.05
  requirement of use 8.11
  rights conferred by a Community trade mark 9.04
  scope of Article 115(4) 2.36
  search of Community register requirement 2.40
  time limits 3.24
  Title structure 2.30, 2.43, 2.49
  TRIPS Agreement, compatible with 2.17

Community Trade Marks (CTMs)
  appeals/review by General Court/Court of Justice 2.44–2.46
  assignment 2.33
  background 2.04
  enforcement/Court proceedings *see* **enforcement proceedings**
  infringement 2.47
  and judicial review *see* **judicial review**
  languages 2.34–2.38
  licensing 2.33
  limitations of effects 9.07
  national trade marks, taking into account in CTM system 2.23
  office proceedings 2.39–2.46
  procedural matters 2.34–2.38
  reform package 13.10
  reproduction in dictionaries 9.05
  rights in rem, establishing 2.33
  security, given as 2.33
  substantive law 2.31–2.33
  success of 14.02
  validity 2.48, 2.49

comparative advertising 12.02–12.099
  see also **advertising**
  acceptability of additional conditions 12.33
  acronyms 12.48
  Advocate General Opinion
    comparison of shopping baskets 12.95
    contradictions of Article 7(2) of Directive 84/450/EEC 12.28–12.34
    Court taking step back in *L'Oréal* judgment 12.81–12.89
    designations of origin and competitive relationship 12.56–12.59
    interplay between trade marks and comparative advertising 12.07–12.16
    use of similar sign and indispensability challenge 12.68–12.72
  cases of importance
    De Landtsheer Emmanuel 12.54–12.65
    Lidl 12.93–12.99
    L'Oréal v Bellure 12.78–12.92
    O2 12.66–12.77
    Pippig 12.26–12.42
    Siemens 12.43–12.53
    Toshiba 12.05–12.25
  circumstances of case, importance 12.53
  Comparative Advertising Directive 9.37
  comparison of shopping baskets 12.93–12.99
  competitive relationship 12.57, 12.61–12.63
  conditions for 12.19–12.20
  contradictions of Article 7(2) of Directive 84/450/EEC 12.26–12.42
    channels of trade, relevance 12.32, 12.39
    interpretation of Article 7(2) 12.35–12.37
    names of manufacturers, indicating 12.28, 12.38
    parallel imports, challenge to 12.32
    price comparisons, context of 12.34, 12.41
    stricter national standards recommended 12.29–12.31
    test purchases, context of 12.33, 12.40
  Court taking step back in *L'Oréal* judgment 12.78–12.92
  defining 12.18
  delineating 12.07
  designations of origin and competitive relationship 12.54–12.65
    Article 3(a)1(f) 12.59, 12.65
    relevance to a type of product 12.56, 12.60
    scope of Directive (84/450/EEC) 12.58, 12.64
  interplay between trade marks and comparative advertising 12.05–12.25
    delineating comparative advertising 12.07
    misuse of reputation 12.11–12.16
    objective comparisons 12.08–12.10

comparative advertising (*cont.*):
  judgments
    comparison of shopping baskets 12.96–12.99
    contradictions of Article 7(2) of Directive 84/450/EEC 12.35–12.42
    Court taking step back in *L'Oréal* judgment 12.90–12.92
    designations of origin and competitive relationship 12.60–12.65
    interplay between trade marks and comparative advertising 12.17–12.25
    permissive approach of Court, reconfirming 12.45–12.53
    use of similar sign and indispensability challenge 12.73–12.77
  questions 12.86–12.89, 12.91–12.92
  reconfirming permissive approach of Court 12.43–12.53
  reference to a type of product 12.56, 12.60
  relevant public, importance 12.47
  scope of Directive (84/450/EEC) 12.58, 12.64
  significance of benefits 12.50–12.52
    to advertiser 12.52
    to consumer 12.51
  technical function, relevance 12.49
  unfair advantage 12.13–12.15, 12.23–12.24
  use of similar sign and indispensability challenge 12.66–12.77
    indispensability requirement 12.70–12.72
    relationship between Directives 89/104 and 84/450 12.73–12.75
    use of a sign similar to a trade mark 12.76–12.77
compatibility, indicating
  advertiser, activities of 9.341
  concept of 'honest practices in industrial and commercial matters' 9.339–9.340, 9.340–9.350
  context for interpreting Article 6 9.329
  criteria making use necessary 9.342–9.346
  factors for assessing whether use necessary 9.333–9.338
  fundamental criterion for application to Article 6(1)(c) 9.330–9.332
competence of national court
  genuine use requirement 8.43
competition
  Advocate General Opinion
    comparison of *Javico* judgment with *Silhouette* 11.88–11.92
    dominance and intellectual property 11.179–11.182
    function of the sign 11.192–11.204
  Article 36 10.115–10.116
  Article 101, application 11.13–11.97
    interaction with trade mark law 11.13–11.97
    interpretation generally 11.15–11.16
    interpretation of Article 101(1) 11.88–11.91, 11.93–11.96
    interpretation of Article 101(3) 11.92, 11.97
  Article 102, application 11.98–11.214
    interpretation generally 11.15–11.16

  cases of importance
    AstraZeneca 11.138–11.140
    BAT 11.69–11.72
    Bayer Dental 11.76
    Béguelin 11.31–11.32
    Bronner 11.141–11.146, 11.147–11.153
    Campari 11.77–11.84
    Consten & Grundig 11.13–11.25
    Continental Can 11.100–11.105
    Delimitis 11.33–11.48
    Der Grüne Punkt 11.188–11.214
    Groupement de Cartes Bancaires 11.49–11.52
    Hilti 11.127–11.128
    Hugin 11.109–11.111
    importing *Bronner* principles 11.147–11.153
    IMS Health 11.147–11.153
    Javico 11.85–11.97
    Lelos 11.177–11.187
    Magill 11.129–11.137, 11.141–11.146
    Microsoft 11.154–11.167
    Nungesser & EMI 11.53–11.59
    Pronuptia de Paris 11.60–11.68
    Renault 11.125–11.126
    Silhouette 11.85–11.97
    Société Technique Minière 11.26–11.27
    Syfait 11.168–11.176, 11.177–11.187
    United Brands 11.106–11.108
    Völk v Vervaecke 11.28–11.30
    Volvo v Veng 11.119–11.124
  colours 5.208–5.209
  comparative advertising 12.57, 12.61–12.63
  comparison of *Javico* judgment with *Silhouette* 11.85–11.97
  context, relevance 11.31–11.32
  direct applicability 11.12
  and exhaustion of rights, in new regime 10.284
  existence of a right and way right is exercised 11.53–11.59
  franchising agreements 11.60–11.68
    anti-competitive clauses 11.66–11.68
    essential clauses 11.64–11.65
    relevance of specific agreement 11.62–11.63
  function of the sign 11.188–11.214
  goods and services, definition 4.50
  judgments
    comparison of *Javico* judgment with *Silhouette* 11.93–11.97
    dominance and intellectual property 11.183–11.187
    function of the sign 11.205–11.213
  licensing 11.57–11.59
  multiple tasks of European law 11.09–11.11
  object and effect of agreements 11.35, 11.49–11.52
  packaging 5.404
  repackaging
    and parallel imports 10.108–10.109, 10.115–10.116
    repackaging bans, Commission on 11.76
  rights and contract (existence and exercise) 11.55–11.56
  rights of competitors 10.395–10.408
  and risk of confusion 11.71–11.72

Index

rule of reason analysis 11.26–11.27
rules 11.06–11.12
significant effect 11.28–11.30
signs, function of 11.201
and substitution 10.08–10.09
surnames 5.144–5.145
and trade marks
  agreement capable of constituting a threat 11.17
  application of Article 101 11.13–11.97
  application of Article 102 11.98–11.214
  delimitation agreements 11.69–11.75
  dominance 11.98–11.187
  effect of trade mark registration 11.21
  exemption requirements 11.23
  interchangeability criterion 11.100–11.105
  object and effect 11.19
  property, Article 36 and competition provisions 11.22
  quality considerations 11.24–11.25
  relevant product market 11.18, 11.99–11.105
  validity of agreement 11.20
  vertical agreements 11.15–11.16
Treaty provisions 11.06–11.08
unfair 5.865, 5.870–5.871, 5.880–5.883
vertical agreements 11.15–11.16
web of agreements 11.33–11.48
  access clause, relevance 11.41–11.42
  block exemptions 11.43
  definition of relevant market 11.36
  exemptions to rule 11.43
  multifactor tests 11.38–11.40
  national court, role 11.45–11.48
  validity of agreement 11.44

composite trade marks or words
admissibility considerations 5.557
conditions for composite marks 5.561–5.562
defining descriptiveness 5.560
descriptive signs or indications 5.532–5.566
lexical inventions 5.564
perspective for assessing distinctiveness 5.563
procedural paradox 5.539
public interest considerations 5.547–5.548
relative grounds for refusal of registration/ declaration of invalidity 7.314–7.327
scope of appeal 5.540–5.541
suggested way forward 5.555–5.556
unusual juxtaposition 5.564

concepts
versus signs 4.13, 4.36, 4.37

conceptual similarity
global appreciation 7.187
well-known and reputed trade marks 7.597–7.602

conflicts, trade mark *see* **trade mark conflicts**

confusion
see also **relative grounds for refusal of registration/declaration of invalidity; similarity concept**
assessment, relevant time for 7.151–7.152, 7.157–7.160
and association 7.21–7.28, 7.29
and competition law 11.71–11.72
conversion 7.341–7.345
establishing 7.49–7.147
aural similarity 7.72–7.74
challenge to *Lloyd* 7.75–7.88
cumulative similarity/identity conditions 7.55–7.60
global appreciation against a wider context 7.61–7.65
test for comparing the marks 7.66–7.71
geographical indications 12.100–12.116
likelihood of *see* **likelihood of confusion**
in parts of the Community 7.332–7.345
post-sale 7.191–7.192
properly substantial and genuine 7.33–7.36
similarity and distinctiveness 7.20–7.48
  average consumer 7.48
  economic linkages 7.32
  language of provision and principles of Directive 7.26
  positive finding on confusion 7.37–7.44
variation of 14.08

consent concept
and acquiescence 10.386–10.394
assessment 10.307
'clear' consent 10.297–10.313
as Community concept 10.302–10.303
delineating consent 10.304–10.306
developing 10.73
free movement of goods 10.73, 10.86–10.91, 10.291–10.296
and independent rights 10.78
interpretation of concept 10.311
requirement for consent 10.312–10.313
'specific' consent 10.291–10.296

consumers
see also **public interest considerations**
average consumer 5.353, 5.381, 5.791–5.792, 7.48
burden of proof, consumer goods 5.715–5.722
colours 5.223–5.228
comparative advertising, benefits 12.51
of electronic goods, targeting in EU 9.203–9.207
end consumer 8.283–8.302
level of attention of average consumer 5.353, 5.381
protection of 9.56
rights 10.395–10.408
surnames 5.142–5.143
surveys 12.187
trade marks of a deceptive nature 5.855

contributory infringement
and Internet 9.144–9.146

conversion
Community Trade Mark Regulation 2.25
confusion in parts of the Community 7.341–7.345
of a descriptive sign to a mark 6.15

copyright
free movement of goods and new trade mark regime 10.265, 10.272–10.273
and trade marks 4.121

cosmetics
meaning of *Clinique* for 5.866–5.871
and public interest 5.868–5.869
unboxing cosmetic products 9.193–9.194, 9.209–9.210

Index

Council Directive 89/104/EEC to Approximate the Laws of the Member States Relating to Trade Marks (1988) *see* 'Harmonization' Directive (89/104/EEC), as codified (2008/95/EC)
Council Regulation (EC) 40/94 on the Community Trade Mark (1994) *see* Community Trade Mark Regulation (CTMR)
Court of First Instance
  see also General Court (*formerly* Court of First Instance)
  Boards of Appeal 2.46
  confusion, establishing 7.76–7.77
  distinctiveness acquired through use 6.50–6.56, 6.63, 6.68, 6.71, 6.127–6.128
  surname protection 7.201–7.223
  well-known and reputed trade marks 7.550–7.554
Court of Justice of the European Union (CJEU)
  actions against a Community institution for failure to act 3.08
  adjudication on institutional power struggles 3.03
  administrative proceedings, scope 3.61–3.63
  annulment actions by 3.09–3.11
  appeals to 2.45, 2.46, 3.12, 3.69–3.84
    'economic behaviour,' importance 7.514–7.517
    single letters and numerals 5.99–5.106, 5.113–5.121
    slogans, registrability 5.182–5.190
    unfair advantage 7.566–7.574
  application of the law 3.03
  balancing exercises 14.03
  case law prior to 1988 Directive and 1993 Regulation 2.02
  clarification from 3.14, 3.15
  distancing from formal legislative process 3.03
  fine-tuning the principles 7.444–7.451, 14.14
  forms of action
    actions against a Community institution for failure to act 3.08
    actions against Member States in breach of EU law 3.06–3.07
    annulment 3.09–3.11
    appeals 3.12
    references for a preliminary ruling 3.13–3.19
  as a framework institution of the EU 3.02
  as guardian of the Treaties 3.05
  interpretation of the law 3.03
  as interpretive court 14.01
  judicial review and CTMs *see* judicial review
  jurisdiction, exercise of 3.05
  Member States in breach of EU law, action against 3.06–3.07
  multifactor test, favouring of 14.13
  and national courts 3.14–3.17, 4.05
  precedents set by in preliminary ruling process 3.17–3.19
  preliminary ruling, references for 3.13–3.19
  references to 1.02
  Rules of Procedure, adoption 3.03, 3.64, 3.65
  ruling reversed only by Court itself in subsequent cases or by amendment of Treaties 3.04
  as ultimate arbiter for Community trade mark applications 4.06

CTMR *see* Community Trade Mark Regulation (CTMR), 1993
CTMs *see* Community Trade Marks (CTMs)
customs
  seizure by 9.549–9.573
  transit as basis for detention by 9.513.522
Cyprus
  accession to EU (2004) 2.59
Czech Republic
  accession to EU (2004) 2.59

damage to reputation
  see also reputation
  free movement of goods and new trade mark regime 10.308–10.309, 10.350, 10.351–10.352, 10.366–10.368
  and minimum intervention 10.380–10.381
deceptive nature, trade marks of 5.841–5.973
  admissibility considerations 5.843
  advertising messages 5.872–5.877
  assignment of trade marks 5.841–5.858
  commercialization of trade marks 5.844–5.845
  cosmetics 5.866–5.871
  effect on trade and scope of prohibition 5.863, 5.875–5.877
  and free movement of goods 5.859–5.911
  functions of trade marks 5.846
  legislative framework 5.862
  perspective for determining deception 5.847
  procedural considerations 5.583
  proportionality 5.864
  symbol, use of 5.860–5.865
  unfair competition 5.865, 5.870–5.871, 5.880–5.883
delimitation agreements
  Commission on 11.73–11.75
  competition and trade mark law 11.69–11.75
Denmark
  and Community Trade Mark Regulation 2.24
'deposit' systems
  and Community Trade Mark Regulation 2.23
derivative markets
  dominance 11.114
descriptive signs or indications
  adjusting perspective for viewing 5.585–5.586
  autonomy of Community trade mark regime 5.644
  balancing functions with scope of protection 5.599
  burden of proof 5.707–5.722
  challenging of procedural points 5.664–5.698
  COLOR EDITION 5.660
  Community trade marks 5.695–5.698
  composite trade marks or words 5.532–5.566, 5.630–5.632
  Court orders 5.647–5.648, 5.655–5.658
  deconstructing the specification 5.641–5.643
  defining descriptiveness 5.560
  descriptive and lacking in distinctiveness 5.662
  descriptive for a part of the goods 5.663
  ecoDoor 5.663
  free movement of goods 5.699–5.706
  future and potential use matters 5.592
  general principles, setting 5.504–5.531

geographical names 5.504–5.531
German doctrine 5.518–5.519, 5.523
keeping free for others to use 5.587–5.588
KOMPRESSOR PLUS 5.661
limiting scope of reference 5.597–5.598
link between product and geographical indication 5.531
meaning of 'exclusively' 5.572
more than mere sum and its parts neologism 5.609–5.611
multifactor test 5.573–5.574
multiplicity of meanings 5.573–5.574
nuanced approach in *Doublemint* 5.567–5.594
overriding effect of national rules 5.691–5.693
parallel approach 5.595–5.632
peculiarity of Benelux 5.608, 5.615
Photos.com 5.662
practices of national offices and registrability 5.602
public interest considerations 5.524, 5.547–5.548
recent case law 5.659–5.663
registrability in other Member States 5.616
registration process 5.613–5.614
restating the principles 5.591
restrictions in other jurisdictions 5.589
right to request invalidation 5.660
roadmap for assessing registrability 5.600–5.601
same reasoning for all types of sign 5.604
specifications and disclaimers 5.617–5.619, 5.641–5.643
thorough examination procedures 5.620
time considerations 5.694

detriment, likelihood of
and appeals to Court of Justice 3.71

device marks, absence of distinctiveness
BEST BUY 5.501–5.503
General Court 5.497
judgments 5.498–5.500
Louis Vuitton's lock device mark 5.496–5.500
OHIM decisions 5.496

devoid of any distinctive character 5.16–5.503
absence of justification 5.402–5.404
actual distinctive character 5.354–5.356
alternatives, relevance 5.315–5.320
appeals 5.82–5.83, 5.441–5.443
appraisal of facts and new pleas 5.32–5.33
assessment of distinctive character 5.44–5.46, 5.362–5.370
availability, need to preserve 5.357–5.360
average consumer's level of attention 5.353, 5.381
biometrical identification 5.65
burden of proof 5.76
versus capable of distinguishing 4.157
chocolate in animal shapes 5.492–5.495
colours, distinctiveness 5.200–5.228
combinations of colours 5.229–5.237
considering mark as a whole 5.384–5.386
context for determining distinctiveness 5.393–5.396, 5.406–5.413
criteria concerning use of a trade mark 5.387
critical time for assessing distinctive character 5.346–5.349
date for assessing distinctive character 5.382

definition of goods and services 4.09, 4.10, 4.29, 4.157
descriptive and lacking in distinctiveness 5.662
descriptiveness, assessing first 5.26
device marks 5.496–5.503
distinctive character and perceptible differences 5.22
distinctiveness of abbreviations 5.84–5.94
effect of registrations in other Member States 5.313–5.314
frosted bottle cases 4.484–4.491
functionality of colours 5.238–5.247
grounds of appeal 5.27–5.30
inadmissibility 5.32–5.33
interests of competitors 5.404
monopolization argument 5.417–5.426
non-discrimination principle 5.50–5.51
overall impression 5.74–5.75, 5.268–5.269, 5.436–5.440
packaging 5.301–5.314, 5.305–5.308, 5.389–5.426, 5.460–5.483
permissive perspective 5.40–5.43
perspective for determining registrability 5.23–5.24
practice of Office as 'precedent' 5.31
registration of comparable marks 5.73, 5.77
responsibility of sign 5.79–5.81
shapes 5.248–5.314, 5.414–5.416, 5.427–5.459
significance of similar products 5.351–5.352
single letters and numerals 5.95–5.128
slogans 5.146–5.199
statutory interpretation 5.34–5.36
surnames, no special conditions for 5.129–5.145
test for assessing distinctive character 5.309–5.312
three-dimensional trade marks, level of distinctiveness required 5.399–5.401
washing tables cases 5.321–5.388

dilution
assessment of detriment 7.495–7.498
blurring 7.476–7.480, 7.482–7.484
existence of a link 7.488–7.494
free riding 7.474–7.475, 9.257–9.259
and infringement 7.467–7.473
Internet and trade marks 9.254–9.256
relative grounds for refusal 7.458–7.507
repercussions 7.499–7.507
standard and burden of proof 7.486–7.487
tarnishment 7.481, 9.254, 9.259

Directive, Trade Mark *see* **'Harmonization' Directive (89/104/EEC), as codified (2008/95/EC)**

discrimination
non-discrimination principle 5.50–5.51
origin, based on 10.22–10.24
product characteristics, based on 10.30–10.32

distinctiveness
abbreviations 5.84–5.94
actual distinctive character 5.354–5.356
arbitrary addition and technical result 4.161
assessment of distinctive character 5.309–5.312, 5.362–5.370, 5.382
versus attractiveness 5.808–5.818

distinctiveness (*cont.*):
  capable of distinguishing 4.02, 4.21–4.23,
    4.41–4.42, 4.156–4.175, 4.172–4.175
    versus devoid of distinctive character 4.157
    principles, setting 4.156–4.171
  colours 5.200–5.228
    acquired through use 6.87
    competition considerations 5.208–5.209
    distinctive character of colour per se 5.222
    public perception, importance 5.223–5.228
  confusion, similarity and distinctiveness 7.20–7.48,
    7.45–7.47
  context for determining 5.393–5.396,
    5.406–5.413
  continuum of distinctiveness 4.167–4.169
  date for assessing distinctive character 5.382
  Directive provisions, limited effect 4.172–4.175
  distinctive character acquired after date
    of application for registration/date of
    registration 4.09
  distinctive character and perceptible
    differences 5.22
  enhanced distinctiveness, role in likelihood of
    confusion 7.126–7.128
  essential function of a trade mark 4.163
  functionality 4.42, 4.43–4.44, 4.46
  inherent versus acquired 6.40, 6.49
  Internet and trade marks 9.254–9.256
  as key to obtaining trade mark protection 4.02
  level for three-dimensional trade
    marks 5.399–5.401
  linking with concept of sign 4.21–4.23, 4.41–4.42
  loss of distinctive character 7.154–7.156
  no distinction between different categories of trade
    marks 4.164–4.166
  potentiality and actuality 4.160
  presumption of 7.100–7.113
  and reputation 9.25
  sign or mark devoid of any distinctive character *see*
    devoid of any distinctive character
  specific, misappraisal of 5.253–5.260
    facts relating to distinctiveness 5.261–5.264
    as result of applying excessively stringent
      criteria 5.255–5.258
    as result of taking view that the shapes were
      usual 5.259–5.260
    sign as a whole 5.253–5.254
  surnames, distinctive character 5.135–5.137
  universally applicable concept of distinctive
    character 6.39
  use, acquired through *see* **distinctiveness acquired
    through use**
  word marks 7.134–7.140
distinctiveness acquired through use
  see also **distinctiveness**
  acquired distinctive character in the
    Benelux 6.90–6.120
    general criteria for applying distinctiveness/
      descriptiveness 6.97–6.104
    language considerations 6.115
    territorial scope of assessment 6.105–6.115
    Uniform Benelux Law 6.113

Advocate General Opinion
  acquired distinctive character in the
    Benelux 6.96–6.115
  assessment test 6.07–6.12
  combined use 6.39–6.48
  sales figures 6.57–6.62
  use as a mark 6.27
assessment test 6.04–6.24, 6.30
  evidence and overall assessment 6.11, 6.18–6.24
  meaning of 'distinctiveness acquired through
    use' 6.13–6.17
  multifactor 6.18, 6.19–6.24
balancing exercises, reliance on 6.65
case details/order of reference
  evidence of acquired
    distinctiveness 6.144–6.146
  relevant point in time for determining
    distinctiveness 6.124–6.126
cases of importance
  Erpo Möbelwerk 6.39
  Europolis 6.90
  Kit Kat/Nestlé 6.36–6.49, 6.66
  Lindt & Sprüngli 6.139–6.143
  Oberbank & Banco Santander 6.144–6.162
  Philips 6.25–6.35, 6.66, 6.78
  Storck I 6.50–6.72
  Storck II 6.73–6.89
  Windsurfing Chiemsee 6.04–6.24, 6.30, 6.78,
    6.79, 6.102, 6.118, 6.148
combined use 6.36–6.49
competition elements 6.22
concept of use 6.44
conclusions 6.156–6.162
conversion of a descriptive sign to a mark 6.15
electronic goods/telecommunications
  services 6.125
equal treatment of marks 6.17
evidence of acquired distinctiveness 6.139–6.143
  burden of proof 6.153–6.155, 6.159–6.162
  differentiation of degree of distinctiveness 6.148
  evidence in general 6.148, 6.149
  expert opinion 6.11
  geographical extent 6.142
  opinion surveys 6.03, 6.23, 6.146, 6.148, 6.149,
    6.151, 6.156–6.157
  type of evidence required 6.11
geographical extent 6.80–6.82, 6.86–6.89, 6.142
geographical indications 6.14
geographical name 6.20
'identify' versus 'distinguish' 6.100
inherent versus acquired distinctiveness 6.40, 6.49
issues to be resolved 6.02, 6.03
judgments
  acquired distinctive character in the
    Benelux 6.116–6.120
  assessment test 6.13–6.24
  combined use 6.49
  Court of First Instance 6.50–6.56, 6.63, 6.68,
    6.71, 6.127–6.128
  evidence of acquired distinctiveness 6.147–6.155
  sales figures 6.50–6.56, 6.63–6.72
  use as a mark 6.28–6.35

Index

link with a particular undertaking, establishing 6.11
manner of proving distinctiveness 6.02
meaning of 'distinctiveness acquired through use' 6.13–6.17
multifactor test 6.18, 6.19–6.24
multiple and sole users 6.35
'need to leave free' doctrine 6.07, 6.13
non-verbal marks 6.87
packaging 6.54, 6.56
percentages measures 6.10, 6.23
picture of product 6.68
procedural issues 6.03
public interest considerations 6.100
relevant class of persons identifying maker of the product 6.15, 6.16, 6.101
relevant point in time for determining distinctiveness 6.59–6.62, 6.69–6.72, 6.121–6.138
   case backgrounds 6.124–6.126
   evidence of acquired distinctiveness 6.152–6.155, 6.158
   judgments 6.127–6.138
   'legitimate expectations' 6.129
   'logic of the system' 6.129
   point of sale 6.61
   post-sale 6.62
relevant public 6.09, 6.10
sales figures
   and advertising expenditure 6.50–6.72
   evidence of use 6.76–6.79
   geographical extent 6.80–6.82, 6.86–6.89
   market share 6.84–6.85
   picture of product 6.68
   relevant point in time for determining distinctiveness 6.59–6.62, 6.69–6.72
   and territorial scope of distinctiveness acquired through use 6.73–6.89
   three-dimensional signs 6.57–6.58, 6.64–6.67
shapes 6.26, 6.27, 6.32, 6.55
statutory provisions of Directive and Regulation 4.02, 6.01–6.03
substantive issues 6.03
territorial scope 6.03
three-dimensional signs 6.57–6.58, 6.64–6.67
'trade circles' 6.06
use as a mark 6.25–6.35
   monopolization argument 6.29, 6.35
   public addressed by the mark 6.32
   specific and reliable data requirement 6.31
   as a trade mark 6.33
word marks 6.95, 6.97, 6.98, 6.99
domain names and trade marks 12.153–12.160
bad faith 12.155, 12.157–12.159
   generic terms and bad faith 12.157–12.160
   Internetportal 12.153–12.160
multifactor test 12.159
dominance
see also **competition**
banana market 11.106–11.108
competition 11.98–11.114
crossing market boundaries 11.112–11.113

derivative markets 11.114
and exclusivity 11.115–11.118
and intellectual property 11.115–11.187
   abusive conduct, factors establishing 11.136–11.137
   anti-competitive exploitation of a patent 11.127–11.128
   applicable standard 11.158–11.159
   exclusivity 11.115–11.118, 11.129–11.137
   exporting *Magill* principles 11.141–11.146
   importing *Bronner* principles 11.147–11.153
   indispensability requirement 11.157
   interoperability 11.154–11.167
   lenient approach 11.125–11.126
   media player bundling 11.164–11.167
   monopolization 11.134–11.135
   prolonging patent rights 11.138–11.140
   refusal to license an IP right 11.160–11.163
   refusal to supply 11.168–11.176
   reversing the order 11.121–11.124
   relevant market 11.99–11.105
   repackaging and parallel imports 10.108–10.109
   spare parts 11.109–11.111
due cause concept 7.584–7.596
balancing exercise 7.591–7.593
conditions for establishing due course 7.594–7.596
durability requirement
graphical representation 4.38, 4.39, 4.101

ECJ (European Court of Justice) *see* **Court of Justice of the European Union (CJEU)**
'economic behaviour,' importance
relative grounds for refusal 7.508–7.524
electronic goods
see also **Internet and trade marks; keywords, use by advertisers**
distinctiveness acquired through use 6.125
electronic market platforms
see also **Internet and trade marks; keywords, use by advertisers**
advertising on online marketplace and products offered for sale 9.211–9.213
consumers in EU, targeting 9.203–9.207
cross-territorial reach of Internet 9.197
display of trade marks on online marketplace 9.214
and keywords 9.186–9.221
measures against online operators 9.218–9.221
operator liability 9.215–9.217
paid Internet referencing service 9.195–9.196
private and business sellers 9.202
products offered for sale and advertising on online marketplace 9.211–9.213
service provider liability 9.198–9.200
testers and dramming products 9.192, 9.208
unboxing cosmetic products 9.193–9.194, 9.209–9.210
emblems
trade mark including 4.09
enforcement proceedings 2.47–2.58
see also **infringement; trade mark conflicts**
adequacy of 'national' measures 9.446–9.449
border measures 9.421–9.436, 9.485–9.493

enforcement proceedings (*cont.*):
  Brussels Convention (1968) 2.50
  civil 2.47, 2.48, 9.414–9.484
  Community Trade Mark Regulation
    (CTMR) 2.49, 2.50, 9.414–9.486
  Community Trade Marks (CTMs) 2.47–2.58,
    9.409–9.495
  criminal 2.47
  and infringement 2.47, 9.474–9.484
  injunctive relief 9.437–9.454
  law applicable to sanctions for
    infringements 9.474–9.484
  national borders, effect 9.421–9.436
  'special reasons' and national
    provisions 9.444–9.445
  'special reasons' condition 9.440–9.443
  territorial scope of prohibition 9.455–9.473
  validity of CTMs 2.48, 2.49
enlargement of European Union 2.05, 2.59–2.61
  accession of Member States
    Austria (1995) 2.59
    Bulgaria (2006) 2.59
    Cyprus (2004) 2.59
    Czech Republic (2004) 2.59
    Estonia (2004) 2.59
    Finland (1995) 2.59
    Greece (1981) 2.05
    Hungary (2004) 2.59
    Latvia (2004) 2.59
    Lithuania (2004) 2.59
    Malta (2004) 2.59
    Poland (2004) 2.59
    Portugal (1986) 2.05
    Romania (2006) 2.59
    Slovakia (2004) 2.59
    Slovenia (2004) 2.59
    Spain (1986) 2.05
    Sweden (1995) 2.59
  and Directive 2.60
equal treatment principle
  trade mark conflicts 3.107
equality proviso
  parallel imports 10.36–10.37
Estonia
  accession to EU (2004) 2.59
European Central Bank (ECB)
  seat of Office (Germany) 2.05
European Commission
  application of Article 101(3) by 11.77–11.84
  on delimitation agreements 11.73–11.75
  Memorandum on an EEC Trade Mark
    (1976) 2.03, 2.04
  preliminary procedure performed by 3.06
  proceedings against Member State 3.07
  on repackaging bans 11.76
  trade mark reform 13.07–13.14
European Court of Human Rights (ECtHR)
  see also Budweiser judgments
  analysis 12.240–12.246
  dissenting opinions 12.245–12.246
  on geographical indications, trade marks and
    property rights 12.230–12.246

rights arising from an application for a trade mark
    registration 12.241–12.242
  trade mark applications and concept of
    'possessions' 12.243–12.244
European Court of Justice (ECJ) *see* **Court of Justice
    of the European Union (CJEU)**
European Economic Area (EEA)
  goods put on market in 10.314–10.317
European Medicines Agency
  seat of Office (United Kingdom) 2.05
European Patent Convention (EPC)
  and judicial review 3.24
European Patent Office (EPO)
  languages 2.05
European Union (EU)
  see also **European Central Bank (ECB);
    Member States**
  confusion in parts of the Community 7.332–7.345
  as contracting party of Protocol to Madrid
    Agreement 2.18
  enlargement 2.05, 2.59–2.61
  territory, unitary trade mark right effective
    throughout 2.20
  trade mark law *see* **trade mark law (EU)**
evidence
  see also **burden of proof**
  of acquired distinctiveness 6.139–6.143
    burden of proof 6.153–6.155, 6.159–6.162
    differentiation of degree of
      distinctiveness 6.148
    evidence in general 6.148, 6.149
    expert opinion 6.11
    geographical extent 6.142
    opinion surveys 6.03, 6.23, 6.146, 6.148, 6.149,
      6.151, 6.156–6.157
  of distinctive character 5.274–5.277
    meaning 5.278–5.279
  in general 6.148, 6.149
  likelihood of confusion 14.07
  new, rejection of 7.227–7.228
  new/additional evidence submitted in first instance
    units before that instance outside of properly
    set time limits 3.41, 3.43, 3.44, 3.46, 3.47,
    3.48, 3.50
  of use
    and burden of proof 8.58–8.71
    sales figures 6.76–6.79
ex officio **examination, relinquishing**
  and Community Trade Mark Regulation 2.24
exclusivity
  and dominance 11.115–11.118
exhaustion of rights
  and advertising 10.257
  and Community Trade Mark Regulation 10.285
  and competition policy 10.284
  conferred by a trade mark, in new
    regime 10.146–10.147
  and Directive 10.136
  Internet and trade marks 9.180–9.185
  limitations to rights 9.281–9.282
  new trade mark regime 10.136, 10.137–10.138,
    10.146–10.147

principle of EU-wide exhaustion of national IP
  rights 2.02
and repackaging 10.137–10.138
territorial scope 10.274–10.290
trade mark reform exceptions 13.32

failure to act
actions against a Community institution by CJEU
  for 3.08
families of marks
global appreciation 7.328–7.331
financial penalties
Member States 3.07
Finland
accession to EU (1995) 2.59
First Council Directive 89/104/EEC to Approximate the Laws of the Member States Relating to Trade Marks (1988) *see* **'Harmonization' Directive (89/104/EEC), as codified (2008/95/EC)**
franchising agreements 11.60–11.68
anti-competitive clauses 11.66–11.68
essential clauses 11.64–11.65
relevance of specific agreement 11.62–11.63
free movement of goods
see also **goods and services; products**
and Article 3(1)(c) 5.699–5.706
bilateral agreements and geographical
  indications 12.162–12.174
broadening scope of principle 10.19
consent concept 10.73, 10.86–10.91, 10.291–10.296
and deceptive use 5.859–5.911
  cosmetics 5.866–5.871
  effect on trade and scope of prohibition 5.863,
    5.875–5.877
  legislative framework 5.862
  proportionality 5.864
  unfair competition 5.865, 5.870–5.871,
    5.880–5.883
and exercise of trade mark rights 7.98–7.99
and intellectual property
  existence–exercise dichotomy 10.61–10.64
  independent rights 10.67–10.70
  specific subject-matter of the right 10.65–10.66
and new trade mark regime
  absence of prior notice, consequences 10.371
  admissibility considerations 10.266
  adverse effect on the original condition of the
    product 10.184–10.186
  application of Articles 34 and 36 10.272–10.273
  applying the principles 10.159–10.167
  Article 7 10.117–10.408
  Article 7(1) 10.276–10.280
  artificial partitioning of the markets between
    Member States 10.179–10.183
  burden of proof 10.148–10.149, 10.209, 10.356
  case law 10.176–10.178
  clear identification of importer and
    manufacturer 10.359
  commercial policy considerations 10.282–10.283
  'competence' of Directive 10.281
  conditions of *Bristol Myers Squibbs* and
    overstickered products 10.342–10.345

consent and acquiescence 10.386–10.394
consumer rights, competitor rights and
  markets 10.395–10.408
copyright considerations 10.265, 10.272–10.273
damage to reputation 10.308–10.309, 10.350,
  10.351–10.352, 10.366–10.368
Danish cases 10.118–10.124
derogation from Article 5(1) 10.279–10.280
and Directive 10.117–10.197, 10.276–10.280, 10.286
disclosure 10.378–10.385
effect of Directive in national legal order 10.286
effect of giving notice 10.353–10.355
exceptions to general principle 10.258–10.259,
  10.268–10.271
exhaustion of rights 10.136, 10.137–10.138,
  10.146–10.147, 10.257, 10.267, 10.284, 10.285
factors for assessing risk of significant
  damage 10.263–10.264
fundamental interests protected by trade mark
  rights 10.139–10.140
general propositions 10.160–10.162, 10.164
German cases 10.125–10.132
goods put on the market in the
  EEA 10.314–10.317
identifying the issues 10.150–10.158
inappropriate presentation and
  reputation 10.191–10.192
interpretation of Article 7(1) 10.171–10.172
interpretation of Article 7(2) 10.173–10.186
legal contexts 10.338–10.339
main criteria for application of Article 36 10.141
manufacturer, indication of 10.190
necessity factors 10.203–10.206,
  10.346–10.349, 10.357
no adverse effect on condition of product 10.358
notice 10.361
notification duty 10.382
offering testers and putting goods on the
  market 10.328–10.333
partitioning the market 10.142–10.144,
  10.179–10.183, 10.241–10.247
presentation not damaging to reputation
  presentation 10.360
prior notice 10.145, 10.370, 10.371
procedural peculiarity 10.256
rebranding and necessity 10.204–10.205
reformulating *Bristol Myers Squibbs* 10.340
rejecting intention requirement 10.201–10.202
remaining requirements 10.187–10.193
repackaging 10.133–10.135, 10.137–10.138,
  10.145, 10.188–10.189, 10.212–10.228,
  10.334–10.371
replacing the trade mark and necessity
  requirement 10.198–10.213
reputation and functions of trade
  marks 10.260–10.264
role of Court 10.337
six questions of 'essence' 10.341–10.361
specific consent 10.291–10.296
specific rulings 10.163, 10.165–10.167
trade mark infringement and policing channels
  of trade 10.229–10.251

free movement of goods (*cont.*):
  and parallel imports 10.19, 10.54
  rationale 10.54
  and trade mark law
    changing direction 10.83–10.85
    competition and Article 36 10.115–10.116
    compulsory licence 10.81–10.82
    consent and independent rights 10.78
    consent concept 10.73, 10.86–10.91
    essential function and specific subject matter of trade marks 10.71–10.72
    lack of protection 10.79–10.80
    restrictive approach 10.74–10.77
    role and function of trade marks 10.86–10.91
    voluntary assignment 10.92–10.97
free riding
  dilution 7.474–7.475, 9.257–9.259
functionality
  aesthetic 5.835
  broad concept 14.04
  colours 5.238–5.247
  company names 9.384
  graphical representation 4.137–4.140
  logos 11.198–11.200
  shapes 4.03, 5.759–5.840
  signs 4.42, 4.43–4.44, 4.46, 4.51, 4.52
    competition issues 11.201, 11.212–11.213
    and dominance 11.188–11.214
    exclusivity 11.209–11.211
    logos 11.198–11.200
    proportionality 11.214
    'reasonable time' claim 11.202–11.204
    trade mark agreement 11.194–11.197
  trade marks
    deceptive use 5.846
    essential function of a trade mark 4.163, 9.53, 10.71–10.72, 10.86–10.91
    free movement of goods and trade mark law 10.71–10.72
    indications of origin 2.08, 9.53
    Internet environment 9.159
    keywords, effect 9.156
    monopolization argument 4.49

General Agreement on Tariffs and Trade (GATT)
  trade mark law 2.06
General Court (*formerly* **Court of First Instance**)
  decisions reviewed by 2.45, 3.12
  device marks, absence of distinctiveness 5.497
  permissive approach of 7.511–7.513
  powers to annul/alter decisions by Board of Appeal of OHIM 3.56–3.57
  Rules of Procedure 3.03, 3.64
  setting aside of judgment of 3.12
  slogans, registrability 5.180–5.181
genericity considerations/generic terms
  co-existence between trade marks and geographical indication protection 12.114–12.116, 12.126–12.129
  concept of genericity 12.134–12.137
  generic terms as earlier rights 12.160

use of trade marks 8.259–8.302
  cases 8.260–8.302
  differences of perception 8.260–8.282
  relevant public 8.260–8.282
genuine use requirement 8.14–8.125
see also **use of trade marks**
  advertising 8.106–8.108
  Advocate General Opinion 8.19–8.33, 8.83–8.88, 8.100–8.108
  and appeals to Court of Justice 3.71
  case details/order of reference
    evidence of use and burden of proof 8.58–8.61
    promotional items 8.97–8.99
    quantity not relevant 8.44–8.46
  competence of national court 8.43
  complementary services offered free of charge 8.115–8.125
  concept 8.34–8.40
  criteria and types of use 8.49–8.55
  directly related goods and services 8.42
  evidence of use and burden of proof 8.58–8.71
  'genuine' requirement 8.25–8.33
  guarantee of origin 8.100–8.102
  integral parts 8.41
  interpretation of use 8.22–8.24
  judgments 8.34–8.43, 8.66–8.71, 8.89–8.93, 8.109–8.114
    of Court of First Instance 8.62–8.65
  legislative framework 8.19–8.21
  minimal use 8.72–8.74
  principles 8.14–8.43
  promotional items 8.96–8.114
  quantity not relevant 8.44–8.57
  reasoned order of Court 8.47–8.57
  reference market, use of mark in 8.103–8.105
  uniform interpretation 8.34
  use after filing application for revocation 8.56–8.57
  use with or without profit 8.75–8.125
    non-profitable activities 8.76–8.95
    respective arguments 8.81–8.82
geographical indications
see also **origin**
  as absolute ground for refusal 12.138–12.152
    scope of prohibition 12.143–12.148
    temporal application of Regulation 110/220 12.140–12.142
    and Trade Marks Directive 12.149
  Advocate General Opinion
    co-existence between trade marks and geographical indication protection 12.118–12.122
    consumer confusion and a misappropriation rationale 12.106–12.111
  bilateral agreements and free movement of goods 12.162–12.174
  cases of importance
    Bavaria 12.117–12.133
    Budweiser 12.162–12.174
    Cognac II 12.138–12.152
    Feta 12.100–12.116
    Grana Padano 12.134–12.137

Index

co-existence between trade marks and geographical indication protection 12.117–12.133
consumer confusion and a misappropriation rationale 12.100–12.116
distinctiveness acquired through use 6.14
genericity considerations
    co-existence between trade marks and geographical indication protection 12.114–12.116, 12.126–12.129
    concept of genericity 12.134–12.137
geography and product characteristics 12.113
judgments
    co-existence between trade marks and geographical indication protection 12.123–12.133
    consumer confusion and a misappropriation rationale 12.112–12.116
    geographical indications as absolute ground for refusal 12.138–12.152
products, association with 5.531, 12.178–12.179
protected geographical indication (PGI)
    effect of registration on pre-existing trade marks 12.121–12.122
    reputation, trade marks and PGIs 12.130–12.133
    validity of registration 12.118–12.120
protection framework 12.101–12.103
    history of *Feta's* protection 12.104–12.105
'simple and indirect' vs. 'qualified' 12.177
social aspects of agriculture 12.124–12.125
validity of protected geographical indication (PGI) registration 12.118–12.120
wines or spirits 4.10

Germany
and Community Trade Mark Regulation 2.23
descriptive signs or indications 5.518–5.519, 5.523
Patent and Trade Mark Office (GPTO) 5.85, 5.86

get-up imitation
composite marks 7.314–7.327
unfair advantage 7.545–7.547

global appreciation 7.179–7.348
see also **confusion; relative grounds for refusal of registration/declaration of invalidity**
aural similarity 7.72–7.74
challenge to *Lloyd* 7.75–7.88
comparison of goods or services 7.141–7.147
composite marks 7.297–7.327
conceptual similarity 7.187
cumulative similarity/identity conditions 7.55–7.60
delimiting the dispute 7.57, 7.59
dominant elements 7.95–7.97, 7.239–7.249
enhanced distinctiveness, role in likelihood of confusion 7.126–7.128
establishing confusion 7.49–7.147
exercise of trade mark rights and free movement of goods 7.98–7.99
foreign equivalents 7.129–7.133
likelihood of confusion test 7.58, 7.60, 7.126–7.128
multifactor assessment, distinctiveness as part of 7.114–7.125
pharmaceuticals/role of professionals 7.284–7.296
presumption of distinctiveness 7.100–7.113

similarity between a figurative and a word mark 7.89–7.99
surname protection 7.198–7.238
tests 7.49, 7.50–7.54
against a wider context 7.61–7.65

global assessment test
identity, establishing 7.13

goods and services
see also **free movement of goods; retail services**
Advocate General Opinion
    capable of distinguishing 4.158–4.161
    definition of for which mark registered 4.178–4.184, 4.201–4.217
    graphical representation 4.84–4.94, 4.112–4.121, 4.120, 4.133–4.143, 4.151–4.154
    signs 4.31–4.52
cases of importance
    Apple Store 4.63–4.75
    Dyson 4.11–4.62
    Heidelberger Bauchemie 4.39, 4.148–4.155
    IP Translator 4.190–4.244
    Libertel 4.17–4.19, 4.131– 4.155, 4.151, 4.155
    Nichols 4.24
    Philips 4.21–4.23, 4.156–4.171
    Postkantoor 4.20, 4.21, 4.172
    Praktiker 4.176–4.189
    Shield Mark 4.106–4.130, 4.151
    Sieckmann 4.13, 4.16, 4.77–4.105, 4.106, 4.116, 4.124, 4.151, 4.206
colours *see* **colours**
comparison 7.141–7.147
complementary services 8.115–8.125
custom-free zones and original goods 9.521–9.537
definition of for which mark registered 4.176–4.264
    Advocate General Opinion 4.178–4.184
    case law, factual setting/questions referred 4.177
    judgment 4.185–4.189
    OHIM President, Communication No 4/03 4.192–4.197, 4.211
    registration of service marks for retail services 4.176–4.189
    specification, clarity and precision requirements 4.190–4.244
    verbal description 4.207
design of retail store connected with products on sale 4.63–4.75
distinctiveness requirement *see* **distinctiveness requirement**
establishment where services carried out 4.63–4.65
extending concept of 'service' to retailing of applicant's own goods 4.75
genuine use requirement 8.42
goods destined to be exported 9.267
goods out of production 8.208–8.215
goods put on the market in the EEA 10.314–10.317
graphical representation *see* **graphical representation**
grounds for refusal, revocation or invalidity relating to only some of 8.09
historical perspective 4.04, 4.05

goods and services (*cont.*):
  identical, effect on rights of trade mark proprietor 'requirement' 9.30–9.121
  judgments
    capable of distinguishing 4.167–4.171
    definition of for which mark registered 4.185–4.189, 4.218–4.232
    graphical representation 4.95–4.105, 4.122–4.130, 4.144–4.147, 4.155
    signs 4.53–4.62, 4.66–4.75
  keyword use 9.154–9.155
  limitations to rights
    principles 9.272–9.307
    role of Court 9.279
    use of mark in relation to goods 9.280–9.283
    use of mark in relation to services 9.284–9.290
  nature of goods themselves 5.823–5.826
    expansive approach 5.831–5.834
  Nice Agreement and Classification 4.70, 4.191, 4.192, 4.203, 4.209, 4.210
    Class 9 4.28, 4.204
    Class 35 4.63
    Class 41 4.75, 4.199
  original
    and competing 9.173
    and custom-free zones 9.521–9.537
    and toys 9.78, 9.359–9.360
  packaging and establishment of services 4.65, 4.67, 4.74
  quality considerations 9.283
  second-hand goods 9.180, 9.182, 9.183, 9.299–9.302
  sensory perception requirement 4.13, 4.16, 4.36
  signs *see* **signs**
  statutory provisions of Directive and Regulation 4.08–4.10
  use of marks for goods/services for which registered 8.207–8.215
goodwill 9.232, 14.09
graphical representation
  see also **goods and services; signs; sounds**
  accessibility 4.38, 4.100
  capable of being represented graphically 4.76–4.155
  clarity and precision requirements 4.38, 4.99, 4.105, 4.115
  colours 4.141–4.143, 4.145–4.147
  conditions for fulfilling requirement 4.77, 4.90, 4.98–4.102
  Directive, context of 4.95–4.96
  durability 4.38, 4.39, 4.101
  function 4.137–4.140
  historical ability to obtain registration 4.04
  intelligibility 4.38, 4.100
  legal certainty 4.40, 4.89
  limitation of scope of reference 4.113, 4.122
  linking with concept of sign 4.21–4.23
  non-visual signs 4.76, 4.77
  objectivity 4.38, 4.102
  public policy considerations 4.131–4.155
  scents 4.77, 4.79, 4.88, 4.91–4.94, 4.103–4.105
  self-containment 4.38, 4.100
  and shape 4.13
  signs, requirements for 4.38–4.40
  of sounds 4.116–4.119
  trade marks as communicators 4.85
  unequivocality 4.102
  viewpoint of individual sensing the sign 4.86–4.87
  visual signs 4.76, 4.88
  wider policy considerations 4.120
Greece
  accession to EU (1981) 2.05
  and Community Trade Mark Regulation 2.23
guarantee of origin
  use as 8.100–8.102

'Harmonization' Directive (89/104/EEC), as codified (2008/95/EC) 2.07–2.13
  see also **absolute grounds for refusal of registration/declaration of invalidity; relative grounds for refusal of registration/declaration of invalidity**
  adoption (1988) 2.05
  aim 2.07
  Article 6 defences 9.175–9.176
  Article 7(1) 10.276–10.280
    questions 10.311
    scope, derogation from Article 5(1) 10.279–10.280
    territorial scope 10.287–10.289
    wording and legislative history 10.277–10.278
  'competence' 10.281
  confusion, similarity and distinctiveness 7.26
  and Court of Justice jurisprudence 3.113, 3.114
  definition of a trade mark 4.08
  design of retail store connected with products on sale 4.63, 4.65, 4.67, 4.68, 4.69, 4.71, 4.72, 4.74
  distinctiveness acquired through use 6.01–6.03
  effect in national legal order 10.286, 10.290
  and enlargement of EU 2.60
  and exhaustion of rights 10.136
  free movement of goods and new trade mark regime 10.117–10.197, 10.236, 10.276–10.280
  functions of trade marks 4.163
  general scope 2.12
  goods and services
    capable of distinguishing 4.172–4.175
    definition of for which mark registered 4.176, 4.177, 4.181, 4.201, 4.208, 4.210, 4.215
    general provisions 4.08–4.10
    graphical representation 4.82, 4.95–4.96, 4.97
  grace period 8.218
  graphical representation 4.82
    colours 4.132
    context of Article 2 4.95–4.96
    non-visual signs 4.97
    sounds 4.111
  grounds for which an application may be refused/registration declared invalid 4.09
  identical signs and goods or services, effect on rights of trade mark proprietor 'requirement' 9.34–9.36
  interaction with Regulation 2.62, 3.114
  interpretation of provisions in context 3.113

justification of non-use 8.234
and keywords 9.150–9.164
limitations of effects of a trade mark 9.03
limitations to rights 9.275–9.278, 9.291
list of examples (Article 2) 4.24
    interpretation 4.61, 4.65, 4.72
    non-exhaustive character of 4.25
    open-ended 4.02
    'sign' requirement 4.56, 4.57
mandatory provisions 2.10
matters left to discretion of Member States 2.13
national law provisions established by 2.09
open-ended nature of 4.02, 4.04
optional provisions 2.11
Recitals 2.08
reforms 13.43–13.44
relative grounds for refusal 7.06
requirement of use 8.06–8.10
rights conferred by a trade mark 9.02
signs
    functionality requirement 4.43–4.44
    lack of definition 4.02
    shapes 4.45–4.48
and TRIPS Agreement 4.48
wording and legislative history
    of Article 7(1) 10.277–10.278

honest practices in industrial and commercial matters
compatibility, indicating 9.339–9.340, 9.347–9.350

Hungary
accession to EU (2004) 2.59

Implementing Regulation (Commission Regulation (EC) No. 2868/95 of 13 December 1995 implementing Council Regulation (EC) No. 40/94 on the Community trade mark)
see also **Community Trade Mark Regulation (CTMR)**
definition of for which mark registered 4.203, 4.204, 4.213
intervention by legislature 3.25
opposition proceedings 3.43
Rules 3.42
time limits 3.24

importing
see also **parallel imports; transit**
of counterfeit products through the mail 9.574–9.585

infringement
see also **trade mark conflicts**
clash between 'third party' concept and registered trade marks 9.08–9.19
contributory 9.144–9.146
criteria for establishing 9.268
dilution, proof of 7.467–7.473
and enforcement proceedings 2.47, 9.474–9.484
and policing channels of trade 10.229–10.251
    Article 34, applicability 10.237
    essential principle of Court jurisprudence 10.238
    general principles 10.233
    legislative content of Directive 10.236
    partitioning the market 10.241–10.247
    pharmaceuticals and whisky 10.239
    repackaging 10.234–10.235
    reputation considerations 10.240
seizure of infringing goods 9.485–9.486
transit as 9.508–9.514, 9.536–9.548
and use by search engine 9.131–9.132

injunctions
enforcement proceedings 9.437–9.454
whether local reputation sufficient for obtaining 7.383–7.387

integral parts
genuine use requirement 8.41

intellectual property (IP)
and bundling 11.154–11.167
cooperation between OHIM and national offices 13.12
and dominance 11.115–11.187
    abusive conduct, factors establishing 11.136–11.137
    anti-competitive exploitation of a patent 11.127–11.128
    applicable standard 11.158–11.159
    exclusivity 11.115–11.118, 11.129–11.137
    exporting *Magill* principles 11.141–11.146
    importing *Bronner* principles 11.147–11.153
    indispensability requirement 11.157
    interoperability 11.154–11.167
    lenient approach 11.125–11.126
    media player bundling 11.164–11.167
    monopolization 11.134–11.135
    prolonging patent rights 11.138–11.140
    refusal to license an IP right 11.160–11.163
    refusal to supply 11.168–11.176
    reversing the order 11.121–11.124
exhaustion of national rights 2.02
and free movement of goods 10.57–10.70
    existence–exercise dichotomy 10.61–10.64
    independent rights 10.67–10.70
    specific subject-matter of the right 10.65–10.66
refusal to license an IP right 11.160–11.163
trade marks and other IP rights 4.49–4.50, 14.06
transit 9.511–9.512

intelligibility requirement
graphical representation 4.38, 4.100

***inter partes* proceedings**
language of applications 2.34

intermediaries, use by
case details/order of reference 9.115–9.117
reasoned order of Court 9.118–9.121

Internet and trade marks
see also **electronic market platforms; keywords, use by advertisers**
advertisements, display of 9.136–9.140
Advocate General Opinion
    electronic market platforms, and keywords 9.191–9.200
    Google France approach in a non-Internet environment 9.264–9.298
    Interflora case 9.227–9.237
    new market context 9.128–9.143
    and oral procedures 9.238

Internet and trade marks (*cont.*):
Article 6 defences 9.175–9.176
case details/order of reference
electronic market platforms and
keywords 9.186–9.190
Google France approach in a non-Internet
environment 9.262–9.263
Interflora case 9.222–9.224
new market context 9.122–9.127
cases of importance
BergSpechte 9.170–9.171
Eis.de 9.169
Frisdranken Industrie Winters BV v Red Bull GmbH 9.262–9.271
Google 9.122–9.143
Interflora 9.222–9.261
L'Oréal v eBay 9.186–9.221
Portakabin 9.172–9.185
contributory infringement 9.144–9.146
cross-territorial reach of Internet 9.197
dialogue between CJEU and national court 9.224–9.226
dilution 9.254–9.256
distinctiveness 9.254–9.256
essential function of a trade mark 9.159
exhaustion 9.180–9.185
Google principles 9.169
extending 9.170–9.185
Google France approach in a non-Internet environment 9.262–9.271
infringement and use by search engine 9.131–9.132
judgments
electronic market platforms, and keywords 9.201–9.221
Google France approach in a non-Internet environment 9.269–9.271
Interflora case 9.238–9.259
keywords, use by advertisers 9.149–9.168
measures against online operators 9.218–9.221
misspelt trade marks 9.172, 9.174
new market context 9.122–9.143
new test, parameters 9.177–9.179
online marketplace, advertising on 9.211–9.213
operator liability 9.215–9.217
original and competing goods 9.173
private and business sellers 9.202
service provider liability 9.165–9.168, 9.198–9.200
and trade marks with reputation 9.141–9.143
invalidity
see also **absolute grounds for refusal of registration/ declaration of invalidity; relative grounds for refusal of registration/declaration of invalidity**
establishment *a posteriori* 8.10
grounds for, relating to only some of the goods or services 8.09
investment
and adverse effect 9.251–9.253
Ireland
and Community Trade Mark Regulation 2.23

judicial review
see also **Court of Justice of the European Union (CJEU)**
cases of importance
Anheuser-Busch Inc 3.44–3.47, 3.111
Baby Dry 3.22
Bimbo 3.84
Centrotherm 3.37–3.39
Edwin 3.87, 3.99, 3.100, 3.104
Jager 3.48–3.53
Kaul 3.28, 3.28–3.35, 3.36, 3.38, 3.39, 3.56
National Lottery 3.87, 3.97, 3.104
New Yorker 3.41
Rintisch v OHIM 3.42–3.43
Volkshandy 3.110
and Community Trade Mark 2.44–2.46, 3.20–3.110
Advocate General Opinion 3.51–3.53, 3.98
annulment of decision for reasons not raised by claimant 3.66
Boards of Appeal *see* **Boards of Appeal**
interrelated issues settled 3.27
judgment of Court of Justice 3.54–3.55
nature of court proceedings 3.56–3.59
new/additional evidence submitted in first instance units before that instance outside of properly set time limits 3.39–3.50
and Regulation 3.67, 3.110
scope of judicial review 3.64–3.68
and OHIM *see under* **Office for Harmonization in the Internal Market (OHIM)**
scope 3.64–3.68

keywords, use by advertisers 9.147–9.168
see also **electronic market platforms; Internet and trade marks**
advertising function 9.161–9.163
allowing advertisers to select 9.133–9.135, 9.147–9.168
in course of trade 9.152–9.153
and electronic market platforms 9.186–9.221
exhaustion of rights 9.181
liable to have adverse effect on functions of the trade mark 9.156
origin function 9.157
in relation to goods or services 9.154–9.155
service provider liability 9.165–9.168
similar to trade marks 9.170–9.171
and trade mark law 9.150–9.164
and transparency in advertising 9.158
unclear messages 9.160

languages
acquired distinctive character 6.115
applications for registration 2.34
Community Trade Mark 2.34–2.38
confusion in parts of the Community 7.332–7.335
Kik decision (2003) 2.35
limited number for Office 2.05
new Member States 2.61
Latvia
accession to EU (2004) 2.59

legal certainty
  graphical representation 4.40, 4.89
letters, single
  appeals 5.99–5.106
  devoid of any distinctive character
    considerations 5.96–5.106, 5.122, 5.125, 5.127
  views of OHIM and General Court 5.96–5.98
licensing
  Community Trade Marks (CTMs) 2.33
  and competition law 11.57–11.59
  compulsory licence 10.81–10.82
  open exclusive/exclusive licences 11.57–11.59
  trade mark reform (new package) 13.37
likelihood of association
  relative grounds for refusal 7.02
  surname protection 7.221
likelihood of confusion
  and appeals to Court of Justice 3.71
  and double-identity protection 14.10
  establishing confusion 7.58, 7.60, 7.126–7.128
  evidence requirement 14.07
  global assessment 9.21
  identity, establishing 7.17
  relative grounds for refusal 7.02, 7.17
  and similarity concept 4.189
  surname protection 7.221
  trade mark as registered, scope of
    protection 9.20–9.29
limitations to trade mark rights 9.272–9.363
  Article 6(1)(b)
    'schematic' classification 9.314–9.316
    scope of 9.308–9.326
    teleological analysis 9.317–9.318
    use in accordance with honest
      practices 9.319–9.321
    wording and context 9.311–9.313
  compatibility, indicating 9.327–9.350
    advertiser, activities of 9.341
    concept of 'honest practices in industrial
      and commercial matters' 9.339–9.340,
      9.347–9.350
    criteria making use necessary 9.343–9.346
    factors for assessing whether use
      necessary 9.333–9.338
  Directive, effect 9.275–9.278, 9.291
  exercise of rights 9.298–9.307
  exhaustion of rights 9.281–9.282
  narrow analysis, in *Adam Opel* 9.351–9.363
    Article 6(1), application to the facts
      in 9.352–9.356
    Article 6(1)(c) 9.357–9.358
    whether specific toy can be described by reference
      to original product 9.359–9.360
  quality considerations 9.283
  repair and maintenance 9.303–9.307
  sale of second-hand goods ads 9.299–9.302
  unauthorized use to inform the
    public 9.293–9.297
  use of mark in relation to goods 9.280–9.283
  use of mark in relation to services 9.284–9.290
Lithuania
  accession to EU (2004) 2.59

logos, use of
  challenging limits of protection 9.59–9.83
  functionality 11.198–11.200
Louis Vuitton's lock device mark
  absence of distinctiveness 5.496–5.500
  General Court 5.497
  judgment 5.498–5.500
  OHIM decisions 5.496

Madrid Agreement Concerning the International
  Registration of Marks 2.06
  Protocol, EU as contracting party of 2.18
  signs 4.64
Malta
  accession to EU (2004) 2.59
manufacturers, indicating names of
  comparative advertising 12.28, 12.38
  free movement of goods and new trade mark
    regime 10.190
market boundaries, crossing
  dominance 11.112–11.113
Member States
  artificial partitioning of the markets
    between 10.179–10.183
  Community trade mark courts 2.48, 2.51
  descriptive signs or indications, registrability
    considerations 5.616
  effect of registrations in other 5.313–5.314
  enforcement action against when in breach of EU
    law 3.06–3.07
  financial penalties 3.07
  infringement of Treaty by 3.07
  languages 2.61
  matters left to discretion of 2.13
  repackaging and parallel imports 10.104
  response to actions by Court of Justice 3.06
  trade marks well-known in 7.353–7.369
  transit from a Member State for a non-Member
    State 9.499–9.509
Memorandum on an EEC Trade Mark (1976),
  European Commission 2.03, 2.04
misspelt trade marks 9.172, 9.174
misuse of reputation 12.11–12.16
  concept of distinguishing marks 12.12
  necessity factors 12.16
  unfair advantage 12.13–12.15
mixed characters assessments
  appeals to Court of Justice 3.71
monopolization argument
  see also **competition; dominance**
  de facto monopoly 11.134–11.135
  distinctiveness
    acquired through use 6.29, 6.35
    and packaging 5.417–5.426
  policy considerations 4.49
multifactor tests
  absolute grounds for refusal of registration/
    declaration of invalidity 5.575–5.580
  first part of test 5.581
  more than minimal 5.584
  second part of test 5.582, 5.583
  distinctiveness acquired through use 6.18, 6.19–6.24

multifactor tests (*cont.*):
   favouring by Court 14.13
   relative grounds for refusal of registration/
      declaration of invalidity 7.114–7.125
musical notation
   graphical representation 4.107, 4.117, 4.118

national courts
   competence of 8.43
   competition 11.45–11.48
   and Court of Justice 3.14–3.17, 4.05
   trade mark conflicts 9.57–9.58
   wishing to apply trusted principles 4.05
necessity requirement
   free movement of goods and new trade mark
      regime 10.203–10.206, 10.204–10.205,
      10.206, 10.221–10.222, 10.224–10.225, 10.226,
      10.346–10.349, 10.357, 10.383–10.385
   misuse of reputation 12.16
   re-boxing style 10.346–10.349
   rebranding 10.204–10.205
   repackaging 10.221–10.222, 10.224–10.225
   and specific subject matter 10.224–10.225
   time for assessing 10.206
   uncertainties 10.221–10.222
New Code of Industrial Property
   compensation for applicants 12.245
   Nice Agreement Concerning the International
      Classification of for the Purposes of the
      Registration of Marks (1957) 4.70
   Class 9 4.28, 6.125
   Class 35 4.63
   Class 36 5.86
   Class 38 6.125
   Class 41 4.75, 4.199
   definitions 4.191, 4.192, 4.203, 4.209, 4.210
   distinctiveness acquired through use 6.125
   goods and services 4.204
non-discrimination principle 5.50–5.51
non-verbal marks
   distinctiveness 6.87
numerals (single), signs consisting of
   appeals 5.113–5.121
   devoid of any distinctive character
      considerations 5.95, 5.107–5.121,
      5.122, 5.125

objectivity requirement
   graphical representation 4.38, 4.102
odours *see* **olfactory signs**
Office for Harmonization in the Internal
   Market (OHIM)
   Administrative Board 2.61
   administrative examination system within 3.20
   administrative proceedings, scope 3.61–3.63
   and appeals to Court of Justice 3.79, 3.80, 3.81
   applications filed at 2.16, 2.34
   Boards of Appeal *see* **Boards of Appeal**
   Budget Committee 2.61
   cancellation actions pending before 2.58
   and Community Trade Mark
      Regulation 2.23, 2.25

   conversion applications filed at 2.25
   cooperation with national IP offices 13.12
   decisions subject to appeal *see* **appeals**
   device marks, absence of distinctiveness 5.496
   disregarding of facts or evidence 'not submitted in
      due time' 3.23
   establishment (1994) 2.14
   examination of facts of its own motion 3.23
   filing of oppositions 2.41
   finances 13.13, 13.46–13.47
   first instance units and Boards of Appeal 3.22
   as focus of interpretation of legislation 2.02
   governance 13.14, 13.48–13.51
   implementing legislation adopted prior to opening
      of 2.15
   and judicial review 3.20, 3.22, 3.23, 3.24,
      3.60, 3.108
      administrative proceedings, scope 3.61,
         3.62, 3.63
      Advocate General Opinion 3.52, 3.53
      appeals 3.79, 3.80, 3.81
      Boards of Appeal 3.30, 3.31, 3.33
      judgment of Court of Justice 3.54, 3.55
      national law, case of 3.86, 3.87, 3.94, 3.95, 3.96,
         3.98, 3.100, 3.102, 3.104
      nature of court proceedings 3.56
      new/additional evidence submitted in first
         instance units before that instance outside
         of properly set time limits 3.41, 3.43, 3.44,
         3.46, 3.47, 3.48, 3.50
   jurisdictional differences with Courts in trade mark
      registration cases 3.60
   languages 2.05, 2.06, 2.34
   location of 2.05, 2.06
   numbers of applications received 2.16
   practice as 'precedent' 5.31
   President, Communication No 4/03
      on 4.192–4.197, 4.211
   proceedings 2.39–2.46
   revoking of registrations of CTMs 2.42
   slogans, registrability 5.179
OHIM *see* **Office for Harmonization in the Internal**
   Market (OHIM)
olfactory signs *see* **scents**
opinion surveys
   distinctiveness acquired through use 6.03, 6.23,
      6.146, 6.148, 6.149, 6.151, 6.156–6.157
'opposition' systems
   and Community Trade Mark
      Regulation 2.23, 2.24
origin
   see also **geographical indications**
   adverse effect and origin function 9.243–9.248
   beyond the origin function 10.252–10.273
   BUD as appellation of origin
      (*Budweiser IV*) 12.213–12.229
   concept 10.25–10.29
   designations of origin and competitive
      relationship 12.54–12.65
      Article 3(a)1(f) 12.59, 12.65
      relevance to a type of product 12.56, 12.60
      scope of Directive (84/450/EEC) 12.58, 12.64

Index

discrimination based on 10.22–10.24
guarantee of 8.100–8.102, 10.111
keywords, use by advertisers 9.157
trade mark functions as indication of 2.08, 9.53

packaging
and Article 7(1)(b) 5.389–5.426
assimilation of appearance with 14.05
and product shape 5.301–5.314
distinctive character 5.460–5.483
distinctiveness acquired through use 6.54, 6.56
and establishment of services 4.65, 4.67, 4.74
repackaging and parallel imports 10.98–10.116

parallel imports
see also **free movement of goods**
Advocate General Opinion
 free movement of goods 10.87–10.90, 10.133–10.167, 10.200–10.213, 10.219–10.223, 10.232–10.247, 10.255–10.265, 10.276–10.286, 10.300–10.309, 10.322–10.324, 10.336–10.361, 10.380–10.382, 10.390–10.391, 10.397–10.401
 repackaging and parallel imports 10.101–10.109
bananas, comparing with other fruits 10.14
beer, comparing with wine 10.10–10.13
cases of importance
 Ballantine 10.229–10.251
 Boehringer 10.214–10.228
 Boehringer II 10.334–10.371
 Bristol Myers Squibb 10.117–10.408, 10.340, 10.342–10.345
 Centrafarm v American Home Products 10.83–10.85
 Codacons 10.50–10.54
 Commission v Ireland 10.55–10.56
 Coty 10.328–10.333
 Davidoff 10.297–10.313
 Dior 10.252–10.273
 Hag-I 10.74–10.77
 Hag-II 10.86–10.91
 Hoffmann-La Roche 10.98–10.116
 Ideal Standard 10.92–10.97
 Martin y Paz 10.386–10.394
 Merck v Stephar 10.79–10.80, 10.228
 Oripharm 10.372–10.377
 Peak Holding 10.318–10.327
 Pharmacia & Upjohn 10.198–10.213
 Pharmon v Hoechst 10.81–10.82
 Sebago 10.291–10.296
 Silhouette 10.274–10.290
 Terrapin 10.78
 Viking Gas 10.395–10.408
 Wellcome v Paranova 10.378–10.385
channels of trade as challenge to 12.32
competition and substitution 10.08–10.09
concept of origin 10.25–10.29
duties and taxes 10.05–10.14
effect and scope of measure 10.21
equality proviso 10.36–10.37
free movement of goods 10.19, 10.54
 broadening scope of principle 10.19
 and intellectual property 10.57–10.70
 and new trade mark regime 10.117–10.408
 rationale 10.10.54
 and trade mark law 10.71–10.116
general principles 10.02–10.56
hallmarks and public interest 10.55–10.56
interrelationship between layers of Community law 10.53
intra-Community and intra-state trade 10.20
judgments
 free movement of goods 10.91, 10.168–10.193, 10.194–10.197, 10.210–10.213, 10.224–10.227, 10.248–10.251, 10.287–10.290, 10.310–10.313, 10.325–10.327, 10.362–10.371, 10.392–10.394, 10.402–10.408
 repackaging and parallel imports 10.110–10.116
labelling requirement 10.50–10.54
legislative framework 10.02–10.04
product similarity issue 10.07
protection of health and life of humans 10.46–10.49
public morality 10.38–10.45
quantitative restrictions 10.15–10.35
 broad principle 10.16–10.17
 concept of origin 10.25–10.29
 discrimination based on origin 10.22–10.24
 discrimination based on product characteristics 10.30–10.32
 effect and scope of measure 10.21
 exception and principle 10.18–10.19
 free movement of goods principle, broadening scope of 10.19
 intra-Community and intra-state trade 10.20
 selling arrangements 10.33–10.35
repackaging 10.98–10.116
vertical application 10.52
whisky, comparing with liqueurs 10.14

parallel national rights
Community Trade Mark Regulation 2.28–2.29

Paris Convention for the Protection of Industrial Property
refusal or invalidation of trade marks 4.09, 4.10

partitioning the market
artificial partitioning of the markets between Member States 10.179–10.183
and Directive 10.142–10.144
marking obligations 10.246–10.247
policing channels of trade 10.241–10.247
removal of identification numbers 10.244–10.245
removal of the word 'pure' 10.242–10.243
replacement of importer's name 10.244–10.245

patents
anti-competitive exploitation of 11.127–11.128
European Patent Office (EPO) 2.05
Unified Patent Court 2.48

pharmaceuticals/role of professionals
attentiveness variable 7.284–7.287
free movement of goods and new trade mark regime 10.239
global appreciation 7.284–7.296

Poland
accession to EU (2004) 2.59

policy considerations
trade marks and other IP rights 4.49–4.50

Portugal
   accession to EU (1986) 2.05
   and Community Trade Mark Regulation 2.23
'possessions' concept
   and trade mark applications 12.243–12.244
precedents
   role in preliminary rulings process 3.17–3.19
   value of 3.105–3.110
precision requirement
   definition of for which mark registered 4.190–4.244
   graphical representation 4.38, 4.92, 4.99, 4.105, 4.115
Preliminary Draft of a Convention for a European Trade Mark (1964), unpublished 2.03
preliminary ruling, references for 3.13–3.19
price comparisons
   comparative advertising 12.34, 12.41
prior notice
   absence of, consequences 10.371
   extent of disclosure 10.385
   free movement of goods and new trade mark regime 10.145, 10.370, 10.371
   and indication of repackaging 10.145
products
   see also **advertising; comparative advertising; goods and services**
   assimilation of appearance with packaging 14.05
   characteristics and geography 12.113
   'concept' behind 5.427–5.443
   counterfeit products through mail, importing 9.574–9.585
   design of retail store connected with products on sale 4.63–4.75
   discrimination based on characteristics 10.30–10.32
   distinctiveness *see* **distinctiveness; distinctiveness acquired through use**
   domestic product market, relevance 10.39
   dramming, and testers 9.192, 9.208
   and geographical indications 5.531
   offered for sale, and advertising on online marketplace 9.211–9.213
   original condition, repackaging affecting 10.112
   picture of 6.68
   quality *see* **quality considerations**
   reference to a type 12.56, 12.60
   relevant class of persons identifying maker of 6.15, 6.16, 6.101
   shapes *see* **shapes**
   similarity between 7.205–7.213
promotional items
   genuine use requirement 8.96–8.114
proportionality
   function of the sign 11.214
   symbol, use of 5.864
proprietor of trade marks
   see also **trade mark conflicts**
   identical signs and goods or services, effect on rights of trade mark proprietor 'requirement' 9.30–9.121
   interests of 9.50–9.51, 9.54–9.55
   use by or with his/her consent 8.216–8.217

protected geographical indication (PGI)
   see also **geographical indications**
   effect on pre-existing trade marks 12.121–12.122
   reputation, trade marks and PGIs 12.130–12.133
   validity of registration 12.118–12.120
Protocol to the Madrid Agreement Concerning the International Registration of Marks
   EU as contracting party to 2.18
public interest considerations
   see also **consumers/consumer perception; relevant public**
   and cosmetics 5.868–5.869
   descriptive signs or indications 5.524, 5.547–5.548
   distinctiveness acquired through use 6.100
   and hallmarks 10.55–10.56
   independence and interdependence 5.05–5.10
   signs or indications that have become customary 5.767, 5.782
public morality
   domestic product market, relevance 10.39
   parallel imports 10.38–10.45
   public policy 10.40–10.43
   public security 10.44–10.45
public policy considerations
   graphical representation 4.131–4.155
   trade marks contrary to public policy 4.09, 4.10

quality considerations
   competition 11.24–11.25
   limitations to trade mark rights 9.283
   public health and guarantee of quality function 10.103
   repackaging and parallel imports 10.103, 10.107
quantitative restrictions 10.15–10.35
   see also **parallel imports**
   broad principle 10.16–10.17
   concept of origin 10.25–10.29
   discrimination based on origin 10.22–10.24
   discrimination based on product characteristics 10.30–10.32
   effect and scope of measure 10.21
   exception and principle 10.18–10.19
   free movement of goods principle, broadening scope of 10.19
   intra-Community and intra-state trade 10.20
   selling arrangements 10.33–10.35

re-boxing
   and necessity 10.346–10.349
rebranding
   conditions 10.207–10.208
   and necessity 10.204–10.205
   and repackaging 10.212–10.213
refusal of application/declaration of invalidity *see* **absolute grounds for refusal of registration/declaration of invalidity; relative grounds for refusal of registration/declaration of invalidity**
registration of trade marks
   see also **Madrid Agreement Concerning the International Registration of Marks; Office for Harmonization in the Internal Market (OHIM)**

Index

applications *see* **applications for registration**
BUDWEISER, international trade mark registrations for 3.44
colours 4.17
and competition law 11.21
concept of use 9.20–9.29
devoid of any distinctive character 5.25, 5.47–5.49, 5.61–5.63
jurisdictional differences between OHIM and Courts 3.60
as key of trade mark protection 4.96
limitations of Trade Mark Registration Treaty 2.06
in other Member States, effect 5.313–5.314
parameters for assessing registrability 5.613–5.614
perspective for determining registrability 5.23–5.24
process 5.613–5.614
protected geographical indication (PGI)
  effect on pre-existing trade marks 12.121–12.122
  validity of registration 12.118–12.120
refusal *see* **absolute grounds for refusal of registration/declaration of invalidity; relative grounds for refusal of registration/declaration of invalidity**
registered trade marks and concept of 'third party' 9.08–9.19
scrutiny of conflicts concerning registration 3.20
surnames 5.134
trade mark as registered, scope of protection 9.20–9.29
use of signs as registered marks 9.63
of variation 8.175–8.182

relative grounds for refusal of registration/ declaration of invalidity
see also **absolute grounds for refusal of registration/ declaration of invalidity**
Advocate General Opinion
  confusion, similarity and distinctiveness 7.22–7.25, 7.31, 7.34–7.35, 7.39–7.40, 7.45–7.46
  global appreciation 7.51–7.52, 7.57–7.58, 7.61, 7.66–7.68, 7.73, 7.78–7.84, 7.142–7.146, 7.186–7.193, 7.224–7.229, 7.242–7.246, 7.254–7.255, 7.265–7.268, 7.273–7.279, 7.291
  identity, establishing 7.10–7.15
  relevant points in time 7.150–7.156, 7.171–7.173
  well-known and reputed trade marks 7.348–7.349, 7.362–7.365, 7.375–7.387, 7.421–7.422, 7.427–7.449, 7.465–7.481, 7.531–7.537, 7.586–7.590
appeals
  'economic behaviour,' importance 7.514–7.517
  grounds of 7.234–7.238
  limiting scope of 7.225–7.226, 7.232–7.233
  unfair advantage 7.566–7.574
aural similarity 7.72–7.74
case details/order of reference
  dilution, proof of 7.459–7.464
  'economic behaviour,' importance 7.509–7.510
  foreign equivalents 7.129
  pharmaceuticals/role of professionals 7.292–7.296
  presumption of distinctiveness 7.100–7.104
  relevant points in time 7.166–7.170
  reputation 'in the Community' 7.371–7.374
  unfair advantage 7.526–7.530, 7.561–7.565
  well-known and reputed trade marks 7.358–7.361
cases of importance
  Adidas 7.417–7.436
  Armafoam 7.332–7.345
  Arsenal 7.182–7.197
  Ballons d'Or/Golden Balls 7.129–7.133
  Bellure 7.525–7.547
  Calvin Klein 7.437, 7.438–7.443, 7.452, 7.457
  Canon 7.29–7.32, 7.61–7.65, 7.141–7.147
  Davidoff v Golkid 7.403–7.416, 7.417–7.425
  Environmental Manufacturing 7.508–7.524
  Ferrero 7.437, 7.444–7.451, 7.452, 7.455, 7.457
  Fincas Tarragona 7.353–7.369
  Flexi Air 7.114–7.125
  Formula One 7.100–7.113
  General Motors 7.346–7.352
  Génesis 7.166–7.178
  Helena Rubinstein 7.560–7.582
  Intel 7.458–7.507, 7.548–7.559
  La Española 7.297, 7.314–7.327
  Levi Strauss 7.148–7.165
  Limoncello 7.297, 7.299–7.304
  Lloyd 7.45–7.47, 7.48, 7.72–7.74
  Lloyd Schuhfabrik 7.33–7.36
  Marca Mode 7.37–7.44
  Matratzen I 7.89–7.99
  Medion 7.239–7.270
  Mühlens 7.75–7.88
  Nasdaq 7.548–7.559
  Pago 7.370–7.402
  Picasso/Picaro 7.182–7.197
  Praktiker 7.271–7.283
  Quicky 7.297, 7.305–7.313
  Red Bull trio 7.583–7.605
  Sabel 7.21–7.28, 7.29, 7.37–7.44, 7.50–7.54, 7.66–7.71
  Seven for all mankind 7.134–7.140
  Travatan 7.284–7.296
  Uniweb 7.328–7.331
  Vedial 7.55–7.60
  Wesergold 7.126–7.128
comparison of goods or services 7.141–7.147
comparison of marks 7.66–7.71
composite marks 7.297–7.327
conceptual similarity 7.187, 7.597–7.602
conflicts with earlier rights 7.06
confusion, similarity and distinctiveness 7.20–7.48
  average consumer 7.48
  confusion and association 7.21–7.28, 7.29
  distinctiveness factors 7.30, 7.45–7.47
  economic linkages 7.32
  language of provision and principles of Directive 7.26
  positive finding on confusion 7.37–7.44
  properly substantial and genuine confusion 7.33–7.36
  similarity and reputation 7.32
  see also **establishing confusion below**

relative grounds for refusal of registration/declaration of invalidity (*cont.*):
  cumulative similarity/identity conditions 7.55–7.60
  dilution, proof of 7.458–7.507
    assessment of detriment 7.495–7.498
    blurring 7.476–7.480, 7.482–7.484
    existence of a link 7.488–7.494
    free riding 7.474–7.475
    relevant public 7.485
    repercussions 7.499–7.507
    standard and burden of proof 7.486–7.487
    tarnishment 7.481
  in Directive 7.06, 7.26
  distinctiveness
    and confusion/similarity 7.20–7.48
    enhanced, role in likelihood of confusion 7.126–7.128
    loss of distinctive character 7.154–7.156
    multifactor assessment, as part of 7.114–7.125
    presumption of 7.100–7.113
    word marks 7.134–7.140
  dominant elements 7.95–7.97, 7.239–7.249
    dominant figurative elements 7.314–7.327
    unclear dominance, all elements counting 7.305–7.313
  dominant figurative elements 7.314–7.327
  due cause concept 7.584–7.596
    balancing exercise 7.591–7.593
    conditions for establishing due course 7.594–7.596
  'economic behaviour,' importance 7.508–7.524
    appeals to Court of Justice 7.514–7.517
    case background 7.509–7.510
    permissive approach of General Court 7.510–7.513
    repercussions 7.518–7.524
  foreign equivalents 7.129–7.133
  get-up imitation 7.314–7.327
  global appreciation 7.179–7.348
    application of *Medion* principle 7.250–7.270
    Article 8(1)(b) considerations 7.129, 7.230–7.231
    aural similarity 7.72–7.74
    challenge to *Lloyd* 7.75–7.88
    comparison of goods or services 7.141–7.147
    composite marks 7.297–7.327
    conceptual similarity 7.187
    confusion in parts of the Community 7.332–7.345
    in context of Article 5(2) 7.426–7.431
    cumulative similarity/identity conditions 7.55–7.60
    dominant elements 7.95–7.97, 7.239–7.249, 7.305–7.327
    enhanced distinctiveness, role in likelihood of confusion 7.126–7.128
    establishing confusion 7.49–7.147
    exercise of trade mark rights and free movement of goods 7.98–7.99
    families of marks 7.328–7.331
    foreign equivalents 7.129–7.133
    likelihood of association 7.221
    likelihood of confusion test 7.58, 7.60, 7.126–7.128, 7.218–7.220
    multifactor assessment, distinctiveness as part of 7.114–7.125
    pharmaceuticals/role of professionals 7.284–7.296
    post-sale confusion 7.191–7.192
    post-sale effect of trade mark 7.189–7.190
    presumption of distinctiveness 7.100–7.113
    retail services 7.271–7.283
    scope of specification 7.222–7.223
    similarity between a figurative and a word mark 7.89–7.99
    similarity between marks 7.214–7.217
    similarity between products 7.205–7.213
    surname protection 7.198–7.238
    targeted public 7.203–7.204
    tests 7.49, 7.50–7.54
    against a wider context 7.61–7.65
  global assessment test 7.13
  identity, establishing 7.08–7.19
  judgments
    confusion, similarity and distinctiveness 7.27–7.28, 7.32, 7.36, 7.41–7.44, 7.47
    of Court of First Instance 7.76–7.77, 7.91–7.94, 7.116–7.120, 7.183–7.185, 7.201–7.223, 7.550–7.554
    global appreciation 7.53–7.54, 7.59, 7.62–7.65, 7.69–7.71, 7.74, 7.85–7.88, 7.91–7.99, 7.105–7.107, 7.116–7.125, 7.130–7.133, 7.147, 7.194–7.197, 7.247–7.249, 7.256–7.264, 7.269–7.270, 7.280–7.283, 7.330–7.331
    identity, establishing 7.16–7.19
    presumption of distinctiveness 7.105–7.107
    relevant points in time 7.157–7.165, 7.174–7.178
    well-known and reputed trade marks 7.350–7.352, 7.366–7.369, 7.388–7.395, 7.414–7.416, 7.423–7.425, 7.430–7.431, 7.482–7.498, 7.538–7.544, 7.591–7.596
  likelihood of association 7.02, 7.221
  likelihood of confusion 7.02, 7.17, 7.218–7.220
  multifactor assessment, distinctiveness as part of 7.114–7.125
  new evidence, rejecting 7.227–7.228
  new trade mark 'package' after April 2015 13.22
  non-negligible word elements that cannot be ignored 7.299–7.304
  pharmaceuticals/role of professionals 7.284–7.296
  prevailing of earlier rights 7.02
  priority limits 7.166–7.178
  in the Regulation 7.07
  relevant points in time 7.148–7.178
    assessment of confusion 7.151–7.152, 7.157–7.160
    loss of distinctive character 7.154–7.156
    post-sale confusion 7.191–7.192
    post-sale effect of trade mark 7.189–7.190
    priority limits 7.166–7.178
    scope of the right/scope of protection 7.153–7.156, 7.161–7.165
    timing of assessment 7.148–7.165
    vigilant conduct requirement 7.163–7.165

Index

and scope of protection 7.153–7.156, 7.161–7.165, 14.07
surname protection 7.198–7.238
trade marks with reputation 7.02
and TRIPS Agreement 7.11
unclear dominance, all elements counting 7.305–7.313
unfair advantage 7.525–7.547
  get-up imitation 7.545–7.547
  in practice 7.560–7.582
well-known and reputed trade marks 7.346–7.602
  ambiguities of cases 7.406–7.408
  conceptual similarity 7.597–7.602
  considering territory as a whole 7.381
  context 7.381, 7.385
  dilution, proof of 7.458–7.507
  due cause concept 7.584–7.596
  'economic behaviour,' importance 7.508–7.524
  fine-tuning the principles 7.444–7.451, 14.14
  free riding 7.474–7.475
  interpretive limits of *Davidoff* 7.417–7.425
  link, relationship with infringement 7.467–7.473
  literal interpretation 7.409–7.410
  mechanical approach 7.438–7.443
  in a Member State 7.353–7.369
  protection gap 7.411–7.413
  putting *Intel* into perspective 7.548–7.559
  reputation, factors for assessing 7.346–7.352
  reputation 'in the Community' 7.370–7.402
  scope of Article 5(2) 7.403–7.416, 7.426–7.431
  similarity and reputation 7.437–7.457
  substantial part of Community 7.381, 7.382
  unfair advantage 7.525–7.547, 7.560–7.582
  use as a trade mark 7.432–7.436
word marks, distinctiveness 7.134–7.140

relevant points in time
assessment of confusion 7.151–7.152, 7.157–7.160
case backgrounds 6.124–6.155, 6.158
distinctiveness, determining 6.59–6.62, 6.69–6.72, 6.121–6.138
evidence of acquired distinctiveness 6.152–6.155, 6.158
judgments 6.127–6.138
'legitimate expectations' 6.129
'logic of the system' 6.161
point of sale 6.61
post-sale 6.62, 7.189–7.190
  confusion 7.191–7.192
scope of right/protection 7.153–7.156, 7.161–7.165
timing of assessment 7.148–7.165
vigilant conduct requirement 7.163–7.165

relevant product market
competition 11.36, 11.99–11.105

relevant public
see also **public interest considerations**
comparative advertising 12.47
dilution, proof of 7.485
distinctiveness acquired through use 6.09, 6.10
generic indications, development into 8.260–8.282

repackaging
see also **packaging**
advanced notice requirement 10.223
affecting original condition of the product 10.112
application of general principles 10.234–10.235
Commission on 11.76
competition 10.108–10.109, 10.115–10.116
concept 10.362–10.363
dominance, trade mark rights and competition 10.108–10.109
and exhaustion of rights, in new regime 10.137–10.138
framing position of the Court 10.220
free movement of goods 10.110, 10.133–10.135
general rule (first repackaging condition) 10.113
  limitations to general rule and three additional conditions 10.114
and guarantee of origin 10.111
indication of 10.188–10.189
manner and style 10.364–10.365
necessity requirement 10.221–10.222, 10.224–10.225
overstickering 10.342–10.345
and parallel imports 10.98–10.116
position in Member States 10.104
prior notice and indication of 10.145
product quality and liability considerations 10.107
public health and guarantee of quality function 10.103
and rebranding 10.212–10.213
scope of Article 36 10.105–10.106

repair and maintenance
limitations to trade mark rights 9.303–9.307

reputation
see also **trade marks**
and appeals to Court of Justice 3.71
'in the Community' 7.370–7.402
damage to 10.308–10.309, 10.350, 10.351–10.352, 10.366–10.368
and minimum intervention 10.380–10.381
and distinctiveness 9.25
factors for assessing 7.346–7.352
free movement of goods and new trade mark regime 10.240, 10.260–10.264
and inappropriate presentation 10.191–10.192
and Internet 9.141–9.143
local, whether sufficient for obtaining an injunction 7.383–7.387
misuse of 12.11–12.16
  concept of distinguishing marks 12.12
  necessity factors 12.16
  unfair advantage 12.13–12.15
and protected geographical indications 12.130–12.133
and similarity concept 7.32, 7.437–7.457
well-known and reputed trade marks 7.346–7.602
  ambiguities of cases 7.406–7.408
  conceptual similarity 7.597–7.602
  considering territory as a whole 7.381
  context 7.381, 7.385
  dilution, proof of 7.458–7.507
  due cause concept 7.584–7.596
  'economic behaviour,' importance 7.508–7.524
  fine-tuning the principles 7.444–7.451, 14.14
  interpretive limits of *Davidoff* 7.417–7.425
  literal interpretation 7.409–7.410

Index

reputation (*cont.*):
  well-known and reputed trade marks (*cont.*):
    mechanical approach 7.438–7.443
    in a Member State 7.353–7.369
    protection gap 7.411–7.413
    putting *Intel* into perspective 7.548–7.559
    scope of Article 5(2) 7.403–7.406, 7.403–7.416, 7.426–7.431
    similarity and reputation 7.437–7.457
    substantial part of Community 7.381, 7.382
    unfair advantage 7.525–7.547, 7.560–7.582
    use as a trade mark 7.432–7.436
retail services
  see also **goods and services; products**
  design of retail store connected with products on sale 4.63–4.75
  extending concept of 'service' to retailing of applicant's own goods 4.75
  global appreciation 7.271–7.283
  registration of service marks 4.176–4.189
revocation of trade marks
  establishment *a posteriori* 8.10
  grounds 8.08, 8.09
  relating to only some of the goods or services 8.09
  use after filing application for 8.56–8.57
rights in rem
  establishing 2.33
  trade mark reform (new package) 13.37
Romania
  accession to EU (2006) 2.59
rule of reason analysis
  competition 11.26–11.27

sales figures
  and advertising expenditure 6.50–6.72
  distinctiveness acquired through use 6.50–6.72, 6.73–6.89
  evidence of use 6.76–6.79
  geographical extent 6.80–6.82, 6.86–6.89
  market share 6.84–6.85
  relevant point in time for determining distinctiveness 6.59–6.62, 6.69–6.72
  and territorial scope of distinctiveness acquired through use 6.73–6.89
  three-dimensional signs 6.57–6.58, 6.64–6.67
sales figures/advertising expenditure
  distinctiveness acquired through use 6.50–6.72
Scandinavian countries
  and Community Trade Mark Regulation 2.23
scents
  and chemical formulae 4.16, 4.79, 4.103
  clarity and precision requirements 4.92
  graphical representation 4.77, 4.79, 4.88, 4.91–4.94, 4.103–4.105
scope of protection
  see also **trade mark conflicts**
  and availability 9.84–9.101
    availability requirement as a limiting factor 9.100–9.101
    impact of 9.93–9.99
  balancing functions with 5.599
  colours 9.26–9.29
  expanding 9.102–9.114
  limiting of 9.31–9.40
  relevant points in time 7.153–7.156, 7.161–7.165, 14.07
  trade marks as registered 9.20–9.29
  types of use remaining outside 14.11
search engines
  and infringement 9.131–9.132
second-hand goods
  advertisements 9.299–9.302
  exhaustion of rights 9.180, 9.182, 9.183
self-containment
  graphical representation 4.38, 4.100
seniority claims
  Community Trade Mark Regulation 2.26–2.27
sensory perception requirement
  signs 4.13, 4.16, 4.36
  sounds 4.114
service provider liability
  Internet and trade marks 9.165–9.168, 9.198–9.200
services *see* **goods and services**
shapes
  see also **three-dimensional signs/trade marks**
  and assimilation of packaging 5.301–5.314
  broad interpretation of 5.796–5.807
  broad perspective 5.282–5.300
  character of 5.248–5.281
  chocolate in animal shapes
    mouse 5.495
    rabbit 5.492–5.494
  criteria for assessing distinctive character of 'product shape' 5.270–5.272
  distinctiveness acquired through use 6.26, 6.27, 6.32, 6.55
  evidence of distinctive character 5.274–5.277
    meaning of the evidence 5.278–5.279
  facts
    appraising 5.273
    relating to distinctiveness, misappraisal of 5.261–5.264
  functional 4.03, 5.759–5.840
  general propositions 5.281
  and graphical representation 4.13
  infringement of right to hearing 5.265–5.266
  misappraisal of distinctiveness 5.253–5.260
    facts relating to distinctiveness 5.261–5.264
    as result of applying excessively stringent criteria 5.255–5.258
    as result of taking view that the shapes were usual 5.259–5.260
    sign as a whole 5.253–5.254
  overall impression 5.268–5.269
  refusal of application/declaration of invalidity 4.09
  right to be heard 5.280
  setting a roadmap 5.289, 5.295–5.300
  and signs 4.45–4.48
  substantial value, giving 5.827–5.828, 5.831–5.834
  sweets 5.444–5.459, 6.51, 6.52, 6.55
signs
  see also **goods and services; graphical representation**
  in abstract 4.20

applications to indicate type 4.126
and colours 4.17, 4.18, 4.19
versus concepts 4.13, 4.36, 4.37
concepts/definitions 4.11–4.75
   breadth of meaning 4.14
   context, relevance 4.17–4.19, 4.69
   legal background to *Dyson* 4.26–4.30
   need for examples 4.14
   pre-*Dyson* jurisprudence 4.11, 4.15–4.25
   resetting the ground 4.53–4.55
   subject matter of application 4.59, 4.60, 4.67
customary, becoming 5.723–5.758
   acronyms 5.745–5.848
   association and distinctive character 5.730–5.733
   attractiveness versus distinctiveness 5.808–5.818
   average consumer 5.791–5.792
   broad interpretation of shapes 5.796–5.807
   case assessment 5.793–5.795
   Court orders 5.753–5.758
   findings of fact/assessment of evidence 5.755–5.758
   functionality/functional shapes 5.759–5.840
   identification of essential characteristics 5.787–5.788
   legal framework 5.766
   legislative framework 5.725–5.726, 5.739
   link with specification 5.723–5.744, 5.740–5.741
   nature of goods and substantive value 5.819–5.840
   non-functional elements 5.789–5.790
   public interest considerations 5.767, 5.782
   relevance of alternatives 5.762–5.764, 5.769
   scope of provisions 5.783–5.786
   single purpose 5.829–5.830
   trade marks, patents and designs 5.762–5.764
   type and strength of association 5.734–5.737
design of retail store connected with products on sale 4.63–4.75
failure of fundamental requirement 4.13
functionality 4.42, 4.43–4.44, 4.46
   competition issues 11.201, 11.212–11.213
   and dominance 11.188–11.214
   exclusivity 11.209–11.211
   logos 11.198–11.200
   proportionality 11.214
   'reasonable time' claim 11.202–11.204
   trade mark agreement 11.194–11.197
fundamental question 4.11–4.14
graphical representation requirement 4.21–4.23, 4.38–4.40
identical, effect on rights of trade mark proprietor 'requirement' 9.30–9.121
lack of definition in Directive 4.02
list of examples (Article 2 of Directive) 4.24
   interpretation 4.61, 4.65, 4.72
   non-exhaustive character of 4.25
   open-ended 4.02
   'sign' requirement 4.56, 4.57
misappraisal of specific distinctiveness 5.253–5.260
   facts relating to distinctiveness 5.261–5.264

as result of applying excessively stringent criteria 5.255–5.258
as result of taking view that the shapes were usual 5.259–5.260
sign as a whole 5.253–5.254
need to preserve availability of 5.371–5.380
not generally capable of being a trade mark 4.22
numerals, consisting of 5.107–5.121
olfactory *see* **scents**
requirements for 4.56–4.62
   fundamental requirement 4.26–4.62
   what constitutes a sign 4.16, 4.32–4.37
same reasoning for all types of sign 5.604
sensory perception requirement 4.13, 4.16, 4.36
shapes, whether beyond 4.45–4.48
similarity between
   and appeals to Court of Justice 3.71
sounds as 4.123
three-dimensional *see* **three-dimensional signs**
trade marks and other IP rights, policy considerations 4.49–4.50
unambiguous representation 4.39
uniform representation 4.39
use
   other than as registered marks 9.64
   as registered marks 9.63
   similar to trade marks 12.76–12.77
viewpoint of individual sensing 4.86–4.87
visible functional features 4.51, 4.52
visual 4.88
of which a trade mark may consist 4.08
similarity concept
aural similarity 7.72–7.74
conceptual similarity 7.187, 7.597–7.602
confusion, similarity and distinctiveness 7.20–7.48
figurative and word marks, similarity between 7.89–7.99
likelihood of confusion 4.189
marks, similarity between 7.214–7.217
parallel imports 10.07
products, similarity between 7.205–7.213
and reputation 7.32, 7.437–7.457
sign and product 14.07
significance of similar products 5.351–5.352
signs 3.71
slogans, registrability 5.146–5.199
DAS PRINZIP DER BEQUEMLICHKEIT example 5.147–5.176
decision on the merits 5.191–5.194
OHIM and Board of Appeal 5.179
'Vorsprung durch Technik' example 5.178–5.199
post 'Vorsprung' events 5.195–5.199
Slovakia
accession to EU (2004) 2.59
Slovenia
accession to EU (2004) 2.59
sounds
see also **graphical representation**
general framework 4.124–4.125
graphical representation 4.106–4.130, 4.116–4.119
methods of representation 4.127–4.130
musical notation 4.107, 4.117, 4.118

sounds (*cont.*):
  onomatopoeia 4.119, 4.128
  policy considerations 4.106–4.130
  precision 4.115
  reference to title of composition 4.119
  as signs 4.123
  as trade marks 4.114, 4.122–4.123
Spain
  accession to EU (1986) 2.05
  and Community Trade Mark
    Regulation 2.23, 2.24
  seat of Office 2.05
spare parts market and dominance 11.109–11.111
  and intellectual property 11.119–11.124
standard of proof
  dilution, proof of 7.486–7.487
substantive law
  Community Trade Mark 2.31–2.33
surnames
  competition considerations 5.144–5.145
  consumer perception 5.142–5.143
  distinctive character 5.135–5.137
  likelihood of association and confusion 7.221
  no special conditions for 5.129–5.145
  protection 7.198–7.238
  registrability of 5.134
  same criteria for all types of marks 5.141
surveys
  Budweiser judgments 12.187
  distinctiveness acquired through use 6.03, 6.23, 6.146, 6.148, 6.149, 6.151, 6.156–6.157
Sweden
  accession to EU (1995) 2.59
sweets, shape
  chocolate in animal shapes
    mouse 5.495
    rabbit 5.492–5.494
  distinctiveness acquired through use 5.444–5.459, 6.51, 6.52, 6.55
symbol, use of
  effect on trade and scope of prohibition 5.863
  free movement of goods and deceptive
    use 5.860–5.865
  legislative framework 5.862
  proportionality 5.864
  unfair competition 5.865

tarnishment
  dilution 7.481, 9.254, 9.259
technical and scientific terms
  burden of proof 5.707–5.714
territory of use 8.126–8.170
  Advocate General Opinion 8.135–8.144
  judgments 8.145–8.157
  legal contexts 8.126–8.131
  variation on theme of use 8.166–8.170
test purchases, context of
  comparative advertising 12.33, 12.40
TFEU *see* **Treaty on the Functioning of the European Union (TFEU)**
'third party' concept
  clash with registered trade marks 9.08–9.19

three-dimensional signs/trade marks
see also **shapes**
  and Article 7(1)(b) 5.456–5.459
  and 'concept' behind a product 5.427–5.443
  distinctiveness 4.45, 4.169–4.171
    acquired 6.55, 6.57–6.58, 6.64–6.67
    level required 5.399–5.401, 5.414–5.416
  sweets 6.51, 6.52, 6.55
toys, use of trade mark in relation to 9.59–9.83
  whether specific toy model can be described
    by reference to original product 9.78, 9.359–9.360
trade mark conflicts
see also **enforcement proceedings; infringement**
  Advocate General Opinion
    availability and scope of protection 9.87–9.92
    challenging limits of protection 9.61–9.71
    clash between 'third party' concept and
      registered trade marks 9.11–9.14
    conflicts between trade marks and trade
      names 9.365–9.370, 9.375–9.382, 9.395–9.398
    counterbalancing exercise 9.44–9.51
    enforcement proceedings 9.426–9.430, 9.439–9.449, 9.460–9.466, 9.477
    expanding scope of protection 9.104–9.106
    identical signs and goods or services, effect
      on rights of trade mark proprietor
      'requirement' 9.34–9.37
    Internet and trade marks 9.128–9.143, 9.191–9.200
    limitations to rights 9.275–9.290, 9.329–9.341
    scope of Article 6(1)(b) 9.310–9.321
    transit 9.501–9.502, 9.509, 9.514–9.516, 9.525–9.527, 9.539, 9.558–9.559
  Article 6(1)(b)
    interaction with Article 3(1)(c) 5.521, 5.525
    'schematic' classification 9.314–9.316
    scope of 9.308–9.326
    teleological analysis 9.317–9.318
    use in accordance with honest
      practices 9.319–9.321
    wording and context 9.311–9.313
  availability and scope of protection 9.84–9.101
    availability requirement as a limiting
      factor 9.100–9.101
    impact of 9.93–9.99
  case details/order of reference
    border measures 9.487–9.489
    challenging limits of protection 9.59–9.60
    clash between 'third party' concept and
      registered trade marks 9.08–9.10
    conflicts between trade marks and trade
      names 9.362–9.364, 9.373–9.374, 9.391–9.394
    counterbalancing exercise 9.41–9.43
    counterfeit products through mail 9.574–9.576
    enforcement proceedings 9.421–9.425
    expanding scope of protection 9.102–9.103
    identical signs and goods or services, effect
      on rights of trade mark proprietor
      'requirement' 9.31–9.33

Index

intermediaries, use by 9.115–9.117
keywords and electronic market
   platforms 9.186–9.190
limitations to rights 9.272–9.274, 9.308–9.309,
   9.327–9.328
new market context 9.122–9.127
registered trade marks and concept of 'third
   party' 9.08–9.10
trade mark as registered, scope of protection 9.20
transit 9.499–9.500, 9.508, 9.513, 9.521–9.524,
   9.550–9.557
cases of importance
   Adam Opel 9.59–9.83, 9.351–9.363
   Arsenal 9.41–9.58
   Bellure 9.102–9.114
   BergSpechte 9.170–9.171
   BMW 9.272–9.307
   Budweiser IV 9.391–9.410
   Céline 9.373–9.392
   Class International 9.521–9.537
   Coty 9.421–9.436
   Davidoff III 9.485–9.486
   DHL 9.455–9.473
   Eis.de 9.169
   Fédération Cynologique 9.08–9.19
   Frisdranken Industrie Winters BV v Red Bull GmbH 9.262–9.271
   Gautzsch (Gartenpavillon) 9.474–9.484
   Gerolsteiner Brunnen 9.308–9.326
   Gillette 9.327–9.350
   Google 9.122–9.143
   Hölterhoff 9.31–9.40, 9.41, 9.45
   Interflora 9.222–9.261
   L'Oréal v eBay 9.186–9.221
   Marca II 9.84–9.101
   Montex-Diesel 9.536–9.548
   Polo/Lauren 9.499–9.509
   Portakabin 9.172–9.185
   Robelco 9.362–9.374
   Rolex 9.513–9.522
   Smirnoff 9.115–9.121
   Specsavers 9.20–9.29
challenging limits of protection 9.59–9.83
   application of legislation to the facts 9.65–9.71
   other uses of sign 9.64
   use of sign as a registered trade mark 9.63
compatibility, indicating 9.327–9.350
   advertiser, activities of 9.341
   concept of 'honest practices in industrial
      and commercial matters' 9.339–9.340,
      9.340–9.350
   context for interpreting Article 6 9.329
   criteria making use necessary 9.342–9.346
   factors for assessing whether use
      necessary 9.333–9.338
   fundamental criterion for application
      to Article 6(1)(c) 9.330–9.332
concept of use 9.20–9.29, 9.45–9.49
conflict between the *jus excludendi* of the
   holder of the earlier trade mark and the
   jus utendi of the proprietor of the subsequent
   registration 9.12

consumer protection 9.56
counterfeit products through mail,
   importing 9.574–9.585
counterbalancing exercise 9.41–9.58
equal treatment principle 3.107
identical signs and goods or services, effect
   on rights of trade mark proprietor
   'requirement' 9.30–9.121
   and Comparative Advertising Directive 9.37
   limiting scope of protection 9.31–9.40
   and Trade Marks Directive 9.34–9.36
intermediaries, use by 9.115–9.121
Internet and trade marks 9.121–9.271
   contributory infringement 9.144–9.146
   electronic market platforms and
      keywords 9.186–9.221
   extending *Google* principles 9.170–9.185
   Google France approach in a non-Internet
      environment 9.262–9.271
   Google principles 9.169–9.185
   Interflora case 9.222–9.261
   keywords, use by advertisers 9.147–9.168
   new market context 9.122–9.143
   see also **Internet and trade marks**
judgments
   availability and scope of protection 9.93–9.101
   border measures 9.490–9.493
   challenging limits of protection 9.72–9.78
   clash between 'third party' concept and
      registered trade marks 9.15–9.19
   conflicts between trade marks and trade
      names 9.371–9.372, 9.383–9.390,
      9.399–9.404
   counterbalancing exercise 9.52–9.56
   counterfeit products through mail 9.577–9.581
   enforcement proceedings 9.431–9.433,
      9.450–9.454, 9.467–9.472, 9.478–9.479,
      9.490–9.493
   expanding scope of protection 9.107–9.111
   identical signs and goods or services, effect
      on rights of trade mark proprietor
      'requirement' 9.38–9.40
   Internet and trade marks 9.149–9.168,
      9.201–9.221
   limitations to rights 9.290–9.307, 9.342–9.350
   scope of Article 6(1)(b) 9.322–9.326
   trade mark as registered, scope of
      protection 9.21–9.28
   transit 9.503–9.506, 9.510–9.512, 9.517–9.519,
      9.528–9.533, 9.540–9.547, 9.560–9.570
limitations to rights 9.272–9.363
   compatibility, indicating 9.327–9.350
   Directive, effect 9.275–9.278, 9.291
   exercise of rights 9.298–9.307
   narrow analysis, in *Adam Opel* 9.351–9.363
   repair and maintenance 9.303–9.307
   sale of second-hand goods ads 9.299–9.302
   scope of Article 6(1)(b) 9.308–9.326
   unauthorized use to inform the
      public 9.293–9.297
   use of mark in relation to goods 9.280–9.283
   use of mark in relation to services 9.284–9.290

trade mark conflicts (*cont.*):
  logos, use of 9.59–9.83
  and national courts 9.57–9.58
  proprietor of trade marks
    identical signs and goods or services, effect on rights of trade mark proprietor 'requirement' 9.30–9.121
    interests of 9.50–9.51, 9.54–9.55
    use by or with his/her consent 8.216–8.217
  scope of protection
    and availability 9.84–9.101
    colours 9.26–9.29
    expanding 9.101–9.114
    limiting of 9.31–9.40
    trade marks as registered 9.20–9.29
  toys, use of trade mark in relation to 9.59–9.83
    whether specific toy model can be described by reference to original product 9.78, 9.359–9.360
  trade mark as registered, scope of protection 9.20–9.29
  trade names and trade marks 9.362–9.410
    acquiescence and honest concurrent use 9.391–9.408
    names performing a distinguishing function 9.373–9.392
  transit 9.494–9.585
    as basis for detention by customs 9.513–9.522
    burden of proof 9.533
    concepts of offering and putting on the market 9.531–9.532
    custom-free zones and original goods 9.521–9.537
    and customs seizure 9.549–9.573
    'importing' concept 9.529–9.530
    law and issues 9.494–9.498
    from a Member State for a non-Member State 9.499–9.509
    no exception for protection of IP rights 9.511–9.512
    through a Member State as trade mark infringement 9.508–9.514
    as trade mark infringement 9.508–9.514, 9.536–9.548
Trade Mark Directive *see* **'Harmonization' Directive (89/104/EEC), as codified (2008/95/EC)**
trade mark law (EU)
  background 2.01–2.06
  Community Trade Mark *see* **Community Trade Mark (CTM)**
  Community Trade Mark Directive *see* **Community Trade Mark Regulation (CTMR)**
  and free movement of goods
    changing direction 10.83–10.85
    compulsory licence 10.81–10.82
    consent and independent rights 10.78
    consent concept 10.73, 10.86–10.91
    essential function and specific subject matter of trade marks 10.71–10.72
    lack of protection 10.79–10.80
    restrictive approach 10.74–10.77
    role and function of trade marks 10.86–10.91
    voluntary assignment 10.92–10.97
  growth 1.01
  'Harmonization' Directive *see* **'Harmonization' Directive**
  history of 'European' trade mark law 2.03
  history prior to 1988 Directive and 1993 Regulation 1.01, 2.02
  interrelationship between layers of Community law 10.53
  and keywords *see* **keywords, use by advertisers**
  prevention of abuse 4.32
  principle of EU-wide exhaustion of national IP rights 2.02
  and TRIPS Agreement 12.194–12.212
trade mark reform (new package)
  April 2015 Compromise 13.15–13.51
  background 13.01–13.06
  Commission proposals 13.07–13.14
  cooperation 13.12, 13.45
  exceptions 13.29–13.37
    exhaustion 13.32
    fair use 13.29–13.31
    intervening rights 13.33–13.34
  exhaustion of rights 10.136, 10.137–10.138, 10.146–10.147, 13.32
  formalities 13.21
  and free movement of goods
    absence of prior notice, consequences 10.371
    admissibility considerations 10.266
    adverse effect on the original condition of the product 10.184–10.186
    application of Articles 34 and 36 10.272–10.273
    applying the principles 10.159–10.167
    Article 7/Article 7(1) of Directive 10.117–10.408, 10.276–10.280
    artificial partitioning of the markets between Member States 10.179–10.183
    burden of proof 10.148–10.149, 10.356
    case law 10.176–10.178
    clear identification of importer and manufacturer 10.359
    commercial policy considerations 10.282–10.283
    'competence' of Directive 10.281
    conditions of *Bristol Myers Squibbs* and overstickered products 10.342–10.345
    consent and acquiescence 10.386–10.394
    consumer rights, competitor rights and markets 10.395–10.408
    copyright considerations 10.265, 10.272–10.273
    damage to reputation 10.308–10.309, 10.350, 10.351–10.352, 10.366–10.368
    Danish cases 10.118–10.124
    derogation from Article 5(1) 10.279–10.280
    and Directive 10.136, 10.146–10.147, 10.169–10.170, 10.276–10.280
    disclosure 10.378–10.385
    effect of Directive in national legal order 10.286
    effect of giving notice 10.353–10.355
    exceptions to general principle 10.258–10.259, 10.268–10.271
    exhaustion and advertising 10.257, 10.267
    exhaustion of rights 10.136, 10.137–10.138, 10.146–10.147, 10.284, 10.285

890

Index

factors for assessing risk of significant damage 10.263–10.264
fundamental interests protected by trade mark rights 10.139–10.140
general propositions 10.160–10.162, 10.164
German cases 10.125–10.132
goods put on the market in the EEA 10.314–10.317
identifying the issues 10.150–10.158
inappropriate presentation and reputation 10.191–10.192
interpretation of Article 7(1) 10.171–10.172
interpretation of Article 7(2) 10.173–10.186
legal contexts 10.338–10.339
main criteria for application of Article 36 10.141
manufacturer, indication of 10.190
necessity factors 10.203–10.206, 10.346–10.349, 10.357
no adverse effect on condition of product 10.358
notice 10.361
notification duty 10.382
offering testers and putting goods on the market 10.328–10.333
partitioning the market 10.142–10.144, 10.179–10.183, 10.241–10.247
presentation not damaging to reputation presentation 10.360
prior notice 10.145, 10.370, 10.371
procedural peculiarity 10.256
rebranding and necessity 10.204–10.205
reformulating *Bristol Myers Squibbs* 10.340
rejecting intention requirement 10.201–10.202
remaining requirements 10.187–10.193
repackaging 10.133–10.135, 10.137–10.138, 10.145, 10.188–10.189, 10.212–10.228, 10.334–10.371
replacing the trade mark and necessity requirement 10.198–10.213
reputation and functions of trade marks 10.260–10.264
role of Court 10.337
six questions of 'essence' 10.341–10.361
specific rulings 10.163, 10.165–10.167
trade mark infringement and policing channels of trade 10.229–10.251
licensing 13.37
other amendments 13.27
procedures in Community trade mark law 13.10
procedures in national trade mark laws 13.11
requirement of use 13.35–13.36
rights conferred 13.23–13.28
rights in rem 13.37
small consignments 13.25–13.26
substantive law 13.09, 13.20
transfers 13.37
transit 13.23–13.24
types of marks 13.20
Trade Mark Registration Treaty
limitations 2.06
Trade Mark Regulation (EC) 40/94 on the Community Trade Mark (1994) *see* **Community Trade Mark Regulation (CTMR), 1993**

trade marks
see also **colours; Community Trade Mark (CTM); distinctiveness requirement; graphical representation; refusal of application/ declaration of invalidity; signs**
applications for registration *see* **applications for registration**
assignments 5.841–5.858
autonomy of Community trade mark regime 5.644
categories, no distinction between 4.164–4.166
colour combinations as 4.152–4.153
commercialization 5.844–5.845
as communicators 4.85
and competition
  agreement capable of constituting a threat 11.17
  application of Article 101 11.13–11.97
  application of Article 102 11.98–11.214
  delimitation agreements 11.69–11.75
  dominance 11.98–11.187
  effect of trade mark registration 11.21
  exemption requirements 11.23
  interchangeability criterion 11.100–11.105
  object and effect 11.19
  property, Article 36 and competition provisions 11.22
  quality considerations 11.24–11.25
  relevant product market 11.18, 11.99–11.105
  validity of agreement 11.20
  vertical agreements 11.15–11.16
and competition law 4.50
composite 7.314–7.327
concept of distinguishing marks 12.12
conflicts *see* **conflicts, trade mark**
consisting exclusively of signs or indications 4.09, 4.10
contrary to public policy 4.09, 4.10
and copyright 4.121
deception of the public 4.09, 4.10
of a deceptive nature 5.841–5.973
  admissibility considerations 5.843
  advertising messages 5.872–5.877
  commercialization of trade marks 5.844–5.845
  cosmetics 5.866–5.871
  effect on trade and scope of prohibition 5.863
  and free movement of goods 5.859–5.911
  functions of trade marks 5.846
  legislative framework 5.862
  perspective for determining deception 5.847
  procedural considerations 5.583
  proportionality 5.864
  symbol, use of 5.860–5.865
  unfair competition 5.865, 5.870–5.871
delineating exclusive rights 12.42
devoid of any distinctive character *see* **devoid of any distinctive character**
Directive *see* **'Harmonization' Directive (89/104/EEC), as codified (2008/95/EC)**
and domain names *see* **domain names and trade marks**
effect of simultaneous protection 14.06
exercise of trade mark rights and free movement of goods 7.98–7.99

891

trade marks (*cont.*):
  exhaustion cases 14.06
  families of 7.328–7.331
  functions
    deceptive use 5.846
    essential 4.163, 9.53, 10.71–10.72, 10.86–10.91
    as indication of origin 2.08, 9.53
    in Internet environment 9.159
    keywords, effect 9.156
    monopolization argument 4.49
  geographical indication 4.10
  infringement *see* **infringement**
    on Internet 14.12
    keywords similar to 9.170–9.171
      see also **keywords, use by advertisers**
  limitations to rights *see* **limitations to trade mark rights**
  misspelt 9.172, 9.174
  national
    reforms 13.11
    taking into account in CTM system 2.23
  non-traditional 4.04
  and other IP rights 14.06
    policy considerations 4.49–4.50
  reform *see* **trade mark reform (new package)**
  registered, EU-wide protection accorded to 2.08
  registered by agents without authorization 9.06
  Regulation *see* **Community Trade Mark Regulation (CTMR)**
  with reputation *see* **reputation**
  revocation
    establishment *a posteriori* 8.10
    grounds 8.08, 8.09
    relating to only some of the goods or services 8.09
    use after filing application for 8.56–8.57
  sanctions for non-use of a trade mark in legal or administrative proceedings 8.07
  for services, acceptance of 4.176
  similarity between 7.214–7.217
    see also **similarity concept**
  sounds as 4.114, 4.122–4.123
  specific subject-matter 10.71–10.72
  substantive law 13.09
  success of Community trade mark 14.02
  and trade names 12.205–12.212
  unauthorized by competent authorities 4.09, 4.10
  unitary character of Community trade marks 2.20, 7.336–7.340
  use as a mark 6.25–6.35
    monopolization argument 6.29, 6.35
    public addressed by the mark 6.32
    as a trade mark 6.33
    well-known and reputed trade marks 7.432–7.436
  use of a sign similar to 12.76–12.77
  use prohibited pursuant to provisions of law 4.09
  well-known and reputed *see* **reputation**
  wines 4.10
trade names
  acquiescence and honest concurrent use 9.391–9.408
  function of company names 9.384
  'honest practices' exception 9.388–9.390
  performing a distinguishing function 9.373–9.392
  as prior rights 12.211
  protecting 12.194–12.212
    requirements for 12.201–12.202
  status 12.200
  and trade marks 9.362–9.410, 12.205–12.212
Trademark Law Treaty (TLT)
  classes of 4.193
transit 9.494–9.585
  see also **parallel imports**
  as basis for detention by customs 9.513–9.522
  burden of proof 9.533
  concepts of offering and putting on the market 9.531–9.532
  custom-free zones and original goods 9.521–9.537
  and customs seizure 9.549–9.573
  from a Member State for a non-Member State 9.499–9.509
  'importing' concept 9.529–9.530
  law and issues 9.494–9.498
  no exception for protection of IP rights 9.511–9.512
  through a Member State as trade mark infringement 9.508–9.514
  as trade mark infringement 9.508–9.514, 9.536–9.548
  trade mark reform (new package) 13.23–13.24
Treaties
  see also **Treaty on European Union (TEU); Treaty on the Functioning of the European Union (TFEU)**
  amendment requirements 3.04
  Court of Justice as guardian of 3.05
Treaty Establishing a Constitution for Europe (Constitutional Treaty), 2004 3.04
Treaty on European Union (TEU)
  and Court of Justice 3.02
Treaty on the Functioning of the European Union (TFEU)
  Article 101, application 11.13–11.97
    interpretation generally 11.15–11.16
    interpretation of Article 101(1) 11.88–11.91, 11.93–11.96
    interpretation of Article 101(3) 11.92, 11.97
  Article 102, application 11.98–11.214
    interpretation generally 11.15–11.16
  and Court of Justice
    actions against a Community institution for failure to act 3.08
    actions against Member States in breach of EU law 3.07
    annulment actions by 3.09–3.11
    enforcement role 3.03
    preliminary ruling, references for 3.13
TRIPS Agreement (Agreement on Trade-Related Aspects of Intellectual Property Rights)
  CTM system compatible with 2.17
  and Directive 4.48
  and graphical representation 4.138
  identity, establishing 7.11
  and trade mark law 12.194–12.212

Index

two-dimensional signs
  historical ability to obtain registration 4.04

unequivocality requirement
  graphical representation 4.102
unfair advantage
  and appeals to Court of Justice 3.71
  application of trade mark law 4.32, 4.49
  comparative advertising 12.13–12.15, 12.23–12.24
  get-up imitation 7.545–7.547
  misuse of reputation 12.13–12.15
  in practice 7.560–7.582
  well-known and reputed trade marks 7.525–7.547, 7.560–7.582
Unified Patent Court
  enforcement proceedings 2.48
unitary character
  Community Trade Mark Regulation 2.20
United Kingdom (UK)
  and Community Trade Mark Regulation 2.23, 2.24
Uruguay Round agreements (1994)
  and setting up of TRIPS Agreement 2.17
use of trade marks
  Advocate General Opinion
    differences of perception 8.287–8.293
    generic indications, development into 8.263–8.277
    genuine use requirement 8.19–8.33
    grace period 8.225–8.229
    justification of non-use 8.239–8.241
    promotional items 8.100–8.108
    territory of use 8.135–8.144
    use with or without profit 8.83–8.88
  case details/order of reference
    combinations of marks 8.190–8.191
    differences of perception 8.283–8.286
    grace period 8.220–8.224
    justification of non-use 8.237–8.238
    multiple marks 8.196–8.198
    promotional items 8.97–8.99
    registration of variation 8.175–8.178
    registration of variation not relevant 8.183–8.184
    territory of use 8.132–8.134
  cases of importance
    Ansul 8.208–8.215
    Bainbridge 8.175–8.182, 8.252–8.253
    La Mer 8.44–8.57
    Leno Merken/ONEL 8.126–8.165
    Lidl 8.219–8.233, 8.236–8.251
    MINIMAX/*Ansul* 8.14–8.43
    Nasdaq 8.115–8.125
    Procordia (BOSTONGURKA) 8.260–8.282
    Radetzky 8.76–8.95
    Rintisch v Eder (PROTI) 8.182–8.189
    Rivella International 8.166–8.170
    Silberquelle 8.96–8.114
    Specsavers 8.196–8.206
    Sunrider 8.58–8.71
    Walzertraum 8.72–8.74
  challenging limits of protection
    possible threats to functions 9.77
  combinations of marks 8.190–8.195
  concept of use 6.44, 9.20–9.29, 9.45–9.49
  criteria concerning 5.387
  display of advertisements 9.136–9.140
  distinctiveness acquired through *see*
    distinctiveness acquired through use
  evidence of use and burden of proof 8.58–8.71
  factors for assessing whether use necessary 9.333–9.338
  generic indications, development into 8.259–8.302
    cases 8.260–8.302
    differences of perception 8.283–8.302
    relevant public 8.260–8.282
  for goods or services for which registered 8.207–8.215
  goods out of production 8.208–8.215
  grace period 8.218–8.233
  as guarantee of origin 8.100–8.102
  judgments
    combinations of marks 8.192–8.195
    differences of perception 8.294–8.298
    evidence of use 8.66–8.71
    generic indications, development into 8.278–8.282
    genuine use requirement 8.34–8.43
    grace period 8.230–8.233
    justification of non-use 8.242–8.251
    multiple marks 8.199–8.206
    promotional items 8.109–8.114
    registration of variation 8.179
    registration of variation not relevant 8.185–8.189
    territory of use 8.145–8.157
    use with or without profit 8.89–8.93
  justification of non-use 8.234–8.258
    proper reasons for non-use 8.236–8.251
  keywords, allowing advertisers to select 9.133–9.135
  minimal use 8.72–8.74
  multiple marks 8.196–8.206
  with or without profit 8.75–8.125
    non-profitable activities 8.76–8.95
  by proprietor or with his/her consent 8.216–8.217
  as registered 8.171–8.206
  registration of a variation 8.175–8.182
  in relation to goods 9.280–9.290
  requirement of use 8.04–8.13
    administrative proceedings 8.07
    case law 8.12–8.13
    Directive 8.06–8.10
    establishment *a posteriori* of invalidity or revocation of a trade mark 8.10
    genuine use 3.71, 8.14–8.125
    grounds for refusal, revocation or invalidity relating to only some of the goods or services 8.09
    grounds for revocation 8.08
    legislative contexts 8.05–8.11
    Regulation provisions 8.11
    sanctions for non-use of a trade mark in legal or administrative proceedings 8.07
  territory of use 8.126–8.170
  toys, in relation to 9.72–9.76

use of trade marks *(cont.)*:
  as trade marks 6.25–6.35
    monopolization argument 6.29, 6.35
    public addressed by the mark 6.32
    use as a trade mark requirement 12.198
    well-known and reputed trade marks 7.423–7.436, 7.432–7.436
  types of use remaining outside scope of protection 14.11
  use of acceptable version 8.171–8.206
  use together with another mark 8.171–8.206

validity of agreement
  competition 11.44
validity of CTMs
  enforcement proceedings 2.48, 2.49
vigilant conduct requirement
  relevant points in time 7.163–7.165

washing tables cases 5.321–5.388
  inlaid tablets 5.339–5.344, 5.388
  significance of similar products 5.351–5.352
  speckled tablets 5.383–5.387
  two-layered tablets 5.324–5.332
web of agreements
  access clause, relevance 11.41–11.42
  block exemptions 11.43
  definition of relevant market 11.36
  exemptions to rule 11.43
  multifactor tests 11.38–11.40
  national court, role 11.45–11.48
  validity of agreement 11.44
wines
  trade marks containing geographical indication 4.10
WIPO *see* **World Intellectual Property Organization (WIPO)**
word marks, distinctiveness 7.134–7.140
  acquired distinctiveness 6.95, 6.97, 6.98, 6.99
World Intellectual Property Organization (WIPO)
  on renewal of national registration 3.44
World Trade Organization (WTO)
  establishment (1994) 2.17
WTO *see* **World Trade Organization (WTO)**